UNIVERSITY OF MARYLAND

College of Agriculture & Natural Resources

MARYLAND MASTER GARDENER HANDBOOK

Published by the

University of Maryland Extension Master Gardener Program:
extension.umd.edu/mg

University of Maryland Extension Gardening:
extension.umd.edu/hgic

Resources • Ask Extension • Videos

JOHNS HOPKINS UNIVERSITY PRESS
Baltimore

University programs, activities, and facilities are available to all without regard to race, color, sex, gender identity or expression, sexual orientation, marital status, age, national origin, political affiliation, physical or mental disability, religion, protected veteran status, genetic information, personal appearance, or any other legally protected class.

CONTRIBUTORS AND ACKNOWLEDGEMENTS

This handbook is dedicated to University of Maryland Extension Master Gardeners who, each day, create a healthier world through environmental stewardship.

The University of Maryland Extension Master Gardener Handbook was produced by the State Master Gardener Program located at the Central Maryland Research and Education Center. The Master Gardener program operates under the University of Maryland Extension, which is part of the University of Maryland College of Agriculture and Natural Resources.

Project Coordinator	Stephanie Pully, State Master Gardener Coordinator
Editor-in-Chief	LeAnn Zotta, Berkshire Communications
Copy Editor	Nancy Klein, Master Gardener and Master Watershed Steward, Howard County, Maryland
Cover Design	Shannon Dyson, M.A., Associate Art Director
Interior Design	LeAnn Zotta, Berkshire Communications
Original Artwork	Don Wittig, University of Maryland Extension Master Gardener
	Raymond Bosmans Professor Emeritus, University of Maryland Extension
	John Davidson, Ph.D., Professor Emeritus Dept. of Entomology, University of Maryland
	Gary Brewer, Ph.D. Chair, Dept. of Entomology, North Dakota State University
	Jean Burchfield Program Management Specialist, University of Maryland Extension
Photo & Illustration Management	LeAnn Zotta, Berkshire Communications
Copyright and ISBN	© 2025 University of Maryland Extension. **978-1-4214-5185-5 (hardcover)** **978-1-4214-5186-2 (ebook)**

This project was a collaborative effort, and we'd like to express our thanks for the valuable support of our colleagues. We are especially grateful to the authors for the information and knowledge contained herein. It is our hope that this collective work will light the way for current and future Master Gardeners.

Ordering Information: If you would like to order a copy of the Maryland Master Gardener Handbook, please visit **extension.umd.edu/mg** (click on Master Gardener Handbook). Bulk orders available.

Corrections or Changes: If you find an error in this handbook, please notify us at **statemg@umd.edu**. Please include the page number and a description of the problem.

Disclaimer: Website addresses referenced in this manual, while accurate when printed, may change without notice.

TABLE OF CONTENTS

1: INTRODUCTION
1.1 About This Handbook 3
1.2 How to Use This Handbook 4
1.3 University of Maryland Extension Master Gardener Program 4

2: TEACHING AND COMMUNICATION
2.1 Teaching Overview 9
2.2 Age-Appropriate Teaching 11
2.3 Communications Overview 12
2.4 Communication Methods 13
2.5 Giving a Great Presentation 20
2.6 Using Mass Media 24
2.7 Teaching Online 27

3: ECOLOGY
3.1 Maryland's Ecology 35
3.2 Maryland's Landscape 39
3.3 Plant and Wildlife Communities 42
3.4 Species Interactions 45
3.5 Species and Populations 48
3.6 Ecosystems 52
3.7 What Is a Wetland? 56
3.8 Why Are Wetlands Important? 59
3.9 Wetland Regulations 60
3.10 How to Preserve Wetlands 61

4: BASIC BOTANY
4.1 Groupings of Plants 67
4.2 Classification of Plants 69
4.3 The Structure of Plants 73
4.4 Reproductive Structures 80
4.5 Pollination 84
4.6 Plant Growth & Development 86
4.7 Regulation of Plant Growth 87
4.8 Plant Selection & Modification 89

5: SOILS AND FERTILIZERS
5.1 What is a Soil? 95
5.2 Soil Solids 96
5.3 Soil Pores 100
5.4 Soil as Entities of Nature 102
5.5 Soils as Natural Capital and Ecosystem Services. 105
5.6 Soils as Hydrologic Buffers 106
5.7 Soils as Biochemical and Chemical Reactors 107
5.8 Soils as Media for Plant Growth 112
5.9 Soil Testing 114
5.10 Soil Health 119

6: PLANT NUTRITION
6.1 Nutrition Essentiality 127
6.2 Nutrient Types 128
6.3 Nutrient Availability 129
6.4 Macronutrients 129
6.5 Micronutrients 133
6.6 Beneficial Non-Essential Nutrients 136

7: COMPOSTING
7.1 Why Make Compost? 141
7.2 How Is Compost Made? 142
7.3 Compost Ingredients 143
7.4 Starting a Compost Pile 146
7.5 What Can Be Composted? 150
7.6 Basic Composting Steps 151
7.7 Troubleshooting Compost 153
7.8 Tips for Using Compost 153

8: INSECT BASICS
8.1 Insects as Part of a Natural System 158
8.2 Insect Structure 158
8.3 Insect Metamorphosis 163
8.4 Insect Classification 164
8.5 Common Landscape Pests 170
8.6 Common Household Pests 175
8.7 Beneficial Insects 176
8.8 Common Non-insect Arthropods 179

9: PLANT DISEASE BASICS
9.1 Impact of Plant Disease 187
9.2 Basic Plant Disease Concepts 189
9.3 Fungi and Plant Diseases 191
9.4 Classification of Plant Pathogenic Fungi 192
9.5 Plant Diseases Caused by Bacteria 200
9.6 Plant Diseases Caused by Phytoplasmas 202
9.7 Plant Diseases Caused by Nematodes ... 203
9.8 Plant Diseases Caused by Viruses 204
9.9 Parasitic Plants 206
9.10 Environmental Diseases 207
9.11 Principles of Plant Disease Control 208
9.12 Biological and Integrated Pest Management (IPM) Controls 210

10: INTEGRATED PEST MANAGEMENT (IPM)
10.1 What is IPM? 213
10.2 IPM Steps 214
10.3 Healthy Plants = Fewer Problems 215
10.4 Taking Action 216

11: PESTICIDE USE AND SAFETY
- 11.1 Pesticide Basics 227
- 11.2 Pesticide Formulations 228
- 11.3 The Pesticide Label........................... 228
- 11.4 Managing Pesticide Risk 233
- 11.5 Proper Application Practices................. 234
- 11.6 Organic Pesticides............................. 236
- 11.7 Pesticides in the Environment................ 238

12: PLANT DIAGNOSTICS
- 12.1 A Systematic Approach for Diagnosing Plant Problems...................................... 243
- 12.2 How Plants Show Symptoms 245
- 12.3 Biotic vs. Abiotic Causes of Plant Problems ... 247
- 12.4 Symptoms and Signs of Plant Diseases 251
- 12.5 Symptoms and Signs of Insect Pests 253
- 12.6 Diagnostic Keys 254

13: WEEDS
- 13.1 Why Are Weeds a Problem? 348
- 13.2 Weed Biology 349
- 13.3 Weed Identification 352
- 13.4 Weed Management........................... 366
- 13.5 Sustainable Weed Maintenance Plan 374

14: LAWNS
- 14.1 Turfgrass Identification 381
- 14.2 Turfgrass Species.............................. 383
- 14.3 Lawn Establishment 389
- 14.4 Cultural Practices for Turf..................... 393
- 14.5 Turfgrass Problems............................ 402
- 14.6 Organic Lawn Care Tips....................... 413
- 14.7 Lawn Alternatives 413

15: HERBACEOUS PLANTS
- 15.1 About Herbaceous Gardens.................. 420
- 15.2 Herbaceous Plant Families 421
- 15.3 Annuals 427
- 15.4 Perennials..................................... 429
- 15.5 Biennials 431
- 15.6 Underground Stems 431
- 15.7 Landscape Design with Herbaceous Plants ... 436
- 15.8 Herbaceous Garden Maintenance............ 439
- 15.9 Sexual Propagation of Herbaceous Plants..... 442
- 15.10 Asexual Propagation of Herbaceous Plants ... 443

16: WOODY PLANTS
- 16.1 Planning and Site Selection 457
- 16.2 Plant Selection 458
- 16.3 Purchasing Woody Plants..................... 459
- 16.4 Planting Woody Ornamentals 461
- 16.5 Post-Planting Care 464
- 16.6 Woody Plant Maintenance 465
- 16.7 Transplanting Woody Ornamentals 468
- 16.8 Abiotic Problems of Woody Plants 469
- 16.9 Problematic Trees & Shrubs 473
- 16.10 Recommended Woody Plants 475
- 16.11 Ornamental Vines 482
- 16.12 Groundcovers 483

17: PRUNING
- 17.1 Physiology of Pruning 489
- 17.2 Why Prune?.................................... 491
- 17.3 Pruning Tools 493
- 17.4 Pruning Techniques & Terms 494
- 17.5 When to Prune 497
- 17.6 Training Newly-Planted Trees.................. 498
- 17.7 Pruning Mature Trees.......................... 500
- 17.8 Pruning Shrubs................................ 502
- 17.9 Pruning Hedges 502
- 17.10 Pruning Conifers 504
- 17.11 Pruning Other Plants.......................... 504

18: VEGETABLES
- 18.1 Starting a Vegetable Garden 514
- 18.2 Garden Types and Techniques................ 514
- 18.3 Selecting a Garden Site 516
- 18.4 Soil Assessment and Testing.................. 521
- 18.5 Soil Amendments 522
- 18.6 Cover Crops 523
- 18.7 Pollination 525
- 18.8 Vegetable Planting Guide 525
- 18.9 Planting Seed 534
- 18.10 Starting Your Own Transplants 536
- 18.11 Vegetable Garden Maintenance............... 540
- 18.12 Harvesting Vegetables......................... 546
- 18.13 Herbs.. 548
- 18.14 Profiles of Selected Vegetable Crops 556

19: SMALL FRUITS
- 19.1 Cultivar Selection 579
- 19.2 Site Selection and Preparation 580
- 19.3 Planting Small Fruits 582
- 19.4 Small Fruits Maintenance 582
- 19.5 Blueberries.................................... 583
- 19.6 Brambles...................................... 585
- 19.7 Currants and Gooseberries 588
- 19.8 Elderberries 591
- 19.9 Grapes 591

19.10 Hardy Kiwis 593
19.11 Strawberries 595

20: TREE FRUITS
20.1 Tree-Fruit Basics 607
20.2 Planting a Fruit Tree 611
20.3 Mulching and Weeding 612
20.4 Pest and Disease Control 613
20.5 General Pruning Guidelines................ 615
20.6 Pome Fruits: Apple and Pear 616
20.7 Stone Fruits: Peach, Cherry, Plum, Apricot, Nectarine.................................. 623
20.8 Fig Trees 627

21: NATIVE PLANTS
21.1 Why Choose Native Plants? 637
21.2 How to Choose Native Plants 640
21.3 Maximizing Native Plant Performance 640
21.4 Recommended Native Plants for Maryland..... 641

22: INVASIVE PLANTS
22.1 About Invasive Species 647
22.2 Invasive Species: Non-Plant 649
22.3 Invasive Species: Plants 652
22.4 Invasive Control Methods.................. 654
22.5 Common Invasive Plants of Maryland......... 655

23: INDOOR PLANTS
23.1 Selecting Indoor Plants..................... 669
23.2 Requirements for Healthy Indoor Plants 669
23.3 Maintenance Tips 674
23.4 Repotting Indoor Plants 675
23.5 Moving Indoor Plants Outdoors............ 677
23.6 Bringing Plants Back Indoors 678
23.7 Indoor Plant Pest and Disease Diagnostics 678
23.8 Toxic Indoor Plants 679

24: PLANT PROPAGATION
24.1 Sexual Propagation 684
   24.1a About Seeds 684
   24.1b Preparing Seeds for Germination........... 687
   24.1c Starting Seeds Indoors 691
   24.1d Starting Seeds Outdoors 696
24.2 Growing Transplants 697
24.3 Asexual Propagation 699
   24.3a Cuttings.................................. 699
   24.3b Layering 701
   24.3c Division and Separation 703
   24.3d Grafting and Budding 704

25: CONTAINER GARDENING
25.1 Raised Beds 712
25.2 Choosing Container Plants 713
25.3 Choosing the Right Container............. 715
25.4 Growing Media for Containers 719
25.5 Potting and Repotting 720
25.6 Caring for Container Plants 720
25.7 Container Plant Pest and Disease Diagnostics.. 723
25.8 Container Combination Ideas.............. 723

26: LANDSCAPE DESIGN
26.1 What Is Landscape Design? 732
26.2 Site Analysis and Blob Design............. 733
26.3 Functional Uses of Space 734
26.4 Elements of Design 736
26.5 Principles of Composition 739
26.6 Plant Selection 740
26.7 Finalizing Your Design 740
26.8 Installation 742

27: WILDLIFE AND WOODLANDS
27.1 Woodlands.................................. 748
27.2 Principles of Forestry 751
27.3 Property Inventory 752
27.4 Land Care Practices 755
27.5 Managing a Wildlife Habitat 765
27.6 Attracting Beneficial Insects 771
27.7 Attracting and Feeding Birds 772
27.8 Managing Wildlife Damage 776
27.9 Nuisance Animals 777

28: CONSERVATION LANDSCAPING
28.1 The Bay-Wise Philosophy.................. 798
28.2 The Hydrologic Cycle 801
28.3 Groundwater 803
28.4 Water Pollution............................. 805
28.5 Water Conservation 806
28.6 Stormwater Management 808

29: GARDEN TOOLS AND EQUIPMENT
29.1 Choosing the Right Tools 815
29.2 Hand Tools................................. 817
   29.2a Cutting Tools............................ 818
   29.2b Digging Tools 821
   29.2c Raking Tools 823
   29.2d Maintenance of Hand Tools 824
29.3 Power Tools................................ 825
   29.3a Mowers................................. 826
   29.3b Tillers/Cultivators 827
   29.3c String Trimmers 829

29.3d Leaf Blowers 830
29.3e Lawn Edgers 831
29.3f Chipper-Shredders 831
29.3g Maintenance of Power Tools................. 833
29.4 Garden Accessories........................... 833
29.4a Wheelbarrows and Carts 833
29.4b Trellises, Cages, and Stakes 834
29.4c Watering Equipment 837
29.4d Sprayers 841
29.4e Maintenance of Watering Equipment
       and Sprayers 842
29.5 Other Tools and Accessories 842
29.5a Composting Tools.......................... 842
29.5b Other Accessories 845
29.5c Maintenance of Other Tools and Accessories . 847

30: RESOURCE APPENDIX

Glossary of Terms 851
Table 30-A. Measurement Conversions 885
Freeze Dates and Hardiness Zones................... 886

LIST OF FIGURES 887

LIST OF TABLES.................................... 893

INDEX OF DIAGNOSTIC KEYS 897

INDEX 899

1: INTRODUCTION

Stephanie Pully
Jon H. Traunfeld
Robin Hessey

1 INTRODUCTION

CONTENTS

1.1 About This Handbook 3
1.2 How to Use This Handbook 4
1.3 University of Maryland Extension Master Gardener Program 4

1.1 About This Handbook

Gardens and gardeners are more important than ever. Each and every one of our actions in the garden affects the greater ecosystem and the health of its inhabitants. In an era of global warming, diminishing plant and animal diversity, threatened ecosystems, disappearing habitats, and increased nutrient and pesticide pollution, we realize that everything we do in our landscape counts.

Derwood Demo Garden in Montgomery County

As Maryland becomes increasingly suburbanized, thousands of new landscapes are being carved out of farmland and forests. Most of these landscapes drain into the Chesapeake Bay, one of this country's most productive—yet threatened—estuaries. We now know that erodible soils, misapplied fertilizers, and overused pesticides may easily enter a nearby tributary and ultimately affect the health of the entire Bay.

Fortunately, everyone can be a part of the solution! No matter how big or small your planting space, you can have a positive effect on our ecosystem. The approaches outlined in this book offer solutions for not only healthier ecosystems, but also healthier homes.

Gardening is no longer limited to those with large backyards. In fact, some of the most avid plant enthusiasts grow all their plants indoors! All Marylanders want and need accurate information about planting and caring for their plants and property. They need to know how to create sustainable gardens and landscapes that are successful and productive because they use inherent resources (e.g., backyard compost) and diversity of natural systems (e.g., attracting beneficial insects), rather than purchased fertilizers and pesticides. The University of Maryland Extension Master Gardener Program, with almost 40 years of service to the community, is proud to offer the Maryland Master Gardener Handbook as a guide to home horticulturists across the state and beyond.

This handbook and the Maryland Master Gardener Program are structured to help the average gardener learn how to create and maintain a sustainable landscape by:

- Understanding the interrelationships between soil, air, water, plants, and animals
- Learning to use the right plant in the right place and the importance of native plants
- Learning to build and protect healthy soil and recycle nutrients
- Learning how to conserve and protect water resources
- Growing fruits and vegetables organically
- Correctly diagnosing and solving plant problems through practices that do not harm the environment (i.e., Integrated Pest Management, or IPM)

1.2 How to Use This Handbook

Learning about the natural world and gardening is exciting! This handbook was originally created as a textbook to use for the Master Gardener basic training course, but has become a trusted resource for home horticulturists everywhere. Each chapter has a set of learning objectives to help structure the information. Major topic headings for each chapter are in large, bold type. An extensive table of contents, index, and glossary will also help you locate specific information.

One of our main goals is to present useful tools that help identify and solve pest and plant problems. **Chapter 10: Integrated Pest Management (IPM)** and **Chapter 12: Plant Diagnostics** include numerous self-help diagnostic keys that recommend non-chemical controls. The handbook also includes hundreds of color images to assist you in identifying weeds, invasive species, and plant and pest problems.

1.3 University of Maryland Extension Master Gardener Program

Butterfly weed and swallowtail butterfly

Master Gardener programs are active in all 50 states. They extend the expertise and knowledge of the Land-Grant University System to the general public.

The University of Maryland Extension Master Gardener Program was started in 1978 to provide science-based outreach education to the public on subjects related to environmental horticulture and Integrated Pest Management (IPM). The program trains and guides a large corps of dedicated volunteers, a driving force that helps the University of Maryland Extension (UME) achieve its mission and goals. UME is the outreach education arm of the College of Agriculture and Natural Resources.

In exchange for 40 hours of training by Extension faculty, participants agree to volunteer a minimum of 40 hours to the program during their training/internship year. Master Gardeners typically work in group-directed teams and committees with trainees matched to senior Master Gardeners. Typical activities include:

- Environmental gardening demonstrations
- Plant clinics (e.g., "Ask a Master Gardener")
- Compost demonstration sites
- Certification of Bay-Wise landscapes
- Classes and workshops for the public
- Youth gardening projects
- Technical assistance for community gardening and beautification projects

- Information booths at fairs and festivals
- Therapeutic horticulture programs
- Continuing education

Your purchase of this handbook supports the UME Master Gardener Program. Thank you for your support! For more information on the UME Master Gardener Program visit the website at:

extension.umd.edu/mg

Go to the University of Maryland Extension Gardening website for specific gardening and pest management information: **extension.umd.edu/hgic**. Click on the "Ask Maryland's Garden Experts" link 24/7 to send questions and photos. Your questions will be answered by our Certified Professional Horticulturists.

We hope you find your handbook easy to use and helpful to your Master Gardener activities as well as in your own landscape. ❋

University of Maryland Extension Master Gardener Vision
A healthier world through environmental stewardship.
• • • • •
University of Maryland Master Gardener Mission
Support the University of Maryland Extension mission by educating Maryland residents about safe, effective and sustainable horticultural practices that build healthy gardens, landscapes, and communities.

AUTHORS

Stephanie Pully, State Master Gardener Coordinator, University of Maryland Extension.

Jon Traunfeld, Center Director, Extension Specialist and Center Director, Extension Gardening, University of Maryland Extension.

Robin Hessey, Certified Professional Horticulturist and former Advanced Training Coordinator for the State Master Gardener Program, University of Maryland Extension.

PHOTOS

Derwood Demo Garden. University of Maryland Extension.
Butterfly weed and swallowtail butterfly. University of Maryland Extension.

2: TEACHING AND COMMUNICATION

Stephanie Pully

2 TEACHING AND COMMUNICATION

CONTENTS

2.1 Teaching Overview 9

2.2 Age-Appropriate Teaching 11

2.3 Communications Overview 12

2.4 Communication Methods 13

2.5 Giving a Great Presentation 20

2.6 Using Mass Media 24

2.7 Teaching Online 27

LEARNING OBJECTIVES

- Develop effective communication skills using multiple media resources
- Understand how to organize and simplify information
- Explain how to prepare and present a program
- Understand the value of publicity and marketing

INTRODUCTION

Teaching is a large part of what Master Gardeners do. There is, however, more to this task than simply talking at the front of a room or showing a PowerPoint presentation. Teaching involves preparation, careful attention to questions and discussion, and a willingness to share and explore. It's also a great way to expand your own knowledge base. It can be hard work, but it's also very rewarding. Your challenge is to make learning informative, fun, and satisfying for both you and your students.

The most effective adult educators are confident in their abilities, accepting of themselves and others, flexible, capable of admitting their limitations, and appreciative of the contributions of others. If this describes you, you are certain to succeed!

2.1 Teaching Overview

This chapter is targeted toward helping you learn how to access information and share it with your students, i.e., communication.

Teaching is simply communication that imparts knowledge, so in order to be a good teacher, you must be a good communicator. That involves three major concepts, which build on each other:

Information. As a Master Gardener, you want to provide practical advice to and share accurate knowledge with members of your community.

Listening. Before you do any teaching, you must first understand the information needs of your community. Good communication is more than just giving information—it is a two-way street.

Preparation. Once you know what needs to be communicated, you can organize your knowledge, resources and materials, practice your presentation, then—and only then—teach your students what they need to learn.

The topic of gardening involves a lot of factual and technical details, making your preparation even more important. Extension is an outstanding resource for teaching materials and guidance, so reach out for assistance as you need it.

Fielding questions

When students are trying to understand new material, they will ask a lot of questions. Maybe they need to better understand a detail or perhaps they are not getting the bigger picture. Give your audience space to ask their questions, and let them finish before giving your answer.

Make sure you understand the question! It is helpful to repeat the question back to the student to 1) ensure that the entire room has heard the question, and 2) give the student a chance to correct or amend the question, if necessary. This tactic also gives you some time to think about the question and how you will answer it.

Listen carefully to questions—the kinds of questions your students ask can help you understand which parts of the material they are comfortable with and where they might be having trouble.

Also try to understand the depth of the question. Is your audience looking for a simple answer, or do they need the complete story? Assessing this before you answer will always result in a better response.

Handling answers

Remember that the student knows different things than you do, and may or may not have a good grasp of plant nomenclature or a particular propagation technique. Try to use vocabulary that is familiar to the student. It can also be helpful to summarize the topic both before and after the conversation; sometimes the repetition itself will make the material more clear.

After answering the question, ask the questioner whether you have responded in a way that is helpful. If you find yourself unable to adequately answer a question because you need to do some research, that's okay! It's always best to give accurate information.

It is always better to give yourself time to offer a good answer than to give a poor answer quickly. If you cannot answer a question during the lesson, make a note of it, get the questioner's contact information and follow up with the answer later.

Use details to inform, not overwhelm

Be concise—say what you need to say—but use concrete details in your examples to create a picture in the mind of your students. Doing so will make the material easier to retain. You will learn to find a balance between staying on point and expanding on a subject; let your audience be the one to indicate whether or not you've provided sufficient information and take your cues from them.

Hands-on engagement "sticks" best

Students of all ages are better able to retain information (and ask better questions) when they are active participants. When designing learning activities, try to incorporate a hands-on component to the lesson. As an example, if you are giving a presentation on pruning, a live demonstration is good, but even better is allowing students to prune a plant themselves.

Not all subject material lends itself to this kind of instruction, but lessons that offer hands-on experience will be more effective in helping the students remember the material. Walks, tours, and field trips give students the chance to learn about a topic in the context of its environment, which results in even greater retention.

2.2 Age-Appropriate Teaching

You may do Master Gardener work with young people, but many times you will be teaching other adults. Children, teens, and adults all approach learning in different ways.

When teaching adults, keep the following in mind:

- Adults are participating by choice.
- Adults are generally more invested in learning and attach more value to the process because it was their idea.
- Adults have a broad base of experience from which to draw and share with others.

Also note that one's previous experiences might lead adult students to make incorrect assumptions about the material they are learning; for example, an amateur gardener may be following outdated wisdom about using pruning paint on freshly-cut wounds. Check with your students often to make sure everyone is on the same page.

Many adults face barriers to learning. Some may have unrealistic goals, or even diminished vision and hearing. Work with your students to find ways around frustration and make the material accessible to everyone. Be aware that:

- Adults are sensitive to failure in learning situations.
- Adults want information to be relevant to their needs and immediately applicable.

- Most adults want to learn how to perform a task or accomplish a goal and will be focused on the steps they need to take.

Adults respond better when the material is presented through the different senses. Try to design your lessons with hands-on experiences that engage as many of the senses (sight, sound, scent, taste, and touch) as possible.

When teaching children, keep the following in mind:

- Younger students have less experience on which to ground new knowledge. Establishing context can be helpful to younger learners.

- Children are motivated to learn through exploration and curiosity. Give younger students the freedom to explore a topic in a way that makes sense to them.
- Children have different strengths and learning styles, so it's great to let children choose how they learn. Some children learn by reading, some by watching, and some by doing. Letting children find their own way will make the lesson more relevant and give the students an opportunity to find their motivation to learn.

It's important to make sure that younger students are comfortable with the current step before moving on to the next.

2.3 Communications Overview

When providing information—in whatever form it takes—be as clear and coherent as possible. Use simple language, avoid slang and jargon, and only use technical language when you need to. If you do use a technical term, be prepared to explain it in terms that are familiar to your audience.

Using technology to communicate

Technology is a tremendous tool for communication. You have access to a world of information at your fingertips and can use technology to send text, pictures, sound, and even video around the world in seconds.

You may choose to use any number of technology applications in your talks and presentations. While technology is incredibly useful and powerful, it can also be complicated and temperamental. Always be prepared with a "Plan B" if something goes wrong. It can be helpful to have a volunteer on standby to help with such emergencies.

Important note about licensing and fair use

You always have the rights to use your own work as a Master Gardener. You have the right to use anything you create, anything you write, or any photographs you take.

When preparing materials for talks, newsletters, or other projects, it often makes sense to use the work of others. You may have found a picture that perfectly shows a flower you want to talk about or a diagram that clearly demonstrates a technique you want to explain.

Often, you will be able to find a picture or a drawing that does a better job than anything you could do or have the time to do. It's very easy to find artistic works on the Internet, but be careful. Just because the image you want to use is available on the Internet does not necessarily mean you are free to use it in your project.

You may need to follow the terms of a license in order to use someone else's work in your project. There are many different licenses

> **Online content reliability**
>
> It's tempting to look for answers on the Internet because searching is easy and takes little time to find a plethora of information. Beware—there is a great deal of incorrect information on the Internet. You should rely only on information sources that have a good reputation, like university websites (URLs ending in ".edu") and affiliated extension programs. These sites are usually good places to look for up-to-date, science-based information.

for artistic works, and they have different requirements. Some licenses will allow you to change the work to suit your purposes, while other licenses will only allow you to use the work intact. Some licenses require you to pay a fee to use the work, while other works are licensed to be used free of charge. Most licenses require some kind of attribution; you will need to credit the original creator of the work in your project. If you are using someone else's work in your project, you need to follow the terms of their license.

The only works you can freely use without any terms are those that have been released into the public domain along with some Creative Commons licenses.

Licensing is a complicated topic. The bottom line: if you are using other people's work in your project, always get written permission, credit the source and maintain good records. You can see examples of Internet citations at the end of most chapters in this book.

2.4 Communication Methods

There are myriad ways to communicate with your gardening community. You may want to combine or change methods, depending upon your audience. Following is a breakdown of all the ways you might communicate with your gardening community and how to apply them.

Writing

One of the best ways to share large amounts of information is through writing. As a Master Gardener, you will have ample opportunity to use your writing skills to help get information to your fellow Master Gardeners and the public.

You can help produce publications about gardening, prepare text for slide presentations, or write newsletters and columns for the local newspaper. (Later in this chapter you will find details on these methods and others.)

Getting organized at the outset will make your writing easier, better, and more fun. It's a lot like pruning—it's easier done when there are no leaves on the tree!

First, build an outline of the topics you want to cover. This will create a structure for what you want to write. It will help you arrange your subtopics, show you where you need to add more (or less) detail, and indicate places in your project where something is missing, and make the project much easier to manage.

A good outline should also naturally suggest a title for your project. A good title should be simple, short, and accurately capture your subject or topic. If your project is an overview, say so in the title. If your project is a focused piece on a particular plant, pruning technique, or any other specific topic, use the title to tell your reader. A good title is important because it is the first thing readers will see, and it is likely to influence whether or not they decide to read on.

Use the title to keep you focused on the overall picture, and use the outline as a map for your project. Develop and explain each topic in your outline. Use references to support what you say, and include a list of references at the end so your reader can learn more. Introduce each topic to help your readers keep track of their progress, and finish each topic with a quick summary to help readers remember what you've written. Try to move through the topics in your project in a logical way so that each topic builds on the last.

You might get stuck sometimes; it happens to everyone. If that happens, step back, look at the overview, and ask, "What am I trying to show the reader in this section?" Another good thing to ask from the readers' perspective is "What do I want my readers to understand after reading this section?" Often, these questions have a simple answer, which can be a good clue as to what you should write next.

If you're really stuck, put your project aside for a while and do something else. When you come back to it, chances are you'll have fresh perspective and insight about how to proceed.

Writing tips

- Keep your writing simple. Try to give each thought its own sentence and each topic its own paragraph(s). Break long sentences into shorter ones. Avoid slang, jargon, or obscure vocabulary. If you need to use technical language, explain it the first time you use it (not all of your readers may be familiar). If a topic is complicated and difficult to explain, consider breaking it up into subtopics so you can build a picture from simpler pieces. Try to find ways to communicate without confusion.

- As you write, don't be afraid to get help. If you are unsure about a term, check it in a dictionary. If you don't know how your project should handle capitalization or punctuation, take a look at a style guide. If you have questions about accuracy, look up the material in a reference work. If you can't find an answer, ask your colleagues for input or advice.

- Good writers use everything they can to make their projects better. You may want to use materials from somewhere else—for example, a photograph, an excerpt, or a statistic that makes your message clearer. Reminder: Always make sure you have permission to use other people's work before you add it to your project, and always give them written credit.

Email

Email is a quick and easy way to answer a single question, broadcast a message to a group, make an announcement, send an urgent request or forward a document. It is an indispensable tool for teachers and communicators and is sometimes the best (or maybe only) way to get out a quick missive to multiple people.

Email tips

- Email is a more relaxed way to communicate; but with so few social cues, it's very easy to misinterpret language. Always be respectful when using email. Try to keep email messages short and limited to one idea or topic.

- If sending a new email, write a subject line that immediately lets the reader know the topic of the email. An email

thread can wander away from the original subject line, so make sure that if the subject changes, the subject line changes along with it.
- When responding to email, always double-check the "To:" and "CC:" fields to make sure you're sending your message to the right person or people.

Multimedia

With multimedia features available on our phones and computers, we can greatly enhance our interactions by using photos and video. Instead of describing a plant over the phone, we can send pictures or video, making identification easier and less prone to error.

There are a lot of options for getting your multimedia online. Your extension office may maintain a website, or you could upload your images or videos to sites like Flickr, YouTube, or Vimeo. Check with the Extension office to find out what's available and whether there are specific policies or guidelines for posting material online.

Social media

Social media is not only a good way to distribute information to an entire community, it is also a great space for small conversations. With social media, you can build an online destination where people can share notes, experiences, and images. This helps to understand how people are gardening in your area, the challenges they face, and how you can help them achieve their goals.

Integrating social media with presentations

Many presenters fear that as they are talking, the entire audience will be staring down at their phones instead of listening to the presentation.

Well, if you can't beat 'em, join 'em! It's difficult for anyone to sit through and listen to an entire presentation without getting bored; people have shorter attention spans than they used to. Get people engaged by using social media before, during, and after your presentation. Here's how:

....

BEFORE YOUR PRESENTATION

Create and share the online event. Facebook, Twitter and Instagram are the most visible platforms to use. If you're a member of LinkedIn (which you should be), you can use that as well. Create a page or post dedicated to your presentation that includes essential information about your presentation:

- What is the event's main subject?
- When is it?
- Where is it?
- Why should they attend/view?
- Note any giveaways/incentives
- Invite questions in advance

You can send individual invites, directly message people and share with whomever you designate.

Come up with a hashtag. Short, sweet and catchy are the keys to a good hashtag. Some of the best ones are also humorous, like #brownthumb911. Once you've determined your hashtag, share it around and ask others to share it with their followers.

Put up advance teaser posts. Starting about a week to 10 days before your event, upload a few images or short-short videos that represent main topics in your presentation. Keep the images and any text very simple, but memorable and intriguing. The idea is to get people curious enough to want to know more.

DURING YOUR PRESENTATION

Plan to record your event. Arrange in advance to have a colleague or friend video your presentation. Afterward, you can post clips to your social media channels and then post links in your accounts for people who may have missed the live event.

Encourage people to use their phone at the outset. This might seem counter-intuitive, but this is a tremendously successful way to spread the word. Ask the audience to comment and share, post videos or photos, whatever they'd like to do. This is very valuable free publicity and will introduce you to many people who may not have known about Master Gardeners. Shared posts are a powerful way to build your audience.

Include info on your slides. There isn't much use in creating social media awareness if people don't know where to find you. Include your Facebook/Twitter/Instagram handle and event hashtag on each slide.

Encourage tweeted questions. This gives the shyer people in your audience a way to speak up without getting stage fright in front of a large group. The anonymity of a tweeted question also gives people the freedom to ask what they want without any judgment.

AFTER YOUR PRESENTATION

Post your own photos and share them. Again, this allows you to reach people who couldn't attend. It is also a good way to refresh people's memories about what they heard.

Encourage questions and comments. Take this opportunity to engage your audience to 1) answer any questions they may have and 2) to solicit feedback on the presentation itself. Did they learn something? Would they recommend it to a fellow gardener? What did you like most/least?

Thank your attendees. Nice manners are always well-received. Always conclude your talk by sincerely thanking people for attending, and that you hope to see them at your next event. If you have a mailing list or newsletter, let people know how to sign up.

Printed materials

Handouts, pamphlets, and "leave-behinds" (informational brochures) offer the opportunity for your audience to receive your message without you being present. They can pick up a printed piece and take the time to absorb it later. Materials like these are also handy for orienting people on a walking tour or letting them know what's next in the program they're attending.

Give careful consideration to the layout and presentation of information and make it easy for your readers to quickly find the information they want. Keep the information in small pieces so they can grasp it easily.

Published articles

Written articles for the local newspaper or community newsletters can be a great way to get your message out to a wide audience. The bigger the town or city, the bigger the exposure—but sometimes small-town papers (both online and print) can be the vehicle that covers the most important ground for you.

Article-writing tips

- Before you write your article, read the target publication to get a feel for the length, tone, and style of writing it uses.
- Use a logical structure to make your article easy to follow. Start with a short paragraph that grabs the reader's interest, then use the next paragraphs to backtrack and clearly tell the story of how the first paragraph came to be. Save the in-depth material for last, then write a conclusion that comes back around to your opening paragraph.
- Submit illustrative photos along with your article that improve its chances for publication.

If enough of your articles are published, you may even consider approaching the publication about writing a regular blog.

Graphics and visual aids

Graphics are an important part of any presentation; no one wants to sit through an all-text program. When used well, graphics can be helpful in expanding and reinforcing written and spoken material. For example, photographs can give context; illustrations can show detail and structure, and charts and graphs can be used to make data easier to understand. Some students process visual information better than spoken word, so using both will greatly improve your chances of getting through.

Graphics tips

- Consider using UME Master Gardener colors, fonts, and appropriate logos.
- When preparing graphics to use as part of a presentation, try to keep them as simple as possible while still conveying your message. A lot of detail will not only be lost when viewed at a distance, it could potentially confuse the viewer.
- Make or choose graphics that show only one subject at a time. Check a graphic's effectiveness with this test question: Does the graphic explain its part of the presentation on its own? If so, you've done a good job.
- Consider the size of the venue and number of people who will be in attendance, and judge the size of the graphics accordingly. Use graphics that are bold and large, and make use of intense color. For every 10 feet of viewing distance away from your graphic, you should increase the letter height by one inch.
- Keep text to a minimum; if a lot of text is required, create a supplemental handout.

Using posters, exhibits, and displays

Posters, exhibits, and displays can supplement a talk or stand on their own as part of a multimedia presentation or booth exhibit. Displays are a good in-person way to get a little bit of information to a lot of people—even passersby.

Display tips

- Keep it simple and limit each display to one topic or idea.
- Develop a story and show your idea or topic over time.
- Make it easy to navigate; use big headings so that people can easily find a section or subtopic.
- Make it easy to read at a distance; use big enough fonts so that someone can comfortably get a sense of the contents of the display from across the room.
- When staffing a display, answer questions simply, clearly, and with a good attitude. Don't be afraid to use the display to point out places that answer the question in more detail. If someone is reading the display, give them space to learn.

Formal speech

As a Master Gardener, you will have many opportunities to share what you know by speaking to others. This can happen by way of a formal presentation to the public, a group discussion, or even a conversation with a passerby while working in a demo garden. Master Gardeners also stage interactive workshops and tours.

Speech can also be used for broadcast by giving a presentation on television, on the radio or recording a podcast. In these formats, it's often more difficult for the audience to ask questions, so always try to be clear and careful when presenting lessons via broadcast.

(See **section 2.5, Giving a Great Presentation,** for a detailed guide to public Master Gardener talks.)

Casual conversation

Another way you can interact with the public is through informal conversations about gardening. When you start conversations with members of the public, keep in mind what they're asking about, what they want to know, and what their goals are.

Some folks may simply want a quick answer to a diagnostic problem, while others may want to have a long conversation about the virtues of tea roses. Listen carefully so you can respond in a way that gives them what they're looking for.

When you're having one of those long conversations, the subject matter can become complex or even go off-topic. As the expert half of the conversation, occasionally check in with the other person to make sure you're adequately answering his/her questions and addressing the topic in which they're interested.

Remember that listening is just as important as talking, and that the ability to listen well and respond on-point is what separates effective communicators from the rest.

Phone

Fortunately, we are no longer limited to just voice communications when using a phone.

18   Maryland Master Gardener Handbook   UME © 2025. All rights reserved.

With smartphone apps, Skype and Zoom (supported by most computers) we can also video-chat. These apps can be invaluable when you need assistance in the field or want to show a particular feature of a plant.

The ability to send a photo with a phone has also revolutionized the way you can answer questions. Being able to see what the caller sees allows you to zero in on the issue and offer a much better answer to the caller's question.

Learn what resources are available to you when answering calls. If you are answering calls at the extension office, get to know what reference materials are available to you there. Be familiar with the materials published by extension and how to order and distribute those materials to help answer questions.

Phone tips

- When the phone rings, try to put aside other tasks so you can concentrate on the caller and what they need. Introduce yourself, and then ask how you can help. Listen to what the caller has to say and what he or she needs.

- Chances are that when people call, they will have questions. Sometimes people may want to ask you a number of questions all at once (so that they don't forget to ask later). One way to cope with this is to get in the habit of taking notes when on the phone; make sure you have paper and pen or a computer handy.

- Before you answer a question, repeat or rephrase the question back to the caller. This will help you give the caller the most accurate information. When you have questions for the caller, repeat or rephrase their answer. This gives the caller a chance to correct any misunderstandings.

- Sometimes you may need to step away from the phone in order to get the caller the information they need. Ask the caller if they can stay on the line. If the caller wants to wait but your research is taking some time, return to the call periodically to let your caller know you're still working on their question and ask if they wish to continue waiting. If the caller needs to go, ask them how they would like you to get in touch with them and make sure you follow up with an answer.

- If you are answering the phone for someone else, be tactful. Protect your colleague's privacy by indicating to the caller that your colleague is unavailable, but do not give details. Offer to take a message. Don't hesitate to confirm the name and number of the caller or ask them to repeat their contact information to make sure you've copied it correctly.

- Only transfer the caller to another person when it's really necessary. Always explain that you are connecting the caller to another person. If the caller does not want to be transferred, offer to call them back.

- You will occasionally encounter difficult callers who may be having a bad day or dealing with a particularly frustrating problem. Remain calm and be kind. Listen and attempt to address the problem the caller is having, not their behavior.
- If the caller persists in being personally abusive, warn the caller that you will terminate the call. If the caller continues to be abusive, terminate the call and immediately note the time of the call and any information you have about the caller. Inform your colleagues about the caller and the nature of the call. You should never remain on a call if you feel at all unsafe doing so.
- When finishing a call, it is always polite to thank the caller. After the call is over, make a note of the call and log the call for Extension records.

Remember that you are representing both yourself and the Extension—a good impression will help build a nice relationship with the caller and serve to uphold the Extension's reputation in the community.

2.5 Giving a Great Presentation

Note: *Master Gardeners should always consult with the county coordinator to ensure that all presentation materials are correct and appropriate.*

A presentation can be as simple as an informal talk with an illustrated handout or two, or as complicated as a multimedia PowerPoint presentation in an auditorium. The key to success for either situation is *preparation.*

BASIC OUTLINE STRUCTURE

Introduction
- What the talk is about
- Use an attention-grabber

Body
- Main topic 1
  - Sub-topic 1
- 2nd major topic
  - 2nd sub-topic, etc.

Conclusion
- Review
- Re-state takeaway message
- No new material

The importance of preparation

Preparation is the most critical part of giving a good presentation. Each time you present, you are taking your audience on a journey to learn something new. Your audience will not know where you're going, but you as the presenter should have a good idea of the route and know your material well enough to guide everyone along.

Good preparation will put you at ease with the material and give you command of it. You'll know how long to talk, when you're running short on time and what to do about last-minute glitches. *Preparing well is the single best thing you can do to set yourself up for success.*

Organizing your presentation

As with writing, organization is an important part of preparing for a presentation. Being well-prepared will mark you as a professional and give you confidence during your talk.

Good organization will also help your students, who will pick up on the patterns in your talk and use that to get ready for new information. Good organization also gives your students context, which will help them place and retain new knowledge. Being organized can go a long way in making your presentation easier to digest and more fun for your students, too.

The easiest way to organize a presentation is to break it into topics. Start with the introduction, move from topic to topic in a logical order, and then end with a conclusion/summary. Don't forget to build in time for a Q&A session at the end!

- First, identify the most important ideas and concepts you want the group to learn. Put them in a logical order. Do not try to cover too much information in the amount of time given to you; it is better to teach a few ideas well than to cover many ideas incompletely. Don't forget that not all people learn the same way, so it's good to use several different methods to explain a single concept. Repeating the material multiple times in various ways will also help students retain the material. Build that into your talk.
- Draft an outline of what you want to teach. Include all of the parts of your presentation: the introduction, your chosen topics, and the conclusion. Read through your outline to see if the order makes sense and whether the right topics are grouped together. Each topic should build on the previous topic. A good outline can also serve as a talking guide for you!
- Use the outline to see how the topics work together. Check to make sure the topics you are presenting are in a good order—each new topic should build on the last. An outline is also useful for developing patterns in your presentation that your students might find helpful.
- Have a rough idea of how your presentation will go. Think about the kinds of questions your students may ask. Are there extra materials you might need to answer a question? If something unexpected happens, like a power outage, can you continue the presentation?
- Craft a strong introduction to begin your talk, one that will grab your audience. Your introduction might be a story, an anecdote, or some piece of interesting information about your topic.
- Let your introduction tell the whole story in broad strokes. Present your topics in order so that each builds on the information from the previous one. Let the conclusion tell the whole story again, but with a focus on the new information.
- Try to move through your topics in a straight line and avoid bouncing between topics. Having a good structure will make it easier for you to move smoothly through your presentation.
- A conclusion should wrap up the presentation by reinforcing the material that was covered. Remind your students what they learned and place it in a broader context—for example, how they might use this information in their own garden—to help them retain the information.

For more detail about crafting your presentation, please see the **Writing** section.

Getting organized is a lot of work. Expect to spend at least four times the length of your presentation in preparation.

Visual aids

If you have a lot of materials to prepare (slides, handouts, video, artwork, etc.), getting ready can take even longer, so start well in advance of your presentation date.

Visual aids can take many forms:

Images: Photos, illustrations, posters, storyboards

Graphics: Charts, graphs, infographics, diagrams and maps

Demos: In-person or online live demonstrations, or recorded video

Electronic presentations like slide shows and webinars (presuming there is power available)

Assessing the room

A few weeks before your appearance, make sure you'll have everything you need to give your presentation. Here are some things you may want to find out:

- **Appropriate furniture.** Will you need a podium? A table for presenting a demo? An easel for a poster?
- **Power outlet and extension cord.** Is there a power outlet available for your laptop? How long will your laptop work without being plugged in? Can the cord be run in such a way that you will not trip over it?
- **Access to light switches.** Do you need to turn the lights off for a PowerPoint presentation, and then back on for a demo? How much control do you have over which lights can be turned on and off?
- **Presentation equipment.** Does the room have a projector and a screen? Is the projector compatible with your laptop? Do you need an adapter?
- **Microphone.** Does the room have a microphone? How does it turn on? Can you give a presentation in the room if the microphone isn't working?
- **Contact information for the venue.** Is someone available to talk to if you need anything or something goes wrong?

The Extension office may have loaners you can borrow if you need to bring equipment to the venue. Check with the Extension for details on what equipment is available and the borrowing policies.

If possible, see where you will be presenting in advance. Give yourself at least 15 minutes to get acquainted with the space.

How big should the room be? One way you can get an idea of how many people are coming to your event is to ask attendees to preregister; this can give you a rough idea of how well your promotional efforts are working and where your attendees are coming from.

Practicing your presentation

Practicing your presentation will help you feel comfortable with the material and give you a chance to note any spots that require extra time or attention, where you need to take a break, and the overall sequence of topics.

Try not to practice your presentation word for word. It's helpful to practice a few key phrases where the information is important, but practicing the entire presentation too much can dull your delivery and make it more difficult for your students to pay attention to the material.

As you practice, keep track of time—it can go by faster than you expect. Set the stopwatch on your phone, especially if you're prone to expounding on topics or going off on tangents.

Presenting your material

Giving a presentation can be a challenge for people who aren't comfortable being the center of attention. It can also be difficult because it's live; there are few opportunities to stop, go back, and correct things. If you find that giving a presentation is stressful, one thing to remember is that everyone in the audience wants you to succeed. They are attending your presentation to hear what you have to say, and they have no interest in making that harder for you.

Start off with any "house announcements," note where the bathrooms are and where any refreshments are located. This is the time

to announce whether you're happy to take questions throughout the presentation, or whether you'd prefer the audience hold their questions until the end.

Start by grabbing your audience's attention with the great introduction you wrote, and then start to follow your outline. That will set expectations for what's to come and help frame the big picture in peoples' mind.

Maintain a welcoming but professional tone. Stories can be a great teaching tool, but be careful about using stories that stray into uncomfortable or contentious subjects (such as politics). Personal stories can be very effective, but try to make the story about your experience and how it relates directly to the material. Treat your audience with courtesy and respect, and trust them to do the same for you.

Check with your audience periodically to make sure that everyone can still hear you and see your visuals. Inform your students often about what's coming up next and remind them what was just presented.

Presenting for long stretches is hard on both the presenter and the audience, so don't skip over any breaks you've planned. This little

> **Reminder**: When answering a question, always repeat it so that everyone can hear it. When you're done answering, check with the audience to make sure you've answered their question to their satisfaction.

"brain rest" also gives your audience a chance to absorb what you've said so far.

As you present, try to keep an eye on the time. Note if there's a clock on the wall you can check while presenting, or leave your watch or phone on the table so you can stay on schedule. Make sure you move through your presentation quickly enough to get through all of the material and not be rushed at the end.

Wrap things up with your conclusion, then open things up for Q&A. Always plan for a Q&A session at the end of your talk, even if you permitted questions throughout your presentation. People who may have been reluctant to "interrupt" you will invariably wait and almost expect the opportunity to ask their question at the end.

After your presentation

After any presentation, take a moment to reflect on how it went. What worked well? What could be better? Did you have fun? Keep notes on how you might change the presentation next time.

If appropriate, ask students for feedback on the presentation. Ask them what they learned. Find out if there are any areas or topics where the students are less confident about the material. Ask your students how they might apply what they've learned so you can see how well they've assimilated the new information.

2.6 Using Mass Media

Using mass media—essentially television, radio, newspapers, magazines, and the Internet—is the quickest (and perhaps most effective) way to reach large and diverse numbers of people.

There are two main ways to access mass media: the free way (publicity, or PR) and the paid way (advertising). Sometimes you can get advertising for free, which is the best of both worlds!

Publicity

Social media can be a very effective (and free) way of notifying your community (or many communities) about your presentation or event, or even the Master Gardener program in general. (See the **Social Media** section in this chapter for detailed information.)

Aside from social media, newspapers (both print and online) are generally the best avenue for publicizing local news and messages.

First, you need to determine the reason anyone would want to be aware of your event. Then you must determine how to get that information to the public.

Begin by creating a local and regional media list of staff writers, freelance writers and reporters who work in the lifestyle or "features" section of the paper, which is where gardening usually lands. Contact each person on your list and describe why that paper's audience needs to know about your event. You will become a writer's best friend if you can write a press release for them, which is essentially doing their job for them. They can copy and paste your release right into their computer if it's written well enough. Once you establish this kind of relationship, you will rarely get a "no" to your proposal for an article.

You can also issue a free press release on your own through websites like **prlog.com**. New to press releases? There are a number of online guides to help you write an effective release. A quick Google search will turn up a number of results.

If the paper has a Community Calendar, you can likely get your event listed there. There are also free websites like **festivalnet.com** and **eventbrite.com** where you can publicize the details of your event at no cost.

Radio, while not as popular as it used to be, can still be a way to reach your local gardening audience. Check to see if your local stations have a gardening segment, and if not, you might want to start developing a relationship with the station's producer to serve as a volunteer resource for them. With a little luck and perseverance, you might be able to turn it into a regular appearance.

Advertising

Advertising is an important part of any communication effort. Building your audience through advertising and promotion makes your message more effective, if you have the resources to support it.

Word-of-mouth is an inexpensive way to build an invested audience, but it is slow and inefficient. Advertising through print media, radio, television, or social media can get your message out quickly, but may not generate much response. It's also very expensive because ads need to run multiple times to make an impact and reach enough people. This is where sponsors can come to the rescue.

A sponsor can be support your advertising efforts by paying some or all of the cost in exchange for a mention, signage, or other credit. You might be able to find sponsors

in your local business community—for example, a local garden center, community development organization, or even local stores, banks, or other members of the commercial sector. Always make sure the sponsorship terms are clearly defined and understood by both you and your sponsors, and that everyone agrees on requirements and responsibilities.

Planning your advertising spot

For an effective outcome, you'll want to consider your audience, prepare a script (or at least a topic outline), and practice your delivery so that you are comfortable with the material. When you practice, consider ways you may need to alter your presentation at the last minute to accommodate changes in time or venue.

Consider your audience. Think about who you want to reach with your presentation and make note of the age, knowledge level, and interest of your target audience. Also think about others you might reach with your presentation and try to develop your presentation to offer them something, too.

Consider the amount of time you have for your presentation. For a 30-second spot, you will only have time to cover one idea. A five-to ten-minute segment might give you enough time to explore one idea in depth or two short topics.

A 30-minute program might have space for one to three topics, depending on your material. Practice your presentation with a timer to be sure you can complete it without rushing.

Producing your content

Production can be a simple or an involved process. Traditional broadcast outlets such as commercial TV and radio stations usually have staff to help prepare you for an on-air appearance and can give you specific guidelines for presenting your material.

Prepare a script or an outline. Write down everything you want to say and the order you want to say it in. Take a look at your outline to see if parts of your presentation are too long or need more material.

If you're promoting an event, consider everything your attendees might need to know, such as:

- Name of the event
- Purpose of the event
- Date/time
- Location and any special instructions for getting to the event
- Is it outdoors or indoors? Is there a rain date? Where can people check to see if an outdoor event has been canceled?
- Information about tickets/admission
- Food and beverage availability, if any

For longer presentations, include a summary section so you can remind your audience of everything you've covered.

If you are presenting on television or video, decide what kinds of visual aids are appropriate. If you will be giving a demo of a technique or showing plant samples, make sure you plan to have everything ready to go when it's time to give your presentation. If you want to bring visual media, like a display board or graphic, give yourself enough time to prepare them in advance (or check with the Extension to see if they already have something you can use). Use visuals that are simple and can be easily read and understood at a distance. Check with the producer to make sure your visuals are in a format they can use.

When practicing with a script, use it to remind you of major points you want to make and particular turns of phrase you want to use. Try not to read verbatim or practice so much that you sound as though you've memorized it. Use the script to keep your place in the presentation and help you maintain a conversational tone when presenting.

Chances are you won't have a lot of time to give your presentation, and time will go by more quickly than you expect. Make a note of which parts of your presentation you can skip without making the presentation confusing; examples and anecdotes are often good to skip if you are pressed for time. Practice your presentation with and without these parts.

Meet with the production staff to go over your script and agree on which parts need emphasis and when to break. Ask the production staff for guidelines as to which clothing works well with the camera (i.e., colors, patterns, etc.), and check to see if they will apply makeup so you can look your best while presenting. The staff is there to help you succeed, so don't hesitate to ask for advice. Your success is also their success.

If you are producing your own television content for public access broadcast, most local studios have staff or volunteers to offer advice or production assistance.

Appearing on-air or live recording

Live presentations add extra challenges. Be clear, concise, and direct when you speak. Stay on topic and avoid rambling or digression; for this medium, you want a solid, simple overview. Do everything you can to avoid "and um," "uh," and "you know." If you know your presentation well enough you shouldn't have to rely on these mental pauses to find your place.

Will other people be appearing in the segment? Be courteous and give everyone a turn to speak, even if you have to sacrifice a little bit of your own material.

When you are ready to present your material, keep the following in mind:

- Time often goes by more quickly than you expect.
- Use simple English, be clear and direct, and avoid slang and jargon.
- Speak slowly and give your audience time to hear what you're saying.
- Keep stories or examples to a minimum and use them only to emphasize or clarify.
- Stay focused; make sure you have time to cover all parts of your presentation.
- Remember to give a summary at the end of your presentation.
- Tell your audience how to obtain additional information and how to find you on social media.
- Remember to relax, smile, and do your best to have fun!

Building your local audience

The best way to develop a following is to offer reliable information on a regular basis. Build the trust of your audience by offering them carefully prepared material that always contains something new or different, and maintain that trust by giving them a schedule they can count on. Once people know when and where they can find you, you and your material will become a habit. This is also how word-of-mouth recommendations get started.

Tip: If you have a recurring presentation like a blog, podcast or a radio segment, produce your content in advance. There will be times when you are very glad you did.

2.7 Teaching Online

While Extension programs were originally created with the idea of reaching people through in-person, hands-on programming, times have certainly changed. We are now living in a digital, technology-laden world!

Although it may be different than in-person programming, teaching programs online has a multitude of benefits:

- Physical space capacity is unlimited. Your audience can be as large as you like!
- Participants who generally do not like asking questions or participating in person may feel more comfortable doing so in an online setting.
- You can share more resources than in an in-person class in the forms of additional PDFs, photos, website URLs, and more.
- You can record sessions for participants to watch later.
- You can have a broader range of speakers and reach a broader audience because they do not have to travel.
- You can make accommodations for accessibility.

Method of delivery

There are two main types of online presentations and courses: synchronous and asynchronous. Here are explanations and examples of each:

Synchronous

- All participants learn together, live, at a designated time
- Content is released on predetermined dates throughout a course
- Presentations are delivered online via video-conferencing software
- Live demonstrations are delivered via a live video streaming service

Asynchronous

- All course content is immediately available
- Participants work through the material on their own time/at their own pace
- Students can independently view pre-recorded videos on YouTube or other sites
- Students can watch and participate in online modules

When choosing which method of delivery to use, consider what fits your audience and topic best. If your topic requires or invites discussion amongst participants, consider hosting it in a synchronous fashion so that participants can discuss topics in real-time. If the lesson has multiple parts or takes a long time to get through, consider asynchronous delivery so participants can take breaks as needed. If you are unsure that your audience will have consistent access to high-speed Internet or wifi, consider asynchronous content.

Planning an online program

Delivery platform. Which platform will you use to host your program? Will it be public, require registration, or require an account? Consider platforms that do not require an account if you would like to have a larger audience.

Promotional materials. How will you advertise your program? Where will you post the materials?

Communication. How will you advertise your program? How will you allow the audience to submit questions before, during, and after the presentation? How will you follow up after the program with additional information? How can participants ask for help to address technical issues during the program?

Program resources. How will you share any pertinent readings or resources with participants? Do you have an outline or notes you can post ahead of time for participants to follow along with?

Submissions. Will participants need to submit any questions, assignments, or other materials? How will you accept and organize those submissions? Do they need to be visible to all participants or should they only be available to the organizers or presenters?

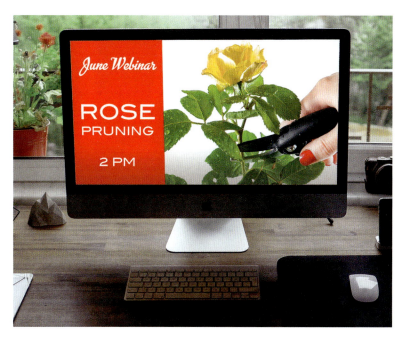

Discussions. Will you allow participants to ask questions during the presentation or after, and if so, how will they be able to ask and have their questions answered?

Evaluations and feedback. How will participants be able to give you feedback on your program?

Accessibility accommodations. Make sure you have a plan to address requests for accessibility, such as low- or no-vision or hearing-impaired participants.

Best practices for online instruction

Each online program will be different, but there are some best practices to keep in mind that work for all online programs:

- Have a host and/or moderator in addition to a speaker. Hosts/moderators can help troubleshoot technical difficulties, mute participants if needed, or handle other tasks that can generally interrupt a speaker's flow. The host/moderator can also help ask questions to the speaker.

- Ask questions out loud, even if they have been typed into a chat box. Participants will not always know how to view the chat box, or may be multi-tasking and listening only. Make sure you read questions out loud so that participants who are not reading will know what you are answering.

- If you plan to record, let participants know both verbally and by typing it into the chat box. Remind participants again when the recording has started. If you are on a platform that allows participants to share video and use a mic, note that they may turn off their video and mute themselves to avoid being recorded.

- Ensure that all participants are muted and their video is turned off to reduce distractions during the presentation.

- Stay on time! Have a plan for responding to questions in case you run out of time.

- Make sure the presenter and host/moderator are prepared in advance. Plug your computer in to the power

source, check your Internet connection, and make sure there are no distractions or loud noises in the background.

- For longer presentations, consider adding some variety such as a change of topic, speaker, pace, or tone. Try adding interactive pieces to the presentation to keep the audience engaged. ❋

Special thanks to Robin Hessey, Certified Professional Horticulturist and former Advanced Training Coordinator for the State Master Gardener Program, University of Maryland Extension.

About your volunteer responsibilities

To maintain Master Gardener certification, volunteers commit to provide 20 hours of volunteer time and 10 hours of continuing education every year.

All UME Master Gardeners are required to record their volunteer activities in the Volunteer Management System (VMS). VMS is used by Master Gardener volunteers to keep an accurate account of their volunteer hours and continuing education, and to report contacts.

Keeping an accurate account of Master Gardener activities is vital to the work of extension. The information that Master Gardeners report is used to monitor the progress of the program, identify needed changes, evaluate the effectiveness and productivity of Master Gardener efforts, and document program impact. To log in, visit: **vms.umd.edu.**

AUTHORS

2024 Edition:
Stephanie Pully, State Master Gardener Coordinator, University of Maryland Extension.

Original authors:
Penn State Extension Master Gardener Program.

REFERENCES

Abbey, T., Adam, S., Ankney, G., Auger, L., Balk, M., Barbercheck, M., Wyble, S. (2016). In Amanda Kirsten (Ed.) *Penn State Extension Master Gardener Manual* (pp. 1-16). University Park, Pennsylvania: Penn State Ag Communications and Marketing. Used with permission.

University of Maryland. Fall, 2020. *Keep Teaching.* University of Maryland website. svp.umd.edu/keepteaching

Rissa Karpov, AliveTek, Inc. *Delivering Content Effectively.* University of Maryland Extension website. lts.umd.edu/Projects/Garden/DeliveringContentEffectively/story_html5.htm

PHOTOS/ILLUSTRATIONS

Hyacinths. Retrieved July 1, 2024 from pixabay.com.

Fauxels, 2019. *Man in Beige Blazer Holding Tablet Computer* [photo]. Retrieved September 12, 2020 from pexels.com.

Boy planting tomato [photo]. Retrieved July 1, 2024 from pixabay.com.

Young man using laptop [photo]. Retrieved September 12, 2020 from pixabay.com.

Conference break-out session [photo]. Retrieved September 12, 2020 from pixabay.com.

Phone with picture of leaf/pest problem [photo]. Retrieved September 10, 2020 from pxfuel.com. Modified.

Millot, A. (1857-1921). Nouveau Larousse illustré, insectes [illustration]. Modified.

Lecturer giving slide presentation [photo]. Retrieved September 11, 2020 from needpix.com

Mass media depiction [illustration]. Retrieved September 13, 2020 from pixabay.com

Woman giving radio interview [photo]. Retrieved September 13, 2020 from pexels.com

Computer screen for rose-pruning webinar. Retrieved October 6, 2020 from pixabay.com

Young woman instructing a video class [photo]. Retrieved October 6, 2020 from pixabay.com

3: ECOLOGY

Sylvan R. Kaufman, Ph.D.

3 ECOLOGY

CONTENTS

3.1 Maryland's Ecology 35

3.2 Maryland's Landscape 39

3.3 Plant and Wildlife Communities 42

3.4 Species Interactions 45

3.5 Species and Populations 48

3.6 Ecosystems 52

3.7 What Is a Wetland? 56

3.8 Why Are Wetlands Important? 59

3.9 Wetland Regulations 60

3.10 How to Preserve Wetlands 61

LEARNING OBJECTIVES

- The influence of local climate and geology on plant and animal communities
- How land-use changes and gardening practices can affect the health of watersheds
- Interactions among plants, animals, and their environment
- How and why plant and animal communities change over time
- How human activities affect the flow of energy and nutrients through the landscape
- The value and function of wetlands in the ecosystem
- Basic characteristics of tidal and non-tidal wetlands

INTRODUCTION

Ecology is the study of how organisms interact with each other and their environment. Whether you garden to grow prize-winning tomatoes, to beautify your landscape, or to attract butterflies, learning the principles of ecology can help you create a healthy, sustainable landscape.

As gardeners we think about the colors and textures plants give to a garden and whether they contribute food or fragrance. We choose where to situate a particular plant thinking about its needs for sun, water, and soil type. We learn to protect plants from pests and diseases and to encourage pollinators and seed-dispersers. The principles of ecology can tie together all of these practices by taking into account:

- The climate and soils of the region
- The adaptations plants will make to grow well under particular conditions
- The helpful and destructive animals or fungi attracted by certain plants
- The cycles of water, energy, and nutrients in our landscape

If you think of your garden and landscape as an ecological system, you begin to see the connections between plants, animals, fungi, bacteria, soils, water, and sunlight.

In this chapter there is a special focus on wetlands because of their importance as ecosystems in Maryland and because of the impact gardening and landscaping can have on water quality and the health of the Chesapeake Bay.

3.1 Maryland's Ecology

To place the state of Maryland in a biological and geological context, we will first look at how global processes affect the state, which other continents share a similar biome, and the climate and geology of the region.

UME © 2025. All rights reserved.

3: Ecology   35

The biosphere

Some processes that affect life in Maryland happen on a global scale, like changes in climate and sea level. In the biosphere—the portions of the Earth that support life—major natural and human-caused changes can have global impacts. For example:

Rises in sea-surface temperatures in the eastern Pacific and low barometric pressure lead to a global weather system called El Niño. Maryland tends to experience wetter than normal winters in El Niño years. Periods with low sea-surface temperatures and high barometric pressure create La Niña, tending to lead to drier winters in Maryland.

The use of chemicals, including chlorofluorocarbons (CFCs - used in refrigeration and air conditioning) were found to be depleting the ozone layer in the 1970s. A global accord to reduce emissions of ozone-depleting chemicals was reached, but levels in the atmosphere still remain high enough that an "ozone hole" (actually a thinning of the ozone layer) happens over the Antarctic and southern South America every year.

Globally, *average temperatures have been rising* faster than normal due to human activities such as the burning fossil fuels and deforestation that release greenhouse gases (carbon dioxide, nitrous oxide, methane, and fluorinated gases). Greenhouse gases trap heat in the Earth's atmosphere. Increasing temperatures are reflected in the revised Hardiness Zone Map. (See references at end of this chapter and the Hardiness Zone Map in the Resource Appendix.)

Sea level continues to rise as global temperatures increase, resulting in more frequent coastal flooding, loss of coastal wetlands, and increased rates of erosion. According to the Maryland Department of Natural Resources (MD DNR), Maryland's sea level has risen by one foot in the last 100 years. This is slightly higher than the global average because the land in our region is slowly sinking due to natural geologic processes. Scientists estimate that sea level will rise another 3.7 feet or more in the next 100 years in Maryland.

Beside increasing temperatures, climate change may also result in more severe storms, more intense heat waves, and an increase in precipitation in this region, but it is difficult for climate models to predict exactly what will occur at the regional level.

Biomes

The biosphere can be divided into biomes (large areas with relatively uniform vegetation). The type of vegetation in a biome is mainly determined by mean annual temperature and precipitation.

The major terrestrial biomes of the world include tundra, desert, grassland, tropical forest, temperate forest, and boreal forests. Maryland is located in the temperate forest biome.

Most temperate forests grow where there are distinct seasons and where there is a moderate amount of precipitation. Temperate forests are not as diverse as tropical forests, but they harbor some of the tallest living organisms, including giant sequoias in North America. Other major temperate forests grow in western Europe, southern South America, and eastern Asia.

Not surprisingly, many popular ornamental non-native woody perennials come from these other temperate forest biomes (e.g., forsythia from eastern Asia and English ivy from western Europe). Houseplants are more likely to come from tropical forest biomes (e.g., philodendron and peace lily) or desert biomes (e.g., crown of thorns and cactus).

The region

Not all of Maryland is forested, and vegetation types differ considerably within the state. At the regional level, vegetation changes because of climactic differences, geology, and topography. In the mountains of western Maryland, higher elevations have colder winters, more snowfall, and slightly cooler summer temperatures. The ancient sandstones and shales of the Appalachian Mountains make up the base of the soils, and forests of hemlock, white pine, and northern hardwoods grow well. On the coastal plain the topography is much flatter, temperatures are slightly warmer, and the soils are formed from deep deposits of sand and gravel or silt from rivers. Mixed loblolly pine and oak forests are common on the coastal plain. Chapter 5 (Soil Properties) contains more information on Maryland's soil types.

Using the geological features of Maryland's landscape, the state can be divided into five physiographic regions (see Figure 3-A).

Appalachian Plateau: Garrett County and Allegany County west from Dans Mountain are characterized by folded bedrock made up of shale, siltstone, and sandstone.

Ridge and Valley: The eastern part of Allegany County and all of Washington County are part of the province where rivers have carved deep valleys through the rock layers.

Blue Ridge: The area of Frederick County between Catoctin Mountain and South Mountain lies within the province, characterized by ridges of quartzite rock.

Figure 3-A. The physiographic regions of Maryland

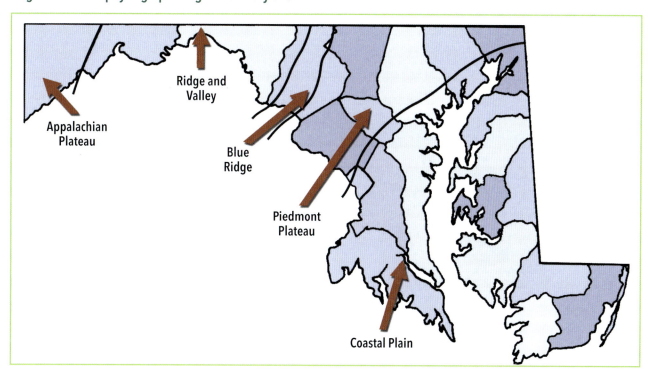

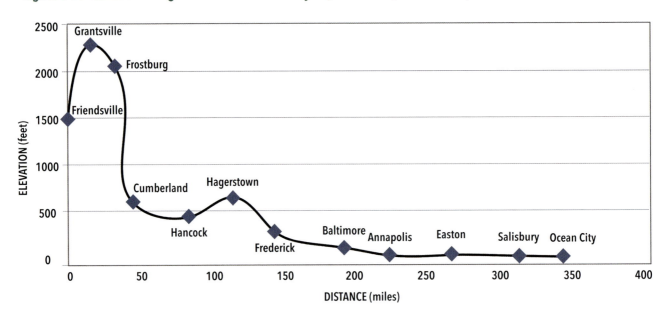
Figure 3-B. Elevation change: Friendsville-Ocean City (I-68 to I-70, then Rte. 50)

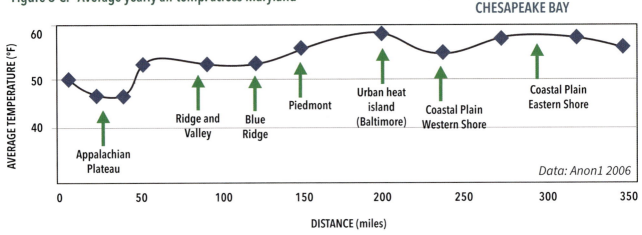
Figure 3-C. Average yearly air temp. across Maryland

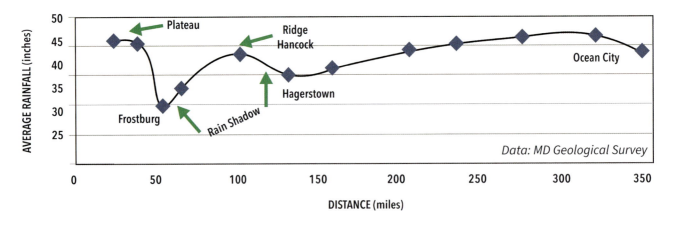
Figure 3-D. Average yearly rainfall across Maryland

Piedmont Plateau: This region runs from the Catoctin Mountains east to the fall line, running through the eastern borders of Montgomery and Howard Counties following roughly along Interstate 95. You can see the change in elevation at the fall line at Great Falls National Park on the Potomac River.

Coastal Plain: Underlain by sediments like sand, gravel, silt, and clay this region stretches east from the fall line to the Atlantic Ocean.

Geography influences differences in climate within Maryland. Maryland is located between 75° to 79° West longitude and 38° to 40° North latitude. At this latitude and longitude the prevailing winds are from the west. We have well-defined seasons, with most plants going dormant in winter (from about November to April), depending on location. Maryland covers an area of 12,303 square miles and is 80% land and 20% water. The land gradually rises as you move west from the Coastal Plain to the Piedmont (see Figure 3-B.)

This change in elevation corresponds with changes in average yearly air temperatures and rainfall (Figs. 3-C, 3-D). Near large urban areas such as Baltimore, there are higher average temperatures as heat radiates from paved surfaces. Less vegetation is present to cool the air. Mountains disrupt air flow causing rain shadows, which are areas on the eastern side of the mountains that receive less rainfall.

These regional geographic, geologic, and climatic differences determine the types of soils in your landscape and the native plant communities. Hardiness zone maps reflect minimum winter temperatures and roughly follow Maryland's changing elevation.

Understanding your soils and the climate of your region will help you to select the right plants for your landscape.

3.2 Maryland's Landscape

To an ecologist, a landscape is an area containing various plant and animal communities or different uses of the land. For example, a residential development with lawns and trees might be surrounded by a ribbon of wooded stream, and an office complex and highways with little to no vegetation.

Watersheds

One way of using natural boundaries to subdivide the landscape is to think about watersheds.

Geologist John Wesley Powell described a watershed as:

> *"…that area of land, a bounded hydrologic system, within which all living things are inextricably linked by their common water course and where, as humans settled, simple logic demanded that they become part of a community."*

Within a watershed, all the water on or under the land drains to one common place. In Maryland, most water drains into the Chesapeake Bay and Atlantic Ocean. In far western Maryland, water from the Youghiogheny watershed drains into the Ohio River and from there to the Mississippi River and Gulf of Mexico. In the southeastern most section of Maryland, water flows into the Atlantic Coastal Bays.

Increasingly, government agencies (such as EPA and MD DNR) collect data based on watershed boundaries. Many communities also have watershed organizations (see the Chesapeake Bay Program and other references at the end of this chapter). Landscaping practices are often connected to water use and cleanliness. Examples of landscaping practices that conserve water include:

- Choosing drought-tolerant plants
- Mulching
- Drip irrigation
- Rainwater collection

Stormwater runoff collects sediments, excess fertilizers, herbicides, pesticides, and other pollutants and carries them into streams and wetlands. Keep water cleaner by:

- Reducing the use of chemicals
- Preventing erosion
- Cleaning up other pollutants
- Slowing the flow of stormwater

From forests to farms

Most of Maryland's watersheds have gone from being forested to a mix of land uses, including residential, industrial, and agricultural. It is important to learn a little about the history of Maryland's landscape to understand how ecological processes have changed over time and how land use affects the ecology of an area:

1600s: 90% of Maryland was forested with a mix of hardwood and pine forests. The Native American Indians cleared small plots of land for agriculture and burned some forests to keep the understory clear of vegetation.

1700s: Extensive deforestation began in the mid-to-late 1700s as settlers cleared fields and iron furnaces consumed wood for smelting iron ore.

1800s: The invention of the steam engine and the circular saw expanded forest cutting into the mountains and valleys. By the mid-1800s, Maryland had lost half its forests. As a result of this massive deforestation, many areas had terrible erosion problems and streams were choked with sediments. Some stream valleys and floodplains are still covered by several feet of sediment.

1900s: The introduction of diseases such as chestnut blight and Dutch elm disease killed off millions of trees. Gypsy moth infestations killed thousands of oak trees. Decreases in fire frequency have favored fire-intolerant species such as red maple and American beech over fire-tolerant species such as loblolly pine and oak.

Agricultural land use began to decline after the Civil War and into the 20th century. Forest conservation initiatives included massive replanting of cutover forests and abandoned farm land. Some land was converted to pine plantations to provide an alternative income source. The soils of abandoned agricultural lands were often depleted of topsoil and compacted by farm machinery, making forest regrowth a slow process. Many regenerating forests have trees with relatively uniform ages.

1950s – present: By 1950, forest cover had reached about 46% in Maryland through natural regeneration and tree planting. Since the 1960s however, forest cover has declined to about 40% as second-growth forests are cut to make way for housing developments, roads, and office parks (MD DNR). The remaining forests continue to mature and fewer new stands of trees grow.

As you will learn in the section on succession, having mixed ages of vegetation can add to the overall biodiversity and stability of an ecosystem. Programs such as Program Open Space, the Forest Conservation Act, Rural Legacy program, and Treemendous Maryland work toward preserving and restoring Maryland's forests.

Urbanization

More than 80% of Marylanders live in urban areas, according to the U.S. Census Bureau. (An urban area is defined as having more than 1,000 people per square mile.) Urbanization has a tremendous impact on ecological processes, and it is important to understand how your landscape is affected:

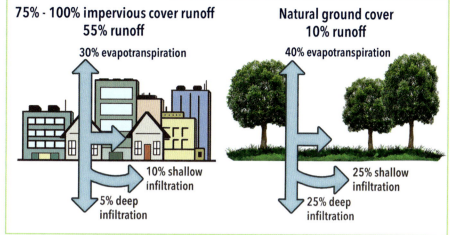

Figure 3-E. Stormwater infiltration and runoff: pervious vs. impervious surfaces

U.S. Environmental Protection Agency, Washington, D.C. "Protecting Water Quality from Urban Runoff." Document No. EPA 841-F-03-003.

Increase in area of impervious surfaces. Because impervious surfaces like roads, roofs, and sidewalks do not let water drain through, runoff increases dramatically. In a forest, only about 10% of the water that falls during a rain storm runs off into streams and wetlands. In a watershed with 10-20% impervious cover, runoff increases to 20%, enough to increase flooding and erosion in stream channels (see Figure 3-E). If you live in an urban or suburban area, think about the amount of impervious cover around your home, such as driveways, sidewalks, patios, and roofs.

Stream channelization. Channelization removes natural curves that slow the flow of water. Urban stream banks are often armored with stone or cement to reduce erosion caused by the faster flowing water. The stormwater runoff, besides being greater in volume, also picks up pollutants that may harm aquatic life. The water in urban streams is often warmer because of the lack of tree cover, and the warmer water causes a change in the species that can live in the stream.

Soil alteration. Soils are often significantly altered in urban environments through compaction, pollution, and topsoil removal. It may be difficult to get plants to grow without amending or even replacing soils. Compacted soils lack air and water spaces and channels for roots to grow through. Often street trees are planted in special artificial soils that hold moisture and air because their roots cannot spread as much as they could in a forest or even a yard.

Changes to plant and animal communities. Habitat becomes divided into smaller and smaller pieces as roads and buildings are constructed. Animals that migrate or have large territories are killed crossing highways or find barriers to movement. Plant populations become fragmented and may have difficulty dispersing their seeds or being pollinated. Some plants and animals adapted to urban environments begin to thrive, displacing more sensitive species.

Forest fragmentation

Think of the urban landscape as a quilt. It consists of patches of forest, backyards, parking areas, abandoned lots, and buildings sewn together by roads, streams, and railway lines (see Figure 3-F).

Large patches will support more species than small patches, and species must have a way to move from one patch to another. If you transform your backyard into a habitat suitable for native plants and wildlife, it provides a tiny refuge. If you convince your neighbors to do the same, you create a larger habitat that might attract migratory birds and a greater diversity of butterflies.

In a community, focusing on preserving high-quality forests and wetlands and connecting them through corridors of green space to other parks and preserves will do more to enhance the environment than preserving scattered small spaces. Tree cover is particularly important in our temperate forest biome because so many plants and animals rely on trees for food and shelter. Forested buffers along streams can act as corridors. Corridors that cross roads should have safe passageways either under or above the road for animals.

Figure 3-F.   Forest fragmentation

Roads and development often isolate patches of natural habitat. Corridors between isolated patches can be formed from rivers or by linking undeveloped areas and parks.

3.3 Plant and Wildlife Communities

This section explores what organisms physically need to survive in a particular place.

What organisms need to survive

Habitat is the physical space that provides the environment and resources needed by a population to survive and reproduce. The habitat for a holly tree would have enough space, nutrients, light, and water to support the growth of the tree. Insects would be essential for pollination because hollies have separate male and female trees. The climate would have to be cold enough in winter to freeze the fruits and make them palatable to birds. Birds ensure that the fruits, with their seeds, are dispersed. So the holly shares its habitat with pollinators, birds, and other plants. The assemblage of all the species in a given area is considered a community.

A garden provides habitat for the plant community you choose as well as for species that choose to make it their home. Suppose you have a community of beans, lettuce, and cucumbers. Each requires some amount of light, water, and nutrients. You may supply water through irrigation and nutrients in the form of fertilizer or compost. Rhizobia bacteria associate with the bean roots enabling them to use nitrogen from the air. Some of the excess nitrogen leaches out of the roots benefitting the lettuce and cucumbers. Mexican bean beetles and cucumber beetles arrive to eat the bean and cucumber plants. Aphids appear and in turn attract ladybugs. A mockingbird drops in to snap up a bean beetle. The lettuce benefits from the shade of the beans and cucumbers. When the lettuce flowers, it attracts pollinators. Your garden has become habitat for a community of plants, insects, bacteria, birds, and more.

Even though all these organisms share a habitat, they do not have exactly the same environmental and resource requirements. A species' niche describes all of the environmental conditions and resources required for it to maintain a viable population. It does not refer to a physical space, but rather to the whole set of conditions under which the species can survive and reproduce.

The idea of a niche was first described by ecologist Robert MacArthur in 1955. MacArthur wanted to know how five different species of warblers could all live together in the spruce forests of the northeastern U.S. All of the warblers are about the same size and all feed on insects. Why didn't they compete with each other for food? MacArthur's observations led him to find that the different warbler species fed in different parts of the spruce tree. For example, the Cape May warbler fed near the tops of the trees, looking for insects in new buds and needles. The bay-breasted warbler fed mainly on interior branches. Later studies showed that because the birds nested at slightly different times of the year, their peak requirements for insects differed and that some of the birds had different feeding strategies, such as chasing flying insects rather than picking them out from among the foliage.

Learning the niche requirements for plants you want to grow will require research on their life cycle, resource needs, and other organisms with which they associate. The ideas of companion planting and intercropping comes from learning which plants' niches complement each other.

Microclimates

In choosing the perfect spot for a plant, it is important to assess the microclimates in your landscape. Microclimates occur when some feature of the landscape creates a difference in temperature, moisture, or sun exposure. On a large scale microclimates are affected by:

Topography. Because cold air flows downhill, valleys can be cooler than ridge tops. But hilltops are exposed to high winds that can dry out plants and cause wind damage.

Large bodies of water. Water moderates temperatures making winter and summer temperatures less extreme.

Urban areas. A heat-island effect occurs in urban areas as buildings and pavements absorb heat and radiate it back into the air at night. Temperatures in winter and summer are hotter in urban areas compared to nearby rural areas.

On a backyard scale, the house, driveway, fences, decks, water features, raised beds, rocks, and soil type affect microclimates. For example, the north side of a house gets less sunlight and has slightly cooler temperatures because of the shade cast by the building. Surface temperatures next to a grassy lawn will be lower than near an asphalt driveway. A rock or fence can provide shelter from wind. Small-scale microclimates are most affected by:

- Aspect: direction a slope or wall faces
- Temperature: presence of vegetation, surface color, and surface evenness
- Water: relative humidity or soil moisture

Water gain/loss

All organisms need water to survive, but they require different amounts and have different ways of obtaining and conserving it (see Figure 3-G). Plants obtain most of their water from the soil through their roots. A few plants, like air plants and other bromeliads, can absorb some of their water from moist air. Plants in dry environments often have adaptations for conserving water, including storing water in their roots, stems, or leaves or reducing evaporation by having small leaves or leaves with hairy or waxy leaf coatings.

Animals obtain most of their water by eating and drinking. Most animals conserve water by finding shelter, but some have special adaptations. The hard shells of beetles help reduce evaporation, and some have an extra waxy coating to reduce water loss. Desert-dwelling kangaroo rats concentrate their urine to retain more water.

Energy and nutrients

All organisms must obtain energy and carbon from some source. Most plants obtain their energy from sunlight and obtain carbon molecules from the air through the process of photosynthesis. During photosynthesis, energy from the sun is used to convert carbon dioxide to carbohydrates. Plants obtain nutrients from the soil through their roots. A few plant families like the pea family (Fabaceae) have bacteria associated with their roots to help the plant obtain nitrogen.

About 90% of plant species associate with fungi called mycorrhizae, which help obtain nutrients for the plant in exchange for the plant providing carbon in the form of sugars to the fungi. You will learn more about the metabolic processes of plants in **Chapter 4** (Botany).

Animals obtain carbon and energy from organic molecules. The organic molecules and nutrients come from whatever food the animal eats. Much of animal behavior centers

Figure 3-G. Water gain/loss in plants and animals

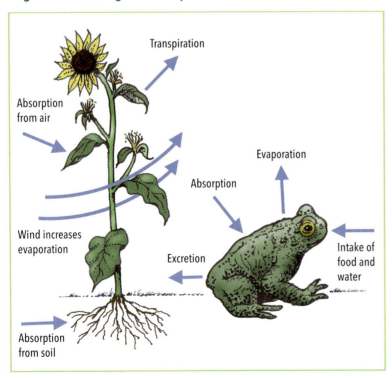

Plants gain water through their roots and sometimes from the air. Animals gain water through what they eat and drink. Plants lose water through evaporation and transpiration, whereas animals lose water through evaporation and excretion.

on the search for food because it costs energy to find and consume it. For example, squirrels will immediately eat sweet, fall-germinating white oak acorns when they find them but will only partially eat or bury the tannin-laden, spring-germinating red oak acorns. They dig up some of the cached acorns when food is scarce in winter/early spring.

Physiology

An organism's physiology determines its needs for energy, water, and nutrients. Adaptations to obtaining and conserving water, energy, and nutrients described above will determine what habitat requirements an organism needs. Matching "the right plant to the right place" means understanding a plant's physiological requirements and matching those to the right habitat. Providing wildlife habitat for specific animals also requires understanding that animal's physiological needs.

3.4 Species Interactions

Organisms never live independently. They all serve different purposes within a community. This section explores the roles species play within the community and how they interact with each other.

Functional groups

Sometimes it is useful to think of different organisms by the functions they perform in the environment. One way to group species is by how they obtain their energy and nutrients:

- *Producers* produce their own energy, e.g., grass
- *Herbivores* eat plants, e.g., rabbits
- *Carnivores* eat other animals, e.g., wolves, river otters
- *Decomposers* feed on dead organic material, e.g., earthworms

You could also group organisms by the type of interactions they have:

- *Mutualists*: interactions benefit both organisms, e.g. bumblebee as pollinator, blue jay as seed disperser
- *Parasites*: one organism benefits by causing harm to another, usually by feeding on it, e.g., ticks and dodder (*Cuscuta* spp.)
- *Competitors*: two organisms compete with each other for limited resources, e.g., gardeners vs. slugs

Think about the groups of species present in your garden. You may have herbivores like cucumber beetles, aphids, and voles. Predators might include spiders, ladybugs, and birds. Decomposers dwelling in the compost include earthworms, fungi, and bacteria. Bumblebees pollinate the tomatoes and peppers. You act as a seed disperser, eating fruits and saving seeds for next year's crops, as well as a competitor to other fruit and seed-eaters.

Native pollinators

Gardening success depends on pollination. In our region, most plants are either wind- or insect-pollinated. Wind-pollinated flowers are often relatively inconspicuous and produce large amounts of pollen. Examples of wind-pollinated plants include pines, oaks, grasses, and ragweed.

There is an incredible diversity of insect pollinators. Native insect pollinators include species of solitary bees, bumblebees, wasps, butterflies, beetles, and flies. Honeybees were introduced from Europe in the early 1600s. The ruby-throated hummingbird acts as one of the few vertebrate pollinators in Maryland. Some pollinators are generalists, pollinating many species of plants, whereas others specialize and pollinate only one or a few plant species.

The economic value of crops pollinated by native pollinators in the United States is estimated at $3 billion per year. Fruits and seeds from insect-pollinated plants provide the major diet for 25 percent of birds and for fruit-eating mammals.

Pollinators often act as a keystone species, a species in a community with a disproportionate impact on its environment relative to its abundance. Habitat loss, pesticides, and diseases are contributing to the decline of native pollinators. You can provide shelter, nesting sites, food, and water to attract and support pollinators (see Table 3-A); you can also minimize the use of pesticides that can kill pollinators.

Changing interactions

Altered and missing functional groups. The species that make up different functional groups often change in urbanized areas, or sometimes functional groups may be missing entirely. Whitetail deer populations have exploded in the last 40 years in part because there are no longer wolves or other large predators to keep their populations in check. These large predators cannot survive in fragmented urban environments. Vehicles driven by people now act as a major accidental predator of deer, birds, and amphibians.

Invasive species. Introduced invasive plants, pests, and diseases have dramatically changed communities in both urban and rural areas. Chestnut blight resulted in oaks and maples becoming more common forest trees. Emerald ash borer has caused a significant decline in ash tree populations in Maryland. Ash trees support 150 species of butterflies and moths alone (Tallamy 2009). Garlic mustard, an introduced species from Europe, covers the forest floor and reduces the growth of tree seedlings. It also alters soil chemistry (Kaufman and Kaufman 2023). These changes could change the long-term regeneration patterns in forests.

Invasive species are successful for many reasons, but one reason is that they have left behind the pests and diseases that recognize them as food. Increasingly, land managers are looking toward biological controls that introduce an insect or disease from the invasive species home range that specifically feeds on the invader, essentially reestablishing a lost interaction. You will learn more about invasive plants in **Chapter 22**.

Table 3-A. Food/shelter requirements for common native pollinators

Pollinator	Food	Shelter
Solitary bees	Nectar and pollen	Nest in hollow stems or tubes; bare patches of well-drained soils; make nests of mud, plant resins, or saps on rocks or bark
Bumblebees	Nectar and pollen	Nest underground, under clumps of grass, or in tree cavities
Butterflies	Larval host plants, nectar, mud puddles for minerals	Shelter in bushes, tall grasses, piles of sticks
Hummingbirds	Nectar, tree sap, insects	Nest in trees, shrubs, and vines. Can provide cotton or willow catkins for nesting material

Gardening practices.
Gardening and farming activities change species interactions, too. Within the garden you create bare ground where weed seeds can germinate. Weeds are often adapted to growing in highly disturbed areas. A crop monoculture is a banquet to pests and diseases that specialize on that crop.

Pesticides can kill beneficial insects as well as insect pests, potentially leading to pest outbreaks. The idea behind Integrated Pest Management (IPM) is to monitor and manage pest populations with minimal pesticide use, preserving natural predator-prey interactions. More about IPM can be found in **Chapter 10.**

Table 3-B. Typical early and late successional species in Maryland

Early: Plants	Late: Plants	Early: Wildlife	Late: Wildlife
Pokeweed	Solomon's Seal	Cottontail rabbit	Flying squirrels
Horseweed	Cranefly orchid	Meadow vole	Wood ducks
Calico aster	Summersweet	Red fox	Spotted salamander
Ragweed	Mountain laurel	Groundhog	Ovenbird
Broomsedge	Hickory	Bluebird	Pileated woodpecker
Blackberry	Oak	Bobwhite quail	Box turtle
Trumpet creeper	Black gum	Bobolink	
Loblolly pine	Dogwood	Deer	
Yellow birch	Sourwood		
Red cedar	American Beech		

Succession

All plant and animal communities change over time. The process of succession is measured by the change in species composition over time within a community (see Table 3-B).

We see succession when an abandoned field gradually becomes a forest or when a shallow pond fills in with plants to become a marsh. Primary succession happens as organisms colonize where there is no pre-existing community, such as on rocks or bare mineral soil. Secondary succession happens when there is a disturbance to an existing community. Designed landscapes undergo succession too as plantings mature, new plants are added, and overgrown plants are removed. Animal communities change in response to changes in the plant community.

Typically, the first colonizers will be annual plants that grow and reproduce rapidly. These are gradually replaced by perennial grasses and other herbaceous plants that are more tolerant of competition. Fast-growing shrubs and trees follow, particularly those whose seeds are dispersed by wind or birds. As trees begin to shade out the sun-loving annuals and perennials, shade-tolerant perennials and tree species establish.

As these late-successional trees mature, the forest species composition may remain relatively constant for a long period of time, until another major disturbance. It can take 100 to 200 years for a mature forest in Maryland to develop from a field.

It is not just species that change over time. The structure of the community becomes more complex as layers of vegetation form. A mature forest has canopy trees, understory trees, and a layer of shrubs and herbaceous plants. These layers of vegetation generally support greater species diversity.

Habitats in transition zones between successional stages and edge habitats tend to support high species diversity. Many animals, such as turkey and deer, use more than one stage to find food and shelter. When designing a garden, consider adding layers of understory trees, shrubs, and perennials to enhance plant and animal diversity.

Natural disturbances

Natural disturbances include volcanic eruptions, landslides, wind, fire, ice storms, and floods, as well as serious pest and disease outbreaks. There are also many human-caused disturbances, such as logging, farming, dredging, mining, pollution, and introduction of invasive species. All these disturbances can result in a different course of succession and formation of a different type of community.

The frequency and intensity of disturbances also has a big effect on succession. Repeated flooding along a river can cause a wet meadow to form rather than a forested floodplain. Human suppression of wildfires has led to less frequent, but more intense, forest fires.

Many human activities mimic natural disturbances. To maintain a meadow (an early successional community) we must mow or burn it to kill off woody plants. Most agricultural crops are annuals that must be planted every year. Cultivation and herbicides kill competing weeds or other self-seeding annuals and perennial plants that seed themselves.

If you want to speed up succession, plant perennials and woody plants that would take longer to arrive and establish if you waited for natural processes to happen.

3.5 Species and Populations

What are species?

In practice, species are groups of individuals that are similar physically, behaviorally, and genetically. Generally, individuals of one species do not interbreed with individuals of a different species either because they are isolated from them geographically, or they have physical or behavioral traits that limit interbreeding.

New species arise through the process of evolution, a change in the gene frequencies of a population over time, and it is this gradual change that makes defining species so difficult.

Evolution and adaptation

Charles Darwin's theory of natural selection, a mechanism for evolution, was largely influenced by his voyage to the Galapagos Islands in 1835. There he observed many very similar finches living on the islands, but varying greatly in the sizes and shapes of their beaks. He proposed that the birds had adapted to eating different food sources on the islands. Under natural selection:

- Offspring are similar to their parents.
- There is some chance variation among individuals and some variation can be passed from parents to offspring.
- More offspring are produced each generation than can be supported by the environment.
- Some individuals have a greater chance of surviving and reproducing than other individuals in the population because they have some physical or behavioral trait that makes them better suited.

Darwin concluded that the finches had evolved into different species because there was competition for food, and individuals who specialized on a different food could have more offspring. Over time the beak sizes changed as, for example, birds with larger beaks could better crack open large seeds and small-beaked birds could better handle smaller seeds.

Shortly after Darwin's voyage, an Augustinian monk named Gregor Mendel discovered through his work on garden peas that genes are the unit of inheritance and that genes come in alternative forms called alleles. Often one allele will be dominant over another, causing the expression of the dominant trait to be more common.

For example, in garden phlox, dark-pink flower color is the dominant color over white. If you have pink and white phlox in your garden, all seedlings with one pink and one white parent will have pink flowers. More recently scientists discovered that other environmentally-controlled molecular factors which influence how genes are read or expressed can be inherited through several generations (epigenetics) (Lind and Spagopoulou 2018) and that genes may be more easily transferred among species than previously thought (horizontal gene transfer) (Quammen 2018).

New species can arise through genetic mutations, but often new species evolve gradually as populations of the same species are isolated from one another. There are many examples of plants that have evolved into different species in the United States because of geographic isolation. Spring beauty (*Claytonia* spp.) is represented by different species in the eastern and western United States.

Isolation does not have to be geographical. Insects normally specializing on one host plant may switch to feed on a new host plant. The offspring of those insects feeding on the new host plant gradually may change over generations into a new species.

Human influences on evolution

Evolution happens over generations, but of course, some insects, bacteria, and viruses can produce many generations in just one year, whereas other organisms like oak trees and elephants take more than 20 years to reproduce. Evolution also relies on a flow of genes carried by individuals (or of pollen and seeds in the case of plants) among populations in the landscape.

Habitat fragmentation leads to restrictions in the ability of organisms to disperse to new areas and to exchange genes among populations. Without the free exchange of genetic material, more species are likely to become inbred and susceptible to pests, diseases, and changes in the environment.

The rate of introduction of new species has increased dramatically through global trade. Intentional introductions of species for horticulture, aquaculture, and the pet trade, plus accidental introduction of species in packing materials, grains, and ballast water lead to changes in evolutionary relationships.

Often new species are introduced without the pests and diseases or competitors that kept them in check in their native habitats, and they become invasive, spreading rapidly in their new environment. Insects and animals here do not recognize the new organisms as food or prey because they do not share an evolutionary history. Over time these relationships often change, but the consequences to native communities could be devastating in the short-term.

Some introduced species with close North American relatives hybridize and lose the specific genetic makeup that made them a distinct species.

Rapid climate change also affects species' ability to adapt. If climate changes faster than species can change their habits to survive warmer, wetter, or drier environments, then the species will go extinct. Many species shift their ranges in response to climatic changes, but plants can only move as far as their seeds are dispersed, and animals must be able to physically move to a new habitat. In increasingly urbanized landscapes it is difficult for species to do that. For those that move up in elevation to cooler environments, they may reach an upper limit if temperatures warm too much.

Agricultural practices have led to changing evolutionary relationships. Some weeds have evolved to mimic crop appearances so they are less likely to be weeded out. Other weeds and insect pests have developed resistance to pesticides. Genes from genetically engineered crops have traveled by pollen to become incorporated into the DNA of wild relatives.

Population dynamics

Populations are groups of individuals of the same species that live in the same place and are at least somewhat isolated or distinct from other populations. For example, a neighborhood is likely to be home to a population of squirrels if it is somewhat isolated from surrounding neighborhoods. To compare populations we look at several attributes:

- *Density*: the number of individuals in a given area
- *Birth rate*: the rate at which new individuals are born
- *Death rate*: the rate at which individuals die
- *Dispersal*: the rate at which individuals leave (emigrate) or arrive (immigrate)
- *Age distribution*: the proportion of individuals of different ages in the population

In plants, the life history of the plant in large part determines the population dynamics. The birth rate is represented by viable seeds produced. Seeds may disperse out of the population or into the population. Pollen may also be carried into and out of the population allowing for gene exchange among populations.

In a population of annuals, all the individuals will be about the same age. Biennials take two years to grow and reproduce before they die. A new population of biennials will have all one-year-old plants, then all two-year-old plants. More mature populations of biennials will start to have a mix of one- and two-year-old plants as seeds collect and form a seed bank in the soil. Some seeds may take more than one year to germinate, leading to a mixed-age population. Perennials live for three or more years, and some may live hundreds of years.

Animals can also have wildly contrasting population dynamics. Compare the life of two-spotted spider mites to that of white-tailed deer. Spider mites can go from egg to adult in 1-3 weeks, depending on temperature. Each female can produce a dozen eggs a day for up to a couple weeks, about 148 eggs over the female's lifespan. Populations explode within just a few warm weeks if there are plenty of leaves around. White-tailed deer females mature within one to two years. Each has one to three fawns a year and lives for 3-5 years on average in the wild, averaging eight fawns over her lifespan.

Resource availability also has a tremendous effect on deer populations. Deer will reproduce earlier, have more offspring each year, and live longer if there are plenty of resources available and few predators.

Population genetics

The life history and population dynamics of species influence the genetic diversity within populations. Pollen and seeds travel different distances, depending upon how they are dispersed, although most seeds land relatively close to the parent plant. For example. wind dispersal distances are affected by:

- The size and weight of the pollen or seeds
- Wind speed and turbulence
- Openness of the environment (e.g., meadow vs. forest understory)
- Height of the plant above the ground

Animal dispersal distances are affected by:

- Length of time to digest fruits
- Average flight or travel distance (e.g., migratory bird vs. box turtle)
- Territory size

Gene flow among populations can keep populations more genetically similar to one another or can introduce new genetic variation. Small populations tend to lose genetic variation. Random events, such as which individuals mate and which offspring survive, can dramatically change the proportions of different genetic traits in a small population through a process called genetic drift. If a population was started by a small number of individuals, the founders are likely to have less genetic diversity than the larger population from which they came, and subsequent matings are likely to occur between genetically-related individuals.

Plant breeding

Gardeners often debate the merits of planting "straight" (open-pollinated) species versus cultivars and hybrids. In agriculture there is increasing interest in the conservation and preservation of a wide variety of cultivars and of a crop's wild relatives so that there will be a source of new genes for future adaptations. Some cultivars and hybrids no longer produce nectar, pollen, or seeds and so they have lost much of their wildlife value.

Straight species are often collected from a natural population; they will have more genetic variation, so some plants may have traits that will allow them to resist new diseases or to adapt to climactic change.

A cultivar is a genetic selection of a plant that is often originally reproduced asexually through cuttings or tissue culture. In this case, individuals of a cultivar are genetically identical. Many crop and ornamental plants are cultivars. For example, on a conventional farm, a field of corn will be a single genetic strain of corn the farmer has selected for its yield, insect resistance, or drought resistance. You might choose to grow 'Rutgers' tomatoes, 'Blue Lake' green beans, and 'Nantes' carrots. Your perennial garden might feature 'Stella d'Oro' daylilies, or *Phlox paniculata 'David.'*

Hybrids are most often crosses between two species. Some hybrids occur in nature, particularly in plants. Sometimes plant hybrids are more vigorous than their parents, but other times are less vigorous or produce no viable seeds. The outcome depends on how the genes from the different species interact.

In horticulture the term "hybrid" is sometimes used to refer to crosses between two cultivars of the same species. Hybrid tomatoes bred for disease resistance are an example of a hybrid between two cultivars of the same species. Pluots and plumcots are hybrids between two species (plums and peaches).

Rare plants in Maryland

More than 600 plant species are on Maryland's rare-plant list, although their degree of rarity varies. Some species may be at the northern or southern limits of their ranges and have only a few populations in Maryland. Others may only occur in Maryland and may also be listed as federally-endangered species. To learn what plants are rare in your county, visit the Maryland Department of Natural Resources website (see the end of this chapter).

Examples of Maryland rare-plant species that can be purchased in nurseries include pink coreopsis (*Coreopsis rosea*) and wild lupine (*Lupinus perennis*).

If a species is rare in your area, avoid planting it in your garden. Although a few plants may not cause harm, they may accidentally introduce a disease that could spread to the wild population and transfer pollen and seeds to the wild population. Botanists trying to conserve rare wild populations need to be able to study the genetics of the wild populations without genes from introduced populations present. Avoid buying any wild-collected rare plants because it is illegal to collect and sell endangered plant species.

3.6 Ecosystems

The concept of an ecosystem brings together the living community and the non-living, abiotic factors influencing that community such as soils, water, nutrients, and climate. The study of ecosystems looks at the flow of energy, water, and nutrients through the living system.

What are food webs?

Earlier in this chapter you read about functional groups that obtain energy in certain ways. Food webs describe how these groups fit together in the ecosystem through their feeding interactions (see Figure 3-H). Energy flows from the producer to the consumer to the decomposers and back to the producers.

Disrupting food webs

Disrupting a food web can lead to one species gaining dominance or to an entirely new community forming in the following ways:

Loss of a keystone species. If a keystone species (or keystone species group such as pollinators) were lost, it would lead to a loss of fruit production in plants pollinated by those pollinators. Birds and other animals that rely on those fruits would disappear. If the pollinators did not recover, plants relying on wind pollination and other forms of pollination would begin to dominate, and those plants would attract their own suite of animal species.

Insect outbreaks. Lack of predators (e.g., birds and spiders) or pathogens can lead to explosive reproduction of insects. If the insects exhaust their food source though, their population will crash. Recent introductions of insects such as the brown marmorated

Figure 3-H. The food web

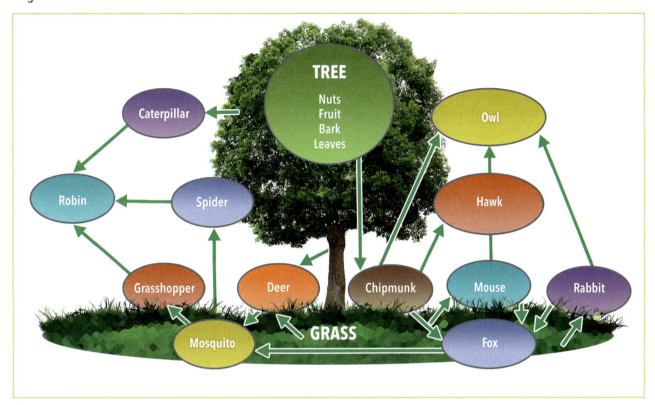

The arrows represent the direction of energy flow through the web.

stink bug and the emerald ash borer can lead to outbreaks because they have no natural enemies outside their home range.

Introduction of invasive plant species. Invasive species often outcompete native plant species for light, water, and nutrients. Changes in the plant community can lead to changes in food sources and types of shelter for animals favoring a different community of animals.

For example, robins experience higher nest predation when nesting in Amur honeysuckle (*Lonicera maackii*) compared to nesting in native shrubs because the architecture of the shrub leads them to build their nests closer to the ground, where they are more accessible to predators. The sugary fruits of invasive shrub honeysuckles are favored by some birds but displace the high fat content fruits of plants like spicebush (*Lindera benzoin*) and viburnum (*Viburnum* spp.) that migratory birds rely on.

Carbon cycle

Carbon occurs mostly as carbon dioxide (CO_2) in the atmosphere, but there are also trace amounts of methane and carbon monoxide. Plants take up carbon in the form of CO_2 in photosynthesis. The uptake is approximately equal to the amount of carbon released through respiration by primary producers, consumers, and decomposers. Carbon becomes stored in terrestrial and aquatic systems for the long-term in fossil fuels, peat, soils, and carbonate rock. For shorter periods, carbon is stored in plant and animal biomass, which is used to produce paper and wood-frame houses.

Carbon dioxide levels in the atmosphere have risen substantially since 1750 due to human activities, primarily the combustion of fossil fuels. Deforestation contributes to CO_2 increases as well, but these are often offset by crop re-growth or new tree cover. The loss of vegetation also results in the release of carbon stored in soils. Although a relatively minor contributor to global CO_2 levels, peat moss for gardening also releases carbon that would have otherwise been in long-term storage.

Rising CO_2 levels have led to:

- Rising temperatures, leading to shifts in species ranges and earlier flowering
- Higher plant growth rates, until water and nutrient limitations are reached
- Increased pollen production, including in ragweed
- Greater toxicity of the oils in poison ivy
- Increased growth of vines

Water cycle

Water plays a critical role in ecosystems (see Figure 3-I). It is necessary for all living organisms and provides important habitat for a huge diversity of fish, amphibians, waterfowl, aquatic insects, and aquatic plants. Water evaporates from lakes, oceans, and rivers and is transpired by plants and respired in every breath animals and plants take. That water condenses in the atmosphere and is returned to earth as rain or snow. Water runs downhill into lakes and rivers. Some of it infiltrates into the ground and is stored there as groundwater, filling in pores in the soil or percolating into underground aquifers. If groundwater reaches the surface through a spring, or just because of a high water table, that water rejoins the surface waters of lakes, streams, and rivers.

In urbanized areas, the flow of water in the landscape has changed because there is less plant cover and more impervious surface area,

Figure 3-I. The hydrologic cycle

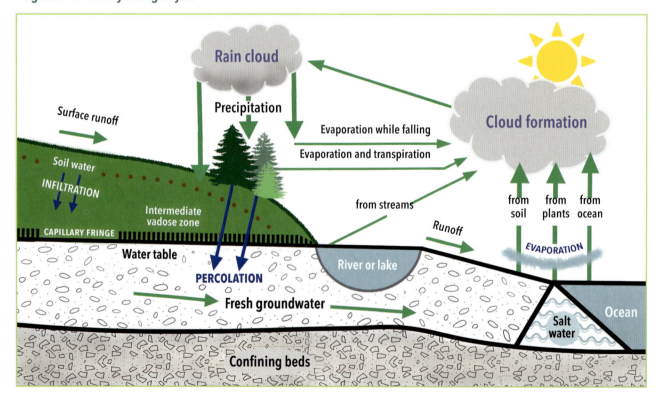

compacted soils, and channelized streams. More water reaches the ground, less soaks into the ground, and greater quantities of polluted water reach wetlands and waterways. Groundwater and water stored in aquifers is used up as people pump water from wells and there is less recharge of groundwater.

Nitrogen cycle

Nitrogen is not the only nutrient important in ecosystems, but it is one of the more complex systems and illustrates what a large effect humans have on ecosystem processes (see Figure 3-J). You will learn about other nutrients important in plant nutrition in Chapter 6.

Nitrogen exists in the atmosphere in gaseous forms. It is fixed or converted to forms usable by plants and animals through the action of bacteria or lightning. Plants mainly take up nitrogen in the form of nitrates. That nitrogen is passed along to animals that consume plants, and when plants and animals die it cycles within the terrestrial system. Some is also lost to the atmosphere as other bacteria convert it back to a gaseous form.

People have significantly altered the nitrogen cycle by:

- Doubling the amount of fixed nitrogen through the production of fertilizer and by planting nitrogen-fixing crops like soybeans
- Burning fossil fuels, adding to gaseous nitrogen (one cause of acid rain)
- Enriching soils with chemical fertilizers, manure, and deposition of atmospheric nitrogen
- Losing biodiversity in ecosystems with plants adapted to low-nutrient soils

Figure 3-J. The nitrogen cycle

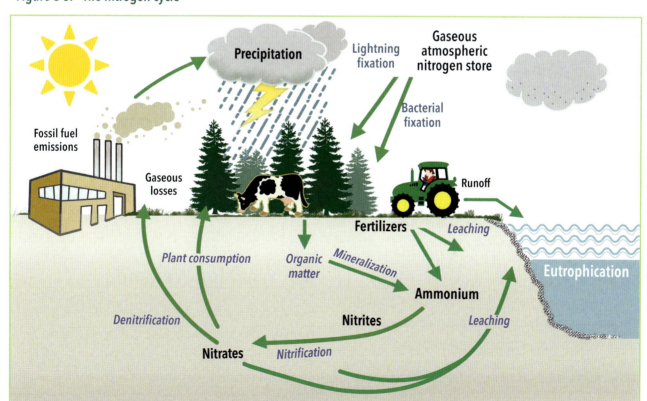

- Increasing nitrate flow in streams and nitrous oxide in the atmosphere through deforestation
- Eutrophying (over-fertilizing water) streams and wetlands with nutrient-enriched runoff

Recycling in the garden

To make your garden a sustainable ecosystem, consider how water, energy, and nutrients are recycled. Composting uses decomposition to keep nutrients on site and avoids the addition of chemical fertilizers (Chapter 7). Cover crops protect soil from erosion by slowing water flow and they add nutrients back into the soil when they are cut or plowed under (Chapter 5). Rain barrels store water for future use. The loose soil and vegetation of gardens helps to slow the flow of rain water and allows water to filter slowly into the soil. Rain gardens help capture and cleanse runoff (see Chapter 28).

Biodiversity in the landscape

Biodiversity is often used as a buzzword, but what does it really mean? Biologists measure biodiversity as the number and distribution of species in an ecosystem. If you have a community with 10 species, but one species is super-abundant and the rest are relatively rare, that community has less biodiversity than a community with 10 species all approximately equal in abundance. Biodiversity can also encompass everything from the diversity of genes to the diversity of ecosystems.

We are still learning about the value of a particular gene, species, or ecosystem, but there are enough critical examples to make preserving biodiversity a high priority:

- A gene could make American chestnut resistant to chestnut blight and return this ecologically and economically valuable tree to our forests.
- Taxol, first extracted from the western yew (*Taxus brevifolia*), provided a new cancer drug. The tree grows best in western old-growth forests threatened by clearcut logging.
- Preserving forested watersheds saves municipalities in New York State millions in water treatment costs.

Ecosystems with more diversity are more resilient to disturbances and are able to recover faster after natural or man-made disasters. They are also more stable over time. Harvard biologist Dr. E. O. Wilson has written eloquently on biodiversity, "We should preserve every scrap of biodiversity as priceless while we learn to use it and come to understand what it means to humanity."

Gardeners can promote biodiversity by including more native plant species in gardens, providing wildlife habitat, and controlling invasive species. Using sustainable gardening techniques that conserve water and energy, minimize the use of pesticides and fertilizers, and re-use materials will have a broad effect on conserving biodiversity in the region, and even worldwide. Volunteering at parks where rare plant communities are protected on-site and at botanic gardens that cultivate endangered plant species from around the world (ex-situ conservation) can also be meaningful contributions.

3.7 What Is a Wetland?

Is a wetland a marsh? Is it a beach? Is it a mucky area in the woods? Is it in a cold or warm region? Is it only near water sources or can it be found in mountainous areas? Is it large or small?

A wetland can be any or all of these. The U.S. Fish and Wildlife Service defines wetlands as:

"...lands transitional between terrestrial and aquatic systems where the water table is usually at or near the surface or the land is covered by shallow water"

Three things define wetlands, and all must be present for an area to be classified as one:

Hydrologic conditions. Land is covered or saturated by water for at least some time during the growing season. It is not necessary for water to be visible in order to identify a non-tidal wetland.

Hydric soils. Soil is wet long enough during the growing season for microorganisms to consume oxygen to the point of making soil anaerobic.

Hydrophytic plants. Plant species are present that have adapted to standing water and anaerobic soils.

Wetland types

There are five major wetland systems:

- Marine (ocean)
- Estuarine (coastal bay)
- Lacustrine (lake)
- Riverine (river)
- Palustrine (marsh/swamp)

Tidal wetlands are influenced by tidal fluctuations. They can be associated with large bodies of salt or brackish water like the Chesapeake Bay, or mostly freshwater rivers like the Potomac and Choptank. Examples of tidal wetlands include:

- Tidal mud flats
- Salt marshes
- Brackish marshes
- Intertidal beaches
- Tidal swamps

Non-tidal wetlands are not influenced by tidal fluctuations and can be riverine or palustrine (shallow freshwater habitats).

Examples of non-tidal wetlands include: freshwater marsh, wet meadow, bog, shrub swamp, wooded swamp, floodplain or bottomland hardwood forest, shallow pond, seepage area, or spring. Even a soggy area near a parking lot or in a highway median can be a wetland.

How to recognize a non-tidal wetland

To identify a wetland, you would assess the characteristics of water, soils, and vegetation.

Water. Water must be present long enough at some point during the year to stress plants and animals not adapted to saturated soils and life in water. Even if water is not currently present, look for evidence of water's presence:

- Water or silt stains on tree trunks or fallen leaves
- Water-carried debris or drift lines around tree trunks (see Figure 3-K)
- Spongy or bog-like soils (see Figure 3-L)

Soils. Wetlands have hydric soils where water fills in between the grains of soil, and the soils are anaerobic (lacking in oxygen). Dig a hole in the soil to look for evidence:

- Anaerobic soil is sometimes indicated by oily gray, blue/gray, or green/gray colors
- If the hole fills up with water, it indicates a high water table or saturated soils
- Red or orange mottling of mineral staining is often present

Figure 3-K. Trapped debris

Figure 3-L. Standing water

- Does the soil smell like rotten egg or sulfur? That's a sign of anaerobic decomposition
- A layer (eight inches or more) of decomposing organic matter on the ground.

Hydrologic records, such as a county soil survey, will also indicate saturated soils.

Plants. Some plants have adapted to anaerobic soils and flooded conditions. Most plants take up oxygen through roots and distribute it through stems and leaves. Wetland plants must use additional strategies to take up oxygen. Coastal plants often have ways of tolerating high salt levels. Wetland plants are called hydrophytes (water-lovers). Look for plants characteristic of wetlands:

- Reeds have oxygen-transporting tubes; water lilies float on top of the water; bald cypress trees have buttressed trunks or pneumataphores (knees) (see Figure 3-M)
- Look for tree roots close to the soil surface, indicating an adaptation to obtain oxygen

- Hypertrophied lenticels (enlarged pores) are often present to increase oxygen uptake
- Fallen trees may have diminished root volume (see Figure 3-N)
- Look for a predominance of plant species indigenous to wet areas (see Figure 3-O)

Wetland plant categories

Obligate wetland plants grow in saturated or anaerobic soils more than 99% of the time:

- Blue flag iris (*Iris versicolor*)
- Cattails (*Typha latifolia*)
- Skunk cabbage (*Symplocarpus foetidus*)
- Bald cypress (*Taxodium distichum*)

Facultative wetland plants occur in wetlands 67 to 99% of the time, and occasionally in uplands:

- Jack-in-the-pulpit (*Arisaema triphyllum*)
- Cardinal flower (*Lobelia cardinalis*)
- Hollow-stemmed Joe Pye weed (*Eupatoriadelphus fistulosus*)
- Common elderberry (*Sambucus canadensis*)

- Spicebush (*Lindera benzoin*)
- Sycamore (*Platanus occidentalis*)

Facultative plants occur in wetlands 34 to 66% of the time:

- Trout lily or dog-toothed violet (*Erythronium umbilicatum*)
- Southern arrowwood (*Viburnum dentatum*)
- Box elder (*Acer negundo*)
- Red maple (*Acer rubrum*)

Facultative upland plants occur in wetlands less than 33% of the time:

- Mayapple (*Podophyllum peltatum*)
- Spring-beauty (*Claytonia virginica*)
- American holly (*Ilex opaca*)
- Tulip poplar (*Liriodendron tulipifera*)

3.8 Why Are Wetlands Important?

Wetlands are an ecosystem within the larger landscape or watershed. About 6% of Maryland's land area is considered wetland and many of those wetlands are part of the Chesapeake Bay watershed. The watershed is 64,000 square miles in area and extends as far north as Cooperstown, NY. Most people in the watershed live just a few minutes' walk from a waterway that drains into the Bay.

The Youghiogheny watershed is home to one of Maryland's rarest wetlands, a boreal peat bog known as Cranesville Swamp. The Atlantic Coastal bays face some of the highest losses of wetlands in the state due to both development and sea-level rise.

Wetlands contribute biological, economic and aesthetic value to our nation, our communities, and to us as individuals.

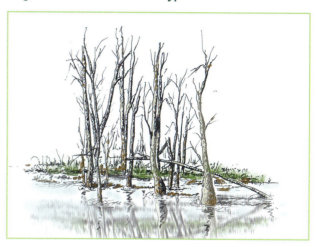

Figure 3-M. Immature bald cypress

Figure 3-N. Fallen tree, diminished roots

Figure 3-O. Skunk cabbage

Benefits of wetlands

Water-quality control. Wetlands help protect the Chesapeake Bay and other watersheds by filtering pollutants, including pesticides, fertilizers, and sediments. They increase groundwater recharge, keep water clean for our streams and lakes, and reduce the cost of treating drinking water.

Flood and erosion control. Wetlands act as buffers, reducing the volume and velocity of floodwaters, mitigating damage from severe storms to streams, agriculture fields, homes, businesses, and infrastructure. They provide a buffer along shorelines to reduce erosion. One acre of wetlands can store 1 to 1.5 million gallons of floodwater (EPA).

Habitat. Wetlands are among the most productive ecosystems in the world, comparable to rain forests and coral reefs. Wetlands provide habitat for an immense variety of species of microbes, plants, insects, amphibians, reptiles, birds, fish, and mammals. This supports Maryland's multi-billion-dollar commercial fishing industry.

Recreation and tourism. Wetlands provide areas for recreational activities such as fishing, hunting, bird-watching, photography, and hiking, as well as educational and research opportunities. Along with tourism, these benefits add to our economy.

Historically, wetlands have been thought of as useless wastelands. Farmers, foresters and developers drained and filled wetlands. Coastal wetlands were dredged and impounded. The public did not recognize the true economic value of wetlands until their contribution to reducing damaging flooding, mitigating pollution, and providing wildlife habitat were better understood.

Mosquito control in wetlands is an ever-controversial topic and has contributed to the loss of many wetlands through draining and filling. Mosquito populations may be controlled to prevent the spread of diseases or to improve quality of life. There are about 50 species of mosquitos in Maryland, not all of which transmit diseases, and some wetland types produce more mosquitos than others. There are also many ways to control mosquitos that do not require eliminating wetlands.

Wetlands are also gained and lost naturally over time. Sea-level rise and coastal erosion results in a decrease in coastal wetland area; beaver create new inland wetlands.

3.9 Wetland Regulations

Overall, Maryland has lost about half of its wetlands since European settlement in the 1600s. Records from the U.S. Fish and Wildlife Service show that Maryland lost 24,000 acres of tidal and nontidal wetlands between 1955 and 1978 and that the Chesapeake Bay watershed lost another 10,000 acres between 1982-1989.

Passage of the Federal Clean Water Act in 1972 and its subsequent amendments have slowed the rate of loss, as has the passage in Maryland of the Nontidal Wetlands Act in 1989. The USDA NRCS reduces wetlands loss on agricultural lands through the Wetland Conservation Provisions and the Wetlands Reserve Easements program.

The Federal Clean Water Act requires a permit in order to discharge dredged or fill material into navigable waters, the complete definition of which includes wetlands. The Maryland Department of the Environment coordinates permit applications for both federal and state permits. Three state acts you are most likely to come across are listed below. Counties may have additional regulations.

The *Maryland Nontidal Wetlands Act* was enacted in 1989 with a goal of "no net loss" of nontidal wetland acreage and function, and requires the State to strive for a net resource gain. It prohibits filling, draining, dredging, and altering native vegetation in non-tidal wetlands (including isolated wetlands) and requires a 25-100' buffer around wetland areas. This Act allows for mitigation, which is the creation, restoration, or enhancement of nontidal wetlands that were lost due to regulated or agricultural activities.

The *Maryland Tidal Wetlands Act* was enacted in 1970 to manage tidal wetlands. It requires a permit or license before any alteration (including dredging or filling, shoreline protection, or putting in pilings) of a tidal wetland can occur and establishes a 25' (sometimes 100') buffer.

The *Chesapeake Bay Critical Area Act* was enacted in 1984 by the Maryland General Assembly and expanded in 2002 to include Maryland's Coastal Bays. It covers land-use policies for land within 1,000 feet of the mean high tide line of any tidal waters, including tidal wetlands. It includes a 100' buffer of natural vegetation.

3.10 How to Preserve Wetlands

Reducing human Impact

As Master Gardeners, encourage wetland conservation through sustainable practices like these:

- Certify your property with the Bay-Wise Landscaping program

Figure 3-P. Beaver damage on tree

- Precipitation that gets on paved surfaces may directly enter wetlands, so don't dump pesticides, oil, or other materials on pavement or in storm drains.
- Don't over-fertilize or allow fertilizers or other lawn products to spill onto the driveway or street. Follow regulations from the University of Maryland.
- Direct water from gutters onto turf or into garden beds instead of onto an impervious surface.
- When landscaping, plant native grasses or forested buffer strips along wetlands on your property.
- Don't collect or remove plants from the wild. Instead, take a picture, identify the plant, and purchase it from a reputable nursery that propagates it.
- Pick up trash in nearby wetlands
- Appreciate the diversity of plant and animal life in wetlands. Listen for tree frogs in the early spring. Look for signs of animals living in the area; tracks of deer, blue heron, raccoon, red fox, skunk, and beaver (see Figure 3-P) are likely to be found in wetlands.

Community involvement

At the community level, some tips to preserve wetlands include:

- Participating in local stream cleanup projects
- Encouraging neighbors to respect wetlands
- Supporting local wetland and watershed protection initiatives
- Encouraging buffers of wetlands strips between streams or coastlines and land-use areas
- Supporting legislation to protect and conserve wetlands
- Reporting destruction of wetlands to the Department of Natural Resources or to your local Riverkeeper. ✸

AUTHORS

2024 EDITION:

Sylvan R. Kaufman, Ph.D., Sylvan Green Earth Consulting, Sante Fe, NM.

ORIGINAL AUTHOR:

(Wetlands section): Maria Malloy, Program Coordinator, University of Maryland Extension.

PUBLICATIONS

Carrol, S. B. and S. D. Salt. 2004. *Ecology for Gardeners.* Timber Press, Portland, OR.

Kaufman, S. and W. Kaufman. 2023. *Invasive Plants: Guide to Identification and the Impacts and Control of Common North American Species, 3rd edition.* Stackpole Books, Mechanicsburg, PA.

Kennedy, Victor S. 2018. *Shifting Baselines in the Chesapeake Bay.* Johns Hopkins University Press, Baltimore, MD.

Kesselheim, A. S. and B. Slattery, 1995. *WOW! The Wonders of Wetlands. An Educator's Guide.* Environmental Concern. St. Michael's, MD. ISBN-10: 1883226074.

Knepper, David A. and Lytton J. Musselman. 2012. *Plants of the Chesapeake Bay.* Johns Hopkins University Press, Baltimore, MD.

Kolbert, Elizabeth. 2015. *Field Notes from a Catastrophe, Man, Nature and Climate Change.* Bloomsbury Publishers, New York, NY.

Lowenfels, J. and W. Lewis. 2010. *Teaming with Microbes, a Gardener's Guide to the Soil Food Web.* Timber Press, Portland, OR.

Molles, M. C. 2019. *Ecology: Concepts and Applications.* McGraw Hill, Boston, MA.

Perlman, D. L. and J. C. Milder. 2004. *Practical Ecology for Planners, Developers and Citizens.* Island Press, Washington, DC.

Quammen, D. 2018. *The Tangled Tree: A Radical New History of Life.* Simon & Schuster, New York, NY.

Slobodkin, L. 2003. A *Citizens Guide to Ecology.* Oxford University Press, New York, NY.

Tallamy, D. W. 2009. *Bringing Nature Home, 2nd Ed.* Timber Press, Portland, OR.

Tiner, R. W, and D.G. Burke. 1995. *Wetlands of Maryland.* U.S. Fish and Wildlife Service, Ecological Services, Region 5, Hadley, MA and. Maryland Department of Natural Resources, Annapolis, MD. Cooperative publication. 193 pp. plus Appendices. fws.gov/wetlands/Documents%5CWetlands-Of-Maryland.pdf

Wilson, E.O. (ed.) 1988. Biodiversity. National Academy of Sciences. Washington, DC. Wilson, E.O. (ed.) 1988. Biodiversity. National Academy of Sciences. Washington, DC.

PHOTOS

Learning Objectives Forest Photo: Retreieved December 2023 from pixabay.com.

ILLUSTRATIONS

3-A: Adapted by LeAnn Zotta from Maryland Geological Survey http://www.mgs.md.gov/geology/index.html.

3-E: *U.S. Environmental Protection Agency, Washington, D.C. "Protecting Water Quality from Urban Runoff." Document No. EPA 841-F-03-003.*

3F-3P: Don Wittig, University of Maryland Extension Master Gardener, Montgomery County.

WEBSITES

Arbor Day Foundation, Revised Hardiness Zone Map. arborday.org/media/mapchanges.cfm

Center for Watershed Protection Center for Watershed Protection. cwp.org

Chesapeake Bay Program. 2023. chesapeakebay.net

Clearwater et al. 2000. *An overview of wetland and water resources of Maryland.* Clearwater et al. 2000. An overview of wetland and water resources of Maryland. mde.state.md.us/programs/Water/WetlandsandWaterways/AboutWetlands/Documents/ mde.state.md.us/assets/document/wetlandswaterways/h2Oresources.pdf

Environmental Protection Agency (EPA), *How's My Waterway* epa.gov/waterdata/hows-my-waterway

Kays, J. S. *Maryland's Forests, Past, Present and Future.* University of Maryland Extension Fact Sheet. extension.umd.edu/sites/extension.umd.edu/files/2021-03/FS627_MDForestsPPF.pdf

Lind, M.I. and F. Spagopoulou. 2018. *Evolutionary consequences of epigenetic inheritance.* Heredity 121:205-209. nature.com/articles/s41437-018-0113-y

Marks, R. 2005. *Native Pollinators.* Fish and Wildlife Habitat Management Leaflet 34. Natural Resources Conservation Service. efotg.sc.egov.usda.gov/references/Delete/2015-11-7/JS-BIOL-34NativePollinators_May2011.pdf

Maryland Department of the Environment (MDE), About Wetlands. mde.maryland.gov/programs/Water/WetlandsandWaterways/AboutWetlands/Pages/index.aspx

Maryland Department of Natural Resources (MD DNR).2023. *Rare, Threatened and Endangered Plants,* dnr.maryland.gov/wildlife/Pages/plants_wildlife/rte/espaa.aspx; *Climate Change and Coastal Conservation,* dnr.maryland.gov/ccs/Pages/habitats_slr.aspx; *Coastal Zone Management Grant,* dnr.maryland.gov/ccs/Pages/funding/czma.aspx; *Forest and Tree Canopy Data for Maryland,* dnr.maryland.gov/forests/Pages/Forest-Tree-Data.aspx; Watershed Associations, dnr.maryland.gov/streams/Pages/watershedAssociations.aspx

Maryland Geological Survey. 2023. *Maryland Geology* mgs.md.gov/geology

Rey et al. 2012. North American Wetlands and Mosquito Control. International Journal of Environmental Research and Public Health 9(12):4537-4605. ncbi.nlm.nih.gov/pmc/articles/PMC3546777/

United States Department of Agriculture Natural Resources Conservation Service (USDA NRCS). 2023. *Wetlands,* nrcs.usda.gov/wps/portal/nrcs/main/national/water/wetlands/

U.S. Environmental Protection Agency (USEPA). 2023. *Wetlands.* epa.gov/wetlands

United States Fish and Wildlife Service (USFWS). 2023. *Wetlands Status and Trends.* fws.gov/wetlands/Status-and-Trends/index.html

Wheeler, J. C. 2003. *Freshwater Use Trends in Maryland*, USGS FS 112-03. pubs.usgs.gov/fs/old.2003/fs-112-03/

Xerces Society. 2023. *Pollinator Conservation Program*. xerces.org/pollinator-conservation; *Habitat Planning,* xerces.org/pollinator-conservation/habitat-restoration/planning

4: BASIC BOTANY

Judith Owen, Ph.D.

4 BASIC BOTANY

CONTENTS

4.1 Groupings of Plants 67

4.2 Classification of Plants 69

4.3 The Structure of Plants 73

4.4 Reproductive Structures 80

4.5 Pollination 83

4.6 Plant Growth & Development 86

4.7 Regulation of Plant Growth 87

4.8 Plant Selection & Modification 89

LEARNING OBJECTIVES

- Plant classifications by life cycle and class
- Plant parts (roots, stems, buds, leaves, flowers, and fruits) and their functions
- The processes of photosynthesis, respiration, and transpiration in plants
- Pollination and reproduction of plants
- How the environment affects plant growth
- The terminology needed to use keys in the identification of leaves
- The binomial system of plant nomenclature
- Categories of genetically modified plants

INTRODUCTION

Botany is the study of plant life. The principles and terminology discussed in this chapter will be necessary to understand this handbook and to communicate plant information effectively. Recognition of plants, diagnosis of plant problems, and recommendations to gardeners all require a sound understanding of the basic structure and processes of plants.

We cannot survive without plants because we cannot manufacture food for ourselves. We must obtain food either directly or indirectly from plants. Plants, on the other hand, can live just fine without us. That is because plants (as well as green algae, cyanobacteria, and a few others) can use light energy, carbon dioxide, and water to make their own food. This is called photosynthesis, and it supports life on our planet. Photosynthesis provides almost all the available oxygen. Oxygen is not only necessary for our respiration, but is also regularly turned into ozone, screening us from harmful ultraviolet (UV) rays of the sun.

We depend on plants for many things besides food. Plants provide fossil fuel, lumber, fibers, medicines, paper, latex, resin, cork, spices, fragrances, and dyes. Plants provide jobs in fields ranging from farming and nursery industries to conservation biology, forest management, landscape design and management, and horticulture, to name just a few.

As gardeners and stewards of the land, we appreciate the aesthetic and therapeutic values of plants as well as their importance in wildlife habitat and the ecosystem benefits they provide.

4.1 Groupings of Plants

There are more than 500,000 species of plants in the world. Throughout history, humans have devised ways to group them into manageable categories. They are classified according to their growth habits, reproductive structures, length of life, uses, or the climates in which they flourish.

Plant growth patterns

Woody plants and herbaceous plants

Plants are either woody or herbaceous. The tissues surrounding a tree will grow in thickness and in strength due to a meristematic tissue called the lateral meristem. This secondary growth is characteristic of woody trees, shrubs, and vines. Herbaceous plants lack this secondary growth and generally die back in winter. For more on woody plants, see **Chapter 16, Woody Plants.**

Deciduous plants and evergreen plants

Woody plants are either deciduous or evergreen. Deciduous plants lose their leaves or needles in winter. Evergreen trees and shrubs have either leaves (broad-leaved evergreens) or needles (needled evergreens). These plants lose and replace some leaves and needles each year.

Monocots and dicots

Flowering plants are divided into two groups based on growth patterns. Seeds may be monocotyledonous or dicotyledonous, depending upon whether they have one or two embryonic leaves. There are additional differences between monocots and dicots (see Table 4-A and Figure 4-A).

Hardiness zones

The USDA classifies plants according to their hardiness, which refers to the lowest temperature the plant will likely withstand. The United States and Canada are divided into 11 zones. Each zone is assigned a number that indicates what the average lowest temperature in that zone is likely to be. (See the **Freeze Dates and Hardiness Zones links** in the Resource Appendix.)

Maryland is in Zones 5b to 8a. If you select plants suited to your hardiness zone, it enhances their ability to flourish.

Table 4-A. Differences between monocots and dicots

Monocots	Dicots
Leaves are narrow and parallel-veined	Leaves are wide and net-veined
Flower parts are in multiples of three	Flower parts are usually in multiples of four or five
Stems have vascular bundles scattered throughout (Fig. 4-A)	Vascular bundles in the stem are arranged in a ring
There is generally no secondary (woody) growth	There may be secondary growth
There is one seed leaf	There are two seed leaves

Figure 4-A. Monocot and dicot stems

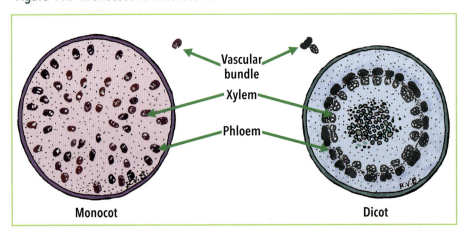

UME © 2025. All rights reserved.

4: Basic Botany   68

Taxonomy

All of these systems are useful. But how do people accurately communicate about plants? The classification system known as taxonomy gives each plant an unambiguous name based on characteristics of the plant. This classification system is examined in the next section.

4.2 Classification of Plants

Latin binomials

Plant names

Each plant is assigned a two-word Latin name that identifies it beyond doubt. The two Latin words together name the species and are known as the binomial. Binomials were designed by Carl Linnaeus in the 18th century. He is considered the "Father of Taxonomy" and named many plants that were sent to him from all over the world.

Binomials are written in italics or are underlined. The first name is the Genus, and it is always capitalized. The second word is the specific epithet, and it is not capitalized. The specific epithet can be thought of as the describer. For example, in *Pieris japonica* and *Spigelia marilandica*, the specific epithet describes its place of origin. In *Yucca filamentosa*, the specific epithet describes a feature of the plant.

Why use Latin binomials?

Plants are often known by more than one common name (see Table 4-B). It can also happen that a common name can actually represent different plants (see Table 4-C). The Latin binomial permits us to communicate with each other without confusion.

Why use Latin? Latin is a dead language, so the meanings of words will not change as they can in a living language. It is understood by people of every nation.

Naming changes

Often there will be a letter or name following the binomial. This refers to the person who identified and named the species. The common garden tomato, *Solanum lycopersicum* L., was named by Linnaeus. The L. may be in parenthesis and followed

Table 4-B.   Same plants–different common names

Genus	Specific epithet	Common names
Liriodendron	*tulipifera*	Tulip tree
Liriodendron	*tulipifera*	Yellow poplar
Liriodendron	*tulipifera*	Tulip poplar
Liriodendron	*tulipifera*	Tulip magnolia
Liriodendron	*tulipifera*	Whitewood

Table 4-C.   Different plants–same common name

Genus	Specific epithet	Common names
Senecio	*cineraria*	Dusty Miller, silver ragwort
Senecio	*candidans*	Dusty Miller, silver ragwort
Senecio	*maritimus*	Dusty Miller, silver ragwort
Cineraria	*maritima*	Dusty Miller, silver ragwort
Centaurea	*maritima*	Dusty Miller, silver ragwort
Centaurea	*cineraria*	Dusty Miller, silver ragwort
Artemisia	*stelleriana*	Dusty Miller, silver ragwort

by a name, as in the purple coneflower, *Echinacea purpura* (L.) Moench. This plant was first named by Linnaeus, but later reclassified by Moench. The classification of plants changes as new information becomes available. The discovery of new species, recent research on DNA and other subcellular structures, or other insight contributes to a refined taxonomy of plants.

Table 4-D. Classification of tomato/purple coneflower*

Kingdom	Plantae (plants)	Plantae
Phylum	Magnoliophyta (flowering plants)	Magnoliophyta
Class	Magnoliopsida (dicotyledons)	Magnoliopsida
Order	Solanales	Asterales
Family	Solanaceae (potato family)	Asteraceae (aster family)
Genus	Solanum (deeply lobed petals)	Echinacea (coneflower)
Species	*Solanum lycopersicum*	*Echinacea purpurea*
	Garden tomato	Eastern purple coneflower

Source: plants.usda.gov/home 2020.

Designations for unknown species or several species

Sometimes the genus is known, but the species is not. The designation "sp." is then used for the specific epithet, as in avocado: *Perseus* sp. If you wish to refer to all the avocado species, you can do so by writing *Perseus* spp. In other words, singular for a species is "sp.", or plural is "spp."

The classification system

The hierarchy arrangement

Every named plant has a binomial. To make this information manageable, plants are further classified into a hierarchy based on their characteristics. Morphology, physiological functions, pollination patterns, microscopic structures, molecular data (and more) all contribute to the grouping of plants.

The plant kingdom contains all the plants on earth and is divided into groups. Each group is called a phylum (also called a division). Phyla (plural) are further divided into classes, then into orders, followed by families. Within families, we find the genus and specific epithet of the plant. This seven-member classification hierarchy is used to categorize every plant known. Two examples are shown in Table 4-D.

Horticultural designations

Using keys for plant identification

A species is generally defined as a group of plants that can successfully interbreed. Subspecies can arise naturally if members of the species are separated geographically and the characteristics of the separated groups of plants start to drift apart. If the physical barrier were removed, however, the plant could once again interbreed. Subspecies are abbreviated as subsp. or ssp. It is written as: *Magnolia macrophylla* **subsp.** *ashei.*

Variety

Sometimes, different-looking plants may arise within a species in the same geographic area. If these are perpetuated, the name of the variety is attached in lower case letters following the specific epithet. It can be written in two ways, as in *Cedrus atlantica glauca* or *Cedrus atlantica* var. *glauca*.

Cultivar

A cultivar is a variety that has been intentionally cultivated for a certain characteristic (cultivated + variety). The cultivar name is then capitalized and placed in single quotes, as in *Malus floribunda* 'Gorgeous'. Horticulturists may refer to a cultivar as a "selection."

Hybrid

A hybrid is a cross between two species or two genera. A hybrid could arise naturally, but most often is produced intentionally by transferring the pollen of one to the stigma of another. The hybrid is given a Latinized name which does not necessarily reveal the parents. This name is preceded by an X after the genus. *Clematis x jackmanii* is a hybrid between *C. lanuginose* and *C. viticella*. When speaking, you would say "Clematis, the hybrid species jackmanii."

Dichotomous keys

To identify a plant, you can use field guides or keys. To use a key, you need to know the parts of a plant and information about the leaves. In a dichotomous key, you will be asked a number of questions. Each question has two or more possible answers. The choice you make directs you to the next question. This process continues until you reach a description of the plant you wish to identify.

A number of plant keys are available online. In addition, a number of plant-identification apps have become available for digital devices.

Figure 4-B. Arrangement of leaves on stem

Alternate — Opposite — Whorled

Leaf identification

Many leaf features are used for identification. Venation, petioles and stipules can be seen in **Figures 4-M** and **4-N**. and 4-N. In this section, we will examine other features of leaves.

- **Arrangement of leaves on a stem.** Leaves are attached to a stem in several different ways (see Figure 4-B). If two leaves are attached at a node, they are opposite. If there is only one leaf at a node, it is alternate. Whorled leaves are three or more leaves at a node.

- **Leaf shape.** The major shapes are lanceolate (black willow), cordate (catalpa), linear (willow oak), elliptical (beech), and ovate (osage orange) (see Figure 4-C.).

- **Leaf margin.** The margin, or edge, of a leaf has many forms; some of these are shown in Figure 4-D. They are entire, undulate (wavy), serrate (toothed), double serrate, crenate (rounded teeth), and lobed (rounded extensions).

- **Leaf bases.** The base of a leaf (see Figure 4-E) is cuneate (wedge-shaped), obtuse (rounded), cordate (heart-shaped), truncate (flat), or oblique (asymmetrical).

- **Leaf tips.** Leaf tips (also Figure 4-E) are acute (pointed), acuminate (a long

Figure 4-C. Leaf shapes

Figure 4-D. Leaf margins

narrow pointed tip), bristle-tipped, truncate (squared), or obtuse (rounded).

- **Simple and compound leaves.** Leaves are simple or compound (see Figure 4-F). Simple leaves are one blade attached to the stem. In a compound leaf, the leaf is divided into leaflets. If these leaflets are again further divided into more leaflets, the leaf is said to be doubly compound. To determine what kind of leaf you have, look for the axillary bud. Leaves have axillary buds, but leaflets do not.

Figure 4-E. Leaf bases (top) and tips

4.3 The Structure of Plants

Cells, tissues, and organs

All organisms are comprised of cells. Cells are a membrane-bound protoplasmic mass where all the functions of the organism are carried out. Plant cells provide structure as well as carrying out the physiological processes.

Cellulose is the component of plant cell walls conferring a rigid structure to the plant. Inside the cell, functions are carried out in specific structures called organelles. Examples of organelles are the nucleus, mitochondria, and chloroplast.

Plant cells are organized into tissues with specialized functions. A tissue is a group of similar cells that perform a particular function. Tissue systems can work together and form organs such as leaves, stems, flowers, seeds, and roots. The basic organs of a plant are seen in Figure 4-G.

Figure 4-F. Simple and compound leaves

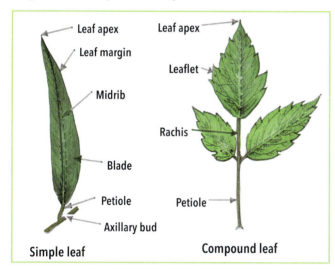

- **Other identification criteria.** Seeds, flowers, bark and twig color, rough or smooth stems, leaf scars, and other features all contribute to the correct identification of a plant.

Figure 4-G. Root and shoot terminology

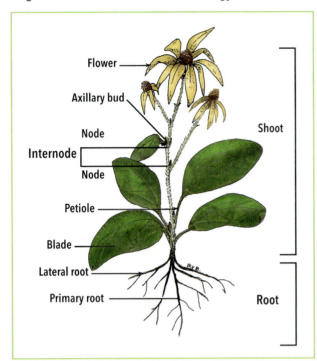

Apical meristems are located at the tips of roots and shoots and are responsible for an increase in length (see Figure 4-H). Shoot apical meristems are also responsible for new leaves, branches, and flowers. At the node, buds form where the petiole joins the stem. These axillary buds are apical meristems that will become new shoots. If the terminal apical meristems are removed, the axillary buds are encouraged to grow. This is familiar to gardeners, who prune the tops of a plant to cause "bushing out" or lateral growth.

Grasses

Most plants grow at the tips due to apical meristems. In grasses, however, the meristems are located near the crown of the plant at a

The leaves, stem, buds, and flowers form the shoot. The point at which a leaf leaves the stem is the node. The length of stem between two nodes is the internode. At the node, an axillary bud may be found. The leaf, also called a blade, may be attached to the stem with its own short stem, which is called a petiole.

The root may consist of a primary root and horizontally-branching lateral roots. The roots and shoots are connected by a continuous vascular system that allows transport and communication between all the plant parts.

Meristems

Meristems are tissues in which cells are actively dividing, resulting in plant growth.

They allow the plant to continue growing throughout its entire life. The cells that develop in a meristem differentiate into the various cell types required in a vascular plant.

Figure 4-H. Meristems

74   Maryland Master Gardener Handbook

node. The blade is pushed upward. This is why grasses can regrow after animals graze and lawns are mowed. For more on grasses, see Chapter 14 (Lawns).

Roots

Roots are the underground part of a plant. They lack nodes, shoots, and leaves. Most roots occur in the top foot of soil. Their depth and number depend on the climate, soil quality, and availability of water.

Functions of roots

Roots have several functions. They anchor the plant, absorb water and nutrients, store food, and support the stem.

Roots anchoring the plant take two forms, a taproot and a fibrous root (see Figure 4-I). Taproots have branching side roots and a main root to access deep sources of water. They are a good strategy for the plant in areas where rainfall is uncertain. Digging up and moving plants with large taproots, however, may be difficult to do without damaging the taproot.

Fibrous roots have no main stem, but many branches. Where water is plentiful, roots may be shallow and not anchor the plant as well

Figure 4-I. Tap root (left) and fibrous root

Figure 4-J. Root anatomy

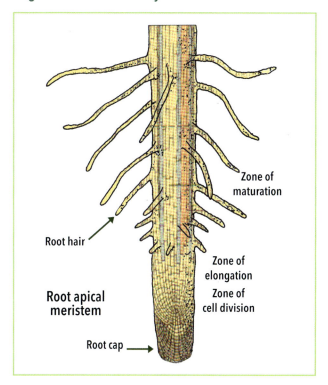

as a deep root. This is why it is better to water plants deeply at intervals, rather than a little each day.

Anatomy of roots

Roots are divided into three zones, as shown in Figure 4-J. The zone of cell division contains the apical meristem. The root cap protects the meristem as the root pushes forward. In the zone of elongation, cells grow and lengthen, extending the root into the soil. Small root hairs are found in the zone of maturation.

This is where water and minerals get absorbed into the plant. Root hairs greatly increase the surface area of the root, enhancing its ability to take up nutrients.

Modified roots

Some roots are modified for a particular function. Aerial roots, such as those found in an orchid, arise from stems and take water from the air, in addition to anchoring the plant. Parasitic roots, such as those of mistletoe, penetrate other plants for their nutrients and water. Roots that store water and food are known as storage roots. Examples are carrots and turnips. They store starch and other carbohydrates. These are just a few examples of modified roots.

Stems

Functions of stems

Stems support the leaves, reproductive structures, and fruit. They contain the vascular system that transports food and water and extend throughout the entire plant. Most importantly, the stem positions the leaves to receive light for photosynthesis.

Transport of nutrients

The stem contains vascular bundles. These are the ducts that are the circulation system of a plant. They are like blood vessels in people. The xylem conducts water and minerals. These nutrients are absorbed by the root and distributed upward to every part of the plant.

The phloem conducts sugars manufactured in the leaves by photosynthesis. These materials are transported downward throughout the plant.

Like roots, stems are modified to perform a variety of functions. The presence of nodes, buds, and occasionally, leaves will identify the structure as a stem.

Stolons are horizontal, above-ground stems, such as those commonly seen in the strawberry (see Figure 4-K). The internodes are long, and a node can set roots and start a new plant. Rhizomes are also modified horizontal stems. These, however, are found underground, as in perennial grasses.

Figure 4-K. Modified stems (stolons, rhizomes, crown)

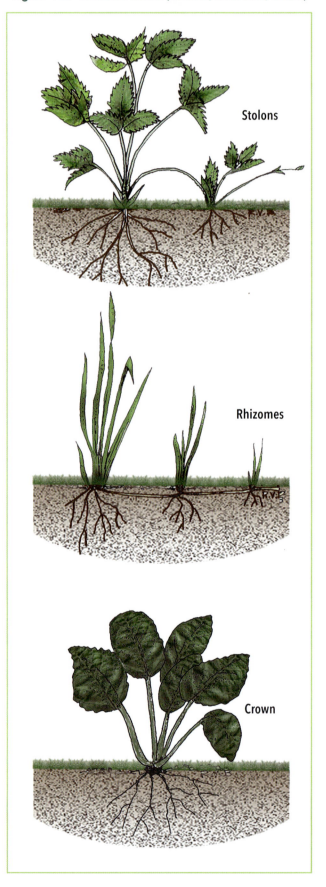

Figure 4-L. Tuber (left) and corm

Stolons and rhizomes are often used to propagate new plants, but are problematic when dealing with an invasive plant species. **(See Chapter 22, Invasive Plants.)**

Crowns, as in cabbage, have leaves and flowers on a stem that has very short internodes. Tubers are underground stems that store starch. The "eyes" of potatoes are axillary buds, formed around the enlarged stem (see Figure 4-L). Corms look like bulbs but are actually stem tissue. (Bulbs are primarily leaf tissue.) The papery tissues on the outside are modified leaves, as in iris, gladiola, and crocuses.

Vascular cambium

Secondary growth in woody plants increases the diameter of the stem due to lateral, or secondary, meristems (see Figure 4-M). This vascular cambium produces phloem, or inner bark, to the outside of the cambium, and xylem (wood) to the inside.

Figure 4-M. Cross-section: woody dicot stem

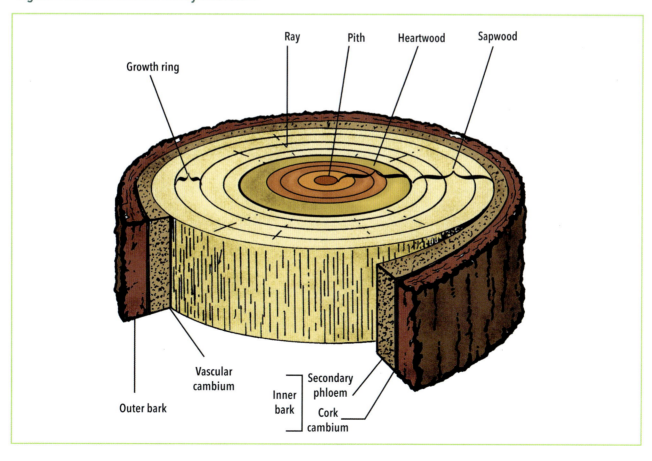

Tree rings

In temperate zones such as Maryland, spring generally provides warm, moist, growing conditions. Xylem produced in the spring has large cells and relatively thin walls. As the growing season progresses, the new cells are smaller and denser.

Dendrology

This change makes it possible to determine the age of a woody plant by counting the annual growth rings in a cross-section (see Figure 4-M). Growth rings also allow dendrologists to monitor past climate conditions.

Heartwood and sapwood

Xylem produced in previous years may still be active in the transport of water and nutrients (sapwood). The older wood in the center (heartwood) becomes non-functional.

Leaves

Functions of leaves

The leaf is the site of photosynthesis. The leaf surface accepts light and regulates the evaporation of water. In general, plants found in shady sites have large leaves to collect the maximum amount of available light. Small-leaved plants, in contrast, are often found in sunny spots.

Attachment to stem

Leaves may be attached to the stem by a short stem of their own known as the petiole. An axillary bud exists at the site where the petiole meets the stem (see Figure 4-O). Sometimes a small leaf is found where the petiole contacts the stem, called a stipule. If no petiole is present, the leaf is called sessile (see Figure 4-O). Sessile leaves may form a sheath around the stem.

Vascular system and venation pattern

The vascular system of the stem continues into the leaves, where we refer to it as veins. Several different vein patterns are seen in leaves and aid in identification (see Figure 4-N). Veins can be parallel (corn), dichotomous, (gingko), pinnately veined (beech), or palmately veined (maple).

Figure 4-O. Attachment of leaves to stem

Figure 4-N. Vein patterns in leaves

Figure 4-P. Stoma

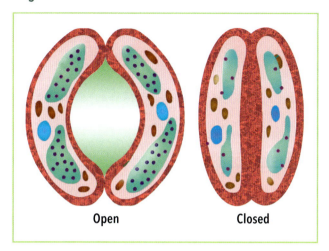

Open Closed

Stomata

Leaves must be able to exchange gasses, just like us. They need to take in carbon dioxide for photosynthesis and release oxygen and water vapor. For this, the leaf has pores called stomata, mostly on the bottom of the leaf. The action of the stomata (singular: stoma) is regulated by guard cells around the pore (see Figure 4-P). When water is plentiful, the guard cells are turgid (full) and in the open position, allowing gas exchange for internal reactions. When there is a lack of water, the guard cells are deflated, closing the pore to reduce the rate of water loss.

A square centimeter of leaf surface can have up to 10,000 stomata. Some aquatic plants, like water lilies, have the stomata on top of the leaf.

Modified leaves

In some plants, leaves have become highly modified to adapt to the environment. Spines are modified leaves that discourage nibbling by animals. In the cactus, the stem has a thick covering and this is where photosynthesis takes place. In this desert adaptation, leaves have less surface area for evaporation as well as a defensive role.

Tendrils, as in the pea, are leaves that are adapted to attach to a supporting structure. Tendrils have specific rates and direction of turn and may respond to touch.

Bracts are modified leaves at the base of a flower. The flowers are small and located at the center, as in the dogwood and the poinsettia. In this case, it is the bracts that attract the pollinators.

Needles are modified leaves. They have a thick outer coat, little surface area, recessed stomata, and specialized cells protecting the vascular system, all adaptations designed for dry wind and cold weather. Needles contain resin, important in wound healing and fire protection.

Figure 4-Q. Cross-section of a bud

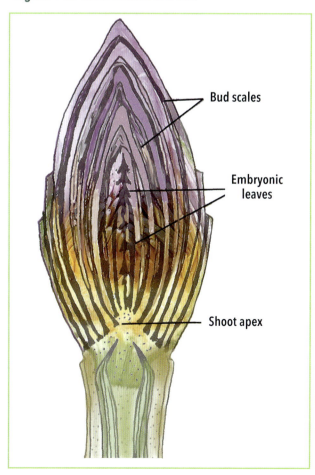

Bud scales

Embryonic leaves

Shoot apex

Buds

A bud is an undeveloped shoot from which embryonic leaves or flower parts arise. Examples include leaf buds and flower buds. Figure 4-Q shows the bud scales that protect the inner embryonic leaves. A tough outer coat protects the bud from insects and the environment. The buds of trees can withstand very low temperatures when dormant.

Buds may be located at the terminals (stem tips) or laterally, in leaf axils. The Brussels sprouts we eat are enlarged axillary buds formed at nodes along the plant's stem. Capers are the immature flower buds of a Mediterranean shrub, *Capparis spinosa* L.

4.4 Reproductive Structures

Angiosperms and gymnosperms

Most existing plant species are flowering plants known as angiosperms. The seeds of angiosperms are enclosed in fruits. Gymnosperms, on the other hand, are non-flowering plants. The most familiar group of gymnosperms is the conifers, which bear cones containing seeds. Conifers generally are evergreen trees with needles (see **Chapter 16, Woody Plants.**)

Flowers

Flowers arise from the apical meristem. You can actually think of the flower as a combination of modified stems and leaves. Figure 4-R is a generalized schematic picture of the cross-section of a flower. The structure of the flower is used in classification of plants and is an aid in identification.

Anatomy of a flower

Flowers have male and female parts. Usually these parts are present in the same flower. They are called perfect flowers. Some plants, like squash, form separate male and female flowers on each plant. We call these plants monoecious (Greek for "one house"). Sometimes, as in the holly, the male and female parts are located on different plants. This is a dioecious plant (Greek for "two houses").

The male part of the flower is the stamen (see Figure 4-R). The stamen consists of the anther, which holds the pollen, and the filament, the stalk that holds the anther position for access by the pollinator.

Figure 4-R. Flower anatomy

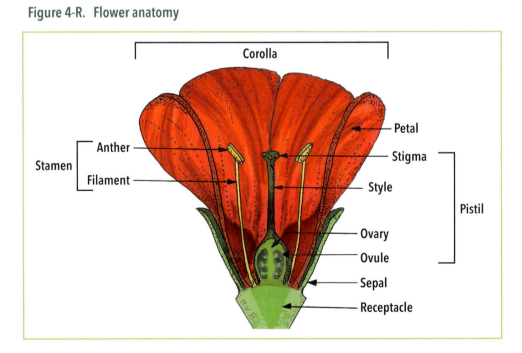

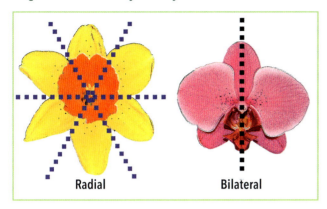

Figure 4-S. Flower symmetry

Figure 4-T. Position of the ovary

The female part of the flower is the carpel. It consists of the stigma, a sticky structure which receives the pollen; the style, which holds the stigma in position; and the ovary. One carpel or several fused carpels in one flower are referred to as the pistil. The ovary contains the ovules that will become seeds when fertilized.

Surrounding this internal structure are the petals. The entire group of petals is the corolla. The petals in the corolla can be either separate or fused. Honeysuckle and morning glory have fused petals. Outside of the petals are the sepals. Sepals are actually modified leaves that protect the bud before it opens. All the parts of the flower are borne on the receptacle. All of these plant parts are useful in identification of the plant.

Symmetry

A flower is either radially or bilaterally symmetrical (see Figure 4-S). A flower is radially symmetrical when there are many planes of symmetry (as in an asterisk: *). A human is bilaterally symmetrical. That is, there is only one plane of symmetry, as in an orchid or a sweet pea flower.

Position of the ovary

The petals attach in different places with respect to the ovary. This is helpful in field identification. If the petals attach at the bottom of the ovary, as in our generalized flower (see Figure 4-R), the ovary is superior. If the petals attach at the top of the ovary, it is inferior. Observe inferior ovaries in squash and iris. Between these two positions, the ovary is semi-superior. If you cut a flower in half, in cross section, it is easy to discover the position of the ovary (see Figure 4-T).

Inflorescence

The arrangement of flowers on the stem is called the inflorescence. Figure 4-U shows some of the most common types of inflorescences. Inflorescences can be complex at times, and can also aid in identification.

Fertilization

Fertilization is different from pollination (see Figure 4-V). Pollination brings the pollen to the right location. Pollen from the anther comes into contact with the stigma.

When the pollen lands on the stigma, a chemical reaction occurs. The pollen then travels down the style into the ovary via a pollen tube. Only when the male pollen unites with the female ovule is the plant fertilized.

Cones

Conifer means "cone-bearing." Most conifers have soft wood. The apical meristem produces a "stem" which becomes the axis of the cone.

Figure 4-U. Inflorescences

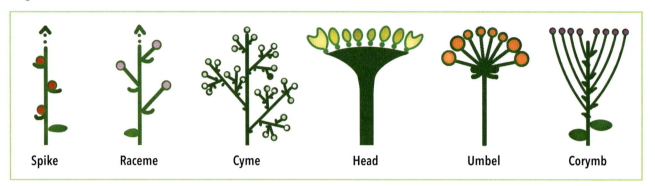

Figure 4-V. Pollination and fertilization

The leaves are modified into scales. At the base of each "leaf" is an axillary bud that becomes the ovule in the female cone. The seed then sits on the woody scale with no protection as in flowers of angiosperms. Male and female cones are most often on the same tree, in different places. Pollen arrives at the female cone by wind or insects.

Seeds

Seeds allow plants plant species to exist through hard times. They can survive extended drought and cold while remaining dormant. The thick outer coat resists decay by bacteria and the elements. Inside, food for the developing embryo is stored. Germination is triggered by light, hormones, water, and other environmental cues.

Anatomy of seeds

The embryo has all the information needed for a new plant (see Figure 4-V). The embryo is protected from weather or dehydration by the seed coat. Endosperm provides food to give the embryo a good start in life. The embryo may have one or two seed leaves.

Germination

Germination occurs when seeds go from a dormant state to actively growing. Water is absorbed into the seed. Some seeds need light to germinate, others require darkness.

If a seed contains only one embryonic leaf, the plant is a monocotyledon. Referred to as monocots, these plants are easily recognized

Figure 4-W. Monocot vs. dicot seed cross-section

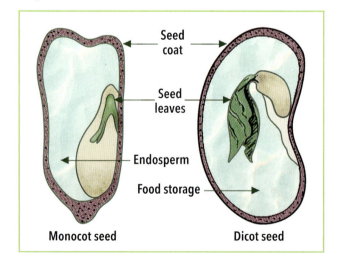

82   Maryland Master Gardener Handbook

by their growth habits. Their vertical leaves with parallel veins appear above the soil, as in corn, oats, or onions.

Dicotyledons, or dicots, have two embryonic leaves. These two seed leaves, or cotyledons, appear above ground. They nourish the seedling and gradually shrink. Then, two "true" leaves appear. It is best to wait for two or four true leaves before setting out seedlings in your garden.

More on monocots and dicots can be found in Section 4.1.

Dissemination

Seeds can be dispersed to locations where they may germinate and will not need to compete with the parent plant for the available resources. They are distributed by wind, seed-eating animals, seed-carrying animals, or water.

Some plants generate few seeds, each one designed for success. Palm trees produce a low number of coconuts, but each one is well protected and highly nutritious. Coconuts will float and are disseminated by water. Maple trees, on the other hand, produce an enormous number of seeds. They depend on the wind for distribution of at least a few seeds to a suitable environment.

Fruit

All flowering plants produce fruit, whether we eat it or not. After fertilization, the ovary develops into the fruit protecting the seed. The flesh of the ovary can provide some nutrition if the seed finds itself in soil that is not so good. Sometimes, the fruit entices other species to transport the seed to another location. The fruit may protect the seed from some diseases or from drying out.

Figure 4-X. Pericarp of the peach

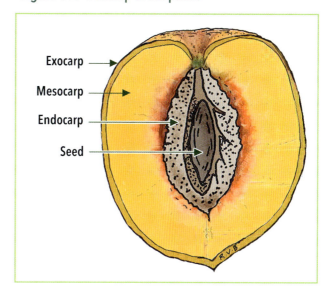

Many of the foods we call vegetables are actually fruits, as they represent the fleshy ovary surrounding the seed(s).

Ovary wall

The ovary wall, or pericarp, is composed of three layers (see Figure 4-X). Each layer can be dry or fleshy, depending upon the type of fruit. The exocarp is the outermost layer, followed by the mesocarp and the endocarp on the inside. Pumpkins and squash have a thick exocarp, and the other layers remain fleshy. Peaches have a hard endocarp (pit) surrounded by soft mesocarp and exocarp.

Simple, aggregate, and multiple fruits

Fruits are classified as simple, aggregate, or multiple. This depends on how many ovaries were involved in their creation. Simple fruits, like peaches and pears, develop from a single ovary. Blackberries form from one flower with multiple carpels, i.e., an aggregate fruit. Pineapples, on the other hand, form from many flowers on one stem, i.e., a multiple fruit.

4.5 Pollination

We love flowers because they are beautiful and sometimes edible. The plant, however, does not care about our tastes; it has one job, and that is to survive. To that end, a seed must be produced, which requires pollination and fertilization.

Pollination strategies

Some plants, like grasses, depend on the wind for pollination. The flowers of wind-pollinated plants are usually small and inconspicuous. Plants that depend on insect or animal pollinators must attract them. They may produce a showy flower, fragrant nectar, pheromones (chemical sex hormones), or sometimes, a disagreeable odor.

Self-pollination

When pollen from a plant falls on its own stigma, whether in the same flower or on another flower on the same plant, it is known as self-pollination. If the plant exists in isolation, or if an insect or animal is not available to aid pollination, the plant species will still survive.

Most plants avoid self-pollination. If the pollen donor and the stigma are on two different plants, there is more genetic variability. Information from both parents stays within the species and the plant has better chances for survival. **(See Chapter 3, Ecology.)**

Plants have evolved several strategies to avoid self-pollination. These include:

- The pollen grains and the carpel develop at different times.
- Male and female structures are on different plants (dioecious).
- There is a built-in mechanism for rejecting pollen from the same plant (self-incompatibility).

Attracting pollinators

Each plant attracts and rewards its chosen pollinators. Flowers are designed so that on the way to the nectar, the pollinator must contact the pollen-containing anthers. Pollen sticks to them and is transferred to the next flower visited.

Birds, moths, beetles, ants, butterflies, mosquitoes, slugs, true bugs, and flies are all important pollinators. Most plants depend on insects. Many of the bees and wasps in our landscape that cause concern for humans are actually excellent pollinators.

Reptiles and mammals can also pollinate. Bats, rodents, lemurs, skinks, lizards, and honey possums are known to pollinate plants in their quest for nectar.

Petal color

The colors of the petals lure pollinators. Flowers pollinated by birds and butterflies tend to be red and yellow and produce lots of nectar, but lack a strong scent. Flowers pollinated in the evening by bats and moths tend to have large pale or white flowers and a strong fragrance.

Bees have vision that is shifted toward the ultraviolet. Flowers pollinated by bees are most often blue, violet, and yellow. Because bees perceive ultraviolet light, they can see color patterns in petals that are not apparent to us. For example, a buttercup looks all yellow to us, but the bee sees a dark center, pointing the way to the nectar. These color patterns are called nectar guides.

Petal shape and location

The nectar must be protected while allowing the pollinator access. Some insects and birds need a landing platform, and the flower has evolved to accommodate the specific weight and size of the pollinator. Other plants depend on hovering birds and insects:

- Snapdragons have a landing platform that triggers the flower to open when a bee of the right size and weight lands on it.
- Butterflies tend to walk around on clusters of small flowers, probing for nectar with their tongues.
- Beetles are attracted to pollen but are rather clumsy. Flowers such as magnolia have large, sturdy petals and wide access to the nectar to accommodate them.
- Wild ginger flowers are at ground level and can be pollinated by slugs, in addition to mosquitoes and gnats.

Nectar may be located at the base of a long tubular flower or in nectar spurs. Hummingbirds and moths are perfectly designed to retrieve this nectar without a landing platform.

Scent

Some pollinators are more attracted to scent than color. The flower scent can be fragrant, distasteful, or undetectable to us. The flowers must be open and releasing scent at the correct time of day to attract the desired pollinators.

Our native pawpaw and skunk cabbage have flowers that smell—frankly—quite disgusting. They are pollinated by flies and other carrion insects that relish the scent.

Flowers like moonflowers, honeysuckle, and yucca release their aroma in the evening to entice bat and moth pollinators. The Saguaro cactus of the southwest has open flowers both day and night to encourage pollination by bees, birds, and bats.

Rewards

Pollinators are not concerned about the future of the plant species. They are in search of nectar and/or pollen as food. Nectar is a high-energy food full of sugars and a small amount of other vitamins and minerals. Pollen is a high-protein food that contains starches and other nutrients. Many species of beetles and bees depend on pollen.

Special pollinators

Many plants are pollinated by more than one species. Other plants and pollinators have evolved to have an exclusive relationship.

Certain orchids require a specific wasp species to pollinate them. To attract the wasp, these orchids mimic a female wasp, tricking the insect into landing on them. (Some orchid species are "cheaters"; they attract a specific wasp with no reward.)

A special relationship exists between the yucca plant and its moth pollinator. Yucca can only be pollinated by moths, and 70 percent of moths only pollinate one yucca species.

Female moths have specialized mouth parts to collect and pack up pollen. She packs this pollen into the stigma then lays her egg in the ovary of a yucca flower. The yucca is pollinated and the larva has nourishment upon hatching.

These are examples of plant/pollinator interdependence. While very efficient, this kind of special relationship is risky. If one of the partners were to become extinct, the other would also disappear.

4.6 Plant Growth & Development

Growth factors

Plant growth factors, also known as plant hormones, are substances produced in one location, but may act in another location. Hormones generally have multiple effects, directing growth and development and responding to environmental stimuli. The major groups of plant hormones are:

- Auxins
- Gibberellins
- Cytokinins
- Ethylene
- Abscisic acid

Auxins

Auxins are a group of hormones that stimulate cell growth and elongation, and participate in plant development, among other things. Auxins are produced in apical meristems. They spread from cell to cell downward through the stem, and suppress growth of the axillary buds. This is called apical dominance. The final shape of a plant is influenced by the number and length of shoot apical meristems. Removal of the terminal bud (pinching back a plant) eliminates the flow of auxins and thus allows lateral buds to sprout.

Gibberellins

Gibberellins promote both stem and cell elongation, and regulate seed germination. They are produced in young roots and leaves. Gibberellins play a role in the development of flowers and fruit and are used in the commercial production of grapes. Application of this hormone will increase the internode length as well as the grape size. Elongated stems permit better air flow and thus reduce disease problems in grapes.

Cytokinins

Cytokinins promote cell division and differentiation. They are synthesized in the roots and enhance axillary bud growth. This counteracts the effects of auxins in apical dominance. Cytokinins also delay the aging of leaves.

Ethylene

Ethylene is a gas that behaves like a hormone. It promotes aging and responds to mechanical stresses such as drought or injury. When plants are touched or exposed to wind, increased ethylene represses growth in length. Ethylene also stimulates fruit ripening and is involved in leaf abscission (dropping of leaves by a deciduous plant). Fruits such as apples and bananas produce large quantities of ethylene. Enclosing a green fruit, such as a tomato, in a bag with some apples will speed the ripening of the tomato.

Abscisic acid

Abscisic acid is produced in leaves, stems, roots and fruit. It establishes dormancy of seeds and buds. It also regulates the closing of stomata when water is limited. This hormone was originally thought to be responsible for abscission of leaves and was named for this effect.

Environmental growth regulators

Light

Light influences plant growth by its quality (wavelength), quantity, and duration (photoperiod). Through the action of hormones, plants may turn toward or away from the light (phototropism). Phototropism and stomata opening are examples of processes affected by the blue component of light. Photosynthesis in plants is most efficient at red- and blue-light wavelengths. Seed germination, flowering, and root growth respond to the red wavelengths of light.

The relative lengths of night and day influence the flowering of some plants. Short-day plants flower only when the day length decreases to a certain extent. Examples are poinsettias and violets. Long-day plants flower in late spring or early summer when the length of the night decreases. Examples of long-day plants are petunias and clover. The flowering of day-neutral plants is independent of day length. Commercial growers can induce flowering by manipulation of day length and/or the application of synthetic hormones. Like people, plants appear to operate on a 24-hour cycle. This circadian rhythm is a complex internal process that regulates the plant's timing of activities. For example, a plant positions the leaves to prepare for daylight and to flower at appropriate times. The plant changes to other metabolic states to conserve energy when the light reactions of photosynthesis subside.

Touch

Plants respond to touch or physical stress several ways. Ethylene production may be increased, changing the growth pattern to respond to the situation. Tendrils will curl around an object they encounter. Roots will grow toward moist soil. Leaves may actually fold up when touched, as in the Mimosa. The Venus flytrap is a well-known example of a plant responding to touch.

Other environmental stimuli

We have seen that hormones, light, and touch all impact the growth of plants. Plants also respond to temperature, the availability of water, gravity, invasion (by fungi, bacteria, or viruses), attack by herbivores (both insect and mammalian), chemical stimuli, and mechanical stresses.

Nutrients

Macronutrients are elements that the plant needs in large amounts for optimal growth. Micronutrients are elements (sometimes called trace elements) needed in small amounts, but with essential roles. For more on plant nutrients, see **Chapter 6, Plant Nutrition.**

4.7 Regulation of Plant Growth

Metabolic processes

Plant growth and development requires three main metabolic processes: photosynthesis, respiration, and transpiration. The plant must maintain an appropriate balance among these processes for optimum health.

Photosynthesis

Photosynthesis is the process by which the plant makes its own food. This makes it possible for non-photosynthetic organisms, like us, to live. The raw materials of photosynthesis are acquired by the plant from the soil (water and minerals) and from the air (carbon dioxide). The energy required is absorbed from the sun by a group of pigment molecules. Chlorophyll and the other pigments are found in special cell organelles called chloroplasts. In the chloroplast, light energy is used to turn the raw materials into simple sugars. Oxygen is a by-product of this reaction that is then released into the atmosphere. (See Figure 4-Y.)

Figure 4-Y. Photosynthesis reaction

$6CO_2$ + $12H_2O$ + light energy ▶▶▶▶ $C_6H_{12}O_6$ + $6O_2$ + $6H_2O$
carbon dioxide, water, sugar, oxygen, water

Leaves are the site of much photosynthesis, presenting a large flattened surface for maximum sun exposure. Stems and other structures may also contain chlorophyll and perform photosynthesis.

Respiration

In order for the plant to benefit from the food that it produces, it must break it down and extract the energy from it. This process is called cellular respiration and occurs in another organelle, the mitochondria. In respiration, sugars and oxygen are broken down into carbon dioxide, water, and energy. This energy is used to build new molecules for growth and to perform the everyday metabolic functions of the plants needed for survival.

Transpiration

Water is absorbed from the soil and transported all around the plant, carrying soil nutrients with it. This is the source of the saying, "Fix the soil, not the plant". After moving into the leaves, water is lost by evaporation from the leaves. This process is known as transpiration and also cools the leaves. The rate of transpiration depends upon the prevailing environmental conditions.

Life cycles

Both woody and herbaceous plants can live for more than one growing season. One way to classify plants is based on the length of their life (see Table 4-E):

- Annuals live for only one growing season. In that season, they flower, set seed, and die. Some garden annuals, like *Celosia* sp. or *Portulaca* sp., drop many viable seeds that germinate readily in the spring.

- Biennial plants live for two seasons. In the first year, they produce leaves, roots, and compact stems. Flowers are produced and seed developed in the second season.

Table 4-E. Plants categorized by lifespan

Name	Definition	Examples
Annual	Lives for one growing season	Sunflower, zinnia, petunia, bean
Biennial	Lives for two growing seasons	Carrot, onion, hollyhock, foxglove
Perennial	Lives for many growing seasons	Liatris, daisy, hosta, deciduous and evergreen trees

- Perennials return year after year. Some of the plant survives the winter and returns in the spring.

4.8 Plant Selection & Modification

Natural selection

In any particular environment, some plants will survive better than others. Even within a species, certain individual plants may survive insect attack or live through a drought. A plant with a particularly colorful flower may better attract a pollinator and thus have a greater chance to propagate itself. These are examples of natural selection, a process of selection by fitness. The well-adapted individuals are most likely to survive and reproduce. This is why genetic diversity is crucial to the survival of species. (See "Pollination" above.)

Artificial selection

For centuries, people have been choosing plants that have desirable qualities. Perhaps they taste better, grow better in the available soil, have a more attractive flower, or resist a certain pest. In fact, many of our food plants have arisen from wild plants after years of selecting for desirable traits (see Table 4-F). Selection by people rather than nature is "artificial selection." Plant breeders do this all the time. They continually choose varieties with some desirable improvement.

Genetic modification

Today, genetic research allows a new method of modifying plants. All living organisms contain DNA, which programs and directs the functioning of that cell. A gene is the region of the DNA that is responsible for a particular function. Genes for specific, desirable traits are inserted into the plant genome. This is often referred to as genetic engineering. These genes may come from another plant species or other organisms, such as insects and bacteria. Not all traits or plants can be handled this way, and much research and experimentation is required to confer a new feature to a plant.

Transgenic plants

When this technology results in a viable plant carrying a new gene, the plant is referred to as a transgenic plant. Many people refer to such a plant as a GMO (genetically modified organism).

Most transgenic plants currently in production were designed to combat weeds, viral diseases, or insects. Research is underway to produce plants with a much wider variety of traits aimed at growers, processors, and consumers, including plants tolerant of environmental stressors such as salinity or drought. Corn, soybean, and cotton are three of our important crops that are likely to contain introduced genes. Not all transgenic plants have

Table 4-F. Wild cabbage/mustard by selection

Food	Selected for	Scientific name
Broccoli, cauliflower	Flower buds, stems	*Brassica oleracea* var. *botrytis*
Brussels sprouts	Axillary buds	*Brassica oleracea* var. *gemmifera*
Kohlrabi	Stem	*Brassica oleracea* var. *gongylodes*
Cabbage	Terminal buds	*Brassica oleracea* var. *capitata*
Collards, kale	Leaves	*Brassica oleracea* var. *acephala*
Chinese kale	Leaves	*Brassica oleracea* var. *alboglabra*
Pak choy	Leaves	*Brassica oleracea* var. *chinensis*

Source: USDA plant profiles and Floridata at **floridata.com**

Table 4-G. Major categories of transgenic plants

Category	Brief description
Insect resistance	A naturally occurring insect toxin (Bt) is found in the soil bacterium *Bacillus thuringiensis*. The gene for this toxin has been inserted into some crop plants to confer resistance to chewing insects.
Viral resistance	A viral protein is overproduced in plants, resulting in resistance to that virus.
Protein production	The genes of proteins important in medicine or industry are inserted into plants for economical production.
Improved nutrition or cooking properties	Oil-producing plants have been altered to provide better nutrition or cooking properties. Rice with elevated vitamin A has been designed but as of this writing, has not been released for a variety of reasons.
Herbicide resistance	Crop plants are made resistant to a synthetic herbicide, simplifying application of herbicides.
Pollen production	Genes are introduced which render plants "male-sterile." This aids in hybrid seed production by alleviating the need to remove or bag male flowers on the desired female plant.

Table 4-H. Issues relating to transgenic plants

Issue	Topics under debate and review
Food safety	<ul><li>Is the nutritional value changed?</li><li>Could introduced proteins, or alteration of existing proteins, trigger an allergy in some people?</li><li>Could a plant that produces a pharmaceutical protein, such as a drug or vaccine, accidentally enter the food supply?</li></ul>
Environmental impact	<ul><li>Could the new trait cause the transgenic plant to become a weed?</li><li>If the trait were to move to a sexually compatible wild relative, could that plant become a weed?</li><li>Could the introduced trait have other types of impacts if it were to move unintentionally into a related wild plant?</li><li>Could the transgenic plant be harmful to non-target organisms or to threatened or endangered species?</li><li>Will the use of antibiotic-resistance genes in transgenic plants contribute to an increased bacterial resistance to antibiotics?</li><li>Are fewer herbicides, or less dangerous herbicides, really used when the herbicide-resistant plants are grown?</li><li>Is soil conservation enhanced by the use of transgenic plants?</li><li>How is the soil microbial community affected by increased use of transgenic plants?</li><li>What will be the impact of insects developing resistance to the toxic proteins produced in transgenic plants?</li></ul>
Social	<ul><li>Should all food containing GMOs be labeled?</li><li>Should a community be made aware of transgenic crops grown in their area?</li><li>Are there special concerns for vegetarians or other groups who may avoid certain foods based on religion or other personal reasons?</li><li>Who benefits from the production of each transgenic plant?</li></ul>

been approved to grow as crop plants. Some are used only for research or do not survive the trials and requirements of the regulatory process. Genetically modified plants are overseen in the federal government by a combined effort of the FDA, USDA, and EPA.

Transgenic plants are used in the production of biologically-active proteins such as enzymes, antibodies, or drugs. This is a very economical way to produce a medically or industrially important protein. When a plant is engineered and farmed to produce a protein used by the pharmaceutical industry, it is referred to as a pharmacrop or plant-based pharmaceutical. The current types of transgenic plants are listed in Table 4-G.

Genetic modification issues

As with any new technology, there are benefits as well as concerns and unanswered questions. The inclusion of new genes in plants that we eat or wear is of global concern and impacts the international production and transport of food.

Each transgenic plant generates specific concerns and has advocates and opponents. Table 4-H lists some of the issues that are currently debated and reviewed. It is important to have a basic understanding of these issues and encourage public dialogue.

Master Gardeners are increasingly called upon to comment on the presence of these crops in our communities or in our food. It is generally accepted that GMO foods are not detrimental to human health, although long-term effects cannot be measured. Master Gardeners are encouraged not to comment on this issue, as there is still research underway to examine the long-term effects of GMO foods. Regardless, the environmental, social and economic impacts must be taken into consideration. The health impacts of some pesticides used in production of GMO plants has in recent years come under scrutiny.

It is worth noting that recent rapid advances in the technology of gene editing will affect the way GMO plants are created. Regulatory agencies will need to adopt new policies to address these new developments.

Current GMO information

The U.S. government maintains a "Unified Biotechnology Website" with information on how biotechnology is regulated in the United States, including specific information and links to the applicable laws and regulations used by USDA, EPA, and FDA in overseeing the technology. In addition, there is a database of all approved organisms and decision documents specific to the individual evaluations. This can be found at:

usbiotechnologyregulation.mrp.usda.gov/ biotechnologygov/home/

Genetically Modified Crops: An overview Shetty, M. J. et al Journal of Pharmacognosy and Phytochemistry 2018; 7(1): 2405-2410. Found at:

phytojournal.com. ✻

AUTHOR

Judith Owen, Ph.D., University of Maryland Extension Master Gardener, Cecil County; currently a Penn State Extension Master Gardener in York, PA.

PUBLICATIONS

Capon, B. 2005. *Botany for Gardeners.* Timber Press. Portland, OR.

Nabors, M.W. 2004. Introduction to Botany. Pearson/Benjamin Cummings, Upper Saddle River, NJ.

PHOTOS

Learning objectives Plant Cells Photo: Hermann Schachner, Creative Commons CC0 1.0 Universal Public Domain Dedication

ILLUSTRATIONS

By Don Wittig, University of Maryland Extension Master Gardener, Montgomery County:

Figure 4-B *Arrangement of leaves on a stem*; Figure 4-C *Leaf shapes*; Figure 4-D *Leaf margins*; Figure 4-E *Leaf bases and tips*; Figure 4-F *Simple and compound leaves*; Figure 4-L *Tuber and corm*; Figure 4-M *Woody dicot stem*; Figure 4-O *Vein patterns in leaves*; Figure 4-W *Cross-section of monocot and dicot seeds*.

By Ray V. Bosmans, University of Maryland Extension:

Figure 4-A *Monocot and dicot stems*; Figure 4-G *Root and shoot terminology*; Figure 4-K *Modified stems*; Figure 4-R *Flower anatomy*; Figure 4-X *Pericarp of a peach*.

Colorization and additional figures by LeAnn Zotta.

WEBSITES

The Ohio State University. *PlantFacts.* plantfacts.org.ohio-state.edu/wiki/

University of Connecticut. *Plant Database.* hort.uconn.edu

USDA. *Plants Database.* fs.usda.gov/managing-land/wildflowers

USDA. *Celebrating Wildflowers.* fs.usda.gov/managing-land/wildflowers

Smithsonian Center for Learning and Digital Access. *Plants and Animals: Partners in Pollination.* learninglab.si.edu/collections/plants-and-animals-partners-in-pollination/er3GDtc6Mx03gqrB#r/

5: SOILS AND FERTILIZERS

Patricia Steinhilber, Ph.D.
Emileigh Lucas, M.S.

5 SOILS AND FERTILIZERS

CONTENTS

5.1 What is a Soil? 95
5.2 Soil Solids 96
5.3 Soil Pores 100
5.4 Soil as Entities of Nature 102
5.5 Soils as Natural Capital and Ecosystem Services 105
5.6 Soils as Hydrologic Buffers 106
5.7 Soils as Biochemical and Chemical Reactors 107
5.8 Soils as Media for Plant Growth 112
5.9 Soil Testing 114
5.10 Soil Health 119

LEARNING OBJECTIVES

- Composition of soils
- The five soil-forming factors and the four soil-forming processes
- Common biochemical and chemical processes in soil
- Nitrogen and phosphorus cycles
- The importance of testing the soil and of interpreting soil test results
- Types of fertilizers and their relative attributes
- Soil health

INTRODUCTION

Soil has many functions on Earth. Soil is the foundation of terrestrial ecosystems and provides most of the nutrients plants require, as well as mechanical support for plant roots.

Soils themselves are complex ecosystems with multiple ecological niches and an immense variety of inhabitants. All three phases of matter on Earth—solids, liquids and gases—are found in soil.

Soil is a very slowly renewable natural resources and requires careful management to preserve its integrity ("health") and protect it from loss and degradation. Rainfall flows through and over soil, so soil management impacts the quality of groundwater and surface water. Well-managed soil leads to healthy plants and clean water.

To read more on this subject, see **Chapter 6, Plant Nutrition.**

5.1 What is a Soil?

Different people think of soils in different ways. It may be thought of as:

- The loose surface material of the Earth in which plants grow (gardeners and farmers)
- The outer layer of the Earth's crust (geologists)
- The "ecstatic skin" of the Earth (writers)
- The interface between the atmosphere, hydrosphere, and lithosphere (ecologists)
- Natural bodies or phenomena of nature (natural scientists)
- The unconsolidated mineral or organic material on the immediate surface of the Earth that serves as a natural medium for the growth of land plants (Soil Science Society of America)

Despite these differences in definitions, one fact remains the same: soils are dynamic, reactive, three-phase ecosystems composed

Figure 5-A. Composition of topsoil when drained

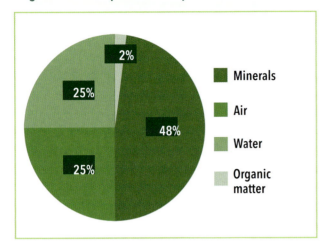

Table 5-A. Major mineral classes in a soil

Mineral class	Particle size	Particle feel
Sands	0.05 – 2 millimeters	Gritty
Silts	0.002 – 0.05 millimeters	Like cornstarch or talcum powder
Clays	≤ 0.002 millimeters	Sticky when wet

The textural class (e.g., clay, sandy clay, clay loam, etc.) affects many properties in the soil. The 12 soil textural classes have been broadly grouped according to their impact on soil properties. Table 5-B shows the groupings and summarizes some of these properties.

Texture and structure

Texture:

- Determined by the proportion of sand, silt, and clay-sized particles in soil

of solids, liquids, and gases. Soil solids may be mineral or organic. The liquid in soil (soil solution) and the gases in soil (soil air) exist in the pore spaces between soil solids.

Figure 5-A shows the proportion of the various components in a typical Maryland topsoil several days after a rainfall.

5.2 Soil Solids

Soil solids, which can be mineral or organic, form the porous matrix (or support system) within which the soil solution and soil air exist.

Mineral solids

Soil minerals exist in various sizes. Table 5-A shows the names and sizes of the main mineral classes in a soil.

Most soils are mixtures of minerals. Soil texture describes the proportion of sand, silt, and clay-sized minerals present in a soil. Twelve textural classes are recognized by USDA based on the percentage of sand, silt, and clay-sized particles in a soil (see Figure 5-B).

Figure 5-B. The 12 soil textural classes

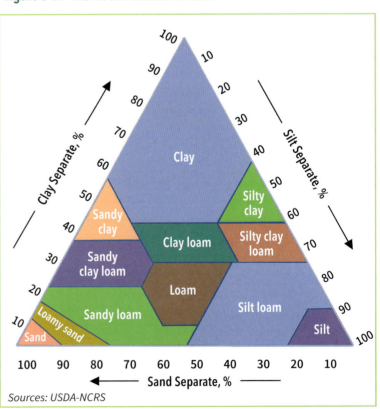

Sources: USDA-NCRS

96 Maryland Master Gardener Handbook   UME © 2025. All rights reserved.

Table 5-B. Effect of soil texture on soil properties

Soil property	Textural class		
	Sand, loamy sand, sandy loam	Loam, silt loam, silt, sandy clay loam	Clay, sandy clay, silty clay, clay loam and silty clay loam
Water and nutrient holding capacity	Low	Moderate	High
Infiltration and drainage	Fast	Moderate	Slow
Leaching potential	High	Moderate	Low
Aeration	Good	Moderate	Poor

- Organic matter plays no role in the determination of texture
- Texture is an inherent, unchangeable property of a soil; it is not altered by soil management practices

Structure:

- The arrangement of soil particles into clumps or aggregates
- Granular or crumb structure is desirable in top soils
- Structure can be improved or degraded as a result of soil management
- Good management results in an abundance of water-stable structures that withstand soil disturbance and the impact of rainfall
- Roots and fungal hyphae entrap soil particles into aggregates and sticky, gummy compounds produced by soil microbes and roots "glue" particles together

Organic solids

Organic matter encompasses all the materials in soils that are or were alive. It exists on a continuum from the living organisms, called biomass, at one end of the spectrum, to dead organisms and the residues of living organisms, and finally to microscopic "protected" material at the other end (see Figure 5-C).

Although organic matter makes up only two to five percent (by weight) of most soils' solid material, it plays a huge role in soil productivity. Soils with adequate organic matter content have a higher capacity to hold water and nutrients that are essential for crop production and a better capacity to supply oxygen for plant roots.

Figure 5-C. Continuum of organic matter in soil

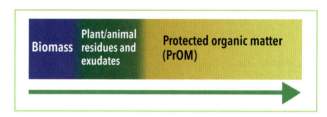

Biomass

Biomass is the living component of the soil. It consists of a range of creatures, as small as microscopic bacteria and as large as worms and other creatures that are visible to the unaided eye. The soil is habitat to more species of organisms than the Earth's surface habitats.

The soil creatures exist in a complex food web, as seen in Figure 5-D. Sources of extensive information on soil organisms are in the Reference section at the end of the chapter.

Figure 5-D. The soil food web

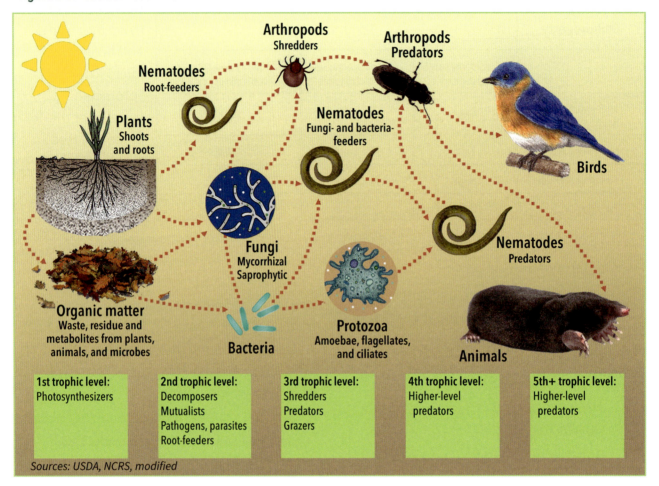

Sources: USDA, NCRS, modified

Functions of biomass

Nutrient cycling

- Microorganisms are the "heavy lifters" in decomposition of organic materials and nutrient cycling
- As the organisms, particularly microorganisms, digest plant and animal materials (referred to as residues), they use what they need and leave the rest behind in plant-available form. This is known as mineralization
- If nutrients, particularly nitrogen, in residues are inadequate for their needs, microorganisms will consume soil nutrients that plants would otherwise use. This is known as immobilization

Creation of biopores

- Larger organisms in the biomass improve soil structure while they move through, consuming plant and animal residues
- Organisms' movement creates channels throughout the soil profile, promoting water infiltration and creating a healthy balance between large pores (which allow rapid infiltration of rainfall and replenishment of oxygen in the root zone) and smaller pores (which store water for plant use and microbial habitat)

Residues and by-products

Residues and by-products include crop residues, dead roots, bodies of soil creatures, and materials that plant roots and soil creatures release or exude into the soil.

Functions of residues and by-products

Fuel and nutrients for soil organisms

- Residues provide the nutrients and energy needed to fuel the soil organisms that comprise the biomass
- Very fine particles of residues, called particulate organic matter or POM, have been shown to be the best source of fuel for soil organisms, and have a rapid turnover rate

Maintenance of soil structure

- The sticky, gummy by-products of residue decomposition hold soil particles together in clumps or aggregates and form the basis for good soil structure
- A soil with good structure allows greater infiltration for rainfall, stores more water for plant growth, and allows for replenishment of oxygen to the root zone
- Soil organisms consuming residues as a food source and producing by-products are builders of soil aggregates, and their presence results in well-structured soils. Maintaining an adequate food source for soil organisms is the key to a healthy soil. This will be discussed in more detail in the Soil Health section.

Protected Organic Matter (PrOM)

Protected organic matter is the stable organic matter in soils. It is the remains of microbial cells that are protected from further breakdown either by being physically sheltered within a microaggregate or bonded onto a clay surface. Some authors call this component of the organic matter "mineral-associated organic matter," or MAOM.

Here's what soil microbiologists have shown about the formation of PrOM (see Figure 5-E):

First, microbes produce enzymes and release them into the soil to break down dead plant and animal tissues. Microbes then reproduce. Eventually, microbes run out of fuel and die. Microbial cells are broken apart (lysed) as they decompose, leading to microbial cell debris also called patchy fragments. Lastly, the patchy fragments can be adsorbed onto soil clays or entrapped with soil aggregates as they form.

Figure 5-E. Protected organic matter (PrOM) formation

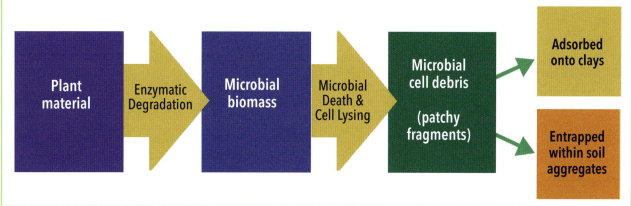

In many soils, PrOM makes up most of the soil organic matter. Because it is protected from breakdown, it is not a good energy or nutrient source for other soil organisms.

The role of humus

The concept of "humus" as a stable part of soil organic matter has endured for more than 100 years. Humification, the process whereby humus is produced, was previously understood to be a process wherein microbes broke down plant and animal residues, leaving recalcitrant materials (or materials that resisted breakdown) that somehow polymerized or combined into large, stable molecules of humus.

Research over the last 25 years has given soil scientists reasons to replace this concept. Using amazing new high-powered analytical tools, research has now shown that humification does not accurately describe what is going on in the soil, as these large stable humus molecules do not naturally exist and were rather an artifact of the technique that was previously used to observe organic matter.

5.3 Soil Pores

Soil pores make up the space between soil solids. The soil solution and soil air exist in the pores. Pores are described by their size and function.

Macropores are large pores which allow for rapid infiltration and drainage of rainfall. These pores are typically drained of water by gravity and filled with air within a day or two after heavy rainfall. They also allow rapid exchange of oxygen and carbon dioxide with the atmosphere.

Mesopores are medium-sized pores which store water against the force of gravity and hold that water in a form that cultivated plants can extract to meet their transpiration needs.

Micropores are small pores that hold water too tightly for most cultivated plants to extract. Micropores are the habitat of soil microbes.

These pores create a microscopic, maze-like network of spaces and channels. Soils need a balance between macropores, mesopores and micropores so plants have adequate water and oxygen in the root zone while maintaining a safe habitat for the smallest of soil organisms even during dry periods.

Soil solution

The soil solution is the liquid component of soil. It is composed of water and dissolved materials, and is the source of nutrients for plants. The soil solution's composition is undergoing constant change during the growing season. For example:

- Fertilization can increase the nutrient content of the soil solution
- The breakdown of plant residues and organic nutrient sources can increase nutrient content
- Plant uptake can reduce nutrient content
- Percolation, the downward movement of water in soil, can move nutrients deeper into soil
- Nutrients associated with soil solids can move into soil solution

Plant growth is optimized by maintaining an adequate quantity of water in soil and by ensuring an adequate level of all plant nutrients in the soil solution.

Table 5-C. Adverse conditions due to soil acidity

Condition	Soil component affected
Inadequate supply of nutrients	Calcium and magnesium may be present in inadequate amounts in acidic soils
Excessive or toxic supply of nutrients or non-essential elements	Aluminum, iron, zinc, manganese, and copper can be present in excessive and even toxic amounts in acidic soils
Nutrients bound in unavailable forms	Phosphorus and molybdenum are so tightly bound to soil clays that they are not available to plants in acidic soils
Inhospitable environment	Bacteria, such as those needed for nitrogen fixation, cannot thrive in acidic soils

Soil pH

A very important characteristic of the soil solution is its pH. pH, a logarithmic scale from 0 to 14, indicates whether the soil is acidic (<7), neutral (7), or basic (>7).

In Maryland, many of our native soils in unimproved condition are acidic. Soil acidity can cause a complex of adverse conditions for plant growth (see Table 5-C). Many gardeners and farmers apply lime to their soil to neutralize the acidity and raise the pH, thus eliminating adverse conditions in the soil solution. Optimal pH ranges for many plant species can be found in the references at the end of this chapter. Information on liming materials is presented later in this chapter.

Soil air

Soil air is similar to the atmosphere in that it contains nitrogen, oxygen, carbon dioxide, and traces of other gases. Soil air, however, is typically higher in carbon dioxide and lower in oxygen than the atmosphere. The amount of

Table 5-D. Atmospheric and soil-air gases after rain

Gas	In the atmosphere	In the soil air
Nitrogen	79%	79%
Oxygen	20.9%	20.6%
Carbon dioxide	0.035%	0.300%

each gas in the atmosphere and in the soil air can be compared in Table 5-D.

The amount of these gases can differ in soil air for two reasons:

- The soil is full of living creatures who are constantly using oxygen and releasing carbon dioxide
- Oxygen moves into the soil and carbon dioxide moves out of the soil through a labyrinthine network of soil macropores

Aerobic and anaerobic conditions

Roots of upland plants and most soil microorganisms need oxygen to survive. They are called aerobic organisms. Some microorganisms and wetland plants can survive (and some even require) the absence of oxygen. These organisms are called anaerobic.

Upland soils (well-drained soils) can become anaerobic under the following conditions:

- Inadequate macropore space.
- High water content because of excessive rainfall, resulting in most pores being water-filled.
- Organic matter additions that cause a flush of microbial growth which then consumes oxygen faster than it can be replenished.

5.4 Soil as Entities of Nature

We can probably all agree that geologic formations such as mountains, rivers, and plateaus are natural phenomena or entities of nature. We recognize that these phenomena differ from place to place because of various factors. Mountains, for example, are different all over the world because they differ in the kind of rocks they are composed of, the environment in which they have existed since formation, and the length of time they have been in existence.

The five soil-forming factors

Soils are also natural phenomena or entities of nature. Soil properties are determined by the source material, or parent material, from which they are forming, the environment in which they are forming, including the length of time they have been in existence, the climate and the landscape position or relief in which they occur, and the organisms that inhabit them. These influences, which are known as the five soil-forming factors, are depicted in Figure 5-F.

Climate

Climate, particularly precipitation and temperature, plays an important role in shaping a soil's properties. The amount, intensity, and type of precipitation will influence how fast parent material breaks down and how fast materials move through

Figure 5-F. The five soil-forming factors

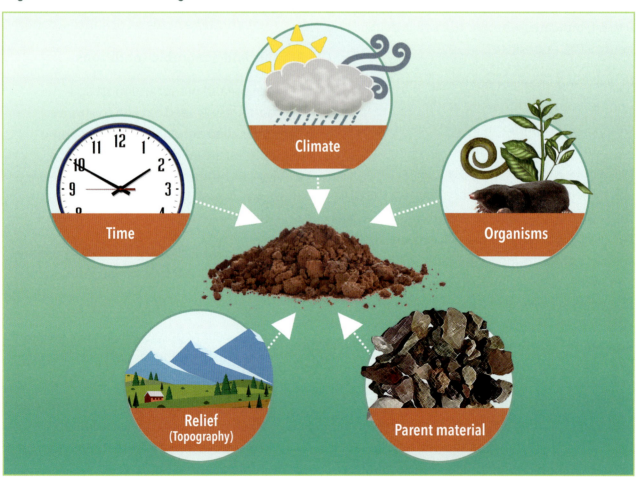

soil. Temperature will influence the rate of chemical reactions and the amount of biological activity in the soil. Temperature also affects the breakdown of parent material through physical freezing and thawing.

Relief (topography or landscape position)

Relief, also called topography and landscape position, includes the slope and aspect (i.e., facing direction, such as north, south, east, or west) of the land. Soils found on hillsides are subjected to loss of topsoil due to water erosion, resulting in thin soils compared to soils at the bottom of a hill. Soils on a north-facing slope will warm up later in the spring compared to soils in other aspects. Cooler temperatures can slow down biological activity and chemical reactions. Flatter slopes will allow more water to infiltrate, thus producing faster chemical reactions and less erosion.

Organisms

Organisms such as animals, microorganisms, and vegetation all affect a soil's properties. Animals and microorganisms travel through the soil and create channels for greater water infiltration. Vegetation eventually falls to the ground and decomposes, thus creating a layer of organic matter on the soil surface. Deep-rooted perennial plants often add much more organic matter into a deeper depth of soil than annual plants and forests.

Time

It takes time, often hundreds, thousands, or millions of years for all of the factors to work together to create soil. Soils in Maryland vary from young soils in flood plains where new parent material has been recently deposited to intermediate-aged soils formed from wind-blown loess deposited after the last glaciation periods approximately 10,000 years ago. Old soils occur in most other areas of the state.

CLORPT

A mnemonic for remembering these factors is CLORPT. This stands for climate, organisms, relief, parent material, and time.

The four soil-forming processes

Soils differ across a landscape because of the five soil-forming factors, but they form as a result of four processes: additions, losses, translocations, and transformations. Table 5-E provides a brief definition for, and examples

Figure 5-G. Soil-forming processes

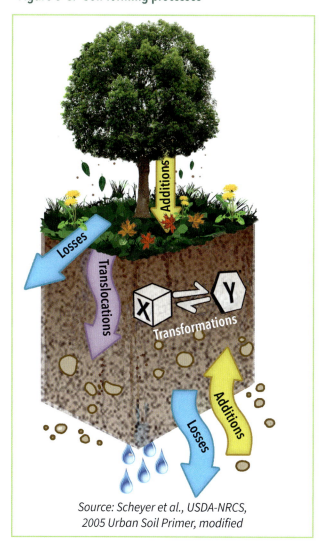

Source: Scheyer et al., USDA-NRCS, 2005 Urban Soil Primer, modified

Table 5-E. The four soil-forming processes

Process	Definition of process	Examples of process
Addition	Materials are added to the soil	• Heat energy is added from the sun • Water is added to the soil during rainfall • Organic matter is added from plant and animal residues • Compost, fertilizers and amendments are added at the soil surface
Loss	Materials are lost from the soil	• Water is lost via evaporation and transpiration • Soil particles and nutrients are lost during erosion • Nutrients are lost due to harvest
Translocation	Materials are moved to another location in the soil	• Calcium and magnesium move downward in the soil with water (known as leaching), making the soil acidic • Clays and organic matter move from the topsoil down to the subsoil with water
Transformation	Materials are changed into another type of material in the soil	• Organic matter is converted to carbon dioxide • Minerals dissolve by weathering • Plant residues are converted to protected organic matter

of, each process. Figure 5-G (on the previous page) illustrates the process graphically.

Soil horizons

Although usually observed only on their surface, soils are actually three-dimensional entities made up of layers or horizons. Horizons can be distinguished from one another by appearance and chemical and physical properties. The most common soil horizons are shown in Figure 5-H.

Soils across the landscape

More than 22,000 different soils have been identified and mapped in the U.S. with approximately 3,000 soils in Maryland alone.

Figure 5-H. Example of a soil profile with the O, A, B, C, and R horizons

O horizon: An organic layer which may be present in forests and other undisturbed locations

A horizon: Known as topsoil; soft, porous, and darker in color than the horizons below it

B horizon: Known as the subsoil; less root and animal activity than the A horizon and often more compact

C horizon: Weathered parent material; very little, if any, root and animal activity

R horizon: Bedrock

Figure 5-I shows a mosaic of soils that occurs across a landscape in Maryland.

If you were to fly northward along the Fall Line, you would see three soils (Chester, Manor, and Glenelg) to your left on the Piedmont Plateau. Although all three soils formed from a similar parent material of weathered rock (micaceous schist in this case) called saprolite, they differ in landscape position. The Chester soil is the one on the top of hillsides; the Manor occurs on the shoulders of hills; and the Glenelg occurs in the level areas at the bottom of slopes. As you might expect, because of the Manor soil's landscape position it is a thinner soil. The Glenelg soil is the deepest because over the millennia it has received additions of soil material from the soils above it.

East of the Fall Line are a number of very different parent materials: sandy sediments; clayey sediments; mixtures of gravel, sand, and clay; and even a silty mantle blown in after the last glaciation period. The soils that make up the landscape here are a result of the parent material in which they formed. Sunnyside soil is found in areas whose soils developed from sandy sediments, and it is high in sand content in all horizons. Christiana soils developed in areas with clayey sediments and have high clay content, especially in the subsoil (B horizon). Both the Chillum and Beltsville soils developed from a silty mantle and have silt loam textures in the A and B horizons; however, the Beltsville soil is deeper.

5.5 Soils as Natural Capital and Ecosystem Services

Natural systems support life-sustaining processes that fulfill the basic needs of all Earth's inhabitants. They can be viewed as natural capital that provides ecosystem services; soils are one of those natural systems. The ecosystem services that soils provide are many and varied:

- Soils are hydrologic buffers as they store and subsequently release water, like a sponge and a faucet.

Figure 5-I. Soil mosaic east/west of the Fall Line

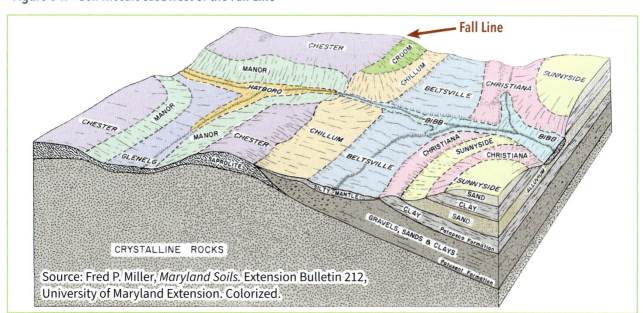

Source: Fred P. Miller, *Maryland Soils*. Extension Bulletin 212, University of Maryland Extension. Colorized.

- Soils are biochemical and chemical reactors, capable of transforming, adsorbing, releasing and storing materials.
- Soils provide mechanical support and nutrition to plants, the ecosystem service with which gardeners are familiar.
- Most of the mineral nutrients required by humans and animals for survival originate in soil.
- Soils are a habitat for an immense array of organisms and house a huge reservoir of genetic diversity.
- Soils shelter seeds until the conditions are favorable for germination, a role that is particularly important in unmanaged ecosystems.
- Soils both emit and absorb greenhouse gasses (carbon dioxide, methane and nitrous oxide) depending upon location and management and can have a role in the mitigation of climate change.
- Soils are the foundation for human infrastructure and hold the record of past civilizations.

5.6 Soils as Hydrologic Buffers

Soils, sometimes called the pedosphere, are the interface between the atmosphere, the lithosphere (Earth), and the water bodies on the Earth's surface (hydrosphere).

Soils play a very important role in the hydrologic (or water) cycle, which is the continual movement of water through the atmosphere, soils, streams, rivers, lakes and oceans, and back to the atmosphere (see Figure 5-J).

Figure 5-J. The hydrologic cycle (soil perspective)

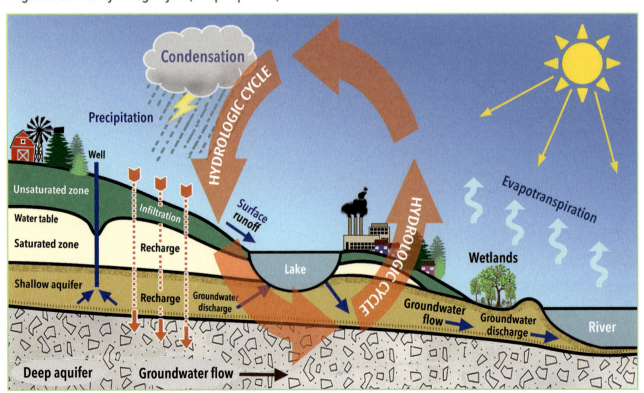

Source: Illinois State Water Survey, modified

Soils absorb rainfall, thus regulating water flow in and through the landscape. As soils are covered with infrastructure and impervious surfaces, soils' capacity to absorb precipitation is eliminated. This can lead to stream degradation and flooding.

Soils store water for plant use and may slowly release it to groundwater. Viewed from these perspectives, soils function alternately as sponges and faucets. Table 5-F provides information on the water-cycle processes as they relate to soils and plants.

5.7 Soils as Biochemical and Chemical Reactors

There are many biochemical and chemical reactions that occur in soils, including cation exchange, adsorption/desorption, and nutrient

Table 5-F. Important hydrologic cycle processes

Process name	Process description	Points to remember
Precipitation	Water falling to the earth as rain, snow, sleet, etc.	Varies in amount and intensity from time to time and from place to place. Maryland receives approximately 40 inches of precipitation a year, much of it in heavy rainfall events
Infiltration	Entry of water into the soil	If precipitation is intense or if the soil is saturated, it may not infiltrate the soil but rather flow over the soil surface as runoff
Percolation	Movement of water through the soil	• Moves nutrients applied on the soil surface deeper into soil to plant roots • Can move nutrients deep into the soil beyond reach of the plant roots (deep percolation) • Groundwater recharge occurs when water percolates all the way to the groundwater
Runoff	Movement of water over the soil surface when precipitation exceeds infiltration	Can carry soil particles (erosion) and soluble nutrients with it
Evaporation	Transformation of liquid water in the soil or water bodies to water vapor	High in warm months and minimal in cool months
Transpiration	Transformation of liquid water to water vapor in plant stomates	High in warm months and negligible when plants are dormant
Condensation	Transformation of water vapor to liquid water	Occurs when air cools and is responsible for formation of clouds and dew
Storage	Water is retained in small and medium pores in the soil	Critical for optimal growth of plants between rainfall events or irrigation
Plant interception	Precipitation that lands directly on plant surfaces where it evaporates and returns to the atmosphere	Under trees, plant interception can prevent up to 50% of precipitation from reaching the soil
Groundwater discharge	Movement of water from the groundwater to a surface body, like a stream or river	Source of water in streams in summertime when rainfall has not occurred for several days

cycling. Cation exchange is a reaction in which soils store certain kinds of materials and readily release them at a later time. Adsorption and desorption are reactions where soils bind other kinds of materials very tightly and release them very slowly. Examples of adsorption include phosphorous bound to iron oxides and organic pesticide molecules bound to organic matter.

Table 5-G. Textural class, clay content, and CEC

Textural class	Range of clay content (%)	Cation exchange capacity (CEC)*
Sand and loamy sands	0 - 15	1 - 5
Sandy loams	15 - 20	5 - 10
Loams and silt loams	0 - 25	5 - 15
Clay loams, sandy clay loams, silty clay loams	20 - 40	15 - 30
Clays, sandy clays, silty clays	> 40	>30

* *cmol/kg or centimoles per kilogram, or an older mode of expression, milliequivalent per 100 grams.*

Finally, nutrient cycling involves nutrients and other elements moving through a sequence of molecular arrangements in the soil-plant-animal-atmosphere system. During some stages in this process, elements may be mobile in soil water or available to plants for growth. At other stages, elements are stable within a solid material or a living organism.

Cation exchange

Clay-sized particles and protected organic matter in soils have negatively charged locations that attract and hold (adsorb) positively charged materials, called cations. The nutrients calcium (Ca+2), magnesium (Mg+2), and potassium (K+) are examples of cations that are held on negatively charged locations on soil materials.

At a later time, when plant uptake has depleted the nutrient content in the soil solution, positively charged nutrients can be released (desorbed) back into the soil solution. This process whereby cations can move back and forth between the soil solution and negatively charged locations on clay-sized particles and protected organic matter is called cation exchange. Cation exchange is critically important because adsorbed nutrients are being held in reserve, thus protected from leaching should heavy rain or excessive irrigation occur.

Cation exchange capacity (often abbreviated as CEC) is a measure of a soil's ability to retain cations and is related to the amount of protected organic matter and clay-sized particles in soils. The higher the clay and protected organic matter contents, the higher the CEC. Table 5-G shows how CEC varies with soil textural class and clay content.

Adsorption

In addition to binding materials via cation exchange, soils can hold materials tightly through the process of adsorption. For example, protected organic matter particles have places on their structures where organic materials like pesticides can be strongly adsorbed. Also, clay-sized iron oxide particles can adsorb phosphorus and molybdenum on their surface.

Nutrient cycling

Many materials in soil, including nutrients, are transformed in soil from one chemical or biological form to another in the soil-plant-animal-atmosphere system. These transformations are often referred to as cycles.

Nitrogen cycle

Nitrogen (N) exists in many forms in soil, water, and the atmosphere. In soil, N can exist in all three phases: solid, liquid, or gas. Nitrogen is also subject to many transformations in soil and water. For these reasons, the nitrogen cycle is the most complicated of the nutrient cycles. A simplified version of the N cycle is shown in Figure 5-K. The different processes that occur in the nitrogen cycle are shown in Table 5-H.

Phosphorus cycle

Phosphorus (P) exists in a variety of forms in the soil; however, unlike nitrogen, phosphorus has no gaseous forms. A simplified version of

Figure 5-K. A simplified version of the N cycle

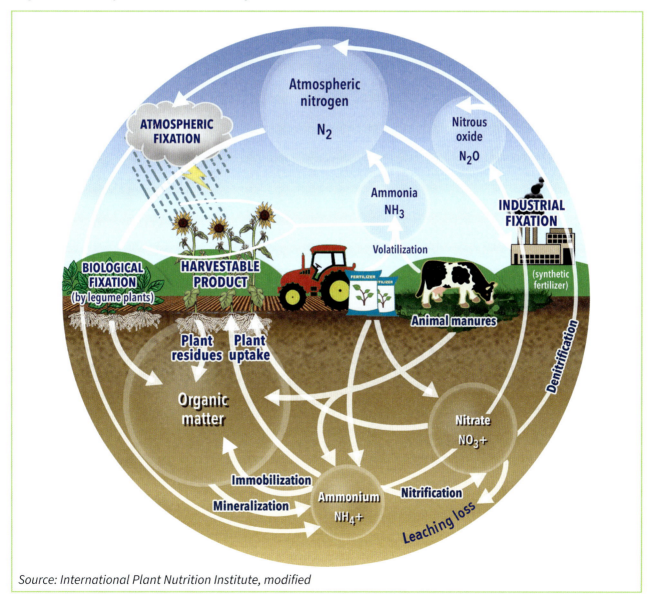

Source: International Plant Nutrition Institute, modified

Table 5-H. Processes in the nitrogen cycle

Process name	Process description	Points to remember
Fertilization	The addition of inorganic (commercial fertilizers) or organic nutrient sources (animal manures, composts, etc.) to soils	Additions of N are required in most cases to ensure optimal plant growth.
Atmospheric fixation and deposition	The addition of N as nitrate dissolved in rainfall or attached to particles (dryfall)	These additions can be substantial in areas with frequent lightning storms or heavy vehicular traffic.
Biological nitrogen fixation	The conversion of N gas to ammonium by organisms	Although the legume-Rhizobia team is the most effective N-fixing couple in nature, other organisms are also able to fix N.
Mineralization	The transformation of organic forms of N to ammonium, an inorganic form	Nutrients tied up in organic molecules must be transformed to an inorganic form before plants can take up substantial quantities.
Immobilization	The uptake of ammonium or nitrate by microbes to meet their nutritional needs	Plants and microbes are in direct competition for available nutrient supplies. If organic sources with a carbon/nitrogen (C:N) ratio greater than 20 are added to soil, immobilization can be anticipated. Avoid applying large quantities of material whose C:N ratio is greater than 20 unless a good nitrogen source is also applied.
Nitrification	The transformation of ammonium-N (NH_4^+) to nitrate-N (NO_3^-)	Requires the action of specialized bacteria that function in soils that are aerobic and have pH greater than 5.5.
Plant uptake	The movement of ammonium or nitrate into plants to meet their nutritional needs	Plants require large amounts of N for optimal growth. The N content of plants typically is 2-5% of their dry weight.
Leaching	The movement of nitrogen by water, usually in the nitrate form, through and beneath root zone	This is usually the most significant loss of N and leads to nitrate pollution of ground water.
Denitrification	The loss of the nitrogen gas, nitrous oxide, from the soil to the atmosphere when soils are anaerobic	This loss is often hard to avoid, as it is highly weather-dependent. Excessive rainfall, poor drainage, or a depression in a growing area can lead to denitrification.
Ammonia volatilization	The loss of N as ammonia gas when ammonium sources of nitrogen are surface-applied	This loss, which can be avoided if the N source is incorporated, is worsened if lime is applied at the same time as an ammonium-N source.
Runoff	Movement of water and dissolved nutrients, like N, over the soil surface when precipitation exceeds infiltration	Runoff losses of N are usually minor compared to leaching losses.
Erosion	The displacement of soil particles by wind or water	Erosion losses of N are usually minor compared to leaching losses.

the P cycle is shown in Figure 5-L.

Table 5-I provides information on the different processes that occur in the phosphorus cycle.

Soils as filters

It is often said that soils make good filters for nutrients and pollutants because they bind materials on their surfaces or because materials are taken up by plants or soil organisms. This is true for some kinds of material but not for others.

Ineffective as a filter

Soils are not effective at holding small negatively-charged ions (anions), like nitrate and chloride. Likewise, they are not effective at holding small negatively-charged non-nutrient ions like bromide or fluoride. Negatively-charged ions are actually repelled by the negatively-charged clay particles in soils. Nitrate and chloride are readily leached because soils cannot "hold" them.

Effective as a filter

Soils are effective at holding cations (positively-charged ions) like calcium and magnesium through the process of cation exchange, and some large anions (negatively-charged ions) like phosphate through the process of adsorption. A soil's capacity to retain material via either process, however, is finite. When all the locations where materials can be held are filled, the soil is saturated for that material and it can retain no more. For example, some soils that have received large amount of P-rich manure for many years get saturated with P and have no additional capacity to adsorb P when it is applied.

Biomass as a filter

Plants and soil organisms take up many materials (nutrients and non-nutrients) into

Figure 5-L. A simplified version of the P cycle

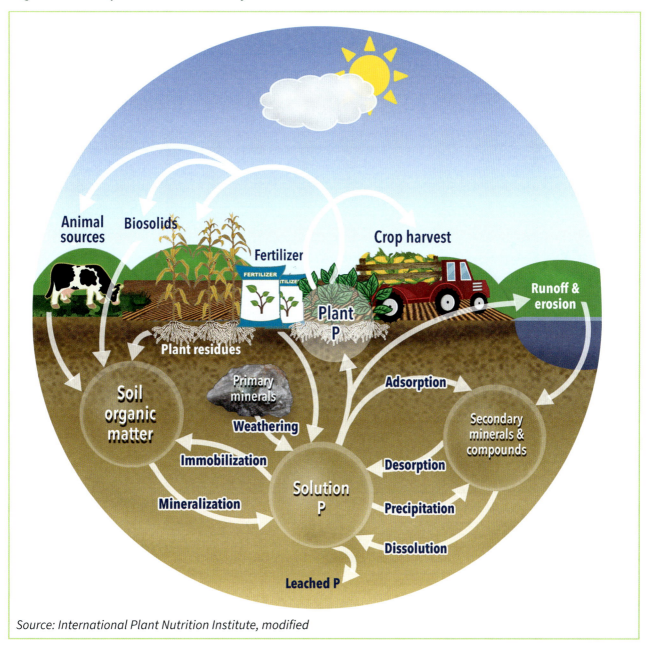

Source: International Plant Nutrition Institute, modified

Table 5-I. Processes in the phosphorus cycle

Process name	Process description	Points to remember
Fertilization	The addition of inorganic or organic nutrient sources to soils	When tests indicate low or moderate levels of plant-available, phosphorus should be applied to ensure optimal plant growth
Adsorption	The binding of phosphate to surfaces of clay-sized soil particles	• The amount of P a soil can adsorb is related to its clay and Al, Fe, and Ca contents • Adsorbed P is not immediately available for plant growth
Desorption	The release of phosphate bound to surfaces of soil particles back into the soil solution	• Desorption occurs when the soil solution becomes limited in, or depleted of, phosphate ions • Phosphorus desorbed during the season is an important source for growing plants
Fixation	The precipitation of soluble phosphate with soluble aluminum, iron, or calcium	• Fixation is the reason that soluble P levels are very low in many soils • Fixed P becomes available for plant growth very slowly as minerals weather
Weathering	The release of phosphate and other nutrients from minerals when they dissolve	In most soils, the amount of phosphate ions released during the weathering of minerals is inadequate to support abundant plant growth
Mineralization	The transformation of organic forms of P (and other nutrients) to an inorganic form (phosphate ion)	Nutrients tied up in organic molecules must be transformed to an inorganic form before plants can take up substantial quantities
Immobilization	The uptake of phosphate ions by microbes or plants to meet their nutritional needs	Plants and microbes are in direct competition for available nutrient supplies
Plant uptake	The movement of phosphate ions into plants to meet their nutritional needs	Plants require substantial amounts of P for optimal growth. P content of plants is typically 0.1-0.5 % of their dry weight
Leaching	The movement of soluble phosphate by water through and beneath the root zone	Under many circumstances, this is usually a minor loss of P but in sandy soils that have been heavily fertilized for many years, leaching has been observed
Runoff	The movement of water and dissolved nutrients, like P, over the soil surface when precipitation exceeds infiltration	Runoff can contain significant amounts of dissolved P, particularly if runoff is flowing over highly fertile soils
Erosion	The displacement of soil particles by wind or water	Erosion can be a major loss of P. Minimizing erosion is very important as both the soil particles and the phosphorus adsorbed onto the particles can cause water quality degradation

their cells while they are alive. When they die, the materials in their cells will again be available to the active transformational possibilities of biogeochemical cycling.

5.8 Soils as Media for Plant Growth

Soils provide water, nutrients, and mechanical support for plants. See **Chapter 6, Plant Nutrition** for more information on plant nutrients in soils.

Optimizing soil pH for plant nutrition

Most soils in the Mid-Atlantic states are acidic in their natural, undisturbed state. The growth of many ornamental and vegetable plants can be improved by raising the pH of the soil. Gardeners can raise the pH of natural and even cultivated soils by the addition of liming materials. Figure 5-M

Figure 5-M. Positive effects of liming on the soil (in relation to plant growth)

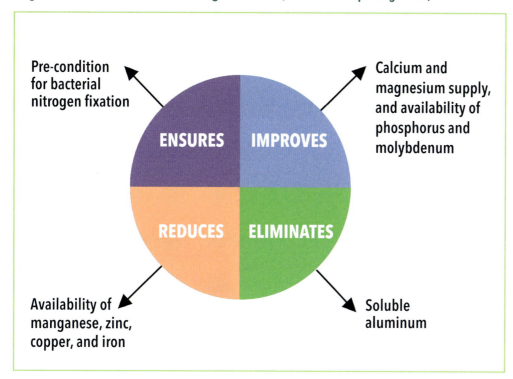

shows how liming materials adjust the soil pH and improve the soil environment and plant growth by:

- Supplying some nutrients
- Making other nutrients more available
- Enhancing growth of bacteria
- Decreasing damaging levels of toxic elements
- Reducing the availability of high concentrations of nutrients that, if high enough, can actually reduce plant growth

Liming material

A liming material is a material that contains calcium and/or magnesium and raises the pH of the soil when applied to the soil. Some liming materials, such as slaked lime and burnt lime, dissolve in the soil solution quickly and adjust the pH quickly, whereas others (limestone and dolomitic limestone) take many months or even years to fully react. The liming potential of these materials is expressed as the calcium carbonate equivalent, also called CCE.

Limestone has a CCE of 100 whereas materials like slaked lime and burnt lime have CCEs greater than 100. This means they have more liming potential per pound of product. The properties of the most commonly used liming materials sold in Maryland are summarized in Table 5-J.

Table 5-J. Common liming materials

Common name of materials	Rate of reaction	Calcium carbon equivalent (CCE)	Conversion factor to pure fine limestone
Limestone (calcium carbonate)	Very slow	100	–
Dolomitic limestone (calcium-magnesium carbonate)	Very slow	109	–
Hydrated lime (calcium hydroxide)	Fast	135	0.74
Burned lime (calcium oxide)	Fast	179	0.56

Lime recommendations are shown on soil test reports, which should be consulted for the recommended amount. Note that lime recommendations are expressed in amounts of pure, fine limestone per unit area. If you use one of the faster-acting, more powerful lime materials, the application rate should be adjusted (see Table 5-J, column 4).

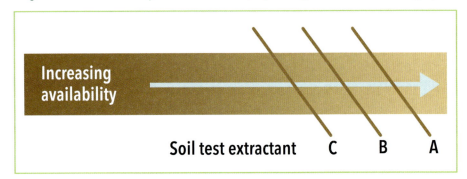

Figure 5-N. Extractability of soil nutrients (depending on extractant strength)

5.9 Soil Testing

Some soils are fertile, which means that they can provide the quantity of each nutrient that plants require at the time they need them. Many soils, however, lack an adequate supply of one or more nutrients. Soil tests were developed to identify situations where nutrient supply is inadequate so a grower or gardener can supplement with either organic or inorganic fertilizers. However, there is no reliable pre-plant soil test for nitrogen because levels can vary widely from week to week during the growing season.

Soils tests are designed to extract some portion of the plant-available forms of nutrients in soils. Plant-available nutrients exist on a continuum, with some portion fully and immediately available and other forms available over a period of days, weeks, or even months.

Soil-testing methodology has developed independently in many states, so growers and homeowners have options in both laboratories and methods. Most methods rely on mixing soils with some kind of chemical solution called an extractant. Some methods use weak chemical extractants (distilled water), like extract A in Figure 5-N; others use stronger ones (acid solutions or acid solutions with other compounds, like extractants B and C, respectively).

Because plant-available nutrients exist in many forms in soils, stronger extractants remove more nutrients than weaker extractants. Do not compare soil test results from one lab to another unless you are sure both labs use the same extractant and express results in the same manner.

Understanding a soil test report

Soil tests typically give information about a measure of plant-available nutrients, relative nutrient status, and nutrient recommendations. Although terminology differs from lab to lab, Table 5-K shows

Table 5-K. Likelihood of improved plant growth

Soil test category	Likelihood of growth improvement if proper nutrients are applied
Very low and low	Very likely
Medium	Likely
Optimum or high	Unlikely
Excessive or very high	Very unlikely

common terminology for soil test reporting and the likelihood of improved plant growth if nutrients are applied. Improvements in plant growth may be more vigorous growth and greater yield.

A sample gardener's soil-test report is shown in Figure 5-O. It features a section that lists the nutrients tested (in the Analysis columns) and the actual laboratory data (in the Result columns).

The bar graph in the middle of the report informs the customer of the relative adequacy of each nutrient or property. This part of the report contains the interpretation of the soil test data.

This type of presentation is very useful to get a quick over view of the nutrient condition of the soil. At a quick glance one can see that phosphorus (P) and potassium (K), two macronutrients, are low while iron (Fe) and manganese (Mn) are high.

At the bottom of the report are the recommendations, which are provided in pounds per 1,000 square feet. Proceeding from left to right, because the pH is medium, the lab recommends 107 pounds of limestone (CaCO$_3$ or calcium carbonate) per 1,000 square feet. The "D" indicates that dolomitic (calcium-magnesium carbonate) lime is recommended because the magnesium is also medium. The phosphate (P$_2$O$_5$) and potash (K$_2$O) are "low" and recommendations

Figure 5-O. Sample soil analysis report

are provided. In this case the lab tested for other nutrients; unfortunately, research on sulfur and the micronutrients (B, Cu, Fe, Mn and Zn) is scarce in Maryland and recommendations for those nutrients provided by this lab are not supported by research.

Nutrients for plant growth

Gardeners have a myriad of fertilizer choices when a soil test indicates a deficiency in one or more nutrients. These choices include commercial synthetic fertilizers, commercial organic fertilizers, compost (homemade or purchased), manure (purchased or from nearby farms), and many others.

What is a fertilizer?

A fertilizer is a material that contains at least one plant nutrient and is registered as a fertilizer by states' department of agriculture. A fertilizer may be a single nutrient source (like sodium nitrate, 16-0-0, which contains only nitrogen) or a mixture of nutrients (like 10-6-4, a common dry fertilizer blend which contains nitrogen, phosphorus, and potassium).

Nutrient guarantee

The nutrient content of a fertilizer is described by its nutrient guarantee. A nutrient guarantee consists of three numbers (i.e., 6-24-24) and can be found on a fertilizer bag or bottle. These three numbers are separated by hyphens and refer to the percent (by weight) of N (nitrogen), P expressed as P_2O_5 (phosphate), and K expressed as K_2O (potash). Figure 5-P shows an example of a nutrient guarantee.

It may seem confusing to express the phosphorus and potassium content of fertilizers in their oxide forms (P_2O_5 and K_2O), considering that these specific forms of phosphorus and potassium are not actually present in fertilizers. This is, however, the traditional manner of labeling fertilizers. Nutrient recommendations are also expressed in their oxide forms.

If additional nutrients are contained in the fertilizer, this information may be indicated in the nutrient guarantee. Additional nutrients (beyond N, P, and K) are expressed on an elemental basis. For example, a bag

Figure 5-P. Nutrient guarantee of a fertilizer

Do not expect the fertilizer guarantee to add up to 100 percent. All nutrients are contained in compounds that contain other elements.

The phosphorus and potassium content of food, water, and biological samples (like blood) is expressed as an element, i.e., phosphorus and potassium, not phosphate and potash. To convert from phosphate to phosphorus and from potash to potassium, use these formulas:

phosphate (P_2O_5) x 0.44 = phosphorus (P)

potash (K_2O) x 0.83 = potassium (K)

of potassium-magnesium sulfate contains sulfur (S) and magnesium (Mg) in addition to potassium. Its guarantee is 0-0-22-22S-11Mg.

Commercial, synthetic, and organic fertilizers

Choosing the appropriate nutrient source to meet plant needs based on a soil test can take some thought. Following is a review of the pros and cons of each type.

Commercial fertilizers

Commercial fertilizers are specifically labeled as a fertilizer and offered for sale. Commercial fertilizers can be organic or synthetic.

Synthetic fertilizers

Synthetic fertilizers are sourced from non-renewable materials. In the case of phosphorus and potassium, the original materials are minerals mined from the Earth's crust and processed. In the case of nitrogen fertilizer, a source of hydrogen is required and it usually comes from natural gas.

Scores of synthetic fertilizers exist. Some, like muriate of potash (0-0-60), urea (46-0-0) and triple superphosphate (0-46-0), supply only a single nutrient while others may provide more than one nutrient. Potassium nitrate (13-0-46) and 10-10-10 are examples of commercial synthetic fertilizers that contain more than one nutrient.

Commercial synthetic fertilizer products are advantageous for several reasons:

Predictability. Each product is relatively uniform, regardless of manufacturer. Thus, ammonium sulfate (21-0-0) will react similarly in the soils regardless of the company that provides it. Additionally, many years of international fertilizer research have been conducted to gain understanding of how fertilizer materials react once applied to soils.

Table 5-L. Nutrient guarantee of synthetic fertilizers

Fertilizer	Nutrient Guarantee
Ammonium sulfate	20-0-0-24S
Potassium nitrate	13-0-44
Sodium nitrate	16-0-0
Urea	46-0-0
Calcium nitrate	16-0-0-22Ca
Superphosphate	0-18-0
Muriate of potash	0-0-60
Sulfur-coated urea (SCU)	40-0-0
Methylenediurea	28-0-0

Availability to the soil. These fertilizers contain nutrients in a readily available form (unless noted). Exceptions are specially-manufactured products that contain slow-release N, like ureaform, sulfur-coated urea, and methylenediurea.

Flexibility. Fertilizers are available that contain only one or two of the three major nutrients. Using these products allows you to apply only those nutrients you need. Examples: If your soil test indicates very high levels of P and K and no P and K are recommended, you can add just the nitrogen that is recommended by using urea (46-0-0).

Some common commercial synthetic fertilizers and their nutrient guarantee are listed in Table 5-L.

Although most commercial synthetic fertilizers contain substantial quantities of soluble or readily-available nutrients, they do not burn plants if applied at the recommended rates. Warning: they should never be applied directly to plants, unless you are using a formulation specifically designed for foliar application.

Over-application or misapplication of any fertilizer material, synthetic or otherwise, can lead to water pollution. It is important to follow soil test recommendations, apply nutrients at recommended rates, and minimize erosion and runoff from growing areas.

Organic fertilizers

The term "organic" is used in two different contexts: 1) origin/type of material, and 2) a specific farming system defined by federal and state regulations.

1) refers to material that was once part of a living organism and is composed of units (molecules) with a carbon backbone (e.g., manures and food-processing wastes like fish meal).

2) refers to a farm-production system that allows the use of some organic and minimally-processed soil amendments and fertilizers.

Not all "organic" soil amendments and fertilizers are organic in that they originate from a living source and are composed of a carbon backbone. Greensand and rock phosphate are classified by regulations as "organic" but do not have a carbon backbone. Chemically, they are actually inorganic or mineral materials.

Conversely, some organic materials, like sewage sludge, are not approved by government agencies for use in "organic" production systems. The Organic Material Research Institute (OMRI) is the agency that certifies products as "organic."

The nutrient content of commercial organic fertilizers is relatively low and quite variable. They may have low nutrient availability and contain a whole suite of nutrients. They often originate as a waste product of animal and crop production and processing industries. For example, blood meal and bone meal both originate from the meat-packing industry. Composted manures originate from animal-production operations.

While all commercial organic fertilizers are labeled with a fertilizer guarantee, the speed with which the nutrients become available for plant growth varies. They also come with an environmental cost, as considerable energy was invested in processing before marketing them as fertilizers. Consider blood meal, a waste product of slaughterhouses. It has been collected, dried and powdered prior to sale. On the plus side, processing animal-based organic fertilizers saves them from being landfilled.

Examples of commercial organic fertilizers and their guaranteed analyses are in Table 5-M.

Some fertilizer companies manufacture products that are mixtures of various organic materials often blended into a compost base for ease of handling.

Table 5-M. Nutrient guarantee of organic fertilizers

Fertilizer	Nutrient Guarantee
Fish meal	4-4-1
Blood meal	12-3-1
Bone meal	4-2-0
Composted cattle manure	1-1-1
Composted yard waste	1-0-1
Chicken litter (dehydrated)	4-3-3

Compost may be produced at home, and manure is often available from local farms. Because they are not formerly labeled and registered, they are not by definition "fertilizers" but they are useful nutrient sources in home landscapes.

Choosing a nutrient source

Choosing the appropriate nutrient source to meet plant needs based on a soil test can take some thought. Some gardeners will only use "organic" fertilizers. In fact, the issue of which product to use in any situation is more complicated. Table 5-N highlights the pros and cons of each type of material.

5.10 Soil Health

In the 1980s and 1990s, a concept called "soil quality" was proposed similar to the concepts of air quality and water quality. By late 1990, the concept evolved into "soil health" and from there the concept has gained in acceptance. The U. S. Department of Agriculture Natural Resources Conservation Service (USDA-NRCS) is encouraging soil-health practices. The Soil Health Institute, a private NGO, offers publications and conferences on soil health. Congress has even held hearings on soil health.

The USDA-NRCS defines "soil health" as the continued capacity of soil to function as a vital, living ecosystem that sustains plants, animals, and humans. The beauty of this concept is that it views soil holistically, assessing biological, chemical, and physical qualities of soil, as visually demonstrated in Figure 5-Q.

Characteristics of healthy soils

Cornell University has published the most comprehensive volume on soil health. Their paradigm is as follows:

- They are fertile; their nutrient status is optimum or sufficient but not excessive
- They have adequate water storage as well as adequate drainage
- They have good tilth (i.e., good structure and are crumbly when moist)
- They have a small population of pathogenic organisms and a large population of beneficial organisms
- They resist degradation and are resilient under adversity due to their good structure

Table 5-N. Pros and cons of nutrient sources

Group	Pros	Cons
Synthetic commercial fertilizers	Predictable behavior; sources can be tailored to recommendations	Production consumes non-renewable resources
Commercial organic fertilizers	Waste products of animal or crop production	Requires knowledge of behavior for informed use; continued use can lead to excessive P and/or K levels
Manures	May be for sale or local and convenient	Requires knowledge of content and behavior for informed use; continued use can lead to excessive P and/or K levels
Compost	May be for sale or local and convenient	Low plant-available nitrogen content; continued use can lead to excessive P and/or K levels

Figure 5-Q. The soil health paradigm

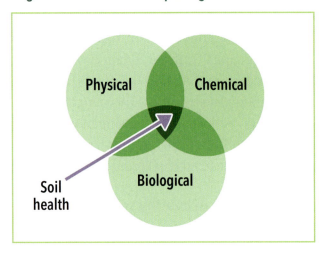

Dr. Douglas Karlan, a retired researcher from USDA Agricultural Research Service who studied soil health, likens soils to a factory and soil organisms as its workers. "Keeping the factory doors open means planting crops that actively grow in early March or crops that still grow until the freeze-up in November."

Cover crops are plants grown for erosion control, nutrient scavenging and maintenance of soil health. Typically planted in late summer or early fall as vegetable and flower gardens decline, they prolong the time when plants are not actively growing.

Choose different plant species whenever possible. Different plant species may exude a variety of exudates. Some may favor the proliferation of some microbe species over others. Different plants may have different root architectures (shallow fibrous roots as opposed to deep tap roots) that enable them to explore different parts of the soil.

Gardeners can choose the cover-crop species that best suits their goals. Forage radish has deep tap roots that can break up compacted soils; legumes fix nitrogen for subsequent plants; grains like rye and wheat

Practices that develop and maintain a healthy soil

Two interrelated practices guide gardeners and farmers in achieving this goal: feeding microbes and protecting soil aggregates.

Feed the microbes year-'round with cover crops. View this as a year-long task so microbes have living plants in both the cool and warm seasons. Research shows that a very substantial part of the carbohydrate fixed by plants is shuttled to the roots and exuded to support the rhizosphere microbes.

Table 5-O. Features of cool-season cover crops

Crop	Winter-killed	Winter-hardy	Root features	Nitrogen-fixer	Notes
Crimson Clover	---	Yes	---	Yes	Supplies nitrogen to next crop
Forage Radish	Yes	---	Deep tap root	---	Alleviates compaction; little spring residue
Oats	Yes	---	---	---	Little spring residue
Wheat	---	Yes	Extensive fibrous roots	---	Good source of soil organic matter
Rye	---	Yes	Extensive fibrous roots	---	Good source of soil organic matter
Hairy Vetch	---	Yes	---	Yes	Supplies nitrogen to next crop
Austrian winter pea	---	Yes	---	Yes	Supplies nitrogen to next crop

have extensive fibrous root systems and produce large amount of below-ground biomass; oats and forage radish are killed by typical winter temperatures thus alleviating a need for termination. Table 5-O (previous page) indicates the features of many of the cool-season cover crops that grow in Maryland.

Cover crops like buckwheat and phacelia can also be grown in the warm season for canopy cover and aggregate protection. Both of these species have the added benefit of supporting pollinators.

Protect soil aggregates from rainfall by maintaining a plant canopy or mulching. Raindrops destroy unprotected soil aggregates. Figure 5-R shows two examples of cover crops and mulching in vegetable beds. Areas were seeded in late August and photos were taken in mid-October. The photo on the left shows oats and winter peas growing through a heavy mulch of dry grass clippings. On the right is a vigorous growth of forage radish. Forage radish is a remarkable crop with a large fleshy edible taproot that loosens compacted subsoil and provides quick canopy coverage and weed suppression in fall and early winter. It is not winter-hardy and very little residue remains in the spring.

Soil productivity beyond nutrients

Soil tests can identify soils with low nutrient status and high acidity. These growth-limiting issues can be addressed with fertilizers and lime, respectively. Some gardeners in Maryland, however, encounter soil-related problems of a non-nutrient nature.

Figure 5-R. Cover crops mulching vegetable beds

Austrian winter pea (left) and oats with grass-clipping mulch

Forage radish

Soil compaction

Soil compaction describes a condition when a soil has low pore space or is very dense.

It is not unusual for the soil around homes to be compacted. Topsoil may have been removed during construction, leaving subsoil at the surface. In addition, use of heavy equipment during construction compacts soil. In the Piedmont region, some subsoils are naturally very compact.

Soil compaction often results in low root-zone oxygen. The addition of organic matter, like compost, helps alleviate compaction. Even better would be an annual fall cover crop. Regardless of the choice of plant species, root growth will incorporate organic matter very effectively throughout the root zone. Decomposition of the roots leads to an increase in macropores space and improved aeration.

Additions of organic material like compost may reduce compaction. However, roots do a much superior job of providing a food source to microbes and exploring soil.

Salt-affected soils

In some counties in Maryland, salt-affected soils have been observed. Some homeowners on the southern Eastern Shore (Dorchester and Somerset Counties) with sites close to the Bay are experiencing poor plant performance due to high salt levels in the soil. This has been attributed to salt-water intrusion into streams and salt spray during severe storms like hurricanes.

Many soil test labs are equipped to determine if a soil is salt-affected. Choosing salt-tolerant plants is an option for homeowners impacted by this condition. ❋

AUTHORS

Patricia Steinhilber, Ph.D., Soil Fertility and Nutrient Management Specialist, retired.

Emileigh Lucas, M.S., Nutrient Management Communications Specialist.

PUBLICATIONS

Moebius-Clune, B.N., D.J. Moebius-Clune, B.K. Gugino, O.J. Idowu, R.R. Schindelbeck, A.J. Ristow, H.M. van Es, J.E. Thies, H.A. Shayler, M.B. McBride, K.S.M Kurtz, D.W. Wolfe, and G.S. Abawi, 2016. *Comprehensive Assessment of Soil Health – The Cornell Framework, Edition 3.2*. Cornell University, Geneva, NY.

Montgomery, David. 2007. *Dirt: the Erosion of Civilizations*. University of California Press, Berkeley, CA.

Nardi, James. 2007. *Life in the Soil: A Guide for Naturalists and Gardens.* The University of Chicago Press, Chicago, IL.

Nardi, James. 2003. *The World Beneath Our Feet*. Oxford University Press, New York, NY.

Orgiazzi, A., Bardgett, R.D., Barrios, E., Behan-Pelletier, V., Briones, M.J.I., Chotte, J-L., De Deyn, G.B., Eggleton, P., Fierer, N., Fraser, T., Hedlund, K., Jeffery, S., Johnson, N.C., Jones, A., Kandeler, E., Kaneko, N., Lavelle, P., Lemanceau, P., Miko, L., Montanarella, L., Moreira, F.M.S., Ramirez, K.S., Scheu, S., Singh, B.K., Six, J., van der Putten, W.H., Wall, D.H. (Eds.), 2016. *Global Soil Biodiversity Atlas*. European Commission, Publications Office of the European Union, Luxembourg.

Scheyer, J. M., and K. W. Hipple. 2005. *Urban Soil Primer*. United States Department of Agriculture, Natural Resources Conservation Service, National Soil Survey Center, Lincoln, NE (soils.usda.gov/use).

Tugel, A.J., A.M. Lewandowski, and D. Happe-vonArb, eds. 2000. *Soil Biology Primer.* Soil and Water Conservation Society, Ankeny, IA.

Wolf, Benjamin, 1999. *The Fertile Triangle:The Interrelationship of Air, Water, and Nutrients in Maximizing Soil Productivity.* Food Products Press, New York, NY.

PHOTOS

Learning Objectives Seedling: subha02, Accessed July 2, 2024 from **pixabay**

ILLUSTRATIONS

Figure 5-B. USDA-NCRS. *Soil textural triangle.*

Figure 5-D. USDA-NCRS. *The soil food web.* Tugel, A.J., A.M. Lewandowski, and D. Happe-vonArb, eds. 2000. Soil Biology Primer. Ankeny, IA: Soil and Water Conservation Society.

Figure 5-G. Scheyer et al., USDA-NRCS, 2005 Urban Soil Primer. *Soil-forming processes.*

Figure 5-I. Miller, Fred P. 1976. *Maryland Soils.* Extension Bulletin 212, University of Maryland Extension, College Park, MD. *Soil mosaic east and west of the Fall Line.*

Figure 5-A, 5-C, 5-E, 5-F, 5-H, 5-J, 5-M, 5-N, 5-P, 5-Q. LeAnn Zotta, Berkshire Communications.

Figure 5-K. LeAnn Zotta, Berkshire Communications. Modified from the International Plant Nutrition Institute. *A simplified version of the N cycle.*

Figure 5-L. LeAnn Zotta, Berkshire Communications. Modified from the International Plant Nutrition Institute. *A simplified version of the P cycle.*

Figure 5-O. Michelle Nelson, Montgomery Parks.

Figure 5-R. Jon Traunfeld, University of Maryland Extension.

WEBSITES

For more detailed information on the parent material of soils in Maryland, go to **mgs.md.gov/geology/**

For information about the soils that exist in an area of interest, consult the soil survey for that county or visit **websoilsurvey.nrcs.usda.gov/app**

Tugel, A.J., A.M. Lewandowski, and D. Happe-vonArb, eds. 2000. *Soil Biology Primer*. **nrcs.usda.gov/wps/portal/nrcs/main/soils/health/biology/**

Soil Science Society of America. **soils.org/about-soils** and **soilsmatter.wordpress.com/**

Dr. Bonnie Basler, Princeton University. *Communication between microbes.* **ted.com/talks/bonnie_bassler_how_bacteria_talk?language=en**

Monterey Institute for Technology and Education. *Determining Soil Texture by Sedimentation.* **youtube.com/watch?v=knrmCbctGEA**

New Mexico State University. *Cation exchange.* **youtube.com/watch?v=HmEyymGXOfI**

VIDEOS

The Soil Science Society of America developed a video series for the International Year of Soil (2015). Search **youtube.com** for "SSSA-International Year of Soil" for the whole series, which includes:

January – Soils Sustain Life

February – Soils Support Urban Life

March – Soils Support Agriculture

April – Soils Clean and Capture Water

May – Soils Support Buildings and Infrastructure

June – Soils Support Recreation

July – Soils are Living

August – Soils Support Health

September – Soils Protect the Natural Environment

October – Soils and the Products We Use

November – Soils and Climate

December – Soils and Culture

6: PLANT NUTRITION

Andrew G. Ristvey, Ph.D.

6 PLANT NUTRITION

CONTENTS

6.1 Nutrition Essentiality 127

6.2 Nutrient Types 128

6.3 Nutrient Availability 129

6.4 Macronutrients 129

6.5 Micronutrients 133

6.6 Beneficial Non-Essential Nutrients 136

LEARNING OBJECTIVES

- Criteria for essentiality
- The "law of the minimum" principle
- Mineral and non-mineral nutrients
- How nutrients get to plant roots
- Macro-, micro- and other beneficial nutrients

INTRODUCTION

Plants are photoautotrophic. That means they have the ability to create organic building materials from sunlight, carbon dioxide, and other inorganic materials. There are basic requirements of nutrition that are required by plants to fully carry out growth and reproductive success.

6.1 Nutrition Essentiality

Arnon and Stout (1939) listed three criteria for essentiality:

1. Required for the completion of the life cycle of the plant
2. Must not be replaceable by another element
3. Must be directly involved in plant metabolism; i.e., it must be required for a specific physiological function

An additional criterion should be included:

4. The element must be required by a substantial number of plant species

In ideal circumstances, plant growth may be limited only by the speed with which biological and genetic processes can take place. In the natural environment, however, plant growth is constrained by many factors, including light, water, temperature, and nutrient availability.

- There are 17 recognized elements that are considered essential for plant growth
- Three elements are non-mineral, which are acquired from the air and water: Carbon (C), Oxygen (O), and Hydrogen (H)
- The other 14 are considered mineral nutrients

Some nutrients addressed in this chapter are not considered essential either because they 1) are not needed by a substantial number of plant species or 2) provide an extra function beyond growth and reproduction.

Liebig's Law of the Minimum

Justus von Liebig, a 19th-century German chemist, developed the "Law of the Minimum" principle, which states that plant growth progresses to the limit imposed by the resource in least relative supply. Liebig suggested that the yield potential of a crop is like a barrel with staves of unequal length (see Figure 6-A).

The truth is that plant nutrition is far more complicated. "Least relative supply" suggests that one nutrient may be needed in far greater supply than another. That nutrient may be in greater supply than any other nutrient, but so much of it is needed by the plant that the

Figure 6-A. Liebig's Law of the Minimum

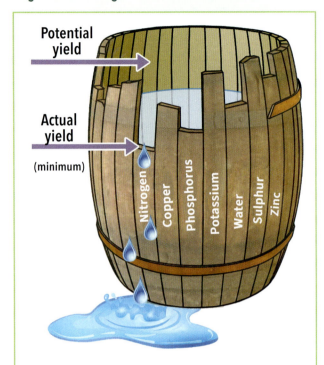

Liebig suggested that the yield potential of a crop is like a barrel with staves of unequal length. The staves represent resources. The capacity of the barrel is limited by the length of the shortest stave (in this case, nitrogen), and can only be increased by lengthening that stave. When that stave is lengthened, another one becomes the limiting factor.

amount available is relatively insufficient for growth (Mills and Jones, 1996).

6.2 Nutrient Types

Non-mineral nutrients

Hydrogen, oxygen, and carbon are considered non-mineral nutrients because they are derived from the atmosphere or water. They are needed by plants in large quantities compared to other nutrients.

Carbon is the most abundant element in plants. It serves as the main building block for all organic compounds, and life itself. Carbon, in the form of carbon dioxide, is reduced and converted to carbohydrates during the process of photosynthesis. Carbohydrates serve as a main medium for storage. The ability to synthesize amino acids, nucleic acids, and lipids from those carbohydrate reserves are processes primarily found in plants and in some bacteria.

Oxygen is a critical element in a process called respiration, during which carbohydrates and other carbon-containing compounds are broken down for energy. Oxygen is also a main element of organic compounds. Oxygen is obtained from the atmosphere and from the breakdown of water during photosynthesis.

Organisms that need oxygen for energy production are called aerobes. Some organisms have other methods for energy production—like fermentation—or they use elements like sulfur or compounds like nitrate in place of oxygen. These are called anaerobes. For many of these organisms, oxygen is toxic.

Hydrogen is also used for carbohydrate production. It is released during photosynthesis when water is split apart.

Mineral nutrients

There are now 14 recognized essential nutrients that exist in mineral form, with nickel being the latest addition. These nutrients are derived either from the soil or the atmosphere and enter the plant through the roots or leaves.

The mineral nutrients are classified as either macronutrients or micronutrients. Macronutrients are required in far greater amounts than micronutrients and are separated into primary and secondary macronutrients.

6.3 Nutrient Availability

Several factors affect the availability of nutrients for plant roots in soil and substrates, like potting media. Plant roots acquire nutrients from the soil in three ways:

1. Mass flow: dissolved nutrients move with water through the soil profile
2. Diffusion: nutrients, dissolved in water, move from higher to lower concentrations in the soil, to the roots
3. Roots can grow to, and proliferate in, areas of high nutrient concentration

Even if the nutrient is present in the soil or substrate, it may not be available for uptake (see term definitions in Table 6-A). One of the most important factors controlling nutrient availability is pH, or the amount of hydrogen ions in an aqueous environment (see Chapter 5, Soil Pores).

Different nutrients have different availabilities in different pH ranges. Other important factors of nutrient availability are cation and anion exchange capacity, which refers to the capacity of a soil or substrate to hold and exchange cations or anions (see Chapter 5, Soil as a Biochemical Reactor). Both are dependent upon the electrostatic charges of the soil particles and the minerals the soils contain.

The following sections provide a description of each nutrient, information about availability in soils, use of the nutrient in the plant, and symptoms of deficiency and toxicity. The nutrients are listed alphabetically. Table 6-B contains a summary of the effects of nutrient deficiency, toxicity, and interaction with other nutrients.

6.4 Macronutrients

Six essential nutrients are considered macronutrients. They are required by plants in relatively large amounts, at levels from 10 to 5,000 times greater than those of many micronutrients (Mills and Jones, 1996). Macronutrients are divided into primary and secondary macronutrients.

- Primary macronutrients include nitrogen, phosphorus, and potassium. They are typically limiting to plant growth and are applied to soil as fertilizer.
- Secondary macronutrients are those that are typically found in soil at sufficient levels to satisfy plant growth. They include calcium, magnesium, and sulfur.

Calcium (Ca)

Calcium comes from weathering of calcium-containing minerals like apatites, gypsum,

Table 6-A. Terms to remember

Term	Definition
Parts per million (ppm)	A metric measurement of concentration 1 ppm = 1 milligram/ kilogram = 1 milligram/liter; 1 ppm = 0.0001%
Uptake (passive)	Process of assimilating minerals and other compounds from soils into the root
Uptake (active)	Process of expending energy to assimilate minerals and other compounds from soils into the root

and carbonates, and is available for uptake as a cation -Ca^{+2} and is most available at a pH just above 7. Free calcium is loosely bound to organic and mineral colloids, available for plant uptake. Calcium is taken up passively in young plant roots and moves through the plant primarily via the xylem during evapotranspiration (Mills and Jones, 1996). Sufficient calcium concentrations in plant leaf tissues range from 0.5 to 1.5% dry weight.

Function

Calcium is mainly found in the cell walls and is responsible for membrane stability and cell wall integrity. Calcium is required for the extension of cell walls during cell growth at shoot and root tips, and enhances pollen tube growth.

Symptoms of deficiency and toxicity

Calcium has limited mobility in plants. Deficiencies are often first expressed in young tissues as reduced growth in root and shoot meristems. During times of drought or high humidity, calcium supply may become deficient. Insufficient calcium in tomato, pepper, and watermelon plants can cause the breakdown of the cell walls of fruits. This is called blossom-end rot.

Toxicity effects are indirect, interfering with magnesium (Mg) and potassium (K) uptake and creating deficiencies of both in the plant. Over-use of calcium-based fertilizers may increase soil pH, rendering phosphorus, iron, manganese, boron, and zinc less available.

Magnesium (Mg)

Magnesium is found in many soil minerals and mineral salts but has little association with organic matter. After weathering from these mineral sources, magnesium is held by soil colloids, mainly clay, and is taken up by plant roots as a cation -Mg^{+2} and is most available at a pH just above 7.

Function

Plants take up magnesium passively and transport it mainly through the phloem. About 15-20% of the magnesium is found in the pigment molecule, chlorophyll. It is a co-factor for important plant enzymes. Normal magnesium concentrations are between 0.15 and 0.4% dry weight.

Symptoms of deficiency and toxicity

Deficiency symptoms appear in older leaves as interveinal chlorosis. There is typically no magnesium toxicity.

Nitrogen (N)

Nitrogen exists in many forms. Globally, the vast majority of nitrogen is in the lithosphere, mostly in igneous rock and some in sedimentary formations. The atmosphere contains approximately 1.9% of the global nitrogen, mostly in the form of N_2 and a very small amount in the form of other nitrogenous compounds. The biosphere contains no greater than 1/50th of 1% of the global nitrogen, most of which is either dissolved in the oceans or pooled in the terrestrial ecosystem, and less than 1% is available to plants as mineral nitrogen in the soil.

Function

Nitrogen is used by the plant in three forms: nitrate (NO_3^-), ammonium (NH_4^+), and to a lesser extent, amino acids. Plants sequester nitrogen into compounds such as amino acids and proteins. The nitrate and ammonium forms of mineralized nitrogen are different in the way they interact with soil and how they are used by plants. The ammonium ion (NH$_4^+$) is a cation. Ammonium can be bound by humic particles or negatively-charged clays. It is more available at neutral pH and less in low pH due to competition with H$^+$. Upon entering the plant root, a hydrogen ion from the ammonium is released, creating ammonia (NH$_3$). Hydrogen ions are released back out of the root, acidifying the soil around the root. Because ammonia is toxic and disrupts the electrochemical balance in cells, the plant must sequester the ammonia immediately. Plants cannot store ammonia, so the immediate result of ammonium uptake is amino acid production.

On the other hand, nitrate is an anion. Nitrate tends to move rapidly through the soil profile. In plants, nitrate is taken up both passively and actively. Uptake of nitrate causes the release of a hydroxyl ion (OH$^-$) out of the roots to the rhizosphere, raising the soil pH. Plants can store nitrate for future use, unlike ammonium. When nitrogen is needed, the plant reduces nitrate to ammonia by the enzymes nitrate reductase and nitrite reductase, in a very energy-intensive process that is driven by sunlight. Once again, the ammonia produced must be sequestered immediately, forming amino acids.

Acid-loving plant species like blueberries and rhododendrons do not effectively reduce nitrate because they produce only small quantities of the reductase enzymes. So the ammonium ion is their primary form of nitrogen nutrition. It is possible that in this way, ericaceous species adapted to, and have become more competitive in, low pH environments where there is little NO$_3^-$ production via nitrification.

Nitrogen is used for a variety of structural and metabolic compounds. Over half of the nitrogen in plants is found in the leaves. Between 15% and 30% of that leaf nitrogen goes into the production of Ribulose 1-5-biphosphate carboxylase (Rubisco), the most abundant enzyme on earth and the key plant enzyme that helps the production of carbohydrates from carbon dioxide (Evans, 1989).

Nitrogen is one of two primary nutrients responsible for nutrient problems in surface waters. The other is phosphorus. It also is a detriment to groundwater and is the primary focus of nutrient management activities. Interestingly, nitrogen can be easily made inert by denitrification processes, rendering it harmless to surface waters. **(See N cycle in Chapter 5.)**

Symptoms of deficiency and toxicity

Nitrogen deficiency symptoms include yellowing and chlorosis of mature leaves, slower plant growth, and increased root:shoot ratios.

Toxicity of nitrogen is primarily from ammonium. It can directly injure plant roots, compete with potassium for root uptake, or acidify the soil, making calcium and magnesium more available.

Phosphorus (P)

Phosphorus exists in soils in several forms, including:

- Minerals that contain phosphorus, like apatites
- Bound in organic material within the soil
- Bound to other elements like Ca, Mg, iron (Fe) or aluminum (Al)

- Adsorbed to soil particles like clay
- In a soluble form and readily available

The availability of phosphorus largely depends upon the minerals in the soil and the pH of the soil. Phosphorus is mainly taken up by plant roots in two forms: $H_2PO_4^-$ and HPO_4^{-2}.

- At high soil pH (above 7), phosphorus tends to be bound to Ca or Mg
- At low pH (below 5.5), phosphorus tends to bind to Fe and Al
- Between the pH of 5.5 and 7, phosphorus is most available to plants so it is a limiting nutrient in many terrestrial systems—that is why it is an important constituent in fertilizers
- In the United States, phosphorus in fertilizers is expressed as phosphate (P_2O_5)
- Because phosphorus is easily bound to soil minerals, plant roots must be in close proximity for uptake

Phosphorus is the second macronutrient that negatively affects surface waters. Unlike N, P is conserved in the environment and can be even more detrimental to water quality than N. While P is often bound to soils, erosion carries P-bound soil particles to surface waters, where it eventually becomes available to feed harmful algal blooms in freshwaters and estuarine systems like the Chesapeake Bay.

Mycorrhizae and P

Many plants use mycorrhizal fungi, which infect the roots and create a symbiotic relationship. This allows the plant to increase the volume of soil that can be exploited for P because the fungal hyphae have a much larger surface area than plant roots. The trade-off is that the mycorrhizal fungi pull carbon resources from the plant. The end result of this infection is positive for both organisms. Interestingly, high phosphorus concentrations in the soil retard mycorrhizal infection.

Function

Phosphorus is the primary energy carrier in cells and is present in many cell structures, including acting as an important component of cell membranes. Phosphorus is incorporated in proteins and nucleotides and regulates many enzyme activities. Sufficient concentrations in plant leaves range from 0.2 to 0.5%.

Symptoms of deficiency and toxicity

Phosphorus deficiency slows growth but increases root:shoot ratio. The belief that high phosphorus fertilization grows roots is incorrect. It is quite the opposite. Older leaves become dark green or purple in color with eventual necrosis of leaf margins. Production of flowers is compromised along with fruit and seeds.

Toxicity has indirect effects upon growth. High phosphorus levels in soil interfere with iron availability and decrease the uptake of copper and zinc.

Potassium (K)

Like phosphorus, potassium exists in many forms in soils. Much of it is tightly bound to soil colloids and is unavailable to plants. Plants take up potassium in large amounts compared to all other nutrients, except for nitrogen. Potassium is important for efficient nitrate-N uptake, and use of nitrate-N increases K uptake. Ammonium-N use may depress K uptake in soil.

Function

In plant tissue the N:K ratio is close to 1:1. When in the plant, potassium helps maintain a variety of plant metabolic activity mainly by regulating water status and the opening and closing of stoma. Potassium aids in carbohydrate transport and cellulose production.

Symptoms of deficiency and toxicity

Because potassium is mobile in the plant, deficiencies initially show in older growth as yellowing leaf edges with eventual leaf edge necrosis known as "scorch." Because potassium is involved with cellulose production, deficiencies also show as stem weakness and disease sensitivity.

Taste and quality of fruit is negatively affected when K is deficient.

There is typically no potassium toxicity in plants, but when potassium is in abundance, it can reduce the availability of Mg and Ca.

Sulfur (S)

In soil, the majority of sulfur is found in organic form, and to a lesser extent mineral form. Plant roots actively take up sulfur primarily as sulfates (SO_4) although some atmospheric sulfur may be acquired through foliage. Sulfur is immobile in plants.

Function

Plants utilize sulfur in amino acids, proteins, vitamins, and other plant compounds like glycoside oils that give onions and mustards their characteristic flavors. Sulfur also activates certain enzyme systems. Leaf-tissue sulfur concentrations are typically between 0.15 and 0.5% of dry weight.

Symptoms of deficiency and toxicity

Sulfur deficiency symptoms appear similar to those of nitrogen deficiency but show up on younger leaves first, because sulfur is not mobile once incorporated in the plant. There are rarely issues of toxicity.

6.5 Micronutrients

Micronutrients, or trace elements, are those elements that are required by the plant in quantities far less than macronutrients. Micronutrient deficiencies are not uncommon, and many times are due to soil pH levels.

In most cases a correction of soil pH and the yearly addition of organic matter will alleviate micronutrient deficiencies in most mineral soils. When a suspected micronutrient deficiency is severe and persistent, it may be advisable to submit a soil sample for a full spectrum test of major and minor nutrients. There are eight recognized essential micronutrients.

Boron (B)

Like calcium, boron moves into the plant, passively taken up in solution by the roots via transpiration.

Function

In the plant, boron moves with water in the xylem. Boron serves many roles in plants: from cell growth, including division, differentiation, and elongation, to cell processes like carbohydrate metabolism. Most boron is concentrated at growth areas, including reproductive structures. A sufficient concentration of boron in plants is about 0.002%, or 20 ppm.

Symptoms of deficiency and toxicity

Boron deficiencies are very common and may be caused by drought or high humidity. Because boron is associated with cell growth, deficiencies usually show up in new growth as wrinkled and withered leaves, with tip death soon after. In areas with boron deficiency, apply 6-7 level tablespoons of borax/1000 sq. ft. of garden area. Deficiencies are more often seen in sandy soils on the Coastal Plain.

Toxicity can develop quickly, and the difference between deficient and toxic is small. Boron toxicity is characterized by yellowing of the leaf tips, interveinal chlorosis, and leaf-margin scorching. Toxicity usually occurs with over-use of boron-containing fertilizers.

Chlorine (Cl)

Chlorine naturally occurs in soil minerals and is made available to roots through natural weathering. Chlorine is taken up by the plant both actively and passively, depending on soil concentrations: uptake is active when low and passive when high (White and Broadley, 2001).

Function

Chlorine is utilized in several processes of photosynthesis and is readily mobile throughout the plant. Sufficiency levels in plants are at 50 ppm.

Symptoms of deficiency and toxicity

Deficiencies are uncommon; toxicity symptoms appear as yellowing/burning leaf tips, with interveinal areas becoming bleached, scorched, and necrotic in severe cases.

Copper (Cu)

Copper is optimally available in slightly acidic conditions, where the copper ion exchanges with other cations held by soil particles. Root uptake is active and copper moves in the xylem, in combination with amino acids and other nitrogenous compounds. Once inside the plant, copper is not mobile.

Function

Copper works together with enzymes in metabolic activities and photosynthesis. Sufficiency in leaves is about 5 ppm.

Symptoms of deficiency and toxicity

Deficiencies of copper show up on the youngest leaves first, with depressed and twisted growth. New leaves appear pale along the margins but green at the end of the veins. Spotty necrosis occurs in the leaf margins and stems may become distorted and twisted. Toxic levels of copper induce iron deficiency and depressed root growth.

Iron (Fe)

Iron is ubiquitous in many soils, yet availability depends on soil chemistry. Iron is actively taken up by the plant and is transported by the xylem to the leaves. Some plants are able to make iron more soluble and available by acidifying the rhizosphere.

Function

Iron is used in several metabolic enzymes, especially those related to respiration and photosynthesis. Sufficiency in most plants is at 50 ppm.

Symptoms of deficiency and toxicity

Deficiency is similar to magnesium symptoms, but occurs on the youngest leaves first, because iron is not mobile in the plant once assimilated. Toxicities are rare but may produce manganese deficiency, as iron interferes with manganese uptake.

Manganese (Mn)

Manganese is found in soils derived from various iron-containing minerals and manganese oxides. Availability depends upon pH and organic colloid content. Low pH makes manganese soluble enough to leach through the soil profile. Manganese is transported in the xylem and delivered to meristematic tissue, and is not mobile.

Function

Manganese is used as a co-factor for many metabolic enzymes and is important to photosynthesis and antioxidant activity. Sufficiency in most plants ranges between 10 and 50 ppm.

Symptoms of deficiency and toxicity

Deficiency symptoms appear as interveinal chlorosis, similar to iron and zinc. Toxicity occurs in acid soil conditions when manganese is most available. Toxicity varies among plant species. Plants associated with acid soils are naturally tolerant to high manganese concentrations. Symptoms appear as dark purple or brown spots within the leaf margins and/or leaf tip necrosis. Severe toxicity results in stunted and yellowed meristems.

Molybdenum (Mo)

Unlike many micronutrients, molybdenum becomes more available in higher pH soils. Uptake is inhibited by sulfate and promoted by phosphate. When molybdenum is taken up by the plant, it is transported through the xylem or phloem. It is relatively mobile in the plant.

Function

Upon entry into the plant, it is sent directly to the leaf. There, Mo is used for nitrate reduction, one of two important physiological steps that make nitrate usable in the plant. Sufficient concentration of molybdenum in plant tissue is 0.20 ppm dry weight.

Symptoms of deficiency and toxicity

Because molybdenum is essential for nitrate reduction, a deficiency in molybdenum manifests as a nitrogen deficiency, starting with leaf chlorosis in older leaves, then leaf-margin wilting, with eventual leaf death and then meristem death. Toxicity is rare in soils, and plants can tolerate relatively high levels.

Nickel (Ni)

Nickel is the newest recognized essential plant nutrient. Nickel is relatively common in soils at concentrations much greater than required for plant growth. The requirement of nickel had not been known because impurities in irrigation water and fertilizers supplied the very low requirements of this nutrient.

Function

Little is known about nickel uptake in plants. It is required for the enzyme urease to metabolize urea, releasing the ammoniacal nitrogen for plant use. Nickel is also required for iron absorption, seed production, and germination.

Symptoms of deficiency and toxicity

Deficiency symptoms include rounded, blunt, and slightly curled leaves known as "mouse-ear." This condition is seen on spring growth and results from toxic accumulation of urea. At a level of 100 ppm or higher, nickel is considered to be phytotoxic.

Toxicity is more likely than deficiency, especially where industrial waste is concentrated. Symptoms include severely stunted growth; young leaves show chlorotic iron-deficiency symptoms, followed by severe necrosis, collapse, and death.

Zinc (Zn)

Zinc is present in sulfide and silicate minerals and also in organic matter. It is most available in low-pH soils. Zinc is actively taken up by plants and transported through the xylem.

Function

Zinc is used for several metabolic functions, including auxin production, protein synthesis, enzyme activity, and carbohydrate metabolism and regulation. Zinc is necessary for chlorophyll production and may enable plants to tolerate colder temperatures. A sufficient concentration in leaves is about 20 ppm dry weight.

Symptoms of deficiency and toxicity

Deficiency symptoms can be species-specific. Common symptoms include interveinal chlorosis on older leaves and shortened internode length.

Toxicity may occur in soils with a pH of less than 5 or where municipal sludge has been added to soils. Toxicity concentrations are species-dependent. Excessive zinc can interfere with iron uptake, and excessive phosphorus can interfere with zinc uptake and metabolism within the plant (Mills and Jones, 1996).

6.6 Beneficial Non-Essential Nutrients

There are several beneficial elements that are not considered essential for all plant species but are required by certain species to carry on specific physiological functions.

Silicon (Si)

Silicon is the most abundant element in soil next to oxygen, comprising more than 25% of the earth's crust. In soils, the soluble form of silicon exists as silicic acid (H_4SiO_4) at concentrations that may be as great or greater than phosphorus concentrations. Many plants are known to utilize silicon.

Cobalt (Co)

Cobalt is needed by leguminous plants for Rhizobium bacteria symbiosis. Rhizobium requires cobalt for the fixation of inert atmospheric nitrogen (N_2) to the usable ammonium NH_4^+ form.

Vanadium (V)

Vanadium has been shown to partially replace molybdenum's functions in plants (Mills and Jones, 1996). ❋

Table 6-B. **Macronutrients and micronutrients** (as they relate to plant growth)

Macronutrient	Form	Deficiency/Symptoms	Toxicity	Nutrient interactions
Calcium (Ca)	Ca^{+2}	Younger leaves: reduction in meristem growth	Indirect effects upon growth	Creates interference in uptake of Mg and K
Magnesium (Mg)	Mg^{+2}	Older leaves: interveinal chlorosis	Indirect effects upon growth	Creates interference in uptake of Ca and K
Nitrogen (N)	NO_3^- NH_4^+	Older leaves: light green to yellowing foliage with stunted growth. Leaf necrosis and death in severe deficiencies	**From nitrate:** none **From ammonium:** stunted root growth and death, wilting, foliar chlorosis, and necrosis	**From nitrate:** deficiencies of P, S, and Cl⁻ **From ammonium:** deficiencies of K, Ca, and Mg from soil acidification
Phosphorus (P)	H_3PO_4 $H_2PO_4^-$ HPO_4^{-2}	Older leaves: become dark green or purple with eventual necrosis of leaf margins; less flower production	Indirect effects upon growth	Creates interference in uptake of Fe, Cu, and Zn
Potassium (K)	K^+	Older leaves: yellowing edges, "scorch," weakness, and disease sensitivity	Indirect effects upon growth	Creates interference in uptake of Ca and Mg
Sulfur (S)	SO_2^{-4}	Younger leaves: similar to nitrogen deficiency	None	None

Micronutrient	Form	Deficiency/Symptoms	Toxicity	Nutrient interactions
Boron (B)	H_3BO_{3+} $H_2BO_3^-$ $B_4O_7^{-2}$	Younger leaves: wrinkled and withered leaves, tip death	Yellowing of the leaf tips, interveinal chlorosis, and leaf margin scorching	Necessary for P nutrition; K upsets Ca:B ratio
Chlorine (Cl)	Cl^-	Uncommon	Yellowing and burning of leaf tips, interveinal chlorosis	Interferes with NO_3^- uptake if over-applied
Copper (Cu)	Cu^{+2}	Younger leaves: depressed and twisted growth	Interveinal chlorosis	Interferes with Fe uptake if over-applied
Iron (Fe)	Fe^{+2}	Younger leaves: interveinal chlorosis	Interveinal chlorosis	Interferes with Mn uptake if over-applied
Manganese (Mn)	Mn^{+2}	Younger leaves: interveinal chlorosis	Dark purple or brown spots within leaf margins and/or leaf-tip necrosis	Interferes with Fe uptake if over-applied
Molybdenum (Mo)	MoO_4^{-2}	Similar to N deficiency	Rare; possible Cu-deficiency symptoms	Interferes with Cu uptake if over-applied
Nickel (Ni)	Ni^{+2}	Blunt and slightly curled leaves (i.e., "mouse-ear")	Stunted growth; young leaves show iron deficiency, followed by severe necrosis, collapse, and death	May interfere with Fe uptake at toxic levels
Zinc (Zn)	Zn^{+2}	Can be species-specific. Common symptoms: interveinal chlorosis on older leaves and shortened internode length	Interveinal chlorosis	Interferes with Fe uptake if over-applied. Excessive P interferes with Zn uptake

AUTHOR

Andrew G. Ristvey, Ph.D., Extension Specialist, Commercial Horticulture, University of Maryland Extension.

PUBLICATIONS

Arnon, D. J., and P. R. Stout. 1939. "The Essentiality of Certain Elements in Minute Quantity for Plants with Special Reference to Copper." *Plant Physiology.* 14:371-375.

Evans, J. R. 1989. "Photosynthesis and the Nitrogen Relationships in the Leaves of C3 Plants." *Oecologia.* 78:9-19.

Mills, H. A., and J. B. Jones, Jr. 1996. *Plant Analysis Handbook II: A Practical Sampling, Preparation, Analysis and Interpretation Guide.* MicroMacro Publishing Inc., Athens, GA.

Wallace, T. 1951. *The Diagnosis of Mineral Deficiencies in Plants by Visual Symptoms.* Second edition. H.M. Stationary Office, London.

White, P. J., and M. R. Broadley. 2001. "Chloride in Soils and its Uptake and Movement within the Plant: A Review". *Annals of Botany.* 88: 967-988, 2001.

ILLUSTRATIONS

Main Chapter Photo: **Miha Creative** via Adobe Stock.

Figure 6-A. Adapted by LeAnn Zotta from *Liebig's "Law of the Minimum" principle* - public domain.

7: COMPOSTING

Rachel J. Rhodes, M. S.
Courtney Coddington, M. S.

7 COMPOSTING

CONTENTS

7.1 Why Make Compost? 141

7.2 How Is Compost Made? 142

7.3 Compost Ingredients 143

7.4 Starting a Compost Pile 146

7.5 What Can Be Composted? 150

7.6 Basic Composting Steps 151

7.7 Troubleshooting Compost 153

7.8 Tips for Using Compost 153

LEARNING OBJECTIVES

- What compost is
- The benefits of composting
- The composting process, including the six essential components
- How to start a compost system
- How to troubleshoot composting problems
- Uses for finished compost

INTRODUCTION

Compost is a dark, crumbly, earthy-smelling material produced by the natural decomposition of leaves, grass clippings, and many other organic materials. It is much like the organic matter existing on top of and in all soil, and can be made by just about any gardener or homeowner.

Compost piles are started and maintained by humans, but are naturally created by microbes and soil organisms which break down plant and animal remains as part of the decomposition process. This activity is part of the larger processes of nutrient-cycling and soil-building that happen within any ecosystem.

Compost expedites the natural cycle to produce an excellent soil amendment for the landscape. Finished compost contains major and minor elements, other compounds necessary for plant growth, and organic matter which improves soil structure.

7.1 Why Make Compost?

There are very important reasons to incorporate compost into your landscape:

Composting reduces the amount of material going to landfills. Municipal waste is composed of 6% yard waste, 22% food waste, and 13% paper, most of which can be composted (U.S. EPA, Office of Solid Waste, 2017). Disposing of yard waste in landfills is expensive and lacks environmental sustainability and burning organic materials releases pollutants that weaken fragile ecosystems. Composting provides a more environmentally friendly alternative than either of these methods.

Backyard composting is cost-effective. Some Maryland jurisdictions impose special taxes on homeowners for yard waste disposal. Compost instead! Composting produces a valuable and free soil amendment, saving money that would otherwise be spent on items like peat moss and fertilizer. Compost improves soil tilth, aeration, water-holding capacity, and feeds the soil with a wide range of macro- and micronutrients. Most Maryland landscapes benefit from regular additions of compost.

Compost suppresses some soil-borne diseases. Populations of some microbes in compost may out-compete pathogens for food and habitat while others attack or repel plant pathogens.

Composting is good for the environment, plus it's fun, educational, and something in which the whole family can participate.

7.2 How Is Compost Made?

The composting process

The gardener's goal is to manage the materials and environmental conditions in the pile to facilitate the quick and complete breakdown of organic matter. A simplified composting equation is shown in Figure 7-A.

This cycle can be guided through several stages, each requiring actions from the gardener to move the process along and ensure that the ingredients remain in balance, which keeps the cycle going. By managing the six factors of effective composting, any gardener can successfully turn yard waste and kitchen scraps into valuable compost.

Note: The term "compost pile" is often used generically in this chapter to mean any type of composting system, either simple or complex.

The compost cycle

The compost cycle can be observed over four main stages of activity. Each stage is identified by changes in the pile's core temperature.

6 FACTORS OF EFFECTIVE COMPOSTING

1: Microorganisms that digest organic matter
2: Air ⎤
3: Water ⎬ Required by the microorganisms
4: Food ⎦
5: Size of the food particles
6: Volume of the pile

Stage 1: Psychrophilic bacteria, the bacteria that are capable of working in the lowest temperature range, are usually the first to begin decomposing material. They work efficiently at 55° but can continue to decompose material at temperatures as low as 0°.

As they begin breaking down material in the pile, their activity creates heat that will begin to raise the temperature of the compost pile to Stage 2, which is the temperature range that recruits mesophilic bacteria. These bacteria only give off a small amount of heat that often gets overshadowed by heat lost to the environment. At this stage it is necessary to manage heat loss in order to reach Stage 2. Proper pile construction/ containment and adding the right ratio of ingredients to keep the microbial activity going strong will achieve that goal.

Figure 7-A. Simplified composting equation

COMPOST FACT: There are approximately 5 billion microbes in 1 gram of soil!

Stage 2: When temperatures range between 40º-110º, the pile is in Stage 2. Mesophilic bacteria will work most efficiently at a temperature range of 70º-90º and will complete most of the decomposition work in the composting process. If a compost pile is maintained and monitored correctly, mesophilic bacteria populations can thrive and eventually create enough heat to bring the compost pile into the Stage 3 temperature range of 104º-170º.

Stage 3: The compost pile will recruit thermophilic bacteria, which thrive on heat. During this stage, the pile will need to be turned and fed new materials to support the fast-working thermophiles. These bacteria work quickly to digest materials; their activity will peak after four to seven days if the pile is not carefully managed. Monitoring and adjusting temperature and moisture during Stage 3 can extend the activity of the thermophilic bacteria another week, or longer, if the pile is large enough. Once the Stage 3 activity peaks at 160º-180ºF, the temperature will begin cooling down and enter Stage 4.

Stage 4: The materials take on a uniform brown color instead of greens and yellows. At this stage most bacterial work is finished. Other decomposers and soil organisms begin to appear as the temperature stabilizes. It is common to see fungi, cobweb-like growths produced by actinomycetes, and invertebrates.

The time it takes for the composting process to complete depends upon the six main factors mentioned on the previous page: microorganisms, air, water, food (ingredients), the particle size associated with those ingredients, and the size of the pile. The maintenance of the pile will also impact the speed of the process.

7.3 Compost Ingredients

The microbial decomposers

Bacteria, fungi, and other microbes are the key players in composting (see Figure 7-B). These organisms "feed" on organic matter and use the carbon and nitrogen it contains to grow and reproduce. The heat generated by the compost pile is a result of microbial activity. Microbes are active in small numbers at temperatures just above freezing, but are most efficient at 130º–140º F. They are assisted by many larger organisms like earthworms, slugs, snails, millipedes, sow bugs, and various insect larvae that feed on plant and animal matter in the soil. These same organisms are responsible for the decay of both forest floor litter and the corn stubble in a farmer's field.

Carbon/nitrogen

Composting microbes use carbon for energy and nitrogen for growth (protein synthesis). These two elements can be found in the organic matter a gardener adds to the pile. Organic matter comes in two broad forms:

Green materials include fresh grass clippings, weeds, kitchen waste, and farm manure. These are high in nitrogen and moisture, but low in carbon. They are also high in readily-digested sugars and starches.

Brown materials include mature woody materials, fallen leaves, straw, wood chips, and sawdust. These are high in carbon (mostly cellulose and lignin), low in moisture, and slow to break down.

A blending of equal parts (by volume or weight) of green and brown materials gives the decomposers an ideal diet.

Figure 7-B. The compost-pile food web

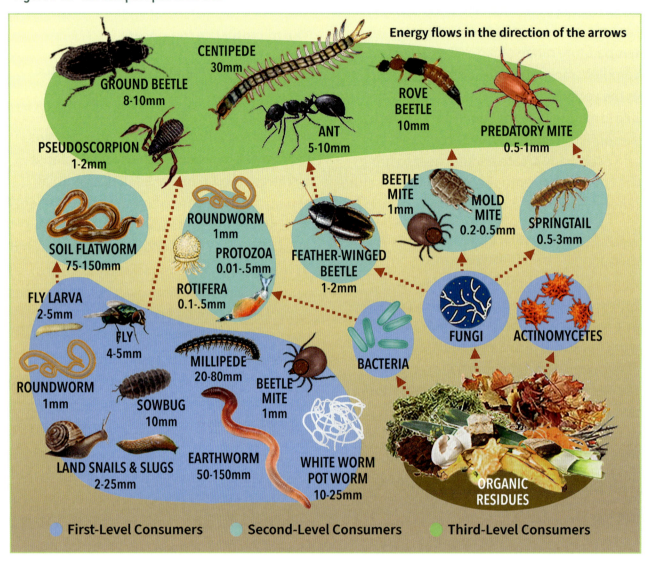

Water and oxygen

Most life forms require oxygen and water to grow and reproduce. The microorganisms that produce compost are no different. You can control the content and movement of air and water in the composting system to enhance the activity of the fungi and bacteria.

Composting occurs both with oxygen (aerobic) or without it (anaerobic). Microbes exist under both of these conditions, but aerobic composting is faster and more effective. Anaerobic microbes compost by fermentation, which results in the formation of foul odors, acids, and alcohols that can harm plants in the garden. Aerobic composting is essentially odorless when done properly.

Oxygen is often the principal factor limiting the complete breakdown of ingredients. Reviving the microbes with fresh air will cause the pile to reheat. This is typically done by turning or inverting the pile with a garden fork or pitchfork. Turn by slicing down through the pile and inverting each slice. The goal is to shift materials from the outer parts of the pile closer to the center for better decomposition and to incorporate oxygen.

Air flow may also be limited by too much finely-chopped material and compaction that results from an overly large pile. Adding coarse materials like dead leaves, straw, or fine twigs when building the pile (and when periodically turning the pile) will also improve aeration.

Microbes function best when composting materials are about as damp as a wrung-out sponge and have numerous air passages. Very wet or dry conditions will adversely affect the moisture and air balance in the compost pile.

Moisture is important because microbes can only break down moist materials. If the organic materials are too dry, the process will slow and most of the decomposers will go dormant. The same result occurs if the materials become too wet. Air is pushed out of the pile, aerobic microbes die off, nutrients are lost, and unpleasant odors develop.

An easy way to determine moisture content is to occasionally squeeze a handful of composting material. If nothing comes out, the material is too dry. If the material oozes between your fingers, it is too wet. You can dry out wet compost by mixing the pile or incorporating coarse materials like leaves, straw, or sawdust. To adequately wet a dry pile, turn the material and add water gradually until it is properly moistened.

Particle size

The organisms responsible for decomposition work on the surface of the organic matter. You can increase the surface area by shredding or chopping the material to be composted into smaller pieces. Although this is not essential, it does speed up the process. Remember, however, that material which is too fine may mat together, restrict air flow, and thereby slow decomposition.

Table 7-A. Compost measurement conversions

1 bushel	8 dry gallons
1 bushel	1.24 cubic feet
1 cubic foot	6.4 dry gallons
20 bushels	158 dry gallons
55-gallon drum	7.35 cubic feet
55-gallon drum	5.93 bushels

For a typical single bin:
3 feet wide x 3 feet tall x 3 feet deep = 27 cubic feet
27 cubic feet - 1 cubic yard
1 cubic yard = 202 gallons - 25.25 bushels

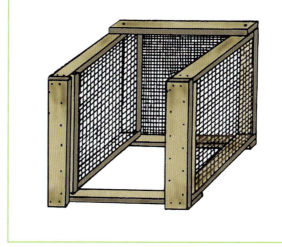

Pile volume

A compost pile should be at least three feet wide by three feet long by three feet high (one cubic yard), but no higher or wider than five feet by five feet. A smaller pile may not have sufficient critical mass to heat up and stay hot. A pile higher or wider than five feet is difficult to manage and may not allow sufficient aeration in the center.

Note: If you use an enclosed compost barrel or bin, follow manufacturer's instructions regarding optimal volume.

7.4 Starting a Compost Pile

Locating your pile

- Situate the pile on a level spot. This reduces the chance of water runoff leaching nutrients from the compost.
- Place the pile near the garden or where the raw material is generated and the end product will be used.
- Choose a spot that is accessible but inconspicuous so that it is not a focal point of your landscape.
- Be respectful of adjacent neighbor's properties, as compost piles are often considered unsightly or a potential source of pests.
- Keep the pile away from wooden buildings to avoid attracting termites.
- Avoid locating the pile near trees and shrubs that could send their roots into the nutrient-rich pile.
- Make sure a water source is nearby to help maintain the moisture level.
- Allow sufficient room to stockpile ingredients (especially extra "browns"), to turn the pile, and to store finished compost.
- A full-sun site is not necessary because the decomposition process is driven by microbes, not the sun. Full sunlight may also increase the need to address moisture levels and temperature, as the heat from direct sunlight could dry out or overheat your pile.
- Be sure to check HOA, neighborhood, city or other ordinances to make sure composting is allowed in your area. Certain types of composting may be either limited or prohibited.

Composting methods

To help determine which method is right for you and your landscape, see **Table 7-B.**

A simple pile

A pile design is the most basic composting method. Simply mound equal amounts of greens and browns into a pile, and when there is enough material, occasionally turn the pile and keep it moistened to perpetuate the composting process.

Composting bins

Bin systems are typically designed as a divided row of boxes or bins, which hold successive stages of compost. They can be made from numerous materials like woven wire fencing (hog, chicken, or turkey wire, hardware cloth, chain-link), wood slat fencing (snow fence), cement blocks, bricks, pallets, or scrap lumber.

Good air movement from both the sides and the top is necessary for oxygen to aid the microbial processes. Constructing the bins with slatted or mesh sides is the most effective way of creating good air flow. One side of the enclosure should be open for turning and removing finished compost (see Figure 7-C).

A large number of manufactured, free-standing bins (often from recycled plastic) are available commercially. Material longevity is important to consider with respect to

Figure 7-C. A three-bin compost setup

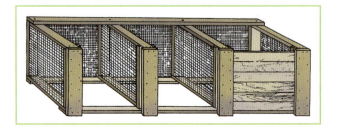

monetary and time investment, as untreated wood materials are easy to use but decay in a few years. Treated lumber may be used, so long as the lumber was not preserved using Chromated Copper Arsenate (CCA), which is not recommended for use with anything that could be a component of food production. Alkaline Copper Quaternary (ACQ) is a safer, water-based alternative for preserving lumber that is typically available to the public.

A sequence of several "turning" piles in a row allows a gardener the ability to move composting material from one bin to the next on a regular basis. Turning piles are most appropriate if you have a large volume of material and the desire to make high-quality compost in a short time. A row of three bins (see Figure 7-C) or piles can be quite effective, with the first unit holding compost that is actively working. Use the middle unit to hold compost close to completion and the third to finish and store compost before use.

Additional bins can be constructed as holding areas for raw materials before mixing.

Tumblers/barrels

Tumbler units (see Figure 7-D) work best where space is limited, appearance is important, or where unwanted pests might be attracted to the compost materials (i.e., kitchen scraps). Tumblers and barrels typically hold about six to eight cubic feet of material. When the drum is rotated, the material is mixed and aerated.

Tumblers can either be purchased or constructed at home, typically using 55-gallon plastic food-grade containers.

To use tumblers effectively, it is important to:

- Initially load the barrel to capacity before rotating

Figure 7-D. Typical compost tumbler

- Maintain a C:N ratio of 25-40:1 (see Table 7-C)
- Avoid excess moisture; only add enough water to reach a "damp-sponge" feel
- Rotate the tumbler several times a week to keep the ingredients aerated
- Monitor the pile temperature to determine further maintenance and finishing requirements

During the heat of the summer a tumbler can overheat and become anaerobic. Keep a close eye on it during temperature swings.

Tumblers are difficult to manage in winter because the contents are elevated and frigid air can circulate 360° around it. The compost will freeze solid more quickly than it would in an on-the-ground composter. Plan to have your composting finished by late fall, or use an alternative composting method in winter.

For continual composting it may be necessary to have one tumbler for adding material and one for processing.

Figure 7-E. Trench composting

Trenching and incorporation

Trenching and incorporation are simple methods typically used for composting food scraps. These methods are best for keeping rodents and other animals at bay.

Dig a hole or long trench deep enough to mask the scent of the kitchen scraps, which is what attracts unwanted animals. Load ingredients into the trench and cover thoroughly with about six to eight inches of soil (see Figure 7-E). The ingredients decompose in place and release nutrients as they decompose. Ingredients are best added as shredded particles rather than whole chunks.

If you would rather forego digging a trench, you can simply dig random small holes, incorporate batches of scraps directly into the garden, and backfill with soil.

Vermicomposting

Vermicomposting involves feeding kitchen scraps and small amounts of "greens" to worms that are housed in an aerated container, called a worm bin (see Figure 7-F).

Worm bins are compact structures that can be kept conveniently indoors or in a sheltered area near the home that is not exposed to freezing temperatures.

Redworms are typically used because they can digest two-thirds of their weight in material daily and reproduce every week. Redworms can be purchased through online suppliers.

To start the process, add worms to a perforated tray that is full of moistened bedding material (shredded paper, coir, and/or shredded leaves), kitchen scraps and small amounts of yard waste. These ingredients are processed by the worms until much of the material in the tray is castings (excrement). Once a tray is finished, start a new one and nestle it down into the compost in the first tray. The holes in the bottom of the trays allow airflow, but also let worms migrate upward into the newly-charged tray. After a couple of days, remove the first tray and harvest the compost. Repeat the process for fresh compost.

Figure 7-F. Vermicomposter

Table 7-B. Composting system comparison

System Type	Cost	Composting Rate	Notes
-- Yard Waste --			
Pile	None	Slow if not turned (6 months-2 years)	Very low maintenance; okay where aesthetics are not a concern.
Tumbler	Moderate-high; less if using scrap and recycled materials	Fast (minimum of 3 weeks)	Materials are turned from bin to bin. Good for large yards.
Mulch	Low	Usable immediately, but material should be shredded / mixed	Materials can be incorporated at the end of the season.
Directly mixed into soil	Low	Slow to medium	Okay to chop and mix small quantities of grass clippings or spent plants into garden soil. High carbon materials (leaves) can produce a nitrogen deficiency.
Commercial bin	High	Fast (minimum of 3 weeks)	Take finished compost from bin bottom or screen and used as needed. Occasionally turn or stir materials to speed process.
-- Kitchen Waste --			
Trench	None	Fast (minimum of 2 weeks)	Bury wastes 8-12 inches deep in garden bed.
Trash can composter	Low	Slow (faster if turned)	Drill holes in sides and bottom. Raise can up on blocks. Position a length of perforated rigid pipe vertically through the lid. This "chimney" will help speed up the process.
Worm bin	Medium	Fast (minimum of 4 weeks).	Can be done inside or outside. Excellent project for children.
Barrel or drum turning unit	High	Fast (minimum of 4 weeks)	Can be purchased or constructed at home.

Source: Adapted from *Composting: Wastes to Resources,* by Jean F. Bonhotal and Marianne E. Krasny.

Composting tools

There are a number of tools which will aid in the compost process. Specially designed compost turners or aerators aid in turning the compost pile, as will a pitchfork or garden fork (see Figure 7-G). A temperature probe is essential to ensure that temperatures are high enough (140°F) to kill pathogens and seeds.

A wide range of shredders and chippers are available. Consider the amount of material you plan to handle when deciding whether or not to purchase such equipment. Also ask yourself

Figure 7-G. Pitchfork

how often you will use the equipment in any one season.

Pruning shears, string trimmers, lawn mowers, machetes, and hatchets are adequate to cut up most yard waste. An easy way to shred fallen leaves is to mow them before raking. You can collect the shredded leaves directly with a mower-bag attachment. If a mower bag is not available, rake the leaves to the compost area and run your lawn mower through them with the discharge shoot directed towards the pile.

Finished compost may have varying particle sizes. A compost sifter (see Figure 7-H) can be used to separate out the finished particles from the larger (unfinished) chunks. Place the sifter over a wheelbarrow or bin and add a few shovelfuls of compost. Shake the sifter and the finished compost will fall through the screen. Simply add the larger chunks back to the pile.

See **Chapter 29, Garden Tools and Equipment**, for more information about composting tools.

Figure 7-H. Compost sifter

7.5 What Can Be Composted?

Adding the right kind of materials and properly balancing them is the overall goal. The finer focus should be on perfecting the C:N ratio (see Table 7-C). This ratio is an important factor for promoting the ideal environment to allow bacteria to easily decompose organic matter. The C:N ratio is calculated as:

$$\text{C:N ratio} = \frac{\text{weight of biodegradable C}}{\text{weight of organic N + ammonium N + nitrate N}}$$

Microorganisms in compost use carbon (browns) for energy and nitrogen (greens) for protein synthesis. The proportion can vary; the microbes will function well at C:N ratios from

Table 7-C.   C:N ratios of common ingredients

Low-carbon nitrogen levels	
Vegetable waste	12-25:1
Grass clippings	25:1
Cow manure	12-25:1
Horse manure	25:1
Horse manure w/ litter	35:1
Poultry manure	10:1
Poultry manure w/ litter	13-18:1
High-carbon nitrogen levels	
Dead mature leaves	25-50:1
Corn stalks	50:1
Pine needles	50:1
Straw	50-100:1
Tree bark	30-50:1
Paper	100-130:1
Wood chips/sawdust	100-500:1

Table 7-D. What (and what not) to compost

YES		NO	
Bread	Coffee grounds	Bones	Vegetable oil
Egg shells	Evergreen needles	Cat or dog manure	Dairy: Cheese, milk, etc.
Fruit/vegetable peels, scraps and rinds	Grass/shrub clippings (untreated)	Beef, pork or chicken meat	Fish scraps
Farm-animal manure	Paper, cardboard	Grease or lard	Tea bags / coffee filters
Sawdust (small amounts)	Sod (turn upside-down)	Mayonnaise	Onions/garlic (repel worms)
Soil (very small amounts)	Spent plants (undiseased)	Glossy paper	Cooked foods
Straw/hay/corn stalks	Used tea leaves	Diseased or infested plants	Peanut butter
Fallen tree leaves	Pinecones, small twigs	Salad dressing	Cat litter
Wood ash (very small amounts)	Weeds (no flowers/seedheads)	Dryer lint (contains plastic)	Invasive plants
Citrus rinds	Potting soil	Lime	Starters (unnecessary)

25:1 to 40:1. A mixture of materials containing 30 parts of carbon to 1 part of nitrogen is considered ideal. Most organic materials do not fit the 30:1 ratio exactly, so different materials are combined. With the proper mix, microbes and other digesters will quickly start working to make compost for you. Finished compost has a C:N ratio of 20-25:1.

Ideally, begin your composting system with a large supply of organic matter. Practically any plant material can be composted.

Some material should not be composted at all (see Table 7-C). Do not add:

- Plants from the flower and vegetable garden that are infected with diseases.
- Weeds that have produced seed heads or that spread by stolons or rhizomes.
- Cat and dog droppings, because they may contain two dangerous organisms: *Toxoplasma gondii* and *Toxocara cati*, which are extremely harmful to immunocompromised people.
- Fat of any kind.
- Dairy, poultry, fish or meat products.
- Coated or treated paper, as it may contain chemicals that could inhibit decomposition and/or plant growth.

7.6 Basic Composting Steps

No two compost piles are exactly the same and there is no single "correct" set of composting techniques that gardeners should follow. Select your methods based on your circumstances. That said, some tips may help you compost more effectively:

- Mix materials vs. layering

- To speed up the process add an extra nitrogen (e.g., cottonseed meal, blood meal) source at each turning
- Monitor the temperature regularly with a temperature probe
- Use a tarp to help manage your pile; it can protect against too much rain and keep moisture in during dry spells
- Do not turn the pile in winter because this allows too much heat to escape and slows decomposition

MAKING "FAST COMPOST"

Fast composting is labor-intensive because of the time needed to gather, store, and prepare adequate quantities of materials and manage the operation. Having more than one bin simplifies things, as you can simply transfer materials to an adjacent bin at each turning.

Chop or shred the organic matter before adding it to the pile. Mechanical chippers or shredders are most effective but a lawn mower, pruners, a machete or a hatchet can be used as well. Shred paper before adding to your pile.

Charge (completely fill) your bin all at once to create rapid heating, which speeds the process.

Turn the pile after three days. Lots of steam should arise in the summer. If the pile is not heating, check "Troubleshooting Tips" (see Table 7-D) for a possible causes and solutions.

The "fast" method generates very high temperatures of about 160°F. This is high enough to kill most weed seeds and disease organisms, but temperatures above 160° kill composting microbes as well. After two weeks of regular turning, the temperature will have dropped as the composting process slows. The compost will be brown and crumbly, and have an earthy smell. Age the compost for two more weeks before using around plants.

Finished compost

Compost is ready when its temperature has decreased to slightly above air temperature and turning the pile fails to raise its temperature. Finished compost is dark and fairly homogeneous, although you will see pieces of the original ingredients.

Composted material taken directly from the pile will contain particles of many sizes. This is fine, as even under optimal conditions the process may not be absolutely complete in a single season. Sift out larger pieces or leave them in; they will not harm the bed.

Keep finished compost dry to prevent nutrient-leaching and anaerobic digestion. Compost that becomes water-logged or is stacked over three feet high may become anaerobic, producing harmful alcohol and methanol.

FIVE WAYS TO HANDLE LEAVES

1. Compost them in the fall, adding a shovelful of finished compost per bushel
2. Spread them on bare ground and around trees, shrubs, and perennial beds
3. Incorporate directly into soil; add a nitrogen source to prevent nitrogen tie-up
4. Bag them, adding a few shovelfuls of finished compost to each large bag. Moisten, make ventilation holes and over-winter them. In the spring they should be largely decomposed.
5. Shred* well with a mower and leave them on the lawn (max. of ½-inch deep).

Shredding leaves will reduce the volume, hasten decomposition, and make them easier to manage

7.7 Troubleshooting Compost

If your compost is not "cooking" or has a foul odor, there is a simple remedy. See Table 7-D to properly identify the problem and solution.

7.8 Tips for Using Compost

Soil application

Compost can be incorporated into garden soil at a rate of between 25 to 50 bushels per 1,000 square feet of area, a ½- to 1-inch layer of compost uniformly spread over the entire surface. (See Figure 7-I for the formula.)

Mix compost into the top six to eight inches of soil. You can apply it every year, but no more than a ¼- to ½-inch layer of screened compost should be spread on turf each year.

It is sometimes necessary to add additional nitrogen to soils when incorporating raw organic materials with high C:N ratios, e.g., tree leaves. Soil microbes will use up nitrogen as they digest the organic matter, creating the potential for nitrogen deficiency in your lawn or plants. Add about ½ cup of a 10% nitrogen fertilizer per three bushels of leaves to help reduce the demand on soil nitrogen levels.

As a mulch

Coarse-textured compost, particularly coarse leaf compost, can also be used as an organic mulch on the soil surface. Organic mulches are valuable because they:

- Reduce rainfall runoff
- Decrease water evaporation from the surface

Table 7-E. Troubleshooting compost issues

Problem	Possible causes	Solutions
Rotten odor	<ul><li>Excess moisture</li><li>Compaction</li><li>Other anaerobic conditions</li></ul>	<ul><li>Cover pile during rainy spells</li><li>Turn pile</li><li>Make pile smaller</li></ul>
Ammonia odor	<ul><li>Too much nitrogen (lack of carbon)</li></ul>	<ul><li>Add high-carbon material, such as sawdust, wood chips, or straw</li></ul>
Low pile temperature	<ul><li>Pile too small</li><li>Insufficient moisture</li><li>Poor aeration</li><li>Lack of nitrogen</li><li>Cold weather</li></ul>	<ul><li>Make pile bigger, insulate sides and top with an extra layer of material like straw</li><li>Add water while turning pile</li><li>Turn pile</li><li>Mix in nitrogen sources such as grass clippings or manure</li></ul>
High pile temperature (160°F)	<ul><li>Pile too large</li><li>Insufficient ventilation</li></ul>	<ul><li>Reduce pile size</li><li>Turn pile</li></ul>
Pests: rats, raccoons, insects	<ul><li>Presence of meat scraps or fatty food waste</li></ul>	<ul><li>Remove meat and fatty foods from pile or cover with a layer of sawdust</li><li>Build an animal-proof compost bin, or turn pile to increase temperature</li></ul>

Figure 7-I. Figuring the application rate

TO COVER A 200 SQUARE-FOOT BED WITH 2 INCHES

200 s.f. X 0.16 ft. = 33.33 cu. ft. (1 cu. yd. = 27 cu. ft.)

33.33 cu. ft. / 27 = 1.2 cu. yd.

YOU WILL NEED 1.2 CUBIC YARDS OF COMPOST

- Keep soils cooler in summer
- Keep soils frozen in winter and reduce plant heaving
- Prevent soil erosion
- Make soil easier to cultivate
- Prevent soil splashing, keeping fruit and flowers clean
- Help control weeds
- Present an attractive surface covering

Organic mulch should be no more than two to three inches thick around trees and shrubs. A slightly deeper layer is effective on shallow-rooted, acid-tolerant plants like azaleas.

Never allow mulch to contact tree or shrub trunks. The moisture-holding quality of the mulch may cause bark rot, killing the plant.

For potting

Compost can also be used as a growing medium for outdoor potted plants. No more than ½ of the mix should be compost. Pots filled entirely with compost tend to dry out. To minimize this problem, fill the bottom and sides of your containers with compost and reserve the middle of the pot for garden soil that can hold water more tightly.

It's best not to re-use compost a second season for growing potted plants. Weathering will cause particle size to decrease, leading to poor aeration and inhibited root growth. Instead, spread it around garden plants. ❋

AUTHORS

Courtney Coddington, M.S., Assoc. Agent, Master Gardener Program, University of Maryland Extension.

Rachel J. Rhodes, M.S., Senior Agent, Master Gardener Program, University of Maryland Extension.

PUBLICATIONS

Dindal, Dr. Daniel L. 1990. *Soil Biology Guide.* Wiley-Interscience.

ILLUSTRATIONS

Figure 7-B. Adapted by LeAnn Zotta from "Food Web of the Compost Pile," by Dr. Daniel L. Dindal, Distinguished Teaching Professor Emeritus, State University of New York College of Environmental Science and Forestry.

Colorization and other figures by LeAnn Zotta.

8: INSECT BASICS

Emily Zobel, M. S.

8 INSECT BASICS

CONTENTS

8.1 Insects as Part of a Natural System 158

8.2 Insect Structure 158

8.3 Insect Metamorphosis 163

8.4 Insect Classification 164

8.5 Common Landscape Pests 170

8.6 Common Household Pests 175

8.7 Beneficial Insects 176

8.8 Common Non-insect Arthropods 179

LEARNING OBJECTIVES

- The role insects play in the natural system, and how they affect humans
- Basic anatomy of insects
- Different life cycles and life stages of insects
- The orders and characteristics of insects encountered in the garden and home

INTRODUCTION

Insects are the most prolific group of animals in the world. They are extremely adaptable and can be found in a wide range of habitats, from deserts and mountain tops to freshwater lakes, rivers and streams—even along ocean shorelines. There are more than 100,000 insect species in North America alone.

The vast majority of insects are beneficial or harmless to humans; they pollinate crops and provide food for wildlife, including small mammals, reptiles, amphibians, birds, and fish. Fewer than 10 percent are considered pests. Some pest species may cause damage to crops, ornamental trees and plants, stored products, fabrics, and other items; others impact human and animal health by transmitting diseases.

Insects are part of the animal kingdom, which is divided into phyla. Insects are in the phylum *Arthropoda*, which is subdivided into classes. Some defining characteristics of phylum *Arthropoda* are:

- Segmented bodies with bilateral symmetry
- Jointed appendages
- An exoskeleton, which requires periodic shedding/molting to grow
- Internal structures that includes a "heart" running along the upper or dorsal part of the body and a nerve cord along the lower or ventral part of the body
- Cold-blooded, so their body temperature and vital function depend on the ambient temperature of the environment. This is why many insects are most active during warmer parts of the day and warmer months of the year.

Examples of other non-insect arthropods:

- Crustaceans: Crabs, shrimp, lobster, barnacles
- Myriapoda: Millipedes, centipedes
- Arachnida: Spiders, ticks, mites, harvestmen, scorpions

Table 8-A. Examples of arthropod classes

Class	Examples	Pairs of legs
Crustacea	Crayfish, sowbugs	5
Arachnida	Spiders, mites, ticks	4
Diplopoda	Millipedes	2 pairs/segment
Chilopoda	Centipedes	1 pair/segment
Insecta	All insects	3

Insects differ from other arthropods in that they have:

- A body divided into three regions (head, thorax, and abdomen)
- Three pairs of legs located on the thorax
- One pair of antennae

Classes are further divided into orders, then families, genera, and species (**see Chapter 4, Botany**). As scientists continue to study animals and plants, and their evolution, classification groups can be created, rearranged, changed, and combined. There are currently 31 orders of insects, which are described in **Table 8-C** (p. 182).

8.1 Insects as Part of a Natural System

Figure 8-A. Dung beetle

Insects play an essential part in the food web. They are often the first level that consumes plants. Conversely, they also serve as food for other animals such as birds, reptiles, amphibians, and small mammals. In many countries insects are eaten by humans as a primary source of protein.

Insects play a crucial role as decomposers that aid in the recycling and disposal of waste in the environment. They feed on and break down things like dead wood, leaf litter, dead animals and dung (see Figure 8-A). Without insects, dead animals and plants would accumulate in our environment, creating health issues for humans and wildlife.

Along the same lines, insects help maintain ecological balance by keeping other insect, animal, and plant populations at a manageable level. Some are predatory or parasitic on other insects and animals, including people. Through predation, parasitism, and disease transmission, insects help maintain the environmental community structure, composition, and balance.

Insects pollinate many of our crops and native plants. Some insects are generalists and will pollinate many different plants; others are more specialized and have co-evolved only to pollinate one group of plants, or, in extreme cases, only one plant species. For example, the cacao plant is only pollinated by a few species of small flies called chocolate midges.

Insects also "manufacture" products we enjoy and rely upon, such as honey, beeswax, lacquer, and silk.

8.2 Insect Structure

All adult insects possess the following characteristics: three body regions, three pairs of legs, one pair of antennae, and zero, one or two pairs of wings.

Exoskeleton

The insect body is supported by an outer skeleton or exoskeleton, which also serves as a: protective covering over the body; a surface for muscle attachment; a water-tight barrier; and a sensory interface with the environment.

The exoskeleton is made up of layers (see Figure 8-B). The top layer is the epicuticle, which is thin and covered in wax. It serves as a barrier to movement of water into or out of the insect's body.

Figure 8-B. Insect exoskeleton layers

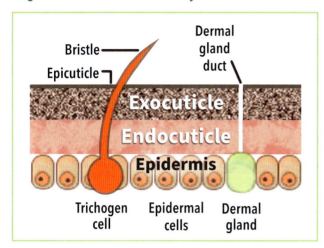

Under the epicuticle is the procuticle, which is made up of layers of microfibers of chitin, oriented at slightly different angles. Having thin layers at different angles prevents a stretch or crack at the surface from progressing downward and becoming lethal. The procuticle is divided into two parts: the hard, outer exocuticle, and a soft, inner endocuticle. In addition to chitin, these layers have a mixture of other proteins that affect the cuticle's flexibility and rigidity. They vary based on species and location on the body.

Under the procuticle is the epidermis, which produces the overlying layers of the cuticle and the basement membrane, which in turn separates the exoskeleton from the rest of the insect's body cavity.

The cuticle of each segment is formed into several hardened plates called sclerites, which are separated by infolds to give them flexibility. The cuticle of the immature stage is not usually as hardened as that of the adult. Insects and other arthropods must molt their exoskeleton in order to grow.

During molting, the cuticle separates from the epidermal cells. A special molting fluid is secreted into that space which breaks down the old cuticle so the insect can absorb and reuse it to make the new endocuticle. Meanwhile, the epidermal cells begin to produce the new cuticle. Once ready, the insect will suck in air to expand its body cavity, causing a crack or split in the old exoskeleton along pre-determined lines, enabling it to wriggle out. Once out, the insect will continue to pump in air to expand and stretch the new

Figure 8-C. Grasshopper structure: Head, thorax and abdomen

Figure 8-D. Insect head with chewing mouthparts

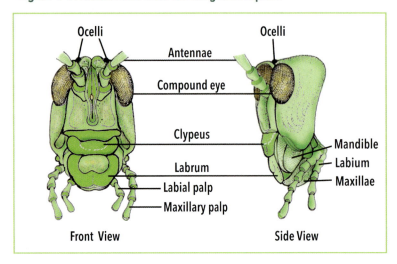

exoskeleton, which is soft and flexible, before it hardens. During this period, the insect cannot move.

Insects have three body regions: the head, thorax, and abdomen (see Figure 8-C). The head is where most of the insect's sensory organs are located, while the thorax is where appendages for movement are found. The abdomen holds many of the internal organs.

Head

Mouthparts (see Figure 8-D) vary in form and function and are located on either the anterior or ventral part of the head. The basic parts are:

Labrum. The plate that serves as an upper lip in insects with chewing mouthparts. Helps to pull food into the mouth.

Mandible (see Figure 8-E). The first pair of feeding appendages, analogous to a jaw. Used to chew, cut, and tear food, to carry things, to fight, and to mold wax. Moves from side to side rather than up and down.

Maxillae. The second pair of feeding appendages, used for food handling and sensing. More complicated than the mandibles but work in the same manner. May have a pair of sensory palps (small segmented appendages).

Hypopharynx. A tongue-like structure that helps mix food and saliva.

Labium. Analogous to a lower lip. Its function is to close the mouth below or behind. May have a pair of sensory palps.

The mouthpart structure gives clues to food type and feeding behaviors of that insect (see Figure 8-F).

Chewing. Unlike humans, insects chew by laterally moving their mandibles. Similar to other animals' teeth, the size and shape of an insect's mandibles can hint about the type of food they chew (see Figure 8-E). Predatory insects have sharp mandibles while herbivorous insects have flat, dull mandibles.

Siphoning. Butterflies and moths have a sucking mouthpart that features a proboscis, used for sucking up nectar into the mouth or oral cavity. When feeding, the proboscis is uncoiled and extended.

Piercing-sucking, rasping-sucking. Found in a variety of insects such as herbivorous and

Figure 8-E. Mandible types

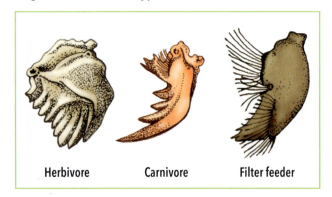

160   Maryland Master Gardener Handbook   UME © 2025. All rights reserved.

Figure 8-F. Modifications of insect mouthparts

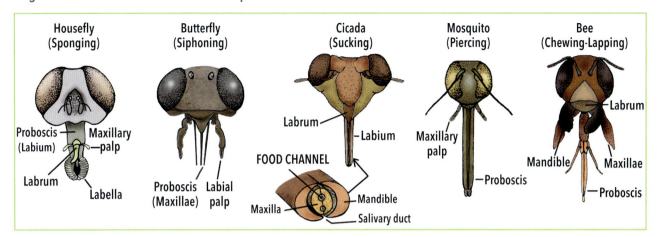

predaceous bugs and mosquitoes. Mandibles and maxillae are formed into stylets that are enclosed by the labium. Once the stylets penetrate, a secretion is injected to dissolve tissue, which acts as a toxin in predatory species or as an anticoagulant for mosquitoes.

Chewing-lapping. Found in adult honeybees and bumblebees. Mouthparts are modified to utilize liquid food, honey, and nectar. A central "tongue," i.e., proboscis, is used to draw liquid into the body. The mandibles are not used for feeding but function to cut floral tissue to gain access to nectar, for defense, and for manipulating wax.

Sponging. Found in adults of specialized flies. During feeding the proboscis (modified labium) is lowered and salivary secretions are pumped onto the food. The dissolved or suspended food then moves by capillary action into the pseudotracheae (sponge) and is ingested. There may be sharp teeth on the pseudotracheae to rasp flesh and draw up blood. The labella is the fleshy distal end of the labium that functions as a sponge-like organ to sop up liquids.

The mouthparts of insect larvae (immature insects with complete metamorphosis) tend to be chewing, regardless of the type the adult possesses. Nymphs (immature insects with gradual metamorphosis) tend to have the same type of mouthparts as the adults. Some adult insects have non-functional mouthparts. These species have short adult lives, living only long enough to mate and lay eggs.

Eyes of insects can vary across and within an insect order and during an insect life cycle. Many mature insects have two compound eyes that are made up of multiple separate lenses. In addition to the two compound eyes, some insects also have one, two, or three simple eyes called ocelli. These are typically found on the top of the insect's head and are used for light detection. Some insects, such as fleas and springtails, only have ocelli. Others will have ocelli during their larval stages and compound eyes in adulthood.

Antennae (see Figure 8-G) are located on the front of the head. They are extremely variable in size, shape, and number of segments. Many insect groups have unique antennae, which is useful in the identification process.

Antennae are used to sense odors or pheromones, which help insects find food, water, a mate, and egg-laying sites. In some insect groups, male insects have larger, flashier antennae to help attract a mate.

Figure 8-G. Insect antennae types

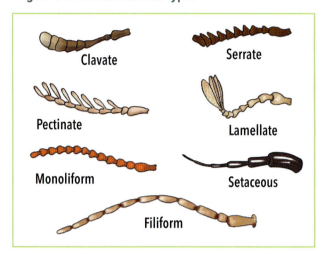

Thorax

The thorax is the second body region. It is divided into three segments: prothorax, mesothorax, and metathorax. The thorax is the region in charge of movement.

Each of the three segments has a pair of legs. If present, most adult insects have two pairs of wings, which are attached to the mesothorax and metathorax. The exceptions are true flies (order *Diptera*) and twisted wing insects (order *Strepsiptera*), which only have one pair of wings. Some insects have a pronotum, which is a prominent plate-like structure that covers all or part of the dorsal surface of the thorax.

Legs are located on the thorax, with each segment having one pair (see Figure 8-H). Most insects have legs but there are a few exceptions, such as maggots (immature flies) and female adult scale. The legs are used for walking, jumping, or running but may be modified for other activities such as grasping, digging, and swimming. The variation in leg shape and function can be useful in identification. Immature insects such as caterpillars may also have short abdominal legs called prolegs. These are not considered to be "true" legs because they are not segmented. Insect feet are called tarsi and are also segmented. They may have claws and pads to aid in gripping a surface or food.

Wings vary significantly in size, shape, and texture, depending on the insect (see Figure 8-I). Most adult insects have two pairs; others only have one pair, or none. Wings, if present, are located on the second and third thoracic segments. Most are membranous or transparent; some are leather; others are covered with hairs or scales. The fore wings and hind wings can be similar or different, but all have veins. Their pattern or arrangement is called venation and is different for each

Figure 8-H. Leg adaptations of selected insects

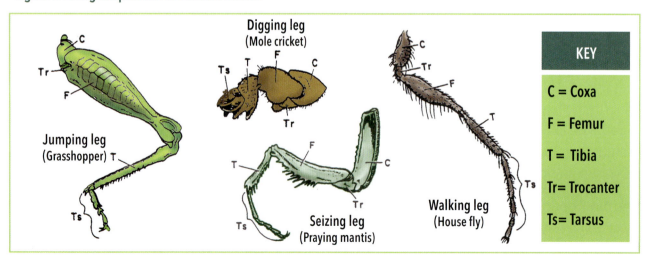

Figure 8-I. Insect wing types

species. Venation is a crucial characteristic in classification and identification.

Many insect order names end in "ptera," which comes from the Greek word meaning "with wings." For example, *Hemiptera* means half-winged, *Hymenoptera* means membrane-winged, *Diptera* means two-winged, and *Isoptera* means equal wings.

Abdomen

The abdomen is the third body region and contains the digestive system, the excretory system, and the reproductive system (in adult insects). The abdomen may have up to 12 segments.

Tiny openings known as spiracles are usually found along the thorax, but are also found on the abdomen in medium to large-sized insects. Spiracles are attached to a tracheal system, which aids the insect in gas exchange.

Some insects have a pair of appendages at the end of the abdomen which may be associated with either reproduction or defense. These appendages may be short (grasshoppers), long and delicate (mayflies), or curved and pincer-like (earwigs). Immature insects like caterpillars and sawfly larvae may have prolegs along their abdomen, which help with movement. Aquatic nymphs may have segmental gills along their abdomen.

8.3 Insect Metamorphosis

There are two types of insect metamorphosis: gradual (incomplete) and complete (see Figure 8-J). Both require the immature insect to undergo a series of molts. Each time an insect molts, it gets a little larger. Depending on its metamorphosis type, it may also change in other ways. Each molt represents the end of one growth stage (instar) and the beginning of another. The growth sequence is denoted as first instar, second instar, etc. In some insect species the number of instars is constant (typically from 3 to 15), but in others it may vary in response to temperature, food availability, or other environmental factors.

Gradual metamorphosis includes three life stages: egg, several nymphal instars, and adult. The nymphs resemble adults in appearance and differ mostly in size, coloration, and wing development. If the adult stage has wings, they will develop externally and can be seen as wing pads on fourth-fifth instar nymphs. Some examples of insects with incomplete metamorphosis include grasshoppers, aphids, stink bugs, and praying mantises.

Complete metamorphosis typically appears quite differently. There are four life stages: egg, several larval instars, pupa, and adult. Larvae and adults might have different habitats, food sources, and behaviors.

During pupation the insect does not feed or move much; the larval structures break down and adult structures are formed, resulting in changes in the insect's mouthparts, legs,

Figure 8-J. Gradual vs. complete metamorphosis

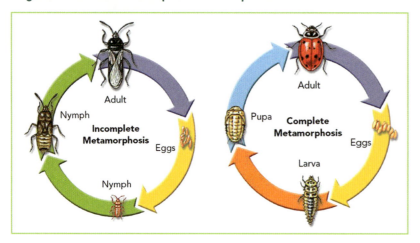

body shape, and wing formation. If the adult stage has wings, they develop internally. Some examples of insects with complete metamorphosis include beetles, bees, wasps, ants, butterflies, and flies.

8.4 Insect Classification

The information below describes insect orders commonly found in the garden and landscape. A summary of all insect orders can be found in **Table 8-C** at the end of this chapter.

Insects with gradual metamorphosis

Order Odonata: Dragonflies and damselflies

Adults: Large eyes, robust thorax, long and slender abdomen, small and bristle-like antennae. Two pairs of wings: elongate, with many veins. May or may not be patterned. Dragonflies hold wings horizontally at rest while damselflies fold them over the back.

Nymphs: Aquatic, with a modified scoop mouth for capturing prey.

Chewing mouthparts: Adults and nymphs are predatory, feeding on insects and other aquatic organisms.

Habitat: Commonly found near bodies of water.

Order Dermaptera: Earwigs

Adults: Elongate, flattened, brown color. Thread-like antennae. Two pairs of wings; front pair is short and leathery, hind pair is membranous and folds like a fan under front wings. Pair of forceps-like pincers at the rear.

Nymphs: Resemble adults but are smaller, with wings reduced in size or absent.

Chewing mouthparts: Feed on plant material. Scavengers and sometimes predators.

Figure 8-K. Dragonfly and damselfly

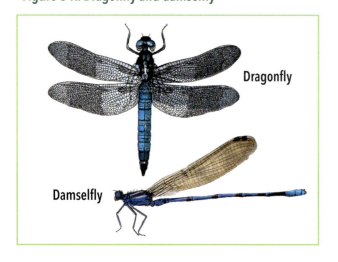

Figure 8-L. Earwig

Habitat: Nocturnal. Hide during the day in leaf litter, mulch, or under bark. May be good nocturnal predators of aphids.

Order Orthoptera: Grasshoppers, katydids, and crickets

Adults: Elongate. May be narrow or flattened; color is variable. Hind legs are modified for jumping. Wings: two pairs, front pair generally long, narrow, and leathery; hind pair is broad, many-veined, and usually folded under front wings when at rest. Some wings reduced in size.

Nymphs: Resemble adults but are smaller, with wings reduced in size or absent.

Chewing mouthparts: Plant feeders.

Habitat: Trees, shrubs, herbaceous vegetation, and indoors.

Figure 8-M. Grasshopper, katydid and cricket

Katydids, also known as bush crickets, are usually green and camouflaged to blend in with foliage. They can be distinguished from other orthopterans by their very long, thin antennae, which can be as long as or longer than the body. Females typically have a flattened sword-like ovipositor and their wings are held vertically over body (like the roof of a house).

Order Blattodea: Cockroaches and Termites

Cockroaches:

Adults: Usually dark brown/reddish in color with a flattened oval body, long antennae. Head is usually concealed by the pronotum. Can be winged or wingless; if winged, wings are held flat over the back.

Figure 8-N. Cockroach and termite

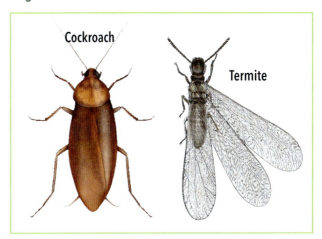

Nymphs: Resemble adults, with no or reduced-size wings.

Chewing mouthparts: Omnivorous scavengers.

Habitat: Only a handful of species are considered household pests. Most native species live in woodlands and are not pests.

Termites (*infraorder* Isoptera):

Adults (workers): Whitish, wingless, or wing buds, with short bead-like straight antennae, and a broad waist.

Adults (swarmers): Dark brown, with two pairs of nearly identical wings that are longer than the body.

Nymphs: Resemble workers, but are smaller and wingless.

Chewing mouthparts: Wood feeders (structural pests).

Habitat: Eusocial with a caste social structure. Colony forms in the soil. When infesting a structure, termites construct mud tubes to maintain soil contact for moisture and moving food to the colony. Eastern subterranean termites are most common in the mid-Atlantic.

Order Mantodea: Mantids

Adults: Triangular head, large compound eyes with three ocelli. Often has elongated prothorax. Large raptorial forelegs. Front wings are leathery; hind wings are membranous. When at rest, wings fold over the back.

Nymphs: Resemble adults, but smaller with wings reduced in size or absent.

Chewing mouthparts: Predatory.

Habitat: Worldwide in locations with ample vegetation and mild winters. Prefer gardens, forests, and densely vegetated areas.

Order Hemiptera (in general):

Adults: Winged adults lay eggs and feed actively on plants and other insects.

Figure 8-O. Praying mantis

Nymphs: In most cases resemble adults, but smaller with wings reduced in size or absent.

Piercing-sucking mouthparts: Beak-like mouth.

Habitat: May be either terrestrial or aquatic.

Figure 8-P. Brown marmorated stink bug

The brown marmorated stink bug is a common garden pest, overwintering in homes, buildings, and warehouses. It is distinguished from our native brown stink bugs by the white bands on its legs and antennae, rounded shoulders and alternating dark and light bands along the abdomen edges.

Suborder Heteroptera: True bugs

Large, widely-distributed group that includes water bugs, lace bugs, stink bugs, bed bugs, assassin bugs, and plant bugs.

Adults: Size can be ⅛-inch to more than two inches. Body is oval to long and narrow. Wings: two pairs (if present). Basal portion of front pair is thick and leathery; apical portion is membranous. Hind wings are membranous and shorter than front wings. When at rest, wings fold over the back, creating an X-shape. Long antennae and well-developed eyes.

Nymphs: Appear like miniature wingless adults.

Piercing-sucking mouthparts: Predatory, plant, or blood feeder. Plant-feeding damage looks like stippling on leaves and/or starburst on fruit.

Habitat: May be either aquatic or terrestrial.

Figure 8-Q. Cicada and leafhopper

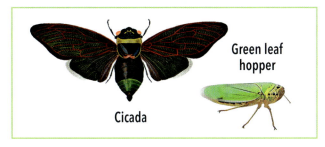

Suborder Auchenorrhyncha: Cicadas, leafhoppers and plant hoppers

Adults: Active flyers and jumpers. Antennae are short and bristle-like, with mouthparts arising from the back of the head. Adult tarsi have three subsegments. Some are pests and can transmit diseases.

Nymphs: Resemble adults but lack ocelli. May have fewer tarsal segments. Wing buds develop only in their later instars.

Piercing-sucking mouthparts: Feed on the xylem and phloem of plants. Some produce honeydew.

Habitat: Occur in all regions except Antarctica. Species-rich in the tropics.

Suborder Sternorrhyncha: Psyllids, whiteflies, aphids, adelgids, scale insects, and mealybugs

Adults: Small to tiny; many need a hand lens to see. Some are pests and can transmit diseases. Many are wingless. Some scale insects lack legs and antennae. Relatively sedentary habits. May be winged or wingless. Bear nymphs daily.

Nymphs: Slight differences from adult; have large front legs for tunneling.

Chewing mouthparts: Plant feeders; produce honeydew.

Habitat: Distributed worldwide. Can be a major farm crop pest as well as an ornamental pest in the home landscape.

Order Thysanoptera: Thrips

Adults: Tiny (>3/16-inch), slender-bodied. Color varies from yellow to black; may be winged or wingless. If winged, they have two long, narrow pairs, fringed with hairs. Short antennae.

Nymphs: Resemble adults, but smaller with no wings or reduced size.

Rasping-sucking mouthparts: Plant feeders, gall formers, plant-disease vectors, predators, and fungal feeders.

Habitat: About equally divided between plant litter, flowers, and green leaves. Appear throughout the world.

Figure 8-R. Aphid

Figure 8-S. Thrip

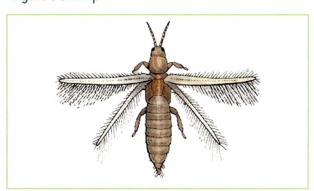

UME © 2025. All rights reserved.

Insects with complete metamorphosis

Order Neuroptera: Alderflies, dobsonflies, fishflies, snakeflies, lacewings, antlions, owlflies

Figure 8-T. Adult lacewing

Adults: Soft-bodied, ½-inch to two inches or more. Two pairs of membranous wings with many veins, held roof-like over body. Antennae long. Color varies from green to brown.

Larvae: Most are predaceous with sickle-like mouthparts; some are aquatic.

Chewing mouthparts: Predatory, non-feeding or feed on pollen and nectar.

Habitat: Common worldwide, with multiple families. Usually found in live vegetation.

Order Coleoptera: Beetles and weevils

Adults: Size varies from less than 1/32-inch to more than seven inches. Body is hard; round to elongate. Color is highly variable. Two pairs of wings: front pair is hardened or leathery and rigid (known as elytra); hind wings are membranous and fold under front wings. Antennae are clubbed, serrated, feathery, bead-like, or thread-like.

Larvae: Soft-bodied, with a head capsule, three pairs of legs on thorax, no legs on abdomen. (Weevil larvae lack legs on thorax.) Some larvae are C-shaped grubs; others are elongated. Very active.

Figure 8-U. Vine weevil and carrion beetle

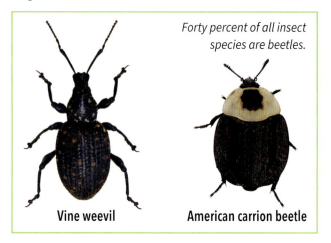

Forty percent of all insect species are beetles.

Vine weevil   American carrion beetle

Chewing Mouthparts: Plant feeders, predators, scavengers, and parasites.

Habitat: Extremely variable; this order occupies nearly all places insects are found.

Order Lepidoptera: Moths and butterflies

Adults: One quarter-inch to more than two inches, soft-bodied, elongate. Color is highly

Figure 8-V. Pipevine swallowtail butterfly

Figure 8-W. Promethea silkmoth

variable. Antennae are long and slender, sometimes plumose; always knobbed apically in butterflies. Two pairs of membranous wings, mostly or entirely covered with scales.

Larvae: Soft-bodied, of variable size. Three pairs of thoracic legs, five or fewer pairs of abdominal prolegs (short and fleshy with tiny apical hooks). Lack compound eyes, but have a group of small ocelli on each side of head. Many have hairs or spines, and color varies.

Pupae: Some wrap in silk cocoons. Butterfly pupae are called chrysalids, which may be sculptured and brightly colored. Moth pupae are smooth and brown.

Mouthparts: Adults use a proboscis mouth (when present) to feed on nectar and other liquid food. Larvae/caterpillars have chewing mouths and mainly feed on plant material.

Habitat: Larvae are pests and can be leaf miners, borers, and gall-makers.

Order Diptera: Flies

Adults: Less than ⅛-inch to more than one inch long. Color varies from black to iridescent blue. Usually small and soft-bodied. One pair of membranous wings. Hind wings are reduced to small knobs called halteres.

Larvae: Legless and wormlike (maggots). Head capsules may be well-developed in primitive flies but non-existent in advanced flies.

Piercing-sucking or sponging mouthparts: Adults feed on nectar sap; some are blood feeders, many are predaceous. Larvae may be predaceous, scavengers, or feed on plant tissue.

Habitat: Larvae occur in a wide variety of habitats, many in aquatic surroundings. Some feed within plant tissue as leaf miners,

Figure 8-X. Black onion fly

In all true flies the second pair of wings has been reduced to small knobs called halteres (see above), which help the insect balance during flight.

borers, or gall formers. Predaceous larvae live in water, soil, under bark or stones, or on vegetation. Many species feed on decaying plant or animal matter during the larval stage.

Order Hymenoptera: Sawflies, ants, wasps, and bees (in general)

Adults: Less than ⅛-inch to several inches. Color is variable. Two pairs of membranous wings (hind smaller than front). Ovipositor well-developed; some modified into stinger for offense and defense. Only females can sting.

Larvae: Grub-like, maggot-like, or caterpillar-like (sawflies).

Chewing mouthparts: Bees have a modified tongue-like structure. Adults feed on nectar, honey, pollen, and plant tissue. Many are predaceous. Larvae may be predaceous, or feed on plant tissue.

Habitat: Many are important pollinators. May be solitary or have social structure ranging from simple to complex. Aerial or ground nest.

Figure 8-Y. Insects from the order *Hymenoptera*

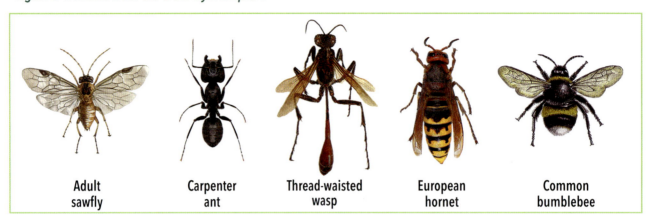

Adult sawfly | Carpenter ant | Thread-waisted wasp | European hornet | Common bumblebee

Specific notes on Order *Hymenoptera*:

Sawflies: Adults are wasp-like but do not have narrow waist. Some are brightly colored. All measure usually less than one inch. The larvae are caterpillar-like, with six or more pairs of prolegs and feed externally on plant foliage.

Ants: Appear worldwide. Size is variable. Ants can be carnivores, scavengers, and plant feeders. Reproductive forms have wings; workers do not. Complex social structure.

Wasps and hornets: These include parasitic *Hymenoptera*, some with very long ovipositors. Both hornets and yellowjackets are nest-builders (aerial and ground). Some are solitary nesters; most all are predatory.

Bees: Generally robust and active. Most are hairy. May be social or solitary. All are important pollinators.

8.5 Common Landscape Pests

The following groups of insects are commonly found in gardens and the home landscape. These groups can be made up of one or more families of insects (see Figure 8-Z).

Whiteflies (*Hemiptera: Sternorrhyncha*) are small insects (approximately 3/16-inch) that resemble tiny white moths. They are commonly found feeding on undersides of leaves and will take flight when the leaves are disturbed. Nymphs are wingless and active during their first instars but will be sessile (attached and not capable of moving) and resemble scales. Examples: greenhouse whitefly, silverleaf whitefly.

Aphids (*Hemiptera: Sternorrhyncha*) are small, soft-bodied insects with a pair of cornicles (tubular structures) at the rear of the abdomen. They can be winged or wingless.

Figure 8-Z. Common landscape pests

Whitefly | Aphid | Psyllid | Scale | Mealy bug | Leafhopper

Generally feed on young shoots or leaves of plants. They can reproduce by way of parthenogenesis (asexual reproduction) and may be a mixture of winged and wingless. Examples: green peach aphid, woolly apple aphid, giant bark aphid.

Psyllids (*Hemiptera: Sternorrhyncha*) resemble miniature cicadas and are sometimes called jumping plant lice. Their feeding can cause leaves to cup, or form galls. Each kind of psyllid feeds on only one plant species or closely related group of plants. Examples: boxwood psyllid, hackberry psyllid.

Scale insects (*Hemiptera: Sternorrhyncha*) are very diverse. They are ⅛- to ⅓-inch long. Some scales feed on only certain plant species, whereas others feed on a wide range of plants. They appear as raised bumps on twigs and branches and can be scraped off. The females are wingless and usually immobile. Males will have one pair of wings. Their immature stage is commonly called the 'crawler' stage because this is when the scale can walk about on plants to find new feeding sites.

Generally, they are divided into two categories: armored (hard) scales and soft scales.

Armored scales tend to be flat, circular, elongate, or oyster-shell-shaped and vary in color. They do not produce honeydew. Common examples: San Jose scale, euonymus scale, elongate hemlock scale.

Soft scales are convex in shape with a waxy or cottony appearance. They produce honeydew and are common pests of houseplants. Examples: Indian wax scale, tortoise scale, calico scale.

Mealybugs (*Hemiptera: Sternorrhyncha*) are smaller, oval, and are covered with tufts of dusty white wax. They can be found at rest or slowly crawling on the undersides of leaves or stems. Examples: long-tailed mealybug, taxus mealybug.

Leafhoppers (*Hemiptera: Auchenorrhyncha*) are about ⅛- to ¼-inch long, slender with angular heads, and hold the wings roof-like over the back. Most pest species are green with some color banding. Some species may transmit xylem-fastidious bacteria capable of causing scorch-like symptoms on plant leaves. Leafhoppers also produce honeydew.

Caterpillars (*Lepidoptera*) feed on the leaves of plants throughout the season. Generally, most species do not cause significant damage and will not require control except on young trees or if heavy defoliation occurs. See Figure 8-AA for examples of common pest caterpillars.

Figure 8-AA. Pest caterpillars (maximum length)

The larvae of several species of clearwing moths are boring pests in woody ornamental, fruit, and vegetable plants. Clearwing moths are delicate, day-flying moths that resemble wasps. Larvae are creamy-colored with brown heads. Female moths lay eggs in cracks, crevices, and rough or wounded areas on the host plant's bark or stem. The newly-hatched larva bore into the bark, stem, cambium, or heartwood of the host, where it will stay until it is ready to pupate. Some species pupate under the bark, and others drop down and pupate in the soil.

Signs and symptoms of borer damage include holes, frass (insect droppings), leaf-yellowing, and dieback. While some borers are attracted to a range of hosts, most attack only certain kinds of trees and shrubs.

Examples (see Figure 8-BB): Squash vine borer, lesser peach tree borer, dogwood borer, lilac/ash borer (depending upon which it attacks).

The Mid-Atlantic area does have a few species of "stinging" caterpillars. Unlike bees and wasps, these caterpillars don't have real stingers, but rather have venomous spines that run down their body. Stinging caterpillars are generally not encountered in large numbers and are not aggressive. They feed mainly on native trees and shrubs in wooded areas. If found, they should not be touched. They can be scooped up in a cup with cardboard and

Figure 8-CC. Stinging caterpillars

Puss caterpillar   Saddleback caterpillar   Io moth caterpillar

moved out of the garden. Examples (see Figure 8-CC): Puss caterpillar, saddleback caterpillar, Io moth caterpillar.

Sawfly larvae (*Hymenoptera*) are often regarded as pests, while the adult is considered neutral. Sawfly larvae resemble caterpillars (Lepidoptera) in appearance; however, they have six or more pairs of prolegs on their abdomens (see Figure 8-DD). They often engage in gregarious behavior by feeding in groups, which may cause part or the whole plant to become defoliated. Examples: rose

Figure 8-DD. Butterfly vs. sawfly larva

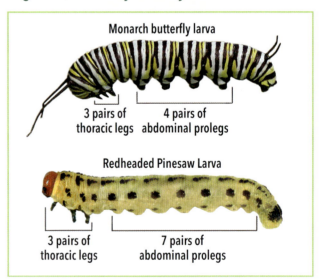

Caterpillars have five or fewer pairs of prolegs, which also have a circle of hooks on the bottom of each leg. Sawfly larvae have six or more pairs of prolegs.

Caterpillars can also have more than one set of ocelli (primitive eyes) whereas sawfly larvae have one set.

Use the number of fingers on your hand as a convenient identification tool.

Figure 8-BB. Common borers

*Depending upon which is being damaged

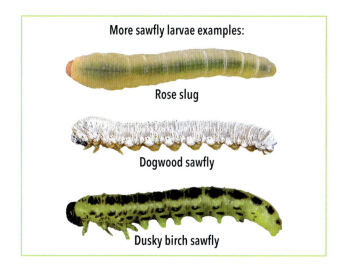

More sawfly larvae examples:
Rose slug
Dogwood sawfly
Dusky birch sawfly

slug, redheaded pine sawfly, dogwood sawfly, and dusky birch sawfly.

Scarab beetles (*Scarabaeidae*) is a large, diverse group of beetles. While many of the beetles found in this family are herbaceous and feed on landscape plants, making them a pest, others play beneficial roles such as being scavengers that recycle dung, carrion, or decaying plant material. Larger charismatic beetles such as rhinoceros beetles, Hercules beetles and Goliath beetles are also found within this family.

Scarab beetles (see Figure 8-EE) have stout-bodies that range in size from 1/16-inch to just over 6 inches depending on the species. They have lamellae (clubbed) antennae that can be compressed into a ball or fanned out.

Their larvae, commonly called grubs, are C-shaped and pale yellow or white (see Figure 8-EE). Grubs can often be identified by looking at their anal slit and the hair pattern found on the underside of the last segment of their abdomen. Grubs are considered pests due to their feeding on turfgrass roots. Examples of pest species: Japanese beetles, June beetle, rose chafer beetle.

Longhorn beetles (*Cerambycidae*) get their name because adults have extremely long antennae, often as long as or longer than the beetle's body. The larvae of most longhorned beetles are wood boring and called a roundheaded borer because they make a round hole in the wood (see Figure 8-FF).

The female will lay her eggs on the bark of a tree or stem of a plant, and when they hatch, the larvae will burrow into the plant. The larvae will feed on the tree's inner bark, then

Figure 8-EE. Scarab beetles and larvae (grubs)

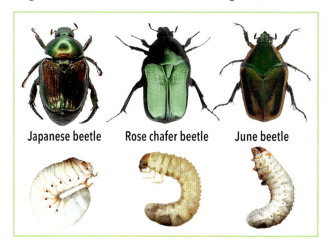

Japanese beetle | Rose chafer beetle | June beetle

Figure 8-FF. Asian longhorned beetle/damage

Banded hickory borer | Flower longhorn beetle

bore into the sapwood or heartwood before making a chamber for pupation.

The majority of roundheaded borers infest dead, dying, or highly stressed trees. There are a few species that infest healthy or slightly weakened trees. Examples: Asian longhorned beetle, banded hickory borer, flower longhorn beetle.

Jewel beetles or metallic wood-boring beetles (*Buprestidae*) get their name from the adult beetles' metallic coloration. Adults are elongate and oval in shape with short antennae, and can range in size from ¼- to 2½-inches long. Their hardened forewings nearly or entirely cover their abdomen.

The larvae are wood-boring and are called flatheaded borers due to their head shape. They create "D" shaped holes. Examples: emerald ash borer, flatheaded appletree borer, sculptured pine borer (see Figure 8-GG).

Similar to roundheaded borers, most flatheaded borers infest dead, dying, or highly stressed trees. The holes made by boring insects also allow for water, fungi, bacteria, and other small organisms to enter and further weaken and decompose the tree.

Invasive wood-boring insects often have high ecological and economic costs associated with them. Their new environment lacks natural enemies to control their population, and native trees may not have the defenses needed to combat them.

Leaf beetles (*Chrysomelidae*) feed on plant foliage either as adults, larvae, or both. This is a large group of beetles, with a lot of variation in size and color. The adult beetles are small to medium in size, with a dome-shaped abdomen.

Larvae are usually soft-bodied and vary in shape depending on their feeding habits. Some feed on the surface of the leaf, while other species are leaf miners. Adult feeding damage appears as small shot holes or skeletonization of the lower side of the leaf. Examples: locust leaf miner, elm leaf beetle, spotted cucumber beetle, and imported willow leaf beetle (see Figure 8-HH).

Figure 8-GG. Metallic wood borer and damage

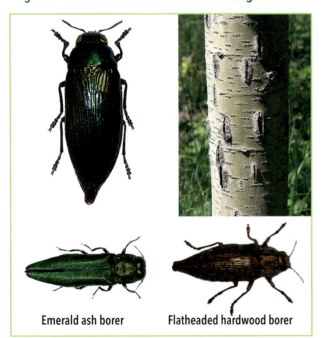

Figure 8-HH. Leaf beetles

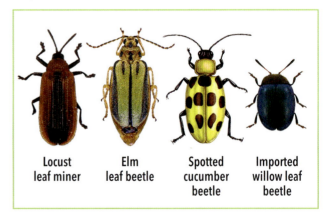

8.6 Common Household Pests

The following groups of insects are commonly found inside homes and buildings, and are considered pests.

Ladybird beetles, boxelder bugs, crickets, and brown marmorated stink bugs will enter buildings in the fall, searching for a location to overwinter. These insects can be swept up and tossed back outside or, in the case of invasive insects such as the brown marmorated stink bug, can be killed by placing them in a container of soapy water. To prevent them from entering, caulk up all holes, and make sure that window screens fit tightly. (See illustrations of **ladybird beetle** (page 170), **cricket** (page 157), and **brown marmorated stink bug** (page 158).

Figure 8-II. Boxelder bug

Silverfish and firebrats (*Zygentoma*): Adults are one inch long, elongate, wingless, and have three tail-like appendages at the end of their abdomen. The nymphs resemble adults but are smaller. They have chewing mouthparts and feed on starchy substances including glue, linens, silks, paper, vegetables, and starchy food. They are very active and run rapidly. Silverfish are grey and prefer cold, damp areas, while firebrats (see Figure 8-JJ) are tan and prefer warm environments.

Figure 8-JJ. Firebrat

Termites (*Isoptera*) are beneficial when they help reduce wood in the ecosystem by feeding on old roots, tree stumps, and fallen tree limbs, but become pests when they feed on the structural timbers in buildings. The Eastern subterranean termite is the most common pest species in the mid-Atlantic region.

Termites are social insects that live in underground colonies and have specialized castes to perform specific colony functions. Worker termites are whitish, wingless, or with short wing buds. They have short bead-like straight antennae and broad waist. Swarmer termites are dark brown and have two pairs of nearly identical wings that are longer than the body. Termite nymphs resemble workers but are smaller and wingless.

Figure 8-KK. Flying ant vs. termite swarmer

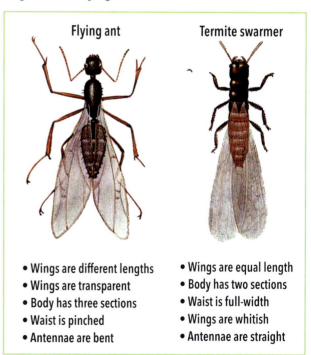

Flying ant
- Wings are different lengths
- Wings are transparent
- Body has three sections
- Waist is pinched
- Antennae are bent

Termite swarmer
- Wings are equal length
- Body has two sections
- Waist is full-width
- Wings are whitish
- Antennae are straight

Fleas (*Siphonaptera*): Adults are less than ⅛-inch long, reddish-brown in color, are

Figure 8-LL. Flea

laterally flattened, wingless, and feed on the blood of a host. They undergo complete metamorphosis. The larvae are tiny, whitish, and legless and live in carpet. Larvae feed on dried blood and move to dark areas, such as under furniture, to pupate. Flea bites tend to develop an itchy red bump.

Bedbugs (*Hemiptera*): Adult bed bugs are about 3/16-inch long and reddish-brown, with oval, flattened bodies. Nymphs look like smaller adults. The common bed bug (*Cimex lectularius*) prefers feeding on humans but will bite other warm-blooded animals, including dogs, cats, and rodents. Bed bugs are active mainly at night and tend to hide during the day in tiny crevices. They are efficient hitchhikers and are easily transported into dwellings on luggage, clothing, beds, furniture, and belongings. Bed-bug bite symptoms vary from person to person, but most develop an itchy red welt within a day or so of the bite. Bed bugs do not transmit any diseases.

Figure 8-MM. Bedbug

8.7 Beneficial Insects

The majority of insects are beneficial to humans, either directly or indirectly. Directly beneficial insects include pollinators and biological controllers of pest species.

Some nuisance species also play critical ecological roles. For example, many people consider paper wasps to be pests due to the potential risk of getting stung, but they are great biological control agents and pollinators in the garden.

Pollinators

Pollination is the movement of pollen grains from the male anther of a flower to the female stigma of a flower to reproduce and create seeds. While some plants are pollinated by wind and rain, most of our showier flowering plants rely on animals or pollinators to aid pollen movement (see Table 8-B).

Bees are the most well-known insect pollinators. Wasps, ants, flies, beetles, butterflies, and moths also pollinate many of our garden and landscape plants. Bats, rodents, and birds also serve as pollinators.

Figure 8-NN. Carpenter bee

Some pollinators visit many flowering plants, while others are specialists that concentrate on a single plant. Pollinators do not purposely transfer pollen but rather are often eating or collecting pollen or nectar as food for themselves or their colony when pollen grains attach themselves to the animal's body. Some plants attract pollinators by giving off pheromones or chemical odors that mimic other food sources or mating hormones.

Most flowering plants require pollination in order to reproduce, but studies have shown that even self-pollinating plants have an increased yield when pollinators are present.

Table 8-B. Examples of insect-flower pollination

Insect	Flower Characteristics	Flowers Pollinated
Bees: honeybee, sweat bee, bumblebee, carpenter bee, mason bee	Open during the day Nectar-producer Brightly colored with petals that are usually blue or yellow or a mixture of these (bees cannot see red) Sweet or minty fragrance Provide landing platforms Often bilaterally symmetrical (one side of the flower is a mirror image of the other) Flowers are often tubular with nectar at base of tube	Snapdragon Bee balm Cosmos Coneflowers Zinnias Asters Goldenrod
Moths and butterflies: hawk moth, swallowtail butterfly, skipper, geometer moth	Open during the late afternoon or night Nectar-producer Clusters of flowers with landing platforms	Morning glory Tobacco Yucca Gardenia Peacock flower
Beetles: blister beetle, soldier beetle, scarab, longhorned beetle	Bowl-shaped flowers White to dull white or green Smell fruity, spicy, sweet or fermented Open during the day Nectar producers May be large solitary flowers or clusters of small flowers	Magnolias Pond lilies Goldenrod Tulip trees Spicebush Yarrow Sunflower
Flies: bee fly, flower fly, tachinid fly	Pale and dull to dark brown, green or purple Putrid odor (like rotting meat) or smell like carrion, dung, humus, sap, or blood Nectar guides not present Flowers are funnel-like or complex traps	Jack-in-the-pulpit Paw paw Skunk cabbage Cacao trees

Biological controllers

Biological control agents are insects, spiders, other arthropods, and pathogens that help control pest populations. They do this by consuming the pest directly (predation) or by using the pest insect as a food source for their young (parasitism). More information about the use of beneficial insects for biological control in the garden and home landscape can be found in **Chapter 10** (IPM).

Parasitoids is the term given to insects—mainly wasps and flies—which have larvae that live inside a host and end up killing it. Parasitoids differ from insects such as fleas or lice that live on a host but don't kill it.

Figure 8-OO. Hornworm covered with wasp pupa

The braconid wasp is a very common parasitoid in the home landscape. Most gardeners will never see the adults or larva, but will often find hornworm caterpillars covered with wasp pupa. A female wasp lays eggs just under the skin of the hornworm; the eggs hatch and the larvae feed on the hornworm's insides. Mature larvae eat their way out of the caterpillar and spin a cocoon on its outer skin. Adult wasps emerge from the cocoons and the weakened hornworm dies.

Female parasitoids will lay their eggs either on or inside of a host insect (egg, immature, or adult). Once the larva hatches it feeds on the host. Some parasitoids pupate inside the host while others do so outside of the host. Most adult parasitoids feed on pollen and nectar.

Unlike predator insects, parasitoids are more host-specific. While parasitoid larvae can not be seen while in the host, you can find examples in your garden, such as mummy aphids with exit holes or hornworm caterpillars with white cocoons on them (see Figure 8-OO). Examples of common parasitoids include: tachinid flies, braconid wasps, and ichneumon wasps. **See Chapter 10** (IPM) for more information about parasitoids.

Ladybird beetles (*Coccinellidae*), also known as ladybugs, are generalist predators that feed on small insects such as aphids, spider mites, and scales. They overwinter as adults and emerge in the spring. After feeding, they mate. Females will lay a cluster of eggs near prey. Eggs are 1/16- to 1/8-inch in size, elongate oval, and yellow or white. Larvae are black to gray with yellow-to-orange markings. The body will be tapered from front to rear and may have tubercles with spines along the back. Adults vary in size and coloration, depending upon species. Smaller species tend to be black with red or yellow spots, while the larger species are red-pink-orange with black spots.

Green lacewings (family *Chrysopidae*) and brown lacewings (family *Hemerobiidae*) get their name from their heavily veined and membranous wings, which create a pattern similar to lace or a net. The adults are about ½-inch in length. Green lacewing eggs are laid as a single egg at the end of a thread to prevent predation and cannibalism. Brown lacewing eggs are not stalked.

Figure 8-RR. Lacewing larva

Lacewing larvae are ferocious predators of many soft-bodied insects including aphids, scale insects, mealybugs, caterpillars, and insect eggs.

Both the adults and the larvae are predatory, feeding on small insects like aphids. Adults also feed on honeydew, nectar, and pollen. The larvae are 1/8- to 3/8-inch long and are brown to gray, with long curved mandibles.

There are several species of **predatory stink bugs** (family *Pentatomidae*), but the most common ones found in the garden are the spined soldier bug (*Podisus maculiventris*) and the two-spotted stink bug (*Perillus bioculatus*). The adult spined soldier bugs are about ¼-inch in size, light brown, and flattened with a spine on both sides of the thorax.

Figure 8-QQ. Two-spotted stink bug

Figure 8-PP. Adult ladybird beetle and larva

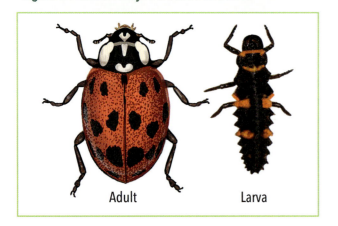

Adult   Larva

178   Maryland Master Gardener Handbook

Both the adult and nymphs are predaceous and have been known to attack prey larger than themselves. Adult two-spotted stink bugs come in both a red and tan coloration. They have two distinctive spots on the top of their thorax and keyhole-shaped marking on their back (see Figure 8-RR). The nymphs will have a red, orange, or tan circle shape on their abdomen with black spots around the edge.

Flower flies (family *Syrphidae*) are often confused with bees due to their brown abdomen with yellow-orange bands and habit of hovering around flowers. Adults range in size from ¼- to ½-inch, have large eyes, and only one pair of membranous wings, in contrast to bees, which have two pairs of wings (see Figure 8-SS). Larvae are ⅛- to ¼-inch long maggots that vary in color from green to brown. Mouthparts consist of two retractable hooks. The larvae are predaceous while adults feed on pollen.

Figure 8-SS. Flower fly

8.8 Common Non-insect Arthropods

Mites (subclass *Acari*) are tiny and soft-bodied arthropods, with one body region and no antennae. Mites are a large, diverse group that span several different orders. Most mites have six legs as larva and eight legs as nymphs and adults, but some, such as the eriophyid mites, only have four legs during their life cycle.

Mites feed on a variety of things. Some are herbaceous, while others are predatory, and others can be parasitic on other arthropods or animals. Herbaceous mite feeding causes a stippled appearance to leaf surfaces, making the leaves appear silver or bronze. Feeding may also create galls on leaves or witches' broom on stems and flower buds. Spider mites will cover host plants with fine strands of webbing in addition to feeding damage Figure 8-TT). Common mites: varroa mite, two-spotted spider mite, rust mites, spruce spider mites.

Figure 8-TT. Spider mite webbing

Ticks (*Ixodidae*) are obligate blood-feeders with one body region and no antennae. They have six legs as larvae, eight legs as nymphs and adults. All life stages of ticks feed on blood. They can feed on humans and other mammals, reptiles, birds, and amphibians. Ticks find a host by waiting for them on the tips of leaves or grass blades with their front pairs of legs held out. When a host brushes the leaf, the tick climbs on and searches for an area to feed. There are two types of tick: hard tick and soft ticks.

Hard ticks have a tough dorsal plate called a scutum, and their mouthparts are visible from above (see Figure 8-UU). They generally have three hosts and take at least a year to complete their life cycle.

Figure 8-UU. Deer tick

Soft ticks lack a scutum, are soft-bodied, and their mouthparts are not visible from above.

Ticks can transmit several diseases, such as Lyme disease, Rocky Mountain spotted fever, and tick paralysis, but most tick bites do not result in illness. To prevent bites, wear pants and long sleeves when in habitats such as woods, leaf litter, or grassy meadows.

Clothing and shoes can be treated with permethrin for extra protection (always read and follow the instructions when using chemical controls). DEET can be applied to open skin areas, but should not be applied under clothing or on pets. A lint roller is also a great way to remove ticks from clothing, as is washing in hot water and drying on high heat.

Spiders (order *Araneae*) have two distinct body regions (cephalothorax and abdomen), eight legs, and chelicerae with fangs (see Figure 8-VV). Their spinnerets, which extrude silk, are located on the underside of their abdomen. They vary in size and color. All are predators. Spiders are neither aggressive nor dangerous and rarely bite. They are important predators in our gardens because of the large number of insects they eat.

Figure 8-VV. Garden spider

Millipedes (class *Diplopoda*) are elongated, with 11 or more rounded body segments. There are two pairs of short legs on most body segments, and two short antennae located on the head (see Figure 8-WW). They are slow-moving and are found in damp locations such as under mulch, leaf litter, and dead plant debris, or in cracks and crevices. They feed on fungi and decaying organic matter, making them beneficial as "recyclers" in the environment and landscape.

Millipedes often invade crawl spaces, damp basements, and first floors of houses during the fall when searching for overwintering sites. Millipedes are not harmful and don't bite or sting. They do not attack people, property, possessions, or pets. When threatened, millipedes will curl into a ring and release an obnoxious smelling fluid. This fluid can be a minor irritant to the eye, so wash your hands thoroughly after touching a millipede.

Figure 8-WW. Centipede (top) and millipede

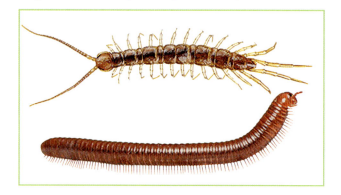

Centipedes (class *Chilopoda*) are elongated flattened arthropods with one pair of legs per body segment, and a pair of long slender antennae that extends forward from the head (see Figure 8-WW). They vary in length from one to several inches, depending on the species. Centipedes are fast-moving and tend to be active at night. Most are predators, feeding on numerous other arthropods. They can be found outside in damp areas such as under mulch, leaf litter, logs, and rocks.

The house centipede is commonly found in basements, storage areas, laundry rooms, garages, and bathrooms. They have a "hairier" appearance than centipedes found outdoors.

Although all centipedes have poison glands and the means to inject their venom, bites are rare and typically do not cause more than temporary, localized pain. Centipedes do not carry serious diseases and do not damage food or belongings in the home.

Table 8-C. Insect characteristics by order

Order	Common Name	Metamorphosis	Mouthparts
Protura	Proturans	Gradual	Chewing
Diplura	Two-pronged bristletails	Gradual	Chewing
Collembola	Springtails	Gradual	Chewing
Archaeognatha or Microcoryphia	Jumping bristletails	Gradual	Chewing
Zygentoma	Silverfish, firebrats	Gradual	Chewing
Ephemeroptera	Mayflies	Gradual; nymphs aquatic	Nymph: chewing Adult: vestigial
Odonata	Dragonflies, damselflies	Gradual; nymphs aquatic	Chewing
Blattodea	Cockroaches, termites	Gradual	Chewing
Mantodea	Mantids	Gradual	Chewing
Dermaptera	Earwigs	Gradual	Chewing
Plecoptera	Stoneflies	Gradual; nymphs aquatic	Chewing
Orthoptera	Grasshoppers, crickets, katydids	Gradual	Chewing
Phasmatoptera	Walking stick, leaf insects	Gradual	Chewing
Embioptera	Webspinners	Gradual	Chewing
Zoraptera	Angel Insects	Gradual	Chewing
Notoptera	Ice crawlers, heelwalkers	Gradual	Chewing
Psocoptera	Booklice, barklice	Gradual	Chewing
Mallophaga	Chewing lice	Gradual	Chewing
Anoplura	Sucking lice	Gradual	Sucking
Hemiptera	True Bugs	Gradual	Sucking
Thysanoptera	Thrips	Gradual	Rasping-sucking
Neuroptera	Dobsonflies, fishflies, alderflies, lacewings, antlions	Complete	Chewing
Siphonaptera	Fleas	Complete	Chewing
Strepsiptera	Twisted-winged parasites	Complete	Vestigial
Raphidioptera	Snakeflies	Complete	Chewing
Mecoptera	Scorpionflies	Complete	Chewing; beak-like
Trichoptera	Caddisflies	Complete; larvae aquatic	Chewing; reduced
Lepidoptera	Moths, butterflies	Complete	Larvae: chewing; Adult: sucking or vestigial
Diptera	Flies	Complete	Sucking
Coleoptera	Beetles	Complete	Chewing
Hymenoptera	Sawflies, ants, wasps, bees	Complete	Chewing, chewing- sucking

Table 8-C. Insect characteristics by order (continued)

Order	Wings	Usual size	Habitat
Protura	Wingless	Tiny	In soil or leaf litter
Diplura	Wingless	Tiny	In soil or leaf litter
Collembola	Wingless	Tiny	In soil or leaf litter
Archaeognatha or Microcoryphia	Wingless	Small	In soil or leaf litter
Zygentoma	Wingless	Small	In leaf litter, buildings
Ephemeroptera	2 pairs: Membranous	Medium	Near water
Odonata	2 pairs: Membranous	Large	Near water
Blattodea	Wingless or 2 pairs: Cockroaches: front leathery, hind membranous. Termites: both pairs membranous.	Small to medium	On ground, wood or buildings
Mantodea	Wingless or 2 pairs: Front leathery, hind membranous	Medium to large	On vegetation
Dermaptera	2 pairs: Front short, leathery; hind membranous, fan-like	Small to medium	In leaf litter, plants
Plecoptera	2 pairs: Membranous	Medium	Near water
Orthoptera	Wingless or 2 pairs: Front leathery, hind membranous	Large	On ground or vegetation
Phasmatoptera	Wingless or 2 pairs: Front leathery, hind membranous	Medium to large	On ground or vegetation
Embioptera	Wingless or 2 pairs: Membranous	Small	On ground, underground, under rocks or loose bark
Zoraptera	Wingless or 2 pairs: Membranous	Small	In rotting wood
Notoptera	Wingless	Small	On top of mountains and the edges of glaciers
Psocoptera	Wingless or 2 pairs: Membranous	Small	In leaf litter, buildings
Mallophaga	Wingless	Small	On birds or mammals
Anoplura	Wingless	Small	On mammals
Hemiptera	Wingless or 2 pairs: All membranous or front leathery	Tiny to medium	On leaf litter, vegetation, in water
Thysanoptera	Wingless or 2 pairs: Fringed wings	Tiny	In leaf litter or on vegetation
Neuroptera	2 pairs: Membranous	Medium to large	On vegetation
Siphonaptera	Wingless	Tiny	On birds or mammals
Strepsiptera	Females wingless, males 1 pair	Tiny	In other insects
Raphidioptera	2 pairs: Membranous	Medium	On vegetation
Mecoptera	Wingless or 2 pairs: Membranous	Medium	In leaf litter or on vegetation
Trichoptera	2 pairs: Membranous	Small to medium	Near water
Lepidoptera	2 pairs: Scale-covered	Minute to large	On vegetation
Diptera	1 pair: Front membranous, hind modified into halteres	Small to large	On vegetation, other habitats
Coleoptera	2 pairs: Front harden (Elytra), hind membranous	Small to large	All habitats
Hymenoptera	Wingless or 2 pairs: Membranous wings	Tiny to large	On ground or vegetation

AUTHOR

Emily Zobel, M.S., Senior Agent Associate, Master Gardener Program, University of Maryland Extension.

PUBLICATIONS

Borror, D. J. and R. E. White. 1998. *A Field Guide to Insects, America North of Mexico.* Peterson Field Guide Series. Houghton Mifflin Company. Boston, MA. ISBN-10: 0395911702.

Covell, Jr., C. V. 1984. *A Field Guide to Moths, Eastern North America*. Peterson Field Guide Series. Houghton Mifflin Company. Boston, MA. ISBN-10: 0395260566.

Chu, G. S. and L. K. Cutkomp. 1992. *How to Know the Immature Insects, 2nd Ed*. Wm. C. Brown Communications, Inc. Dubuque, IA. ISBN-10: 0697055965.

Cranshaw, W. 2017. *Garden Insects of North America*. 2nd Ed. Princeton University Press. Princeton, NJ. ISBN-10: 0691167443.

Dreistadt, S. H. and M. L. Flint. 2004. *Pests of Landscape Trees and Shrubs: An Integrated Pest Management Guide.* University of California, Division of Agriculture and Natural Resources, Publication 3359. University of California. Oakland, CA. ISBN-10: 1601078641.

Eaton, K. and E.R. Kaufman. 2007. *Kaufman Field Guide to Insects of North America.* Houghton Mifflin Company. Boston, MA. ISBN-10: 0618153101

Klots, A. B. 1979. *A Field Guide to The Butterflies of North America, East of the Great Plains.* Peterson Field Guide Series. Houghton Mifflin Company. Boston, MA. ISBN-10: 0395078652.

Rogers, Kara. "Katydid". *Encyclopedia Britannica*, 29 Mar. 2019, britannica.com/animal/long-horned-grasshopper.

Triplehorn, C. A. and N. F. Johnson. 2005. *Borror and DeLong's Introduction to the Study of Insects, 7th Ed.* Saunders College Publishing. Philadelphia, PA. ISBN-10: 0030968356.

Wagner, D. L. 2005. *Caterpillars of Eastern North America.* Princeton University Press. Princeton, NJ. ISBN 0691121435.

White, R. E. 1983. *A Field Guide to the Beetles of North America.* Peterson Field Guide Series. Houghton Mifflin Company. Boston, MA. ISBN-10: 0395910897.

Woodbury, E. N. 1994. *Butterflies of Delmarva*. Tidewater Publishers. Centreville, MD. ISBN-10: 0870334530.

Zim, H. S. and C. Cottam. 2001. *Insects. Golden Guide.* Saint Martin's Press. New York, NY. ISBN 1582381291.

PHOTOS

Main Chpater Photo: Stephanie Pully, University of Maryland Extension.

Figure 8-V: Photo by Greg Hume, adapted by Stephanie Pully.

Figure 8-FF: Asian longhorned beetle damage - Leslie J. Mehrhoff, University of Connecticut, Bugwood.org. Banded hickory beetle: Christina Butler via Flickr. Flower longhorn beetle: Katja Schulz via Flickr.

Figure 8-NN: Department of Entomology, University of Maryland

Figure 8-SS: National Park Service.

Figure 8-TT: Photograph by Eran Finkle, distributed under a CC-BY 2.0 license. https://flickr.com/photos/finklez/37545597702

ILLUSTRATIONS

LeAnn Zotta: Figures 8-A - 8Z (Except 8-V).

LeAnn Zotta: Figures 8-AA, 8-BB, 8-CC, 8-DD, 8-EE, 8-FF, 8-GG, 8-HH, 8-II, 8-JJ, 8-KK, 8-LL, 8-MM, 8-OO, 8-PP, 8-QQ, 8-RR, 8-TT, 8-UU, 8-VV.

9: PLANT DISEASE BASICS

David Clement, Ph.D.

9 PLANT DISEASE BASICS

CONTENTS

9.1 Impact of Plant Disease 187

9.2 Basic Plant Disease Concepts 189

9.3 Fungi and Plant Diseases 191

9.4 Classification of Plant Pathogenic Fungi 192

9.5 Plant Diseases Caused by Bacteria 200

9.6 Plant Diseases Caused by Phytoplasmas 202

9.7 Plant Diseases Caused by Nematodes 203

9.8 Plant Diseases Caused by Viruses 204

9.9 Parasitic Plants 206

9.10 Environmental Diseases 207

9.11 Principles of Plant Disease Control 208

9.12 Biological and Integrated Pest Management (IPM) Controls 210

LEARNING OBJECTIVES

- Types of pathogens that can cause plant diseases
- Conditions necessary for plant disease to occur
- Common symptoms and signs of plant disease
- How cultural and environmental conditions cause plant problems
- Strategies for managing disease problems

INTRODUCTION

Plant pathologists study plant diseases caused by fungi, bacteria, viruses, parasitic plants, and nematodes. Pathologists also examine how diseases spread, the disease cycle, and the best control options. The study of plant pathology also includes plant disorders caused by nutrient imbalances, air pollution, and unfavorable growing conditions.

Plant diseases have had profound effects on humankind through the centuries as evidenced by Biblical references to blasting and mildew of plants. The Greek philosopher Theophrastus (370-286 BCE) was the first to describe maladies of trees, cereals, and legumes that we today classify as leaf scorch, rot, scab, and cereal rust. The Romans were also aware of rust diseases of their grain crops. They celebrated the holiday of Robigalia, which included sacrifices of reddish-colored dogs and cattle in an attempt to appease the rust god Robigo.

With the invention of the microscope in the 17th century, fungi and bacteria associated with plants began to be investigated. In 1665, Robert Hooke published the first illustration of rust on a rose leaf.

Advances in the study of disease life-cycles were hampered by the widely held belief of "spontaneous generation," a theory that considered pathogenic microorganisms as products of disease rather than causal agents of disease.

The devastating epidemics of late blight of potato in Ireland in 1845 and 1846 dramatized the effect of plant diseases on humans. Tragically, these epidemics caused famine and death for more than a million people and resulted in a loss of nearly a third of Ireland's population between 1845 and 1860.

In 1861, German botanist Anton De Bary proved that a fungus, *Phytophthora infestans*, was the causal agent of late blight of potato. This was a milestone in the study of plant disease because it showed that a fungal pathogen was the *cause* of the disease.

Two years later, Louis Pasteur proposed his germ theory of disease which finally disproved the theory of spontaneous generation. This milestone essentially changed the way modern science investigated the diseases of all living organisms.

9.1 Impact of Plant Disease

A few examples of plant-disease epidemics that have resulted in devastating plant losses in the United States include:

Figure 9-A. Close-up of chestnut blight

- Chestnut blight, introduced in 1904, which has virtually eliminated American chestnut trees from North America
- Citrus canker, introduced in 1910 (and a closely-related bacterium called citrus bacterial spot, discovered in 1984) have destroyed millions of citrus trees
- White pine blister rust, introduced in 1912, has caused large economic losses in the timber industry
- Dutch elm disease, introduced in 1930, has decimated large numbers of elm trees from the East Coast to the Midwest
- Oak wilt, first reported in 1944, continues to destroy large numbers of oak trees from the East Coast to the Midwest
- Dogwood anthracnose, first reported in the northeast in 1978 (not as common now)
- Dogwood powdery mildew became widespread in 1994 and continues to cause extensive decline
- Sudden oak death, discovered in 2000 in dying California trees, periodically arrives on nursery shipments but is not currently established in Maryland landscapes
- *Ralstonia solanacearum race* 3 biovar 2, introduced in 2003 on greenhouse geraniums
- Asian soybean rust, introduced in 2004 by hurricanes
- Impatiens downy mildew, first reported in 2004
- Basil downy mildew, first reported in 2007
- Brown rot on Kwansan cherries, first reported in 2009
- Thousand cankers disease of black walnut, first reported in 2010
- Boxwood blight, first reported in 2011
- Beech leaf disease, first reported in 2012

As a direct result of severe disease losses from imported diseased plant material, Congress in 1912 passed plant quarantine laws to intercept diseased plant products before they could threaten our agriculture. The Agricultural Plant Health Inspection Service (APHIS) has quarantine inspectors stationed at points of entry into the U.S. such as airports and shipping ports, as well as certain interstate points to intercept plant products likely to introduce new plant pathogens.

In 2002 the National Plant Diagnostic Network (NPDN) was established. The network is a collective of Land Grant University plant disease and pest diagnosis facilities across the U.S.

Lead universities have been designated to represent regional needs. The National Agricultural Pest Information System

(NAPIS), located at Purdue University, has been designated as the central repository for archiving data collected from the various regions.

9.2 Basic Plant Disease Concepts

There are many ways to describe or define plant disease, but simply put, it is:

Profound physiological and morphological changes that cause a disruption of normal plant function over time.

Conversely, a healthy plant is one that can carry out its physiological functions to the best of its genetic ability.

Symptoms are the visible reactions of a plant to a disease and may suggest a cause. Disease symptoms might include:

- Wilting
- Necrosis
- Abnormal coloration
- Abnormal cellular growth
- Cankers
- Galls
- Defoliation
- Fruit drop
- Damping off
- Stunting

It is important to remember—and frustrating at times—to realize that different disease agents can cause similar symptoms on the same host, or even simultaneous mixed infections in the host plant. An equally important point is that plant damage caused by insect or mite feeding, or environmental conditions, can also cause "disease-like" symptoms on plants.

Figure 9-B. Examples of disease symptoms

Botryosphaeria dieback on rhododendron

Bacterial leaf scorch on oak

Signs are the visible parts of the pathogen or its products seen on the host that can be used to identify the pathogen. Examples of common disease signs include:

- A white coating of powdery mildew on leaves
- Mushroom growth on a tree limb
- Droplets of bacterial ooze on a fruit-tree twig
- Nematode cysts on plant roots
- Dark fungal fruiting bodies in leaf lesions

Plant disease causes

A pathogen is any organism that can incite a disease. Pathogens cause infectious diseases that can spread from an infected plant to a healthy plant.

Proof that an organism is a pathogen has to be verified through a set of procedures called Koch's Postulates. Robert Koch was a German microbiologist who set up a series

Figure 9-C. Examples of disease signs

Powdery mildew

Leaf spot

of postulates in 1876 to prove that anthrax disease of cattle was caused by a bacterium. Examples of pathogens that cause infectious diseases are:

- Bacteria
- Fungi
- Viruses
- Nematodes
- Parasitic plants

Plant diseases can also be caused by noninfectious or nonliving factors. Causes of disease by nonliving factors include:

- Unfavorable growing conditions
- Mineral deficiencies
- Air pollution

Figure 9-D. Examples of plant disease causes

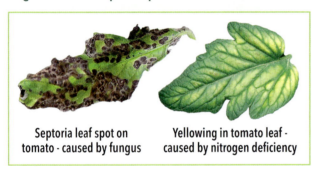

Septoria leaf spot on tomato - caused by fungus

Yellowing in tomato leaf - caused by nitrogen deficiency

Some pathogens are restricted to a single plant species, whereas others can infect an entire plant genus. Others can attack a large number of hosts, spanning many plant genera.

There are also several levels of parasitism that pathogens can have with their hosts:

- When a pathogen is capable of infecting a plant, the plant is considered susceptible to that pathogen
- If a pathogen cannot infect a plant, the plant is considered resistant to that pathogen
- Plants can vary in their response to pathogens, from complete resistance to partial resistance
- Pathogens can vary in their degree of virulence on a susceptible plant, ranging from highly virulent to weakly virulent

Inoculum and pathogen spread

Inoculum is any part of the pathogen that can cause infection. Examples of inoculum include:

- Fungal spores
- Fungal mycelium
- Bacterial cells
- Virus particles
- Nematode eggs

An inoculum that survives the winter and causes the original infection in the spring is called primary inoculum. A secondary inoculum causes additional infection throughout the growing season.

An inoculum is sometimes present at the site where a plant is grown, or it can be introduced from an outside source. Examples of inocula already present at a planting site would include pathogens that overwintered on perennial weeds. Examples of an introduced inoculum would include plant material such as infected seeds or inocula brought in by insect vectors.

Inocula can be disseminated passively by wind, rain, insects, and people. It can be disseminated actively when, for example, nematodes or water-mold zoospores swim through water in the soil toward plant roots.

Pathogen survival

In order to remain viable, pathogens must have a survival strategy when their host plants

An important concept to remember

Only a fraction of any pathogen's inoculum will ever land on a susceptible host. Most pathogens produce a tremendous surplus of inoculum.

are dormant or absent. In perennial plants, pathogens can survive in infected plant parts such as roots, bulbs, stems, and bud scales. Annual plants, however, die at the end of the growing season and pathogens must survive plant debris, the soil, insect vectors or seeds, or form resistant resting structures.

Host-pathogen interactions

The interactions of the three components of disease may be diagrammed as a disease triangle (see Figure 9-E). Plant disease occurs when a susceptible plant is infected by a pathogen under environmental conditions that favor disease. Each of these three components can affect the amount of disease that occurs. For example:

- A plant can have varying levels of pathogen resistance or may be at a nonsusceptible growth stage for infection
- The pathogen may vary in its virulence to the host, or may not be present
- Fluctuations above or below the optimum temperature and humidity level needed for infection can affect disease severity
- The weather can affect pathogen dispersal by wind or rain and can alter the migration of insect vectors

9.3 Fungi and Plant Diseases

See Chapter 9 for more information about pests and disease, and Chapter 12 for details about signs, symptoms and disease control.

Fungi

The study of fungi is called mycology. Fungi are organisms that are mostly microscopic although some produce large structures such as toadstools or mushrooms. Because fungi lack chlorophyll they cannot manufacture their own food and must draw sustenance from other living things.

Figure 9-E. Plant disease triangle

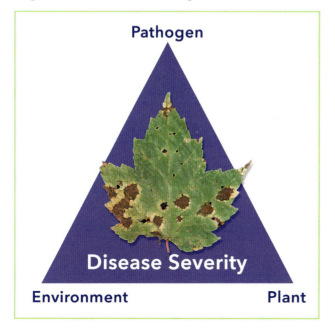

Figure 9-F. Mushroom mycelium

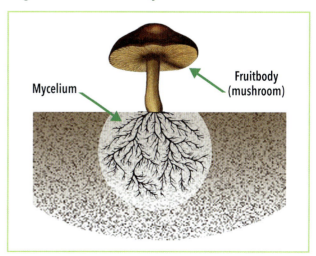

Current estimates are still being investigated, but with molecular biology techniques, approximately 11.7 to 13.2 million fungal species are estimated. Only around 150,000 have been described to date. Most are either beneficial or benign, and only about 19,000 cause plant diseases.

Fungi grow as microscopic filaments called hyphae, which branch in all directions. Many hyphae are collectively called mycelium. Specialized aggregates of mycelium with a hard rind, known as sclerotia, enable some fungi to survive unfavorable conditions.

Fungi reproduction

The main reproductive unit of fungi are spores, often formed in specialized structures on the mycelium. Fungi can be identified by their spore morphology and spore-bearing structures. Fungi can also reproduce by regenerating from pieces of mycelium.

Asexual spores involve no genetic changes and are simply a means of dispersal or survival. Asexual spores are called conidia, usually carried by wind. In some cases insects can serve as vectors.

Sexual spores are very different from asexual spores produced by the same fungus, and are often produced at just one point in the life cycle. They result from a recombination of genetic material and spur genetic variation that enables a fungal species to adapt to a variety of conditions. This recombination may also result in new fungal strains that can overcome a plant's disease defenses or develop resistance to chemical controls.

9.4 Classification of Plant Pathogenic Fungi

Fungi-like organisms

Asexual spores can be of several types. Water molds such as *Pythium*, *Phytophthora*, and the

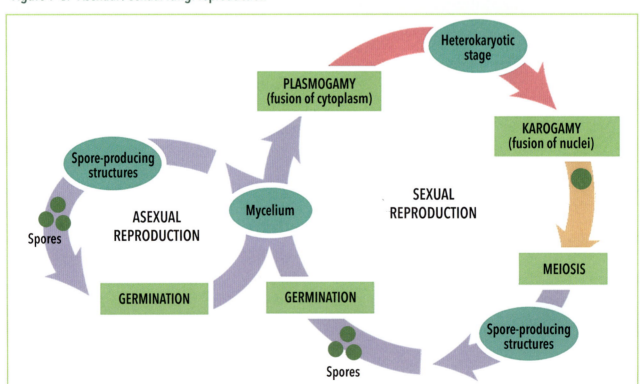

Figure 9-G. Asexual / sexual fungi reproduction

downy mildews produce two kinds of asexual spores called sporangia and zoospores. Sporangia may germinate directly or, depending upon moisture and temperature, produce motile zoospores that swim in water to find a suitable plant host.

Although technically not considered fungi by modern taxonomists, these organisms are called water molds because of their dependence upon wet conditions for reproduction and growth. Water molds reproduce asexually by zoospores contained within a structure called a zoosporangium. They form thick-walled sexual spores called oospores, which can survive adverse conditions.

The genera *Pythium* and *Phytophthora* are two important members of the water mold group. *Pythium* typically causes damping-off diseases of landscape bedding and indoor plants as well as seed decay, root rots, and blights on turf grass. Excess water is the usual cause.

Phytophthora is famous for late blight of potato, root diseases, and lately, sudden oak death. Dispersal is by transport of infected plants or soil and by water contaminated with zoospores. Some *Phytophthora* species can spread by aerial dispersal of sporangia.

The genus *Albugo* is called a white rust because of the white pustules formed on diseased plants. An example of a disease caused by *Albugo* is white rust of crucifers.

The downy mildews are obligate parasites and disperse their zoosporangia by wind. Examples of diseases in this group include:

- Cucurbit downy mildew caused by Pseudoperonospora
- Downy mildew on impatiens caused by Plasmopara
- Downy on basil caused by Peronospora

Zygomycetes: the Bread Molds

The fungal zygomycetes are called the bread molds after one of the principle organisms in the class, *Rhizopus*, which is frequently seen on moldy bread. These fungi don't produce motile zoospores but still encase their spores in a sporangium. The sexual spore is called a zygospore. These fungi produce mycelium without crosswalls, called septa.

Ascomycete: the Sac Fungi

The ascomycetes are referred to as the sac fungi because the sexual spores (ascospores) are enclosed in a sac called the ascus. The ascus can be exposed or naked or formed within a fruiting body called an ascocarp. Flask-shaped ascocarps are called perithecia.

Ascocarps that are open and saucer-shaped are called apothecia. Ascocarps can also be in mushroom form, such as a morel. This is a large assemblage of fungi with many widely differing morphologies and characteristics. These fungi produce well-developed septate mycelium and can be distinguished by their characteristic spore morphologies.

ONE FUNGUS = ONE NAME

This classification system has recently gained acceptance because of advancements in the grouping of fungi based on genetically-related groups, independent of reproductive and morphological characteristics.

Basidiomycetes

The basidiomycetes are called the club fungi because they produce their sexual spores, called basidiospores, within a microscopic club-shaped structure called a basidium. This group of fungi produces some of the largest fruiting structures in the fungal kingdom, appearing in the form of fleshy fruiting bodies called mushrooms, puffballs, and conks. These fleshy fungi can be associated in beneficial relationships with tree roots as mycorrhizal fungi.

Many of these fungi have complex life cycles. For example, many of the rust fungi must infect two unrelated plant genera to complete their reproductive cycle.

Many basidiomycetes cause root rots and wood decay diseases in trees. Both the rust and the smut fungi are obligate parasites and cause some of the most destructive crop diseases known, causing famines and large food losses throughout recorded history.

Common fungal diseases

Boxwood blight

Boxwood blight is caused by the fungus *Calonectria pseudonaviculata*. In 2011 professionals in the horticulture industry were informed of this disease but outbreaks were scattered. The rainy 2018 season greatly increased the spread of the disease and it is now more noticeable in Maryland landscapes.

On a few occasions, boxwood blight has been observed on Japanese spurge (*Pachysandra terminalis*) in Connecticut and on sweetbox (*Sarcococca* sp.) in Maryland and Virginia. Essentially, boxwood blight occurs up and down the east coast but is moving west.

Figure 9-H. Boxwood blight

Boxwood blight will infect all boxwoods grown in landscapes; however, some cultivars, especially English and American, are more susceptible than others.

Management strategies:

- Avoid planting new boxwood plants in your existing landscape
- Do not buy holiday boxwood wreaths
- Inspect new plants carefully; ask if plants have been grown in a certified "cleanliness program"
- Watch newly-planted boxwoods carefully for disease symptoms
- Choose more resistant cultivars if available
- If disease is identified, immediately remove and bag infected plants/fallen leaves; do not compost
- Launder all clothing, gloves, and shoes, and sanitize gardening tools

Removal of the plant will not guarantee eradication of the pathogen because it can survive in the soil for many years. Fungicide sprays have shown some disease suppression, but these treatments require repeated application throughout the season and do not eradicate the blight.

Consider replacement of boxwoods with non-susceptible plants such as hollies and conifers.

Southern blight on groundcovers

Southern blight is caused by the fungus *Sclerotium rolfsii*, which can attack any herbaceous perennial. It is active only during hot weather, so plants can grow well in infested soil during most of the growing season and only become damaged during the hottest part of the summer.

The first symptoms seen are wilting and collapse of individual stems or entire plants. Close inspection of the stem at the soil line reveals white mycelium (strands of fungus growing on the stem and mulch or soil surface) and small (⅛ to 1⁄16 inch), tan spherical sclerotia that resemble mustard seeds. They are white when first formed and gradually turn brown over several days. Roots of infected plants are unaffected. Cortical decay of the stem at the soil line is common during hot, humid weather.

Southern blight is commonly found on lysimachia, ajuga, and groundcover thymes. It is capable of blighting most herbaceous perennials, vegetables, annuals, herbs, and even turf and woody plants.

Management strategies

- Removed wilted and blighted plants and plant parts immediately; do not compost because the sclerotia of this fungus may survive the composting process

Figure 9-I. Southern blight on delphinium

- Reduce the number of sclerotia surviving in the upper few inches of soil during the season and clean all debris in the fall
- Deep plowing can provide good control by burying the sclerotia

Volutella blight on pachysandra

The symptoms of this fungal disease on pachysandra include brown or black spots on leaves that may enlarge and blight the entire leaf or stem. Infected plants may turn black and become soft. In wet weather pink spores will be visible on infected surfaces. Under drier conditions the brown spots may have a bull's-eye appearance or concentric rings.

Figure 9-J. Volutella blight on pachysandra

Management strategies

- Avoid overhead irrigation, which will promote faster leaf-drying
- Thin plantings by selectively pruning infected leaves with a lawn mower set at the highest setting, or a string trimmer
- Removal of fallen debris with a leaf blower and cleanup of old leaves helps to reduce the amount of trapped moisture and promotes faster drying of the planting bed

Rust diseases of junipers (cedar), apples, hawthorns, and quince

Cedar apple rust, quince rust, and hawthorn rust are caused by fungi in the genus *Gymnosporangium*. These rust fungi require two types of plants, a pomaceous plant and a cedar, with which to complete their life cycle.

Juniperus virginiana, the Eastern red cedar, is the most common rust-susceptible cedar in Maryland. In moist spring weather, gelatinous masses of reddish-orange fungal spores are produced on infected junipers. Peculiar round leaf galls, twig galls, cankers, and twig dieback occur on cedar hosts. Fungal spores produced on one type of host plant are carried by wind to infect the other.

Figure 9-K. Cedar apple rust on juniper and apple

These rusts damage many popular ornamental plants (e.g., apple and crabapple, serviceberry, hawthorn and ornamental pears). Colorful leaf spots and twig and fruit malformations (as well as twig cankers) are produced on pomaceous plants. Highly susceptible, heavily infected pomaceous plants may be defoliated by midsummer. Leaf spots are conspicuous; the loss of leaf area due to spotting and defoliation reduces tree vigor, decreases yields, and makes the plants more susceptible to winter injury and other diseases.

Most infected fruit drops in June, whereas the remainder may be misshapen, cracked, and subject to secondary fruit rots. Quince rust galls on twigs may result in branch dieback and distorted growth. On cedar hosts, galled leaves and twigs may die back, resulting in distorted growth. Perennial rust cankers may cause witches' brooms (abnormal, massed, brush-like development of many weak shoots arising at, or close to, the same point) and large swollen cankers.

Management strategies

- Select resistant pomaceous varieties.
- Do not plant susceptible apple varieties near susceptible junipers. A distance of one to two miles greatly reduces infection (impractical in areas where eastern red cedar is common).
- Hand-pick and destroy cedar galls by April 1, before spore-producing tendrils are formed.
- Cedar galls are easiest to see in wet weather when the orange spore tendrils are extruded.

Canker diseases

A large percentage of the cankers that cause dieback occur on shade trees. These are more

Figure 9-L. Botryosphaeria canker on rhododendron

common on stressed trees planted in marginal sites or on poorly maintained trees.

Young cankers are slightly darker than adjacent healthy bark and appear slightly sunken. As cankers enlarge they kill the living woody tissue within the branch or trunk.

Canker growth may cause the bark along the edges to crack and fall away, exposing the dead wood underneath. After a canker enlarges enough to girdle a branch or trunk, the portion beyond the canker dies.

Small twigs are killed more quickly than larger branches. Symptoms may include progressive upper branch dieback, disfigured branch growth, or target-shaped areas on trunks with concentric rings of dead bark. Examples of fungi that cause cankers in the landscape include *Nectria*, *Cytospora*, *Phomopsis*, *Monochaetia*, *Fusarium*, and *Botryosphaeria*.

Management strategies

- There are no chemical controls for cankers and they cannot be stopped once they become extensive
- The only control is to remove affected branches and prune to healthy wood
- To help prevent cankers, water and fertilize stressed trees during drought to promote better tree vigor

Root and wood-decaying fungi

Common fungal examples include the genera *Armillaria, Ganoderma, Laetiporus*, and *Inonotus,* which cause root and wood rots that result in dieback and decline symptoms on trees.

The outward signs of trunk and limb rots are basidiocarps that emerge from the tree trunk or branches. Basidiocarps are the fruiting body of the decay-causing fungi. They can be fleshy mushroom-like structures that appear annually, or hard, flat, shelf-like, triangular, or shell-shaped perennial structures that grow a new layer each year as the rot progresses. Colors range from white to brown or pale gray. *Laetiporus sulphureus* produces sulfur yellow to bright orange basidiocarps on ash, beech, cherry, maple, oak, and tulip poplar trees.

Basidiocarps of trunk and limb rots are found anywhere on the trunk or large branches. Basidiocarps located on the trunk near ground level may be the symptom of root rot or trunk rot. To determine whether it is a trunk or root rot, look for other symptoms. Because

Figure 9-M. Ganoderma fungi

the heartwood of a tree is not involved in translocation or storage of sap, there may be no other exterior symptoms of trunk rot. Root rots often cause dieback and other symptoms because they disrupt translocation of sap.

Wood rots cause wood to decay via a number of chemical and physical reactions. Infection usually occurs when the fungus gains entry through pruning wounds, frost cracks, fire scars, or broken branches. As the wood decays, cellulose predominates. The end result is brittle, stringy, or crumbly heartwood, which may fracture across the grain or into cubical chunks, depending upon the type of wood rot.

Management strategies

- Consult a certified arborist to determine the extent of the rot as soon as you see any basidiocarps
- There are no chemical cures for trunk and limb rots, but they can be prevented by proper maintenance practices such as pruning

Powdery mildews

Powdery mildew is the common name for the disease and symptoms caused by a closely related group of fungi. These fungi grow on the upper and lower leaf surfaces, young stems, and shoot tips of plants. As they grow, they produce microscopic chains of spores that give infected areas their characteristic white powdery appearance. These white spores are a sign of the powdery mildew fungus.

The fungi parasitize the tissues of the plant, causing a decline in its vigor. They also block light needed for photosynthesis. Infection is rarely lethal but does cause leaf yellowing and browning, leaf distortion, early fall

Figure 9-N. Powdery mildew on a squash plant

coloration, premature leaf drop, blemished or aborted flowers, and slower-than-normal growth.

The optimum conditions for powdery mildew development are warm days followed by cool, humid nights. Dry daytime weather allows spores to spread to other plants on air currents. On a cool evening they absorb enough moisture from the air to germinate and cause infection. The entire powdery mildew life-cycle can take place in less than a week under ideal conditions, and many overlapping infection cycles can occur within a single growing season.

Management strategies

- Select plants that are resistant to powdery mildew
- Place susceptible plants where there is adequate sunlight and good air circulation to reduce humidity levels, and properly space plants to avoid crowding
- Pruning/pinching back for better air circulation may also help

- If the disease is severe, use registered fungicides or horticultural oil products specifically formulated to combat powdery mildew

Ascomycetes of dogwood

Powdery mildew (*Microsphaera* and *Phyllactinia*) has become a more severe and widespread problem for dogwoods in recent years. It appears as a powdery white coating on the leaves from early summer through fall.

In some years the powdery appearance is less evident. Under severe conditions, the new leaves can exhibit leaf scorch, twisting, distortion, and smaller than normal growth.

Figure 9-O. Powdery mildew on lilac

Older infected leaves often develop purple blotches that progress to dead areas. Infections cause the loss of water and photosynthetic leaf area which weakens trees and reduces growth.

Management strategies

- Select powdery mildew-resistant cultivars of flowering dogwood such as 'Appalachian Joy', 'Jean's Appalachian Snow', 'Karen's Appalachian Blush', and 'Kay's Appalachian Mist'
- Place susceptible plants where there is adequate sunlight and good air circulation to reduce humidity, and properly space plants to avoid crowding
- Prune dogwoods in late fall/early winter (November-December) or after the trees are finished flowering in the spring
- For severe symptoms (especially on young trees) apply a fungicide labeled for powdery mildew on dogwood
- Spray at bud break in the spring, followed by additional sprays every two weeks as needed throughout the season

Miscellaneous mushrooms, mushrooms associated with decomposition, bird's nest fungi, and artillery fungi in the landscape

Commonly used organic mulches, such as wood chips and bark, decompose over time and the primary organisms responsible are bacteria, fungi, and protists. These organisms derive nutrition from the cellulose, lignin, and other organic compounds in the mulch. Some organisms, such as slime molds, feed on the bacteria and other organisms in the mulch.

Fungi associated with organic decomposition are not harmful to landscape plants, but their presence can draw questions from curious observers. Many mushroom species can be associated with decomposing mulch. One of the more interesting groups is called stinkhorns because of the foul odor they produce. Flies are typically attracted to them and assist in spore dispersal. One of the most common examples in mulched landscapes is the dog stinkhorn, *Mutinus caninus*.

Slime molds are now considered protists. The genera *Fuligo* and *Physarum* often start out as brightly colored, sticky masses on the surface of the mulch before they become dry

Figure 9-P. Bird's nest fungi on mulch

and crusty. They produce their dust-like black spores within these structures.

Bird's nest fungi in the genera *Cyathus* and *Crucibulum* produce structures that resemble small cup-like structures that are referred to as "bird's nests" because of the egg-like masses of spores found within. These spore masses are propelled by raindrops and contain a sticky material that can attach to leaves, fence posts, and other structures.

Artillery fungi in the genus *Sphaerobolus* are a smaller type of bird's nest fungus that orients towards light or bright surfaces. The cups are cream to orange-brown and contain a single spore mass. The spore masses are released under pressure and can be propelled up to 20 feet away. The sticky masses, which resemble tar specks,adhere to buildings, cars, and leaves and can be very difficult to remove. Although not necessary, management strategies include removal of the organisms and the use of alternatives to organic mulches.

9.5 Plant Diseases Caused by Bacteria

Bacteria are simple single-celled organisms that are microscopic. Out of the many millions of bacterial species yet to be discovered, only about 30,000 have been described. Of these, only about 150 species have been shown to be plant pathogenic.

Most of these bacteria are enveloped in a protective layer of viscous gummy material and most also have flagella that are distributed in various patterns over the cell wall.

Bacteria multiply and divide asexually by binary fission, which means reproduction by splitting into two equal halves. Bacteria can go through this process very rapidly, and under favorable conditions may divide every 20 minutes. At this doubling rate of reproduction one bacterium could produce one million bacteria in about 10 hours.

Bacteria invade plants through wounds or natural openings, such as lenticels or stomata. Wounds can occur from cultivation practices and from nematode or insect feeding. Bacteria can be spread from plant to plant by soil, water, infected seeds or plant parts, pruning tools, and insects. Most plant pathogenic bacteria develop in their host but have the ability to also remain active for a period of time on plant debris. In some cases they can survive in the soil.

Currently there are 12 major plant bacteria genera along with two phytoplasma genera. Within each genus there are numerous species and subspecies, or pathovars. Bacterial pathogens are often separated by differential growth media, flagellar arrangement, chemical composition of their cell walls, nutrition requirements, and serological techniques.

Common bacterial diseases

Bacterial leaf scorch

Bacterial leaf scorch is a relatively new disease of shade trees and affects a large number of plants including elm, oak, sycamore, maple, mulberry, and hickory. Symptoms typically appear in mid- to late summer on lower branches as irregular marginal browning on interior leaves. Symptoms progress along the branch towards the tip. Symptoms will occur every year and progress through the crown. Scorched areas may have a yellow halo around them depending on the tree species. Reduced growth and dieback are also common in severely infected plants. These symptoms are sometimes mistaken for drought, environmental stress, or other diseases.

Figure 9-Q Bacterial leaf scorch on maple and elm

Bacterial scorch symptoms differ from drought scorch symptoms, in that they appear first on the lower branches and on the older interior leaves. Drought scorch symptoms will be more uniform and will first appear near the upper branches and on the younger leaves near the tips of the branches.

Management strategies

- There are no treatments for bacterial leaf scorch, but tree life may be prolonged if symptomatic branches and dead wood are pruned out promptly.
- Antibiotic trunk injections have shown promise, but they only relieve symptoms and don't provide a permanent cure.

Fire blight

Fire blight is a serious bacterial disease of plants in the rose family. The most commonly damaged plants in the landscape are apple, cotoneaster, firethorn, hawthorn, mountain ash, quince, and pear. The full list of susceptible plants includes more than 130 plant species.

Other plants that can be infected include chokeberry, kerria, photinia, serviceberry, and spirea. The first symptoms usually appear on the blossoms as they quickly droop, shrivel, or turn brown. The disease progresses from the blossoms into the twigs and branches. The very tips of branches often droop or characteristically curl over to give a hooked appearance. The affected leaves turn dark brown to black and stay attached to the branch, giving the appearance of scorching.

Figure 9-R. Fire blight on apple tree

With few exceptions, the disease moves more slowly in woody tissue, often moving down to the base of a branch where it forms a lesion or canker. The color of the infected wood beneath the bark often is a reddish brown.

The most damaging cankers are those formed on the main stem or base of the plant because they often girdle and kill the plant. During wet weather, droplets of bacterial ooze form on the surface of cankers and can be spread to other plants by wind, rain, birds, humans, or insects.

The most common insects to spread the disease are pollinators, such as bees and flies. The bacteria overwinter at the margins of cankers and become active again in spring.

Management strategies

- Select resistant plant varieties
- Avoid overfertilizing, which creates excessive succulent growth that is more susceptible to infection
- Control insect populations with appropriate insecticides
- Copper fungicides can be applied in early spring to slow down infections
- Prune out infected branches eight to 12 inches below any visible symptoms
- Don't prune infected shoots back to a healthy branch; leave a four- to five-inch stub that can be pruned off during winter dormancy

9.6 Plant Diseases Caused by Phytoplasmas

Phytoplasmas can be described as bacteria without rigid cell walls. These organisms were first seen with an electron microscope in 1967. Phytoplasmas are spread by leafhopper, planthopper, and psyllid insect vectors, as well as by grafting and dodder.

Common phytoplasma diseases

Aster yellows

Aster yellows causes a general yellowing and stunting of the plant. Often there are other symptoms on older plants, such as formation of witches' brooms, abnormal production of adventitious roots (roots coming out of stem tissue), and malformed flowers with petals that wilt and die back and are often abnormally green in color, especially in *Echinacea* and *Rudbeckia* flowers.

Figure 9-S. Aster yellows

This disease is spread in the field by the aster leafhopper. Aster yellows survives in many weed hosts, and leafhoppers feeding on infected weeds can spread the disease to healthy crop plants. Perennials infected with aster yellows generally die within the first season of infection.

Management strategies

- Prevention is the best management practices for phytoplasmas such as aster yellows, as there is no cure
- Inspect new and established plants for abnormal coloration or stunted growth
- Submit plant samples for testing and destroy any infected plants immediately to prevent spread
- Weed control helps eliminate infection sources

9.7 Plant Diseases Caused by Nematodes

Plant parasitic nematodes are very tiny (.007-.15-inch) worms. There are also many other free-living or non-plant feeding nematode species found in every kind of habitat. All plant parasitic nematodes have a needle-like structure called a stylet. The stylet is located in the nematode head and is used to puncture plant cells so that the nematode can consume the cellular contents.

Nematodes can be classified as either:

Endoparasites, which burrow into tissues and feed internally on a plant

Ectoparasites, which feed from the surface on plant tissues

Both nematode types may also be further classified as either migratory or sedentary. Migratory forms are mobile throughout all stages in their life cycle except the egg stage. Sedentary forms enlarge and become immobile once they start to feed.

Soil nematodes cause damage to root tissues and interfere with the uptake of water and nutrients from the root to the shoot. In addition, nematodes sometimes inject toxic substances into the cells they feed on, which further disrupt cellular function.

Certain plant parasitic nematodes can serve as virus vectors. Others cause severe enough feeding wounds to allow other soil pathogens, such as fungi and bacteria, to gain entry into damaged plants.

Some nematodes have broad host ranges whereas others attack very specific plants. Many nematode species can also survive and complete their life cycles on weeds.

Nematodes have large food reserves that allow them to survive for as long as a year without a host and even overwinter in frozen soil.

Common nematode diseases

You should suspect one or more of the nematodes that reside in soil and feed on plant roots when plants fail to establish, are stunted, wilt in hot weather, then decline and die. Carefully dig the plant and wash the roots.

The most common root-infecting nematode in herbaceous perennials is the root knot nematode (caused by several species *of Meloidogyne*). Root knot nematodes enter the roots as tiny larvae, causing swellings (root knots) that can be easily seen. Infected plants show small to large swellings (knots) on the roots. The root system may be much reduced in size and have secondary decay.

Figure 9-T.   Root knot nematode on a tomato plant

Plants commonly damaged by root knot nematodes include: *Acanthus* (bear's breeches), Japanese anemone, *Astilbe*, *Campanula poscharskyana*, *Cimicifuga* species (snake root), *Geranium* species (cranesbill), *Ligularia*, *Lobelia*, *Lythrum*, *Salvia*, *Stachys* (lamb's ear), and *Veronica* (speedwell).

There are nearly 4,100 species of plant parasitic nematodes reported to date. About 25 other genera of nematodes can damage herbaceous perennials if present in large enough numbers, but do not produce symptoms that are diagnosed as nematode damage. Soil and tissue testing are the only accurate methods to determine that nematodes are the cause of plant injury.

Foliar nematodes produce off-color areas in the foliage that progress to leaf blight by mid-summer. The most common species found in herbaceous perennials is the strawberry leaf nematode, *Aphelenchoides fragariae*. Early in the season the nematodes feed on young shoots and leaves before entering the leaf, where they feed between the veins. The most common symptom is discoloration, bounded by leaf veins. Parallel-veined plants (e.g., hosta) develop long streaks of discolored tissue.

Management strategies

- Destroy any infected plants as soon as symptoms are confirmed
- One management option is to remove susceptible plants for several growing seasons
- Some "green manure" crops (cover crops) have good suppressive activity against root knot

9.8 Plant Diseases Caused by Viruses

Plant viruses differ from all other plant pathogens. They are not made up of cells and can only be seen with an electron microscope. Because viruses are not cellular, they do not have Latin names but are named with common names from the first host in which they were studied. Individual viruses are referred to as virus particles or virions.

Viruses are composed of a small piece of either DNA or RNA encapsulated inside a protein coat, or capsid. Although many viruses consist of one type of virion that contains all the genetic information needed for the virus to function, some viruses split their genome among several particles.

Viruses are unique in that they have none of the attributes of cellular pathogens. They can reproduce inside living cells, spread within infected plant tissues, and spread to other plants by vectors.

Viruses do not divide or produce any kind of reproductive structures, such as spores. Instead, viruses multiply by taking control of the plant cell, forcing it to manufacture more virus particles. Viruses cannot be cultured on artificial media because they need living cells to multiply. Serological tests and molecular biological techniques are currently the most common methods used to detect viruses.

Viruses in nature rely on vectors to spread from plant to plant. They can be spread by vegetative propagation, sap, seeds, pollen, insects, mites, nematodes, fungi, and parasitic plants. Viruses can be spread relatively long distances in insect vectors, such as aphids carried on the prevailing winds.

Most plant viruses cause systemic infections, and there is no cure for infected plants. Viruses do not kill cells by consuming them. Instead, they disrupt normal cellular processes and eventually cause abnormal cellular function.

In addition to typical viruses there are disease agents called viroids, discovered in 1971 by T. O. Diener. They are small, naked, circular pieces of single-stranded RNAs capable of infecting plants. Viroids seem to be the smallest nucleic acid molecules known to infect plants, with symptoms that resemble those of typical virus infections.

Common virus diseases

In Maryland, the most commonly encountered virus in perennials and vegetables is cucumber mosaic virus. Other confirmed viruses include alfalfa mosaic, arabis mosaic, tobacco etch, tomato spotted wilt, tobacco ringspot, tobacco mosaic, impatiens necrotic spot, rose rosette, and tomato ringspot. Many others are probably present but not yet confirmed.

Cucumber mosaic virus (CMV) infects many different plants and is a worldwide problem in perennials. CMV has many strains and typically causes stunting, distortion, and a mosaic pattern on leaves and flowers. CMV is primarily spread by aphids from plant to plant and infects many weeds that serve as reservoir hosts for infection of perennials. CMV can also be spread in infected sap by people handling infected and healthy plants simultaneously.

Tobacco mosaic virus (TMV) is very common and also worldwide. TMV has a wide host range and high potential for spread in production facilities. It infects more than 150 plant genera, including many ornamentals. The most common symptom of TMV is a mosaic pattern of dark green and light green areas on infected plant leaves. Infected sap, grafting, dodder, and seed spread TMV; insects do not.

The most common means of transmission is by people handling infected and healthy plants simultaneously.

Impatiens necrotic spot virus (INSV) was described as a distinct virus in the tospovirus group in 1991.

INSV is related to another tospovirus called tomato spotted wilt virus (TSWV). Both have a very wide host range that includes many popular ornamentals. Symptoms can include necrotic streaks, spots, rings, and lines on leaves and stems; distorted flowers, stems and leaves; general stunting, and bud drop. Black, brown, reddish, or yellowish concentric rings, though not always present, are also symptoms of infection.

Both viruses are transmitted by at least five species of thrips. The Western flower thrip is currently the most common species on ornamentals. Only immature larval thrips can acquire the virus from an infected plant and are then able to transmit the virus for the life of the thrips (12 to 44 days). Virus spread occurs by movement of infected thrips to healthy plants by crawling or jumping, or on air currents within greenhouses or fields. Infected stock plants used for propagation and weeds that remain between crop cycles are possible sources of the virus.

Figure 9-U. Common viral plant diseases

Cucumber mosaic virus (CMV)   Tobacco mosaic virus (TMV)   Impatiens necrotic spot virus (INSV)

Tobacco ringspot and **tomato ringspot** viruses are transmitted by nematodes in the genera *Longidorus*, *Paralongidorus*, and *Xiphinema*, and also by infected sap. The nematodes acquire the virus by feeding for a few hours on infected plants (frequently weed species growing next to the crop). They can then continue to transmit virus for several months.

In some cases, infected seed can be the culprit. Initially, virus-infected plants show severe symptoms of necrosis, mosaic, and ring spots on the foliage. On perennial hosts that survive to the following growing season, foliar symptoms become less obvious or may disappear entirely.

Management strategies

- There is no cure for infected plants; remove and discard them
- Eliminate weeds and plant debris that can act as reservoirs where aphids, larval thrips, and nematodes can acquire viruses
- If you use tobacco products, wash your hands with a phosphate detergent or soap before handling plants

Rose rosette disease (RRD) infects multiflora as well as ornamental roses. The initial symptoms are reddening of the stems and stunted growth. Sometimes there is a proliferation or clustering of stems with excessive soft pliable thorns. The flowers may also abort. Infected roses may die within two years.

The disease is transmitted by an eriophyid mite and by grafting. Mites can be carried by wind currents from infected roses to healthy plants downwind. Multiflora roses serve as the main source of infection in ornamental plantings.

Management strategies

- Early detection is critical to prevent further spread, as there are no pesticides for this disease
- Infected roses should be removed promptly because this disease is systemic and resides in the roots, which puts nearby roses at risk
- Remaining roses should be closely monitored for symptoms; multiflora roses should be removed from the vicinity as they are a disease carrier
- Ornamental plantings should be placed upwind of multiflora roses and spaced so their foliage will not touch

9.9 Parasitic Plants

Several seed plants are capable of parasitizing other plants. Examples of these include dodder, mistletoe, witchweed, beech drops, and broomrape. Dodder and mistletoe attach to aerial portions of a plant, while witchweed, beech drops, and broomrape attach to plant roots. In Maryland and Delaware, mistletoe and dodder are the only parasitic plants common in home gardens.

Mistletoe is evergreen and grows on shade trees such as oak and red maple. Dodder is a thread-like, parasitic, annual vine with scale-like leaves. Seeds germinate in the spring and early summer. The young seedlings develop a temporary root system until the dodder attaches to a host plant. Modified roots penetrate the host plant and attach to the plant's vascular system to extract nutrients.

Dodder grows rapidly, envelopes its host, and forms large mats. The flowers are small, white or pink, and found in many clusters. The fruit is a tiny capsule that usually contains four seeds.

Seeds persist in the soil for a long time. Plants are killed by the first frost.

There are many species of dodder throughout the country. It can be a problem in landscapes and nurseries. Host plants include clover (and other legumes), many herbaceous plants, chrysanthemums, azaleas, and cranberries.

Management strategies

- Hand-pull and dispose of dodder as soon as you notice it
- Pre-emergent herbicides can be used to control dodder before it germinates

Figure 9-V.   Dodder (cuscuta) on ground cover

9.10 Environmental Diseases

Diseases caused by environmental factors are not contagious, but they can cause substantial plant damage. In general, most environmental problems are caused by deficiencies or excesses of normal factors that support life.

Temperature effects

Plants may be damaged by very high or very low temperatures. Rapid temperature changes are most likely to cause injury. Damage by late frosts includes freeze injuries to fruit buds of peaches, cherries, apricots, and strawberries. Low temperatures in winter can cause bark splitting or frost cracks on the sunny side of many tree species in the landscape.

Tropical indoor plants are prone to low-temperature injury both in the home and while in transport. Cold-injury symptoms usually show up as blackening of the tissues about a week after the injury occurs.

High-temperature injury includes sunscald on indoor plants that are moved outdoors before the plant has had time to acclimatize itself to sunlight. Fleshy vegetables, such as tomatoes, peppers, and eggplant, will also show sunscald injury in the home vegetable garden.

Moisture effects

Excessive moisture and drought both damage plants. Poor drainage results in root decay because of reduced oxygen levels in the root zone and results in wilting and death of the leaves and shoots. Proper drainage is important to outdoor plants as well as indoor plants. More houseplants suffer from overwatering practices than for any other reason.

Another type of damage that sometimes occurs under excessive moisture conditions is swelling or oedema, which appears as numerous swollen bumps on the lower side of leaves.

Following the swelling, the area turns brown and becomes corky in texture. This damage is common on certain herbaceous plants such as geraniums. Drought injury causes wilting, scorch of the foliage, and stunting as well as loss of flowers and fruit.

Figure 9-W. Common diseases/disorders caused by environmental factors

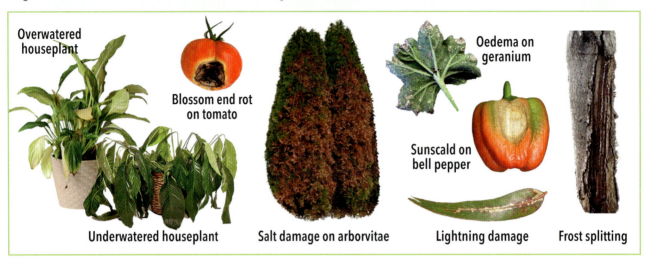

Nutritional effects

Plants require both macro- and micronutrients to maintain healthy growth. Lower than optimum levels of nutrients usually result in growth reduction. Chronic nutrient deficiency can result in severe decline or death in extreme situations. Some minerals and salts can interfere with normal metabolism and are toxic if present in high concentrations.

A common problem in home gardens is blossom-end rot of tomatoes and peppers caused by a localized calcium deficiency in the fruits brought on by water stress (too much or too little) or excessive amounts of nitrogen fertilizer, either of which reduces the uptake of calcium from the soil.

Air pollution

Plants are damaged by ozone, sulfur dioxide, hydrogen fluoride, nitrogen dioxide, and peroxyacetyl nitrate (PAN). Some of these pollutants, such as sulfur dioxide and hydrogen fluoride, are produced directly from industrial sources, while others, such as ozone and PAN, are produced as secondary by-products of photochemical reactions.

Hydrocarbons released from cars in heavily populated areas result in the production of both ozone and PAN. These gases enter plants through their stomata and cause characteristic bronzing symptoms on leaves.

9.11 Principles of Plant Disease Control

Gardeners constantly encounter a variety of plant diseases and naturally want to know which control measures are most effective. Unfortunately, by the time the disease symptoms appear it is often too late to reverse the damage. In some cases there are simply no acceptable control measures available short of plant removal.

Diagnosis of the disease can allow planning for a control method to prevent the disease next season. The various controls for diseases can be classified as:

- Exclusion strategies
- Inoculum reduction methods
- Chemical controls
- Biological controls
- Resistant plants

- Integrated pest management (IPM) strategies, which may incorporate any or all of these methods

Exclusion

Exclusion strategies try to preclude a pathogen from entering an area. On a national scale, this involves quarantine laws and plant inspectors stationed at points of entry into the country. On a homeowner scale, it means purchasing disease-free plants and carefully inspecting plants prior to planting.

Many fruit catalogs advertise disease-free plants or virus-indexed plants that are certified virus-free. Seeds and bulbs can be similarly certified. Whenever a plant is divided or propagated asexually, the parent plant should be certified disease-free.

Inoculum reduction

Inoculum reduction involves the elimination, removal, or reduction of plant pathogens. Many gardeners practice this by plant removal, pruning, removal of fallen fruit or leaves, and the use of soil amendments that favor microflora that is antagonistic to the pathogen.

Chemical controls

Some plant diseases can be controlled chemically with fungicides and bactericides. There are no nematicides registered for homeowners and there are no chemicals that will kill viruses.

Most fungicides are preemptive in nature, which means that they have to be applied before a pathogen infects a plant. A few of the newer fungicides can be applied after infection for disease control. It is often too late to spray once you notice any disease symptoms. If you diagnose the disease this season, you can plan for control next season.

Fungicides classified as "multi-site toxicants" are broad-spectrum surface protectants. These chemicals disrupt a wide variety of life processes in the fungal cell and resistance is seldom a problem in normal use.

"Single-site toxicants" have a narrower spectrum of activity and often have systemic and eradicant activity. They predominantly act on a single metabolic site inside the fungal cell. Development of resistant fungal populations can be a limiting factor in the use of these compounds.

A third category of fungicides is a collection of products that protect plants through mechanical means, host plant defense induction, or undefined modes of action.

Some diseases, such as anthracnose, are difficult to chemically control on large trees. Some plants may be difficult to grow without a spray schedule. The best long-term solution may be to replace high-maintenance plants with disease-resistant cultivars.

Resistant plants

The use of disease-resistant plants in the landscape is the best way of preventing problems and is a very effective Integrated Pest Management (IPM) technique for reducing plant damage. Often it is easier to replace problem-prone plants than to treat for problems after they repeatedly occur. When choosing landscape plants, consult nurseries, garden magazines, and websites for current information of disease-resistant cultivars.

9.12 Biological and Integrated Pest Management (IPM) Controls

Biological control of plant pathogens involves the use of antagonistic microorganisms either before or after infection occurs. Some of the work that has shown success is biocontrol of crown gall using beneficial antagonistic bacterial strains, which produce an antibiotic specific to the related crown gall bacterium.

Commercial biological control agents are available as seed treatments and soil amendments to protect plants against soil pathogens. Currently the bacterial species in *Bacillus, Pseudomonas* spp., and *Trichoderma* spp. are being applied to combat plant pathogens in commercial production systems.

IPM strategies integrate techniques such as pathogen exclusion, inoculum reduction, chemical control, and resistant cultivars. IPM procedures rely on minimal pesticide use and require a thorough understanding of a pathogen's life cycle in order to effectively target controls. **See Chapter 10** for more information about IPM and **Chapter 12** for diagnostic information about signs, symptoms and control of plant diseases. ❋

AUTHORS

David Clement, Ph.D., Plant Pathologist, University of Maryland Extension.

PUBLICATIONS

Agrios, G. N. 2005. *Plant Pathology, Fifth Edition*. Elsevier Academic Press. Burlington, MA. ISBN-10: 0120445654.

Pirone, P. 1978. *Diseases & Pests of Ornamental Plants,* 5th ed. Wiley Press. New York, NY. ISBN-10: 0471072494.

Gill, S., R. Cloyd, J. Baker, D. Clement, and E. Dutky. 2006. *Pests & Diseases of Herbaceous Perennials: The Biological Approach*. 2nd ed. Ball Publishing. Batavia, IL. ISBN-10: 1883052505.

Horst, R. K. 1990. W*estcott's Plant Disease Handbook*, 5th ed. Van Nostrand Reinhold. New York, NY. ISBN-0-442-31853-7.

Sinclair, W. and H. Lyon. 2005. D*iseases of Trees and Shrubs,* 2nd ed. Cornell Press. Ithaca, NY. ISBN-10: 0801443717.

Schumann, G. 1991. *Plant Diseases: Their Biology and Social Impact.* APS Press. St. Paul, MN. ISBN-10: 0890541167.

Tattar, T. 1989. *Diseases of Shade Trees*. Elsevier Academic Press. Burlington, MA. ISBN-10: 0126843511.

PHOTOS

Main Chaper Photo, Figure 9-R: JonTraunfeld, University of Maryland Extension.

Figures 9-A, 9-I, 9-K, 9-M, 9-N, 9-P, 9-S: University of Maryland Extension

Figure 9-H, 9-J, 9-L: Dave Clement, University of Maryland Extension.

Page 179: Spider mite webbing. Flickr attributed: Eran Finkle.

Figures 9-O, 9-T **Pixabay.com**.

ILLUSTRATIONS

Figures 9-B, 9-C, 9-D, 9-E, 9-F, 9-G 9-Q, 9-U. LeAnn Zotta.

10: INTEGRATED PEST MANAGEMENT (IPM)

Jon Traunfeld
David Clement, Ph.D.

10 INTEGRATED PEST MANAGEMENT (IPM)

CONTENTS

10.1 What is IPM? 213

10.2 IPM Steps 214

10.3 Healthy Plants = Fewer Problems 215

10.4 Taking Action 216

LEARNING OBJECTIVES

- The principles and practices of integrated pest management (IPM)
- Techniques for preventing insect and disease problems
- Understanding when to take action and which actions to take, if any
- Cultural, physical, chemical, and biological management strategies for managing pests, as well as beneficial insects

INTRODUCTION

Integrated pest management (IPM) represents a common-sense approach to pest control. It involves an understanding and careful examination of all factors (and their interrelationships) influencing plant growth. These include soil, water, air, nutrients, insects, diseases, landscape design, weeds, animals, beneficial organisms, weather, and cultural practices. The IPM goal is to manage problems at acceptable levels rather than attempting to eliminate them.

In many cases, you can prevent pest problems by selecting the appropriate plant species for your particular site and providing the best possible growing conditions. Regular observation of the plants in your landscape is critical in helping you to decide whether or not a problem requires corrective action.

You need knowledge, skill, and experience to use IPM principles and correctly diagnose plant problems. This chapter is a starting point for learning how to prevent and manage plant and pest problems. Too often, gardeners assume that plant problems are caused by pests and diseases that require chemical control. In fact, many plant problems are caused by cultural and environmental factors, and most of the insect pests and diseases found in home landscapes can be managed successfully without chemical pesticides.

IPM research and education is a principal mission of the United States Department of Agriculture and the University of Maryland's College of Agriculture and Natural Resources. Master Gardeners play a critical role in educating the public about IPM and helping residents and communities solve plant and pest problems.

10.1 What is IPM?

The term Integrated Pest Management was introduced in the late 1960s. Different aspects of IPM, such as the introduction of predators and parasites to reduce a pest population, had been known and used for some time. The full IPM concept developed, in part, as a reaction to the limitations and problems associated with chemical pesticides. These include accumulation in the food chain (e.g., DDT), pest resistance, secondary pest build-up, non-target injury pollinator losses, human health risks, and potential water, air, and soil pollution.

IPM is a knowledge-based, holistic approach to managing pests at an acceptable level. It emphasizes biological, cultural, and physical methods to prevent and manage problems. Least-toxic pesticides may also be warranted.

The impact of your gardening and pest management decisions often extends far beyond your property lines. The IPM approach compels you to consider your landscape as part of the larger community ecosystem to manage responsibly.

An important educational component of IPM is desensitizing people to insects and minor plant injury from diseases and pests. For example, hundreds of native insect species, especially caterpillars, feed on native plants. Plants and herbivores have co-evolved to create a durable ecosystem. Caterpillars don't typically defoliate or kill host plants because their populations are kept in check by disease and other critters. Accepting the presence and activities of these plant-feeders is a critical first step in reducing unnecessary pesticide use and creating healthier landscapes.

10.2 IPM Steps

- **Know your backyard environment.** One-half of all plant problems are not caused by living organisms (biotic), but by cultural and environmental factors (abiotic). Learn about the plants, insects, diseases, and wildlife in your backyard and community. This information can be found in books, Extension publications, websites, from your own experiences and those of your fellow gardeners.

- **Learn about your plants.** Before you can recognize or prevent problems, you need to become familiar with your plants' growth habits and necessary conditions for good growth. Learn which plants are native and which are exotic, which are prone to serious pest problems, and which are better adapted to conditions in your area.

- **Learn to tolerate some damage.** Most healthy herbaceous and woody plants can tolerate 20% to 30% defoliation without suffering long-term damage or yield reduction.

- **Keep a notebook**. Record observations, successes, and failures. Update your notebook regularly and refer to it often to avoid repeating mistakes.

- **Prevent plant problems.** The best management method is prevention. When you focus your time, attention, and efforts on growing the right plant in the right place in the right way, you can greatly reduce plant problems. See Healthy Plants = Fewer Problems for more details on keeping plants healthy.

- **Monitor plants regularly.** Check for pests and plant problems by closely observing visible plant parts. Use a magnifier or hand lens for a larger view. Be sure to flip leaves over and examine the undersides. Be prepared to get on your hands and knees to do a thorough job. Some pests, like slugs, are mainly active at night. Weekly inspections of your garden will catch most problems before they get out of hand.

- **Learn not to panic when observing symptoms.** Is the problem serious, is it getting worse, and is the plant in grave danger?

- **Diagnose accurately.** Where you observe pests or disease symptoms, identify the culprit and learn the life cycle, habits, characteristics, damage potential, and best time to take action. Correct identification of pest or plant problems is critical.

- **Take action if necessary.** Manage the problem using physical and cultural methods first. Apply a least-toxic pesticide as a last resort. For home gardeners, control measures often begin when pest injury reaches an "aesthetic threshold"—the point at which any additional damage to plant appearance cannot be tolerated. Many insect pests and diseases cause only minor injury and can be ignored.

- Evaluate the effectiveness of the actions and continue to monitor and learn. And don't forget to enjoy your garden!

10.3 Healthy Plants = Fewer Problems

Plant management

- Make a plan of your existing landscape and identify the location of your plants and trees.
- Note which look healthy and which seem to have problems.
- Know what your plants should look like. Are they growing normally?
- Be willing to remove plants with chronic problems (e.g., azaleas grown in full sun often have severe lacebug problems).
- Replace problem plants with those better adapted to your region and specific planting sites. Check gardening references and reputable local nurseries for ideas.

- Select disease- or insect-resistant varieties. Purchase healthy, certified, and disease-free transplants and nursery stock.
- Plant at the right time.
- When planting new plants—especially plants grown in containers—loosen and spread the root system to encourage growth out into the surrounding soil.

Soil quality

- Improve soils high in clay or sand by incorporating compost prior to planting shrubs and trees. This should be done over the entire area where roots will be growing, not just in the planting hole.
- Incorporate organic matter in annual and perennial beds on a regular basis.
- Take a soil test every three years and adjust the pH accordingly.
- Fertilize only as needed to maintain vigor. Trees and shrubs typically grow well with little or no fertilizer. Over-fertilized plants produce excessive succulent growth that is attractive to sucking insect pests. Aphids and spider mites will reproduce at a faster rate on over-fertilized plants.

Mulches and water

- Maintain even soil moisture.
- Avoid overhead watering and splashing soil onto plants, which can then spread soil-borne pathogens onto lower leaves. Water early so plants dry thoroughly by nightfall.
- Water trees and shrubs slowly and deeply. Newly planted trees and shrubs have small, limited root zones and need water near the base of the main trunk

or stem. Conversely, older, established root zones can extend horizontally two to three times the height of the tree beyond the dripline. Check the depth of soil moisture after irrigation by inserting a stick or screwdriver in the soil.

- Water newly planted trees and shrubs deeply (two inches of water) every one to two weeks (as needed) until they become established.
- Use drip irrigation and soaker hoses where practical.
- Prevent weed growth. Weeds rob plants of moisture and nutrients and are alternate hosts for pests and diseases.

Other cultural practices

- Prune to increase air circulation, which encourages more rapid drying of foliage.
- Prune out diseased plant parts to help save the whole plant.
- Avoid accidental root pruning caused by hoeing and tilling.
- Don't work with plants when foliage is wet; you could spread disease.

10.4 Taking Action

Even the most diligent and well-informed gardeners will face plant problems that require some action to prevent further injury. Pests, weather, soil conditions, or other factors may be the culprit. Use the tips below to make good decisions about when to take action:

- You have less time to make a control decision on seedlings, transplants, and newly planted trees and shrubs. Many pests and diseases do not need to be controlled on healthy, mature plants.
- Site and/or cultural conditions may need to be modified to correct environmental problems.
- Judgments are based on aesthetics, plant value, and actual threat to the plant's health: to structures (e.g., carpenter ants), or to personal safety (e.g., hazardous trees). Monitor pest or disease progression carefully.
- Set realistic thresholds for insects and diseases. It is very important to identify the pest or disease and become familiar with its life cycle. Ignore minor pests and focus instead on serious threats. For example, Eastern tent caterpillar feeding occurs early enough in the season for cherry trees to refoliate without causing harm to the tree.
- Sometimes by the time you observe the disease or insect damage, it is too late to do anything about the problem until next season.
- Treatment decisions depend on the type of plant. If a plant is easy to replace, such as an annual, just replace it. Plants that continue to grow throughout the season will often outgrow the pest or disease damage, such as locust leafminers on locust and leaf anthracnose disease on sycamore.
- Once you have identified the problem and determined that it requires corrective action, select a control strategy. Always choose the least toxic solutions first, such as such as hand-removal of pests, changing watering practices, pruning out damage, and encouraging beneficial insects.
- In some cases, it is appropriate to spot-treat with pesticides. When possible, select the least toxic materials (i. e.,

bio-rational pesticides) because they are less likely to harm beneficial organisms and they degrade quickly. Some examples are Bt (*Bacillus thuringiensis*), insecticidal soap, and horticultural oil. Horticultural oil can be used for both insect and disease management.

- In contrast, residual broad-spectrum pesticides usually affect many non-target organisms and persist for a long time in the environment.

Biological control

It is important not to view all creatures in your landscape as pests. Hundreds of different insects, spiders, and other beneficial microorganisms, such as soil fungi and bacteria, inhabit even the smallest yards. Together with your plants they comprise your unique backyard ecosystem. Some insects may be occasional feeders on favorite garden plants but will not become damaging pests.

For example, aphid-feeding in the spring alarms many gardeners. Natural enemies in the form of predators and parasites are often close behind, cleaning up local infestations in a few weeks.

- Predators attack and consume pests directly. They are usually larger and more active than the prey they eat. For example, insect predators tend to move rapidly and have large eyes and forward-pointing mouthparts.
- Parasites use pests as food sources for their young. For example, insect parasites lay their eggs in, on, or near the pest insect. The offspring then grow in or on the host, eventually killing it.

Predatory and parasitic insects are often collectively referred to as natural enemies, beneficial insects, or "beneficials." It is important to remember that many other beneficial organisms, such as birds, reptiles, earthworms, and nematodes, also exist in your yard.

Common insect predators

Ladybird beetles (Figure 10-A)

"Ladybugs" are predators of aphids, mealybugs, and other small insects. Adults vary in size from ⅛- to ⅜-inch long. The color ranges from all black to black with red to yellow spots, or red to orange with black spots, or grayish with black spots. There are more than 30 species in Maryland. Immatures are ⅛- to ⅜-inch long, alligator-like, and segmented, usually with short bristles on their body. The color is usually gray to black with yellow to orange markings. Eggs are usually yellow, oval, and laid upright in clusters on leaf undersides. It is not necessary to buy and release ladybird beetles; they will come on their own as long as you have a diverse landscape and residual insecticides are not sprayed.

Figure 10-A. Ladybird beetle (ladybug, lady beetle)

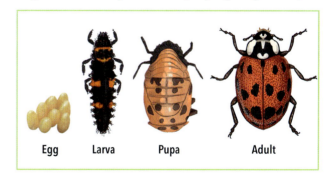

Egg   Larva   Pupa   Adult

Lacewings (Figure 10-B)

Predators of aphids and other small insects. Adults are ½- to ¾-inch long, green or brown, with small heads and large eyes. The transparent wings are longer than the body and have a fine network of veins. Larvae are spindle-shaped, yellow-brown, and mottled.

They have spines along their sides and long, curved mouthparts. Green lacewing eggs are laid on the ends of long, fine stalks, often attached to leaves or twigs. Lacewings are available commercially.

Figure 10-B.   Lacewing life cycle

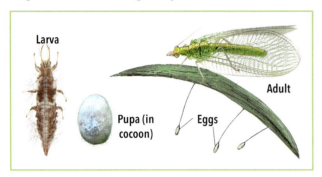

Syrphids or flower flies (Figure 10-C)

Aphid predators. Adults are ⅛- to ⅝-inch long. They resemble bees with yellow-black or white-black striped abdomens. Adults are often seen feeding on flower nectar. Larvae are grayish or greenish maggots and feed on aphids. Adult females lay eggs around aphid colonies and may be seen flying around aphid-infested plants. Not available commercially.

Figure 10-C.   Syrphid (hover fly, flower fly)

Praying mantids (Figure 10-D)

Large general predators. They will eat anything they happen upon, including each other. The adults are 2½ to four inches long, green or brown with long bodies, large eyes, and papery wings. Front legs are enlarged and adapted for grabbing prey. Immatures resemble adults but are smaller and wingless. Female mantid lays eggs in frothy masses glued to stems and twigs. They are straw-colored and resemble foam. Buying and releasing mantids is not recommended.

Figure 10-D.   Praying mantid

Ground beetle (Figure 10-E)

Large general predators. Adults are one inch or less in length, fast-moving, iridescent bluish-black in color. They hide under rocks and other objects during the day. Larvae are elongated and dark brown-black with large heads. They are not available commercially.

Figure 10-E.   Ground beetle

Predatory mites (Figure 10-F)

Widely used as biological-control organisms. They are the same size or larger than spider mites and move rapidly. The color may be white, tan, orange or reddish. Predatory mites are available commercially; the supplier can suggest the species and quantity to buy.

Figure 10-F. Predatory mite

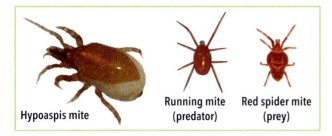

Figure 10-H. Parasitic wasp and aphid host

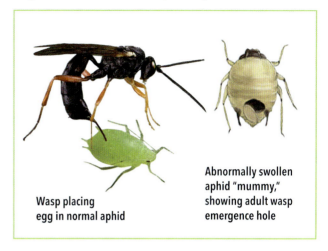

Other natural predators (Fig. 10-G)

Assassin bugs, predatory bugs, aphid midges, lightning bugs, dragon and damselflies, predatory wasps, and spiders also control pests in your landscape.

Common insect parasites

Parasitic wasps (Figure 10-H and 10-I)

This sizable group of small-to-large wasps parasitize a variety of caterpillars, beetle larvae, flies, aphids, and other insects. Adults are slender, aphid-sized black or yellowish-to-brown, with a pinched waist and clear wings. Some females may have very long ovipositors or "stingers," but they cannot sting people.

The female wasp uses her ovipositor to insert eggs into host insects. The larvae hatch, feed, and eventually kill the host. Some will pupate inside the host, while others will spin cocoons on or near a dead or dying host. They can parasitize a host insect at all life stages, but eggs and larvae stages are the most common.

Parasitic wasps are specialists and only prey on one species or genus of host insects. Common examples seen in the garden include parasitized aphids and hornworms. A parasitized aphid remains attached to the plant and eventually turns into a "mummy" that is swollen, brown, and papery in appearance. Close examination may reveal a small exit hole chewed in the mummy's back from which the adult wasp emerged.

Parasitized hornworms are often seen with many white, silken cocoons attached to their bodies.

Figure 10-G. Other natural predators

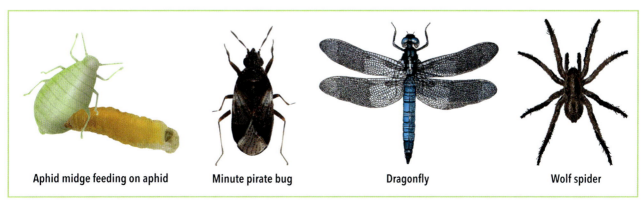

Figure 10-I. Life cycle of a parasitic wasp

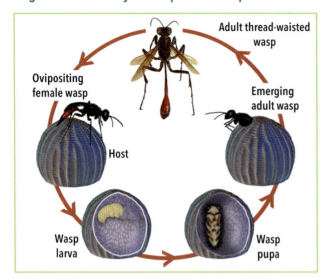

Figure 10-J. Parasitic nematode - borer host

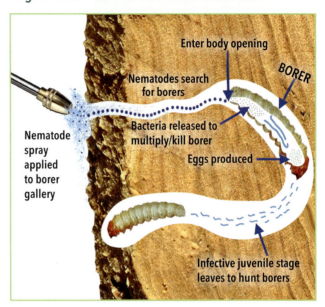

Several species of egg and larval parasitic wasps are available commercially but usually are not needed in the home garden because naturally-occurring parasites will find a host on their own.

Beneficial organisms

Parasitic nematodes (Figure 10-J)

Parasitic nematodes are tiny worms that are not harmful to humans, animals, nor plants. They occur naturally (mainly in soils) and can be purchased to control the larva of some pests, like grubs, borers, and cutworms.

Two types are available commercially: Steinernema (Sc) and Heterorhabditis (Hb). Sc nematodes work on insects that feed near the soil surface or inside plants, whereas Hb nematodes can move through the soil profile to attack certain beetle grubs. Follow package directions for appropriate storage and application techniques.

To conserve and protect beneficial organisms in your garden or landscape:

- Provide water, food, cover, nesting places, and diversity of flowering plants.

- Reduce or eliminate pesticide use or switch to careful timing of bio-rational nonresidual pesticides, such as insecticidal soaps, horticultural oils, and botanical pesticides that have short-term effects on beneficials populations (compared to synthetic pesticides).

- Maintain a diverse habitat for adult beneficials by growing a wide variety of annual and perennial flowers that bloom throughout the season (see Table 10-A).

- Provide water by misting or wetting down plants and mulch, which cools the area during hot weather.

- Leave shallow, open containers or basins of fresh water on the ground in shade for birds, toads, frogs, turtles, snakes, spiders, and insects.

- A diverse habitat of trees, shrubs, plants, and mulch can provide shelter, hiding places, and overwintering sites for beneficials (straw mulch is especially attractive to spiders).

Table 10-A. Plants with flowers that attract/feed beneficial insects

Umbelliferae family	Carrot, yarrow, Queen Anne's lace, dill, anise, fennel, coriander, parsley
Compositae family	Zinnia, marigold, aster, daisy, mum, black-eyed Susan, coneflower, coreopsis
Labiatae family and perennial herbs	Mountain mints, anise hyssop, thyme, sage, oregano, bee balm, basil
Brassicaceae	Arugula, broccoli raab, Asian greens
Other plants	Salvia, alyssum, wallflower, buckwheat, nasturtium, poppy, many wildflowers

Physical strategies

Removal of plant parts. Removing and disposing of badly damaged plants or plant parts may minimize the problem on adjacent plants and prevent recurrence. For example, removing the lower leaf stems can prevent the upward spread of early blight in tomato. Bean plants that are heavily infested with Mexican bean beetle can be cut off at ground level and sealed up in black plastic bags. This will disrupt the beetles' life cycle, thus reducing damage to the second or third crop of beans.

Barriers. Fences deter rabbits, groundhogs, deer, and other plant feeders. Floating row covers are excellent for excluding insect pests. Other tactics include paper collars for cutworms and diatomaceous earth for slugs. A product containing kaolin clay, mixed with water and sprayed on plants, creates a film barrier that can suppress some pest insect species.

Late fall or early spring tillage. Many pests and diseases overwinter in the crop debris of host plants or in the soil around host plants. Tilling can disrupt pest habitats.

Water stream. A strong hose spray may temporarily dislodge mites, aphids, and other pests. Be careful not to damage plants.

Hand-picking. Pick off adult and immature insects and egg masses. Pests can be squashed or dropped into a container of soapy water.

Cultural strategies

Properly space plants to encourage good air circulation. Correct spacing creates better airflow around leaves and stems, reducing the risk of foliar diseases.

Grow pest-resistant/tolerant plants. When selecting plants, check online sources and gardening catalogs for those with resistance or tolerance to pests/diseases. Many native plants are better adapted to Maryland conditions and are tolerant of pests and diseases.

Time your seeding and planting. Some pests can be circumvented by growing vulnerable plants when damage is least likely. For example, delaying planting of crops in the squash family can reduce injury from cucumber beetle, squash bug, and squash vine borer.

Plant in raised beds. This can help reduce root-rot problems and promote stronger root growth. It's especially helpful where soils are compacted and poorly drained.

Inter-plant your garden and landscape. Use borders of herbs, annuals, and perennials to attract beneficial insects and pollinators. Mixed plantings (polyculture) create a more diverse and stable ecological landscape.

Rotate crops. Refrain from planting the same plants in the same place every season. Rotate crops that are prone to pests and diseases.

Harvest promptly and regularly. Don't allow fruits and vegetables to become over-ripe; they become more vulnerable to insect and disease problems.

Practice good garden sanitation. Remove and dispose of diseased or infested plant parts and dead plants. Rake up and dispose of diseased leaves and fruits. Clean up and compost uninfected garden debris in the fall.

Chemical strategies

Synthetic pesticides, organic plant compounds, or natural organisms should be used as a last resort after physical, cultural, and biological controls have been attempted.

Broad-spectrum residual insecticides should never be relied upon as the primary management strategy. Residual pesticides remain effective in the environment for days, weeks, or months, impacting beneficial organisms as well as pests.

Except for some serious tree-fruit pests, pesticides should not be applied on a scheduled or preventive basis. Use bio-rational pesticides when possible; they produce smaller negative impacts on the ecosystem. These include copper and sulfur for controlling diseases, and insecticidal soap, horticultural oil, and botanical insecticides (such as neem) for controlling insect pests.

Note that organic pesticides like the pyrethrins can have negative ecological impacts because they also kill beneficials. Often, the best approach is to focus on prevention for next year.

When to act

One or more of the following factors could trigger the decision to apply a pesticide:

- There is an identifiable and serious pest causing the symptom(s)
- Damage is unacceptable (subjective)
- Beneficials aren't controlling the pest
- It's a recurring problem
- It's a specimen plant
- All else has failed
- The pesticide will likely be effective
- One or two applications can prevent an anticipated problem (e.g., crabgrass, black rot of grapes)

See **Chapter 11, Pesticide Use**, for more information about pesticides, and **Chapter 12, Plant Diagnostics** for more information about identifying and treating plant pest and disease problems. ❊

AUTHORS

Jon Traunfeld, Center Director, Extension Specialist and Center Director, Extension Gardening, University of Maryland Extension.

David Clement, Ph.D., Extension Specialist in Plant Pathology & Commercial Horticulture, University of Maryland Extension.

PUBLICATIONS

2024 Edition adapted from the Maryland Master Gardener Handbook, 1996.

ILLUSTRATIONS

Figure 10-A *Ladybird beetle life cycle*; Figure 10-B *Lacewing life cycle*; Figure 10-C *Syrphid life cycle*; Figure 10-F *Predatory mite*; Figure 10-G *Other natural predators*; Figure 10-H *Parasitic wasp and aphid host*; Figure 10-I *Life cycle of a parasitic wasp*; Figure 10-J *Parasitic nematode - borer host*. By LeAnn Zotta, Berkshire Communications.

Figures 10-D: zcy via Adobe Stock.

Figure 10-E: Grafvision via Adobe Stock.

PHOTOS

Main chapter photo: NY State IPM Program at Cornell University. Freely distributed via Flickr under a CC license.

11: PESTICIDE USE AND SAFETY

Courtney Coddington

11 PESTICIDE USE AND SAFETY

CONTENTS

11.1 Pesticide Basics 227

11.2 Pesticide Formulations 228

11.3 The Pesticide Label 228

11.4 Managing Pesticide Risk 233

11.5 Proper Application Practices 234

11.6 Organic Pesticides 236

11.7 Pesticides in the Environment 238

LEARNING OBJECTIVES

- The different types of pesticides and how they work
- The components of a pesticide label
- How to guide clients in responsible pesticide selection and usage, if/when appropriate

INTRODUCTION

A pest can be any plant disease, weed, or animal pest (e.g., insect, nematode, bird, or mammal) that causes damage or economic injury to desirable plants, pets, human health, structures, etc. A pesticide is a chemical substance that kills or controls pests. While the suffix "cide" means "to kill," chemicals used to attract, repel, and regulate growth and function are also classified as pesticides under U.S. government regulations.

Pesticides may be a necessary tool when pest populations reach a level that causes economic injury and non-chemical methods fail to provide adequate control.

While it is rarely possible or desirable to eradicate every individual pest across large areas of infestation, pesticides can be part of an integrated pest management (IPM) plan to control or manage pest populations and keep them below a damage threshold (a tolerance). To learn more about IPM, see Chapter 10.

11.1 Pesticide Basics

A pesticide can be categorized in three ways:

- By how it should be used
- By how it affects the pest
- By how it works

The term "pesticide" is the broadest level of categorization. Other terms like "insecticide," "fungicide," and "herbicide" are ways of further describing a pesticide and how it should be used. An herbicide is always a type of pesticide, but not all pesticides are herbicides.

There are many categories of pesticides that are named based upon the pests that they are intended to impact:

- Acaricides (miticides): mites and ticks
- Bactericides: bacteria
- Fungicides: fungi
- Herbicides: weeds and other undesirable plants
- Insecticides: insects and related arthropods
- Molluscicides: mollusks like slugs and snails
- Nematicides: nematodes
- Rodenticides : rodents

Pesticides are also commonly grouped by how they affect the target pest. Familiarity with these additional categories can be useful when searching for specific pesticides at a local garden center.

- **Repellents** keep pests away by means of an unattractive scent or taste, or ingredients that mimic the presence of a natural predator.

- **Attractants** lure pests with pheromones or hormones.
- **Antitranspirants** or **antidesiccants** reduce water loss from plants and protect them from winter damage, drought, wind burn, and transplant shock.
- **Contact poisons** kill pests simply by touching them.
- **Stomach poisons** kill pests when ingested.
- **Systemics** circulate through the animal/plant's natural blood/sap flow, distributing the toxicant from the point of application throughout the entire host animal or plant.
- **Fumigants** are gases that kill when inhaled or otherwise absorbed by pests.
- **Selective pesticides** work against certain kinds of plants or animals. For example, 2,4-D (used for lawn weed control) kills broadleaf plants but leaves the grass unharmed.
- **Nonselective** or **broad-spectrum pesticides** kill most plants or animals in a class. For instance, nonselective insecticides kill both insect pests and beneficial insects; nonselective herbicides kill both grasses and broadleaf plants.

Lastly, pesticides can be grouped by function or "mode of action" (MOA)—how they specifically work to impact target pests.

For example, some insecticides act by exciting nerve and muscle targets within an insect. These are generally fast-acting and among the most common MOAs for current insecticides.

Another type are insect growth regulators (IGRs) that mimic growth hormones and disrupt the normal growth, development, and reproductive cycle of an insect. IGRs target population dynamics and typically take longer to show noticeable effects.

Insect pest populations exposed to a single insecticide will, over time, naturally develop resistance to that insecticide. Farmers and growers can slow resistance development by alternating pesticides with different MOAs.

11.2 Pesticide Formulations

Formulation describes the physical state of a pesticide and determines how it will be used. Pesticides are rarely applied full strength.

The chemical in the pesticide formulation that actually kills or controls the pest(s) is termed the "active ingredient." Any other chemical(s), those which have no pesticide activity, or which are used to formulate or apply, are called "inert ingredients." Note that under this definition, "inert ingredient" can have effects of its own; it simply does not contribute directly to control of the pest. In fact, inert ingredients may have the potential to cause adverse effects (on humans, other animals, or plants, as well as the pest). See Table 11-A for a list of common pesticide formulations.

11.3 The Pesticide Label

All of the printed information about a pesticide product—including the label, brochures, and flyers from the company or its agents—is called labeling. The label that is printed on or attached to a container of pesticide will describe how to correctly use the product and which special safety measures need to be taken.

The pesticide label is the sum of knowledge about the active and inactive ingredients. Its contents are obtained by the registrant and regulators by testing for efficacy, environmental fate, and toxicological effects. It is a legal document; each product must be used only in accordance with the directions on its label.

In some cases a product may have an abbreviated label, where the full or extended label can be accessed via the website of either the manufacturer or the regulating government agency.

See Figure 11-A for a sample organic label diagram. Specific parts of a pesticide label include:

A **Brand name.** Each company uses brand names to identify its products, which are always prominently displayed on the package front. It is not uncommon for a company to use the same brand name (or one with very small differences) for products containing different active ingredients.

Type of formulation. The same pesticide may be available in more than one formulation.

B **Ingredient statement.** The label must list the names and amounts of the active ingredients and inert ingredients in the product.

Common name and chemical name. Active ingredients have complex chemical names derived from their composition. Some have

Table 11-A. Common pesticide formulations

Emulsifiable concentrates (EC or E)	The active ingredient is mixed with an oil base (often listed as "petroleum derivatives") to form an emulsion that is easily diluted with water. Do not freeze ECs, which can break down the emulsifier. Easily absorbed through the skin.
Solutions (S)	Referred to as RTUs (ready-to-use) because they are pre-mixed with water in a spray bottle. More expensive, but eliminate the need for mixing, thereby reducing exposure and health risks.
Flowables or liquids (F or L)	Mixed with water to form a suspension in a spray tank.
Aerosols (A)	Very low concentrate solutions, usually a fine spray sold in (expensive) aerosol cans.
Dusts (D)	Active ingredients are added to a fine, dry inert powder or talc. Dusts are subject to drifting and are easily inhaled.
Wettable powders (WP or W)	Combine the active ingredient with a fine powder. They are intended to be mixed with water. Continuous agitation is required to maintain a suspension, making it difficult for home gardeners to use. Easy to inhale during mixing.
Granules (G)	Active ingredients are added to coarse particles (granules) of inert material such as fired clay.
Soluble powders (SP)	The active ingredient is in a powder form that fully dissolves in water.
Baits (B)	Active ingredients are added to an edible or attractive substance. Used to control slugs, snails, or small ground insects and rodents.
Adjuvants	Chemicals are added to a formulation or mixture to improve its performance and safety. Often include a surfactant.
Surfactants (surface-active agents)	Reduce the surface tension between two dissimilar materials, such as a spray film and a solid surface. Surfactants act as spreading, sticking, and wetting agents.

also been given a shorter common name to make them easier to identify. Different brands may actually contain the same active ingredients, which can be determined by carefully comparing the common or chemical names on the label.

C Registration number. This number must appear on every conventional pesticide label. It shows that the product has been approved by the U.S. Environmental Protection Agency (EPA) for the uses listed on the label.

D Establishment number. The establishment number tells which factory made the chemical.

E Net contents. The net contents tells how much is in the container. This can be expressed in gallons, pints, pounds, quarts, or other units of measure.

F Name and address of manufacturer. The law requires the maker or distributor of a product to print this information on the label.

G Signal words and symbols. Some pesticides may be toxic to humans. You can tell how acutely toxic a product is by reading the signal word and symbol on the label (see Table 11-B). Note that these ratings apply only to acute toxicity (i.e., risk of poisoning or death within 24-48 hours).

Highly toxic pesticides may display a skull and crossbones on the label and are not available to home gardeners without a pesticide applicator license. All such products must bear the statement "Keep Out of Reach of Children."

In some pesticide literature, the term LD_{50} is used to give an indication of toxicity. LD_{50} stands for lethal dosage necessary to kill 50% of a test population of animals. The numbers after the 50 represent the milligrams (mg) of the substance per kilograms (kg) of body weight necessary to kill 50% of the test population. The lower the LD_{50} value, the more poisonous the pesticide.

For example, an LD_{50} of 5 is more poisonous than an LD_{50} of 200 because only 5 mg of the first substance per kg of body weight are necessary to kill 50% of the test population, whereas the second product would require an exposure of 200 mg per kg to cause 50% death.

Chemicals may also have long-term, or chronic, effects. Chronic toxicity is measured differently and cannot be rated simply. The signal word is a good indicator of how acutely toxic a product is, but it does not indicate anything about the product's potential to cause long-term effects. Remember that even a product bearing the "Caution" label may have the potential to cause chronic effects if exposure is not minimized.

Table 11-B. "Signal words" on a pesticide label

CATEGORY	SIGNAL WORD	LD_{50} RANGE	HUMAN TOXICITY
Category I	DANGER: POISON	0-50 mg/kg	Highly toxic
Category II	Warning	50-500 mg/kg	Moderately toxic
Category III	Caution	500-5000 mg/kg	Slightly toxic
Category IV	Caution	Over 5000 mg/kg	Relatively non-toxic

Conversely, a product that is an acute toxicity hazard may have no known chronic effects associated with it. The best way to avoid any potential for either acute or chronic effects is to read and follow all label directions, including use of protective equipment.

H **Statement of practical treatment.** If swallowing or inhaling the product, or getting it in the eyes or on the skin would be harmful, the label contains emergency first-aid measures and states the types of exposure which require medical attention.

Figure 11-A. Sample pesticide label

The pesticide label is the most important information you can take to the doctor when someone has been poisoned. The appropriate treatment differs depending on the active ingredients, so without the label it is difficult for the physician to help.

I **Precautionary statement.** A section with a title similar to "Hazards to Humans and Domestic Animals" describes the ways in which the product may be poisonous or harmful to humans and animals. It also describes any special steps necessary to avoid harm, such as the type of protective equipment needed. If the product is highly toxic, this section informs physicians of the proper treatment for poisoning.

J **Environmental hazards.** This portion of the label explains how to avoid damage to the environment. Some examples:

- "This product is highly toxic to bees exposed to direct treatment or residues on crops."
- "Do not contaminate water when cleaning equipment or when disposing of wastes."
- "Do not apply where runoff is likely to occur."

K **Bee hazard.** Many chemical labels may now include a separate section for effects on pollinators, or "beneficial insects." Read this section carefully and refer to the full or extended label for details and application instructions.

In some cases—even when the label may claim a product is "safe for beneficials"—government regulations may only have required testing for impacts on honey bees (*Apis mellifera*) and certain species of beneficial predatory insects like ladybird beetles. Because the testing required for product registration is extensive and costly, there may not be any data indicating whether or not the product can cause harm to other species of bees or beneficial insects.

It is also important to note whether a specific life stage of a beneficial is affected. In many cases adult honey bees and adult lepidopterans (moths and butterflies) may not be affected but the juvenile stages of either are highly susceptible. In these cases, application timing and targeting is extremely important.

An insecticide that is considered "reduced risk" may only be evaluating the level of risk to the human applicator. A label claim of "Safe for Non-target Organisms" can be misleading because it could be referring only to the risk to humans, other mammals, fish, and/or birds. For instance, a pesticide designed to kill insects may have reduced risks to mammals but may very likely indiscriminately kill non-target insects or insect life-stages.

An example is Bt (*Bacillus thuringiensis*). Bt is an effective and useful reduced-risk pesticide. Its MOA is insect-specific in that mammals, birds, and fish lack the ability to activate the toxin. Bt is very effective at killing pest caterpillars (especially early instars). The pesticide does not, however, distinguish between the caterpillar of a tobacco hornworm (pest) or a monarch butterfly (beneficial). Therefore, careful consideration must be given to all relevant factors before selecting and using a pesticide.

L **Physical and chemical hazards.** This section lists specific fire, explosion, or chemical hazards the product may pose.

M **Directions for use.** This part of the label usually includes:

- The pests the product will control
- The crop, animal, or site the product can be used on
- How the product should be applied
- How much of the product to use
- Where and when it should be applied

Pre-harvest periods. When pesticides are used on food crops, there may be a period of time that must pass from the time of application until it is safe to pick and eat the crop. Known as the pre-harvest interval, or PHI, and expressed as "days to harvest," this is the time required for the pesticide residue to be reduced below the level of concern.

The PHI is often listed as a number in parentheses following the crop name. (Because neem oil is an organic and low-risk pesticide, no PHI is shown on this label.)

Fruits and vegetables that have been treated with a pesticide should be rinsed with clean water to remove or reduce surface residue. Rinsing will not remove any residues that may have been absorbed into the plant, but if the PHI has been observed, these residues should be at or below any level of concern for human safety.

N **Misuse statement.** This section states that it is a violation of federal law to use a product in a manner inconsistent with its labeling. In addition to being illegal, misuse can result in harm to people, pets, other animals, and/or the environment.

O **Storage and disposal directions.** Every pesticide should be correctly stored and disposed. This section provides information about storing and disposing of the product.

MARYLAND'S PESTICIDE REGULATIONS

The Maryland Department of Agriculture (MDA) is responsible for regulating pesticides in the state, including "minimum risk" pesticides (a legal term under Section 25(b) of the main pesticide law in the U.S.).

If a product does not bear a registration number, its legal status in Maryland can be determined by looking the product up on the MDA website.

Pesticides and the law

The registration and use of pesticides in all states are governed by the EPA and by the Department of Agriculture of each state. Under the amended Federal Insecticide, Fungicide and Rodenticide Act (Federal Environmental Control Act of 1972), it is illegal to use a pesticide on a crop or site unless it is listed on the label. You may not exceed the given rate of application on the label. Any use of pesticide in a manner not in accordance with the label is a violation of the law. Fines and other penalties vary according to specific parts of the laws broken.

Under state law you are liable for the misuse of pesticides on your property. Recent court rulings extend your liability to include misuse by commercial applicators you hire. Serious misuse by gardeners usually results from drift or leaching of a pesticide onto non-target plants, direct treatment of a plant with the wrong pesticide, or improper pesticide storage.

11.4 Managing Pesticide Risk

The risks associated with pesticide usage can be difficult to measure. Risk is determined by a combination of innate toxicity of the product and likelihood of exposure in a given situation.

There is some level of risk associated with the use of any pesticide, even organic pesticides. The signal words "caution", "warning", and "danger" can help you determine the acute toxicity of a product but acute toxicity is not the only factor when it comes to determining risk. A low-toxicity product used without attention to proper personal protective equipment (PPE) and application can pose the same risk to both applicator and environment as a high-toxicity product used properly.

Some pesticides may have the potential to cause certain chronic or delayed effects. Some of the label directions and limitations are specifically aimed at protecting against such effects. Measures might include the type of PPE required, limits on the amount of product that can be applied at one time, or limits on the frequency of use.

The relationship between toxicity and exposure is key to assessing and minimizing the risk of using a specific product in a specific situation. To mitigate risk, choose products with the lowest possible toxicity and limit exposure of non-target organisms and habitats, including wildlife, water sources, and the applicator. "Target and Timing" are important considerations to remember.

Target the application. Those applications which place the product only where a pest is present (rather than across an entire crop or landscape) limit the exposure of non-targets to pesticide products.

Time the application. Timing can help reduce the exposure to non-target organisms as well, especially when protecting pollinating species. Pollinators visit plants when they are in flower, so avoid applying pesticides to plants that are flowering. Also, some pesticides are most effective only during particular stages in the pest's life cycle. Time pesticide applications for maximum efficacy so that repeated applications are less likely to be necessary.

11.5 Proper Application Practices

See Table 11-C for a list of common terms used regarding the application of pesticides.

Before you apply:

- Read the label each time you use a pesticide, even if you have read it before.
- Use equipment as directed to prevent over-application or spills. The same sprayer can be used for insecticides and fungicides if it is thoroughly washed between uses. To avoid accidental plant injury, herbicides should be applied with a separate sprayer.
- If you apply pesticides through garden-hose connections to sprayers, use an anti-siphon device, which will prevent backward flow of the water and pesticide into the water source.
- Put on the correct personal protective equipment (PPE).
- Frequently check for any leaks in spray equipment.
- When measuring and mixing pesticides, work on a flat, stable surface.
- When using concentrates, mix up only enough for a single application. Don't attempt to store mixtures.
- Only apply pesticides in early morning or evening, on days with low winds and temperatures below 85°F.
- Clear all people, pets, and livestock from the area.

Table 11-C. Terminology: pesticide application

Broadcast	Uniform application by scattering or spraying a pesticide over the entire crop or a relatively large area of the site
Spot treatment	Application to a small section or area of a crop or site
Dip	Immersion of a plant or animal into a pesticide
Directed	Targeting the pesticide to a particular portion of a plant, animal, or structure
Drench	Saturating the soil or plant part with a pesticide
Foliar	Application to the leaves of plants
In furrow	Application to or in the furrow in which a plant is growing
Side dress	Application along the side of a crop row
Injection	Forcing a pesticide into a plant, animal, building, other structure, or the soil
Pre-plant	Use before a crop is planted by applying treatment to soil
Pre-emergent	Use before plants emerge from soil (may be designed to prevent germination)
Post-emergent	Use after crop or weeds have germinated and emerged from the soil (may be selective or non-selective)

During application:

- To minimize drift, spray at a low pressure using a large nozzle opening with a coarse spray (large spray droplets). If moderate or high winds come up while you are working, stop immediately.
- Never apply pesticides to bare ground or eroded areas unless the label specifies that it may be used on bare ground.
- Volatile herbicides (chemicals that are prone to changing into a gaseous state) like 2,4-D should not be used near highly sensitive plants like grape and tomato.
- Never apply pesticides near wells, ponds, streams, marshes, or other surface water that could be contaminated.

After you apply:

- Keep people and pets away from the area until the product has dried or the dust has settled, or longer if the product label specifies a time.
- Never transfer leftover pesticides to other containers.
- If you have excess mixture, spray it over an area for which it is labeled until the sprayer is empty.
- Thoroughly clean all spray equipment inside and out with clean water after use. Flush the hoses and nozzles.
- Do not dump the rinse water in one place; spray it over a broad area (for which the product is labeled) so that the pesticide will be further diluted.
- NEVER RINSE PESTICIDES DOWN THE DRAIN OR THE TOILET!

Figure 11-B. Pesticide caution label

Storage and disposal

- Store all pesticides in a locked cabinet, out of reach of children and pets. Protect pesticides from temperature extremes; some can be damaged by freezing, and others can be altered by heat. Heat and cold can also contribute to the breakdown of the product.

- When possible, only purchase the amount of pesticide you expect to use during the current growing season. Write the year on the container. Pesticide shelf life varies widely and depends upon the type of formulation, type of container, and the storage conditions. Pesticides are best stored at room temperature.

- Follow the storage instructions on the label, whether using a ready-to-use (RTU) or concentrate. Contact the pesticide manufacturer or the National Pesticide Information Center if questions arise about the storage or efficacy of a product.

- The best way to dispose of leftover pesticide is to use it up according to label directions. Rinse out used containers of liquid pesticide and pour the rinse water into a spray tank. Rinse three times, allowing 30 seconds to drain between each rinse. Spray the rinse water on plants listed on the label.

- Wrap empty pesticide containers in newspaper and place in the trash.

- Never re-use empty pesticide containers and never allow children to play with empty containers. If possible, puncture or break the containers before disposal so they cannot be reused by others.

- Do not burn paper containers. Call your local landfill or Department of Public Works to learn their policies for accepting unused pesticides.

11.6 Organic Pesticides

Biopesticides

Biopesticides are labeled and regulated like other pesticides but are made of living things, come from living things, or are found in nature. They are often targeted in their activity, which greatly reduces their toxicity (and therefore risk) to non-target organisms.

Biopesticides include microbes such as bacteria and fungi. These are typically considered biological controls in an IPM program (rather than chemical pesticide controls) but for the sake of EPA pesticide regulations they are considered pesticides.

Minimum-Risk Pesticides (MRPs)

This is a special pesticide category that does not require EPA registration before being sold in the U.S. There is a list of active and inert ingredients that qualify a product as minimum risk; such products may not contain any ingredient not on the list. Many minimum-risk pesticides are considered organic.

Some examples of approved active ingredients are cedarwood oil, citronella, corn gluten, garlic, dried blood, potassium sorbate, malic acid, white pepper, and zinc metal. Note that some of these ingredients are not allowed in food production.

As with organic pesticides, applicators should use care to protect themselves and non-target organisms/habitats from incidental exposure. MRPs may be permitted for use but this does not guarantee efficacy. Before using or recommending an active ingredient, be sure to research and understand how effective the product is at controlling the target pest.

Organic pesticides

A wide array of organic pesticides is available to the public, ranging in toxicity from very mild to dangerous. Many people assume that the word "organic" means that no pesticides are used in growing plants or animals, but there are pesticides that are permitted for use in organic growing and landscape care.

Organic pesticides are derived from natural (versus synthetic) substances and meet the USDA requirements for organic labeling. Being designated an organic pesticide does not guarantee low acute toxicity, lack of potential chronic or delayed effects, or mean that a product is "safer." In fact, not all natural substances are permitted in organic agriculture; naturally-occurring chemicals like arsenic, strychnine, and tobacco dust are not allowed.

The EPA prohibits the use of terms like "non-toxic," "natural," "safe," or "green" on pesticide labels in order to prevent the impression that a certain pesticide is "safe to use" while other pesticides are not.

All pesticides are intended to kill living organisms and inherently have some level of toxicity; safe use is dependent upon following the label directions and using proper care. When choosing an organic pesticide, be sure to assess the toxicity for the situation (e.g., some products are less toxic to humans but very toxic to wildlife) and avoid assumptions about the safety of a product. Try to minimize exposure when using organic products just as you would a more toxic product.

Following are descriptions of organic-pesticide categories:

Plant-derived. Such products are less persistent in the environment and break down quickly in sunlight, so timing must be more precise and multiple sprays may be required. Plant-derived pesticides are not necessarily less toxic than synthetics. Examples: neem and pyrethrum.

Mineral-based. These pesticides are inorganic materials, primarily from mined materials. Sulfur and copper are still widely used in either the elemental form (flowers of sulfur) or in combination with other materials (e.g., Bordeaux mixture, which is comprised of lime, copper sulfate, and water). Agricultural-grade diatomaceous earth (DE) contains the skeletal remains of diatoms and lacerates (soft-bodied pests like cutworms and slugs). Make sure you purchase natural or agricultural-grade DE, and not swimming-pool grade.

Soaps and oils. Soaps and oils are contact materials that break down quickly and are relatively nontoxic to humans, pets, and wildlife.

Soaps are mild poisons that kill by penetration and disruption of the cellular membranes of soft-bodied insects. Oils suffocate soft-bodied insects by plugging the spiracles used for breathing. They are also effective at killing insect eggs. Research has shown oil to be an effective control of diseases such as powdery mildew and rust fungi on selected plants.

Both soaps and oils can cause toxicity when sprayed on sensitive plants or plants that have already suffered significant feeding damage. In addition, soaps and oils should be target-sprayed where the pest occurs and applied in the morning when temperatures are not expected to exceed 85°F.

Lightweight summer and horticultural oils can be sprayed on foliage but dormant oils should never be sprayed on developing buds or foliage. Oil- and sulfur-based sprays (including some fungicides) should not be sprayed within 14 days of one another.

Microbials. These pesticides are derived from microorganisms. *Bacillus thuringiensis* (Bt) is the most common microbial pesticide in use. Different strains are available that can control various beetle, caterpillar, and mosquito pests. *Bt kurstaki* (Btk) works best to control young caterpillar larvae.

Spinosad is an effective insecticide derived from spinosyns, metabolites of a soil microorganism.

11.7 Pesticides in the Environment

Environmental fate

Like other synthetic and naturally-occurring chemicals, pesticides may be transferred around the environment, depending on innate characteristics of the pesticide and conditions at the site of application. Adsorption is the process whereby chemicals are bound to surfaces by physical or chemical attraction.

Absorption is the process whereby chemicals are transported from surfaces into the insides of plants and animals. Depending on their innate characteristics, pesticides may be tightly adsorbed to surfaces of plants, animals, soil, or structures, or they may be easily absorbed inside plants and animals.

Movement in air

Air currents may carry pesticides as vapors, spray droplets, dusts, or solid particles. "Drift" refers to the movement of pesticides on air currents. Generally, the smaller the particle size, the more likely it is that drift will occur. High temperatures also increase the tendency of pesticides to drift. As the air heats up, it can carry vaporized molecules of pesticide with it, moving them long distances off-site. Drift of pesticides moves them away from the intended target and may result in harm to plants, beneficials, other wildlife, or humans. Water sources may be contaminated if drift moves over them and residues are redeposited in the water.

Movement in water

Most movement of pesticides in water takes place through either runoff, i.e., surface movement off the application site, or through leaching or movement down through the soil. Runoff occurs before the residue has had a chance to be absorbed into plants or adsorbed onto surfaces (which may include plant surfaces). Pesticides that are water-soluble are more likely to be subject to runoff and leaching.

Pesticide degradation

Degradation of pesticides in the environment takes place mainly through the actions of heat, sunlight, and microbes. Pesticides applied indoors are less exposed to these factors and may remain on surfaces for longer periods of time than the same pesticide applied outdoors. Pesticide labels reflect this fact, as some pesticides are registered for use on crops, lawns or landscapes but not inside due to their much longer indoor half-life.

Once a pesticide is absorbed into an organism, it is subject to the organism's own degradation processes. Each organism has its own set of enzymes that transform the pesticide to other forms (metabolites) and ultimately excrete the pesticide and/or its metabolites. These metabolites are usually less toxic to the organism than the parent compound, but several different metabolites may be formed in the process of degradation, and some of them may actually be more toxic than the parent compound. Chemicals that are more fat-soluble, or lipophilic, are stored, whereas those that are water-soluble are excreted.

In plants, storage sites include lipid-rich plant parts such as seeds. Excretion of water soluble metabolites occurs through transpiration. In animals, lipophilic pesticides are stored in body fat, including the fat in mammal milk; water-soluble pesticides are excreted in urine.

Most pesticides in use today are water-soluble. They are more quickly metabolized, and are excreted in the urine within hours or days after exposure. Exposure to a large dose, such as a spill, may overwhelm the body's ability to excrete the pesticide, and serious illness or injury could occur. Exposure to repeated doses of small amounts is also of concern because of the potential for chronic effects.

Spills and misapplication

Do not hose down pesticide spills, as this will spread the pesticide and could carry it into storm drains or sewers, ultimately leading to contamination of streams, rivers, or the Chesapeake Bay. Instead, control and contain liquid spills by applying an absorbent material such as cat litter or vermiculite on top of the spill, and then sweeping the material into a heavy-duty trash bag. For spills of most consumer pesticides, the material may be disposed of in a sanitary landfill. Larger spills, or those involving high-concentrate materials, might have to be treated as hazardous waste.

When cleaning up a spill, wear chemical-resistant gloves as well as long pants and a long-sleeved shirt. The manufacturer can be called for advice or assistance, if necessary. The manufacturer's telephone number is required to appear on the product label.

If you accidentally use a pesticide on a site for which it is not labeled (e.g., using a pesticide labeled for ornamentals on vegetables), do not eat the crop. The label won't carry information such as proper application rate or pre-harvest interval, and it is possible that residues of the pesticide could cause harm if consumed.

Pesticides and surface water

The Chesapeake Bay and Maryland's rivers, ponds, lakes, and streams are home to a myriad of wildlife. Contamination of surface

Figure 11-C. Phytotoxicity on cucumber leaf

waters can cause direct kills of wildlife and indirectly affect them through loss of suitable habitat and/or food sources.

Because surface water is a significant source of drinking water in Maryland, pesticide contamination could also have adverse implications for human health.

Runoff is the main method through which surface waters may become contaminated. The slope, soil characteristics, and vegetative cover, as well as rainfall amount also affect surface-waters contamination.

Grasses, shrubs, and trees along waterways provide sites for pesticides to adsorb and help prevent runoff. Following **proper application practices** also helps prevent runoff contamination.

Pesticides and groundwater

Groundwater exists in bedrock cracks and spaces between soil granules. Cleaning up contaminated groundwater is extremely difficult, if not impossible.

If pesticides leach into sandy soil or other soil with little organic matter to bind the pesticides, they may reach groundwater before being completely detoxified by microbial degradation. Labels of pesticides with high water solubility, low capacity for adsorption to soil particles, and/or are persistent, provide directions on how to avoid groundwater contamination.

Groundwater contamination can also occur directly when application is too close to wells or near wells with broken casings. ❋

AUTHOR

Courtney Coddington, Former Agent Associate for Home Horticulture, University of Maryland Extension.

PUBLICATIONS

Adapted in part from the *Penn State Master Gardener Manual*.

WEBSITES

EPA regulations. epa.gov/laws-regulations/summary-federal-insecticide-fungicide-and-rodenticide-act

National Pesticide Information Center: 1-800-858-7378 or npic.orst.edu/

Insecticide Resistance Action Committee. *Online Classification.* irac-online.org/modes-of-action/

Insecticide Resistance Action Committee. Insecticide resistance management. cals.arizona.edu/crops/pdfs/IRAC%20MOA%20brochure_v4%202_Oct10.pdf

U.S. Environmental Protection Agency. epa.gov/pesticides

University of Maryland Pesticide Education and Assessment Program. pesticide.umd.edu

University of Maryland Pesticide Information Leaflet Series. pesticide.umd.edu/pesticide-information-leaflets1.html

PHOTOS

Main chapter photo and Figure 11-C. Jon Traunfeld, University of Maryland.

12: PLANT DIAGNOSTICS

Jon Traunfeld
David Clement, Ph.D.
Emily Zobel
Debra Ricigliano

12 PLANT DIAGNOSTICS

CONTENTS

12.1 A Systematic Approach for Diagnosing Plant Problems 243

12.2 How Plants Show Symptoms 245

12.3 Biotic vs. Abiotic Causes of Plant Problems 247

12.4 Symptoms and Signs of Plant Diseases 251

12.5 Symptoms and Signs of Insect Pests 253

12.6 Diagnostic Keys 254

LEARNING OBJECTIVES

- How to approach diagnosing a plant problem
- How plants show symptoms
- How to know the difference between biotic and abiotic plant problems
- How to identify disease and insect problems, and what to do about them

INTRODUCTION

Timely diagnosis of plant problems can help keep your landscape and gardens beautiful and productive. It can also prevent expensive removal and replacement of damaged plants. Determining the cause of plant problems requires an inquisitive, investigative approach combined with careful observation; it also requires the ability to put all the pieces together to reconstruct the event(s) that produced the plant damage.

An accurate diagnosis must be made before corrective action can be taken. Even if no corrective measures are available, or if it is too late to fix the problem this growing season, an accurate problem diagnosis will correctly guide future management solutions.

The probability of a correct diagnosis based on only one or two symptoms is low. Similarities of symptoms produced on the same plant by completely different factors frequently make the use of symptoms alone inadequate.

In diagnosing plant problems, you can follow a series of deductive steps to gather information and clues from the big-picture situation down to the specific plant or plant part. Through this systematic process of deduction and elimination, you may be able to narrow down the most probable causes of the damage.

12.1 A Systematic Approach for Diagnosing Plant Problems

Define the problem

Check plant identification and characteristics to establish what the "normal" plant would look like at this time of year. Describe the "abnormality" (e.g., the symptoms and signs).

Take a history of the plant:

- Plant name (common and Latin, if possible)
- How long the plants has been in its current spot, when it was planted (or transplanted), and the age of the plant
- The plant source (nursery-grown, relocated from another site, grown from seed or cuttings)
- The type of plant production (container, bare-root, balled and burlapped)
- The size of the planting and percentage of plants affected
- Site and soil conditions
- Plant location (full sun or shade, low or high ground, dry or wet site)
- Planting technique

Now think about the plant's symptoms:

- Try to establish when the problem was first noticed
- Determine the distribution of symptomatic plants (e.g., single, scattered, or grouped)
- Determine the part of the plant where initial symptoms occurred
- Examine the entire plant in relation to drainage observations or if water collects there (e.g., is the plant between a sidewalk and a road? Is the plant fully established in the landscape or garden? Has it put on normal growth? What else could have contributed to the problem?)

Look for patterns

Selective symptom patterns or a more random pattern (e.g., specific leaf spots on one or only a few plant species) indicate living, or biotic, factors such as pathogens and insects.

A broad damage pattern (e.g., leaf scorch on several species) or a uniform injury pattern on the plant may indicate abiotic factors (e.g., mechanical, physical, or chemical).

Note progression of the damage pattern:

- A sequence of events over time causing symptoms on a plant indicates damage caused by living (biotic) organisms.
- Damage that occurs but does not spread within the plant, or a quick, one-time event often indicates non-living (abiotic) factors.

Determine the causes of the plant problem

Is it biotic?

- Symptoms and signs of diseases
- Symptoms and signs of insects, mites, or other animals

FINALIZING THE DIAGNOSIS

1. Keep an open mind.
2. Avoid "guilt by association." A given insect, animal, or disease may not be the cause of the problem or the symptoms.
3. Closely examine the roots, shoots, trunk, and leaf undersides (use a hand lens if necessary). Look for physical evidence such as plant injury, changes in site conditions, soil compaction, or construction or lawn mower injury.
4. At least half of all observed landscape problems are not caused by insects or diseases. Try to eliminate other causal factors first.
5. A symptom in one part of a plant may indicate a problem in a different part. For example, leaf yellowing and scorching may be caused by root damage.
6. What appears to be one problem could actually be many, such as poor soil drainage, extreme weather, air pollution, pests, diseases, and herbicide drift.
7. All plants go through periods of growth, maturity, and decline; and life-span varies greatly. Plants grown in urban conditions generally have shorter lives. Once mature trees begin to decline, there is often no way to reverse the process. White pines and oaks are common examples of plants that are difficult to rejuvenate after decline symptoms begin.
8. Many pests and diseases are plant-specific. Symptoms affecting more than one plant species or genus may indicate cultural and environmental problems.

Or is it abiotic?

- Mechanical injury
- Weather/temperature/light extremes
- Pesticide/pollutant phytotoxicities
- Nutritional disorders
- Damage patterns in adjacent plants
- Injury patterns on individual plant

Check references for known pests or diseases. Get confirmation from a reliable source, such as Extension publications and websites.

See the inset on the previous page to guide you in synthesizing the information you've collected.

12.2 How Plants Show Symptoms

Normal vs. abnormal needle or leaf drop

Evergreen plants normally retain their leaves or needles for several years, but eventually they fall. This drop is usually gradual and production of new leaves obscures the loss of older leaves.

Normal: Needle or leaf drop is confined to older (inner) leaves and is gradual. Unfavorable growing conditions, such as drought, may accelerate leaf drop so that it becomes apparent and concerning (see Figure 12-A.)

Abnormal: Loss of new (outer) needles or leaves is a serious problem. Drop of current year's leaves may result from a pathogen or insect attack, nutrient deficiencies or toxicities, chemical deficiencies or toxicities, or failure to establish. Pest problems often produce canopy-thinning over time (see Figure 12-B.) Rapid defoliation can also happen with diseases such as boxwood blight and oak wilt. The opposite is also true with the bacterial disease fire blight, which causes rapid dieback but the leaves remain.

Figure 12-A. Normal vs. abnormal needle drop

Normal fall browning/drop of interior needles | Browning on branch ends is abnormal

Needle damage

Death of the tips of conifer needles in a uniform pattern usually indicates an abiotic factor. Air pollutants and drought cause tip burn on conifers as do certain soil-applied herbicides or excess fertilizer. In these cases, all needles of a specific growth period are usually affected, and usually the same length on each needle is affected.

Damage to leaves or needles by living organisms, such as fungi and insects, usually occurs in a specific pattern or sequence.

Needle symptoms often appear straw yellow or light tan in color, and disease signs such as black fruiting bodies embedded in the needles may be present. These diseases usually have a multiple-year life cycle.

Leaf symptoms caused by rapid blighting of anthracnose fungi can show dark brown or black leaf blotches and disease signs such as black fruiting bodies along the veins.

Plant canopy damage

Entire or major portion of top dying: If all or a major portion of a plant dies, suspect a problem with the roots or damage to the vascular system of the trunk. Sudden decline is generally caused by an abiotic factor, such as a toxic chemical in the soil or drastic climatic

Figure 12-B. Canopy loss and branch death

Partial canopy loss due to drought | Branch death caused by borers

Figure 12-D. Shoot dieback

Shoot dieback caused by a frost crack | Shoot dieback with anthracnose

changes, such as freezing or drought (see Figure 12-B.)

Gradual decline of the entire plant or a major portion of it could be caused by living factors such as root rot, wilt disease, insect borers, or chewing damage to the stem from animals such as voles. Slow changes in environmental and cultural factors can also cause general plant decline.

Branch death: In general, if scattered branches decline and gradually die, suspect a living organism such as a canker pathogen, shoot blight, or borers (see Figure 12-B.) If a branch dies suddenly, and especially if affected branches are concentrated on one side, suspect an abiotic factor such as weather (e.g., wind or snow), animal damage, or chemical drift. An exception might include a soil wilt fungus such as Verticillium that can cause a one-sided wilt.

Shoot dieback

Shoot dieback caused by abiotic factors: Look for physical changes such as cracking, girdling, and loose bark. Freeze damage can cause dieback on non-hardy plants.

Shoot dieback (blight) caused by biotic factors: Gradual decline of shoots and retention of dead leaves may indicate a biotic factor (see Figure 12-D.)

- The margin between affected and healthy tissue is often irregular and sunken. There may be small, pin-like projections or bumps over the surface of the dead bark, which are fruiting bodies of pathogenic fungi.

- Boring insects and bacterial diseases, such as fire blight, can also cause rapid shoot dieback.

- Foliar-applied chemical spray injury produces a uniform pattern of spots over the leaf surface. Spots may resemble paint splatter and may be variable sizes. The color is usually uniform across the spots, with no target patterns, fruiting bodies, or halos. Spots are not restricted by veins (see Figure 12-C.)

- The margin between affected and healthy tissue is usually sharp. The injury pattern does not spread with time or move to undamaged plants.

Figure 12-C. Leaf damage pattern - chemical injury

246 Maryland Master Gardener Handbook   UME © 2025. All rights reserved.

- Drift injury from volatile chemicals, such as 2,4-D, produces leaf deformities. Glyphosate injury can carry over multiple years.
- Toxic chemicals taken up through roots, polluted air (typically causing necrotic stippling), and heat or moisture stress cause systemic injury that results in scorching (necrosis) of leaf margins and veins or malformed foliage.

12.3 Biotic vs. Abiotic Causes of Plant Problems

What causes plant problems?

Plants can be damaged by either biotic or abiotic factors:

Biotic (living) organisms. These include pathogens (e.g., fungi, bacteria, viruses, and nematodes) and pests (e.g., insects, mites, mollusks, and rodents).

If you suspect a living organism, look for signs and symptoms to determine whether it is a pathogen or a pest. If the evidence suggests a pathogen, try to distinguish amongst fungal, bacterial, viral, and/or nematode pathogens. If the evidence indicates damage by an insect or other animal, try to distinguish between sucking, boring, mining, and/or chewing types.

Abiotic (non-living) factors. These include mechanical (e.g., breakage and abrasions), physical/environmental (e.g., lightning; extremes of temperature, light, moisture, or oxygen), and chemical factors (e.g., phytotoxicities and nutritional disorders).

If evidence indicates that the damage is being caused by an abiotic factor, you should first determine whether initial damage is occurring in the root system or above ground. Then attempt to determine if the damage is from mechanical, physical, and/or chemical factors.

Is it a biotic or abiotic problem?

Observing the pattern of symptom development will help you distinguish between living and non-living factors:

- Living organisms usually multiply and cause greater symptom severity over time.
- Abiotic factors generally cause plant damage at a given point in time. For example, leaf tissue damaged by a phytotoxic chemical is immediate and does not spread. Exceptions include compacted soil or extended drought that causes chronic damage.

Distinguish among biotic factors

To further identify which subcategory of living factor caused the damage requires a close examination of the observable symptoms and signs:

Symptoms are changes in the growth or appearance of the plant in response to feeding or parasitism. Wilting, necrotic tissues, chlorosis, galls, leaf distortion, and chewed or notched leaves are examples of leaf symptoms. Many damaging factors can produce the same symptoms, so symptoms are not always definitive. For example, off-color foliage can be caused by numerous factors, including aphids and root-rot organisms.

Signs are the observable presence of the actual organism or evidence directly related to it. For insects, these include the actual insect, eggs, cast skins, excrement (frass), and webbing. For diseases, signs are the actual pathogen which include fungal fruiting bodies and mushrooms. Signs can be used to identify the specific living organism that produced the plant damage.

A combination of clues from both symptoms and signs is required for preliminary distinction between pathogen and insect-mite damage. Differentiating between bacterial and fungal pathogens is not always clear cut, but certain symptoms are distinctive (see section 12.4, Symptoms and Signs of Plant Diseases.)

Distinguish among abiotic factors

Uniform and repeated patterns of damage in the planting over multiple species or on the individual plant indicate an abiotic factor. Abiotic factors may be mechanical, physical (environmental), or chemical.

Mechanical factors

Plant damage caused by site or grade changes (construction damage), transplanting damage, lawn mower/string-trimmer injury, abrasion, breakage, and bruising is considered mechanical damage.

Close visual examination will reveal if the stems or roots have been broken or girdled or if the leaves have been bruised, punctured, or broken. For example, if a large balled-and-burlapped tree is dropped while being transplanted and the stem is broken, rapid wilting of the plant above the break will occur. Examine the plant site for signs of recent excavation, construction, or paving.

Physical (environmental) factors

Environmental factors include site conditions (e.g., heavy clay) or weather changes that cause extremes of temperature, light, moisture, or wind. The primary sources of diagnostic information are damage patterns and weather records to pinpoint the time and location of weather extremes.

Figure 12-E. Heat damage (l) and frost damage (r)

Extreme heat. The highest leaf temperatures will occur in the early afternoon when the sun is located in the southwest. Lethal leaf temperatures will occur mostly on unshaded leaves on the outer surface of the plant canopy on the southwest side. Most severe damage occurs on leaves most exposed and furthest from the vascular source of water (e.g., outer leaves, leaf tips, and interveinal areas). See Figure 12-E.

Extreme cold. Damage will occur on the least hardy plants, and will be most severe on the least hardy tissues of those specific plants. Terminal buds are the first plant parts to achieve cold hardiness during fall acclimation. The branch crotches are often the last tissues to achieve cold hardiness. With time, the lower regions achieve hardiness. If warm temperatures induce deacclimation (in the early spring), the terminal buds are first to become less cold-hardy. Plants vary greatly in their cold tolerance.

On a given structure (e.g., leaf or bud), the damage will be death of exposed, non-hardy tissues in a recognizable (repeated) pattern:

- **Frost damage** can be light to severe, depending on exposure. For example, heavy frost on deciduous tree leaves or conifer needles in the spring will uniformly kill all tissue of a given age from the tip of the branch back; light frost damage may be superficial on leaf surfaces, causing a light-colored tan or bleached appearance.
- **Frost cracks** are longitudinal separations of the bark and wood, generally on the southwest side of the trunk. They occur during periods of wide daily temperature fluctuations.
- **Freezing death** of dividing cells on outer portions of leaf folds inside the bud will cause distorted or lace-like leaf blades. This is a result of non-uniform cell division and growth during leaf expansion (see Figure 12-E).
- **Cold damage to the root system** is primarily a concern with container-grown plants. The root temperature fluctuates more and can reach lower temperatures than native soil. Damaged roots, especially near the container edge, appear blackened or spongy with little new growth. Above-ground symptoms will not usually be evident until new shoot growth in the spring. Leaves may emerge smaller than normal because of the restricted uptake of water and nutrients caused by the damaged root system. Plants may wilt or defoliate as air temperatures rise, causing water loss from shoots and leaves to exceed root-uptake capacity.

Light extremes. Plants need time to acclimate to environmental change and tend to respond adversely to rapid environmental changes. A sudden change from low to high light intensity

Figure 12-F. Plants affected by chemical factors

Salt damage to turf

Sulfur deficiency on corn

will result in destruction of the chlorophyll pigments in the leaf (yellowing and necrosis = sunburn).

Conversely, a sudden change from high to low light will result in reduced growth and leaf drop; new leaves will be larger. "Sun leaves" are smaller, thicker, and lighter green than "shade leaves." Flowering will be reduced, delayed, or absent under low light.

Oxygen and moisture extremes. A water-logged root system results in oxygen deficiency because air in soil pores is displaced by water. Without oxygen, root growth comes to a standstill. Water and nutrient uptake are restricted, with subsequent wilting and nutritional deficiency symptoms occurring on the above-ground portions of the plant. Drought and water-logging produce many of the same symptoms, including chlorosis, abscission (dropping) of older leaves, and necrosis on leaf tips and interveinal regions of recently expanded leaves.

Chemical factors

A generally uniform pattern of damage occurring over several plant species and over a relatively large area indicates an abiotic factor, such as a chemical phytotoxicity. Patterns of chemical injury symptoms vary depending on whether the chemical causes damage on contact or is absorbed by the plant.

- **Direct foliar contact** with pesticides and fertilizers causes chlorotic/necrotic spotting, especially interveinally, and along leaf edges.
- **Chemical and fertilizer contact** with the root system can damage roots and produce general symptoms such as reduced growth, wilting, and nutrient deficiency (see Figure 12-F). Direct contact with excess fertilizer salts can actually draw moisture from roots, causing dessication. In severe cases, wilting can occur even though the soil is wet. Lower leaves generally wilt first, followed by marginal leaf-browning. Many factors injuring or inhibiting root growth may produce similar shoot symptoms: nematodes, soil compaction, cold weather, nutritional disorders, and certain herbicides.

Nutrient ions that are immobile in plants:

- Several nutrient ions are translocated upward in the xylem, incorporated in plant tissue, and made immobile. When deficiencies develop in the root zone, they cannot be withdrawn and translocated through the vascular system to new growth.
- Boron and calcium are very immobile. Deficiency symptoms appear first on new growth; with severe deficiencies, the terminal bud dies.
- Iron, manganese, zinc, copper, and molybdenum are also relatively immobile and deficiency symptoms are most pronounced on new growth.
  - Iron deficiency causes interveinal chlorosis on young leaves, with only large veins remaining green. It may also be induced by high soil pH.
  - Manganese deficiency causes interveinal chlorosis with smallest veins remaining green, producing a checkered or finely netted effect. Grey or tan necrotic spots usually develop in chlorotic areas. The dead spots of tissue may drop out of the leaf, giving it a ragged appearance.

Nutrient ions that are mobile in plants:

- Different nutrient ions are mobile in the phloem. If these become deficient in the root zone, they may be withdrawn from the older plant tissue and translocated in the phloem to the new growth. In such situations, deficiency symptoms will first occur on the older leaves.
- These nutrients include nitrogen, phosphorus, potassium, magnesium, chlorine, and, in some plants, sulfur.

(See **Chapter 6, Plant Nutrition**, for a chart of nutrient deficiency and toxicity symptoms.)

Herbicides that are translocated:

- Phloem-translocated herbicides, whether absorbed by roots or shoots, travel to the meristems, causing injury to new leaves and roots. These tissues will be discolored or malformed and injury may persist for several sets of new leaves. Symptoms, including bending and twisting of leaves and stems, are evident almost immediately after application. Examples include 2,4-D, dicamba, glyphosate, and sethoxydim.

Figure 12-G Fungal disease

Figure 12-H. Bacterial disease

Figure 12-I. Viral disease

12.4 Symptoms and Signs of Plant Diseases

*(See **Chapter 9, Plant Disease Basics**, for more detailed information.)*

Fungal diseases

Leaf spots caused by fungi generally have distinct margins (see Figure 12-G). In many cases, they are circular with concentric rings, resulting from growth of the mycelium from the center point of initial infection outward. Leaf spots may coalesce and cause leaf blights.

The margins of fungal leaf spots and stem lesions are usually dark, and the centers can be tan to brown. Leaf veins do not limit spots because mycelium can grow around veins. Root rot and vascular wilt cause gradual wilting of the above-ground shoots.

The most distinguishing clue of a fungal disease is the presence of signs such as mycelium and fruiting bodies of the fungus itself. The mycelium may cover the surface with light-colored growth as in the powdery and downy mildews, or may be a densely growing covering of spore-bearing structures as in gray mold (*Botrytis*) or brown rot. The fruiting bodies range in size from microscopic to those easily detected with the naked eye. They are found within the leaf spot or stem rot area and may be dark or brightly colored, such as the rust fungi. Each type of fungus has its own characteristic structures which enable plant pathologists to identify them.

Bacterial diseases

Unlike fungi, bacteria do not actively penetrate healthy plant tissue. They enter through wounds or natural openings, such as leaf stomata or twig lenticels. Once bacteria enter the plant, they reproduce rapidly, killing the plant cells. In some cases, as in crown gall, bacteria cause plant tissues of stems or leaves to grow abnormally. Bacterial leaf spots are often angular because they are initially limited by leaf veins (see Figure 12-H). Infected tissue may appear oily or water-soaked, and may have a foul odor.

Lesions may enlarge and develop into a general blight. In some cases, bacteria can plug the water-conducting tissue and cause yellowing, wilting, browning, and dieback of leaves, stems, and roots (e.g., bacterial wilt of cucumber, summer squash, and melon).

Viral diseases

Viruses are "submicroscopic" entities that infect individual host-plant cells. Once inside a plant cell, they are able to infect other cells. Viruses are obligate parasites; they can only replicate themselves within a host's cell. Because the virus commandeers the host cell to manufacture viruses identical to itself, the plant cell is unable to function and grow normally. In nature, most viruses are spread by insects, mites, and nematodes. The symptoms of most virus diseases fall into four categories:

- **Lack of chlorophyll formation in normally green organs.** Foliage may be mottled green and yellow, or develop a general mosaic pattern. Vein clearing can be a symptom of some viral diseases. The veins have a somewhat translucent or transparent appearance. Vein banding is another symptom, producing a darker green, lighter green, or yellow band of tissue along the veins.
- **Stunting or other growth inhibition.** The reduction in photosynthesis (because of less chlorophyll) leads to shorter internodes, smaller leaves and blossoms, and reduced yield.
- **Distortions of leaves and flowers.** Witches'-brooms or rosettes result from non-uniform growth within a tissue or uncontrolled growth.
- **Necrotic rings or lesions.** Dead sections of leaves are frequently an attempt by the plant to limit virus spread within its tissues (see Figure 12-I).

Nematode diseases

Disease symptoms can be divided between root and foliar nematodes:

- Root feeding nematodes will cause root damage that will typically cause stunting and off color symptoms. Root knot nematodes will cause a galling and abnormal swelling of the root tissues.
- Foliar nematodes feed within the leaf and will usually stay between the leaf veins. On parallel veined plants, the feeding symptoms will be stripes of necrotic or chlorotic tissue compared to a more net-like appearance on most other plants.

Phytoplasma diseases

Phytoplasma disease symptoms may include:

- Abnormal greening of the flowers, also called virescence.
- Green leaf-like growths within the flower, called phyllody.

Figure 12-J. Chewing damage (Sawfly)

Figure 12-K. Sucking insect damage (mealybug)

- A proliferation or a tight, bushy growth of shortened shoots, called witches'-brooms.
- Whole-plant symptoms may include off-color, undersized foliage. Commonly infected flowering plants include echinacea, aster, petunia, snapdragon, chrysanthemum, and marigold.

12.5 Symptoms and Signs of Insect Pests

See **Chapter 8, Insect Basics,** and **Chapter 10, IPM,** for more detailed information about insects and their controls.

The location and type of damage (e.g., by chewing or sucking mouthparts) are the most important clues to determine insect-caused injury and identify the responsible insect. It's important to know an insect's life cycle when attempting to diagnose a potential problem. Insects with incomplete life cycles (e.g., plant bugs) are often most damaging in the adult stage. Insects with complete life cycles (e.g., moths and beetles) are often most damaging in the larval stage.

Chewing damage

Symptoms of chewing/rasping damage include:

- Entire leaf blade consumed, with only the mid-vein left (caterpillars, beetles, and webworms (see Figure 12-J).
- Distinct portions of leaves are missing, such as notches cut from the leaf margin (black vine weevil adult); circular holes cut from the leaf margin (leaf cutter bees); or small, randomly scattered holes in leaves (beetles, weevils, grasshoppers).
- Leaf surfaces damaged ("skeletonized") by beetle larvae and thrips.
- Leaves "rolled" into a tube or tied together with silken threads (often leafrollers or leaf miners).

Sucking or rasping damage

In addition to direct mechanical damage from feeding, some vascular-feeding insects cause damage by injecting toxic substances when feeding. This can cause symptoms ranging from simple stippling of the leaves to disruption of the entire plant.

- Flecking or stippling results from limited diffusion of the toxin and localized destruction of the chlorophyll by the enzymes injected at the feeding site. Aphids, leafhoppers, and various bugs are commonly associated with this injury.
- Leaf curling or puckering is caused by severe infestations, especially by aphids (see Figure 12-K).
- Damaged and split twigs are due to egg laying (ovipositing) by sucking insects such as tree hoppers and cicadas.
- Leaves covered in shiny honeydew or black sooty mold suggest an outbreak of aphids, planthoppers (including spotted lanternflies), leafhoppers, mealybugs, or soft-scale insects. Sooty mold is unsightly but harmful only in that it can obstruct the plant's photosynthetic ability. Signs of sucking damage can resemble heat or drought stress.
- Root, stem, and branch feeders can cause a general decline of the entire plant or a section of a plant as indicated by poor color, reduced growth, and dieback (e.g., scales and mealybugs).

Other insect damage

- Leaf miners feed between the upper and lower leaf surfaces. If you hold the leaf up to a light, you can see the insect or frass in the damaged area, which will be discolored or swollen (e.g., boxwood, holly, birch, and elm leaf miners).

- Petiole and stalk borers burrow into the petiole near the base or blade of the leaf. Tissues are weakened and the leaf falls in early summer.

- Borers feed under the bark in the cambium tissue or in the solid wood or xylem tissue of trees and shrubs. Damage is often noticed because of a general decline of the plant or a certain branch, holes in the bark, and an accumulation of frass or pitch (e.g., raspberry-crown borer).

- An assortment of insects may cause galls and swellings on leaf and stem tissue (e.g., aphids, wasps, midges, and azalea leaf gall).

- Root feeders are larval stages of weevils, beetles, and moths. They cause general decline of the plant through chewed areas of roots (e.g., Japanese beetle and root weevil).

- Spider mites are arachnids with sucking mouth parts and eight legs. Damage is often a characteristic stipple pattern on leaves which then become pale on the underside. Severe infestation causes leaf bronzing and death. Mite presence may be indicated by "dirty" foliage and fine webbing on the leaf underside, mixed with eggs and frass. Eriophyid mites cause distorted new growth, rolled leaf margins, and swollen leaf veins.

- Slug and snail feeding on low-growing foliage resembles skeletonizing. "Silvering" and slime trails on foliage are signs of these pests.

- Rodents (e.g., mice, voles, squirrels, and rabbits) chew bark and cambium tissue on small trees and shrubs. Teeth marks are a sign of feeding.

- Birds, like the yellow-bellied sap-sucker, sometimes make even rows of holes in tree trunks. ❋

12.6 Diagnostic Keys

The diagnostic keys on the following pages will help you identify common abiotic (cultural and environmental) and biotic (pests and diseases) plant problems. For a full list of the keys and their page numbers, please see the Index of Diagnostic Keys.

Key 12-A.   Abiotic Problems of Herbaceous Ornamentals and Vegetables

LEAF YELLOWING

12.A1 Senescence - broccoli raab

Older leaf drop (senescence). Normal for bottom leaves to yellow and drop as the plant ages.

12.A2 Over-watered tomato

Excessive moisture. Yellowing caused by poorly-drained soil/site conditions.

12.A3 Spindly basil

Insufficient sunlight. Shoots become pale yellow-green, long, and spindly ("leggy").

12.A4 Magnesium deficiency

Nutrient deficiency. Interveinal yellowing indicates a potassium, magnesium, iron, or manganese deficiency.

12.A5 Pollution - watermelon

Air/ozone pollution. Speckled yellowish upper leaf surface; undersides may look silver.

LEAF SPOTS/BLOTCHES

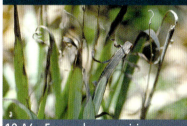
12.A6 Freeze damage - iris

Frost or freeze damage. Water-soaked blotches may darken/turn black.

12.A7 Chemical drift - tomato

Herbicide or pesticide drift. Random pattern of white/light-colored spots and damage on adjacent plants of different species.

LEAF CURLING/DISTORTION

12.A8 Chemical damage - tomato

2,4-D damage. Grapes, tomatoes, squash, and beans are most sensitive. Damage is on new growth. Leaves are narrow, twisted, and crinkled.

12.A10 Drift damage - strawberry

Herbicide damage. Caused by glyphosate or dicamba chemical drift or a tainted sprayer. Leaf yellowing, mottling, curling, and cupping. Damage may follow the leaf veins.

12.A9 Drought stress - viburnum

Water stress. Lower leaves curl first and may brown if drought persists.

12.A11 Heat stress - tomato

Heat stress. Lower leaves curl during hot, dry weather. Use a shade cloth if possible.

continued on next page

continued from previous page

Key 12-A. Abiotic Problems of Herbaceous Ornamentals and Vegetables

LEAF BLISTERS

12.A12 Edema - hibiscus

Small blisters on leaf surface turn dark and appear crusty. Edema can occur on many plants, especially cabbage, yew, and vine geraniums. Develops on wet soils when warm days are followed by cool nights. Maintain even soil moisture and increase air flow around plants.

LEAF SCORCH/LEAF-TIP BURN

12.A13 Drought stress - houseplant

Drought stress. Leaf margins are affected first. Problem is more severe on outside leaves near the top of the plant.

12.A14 Chemical burn - muskmelon

Pesticide burn (phytotoxicity). Caused by soaps/oils. Ranges from random irregular spots up to entire leaf burn.

12.A15 Salt burn -broccoli

Fertilizer burn, salt spray. Leaf-margin burn is from excessive salt uptake and/or grayish spots from direct foliar contact with fertilizer.

12.A16 Lack of calcium - lettuce

Calcium deficiency. Occurs most often on lettuce, cabbage, and Brussels sprouts. Test soil pH and adjust accordingly. If problem persists, mix a small handful of gypsum or ground limestone with soil under the plant.

12.A17 Chlorine burn

Chloride toxicity. Leaves yellow or brown at the tips. Usually from swimming pool drainage and de-icing salts. Divert pool water and ice-melt runoff away from root zones. Irrigate to leach salt out of plant roots.

PLANT WILT

12.A18 Frost-kill - begonia

Cold/frost damage. Occurs after freezing temperatures. Leaves, flowers, and fruit suffer cell damage and soften.

12.A19 Heat stress - bee balm

Drought/heat stress. Leaves cannot transpire water fast enough. Newer growth wilts first.

12.A20 Waterlogged poppy

Excessive rain or over-watering. Poorly drained soils cause death from lack of oxygen because the water displaces the oxygen in the soil. Leaves wilt, turn yellow, and fall off. New transplants may be saved by digging up, partially drying out, and then replanting them.

continued on next page

continued from previous page

Key 12-A. Abiotic Problems of Herbaceous Ornamentals and Vegetables

BROKEN BRANCHES/SPLIT STEMS

12.A21 Waterlogged watermelon

Excessive water or sudden changes in soil moisture. Too much water can cause stem-splitting. Use mulches to maintain even soil moisture.

12.A23 Mature peppers

Mature plants with a heavy fruit load. Peppers are especially prone to branch-breaking. Keep plants pruned and supported with stakes. Promptly pick fruit when ripe to remove weight from plant.

12.A22 Hail damage - tomato

Species or cultivar characteristic. Weakness may be inherent in the plant. Storms may break branches and cause tall plants to fall over.

FAILURE TO FLOWER/BLOSSOM DROP

12.A24 Winter burn - strawberry

Winter damage to perennials. Protect overwintering crowns with a thick mulch layer.

12.A27 Overcrowded carrots

Insufficient sun or plants are spaced too closely. Plant according to recommended spacing and/or thin seedlings.

12.A25 Cauliflower "buttoning"

High spring temperatures. Can cause cauliflower plants to produce small "button" heads or heads that separate

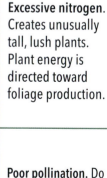
12.A28 Excessive nitrogen - tomato

Excessive nitrogen. Creates unusually tall, lush plants. Plant energy is directed toward foliage production.

12.A26 Failed tomato blossoms

Excessively high or low temperatures, and/or drought stress. Overhead watering and/or shading help on very hot days.

12.A29 Aborted pepper blossom

Poor pollination. Do not use insecticides during the bloom period, especially in the morning when bees are active.

continued on next page

continued from previous page

Key 12-A.   Abiotic Problems of Herbaceous Ornamentals and Vegetables

FAILURE TO FRUIT/FRUIT DROP

12.A30 Failed chile blossom

Excessively high or low temperatures. Extremes can kill pollen, inhibit fertilization, and cause small fruits to abort.

12.A31 Low fruit set - cucumber

Drought stress or excessive water. Mostly leaves with little fruit. Overhead watering and shading may help on very hot days.

12.A32 Competing vegetables

Insufficient sun or plants spaced too closely. Locate in a sunnier spot next season and space plants correctly.

12.A33 Excessive nitrogen - tobacco

Excessive nitrogen. Unusually leafy plants may fail to produce any fruit.

12.A34 Poorly pollinated squash

Insufficient pollination. Caused by a lack of insect pollinators (especially on plants with separate male and female flowers). Don't spray insecticides during bloom period, particularly in the morning when bees are active.

PLANT BOLTS/FLOWERS/GOES TO SEED

12.A35 Bolted spinach

Drought stress. Use mulches to maintain even soil moisture and help cool the plant.

12.A36 Cilantro gone to seed

Excessive light. Short-day plants (e.g., spinach, cilantro) "bolt" when days get longer. Plant "slow-bolt" varieties and/or plant earlier.

12.A37 Flowering broccoli

Cold or hot temperatures. Spring-planted biennials (e.g., broccoli, lettuce, parsley) may suffer stress. Use a row cover over early biennial crops. Select short-season, stress-tolerant cultivars. Plant broccoli and cauliflower in the fall for better results.

continued on next page

continued from previous page

Key 12-A.   Abiotic Problems of Herbaceous Ornamentals and Vegetables

EXTERIOR FRUIT DISCOLORATION/DEFORMITY

12.A38 Frozen tomatoes

Frost/freeze damage. Fruit softens and may turn black. In summer heat, symptoms can occur during fruit growth and harvest.

12.A39 "Catfacing" - tomato

Cold temperatures. Low temperatures before and during bloom cause "catfacing" in tomatoes. Harden off tomato plants and set them out after your local frost-free date.

12.A40 Split cabbage

12.A41 Concentric cracking - tomato

12.A42 Split - heirloom tomato

Cracking.

Excessive nitrogen: Avoid high-nitrogen fertilizers and maintain an even growth rate.

Excessive moisture: Can cause cabbage heads to split and radial/concentric cracking of tomatoes and other vegetables. Use mulches to maintain even soil moisture.

Varietal trait: Large-fruited tomatoes are more susceptible to cracking.

12.A43 Blossom end-rot - tomato

12.A44 Blossom end-rot - tomato

Blossom-end rot. Dark, leathery, sunken areas on blossom-end of peppers, tomatoes, and squash caused by environmental stress and lack of calcium in cell walls. Keep plants well-watered and mulched. Check soil pH and amend accordingly. Mix 1/4 cup of gypsum or ground limestone into each planting hole in spring. Avoid high-nitrogen fertilizers.

12.A45 Sunscald - tomato

Sunscald. Yellow or pale, wrinkled, sunken areas on areas of fruit that are exposed to full sun. Occurs where plants become defoliated.

12.A46 Poor curcurbit pollination

Poor pollination. Results in puffiness of tomatoes and malformed cucurbit fruits. Exacerbated by very high or low temperatures, insufficient light, and lack of pollinators.

continued on next page

continued from previous page

Key 12-A.   Abiotic Problems of Herbaceous Ornamentals and Vegetables

EXTERIOR FRUIT DISCOLORATION/DEFORMITY

12.A47 Green shoulder - tomato

Green shoulder on tomato. Varietal problem that occurs on large-fruited varieties in dense plantings.

12.A50 Malformed carrots

Distorted root crops. Caused by clayey soil, inconsistent moisture, and other stressors

12.A48 Green shoulder - carrot

Green shoulder on carrot, potato, and onion. Caused by sun exposure (chlorophyll production). Keep soil hilled over edible plant parts.

12.A51 Sunscald- pepper

Sunscaled of fruits. Occurs when fruits are unprotected by foliage due to poor plant growth or foliar disease.

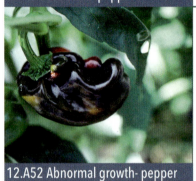
12.A52 Abnormal growth- pepper

Abnormal growth. Common for some fruits to have abnormal shapes due to genetic and envrionmental factors, including poor pollination.

12.A49 Potato (top) and turnip

Misshapen tubers and roots. Alternating wet/dry conditions can causes knobbiness, cracking, and cavities in potatoes and turnips. Use mulches to maintain even soil moisture and add organic matter to loosen clayey soils.

INTERIOR FRUIT DISCOLORATION/DEFORMITY

12.A53 Hollow heart - celery

Boron deficiency. Causes hollow heart in celery and cabbage. Lime soil to maintain proper pH. For sandy soils low in boron, incorporate 6-7 tablespoons of borax annually per 1,000 sq. ft.

12.A54 Graywall - tomato

Potassium deficiency. Tomatoes ripen unevenly inside and out. As fruit matures, the yellow areas may turn gray ("graywall").

continued on next page

continued from previous page

Key 12-A.   Abiotic Problems of Herbaceous Ornamentals and Vegetables

INTERIOR FRUIT DISCOLORATION/QUALITY PROBLEMS

12.A55 Seeds sprouting in tomato

Seeds germinating inside fruit. Results from a breakdown or absence of germination inhibitors in fleshy fruits. May also occur in late-season fruit.

12.A59 Watery tomatoes

Watery produce. Cold weather and low sunlight can cause this. October-harvested tomatoes and muskmelons are often poorly flavored.

12.A56 Tomatoes won't ripen

Failure to ripen. A late-season problem caused by cold temperatures, insufficient ripening time, low sunlight, crowded plants, and/or a varietal characteristic.

12.A60 Overly-hot poblano pepper

Excessive pungency. Hot, dry weather makes radishes spicy and cucumbers bitter, and increases chile-pepper heat. Maintain adequate irrigation.

12.A57 Unevenly ripe tomato

Uneven ripening. See "Failure to ripen" causes (12.A56). Uneven ripening is generally more severe on large-fruited tomato varieties.

12.A61 Drought-stressed cabbage

Bitter-tasting vegetable crops. Caused by heat stress, drought stress, or the plant being over-mature.

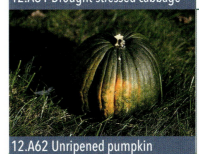
12.A62 Unripened pumpkin

Harvesting too early. Harvest pumpkins and winter squash when fully colored with a rind that a fingernail can't dent

12.A58 Overmature lettuce

Bitter or tough edible plant parts. Can be caused by hot, dry weather or over-maturity. Brassicas and leafy greens need a continuous source of water and nutrients for optimum growth and succulence. Plant and harvest at appropriate times.

12.A63 Tomato bred for shelf life

Little or no flavor. Some produce tastes better (or worse) due to its genetics. Many hybrids have reduced flavor and fragrance compounds.

Key 12-B. Abiotic Problems of Woody Ornamentals, Small Fruit Plants, and Fruit Trees

POOR GROWTH/FAILURE TO ESTABLISH

12.B1   Palm in wrong climate

Species or variety not adapted to the area. See **Chapter 16, Woody Plants,** for more information.

12.B2   Root-bound cypress

Poor plant stock. Plant is pot-bound, weak, or has dead roots. Inspect plants closely prior to purchase and planting.

Lack of proper care or maintenance. Over/under-watering or "volcano" mulching. Keep plants evenly watered during establishment.

12.B3   "Volcano" mulching

12.B4   Tree watering bags

Poor site conditions. Heavy clay or poorly-drained soil; low fertility; lack of soil moisture at planting, especially fall-planted evergreens. Modify the soil. Locate plantings for proper light, and regularly irrigate dry sites.

12.B5 Dogwood planted too deep

Poor planting. Planting too deep causes issues for many woody landscape plants. The top of the root ball should be about an inch above grade. Cut or spread circular root growth to encourage root establishment. Poor soil preparation or excessive mulch also impede establishment.

MATURE TREE DECLINES

12.B6   Apple tree dying of old age

Natural or premature senescence. All plants have an expected life span (urban conditions frequently shorten life expectancy).

Compacted soil. Ask contractors to lay plywood sheets to avoid compaction. Don't allow heavy equipment near root zone.

12.B7   Compacted tree roots

12.B8   Severed tree roots

Severed or damaged roots. Caused by heavy equipment or poor soil drainage, sometimes followed by drought.

12.B9   White pine decline

White pine decline. Needle browning, weak foliage, and bark-wrinkling. Associated with compacted or heavy clay soils and high soil pH.

continued on next page

continued from previous page

Key 12-B. Abiotic Problems of Woody Ornamentals, Small Fruit Plants, and Fruit Trees

SUDDEN DEATH

12.B10 Root rot - hibiscus

Root rot. Plant in well-drained soil; purchase disease-free and/or resistant varieties.

12.B11 Compacted soil

Compacted soil (from construction equipment). Ask contractor to lay down plywood sheets to avoid compaction.

12.B12 Trees killed by drought

Severe drought damage. Keep plants well-watered during the first two years of establishment and during severe drought. Failure to do so risks loss of the plant. Sometimes the plant will go dormant and appear dead, but revive the next season.

LEAF/NEEDLE YELLOWING/DISCOLORATION

12.B13 Iron-deficient strawberry

Iron, magnesium, or manganese deficiency. Occurs in high-pH soils with acid-loving plants/conifers. New growth is slow; foliage may be small and sparse, with premature leaf drop. Do a soil test and adjust pH.

12.B14 Nitrogen-deficient grape

Nitrogen deficiency. Older leaves or needles are uniformly yellow, or margins turn odd colors. Fertilize with an appropriate nitrogen source to restore proper color.

12.B15 Over-watered arborvitae

Excessive water: leaves uniformly yellow and drop. Modify soil for better drainage (especially yews).

12.B16 Rose - insufficient sun

Insufficient light. Plant grows long, spindly shoots and displays pale green or yellowing leaves. If possible, move to a sunnier location.

12.B17 Normal yellowing/drop

Fall coloration. On pines and other evergreens, inner needles turn yellow and drop. This is a natural occurrence.

continued on next page

continued from previous page

Key 12-B. Abiotic Problems of Woody Ornamentals, Small Fruit Plants, and Fruit Trees

LEAF/NEEDLE BROWNING

12.B18 Acid rain in pine forest

Pollution. Foliage may be flecked, thin, and/or stunted with premature needle or leaf drop. Effects are most severe on conifers; damage may appear as brown, dead areas or chlorotic bands.

12.B19 Salt damage - boxwood

Fertilizer or salt damage. Tips of conifer needles brown first. Boxwoods are particularly sensitive to salt. Damage is often observed along streets and sidewalks. Salt damage to deciduous trees may appear when new growth resumes.

12.B20 Winter burn - azalea

Winter burn (evergreens). Browning occurs on the windward side. Install windbreaks and water during dry periods in fall.

12.B21 Drought-damaged cherry

Drought stress. First observed on newer growth. Keep trees well-watered during dry spells, in late fall, and over the winter.

12.B22 Natural gas exposure

Natural gas leak. Newer leaves are affected first. Foliage turns brown and crispy. Roots appear black.

12.B23 Herbicide injury

Herbicide damage. Symptoms may be seen on adjacent plants and on different species.

12.B24 Urine damage - boxwood

Cat or dog urine. Leaves and needles eventually brown. Injury appears low on the plant/tree. Irrigate to reduce salt levels and relieve leaf burn.

LEAF SPOTS/BLOTCHES

12.B25 Pesticide burn - bean

Burning from herbicide, salt, pesticide, or fertilizer. Light-colored spots appear, either in a random or organized pattern.

12.B26 Sunburn - avocado plant

Sunburn. Yellow, brown, or white areas appear on upper sides of leaves as the result of excessive sunlight or heat, or insufficient water.

continued on next page

continued from previous page

Key 12-B.   Abiotic Problems of Woody Ornamentals, Small Fruit Plants, and Fruit Trees

PREMATURE FALL COLOR/LEAF DROP

12.B27 Leaf scorch

Drought/heat stress, poor site conditions, winter damage to crowns and roots. Modify site conditions or adjust cultural practices to reduce stress.

12.B28 Tree growing in poor soil

Root dieback. May occur due to thin or rocky soil, road salt, poor planting techniques, or even drought from the preceding season.

WILTING FOLIAGE

12.B29 Cold injury - magnolia

Root damage caused by freeze, drought, or mechanical injury. Lay down a thick organic mulch in late fall. Keep mulch away from stems and trunks.

12.B30 Wilting Japanese stewartia

Naturally dry site or insufficient watering. Affects newly transplanted trees and shrubs. Keep young plants well-watered until established.

12.B31 Drought stress

Drought stress. First occurs on newer growth. Foliage droops or drops prematurely. May lead to twig and limb dieback. Provide water in summer and fall.

12.B32 Walnut wilt - spruce

Walnut wilt. Affects many woody plants in the vicinity of walnut trees, especially rhododendrons and azaleas. Walnut (*Juglans* spp.) roots contain a chemical (juglone) that may suppress the roots and stunt the growth of other plants that come in contact with the walnut roots.

12.B33 Dry soil

Heavy clay soils. Dense, clayey soils impede root growth and limit water and nutrient uptake. Modify the site conditions and amend the soil.

continued on next page

continued from previous page

Key 12-B.   Abiotic Problems of Woody Ornamentals, Small Fruit Plants, and Fruit Trees

LEAF MARGINS TURN BROWN

12.B34 Pesticide burn - rose

Pesticide burn. Leaf margins are affected first. Leaves are most susceptible when temperatures exceed 85°F and/or tree is otherwise stressed. Spruce, maple, and arborvitae are more sensitive to oil sprays. Copper and sulfur fungicides may cause leaf burn on certain fruit trees and small fruit plants. Concentrates are more likely to burn than wettable powders.

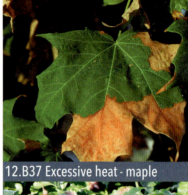
12.B37 Excessive heat - maple

Drought stress/very high temperatures. Scorch appears first near branch tips. Keep susceptible plants watered and use a shade cloth if possible during hot spells.

12.B35 Fertilizer burn - blueberry

Fertilizer burn and salt spray. Random, irregular spots or entire leaf burns appear. Marginal leaf burn is from roots contacting excessive salts.

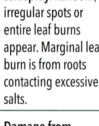
12.B38 Sunburned leaf margins

Sunburn. Yellow, brown, or white areas develop on upper sides of leaves. Caused by excessive sunlight and heat, and insufficient water.

12.B36 Herbicide injury

Damage from lawn herbicides. Symptoms from fall-applied herbicides may not appear until spring. Includes glyphosate.

12.B39 Salt-damaged holly

Chloride toxicity: Leaves yellow and brown at the tips. Typically from swimming pool drainage and de-icing salts. Divert swimming pool water and ice melt runoff away from root zones. Irrigate to reduce salt levels.

INJURED/DEAD LIMBS/TWIGS

12.B40 Wind damage

Ice, wind, or hail damage. Cankers may develop. Small twigs may be bitten off by squirrels for nest-building. Prune out affected parts.

12.B41 Tree broken off at union

Failure of graft union. Incompatible scion wood and rootstock. Determine compatibility prior to planting. There is no remedy.

continued on next page

continued from previous page

Key 12-B.   Abiotic Problems of Woody Ornamentals, Small Fruit Plants, and Fruit Trees

TWIG/BRANCH DIEBACK

12.B42 Mechanical injury

Root damage, freeze, drought, or mechanical injury. Prune out all affected areas and keep plants well-watered. Lay down thick organic mulch in late fall, keeping it away from stems and trunks. Mulch to remove the need for trimming with lawn equipment.

12.B43 Salt runoff damage

Herbicide and de-icing salt damage. Divert ice-melt runoff away from root zones and do not use herbicides in the vicinity of valued plants. Spray only on windless days.

12.B44 Poor drainage

Wet, poorly drained soil. Select suitable, well-drained planting sites.

TREE BARK/TRUNK PROBLEMS

12.B45 Vertical frost crack

Vertical bark cracking. Frost/freeze cracks or sunscald are due to freezing/thawing of water in tree. Wrap vulnerable trunks or paint with interior latex paint.

12.B46 Tree stake-strap injury

Bark is scarred or gouged. Caused by lawn/construction equipment. Mulch to avoid trimming. Remove tree collars after 1 year.

12.B47 Gummosis - plum

Bark oozes sap. Likely gummosis that occurs on peach, cherry, and plum. Caused by insect pests, diseases, or environmental stresses.

12.B48 Tree suckers

Water sprouts or suckers appear. Caused by stress or removal of large limbs. Promptly pull or cut all water sprouts at point of attachment.

12.B49 Rootstock suckers

Bulging graft union. Normal on grafted trees. Remove all suckers below the graft union or suckers may outgrow the desired scion stock.

12.B50 Root girdling

Girdling roots. Occurs in container-grown plants or trees in clayey soil. Can often be removed with a chisel. Loosen pot-bound roots before planting.

continued on next page

continued from previous page

Key 12-B.   Abiotic Problems of Woody Ornamentals, Small Fruit Plants, and Fruit Trees

NEWLY PLANTED TREES/SHRUBS FAIL TO BLOOM

12.B51 Immature apple

Plants have not matured sufficiently to reproduce. Check references and nurseries to determine average age for blooming.

12.B52 Non-blooming hydrangea

Environmental stress. Poor site conditions or excessive shading can cause failure-to-bloom. Consider transplanting to better location.

ESTABLISHED TREES/SHRUBS FAIL TO BLOOM

12.B53 All leaves, little fruit

Trees growing too much vegetation, causing delayed or sparse fruiting. "All leaves and no fruit" can be remedied by minimizing dormant pruning and ceasing the application of high-nitrogen fertilizer. Spread the scaffold branches at wider angles to induce more fruit-bud formation.

12.B54 Environmental stress

Stress. Drought, wet soil, insect and disease damage, low-light conditions. Provide proper care and maintenance.

12.B55 Lilac pruned in fall

Fall pruning. This can remove flower buds. Prune spring-flowering trees and shrubs immediately after bloom period (e.g., dogwood, azalea, forsythia).

DAMAGED BUDS/BLOOMS

12.B56 Blooms damaged by frost

Winter-kill of buds, spring frost damage to buds and flowers, or low-temperature damage. Trees may leaf out without flowering (leaf buds are hardier than flower buds). Avoid planting in low areas or frost pockets.

12.B57 Sulfur-oil overspray-grape

Misuse of pesticides. Do not overspray, which can damage buds and blooms. Do not spray when the temperature is below 40°F. Do not spray dormant oil on open blooms. Always follow label directions.

continued on next page

continued from previous page

Key 12-B. Abiotic Problems of Woody Ornamentals, Small Fruit Plants, and Fruit Trees

BLOSSOM DROP

12.B58 Blooms blown off peach — **Stressful conditions.** Drought, wind, and low temperatures can cause blossom-drop; prevention is difficult.

12.B59 Blossom drop - no bees — **No pollenizer or low bee activity.** Most apple, pear, and nut trees require another variety to be planted nearby. Cool, wet weather deters bees.

12.B60 Spraying during bloom — **Spraying insecticides during bloom.** Broad-spectrum insecticides kill pollinators.

12.B61 Too much nitrogen — **Over-use of nitrogen fertilizers prior to bloom period.** Reduce applications of high-nitrogen fertilizers.

FAILURE TO FRUIT

12.B62 Damaged blooms — **Spraying dormant oil or insecticides on open blooms.** Doing so can kill blooms/pollinators and reduce fruiting.

12.B63 Too much nitrogen — **Over-use of nitrogen prior to bloom period.** Reduce applications of high-nitrogen fertilizers.

12.B64 Unthinned crop — **Biennial bearing.** Failure to thin fruits. Some cultivars are more prone to biennial bearing. See **Chapter 17** for pruning help.

12.B65 Over-pruning - apple — **Severe pruning.** This will reduce the number of blooms. Do not prune out fruit-bearing wood during the dormant season.

12.B66 Male holly plant — **Male plant.** Both male and female plants are required for pollination. Includes hollies, gingko, and skimmia.

12.B67 Low temps - scarce fruit — **Low-temperature damage.** Leaves may develop with few or no blooms. Expect a smaller harvest.

12.B68 Blooms killed by frost — **Winter-kill of buds or frost damage.** Avoid planting in low areas.

12.B69 Pollenizers are required — **No pollenizer or low bee activity.** Most apple, pear, and nut trees need another variety to fruit. Cool, wet weather deters bees.

continued on next page

continued from previous page

Key 12-B. Abiotic Problems of Woody Ornamentals, Small Fruit Plants, and Fruit Trees

UNDERSIZED FRUIT

12.B70 Failure to thin fruit

Failure to thin or prune properly. Thin to reduce number of fruits or blossoms, which directs the tree's energy to produce larger fruits.

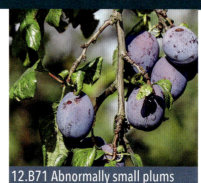
12.B71 Abnormally small plums

Low soil fertility or drought. Follow soil test recommendations and irrigate during critical periods, such as at fruit-set and during growth.

DEFORMED FRUIT

12.B72 Catfacing - pear

"Catfacing." Caused by cold temperatures at pollination time or insect damage when fruit is small. Unsightly but edible.

12.B73 Hail damage - apple

Hail damage. Scars/dents can be observed on the fruit but it is not always punctured. Damage is purely cosmetic and fruit is edible.

CRACKED/SPLIT FRUIT

12.B74 Split peach

Excessive moisture during ripening or overripened fruit. Pick ripened fruit promptly and use mulch to maintain even soil moisture.

12.B75 Nutrient-deficient cherry

Nutrient deficiency. Lack of calcium or boron can weaken fruit skin.

FRUIT EXUDES SAP

12.B76 Peach oozing sap

Fruit grows too quickly. Mainly occurs on peaches. Sap oozes from splits. Damage is cosmetic and the fruit is edible. Use mulches to maintain even soil moisture.

12.B77 Oozing - pruner nick

Mechanical injury. Garden tools can nick the fruit and cause oozing. Take extra care with sharp tools around ripe fruit.

continued on next page

continued from previous page

Key 12-B.   Abiotic Problems of Woody Ornamentals, Small Fruit Plants, and Fruit Trees

EXTERNALLY-DAMAGED FRUIT

12.B78 Sunscald - raspberry

Sunscald. Can cause white, tan, or brown sunken areas on exposed surfaces. May alter fruit flavor. Remove and discard affected fruit.

12.B80 Roughly-handled peaches

Mechanical injury. Many fruits bruise easily as the result of contact with branches, pickers, or rough handling.

12.B81 Russeting - apple

Pesticide burn. Captan®, sulfur, and horticultural oil sprays may produce russeting on sensitive varieties.

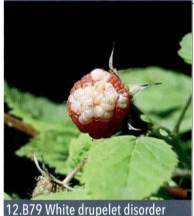
12.B79 White drupelet disorder

High daytime temperatures. Can cause individual bramble fruit drupelets to turn white (i.e., white drupelet disorder). Plant red raspberries where they will receive late-afternoon shade.

12.B82 Hail damage - pear

Hail. Can cause scarring, indentations, and/or small, rough areas on fruit skin. Fruit remains edible.

INTERNALLY-DAMAGED FRUIT

12.B83 Internal browning-drought

Environmental stress. Drought, waterlogging, and high and low temperatures during ripening, harvesting, and handling can create browning.

12.B85 Pear picked too late

Over-mature fruit. Pick ripened fruit promptly. To avoid internal discoloration of pears, pick when green and allow to ripen off the tree.

12.B84 Calcium-deficient apple

Calcium, boron, or magnesium deficiency. Associated with a wide range of fruit disorders. More likely on sandy soils. Test for these micronutrients and amend accordingly.

12.B86 Freeze damage - plum

Freeze damage. Fresh-eating quality will be diminished but fruit can still be used in purées and preserves.

UME © 2025. All rights reserved.   12: Plant Diagnostics   271

Key 12-C. Seedling and Transplant Problems

POOR GERMINATION

12.C1 Frost on soil

Cold soil. Seeds (especially corn and bean) rot in cold, wet soil. Determine the germination requirements of the crop and plant when soil is warm enough. Pre-sprout seed if appropriate.

12.C2 Seedlings in clayey soil

Clayey soil. Seedlings can't easily penetrate the crusted surface. Amend the furrow and cover seeds lightly with compost. Create raised beds and pre-sprout seeds.

12.C3 Dry soil stalls germination

Dry soil. Keep seed beds moist but not soggy. Add compost to help retain moisture if soil is very sandy.

12.C4 Seeds planted too deep

Seeds are planted too deeply. Rule of thumb for seeding depth: 2 to 3 times the seed diameter.

12.C5 Seeds washed out by rain

Seeds displaced or washed away by heavy rain. Re-plant seeds on more level ground.

12.C6 Old seeds

Seeds are not viable. Buy seed packed for the current year. Pre-test germination of questionable seeds.

12.C7 Late blight on tomato

Fungal disease. "Damping off" water molds include pythium, rhizoctonia, and phytophthora. Use a well-drained, sterile growing medium and allow the surface to dry between waterings.

12.C8 Pre-sprouted peas

Species characteristic. Some seeds benefit from pre-sprouting (e.g., spinach, okra, parsley). Soak slow-germinating seeds overnight or scratch with sandpaper to soften/degrade the seedcoat.

12.C9 Wireworm, a seed-eater

Insect feeding. Uncover seeds and check for insect injury. Hand-pick culprits and re-seed if needed.

12.C10 Bird eating seed

Wildlife feeding. Birds and other animals may uncover and eat seeds. Protect seeds with floating row cover or board.

continued on next page

continued from previous page

Key 12-C.   Seedling and Transplant Problems

LEAF DAMAGE/DISCOLORATION

12.C11 Flea beetle leaf damage

Small holes in leaves. Flea beetles: Tiny, dark, shiny insects jump when disturbed and produce a shotgun feeding pattern. Use a row cover.

12.C12 Cutworm leaf damage

Cutworms: Young larvae chew irregular holes in leaves. Install plant collars to deter them.

12.C13 Slug leaf damage

Slugs: Can do serious damage. Install plant collars. Iron-phosphate slug baits are safe to use in a vegetable garden.

12.C14 Frostbitten leaf tips

White-tipped leaves. Caused by frost damage. Plants were seeded or set out too early, with insufficient hardening-off time.

12.C15 Cold damage - transplant

White-tan spots on leaves. Leaves eventually turn brown and papery. Caused by sunburn, cold, and/or wind damage. Harden off seedlings before planting.

12.C16 Wildlife damage

Leaves/stems chewed. Deer, rabbits, groundhogs, birds, earwigs, and slugs can all cause this damage. Rabbits make a clean cut vs. a deer's ragged cut. Use a deer/rabbit repellent or plant collars.

12.C17 Spider mite yellowing

Leaf yellowing. Spider mites: Cause fine stippling. Use insecticidal soap, pyrethrum spray, or predatory mites.

12.C18 Whitefly adults and nymphs

Whiteflies: They will scatter when a plant is disturbed. Control with insecticidal soap or pyrethrum-based insecticide.

12.C19 Nitrogen deficiency

Pale green leaves. Lack of nitrogen or sunlight. Cool soils reduce nutrient uptake. Apply a liquid fertilizer.

12.C20 Phosphorus deficiency

Purple leaves. Cold damage or phosphorous deficiency. Low soil temps prevent phosphorous uptake by roots. Apply a liquid fertilizer.

continued on next page

continued from previous page

Key 12-C. Seedling and Transplant Problems

STUNTED GROWTH/SEEDLING FAILURE

Stunted growth. Caused by cold soil and cool air temperatures. Avoid planting too early. Try warming the soil with black plastic. Harden off plants before transplanting. Fertilize with a liquid fertilizer.

12.C21 Stunted growth

Plants cut at the soil line. Cutworms are night-feeding caterpillars that eat through stems at ground level. Place paper collars around individual plants. Early spring tilling may help.

12.C22 Cutworm damage

Seedlings won't grow. Slugs and snails are night feeders that often leave distinctive slime trails. Lay down abrasive barriers (e.g., diatomaceous earth, coarse sand, oyster or crab shells).

12.C23 Slug damage

Newly-emerged tender seedlings are eaten. Rabbits, squirrels, chipmunks, and/or cutworms are present. Use a floating row cover, fencing, or hot pepper flakes to deter them.

12.C24 Rabbit damage - pine

Desiccation. Seedlings are weak. Leaves turn dry and pale in cool wind due to too much or too little moisture. Plant in well-drained soil.

12.C25 Wind desiccation

Weak stems in young plants. Possibly seed corn/vegetable maggots, small white grubs that feed on young vegetable plants and germinating seeds. May introduce rot. Do not plant too early or deeply. Use a row cover or collars. Add organic matter in fall.

12.C26 Seed corn maggot in onion

Tunneling in roots and stems of corn, bean, and curcubit seedlings. Southern corn rootworm (cucumber beetle larvae) are 2-in. long, with a whitish body and brown head. Plant extra and use a row cover.

12.C27 Southern corn rootworm

Seedlings fall over and die. Damping-off disease causes tap roots and lower stems to shrivel and darken. Use a sterile, well-drained medium and allow surface to dry before watering. Avoid planting in poorly-drained soils.

12.C28 Damping-off disease

274 Maryland Master Gardener Handbook   UME © 2025. All rights reserved.

Key 12-D. Pests and Diseases of Shade Trees

LEAVES EATEN/CHEWED

12.D1 Spongy moth larva (top)/adult

Spongy moth. An early- to mid-season caterpillar. Control on oaks. Other early-season caterpillars include Eastern tent caterpillar and cankerworms ("inchworms"). Treat with *Bacillus thuringiensis* (Bt) or hand-pick when small. May need a residual insecticide if damage is severe.

12.D2 Mid-/late-season caterpillars

Oakworm, fall webworm, and mimosa webworm. No control is fnecessary on these mid- to late-season caterpillars except on young trees or if heavy defoliation is occurring.

12.D3 Japanese beetle feeding

Leaf-feeding beetles. These include Japanese beetles, chafers, locust leafminers, and elm-leaf beetles. May need a residual insecticide if damage is severe.

12.D4 Sawflies - dogwood

12.D5 Redheaded pine sawfly

Sawflies. Affect dusky birch, ash, and dogwood trees; and deciduous plants. Redheaded pine sawfly attacks conifers. Avoid poorly-drained soils. Hand-picking caterpillars and sawflies can adequately control small populations on young trees. May need a residual insecticide if damage is severe.

WEBBED/TENTED FOLIAGE

12.D6 Tent caterpillars

Tent caterpillars, webworms, leafrollers, and leaf tiers. Insects live in webbed leaves or silken tents and are an important food source for baby birds. If many are present, use Bt when caterpillars are small. Knock down or prune webs from terminal branches and destroy/burn.

12.D7 Bagworms - pine

Bagworms. Caterpillars feed on foliage and build protective silk bags covered with host-plant material. Spray with Bt when bags are small (mid-June to mid-July). Hand-pick and destroy bags during fall and winter.

continued on next page

continued from previous page

Key 12-D.   Pests and Diseases of Shade Trees

LEAF DISTORTION/STIPPLING

12.D8 Leafhopper stippling - apple

Leaf surface / Leaf underside

12.D9 Spider mite stippling

Leafhoppers. Pale green to white wedge-shaped insects cause curling and stunting of terminal leaves, especially on maples. Coarse white stippling appears between veins. Whitish cast skins are usually present on underside.

Spider mites. Very tiny "period-sized" insects appear on leaf undersides. Leaves yellow, then turn brown and drop prematurely. Webbing may be seen. Usually impractical to spray large trees, but if control is needed, use insecticidal soap or horticultural oil to minimize adverse effects on natural enemies. Direct the spray toward the leaf underside. Releasing predatory mites to control spider mites is another option on small trees.

12.D10 Aphid leaf-cupping

12.D11 Spotted lanternfly

12.D12 Lacebug larva stippling

Aphids. Large populations can cause leaf twisting and curling. Control is usually unnecessary, but for severe infestations, treat as for spider mites (see 12.D9).

Plant bugs/ planthoppers. Green or brown, about 1/4-in. long. They cause leaf distortion, especially on sycamore and honeylocust. No control needed. Spotted lanternfly (SLF) is planthopper that causes sooty mold/honeydew/ on plants and the ground. SLFs may contribute to decline but not death. Scrape off overwintered eggs; smash adults and nymphs.

Lacebugs. Insects are 1/8- to 1/4-in. long, with lacy wings. They feed on the lower leaf surface, leaving black fecal spots. Stippling on upper leaf surface is white. Especially affect azaleas, sycamore, hawthorn, and serviceberry. Spray leaf undersides with insecticidal soap.

continued on next page

276   Maryland Master Gardener Handbook   UME © 2025. All rights reserved.

continued from previous page

Key 12-D.   Pests and Diseases of Shade Trees

GROWTHS/COATINGS ON LEAVES

12.D13 Spittlebug - oak

Spittlebugs. Small sucking insects covered with spittle produce a whitish frothy material on foliage. They feed on terminal twigs of host plants. Control is generally not warranted.

12.D14 Galls

Galls. Growths on leaves may be raised nodules; some may be fuzzy. Produced by eriophyiid mites (generally not visible to the naked eye), gall midges, and gall wasps. Galls may be various colors and shapes. Control is generally not needed. Dormant-season oil sprays may help reduce overwintering mite populations.

12.D15 Rust - oak leaf

Rust diseases. Upper leaf surfaces turn yellow or brown and infected leaves may drop prematurely. Rusty-colored spores are usually on lower leaf surfaces. Replace with resistant varieties.

12.D16 White pine aphids

Aphids. Small, soft-bodied insects chew young shoots, leaves, and bark (giant bark aphids), creating a sticky honeydew upon which black fungi (sooty mold) grow.

Brown soft scale

Calico soft scale

12.D17 Soft scales

Soft scales. Appear as raised bumps on twigs and branches. Healthy plants can tolerate moderate populations of scales. If high populations are present, spray when plants are dormant with a horticultural oil. Sooty mold may be washed off to increase photosynthesis.

12.D18 Powdery mildew - dogwood

Powdery mildew. A white leaf coating that may cause distortion. Fungicides may be warranted on crabapple and dogwood. Rake up leaves in the fall. Check horticultural oil label for powdery mildew control.

continued on next page

continued from previous page

Key 12-D. Pests and Diseases of Shade Trees

LEAF YELLOWING/BROWNING/WILTING

Armored scales. Hard scales form encrustations on branches; can be scraped off. Prune out branches with severe symptoms.

12.D19 Oystershell scale

Soft scales. Appear as raised bumps on twigs and branches. Can be scraped off. Honeydew and sooty mold may be present. Prune out branches with severe symptoms.

12.D20 White peach scale

Spider mites. Very tiny insects appear on leaf undersides. Leaves yellow, then brown and drop prematurely. Usually impractical to spray large trees. If control is needed, use insecticidal soap or horticultural oils to minimize adverse effects on natural predators, or consider releasing predatory mites.

12.D21 Boxwood mites

Root/wood rots. Many fungi cause wood decay and form fruiting bodies (like mushrooms) on branches/trunk. Infected trees should be removed. Promptly remove single infected branches.

12.D22 Armillaria wood rot - oak

Verticillium wilt. Scrape branches for signs of vascular browning that indicates VW. No sprays are effective. Prune out wilted/dead branches and irrigate during dry spells. Avoid root damage from salt or cultivation. Select resistant varieties. Trunk injections may work for old trees.

12.D23 Verticillium wilt

Cankers. Caused by various fungi. Common genera include cytospora, botryosphaeria, nectria, and phytophthora. Dark, elongated lesions with roughened bark. No chemical control is available. Water during drought and prune out affected branches if practical.

12.D24 Botryosphaeria canker

Borers. Insects make holes and tunnels in branches. Prevent infestations by keeping trees healthy.

12.D25 Peach tree borer

continued on next page

continued from previous page

Key 12-D.   Pests and Diseases of Shade Trees

LEAF SPOTS/DISCOLORATION

Locust leafminer

Serpentine leafminer

Birch leafminer

Elm leafminer sawfly

12.D26 Various leafminers

Serpentine trails or blotches in leaves. Various leafminers (grubs, maggots, small caterpillars, or sawflies) feed between the upper and lower leaf surfaces. Control is difficult on large trees. Identify the tree to identify the pest. Control if damage is severe. 'Heritage' birch is resistant to birch leafminer. Locust leafminer is usually only a problem on black locust and does not require control.

Fire blight - crabapple

Twig blight - peach

Shothole disease - cherry

12.D27 Leaf blights

Leaf blights (anthracnose). Leaf spots/blotches cover the leaf surface. Defoliation can occur if severe. Twigs and branches may also be killed. Registered fungicides may be needed for young trees or severe cases. Prune dead twigs and branches in dry weather and remove all leaves in the fall. Control is impractical on large trees; replace with resistant varieties.

Maple
Sycamore
Oak
12.D28 Shade-tree anthracnose

Leaf-spot diseases Sometimes called shade-tree anthracnose. Damage is isolated. Entire leaves may be blighted during wet weather and cause severe defoliation (especially on sycamore, oak, dogwood, and maple). Treat as for leaf blights (see 12.D27).

12.D29 Bacterial leaf scorch

Bacterial leaf scorch. Affects interior and bottom leaves first. Scorched areas may have a yellow border. Immediately prune out infected branches well below the last scorched leaf. Remove trees with extensive dieback.

12.D30 Eyespot gall - maple

Eyespot gall (maple). Yellow, slightly raised area ringed in red appears on upper leaf surface. Control is not necessary.

12.D31 Tulip tree gall

Tulip tree spot gall. A minor poplar pest gall with purplish spots, 1/8-in. diameter. Control is not necessary.

continued on next page

continued from previous page

Key 12-D. Pests and Diseases of Shade Trees

TWIG/BRANCH PROBLEMS

12.D32 Botryosphaeria - E. redbud

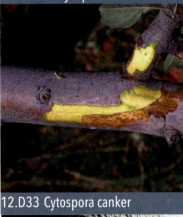
12.D33 Cytospora canker

Twig/branch dieback. Botryosphaeria rots: Caused by various fungi, especially when the tree is otherwise weakened. Dark, elongated lesions with roughened bark. No chemical control is available. Water during drought and prune out affected branches if practical. Keep lawn equipment from injuring bark.

Cankers: Caused by various fungi. Common genera include cytospora, botryosphaeria, nectria, and phytophthora. Cause long, dark lesions with roughened bark (excessive resin flow on conifers). No chemical control is available. Maintain adequate irrigation during drought. Prune out affected branches where practical. Do not compost diseased prunings. Keep lawn equipment from injuring bark.

12.D34 Phytophthora basal canker

12.D35 Armored scale dieback

12.D36 Insect borer tunnels

12.D37 Cicada bark damage

12.D38 Twig girdler

12.D39 Twig chewed by squirrel

Armored scales: Appear as encrustations on branches, especially oak. Prune out affected branches. Apply dormant oil before bud break.

Borers: Various borers create holes and tunnels in branches. Deter them by keeping trees healthy.

Cicadas: Create deep slits in bark during egg-laying activity which weakens twigs. In most years, damage from cicadas is minor and no control is necessary.

Small twigs on the ground.
Twig girdler: Fallen twigs have ends that seems to be evenly filed off. Dispose of fallen twigs with chewed ends in the fall.

Squirrels: Chew the twigs off for nest-building material. Twigs are chewed roughly on an angle.

continued on next page

continued from previous page

Key 12-D. Pests and Diseases of Shade Trees

TWIG/BRANCH PROBLEMS

12.D40 Fire blight - crabapple

Rapid dieback of branches, shoots, or blooms. Caused by fire blight, a bacterial disease that infects fruit trees more than shade trees. Fruit will blacken/brown. Plant looks scorched. Prune out infected branches a foot below damage. Remove suckers. Reduce nitrogen fertilization. For severe infections, apply copper spray.

12.D41 White-oak borer frass

Frass in branch crotches, on bark, or at base of tree. White larvae make shallow tunnels under bark and push frass (excrement) out through holes. Keep mulch away from trunk.

12.D42 Bracket fungi

Fungal growths or mushrooms. Indicates extensive interior decay/root rot. Have large trees inspected by a certified arborist to determine severity and remove the tree if necessary.

12.D43 Gall wasp

Hard growths on twigs. Twig/stem galls are caused by gall wasps. May cause dieback. Prune out galls as they form, especially on pin and willow oak.

12.D44 Crape myrtle bark scale

Whitish-cottony bumps or fluff on twigs and branches. Soft-scale egg masses, like crape myrtle bark scale or woolly aphids. Healthy plants can tolerate moderate populations. If needed, spray when dormant with horticultural oil.

12.D45 Witches' broom

Proliferation of branches or dense bushy growth (witches' broom). Indicates eriophyiid mites; fungal, viral, or phytoplasma diseases; and/or mistletoe. Prune out affected areas.

12.D46 Antler rubbing on sapling

Deer feeding and antler rubbing. Deer netting and electric fences are effective. Repel deer by hanging bar soap, human hair, or blood meal in a mesh bag.

Key 12-E.   Pests and Diseases of Evergreen Trees

NEEDLE YELLOWING/SPOTS/DISCOLORATION

12.E1   Spruce spider mite damage

Spruce spider mites. Very tiny, "period-sized" insects cause tree yellowing from the bottom up, mostly in spring and fall. If needed, use insecticidal soap or horticultural oil.

12.E5   Soft scale - yew

Soft scale (spots). Look for white, brown, or gray scale and scrape off. Use insecticidal soap or horticultural oil if problem is severe.

12.E2   Spruce bud scale

Soft scale (yellowing). Raised bumps on twigs can be scraped off. May also see honeydew and sooty mold, which can be hosed off.

12.E6   Needle cast

Needle cast: Dark-brown to black spots cause early needle drop. Diseases include lophodermium, ploioderma, cyclaneusma, lophodermella; rhizosphaera, isthmiella, Swiss needle cast, and rhabdocline. Fungicide control (with a registered fungicide) may be warranted.

12.E3   Armored scale - magnolia

Armored scale. White scale-covers on needles, or yellow in heavy infestations. Apply horticultural oil at the dormant rate during the dormant season.

12.E7   Needle rust - spruce

Needle rust: Powdery orange-yellow spots. Avoid using lawn sprinklers and prune out/destroy witches' brooms.

12.E4   Spider-mite stippling

Needle stippling. Spider mites cause pinpoint yellow spots on conifer needles. Tap branches on white paper to confirm their presence. If control is needed, use insecticidal soap or horticultural oils to minimize adverse effects on natural predators, or consider releasing predatory mites.

12.E8   Leafminer trails

Serpentine trails or blotches in leaves on hollies and magnolias. The larvae of various leafminers feed between the upper and lower leaf surfaces. Pick off affected leaves.

continued on next page

continued from previous page

Key 12-E.   Pests and Diseases of Evergreen Trees

OTHER EVERGREEN NEEDLE PROBLEMS

12.E9 Spruce mite damage

Needle drop. Spruce mites: Control on small trees with insecticidal soap or horticultural oils and/or release predatory mites.

12.E10 Rhizosphaeria needle cast

Needle diseases: Examine fallen needles for needle cast diseases. A fungicide treatment may be warranted on young trees.

12.E11 Pine leaf aphids

Sooty mold/ honeydew. Aphids: Small green insects feed on needles. Use insecticidal soap or horticultural oil.

12.E12 Pine tortoise scale

Pine tortoise scale: Appear as raised bumps on twigs. Ants, honeydew, and sooty mold present near branch terminals. Control with dormant oil.

12.E13 Pine spittlebugs

Frothy mass. Pine spittlebugs are soft-bodied insects that feed under spittle masses. Present in May and June. Light infestations cause no damage; heavy infestations may kill Scotch pine. Spray with a residual insecticide in May.

12.E14 Sawflies

Needles chewed, eaten, or webbed. Sawflies: Resemble caterpillars, feed in groups. Hand-pick and destroy.

12.E15 Evergreen bagworm

Bagworms: Look for bags constructed of needles, attached to branches. Spray with Bt when bags are small, from mid-June to mid-July. Hand-pick and destroy bags during the fall and winter.

12.E16 Pine tube moth

Pine tube moth: Look for a bundle of needles webbed together into a tube. Control is rarely necessary. Hand-pick and destroy the tubes.

12.E17 Pine webworm

Pine webworm: Young caterpillars mine needles and later make nests of silk and frass around terminal twigs. Hand-pick and destroy.

12.E18 Hemlock woolly adelgid

White material on needles near bark. Pine bark adelgid and Hemlock woolly adelgid produce a fluffy white wax at base of needles in spring. No control necessary.

continued on next page

continued from previous page

Key 12-E. Pests and Diseases of Evergreen Trees

TWIG AND BRANCH PROBLEMS

12.E19 Pine wilt nematode

Wilting. Pine wilt nematodes cause sudden drying out; branches become brittle. No chemical control. Remove dead and dying trees. Avoid planting trees on dry sites that contribute to stress conditions.

12.E23 Sphaeropsis - pine

Branch dieback. Sphaeropsis tip blight: Lower branches die first. Water during drought. Use a registered fungicide on new growth in spring. Remove damaged trees.

12.E20 White pine decline

Poor growth. White pine decline: wrinkled bark on young branches, thin weak foliage. No chemical control. Remove dead and dying trees.

12.E24 Bark beetle holes

Bark beetles/borers: Look for holes. These are stress-related pests and insecticides are not effective. Remove dead/dying trees. Reduce stress on existing trees with adequate watering.

12.E21 Procera root rot

Procera root rot: Causes resin flow at soil line (primarily pines). Avoid planting too deeply or in poorly drained soils. Control insects that spread the disease.

12.E25 Cedar apple rust

Rust diseases: Cause swollen areas on trunk or branches, orange-yellow blister-like or gall-like areas on bark. Remove alternate hosts where practical. No chemical controls are available.

12.E22 Antler rubbing damage

Bark stripped from trunk or branch/shoots chewed. Caused by deer feeding/or antler rubbing. Worse during very cold, snowy winters. Deer netting and electric fences are effective. Repel deer by hanging small bars of soap, human hair, or blood meal in mesh bags.

12.E26 Canker dieback - cedar

Cankers: Common fungi include cytospora, seiridium, phomopsis, kabatina, sphaeropsis, cenangium, and botryosphaeria. Cankers cause dark, elongated lesions with roughened bark and excessive resin flow.

continued on next page

continued from previous page

Key 12-E. Pests and Diseases of Evergreen Trees

DEAD TERMINALS

12.E27 Pine tip moth

Pine shoot and tip moths. Tan to brown caterpillars bore into and kill terminal growth. Prune and destroy affected terminals.

12.E29 White pine weevil

White pine weevil. Adults (brown, 1/4-in., 2 white spots) and larvae (white, 3/8-in., brown heads) feed in terminal leader. In June, prune out and bag up affected terminals.

12.E28 Sphaeropsis tip blight

Sphaeropsis tip blight. Creates excessive pitch on pine terminals and pinpoint needle spots. Water during droughts. Spray a registered fungicide on new growth in spring. Remove severely damaged trees.

12.E30 Cenangium twig blight

Cenangium twig blight. Stressed pine needles redden and terminal buds die. Water during droughts. Prune affected areas during dry weather.

Key 12-F. Pests and Diseases of Evergreen Shrubs

LEAF/NEEDLE YELLOWING

12.F1 Spider mites

Spider mites. Examine lower leaf/needle surfaces for presence of spider mites. Use insecticidal soap or horticultural oils to minimize adverse effects on natural predators. Direct spray toward the lower leaf/needle surfaces.

12.F2 Scale damage - camellia

Armored scales. Encrustations on branches can be scraped off. **Soft scales.** Raised bumps on twigs and branches can be scraped off. Prune out branches with severe symptoms and spray with horticultural oil during dormancy.

continued on next page

continued from previous page

Key 12-F.   Pests and Diseases of Evergreen Shrubs

LEAF/NEEDLE YELLOWING (continued)

12.F3 Whiteflies

Whiteflies. Tiny white insects fly up when plant is disturbed. Naturally controlled by parasites and predators. If severe, spray leaf undersides with insecticidal soap, pyrethrum, or a combination of both.

12.F4 Borer damage

Borers. Create holes/tunnels in branches. Prune out infested areas. Prevent borer infestations by keeping shrubs healthy.

12.F5 Rhododendron root rot

Root rots. General decline of plant; scattered dieback. Remove plant. Improve drainage if replanting in the same area. Prune out affected areas. Fertilization can encourage new growth if enough healthy roots are available to take up nutrients.

12.F6 Normal fall color of azalea

Fall coloration. Inner needles or leaves turn yellow and drop. This is a natural occurrence and no treatment is needed.

12.F7 Scale - juniper

Yellow spots on needles. Scale causes yellowing on leaves and needles. They will simply scrape off. Control if needed with insecticidal soap or horticultural oil during dormancy to minimize effects on natural predators.

12.F8 Boxwood blight

Whole areas of plant turn brown and defoliate. Boxwood blight is a fungal disease caused by the fungal species *Calonectria pseudonaviculata*. Spores are spread by insects, animals, and garden tools and can survive in the soil for years. A lab test is necessary for diagnosis. Contact your local Extension for detailed advice.

continued on next page

continued from previous page

Key 12-F.   Pests and Diseases of Evergreen Shrubs

LEAF SPOTS/STIPPLING/DISCOLORATION

12.F9   Entomosporium leaf spot

Leaf-spot diseases. Can occur in wet weather and blight entire leaves, causing defoliation. Leaf spot on photinia is a concern, but is not generally a serious problem on evergreen shrubs.

12.F10 Powdery mildew

White coating on leaves. Caused by powdery mildew, a white surface growth that may cause distortion. Early powdery mildews are more damaging. Plant resistant cultivars (crabapples, dogwoods). Rake up and dispose of leaves in the fall. Check horticultural oil labels for powdery mildew control.

12.F11 Lacebug damage - azalea

White stippling on upper leaf, with black fecal spots on the leaf underside. Lacebugs are likely the cause. Spray insecticidal soap on leaf undersides.

12.F12 Leafminer damage

Serpentine trails or blotches on leaves. Various leafminer larvae feed between the upper and lower leaf surfaces, especially on holly and boxwood. Pick off affected leaves.

12.F13 Virus - camellia

Leaf mottling. Usually caused by a virus. Leaves become mottled with yellow and green and may show distortion. No chemical controls are available. Prune out affected branches or remove the entire plant if severe.

12.F14 Phytophthora rot

Leaves/needles turn brown. Check for abiotic causes first. Usually caused by drought, but can also be due to an infection in the root system (Phytophthora rot). Roots will be brown or orange. The only treatment is to improve drainage or plant resistant varieties.

continued on next page

UME © 2025. All rights reserved.   12: Plant Diagnostics   287

continued from previous page

Key 12-F. Pests and Diseases of Evergreen Shrubs

TWIG AND BRANCH PROBLEMS

Whitish, cottony material on twigs and branches. Woolly aphids: Honeydew and sooty mold may be present. Healthy plants can tolerate moderate aphid populations.

12.F15 Woolly aphids

Soft scale egg masses: Mostly unsightly, but the plant can usually tolerate it. If needed, spray during dormancy with horticultural oil.

12.F16 Soft scale egg masses

European hornet damage

Vole damage

12.F17 Bark-stripping examples

Bark stripped or girdled. European hornets: Will strip bark off branches for nesting material. No controls are usually necessary.

Voles (meadow mice): Rodents chew on bark and roots of shrubs, especially boxwoods and junipers. Keep mulch away from trunks and lower stems in winter. Use baited snap-traps if necessary.

12.F18 Deer feeding

Bark stripped from trunk or branch/shoots chewed. Caused by deer feeding.antler rubbing. Worse during very cold, snowy winters. Deer netting and electric fences are effective. Repel deer by hanging small bars of soap, human hair, or blood meal in mesh bags.

12.F19 Mushrooms on branch

Fungal growths or mushrooms on branches or trunk. Decay fungi are evidence of extensive interior decay or root rot. Hand-pick affected parts. Plant resistant cultivars.

12.F20 Clearwing borer larva

Frass around wounds and bark cracks. The white larvae of clearwing borers make shallow tunnels under the bark and push frass out through holes. Frass accumulates in branch crotches, bark, and base of shrub. Prune out infested branches.

continued on next page

continued from previous page

Key 12-F.   Pests and Diseases of Evergreen Shrubs

TWIG AND BRANCH PROBLEMS (continued)

12.F21 Armored euonymus scale

Scattered twig/branch dieback. Armored scales: Scrape off or prune out encrustations on branches. Apply horticultural oil before bud break in the spring.

12.F22 Bark damage by cicada

Cicadas: Deep slits made in bark during egg-laying causes twigs to break easily in windy weather. No control is necessary. **Borers:** Borers can also create holes and tunnels in branches. Keep shrubs healthy.

12.F23 Canker and root rot (Canker - rhododendron; Verticillium wilt - boxwood)

Phytophthora root rot/dieback and Botryosphaeria cankers: Foliage fades, yellows, browns, or wilts. Damage is often scattered in the canopy of rhododendrons and azaleas. No controls are available. Promptly prune out affected branches. **Verticillium wilt:** Can occur on aucuba, barberry, boxwood, camellia, magnolia, and photinia. No sprays are effective. Prune out affected branches.

12.F24 Leaf blight

Rapid dieback of leaves/branch tips. Promptly prune out infected branches.

12.F25 Fire blight on contoneaster

Fire blight: on contoneaster quickly blackens/kills terminals. Leaves remain attached. Prune out infected parts. Reduce or cease nitrogen applications.

12.F26 Juniper twig blight

Juniper twig blights: Caused by phomopsis and kabatina. Choose resistant varieties for kabatina. Remove severely diseased plants.

12.F27 Juniper tip midge

Juniper tip midge and leaflet miners: Tips are mined out. Small caterpillars may be present. Prune out infested tips in the dormant season.

continued on next page

continued from previous page

Key 12-F.   Pests and Diseases of Evergreen Shrubs

OTHER EVERGREEN SHRUB PROBLEMS

12.F28 Sooty mold

Sooty mold/honeydew. Small, soft-bodied aphids or soft scales (raised bumps on twigs and branches) are easily scraped off. Healthy plants can tolerate moderate populations of both. If needed, spray with horticultural oil during dormancy.

Holly berry midge

Pyracantha scab - holly

12.F29 Berry discoloration

Discoloration of berries or fruit. Holly berry midge: Berries stay green in the fall. Controls are not available.

Pyracantha scab: Berries turn black. Select resistant varieties.

12.F30 Wilt due to drought

Wilting. Lack of water, wood-boring beetles, root rots/canker, or extensive mechanical injury to the trunk or roots can cause wilting. Prune out affected branches or stems.

12.F31 Ovulinia petal blight

Flower issues. Ovulinia petal blight: Small, water-soaked spots enlarge rapidly, causing flowers to collapse and feel slimy. Some cultivars are more resistant.

12.F32 Exobasidium gall - azalea

Exobasidium flower gall: Swollen or puffy areas on buds, petals, or new leaves. No chemical controls are effective. Prune out infected leaves or hand-pick and remove galls. Some cultivars are more resistant.

12.F33 Boxwood psyllid

Leaf cupping or distortion. Boxwood psyllid: Causes cupping of terminal leaves in the spring. Control is only necessary for heavy infestations. Spray with horticultural oil or insecticidal soap in April and May.

12.F34 Herbicide injury

Herbicide toxicity: When all biotic causes have been ruled out, the problem may be glyphosate injury (Roundup®) that has reached the roots.

continued on next page

continued from previous page

Key 12-F. Pests and Diseases of Evergreen Shrubs

OTHER EVERGREEN SHRUB PROBLEMS (continued)

12.F35 Ugly nest caterpillar

Webbed or tented foliage. Ugly nest caterpillar: Insects are yellowish or greenish with black heads and construct dense nests by webbing twigs and leaves together. If many are present, use Bt when the caterpillars are small.

12.F36 Juniper webworm

Juniper webworm: Insects with tan and brown stripes and black heads cause yellowing, then web branches together and feed inside the webbing. Prune out dead branches. Pull open webbed branches and look for active caterpillars. Use Bt if caterpillars are small.

12.F37 Bagworm

"Bags" appear on branches. Bagworms feed on foliage and construct silk bags covered with host-plant material for protection. Spray with Bt when bags are small, from mid-June to mid-July. Hand-pick and destroy bags during fall and winter.

Euonymus caterpillar

Viburnum leaf beetle

Leaf-notching weevil

12.F38 Leaf-chewers/notchers

Leaves eaten or chewed. Caused by early- and late-season caterpillars, sawflies, leaf-feeding beetles, or leaf-notching weevils. Apply Bt when early-season caterpillar larvae are small. Hand-pick large caterpillars, sawflies, and beetles.

12.F39 Crown gall

Stem galls. Crown gall is a bacterial disease that causes growths of abnormal tissue along the stem. Prune out affected areas or remove plant.

12.F40 Juniper spittlebug

Whitish, frothy mass on foliage. Spittlebugs: Small sucking insects that feed on terminal twigs of host plants. Remove manually or spray with an insecticidal soap.

UME © 2025. All rights reserved.

12: Plant Diagnostics 291

Key 12-G.   Pests and Diseases of Deciduous Shrubs

LEAF YELLOWING

12.G1   Spider mites - rose

Spider mites. Tiny insects appear on leaf undersides. Leaves yellow, then brown, and drop prematurely. Webbing may appear. Treat with insecticidal soap or horticultural oil and/or release predatory mites.

12.G2   Stem gall - forsythia

Stem galls. Enlarged growths on stems or branches. Prune out affected parts.

12.G3   Root rot - forsythia

Root rot. General decline of plant, scattered dieback. Remove plant. Improve drainage if replanting in the same area.

12.G4   Armored scale close-up

Armored scales: Encrustations on branches can be scraped off.

Soft scales: Raised bumps on twigs and branches can be scraped off. Sooty mold and honeydew may be present. Prune out branches with severe symptoms and spray with horticultural oil during dormancy.

12.G5   Whiteflies

Whiteflies. Tiny white insects fly up when plant is disturbed. Control with parasites and predators. If severe, spray leaf undersides with insecticidal soap or pyrethrum.

12.G6   Borer damage - lilac

Borers: Create holes/tunnels in branches. Prune out infested areas. Beneficial nematodes may be sprayed on lilac or rhododendron for clearwing borers.

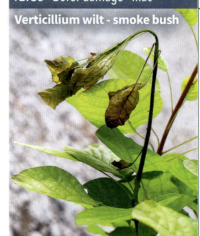
Verticillium wilt - smoke bush

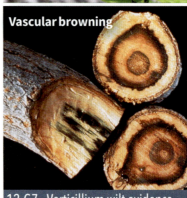
Vascular browning
12.G7   Verticillium wilt evidence

Verticillium wilt: Foliage fades, yellows, browns, or wilts; often scattered throughout the canopy. Scrape twigs and branches to look for vascular browning (left). Sprays are ineffective. Prune out wilted/dead branches and keep watered. Avoid root damage from salt or cultivation. Select resistant alternative varieties. Fertilization can spur new growth if enough healthy roots remain to take up nutrients.

continued on next page

continued from previous page

Key 12-G.   Pests and Diseases of Deciduous Shrubs

LEAF SPOTS/STIPPLING/DISCOLORATION

12.G8   Spider-mite stippling

Tiny yellow spots on leaf underside. Spider mites: Leaves turn yellow, brown, and drop prematurely. Treat with insecticidal soap or horticultural oil, or release predatory mites.

Leaf-spot diseases. In cool, wet weather, leaves may contract blight, develop spots, and drop. **Black spot:** Leaves develop black spots and yellow areas. Control with a registered preventive fungicide and remove fallen leaves.

12.G9   Lace bugs - chokecherry

White stippling on upper leaf, black fecal spots on underside. Lacebugs: Spray insecticidal soap on leaf undersides.

12.G13   Black spot - roses

12.G14   Cercospora - yucca

Cercospora: Commonly seen on hydrangeas but is not a threat. Causes discrete spots with tan-to-brown centers, surrounded by a darker border. Remove infected leaves in the summer and fall.

12.G10   Leafminer damage - lilac

Serpentine trails or blotches on leaves. Various leafminer larvae feed between the upper and lower leaf surfaces. Pick off affected leaves.

12.G11   Bacterial leaf blight

Black leaves. Bacterial leaf blight affects young leaves, turning them black (especially lilac). Promptly prune out infected branches.

12.G12   Mottle/mosaic patterns

Leaf mottling. Viruses causes leaves to become mottled yellow and green. No chemical controls are available. Prune out affected branches or remove entire plant.

12.G15   Powdery mildew - lilac

White coating on leaves. Powdery mildew, a white surface growth on leaves that may cause distortion. Control is not usually needed.

continued on next page

continued from previous page

Key 12-G.   Pests and Diseases of Deciduous Shrubs

TWIG AND BRANCH PROBLEMS

12.G16 Armored euonymus scale

12.G17 Cicada

12.G18 Canker - rhododendron

Scattered twig/branch dieback. Armored scales: Small encrustations on branches. Scrape them off or prune out affected branches. Apply horticultural oil before bud break in the spring. **Borers:** Holes and tunnels in branches. Keep trees healthy. **Cicadas:** Deep slits made in bark during egg-laying causes twigs to break easily in windy weather. No control is necessary. **Verticillium wilt, cankers, and root rot:** Foliage fades, yellows, browns, or wilts, often scattered throughout the canopy. Mostly a problem on lilacs. No sprays are effective. Prune out wilted/dead branches and keep watered. Avoid root damage from salt or cultivation. On problem sites, select resistant alternative shrub varieties. Fertilization can encourage new growth if enough healthy roots are available to take up nutrients.

12.G19 European hornet damage

Bark stripped or girdled. European hornets (large hornets with dark brown and orange markings) will take strips of bark off branches for nesting material. No controls are usually necessary.

12.G20 Deer feeding

Bark stripped from trunk or branch/shoots chewed. Caused by deer feeding/antler rubbing. Worse during very cold, snowy winters. Deer netting and electric fences are effective. Repel deer by hanging small bars of soap, human hair, or blood meal in mesh bags.

12.G21 Crown gall

Stem galls. Crown gall is a bacterial disease that causes growths of abnormal tissue along the stem. Prune out affected areas or remove plant.

continued on next page

continued from previous page

Key 12-G. Pests and Diseases of Deciduous Shrubs

TWIG AND BRANCH PROBLEMS (continued)

12.G22 Clearwing borer damage

Frass around wounds and bark cracks. Clearwing borers: white larvae make shallow tunnels under the bark and push frass out through holes. Frass accumulates in branch crotches, bark, and base of shrub. Prune out infested branches. Beneficial nematodes may be sprayed on infested areas of branches and stems.

12.G23 Woolly aphids

12.G24 Soft scale egg masses

Whitish, cottony material on twigs and branches. Likely woolly aphids or the egg masses of soft scales. Honeydew and sooty mold may be present in the case of aphids. Healthy plants can tolerate moderate populations of both. If needed, spray during dormancy with horticultural oil.

12.G25 Mushroom on branch

Fungal growths or mushrooms on branches or trunk. Decay fungi: reproductive structures are visible evidence of extensive interior wood decay or root rot. Remove affected branches or plants.

12.G26 Witches' broom - rose

Proliferation of branches or dense bushy growth (witches' broom). Indicates eriophyiid mites; fungal, viral, or phytoplasma diseases; and/or mistletoe. Prune out affected areas to avoid spreading the pathogen.

12.G27 Wilt due to drought

Wilting. Lack of water, wood-boring beetles, root rots, or extensive trunk damage can cause wilting. No chemical controls are available. Prune out affected branches or stems. If the cause is drought, water deeply during dry spells.

continued on next page

UME © 2025. All rights reserved.

12: Plant Diagnostics   295

continued from previous page

Key 12-G. Pests and Diseases of Deciduous Shrubs

OTHER DECIDUOUS SHRUB PROBLEMS

12.G28 Euonymus caterpillar

Webbed or tented foliage. Often caused by euonymus caterpillar. If many insects are present, use Bt when the caterpillars are small.

12.G29 Sooty mold-crape myrtle

Sooty mold/honeydew. Small, soft-bodied aphids or soft scales (raised bumps on twigs and branches) are easily scraped off. Healthy plants can tolerate moderate populations of both. If needed, spray with horticultural oil during dormancy.

12.G30 Bagworm - hawthorn

Bags made of plant material on branches. Bagworms feed on foliage and construct protective silk bags covered with host-plant material for protection. Spray with Bt when bags are small, from mid-June to mid-July. Hand-pick and destroy bags during fall and winter.

Tussock caterpillar larva
Flea beetle larvae
Sawfly larva
12.G31 Late-season pests

Leaves eaten or chewed. Caused by early- and late-season caterpillars, sawflies, or leaf-feeding beetles. Control with Bt (a biologic insecticide) when caterpillar larvae are small. Hand-pick large caterpillars, sawflies, and beetles.

12.G32 Spittlebugs

Whitish, frothy mass on foliage. Spittlebugs: Small sucking insects that feed on terminal twigs of host plants. Remove manually or spray with an insecticidal soap.

12.G33 Thrip damage - rose bud

Flower issues. Thrips: Cause white or brown streaks and blotches on blossoms.

12.G34 Japanese beetles - rose

Japanese/chafer beetles and rose slugs: feed on buds and flower petals. Use a residual insecticide.

12.G35 Petal blight - camellia

Botrytis petal blight: Small, discolored spots enlarge and turn entire flower brown. Deadhead flowers.

Key 12-H.   Pests and Diseases of Annuals and Perennials

LEAF SPOTS/DISCOLORATION/DAMAGE

12.H1   Aphid damage - Asclepias

12.H2   Stem borer - coneflower

12.H3   Verticillium wilt-sunflower

12.H4   Southern blight - hosta

12.H5   Mottling - pokeweed

Leaf yellowing; foliage fades, yellows/browns. Caused by aphids, spider mites, stem galls, borers, mealybugs, root rots, whiteflies, verticillium wilt, and Southern blight. Examine lower leaf surfaces for spider mites or whiteflies. Examine twigs and branches for scale covers or borer holes. Scrape base of stem near soil line to look for evidence of vascular browning. Light infestations do not require control. For heavy to moderate mite infestations, consider releasing predatory mites instead of spraying, as heavily damaged plants can be injured by insecticides during hot, dry weather. Remove diseased plants and prune back affected sections.

Leaf mottling. Viruses cause foliage to appear mottled green and yellow. Plants may be stunted. Remove infected plants.

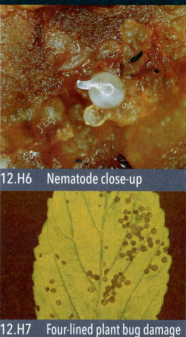
12.H6   Nematode close-up

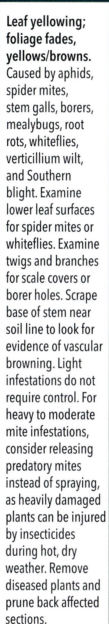
12.H7   Four-lined plant bug damage

12.H8   Harlequin bug

12.H9   Leafhopper - Virginia creeper

Leaf spots or blotches. Caused by various fungi, bacteria, foliar nematodes, and plant bugs.
Four-lined plant bugs: 1/3-in. long, yellowish green with black stripes. Nymphs are bright orange. Feeding causes perfectly circular spots.
Harlequin bugs: red and black, shield shaped. Feeding causes white and yellow blotches on leaves. Remove spotted leaves. Improve air circulation to prevent leaf diseases. Plants can tolerate heavy bug feeding but if damage is severe, use a pyrethrum-based insecticide.

Leaf stippling. Leafhoppers, plant bugs (especially four-lined): nymphs and adults feed on lush spring growth, causing yellow stipples that may become necrotic black blotches. Stunting may occur. Most plants will outgrow the damage later in the season. If necessary, replace heavily damaged annuals.

continued on next page

continued from previous page

Key 12-H. Pests and Diseases of Annuals and Perennials

LEAF SPOTS/DISCOLORATION/DAMAGE (continued)

12.H10 Leaf scorch

Leaf scorch. Abiotic stresses, spider mite, whitefly, and thrip-feeding can all cause scorch. Symptoms can occur along leaf margins or between veins. Immediately prune out infected stems. Use chemical sprays only when necessary and always follow package directions to avoid toxicity.

12.H11 Rust - snapdragon

Orange-yellow spots on leaves and stems. Rust fungi causes orange-colored spots on leaves and stems (e.g., snapdragon and hollyhocks).

12.H12 Leafminers

Light-colored tunnels or blotches (mines) in leaves. Leafminer larvae feed between the upper and lower leaf surfaces (e.g., aquilegia or columbine). Pick off infested leaves.

12.H13 Earwig damage

12.H14 Sawfly damage

12.H15 Slug damage - violets

Leaves eaten/chewed. Caused by caterpillars, slugs, sawflies, leaf-feeding beetles and weevils, grasshoppers, and earwigs. Control caterpillars when larvae are small using the effective biological insecticide Bt. Hand-pick large caterpillars, sawflies, and beetles off plants. Slugs may be controlled with diatomaceous earth or baits, or by removing excess mulch.

12.H16 Powdery mildew - phlox

White powdery coating. Powdery mildew fungi grow on the leaf surface (e.g., monarda and phlox). Check horticultural oil labels for powdery mildew control listings. Select resistant cultivars.

continued on next page

continued from previous page

Key 12-H. Pests and Diseases of Annuals and Perennials

WHOLE-PLANT PROBLEMS

12.H17 Aphid infestation- Asclepias

12.H18 Striped leafhopper

12.H19 Broad-headed Sharpshooter

12.H20 Virus- gerbera

Twisted/distorted plant growth.
Aphids: small, soft-bodied insects on young growth, stems, and leaves. Aphids are usually controlled by beneficial insects like parasitic wasps. Reduce heavy infestations of aphids and treehoppers with insecticidal soap to conserve beneficials and natural predators.
Leafhoppers: Commonly-seen, small jumping insects that vary widely in shape and color. Some are wildly colorful; some resemble thorns. Treat heavy infestations with insecticidal soap or neem oil.
Viruses: Foliage appears mottled green and yellow. Plants may be stunted. There are no controls for viruses. Remove infected plants; do not dispose of in your compost pile.

12.H21 Southern blight-hosta

12.H22 Rhizoctonia blight

Blights. Southern blight, Rhizoctonia web blight: Foliage wilts/collapses and turns brown or black. Plants may be killed. Improve soil drainage and air circulation. Pull mulch away from stems.

12.H23 Verticillium wilt-sunflower

12.H24 Vole damage - Joe Pye

Wilting. Various root rots (e.g., verticillium wilt and Southern blight), stem cankers, borers, aphids, plant hoppers, and root-feeding insects and rodents can cause wilt. Rule out abiotic causes (see Keys 12-A and 12-B). Examine plants carefully for signs of boring activity, such as frass and stem holes. Carefully dig up a plant to observe any root symptoms. Remove infested, rotten portions from perennials and replant remaining healthy sections.

UME © 2025. All rights reserved.

12: Plant Diagnostics

Key 12-I.   Pests and Diseases of Solanaceous Crops (Tomato, Eggplant, Pepper, Potato)

FOLIAGE SYMPTOMS

12.I1   Potato leafhopper

Yellowing leaves. Leafhoppers: Small, green, wedge-shaped insects can spread viruses that yellow plant leaves. Cover plants with a floating row cover after seeding or transplanting.

12.I2   Stippling - eggplant

Fine yellow stippling. Spider mites: Visible with the eye or a hand lens. Severely damaged plants are further injured by insecticides (including soaps and oils).

12.I3   Fusarium wilt - tomato

12.I4   Fusarium wilt - tomato

Leaf/stem wilt. Fusarium wilt is most common on tomatoes. Plant wilts from bottom up but recovers at night. Plant will eventually die. Bacterial wilt causes a more rapid top-down wilt. Discolored stem tissue is present in all wilt diseases. Dispose of infected plants (do not compost) and choose resistant varieties. Rotate solanaceous plants or grow in containers.

12.I5   Early blight - tomato

12.I6   Septoria leafspot

12.I7   Bacterial spot - pepper

Irregular yellow spots with a bull's eye "halo." Caused by early blight (fungal leaf spot disease). Infection begins on lower leaves. Septoria leaf spot is another fungal disease that produces small, circular spots with a dark border. Early blight lesions are larger than Septoria leafspot. Both are very common and often occur simultaneously on tomato. Increase plant spacing and mulch to keep wet soil from splashing up. Prune lower leaf stems up to one foot from the ground and avoid overhead watering. Use a fixed-copper fungicide if disease becomes severe.

Water-soaked leaf blotches on pepper leaves. Bacterial spot can be controlled with a fixed-copper spray. Increase spacing between plants to improve air circulation. Spread mulch around plants and avoid overhead watering.

continued on next page

300   Maryland Master Gardener Handbook   UME © 2025. All rights reserved.

continued from previous page

Key 12-I. Pests and Diseases of Solanaceous Crops (Tomato, Eggplant, Pepper, Potato)

FOLIAGE SYMPTOMS (continued)

12.I8 Late blight potato

12.I9 Late blight tomato

Late blight on potato and tomato. This fungal disease causes dark brown blotches to appear on leaf tips and margins and enlarge rapidly, producing a water-soaked appearance. Use a fixed-copper spray or other registered fungicide. Avoid overhead watering. Plant resistant cultivars and certified disease-free potato seed. Discard severely diseased plants (do not compost).

12.I10 Leaf curling - aphids

Leaf curling/distortion. Aphids/leafhoppers: Soft pink or green insects appear on young growth. Natural predators and parasites usually control aphids. In severe cases, apply neem oil or spinosad.

12.I11 Leaf curl virus - tomato

Viruses: Mottled, deformed leaves (more common on peppers and potatoes). Pull out and discard virus-infected plants. Do not compost.

OTHER SOLANACEOUS CROP PROBLEMS

12.I12 Bacterial potato scab

Tuber diseases of potato: Discard infected tubers. Do not compost. Plant certified seed pieces.

12.I13 Potato tuberworm

Potato tuberworm: Small, pink-white caterpillar tunnels in all plant parts. Use row covers and keep tubers covered with soil and mulch. Discard infested plants.

12.I14 Blackleg potato disease

Blackleg (potato): Plant blackens above and below soil line. Pull out infected plants. Choose certified seed pieces.

12.I15 Southern blight - tomato

Southern blight (tomato/pepper): Brown-black cankers appear on lower stem. Dispose of infected plants and rotate crops.

Key 12-J.   Pests and Diseases of Cucurbits (Cucumber, Squash, Melon)

FOLIAGE SYMPTOMS

12.J1 Spider-mite stippling

Fine yellow stippling on leaf undersides. Spider mites can appear as "dirt" on leaf undersides. Plants with severe mite damage are further injured by insecticidal sprays, including soaps and oils.

12.J2 Cucumber mosaic virus

Mottling and/or leaf distortion. Caused by fungal and bacterial viruses. Pull out and dispose of infected plants (do not compost). Control weeds, aphids, and cucumber beetles; choose virus-resistant varieties.

12.J3 Ringspot

Ringspot. Ringspot virus damages summer and winter squash, but affects other cucurbits only mildly. Ringspot is transmitted by nematodes and can overwinter on weeds. Remove plants and fallen leaves. Do not compost.

12.J4 Leaf curling - watermelon

12.J5 Leaf cupping

Leaf curling, cupping, and/or distortion. Aphids sucking sap make leaves curl downward, turn brown, and eventually die. Naturally-occurring parasites and predators usually keep aphid populations in check, but watch plants because aphids often transmit viral diseases.

12.J6 Squash bug

12.J7 Squash bug eggs

Tiny yellow-green leaf spots. Squash bugs lay golden-brown oval eggs in clusters on the leaf surface and underside. Adults and nymphs suck sap, resulting in pale yellow-green leaf spotting. Hand-pick eggs and use a floating row cover (remove during the bloom period to ensure pollination). If needed, apply a registered organic insecticide such as pyrethrum.

continued on next page

continued from previous page

Key 12-J. Pests and Diseases of Cucurbits (Cucumber, Squash, Melon)

FOLIAGE SYMPTOMS (continued)

12.J8 Downy mildew

Downy mildew. Creates yellow spots on surface and downy, grayish spots on underside (mostly on cucumber, squash, pumpkin, and melon). Starts on older leaves in early summer. Dispose of infected plants and choose resistant varieties.

12.J9 Powdery mildew - squash

Powdery mildew. Starts in mid-summer on older leaves. Can spread rapidly, causing plants to yellow/die. Dispose of infected plants and choose resistant varieties.

12.J10 Bacterial leaf spot

12.J11 Gummy stem blight

Circular or irregular dark spots on leaves/stems. Fungal or bacterial diseases: Use resistant varieties and dispose of infected plants.

Gummy stem blight: Stem blackens at the soil line, primarily on muskmelon and watermelon. Plant resistant varieties and dispose of infected plants.

12.J12 Spotted cucumber beetle

12.J13 Striped cucumber beetle

Chewed leaves, flowers, or stems/stalks. Cucumber beetles: Yellow-green insects with black stripes or spots feed on all plant parts. Damage is less severe after bloom period. Cover with a floating row cover. Remove during bloom time to ensure pollination or use a registered organic insecticide after transplanting or seedling emergence. Discard all plant debris in the fall.

12.J14 Squash beetle adult/larva

Squash beetle: A dark orange, humpbacked beetle with dark spots. Feeds between leaf veins. Hand-pick eggs, larvae, and adults. Use a floating row cover on young plants and remove it when plants begin to bloom to ensure pollination.

continued on next page

continued from previous page

Key 12-J.   Pests and Diseases of Cucurbits (Cucumber, Squash, Melon)

WILTING

12.J15 Squash vine borer adult

12.J16 Squash vine borer larva

Squash vine borer. A small, cream-colored caterpillar with a brown head. Adult female is large, reddish, and wasp-like; eggs are laid on stems and leaf stalks. Sawdust-like frass (excrement) may be seen where larvae bore into lower stems. Use a razor to slit stem, remove borer and mound soil over wound. Use a floating row cover, but remove during bloom time. Do not spray insecticides when bees are active.

12.J17 Bacterial wilt - pumpkin

12.J18 Bacterial wilt - cucumber

Bacterial wilt. Mostly affects melon and cucumber. Spread by cucumber beetles. To confirm diagnosis, cut a wilted stem in half, close to plant base. Rejoin the cut surfaces, then pull apart again. If sticky "threads" appear, it is bacterial disease. Choose resistant varieties like 'County Fair.' Use a floating row cover but remove during bloom time. If severe, use a registered organic insecticide except when bees are active.

FRUIT PROBLEMS

12.J19 Pickleworm damage

Holes in fruit. Look for late-season pickleworm or squash vine borers, especially on pumpkin. Remove affected fruit.

12.J20 Anthracnose - melon

Water-soaked or dry, sunken, black or brown spots. Caused by fungal and bacterial diseases. Plant resistant varieties. Keep plants mulched and discard infected fruit.

12.J21 Cucumber beetle damage

Surface feeding or scraping injury. Cucumber beetles are likely. Dispose of affected fruit.

12.J22 Choanephora rot - squash

Fuzzy gray/black growth on squash and pumpkin blossoms and young fruit. Choanephora wet rot occurs during wet spells. Remove blossoms that stick to young fruit and discard infected blossoms and fruit.

Key 12-K.   Pests and Diseases of Brassicas (Broccoli, Cabbage, Collard)

FOLIAGE SYMPTOMS

12.K1   Leaf spot - cabbage

Bacterial leaf spots. Disease causes spots to form on the leaves; spots are initially small and turn dark brown or purple as they grow larger. Leaves can look raggedy. Mulch around plants to prevent soil splashing up on plants. Rotate crops.

12.K2   Harlequin bug - cabbage

Harlequin bug. Red and black shield-shaped adults and nymphs suck plant sap. Eggs are black and white and barrel-shaped. Hand-pick eggs and adults. Use floating row covers and remove all debris where infestations are severe.

12.K3   Downy mildew - cabbage

Downy mildew. Light yellow-green spots appear on leaf surfaces. Whitish-gray, fuzzy mold develops on lower leaf surface during extended periods of moist weather. Pull out and discard infected plants and choose resistant varieties.

12.K4   Aphids - cabbage

Aphids. Clusters of gray, black, or green insects suck plant sap, causing leaves to curl, yellow, or lose color. Natural parasites and predators keep aphids in check.

12.K5   Black rot - turnip

Black rot. Produces dark yellow-brown, wedge-shaped lesions and black leaf veins. Pull up and dispose of badly infected plants. Select resistant varieties.

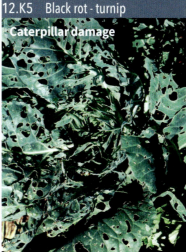

Caterpillar damage

Flea beetle damage

12.K6   Cabbage leaf holes

Holes in leaves. Various caterpillars chew ragged or smooth holes. Use floating row covers, hand-pick eggs and larvae, or spray Bt products when larvae are young. Tiny, dark, shiny flea beetles chew small holes in a scatter-shot pattern. Insects jump when disturbed. Use floating row covers to keep beetles out. Chinese cabbage is more severely affected than other types.

continued on next page

continued from previous page

Key 12-K.   Pests and Diseases of Brassicas (Broccoli, Cabbage, Collard)

FOLIAGE SYMPTOMS (continued)

12.K7   Blackleg - cabbage leaf

Wilting. Can be caused by blackleg disease or cabbage maggots. Pull and discard infected plants. Use a floating row cover for cabbage maggot. Rotate crops and plant resistant varieties.

12.K8   Fusarium - broccoli

Fusarium yellows. Appears mostly on cabbage. Plants are stunted, with purple or yellow leaf margins. Pull out and discard badly infected plants. Select resistant varieties.

HEAD/FLORET PROBLEMS

12.K9   Soft rot - cabbage

Soft spots/rot. Caused by fungal and bacterial diseases, more often on overly-mature plants. Remove infected plant parts. Grow brassicas in well-drained soil and rotate crops.

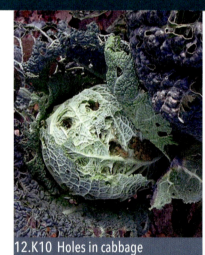

12.K10 Holes in cabbage

Holes in heads or florets. Caused by various caterpillars, which chew holes in leaves first. Cover plants with a floating row cover. Hand-pick eggs and larvae or spray with Bt when larvae are young.

ROOT PROBLEMS

12.K11   Maggots in cabbage root

Holes or tunnels. Cabbage maggots create brown grooves on root surfaces. Tunnels are slimy. Maggot feeding can lead to blackleg and soft rots. Discard infested roots and dispose of plant debris. Use a floating row cover over the bed. Avoid spring manure applications.

12.K12   Club root - cabbage

Swollen root formations. Caused by club-root, root-knot nematode, or fungal disease. Pull out and discard infected plants and rotate crops. Plant resistant varieties. For club root, work in 3 to 5 lbs. hydrated lime per 100 sq. ft. before planting.

Key 12-L.   Pests and Diseases of Legumes (Bean, Pea)

LEAF/STEM SYMPTOMS

12.L1   Root aphids - bean root

Leaves yellow, general plant decline. Root aphids are small, white insects that feed in clusters on plant roots. Pull out and dispose of plants. Till soil and replant with a different family.

12.L2   Fusarium wilt - bean leaf

Wilting. Various root rots, fusarium wilt. Accompanied by lower-leaf yellowing, stunting, and internal stem discoloration. Pull and discard infected plants. Plant resistant varieties on ridges in well-drained soil, and rotate crops.

12.L3   Dry rust - bean

Yellow spots, red-brown pustules. Rust causes rust-colored spots with yellow halos. Remove all debris at season's end. Select resistant varieties.

12.L4   Powdery mildew - pea

White coating on leaves and pods. Powdery mildew may distort pods. Some bean varieties are sensitive to sulfur fungicidal sprays; check horticultural oil labels for powdery mildew control directions.

12.L5   Fusarium - broccoli

Discoloration of roots and stem. Various fungal root rots infect slow-growing, stressed plants. Discard infected plants. Plant on ridges or raised beds in well-drained soil, and rotate crops.

12.L6   Blight - bean

Dark spots/blotches. Various fungal and bacterial leaf blights. Remove all plant debris at season's end. Plant resistant varieties in well-drained soil. Space plants for improved air circulation.

12.L7   Downy mildew - soybean

White, moldy growth on leaves, stems, and pods. Downy mildew is a dry rot, while white mold and pod blight produce water-soaked spots. Pull and discard infected plants. Rotate crops and choose resistant varieties.

12.L8   Mite stippling - bean

Leaf stippling. Spider mites cause pale yellow or bronze discoloration. Plants eventually brown and die. For severe infestations, consider releasing predatory mites.

continued on next page

UME © 2025. All rights reserved.

continued from previous page

Key 12-L.   Pests and Diseases of Legumes (Bean, Pea)

LEAF/STEM SYMPTOMS (continued)

Cupping caused by aphids

Ladybug predator

Leafhopper damage

Leafhoppers

Common bean mosaic

Leaf and stem distortion. Aphids: Small, soft-bodied insects are light-green to black and feed in clusters. Their feeding causes cupping, yellowing, and distortion/curling of young leaves. Aphids may also spread viral diseases. Natural predators and parasites are usually sufficient to control pest populations. Other control options include insecticidal soap and use of a floating row cover.

Potato leafhopper: On beans, damage appears as leaf-margin curling, browning, and eventual wilting. Use a floating row cover, or pyrethrum or neem oil spray for severe/large-area infestations.

Viral diseases: Leaves may become yellowed or mottled. Plants may be stunted or wilted. Pull out and discard infected plants, and remove all plant debris. Choose resistant varieties.

12.L9   Leaf/stem issues

Mexican bean beetle/larva

Bean leaf beetle

Flea beetle

Grasshopper damage

Chewed leaves and stems. Mexican bean beetle: Adults and nymphs skeletonize leaves. Yellow oval-shaped eggs are laid on leaf undersides. Hand-pick eggs, larvae, and adults. Use a floating row cover.

Bean leaf beetle: Creates rounded holes in leaves. Remove and discard infested plants. Bt sprays can be effective against young caterpillars.

Flea beetle: Chews tiny, round holes in leaves. Small, dark, shiny beetles jump when disturbed. Use a floating row cover.

Grasshopper: Chews large ragged holes in leaves (mid- to late-summer). Use a floating row cover.

12.L10   Chewing damage

continued on next page

continued from previous page

Key 12-L.   Pests and Diseases of Legumes (Bean, Pea)

POD SYMPTOMS

Holes chewed in pods. Various caterpillars (corn earworm, corn borer, and gray hairstreak). Hand-pick pests. Use a floating row cover or registered Bt insecticide product.

12.L11 Holes in bean pods

Spots on lima pods. Stink bugs are shield-shaped bugs that feed on pods, leaving white/yellow spots. Damage is usually superficial. Hand-pick pests.

12.L13 Stink bug damage

Tiny grubs inside seed. Bean and pea weevil or cowpea curculio (also on lima). Sometimes occurs on saved/stored bean seed. Discard all plant debris at season's end. Use a floating row cover.

12.L12 Cowpea curculio beetle

Lima seed rot. Fungal disease attacks seeds already damaged by stink bugs. Remove all foliage and fallen debris at the end of the season to prevent stink bugs from overwintering.

12.L14 Lima bean seed rot

Key 12-M.   Pests and Diseases of Sweet Corn

LEAF/STALK SYMPTOMS

Dark spots, blotches, and streaks. Various fungal diseases. Remove and dispose of infected debris; plant resistant varieties.

12.M1 Holes in bean pods

Small, rust-colored pustules. Rust thrives in cool, humid air. Oxalis is an alternate host for this disease. Dispose of infected plants and choose resistant varieties.

12.M2 Corn rust

Round holes. Shotholes in leaves and stalks are caused by European corn borer. Pale-pink or brownish caterpillars have a dark brown head and are about 1 in. long. Hand-pick cream-colored egg masses off of the leaf underside. Remove and dispose of all plant debris to prevent overwintering.

12.M3 European corn borer moth and larva

Key 12-M.   Pests and Diseases of Sweet Corn

LEAF/STALK SYMPTOMS (continued)

12.M4 Stewart's bacterial wilt

Stunting/wilting. Stewart's bacterial wilt causes yellow streaking. Margins have irregular brown areas. Transmitted by flea beetles; more severe on young plants. Remove plants and debris. Till soil in late fall to disrupt beetle habitat, and plant resistant varieties.

12.M5   Flea beetle damage

Holes chewed in leaves. Tiny black flea beetles jump when disturbed and chew small, round holes. They also spread bacterial wilt. Corn earworm and fall armyworm produce irregular holes and notching in leaf margins. Can also be caused by grasshoppers.

EAR DAMAGE

12.M6 Corn smut

Fleshy galls. Smut is a soil-borne fungus that produces white fleshy growths with dark powdery spores. Also appears on leaves, stalks, and tassel. More severe in dry season. Remove and destroy growths to prevent galls and powder from reaching the soil. Plant resistant varieties.

Corn ear worm

Army worm

Sap beetle damage

Wildlife damage

12.M8   Corn kernel damage

Kernel damage. Corn ear worms feed on the tips of ripening ears. Army worms and corn borers enter the ear at base, side, or tip. Sap beetles are small, round, and black and feed on exposed and damaged kernels. Birds, rats, raccoons, squirrels, and deer also feed on ears. Harvest when silk turns brown and kernels are plump. Tip damage can be cut off. Pull and discard badly damaged ears. Insecticides are ineffective once damage is seen. Select cultivars with long husks that provide good tip coverage.

12.M7 Japanese beetle - corn silk

Corn silk chewed. Japanese or cucumber beetle damage. Pollination may suffer if damage is early in silking. Hand-pick pests or spray with a registered organic insecticide. Use Bt or mineral oil on silks to control young caterpillars.

Key 12-N.   Pests and Diseases of Sweet Potato

FOLIAGE SYMPTOMS

12.N1 Holes in sweet potato leaf

Holes chewed in leaves. Caused by sweet potato flea beetle or tortoise beetle. Not a serious problem. Plants will outgrow damage.

12.N2   Spots - sweet potato leaf

Spots and blotches. Caused by various fungal diseases. Damage is usually minor. No controls are necessary.

ROOT SYMPTOMS

12.N3 Spots - sweet potato skin

Black or brown spots on skin. Discoloration extends below ground. Caused by fungal diseases. Select resistant varieties and buy certified, disease-free seed. Do not store infected roots.

12.N5   Holes in sweet potato

Small holes. Holes can be shallow or deep. **Wireworm:** shiny slender worms up to 1 in. long; late season pest. Adult is a click beetle. Remove crop debris at season's end and till soil. Rotate crops.

12.N4   Scurf - sweet potato

Irregular brown spots on skin. Discoloration does not extend below ground. Caused by scurf (fungal disease). Peel off affected skin. Plant certified, disease-free slips.

12.N6   Vole damage

Chewing marks. Caused by voles (meadow mice). Install baited snap traps around the planting bed.

Key 12-O.   Pests and Diseases of Alliums

LEAF/STALK SYMPTOMS

12.O1 White mold - onion

Yellow leaf tips. Caused by white rot, which can also cause yellowing, wilting, or encourage maggots (12.O2). Pull and discard damaged plants. Rotate crops.

12.O2 Onion maggot damage

Wilting. Small, white onion root maggots tunnel into shallot and onion. Space plants farther apart and use row covers. Do not use fresh manure.

continued on next page

continued from previous page

Key 12-O.   Pests and Diseases of Alliums

LEAF/STALK SYMPTOMS (continued)

Water-soaked spots; lesions turn purple with yellow haloes. Purple blotch is a fungal disease that overwinters in plant debris. More severe in wet weather. Discard infected plants. Plant in raised beds and rotate crops.

12.03   Purple blotch - onion

Thrip damage

Botrytis blight

Downy mildew

White flecking or streaking. **Thrips** create long, white streaks. **Botrytis leaf blight** causes white specks that expand. Leaves die back from tip. Treat as for thrips. **Downy mildew** starts on older leaves. White or purplish mold develops in cool, moist weather. Treat all conditions by discarding infected plants. Choose resistant varieties and rotate crops. Increase spacing between plants.

12.05 White streaks - onion

Lines of white dots/blotches. Caused by allium leafminers. Remove infested plants and use floating row covers in April/May and Sept./Oct.

12.04 Allium leafminer damage

BULB DAMAGE

Bulbs are soft/discolored. White rot is a fungal disease that can spread underground from plant to plant and persists in the soil for many years. Rotate allium crops. Use disease-free garlic seed stock.

12.06 White rot - garlic

Larvae pupate in bulbs. Allium leafminer damage. Females insert eggs in leaves; larvae feed inside leaves and migrate to plant base. All alliums are vulnerable. Remove infested plants and use floating row covers in the future.

12.07 Allium leafminer pupae

Key 12-P.   Pests and Diseases of Asparagus

FOLIAGE/STEM SYMPTOMS

12.P1   Low plant vigor

Low plant vigor. Caused by over-harvesting, deep cultivation, weed competition, low soil fertility, or an old planting. See **Chapter 18, Vegetables.**

12.P3 Asparagus fern rosetting

Stunting or rosetting of ferns. Small, green asparagus aphids feed in clusters in leaf axils. Remove and destroy all ferns in the fall.

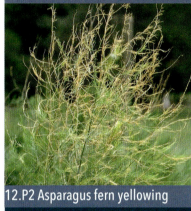
12.P2 Asparagus fern yellowing

Tops yellow/brown and die back. Rust (fungal disease) causes reddish-brown, orange, or black pustules on stems and leaves. Cut tops close to the ground in fall. Plant resistant hybrid varieties.

12.P4 Asparagus beetle larva

Chewed foliage. Asparagus beetles are active all season. Adults are 1/4-in., blue-black, with a red area behind the head. Larvae are 3/8-in., gray-green grubs. Hand-pick both.

SPEAR PROBLEMS

12.P5   Weak, spindly spears

Spindly spears. Fusarium wilt and crown rot cause internal stem/shoot discoloration. Remove infected plants. Plant resistant varieties. **Crowns buried too deeply** or in heavy clay soil: see **Chapter 18, Vegetables.**

12.P7   Tough spears

Tough or deformed spears. Harvested too late or low soil fertility. Side-dress plants with fertilizer in early spring. Weed carefully so as not to damage crowns.

12.P8   Asparagus rust

Red/brown discoloration. Caused by rust. Cut out infected spears. Plant resistant hybrid varieties.

12.P6   Asparagus beetle

Feeding evidence, brown scarring. Asparagus beetle: Wash off dark-brown eggs in spears. Hand-pick adults and larvae. **Slugs, snails:** New spears are chewed. Look for slime trails; hand-pick at night. Lay down coarse sand.

12.P9   Frost injury to spears

Drooping, shriveled spears. Phytophthora root rot (crown rot) is common in wet seasons. Can also be caused by frost injury.

Key 12-Q. Pests and Diseases of Other Vegetable Crops

LETTUCE • SPINACH • BEET • SWISS CHARD

12.Q1 Rabbit damage - beet

Leaves chewed. Caterpillars, leaf-feeding beetles, and slugs: Hand-pick or use a floating row cover. **Flea beetles** (on spinach): Small, round, scatter-shot holes. Larvae may mine leaf undersides. Use a floating row cover. **Rabbits and other wildlife pests:** Fence out large pests. Sprinkle blood meal or crushed hot pepper flakes around plants.

12.Q3 Cercospora leaf spot - lettuce

Older leaves turn yellow or brown. Various fungal diseases (soil-borne): May cause damping-off or wet rots. Discard infected plants. Select resistant varieties and plant in well-drained soil or raised beds. **Leafhoppers:** Small, wedge-shaped insects can transmit viruses. Use a row cover.

12.Q2 Leafminers - beet

Brown spots, blotches, or trails on leaves. Leaf miners: Tiny white maggots produce serpentine or blotch mines by feeding between leaf surfaces. Use a row cover. Remove damaged leaves/plants.

12.Q4 Leaf roll virus - spinach

Stunted plants, leaves curled and yellowed. Virus diseases: Pull out infected plants. Select resistant varieties. **Aphids** (usually green): Can transmit viruses. Pull badly damaged plants. **Tarnished plant bug:** Brownish, 1/4-in., shield-shaped insect. Use a row cover.

CARROT • PARSNIP • PARSLEY • RELATED CROPS

12.Q5 Septoria leaf spot

Tan to dark spots on leaves. Plant bugs: suck sap and inject a toxin that produces small spots. Use a row cover; they move fast and are hard to kill with insecticides. **Fungal and bacterial diseases:** Discard infected plants. Select resistant varieties. Increase plant spacing and avoid overhead watering.

12.Q6 Aster yellows phytoplasma

Stunted plants, leaf yellowing. Leafhoppers and tarnished plant bug: Use a floating row cover. **Virus diseases:** Select resistant varieties. **Root-knot nematode:** Select varieties that make short storage roots. Rotate crops and practice good sanitation.

continued on next page

continued from previous page

Key 12-Q.   Pests and Diseases of Other Vegetable Crops

CARROT • PARSNIP • PARSLEY • RELATED CROPS (continued)

12.Q7 Leafhopper damage — **Yellow, stippled leaves.** Leafhoppers: small, wedge-shaped insects that suck sap and transmit viruses. Use a row cover.

12.Q9 Swallowtail caterpillar — **Chewed foliage.** Caused by swallowtail and other caterpillars; and carrot weevil adults. Hand-pick pests or use a row cover.

12.Q8 Root-knot nematode — **Misshapen, forked, small knots; hairy roots. Root-knot nematode:** Discard infested roots. Select varieties that make short storage roots. Sow in raised beds. **Carrot rust fly:** Use a floating row cover. Control weeds in and around garden.

12.Q10 Carrot weevil damage — **Root tunneling. Carrot weevils:** Creamy-white grubs create zigzag tunnels. Don't allow carrots to overwinter. **Carrot rust fly:** Tunnels have rotted, rust-colored tissue. Maggots are white. Use row covers, rotate crops, control weeds.

Key 12-R.   Pests and Diseases of Pome Fruits (Apple, Pear)

FOLIAGE SYMPTOMS

12.R1 Green apple aphids — **Leaves curled, twisted, or rolled.** Caused by green apple or rosy apple aphid. Sooty mold may grow on honeydew. Aphids spread fire blight. Spray hard with water to dislodge them. Reduce nitrogen applications.

12.R3 Powdery mildew - pear — **White-gray powdery mildew.** Select resistant varieties. Remove damaged shoots and prune to improve air flow. If this was a problem last year, spray with wettable sulfur at bloom or check horticultural oil labels for control.

12.R2 Sooty mold - pear — **Black splotches.** Sooty mold from aphid, scale, or pear psylla feeding. Spray dormant oil at bud swell. Remove water sprouts throughout growing season.

12.R4 Spongy moth — **Leaves chewed.** Caused by spongy moth larvae and other caterpillars from May-June. Hand-pick or spray young larvae with a Bt product.

continued on next page

continued from previous page

Key 12-R. Pests and Diseases of Pome Fruits (Apple, Pear)

FOLIAGE SYMPTOMS (LEAF SPOTS)

12.R5 Pear leaf blister damage

Pear leaf blister mite. Small green or yellow pimples turn into reddish-brown blisters on apple and pear. Tiny white or light-red mites can be seen on leaf undersides with a hand lens. Apply a dormant oil spray in early spring.

12.R6 Cedar apple rust

Cedar apple rust. A fungal disease that causes bright yellow spots with orange or black center. Plant resistant varieties. Do not plant cedar trees, the alternate host of the disease. If possible, remove galls from nearby cedar trees in spring, which range from the diameter of a nickel to a quarter. In wet periods, these galls may produce orange "horns."

12.R7 Black rot symptom

Black rot. A fungal disease also called frogeye leaf spot. Small purple spots become light tan with brown borders. Often associated with fruit mummies (shriveled fruit that remains on the tree from last season). "Frogeye" leaf spots often occur below fruit mummies.

12.R8 Apple scab

Spider mite damage

Fire blight

12.R9 Leaf yellowing/browning

Apple or pear scab. These fungal diseases cause olive-brown, velvety spots on leaves. Plant resistant varieties. Rake up and discard all leaves, fruits, and debris.

Leaves yellowing or browning. Spider mites: Period-sized pests feed on leaf undersides, causing stippling and bronzing. Damage is more severe during hot weather. Spray with dormant oil pre-bloom. Avoid broad-spectrum insecticides that kill predators and often worsen the problem. **San Jose scale:** Tiny yellow crawlers feed on leaf surfaces. Spray with dormant oil pre-bloom. **Fire blight:** Entire leaves turn brown, but do not fall off. Plant resistant varieties. Prune out infected parts using the ugly-stub pruning method (see inset at end of this section). Otherwise, perform dormant pruning of cankers. For severe cases, spray Bordeaux mixture or fixed-copper spray at green-tip stage. Reduce or eliminate nitrogen applications.

continued on next page

continued from previous page

Key 12-R. Pests and Diseases of Pome Fruits (Apple, Pear)

SHOOTS, TWIGS, AND BRANCHES

12.R10 Shepherd's crook

Shoots bend into a "shepherd's crook;" sunken black or wine-colored cankers. Caused by fire blight. See 12-R9 for treatment.

12.R11 Vole damage - pear

Roots and base of young trees chewed. Voles and rabbits nest under cover around trunks. Keep area mowed and mulch pulled back from trunk. Place tree guards (18-in. tall cylinders of hardware cloth) around trees and 2-3 in. below soil line. Use traps to reduce vole population.

12.R12 Flatheaded appletree borer

Trunk/larger branches show wood-boring damage. Metallic, 1/2- to 3/4-in. borers tunnel in cambium tissue. Young trees are more susceptible. Use tree wrap and mulch, and keep trees watered.

12.R13 Lecanium scale

Rough bark and clusters of hard, gray specks. Lecanium scales are reddish-brown to black, seen on young wood. Could also be San Jose scale (see 12-R9). Spray with dormant oil and prune out damaged wood.

FRUITS

12.R14 Apple maggot damage

Apples dimpled; brown trails or streaks in flesh. Small white apple maggots tunnel through fruit. Worse on thin-skinned and early varieties. Discard all drops. Hang 4-5 sticky red sphere traps on outer branches to capture adult flies.

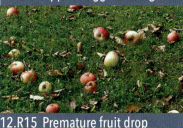

12.R15 Premature fruit drop

Premature drop. Caused by various insect pests. Open and inspect drops to identify pest(s). Promptly discard all drops.

Codling moth larva

Codling moth adult

12.R16 Root-knot nematode

Small holes at blossom end; dark frass kicked out. Codling moth larvae are 1/2-in. long, cream-pink with a brown head. They begin feeding 2-4 weeks after full bloom. Spray insecticide at late petal-fall. Discard all drops and damaged fruit on the tree. Wrap 6-in. strips of cardboard or burlap around trunk and large limbs in Aug. Check wrapping in Dec. and discard any trapped larvae/pupae.

continued on next page

continued from previous page

Key 12-R. Pests and Diseases of Pome Fruits (Apple, Pear)

FRUITS (continued)

12.R17 Plum curculio - apple

Plum curculio larva

Plum curculio adult / Bitter rot

Tan-brown, crescent-shaped scars. Plum curculio larvae tunnel into core. Yellow-white grub with a brown head is 1/4-in. long. Adult is a small black beetle with a long snout. Eggs are laid under the scar. Spray insecticide on first warm days after petal fall. Cool, wet weather at petal fall makes control more difficult. Monitor the adult population by striking branches with a padded broom and collecting curculios on a light-colored tarp.

Scab

Fire blight
12.R18 Spots on fruit

Spots. Can be caused by various diseases such as bitter rot (sunken, brown-black spots that enlarge); scab (velvety, olive-brown spots that become cork-like); fire blight (brown spots, fruit eventually shrivels); or San Jose scale (small, red-purple spots with a light-colored center). For all of these, dispose of all infected fruit, prune out dead wood, remove brush, and plant resistant varieties.

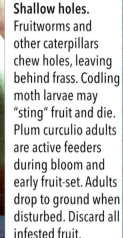
12.R19 Codling moth damage

Shallow holes. Fruitworms and other caterpillars chew holes, leaving behind frass. Codling moth larvae may "sting" fruit and die. Plum curculio adults are active feeders during bloom and early fruit-set. Adults drop to ground when disturbed. Discard all infested fruit.

12.R20 Sooty blotch - apple

Circular clusters of tiny, black specks and small, sooty smudges. Fly speck, sooty blotch, and sooty mold on pear are common, late fungal diseases. Damage can be rubbed or peeled off. Dip fruit in a 10% bleach solution.

12.R21 Deformed apple

Deformed fruit. Caused by early infection of buds; aphids feeding on buds; tarnished plant bug and other insect pests. Control insect and disease pests and remove all affected fruit.

12.R22 Hornet on apple

Insects hover around ripe fruit. Yellow jackets, hornets, and sap beetles feed on ripe fruit. Do not allow fruit to over-mature. Pick up drops.

continued on next page

continued from previous page

FIGHTING FIRE BLIGHT WITH THE "UGLY-STUB" PRUNING METHOD

The fire blight bacterium is a systemic pathogen that moves rapidly into healthy tree tissue. Backyard orchardists are often unaware that pruning infected shoots and limbs during the growing season can further spread the disease. Follow these pruning guidelines:

- Use very sharp pruning tools to remove infected limbs 8 to 12 inches below visible symptoms.

- Do not make the cut back to a healthy limb or spur, but leave a naked ("ugly") stub. (The bacterium will colonize the ends of these pruning cuts and produce cankers, which serve as a source of inoculum for continued infection).

- Mark the stubs to make it easier to locate them. Remove and dispose of the "ugly stubs" during dormant pruning (November-January).

Adapted from: Steiner, P.W. "Ugly Stub" Procedure for Removing Fire blight Symptoms. Extension Fruit Pathology Mimeo. University of Maryland.

Key 12-S.   Pests and Diseases of Stone Fruits (Peach, Cherry, Plum, Apricot)

FOLIAGE SYMPTOMS

12.S1   Powdery mildew

White-gray powder on leaves and buds. Caused by powdery mildew. Remove damaged shoots and prune to improve air flow. If this was a problem the previous year, spray with wettable sulfur at bloom or check horticultural oil labels for control. Select resistant varieties. Also occurs on fruit.

12.S2   Japanese beetle damage

Leaves chewed. Caused by caterpillars or Japanese beetles, which skeletonize leaves. Hand-pick pests. If severe, use a registered insecticide.

12.S3   Peach leaf curl

Leaves curl and pucker. Peach leaf curl is a fungal disease that appears on unfolding leaves in spring. Leaves are thickened, malformed, and brightly colored (purple, red, and orange). Apply a pre-bloom fungicide such as lime-sulfur on all tree parts.

12.S4   Bud damage by plant bug

No buds/damaged buds. Frost damage, improper pruning, and feeding by plant bugs can cause injury to buds. Mow or pull weeds to deter plant bugs.

continued on next page

continued from previous page

Key 12-S.   Pests and Diseases of Stone Fruits (Peach, Cherry, Plum, Apricot)

FOLIAGE SYMPTOMS (continued)

Peach aphids

Verticillium wilt

Leaf yellowing. Green peach aphid: Leaves curl, yellow, and drop. Aphid honeydew can cause on foliage. Spray a water stream at aphids and apply a dormant-oil spray at bud swell. **Spider mites:** White flecks or stippling; leaves brown and die. Worse in hot, dry weather. Apply a dormant-oil spray at bud swell. **Cankers, phytophthora, and verticillium wilt:** Dispose of infected plants. Plant certified stock in well-drained soil.

12.S5   Stone fruit leaf yellowing

Bacterial spot - peach

Cherry leaf spot

Nitrogen deficiency - cherry

Leaf spots. Bacterial spot (peaches): Small, angular spots appear between veins. Spots are green, turn purple, and finally brown. **Scab (peaches):** Small, olive-green spots. **Cherry leaf spot:** Small, purple spots. Leaves develop holes, turn yellow, and often drop. **Plum leaf spot:** Similar to cherry leaf spot, but spots are smaller. **Nitrogen deficiency:** Red spots appear on yellowing leaves. Promptly rake up and dispose of all infected leaves.

12.S6   Stone fruit leaf spots

SHOOT, BRANCH, AND TRUNK PROBLEMS

Gummosis caused by borer

Peach tree borer adult

Gum oozes from trunk base or lower branch crotches. Peach tree borers are 1½-in. white larvae with a brown head. Female adult is a large, blue-and-orange, clear-wing moth. Larvae feed beneath bark and overwinter. Sawdust-like frass may be seen. Spear larvae in the holes with a thin wire. Use insecticide on the trunk. One or two borers can kill a tree.

12.S7   Peach tree borer damage

Dark, sunken cankers. Gummosis may be seen. Cankers are caused by various fungal and bacterial diseases (especially Cytospora canker). Prune and dispose of infected wood below damage, then prune for better air flow. Do not leave stubs. Avoid fertilization after mid-July. Apply interior white latex paint to trunk and large branches after leaf fall.

12.S8   Cytospora canker - apricot

continued on next page

continued from previous page

Key 12-S.   Pests and Diseases of Stone Fruits (Peach, Cherry, Plum, Apricot)

SHOOT, BRANCH, AND TRUNK PROBLEMS (continued)

12.S9 Peach tree shoot damage

Peach shoots wilt and die. Oriental fruit moth larvae are 1/2-in., gray-white with a black head. They bore several inches into new shoots and overwinter in soil under the tree. Prune out and dispose of wilted tips 6 in. below visible damage. Spray an insecticide at petal fall.

12.S12 Lecanium scale

Small, reddish-brown and black bumps on 1- to 3-year-old wood. Lecanium scale is noticeable from May through July. Crawlers feed on foliage after hatching in July. Apply a dormant-rate horticultural oil spray before bud break.

12.S10 Rabbit damage to trunk

Roots and base of young trees are chewed. Voles and rabbits nest under cover around trunks. Keep area mowed and mulch pulled back from trunk. Place tree guards (18-in. tall cylinders of hardware cloth) around trees and 2-3 in. below soil line. Use traps to reduce vole population.

12.S13 Sooty mold

Trunk coated in honeydew/sooty mold. Spotted lanternfly feeding by a large population may stunt growth and reduce yields. Scrape overwintered egg masses; smash adults and nymphs.

12.S11 Black knot - cherry

Black, gnarled swellings. Black knot is a fungal disease of plum and cherry that causes fungal galls. Prune out and dispose of infected wood in very early spring, 3 in. below visible damage. Plant resistant varieties.

12.S14 Shothole borer gummosis

Many small, round holes in twigs and branches. Shothole borer is a bark beetle that overwinters in twigs. Gum may be present. Promptly dispose of infested branches. Painting tree trunks with white water-based latex paint can help repel adults, especially on young trees.

continued on next page

continued from previous page

Key 12-S.   Pests and Diseases of Stone Fruits (Peach, Cherry, Plum, Apricot)

FRUIT PROBLEMS

12.S15 Stone-fruit spots

Spots on fruit.
Brown rot: Small, circular, light-brown lesions expand on ripening fruit. Gray spores appear in moist conditions. Do not allow fruit to over-mature. Promptly dispose of infected fruits and "mummies" on trees and on the ground. Spray fungicides at bloom and as fruit begins to color. A post-harvest 1- to 2-min. dip of fruits in a 10% chlorine bleach solution will kill surface spores. **Peach scab:** Numerous small, greenish, circular spots on fruit surface turn brown-black and velvety. Dispose of infected fruit and harvest prior to full ripeness. **Rhizopus soft rot:** A fungal disease that develops after harvest and is similar to brown rot. Favors heat and humidity. Fruit become soft and covered with whisker-like growth. Avoid bruising/injuring fruit and practice good orchard sanitation.

12.S16 Catfacing- peach

Deformed fruit.
True bug feeding: Fruit remains edible. Control weeds around the planting to deter bugs. **Plum pockets:** This fungal disease causes plums to become elongated and misshapen. Apply a liquid lime-sulfur spray at bud swell.

12.S17 Bird damage - cherries

Fruits pecked, torn, or removed. Bird and squirrel feeding: Harvest fruit before fully ripe. Netting can help but may be impractical for larger trees.

12.S18 Plant bug scarring

Fruits chewed or scarred. Plant bug feeding affects young fruits. Dispose of damaged fruits and control weeds around the planting.

12.S19 Oriental fruit moth damage

Fruits exude gum. Oriental fruit moth larvae bore at stem end. Dispose of infested fruit. Cultivate very shallowly around tree base 2 weeks before bloom.

Insects hover around ripe fruit. Yellow jackets, hornets, and sap beetles feed on overripe fruit. See 12.R22.

Premature fruit drop. Feeding damage by insect pests such as cherry fruit worm. See 12.R15 for controls.

Key 12-T.   Pests and Diseases of Small Fruits

FOLIAGE SYMPTOMS

Aphids

Spider mite damage

Leafhopper damage

12.T1   Leaf-yellowing causes

Leaves yellowing. Aphids: Leaves also curl and crinkle, and drop. Sooty mold may develop. Natural predators usually control the pests. A hard water spray will dislodge aphids. **Spider mites:** Cause white or yellow flecks. Leaves bronze, brown, and die. Monitor plants in hot, dry weather. Spray with horticultural oil or insecticidal soap when mites are first seen. Don't spray if feeding injury is severe or temperatures are over 85°F. **Leafhoppers:** Tiny sap suckers cause white-yellow blotching on leaf margins. Can spread diseases.

12.T2   Mottling - blackberry leaf

Green and yellow mottling, stunted plants. Caused by viral diseases. Purchase certified, virus-free plants. Prune out infected canes; if more than 20% are infected, remove plant. Dig up and remove related wild bramble and control aphids.

12.T3   Powdery mildew - grape

Grayish-white, powdery growth on leaves. Caused by powdery mildew Check horticultural oil labels for control.

12.T4   Strawberry leaf spot

Leaf spots. Caused by various fungal leaf-spot diseases. Rake up and discard infected leaves.

12.T5   Leafroller - strawberry

Leaves rolled together with small caterpillars feeding inside. Leafrollers are the cause. Prune out and dispose of damaged foliage and pests.

12.T6   Japanese beetle- raspberry

Leaves chewed. Various caterpillars: Hand-pick pests or use a row cover. **Japanese beetles:** Skeletonize leaves, especially brambles. Hand-pick beetles. Spray spinosad or neem oil if severe.

12.T7   Root-knot nematodes

Plant wilts; leaves may yellow. Various root-rot/wilt diseases: Remove infected plants and plant certified stock in well-drained soil. **Root-knot nematodes:** Gall-like growths appear on roots. Remove affected plants and replant elsewhere.

continued on next page

continued from previous page

Key 12-T.   Pests and Diseases of Small Fruits

OTHER SMALL FRUIT PROBLEMS

12.T8 Vole damage

Roots, crowns, and lower stems chewed. Voles and rabbits nest in mulch, weeds, and plant debris. Keep the area mowed and mulch pulled back from crowns. Use traps to reduce vole population.

12.T9 Deer eating raspberry

Shoots chewed/girdled, bark stripped. Deer feeding. Install 8' fencing and repel deer by hanging mesh bags containing soap bars, human hair, or blood meal on plants.

12.T10 Wasp on grapes

Flying insects hovering around ripe fruit. Yellow jackets, other wasps/hornets, and sap beetles: small black beetles feed on overripe fruit. Do not allow fruit to over-mature.

12.T11 Weedy garden patch

Low plant vigor and fruit yield. Overcrowded plants, weed competition, "wet" feet, winter damage, low soil fertility, and low light conditions can all contribute. See **Chapter 19, Small Fruits.**

12.T12 Botrytis - blackberry

Ripe fruit rots; gray, fuzzy mold develops. Botrytis (gray mold): this fungal disease is worse during humid, wet weather. Do not allow fruit to over-mature. Dispose of all infected fruit. Prune to increase air flow. Fungicides are not effective once symptoms are observed.

12.T13 Spur blight - raspberry

Dark lesions along canes and branches; dieback. Caused by fungal diseases. Prune and dispose of infected plant parts. Plants may need replacing.

12.T14 Berries covered by tulle

Fruits pecked, torn, or removed. Bird and rodent damage. Place netting over plants 2 to 3 weeks prior to ripening. Deter them with iridescent silver and red streamers over the plant.

12.T15 Crown galls - blackberry

Galls at base of plant, on roots, and on canes. Crown and cane galls are spongy, rough swellings that become dark and woody with age. Dispose of the plant.

continued on next page

continued from previous page

Key 12-T.   Pests and Diseases of Small Fruits

OTHER SMALL FRUIT PROBLEMS

12.T16 Botrytis - strawberry

Dieback of shoot tips and blooms. Botrytis is a fungal disease that is more severe in cool, wet springs. Brown discoloration spreads down shoots and twigs. Blossoms look water-soaked. Reduce nitrogen feeding in spring and prune to increase air circulation. Prune out and remove all infected plant parts.

12.T17 Mummy berry

Berries turn red or tan as they ripen, and become hard and shriveled. Buds, blossoms, shoot tips, and leaves brown/wither. Caused by mummy berry. A powdery mass of spores may appear on plants. Prune out infected parts, collect all fallen fruit "mummies," and dispose of them. Buy resistant varieties.

BRAMBLES

12.T18 Anthracnose - raspberry

White or tan spots with purple borders on canes, followed by dieback. Caused by anthracnose (fungal) infections. Space canes and prune for better air flow. Prune out badly infected canes. Apply a dormant spray of liquid lime-sulfur. Remove nearby wild bramble plants.

12.T19 Spotted-wing drosophila

Damaged fruits. Spotted-wing drosophila and other fruit flies have tiny white larvae that feed in blueberry and raspberry fruits. Harvest promptly. Pyrethrin and spinosad can help control infestations.

12.T20 Blackberry rust

Blister-like, red-orange pustules form on leaf underside. Rust: a group of several fungal diseases mainly found on blackberries and black raspberries. Promptly remove and dispose of affected plant parts. Remove wild brambles in vicinity. Plant resistant varieties from certified stock.

12.T21 Verticillium wilt

Stunted shoots yellow, wilt, and die. Verticillium wilt, primarily on black raspberries. Most severe in cool, moist spring weather. Dispose of infected plants. Plant certified nursery stock.

continued on next page

continued from previous page

Key 12-T.   Pests and Diseases of Small Fruits

BRAMBLES (continued)

12.T22 Cane/spur blight - raspberry

Primocanes (new canes) and floricanes (fruiting canes) develop brown-purple lesions, wilt, and die. Cane and spur blight (fungal diseases): infects recently pruned canes. More prevalent on black raspberries. Prune during dry weather for increased air circulation. Promptly remove dead canes after fruiting. Apply a dormant spray of liquid lime-sulfur when buds are half-green at the tips.

12.T23 Cane borers

Plant becomes weak; individual canes wilt and die. Crown and cane borers: Larvae feed inside canes and crowns. Prune out and dispose of old and damaged canes below damage. **Raspberry cane borers:** Slender 1/2-in. long black beetles begin feeding in shoot tips in June and may reach the crown by fall. Remove wilted shoot tips in mid-summer. Dispose of old and affected canes below the damage.

GRAPES

12.T24 Black rot - grape

Brown spots on leaves; grapes turn black, shrivel, and stay attached. Black rot is the most serious problem for home growers. Fruit is most susceptible when pea-sized, but infections can continue until fruit begins to ripen. Dispose of all affected plant parts, especially "mummies." Prune to improve air flow. Spraying registered fungicides after new growth in spring can greatly reduce severity.

12.T25 Botrytis - grape

Ripe grapes rot on the vine. Botrytis (bunch rot) is a fungal disease that enters breaks in grape skins. Most likely to occur near harvest time but can occur any time during the season. Remove all affected clusters. Prune to increase air circulation. Maintain even soil moisture and avoid overhead watering. Spraying a registered fungicide during bloom and 2-3 weeks before harvest can greatly reduce severity.

continued on next page

continued from previous page

Key 12-T.   Pests and Diseases of Small Fruits

GRAPES (continued)

12.T26 Downy mildew on leaf

Small yellow spots on upper leaf surfaces. Downy mildew also displays white cottony growth on the undersides of the spots. Plant resistant varieties.

12.T27 Spotted lanternfly

Honeydew/sooty mold on leaves/canes. Spotted lanternflies weaken vines, which affects hardiness, yields, and may cause death. Scrape off overwintered eggs; use fine-mesh netting.

12.T28 Grape flea beetle

Small holes chewed in buds and leaves. Small, black flea beetle adults and larvae are damaging.

12.T29 Grape berry moth

Individual berries are webbed together by silk threads. Grape berry moths make visible entrance holes. Discard infested fruit.

12.T30 Grape tumid gall

Small, rough green or red galls on leaves. Grape tumid galls are red. Grape phylloxera are small, aphid-like insects that produce green galls on leaves and roots. Plant varieties that are grafted onto resistant rootstock.

12.T31 Grape cane girdler

Canes are scarred or girdled. Grape cane girdlers are 1/8-in. long black weevils that chew holes in cane ends and overwinter in them. Prune to 6 in. below the damage.

12.T32 Spotted-wing drosophila

Damaged fruits. Caused by spotted-wing drosophila and other fruit-fly species. Tiny white larvae also feed in blueberry and raspberry fruits. Harvest promptly. Organic insecticides (e.g., pyrethrins and spinosad) can help.

STRAWBERRIES

12.T33 Spittlebug nest

Small, white, frothy masses on stems and leaves. Small orange-green spittlebug nymphs suck sap under the spittle. An early-season issue; no controls needed.

12.T34 Flea beetle damage

Holes chewed in leaves. Flea beetles are tiny, dark insects that jump when disturbed. Larvae and adults feed on flowers, leaves, and young fruit. Use a floating row cover.

continued on next page

continued from previous page

Key 12-T.   Pests and Diseases of Small Fruits

STRAWBERRIES (continued)

12.T35 Slug/cutworm damage — Cutworm damage / Slug damage

Damaged fruits. Slugs: Look for trails. Remove breeding/hibernating habitat. Install a row cover, but remove it when plants start to flower. **Cutworms:** Make large, clean holes. Control with diatomaceous earth (DE). **Sap beetles:** Small black insects feed on overripe fruit. **Tarnished plant bug:** Causes "button berry" (i.e., small, woody, and knobbed fruits.

12.T36 Plant bug scarring — Pythium rot / Strawberry aphid

Stunted, weak plants. Various root- and crown-feeding insects: Do not plant in newly tilled grass or sod. Avoid poorly drained soil. Plant in raised beds. **Viral diseases:** Remove infected plants and replace with virus-indexed plants. Control leaf-feeding insects (e.g., leafhoppers, aphids) that spread virus diseases.

Key 12-U.   Pests and Diseases of Nut Trees

FOLIAGE/WOOD SYMPTOMS

12.U1 Walnut caterpillar

Holes chewed in leaves. Often caused by walnut caterpillars, which are hairy and feed in clusters in mid-summer. No control is necessary.

12.U2 Hickory galls

Wart-like growths on exposed roots and lower trunk. Crown gall (bacterial disease) will cause the tree to decline and die prematurely. No controls are available. Avoid mechanical injury to tree trunk and roots.

12.U3 Pecan scab

Spots/blotches on leaves. Caused by insects and diseases. Pecan scab produces dark-olive to black spots. Dispose of fallen leaves.

12.U4 Dieback on walnut

Wilted, water-soaked foliage. Weevil larvae bore into shoots, causing dieback. Promptly prune wilted shoots.

12.U5 Thousand cankers - walnut

Branch dieback. Canker diseases: Remove diseased/damaged wood during dormancy.

continued on next page

continued from previous page

Key 12-U.   Pests and Diseases of Nut Trees

NUT PROBLEMS

Failure to bear. Immature tree: Most nut trees need 6-10 years to produce. **Biennial bearing pattern:** Heavy crops followed by crop failure. Selectively prune and use less fertilizer. **Lack of cross-pollination:** Always plant two or more compatible varieties of the same species. **Overfertilization:** Tree has mostly leaves but few/no nuts. Reduce nitrogen use. **Poor soil drainage, low soil fertility:** Nut trees need deep, well-drained soil. **Spring freezes:** Bud development is poor or non-existent. **Defoliation:** Identify and control serious insect or disease problems. **Not adapted to Maryland:** Pecan trees rarely produce consistent crops, especially on the Western Shore.

12.U6   Failure-to-bear examples

Premature drop. Poor pollination, insects, diseases, drought, and cold: Examine drops for insects. Dispose of diseased and infested nuts.

12.U7   Premature hickory nut drop

12.U8   Poor nutmeat development

12.U9   Damaged nutmeats

Shells are empty or poorly filled. Poor pollination: Cool/rainy during bloom period; short bloom period; low bee activity. **Spring frost/freeze:** Buds fail to develop. **Growing season too short/cool:** Match varieties to the climate. **Micronutrient deficiency:** Boron, zinc, iron, copper, magnesium, and calcium are essential. Test the soil and follow lab recommendations. **Drought:** Keep trees watered.

Nutmeats are discolored or chewed. Walnut husk fly: Larvae feed on green husks. Females lay eggs in mid-summer. Dispose of all fallen nuts. **Walnut curculios:** Dark brown, long-snouted weevils. Females lay eggs on twigs and young nuts. Larvae bore into nutmeats. Pecan and chestnut weevils are similar. Lay down a tarp and tap branches with a padded broom. Adults will drop. Do not leave nuts on the ground.

Key 12-V.   Pests and Diseases of Turfgrass

See **Chapter 14, Lawns,** for detailed information about turfgrasses.

SPOTS/DISCOLORATION OF BLADES/TURF AREAS

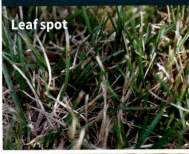

Leaf spot

Leaf spot close-up

Dollar spot

Brown patch close-up

Brown patch

12.V1   Turf leaf-spot examples

Leaf spots. Dollar spot: Leaf lesions have a dark border and hourglass-shaped spots. Common in late spring. Avoid drought stress; prevent thatch buildup and soil compaction. Maintain adequate nitrogen (N) levels by following the Univ. of Maryland Extension (UME) guidelines. **Brown patch (BP):** Most common disease of tall fescue. Blades have elongated lesions with chocolate-brown margins. Entire leaves may brown and thin. Diseased blades can be scattered through the lawn, causing thinning/browning. Occurs when temperatures are 85°+ (day) or 68°+ (night), and relative humidity is high. Mow at proper height. Avoid using water-soluble or quick-release N fertilizer in the spring. In late summer or early fall, overseed or reseed bare areas. Follow UME guidelines.

12.V2   Red thread

Pink-reddish blades. Caused by red thread. Thread-like growths extend beyond leaf blades, appearing in patches. Occurs in spring and fall on fine fescue, perennial ryegrass, and tall fescue. Maintain adequate nitrogen fertilizer levels by following UME guidelines.

12.V3   Slime mold on grass blades

White, gray, brown, purple, or black spore masses suddenly appear on blades. Caused by slime mold. Young spore masses are sticky, but when dry can be easily rubbed off. Warm weather and high moisture favor slime mold reproduction. Remove masses with a strong stream of water, mowing, or raking.

12.V4   Powdery mildew

White coating on blades. Powdery mildew occurs on shaded bluegrass in the fall, but can affect tall fescue. Avoid excess N and drought stress. Increase mower height and re-seed with resistant cultivars.

continued on next page

continued from previous page

Key 12-V.   Pests and Diseases of Turfgrass

See **Chapter 14, Lawns,** for detailed information about turfgrasses.

SPOTS/DISCOLORATION OF BLADES/TURF AREAS (continued)

12.V5 Nitrogen deficiency

Large areas of yellowing grass. Most likely an N deficiency, but also check for a potassium deficiency, pest infestation, or disease of blades or roots. Keep lawn properly fertilized and watered.

12.V6 Sooty mold

Black coating on blades. Occurs primarily in spring or fall after rain. Blades remain green underneath. Sooty mold is not harmful. Wash off soot with a hose, or mow.

12.V7 Lawn rust examples (Orange lawn rust / Yellow lawn rust)

Red, orange, or yellow powder on blades. Rust diseases cause turf to appear yellow or reddish from a distance. Fungal spores rub off on hands, shoes, and clothing. Rust is favored by temperatures between 70-75°F with high humidity, heavy dew, or rain. Rust can infect most grass species in Maryland. Maintain adequate nitrogen levels by following **UME guidelines.**

12.V8 Sod webworm damage

Irregular brown patches with white moths flying low. Sod webworms may be found at the base of the blades and in thatch. They are active from June-July. Reseed with an endophyte-containing type like tall fescue, or spray with Bt.

12.V9 Iron chlorosis

Pale green to golden yellow turf. Chlorosis is an iron or nitrogen deficiency. Yellow streaks may form parallel to leaf veins. Maintain nutrient levels in soil.

12.V10 Herbicide injury

Banded streaks or irregular patterns. Fertilizer or chemical injury may cause grass to be stimulated at the margins. May kill the crown tissue. Calibrate spreaders and sprayers for uniform and accurate application.

12.V11 Drought stress

Turf appears dry and bluish-green. Grass wilts and footprints remain after walking on turf. Caused by drought. Water the lawn.

continued on next page

continued from previous page

Key 12-V. Pests and Diseases of Turfgrass

See **Chapter 14, Lawns,** for detailed information about turfgrasses.

SPOTS/DISCOLORATION OF BLADES/TURF AREAS (continued)

12.V12 Summer patch

Circular, straw-colored patches. Summer patch causes round patches from 3- to 12-in. across. Occurs in bluegrass and fine fescue lawns 2 years or older, from July to Sept. Avoid excessive N, especially in spring. Use slow-release N sources. Increase mowing height, avoid frequent waterings, and reduce thatch.

12.V13 Dog urine spots

Straw-colored patches ringed by dark-green turf. Dog urine may resemble some diseases. May kill the crown tissue. Heavy irrigation will promote recovery.

12.V14 Chinch bug and damage

Localized yellow or brown area. Tiny chinch bugs are black with shiny white wings. They are found on grass crowns and stems. Damage usually occurs in sunny, well-drained locations. Reseed with grasses with high levels of endophyte, such as tall fescue. Often controlled by natural predators.

12.V15 Fairy rings

Rings/arcs of dead or green grass. Mushrooms may be present. Fairy rings are bordered by darker green grass. More common on droughty sites and poorly-nourished turf. Occurs on all turf types. Frequently aerate, maintain adequate nitrogen levels, and water during dry spells.

12.V16 Dead grass over landfill

Patches of dead or dormant grass. Can be caused by buried debris, insect injury, or thick thatch. Often follows a dry period. Determine the cause and treat accordingly.

12.V17 Oil spill from mower

Black or dark spots or patches. Caused by oil or gasoline leakage from lawn equipment. Small gasoline spills can be flushed with water. A severe leak/spill of oil or gas requires replacing the soil.

12.V18 Chlorine damage

Yellow patches near a pool. Chlorine damage from pool water. Leach chlorine through the soil with water and replant.

continued on next page

332 Maryland Master Gardener Handbook UME © 2025. All rights reserved.

continued from previous page

Key 12-V. Pests and Diseases of Turfgrass

See **Chapter 14, Lawns,** for detailed information about turfgrasses.

OTHER TURF PROBLEMS

12.V19 Chafer grub

Turf comes up easily, showing lack of roots. C-shaped white grubs are seen in soil from June-Sept. Can be severe on bluegrass, ryegrass, and fine fescues. Reseed in the fall with a tolerant species like tall fescue or zoysia.

12.V23 Mushrooms in lawn

Mushrooms pop up in lawn. Fungi can appear after wet weather. Mushrooms feed on dead organic matter (e.g., roots, stumps). There is no practical way to eliminate mushrooms. Pick or rake them up.

12.V20 Billbug grubs

Turf blades pull out easily. Billbugs are light tan, legless grubs found near crowns and roots from June-Aug. Water and fertilize grass to stimulate regrowth. Reseed with tall fescues. If needed, use an insecticide from April to mid-May.

12.V24 Moss growing in grass

Green "carpet" grows on bare soil or under thin grass. Moss grows in poorly drained or compacted areas and is more severe in shade. Improve drainage and establish a thicker lawn. Aerate compacted areas and increase light.

12.V21 Algae growing on soil

Black or greenish crust on soil. Algae grows on bare soil or thin turf where soil is poorly drained or compacted. Usually more severe in shade. Improve drainage and establish a thicker lawn. Aerate soil and increase sunlight.

12.V25 Tawny mining bee nest

Holes in the ground; bees flying low over lawn. Mining, digger, or ground bees nest underground. They seldom sting and are active for 2-4 weeks. They are important pollinators; tolerate their brief activity or thicken the lawn to deter nesting.

12.V22 Scalped grass

Grass on high spots looks scalped. Caused by mowers. Level the terrain, raise the mower blade, or change mowing direction.

12.V26 Dull mower blade damage

Ragged blade tips. Tips appear gray, then turn tan. Keep mower blade sharp to avoid blade injury.

Key 12-W. Pests and Diseases of Indoor Plants   (See Key 12-X for common household pest identification)

See **Chapter 23, Indoor Plants,** for detailed information.

FOLIAGE/FLOWER SYMPTOMS

Aphids

Spider mites/webbing

Mealybugs

Whiteflies

Brown scale

12.W1 Indoor plant leaf symptoms

Leaf yellowing; foliage fades, yellows, browns, or wilts. Aphids: Small, soft-bodied insects are found on leaves, stems, and flower buds. **Spider mites:** Tiny pests feed on lower leaf surfaces. Webbing may be visible. **Mealybugs:** White, cottony insects. **Whiteflies:** Adults are tiny white insects that fly from the plants when disturbed. Immature stages are found on lower leaf surfaces. **Brown soft-scale and hemispherical scale:** Raised black or brown bumps on leaves and stems. Regularly rinse plants with water to keep down pest problems. Use a registered houseplant spray to control pests but note that plants that are already damaged can be injured further by insecticidal sprays. Remove diseased plants from their pots, cut out infested/rotten portions, and replant remaining healthy sections. Take cuttings and root them in sterile potting mix. Discard severely damaged plants.

12.W2 Leaf spot - prayer plant

Leaf spots and blotches. Caused by water spots, sunburn, fungi, or bacteria. Remove spotted leaves and improve air circulation. Keep water off the foliage of sensitive plants.

12.W3 Mottling - philodendron

Leaf mottling. Caused by viruses. Foliage appears mottled green and yellow. Plants may be stunted. Discard plant.

12.W4 Leaf scorch - avocado

Leaf scorch. Caused by overfertilization and lack of water. Symptoms occur along leaf margins or between veins. Flush excess fertilizer with water or re-pot with new media.

12.W5 Powdery mildew - poinsettia

White, powdery coating. Powdery mildew. Provide better air flow. Remove affected leaves. Spray with a registered fungicide if severe.

12.W6 Non-flowering Oxalis

Few or no flowers. Low light levels, excessive fertilizer, or cyclamen mites. Relocate plants closer to a light source or add artificial light. Mite-infested plants should be discarded.

continued on next page

334   Maryland Master Gardener Handbook   UME © 2025. All rights reserved.

continued from previous page

Key 12-W. Pests and Diseases of Indoor Plants (See Key 12-X for common household pest identification)

See **Chapter 23, Indoor Plants,** for detailed information.

FOLIAGE SYMPTOMS (continued)

12.W7 "Hitchhiking" pests

Leaves eaten or chewed. Check outdoor plants that are moved inside for pests such as caterpillars, aphids, sowbugs, beetles, weevils, grasshoppers, crickets, slugs, and earwigs. Hand-pick pests and re-pot plants before moving if needed.

12.W8 Mealybugs - areca palm

Fluffy white wax. Mealybugs: White, cottony insects may occur on foliage and in leaf axles, leaf sheaths, roots, and bud scales. Their sap-sucking can cause yellow leaves, stunting, dieback, or death. Use a registered houseplant spray to control them.

WHOLE-PLANT SYMPTOMS

12.W9 Fungus gnats

Flying insects. Whiteflies: Tiny white insects. Use a specific whitefly insecticide. **Fungus gnats:** Tiny black flies fly near plants or light sources. Allow potting media to dry between waterings. Use beneficial nematodes to control larvae.

12.W12 Weak growth

Spindly growth. Low light levels or excessive fertilizer. Relocate plants closer to a light source or add artificial light. Reduce fertilizer over the winter. Irrigate from the top of the pot to leach excess fertilizer salts.

12.W10 Wilting due to over-watering

Wilting. Can be caused by overwatering/root rot, or because the plant is rootbound and needs repotting. Cut out rot and replant remaining plant.

12.W13 Mite damage

Stunted, distorted growth. Aphids: Small, soft-bodied insects. Control with a water stream or registered insecticide. **Cyclamen mites:** Mostly affect flowering plants. Mite- and virus-infected plants are incurable and should be discarded, especially African violets.

12.W11 Root rot - monstera

Soft, discolored roots. Caused by root rots, usually due to overwatering. Discard plant.

UME © 2025. All rights reserved.   12: Plant Diagnostics   335

Key 12-X.   Identification of Indoor Pests

FLYING PESTS

Adult/larva or nymph (not to scale)	Description	Controls
12-X1	**Clothes moth**: Has a ⅜- to 1/2-in. wingspan and buff-colored wings. Larvae are creamy-white caterpillars, measuring up to 1/2-in. long. Found in closets, bedrooms, and attics.	Locate infested fabric or carpet. Check under wool rugs for larvae. Vacuum and shampoo or dry-clean. Store cleaned fabrics in sealed bags/containers or a cedar chest.
12-X2	**Indian meal moth**: Wingspan is ⅝ in., forewings are gray with a reddish-brown tip. Found in the kitchen and pantry. Attracted to light.	Locate infestation and dispose of infested material. Store food in airtight plastic or glass containers or in the freezer. Check stored bird seed, pet food, and dried foods.
12-X3	**Drain fly**: Tiny, gray-black, fuzzy, moth-like insect. Found in bathrooms and near sinks and floor drains.	Clean drains with an enzyme cleaner and manually clean traps. DO NOT pour insecticide down a drain to kill drain flies.
12-X4	**Fungus gnat**: Tiny, black, gnat-like fly. Found flying around houseplants and standing water.	Keep plant saucers dry and allow plants to dry between waterings. Avoid over-fertilization. If necessary, re-pot plants with fresh potting media.
12-X5	**Fruit fly**: Small, tan-colored fly with red eyes. Found in the kitchen.	Store produce in the refrigerator. Rinse cans and bottles for recycling. Ensure that canning containers are well-sealed. Equip windows and doors with tight-fitting (16 mesh) screens to discourage fruit flies.

JUMPING PESTS

12-X6	**Fleas**: Very small, dark brown insect that bites/feeds on human and animal blood. Prefers warm, dark areas of the house.	Thoroughly vacuum carpeting and upholstery, under furniture, and along baseboards. Dispose of bag. Use product containing growth-regulator methoprene to control flea larvae. Control fleas on pets.
12-X7	**Greenhouse camel crickets**: Measure 1 in. or more. Hump-backed, wingless, brown, with long antennae and legs. Found in basement, kitchen/pantry. Attracted to light. Scary-looking, but harmless.	Prevent entry by tightening screens and weather-stripping doors and windows. Dehumidify basements. Keep pet foods and dry food products in tight containers.

continued on next page

continued from previous page

Key 12-X.   Identification of Indoor Pests

JUMPING PESTS (continued)

Adult/larva or nymph (not to scale)	Description	Controls
12-X8	**House or field cricket:** Measures 1 in. or more. Winged, black or brown, usually found in the basement or first floor. Harmless.	Prevent entry by tightening screens and weather-stripping doors and windows. Dehumidify basements. Keep pet foods and dry food products in tight containers.
12-X9	**Springtail:** Tiny (1/8-in. or less), gray to white. Found in bathrooms, around flower pots, or other areas of high humidity. Harmless.	Dehumidify the area. Clean mold and mildew from surfaces. Allow media in potted plants to dry out between waterings or re-pot with fresh media.

WALKING/CRAWLING PESTS

	Description	Controls
12-X10	**Millipede:** 1 in. or longer, dark brown, with many short legs. Usually found in the basement or near an outside entry door.	Prevent entry to home. Weather-strip doors, install new thresholds, and caulk around basement window frames. Dehumidify damp basements.
12-X11	**House centipede:** Over 1-in. long with many long legs. Quick mover. A predatory arthropod that feeds on other insects such as cockroaches. Harmless.	Escort it outdoors. Prevent entry to home. Weather-strip doors, install new thresholds, and caulk around basement window frames.
12-X12	**Spider:** Size is variable, 8 legs, color variable, smooth or hairy, may or may not have a web. A predator that feeds on insects and other spiders. Most are harmless.	Escort it outdoors. Check for other insects in house that may be source of food for spiders. Many enter house in fall. Caulk and seal cracks around doors and windows.
12-X13	**Silverfish or firebrat:** Flattened gray or tan body, about 1/2-in. long with 3 tails. Found in boxes, cabinets, and bathrooms; and near furnaces and other warm areas.	Dehumidify area and store books and papers in sealed containers.
12-X14	**Earwig:** Dark brown, 1/2-in. long, with noticeable pincers on the rear. Will occasionally enter the home but mostly resides outdoors.	Swat or escort it outdoors. Keep debris, mulch, and other hiding places away from the house.
12-X15	**Carpet and cigarette beetle:** Measures 1/4 in. or so. Oval to round; brown, multicolored, or black. Larva are carrot-shaped, furry. Found in closets, bathrooms, and kitchens.	Vacuum thoroughly. Store clean woolens in sealed containers. Dispose of any stored food/spices that have been infested. Store all herbs, spices, and dried foods in airtight containers.

continued on next page

continued from previous page

Key 12-X. Identification of Indoor Pests

WALKING/CRAWLING PESTS (continued)

Adult/larva/egg/nymph	Description	Controls
12-X16	**Pillbug/sowbug:** Measures 1/2- to 3/4-in. long, gray, oval; some roll up into a ball. Pillbugs need a moist environment and die quickly indoors.	Prevent entry to home by weather-stripping doors and thresholds.
12-X17	**Cockroach:** Measure 1/2-in. or longer. Brown to black with long antennae. Found in the kitchen and/or bathroom, often at night.	Have species identified. Sanitation primary control. Use baits containing hydroprene (growth regulator).
12-X18	**Booklice:** Very tiny, tan insects, in or around stored papers and books.	Dehumidify area, store books and papers in sealed containers.
12-X19	**Ant:** Small to large, brown to black, pinched waist, 6 legs. Usually found in the kitchen, occasionally in other rooms.	Identify ant type. Block entry from outdoors. Use bait stations to control ants indoors; granular bait and bait stations are also available for outdoor use.
12-X20	**Bird mite:** Very tiny arachnid that is an external parasite of birds. Will bite humans and animals. They come into house through windows and vents.	Remove bird nests from gutters, vents, and air conditioners. Vacuum mites indoors.
12-X21	**Boxelder bug:** Distinctive red and black insects that appear on the south side of houses and come indoors.	Seal window cracks and screen vents. Control outdoors with a mild soap solution (test on small area to be sure it won't damage siding/plants). Vacuum indoors.
12-X22	**Ladybird beetles:** Color ranges from orange to red, some with spots. Measure about 1/4 in. Ladybird beetles enter around windows and screened porches.	Sweep up indoors and release outside; they are harmless predators of aphids. Seal entry points on the outside of the house.
12-X23	**Clover mites:** Very tiny mites appear in large numbers on sunny exposures, often coming in through windows. Stain red when crushed.	Seal cracks and holes, and vacuum indoors.

Key 12-Y. Identification of Wood-Destroying Pests

Insect/damage	Description	Controls
12.Y1 Subterranean termite	**Subterranean termite:** Small, white, ant-like insects appear in and on wood; the wood becomes soft due to their chewing. Termites create visible mud tubes from the ground to access wood. Damp, punky wood is particularly attractive to termites.	Contact a professional pest-control company.
12.Y2 Termite swarmer	**Termite swarmer:** Dark brown, 1/4-in. long, with 4 wings of equal length. They have a fluttery flight habit. Can appear indoors or outdoors. Swarmers are a reproductive form of subterranean termites, and usually emerge from area of infestation. Swarmers do not cause damage.	Contact a professional pest-control company.
12.Y3 Carpenter ant	**Carpenter ant:** Large brown-to-black insects are 1/4- to 1-in. long, winged or wingless. They are usually found in the house, outdoors, or on trees, often near damaged wood. Carpenter ants do not eat wood, they only nest in it, creating coarse sawdust while nest-building.	Locate nest and treat, repair, or replace damaged wood. Repair water leaks.
12.Y4 Old-house borer	**Old-house borer:** A longhorned beetle. Adults are 5/8- to 1 1/4-in. long, with a slightly flattened black or black-brown body. They attack structural timbers and lumber, creating oval holes and powdery sawdust. They can be heard making chewing noises.	Determine if the infestation is active. Contact a professional pest-control company.
12.Y5 Powder post beetle	**Powder post beetle:** Many species of powder post beetles exist. The most prevalent Maryland species is *Acantholyctus cornifrons*. They are 1/8-in. or smaller and make round holes. Fine sawdust may be seen. They often attack soft woods, structural timbers, pine flooring, imported furniture, and bamboo fences.	Determine if the infestation is active. Replace damaged wood if possible. Contact a professional pest-control company.

Key 12-Z. Identification of Bees and Wasps

Image	Description	Controls	Image	Description	Controls
12.Z1 European hornet	Large, brown with orange markings. May fly at night. Strips bark from trees and shrubs, especially lilacs. Nests in hollow logs, trees, and outbuildings.	Control is difficult. Locating the nest may be unrealistic if it is near a wooded area.	12.Z6 Carpenter bee	Large, with a shiny black abdomen. Bore 1/2-in. round holes in wood to nest. Males have a spot on face, no stinger. Not aggressive.	Treat holes with insecticide and plug with a wooden dowel. They prefer weathered or unpainted wood, but do not eat it.
12.Z2 Yellow jacket	Black and yellow, 1/2 in., not fuzzy. Aggressive. May nest in ground or a gray, papery sphere attached to a house, tree, or shrub. A problem in late summer-early fall.	Use wasp/hornet spray after dark. If in a wall, do not seal opening to the outside or they may chew through interior walls.	12.Z7 Honey bee	Brown, fuzzy, 1/2-in. Common on flowers; nests in trees, commercial hives, and occasionally in structures.	To remove hives, call a beekeeper. If nesting in a wall, contact a pest-control professional. Promptly remove comb and honey after treatment.
12.Z3 Bald-faced hornet	Black with white or yellow markings, 1-in. long legs, narrow waist. Nest in a gray, papery sphere in a tree or shrub.	If near an entry or high-traffic area, use wasp/hornet spray after dark. Do not shine light directly on the nest opening.	12.Z8 Ground bee	Small, fuzzy bees that nest in loose soil in lawns and on banks.	Males have no stinger. They establish a mating territory over the course of a few weeks and only appear threatening. No control necessary.
12.Z4 Paper wasp	Brown with various markings, 1 in. Long, thin legs; narrow waist; nest in a papery nest attached to eaves or porch. Generally not aggressive.	Control is usually not necessary. If near an entry or high-traffic area, use a wasp/hornet spray after dark.	12.Z9 Cicada killer	Large, black, with yellow or white markings on abdomen. They hover above the lawn and nest in loose soil. Not aggressive.	No control necessary.
12.Z5 Bumble bee	Species range from medium to large. Black and yellow stripes, hairy. Common around flowers. Nest in the ground.	Bumble bees are important pollinators.	12.Z10 Scoliid wasp	Blue-black wasp with a yellow stripe on each side, 5/8-in. long. They fly over the lawn during the day. Not aggressive.	A beneficial parasite of white grubs.

AUTHORS

Jon Traunfeld, Extension Specialist and Center Director, Home & Garden Information Center, University of Maryland Extension.

David Clement, Ph.D., Plant Pathologist, HGIC, University of Maryland Extension.

Emily Zobel, Agent Associate, Dorchester County MG Coordinator.

Debra Ricigliano, Lead Horticulturist, University of Maryland, College of Agriculture and Natural Resources, HGIC, retired.

PUBLICATIONS

Main text adapted in part from: J . L. Green. 2000. *A Systematic Approach to Diagnosing Plant Damage.* Horticulture Department, Oregon State University, Corvallis, OR.

2002 ed. Diagnostic Keys, adapted from the *Maryland Master Gardener Handbook*, 1996.

Agnello, A. and G. Chouinard, A. Firlej, W. Turechek, F. Vanoosthuyse, and C. Vincent. 2006. *Tree Fruit Field Guide.* Natural Resource, Agriculture, and Engineering Service (NRAES). Ithaca, NY. ISBN 1-933395-02-8.

Brown-Rytlewski, D., ed. 2007. *A Pocket Guide for IPM Scouting in Woody Landscape Plants*. Michigan State University Extension. East Lansing, MI.

Caldwell, B., E. B. Rosen, E. Sideman, A. Shelton, and C. Smart. 2005. *Resource Guide for Organic Insect and Disease Management*. Cornell University. Geneva, NY.

Chase, A. R., M. Daughtrey, and G. W. Simone. 1995. *Diseases of Annuals and Perennials*. Ball Publishing. Batavia, IL. ISBN 188305208-4.

Childs, R. D., D. C. Swanson, and Dr. R. F. Kujawski. 2002. *Cultural Practice Problems of Trees and Shrubs in the Landscape and Nursery*. University of Massachusetts Extension. Amherst, MA.

Cloyd, R. A., P. L. Nixon, and N. R. Pataky. 2004. *IPM for Gardeners.* Timber Press. Portland, OR. ISBN 0-88192-647-7.

Cranshaw, W. 2004. *Garden Insects of North America*. Princeton University Press. Princeton, NJ. ISBN 0-691-09561-2.

Davidson, J. A. and M. J. Raupp. 1999 (revised). *Landscape IPM. Guidelines for Integrated Pest Management of Insect Pests on Landscape Trees and Shrubs*. Bulletin 350. Maryland Extension. College Park, MD.

Drooz, A.T., ed. 1989. *Insects of Eastern Forests.* USDA, Forest Service. Misc. Publ. 1426. U.S. Department of Agriculture, Forest Service. Washington, DC.

Gill, S., R. A. Cloyd, J. R. Baker, D. L. Clement, and E. Dutky. 2006. 2nd ed. *Pests & Diseases of Herbaceous Perennials.* Ball Publishing. Batavia, IL. ISBN 1-883052-50-5.

Hoffmann, M. P. and A. C. Frodsham. 1993. *Natural Enemies of Vegetable Insect Pests.* Cornell Cooperative Extension. Ithaca, NY.

Howitt, A. H. 1993. *Common Tree Fruit Pests.* North Central Regional Publication No. 63. Michigan State University Cooperative Extension Service, East Lansing, MI. ISBN 13: 9781565250062.

Jaynes, R. A. 1979. *Nut Tree Culture in North America*. Northern Nut Growers Association, New Carlisle, OH.

Johnson, W. T. and H. H. Lyon. 1991. *Insects That Feed on Trees and Shrubs*. Cornell University. Ithaca, NY. ISBN-13: 9780801426025.

Jones, A, L. and T. B. Sutton. 1996. *Diseases of Fruit trees in the East.* Michigan State University Extension. East Lansing, MI. ISBN 1-56525-010-9.

Krischik, V. and J. Davidson. 2004. *IPM (Integrated Pest Management) of Midwest Landscapes.* Minnesota Agricultural Experiment Station. Saint Paul, MN.

MacNab, A. A., A. F. Sherf, and J. K. Springer. 1983. *Identifying Diseases of Vegetables.* Pennsylvania State University College of Agriculture. University Park, PA.

Moorman, G. W. 1997. *Scouting and Controlling Woody Ornamental Diseases in Landscapes and Nurseries.* Pennsylvania State University College of Agriculture. University Park, PA.

Olkowski, W., S. Daar, and H. Olkowski. 1996. *Common Sense Pest Control.* The Taunton Press. Newtown, CT. ISBN 1561581496.

Sherf, A. F. and A. A. McNab. 1986. *Vegetable Diseases and Their Control.* John Wiley & Sons, New York, NY. ISBN: 978-0-471-05860-1.

Sinclair, W. and H. Lyon. 2005. *Diseases of Trees and Shrubs.* Cornell University Press. Geneva, NY. ISBN: 0801443717.

Smith, E. H. and R. C. Whitman. 1992. *NPCA Field Guide to Structural Pests.* National Pest Control Association. Dunn Loring, VA.

PHOTOS (entries marked with an * denote an affiliation with bugwood.org)

UMD Extension: Figures 12-B (canopy loss), 12-D, 12-E (heat damage), 12-H, 12-I, 12-J. Steven Rettke, Rutgers Cooperative Extension: Figure 12-B. Ekaterina via Adobe Stock: Main chapter photo. S. Carroll, used with permission: Figure 12-A. Robert Wick, University of Massachusetts, Bugwood.org*: Figure 12-C. LeAnn Zotta, Berkshire Communications, Generated via AI: Figure12-F. David B Langston, University of Georgia*: Figure 12-G. Jeffrey W. Lotz, Florida Department of Agriculture and Consumer Services*: Figure 12-K. Wikimedia: Figure 12-E (begonia frost damage).

Diagnostic Keys:

Key 12-A: UMD Extension: 1, 5, 6, 7, 8, 9, 10, 11, 13, 14, 15, 19, 21, 23, 24, 25, 26, 27, 28, 29, 30, 32, 34, 35, 39, 40, 41, 42, 44, 45, 47, 50, 51, 52 (M. Talabac), 54, 56. Public domain: 4, 35, 43. Wikimedia: 18, 37, 49 (cracked turnip). Wikimedia attributed: Mariuszjbie: 31, Alandmanson: 61. Flickr attributed: Andrea_44: 20, Dwight Sipler: 22, mykhal: 55. Flickr free license: 33, 43, 58, 62. Jeffrey W. Lotz, Florida Department of Agriculture and Conusmer services, Bugwood.org.*: 12. David B Langston, University of Georgia*: 16. William Jacobi, University of Colorado: 17. R.J. Reynolds Tabacco Company*: 33. Peakpx: 49 (potato). Pixnio.com: 63. Pixabay.com: 60. Pxfuel.com: 36. Pxhere.com: Robert Couse-Baker: 38. LeAnn Zotta: 3, 46, 48, 53, 57, 59. Steph Pully via Adobe Firefly: 2.

Key 12-B: UMD Extension: M. Talabac: 2, 7, 12, 52, 66; 4, 15, 17, 20, 23, 25, 26, 27, 28, 29, 30, 31, 33, 34, 35, 39, 41, 42, 43, 45, 49, 50, 54, 68, 75, 76, 77, 81. Public domain: 38, 71. Flickr free license: 7, 8, 10, 13. Flickr attributed: Apple and Pear Australia, Ltd: 82. Wikimedia attributed: Famartin: 21, 40; SB_Johnny: 32. Mary Ann Hansen, Virginia Polytechnic Institute and State University*: 5. Nicole Ward Gauthier, Department of Plant Pathology, University of Kentucky Cooperative Extension Service: 9. Peter Bedker*: 11. Neil Bell, Oregon State University: 14. Susan Phillips, WHYY News: 22. Joseph OBrien, USDA Forest Service*: 36. Robert L. Anderson, USDA Forest Service*: 37. Kirill Gorlov via Adobe Stock: 44. Rob Flynn*: 48. Whitney Cranshaw, Colorado State University*: 72, 78, 79. H.J. Larson*: 80. 5 Brothers Landscaping: 3, 62, used with permission. Susan Poizner, Orchardpeople.com: 6, 47, 65, used with permission. Pixnio.com: 1, 74. Pxhere.com: 53, 69, 70. LeAnn Zotta: 16, 19, 55, 56, 57, 83, 84, 85. Adobe Stock: Farantsa: 24; Polarpx: 51; encierro: 60; bisa2bisa: 61; vie_art: 64. Steph Pully via Adobe Firefly: 58, 59, 63.

Key 12-C: UMD Extension: 7, 13, 14, 15, 20, 22, 25, 28; K. Baligush: 16; C. Carignan: 18. Flickr attributed: Katja Schulz: 9. Howard F. Schwartz, Colorado State University*: 2. Janet Knodel, NDSU Extension: 11. Frank Peairs, Colorado State University*: 23. John Ghent*: 24. USDA ARS Photo Unit, USDA Agricultural Research Service*: 27. Dr. Whitney Cranshaw, Colorado State University*: 26. R.J. Reynolds Tobacco Company , R.J. Reynolds Tobacco Company*: 12, 21. needpix.com: 3. wikigardener.com: 19. Pexels.com: 8. Pxhere.com: 10. LeAnn Zotta: 1, 6. Steph Pully via Adobe Firefly: 4, 5.

Key 12-D: UMD Extension: M. Talabac: 4; P. Shrewsbury: 6; S. Klick: 7, 35; K. Baligush: 31. UMD Extension Faculty: 1, 2, 3, 8, 10, 11, 12, 17, 18, 19, 20, 21, 22, 23, 24, 25, 26, 27, 29, 30, 36, 40, 42, 46. Flickr free license: 4, 7, 8, 18, 20, 22, 26 (serpentine leafminer). Erich G. Vallery, USDA Forest Service- SRS- 4552*: 2 (oakworm). Albert (Bud) Mayfield, USDA Forest Service*: 5. Dr. Whitney Cranshaw, Colorado State University*: 9, 13, 14, 26 (leafminer adult). R. L. Anderson, USFS*:15. Edward Sikora, Auburn University*: 27 (twig blight). Nancy Gregory, University of Delaware*: 28. John A. Weidhass, Virginia Polytechnic Institute and State University*: 16. Mary Ann Hansen, Virginia Polytechnic Institute and State University: 32. H.J. Larsen*: 33. Edward L. Barnard, Florida Department of Agriculture and Consumer Services*: 34. John Ghent*: 37. William M. Brown Jr.*: 45. Clemson University - USDA Cooperative Extension Slide Series *: 38. USDA Forest Service - North Central Research Station, USDA Forest Service*: 39. James Solomon, USDA Forest Service*: 41. Helene Doughty, Virginia Polytechnic Institute and State University*: 44. Ronald F. Billings, Texas A&M Forest Service*: 43.

Key 12-E: UMD Extension Faculty: 1, 4, 6, 8, 9, 10, 16, 18, 19, 22, 23, 24, 26, 27, 28. UMD Extension: S. Klick: 3, 15; D. Clement: 5. Dr. Whitney Cranshaw, Colorado State University*: 11. Lacy L. Hyche, Auburn University*: 12. Steven Katovich*: 2, 7, 13, 14, 17, 29. Nicole Ward Gauthier, Department of Plant Pathology, University of Kentucky Cooperative Extension Service: 20. R. L. Anderson, USFS*: 21, 30. Joseph OBrien, USDA Forest Service*: 25.

Key 12-F: UMD Extension M. Talabac: 4, 15; K. Baligush: 19; S. Klick: 36, 37. UMD Extension Faculty: 1, 5, 6, 7, 11, 16, 21, 24, 25, 29, 30, 31, 32, 34, 35, 38, 39. Flickr free license: 14. Flickr attributed: Matt Borden: 13. USDA Cooperative Extension Slide Series Bugwood.org: 2. Dr. Whitney Cranshaw, Colorado State University*: 3, 20, 27, 40. Adria Bordas, Virginia Polytechnic Institute and State University*: 8. Don Ferrin, Louisiana State University Agricultural Center*: 9. Robert Lambe, Virginia Polytechnic Institute and State University*: 10. Gyorgy Csoka, Hungary Forest Research Institute*: 12. Robert L. Anderson, USDA Forest Service*: 17, 26. Randy Cyr, Greentree*: 18. John Ghent*: 22. Elizabeth Bush, Virginia Polytechnic Institute and State University*: 23. Joseph OBrien, USDA Forest Service*: 28. Daniel Herms, The Ohio State University*: 33.

Key 12-G: UMD Extension: M. Talabac: 4; D. Clement: 8; S. Klick: 30. UMD Extension Faculty: 12, 13, 14, 15, 16, 18, 19, 20, 21, 24, 25, 27, 28, 35. Flickr free license: 18, 33. Dr. Whitney Cranshaw, Colorado State University*: 5, 9, 34. Eric R. Day, Virginia Polytechnic Institute and State University*: 1. Mary Ann Hansen, Virginia Polytechnic Institute and State University*: 3, 26. James Solomon, USDA Forest Service*: 6, 22. Gyorgy Csoka, Hungary Forest Research Institute*: 10, 31 (sawfly larva).. Elizabeth Bush and Helene Doughty, Virginia Polytechnic Institute and State University*: 11 and 29. Daniel Herms, The Ohio State University*: 17. Joseph Berger*: 23. Petr Kapitola, Central Institute for Supervising and Testing in Agriculture*: 32. Steven Katovich*: 31 (tussock caterpillar). Lacy L. Hyche, Auburn University*: 31 (beetle larvae). LeAnn Zotta: 2. Adobe Stock: 7monarda: 7 (smokebush). USDA Forest Service- Northeastern Area*: 17 (verticillium wilt).

Key 12-H: UMD Extension: D. Clement: 5, 6, 11, 16, 17, 19; K. Baligush: 18; G. Rosenkranz: 24. UMD Extension Faculty: 1, 2, 4, 14, 15, 20, 21, 22. Howard F. Schwartz, Colorado State University*: 3, 23. John A. Weidhass, Virginia Polytechnic Institute and State University*: 7, 12. Dr. Whitney Cranshaw, Colorado State University*: 8, 9, 13.

Key 12-I: UMD Extension: 3, 4, 5, 7, 10, 12, 15. Public domain: 13, 14. Flickr free license: 2. Frank Peairs, Colorado State University*: 1. Howard F. Schwartz, Colorado State University*: 8. William M. Brown Jr.*: 6. Edward Sikora, Auburn University*: 9. University of Georgia Plant Pathology, University of Georgia*: 11. Merle Shepard, Gerald R.Carner, and P.A.C Ooi, Insects and their Natural Enemies Associated with Vegetables and Soybean in Southeast Asia, Bugwood.org: 13. Liudmila via Adobe Stock: 14.

Key 12-J: UMD Extension: 3, 4, 6, 9, 10, 12, 14, 15, 16, 18. Public domain: 2. Flickr free license: 20. Wikimedia attributed: Rasbak: 10. Dr. Whitney Cranshaw, Colorado State University*: 1, 7, 13, 21. Don Ferrin, Louisiana State University Agricultural Center*: 8, 11. Howard F. Schwartz, Colorado State University*: 5, 10, 17, 22. Alton N. Sparks, Jr., University of Georgia: 19.

Key 12-K: UMD Extension Faculty: 12. Flickr free license: 3. Cynthia Ocamb, Oregon State University Extension: 7. Flickr attributed: JIRCAS Library: 9. Elizabeth Bush, Virginia Polytechnic Institute and State University*: 1. Russ Ottens, University of Georgia*: 2. Alton N. Sparks Jr.: 4. Jackie Mullen, Auburn University, Bugwood.org.: 5. Dr. Whitney Cranshaw, Colorado State University*: 6. M.E. Bartolo*: 8.

Key 12-L: UMD Extension: 1, 9, 10. Flickr free license: 4. Howard F. Schwartz, Colorado State University*: 2, 3, 5, 6. Clemson University - USDA Cooperative Extension Slide Series*: 7, 12. Dr. Whitney Cranshaw, Colorado State University*: 11, 8. Thomas Kuhar, Virginia Polytechnic Institute and State University: 13. Robert Lambe, Virginia Polytechnic Institute and State University*: 14

Key 12-M: UMD Extension: 2, 5, 6, 8, Alan Leslie: 8 (wildlife damage). William M. Brown Jr.*: 1. Eugene E. Nelson, Bugwood. org: 8 (sap beetles). Frank Peairs, Colorado State University, Bugwood.org and Clemson University - USDA Cooperative Extension Slide Series *: 3. Mary Ann Hansen, Virginia Polytechnic Institute and State University*: 4. Adam Sisson, Iowa State University*: 7.

Key 12-N: UMD Extension: 4, 5. Dr. Whitney Cranshaw, Colorado State University*: 1. Howard F. Schwartz, Colorado State University*: 2. Domainice via Adobe Stock: 3. Dave Townsend, Growingthehomegarden.com: 6.

Key 12-O: UMD Extension: 2,6. Howard F. Schwartz, Colorado State University*: 1, 3, 5. Flickr free license: Pontiac onion (inset). Lawrence Barringer, Pennsylvania Dept. of Agriculture*: 4, 7.

Key 12-P: UMD Extension: 1, 2, 7, 8, 9; M. Talabac:4; S. Pully: 7. Dr. Whitney Cranshaw, Colorado State University*: 3. Flickr attributed: awyatt: 5. iredding01 via Adobe Stock: 6.

Key 12-Q: UMD Extension: 1, 2, 7. Public domain: 3. Flickr free license: 8. Flickr attributed: F Delventhal: 9. Dr. Whitney Cranshaw, Colorado State University*: 6, 10. Howard F. Schwartz, Colorado State University*: 4. Clemson University- USDA Cooperative Extension Slide Series*: 5.

Key 12-R: UMD Extension: 6, 7, 8; M. Talabac: 9; 10, 13, 16, 17, 18. Public domain: 5. hjschneider via Adobe Stock: 2. Edward Sikora, Auburn University*: 9 (fire blight). James Solomon, USDA Forest Service*, 12. Dr. Whitney Cranshaw, Colorado State University*: 1, 14. Clemson University - USDA Cooperative Extension Slide Series *: 3, 17 (plum curculio larva and adult), 20. Haruta Ovidiu, University of Oradea*: 4. Minnesota Department of Natural Resources - FIA , Minnesota Department of Natural Resources*: 11. Pxhere.com: 15. Gyorgy Csoka, Hungary Forest Research Institute*: 16 (codling moth adult). Elizabeth Bush, Virginia Polytechnic Institute and State University and University of Georgia Plant Pathology , University of Georgia*: 18. Eugene E. Nelson*: 19. Adobe Stock: Dmytro Bel'maz: 21. Flickr attributed: Dirk Fokken: 22.

Key 12-S: UMD Extension: 3, 6 (nitrogen deficiency), 7, 11, M. Talabac: 12, 13; 15 (brown rot and peach scab); S. Gill:16. Flickr attributed: Chris Fannin: 2. Dr. Whitney Cranshaw, Colorado State University*: 4, 5. H.J. Larsen: 5 (Verticillium wilt). University of Georgia Plant Pathology , University of Georgia*: 6 (bacterial spot), 15. Elizabeth Bush, Virginia Polytechnic Institute and State University*: 6 (cherry leaf spot). Susan Poizner - orchardpeople.com: 8. Clemson University - USDA Cooperative Extension Slide Series *: 9. Garden Fancy blog with permission: 10. Carroll E. Younce, USDA Agricultural Research Service*: 14. Catherin Lindell, Michigan State University Extension: 17. Jonas Janner Hamann, Universidade Federal de Santa Maria (UFSM)*: 19. Adobe Stock: Tunatura: 1.

Key 12-T: UMD Extension: 1, 7, 9, 11, 12, 14, 16, 20, 22, 23 (cane borer damage), 24, 30, 34, 36; M. Talabac: 6, 33. Public domain: 35 (slug damage). Dr. Whitney Cranshaw, Colorado State University*: 1 (aphids), 28. Pixnio.com: 10. Curtis Swift, Colorado State University*: 4. Mark Bolda, University of California Natural Resources: 5. Mary Ann Hansen, Virginia Polytechnic Institute and State University*: 8, 13. Eric Coombs, Oregon Department of Agriculture*: 15. Edward Sikora, Auburn University*: 16. University of Georgia Plant Pathology , University of Georgia*: 17, 23 (borer larva), 25, 26. Charles Drake, Virginia Polytechnic Institute and State University*: 18. Hannah Burrack, North Carolina State University*: 19. Lawrence Barringer, Pennsylvania Department of Agriculture*: 27. Rufus Isaacs, Michigan State University Extension: 29. Ric Bessin, University of Kentucky College of Agriculture: 31. J. Obermeyer, Purdue Extension Entomology: 32. Clemson University - USDA Cooperative Extension Slide Series. Bugwood.org: 35 (cutworm damage). Jeffrey W. Lotz, Florida Department of Agriculture and Consumer Services*: 36 (strawberry aphid). Adobe Stock: kazakovmaksim: 2; lassi meony: 3; Amelia: 21.

Key 12-U: UMD Extension: K. Baligush: 4, 7, 8 (walnuts). Flickr free license: 6 (black walnut). Public domain: 8 (drought stress). Flickr attributed: Noj Han: 6 (frozen bud). Dr. Whitney Cranshaw, Colorado State University*: 5, 9 (Walnut husk fly larva). Jerry A. Payne, USDA Agricultural Research Service*: 1. Joseph OBrien, USDA Forest Service*: 2. Rob Flynn*: 3. University of Georgia Plant Pathology , University of Georgia*: 8 (magnesium deficiency). Louis Tedders, USDA Agricultural Research Service*: 9 (pecan curculio damage). Florida Division of Plant Industry , Florida Department of Agriculture and Consumer Services*: 9 (Walnut husk fly).

Key 12-V: UMD Extension: M. Talabac: 11, 22, 26; D. Clement: 16; K. Baligush: 17; P. Shrewsbury: 19. UMD Extension Faculty: 1 (leaf spot, all brown patch images), 3, 4, 5, 6, 7 (orange lawn rust), 8, 9, 10, 12, 13,14, 15 (mushroom fairy ring), 20, 21, 24. Flickr attributed: Kris Lord: 2; Andrena Fulva: 25. pxhere.com: 23. Clemson University- USDA Cooperative Extension Slide Series*: 1 (leaf spot close-up). Mary Ann Hansen, Virginia Polytechnic Institute and State University*: 1 (dollar spot). Clarissa Balbalian, Mississippi State University*: 7. William M. Brown Jr.*: 15. Steph Pully via Adobe Firefly: 18.

Key 12-W: UMD Extension: 1 (aphids, mealybugs, brown scale); C. Carignan: 1(whiteflies); 2, 4, 5; M.Talabac: 6, 7 (stick insect), 9, 11, 12; K. Baligush: 10; 13. Public domain: 7 (snail), 8. Wikimedia attributed: Paramecium: 1 (spider mite webbing); Forest and Kim Starr: 3.

Key 12-X: UMD Extension: 1 (clothes moth larva), 6 (flea larva), 10 (millipede adult), 15 (black carpet beetle larva), 18, 22 (multicolored Asian lady beetle larva). Wikipedia: Katja ZSM: 6 (adult flea); Bruce Marlin: 11 (house centipede adult); Christian Fischer: 13 (silverfish adult). Wikimedia: 2 (Indian meal moth larva). Flickr attributed: Patrick Clement: 1 (clothes moth adult); Andy Reago & Chrissy McClarren: 2 (Indian meal moth adult), Erik Burton: 4 (fungus gnat adult); Eran Finkle: 17 (cockroach egg mass); Brian Gratwicke: 19 (ant adult). Florida Division of Plant Industry, Florida Department of Agriculture and Consumer Services*: 5 (fruit fly larva). Katja Schulz: 5 (fruit fly adult). Whitney Cranshaw, Colorado State University*: 4 (fungus gnat larva), 20, 21 (boxelder bug nymphs). Joseph Berger*: 8, 9, 14, 15 (carpet beetle adult), 16 (pillbug adult), 21 (boxelder bug adult). Clemson University- USDA Cooperative Extension Slide Series*: 2 (Indian meal moth larvae), 7 (camel cricket adult), 17 (German cockroach adult). Eugene E. Nelson*: 12. Walter Baxter: 19 (ant larvae). Gyorgy Csoka, Hungary Forest Research Institute*: 22 (multicolored lady beetle adult). Rayanne Lehman, Pennsylvania Department of Agriculture*: 23. Matt Bertone, NC State University: 3 (adult and larva).

Key 12-Y: UMD Extension: M. Talabac: 1 (termite damage); 2. Scott Bauer, USDA Agricultural Research Service*: 1. Whitney Cranshaw, Colorado State University*: 3 (winged carpenter ants). Daniel H. Brown, USDA Forest Service*: 3 (carpenter ant damage). Gyorgy Csoka, Hungary Forest Research Institute*: 4. USDA Forest Service - Wood Products Insect Lab, USDA Forest Service, Bugwood.org: 5 (powder post beetle damage). Matt Bertone, NC State University: 5 (powder post beetle).

Key 12-Z: UMD Extension: M. Talabac: 1,3, 6, 8; S. Klick: 2; 4; D. Clement: 5. Flickr attributed: Bob Peterson: 10. Dr. Whitney Cranshaw, Colorado State University, Bugwood.org: 7. Nancy Hinkle, University of Georgia*: 9.

OTHER RESOURCES

For updates on new, emerging, and invasive plant pests please see: extension.umd.edu/resources/yard-garden/invasive-species/invasive-insects

13

13: WEEDS

Kelley Oklesson

Josef Mudd

13 WEEDS

CONTENTS

13.1 Why Are Weeds a Problem?..348

13.2 Weed Biology 349

13.3 Weed Identification 352

13.4 Weed Management 366

13.5 Sustainable Weed Maintenance Plan...374

LEARNING OBJECTIVES

- Weed biology and ecology
- Characteristics and examples of annual, biennial, and perennial weeds
- How to identify common weeds
- Non-chemical weed management techniques
- Herbicides and management techniques

INTRODUCTION

Weeds are often defined as plants that grow where they are not wanted. Although a home gardener may think a few violets or dandelions are attractive wildflowers in the lawn, a neighbor or a golf course manager might strongly disagree and consider them an eyesore or a potential invader.

Technically, a weed is defined as *any plant that adversely affects the use, economic value, and/ or aesthetic aspect of the lands and waters it infests.*

Even desirable plants can be considered weeds when they're growing in the wrong location. For example, the kernels from a few unharvested ears of corn may overwinter, germinate in the middle of a tomato patch the following year, and be considered a weed. A plant like bermudagrass can be excellent forage for livestock or used as a tough, drought-tolerant turf grass, but it can be extremely difficult to manage when it creeps over from the neighbor's yard into your flower beds. Even when you seed the lawn with a rotary spreader, some grass seed is likely to end up in a flower bed and the resulting seedlings would be considered weeds.

The weed level you're willing to tolerate in a home lawn or garden is an aesthetic judgment that is also highly subjective. There are no "weed police" to demand that you maintain a perfectly weed-free yard.

There are, however, some weeds that are so aggressive they can invade minimally-managed areas. They can interfere with native species and the functioning of natural environments like forests, marshes, and wetlands. These plants are called invasive species and are discussed in more detail in Chapter 22.

The terms "invasive" and "exotic" often are confused. Exotic species are not native to the region, but that doesn't mean they are all invasive. Invasive species are a small subset of the exotics that can cause economic or environmental harm, or harm to human health. Even native plants, such as poison ivy, pokeweed, ragweed, violet, yellow nutsedge, and greenbriar, can be major weeds.

Weeds *can* have redeeming characteristics. Some are edible (dandelion, purslane, wintercress, lamb's-quarter, and pigweed); others are attractive wildflowers and contain natural dyes; and many provide food and shelter for wildlife. With experience you'll learn which plants can be allowed to grow and which should be quickly eradicated before they take over your garden or neighborhood.

13.1 Why Are Weeds a Problem?

Many of the plants we refer to as weeds are simply part of the natural ecological process called "plant succession" (see Figure 13-A). Disturbed soils are colonized by pioneer plants which are gradually replaced by different species over a period of 50 to 100 years until the natural climax vegetation is reached. Many pioneer plants are annuals, which in time are followed by perennial grasses and broadleaf plants, then woody shrubs, and finally the climax vegetation. In the Mid-Atlantic region, the climax vegetation is generally a hardwood forest primarily composed of oak and hickory. We used to have a chestnut-dominated forest composition but chestnut blight and over-harvesting shifted our forests to oak-hickory. In other regions it might be prairie, conifer, or tropical rain forest.

In the Mid-Atlantic region, if you stopped pulling weeds, mowing grass, and applying herbicide, your landscaped yard would become a forest in fewer than 50 years. By maintaining lawns, landscapes, or crops, we create artificial settings. Stopping the natural process of plant succession requires constant input of energy, whether it is hand-and-knees labor, mulching, tillage, or herbicide applications. This is true whether you're a gardener, farmer, or right-of-way manager.

Weeds are opportunists that compete with desirable plants for light, water, nutrients, and space. Some weeds feature rapid root growth that very efficiently extracts water and nutrients from the soil. Others form tall, dense leaf canopies that absorb light and shade less competitive plants.

We often think that weeds drive out desirable plants, but in many cases the weeds are simply indicators of unsuitable growing conditions for the desired species. For instance, compaction, low fertility, poor drainage, or too much shade can drastically reduce turf growth, but certain weeds tolerate these conditions well. You may need to correct these problems or consider replacing the turf with shade-, drought-, or moisture-tolerant plants, ground covers, or pathways where appropriate.

Weeds can reduce the quantity and quality of flowers and vegetables in the garden and can also compete with turfgrass. From an agricultural perspective, weeds cause yield, quality, and efficiency losses. Yield losses may exceed 50% and products may not be saleable if cows' milk is contaminated by garlic flavor or there are weedy stems in leafy salad greens.

Figure 13-A. Plant succession (section elevation)

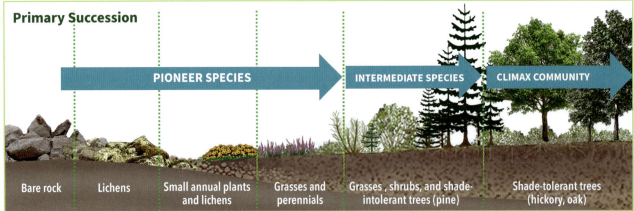

Weeds may harbor pests such as insects, nematodes, diseases, and rodents. Perennial weed species can become an overwintering shelter for some pests which can then easily move on to desirable plants the following spring.

Hazards to humans and animals resulting from weeds can include insect stings; dermatitis from poison ivy contact with skin, clothes, or pets; allergies to pollen from ragweed and others; and poisoning from ingesting plants like deadly nightshade, poison hemlock, or pokeweed.

13.2 Weed Biology

Understanding the biology of weeds helps to identify their weakest point and attack them at the most opportune time. Of particular importance are life cycles, means of reproduction, and seed dispersal mechanisms.

Life cycles

Annuals

Annuals complete their life cycle in one year or less (see Figure 13-B). Annuals can be further divided into two groups: summer and winter. Summer annuals germinate from the seed in the spring, mature in summer, and form new seed and die before winter. Examples include crabgrass, ragweed, and lamb's quarter. Winter annuals germinate in the fall, survive winter's cold, grow in spring, and die before summer. Examples include chickweed, henbit, and annual bluegrass.

Biennials

Biennials live more than one year, but less than two years (see Figure 13-C). In the first year, they germinate, develop a strong root system, and form a rosette of leaves close to the ground. In the second year, the plant grows vigorously and becomes more upright. The foliage may change shape and the plant will "bolt" by sending up a tall stalk with flowers followed by seeds and death of the plant by fall. Biennial weeds include mullein, garlic mustard, Queen Anne's lace, and bull thistle.

Perennials

Perennials live for more than two years and return year after year from an overwintering root system (see Figure 13-C). Most perennials can produce seed but for many species, reproducing vegetative storage organs such as rhizomes, stolons, tubers, and taproots is the dominant means of reproduction and spread. Perennial weeds include dandelion, pokeweed, Canada thistle, and bermudagrass.

Figure 13-B. Life cycle of annual weeds

Figure 13-C. Life cycle of perennial and biennial weeds

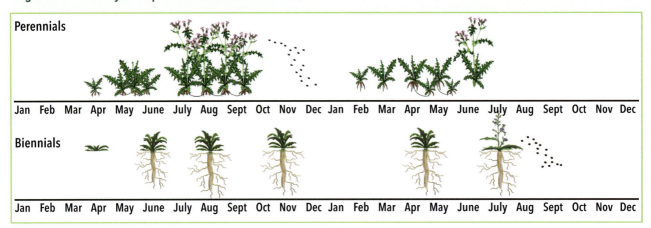

Carbohydrate reserves in the roots of perennials provide a strong competitive advantage for early-season top and root growth that can rapidly capture nutrients, water, space, and light. Repeated mechanical removal of top growth by weeding, pruning, or hoeing can be used to interrupt the life cycle of perennial weeds. If left to grow undisturbed, the above-ground and below-ground parts of perennials increase in size with each successive year. Destroying the root system is essential for full control.

Means of reproduction

A single weed plant can make thousands of seeds per year, so imagine a garden full of weeds making millions of seeds (see Table 13-A). Preventing, or at least minimizing, the production of weed seeds can be one of the most important steps in weed control. The practice of hoeing (shallow cultivation) also effectively cuts off weed shoots from their roots, which disrupts seed production.

Seed longevity (dormancy)

Not all seeds will germinate the following season, even if conditions are favorable. The seeds of many species can remain dormant for extended periods of time in the soil (see Table 13-B). Spreading germination viability over many years reduces the chance of offspring being wiped out by unfavorable growing conditions in any single growing season.

Table 13-A. Production of weed seeds per plant

Canada thistle (per stem)	680
Dandelion	15,000
Foxtail	32,000
Lamb's-quarter	72,000
Pigweed	117,000
Common mullein	223,000
Stevens, O.A. 1954. *Weed Seed Facts*. H.D. Agric. Coll. Ext. Cir. A-128, 4pp. Stevens, O.A. 1957. *Weights of Seeds and Numbers Per Plant*. Weeds 4:46-55.	

Table 13-B. Longevity of buried weed seeds

Weed name	Years
Chickweed	10
Canada thistle	10 - 20
Pigweed	20 - 40
Curly dock	80
Harrington, J.F. 1972. *Seed storage and longevity*. Pp. 145-245 in T.T. Kozlowski (ed.) *Seed Biology*. Academic Press, New York.	

The reservoir, or collection of seeds in the soil, is called the seed bank (example). Deposits to the seed bank are made by weed seeds produced at the site each year plus any added by wind, animals, humans, machines, imported materials, and stormwater runoff. Withdrawals from the seed bank occur through seed germination, predation (rodents, birds, insects), and decay. Tillage and earthworms can move the seeds up and down within the soil profile. Seed banks in lands farmed for more than 30 years range from 100 to 600 million weed seeds per acre, due in large part to conventional tilling.

The combination of high seed production, seed dormancy, and a nearly endless reservoir of weed seeds have led to the old-time saying, "one year's seeding equals seven year's weeding." Clearly, it is extremely important to prevent weeds from going to seed.

Seed dispersal mechanisms

Many seeds have specialized adaptations that help in their dispersal over long distances where they can establish life in new locations (see Figure 13-D). Some species have structures that improve their ability to travel by wind. A few examples are dandelion, groundsel, Canada thistle, and milkweed. Other seeds, such as chickweed, are adapted for traveling in water and float downstream, especially in stormwater runoff. Some have hook-like appendages that attach to clothing and animal fur, such as burdock. Others, ingested by birds, rodents, deer, and domesticated farm animals, may pass through the digestive tract intact and be ready to germinate, such as porcelain berry.

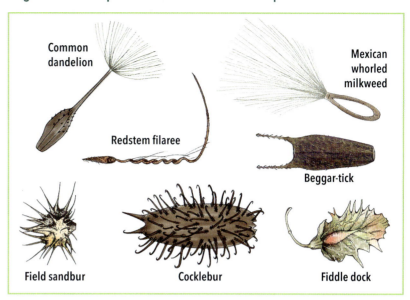

Figure 13-D. Adaptations that aid weed seed dispersal

Humans also move weeds, both intentionally and accidentally. Many ornamental and medicinal plants have been purposely introduced over the years through use in agricultural commerce, and even today horticulturists search the world for new and exciting plants. Some of them become naturalized or invasive long after their introduction. Examples include purple loosestrife, kudzu, and multiflora rose.

Many other species have been introduced and dispersed purely by accident. Weed seeds or root parts may be transported with crop seed, animal waste products, soil, nursery stock, or construction equipment. Many European weeds (e.g., chickweed, dandelion, and crabgrass) were introduced both intentionally and accidentally by early colonists.

Several state and federal laws have been enacted to limit the intentional or accidental introduction and movement of weed species. The Federal Seed Act of 1939 regulates interstate and foreign commerce in seed to protect purchasers from buying mislabeled crop seed or seed contaminated with weed seeds. The Federal Noxious Weed Act of 1974 regulates the introduction of weeds of foreign origin into the U.S. It authorizes inspections at ports of entry, weed surveys within the U.S., and necessary eradication and quarantine measures to prevent the spread of a noxious weed. Individual states have noxious weed laws that are designed to protect local concerns.

In Maryland, seven species have legal status as noxious weeds: johnsongrass, shattercane, certain thistles (Canada, musk, plumeless, and bull), and multiflora rose. For more information about noxious weeds, see **Chapter 22, Invasive Species.**

Maryland has established an Invasive Species Council (MISC) that addresses all types of invasive organisms (e.g., vertebrates, invertebrates, plants, and pathogens). They take an educational/voluntary versus a regulatory approach to invasive species management.

MISC has developed a list of "Species of Concern" to Maryland. Some of the plant species listed are clearly recognized as horrendous weeds, whereas others are controversial ornamental plants that can naturalize well beyond the confines of the garden. Consult the **MISC website** for the current list.

13.3 Weed Identification

Learning to identify weed species, especially aggressive invaders, before they become widely established is critical for determining the best management techniques. The species listed in Table 13-C are the most common weeds found in Maryland lawns and landscapes. See Table 13-D for identifying features of weedy grasses. For additional species, images, and identification help, see the **additional resources** at the end of this chapter.

Table 13-C. Common lawn and garden weeds   * denotes invasive plant

Image	Plant name/origin	Biology	Description
	13C.1 **Dandelion** *Taraxacum officinale* Aster family (Asteraceae) Eurasia	Perennial	Reproduces by seed. Summer rosette of leaves is 3-10 in. long with a high degree of leaf variability, ranging from deeply cut to almost entire. Milky sap when broken. Yellow ray flowers are borne on leafless, hollow stalks. Wind-blown seeds. Fleshy taproot.
	13C.2 **Chicory** *Cichorium intybus* Aster family (Asteraceae) North America	Perennial	Sprouts from a basal rosette, similar to dandelions. Leaves are lanceolate, toothed, and rough on the upper and lower surfaces. Erect, wiry, branching stems up to 3 ft. tall carry bright-blue ray flowers 1 in. across in leaf axils and at ends of branches.

continued on next page

continued from previous page

Table 13-C. Common lawn and garden weeds

* denotes invasive plant

Image	Plant name/origin	Biology	Description
	13C.3 **Broadleaf plantain** *Plantago major* Plantain family (Plantaginaceae) North America	Perennial	Similar to buckhorn plantain. Has a basal rosette of broad, oval leaves with 5-7 nearly parallel veins. Small flowers cluster along tan-green, erect, leafless stalks that are shorter than 1 ft. tall.
	13C.4 **Buckhorn plantain** *Plantago lanceolata* Plantain family (Plantaginaceae) Europe	Perennial	Reproduces by seed. Has a basal rosette of narrow, lanceolate leaves having nearly parallel veins. Fibrous roots. Small clusters of flowers in a tan-green head on erect, leafless flower stalks less than 1 ft. tall.
	13C.5 **Mouseear chickweed** *Cerastium vulgatum* Pink family (Caryophyllaceae) Eurasia	Perennial	Prostrate plant that forms dense, low clumps with hairy leaves and stems. Leaves are opposite and spoon-shaped. Growth habit is similar to common chickweed but is perennial and hairy, and roots at nodes. Common in turf.
	13C.6 **Ground ivy, creeping charlie** *Glechoma hederacea* Mint family (Lamiaceae) Eurasia	Perennial	Low, creeping, invasive plant that roots at nodes. Distinct odor when crushed. Square stems. Leaves are opposite, scalloped, rounded to kidney-shaped, and 1/2 to 1½ in. across. Flowers are lipped, purplish-blue in whorls in upper leaf axils. Tolerates shade and close mowing.
	13C.7 **Common blue violet** *Viola papilionacea* Violet family (Violiaceae) North America	Perennial	Low-growing, less than 1 ft. from basal crown. Heart-shaped leaves. Flowers are blue to violet, occasionally white, on leafless stalks. Thrives in moist, shady sites, but withstands drought once established. Tolerates close mowing.
	13C.8 **White clover** *Trifolium repens* Bean family (Fabaceae) Eurasia, possibly North America	Perennial	Low-growing, less than 1 ft. tall. Roots at nodes. Reproduces by seed and creeping runners. Leaves are composed of three leaflets (trifoliate), most with a pale triangular mark. Each ½-in. flower head is a cluster of many white or pink-tinged pea-like flowers. Tolerates close mowing.

continued on next page

continued from previous page

Table 13-C. Common lawn and garden weeds

* denotes invasive plant

Image	Plant name/origin	Biology	Description
	13C.9 **Yellow wood sorrel** *Oxalis stricta* Woodsorrel family (Oxalidaceae) Europe	Perennial	Grows 4-18 in. tall from seeds or slender rhizomes. Trifoliate leaf arrangement is similar to white clover or black medic, but leaflets are distinctly heart-shaped. Leaves are pale green to purplish. Yellow flowers have 5 petals. Seeds are explosively ejected from a pointed, erect seed capsule. Tolerates shade and mowing.
	13C.10 **Indian mock strawberry** *Duchesnea indica* Rose family (Rosaceae) Asia	Perennial	Low, trailing perennial, less than 1 ft. tall. Stolons root to form a chain of new plants. Trifoliate leaves have rounded teeth. Flowers have 5 yellow petals followed by strawberry-like fruit. Tolerates shade and close mowing.
	13C.11 **Bulbous buttercup** *Ranunculus bulbosus* Buttercup family (Ranunculaceae) Eurasia	Perennial	Features a basal rosette of 3-lobed leaves, arising from a corm. Flowers are bright yellow with 5-7 shiny petals on erect, somewhat hairy stems. Poisonous to livestock. Tall buttercup and creeping buttercup are also common.
	13C.12 **Lesser celandine*** *Ranunculus ficaria* Buttercup family (Ranunculaceae) Europe	Perennial	Herbaceous invasive grows to 3-9 in. tall in moist, wooded floodplains. Introduced as an ornamental plant with shiny, dark green, kidney-shaped leaves. Flowers have glossy, bright yellow petals in early spring. Entire plant goes dormant in summer. Spreads by finger-like tuberous roots.
	13C.13 **Red sorrel** *Rumex acetosella* Buckwheat family (Polygonaceae) Eurasia	Perennial	Creeping perennial grows up to 2 ft. from rhizomes. Arrowhead-shaped leaves are less than 4 in. with prominent basal lobes. Membranous ocrea at base of petioles. Male and female flowers are produced on separate plants, in panicles. Mature panicles appear reddish. Tolerates poor soil and close mowing.
	13C.14 **Curly and broadleaf dock** *Rumex crispus and R. obtusifolius* Buckwheat family (Polygonaceae) Europe	Perennial	Features a large, yellowish taproot with basal rosettes of 6-12 in. leaves. Prominent ocrea surrounds the stem at the base of each leaf. Flowering green stalks grow to 3 ft. tall, turn rusty brown, and persist through winter. Leaves of curly dock are long and narrow with wavy (curly) margins. Broadleaf dock leaves are wider and less wavy.

continued on next page

continued from previous page

Table 13-C. Common lawn and garden weeds

* denotes invasive plant

Image	Plant name/origin	Biology	Description
	13C.15 **Mugwort*** *Artemisia vulgaris* Aster family (Asteraceae) Old World	Perennial	Clump-forming perennial spreads by extensive rhizomes. Leaves are pinnatifid, deeply dissected and similar to ragweed but strongly scented, like chrysanthemum. Flowers are inconspicuous in terminal leafy spikes. Grows to 4 ft., but tolerates close mowing and cultivation.
	13C.16 **Canada thistle*** *Cirsium arvense* Aster family (Asteraceae) Eurasia	Perennial	Clump-forming weed grows to 2-5 ft. Spreads by fleshy, creeping rhizomes. Leaves are long and narrow, alternate, and irregularly lobed with spiny margins. Spineless stem. Lavender disk flowers are followed by fluffy pappus capable of floating long distances in the wind.
	13C.17 **Horsenettle** *Solanum carolinense* Nightshade family (Solanaceae) North America	Perennial	Grows 1-3 ft. tall from deep rhizomes. Leaves are large, wavy, and alternate. Spines appear on upper and lower midrib of leaves and on stems. Flowers are 5-petaled, potato-like, white to pale lavender in color. Yellow, rounded berries persist through the winter.
	13C.18 **Bittersweet nightshade** *Solanum dulcamara* Nightshade family (Solanaceae) Eurasia	Perennial	Semi-woody vine grows to 2-10 ft. Leaves are dark green and variable, some ovate to oval, others ovate with 2 basal lobes. Flowers are 5-petaled, purple to white, and similar to potato. Berries measure 3/8 in., turning from green to bright red. Unpleasant odor and poisonous.
	13C.19 **Field bindweed** *Convolvulus arvensis* Morning glory family (Convolvulaceae) Eurasia	Perennial	Deep fleshy rhizomes. Leaves are arrow-shaped, alternate on trailing or climbing stems. White-to-pale-pink funnel-shaped flowers are up to 1½ in. across. Often confused with annual morning glories or hedge bindweed.
	13C.20 **Hedge bindweed** *Convolvulus sepium* Morning glory family (Convolvulaceae) Eurasia	Perennial	Deep, fleshy rhizomes. Often confused with annual morning glories or field bindweed. Compared to field bindweed, leaves and flowers are larger, leaf bases are cut square, and hedge bindweed is more likely to climb than trail.

continued on next page

continued from previous page

Table 13-C. Common lawn and garden weeds　　　　　　　　　　　　　　　　　　　　　　　　* denotes invasive plant

Image	Plant name/origin	Biology	Description
	13C.21 **Common milkweed** *Asclepias syriaca* Milkweed family (Asclepiadaceae) North America	Perennial	Fleshy rhizomes. Exudes milky sap when broken. Leaves are larger than hemp dogbane, opposite, oblong, margins entire, prominent white midrib. Stems are erect, 2-4 ft., not branched. Large, fragrant rounded clusters of purplish-pink to white flowers attract insects. Large, teardrop-shaped pods contain many silky-haired seeds that disperse in the wind.
	13C.22 **Hemp dogbane** *Apocynum cannabinum* Milkweed family (Asclepiadaceae) North America	Perennial	Fleshy rhizomes. Exudes milky sap when broken. Leaves are smaller than milkweed, opposite, oblong, margins entire, prominent white midrib. Stems are erect, 2-4 ft., branched. Clusters of greenish-white flowers. Long, slim pods (in pairs) contain many seeds with silky hairs that disperse in the wind.
	13C.23 **Common pokeweed** *Phytolacca americana* Pokeweed family (Phytolaccaceae) North America	Perennial	Large 3-8-ft. weed resembles a small tree. Grows from seeds or the large, red-tinged, fleshy taproot. Leaves are light green, alternate, smooth, lanceolate to egg-shaped, often reddish on the underside. Stems are reddish. Small, white flowers appear in long, purple-stemmed, hanging clusters. Berries are green at first, turning glossy, dark purple, leaving a purple-red stain. Poisonous.
	13C.24 **Multiflora rose*** *Rosa multiflora* Rose family (Rosaceae) Asia	Perennial	Perennial shrub with thorny, arching stems that can root at the tips. Compound leaves with 5-7 toothed leaflets and stipules at base of leaf stalk. Fragrant, white, 5-petaled rose flowers in May-June are followed by small orange-red hips that remain through winter. Invades pastures, roadsides, and forests.
	13C.25 **Wineberry*** *Rubus phoenicolasius* Rose family (Rosaceae) Eastern Asia	Perennial	Perennial shrub reaches 3-6 ft. with arching stems that can root at the tips. Stems and petioles are covered in dense, reddish glandular hairs and prickles. Leaves are alternate, divided into three leaflets, broadly ovate with pointed tips, serrated margins. Undersides have dense white hairs. Small white flowers are followed by raspberry-like red fruits in summer.
	13C.26 **Japanese knotweed*** *Polygonum cuspidatum* Buckwheat family (Polygonaceae) Eastern Asia	Perennial	Shrubby, herbaceous weed grows to 10 ft. Leaves are 6-in. long by 3-in. wide, oval with smooth margins. Stems are similar to bamboo, but on newer foliage a membranous sheath surrounds the area where stem and leaf meet. Flowers are small, green-white in spikes along the stems. Small, greenish, triangular fruits. Reproduces from heavy rhizomes.

continued on next page

continued from previous page

Table 13-C. Common lawn and garden weeds

* denotes invasive plant

Image	Plant name/origin	Biology	Description
	13C.27 **Autumn olive*** *Elaeagnus umbellata* Olive family (Eleagnaceae) China and Japan	Perennial	Deciduous woody shrub grows to 20 ft. Leaves, stems, and fruit have silvery to rusty scales. Leaves are egg- to lance-shaped, smooth margins, alternate, silvery underside. Creamy-white to yellow flowers are fragrant. Abundant ¼-in. red fruit with scales.
	13C.28 **Amur, Tartarian honeysuckle*** *Lonicera maackii, L. tatarica* Honeysuckle family (Caprifoliaceae) Eastern Asia	Perennial	Deciduous woody shrub, upright, grows to 5-15 ft. tall. Leaves are oval to egg-shaped and opposite. Slightly fragrant white-to-pinkish flowers are borne along the stem in leaf axils in spring. Red berries appear in pairs in axils.
	13C.29 **Yellow nutsedge** *Cyperus esculentus* Sedge family (Cyperaceae) North America	Perennial	Grows from small nutlets (tubers) attached to rhizomes. Leaves are shiny, yellow-green, narrow, and grass-like. Stems are 3-sided, triangular in cross-section. No ligule or collar region.
	13C.30 **Wild garlic** *Allium vineale* Lily family (Liliaceae) Eurasia	Perennial	Grows from bulbs. Grass-like, hollow leaves, round in cross-section. Foliage and bulbs smell like onion or garlic. May produce aerial bulblets. If mowed, plant produces clusters of many underground bulbs. Wild onion is similar, but leaves are flat in cross-section.
	13C.31 **Star-of-Bethlehem** *Ornithogalum umbellatum* Lily family (Liliaceae) Europe and North Africa	Perennial	Grows from bulbs in dense clumps. Dark-green, grass-like leaves are less than 12 in. long, with a whitish midrib similar to crocus. Ornamental 6-petaled white flowers. Can tolerate shade and close mowing.
	13C.32 **Giant hogweed*** *Heracleum mantegazzianum* Carrot family (Apiaceae) Eurasia	Perennial	**Red Alert.** Rare, but serious, plant of regulatory concern. Huge plant reaching 10-15 ft. Leaves are 4 ft. across, deeply divided and variable. Stems are purple-spotted, hairy, and hollow. Flat-topped, branching flower clusters up to 1 ft. wide are composed of many small white flowers. Plant sap causes serious skin blisters.

continued on next page

continued from previous page

Table 13-C. Common lawn and garden weeds

* denotes invasive plant

Image	Plant name/origin	Biology	Description
	13C.33 **Speedwell** *Veronica* spp. Figwort family (Scrophulariaceae) Eurasia	Perennial or annual	All species are creeping prostate plants with small, rounded leaves, toothed at the margins. Flowers are light-blue to white with 5 petals. Fruit is a heart-shaped capsule.
	13C.34 **Japanese honeysuckle*** *Lonicera japonica* Honeysuckle family (Caprifoliaceae) Eastern Asia	Woody perennial vine	Climbing or trailing vine girdles young plants. Leaves are opposite, shape is variable. Oval shape with entire margins mid-late spring, but deeply-lobed early. Deciduous in cold climates, semi-evergreen to evergreen in warmer areas. Flowers are fragrant, white-to-creamy pairs arising from leaf axils. Black berries in pairs.
	13C.35 **Greenbriar** *Smilax* Lily family (Liliaceae) North America	Woody perennial vine	Can form impenetrable thickets. Climbs by tendrils attached to the petiole. Stems are bright green with sharp prickles. Shiny, bright-green leaves are alternate, rounded to heart-shaped, with smooth margins and parallel veins. Bears blue-black berry-like fruits.
	13C.36 **Poison ivy** *Toxicodendron radicans* Cashew family (Anacardiaceae) North America	Woody perennial vine	Contains urushiol in all plant parts, which causes inflammation, blisters, and severe itching. Urushiol remains in winter and even after plant death. Climbs by aerial roots that form hairy, fibrous ropes. Vining habit in shade, bush-like in sun. Leaves have 3 glossy 2-4-in. leaflets, margins are variably toothed, lobed, or nearly entire. Gray-white berries. Bright red fall color. Tolerates shade.
	13C.37 **Virginia creeper** *Parthenocissus quinquefolia* Grape family (Vitaceae) North America	Woody perennial vine	Stems trail or climb by tendrils with adhesive discs. Leaves are alternate, palmately compound, usually with 5 leaflets but sometimes 3 or 7, football to egg-shaped, margins toothed. Flowers are greenish, in clusters. Blue-black berries. Often mistaken for poison ivy (which has only 3 leaflets and gray-white berries).
	13C.38 **Trumpet creeper** *Campsis radicans* Trumpet creeper family (Bignoniaceae) North America	Woody perennial vine	Stems grow 20-40 ft., trailing or climbing by aerial roots. Leaves are opposite, pinnately compound, with 7-15 toothed leaflets. Flowers are orange, 2 in. long, and trumpet-shaped in terminal clusters, followed by 4-6-in. long slender seed pods.

continued on next page

continued from previous page

Table 13-C. Common lawn and garden weeds

* denotes invasive plant

Image	Plant name/origin	Biology	Description
	13C.39 **Kudzu*** *Pueraria lobata* Bean family (Fabaceae) Japan	Woody perennial vine	Deciduous, aggressively invasive vine that can grow to 100 ft., engulfing entire trees. Broad trifoliate leaves may be lobed or entire. Lavender-purple flowers are pea-like and appear in clusters. Massive root system spreads vegetatively.
	13C.40 **Porcelainberry*** *Ampelopsis brevipedunculata* Grape family (Vitaceae) Asia	Woody perennial vine	Similar to wild grape, it climbs by tendrils. Leaves alternate, dark green and maple-shaped with toothed margins, varying from slightly lobed to deeply cut. Berry colors may include lime green, turquoise-blue, lavender, and purple all in the same cluster.
	13C.41 **Oriental bittersweet*** *Celastrus orbiculatus* Stafftree family (Celastraceae) Asia	Woody perennial vine	Climbing, deciduous invasive. Leaves are rounded to obovate, alternate, simple with bluntly toothed margins. Inconspicuous flowers are followed by green-to-yellow fruits that burst open to display orange-red seeds that persist after fall leaf drop.
	13C.42 **Garlic mustard*** *Alliaria petiolata* Mustard family (Cruciferae) Europe	Biennial	Invasive species prefers shady forests and floodplains. Round to kidney-shaped leaves in rosettes the first year; the following spring, forms erect 1-4-ft. shoots with more triangular leaves. Begins flowering and dies by summer. Terminal spikes of white 4-petaled flowers. Mustard-like seeds are produced in long, slender, upright capsules.
	13C.43 **Bull thistle*** *Cirsium vulgare* Aster family (Asteraceae) Eurasia, but widespread in U.S.	Biennial	Produces a rosette in the first season. Leaves are deeply cut, hairy, and spiny with needle-like tips. Prickly wings and spines on stems. Purple disk flowers are 1-2 in. in diameter.
	13C.44 **Common mallow** *Malva neglecta* Mallow family (Malvaceae) Europe	Biennial and annual	Grows to 1 ft. tall. Leaves are alternate, rounded, palmately veined with toothed margins on long petioles. Flowers are 5-petaled, pale lavender to white. Button-like fruit is similar to hollyhock.

continued on next page

continued from previous page

Table 13-C. Common lawn and garden weeds   * denotes invasive plant

Image	Plant name/origin	Biology	Description
	13C.45 **Star chickweed, common chickweed** *Stellaria media* Pink family (Caryophyllaceae) Eurasia	Winter annual	Prostrate, creeping, light-green mats in turf, landscape, and vegetable gardens. Grows to 3-6 in. in sun, up to 18 in. in shade. Young leaves are smooth, opposite, egg-shaped, pointed at tip. Five white deeply-lobed petals give the appearance of 10 petals. Similar to mouseear chickweed, but neither perennial nor hairy. Common in turf.
	13C.46 **Henbit** *Lamium amplexicaule* Mint family (Lamiaceae) Eurasia, Northern Africa	Winter annual	Grows to less than 12 in. Square stems. Leaves are opposite, scalloped, and rounded. Lower leaves have petioles, upper leaves half-encircle the stem. Pinkish-purple lipped flowers appear in whorls in the axils of upper leaves. Tolerates close mowing.
	13C.47 **Red (purple) deadnettle** *Lamium purpureum* Mint family (Lamiaceae) Eurasia	Winter annual	Square stems. Leaves are opposite, pointed, and overlapping near top of stem. Leaves often appear with purple coloring. Pinkish-purple lipped flowers are borne at top of plant. Tolerates close mowing.
	13C.48 **Hairy bittercress** *Cardamine hirsuta* Mustard family (Cruciferae) Old World	Winter annual	Features a basal rosette of pinnate leaves, 1-3 pairs of leaflets with terminal, larger leaflet. Tiny 4-petaled white flowers appear in clusters at the top of stems, followed by slender, upright seed capsules. Capsules pop explosively. Tolerates shade and close mowing.
	13C.49 **Common groundsel** *Senecio vulgaris* Aster family (Asteraceae) Europe, Northern Africa, Asia	Winter or summer annual	Erect, multi-branched. Grows to 6-18 in. tall. Leaves are irregularly toothed, deeply lobed to dissected, somewhat fleshy. Flower heads have many yellow disk flowers followed by fluffy pappus which aids in seed dispersal by wind.
	13C.50 **Knawel** *Scleranthus annuus* Pink family (Caryophyllaceae) Eurasia	Winter or summer annual	Prostrate plant stays under 1 ft. Multi-branched, forming dense clumps of light blue-gray foliage. Leaves are very small, linear, and sharply pointed. Flowers are inconspicuous. Found mostly on dry, sandy, infertile soils.

continued on next page

continued from previous page

Table 13-C. Common lawn and garden weeds   * denotes invasive plant

Image	Plant name/origin	Biology	Description
	13C.51 **Horseweed** *Conyza canadensis* Aster family (Asteraceae) North America	Winter or summer annual	Germinates in fall or spring. Erect, 3-6-ft. tall plant, generally unbranched except at top. Hairy leaves are long and narrow with toothed margins, whorled around hairy stems. Many small, white ray and yellow disk flowers. Seeds are spread by the wind. Glyphosate-resistant in some areas.
	13C.52 **Black medic** *Medicago lupulina* Bean family (Fabaceae) Europe, Western Asia	Summer annual	Prostrate plant generally less than 6 in. tall. Trifoliate leaf arrangement is similar to white clover (oxalis). Leaflets are dark green, stems downy. Center leaflet has a short petiole. Features clover-like clusters of tiny, yellow, pea-shaped flowers. Often appears in dry, sunny, closely-mowed sites.
	13C.53 **Common purslane** *Portulaca oleracea* Purslane family (Portulacaceae) Western Asia	Summer annual	Prostrate plant forms low mats less than 1 ft. tall. Stems and leaves are thick, succulent, light-green to maroon on undersides and older portions. Flowers are yellow, with 5 petals at tips of stems.
	13C.54 **Carpetweed** *Mollugo verticillata* Carpetweed family (Aizoaceae) Tropical America	Summer annual	Prostrate plant forms low, circular mats. Narrow leaves appear in whorls of 3-8 at each node. Very small white flowers. Grows flat and carpet-like when young.
	13C.55 **Prostrate knotweed** *Polygonum aviculare* Buckwheat family (Polygonaceae) North America	Summer annual	Prostrate plant has dull, blue-green leaves, alternate, small, elliptical to oblong and less than 1 in. long. Short petioles have a conspicuous ocrea sheathing the stem at the leaf base. Very small white-to-pinkish flowers. Similar to spurge, but without milky sap. Tolerates dry, compacted areas and close mowing.
	13C.56 **Prostrate spurge** *Euphorbia supina* Spurge family (Euphorbiaceae) America	Summer annual	Prostrate, mat-forming plant. Stems and foliage release milky sap when broken. Leaves are opposite and oblong, often with a dark maroon spot on the upper surface and dark maroon below. Inconspicuous flowers in leaf axils. Similar to prostrate knotweed. Tolerates dry soils and close mowing.

continued on next page

continued from previous page

Table 13-C. Common lawn and garden weeds

*denotes invasive plant

Image	Plant name/origin	Biology	Description
	13C.57 **Hairy galinsoga** *Galinsoga ciliata* Aster family (Asteraceae) South America, Central America	Summer annual	Grows 1-2 ft. tall with erect, branching stems. Leaves are opposite, egg-shaped, with pointed tip, toothed margins, and covered with coarse hairs. Numerous small flowers appear in terminal clusters with 4-5 white rays surrounding yellow disk centers.
	13C.58 **Daisy fleabane** *Erigeron annuus* Aster family (Asteraceae) North America	Summer annual	Spring blooming plant grows 1-3 ft. tall. Leaves are hairy with toothed margins. Lower leaves are ovate, upper leaves are more lanceolate. Stems are hairy, branching at top. Aster-like 1/2-1-in. flower heads have 40-60 white-to-pink ray flowers, surrounding yellow disk flowers.
	13C.59 **Common ragweed** *Ambrosia artemisiifolia* Aster family (Asteraceae) North America	Summer annual	Erect and branching, grows 1-4 ft. Leaves are pinnatifid, deeply dissected, fern-like. Green flowers are inconspicuous, in terminal clusters. Ragweed pollen is the primary cause of hay fever. Foliage is similar to mugwort, but is not chrysanthemum-scented and does not grow from rhizomes.
	13C.60 **Common lamb's-quarter** *Chenopodium album* Goosefoot family (Chenopodiaceae) North America, Eurasia	Summer annual	Erect, 2-5 ft. tall, branching plant has whitish, mealy or waxy coating on newest leaves. First leaves are opposite, later are alternate, egg-shaped, and irregularly toothed. Individual green flowers are inconspicuous but clustered in large terminal panicles. Stem often shows pink to red vertical stripes.
	13C.61 **Redroot pigweed** *Amaranthus retroflexus* Amaranth family (Amaranthaceae) Tropical America	Summer annual	Erect, 2-5-ft. branching weed. Leaves are alternate, egg-shaped, dull green to reddish. Small greenish flowers appear in dense, stiff terminal panicles. Smooth pigweed (*Amaranthus hybridus*) is also common.
	13C.62 **Pennsylvania smartweed** *Polygonum pensylvanicum* Buckwheat family (Polygonaceae) North America	Summer annual	Grows 1-4 ft. Leaves are alternate, lanceolate, with smooth margins, sometimes with a purplish thumbprint marking the 2-3-in. leaf. Conspicuous ocrea surrounds the point where petiole meets stem. Pink flowers appear in spike-like clusters.

continued on next page

continued from previous page

Table 13-C. Common lawn and garden weeds

* denotes invasive plant

Image	Plant name/origin	Biology	Description
	13C.63 **Common cocklebur** *Xanthium strumarium* Aster family (Asteraceae) Eurasia, Central America, North America	Summer annual	Large 2-4-ft. plant with rough, sandpapery, maple-shaped, alternate leaves. Stem is often purple-spotted. Inconspicuous green flowers appear in leaf axils followed by distinct ½-in. prickly burs with hooks.
	13C.64 **Velvetleaf** *Abutilon theophrasti* Mallow family (Malvaceae) India	Summer annual	Erect, 2-5-ft. plant with velvety leaf and stem surfaces. Leaves are simple and heart-shaped with finely-toothed margins, covered in velvety soft hairs. Yellow 5-petaled flowers appear in leaf axils, followed by button-like fruit similar to hollyhock.
	13C.65 **Jimsonweed** *Datura stramonium* Nightshade family (Solanaceae) Possibly Central America	Summer annual	Erect, 2-4 ft., branching habit. Large leaves are coarsely toothed, wavy margins, alternate. Lavender flowers are either large and funnel-shaped on purple-stemmed plants, or white on green-stemmed plants. Walnut-sized seed pods are covered with sharp spines. All parts have a strong, unpleasant odor and are poisonous.
	13C.66 **Ivyleaf morning glory** *Ipomoea hederacea* Morning glory family (Convolvulaceae) Tropical America	Summer annual	Climbing or trailing vine. Leaves are ivy-shaped, covered in erect hairs. Flowers are funnel-shaped, sky-blue, purple or white. Grows from seeds, not from rhizomes like bindweeds.
	13C.67 **Pitted morning glory** *Ipomoea lacunosa* Morning glory family (Convolvulaceae) Tropical America	Summer annual	Climbing or trailing vine. Leaves are variable from heart- to somewhat ivy-shaped, alternate, nearly hairless, often with purplish coloration of leaves and stems. Flowers are small, white, and funnel-shaped. Grows from seeds, not from rhizomes like bindweeds.
	13C.68 **Tall morning glory** *Ipomoea purpurea* Morning glory family (Convolvulaceae) Tropical America	Summer annual	Climbing or trailing vine. Leaves are heart-shaped, alternate, and smooth-edged. Funnel-shaped flowers are white to purple. Grows from seeds, not from rhizomes like bindweeds.

continued on next page

continued from previous page

Table 13-C. Common lawn and garden weeds

* denotes invasive plant

Image	Plant name/origin	Biology	Description
	13C.69 **Asiatic dayflower** *Commelina communis* Spiderwort family (Commelinaceae) Tropical America	Summer annual	Monocot that resembles a dicot. Lanceolate leaves have parallel veins and no petioles. Leaf blades clasp stem at base. Stems and leaves are fleshy. Flowers have 2 large blue petals above a smaller white petal.
	13C.70 **Mile-a-minute*** *Polygonum perfoliatum* Buckwheat family (Polygonaceae) Asia	Summer annual vine	Summer annual vine grows 10-15 ft. Leaves are light green and triangular. Petioles and stems have recurved spines. Prominent leaf-like sheath encircles stem at base of petiole. Inconspicuous flowers. Fruit appears in a metallic blue berry-like cluster. Tolerates shade.
	13C.71 **Field dodder** *Cuscuta pentagona* Morning glory family (Convolvulaceae) North America	Summer annual vine	Parasitic vine germinates from seed. Thread-like, yellow-orange stems twine over host plants. Roots are modified to penetrate then draw nutrients and water from the host. Leaves are inconspicuous. Flowers are small, whitish, and appear in clusters.

Table 13-D. Vegetative identification of weedy grasses

* denotes invasive plant

		Plant name/origin	Auricle/bud shoot	Ligule/sheath	Blade	Seed-head	Comments
		Barnyardgrass *Echinochloa crus-galli* Europe	Absent/Rolled	Absent/Glabrous Flattened	Glabrous	Coarse branched panicle	Erect summer annual. Grows to 4 ft. One of the few grasses without a ligule.
		Crabgrass, Large *Digitaria sanguinalis* Europe	Absent/Rolled	Membranous/1-2 mm Hairy Nearly round	Wide, hairy above and below. 1st leaf is short, blunt, and wide.	3-5 finger-like spikes	Summer annual. Grows to 2 ft. Decumbent growth; swollen nodes; may root at nodes; tolerates close mowing.
		Crabgrass, Smooth *Digitaria ischaemum* Europe	Absent/Rolled	Membranous/1-2 mm Smooth Nearly round	Wide, slightly hairy at leaf base. 1st leaf is short, blunt, and wide.	3-5 finger-like spikes	Summer annual. Grows to 2 ft. Decumbent growth habit; swollen nodes; tolerates close mowing.
		Johnsongrass* *Sorghum halepense* Mediterranean	Absent/Rolled	Membranous/2 mm Glabrous Nearly round	6-20 in. x ½-1½ in. Glabrous, rough margins, prominent white midrib.	Large, open panicle, purplish hue	Perennial. Grows to 6 ft. Coarse-textured. Thick, creeping rhizomes form large clumps; noxious.

continued on next page

continued from previous page

		Plant name/ origin	Auricle/ bud shoot	Ligule/ sheath	Blade	Seed-head	Comments
		Goosegrass *Eleusine indica* Old World	Absent/ Folded	Membranous/ <1 mm Hairy at top Distinctly flat	5-10 mm. Hairy near base, above blade, collar margins.	Coarse branched panicle	Summer annual to 2 ft. Light-green/white at stem base. Tolerates close mowing.
		Annual bluegrass *Poa annua* Eurasia	Absent/ Folded	Membranous/ 1-2 mm Flat, smooth Round to acute	Wide, hairy above and below. 1st leaf is short, blunt, wide.	3-5 finger-like spikes	Summer annual to 2 ft. tall. Decumbent growth habit; swollen nodes; may root at nodes; tolerates close mowing.
		Orchardgrass *Dactylis glomerata* Europe	Absent/ Folded	Membranous/ >2 mm Center peaked Distinctly flat	2-3 mm. Smooth above, below, on margins. Light blue-green with a canoe-shaped leaf tip.	3-5 finger-like spikes	Winter annual. <1 ft. Likes cool, moist conditions. Tolerates shade/close mowing.
		Japanese Stiltgrass* *Microstegium vimineum* Asia	Absent/ Rolled	Membranous/ >1 mm Hairs on back Hairy at top	Light green, pointed, whitish midrib divides leaf unequally.	Fine, slender, spike-like panicle	Summer annual to 2 ft. Invasive. Roots at nodes. Tolerates shade/close mowing.
		Nimblewill *Muhlenbergia schreberi* North America	Absent/ Folded	Membranous/ >1 mm Loose Not hairy	Short, not hairy. Has flat-topped appearance when mowed.	Fine, slender, spike-like panicle	Spreading perennial to 1½ ft. tall. Slow to green in spring, browns early; fresh scent; tolerates shade/close mowing.
		Giant foxtail *Setaria faberi* China	Absent/ Rolled	Somewhat hairy. Fringe of hair may be fused at base. Margin hairy.	Short hairs on upper surface. Smooth below.	Bristly, spike-like foxtail	Summer annual up to 5 ft. tall. Leaves and seed head arch. Hair on collar, rough margins.
		Fall Panicum *Panicum dichotomiflorum* North America	Absent/ Rolled	Fringe of hairs. Glabrous, glossy when mature, velvety when 3 leaves or fewer.	15-20 mm. Glabrous, with long, fine hairs below on young leaves.	Large, delicate panicle	Summer annual to 5 ft. Stems bend at joints; lower nodes enlarged. Prominent white midrib as plant matures.
		Bermudagrass *Cynodon dactylon* Africa	Absent/ Rolled	Fringe of hairs. Round to flat, mostly smooth. Hair on collar margin.	2-5 mm wide. Smooth to rough, few longer hairs near base; hair on collar margin.	3-7 finger-like spikes	Perennial to 2 ft. Spreads aggressively by strong, wiry stolons. Tolerates close mowing. Dormant/brown in winter.
		Quackgrass *Agropyron repens* North America	Long/ Clasping	Membranous < 1 mm Glabrous or hairy	Glabrous or sparsely hairy. Dull blue-grayish-green coloring.	Terminal spike with alternating spikelets	Perennial to 3 ft. Sharp-tipped rhizomes. The only common grass with both clasping auricles and rhizomes.
		Tall fescue *Festuca arundinacea* Europe	Small Short Hairy Rolled	Membranous < 1 mm Round Smooth	Smooth to rough above, glossy below; distinct ridges run down leaf length.	Panicle	Perennial to 3 ft. tall. Clump-forming. Fibrous root system. Coarser than bluegrass or fine fescues.

UME © 2025. All rights reserved.

13: Weeds 365

13.4 Weed Management

Managing weeds is a continuous process. Success requires knowledge of weed identification and biology, understanding management options, and implementing a combination of effective methods. Managing weeds in your lawn and landscape often involves three approaches:

Prevention. Avoid the introduction or establishment of specific weed species in areas that are not currently infested. The scale of prevention can be as local as an individual portion of a yard or as broad as a state or nation. For example, although you may have Canada thistle in a flower bed in the front yard, you will want to prevent it from becoming established in additional flower beds throughout your property.

Eradication. Kill or completely remove all seeds and vegetative parts of a particular species from a site so it cannot reappear without reintroduction. Eradication can be expensive and time-consuming, so it is most appropriate for weeds that are 1) new to a particular site, or 2) invasive species such as giant hogweed, kudzu, and purple loosestrife that have potential to do serious harm to humans or the environment, and would be even more difficult to control after becoming well established. Eradication can also be practiced on a local or wide scale.

Suppression. Reduce the weed population to a level that can be tolerated in economic or aesthetic terms. Suppression is an appropriate degree of management for weeds such as crabgrass and dandelion, which are ubiquitous in every yard throughout the state.

Modeling weed management after the Integrated Pest Management (IPM) approach manages weeds in an economically and environmentally sound manner. These include biological, cultural, mechanical, and chemical methods. See Chapter 10, IPM, for more info.

Biological management

In their place of origin, plants are plagued by a mixture of predators and pathogens that keep them in balance with their environment. When the plant is brought to a new location, the natural enemies may be left behind, allowing the plant to grow unchecked and become a "weed."

To initiate a biological control program, scientists go back to the country of origin, locate a plant's natural enemies, bring them to the U.S. under strict quarantine regulations, and test to insure they will not transfer to other host plants. If the biocontrol agent meets strict criteria, it can be released in hopes of establishing populations that will help keep the weed in check. Eradication is generally not the goal because some host plants are necessary for the survival of the biocontrol organism.

Biological control methods are typically executed by government agencies managing exotic invasives that may cause environmental, economic, or aesthetic harm. Biological control projects in Maryland and surrounding areas have included using a weevil for musk thistle, a rust for yellow nutsedge, a beetle for purple loosestrife, and a weevil for mile-a-minute.

Cultural and mechanical management

Cultural and mechanical practices have been the primary means of weed control for centuries. Today, gardeners often overlook the value of these practices and instead reach for a container of herbicide for convenience. Cultural and mechanical practices focus on prevention, avoidance, and suppression of weeds. Using IPM methods can help manage weeds with the use of chemicals being the last option. The following practices are the proper way to implement a successful IPM program.

Competitive lawns and landscapes

Use all means possible to increase the ability of desirable plants to compete with weeds. This includes selecting well-adapted varieties; improving fertility, pH, and soil structure (**See Chapter 4, Botany**); watering deeply rather than merely sprinkling; and mowing turf properly (**see Chapter 14, Lawns**). If you have ongoing problems with weeds in a particular setting, it's possible there are underlying causes such as soil compaction, too much shade, or waterlogged soils that are unfavorable for the growth of desirable plants. You may need to address these problems first.

Plant spacing and bed density

Maintaining the thickness of desirable plant canopies by closely spacing plants will help reduce weed growth in groundcovers, turf, and flower and vegetable beds. Trees and shrubs need to be planted to accommodate their mature size needs. Installing small and young materials will require more attention to weed maintenance due to their small root and foliage structure. Perennials can be planted densely as a groundcover. Prevent pest problems by:

- Selecting pest-resistant species and cultivars and maintaining proper bed density by designing with dense plantings and/or groundcovers.

- Adding or replacing plants as needed in existing landscapes to maintain density.
- Discontinuing the use of Tier 2 invasive plants (see the **MDA website**) and either removing or managing the life cycle of Tier 1 and 2 invasive plants in existing landscapes.

Weed prevention and sanitation

The focus should be on keeping weeds you already have from going to seed. Many techniques to help you do this are mentioned later in this chapter. Remember that every weed that goes to seed means more work for you next year. You may need to put in extra effort in the first few years, but gradually good weed management will pay off with fewer future problems.

Take measures to avoid the introduction of new weeds into the garden:

- Select clean seeds and plants. When purchasing plants, check the containers and root balls for weeds. If they contain difficult-to-control species like thistle, mugwort, or bermudagrass, you may want to avoid buying plants from that particular source.

- Any time new soil, mulch, or manure is brought to a site, there is the potential for introducing weeds, unless the product has been properly sterilized or composted. Evaluate the risk. Soil and manure may contain lots of seeds, whereas hardwood bark and pine needles generally have fewer.

- Use straw, not hay. Straw is composed of the stems of wheat or barley that have been harvested for grain and contain few weeds. Hay is a mixture of forages and weeds and may harbor many seeds.

- Tractors, tillage implements, grading equipment, and mowers can readily transport weed seeds and vegetative parts from one location to another. Always clean equipment before moving to a new site.
- Compost all yard waste and animal manure to kill weed seeds. It's all right to put vegetative parts of weeds into the compost, but don't include seed heads or perennial roots unless you're sure the temperature will get high enough to kill them (above 140°F).

Physical and mechanical disturbance

Hand-weeding works well for small, annual weeds, but with larger annuals and almost all perennials, the roots may break off in the soil and allow the plant to grow back from the root. Control will be poor on spreading perennials like Canada thistle, mugwort, and bermudagrass. Hand-weeding is best done after a rain when the soil is moist and weeds come up more easily.

Shallow cultivation is another method of disrupting shoot production and starving out weeds. Using a scuffle hoe, sever weed stems from the root by cultivating the soil to a depth of just one to two inches. (See Figure 13-E.) A hoe is meant to sever young weeds at the soil line and disturb soil as little as possible. It is not a digging tool, nor is it good for perennial weeds whose roots are deep. A hoe works best when the weather is hot and dry, and soil is firm. For very small annual weeds without a large root system, cutting at the soil line and leaving the tops on the surface is sufficient. The advantage of hoeing over rototilling is that it causes minimal soil disturbance, so few new seeds are brought to the surface.

In limited situations where a pernicious perennial weed such as Canada thistle, quack grass, or yellow nutsedge has invaded an area, it may be possible to starve the root system by repeatedly cutting all top growth at the soil level throughout the growing season.

Tillage includes digging, cultivating, rototilling, discing, and plowing. Historically, prior to the development of herbicides, tillage was the primary method of weed control. Tillage distributes weed seeds throughout the soil profile, burying some seeds while bringing others to the surface where conditions are ideal for germination. Tillage is effective for destroying young annual weeds, but with perennials, chopping the roots into smaller pieces can actually increase the number of plants and spread them around. Regrowth can occur from buds on small pieces of root. Therefore, management must be directed toward destruction of the root system. Soil disturbances should be kept to a minimum to reduce organic matter loss, soil erosion, damage to soil structure, and disruption of the soil food web.

A less practical offshoot of tillage is to do it frequently and repeatedly. After each tilling, carbohydrate reserves in the roots are used to

Figure 13-E. Shallow cultivation

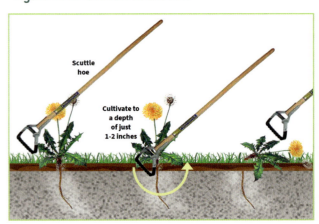

produce new shoots. Reserves are gradually depleted. For complete starvation and death, tillage may need to be repeated every 10 to 14 days for the entire growing season. If not done often, carbohydrate reserves will be replenished and root segments will continue to increase in number and spread.

Mowing can suppress many annual and perennial weed species. In nature, low-growing or mower-tolerant species will grow vegetatively or simply set seed at low heights (e.g., white clover or crabgrass in turf). In non-turf or minimally managed areas, repeated mowing will favor low-growing broadleafs and grasses, and discourage taller-growing herbaceous and woody plants. Mowing stimulates new branches or tillers, which can deplete root reserves if done frequently and can reduce seed production.

Mulching

Mulch is very effective in the home landscape as a physical barrier to prevent weed germination and smother newly emerging plants. Mulch works by preventing sunlight from reaching the soil surface and by exhausting the food reserves of young seedlings before they become established.

Organic mulches include straw, wood chips, bark, shredded leaves, grass clippings, and newspaper. Coarsely textured nuggets or chips provide a less hospitable environment for germinating weed seedlings than finely shredded mulches. A mulch layer two to three inches thick is sufficient for weed control and moisture retention. Alternatively, laying down a few sheets of newspaper can reduce the amount of mulch needed. Using excessive amounts of mulch is unnecessary and unhealthy for plants.

Mulch gradually decays and weed seeds may be deposited on top by wind, birds, mowers, or blowers so application must be repeated to maintain weed suppression. If chickweed and bittercress are major problems, apply new mulch in late summer to early fall. If crabgrass or other summer annuals are the focus, then apply mulch in winter to early spring.

Synthetic mulches such as black plastic will control most weeds. However, some perennials, especially nutsedge and quackgrass, can puncture and grow through plastic.

Clear plastic may be used to warm the soil and speed the time to harvest, but does not stop weed growth. Black polyethylene mulches that are impervious to water may need drip irrigation installed beneath and are best suited to vegetable crops grown in rows. Black polyester landscape fabrics allow water and air to penetrate so are more suitable for landscape uses. Synthetic mulches can be covered with a one- to two-inch layer of organic mulch to slow breakdown by ultraviolet light and to improve the overall appearance.

Gravel, rocks, shredded rubber tires, and pre-formed rubber mats are some other types of mulches that can reduce weeds. A problem with these more permanent types of mulches is that any clippings, leaves, or soil that end up on top of them provide a substrate for future weed growth. Consider using larger three- to five-inch riverstones rather than small gravel so that organic materials can be easily removed with a blower.

Edging/physical barriers

Installing plastic or metal edging at least four inches deep and two to three inches high can help stop but not totally prevent stoloniferous spreading grasses, like bermudagrass or zoysiagrass, from invading your landscape beds. No-mow strips made of paver, brick, or concrete will also discourage the grass and allow vertical cutting or spot treating of stolons and rhizomes creeping into beds.

Flame

Portable propane flamers can be used to kill small annual weeds. A flame is aimed at the weed long enough to cause cells to rupture. The weeds don't catch fire, but appear wilted. (Rapid death by flame, vinegar, or other contact chemical is often referred to as "burning" the tops of weeds.) The heat won't penetrate the soil enough to kill perennial roots. Be cautious when flame weeding during dry periods and around flammable mulches. Pouring hot water on plants has much the same effect.

Stale seedbed

Enormous numbers of weed seedlings will emerge from freshly tilled soil, but many can be destroyed with a stale seedbed approach. Till the soil and allow a flush of weeds to germinate, then kill the seedlings with herbicide, flame, or a very shallow (<1 inch) cultivation. Wait for another flush of seedlings and kill again. After several cycles, the number of seedlings will be dramatically reduced. In the final step, plant with as little soil disturbance as possible so that new weed seeds are not brought to the surface.

Solarization

This method is often recommended in organic references and can be effective where temperatures are very high for much of the year. Till moist soil thoroughly, cover with clear plastic, seal the edges, and let set for several weeks. Heat from the sun will kill many seeds, pathogens, and insects in the top four to six inches of soil. In Maryland, temperatures are only high enough during the summer peak for this process to be even marginally effective.

Chemical management

Herbicides are pesticides that kill plants. In 2001, seven of the top ten pesticides used in the home and garden sector were herbicides (USEPA). According to EPA estimates, between 24 and 41 million pounds of herbicide-active ingredient were applied to home grounds annually. The top two herbicides by volume were 2,4-D (many trade names) and glyphosate (Roundup®).

Herbicides may be used when cultural and mechanical practices have not been successful and weeds threaten to overtake desirable species. It is essential to identify weeds and select herbicides that are safe on the desirable plants. Choosing the wrong product for the job, using excessive rates, or misapplying herbicides may damage or kill desirable ornamental or edible plants in the landscape.

Herbicide use and safety

- The label is the law. Be sure to read, understand, and follow the label directions for proper use of these chemicals. Accurate rate calculations and equipment calibration are essential for some types of herbicide application, especially selective herbicides, and the margin of error can be rather low. The label also contains other important safety and use information. Read it carefully! The safety data sheet (SDS) describes the proper response to accidental spills or exposure to the chemical in question.

- Proper personal protective equipment (PPE) requirements for the safe use of an herbicide product also appear on the label. Examples of PPE include gloves, long pants, a long-sleeve shirt, eye protection, and a face shield.

- Additional precautions should be taken when mixing chemicals even when wearing PPE. Do not stand directly over the application equipment, and don't leave it unattended.

- Pay careful attention to the environmental precautions section of the label, which will alert you to which ecosystems may be negatively impacted by application of the product, along with any use restrictions (do not use in proximity to waterways).

- Always dedicate a separate sprayer for herbicides only and triple-rinse with a strong detergent between applications. Dispose of the rinse water in areas consistent with label use. Do not use the herbicide sprayer for insecticides or fungicides because herbicide residues may injure sensitive plants.

- Use spot treatments rather than broadcast applications whenever possible. You'll reduce the amount of herbicide in the environment and reduce the chances of injury to non-target species.

Herbicide types

Herbicides may be classified by their selectivity, movement in plants, timing, and application method. Nonselective herbicides kill or injure all plants, whether they are broadleafs or grasses. Glyphosate, diquat, and vinegar are nonselective. Selective herbicides kill or damage certain plant species without

ABOUT HERBICIDE NAMES

There are three names associated with each herbicide:

- *The chemical name* is a complex technical description of the active ingredient.

- *The common name* is a simpler version of the chemical name. Each active ingredient has only one approved and accepted chemical name and one common name.

- *A trade name* is used by a company for marketing purposes. There may be many trade names for a single common name.

For example, the chemical name N-(phosphonomethyl) glycine is the chemical name for an active ingredient with the common name glyphosate, which is sold by various companies under trade names such as Roundup®, Kleenup®, and Accord.

Another example is 2,4-dichlorophenoxy acetic acid with the common name of 2,4-D. It kills dicots, but not grasses. There are hundreds of trade names of products containing 2,4-D alone or in combination with other products. Some of the more common trade names are Aqua-Kleen®, Barrage®, Lawn-Keep®, and Malerbane®.

Brand names and packaging are constantly changing, so referring to herbicides by their common name greatly simplifies figuring out which ones will work on which weeds.

seriously harming others. For example, 2,4-D selectively controls broadleaf weeds growing in turf without damaging the grass. Selectivity may be due to differences in morphology, absorption, translocation, or physiology between the species.

Contact. These products affect only the portion of the green plant tissue to which they are applied. They can "burn down" the tops, but they cannot move within the plant's vascular system and control the roots, rhizomes, or tubers of perennials. Repeat applications are necessary to control regrowth from roots. Thorough spray coverage is important because the product cannot move within the plant. Contact herbicides generally kill quickly, often within hours of application. Vinegar and pelargonic acid (Scythe®) are examples of contact herbicides.

Systemic. This type of herbicide moves within the plant's vascular system (see Figure 13-F). In the spring, nutrients and energy necessary for plant growth are being translocated upward to new foliage. Systemic herbicides applied to new spring growth will move upward, killing foliage, but not the roots. Systemic herbicides applied to mature foliage later in the summer and fall will be translocated downward into the roots. It is essential to have downward movement to kill the extensive root systems of perennial weeds. Systemic herbicides may require several days or even weeks to be fully translocated throughout the plant and for death to occur. Glyphosate (Roundup®) is a non-selective, systemic herbicide, whereas 2,4-D, dicamba (Banvel®), and sethoxydim (Vantage®) are selective, systemic herbicides.

Application timing

Another important herbicide classification refers to the timing of application relative to weed and crop germination. Post-emergent herbicides are applied directly to the foliage of weeds after they have germinated. Post-emergent products may be selective (2,4-D) or nonselective (glyphosate). Post-emergent products work best when the target plants are actively growing. Pre-emergent herbicides are applied before weeds begin to germinate.

Figure 13-F. Systemic herbicide translocation

This may be before or after the desirable plant has emerged. Rainfall or irrigation washes the herbicide into solution where it forms a barrier in the top inch of soil. As weed seeds germinate, they grow through the treated zone, absorbing herbicide that inhibits development of roots and further growth.

The persistence of pre-emergent herbicides in soil is referred to as residual activity. Do not disturb the treated zone or residual activity will be lost. (See Figure 13-G.)

Herbicides work best when plants are actively growing under good conditions with adequate rainfall and not injured by frost. Foliar herbicides need time to be absorbed into the plant, so check the weather forecast for rain before making an application. Always spray herbicides when there is no wind. The slightest breeze may carry droplets of the herbicide onto sensitive plants nearby.

Organic herbicides

As the demand increases for organic alternatives to synthetic herbicides, new products are under development. Most may need to be reapplied but have low toxicity to the environment. The label still needs to be respected as in the case of the inorganic herbicides. They don't all work on every weed, so know your weeds, and read the label.

Pelargonic acid naturally occurs in many different plants and has little or no toxicity to the environment. It is a post-emergent, non-selective herbicide. It's mainly used to kill the vegetative shoots of a plant, or top-kill. Reapplication may be necessary.

Acetic acid (vinegar) and **citric acid** (naturally occurring in citrus fruits) are both post-emergent, non-selective herbicides that work by breaking down plant cell walls. They can be used as contact herbicides for killing small annual broadleaf weeds and young grasses. Perennials and large annuals may exhibit some "burndown" of top growth, but the roots will re-grow and may require repeated applications to completely kill the plant.

Familiar household strength vinegar is 5% acetic acid, but the concentrations that are shown to be effective for weed control have been between 10% and 20%. Concentrated forms of acetic acid may cause severe burns and permanent corneal injury, resulting in blindness. Protective eye wear and gloves are an absolute must when handling the concentrate.

Figure 13-G. Residual barrier

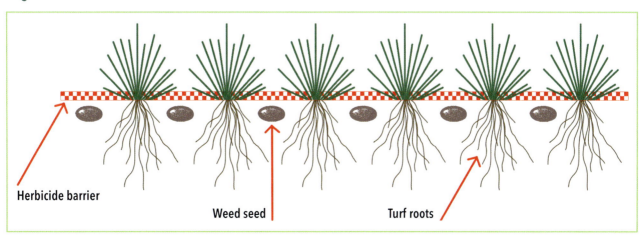

Iron-based herbicide is a selective post-emergent with low toxicity to the environment. Repeated applications may be necessary to completely kill plants. Broadleaf weeds take up iron more readily than turf grass and reach an iron toxicity level faster than grass.

Corn gluten meal is a non-selective, pre-emergent herbicide, which means it does not impact weeds that have already germinated. It has low toxicity in the environment. Reapplication may be necessary to prevent weed seeds from germinating. Buyer beware, corn gluten meal contains 9%-10% nitrogen which can feed both the grass and weeds. The recommended corn gluten rate of 20 lb./1,000 square feet provides approximately 2 lb./1,000 square feet of nitrogen.

13.5 Sustainable Weed Maintenance Plan

The key to keeping weeds at bay is to establish a garden with short-term maintenance requirements that will eventually reduce long-term maintenance chores. Following is a plan for homeowners to understand the process and control weeds without herbicides.

Site analysis

First, get an overview of your existing plants:

- Which plants do you currently have? Identify and list them.
- Are any of your plants dead, declining, decayed, displaced, invasive, or ones you want to remove? Identify which plants need to be removed and/or relocated.
- Did any of the plant removals change the original site conditions? For example, if you removed a tree, the light levels or hydrology for the surrounding plants could change.
- Replace plants with natives whenever possible.

Prioritization

- Identify which areas of your garden are most important to you. Assess the resources (time and money) it will require throughout the year for you to keep those areas planted densely, irrigated as needed, and relatively weed-free.
- Assess what is actually achievable, given the resources available to you. If you are overly ambitious and bite off more than you can chew, you will likely end up needing to hire a landscaper to help with the maintenance chores. If you do outsource the maintenance, make sure the landscaper understands how to maintain the garden using the sustainable practices outlined in the following Implementation section.

Implementation

Garden maintenance is all about time management. It can be done quickly and frequently, or less often with more time allotted. Make a commitment to one method or the other and stick to a regular schedule rather than doing it on an *ad hoc* basis.

- Establish and maintain dense plantings like native groundcovers. They will effectively crowd out weeds and replace the need for purchased mulch with "green mulch." Establishment can be a two- to three-year process, so be patient and persistent and eventually the weeds will diminish, if not disappear altogether.

- Succession-plant. Keep your garden constantly and fully planted to shade the soil, allowing fewer weed seeds to germinate. To cover an area quickly, choose a plant with edible leaves and generously sow the seed in a patch rather than a row. Thin plants with garden snips instead of pulling them out, which creates a kind of a microgreens cover crop that fends off weeds. Follow spring lettuces and cold crops with hot-weather vegetables, then back to cold crops. Intersperse flowering ornamentals wherever you see fit. When your perennials die back, fill in the bare spots with annuals.

- Always plant a cover crop. Someone once said that you can either plant a cover crop or nature will plant one for you: weeds. Millet, buckwheat, and sorghum do well in summer bare spots as long as they're kept watered. When the cool weather arrives, plant cover crops like mustard, rye, winter wheat, tillage radishes (nature's soil aerator), Austrian peas, or crimson clover. These will probably die off on their own if the temperatures are cold enough, but if they persist, just pull them up and leave them as mulch until spring.

- Prevent weeds in the first place. Cover your garden area with four inches of compost each year. This not only significantly improves the soil and helps retain water, but it's like pulling a shade down that prevents light from germinating the weed-seed bank that resides in the soil. Square-foot gardening is one example; you might also underplant a tall species like sunflowers or corn with a ground-hugging melon vine to shade the soil. This practice also helps conserve water.

- Your compost can contain weed seeds, as can manure. The wind and birds can also carry weed seeds. While your weeding chores will always be part of your gardening routine, you can actually design your garden to make weeding faster and easier. Plant in neat rows with enough spacing between plants to accommodate a hoe. You can hoe through multiple rows in a snap rather than hoeing around individual plants.

- Keep after the weeds in the garden and don't let them go to seed. Some weed species can release thousands of seeds from just one plant! Spot-spray lawn weeds with an organic herbicide or manually pull them. Do a periodic soil test for nutrients to keep plants growing—bare spots created by stunted/weak plants that aren't growing well hold the door open for weeds.

Lawn weeds

As for managing lawn weeds, the key is to maintain healthy, dense turf. A thin, weak lawn is much more prone to weed infestation. To keep turf strong, fertilize cool-season grasses in the fall rather than spring when it favors the weedy summer annuals. Mow high to keep grass growing strong. Never take off more than one-third of the height at a time.

Water deeply as opposed to frequent, light sprinkling, which encourages weed-seed germination. If weeds begin to encroach, spot-treat small patches rather than the entire lawn, if possible. ✻

Additional weed identification and management resources

CD:

Weed identification CD: Richard Old. XID Services, Inc. *1200 Weeds of the 48 States and Adjacent Canada – Interactive Database for Identifying Weeds*. UPC: 9781450736862.

Websites:

Maryland Dept. of Agriculture Plant Protection and Weed Management	mda.maryland.gov/plants-pests/Pages/plant_protection_weed_management.aspx
Virginia Tech Weed Identification	weedid.cals.vt.edu
New Jersey Weed Gallery	njaes.rutgers.edu/weeds/
USDA Plants Database	plants.sc.egov.usda.gov/home
Weed Science Society of America	wssa.net
The Nature Conservancy Weed Control Methods Handbook: Tools and Techniques for Use in Natural Areas	invasive.org/gist/products/handbook/methods-handbook.pdf
Cornell Organic Weed Mgmt.	weedecology.css.cornell.edu/manage/
Cornell Poisonous Plants	poisonousplants.ansci.cornell.edu
Poisonous Plants of N. Carolina	ncpoisoncontrol.org/types-of-poisons/plants-and-mushrooms/poisonous-plants
Maryland Invasive Species Council	mdinvasives.org
Plant Invaders of Mid-Atlantic Natural Areas - National Park Service, US Fish & Wildlife	invasive.org/alien/pubs/midatlantic/midatlantic.pdf
Biological Control of Invasive Plants in the Eastern U. S.	invasive.org/eastern/biocontrol/
National Invasive Species Information Center	invasivespeciesinfo.gov
Crop Data Management Systems (Pesticide labels and MSDS)	cdms.net/manuf/manuf.asp

Disclaimer: Mention or display of a trademark, proprietary product, or firm in either text or figures does not constitute an endorsement by University of Maryland Extension and does not imply approval to the exclusion of other suitable products or firms.

AUTHORS

Original author: Betty Marose, IPM Specialist, University of Maryland Extension, retired.

2024 Edition:

Kelley Oklesson, PLA, LEED AP, CBLP I and II, CPH, ASLA and Lecturer (Landscape Architecture) University of Maryland.

Josef Mudd, Master Gardener Volunteer, University of Maryland Extension.

PUBLICATIONS

Brown, M.L. and R.G. Brown. 1984. *Herbaceous Plants of Maryland*. Port City Press. Baltimore, MD. ISBN 84-072042.

Brown, M.L. and R.G. Brown. 1972. *Woody Plants of Maryland.* Port City Press. Baltimore, MD. ISBN 70-184336.

Crafts, A.S. 1975. *Modern Weed Control.* University of California Press. Berkeley, CA. ISBN 0-520-027337.

Corson, C 2016. *Sustainable Landscape Maintenance Manual for the Chesapeake Bay Watershed.* Chesapeake Conservation Landscape Council.

Table 13-B: Harrington, J.F. 1972. *Seed storage and longevity.* Pp. 145-245 in T.T. Kozlowski (ed.) *Seed Biology.* Academic Press, New York.

Klingman, G.C. and F.M. Ashton. 1982. *Weed Science: Principles and Practices.* 2nd Edition. John Wiley & Sons, Inc. Hoboken, NJ. ISBN 0-471-08487-5.

Lorenzi, H.J. and L.S. Jeffery. 1987. *Weeds of the United States and Their Control.* Van Nostrand Reinhold Co, Inc. New York, NY. ISBN 0-442-25884-4.

McKenny, M. and R.T. Peterson. 1998. *A Field Guide to Wildflowers : Northeastern and North-Central North America* (Peterson Field Guides). Houghton Mifflin. Boston, MA. ISBN 10: 0395911729.

Newcomb, L. 1989. *Newcomb's Wildflower Guide.* Little, Brown and Company. Boston, MA. ISBN 10: 0316604429.

Phillips, C.E. *Field Manual No. 2. Some Grasses of the Northeast; A key to their identification by vegetative characters.* University of Delaware. Agricultural Experiment Station. Newark, DE. (No date exists on the publication.)

Radosevitch S., J. Holt, and C. Chersa. 1997. *Weed Ecology: Implications for Management.* John Wiley & Sons, Inc. Hoboken, NJ. ISBN 10: 0471116068.

Table 13-A: Stevens, O.A. 1954. *Weed Seed Facts.* H.D. Agric. Coll. Ext. Cir. A-128, 4 pp.

Table 13-A: Stevens, O.A. 1957. *Weights of Seeds and Numbers Per Plant.* Weeds 4:46-55. Anderson, W.P. 1977. Weed Science: Principles. West Publishing Co. Eagan, MN. ISBN 0-8299-0084-5.

Uva, R.A., J.C. Neal, and J.M. Ditomaso. 1997. *Weeds of the Northeast.* Cornell Press. Ithaca, NY. ISBN 10: 0801483344.

PHOTOS

Main Chapter Photo, 13C.1, 13C.6, 13C.30, 13C.33, 13C.43, 13C.47, 13C.48, 13C.49, 13C.64, 13C.65. Rachel Rhodes, University of Maryland Extension.

13C.2, 13C.15, 13C.25, 13C.70. Jon Traunfeld, University of Maryland Extension.

13C.3. Michael Shephard, USDA Forest Service, Bugwood.org

13C.4, 13C.11. Andreas Rockstein via Flickr.

13C.5, 13D.10. John D. Byrd, Mississippi State University, Bugwood.org.

13C.7 Jack Pearce via Flickr.

13C.8, 13C.12, 13C.26, 13C.38, 13C.40. Miri Talabac, University of Maryland Extension.

13C.9, 13C.18. Rob Routledge, Sault College, Bugwood.org

13C.10. **Dr. Boli** via Flickr

13C.13, 13C.28, 13C. 31, 13C.39, 13C.42. Leslie J. Mehrhoff, University of Connecticut, Bugwood.org

13C.14, 13C.29, 13C.36, 13D.13. Steve Dewey, Utah State University, Bugwood.org

13C.16, 13C.20, 13C.50, 13C.52, 13C.53, 13C.56, 13C.59, 13C.61, 13.D6, 13D.7. University of Maryland Extension.

13C.17, 13C.35, 13D.14. James H. Miller & Ted Bodner, Southern Weed Science Society, bugwood.org

13C.19, 13C.68, 13D.1, 13D.2. Howard F. Schwartz, Colorado State University, Bugwood.org

13C.21, 13C.37 Stephanie Pully, University of Maryland Extension.

13C.22, 13C.27. James H. Miller, USDA Forest Service, Bugwood.org

13C.23. Public domain via Flickr.

13C.24, 13C.41. James R. Allison, Georgia Department of Natural Resources, Bugwood.org

13C.27. James H. Miller, USDA Forest Service, Bugwood.org

13C.32. Terry English, USDA APHIS PPQ, Bugwood.org

13C.34. Chuck Bargeron, Universtiy of Georgia, Bugwood.org

13C.36, 13C.71, 13D.12. Charles T. Bryson, USDA Agricultural Research Service, Bugwood.org

13C.44, 13C.55, 13C.57. Bruce Ackley, The Ohio State University, Bugwood.org

13C.45. **Robert Flogaus-Faust** via Wikimedia

13C.51. Forest and Kim Starr, Starr Environmental, Bugwood.org

13C.54. Debra Ricigliano, University of Maryland Extension, retired

13C.58. Cbaile19 via Wikimedia, Public domain

13C.60. Bonnie Million, Bureau of Land Management, Bugwood.org

13C.62. **Gilles Ayotte**, Laval University, Wikimedia.

13C.63. Jan Samanek, Phytosanitary Administration, Bugwood.org

13C.66. Billy Craft, Bugwood.org

13C.67, 13C.69. Sekh Sayantan, Bugwood.org

13D.3. Joseph Berger, Bugwood.org

13D.9. Tim Murphy, University of Georgia, Bugwood.org

13D.11. **Blake Bringhurst** via Wikimedia.

ILLUSTRATIONS

Figure 13-E. LeAnn Zotta, Berkshire Communications.

Figure 13-F, 13-G. Don Wittig, University of Maryland Master Gardener, Montgomery County, retired. Colorization by LeAnn Zotta.

Table 13-D illustrations (except Japanese stiltgrass). CE Phillips, University of Delaware, used with permission. Japanese stiltgrass: Ray V. Bosmans, University of Maryland Extension, retired.

14: LAWNS

Geoffrey Jordan Rinehart

14 LAWNS

CONTENTS

14.1 Turfgrass Identification 381
14.2 Turfgrass Species 383
14.3 Lawn Establishment 389
14.4 Cultural Practices for Turf 393
14.5 Turfgrass Problems 402
14.6 Organic Lawn Care Tips 413
14.7 Lawn Alternatives 413

LEARNING OBJECTIVES

- Turfgrass identification terminology
- Recommended turfgrass species for Maryland
- Lawn establishment practices: seeding, sod, and site preparation
- Cultural practices: fertilizing, mowing, watering, thatch control, aeration, and liming
- Common lawn problems: weeds, insect pests, diseases, and abiotic disorders

INTRODUCTION

Lawns are an integral part of Maryland landscapes. In addition to enhancing a home, lawns provide practical benefits. A healthy lawn increases property values, controls soil erosion, filters pollution from runoff, moderates summer ground temperatures, and adds oxygen to the air.

On the other hand, misapplication of pesticides and fertilizers on lawns contributes to pollution of the Chesapeake Bay. Correct timing, selection, and application rates of these products can greatly reduce their negative impact on the health of the Bay.

Proper cultural practices that encourage a healthy lawn are also essential.

14.1 Turfgrass Identification

Turfgrass terminology

Figures 14-A through 14-G illustrate the vegetative parts of a grass plant and provide tips on what to look for when identifying a given type of grass.

Always use more than one plant and structure for identification because vegetative characteristics can vary depending upon environmental conditions or cultivar.

Figure 14-A. Parts of a grass plant

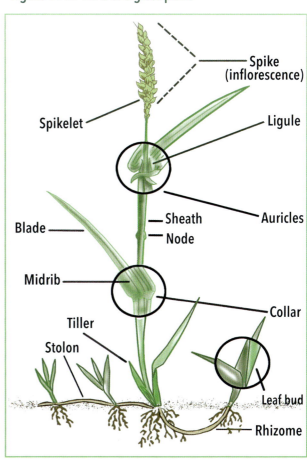

Leaf blade

The upper flattened portion of a grass leaf (see Figure 14-B).

- Is the texture fine, medium, or coarse?
- Are veins prominent?
- What shade of green is the blade?
- Is the blade smooth (glabrous) or hairy (pubescent)?
- Is the tip of the blade sharply pointed, boat-shaped, or blunt and round?

Leaf sheath

The lower portion of a leaf (the part that encircles the stem) (see Figure 14-C).

- Is the sheath cylindrical or compressed?
- Is the sheath closed or open, or do the margins overlap?

Vernation

The arrangement of new leaves within the older leaf sheath (see Figure 14-D). Is the leaf folded or rolled when it emerges?

Collar

The band at the junction of the blade and sheath (see Figure 14-E). Is the collar divided, broad, or narrow?

Ligule

The appendage on the inner side of a grass leaf at the junction of the blade and the leaf sheath (see Figure 14-F).

- Is the ligule absent, membranous, or hairy?
- What is the size and shape of the ligule?
- What does the upper ligule edge look like? Is it smooth, notched, or hairy?

Figure 14-B. Leaf blade shapes and textures

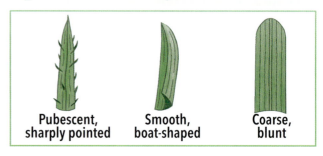

Figure 14-C. Leaf sheath types

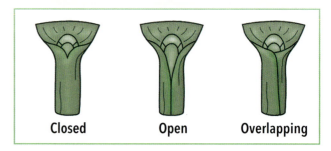

Figure 14-D. Vernation types

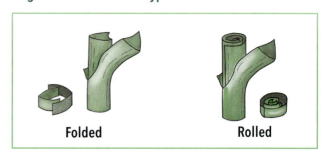

Figure 14-E. Collar types

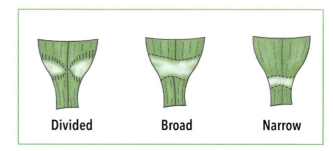

Figure 14-F. Ligule types

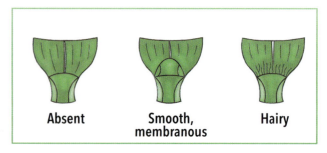

Auricle

Auricles are appendages occurring in pairs at the base of the blade (see Figure 14-G).

- Are auricles present or absent?
- If present, are the auricles small (rudimentary) or prominent (claw-like)?

Growth habit

Growth habit refers to the orientation of shoots (see Figure 14-H).

- Is the plant erect or lying down (decumbent)?
- Are there lateral shoots such as rhizomes (underground stems), stolons (above-ground stems), or only tillers?

14.2 Turfgrass Species

Maryland is located in an area referred to as the "transition zone." Within this zone, neither cool-season nor warm-season turfgrasses perform well during the entire year. Cool-season grasses will go dormant during a dry, hot summer and warm-season grasses go dormant after the first frost in the fall.

Either cool-season grasses or cold-tolerant warm-season grasses (e.g., zoysiagrass or cold-tolerant bermudagrass varieties) are recommended for most home lawns in Maryland. For lawns in the lower Eastern Shore counties, zoysia is a viable choice as an alternative to cool-season grasses, and improved cold-tolerant varieties of bermudagrass can be planted with success.

Cool-season turfgrasses include species that are adapted to most areas of Maryland:

- Maximum growth occurs during cool spring and fall weather.

Figure 14-G. Auricle types

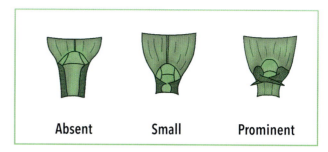

Figure 14-H. Grass growth habit

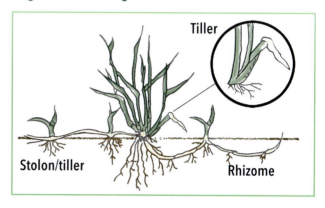

- May become semi-dormant during hot and/or dry periods in summer.
- Examples: turf-type tall fescue, fine fescues, and Kentucky bluegrass.

Warm-season turfgrasses include species that are best adapted to all areas except Western Maryland:

- Maximum growth occurs during hot weather; grass is dormant during the fall, winter, and early spring.
- Excellent heat- and drought-tolerance.
- Examples: zoysiagrass and bermudagrass.

Tall fescue *(Festuca arundinacea L.)*

Tall fescue forms a persistent and durable turf for home lawns, parks, playgrounds, and athletic fields. It is commonly used in other low-maintenance situations such as utility areas, highway medians, airstrips, and fairgrounds. Recommended for most homeowner sites.

Many new and improved varieties (called "turf-type tall fescue") have a finer texture, high tiller densities, and a darker green color than the older, coarse-textured, light-green varieties such as "Kentucky 31" and "Alta." Dwarf varieties are currently in demand for their reduced height and increased tiller densities. Although some of these varieties are used successfully, the slower rate of growth may cause delayed recovery from disease, insects, and wear.

Figure 14-I. Tall fescue

Of the cool-season turfgrasses, tall fescue is the most tolerant of heat and drought due to its ability to form a deep root system. It is also the most resistant to disease and insect damage, but only has fair recovery potential. It produces a minimal amount of thatch.

It performs well in open, sunny areas and is moderately shade-tolerant (requires about four hours of direct sunlight). It is more shade-tolerant than Kentucky bluegrass and perennial ryegrass. It grows best in well-drained soil.

Identification features:

Leaf blade: K-31 is medium to coarse; turf-types are medium-textured, medium-dark green color, 5 mm to 10 mm wide; flat blades

Vernation: rolled
Collar: broad, divided
Ligule: membranous
Auricles: short, blunt
Growth habit: bunch-type, tillers

Fine fescues *(Festuca spp.)*

Fine fescues are used for low-maintenance areas such as slopes, rights-of-way, and vacation homes. Of the cool-season species, these are the most tolerant of shady sites.

These species are narrow-leaved. The most common turf-type fine fescues include creeping red fescue (*Festuca rubra* L.), chewings fescue (*Festuca rubra* var. *commutata*), hard fescue (*Festuca trachyphylla*), and sheep fescue (*Festuca ovina* L.).

Of these, hard fescue has been found to perform the best of all of these species in University of Maryland trials.

Expect an attractive, uniform stand of turfgrass that is compatible in mixtures with most cool-season turf. As a group, they tolerate low-fertility soils, low pH, droughty soils, and shaded conditions.

Figure 14-J. Fine fescue

Fine fescues are not well-adapted to high heat, humidity, poorly-drained sites, or high-traffic areas such as athletic fields and playgrounds.

They do not tolerate high rates of nitrogen fertilizer and require periodic dethatching.

Identification features:

Creeping red fescue

Leaf blade: fine texture, 1.5 mm to 3 mm wide, medium-dark green

Vernation: folded

Collar: narrow

Ligule: membranous, .5 mm long, truncated

Auricles: absent

Growth habit: creeping

Chewings fescue

Similar to creeping red fescue but with a non-creeping growth habit.

Hard fescue, Sheep fescue

Leaf blade: fine texture, medium-dark green

Vernation: folded

Collar: broad, divided, without hairs

Ligule: membranous, .3 mm long, rounded

Auricles: rounded

Growth habit: non-creeping, bunch-type

Kentucky bluegrass *(Poa pratensis L.)*

Performs best in well-drained soils and open, sunny sites. Does not tolerate poorly drained soils or heavily shaded areas. Is cold-tolerant, wear-tolerant, and moderately heat- and drought-tolerant. Has superior recuperative potential compared to most other cool-season turfgrasses.

Requires a higher amount of nitrogen (N) fertilizer than other cool-season turfgrasses and is more susceptible to disease and insect infestations, like white grubs. Is considered to be a high-maintenance turf in Maryland.

Fine-fescue facts

- Creeping red fescue produces rhizomes, allowing it to fill in thin areas of turf and to make a good recovery from injury. This species has good seedling vigor compared to hard and sheep fescues.

- Hard fescue has received much attention in recent years for its tolerance of low-fertility soils and drought. Its major disadvantage is its relatively slow rate of germination and establishment.

- Sheep fescue is a bunch-type grass used primarily in low-maintenance situations. It is the least-used of the turf-type fine fescues.

- Chewings fescue lacks strong rhizome development but has greater tolerance for low mowing.

Produces a significant amount of thatch, so periodic dethatching is necessary.

Slower to become established and to germinate than most other turfgrasses (requiring up to three weeks for emergence).

Due to its production of underground rhizomes, is commonly used in sod production.

Figure 14-K. Kentucky bluegrass

Identification features:

Leaf blade: V-shaped or flat, boat-shaped tip, medium-to-fine texture, medium- to dark-green color

Vernation: folded

Collar: broad, divided

Ligule: membranous

Auricles: absent

Growth habit: spreading-rhizomatous

Perennial ryegrass *(Lolium perenne L.)*

Grows best in neutral to slightly acidic well-drained soils. Commonly used in grass-seed mixtures because of its quick germination rate.

Very susceptible to turf diseases such as gray leaf spot. *Perennial ryegrass is not a recommended turfgrass species for home lawns in Maryland.*

Identification features:

Leaf blade: flat, 2 mm to 5 mm wide, medium texture, medium- to dark-green color

Vernation: folded

Collar: broad, divided

Ligule: membranous

Auricles: small, claw-like

Growth habit: bunch-type

Figure 14-L. Perennial ryegrass

Bermudagrass

A warm-season species that grows best from mid-May through mid-August. Forms an attractive lawn turf in southern portions of the state, particularly the lower Eastern Shore. Produces extensive rhizomes and stolons that readily root at the nodes and spread rapidly, giving it good recuperative potential. Can also spread into unwanted areas (like neighbors' yards or garden beds).

Figure 14-M. Bermudagrass

Most varieties are planted either by sprigs or sod. Sprigging takes longer to establish. Top varieties for Maryland include 'Latitude 36', 'Iron Cutter', and 'Tahoma 31'. Cost of establishment is typically high, but is quick to take hold in warm weather.

Moderately drought-tolerant once established. Performs best under moderate moisture levels in fertile, well-limed soils. Does not tolerate poor drainage or shade.

Dethatch in early summer when thatch measures one inch. Do not apply fertilizer past mid-August. Grass goes dormant (turns a straw-brown color) after fall frost and does not green up until mid- to late spring.

Identification features:

Leaf blade: flat, stiff, 2 mm to 3 mm wide, medium-textured, glabrous to slightly hairy

Vernation: rolled

Collar: narrow, continuous, glabrous and hairy on margins

Ligule: a ring of white hairs

Auricle: absent

Growth habit: Spreads by stolons and rhizomes. Inflorescence measuring 3 cm to 10 cm long consists of three to seven spikes in a single whorl with a fingerlike arrangement.

Zoysiagrass *(Zoysia japonica L.)*

Warm-season species shows optimum growth during periods of high temperatures. The recommended time to fertilize is in mid- to late spring and in mid-summer. Fertilizer should not be applied past mid-August.

Forms an attractive turf in central portions of the state and the Eastern Shore. Produces extensive, thick stolons that spread rapidly, giving it good recuperative potential. Can also spread into areas where it is not wanted (like neighboring yards and flower beds).

Figure 14-N. Zoysiagrass

Drought-tolerant once established. Performs best under moderate moisture levels on fertile, well-limed soils. Will not tolerate poor drainage or shade. Produces an abundant amount of thatch. Dethatching should be done in early summer when thatch becomes thicker than one inch.

Goes dormant (turns a straw-brown color) after frost in the fall and does not green up until mid- to late spring.

While some varieties can be seeded, zoysia is propagated vegetatively in late spring through July by planting sod plugs, sprigs, or sod.

Table 14-A. Characteristics of turfgrass species

Species	Days to germinate	Full sun	Shade	Drought tolerance	High-traffic tolerance	Insect/disease resistance
Turf-type tall fescue	7-14	Excellent	Fair	Excellent	Good	Good
Fine fescue	7-14	Good-fair	Excellent-good	Good-fair	Poor	Good
Kentucky bluegrass	12-21	Excellent	Fair-poor	Good	Very good	Fair-poor
Perennial ryegrass	5-10	Excellent	Fair-poor	Poor	Good	Poor (fair if seeds contain endophytes*)
Bermudagrass	n/a	Excellent	Very poor	Excellent	Excellent	Good
Zoysiagrass	n/a	Excellent	Poor	Excellent	Excellent	Good

*Endophytes are beneficial fungi or bacteria that live within plant tissue. Perennial ryegrass and fescue turf with high endophyte levels are more drought-resistant and less prone to damage from sod webworm and chinch bugs.

The cost of establishment is typically high and zoysiagrass can be slow to establish. The time required depends upon plug size, competition from other grasses, weeds, and the growing environment. The quickest establishment is with four-inch plugs, or, better yet, sod. Three to six years may be required to develop a solid stand of 'Meyer' zoysiagrass planted as plugs.

Identification features:

Leaf blade: flat, stiff, 2 mm to 4 mm wide, medium-textured

Vernation: rolled

Collar: broad, continuous, with long hairs

Ligule: a fringe of hairs

Auricle: absent

Growth habit: spreads by stolons and rhizomes

Recommended turfgrass cultivars

During the last decade, numerous new turfgrass cultivars have been developed and released by turfgrass seed breeders. Although many of them are adapted to the environmental conditions in other regions of the country, some are not well-adapted to the difficult environmental conditions that occur in the transition zone, which includes Maryland and Virginia. To identify cultivars that will perform well in this region, extensive cultivar trials are conducted each year at the University of Maryland and Virginia Tech.

The cultivar performance data are reviewed annually at a joint meeting of university researchers and representatives of the Departments of Agriculture of both states. The use of recommended cultivars usually results in a turfgrass stand of higher quality and density, greater stress tolerance, lower nutrient requirements, less water usage, fewer pest problems, and less pesticide use.

About common turfgrass cultivars

- Cultivars recommended here have been evaluated for performance in Maryland and Virginia.
- Maryland Certified Sod must consist of only recommended cultivars.
- Recommended cultivars provide better quality turf and improve ground cover.
- Recommended cultivars often have lower fertilizer, water, and pesticide needs.

Turfgrass species with reduced nutrient requirements (especially nitrogen) have attracted great interest in recent years. The two recommended turfgrasses with the lowest nitrogen requirements are the fine fescues and zoysiagrass. Turf-type tall fescue has intermediate requirements. Kentucky bluegrass and bermudagrass generally have the highest nitrogen requirements but several Kentucky bluegrass cultivars provide fair performance with reduced nitrogen fertility and other maintenance inputs.

Publication TT-77, "Recommended Turfgrass Cultivars for Certified Sod and Professional Seed Mixtures," contains a comprehensive list of the tested turfgrass cultivars that have performed well in trials in both Maryland and Virginia over at least a two- to three-year period.

Although geared toward professional turf managers and sod producers, this publication is an excellent reference for homeowners who want a list of the most current, proven cultivars of turfgrass available. It should be noted that it is difficult for homeowners to find these cultivars and it may be necessary to consult a respected landscaping company to obtain the desired cultivar.

14.3 Lawn Establishment

The quality and success of a new lawn depends on the time, effort, and expense homeowners are willing to devote to proper planning and site preparation.

A number of basic steps should be taken to ensure successful establishment. If any of these steps are omitted or done improperly, the resulting lawn may be thin and/or deteriorate over time. Unfortunately, many new lawns are started on ground that has been stripped of topsoil, is rocky, and contains little or no organic matter. See the **Site preparation section** for complete step-by-step directions.

Soil testing

First, do a soil test. This step is critical to a new turf project, whether it be seeding bare ground or laying sod.

- The test results will indicate the soil's pH and lime requirements, as well as the amounts of phosphorus, potassium, and organic matter present in the soil. Fertilizer and liming recommendations will be included if relevant.

- Soil pH should be between 5.8 to 6.8 for optimal turf growth.

- Soil testing information is found in **Publication HG 110,** "Selecting and Using a Soil Testing Laboratory," and "**Soil Testing Lab Comparison.**" These publications are available from your county extension office and online.

Site preparation

Site preparation is the same for seeding and laying sod. After the lawn is established it is difficult and costly to try to improve the soil, so it's best to properly prepare the site before you seed or sod.

First, test your soil. Don't amend it just yet.

Rough grade. Rough grading involves removing all debris, including large stones or wood left by construction work. Where topsoil will be replaced or augmented, grade the area to the contour of the desired finished grade first. Slope soil away from buildings to prevent water problems. Steep slopes should be terraced, contained with a retaining wall, or planted with a low-maintenance ground cover.

Lime according to soil test results. Grass growth will be unsatisfactory if the soil pH is not in the 5.8-6.8 range. If the soil is too acidic, work the recommended amount of ground or pelletized limestone into the top four to six inches of soil. If soil test results are not available when you are ready to seed, postpone liming until you know the pH level.

Apply basic fertilizer. The lab's soil test report will indicate any nutrient deficiencies and provide recommendations. Follow the fertilizer and lime recommendations for all nutrients except nitrogen. For nitrogen, follow the University of Maryland Extension

Table 14-B. Seed rate for new and established lawns

Species	New lawn	Overseeding
Turf-type tall fescue	6-8 lbs. per 1,000 sq. ft.	3-4 lbs. per 1,000 sq. ft.
Fine fescue	4-5 lbs. per 1,000 sq. ft.	2-2 1/2 lbs. per 1,000 sq. ft.
Kentucky bluegrass	2-3 lbs. per 1,000 sq. ft.	1-1 1/2 lbs. per 1,000 sq. ft.

recommendations for nitrogen found in Tables 14-E and 14-F.

Failure to correct a soil phosphorus deficiency or low soil pH is a common reason for poor establishment. If a soil test cannot be done before seeding, apply a starter fertilizer on the seedbed. (A starter fertilizer has a high level of phosphate relative to the nitrogen and potash.) In accordance with the Fertilizer Use Act of 2011, turf fertilizer containing phosphorous can only be used if the measured phosphorous level is low, a new lawn is being established, or the lawn is being repaired or reestablished.

Incorporate organic matter, if necessary. This step is more important on lawns to be seeded on sites that have been stripped of topsoil, such as new construction. Work organic matter into your soil along with the lime (if required) and fertilizer. Avoid overtilling or tilling wet soil, which can damage the soil structure. Apply the lime and fertilizer, in separate applications, with a lawn spreader to ensure they are distributed evenly. Sources of organic matter include leaf compost, composted sewer sludge, well-rotted manure, and mushroom compost. Apply approximately two inches of organic matter evenly over the area. Till the amendments into the top four to six inches of soil. After tilling, it is advisable to allow the soil to settle for several days before seeding or use a sprinkler to apply about an inch of water over the area.

Finish-grade. Rake area to finish-grade just before seeding. Make sure all low spots are filled in.

Fertilize. Just prior to seeding, make a light fertilizer application at a rate of one-half lb. of phosphorous/1,000 square feet, preferably a slow-release fertilizer. Do not apply after June 1 for a spring seeding or later than six weeks after the first frost for a fall feeding. In the fall all fertilizer applications need to be made by November 15.

Distribute seed. Divide the total seed quantity into two equal parts. Sow half the seed in one direction and the second half at right angles to the first, using a mechanical seeder or spreader.

Rake lightly. Rake lightly with a metal rake; use a seed roller or even footsteps to firm soil around the seed. Seed should not be covered with more than one-quarter inch of soil.

Topdress. Cover the seeded area with weed-free straw or compost. Light amounts of straw (some soil showing through the mulch) may be left on the area to naturally decompose.

Seeding

Timing is crucial when sowing grass seed. Late summer to early fall (late August to mid-October) is the recommended time for seeding cool-season grasses. Warm soils and moderate air temperatures encourage seed germination and there is less competition from weeds. If autumn leaf drop is a concern, seeding should be done in late August or early September.

The second-best time for seeding is early March through early April. Seed planted at other times tends to fail, usually because of weed competition and weather.

Mixtures and blends of grass seed

Seed is commonly sold in mixtures or blends. A mixture is a combination of two or more grass species, such as turf-type tall fescue and Kentucky bluegrass. A blend is two or more cultivars of the same species. Mixtures and blends are popular because they increase the genetic diversity of the lawn. Certain grass species and cultivars are more susceptible to disease and insect problems; using mixtures and blends increases the turf's ability to resist diseases and overcome insect infestations. Mixtures are also used if growing conditions vary within the yard.

Choosing and buying seed

Select a high-quality seed mixture that is adapted to the site conditions (e.g., tall fescue for sunny areas and fine fescue for shade) and intended use of the turf. Poor-quality seed may have a low germination rate and contain weed seeds and/or undesirable grass species. Certified seed is the highest-quality seed for homeowners to purchase and is recognizable by its blue "Certified" tag. If the species in the seed mixture are not adapted to your conditions, the resulting stand may become thin and subject to weed encroachment.

When purchasing turfgrass seed, read the label to determine the kind, amount, and quality of seed in the container. All retail seed is required by law to bear a label indicating basic information about its quality, which is regulated by the Maryland Department of Agriculture. The basic information on the label should include, at a minimum:

- Name and address of labeler (the party responsible for the container's contents)

Table 14-C. Sod vs. seed comparison

	SOD	SEED
ADVANTAGES	Can be installed any time as long as the ground is not frozen and daytime temperatures are below 95°F.	Lower initial cost.
	Faster establishment and immediate results.	Desired cultivars of turfgrass can be sown.
	Quicker erosion control. Can be used successfully on steep banks or culverts.	Can be more easily done in smaller sections if only a part of the lawn needs repair.
	Fewer problems with weed encroachment.	Greater flexibility in planting a mixture for specific site conditions (e.g., a mixture that performs better in shade or high-traffic areas).
DISADVANTAGES	Higher initial cost.	Limited period for establishment. Seed should be sown in late summer-early fall for greatest success.
	Limited choice of turf cultivars.	Daily watering is necessary, sometimes twice a day, depending upon weather conditions during the initial establishment period.
	More labor required for installation.	Takes longer for lawn to establish. Seeded areas need to be restricted from use for up to 2 months. Heavy rains can wash away seed in the interim.
	Not always readily available.	Greater chance of weed encroachment during establishment.

- Lot number (allows the contents to be traced to the original source of production)
- Kind and variety of turfgrass seed, listed in order of predominance
- Percentage by weight of pure seed of each species and variety (percentage purity)
- Germination percentage (percentage of viable seed)
- Percentage by weight of other crop seed
- Percentage by weight of weed seed (should be less than .5 percent)
- Percentage of undesirable grass seed (should not contain any)
- Percentage by weight of inert matter (mostly chaff)
- Date of the germination test

Seed-sowing

After doing the work to properly prepare the planting site, divide the required total amount of seed into two parts. Apply one-half in one direction (north/south) and the remainder in the opposite direction (east/west). *Seed-soil contact is essential. Before overseeding, use a core aerator or a slit seeder.*

Sod-laying

Sod produces mature turf in days rather than the months required to establish turf from seed. Most sod consists of Kentucky bluegrass, although some growers do produce tall fescue, fine fescue, and zoysia sod.

Certified sod is high quality and is produced under the supervision of the Maryland Department of Agriculture. Production fields must be inspected before being seeded and at periodic intervals prior to sale of the sod. Certification gives assurance of the sod's genetic purity, and the inspection program demands that cultural practices be carried out to ensure that the sod is free of weeds, undesirable grasses, insects, and diseases.

Successful sod-laying tips

Sod quality, soil preparation, and how you lay the sod will determine its performance.

- Sod should be dense, with sufficiently developed roots, so it does not fall apart when harvested and transported. The more mature the roots, the thinner the sod can be cut without deteriorating. High-quality sod should have a root and soil thickness of .5 to .75 inch.
- Sod should be laid immediately after delivery. If it needs to be held for several days before installing, spread it out in a cool, shaded area, grass side up, and keep it moist. Never store it in the sun.
- Lay the first strip of sod in the direction of the longest side of the area. Lay the next strip offset from the first so the joints between the pieces are staggered, similar to the way you would lay bricks.
- On a slope, keep strips perpendicular to the slope and secure each strip with stakes until root development is strong enough to hold the sod in place.
- Edges should be tightly fitted against adjacent strips as each strip is laid and then lightly tamped or rolled to ensure good contact with the soil.
- Fill any openings that remain from irregular shapes with sod pieces that are custom cut with knife or spade to minimize bare spots.
- Use a knife or spade to trim off any excess sod, straighten strips that may

be uneven, or custom-cut around irregularly-shaped landscape beds or hardscape features.

- Immediately after installing, water thoroughly to wet the soil to a four- to six-inch depth. During the initial rooting period (usually two to three weeks), irrigate daily to maintain adequate soil moisture but do not water to the point where water is running off the site. Do not allow the sod to wilt or dry during this period.
- Rolling the sod with a weighted, water-filled roller can be beneficial to help smooth out minor imperfections of the final grade.

Renovation and overseeding

If there is severe weed encroachment, begin complete renovation in August to allow ample time for reseeding. Spray the existing lawn with a non-selective herbicide to kill the entire area. Two or three applications might be necessary if you are killing a perennial grass weed such as bermudagrass or nimblewill. To prepare the site for planting, mow the dead plant material as low as your mower will allow, then follow the same steps for lawn establishment.

Overseeding is performed to repair minimal damage sustained in the summer, to improve the overall quality of lawn, and to thicken up lawns to minimize weeds. It is necessary to core aerate or to use either a vertical mower or a slit seeder when overseeding. Overseeding should be done between late August and October 1 on cool-season lawns.

It's time to overseed when there is ...

- A weed infestation (30-40 percent weeds) or infestation of a perennial grass weed such as bermudagrass
- Insect and/or disease damage
- Drought damage
- Shade-caused thinning
- Heavy foot-traffic damage
- Negative cultural impact (e.g., improper fertilization or mowing too short)
- A desire to convert an existing lawn to an improved cultivar or species

14.4 Cultural Practices for Turf

Turf fertilizers

Fertilizing is an essential element in maintaining a healthy lawn that is better able to resist insects and disease and crowd out weeds. Fertilizer provides both macro- and micronutrients that encourage active turf growth.

- Fertilizer should be applied according to a schedule during active growth, which is when grass plants best absorb the nutrients.
- Approximately two-thirds of annual cool-season turfgrass fertilizer should be applied in fall. Warm-season turfgrasses are fertilized in the late spring through summer.
- Nitrogen is the nutrient required in the greatest amount. Recommendations are based on the amount of nitrogen needed or "pounds of nitrogen per 1,000

square feet." The recommendation is a maximum of .09 lbs. of nitrogen per 1,000 square feet applied at each application (based on the Fertilizer Use Act of 2011).

- Nitrogen helps maintain high turf density. During the fall, nitrogen encourages the growth of a deep root system in cool-season grasses. This is key to a healthy lawn that can withstand drought and recover from stress.

- Always buy fertilizer on the basis of its quality rather than on bag size and price. Value depends on the amount of plant nutrients contained in the bag and the source of the nitrogen-carrying portion of the fertilizer.

- The three prominent numbers found on every type of fertilizer comprise the guaranteed analysis. The numbers represent the percentage of nutrients (by weight) in the bag. In order, the numbers refer to nitrogen, phosphorus, and potassium (N, P, K). For example, a 32-0-4 fertilizer contains 32 percent nitrogen, 0 percent phosphorus, and 4 percent potassium. If the phosphorous level in soil is high or excessive on established lawns (10 years or older), use a zero-P fertilizer.

Combination fertilizers

Weed-and-feed products (fertilizers combined with a selective herbicide) are commonly available to homeowners. Although convenient, they often lead to over-fertilization and application at the wrong time of year. It is best to fertilize and treat weeds or insects (e.g., perennial weeds, white grubs) separately. Use products labeled specifically for the problem.

Starter fertilizers

Starter fertilizers are formulated for starting or renovating a lawn. They are higher in phosphorus. The nitrogen applied during a "starter fertilizer" application should be included in the total amount of nitrogen that is being applied for the year. After two to three cuttings, a modest amount of additional fertilizer (.25 lb.-.5 lb. nitrogen/1,000 square feet) should be applied to the new turfgrass to continue to encourage strong establishment. (See Tables 14-E and 14-F.)

Nitrogen sources

The ideal fertilizer program provides for uniform turfgrass growth over the entire growing season. Although this ideal is never fully reached because of temperature and moisture fluctuations, the types of nitrogen-carrying materials in a fertilizer are important in achieving steady, season-long growth.

Nitrogen sources are divided into two broad groups: quick-release and slow-release. Slow-release sources include both inorganic and organic sources of nitrogen. The Fertilizer Use Act of 2011 requires that at least 20 percent of the total nitrogen in lawn fertilizers be slow-release if nitrogen is applied at the full, allowable rate (i.e., only .7 lb./1,000 square feet out of .09 lb./1,000 square feet can be "quick release" or "water-soluble" nitrogen).

Quick-release nitrogen

Quick-release, or water-soluble, nitrogen sources include ammonium nitrate, ammonium sulfate, ammonium phosphate, and urea. Their main attributes include:

- Rapid release of nitrogen, providing almost immediate green-up.

- Lower cost.
- A water-soluble formula.
- Greater tendency to burn (dehydrate) the turf.
- Short-term sudden flush of growth and rapid depletion (three to six weeks) of the available nitrogen.
- Frequent light applications are necessary to obtain uniform growth.
- Higher potential to leach, causing nutrient pollution if over-applied.

Slow-release nitrogen

Slow-release, or water-insoluble nitrogen (WIN), sources include organic products made from previously living plant or animal materials, ureaformaldehyde (urea compounds), isobutylidene diurea (IBDU), methylene urea, and sulfur- or polymer-coated urea. To calculate the percentage of WIN, divide the percentage of water-insoluble nitrogen by the total percentage of nitrogen in the bag and multiply by 100.

The main attributes of slow-release nitrogen sources include:

- The release of a major portion of nitrogen over an extended period.
- Dependency upon microbial decomposition, physical processes, and/or chemical reactions to provide nitrogen in a form that is available to the plant. The activity of soil microorganisms is highly dependent upon soil moisture, pH, and temperature.
- Under high temperatures and adequate moisture, microbial breakdown is accelerated. During high temperatures and low moisture or low temperatures, the breakdown is much slower.
- More expensive per pound of nutrient.
- Less likely to damage the lawn.
- Effects last over a longer period of time.
- Less likely to leach and cause nutrient pollution.

Slow-release inorganic fertilizers

Urea compounds are synthetic nitrogen sources made by the chemical union of urea and formaldehyde. Within a given ureaformaldehyde product, there is a series of chemical compounds with varying degrees of solubility and/or resistance to decomposition.

As the ratio of urea to formaldehyde increases, the length of the methylene urea chains, or

Table 14-D. Starter vs. slow-release fertilizer content

Starter fertilizer 12-24-6		Slow-release fertilizer 18-0-3	
Total nitrogen (N)*	12%	Total nitrogen (N)*	18%
Ammoniacal nitrogen	10%	Ammoniacal nitrogen	4.7%
Urea	2%	Other water-soluble nitrogen	5.3%
Available phosphate	24%	Water-insoluble nitrogen*	8%
Soluble potash	6%	Soluble potash	3%
Ingredients: Sulfur-coated urea, monoammonium phosphate, and muriate of potash.		Ingredients: Dehydrated manure, feather meal, kelp meal, ureaform, ammonium sulfate, and sulfate of potash.	
*It is common for manufacturers to blend multiple nitrogen sources, which can include quick-release and slow-release sources. The Fertilizer Use Act of 2011 requires that at least 20% of the nitrogen in lawn fertilizers be slow-release if the product is applied at the full rate of .09 lb. nitrogen/1,000 sq. ft.			

How much fertilizer will you need?

Focus on these three critical numbers:

1. Pounds of nitrogen per 1,000 sq. ft.*
2. The percentage of nitrogen in the guaranteed analysis
3. The square footage of lawn area

Use the following formula and plug in your own numbers:

(Pounds of nitrogen per 1,000 sq. ft.
÷
The percent of nitrogen in the fertilizer's guaranteed analysis)
X
(The square footage of lawn ÷ 1,000)

= **Amount of fertilizer you will need**

• • • • •

Example: A lawn measures 8,000 sq. ft. and .09 lb. of nitrogen is needed per 1,000 sq. ft. The guaranteed analysis is 26-0-3.

(.09 ÷ .26)   x   (8000 ÷ 1000)
= **You will need 27.7 lbs. of fertilizer**

• • • • •

If the lawn is larger than an acre, convert the area measurement to square feet.

One acre = 43,560 square feet

• • • • •

Never use more fertilizer than needed and always follow the label instructions. Keep leftover fertilizer in a tightly-closed container and store it in a dry environment. Long-term storage is not advisable, so calculate how much fertilizer you'll need beforehand to avoid waste.

See fertilizer schedules in Tables 14-E and 14-F.

---

polymers, decreases. As soil microorganisms decompose these materials, the short-chained compounds break down first, followed in succession by each longer-chained compound. As a result, the nitrogen is released over a relatively long period.

"Standard" ureaform has a urea-to-formaldehyde ratio of approximately 1.3:1. The longest chain materials are called ureaform, which are released the slowest. Ureaform contains about 25 percent water-soluble nitrogen and 75 percent water-insoluble nitrogen. These materials may be applied at higher rates at relatively infrequent intervals. Currently, compounds called methylene ureas (see below) are available commercially. These nitrogen sources have higher urea to formaldehyde ratios (shorter-chained compounds). They contain approximately 75 percent water-soluble nitrogen and 25 percent water-insoluble nitrogen. As the amount of water-insoluble nitrogen decreases, the application rate should be decreased and the frequency of application increased.

Methylene ureas are products that contain intermediate-chain materials and have an intermediate release rate. Fluid ureaformaldehydes containing intermediate-chain methylene ureas are commonly used by the lawn-service industry. These materials generally contain some quick-release nitrogen but are less likely to burn roots than other fluid or liquid nitrogen carriers. Care must be taken not to confuse urea (quickly-available nitrogen) with ureaform or methylene urea products (slowly available nitrogen).

IBDU is an example of a synthetic nitrogen source that depends on moisture for the nitrogen to be released. IBDU has extremely low solubility in water, so nitrogen is released slowly. Because it is relatively unaffected by temperature, it has the advantage of releasing nitrogen during cold weather if adequate moisture is available. IBDU also has been shown to be more efficient (more of the applied nitrogen is recovered by the plant during the year of application) than natural organics or ureaform nitrogen.

Sulfur-coated urea (SCU) is a slow-release nitrogen source made by coating urea prills (i.e., small granules) with molten sulfur. Most SCU products are also coated with a sealant, such as wax, to seal cracks or other imperfections in the sulfur coating. The release of nitrogen is determined by the thickness of the coating. Urea particles with varying thicknesses of sulfur coatings release nitrogen over a relatively long time (six to eight weeks).

SCU does not qualify as water-insoluble nitrogen under accepted definitions and is often labeled with a controlled-release nitrogen (CRN) statement or rate of dissolution statement. The dissolution rate refers to the amount of sulfur-coated urea that will dissolve in water in seven days under laboratory conditions. If an SCU product has a 30 percent dissolution rate, then 30 percent of the nitrogen acts as a quickly available source and 70 percent as a slow-release source.

Slow-release organic fertilizers

These include activated or processed sewage sludge, animal and/or vegetable tankage, manures, various composted products, poultry meal, and cottonseed meal. Natural organic sources vary greatly in their chemical composition. There is a wide variation in the rate of breakdown, although all of them release their nitrogen at a slower rate than the quickly available nitrogen sources.

Table 14-E. Low-input turf fertilizer recommendation

Grass type	Application time	Lbs. of nitrogen per 1,000 sq. ft.
Tall fescue	September + October	.09 - 1.8 lbs. a year: .09 lb. (Sept.) + .09 lb. (Oct.)
Fine fescue	October	.09 lb.
Kentucky bluegrass	September + October	.09 - 1.8 lbs. a year: .09 lb. (Sept.) + .09 lb. (Oct.)
Bermudagrass	May + July	1.8 lbs. a year: .09 lb. (May) + .09 lb. (July)
Zoysiagrass	June	.09 lb.

Note: If clippings are left on the lawn, you may only need 1 application/yr. regardless of your lawn's age. Healthy lawns established longer than 12 yrs. may only need 1 application/yr. Do not apply any fertilizer between Nov. 15 and March 1.

Table 14-F. Optional turf fertilizer application

Grass type	Application time	Lbs. of nitrogen per 1,000 sq. ft.
Tall fescue	Late May or early June	.5 to .09 lb.
Fine fescue	Late May or early June	.5 lb.
Kentucky bluegrass	Late May or early June	.5 to .09 lb.
Bermudagrass	August	.09 lb.
Zoysiagrass	July or August	.5 to .09 lb.

Tall fescue, and particularly Kentucky bluegrass, may need moderate additional applications of fertilizer to maintain density and reduce pest and weed problems. The optional applications may help your lawn if:

- Clippings are bagged/removed
- There is a severe crabgrass problem

- The lawn has low density
- The lawn is heavily used
- There has been pest or other damage
- The lawn was seeded the previous fall
- The previous fall fertilization was missed

When applied to the lawn at recommended rates, fertilizer normally won't threaten groundwater or surface water. If your soil is sandy or if you live in an area with a high water table, use a fertilizer with a high percentage of water-insoluble nitrogen.

The large amount of paved area in cities and suburbs provides a direct route for nutrients and other pollutants to enter streams, rivers, and the Chesapeake Bay. Careful application of fertilizer is one way you can prevent pollution.

Follow these tips to make sure the fertilizer you use stays on the lawn and out of the water:

- Don't apply fertilizer within 15 feet of a body of water (10 feet if you use a drop spreader or rotary spreader with a deflector).
- Do not apply fertilizer near storm drains or drainage ditches.
- Do not apply fertilizer if heavy rain is expected.
- Sweep any fertilizer that lands on the driveway, sidewalk, or street back onto your lawn.
- Use a drop spreader instead of a rotary spreader in restricted spaces, especially when near water, driveways, or walkways. Look for lawn spreaders with an edge guard.
- Fill and wash spreaders over grassy or mulched areas, not on hard surfaces.

Table 14-G. Mowing-height guide

Grass type	Spring-Summer (inches)	Fall-Winter (inches)
Tall fescue	21/2 - 31/2	21/2
Fine fescue	21/2 - 31/2	21/2
Kentucky bluegrass	21/2 - 31/2	2 - 21/2
Bermudagrass	11/2	11/2 - 2
Zoysiagrass	11/2 - 2	2 - 21/2

- Avoid getting fertilizer into natural high drainage areas on your property.
- Never apply to frozen ground or dormant lawns. The Fertilizer Use Act of 2011 prohibits fertilizing lawns between November 15 and March 1.
- Do not use fertilizer to melt ice, and avoid melting products that contain nitrogen. Refer to University of Maryland Extension Publication **FS 707**, "Melting Ice Safely."

Mowing

Proper mowing technique is one of the most important factors in the aesthetic quality and longevity of any lawn. Often it is the most overlooked and mismanaged cultural practice.

The following are important factors to consider when evaluating a mowing program:

Mower height setting

- Low mowing is a major cause of lawn deterioration. Remove no more than one-third of the grass blade each time you mow. For example, to maintain a 2½-inch height, mow before the grass reaches a height of 3½ inches. Mowing to the proper height can reduce weeds by 50 percent to 80 percent in tall fescue and also help reduce disease problems. Mowing the lawn too short will encourage crabgrass infestation.

- Removing larger amounts of leaf surface may result in physiological shock to the plant, cause excessive graying or browning of leaf tips, and greatly curtailing photosynthesis.
- Low mowing also stresses the root system, causing the turf to become weaker and less drought-tolerant.
- Raise the mower height ½-1 inch during hot, dry periods in the summer.

Frequency of cut

- Infrequent mowing allows the turf to grow too tall. Subsequent mowing often removes too much leaf surface and may shock the plants.
- Mow your lawn frequently so that clippings break down rapidly. The accumulation of clippings from grass that has grown too long between cuttings may smother the lawn and provide an environment conducive to disease and insect damage.
- Weekly mowing may not be enough, especially during the peak period of spring growth. Conversely, in a dry summer, mowing every other week may be enough.
- The rate of growth depends on weather, season, soil fertility, moisture conditions, and species.
- Grasscycling (see box to the right) can be practiced on lawns cut at proper intervals.

Equipment maintenance

- Sharpen mower blades at least annually and, if needed, mid-season.
- Be sure to wash mower (top and underside) after each use. Clipping and debris build-up on the undercarriage can lead to less efficient operation of the engine and blade-cutting quality. Wash mower on a lawn or mulch area to prevent clippings and residual oil/gas from being washed into storm drains.
- Conduct engine fluid and spark plug changes based on manufacturer recommended intervals.

Grasscycling

Grasscycling ("mulch mowing") is the simple practice of letting grass clippings decompose on the lawn after mowing. This can also be

Grasscyling tips

- Always mow with a sharp blade and when the lawn is dry. Friction caused by mowing wet grass dulls the blade.
- Mow regularly. Remove no more than one-third of the leaf blade at each mowing. During the spring it may be necessary to mow twice a week.
- Mulching mowers hasten the decomposition process but are not necessary. Check availability of mulching "kits" which can be purchased for some models of lawn mowers. Kits include a plate that blocks discharged chutes, forcing clippings back through the blades. Check your lawn mower manual.
- Avoid over-fertilizing.

done in the autumn to mulch fallen leaves into the lawn and reduce leaf-raking. Grasscyling:

- Helps protect the environment by reducing the amount of grass clippings in the landfill.
- Encourages a healthier lawn by returning both macronutrients and micronutrients to the soil in a slow-release form. This practice can reduce fertilizer use, save time and money, and decrease the amount of runoff into the Chesapeake Bay and its tributaries.
- Eliminates the need to bag or rake grass clippings.
- Does not contribute to thatch buildup or turf diseases. Grass clippings are largely composed of water and decompose rapidly. Microbial decomposition of clippings occurs on soils that are maintained at a pH of 6.0 to 6.8.

Watering

Most established lawns in Maryland do not require much irrigation, except during a hot or a particularly dry summer.

Newly-seeded lawns and lawns established for less than two years should be irrigated. Water if the grass blades begin to wilt, develop a blue-gray color, or show footprints after being walked upon. Newly-seeded lawns should be watered frequently enough to keep seed from drying out until the seed has germinated and grass has started to grow.

Established tall fescue and zoysia grass lawns can go dormant during the summer. Dormancy is an important survival mechanism and lawns will recover quickly when rainfall returns. Dormant lawns continue to protect water quality by holding soil and potential pollutants. Do not fertilize dormant or drought-stressed lawns and adjust mowing height accordingly.

Water in the early morning, ideally by 10 a.m., to avoid evaporation from warmer temperatures and a higher sun angle.

Water slowly to prevent runoff. Use a sprinkler to apply one-half inch of water per watering. To measure how much water is applied within a given time frame, you can place shallow cans in the area and measure the accumulation. Lawns only need one inch of water per week, which can be applied in two applications of ½-inch each.

Frequent, shallow watering, as is sometimes applied with a sprinkler system, tends to keep the upper layers of soil near a point of saturation most of the time. This encourages shallow rooting, disease, and insect problems, as well as damage from foot traffic.

Thatch management

Thatch problems

Thatch is defined as a tightly intermingled layer of partly decomposed stems and roots of grasses that develops between the actively growing green vegetation and the soil surface.

About one-half inch of thatch is good but more than that can decrease the vigor of turfgrasses by restricting movement of water, air, plant nutrients, and pesticides to the soil. During wet periods, it may act as a sponge and hold excessive amounts of water, reducing the oxygen supply to the roots. On the other hand, if thatch becomes dry, it is extremely difficult to re-wet.

Many turfgrass disease organisms and insects (billbugs, chinch bugs, and sod webworm larvae) may be harbored in thatch. Fungicides, insecticides, and fertilizers are less effective because they cannot infiltrate the thatch layer.

Too much thatch also interferes with the proper mowing height of turf. As the thatch layer builds up, mowers tend to ride on the thatch and do not cut at the desired height.

Build-up depends upon several factors. Certain grasses such as Kentucky bluegrass and zoysia tend to thatch much faster than others, some because of their vigorous growth, and others because of the resistance of their tissues to decomposition.

Lawns should be dethatched when the thatch layer is about one-inch thick.

Thatch prevention and removal

To prevent thatch, soil pH should be kept in the 6.5 to 6.8 range, which is most favorable for the microorganisms that decompose thatch. Apply ground limestone when pH levels drop below this range and avoid over-fertilizing turf.

Dethatching a lawn every two years as part of a prevention program results in much less debris and damage to established turf than having to dethatch in a curative program.

Mechanically removing thatch should be attempted only when growth conditions are adequate for rapid recovery of the grass. Dethatch cool-season turf in the fall and warm-season turf in the summer. The health and general vigor of the plant and root system, climatic conditions, and the amount of thatch present determine how much thatch can be removed in one treatment. Healthier turf can tolerate more aggressive thatch removal than unhealthy turf.

When a large amount of thatch is present, it is unwise to attempt to remove all in one treatment. If temperatures are ideal for growth and adequate moisture is available, the treatment can be much more aggressive than under high temperatures and/or low moisture conditions.

Preferred dethatching machines have blades or knives that cut through the thatch into the underlying soil. These machines are called vertical mowers. Avoid spring-tine machines or tines that can be added to a rotary mower blade. They are often inadequate. Proper machines can be rented from hardware stores or equipment-rental companies.

Raking and removal of the dislodged thatch is necessary after using a dethatching machine. This material can be composted.

Aeration

Mechanical aeration alleviates soil compaction in established turf, encourages root growth, and allows lime and fertilizer to enter the soil.

Compaction occurs primarily in the soil surface. A compacted layer as thin as ¼ inch to ½ inch can greatly impede water infiltration and gas exchange between soil and atmosphere.

Core-aerating machines should remove plugs of soil measuring ½ inch to ¾ inch in diameter, two to four inches deep, and about two to six inches apart. This action creates a system of large pores by which moisture and plant nutrients can be taken into the soil. Fall is the best time to aerate cool-season lawns, and June through August is the recommended time to aerate warm-season lawns. Never aerate when a lawn is dormant. A general rule is to aerate only when desirable grasses are growing vigorously.

Soil should be moist, but not wet, before aerating. Irrigate the lawn a few days prior to aerating if the soil has been dry. Soil plugs can be left on the surface of the lawn. They will decompose in a couple of weeks and be chopped up by mowing.

Core aeration should be performed every year on lawns that receive heavy foot traffic. Otherwise, aerating home lawns every two to three years is sufficient.

Aeration can also be done before overseeding. Because the procedure makes holes for the seed to fall into, seed-to-soil contact is greatly improved. Finely decomposed organic matter (compost) can be spread over the area after aeration has been performed to improve seedling growth. No more than one-quarter to one-half inch of organic matter should be applied to avoid damaging the existing turf.

Liming

The optimum pH for turf growth is 6.0 to 6.8. If the pH level falls below 5.5, turf growth will be compromised. Maryland soils tend to become acidic over time, so a soil test should be performed every three years to check the pH and other nutrients. The test results will provide a liming recommendation. If more than 50 lbs. of limestone per 1,000 sq. ft. is recommended, the amount should be split into two applications. For example, if 85 lbs. is needed, apply 50 lbs. immediately then wait six months to apply the remaining 35 lbs.

Limestone should be applied with a lawn spreader. To attain uniform coverage, apply half of the lime in one direction and the remainder in a perpendicular direction.

Lime can be applied almost anytime, but the ideal time is in the fall. The freezing and thawing of the soil over the winter will help to incorporate the lime into the ground. It is not recommended to apply lime when temperatures are above 85°F. or on snow- or frost-covered turf.

Agricultural ("ag") lime, or calcitic lime, is the recommended form of limestone for homeowner use. Pelletized lime is very similar and is easier to spread because it limits the amount of "dust" created when spreading ag lime. Dolomitic lime is recommended for soils that are also low in magnesium. Burnt or hydrated limestone is caustic and not recommended for homeowner use.

14.5 Turfgrass Problems

Weeds

Any management practice that increases the density and vigor of desirable turfgrasses tends to discourage competition from weeds. Studies show that weeds are not prevalent in a dense, healthy, vigorously growing lawn. Weeds are opportunistic; they germinate in thin, weak stands of grass. Cultural practices for controlling summer annual grasses (such as crabgrass) and broadleaf weeds are aimed at shading and crowding the young weed seedlings out by producing a dense turf.

Effective cultural control measures include:

- Proper selection of grass type
- Successful lawn establishment
- Adequate lime and fertilizer
- Proper mowing, watering, aerating, and dethatching
- Insect and disease control

Herbicides are an important tool for weed control but should not be solely relied upon to eliminate weeds. Before selecting a herbicide, assess the amount of weeds in the lawn. A low infestation of some broadleaf weeds, like dandelions, can be hand-pulled. Most home lawns can include a small weed population and still be healthy and attractive. Next, identify the weed to determine the most effective herbicide and application timing.

To prevent future infestations, review cultural practices, along with growing conditions, as the possible reason for weed encroachment. Try to determine how the weed was introduced into the yard and the conditions that favor it. For example, ground ivy is often found in shady areas where shade-intolerant turfgrasses have begun to thin out and decline.

Crabgrass

Crabgrass is one of the most common turf weeds. Two species, hairy or large (*Digitaria sanguinalis L.*) and smooth or small (*D. ischaemum L.*), are found in Maryland. Both are summer annuals. The seed germination period ranges from mid-spring to mid-summer and all plants are killed by the first frost. Abundant quantities of seeds are produced and will be ready to germinate the following season.

To control crabgrass, mow turf to the tallest recommended height in the growing season and follow proper lawn-care practices to encourage a thick, healthy stand of turfgrass. Crabgrass germinates in thin areas of lawns and in compacted, dry, infertile soil.

Do not aerate the lawn during the seed germination period of summer annual weeds. Germination begins when soil temperatures reach 55°F to 60°F for seven to ten consecutive days. This is usually early March to early April on the Eastern Shore, mid-March to mid-April in Central Maryland, and mid-April to mid-May in Western Maryland. Apply a pre-emergent before germination.

Typically, soil temperatures favorable to crabgrass germination are indicated by forsythia bloom (although during long, cool springs, this isn't always the case). For season-long crabgrass control, check the product label to determine if two applications, about six weeks apart, are recommended. Also refer to Publication TT-43, "Herbicides for Crabgrass and Goosegrass Control in Turf."

Post-emergent herbicides for crabgrass control are more effective at controlling young crabgrass (in the one- to three-leaf stage). Table 14-H describes common lawn weeds and how to control them.

Types of herbicides

Selective herbicides

Many pre-emergent and post-emergent herbicides are selective herbicides. This means when used according to label directions, they target specific weeds only, with little or no damage to turf.

Pre-emergent herbicides are applied prior to the germination of weeds. They are commonly used to control annual grass weeds, such as crabgrass. The active chemical forms a barrier in the soil which kills weeds as they germinate. Pre-emergent herbicides need to be watered in soon after they are applied. Use caution if you intend to overseed that season because the pre-emergent will also kill germinating grass seedlings. The only exception is the herbicide Siduron (Tupersan®). Always read and follow the product label.

Table 14-H. Common lawn weeds

Species	Type	Life cycle	Cultural control	Chemical control
Japanese stiltgrass *Microstegium vimineum*	Grassy Table 13-D	Summer annual	Mow or hand-pull before seed set and mow to proper height.	Use pre-emergent crabgrass herbicide approx. 2 weeks earlier than recommended. Spray infested area with a non-selective herbicide in August and reseed.
Annual bluegrass *Poa annua*	Grassy Table 13-D	Winter annual. Light green in early spring. Dies out In hot weather.	Thrives in poorly-drained soils. Improve drainage to discourage it. Mow to proper height.	Apply a pre-emergent herbicide labeled for annual bluegrass in mid-Sept. (if not overseeding).
Bermudagrass *Cynodon dactylon*	Grassy Table 13-D	Perennial. Goes dormant/brown after the first frost.	Begin control when infestation is first detected. Complete eradication of perennial grass weeds is difficult.	Use a non-selective herbicide to either spot-treat or do a complete renovation. Start in early Aug. to allow time to re-treat if regrowth occurs. Seed after treated areas die.
Nimblewill *Muhlenbergia schreberi*	Grassy Table 13-D	Perennial. Goes dormant/brown after the first frost.	Hand-dig small patches.	Same as for bermudagrass.
Yellow nutsedge *Cyperus esculentus*	Sedge 13-C.29	Perennial	Improve drainage. Hand-pulling is difficult because nutlets left behind form new plants.	Treat with a post-emergent herbicide labeled for nutsedge.
White clover *Trifolium repens*	Broadleaf 13-C.8	Perennial	More prevalent in low-fertility soils. Follow nitrogen schedule.	Spot-treat with a liquid broadleaf selective post-emergent herbicide when actively growing in fall or spring, or use a granular herbicide.
Ground ivy, creeping Charlie *Glechoma hederacea*	Broadleaf 13-C.6	Perennial	Hand-pull small areas. Usually creeps along lawn edges, and near trees and shrubs. Follow nitrogen schedule.	Spot-treat with liquid broadleaf selective post-emergent herbicide or a granular herbicide in the fall and spring. Control can require 2-3 applications.
Wild violet *Viola* spp.	Broadleaf 13-C.7	Perennial	Hoe or hand-pull. Seed with shade-tolerant grass such as fine fescue. Follow nitrogen schedule. Mow to proper height.	Spot-treat with liquid broadleaf-selective post-emergent herbicide for wild violets or with a non-selective herbicide and reseed. Control can require 2-3 applications.
Wild garlic *Allium voneale*	Broadleaf 13-C.30	Perennial	Hand-pull when soil is moist. Remove bulb.	Treat with broadleaf selective post-emergent herbicide. Crush foliage before applying for better control.
Common chickweed *Stellaria media*	Broadleaf 13-C.45	Winter annual	Maintain thick lawn by following recommended cultural practices.	Treat with selective post-emergent broadleaf herbicide when actively growing.
Mouseear chickweed *Cerastium vulgatum*	Broadleaf 13-C.5	Perennial	Same as for common chickweed.	Treat with selective post-emergent broadleaf herbicide when actively growing.

For more information and an image, click on the link in the "Type" column.

Post-emergent herbicides are used to control actively growing grass and broadleaf weeds. The foliage of the weed is targeted instead of the soil. To be effective, the chemical needs to be absorbed into the plant itself and moved down to the root system. Avoid mowing the grass for a couple of days before and after the application.

Post-emergent herbicides should not be applied if rain is in the immediate forecast because it will wash the product off the leaves. Some granular products will recommend the turf be wet before application to help the granules adhere to the weeds.

Liquid herbicides can be used effectively to spot-treat weeds instead of treating the entire lawn. Fall is the best time to target established perennial broadleaf weeds such as ground ivy, white clover, wild violets, and wild garlic. Spring is the second-best time to target established perennial weeds and is a good time to try to control young, newly-emerging perennial weeds.

Non-selective herbicides

Non-selective herbicides kill all vegetation they come in contact with and must be applied to vegetation that is actively growing. Most often they are used for complete lawn renovation. Renovation should be considered when a lawn contains 40-50 percent weeds or to control an invasion of a perennial grass weed such as bermudagrass or nimblewill. The recommended time to begin lawn renovation is late summer (late August to mid-September). This will allow ample time to kill the weeds and have time to reseed.

Moss

Moss can sometimes occur in home lawns. It appears when growing conditions are not optimal for turf growth. Moss does not kill the grass but rather moves into areas of weak, thin turf. The key to controlling moss is to improve growing conditions to encourage a thick stand of healthy grass (see Table 14-I).

Table 14-I. Moss causes and controls

Cause	Control/remedy
Low soil fertility	Fertilize on a regular schedule.
Acidic soil	Perform a soil test and apply lime according to the results.
Dense shade from trees and shrubs	Prune surrounding plant material to increase sunlight.
Areas with poor drainage	Improve drainage by adding organic matter to the soil or regrading.
Soil compaction	Core aerate at the appropriate time.
Excessive moisture	Do not overwater.
Poor air circulation	Prune surrounding plant material to increase air flow.
Poor lawn care	Follow recommended cultural practices.
Inappropriate choice of turf species for the site conditions	Plant shade-tolerant turf where appropriate.

Several of these conditions may need to be improved before the moss can be fully eliminated. If the growing conditions cannot be adjusted, consider converting the area to ornamental beds or plant a groundcover. (Refer to the article on **lawn alternatives** on the HGIC website.) Once established, groundcovers may require less maintenance than grass in areas where they are better adapted anyway. Moss itself is considered a low-maintenance groundcover.

Mushrooms

During periods of wet weather, various species of mushrooms can appear in lawns. Mushrooms are the fruiting bodies of a fungus and commonly appear in turf areas where trees were removed. Fungi feed on decaying roots, stumps, and buried logs and can be present many years after the tree is removed. Mushrooms can be unsightly, but they do not harm the turf. No products are labeled to control them. Some species can be poisonous. If necessary, they can be raked up and appropriately disposed of.

Insects

The most damaging turf insect in Maryland is the white grub. Table 14-J identifies and describes the management practices for the most common lawn insects. Table 14-K provides a key to insect damage by symptom. See **Chapter 10, IPM**, for more information about insect management.

Table 14-J. Lawn insect identification and control

Image	Insect	Damage	What to look for	Prevention	Control
Japanese beetle / Oriental beetle / Masked chafer / Asiatic garden beetle	**White grub** Several grub species damage turf, including the larvae of Japanese beetles, Oriental beetles, masked chafers, and Asiatic garden beetles. White grubs are identified by their raster pattern, located on the underside of the abdomen.	Root damage is most evident Aug. to early Oct. Worse in dry summers. Grass gradually thins, wilts, and browns in irregular patches. Birds, skunks, and raccoons dig up grub-infested areas, causing further damage.	Cut a few 1-ft.-square sod sections and look for C-shaped grubs in the top 1-2 in. of soil. If you find an average of 8 grubs or more in a section, chemical control may be necessary. A few grubs are common and need no treatment.	Plant tall fescue (fewer grub issues). Do not over-water lawns during the adult egg-laying and development period (late June-early Sept.). Beetles tend to lay eggs in moist soil. Fertilize in fall to encourage deep roots.	If there were grubs last season, apply an insecticide labeled for season-long grub control in May to prevent a grub infestation later in the summer. *Bacillus popilliae* (Bp) (milky spore) treats only Japanese beetle grubs. For maximum benefit, adjacent lots need to be treated. Research is inconclusive on Bp effectiveness. Entomopathogenic nematodes can provide modest control which may be enough to sufficiently decrease grub populations. If a "rescue treatment" is needed, apply in late summer and re-seed in early fall.
	Green June beetle Larvae can grow to 2 in.	Tunnel/push up small piles of soil.	Tunnels look like earthworm holes. Exit holes are approx. the diameter of a pencil.	Tamp down tunnels and re-seed if needed. Fertilize, mow, and lime as indicated.	Usually not necessary on home lawns.

continued on next page

continued from previous page

Table 14-J. Lawn insect identification and control

Image	Insect	Damage	What to look for	Prevention	Control
	Billbug Adults are dark brown-to-black weevils that emerge in spring after overwintering in thatch/leaf litter. They lay eggs in the stems of grasses in June and July. Larvae are small, white, and legless. They usually pupate in Aug. and emerge as adults soon after.	Larvae feed on the inside of the lower stem, then the crown and roots. Only larvae cause significant damage.	Adults are sometimes observed on paved surfaces during Sept. and Oct. Heat- and drought- stressed turf is first to show damage. Small brown or tan patches (2- to 6-in. across) begin to appear in mid-summer. Look for hollow stems and sawdust-like material at the base of the plants. Larvae are difficult to detect.	Control thatch. Plant resistant turf varieties, especially those containing endophytic fungi (e.g., tall fescue). Maintain a healthy lawn to aid in damage recovery.	Insecticide is not recommended because by the time damage is noticed, it is too late to treat. This pest is not significant enough to warrant preventive treatment in home lawns.
	Mining bee and cicada killer wasp	Burrowing creates soil mounds. Both insects are beneficial.	Either insect flying over the lawn surface.	Irrigate during flying activity and thicken up turf to reduce nesting.	They are pollinators, so tolerate them if possible. No control is needed for mining bees. If cicada killers produce many mounds, spray a labeled lawn insecticide into nest.
	Chinch bug No larval or pupal stage. Insects hatch directly into minute nymphs. Adults have black bodies with white folded wings. Usually 2 generations per yr. They overwinter in leaf litter or thatch.	Chinch bugs feed on leaves by sucking fluids out of the blades, causing yellow or brown patches.	Heat- and drought-stressed turf shows damage first. Adults are seen in thatch layer. Check turf bordering dead areas or place a large can, with both ends removed, a few inches into the soil and fill with water. Any chinch bugs will float to the surface in 10-15 minutes.	Control thatch. Plant resistant turf varieties, particularly those with endophytic fungi (such as tall fescue). Healthy turf can tolerate a low population of chinch bugs without any negative impact.	Natural predators like the big-eyed bug keep populations in check. Chemical control is not recommended for home lawns.
	Sod webworm Larvae grow to 3/4 in. long and have rows of spots on their bodies. Moths are about 1/2-in. long and appear to have a long snout.	Larvae chew leaf blades at the base. Female moths drop eggs over turf as they fly.	Off-white moths flying over turf are visible, as are irregular patches of yellow-brown grass. Areas appear scalped. Damage occurs in mid-summer through early fall.	Plant resistant varieties of turf, specifically endophyte-containing varieties like tall fescue.	Bt (*Bacillus thuringiensis*) can be used to control young larvae. Natural enemies include big-eyed bugs and ground beetles.

Table 14-K. Insect-caused turf problems (by symptom)

Symptom	Possible cause	Control/comments
Turf comes up easily, obvious lack of roots	**White grubs.** Turf can sometimes be rolled up like a carpet. C-shaped grubs are found in soil from June through September. Can be severe on bluegrass, ryegrass, and fine fescue.	Reseed the lawn in the fall with a tolerant turf species such as tall fescue or zoysia.
Turf blades can be pulled easily from sod	**Billbugs.** Light tan, sawdust-like frass in areas of heavy feeding. Small legless grubs found near crowns and roots from June through August.	Water and fertilize grass to stimulate regrowth. Reseed with endophyte-containing tall fescues.
Irregular brown patches with white moths flying over the turf	**Sod webworm.** Brown caterpillars may be found at the base of the blades and in the thatch.	Reseed with grasses having high levels of endophyte, such as tall fescue, or spray with Bt insecticide.
Localized yellow or brown areas	**Chinch bugs.** Tiny black insects with shiny white wings found on crowns and stems. Damage usually occurs in sunny, well-drained locations.	Reseed with grasses having high levels of endophyte, such as tall fescue. Often controlled by natural predators such as big-eyed bugs.

Diseases

Disease pathogens are present in most turfgrass stands. Usually, these organisms exist in a dormant or saprophytic state. (An organism that obtains nutrients from dead organic matter is termed a saprophyte.) Diseases become a problem when environmental conditions become favorable for the buildup of pathogen populations or cause an increase in the susceptibility of the host plant. For disease symptoms to occur, there must be a susceptible host plant, a pathogen (usually a fungus) present, and environmental conditions that allow the fungus to grow and gain an advantage on the host plant. These three factors are known as the "disease triangle."

Different turfgrass diseases can occur under a blanket of snow in the winter, as well as only during the hottest and most humid conditions of midsummer. Too much or too little nitrogen fertilizer can also contribute to a disease problem. Some diseases occur when soils are saturated with water; others occur under periods of drought stress.

Disease management strategies

First, get an accurate diagnosis. It can be difficult because pathogens that cause turf diseases are usually visible only under a microscope. Pathogens will, however, occasionally produce large fruiting bodies, such as mushrooms, spores, or threadlike filaments called mycelium, that can be seen without a microscope. (See Table 14-L.)

More commonly, symptoms (the visible characteristics of the plant which indicate it is diseased) are used for diagnosis. Symptoms can take on a variety of sizes, shapes, and colors and be present on leaf blades or on the crowns and roots (see Table 14-M.) Symptoms also appear on populations of plants and may take the form of circular patches, rings, or irregular areas of blighted turf.

Table 14-L. Common turf diseases

Disease	Symptoms	Favorable conditions	Control/comments
Brown patch Affects all turfgrass, especially tall fescue and perennial rye.	Circular to irregular yellow-brown patches of thinned turf. On individual blades, elongated lesions bordered above and below by tan or chocolate-brown-to-purple bands.	Prevalent June-Sept. when daytime temps are 85°+, nighttime temps are 68°+, and humidity is high. Too much water-soluble fertilizer, especially urea, nitrate, or ammonium, in late spring-summer increases disease probability.	Does not kill the turf crown. Most tall-fescue lawns recover with proper fall fertilization and drier, cooler weather. Do not plant perennial rye. Maintain balanced fertility; avoid heavy spring applications of fertilizer.
Red thread Affects mostly fine fescues and perennial rye, but can also be seen on tall fescue.	Circular or irregular pink/red patches. Gelatinous, reddish fungus grows on leaf blades and sheaths. When blades dry, red, brittle strands extend from blade tips.	Cool, wet weather in early spring or mid-late autumn. Associated with periods of overcast, drizzly weather. Usually more prevalent on under-fertilized turf.	Short-term: Add ½ lb. nitrogen/1,000 sq. ft. to help grass "grow out" of disease. Long-term: Follow a recommended fertilizer schedule.
Dollar spot Affects all species of turfgrass grown in Maryland.	Hourglass-shaped lesions across the blade with whitened centers and dark borders. Produces numerous 2-6-in. spots.	Occurs late spring-fall, is worst in summer. Usually more prevalent on under-fertilized turf. Drought, thatch, and compacted soil increase disease susceptibility.	Follow recommended fertilizer schedule. Aerate and reduce thatch.

Table 14-M. Disease-caused turf problems (by symptom)

Symptom	Possible cause	Control/comments
Leaf spots	**Helminthosporium leaf spot:** Leaf spots with tan centers. Lesions are round or elongated. Turf thins. Common in wet spring weather. Primarily affects bluegrass and ryegrass.	Avoid drought stress and light/frequent watering. Reduce thatch and avoid spring fertilization with soluble nitrogen sources. Reseed with improved turf-type tall fescue cultivars.
	Dollar spot: Leaf lesions with a dark border and hourglass-shaped spots. Affects all turfgrass species, including zoysia.	Avoid drought stress. Prevent thatch buildup and soil compaction. Maintain adequate nitrogen fertility and reseed with improved turf cultivars.
	Brown patch: Elongated lesions with chocolate-brown margins. Leaves may brown and thinning may occur June-Sept. Can be severe on bluegrass, ryegrass, and fine fescue.	Water in early morning and avoid watering lightly/frequently. Avoid excessive nitrogen fertilization.
Pink/reddish color on leaf blades	**Red thread:** Red, thread-like growths extending from leaf-blade tips. Appears in patches and occurs in spring and fall on fine fescue and perennial ryegrass species. Can also affect tall fescue in very cool, wet weather.	Maintain adequate nitrogen fertility levels. Adding ½ lb. nitrogen/1,000 sq. ft. can help to cure symptoms without the use of a fungicide.
Gray to black streaks in leaf blades	**Striped smut:** Leaves split into ribbons and curl. Appears in irregular patches and infects primarily bluegrass in spring and fall.	Avoid drought stress and excessive thatch. Reseed with improved turf cultivars.

continued on next page

continued from previous page

Table 14-M. Disease-caused turf problems (by symptom)

Symptom	Possible cause	Control/comments
Blades covered with red, orange, or yellow powdery material	Rust diseases. Turf may appear yellow or reddish from a distance. Occurs primarily on bluegrass, ryegrass, and zoysia.	Maintain adequate nitrogen fertility levels and reseed with improved turf cultivars. Adding ½ lb. nitrogen/1,000 sq. ft. can help to cure symptoms without use of a fungicide.
Blades covered with a white coating	Powdery mildew. The white coating typically occurs on bluegrass in shady areas during the fall months.	Reduce shade and improve air movement. Avoid excessive nitrogen and drought stress. Increase mowing height and reseed with improved disease-resistant cultivars.
Blades covered with black sooty-like material	Sooty mold. Not harmful. Easily wiped off or removed. Blades remain green underneath. Occurs primarily in spring or fall after rain.	Wash off sooty material with a hose or remove it by mowing.
Rings or arcs of dead or green grass; mushrooms may be present	Fairy rings. Rings or arcs of dead/green grass bordered by zones of darker green. More common on droughty sites and poorly nourished turf. Occurs on all turf cultivars year-'round.	Aerate turf frequently. Maintain adequate nitrogen fertility and adequate water during dry spells.
Circular straw-colored patches	Summer patch. Circular patches from 3-12-in. in diameter. Occurs in bluegrass and fine fescue lawns 2 years or older from July-Sept.	Avoid excessive nitrogen, especially in spring. Use slow-release nitrogen sources. Increase mowing height, avoid light and frequent watering, and reduce thatch.

Cultural control

Cultural control is always the first line of defense against turfgrass diseases. Part of the diagnosis should include addressing the mismanagement of turf, which can contribute to a disease problem. Cultural practices that need to be addressed include:

Mowing. Mowing below the recommended height can place stress on the grass, making it more susceptible to some diseases (especially in the summer months). Every time a mower removes leaf tissue a wound is created though which a pathogen may enter the plant. Sometimes mowing may actually spread the pathogen from one location to another. Mow when turf is dry and make sure that blades are sharp.

Fertilization. Over-fertilization is a common reason for residential lawn diseases. Avoid heavy applications of nitrogen during spring and summer. Lush spring or summer growth can be more prone to certain diseases. Diseases favored by large applications of nitrogen fertilizer include leaf spot, brown patch, pythium blight, stripe smut, and snow-mold diseases. On the other hand, certain diseases such as dollar spot, red thread, pink patch, and rust diseases are more prevalent in low-fertility soils.

Irrigation. Incorrect irrigation contributes to disease problems because most fungal pathogens require frequent watering to infect plant tissue. Evening watering should be avoided if possible because it leaves a film of water on plants for an extended period of time. Watering should be done in early morning.

Thatch. Thatch accumulation results in weakened plants that become more susceptible to diseases and can provide a habitat for disease organisms. An excessive amount of thatch can prevent wetting of the soil and restrict fertilizer from reaching the root system, further weakening the turf.

Compaction. Compaction leads to poor infiltration and reduced oxygen diffusion to the root zone. Some root and crown diseases, such as summer patch and anthracnose, are frequently associated with compacted soils on putting greens.

Air circulation. Areas with poor airflow are prone to diseases such as powdery mildew. Prune trees and shrubs to increase air movement.

Disease-resistant species and varieties

No turfgrass is resistant to all diseases. In Maryland, tall fescue and zoysiagrass tend to be the species most resistant to disease. To increase a turf stand's overall resistance, plant mixtures of different grass species and/or blends of cultivars of an individual species (for cool-season grasses). If a disease damages one cultivar or species, the others will fill the void. Plant shade-tolerant species in areas with reduced sunlight.

Chemical control

Fungicides should be applied only for diseases that kill the roots or crown, such as summer patch. Homeowner use of fungicides should be generally discouraged because many lawn fungi need preventive spraying. By the time the homeowner notices symptoms, it is too late to spray. Multiple applications are necessary and homeowners usually do not own the proper equipment for an effective application. Fungicides are expensive and most of the effective products are available to licensed applicators only. Homeowners can consult with a lawn-care professional for treatment.

Contact fungicides, usually used to control foliar diseases, are only effective for short durations (seven to 14 days), and do not protect new foliage. As a group, they have a broad spectrum of control. Systemic fungicides are absorbed and translocated within the plant. They control foliar, root, and crown pathogens; protect plants for a period of two to four weeks; and protect new growth.

Systemic fungicides tend to encourage pathogen resistance if overused and not rotated consistently.

Abiotic disorders of lawns

The vast majority of turf problems are abiotic (i.e., unrelated to disease or insect organisms). Symptoms can appear similar to those created by disease or insects, but the treatment is very different. Abiotic problems can be tricky to diagnose and require an examination of site conditions, cultural practices, and use of the lawn. Often, by the time damage is noticed, it is too late for treatment and the only solution is to renovate.

To avoid further damage, it is necessary to fix the original cause of the damage. For example, if patches of dead grass appear that are not caused by disease or insects, it is possible that rocks are buried underneath the dead areas. The solution is to dig up the area to search for and remove the debris, and then reseed. See Table 14-N for common abiotic problems.

Table 14-N. Abiotic turf problems (by symptom)

Symptom	Possible cause	Control/comments
Straw-colored patches encircled by a ring of dark-green turf	**Dog urine.** May resemble some turf diseases. May kill the crown tissue.	Watering immediately to dilute the urine can help.
Banded streaks or irregular patterns	**Fertilizer or chemical injury.** Grass may be stimulated at the margins. May kill the crown tissue.	Calibrate spreaders and sprayers for uniform and accurate application of materials. Re-seed areas.
Black or dark "oily" spots or patches	**Oil or gasoline damage.** Fuel or oil leaking from a lawn mower will kill grass.	A severe oil leak/spill requires removal of affected soil. Small gasoline leaks or spills volatilize quickly. Soil should be replaced if saturated.
Large, yellow area near pool	**Chlorine damage.** Pool water has a high chlorine content which can kill grass.	Leach chlorine through soil using water. Replant.
Grass over high spots looks scalped	**Mower injury.** Mower cuts into plant crowns that are exposed.	Adjust terrain, raise mower blade, or change mowing direction.
Shredded blade tips	**Dull mower injury.** Blade tips appear gray and then turn tan.	Sharpen mower blades.
Patches of dead or dormant grass	**Buried debris, insect injury, or thick thatch.** Often follows a dry period.	Check for causes.
Pale green to golden-yellow turf	**Chlorosis.** Iron or nitrogen deficiency. Yellow streaks may form parallel to leaf veins.	Maintain adequate fertilizer levels.
Black or greenish crust on soil	**Algae growth.** Appears on bare soil, thin turf, poorly drained, or compacted areas. Usually more severe in shade.	Increase drainage and establish a thicker stand of turf. Aerate compacted areas and increase sunlight in shaded areas.
Small green plants growing with turf	**Moss.** Appears on bare soil, thin turf, or poorly drained or compacted areas. Usually more severe in shade.	Increase drainage and establish a thicker stand of turf. Aerate compacted areas and increase sunlight in shaded areas.
Turf appears dry and bluish green in color	**Drought.** Footprints remain after walking on turf. Grass wilts.	Irrigate turf.
Turf dies out every year over the summer	**Site conditions.** Grass is either on a slope, or in a full-sun location with poor soil.	Plant site-appropriate groundcover. Aerate and topdress with organic matter to improve soil.
Areas of thinning turf	**High-traffic/compacted soil.** Weeds, most often crabgrass, move into these areas.	Aerate turf at appropriate time more often and reseed regularly/as needed.

14.6 Organic Lawn Care Tips

A working definition of "organic" used by most organic gardeners is "without synthetic chemical fertilizers or pesticides."

Here are tips for organic lawn care:

- Maintain proper soil pH. Perform a soil test every three years and apply lime according to results.
- Fertilize at the proper time. Fall fertilization encourages root growth. Use slow-release fertilizers.
- Irrigate only if necessary. Tall fescue lawns can go dormant in the summer and will recover when rainfall returns and temperatures fall. Only newly-seeded lawns and those less than two years old need irrigation.
- Mow at the proper height and keep your lawn mower blade sharp. Mowing fescue at three to three-and-a-half inches encourages better root growth, increases traffic tolerance, and discourages crabgrass invasion.
- Amend poor soil conditions. Aerate compacted soil, add compost to poor soil, and correct drainage problems.
- Use proper seed for site conditions and buy high-quality seed.
- Core-aerate and overseed in the fall. Consistent overseeding will help maintain lawn density, which helps deter weed encroachment.
- Keeping thatch levels to less than ¾ inch will encourage water and fertilizer infiltration into the soil. Certain disease pathogens and insects thrive in excessive thatch conditions.
- Grasscycle. Mulch-mowing your clippings returns nutrients to the soil and reduces green waste burdens for municipalities and counties.
- Hand-pull weeds, or use chelated iron (Iron hydroxyethylethylene-diaminetriacetic acid, or HEDTA) products for spraying broadleaf weeds.

14.7 Lawn Alternatives

Removing grass and reducing the size of your lawn may be desirable if you:

- Cannot grow turfgrass because of a steep slope, unsuitable soil conditions, or too much shade.
- Have a lawn that is largely unused and would like to devote your time and resources to other purposes.
- Wish to add more diversity to your landscape.

Whatever your motivations are, there are plenty of ways you can replace all or a portion of your lawn (see Figure 14-O for a general planting guide). Here are several options for Maryland residents:

- Groundcovers spread but do not grow tall, so no mowing and little maintenance is necessary. These plants can work well on steep slopes, sharp angles, and narrow driveway strips.
- Perennial evergreen ground covers, with time, can choke out weeds.
- You will need to weed and mulch until your groundcover is established. Use an edge barrier to contain spreading groundcovers and keep a neat appearance.

- Avoid using invasive plants like periwinkles (*Vinca major* and *Vinca minor*), Japanese spurge (*Pachysandra terminalis*), and carpet bugleweed (*Ajuga reptans*).
- Many groundcovers that are Maryland natives are also deer-resistant. See the **recommended groundcovers list** for ideas.

Ornamental grasses

Ornamental grasses are low maintenance, drought-resistant, grow in most soils, seldom require fertilizer, and have few pest or disease problems. Some suggestions:

- Maryland native switchgrass (*Panicum virgatum*), little blue stem (*Schizachyrium scoparium*), and yellow indiangrass (*Sorghastrum nutans*) are three great choices for sunny sites.
- In shady sites, try bottlebrush grass (*Elymus hystrix*) or the grass-like Pennsylvania sedge (*Carex pensylvanica*).
- You can create stunning displays using different textures, heights, and growing habits.
- Foliage should be cut back at least once a year, preferably in the early spring before new growth begins.

No-mow/natural areas

If you have a large area of land (e.g., several acres), consider maintaining only a small lawn

Figure 14-O. Lawn alternative planting guide

close to your home where it is most often used. Leave the more remote areas unmowed and naturalistic. This can save you time and money and result in a beautiful natural landscape that attracts a variety of songbirds, pollinators, amphibians, and other wildlife.

If you leave a portion of your land unmowed it will begin to go through the natural stages of succession. One type of vegetation will follow another: first grasses and other herbaceous plants followed by shrubs, tree seedlings, and mature trees. As you allow an area to go through natural succession, be prepared to manage invasive plants.

Lower-maintenance options

- Fine leaf fescues, such as hard, creeping red, chewings, and sheep fescue, require less frequent mowing than tall fescue. In fact, these grasses should not be mowed during hot, dry summer conditions.

- The grasses mentioned above are recommended for shady conditions. Hard fescue and sheep fescue are the best of the fine fescues for full sun. Left unmowed in the summer months, fine fescues can grow to more than four inches tall and have a clumpy, windswept look.

- Fine fescues are prone to thatch buildup and require periodic dethatching (about every two years). They are also intolerant of heavy foot traffic.

Mulch as a solution

Grass not growing well under a tree? Too much shade and too much competition for water and nutrients from the tree roots will prevent turf from performing well under shade trees.

Add two to three inches of wood mulch under the tree all the way out to the dripline. This will reduce weeds, retain moisture, increase soil fertility and structure, and protect the tree trunk from mower damage. ❈

Recommended groundcovers for Maryland

* = deer-resistant   + = native

Allegheny spurge+ *(Pachysandra procumbens)*

Alum root*+ *(Heuchera americana)*

Ageratum, hardy+ *(Conoclinium coelestinum)*

Barrenwort *(Epimedium spp.)*

Catmint* 'Walkers Low' *(Nepeta x faassenii 'Walkers Low')*

Cinnamon fern* *(Osmunda cinnamomea)*

Creeping thyme* *(Thymus serpyllum)*

Crested iris*+ *(Iris cristata)*

Green-and-gold*+ *(Chrysogonum virginianum)*

Lamb's ears* 'Helene von Stein' *(Stachys byzantina 'Helene von Stein')*

Maidenhair fern*+ *(Adiantum pedatum)*

Mondo grass *(Ophiopogon japonicus)*

Pennsylvania sedge* *(Carex pensylvanica)*

Phlox, creeping+ *(Phlox stolonifera)*

Plumbago* *(Ceratostigma plumbaginoides)*

Sedum 'Angelina' *(Sedum rupestre 'Angelina')*

Solomon's seal, variegated *(Polygonatum odorata)*

Sweet box* *(Sarcococca hookeriana var. humilis)*

Willowleaf cotoneaster *(Cotoneaster salicifolius repens)*

Wild ginger*+ *(Asarum canadense)*

Winter jasmine* *(Jasminum nudiflorum)*

Wood spurge* *(Euphorbia amygdaloides)*

AUTHORS

2024 Edition: Geoffrey Jordan Rinehart, Lecturer, UMD Institute of Applied Agriculture.

Original author: Debra Ricigliano, CPH, Horticultural Consultant, University of Maryland Extension, retired.

Reviewer: Jon Traunfeld, Extension Specialist and Center Director, Extension Gardening, University of Maryland Extension.

PUBLICATIONS

"Turfgrass Identification" section is reprinted with permission from *The Oregon-Washington Master Gardener Handbook*. 1999.

Dernoeden, P. March 2008. TT-43, *Herbicides for Crabgrass and Goosegrass Control in Maryland.* Natural Resource Sciences and Landscape Architecture, University of Maryland, College Park, MD.

Koppenhöfer, A. June 2002. FS1009, *An Integrated Approach to Insect Management in Turfgrass: White Grubs.* Rutgers Cooperative Research & Extension, NJAES, Rutgers, The State University of New Jersey. New Brunswick, NJ.

Potter, M. and D. Potter. Revised June 1999. ENT-10, *Controlling White Grubs in Turfgrass.* Cooperative Extension Service, University of Kentucky, College of Agriculture. Lexington, KY.

Ricigliano, D. HG 101, *Guide to Controlling Weeds in Cool Season Turf; HG 102, Lawn Establishment, Renovation and Overseeding; HG 103, Fertilizer Facts for Home Lawns*. Home and Garden Information Center, University of Maryland Extension. College Park, MD.

Turgeon, A. J. 2002. *Turfgrass Management.* Prentice Hall, Inc. Englewood Cliffs, NJ. ISBN-13: 9780132236164.

Turner, T., D. Funk, and J. Krouse. May 2010. TT-77, *Recommended Turfgrass Cultivars for Certified Sod and Professional Seed Mixtures.* Natural Resource Sciences and Landscape Architecture, University of Maryland, College Park, MD.

WEBSITES

Maryland Turf Council. mdturfcouncil.org

University of Maryland Extension. *Diagnose Lawn Problems in Maryland.* extension.umd.edu/resource/diagnose-lawn-problems-maryland

Duble, Richard L. Turfgrass Specialist, Texas Cooperative Extension. *Bermudagrass, The Sports Turf of the South.* aggie-horticulture.tamu.edu/plantanswers/turf/publications/Bermuda.html

PennState College of Agricultural Sciences. *Home Lawns.* plantscience.psu.edu/research/centers/turf/extension/home-lawns/home-lawn

University of Maryland Extension. *IPM: Prevent, Identify, and Manage Plant Problems.* extension.umd.edu/resource/ipm-prevent-identify-and-manage-plant-problems

GRAPHICS

Main chapter photo: Miri Talabac, University of Maryland Extension. Figures 14A-14H, 14-O: LeAnn Zotta, Berkshire Communications. Figures 14-I-14-N: NC State University Extension. Table 14-J: Japanese beetle, oriental beetle, masked chafer, Asiatic garden beetle, NC State University Extension, used with permission; green June beetle: Clemson University - USDA Cooperative Extension Slide Series, Bugwood.org.; billbug larva: Whitney Cranshaw, Colorado State University, Bugwood.org; billbug adult: Joseph Berger, Bugwood.org.; mining bee: **Charlie Jackson** via Flickr; cicada killer: Suzanne Klick, UME; chinch bug adult: **Christina Butler** via Flickr; cinch bug damage: Dr. Adam Dale, University of FLorida. sod webworm: Dr. David Smitley, Michigan State University Extension.

15: HERBACEOUS PLANTS

Esther Mitchell
Susan Trice

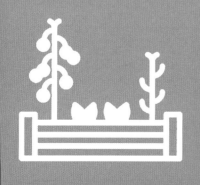

15 HERBACEOUS PLANTS

CONTENTS

15.1 About Herbaceous Gardens 420

15.2 Herbaceous Plant Families 421

15.3 Annuals 427

15.4 Perennials 429

15.5 Biennials 431

15.6 Underground Stems 431

15.7 Landscape Design with Herbaceous Plants 436

15.8 Herbaceous Garden Maintenance 439

15.9 Sexual Propagation of Herbaceous Plants 442

15.10 Asexual Propagation of Herbaceous Plants 443

LEARNING OBJECTIVES

- The differences between annuals, perennials, biennials, and underground stems
- The characteristics of common herbaceous plant families
- Design guidelines for an herbaceous garden
- Maintaining an herbaceous garden
- Propagating herbaceous plants
- Perennial planting guides

INTRODUCTION

Flowers are the horticulturist's reward for hard work. Flower beds and borders enliven the landscape and complement the conventional green landscaping features of trees and shrubs. They visually alter heights and slopes, adding depth and dimension, form and texture, and even fragrance.

Most flowers and herbs are referred to as "herbaceous" because they lack a woody stem. Trees and shrubs are referred to as "woody" because they have branches, twigs, and trunks, but they can flower as well.

There are four main types of herbaceous plants:

An **herbaceous annual** blooms all season but is killed by freezing temperatures. It remains in the garden for only one growing season, although it may self-seed and return to your garden as a "volunteer."

An **herbaceous perennial** is a hardy plant that remains in the garden year-'round for anywhere from three to 100 or more years. The top portion dies back each winter. Perennials seldom bloom for more than a few weeks.

Like annuals, an **herbaceous biennial** is a short-lived plant, but completes its life cycle in two years instead of one. The first year is vegetative growth. The plant flowers and sets seed the second year. Like a perennial, it blooms for a limited period of time.

Bulbs, corms, tubers, and rhizomes fall into the category of underground stems. These perennials bloom once each year for a few weeks in either spring or summer, then die back. A few, like cyclamen, bloom in the fall. They can live for decades with proper care.

A well-designed herbaceous garden can:

- Create a privacy screen or block unattractive aspects of the yard
- Produce an abundance of flowers
- Make your home entrance more inviting
- Make use of an unmowable, steep slope
- Turn a stony outcropping into a beautiful rock garden
- Be a bog garden where it's too wet for a lawn
- Save work by containing perennials that don't require yearly replanting

15.1 About Herbaceous Gardens

The success of the garden will depend on how well the plants you select align with the following conditions in your own environment.

Day length. Day length is usually the most critical factor in regulating vegetative growth, flower initiation and development, and the induction of dormancy. Plants use day length as a cue to initiate growth in spring and prepare them for the cold weather in the fall. Many plants require specific day-length conditions to form flowers.

Light. Light is the energy source for plants. Cloudy, rainy days or shade cast by nearby plants and structures can significantly reduce the amount of light available. Plants survive only where the amount of light is within a range they can tolerate. For example, shade-adapted plants cannot tolerate the bright light of full sun and will burn.

Temperature. Plants grow best within a defined range of temperatures, which is wider for some species and narrower for others. Plants survive only where temperatures allow them to carry on life-sustaining chemical reactions.

Plants differ in their ability to survive cold temperatures. Some tropical plants are injured by temperatures below 60°F. Arctic species can tolerate temperatures well below zero. The ability of a plant to withstand cold is a function of how deep the plant's dormancy is, how well it retains water, and its general health. Wind exposure, bright sun, or rapidly changing temperatures can also compromise a plant's cold tolerance.

Heat tolerance also varies from species to species. Plants that are native to arid tropical regions are naturally very heat-tolerant, while subarctic and alpine plants show very little heat tolerance. High overnight temperatures are often the most limiting factor for plants.

Water. Some plants tolerate drought during the summer but need winter rains. Others need a consistent supply of moisture to grow well. Research the water requirements of the plants you are considering to help you choose those which need a minimum of irrigation to perform well. If you have poorly drained, chronically wet soil, you can select lovely garden plants that naturally grow in bogs, fens, and other wet places.

pH (potential Hydrogen). The pH scale is commonly used to represent hydrogen ion activity (i.e., the potential for hydrogen). The ability of plant roots to take up certain nutrients depends upon pH, which is a measure of the acidity or alkalinity of your soil. Most plants grow best in soils that have a pH near 7.0. Most ericaceous plants, such as azaleas and blueberries, need acidic soil with a pH below 6.0 to grow well.

The solubility of many trace elements is controlled by pH, and only the soluble forms of these important micronutrients can be used by plants. Iron is not very soluble at high pH and iron chlorosis is often present in high-pH soils, even if they contain abundant iron.

Lime neutralizes acidic soil and makes it more alkaline by increasing the pH. Ground limestone (calcium carbonate) can be used, but it's dusty and hard to spread evenly. Dolomite (revitalized lime) is easier to spread. Wood ashes also contain lime and can be used to raise soil pH.

Sulfur makes the soil more acidic by lowering the pH. Elemental sulphur (ammonium sulfate) is the most common material used to acidify soil. Aluminum sulfur and iron sulfate may also be used. See **Chapter 5, Soils and Fertilizers**, for an expanded discussion.

15.2 Herbaceous Plant Families

Most gardeners and landscapers are interested in the plant species and maybe the genus. The next highest order of plant taxonomy is the family. Understanding a plant's family characteristics helps identify what a given plant needs to thrive. These family traits can also definitively identify a plant, which is the first step in diagnosing a problem.

Each family has its own traits, like the number of pistils and stamens in the flower, how they produce seed, or which pH they prefer. Grouping family plants together is smart because the group's horticultural needs are the same, which offers them all a measure of protection from pests and diseases.

Following is a selection of the most common herbaceous plant families.

ASTERACEAE (formerly Compositae)

The daisy family is one of the largest, with more than 32,000 species distributed all over the world.

Astereaceae includes shrubs, perennials, and annuals, but not trees or aquatics. Many are weeds (dandelion and thistle), many are familiar garden flowers (aster, chrysanthemum, and coneflower), and some are edible (lettuce and artichoke).

Leaves, stem, and roots

The leaves of this family are often undivided and spoon-shaped, but are sometimes toothed or divided, and may be prickly. There is often a basal rosette, as in the daisy or dandelion, and there may be leaves on the stem, as in the thistle. The stem itself may be solid or hollow and it, too, may be prickly. The roots may be short and near the surface, as in the daisy, or there may be a long tap root, as in the dandelion or thistle.

Flowers

It is the flowers that give this plant family its original name of Compositae. They are composite, or made up of many individual flowers. These flowers may be regular (disc florets) with all the petals the same size, or irregular (ray florets) with some petals larger than others. Often, the disc florets form the central disc of short flowers, and the irregular ray florets form the outside "petals" with the larger edge on the outside of the flower head. Some members of this family are made up of only disc florets or only ray florets.

Seeds

Each single flower can produce a seed. The flowers sit on a disc surrounded by bracts. After pollination, the seeds grow and mature until they are ripe and ready to be dispersed. In some species, the bracts surrounding the flower open and the seeds are dispersed by the wind. The seed is often attached to its own "parachute," as with the dandelion. In other species, the bracts close over the disc while the seeds mature and the seed case turns brown. When the seeds are ready, they separate from the disc. Seeds of this family are oval and may be flat or rounded. They can be straw-colored, warm brown, or nearly black.

Many members of this plant family do not produce viable seeds. Instead, they produce what looks like a fine seed-head of white fluff which actually has no seed at the bottom of the "parachute." In some cases, there may be a seed case full of ripe brown seeds but they may be flat or bent and spindly, and not viable. Healthy seeds have a slight bulge (even flat seeds), and some are fat and rounded.

ORCHIDACEAE

This is the largest family of flowering plants. There are 880 genera and 30,000+ accepted species. Orchids are irregular monocots.

Leaves, stem, and roots

The leaves are simple, alternate, and undivided, with parallel veins that are usually either in two files or arranged in a spiral around the stem. The leaves of some species have been reduced to scales. The stems are erect and often climbing or trailing. Orchids have roots that are either adventitious, tuberous, fleshy, climbing, or aerial. The main roots are always absent.

Flowers

Fragrant orchid flowers feature three sepals, three petals (one of which is modified into often eccentric forms), three stamens, and one anther. The pollen in the anthers is either waxy or granular. Flowers appear in all colors except black.

Reproductive organs are located in the column. The ovary is inferior (i.e., below the rest of the flower).

Seeds

Orchid seeds depend on fungi, which supply the seed with enough food to germinate and grow. The resulting capsules are dry and dust-like, with no endosperm, and disperse in the wind.

POACEAE
(formerly Gramineae)

Poaceae is a large family of 12,000 grass species and at least 800 genera. Grasses range in size from small annuals (*Poa annua*) to towering timber bamboo (*Dendrocalamus giganteus*).

This is unquestionably the most important plant family as it provides the majority of food for humans and their domesticated animals. In addition to cereal grains (rice, wheat, barley, oats, and corn), grasses are the source of bamboo shoots used in Asian foods, the primary source of sugar (sucrose) from sugar cane (*Saccharum officinarum*), alcoholic beverages from barley malt (beer) and fermented rice (sake), and bamboo timbers for construction.

Perhaps just as important, from an economic point of view, are the suite of taxa used as forage for domesticated animals and the creation of human-dominated environments (turf grasses). Many of these have escaped cultivation and, especially in disturbed areas, have established a strong position amongst our local flora.

Leaves, stem, and roots

Poaceae leaves may be either deciduous or evergreen. All are either alternate or basal, and have a much greater length than width. The leaves feature parallel veins and have a cylindrical sheath that encircles the stem, with a blade above it. The stems have conspicuous nodes where the leaf base is attached.

The stem may grow underground like a rhizome, and is cylindrical with conspicuous nodes and internodes. It can be herbaceous or woody. The roots can vary between adventitious, fibrous, branched, or stilt.

Flowers

Small, reduced flowers appear as tufted or caespitose plants with linear, sheathing leaves. Differs from the Cyperaceae with its round (terete in cross-section) stems, also called "culms." Culms are hollow (neither pithy nor solid) at the internodes, and leaves are arranged in two rows. Sheathing leaf bases are also often "open" or loosely connected to the culm, frequently showing a ligule at the point where the leaf blade meets the sheath. Reproductive structures are distinct in that the inflorescences are made up of spikelets.

Seeds

The ovary consists of three united carpels that form a single chamber. It matures as a single seed called a caryopsis (grain) or, rarely, an achene (a dry seed) or a berry. In contrast to most large families, the fruit is usually not needed for species identification.

EUPHORBIACEAE

Euphorbiaceae is a large family of flowering spurge plants with 240 genera and about 6,000 species. Most are herbs, but some, especially in the tropics, are shrubs or trees. Some are succulent and resemble cacti. This family also includes native weeds, garden ornamentals, and houseplants. Some examples include:

- Sun spurge
- Snow-on-the-mountain
- Croton
- Poinsettia
- Crown-of-thorns

All spurges cause vomiting, nausea, and/or diarrhea if ingested. Simply touching some species, such as crown-of-thorns and poinsettia, can cause skin rashes, blistering, and eye irritation. Even dried castor bean plants retain their poisonous properties.

Large doses of ingested spurge toxin result in intense burning of the mouth, throat, and stomach; uncontrollable salivation; convulsions; and sometimes coma or death. Wear gloves to prune this family and keep your pets and children away from these plants.

Leaves, stem, and roots

Leaves are simple and alternate, positioned along the stem. A few rare species feature leaves that are opposite and whorled. There is a reduction tendency; some are reduced to spines or scales.

The herbaceous, fleshy stems hold a milky latex sap that contains a variety of toxins.

Plants in this family have a tap root.

Flowers

Flowers are usually unisexual, with both male and female flowers appearing on the same plant. There are either no sepals and petals; or five, plus five, 10, or up to 1,000 stamens.

The ovary is positioned superior, and usually consists of three (though sometimes two or four) united carpels with partition walls, forming an equal number of chambers.

All spurges have small, colorful, showy flowers which can sometimes be mistaken for sepals or petals.

Seeds

The ovary matures as a capsule, with one seed per cell. Euphorbia seeds have a limited shelf life and are infrequently available on the retail market.

LAMIACEAE (formerly Labiatae)

The deadnettle family consists mostly of shrubs and herbs, and is distributed worldwide. It includes many well-known herbs (mint, sage, thyme, basil), ornamental plants (coleus, leonotis) and weeds (henbit, ground ivy, self-heal). No trees are in the group.

Leaves, stem, and roots

Lamiaceae stems are often square. The leaves are simple and undivided, in pairs up the stem with each pair at right angles to the last. They are frequently hairy or have scent glands and aromatic foliage.

Flowers

The flowers give this plant family its original name of Labiatae. They have two lips, one of which protrudes more than the other. Generally, the upper lip has two lobes and forms a hood over the lower lip. The lower lip consists of three lobes which form a landing platform for pollinating insects. The flowers occur in whorls or circles round the stem, and each flower protrudes from a pointed calyx.

Seeds

Each single flower can produce four seeds. They form at the base of the flower and develop inside the calyx. There is no seed pod; when the seeds are ripe, they simply roll out of the calyx.

LILIACEAE

The lily family has about 3,500 species distributed throughout the world. They are mainly ornamental plants, but include vegetables of the allium family (onion, garlic, leek, chive) and asparagus. Some species are used medicinally. The majority are herbaceous with a swollen storage organ, but there are also evergreen succulents (aloe) and woody evergreen climbers (lapageria).

Leaves, stem, and roots

Liliaceae leaves are often long and thin with parallel veins arising from the base, or oval with net veins arising along the stem, as in trillium. In extreme cases, the leaves have been reduced to scales (asparagus) or modified to extend into tendrils (gloriosa) or even needles (borya). Many are perennial and have storage organs such as bulbs, corms, or rhizomes. Liliaceae are monocotyledons (i.e., they only have one seed leaf).

Flowers

The flowers are often borne in racemes, although they may also be solitary, as in the tulip. They usually have six petals which may be joined to some degree, may form a tube (*Kniphofia*), may be of different sizes (*Calochortus*) or may all be of equal size and shape. There are nearly always six stamens.

Seeds

The ovary (seed pod) in this family is usually superior (inside the flower) with three chambers, and the seeds are arranged in two rows in each chamber. Seeds of many species are round, flat, and papery, although they may also be black and round.

CACTI

Cacti are distinctive, succulent plants that grow as trees, shrubs, or in the form of ground cover. Most species grow on the ground, but there is also a wide range of epiphytic species. Cacti sizes range from small and round to pole-like and tall.

Cacti are adapted to extremely arid and hot environments, possessing a wide range of anatomical and physiological features that conserve water.

The life of a cactus is seldom longer than 300 years, and there are cacti which live only 25 years (although these flower as early as their second year).

Leaves, stem, and roots

The "leaves" have developed into the prickly spines for which cacti are known. In most species, except for the sub-family of the Pereskioideae, the leaves are greatly or entirely reduced.

NEW LILIACEAE "OFFSPRING"

Many groups of Liliaceae have recently been given their own family status:

Alliaceae
Alstroemeriaceae
Amaryllidaceae
Asparagaceae
Asphodelaceae
Aspidistraceae
Calochortaceae
Colchicaceae
Convallariaceae
Fritillariaceae
Hemerocallidaceae
Hyacinthaceae
Trilliaceae
Zephyranhaceae

Even before these changes, it was difficult to know whether a plant belonged to the lily, iris, or amaryllis family. Here are some points of difference to distinguish them:

Liliaceae: 6 stamens, superior ovary (inside the flower)

Iridaceae: 3 stamens, inferior ovary (behind the flower)

Amaryllidaceae: 6 stamens, inferior ovary (behind the flower)

Cacti stems have evolved into green succulent structures that contain the chlorophyll necessary for life and growth. Nearly all cacti species have a bitter milk-like substance contained within the stem.

The cactus' root system is most often fibrous and shallow, and designed to absorb small amounts of surface moisture.

Flowers

Cactus flowers are large, with a diameter from two to 12 inches. Their colors are often conspicuous and spectacular. Like the cactus' spines and branches, its flowers arise from areoles.

The flowers, mostly radially symmetrical and hermaphrodite, bloom either by day or night, depending upon the species. Many are night-blooming, as they are pollinated by nocturnal insects or small animals, principally moths and bats.

Their shape varies from tube-like to bell-like to wheel-shaped, ranging in size from three-quarters of an inch to 12 inches. Most have numerous sepals (five to 50 or more), and change form from outside to inside, from bracts to petals. They have stamens in great numbers (from 50 to 1,500, rarely fewer).

Seeds

The berry-like fruits may contain just a few seeds or as many as 3,000, which measure one-tenth to five inches long.

MALVACEAE

The Mallow family contains more than 1,000 species, mainly found in South America. The family comprises plants, shrubs, and trees. The species of most economic importance are cotton and okra (*Hibiscus esculentus*). Many hibiscus, abutilon, and hollyhock are grown as garden flowers.

Leaves, stem, and roots

The leaves are alternate, with leafy growths where they join the stem, and they are often hairy. The calyx is composed of five sepals, sometimes joined, with another row of false sepals beneath them. The leaves are either palmate and lobed, divided (hollyhock), or undivided and toothed (hibiscus).

Flowers

The flowers of this family are large and composed of five separate petals, usually rolled up together in bud or dying. The stamens and style (stalk) form a long tube protruding from the center of the flower, and the stigma at the end of the tube is divided.

Seeds

The seed capsule is inside the flower, with five or more parts joined together. The seeds may be hairy (cotton), rounded (hibiscus), flat discs (hollyhock) or even a berry (wax mallow).

SOLANACEAE

The potato family is sizable, with nearly 4,000 species in 90 different genera. They are found in most temperate and tropical regions, with many coming from Australia and Central and South America.

Solanaceae consists mainly of herbs, a few shrubs and trees, along with many of our most well-known food plants, including potatoes, tomatoes, eggplant, and peppers. Popular ornamental plants also belong to this family, including petunia, browallia, and salpiglossis.

There are several poisonous species, namely deadly nightshade, henbane, and thorn apple. The family also includes tobacco. While it is an economically important plant, it contains the highly toxic alkaloid, nicotine.

Leaves, stem, and roots

Members of this family are often climbers or at least scrambling plants, with hairy stems and leaves. The leaves are variable; may be entire or dissected, without stipules; and are usually alternate. The calyx has five parts which may be joined, and it often remains and enlarges around the fruit, as in Cape gooseberry or the Shoo-fly plant.

Flowers

The flowers have five petals and are generally regular in shape. They may be round and flat or star-shaped, but are often bell-shaped or tubular. They usually occur in groups in the leaf axils, although they may be solitary. There are five stamens attached to the corolla tube.

Seeds

The ovary is superior (inside the flower), and the fruit is either a berry or a capsule, often containing many light brown disc-shaped seeds.

15.3 Annuals

Annuals are easy to grow, produce instant color, and bloom for most of the growing season. The main disadvantage of annuals is that you must sow them from seed or set them out as transplants every year, which involves some effort and expense.

Annuals offer you a chance to experiment with color, height, texture, and form. If you make a mistake, it is only for one growing season. Use them to fill in spaces until you install permanent plants or after an earlier perennial or bulb has already faded. Annuals are excellent for extending perennial beds and filling planters, window boxes, and hanging baskets. Examples of annuals include marigolds, petunias, alyssum, and cockscomb.

Life cycle of annuals

Annual flowers complete their life cycle in one growing season, during which time they grow, flower, and produce seed. Although some varieties will naturally re-seed themselves, the parents of each seed are unknown and certain desirable characteristics may be lost.

Snapdragons and cosmos tend to produce a large quantity of seeds that will survive through the winter and produce new plants the following growing season. Other self-seeders such as alyssum, petunia, and impatiens will scatter seed freely, but perhaps in undesirable areas.

Types of annuals

Hardy annuals are the most cold-tolerant; they will take light frost and some freezing weather without dying. In most cases, hardy annuals can be planted in the fall or spring before the last frost date. Examples include calendula, cornflower, foxglove, larkspur, pansy, sweet alyssum, stock, viola, and many dianthus cultivars. Most hardy annuals are not heat-tolerant and usually decline and die with the onset of hot summer temperatures.

Half-hardy annuals will tolerate periods of cold, damp weather but will be damaged by frost. Most half-hardy annuals can be seeded outdoors in early spring because they do not require warm soil to germinate. Seeds or transplants are normally planted after the last spring frost. Examples include baby's breath, bells of Ireland, blue sage, candytuft, cleome, forget-me-not, love-in-a-mist, snow-on-the-mountain, strawflower, and torenia. Many half-hardy annuals decline in the mid-summer heat but may rebloom in late summer or fall.

Tender annuals are native to warm tropical regions of the world. They are sensitive to cold soil temperatures and easily damaged by frost. Most seeds will rot instead of germinate when soil temperatures are below 60°F. Wait two to three weeks after the last spring frost to sow seeds or transplant outdoors. Examples include ageratum, balsam, begonia, celosia, coleus, globe amaranth, impatiens, marigold, morning glory, nasturtium, nicotiana, petunia, scarlet sage, verbena, vinca, and zinnia.

Annuals are sometimes categorized as either cool- or warm-season. Cool-season annuals, such as geranium, petunia, and snapdragon, grow best when daytime temperatures are in the 70s and 80s. Best flower production is in the spring and fall and will likely decline in the middle of a hot summer. Warm-season annuals, such as blue daze, four-o'clocks, and pentas, perform well when the daytime temperatures are in the 80s and 90s and nighttime temperatures are in the 60s and 70s.

Guidelines for purchasing annuals

Annuals can be started from seed, either directly sown or started indoors in late winter. Always check the seed packet to know when to start seeds in your growing zone.

Annuals can also be purchased in a wide range of container sizes—the bigger the plant, the higher the price tag. Smaller, less-expensive annuals grow quickly so if you have a little patience you can save a sizable sum of money.

- Annuals will continuously bloom until frost. Some annuals will even tolerate a light frost and keep growing.
- Choose annuals for their color, foliage, height, and texture. Annuals are an all-purpose fill-in for any empty space.

Figure 15-A. Leggy vs. stocky annual

Always choose short, stocky plants (left) instead of taller, lanky plants (right). The stocky plants will live longer and perform better.

- Buy plants locally if you can. While some annuals are available online, locally-grown plants have a much better chance of thriving because they are already adapted to the local environment.

Planting annuals

Before you plant

Preparing the soil is very important for flowers. Although some annuals can grow and flower in poorly-prepared soil, their performance will be substantially improved if planted in excellent soil. Prepare the flower bed in the fall before next spring's planting.

- Have the soil tested early and adjust the pH if needed. Materials to adjust pH need time to do their work.
- Check and adjust the drainage. To test the drainage, dig a hole about 10 inches deep and fill it with water. The next day, fill the hole with water again and see how long it remains. It should not take longer than eight hours to disappear. If the drainage is poor, dig furrows along the sides of the bed and add soil from the furrows to the bed. This raises the

level of the bed above the soil level, allowing excess water to seep from the bed into the furrows. Prevent soil erosion during rains by surrounding raised beds with wooden, metal, or masonry borders.

- Dig the bed to a depth of eight to 12 inches. Add four to six inches of organic matter to improve the soil structure. In the spring, add fertilizer if necessary. Spade again and rake the surface.

- Be sure you allow enough space for the plant to grow to its full width and height.

Planting a seedling/transplant

- Carefully remove the plant from its pot or cell and gently loosen the root ball so roots can easily reach into surrounding soil.

- Prune away any damaged stems, leaves, or roots. Place the plant in the hole at the same level as it was growing in its container. Backfill the hole and water thoroughly. Check the moisture level daily until the plant is established.

15.4 Perennials

Most flowering perennials prefer moderate weather but some live happily in hot, humid summer climates. Asters, chrysanthemums, and daisies are examples of flowering perennials.

Life cycle of perennials

Perennials are plants that live for three years or longer. Most bloom for only two or three weeks, although their leaves remain until winter sets in. The tops of herbaceous perennials often die in the fall, but the roots survive the winter and send up new growth during the spring. Some herbaceous perennials grow basal rosette foliage (small leaves that grow at the base of the plant, similar to biennials) after the stems die off.

Some perennial plants start to look tired and bloom less profusely after about four years, which is a good time to consider either dividing or replacing them.

Types of perennials

Hardy perennials include flowers, shrubs, and trees and can sometimes live for hundreds of years. Wildflowers are part of this group. Examples include penstemon, astilbe, delphinium, foxglove, helleborus, and daylily.

Tender perennials grown in regions with extreme winters can be considered annuals because they die back after hard frosts in the fall. If you plant tender perennials in containers, you can move them indoors in the fall and they will live through the winter. Examples of tender perennials are impatiens and lantana.

Perennials can be further divided into evergreen and deciduous. Perennials that keep their foliage all year long are evergreen perennials. Deciduous perennials will lose their foliage during the fall or winter and grow it back during the spring.

Guidelines for purchasing perennials

Perennials can be started from seed, either directly sown or started indoors, just like annuals. Perennials can also be purchased either as transplants or bare-root stock. Prices will depend on the size and maturity of the plant.

- Because most perennials bloom for only a short period each year, carefully choose them for their form, foliage, texture, and structure.
- Buy plants locally if possible. If an online company is your only option, order only from reputable mail-order companies. Very low prices may be tempting, but the plants you will receive are likely to be of low quality.
- If your mail-order plants arrive too early, store them at 50°F and keep moist.

If you can buy locally:

- Purchase potted perennials that are bushy, sturdy, and compact rather than big and tall.
- Look for signs of young, new growth and a firm, dense root system.
- Choose plants that are only partially in bloom but have many buds.
- Avoid leggy, droopy plants and those with yellowed leaves.
- Inspect the leaves for insects or diseases.

Planting new perennials

Perennials can be planted any time during the growing season, but try to plant at least a month before winter weather arrives so the roots have time to establish.

Ideally, plant spring-flowering perennials in late summer to early fall; plant perennials that bloom in late summer and fall in the spring. See Table 15-D for a perennial planning and planting chart.

Before you plant

- **Prepare your planting bed.** The process is the same as it is for annuals, but loosen the soil to a depth of 12 to 18 inches (deeper than for annuals). Be sure to add organic matter at planting time because you will not be able to add it later.
- Be sure you have allowed enough space for each plant to grow to maturity and multiply. The inclination is to plant them close together to fill the space, but they need room to expand. Fill in the bed with annuals until your perennials mature.

Don't expect your perennial flowers to look like those pictured on the label in the first year. Your patience and care will be rewarded with increasingly beautiful blooms, year after year.

Planting a perennial seedling/transplant:

- Carefully remove the plant from its pot or cell and gently loosen the root ball so roots can easily reach into surrounding soil.
- Prune away any damaged stems, leaves, or roots. Place the plant in the hole at the same level as it was growing in its container.
- Firm soil around the roots and stem, and water thoroughly.

Planting a bare-root perennial

- Prepare the soil the same as you would for planting a new perennial.
- Identify the place where the roots meet the stem and plant, and situate the plant with that spot slightly above soil level. The soil will settle and the plant will settle along with it. The point is to keep the crown covered.

- Water consistently until new growth sprouts and the plant is established.

Transplanting established perennials

If you need to transplant a perennial, do it on a cloudy day to reduce stress on the plant. It's best to transplant perennials when dormant or just starting to sprout. Early spring or fall are the best times to transplant.

Follow these steps for the best chance of transplanting success:

- Dig the new hole first. Amend the soil with organic matter, if possible.
- Fill the hole with water and let it drain.
- Carefully dig up the perennial to be moved, saving as much of the root ball as possible.
- Settle the transplant into the hole at the same soil level as its previous home. Completely surround the root ball with soil and lightly tamp down.
- Water the transplant, mulch it, and protect it, if needed, with a wind screen.

15.5 Biennials

The life cycle of biennials

Biennial plants perform similarly to annuals but complete their life cycle in two growing seasons instead of one. The first season is focused on growing roots and leaves. Rosette, or basal, foliage (leaves that surround the stem close to the ground) often carry biennials through the winter.

In the second year, biennials grow flowers, which then turn to seed. The plant dies and the seeds will sprout and begin the cycle again in the next growing season. Examples of biennials are forget-me-not, foxglove, pansy, viola, and ragwort.

All biennials are hardy and can be planted as you would annuals.

15.6 Underground Stems

The life cycle of underground stems

Underground stems (bulbs and bulb-like plants) behave much like perennials and have a similar life cycle of spring top growth, flowering, dieback, and re-emergence the following season.

Types of underground stems

The term "underground stems" loosely refers to bulbs (daffodil, garlic), corms (crocus, gladiolus), tubers and tuberous roots (caladium, dahlia), and rhizomes (iris, ginger). They are broadly grouped into spring-flowering (January to May) and summer-flowering (June to September). For purposes of this chapter, they will all be referred to as "bulbs."

The true definition of a bulb can be a bit tricky. A bulb is technically any plant that stores nutrient reserves underground in some part of its anatomy. Although they have differences, all underground stems are below-surface reproductive structures that are capable of creating a whole new plant. (See Figure 15-B.)

Bulbs and bulb-like plants are usually perennials. In general, they are a short, flattened stem that bears fleshy food-storage leaves.

Many bulbs prefer cold climates but some, such as bamboo, prefer warm temperatures. True bulbs have visible storage rings when cut in half. This group can be subdivided into tunicate bulbs and imbricate bulbs. Tunicate

Figure 15-B. Types of underground stems

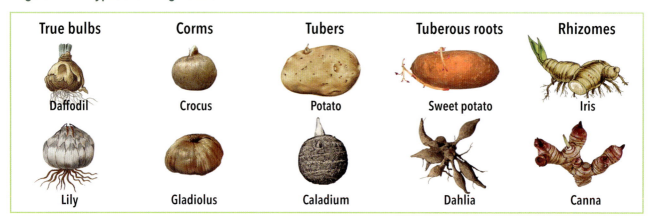

bulbs have a paper-like cover that protects the nutrient storage area. Imbricate bulbs lack this protective cover. Examples of tunicate bulbs are tulips, hyacinths, and daffodils. Lilies are an example of an imbricate bulb.

Corms are defined as an engorged stem base that serves to store nutrients. Corms have a basal plate from where the roots develop at the bottom on the corm. They also have a papery cover (tunic) like tunicate bulbs. Examples of corms are crocus, gladiolus, and tuberous begonia.

Tubers are similar to corms but do not have a papery covering or a basal plate. The roots develop out of small buds located around the tuber. Examples of tubers are anemones, caladiums, and oxalis. Potatoes, sweet potatoes, and the plant known in Mexico and Central America as "yuca" or "cassava" are other examples of tubers.

Rhizomes tend to grow horizontally, underground. Rhizomes can rise up out of the soil and form new plants. For this reason, many rhizome varieties are very invasive. Be careful when choosing plants with rhizomes and where you plant them. Examples of rhizomes are iris, lily-of-the-valley, bamboo, and various turf and ornamental grasses.

Spring-flowering bulbs (January-May)

Including spring bulbs in your garden provides early color before most annuals and perennials bloom. Popular spring bulbs include anemone, allium, crocus, tulip, narcissus/daffodils, and scilla. See Table 15-A for a planting guide of popular bulbs.

October is usually the month for planting spring-flowering bulbs. These bulbs need some time to establish a healthy root system prior to the onset of winter, so do not plant them too late.

Choose bulbs on the basis of color and flower size for specific purposes. For example, small flowers create a natural look while tall or large blooms stand out as specimen plants.

Selecting high-quality spring bulbs is very important because the flower bud has already developed before the bulb is offered for sale. Look for large, plump, firm bulbs—the larger the better. Also check the root base to make sure this area is firm, intact, and free of mold.

Not all bulbs perform equally; some are more reliable than others. The most reliable tulips are the Darwin hybrids and species tulips such as 'Linifolia' and 'Tarda'. These tulips tend to live much longer and are truly perennial in the

Table 15-A. Planting guide for flowering bulbs

Name	Name	Name	Name
Allium — Bulb, Plant in fall, 4-8 in., Hardy	**Cyclamen** — Tuber, Plant in spring, 1-2 in., Hardy	**Glory-of-the-snow** — Bulb, Plant in fall, 3 in., Hardy	**Narcissus** — Bulb, Plant in fall, 4-6 in., Hardy
Begonia, tuberous — Tuber, Plant in spring, ½ in., Lift in fall	**Daffodil** — Bulb, Plant in fall, 6-8 in., Hardy	**Hyacinth** — Bulb, Plant in fall, 4-6 in., Hardy	**Ranunculus** — Tuber, Plant in spring, 2-3 in., Lift in fall
Caladium — Tuber, Plant in spring, 2 in., Lift in fall	**Dahlia** — Tuber, Plant in spring, 2-8 in., Lift in fall	**Hyacinth, grape** — Bulb, Plant in fall, 2-3 in., Hardy	**Scilla** — Bulb, Plant in fall, 1-2 in., Hardy
Calla — Tuber, Plant in spring, 3-5 in., Lift in fall	**Foxtail lily** — Tuber, Plant in spring, 8 in., Lift in fall	**Hyacinth, wood** — Bulb, Plant in fall, 3 in., Hardy	**Spanish bluebell** — Bulb, Plant in fall, 2 in., Hardy
Canna — Rhizome, Plant in spring, 4-6 in., Lift in fall	**Freesia** — Corm, Plant in spring, 3-5 in., Lift in fall	**Iris, bearded** — Rhizome, Plant in fall, 2 in., Hardy	**Toad lily** — Rhizome, Plant in spring/sum., 3-4 in., Hardy
Crocus, fall — Corm, Plant in spring/sum., 2-4 in., Hardy	**Fritillaria, Imperial** — Bulb, Plant in fall, 6 in., Hardy	**Iris, dwarf** — Bulb, Plant in fall, 1-2 in., Hardy	**Tulip** — Bulb, Plant in fall, 6-8 in., Hardy
Crocus, spring — Bulb, Plant in fall, 2-3 in., Hardy	**Gladiolus** — Corm, Plant in spring, 5-6 in., Lift in fall	**Lilies (all)** — Bulb, Plant in spring/fall, 6-7 in., Hardy	**Windflower, Grecian** — Tuber, Plant in spring, 2-3 in., Lift in fall

garden as opposed to many other cultivars with short life spans. *Crocus thomasianus* is a tough, durable crocus that is one of the best species to use either in lawns or areas with compacted soil. This vigorous corm will readily naturalize, even in areas troubled by rodents.

Summer-flowering bulbs (June to September)

This group includes amaryllis, tuberous begonia, caladium, calla lily, colchicum (autumn crocus), dahlia, gladiolus, lycoris, lily, and spider lily. Plant summer-flowering bulbs from April to May (after the last frost) except lily bulbs, which should be planted in late fall.

Planting bulbs

Before you plant

- Keep bulbs cool (60°F-65°F) until planting time.
- Most bulbs need full sun, so select a planting site that will provide at least five to six hours of direct sunlight each day. Bulbs that are left in the ground year after year should have eight to 10 hours of daily sunlight for good flowering.
- Adequate drainage is also an important consideration, as most bulb plants will easily rot if overwatered or planted in wet areas.
- Many soil types are tolerated, but most bulbs prefer soil rich in organic matter. Be prepared to amend clay or poor soils.
- Decide whether you prefer a naturalized appearance or a more formal garden. That will determine how the bulbs should be planted.
- Check the correct planting depth for each bulb with a successful local grower or other good source. Catalogs and reference books can be incorrect, depending upon soil type and condition. In general, the planting hole should be two and one-half to three times the diameter of the bulb. If you plant bulbs too shallowly, you may encourage frost heaving and lose the bulbs. Do not plant bulbs too deeply. Underground stems only have so much energy to grow upward and emerge above the soil to get the light they need to produce their leaves, stems, and flowers.

The planting process

- Prepare the bulb bed to the proper depth. Protect bulbs from wildlife by sprinkling crushed oyster shells in the bed bottom or lining the bed with hardware cloth.
- For individual planting holes, loosen the soil below the depth the bulb is to be planted. Mix a tablespoon of slow-release fertilizer that is high in phosphates, such as bone meal, into each planting hole. Cover with a layer of soil to ensure the bulbs do not contact the fertilizers directly.
- Set the bulb upright, with any roots pointing downward, in the planting hole and cover it with amended soil.

ABOUT SUMMER-FLOWERING BULBS

Before investing any time and money, be aware that many summer-flowering bulbs are not cold-hardy. They will have to be dug up in late fall and properly stored in a frost-free location over the winter.

- If bulbs are being used to naturalize an area, toss them and plant them where they fall to create a random effect.

Bulb maintenance

Foliage

Bulb foliage is very important. Allow the foliage of spring-blooming bulbs to die back on its own. The plants must perform photosynthesis to store food in bulb and form flower buds for the next year. After the leaves turn yellow, cut and remove the stems and foliage of the plants to prevent diseases from infecting next year's plants.

Watering

Normal rainfall usually provides enough moisture for bulbs. A long spell of dry weather, however, will necessitate a weekly soaking until the rain returns. Don't neglect your bulbs after they bloom.

Mulching

In early spring, push mulch away from emerging leaves as soon as danger of severe freezing has passed. If mulch is allowed to interfere with new growth, the shoots may be pale green or colorless and new stems and foliage can get broken.

Fertilizing

After the plants bloom, fertilize them lightly with 5-10-10 fertilizer. Use no more than one pound for a 50-square-foot flower bed. Avoid high-nitrogen fertilizer and be sure to keep fertilizer off the leaves and away from roots, as it will burn them. In addition to 5-10-10 fertilizer, you can use bone meal as an extra source of phosphorus.

Staking

Staking bulbs is sometimes necessary. Some bulb flowers will face in only one direction. Use the stake to orient the flower to face toward the front of the bed.

Deadheading

When flowers fade, cut them off to prevent seed formation. Development of seed pods takes stored food from the bulbs. Deadheading may also promote longer bloom periods. Avoid removing any foliage.

Transplanting bulbs

Many spring-blooming bulbs are best moved in the fall only after the foliage has disappeared. Bulbs dug and moved before foliage fades are useless.

Bulbs can be difficult to locate once the foliage is gone, so install some kind of location marker in the spring to easily locate the bulbs for transplanting in the fall.

Propagating bulbs

Bulbs such as daffodils, snowdrops, and grape hyacinths multiply and should be divided regularly. Others, such as tulips and hyacinths, only replace the old bulb each year.

Bulbs are best divided and transplanted when they are dormant, in late June or July.

Carefully separate clumps or gently remove the small bulblets at the base and replant them according to recommended spacing. Always plant with the roots pointing downward. (See Figure 15-C.)

Storing bulbs

Many summer-flowering bulbs are tender, and must be dug and stored after the leaves have yellowed.

Figure 15-C. Corm with cormlets

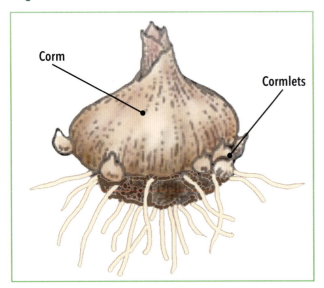

Digging and curing bulbs

Use a spading fork to carefully lift the bulbs from the ground. Wash off any soil that clings to the bulbs, except those which will be stored in pots. Leave the soil on achimenes, begonia, canna, caladium, and dahlias.

Cure the bulbs by spreading them out in a shaded place to dry. Curing typically takes one to three days.

The storing process

When the cured bulbs are dry, store them away from sunlight in a cool, dry basement, cellar, garage, or shed at 50°F to 55°F. Avoid temperatures below 45°F or above 70°F. Be sure air freely circulates around stored bulbs.

Store bulbs with soil around them (achimenes, etc.) in clumps on a slightly moistened layer of peat moss or sawdust. The storage temperature recommendations are the same as for cured bulbs. Rinse the clumped bulbs and separate them just before planting the following spring.

BULB-STORAGE NOTES

- Bulbs can be held temporarily at 60°F to 65°F.
- Don't store bulbs in a garage or any other area where exhaust fumes are present.
- Bulbs purchased in the fall, held over the winter, and planted in spring will not flower.
- Never dig bulbs for transplanting or propagation until after the foliage has yellowed and died back.
- Check bulbs periodically over the winter for mold or dryness.

Never store bulbs more than two or three layers deep as they will generate heat which can cause decay.

15.7 Landscape Design with Herbaceous Plants

Much of the excitement of creating an herbaceous border or flower bed lies in the great flexibility of its design.

One of the first decisions you must make when designing a landscape is to determine the look you want. Do you want it to soothe the soul, evoke happiness, attract birds and pollinators, or simply be versatile from year to year?

Planning a border is best done to scale on graph paper. The hardest task—organizing the selection of plants—can be simplified if only two main mass forms are considered: drifts (elongated groupings of a plant) and clumps (circular groupings of a species or a single large plant, such as a peony). For the best effect, vary the length of drifts and the diameter and height of clumps. Dimensions should always be in proportion to the overall size of the border.

See **Chapter 26, Landscape Design,** for extensive detail about planning for space, color, and function. Always plan your garden before you buy anything to minimize errors and expense.

Assess and amend the planting site

- Monitor the sun's location in the morning, afternoon, and evening and understand where the sun rises and sets in relation to your planting beds.
- Understand the type of soil you have (clay, sand, or loam) and how efficiently it drains. Amend it if necessary.
- Determine the pH of your soil with a soil test and amend it with lime or sulfur, if needed. If you are planting azaleas, rhododendrons, mountain laurel, or other plants that like acidic soil, the top six to 12 inches will likely need amending.

Selecting plants

- Know your **growing zone** and spring and fall frost dates.
- Consider the succession of blooms so that there is always something colorful flowering in your yard (see Table 15-C). Don't forget winter: crocus and helleborus often poke through the snow.
- Choose plants that fit your lifestyle and personality. Your garden is definitely a reflection of you. Know your time constraints and don't plant more than you can care for.

ABOUT CUT FLOWERS

You can often know whether or not a particular flower is good for cutting because it will say so on the plant label.

If the label says "good for drying," the flowers of that plant will be good for cutting as well.

Flowers that last for a week or more are considered best for arrangements. If no one in the house is allergic, bring in flowers with a nice fragrance.

There are many more, but some of the best cut flowers are:

Daffodil • Lily • Sunflower • Peony
Dutch iris • Carnation • Liatris
Snapdragon • Gladiolus • Chrysanthemum
Aster • Zinnia • Sweet William • Sweet pea

- Buy in odd numbers (three, five, seven, or more) and plant in odd numbers for the greatest visual appeal. The exception is a shrub or large perennial that can hold its own without being grouped with other plants.
- Limit plant height to two-thirds the width of the bed or else the bed will look crowded and overwhelmed.
- Another exception is if the planting bed is round. A single large/tall plant can be placed in the center, with medium-height plants surrounding it, and small plants around the outside edge (i.e., in concentric circles).
- Only get enough plants to fill the space. Avoid overplanting/overcrowding, which can cause sun to be shaded out and air circulation to be poor. Check

the plant label to know the mature height and width of the plant, and space accordingly.

- Typical landscapes already have multiple shades of green amongst the trees and shrubs. If you enjoy changing color schemes yearly, you can use annuals. Most gardeners, however, grow tired of planting all annuals each year and decide to add some perennials. Choose the colors you like the most for the perennials (so you won't tire of them), then add annuals to complement those perennial colors. See **Chapter 26, Landscape Design,** for more about color schemes.

- An important growing trend is to plant flowers which attract pollinators. See Table 15-B for colors that attract these beneficial creatures.

Tips for arranging plants

- Waves or curves follow a natural order and are much more pleasing to the eye as opposed to sharp angles, which are more common in formal gardens.

- Establish plants in groups large enough to form irregularly shaped masses of color or texture rather than planting in "single file" or perfect rows.

Table 15-B. Traits of flowering-plant pollinators

	Pollinator							
	Bats	**Bees**	**Beetles**	**Birds**	**Butterflies**	**Flies**	**Moths**	**Wind**
Color	Dull, white, green, or purple	Bright white, yellow, blue, or UV	Dull white or green	Scarlet, orange, red, or white	Bright, including red and purple	Pale, dull to dark brown or purple, flecked with translucent patches	Pale and dull red, purple, pink, or white	Dull green, brown, or colorless; petals absent or reduced
Nectar guides	Absent	Present	Absent	Absent	Present	Absent	Absent	Absent
Nectar	Abundant, somewhat hidden	Usually present	Sometimes present, unhidden	Ample, deeply hidden	Ample, deeply hidden	Usually absent	Ample, deeply hidden	None
Odor	Strong, musty; emitted at night	Fresh, mild, pleasant	None to strongly fruity or fetid	None	Faint but fresh	Putrid	Strong, sweet; emitted at night	None
Pollen	Ample	Limited; often sticky and scented	Ample	Modest	Limited	Modest	Limited	Abundant, not sticky
Flower shape	Regular, bowl-like; closed during the day	Shallow; has a landing platform; tubular	Large, bowl-like (Magnolia)	Large, funnel-shaped; cupped, strong perch support	Narrow, tubular with spur; wide landing pad	Shallow, funnel-shaped, or complex and trap-like	Regular; tubular without a lip	Regular; small with stigmas exerted

- Foundation plants (evergreens and deciduous trees) should be planted first, shrubs second, herbaceous perennials and bulbs third, and annuals last.
- Repeat the same plants within the bed to keep it from looking chaotic.
- Arrange plants by height to allow sun to reach each plant and be able to see, water, and inspect the plants. Short plants (six to 12 inches) should be placed at the front of the garden bed. Medium-height plants (12 to 24 inches) should be planted in the middle of the garden bed, and tall plants (24 to 36 inches) should be planted in the back.
- Offset tall, lanky plants with rounder plants for greater eye appeal.
- You can also arrange and grow herbaceous plants in containers. See **Chapter 25, Container Gardening,** for complete details about container types, potting media, and caring for container plants.

15.8 Herbaceous Garden Maintenance

Preventing weeds

There are four ways for weeds to invade your garden:

- Air
- Transfer from animals or humans
- The soil of transplanted plants
- Plants from a low-end garden center

Weed seeds need sufficient sunlight to germinate and grow. If sufficient sunlight is not available, the presence of weeds in your garden is greatly diminished. See the **Sustainable Weed Maintenance Plan** in Chapter 13.

Mulching

There are three types of mulch:

- Organic: bark, compost, grass clippings, leaves, pine needles, wood chips, peat moss, hay, and straw
- Inorganic: gravel, stones, sand, rubber, and marble chip.
- Films: Black plastic, corrugated cardboard, newspaper, mulching paper, and aluminized paper or foil

Mulch serves to cover bare ground/prevent weeds, conserve moisture around plants, and provide a neat appearance for your garden beds. Some mulching tips:

- Apply mulch around ornamental plants immediately after planting.
- Delay fall mulching until after the ground has frozen (except for new plantings) to discourage rodents from overwintering in it.
- Do not over-mulch as it will suffocate shallow-rooted ornamentals and cause stem decay on trees and shrubs.

Watering

Plants can survive drought to varying degrees. Look for signs of heat/drought stress:

- Upward leaf-curling or rolling
- Leaves begin to yellow and/or brown
- Blossoms or fruit drops from plant
- Interior needle drop on evergreens
- Undersized fruits, vegetables, and nuts
- Produce with an "off" flavor

Secondary problems associated with drought include:

- Blossom-end rot of tomato, bell pepper, squash, and melon
- Increased wildlife activity and subsequent damage
- Increased insect damage

Long-term consequences of drought include:

- Increased potential of attack by borers
- Increased potential for plant diseases
- Root death
- Diminished winter hardiness
- Terminal dieback; dead twigs and branches
- Eventual plant death

Prioritize watering

High priority:

Trees and shrubs. Water young and newly planted trees first. Large, mature shade trees and shrubs need watering at the first sign of wilting or if drought is severe.

Medium-high priority:

Perennials, fruit and nut trees, small fruits and vegetables, and turf younger than one year.

Low priority:

Annual flowers, herbs, ornamental grasses, and established turf.

Pruning, deadheading, and pinching back

Pruning

Pruning improves the shape of a plant, controls its size, and increases its productivity. Use clean, sharp pruning shears to cut plants back and encourage bushiness, and occasionally prune back overgrown stems to create better air flow. Herbaceous plants can be cut to the ground at the end of the season. See **Chapter 17, Pruning,** for instructions.

Deadheading

Deadheading is the process of removing flowers after they have bloomed and faded in order to halt seed production (see Figure 15-D). This practice keeps the plant healthier, conserves its energy, and improves the appearance of both the plant and garden. Regularly deadheading annuals will keep them re-blooming until frost.

If you want the plant to self-sow, stop deadheading blooms at the end of the season so that any remaining flowers can go to seed.

Pinching back

Pinching back can be thought of as a "pre-pruning" task as it is done before the plant blooms. This practice keeps the plant bushy and compact, and delays blooming in mums so they flower at the right time in the fall.

To pinch a plant back, grab the terminal growth or bud at the tip of the plant and literally pinch it off.

Most annuals respond well to pinching back, especially chrysanthemum, coleus, cosmos, snapdragon, and zinnia. Not all plants can or should be pinched back, however, like stock, sunflowers, and cockscomb. Check before you pinch!

Disbudding is a form of pinching back that involves actually pinching off lateral buds as soon as they appear. This action helps direct energy to root development and will result in fewer, but larger, flowers.

Figure 15-D. Perennials that may bloom again after deadheading

How to deadhead flowers with lateral buds

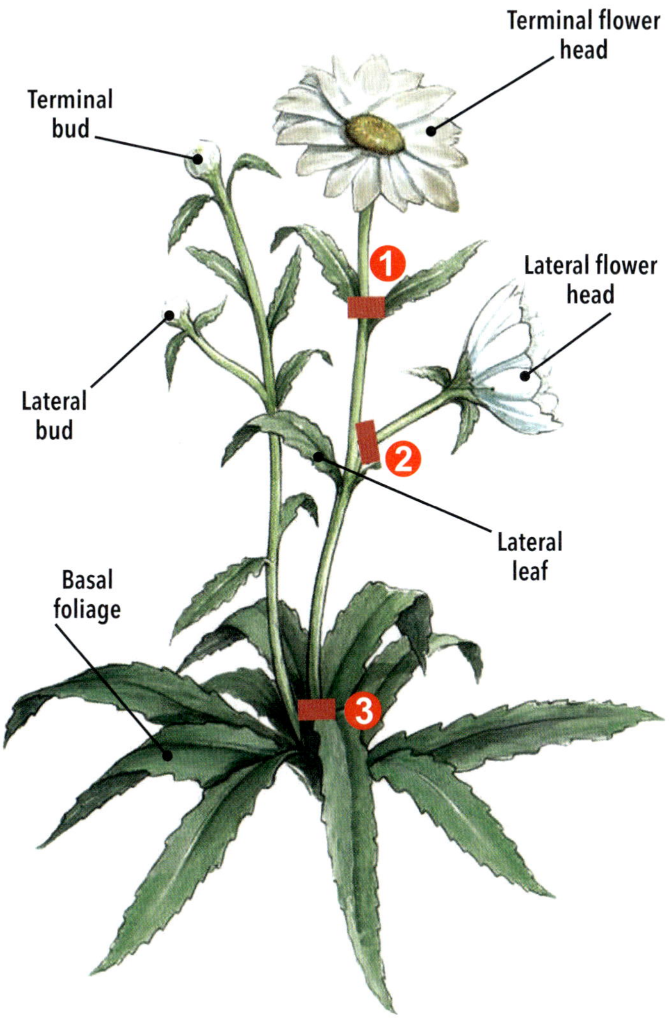

Labels on diagram:
- Terminal flower head
- Terminal bud
- Lateral flower head
- Lateral bud
- Lateral leaf
- Basal foliage

① Cut a fading flower down to a lateral flower, leaf, or bud.

② When the next lowest lateral flower begins to fade, prune it to another lateral flower or bud. Continue until there are no more lateral flowers or buds.

③ When all of the buds have faded/been deadheaded and the foliage starts to look raggedy, prune the entire stem back to the basal foliage (if it is still there).

Common name	Scientific name
Allwood pink	*Dianthus x allwoodii* cvs.
Baby's breath	*Gypsophila paniculata* & cvs.
Bee balm	*Monarda didyma* & cvs.
Blanket flower	*Gaillardia x grandiflora* cvs.
Butterfly weed	*Asclepias tuberosa*
Checker mallow*	*Sidalcea malviflora* & cvs.
Cheddar pink	*Dianthus gratianopolitanus* & cvs.
Columbine	*Aquilegia* spp. & cvs.
Culver's root*	*Veronicastrum virginicum*
Dame's rocket	*Hesperis matronalis* & cvs.
Delphinium*	*Delphinium* spp. & cvs.
False sunflower	*Heliopsis helianthoides* & cvs.
Foxglove*	*Digitalis* spp. & cvs.
Gaura	*Gaura lindheimeri* & cvs.
Geum	*Geum* spp. & cvs.
Globe thistle*	*Echinops ritro* & cvs.
Golden marguerites	*Anthemis tinctoria* & cvs.
Hardy begonia	*Begonia grandis* ssp. *evansiana*
Hollyhock*	*Alcea rosea* cvs.
Italian bugloss	*Anchusa asurea*
Jupiter's beard	*Centranthus ruber*
Lavender	*Lavandula* spp. & cvs.
Lilyleaf ladybell	*Adenophora lilifolia*
Lupine*	*Lupinus* spp. & cvs.
Masterwort	*Astrantia major* & cvs.
Monkshood	*Aconitum* spp. & cvs.
Mountain bluet	*Centaurea montana*
Painted daisy	*Tanacetum coccineum* & cvs.
Patrinia	*Patrinia scabiosifolia*
Penstemon*	*Penstemon barbatus* & cvs.
Phlox	*Phlox paniculata* cvs.
Pincushion flower	*Scabiosa* spp. & cvs.
Purple coneflower	*Echinacea purpurea*
Purple toadflax*	*Linaria purpurea* & cvs.
Rose campion	*Lychnis coronaria* & cvs.
Salvia (perennial)*	*Salvia nemorosa* & cvs.
Shasta daisy	*Leucanthemum x superbum* cvs.
Sneezeweed	*Helenium autumnale*
Spike speedwell*	*Veronica spicata* cvs.
Spiderwort	*Tradescantia x andersoniana* cvs.
Stokes' aster	*Stokesia laevis* & cvs.
Sweet violet	*Viola odorata* & cvs.
Tickseed	*Coreopsis* spp. & cvs.
Yarrow	*Achillea* spp. & cvs.
Yellow corydalis	*Corydalis lutea*

*Allow at least 70% of the stem to flower before deadheading.

15.9 Sexual Propagation of Herbaceous Plants

To get a good start toward raising vigorous flowering annuals or perennials, buy viable seed packaged for the current year. Include some newer varieties that have desirable traits. Seed saved from previous years may germinate slowly and erratically, or produce poor seedlings.

Seed propagation has several advantages over vegetative division:

- Diseases are less likely to be carried over with seed.
- Less common varieties are more often available as seed.
- Seed of species plants (also known as open-pollinated varieties) will come true-to-type; cultivar seeds may not.

See **Chapter 23, Plant Propagation,** for extensive information.

Starting seeds indoors

Keep the seed dry and cool until planted. If seed must be stored, refrigerate packets in an airtight container with one-half inch of powdered milk in it to absorb excess moisture.

When you are ready, organize your pots/cell-packs, media, and distilled water, and then start planting.

- Fill shallow containers with damp, sterile seed-starting mix.
- Generally, plant seeds to a depth of one to three times their diameter. See the seed packet for specific instructions.
- Mist or bottom-water to wet the planting medium instead of watering from overhead, which can disturb the seeds.
- Cover and place the container in warm, light, or dark location, depending upon the plant's requirements.
- As soon as the first green sprout appears, move the container to a cooler, brighter location.
- Ideally, the temperature should be 65°F-68°F and have bright light for 15 hours a day. Fluorescent grow lights work well.
- Protect against damping-off (fungal disease) by allowing air to circulate freely around seedlings.
- Harden off transplants prior to transplanting by setting them outside for successively longer periods each day for about a week before planting. This helps prevent transplant shock.

When to plant seeds

Do not rush to start seeds outdoors or to set out started plants. Delay this until after the last frost date, which you can find on the **National Gardening Association website** by entering your zip code.

Most seeds will not germinate well in soils below 60°F. If the soil is too cold, seeds will remain dormant until the soil warms and they may rot in the interim. There are some cold-loving annuals, like larkspur or Shirley poppies, that can be sown in late fall or very early spring.

Another reason direct-seeded plants fail to germinate properly is because the soil surface has "caked," and water cannot easily penetrate it. To prevent this, sow the seeds in vermiculite-filled furrows.

- Make furrows in soil about one-half inch deep. If soil is dry, water the furrow, then fill it with fine vermiculite and sprinkle with water.

- Make another shallow furrow in the vermiculite and sow the seed at the rate recommended on the package.
- Cover the seed with a layer of vermiculite. Using a nozzle adjusted for a fine mist, thoroughly water the seeded area.
- Keep the seed bed well-watered or cover with a fine mulch (e.g., coir) to keep the sprouting seeds moist.

Thinning

After direct-sown sprouts develop the first pair of true leaves, thin them to the recommended spacing. Thinning allows plants to receive enough light, water, nutrients, and room to develop fully.

If plants have been seeded in vermiculite-filled furrows, excess seedlings can be transplanted to another spot without injury. Zinnias are an exception; transplanted plants will flower as a large, nearly naked corolla with a few colorful petals, a phenomenon referred to as "Mexican hats."

Another exception to the thinning rule is sweet alyssum, an annual which is particularly susceptible to damping-off. To ensure a good stand of plants, sow the seed in hills and do not bother to thin the seedlings.

Your flower show can begin several weeks earlier if you set out transplants rather than sow seeds. Some annuals require a long time to grow before they will bloom and must get an indoor head-start.

15.10 Asexual Propagation of Herbaceous Plants

There are two primary ways to asexually propagate herbaceous plants: division and cuttings.

Division

There are three main reasons to divide perennials:

- To control the size of the plant
- To rejuvenate the plant
- To increase the number of plants

Most perennials left in the same place for more than three to five years are likely to be overcrowded, with dead, unsightly centers. The center of the clump will grow poorly, if at all, and the flowers will be sparse. The clump will have a "doughnut" appearance and, at this point, the plant needs to be divided (see Figure 15-E).

In Maryland, divide spring and summer bloomers after the flowers fade, either in late summer or fall as the foliage dies down. Divide fall-blooming herbaceous perennials in early spring, as soon as the growing tips of the plant have emerged. Dividing this early gives the plant time for the roots to acclimate before hot weather sets in. Spring-divided perennials often bloom a little later than usual.

Some perennials, such as chrysanthemums and asters, may need to be divided every one or two years or they will crowd themselves into non-flowering clumps. Bleeding heart and peonies may never need to be divided unless you want to multiply your stock.

To divide mature clumps of perennials:

- Prepare the area where you plan to put your new divisions before you lift the parent plant.
- It is not advisable to divide perennials on hot, sunny days. Wait for a cloudy stretch of weather, ideally with several days of light rain in the forecast, to help avoid transplant shock.

Figure 15-E. Properly-spaced iris vs. overgrown clump

Figure 15-F. Dahlia garden completely from cuttings

- The day before you divide, thoroughly water the plant to help maintain the root ball and keep it moist when it comes time to dig it up.
- Prune the stems and foliage to six inches from the ground before you dig. Keep only three to five vigorous side shoots from the outer part of the clump. Discard the center of the clump.
- Be careful not to over-divide; too small a clump will not perform very well (if at all) in the first year after replanting.

Cuttings

Many herbaceous plants can be propagated from either tip or root cuttings. In general, tip cuttings are easier for beginners to propagate than root cuttings. For detailed information about all kinds of propagation, please see **Chapter 24, Plant Propagation.**

Tip cuttings

Plants for tip-cutting include dahlia, boxwood, and gardenia (see Figure 15-F). Select new growth and make tip cuttings three to six inches long. Leave all foliage except that which will be below the soil line and treat the base of the cutting with a rooting hormone.

Insert one cutting per pot filled with damp sand and place it in a lightly shaded place. Cover with clear plastic and keep moist.

When cuttings do not pull easily out of the soil, they have begun to root. Make air holes in the plastic sheet or raise it to increase air circulation. This will harden the cuttings.

Root cuttings

Make root cuttings of phlox, baby's breath, and oriental poppy. Dig the plants in spring. Select pencil-size roots; cut them into four-inch sections. Put each piece in a peat pot filled with a mix of two parts sand, one part soil, and one part peat moss. Water thoroughly.

Additional resources:

Native Plants
Invasive Plants
Lawns (grasses)
Attracting Wildlife to Your Garden

Table 15-C. Perennial bloom times (by season)

Spring-blooming	Summer-blooming	Fall-blooming	Winter-blooming
Agapanthus	Alchemilla	Acacia	Acacia
Amaryllis	Allium	Allium	Alstroemeria
Anemone	Alstroemeria	Alstroemeria	Amaryllis
Apple blossom	Amaranthus	Amaranthus	Asiatic lily
Azalea	Aster	Anemone	Carnation
Bird of paradise	Astilbe	Anise hyssop	'Casa Blanca' lily
Brodea	Baby's breath	Asiatic Lily	Chrysanthemum
Calla lily	Bird of paradise	Aster	Cyclamen
'Casa Blanca' lily	Calla lily	Baby's breath	Evergreens
Cherry blossom	Campanula	Bittersweet	Gerbera daisy
Cornflower	Carnation	Carnation	Ginger
Cosmos	'Casa Blanca' lily	Chinaberry	Helleborus
Creeping phlox	Catmint	Chrysanthemum	Holly berry
Daffodil	Chrysanthemum	Cockscomb	Narcissus
Dahlia	Cockscomb	Coreopsis	Orchid
Delphinium	Coneflower	Cosmos	Pansy
Delwood	Coreopsis	Dahlia	Pepperberry
Forsythia	Cosmos	Echinops	Phlox
Freesia	Dahlia	Freesia	Protea
Gardenia	Daisy	Gerbera daisy	Queen Anne's lace
'Gloriosa' lily	Delphinium	Gladiolus	Roses
Heather	Dianthus	'Gloriosa' lily	Star of Bethlehem
Helleborus	Didiscus	Hypericum	Statice
Hyacinth	Euphorbia	Iris	
Iris	Foxglove	Juniper	**Long-blooming**
Larkspur	Freesia	Kalanchoe	Aster (Stokes')
Liatris	Gardenia	Kangaroo paw	Balloon flower
Lilac	Genista	Liatris	Black-eyed susan
Lisianthus	Ginger	Lobelia	Bleeding heart
Narcissus	Gladiolus	Misty Blue	Campanula
Orchid	'Gloriosa' Lily	Obedient plant	Catmint
Peach blossom	Hallaconia	Orchid	Coreopsis
Peony	Heather	Pepperberry	Corydalis
Phlox	Hollyhock	Protea	'Stella D'Oro' daylily
Poppy	Hosta	Queen Anne's Lace	Dianthus
Protea	Hydrangea	Quince	Echinacea
Pussy willow	Hypericum	Rose	Gaillardia
Ranunculus	Iris	Rover	Jupiter's beard
Rhododendron	Kangaroo paw	Rowen berry	Mallow
Rose	Lavender	Salvia	Pincushion flower
Seeded eucalyptus	Liatris	Solidago	Red valerian
Solidago	Lilac	Star of Bethlehem	Sedum
Stephanotis	Lisianthus	Statice	Soapwort
Stock	Obedient plant	Sunflower	Speedwell
Sweet pea	Russian sage	Toad lily	Spiderwort
Tulip	Salvia	Turtlehead	Sunray flower
Viburnum	'Stargazer' lily	Yarrow	Yarrow
Wax flower	Statice	Zinnia	
Zinnia	Yarrow		

The tables on this and the following pages are to help you plan your garden so that there is interest from early spring to late fall and even through the winter.

Table 15-C: Blooms by season

Table 15-D: Comprehensive perennial planning and planting guide

Table 15-E: Annuals for specific environments

Table 15-F: Perennials for specific environments

Table 15-G: Herbaceous plants for drying

Table 15-H: Herbaceous plants with foliage interest

Table 15-D. Perennial planning and planting guide

Key: ☀ = Full Sun ◐ = Part Sun ● = Shade
D = Soil dries quickly
M = Average moisture/good drainage
W = Soil stays evenly moist but not wet

ES = Early spring ESU = Early summer EF = Early fall
MS = Mid-spring MSU = Mid-summer MF = Mid-fall
LS = Late spring LSU = Late summer F = Frost

Note: Plants in containers may bloom up to 4 weeks sooner.

Common name	Scientific name	Bloom color(s)	Bloom time	Height (inches)	Spacing (inches)	Light	Soil
Anemone	*Anemone*	pink shades	MSU-MF	24-48	18-24	☀ ◐	M-W
Aster	*Aster*	purple/pink/blue	ESU-MF	24-48	12-18	☀	M-W
Astilbe	*Astilbe*	pink/peach/black	MSU-LSU	10-48	12-18	◐	M-W
Balloon flower	*Platycodon*	blue/white	ESU-EF	15-40	12-18	☀ ◐	M
Barrenwort	*Epimedium*	pink/white/yellow	LS-ESU	10-30	12-15	◐ ●	M
Bee balm	*Monarda*	purple/red/white	MSU-LSU	30-42	15-20	☀ ◐	M-W
Bellflower	*Campanula*	purple	LS-EF	6-72	10-24	☀ ◐	M
Betony	*Stachy*	white only	MSU-LSU	10-12	12-15	☀ ◐	D-M
Bleeding heart	*Dicentra*	pink/white	ESU-EF	10-36	12-30	☀ ◐ ●	M-W
Boltonia	*Boltonia*	pink/white	LSU-MF	36-60	18-24	☀	D-M-W
Bugbane	*Cimicifuga*	white only	LSU-EF	60-72	24-30	◐	M
Canna	*Canna*	orange/yellow/red/purple/pink	MSU-EF	36-84	24	☀ ◐	M
Catmint	*Nepeta*	blue/purple	MSU-EF	12-48	12-30	☀ ◐	D-M
Colewort	*Crambe*	white only	ESU	60	36-48	☀	M
Columbine	*Aquilegia*	pink/yellow/red/blue	LS-ESU	6-36	12-18	☀ ◐	M
Coral bells	*Heuchera*	pink/red	MSU-LSU	10-24	15-18	☀ ◐ ●	M
Corydalis	*Corydalis*	yellow/blue	MS-EF	8-15	8-12	◐ ●	M-W
Colewort	*Crambe*	pink/white	ES	24-48	36-48	◐	M
Coneflower	*Rudbeckia*	yellow	MSU-MF	24-30	18-24	☀	M
Coneflower (purple)	*Echinacea*	purple/pink	ESU-MF	40	18-24	☀ ◐	D-M
Culver's root	*Veronicastrum*	white only	LSU-EF	48-60	24-30	☀ ◐	M-W
Daylily	*Hemerocallis*	purple/pink/red/yellow	ESU-MF	18-48	15-30	☀ ◐	D-M
Deadnettle	*Lamium*	pink + foliage	ESU-MSU	12	12-18	◐ ●	D-M
Delphinium	*Delphinium*	purple/pink/blue	ESU-MF	24-84	12-30	☀	M

continued on next page

continued from previous page

Table 15-D. Perennial planning and planting guide

Key: ☀ = Full Sun ◐ = Part Sun ● = Shade
D = Soil dries quickly
M = Average moisture/good drainage
W = Soil remains evenly moist but not wet

ES = Early spring ESU = Early summer EF = Early fall
MS = Mid-spring MSU = Mid-summer MF = Mid-fall
LS = Late spring LSU = Late summer F = Frost

Note: Plants in containers may bloom up to 4 weeks sooner.

Common name	Scientific name	Bloom color(s)	Bloom time	Height (inches)	Spacing (inches)	Light	Soil
False sunflower	*Heliopsis*	yellow	ESU-EF	48	18-30	☀	D-M
Ferns	*Ferns*	foliage	ES-F	12-72	12-30	☀ ◐ ●	M-W
Foam flower	*Tiarella*	white only	MS-EF	12-18	12-18	◐ ●	M-W
Foxglove	*Digitalis*	pink/red/white/yellow	ESU-MSU	30-48	12-18	☀ ◐	M
Gayfeather	*Liatris*	purple/pink/white	MSU-EF	24-60	12-18	☀ ◐	D-M
Geranium	*Geranium*	white/peach/red/pink	MS-LSU	8-48	12-24	☀ ◐	M
Globe thistle	*Echinops*	blue/purple	MSU-LSU	30-36	15	☀ ◐	M
Goatsbeard	*Aruncus*	white only	MS-ESU	8-72	12-36	◐	M-W
Globe amaranth	*Gomphrena*	red/orange	MSU-EF	24	12	☀	M
Globe flower	*Trollius*	orange/yellow	MS-ESU	16-24	12-18	◐ ●	M-W
Hollyhock	*Alcea*	pink/red/white/yellow	ESU-EF	48-96	18-24	☀	M
Helenium	*Helenium*	orange/red	LSU-EF	36	15-18	☀	M-W
Heliotrope	*Heliotropium*	purple	ESU-EF	24-26	18	☀	M
Hosta	*Hosta*	+ foliage	MSU-MF	12-48	12-36	◐ ●	D-M-W
Iris, bearded	*Iris x germanica*	all colors	MS-ESU	10-48	18-24	☀	M
Iris, Japanese	*Iris ensata*	pink/purple/red/blue	ESU-MSU	36-48	18-24	☀	M-W
Iris, Siberian	*Iris siberica*	purple/yellow	MS-ESU	10-36	15-18	☀ ◐	D-M-W
Lady's mantle	*Alchemilla*	yellow	ESU-LSU	18	15-18	◐	M
Lavender	*Lavandula*	pink/purple	ESU-LSU	12-36	12-36	☀	D-M
Lenten rose	*Helleborus*	pink/purple/white	ES-ESU	8-18	12-24	◐ ●	M
Lily-of-the-valley	*Convallaria*	white only	MS-ESU	8-12	3-6	◐ ●	M-W
Lilyturf	*Liriope*	purple/white	LSU-EF	20	12-18	☀ ◐ ●	D-M-W
Lobelia	*Lobelia*	purple/red	MSU-EF	36-48	12-18	☀ ◐	M-W
Lupine (Lupine)	*Lupinus*	most colors	ESU-MSU	18-24	15-18	☀	M

continued on next page

continued from previous page

Table 15-D. Perennial planning and planting guide

Key: ☼ = Full Sun ◐ = Part Sun ● = Shade
D = Soil dries quickly
M = Average moisture/good drainage
W = Soil remains evenly moist but not wet

ES = Early spring   ESU = Early summer   EF = Early fall
MS = Mid-spring   MSU = Mid-summer   MF = Mid-fall
LS = Late spring   LSU = Late summer   F = Frost

Note: Plants in containers may bloom up to 4 weeks sooner.

Common name	Scientific name	Bloom color(s)	Bloom time	Height (inches)	Spacing (inches)	Light	Soil
Lungwort	*Pulmonaria*		MS	12	12-18	◐●	M-W
Mallow	*Malva*		MSU-MF	24-48	15-24	☼	M
Meadow rue	*Thalictrum*		MSU-LSU	36-96	12-18	◐	M-W
Mum	*Chrysanthemum*		LSU-MF	14-18	12-24	☼	M
Oriental poppy	*Papaver*		ESU	24-40	15-20	☼	M
Penstemon	*Penstemon*		ESU-EF	18-36	12-18	☼ ◐	D-M
Peony	*Paeonia*		MSU	26-48	18-30	☼	M
Phlox	*Phlox*		ESU-EF	30-40	18-24	☼	M
Pinks	*Dianthus*		MSU-EF	4-18	8-24	☼	D-M
Primrose	*Primula*		MS-MSU	4-24	8-12	◐●	M-W
Russian sage	*Perovskia*		MSU-EF	36-48	24-30	☼	D-M
Salvia	*Salvia*		MS-LSU	18-36	12-18	☼	M
Scabiosa	*Scabious*		MS-F	15-48	12-18	☼	D-M
Sea holly	*Eryngium*		MSU-LSU	24-36	18-24	☼	D-M
Silver mound	*Artemesia*	foliage	ES-F	12-36	12-24	☼	D-M
Solomon's seal	*Polygonatum*	white only	MS-ESU	24	12-18	◐●	M-W
Solomon's seal (false)	*Smilacine*	white/red fruit	ESU-MSU	24-36	12-18	◐●	M-W
Speedwell	*Veronica*		MS-MF	12-24	12-18	☼	D-M
Stokes' aster	*Stokesia*		MSU-EF	20-24	12-18	☼	D-M
Stonecrop	*Sedum*		LSU-EF	18-24	12-18	☼	M
Tickseed	*Coreopsis*		ESU-MF	8-24	8-18	☼	D-M-W
Toad lily	*Tricyrtis*		EF-MF	15-24	12-15	◐●	M
Valerian	*Centranthus*		ESU-EF	36	12-18	☼ ◐	D-M
Virginia bluebells	*Mertensia*		ES-MS	18	12-18	◐●	M

continued on next page

continued from previous page

Table 15-D. Perennial planning and planting guide

Key: ☼ = Full Sun ☽ = Part Sun ● = Shade	ES = Early spring	ESU = Early summer	EF = Early fall
D = Soil dries quickly	MS = Mid-spring	MSU = Mid-summer	MF = Mid-fall
M = Average moisture/good drainage	LS = Late spring	LSU = Late summer	F = Frost
W = Soil remains evenly moist but not wet	Note: Plants in containers may bloom up to 4 weeks sooner.		

Common name	Scientific name	Bloom color(s)	Bloom time	Height (inches)	Spacing (inches)	Light	Soil
Waxbells	*Kirengeshoma*	yellow	LSU-EF	36-48	36-48	☽	M
Wild ginger	*Asarum*	foliage	ES-F	6	8-12	●	M
Wild indigo	*Baptisia*	yellow, blue	ESU	36-48	18-30	☼	M
Yarrow	*Achillea*	purple, pink, red, peach, yellow	MSU-EF	24-48	12-18	☼	D-M

Table 15-E. Annuals for specific environments

Tender annuals

Common name	Scientific name	Common name	Scientific name
Ageratum	*Ageratum houstonianum*	Morning glory	*Ipomoea tricolor*
Amaranth	*Amaranth* spp.	Nasturtium	*Tropaeolum majus*
Balsam	*Impatiens* spp.	Petunia	*Petunia x hybrida*
Celosia	*Celosia cristata*	Salvia	*Salvia* spp.
Coleus	*Solenostemon scutellarioides*	Verbena	*Verbena x hybrida*
Flowering tobacco	*Nicotiana alata*	Vinca	*Catharanthus roseus*
Impatiens	*Impatiens wallerana*	Wax begonia	*Begonia semperflorens-cultorum*
Marigold	*Tagetes* hybrids	Zinnia	*Zinnia elegans*

Heat-drought-tolerant annuals (*=extra-tolerant)

Common name	Scientific name	Common name	Scientific name
Black-eyed susan	*Rudbeckia hirta*	Marigold	*Tagetes* hybrids
Blanket flower	*Gaillardia pulchella*	Morning glory*	*Ipomoea tricolor*
Celosia	*Celosia cristata*	Nierembergia	*Nierembergia hippomanica*
Cleome	*Cleome hassleriana*	Petunia	*Petunia x hybrida*
Cornflower	*Centaurea cyanus*	Pincushion flower	*Scabiosa atropurpurea*
Cosmos	*Cosmos bipinnatus*	Phlox (annual)	*Phlox drummondii*
Four o'clock*	*Mirabilis jalapa*	Rocket larkspur	*Consolida ambigua*
Flowering tobacco	*Nicotiana alata*	Rose moss	*Portulaca grandiflora*
Geranium	*Pelargonium x hortorum*	Scarlet sage	*Salvia splendens*
Gerber daisy	*Gerbera jamesonii*	Sunflower*	*Helianthus annus*
Globe amaranth	*Gomphrena globosa*	Verbena	*Verbena x hybrida*
Licorice plant	*Helichrysum petiolatum*	Zinnia*	*Zinnia elegans*

Part-shade annuals

Common name	Scientific name	Common name	Scientific name
Balsam	*Impatiens balsamina*	Nasturtium	*Tropaeolum majus*
Browallia	*Browallia speciosa*	Pansy	*Viola x wittrockiana*
Calendula	*Calendula officinalis*	Petunia	*Petunia x hybrida*
Coleus	*Solenostemon scutellarioides*	Snapdragon	*Antirrhinum majus*
Cornflower	*Centaurea cyanus*	Sweet alyssum	*Lobularia maritima*
Forget-me-not	*Myosotis sylvatica*	Sweet pea	*Lathyrus odoratus*
Flowering tobacco	*Nicotiana alata*	Wallflower	*Erysimum cheiri*
Impatiens	*Impatiens wallerana*	Wax begonia	*Begonia semperflorens-cultorum*
Lobelia	*Lobelia erinus*	Wishbone flower	*Torenia fournieri*

Table 15-F. Perennials for specific environments

Perennials for normal shade (*=can become invasive)

Common name	Scientific name	Common name	Scientific name
Bishop's cap	*Epimedium x rubrum*	Martagon lily	*Lilium martagon*
Bleeding heart	*Dicentra spectabilis*	Plantain lily	*Hosta* spp.
Bugleweed *	*Ajuga reptans*	Primrose	*Primula* spp.
Coral bells	*Heuchera sanguinea*	Shooting star	*Dodecatheon meadia*
Foamflower	*Tiarella cordifolia*	Sweet woodruff	*Asperula* spp.
Green & Gold	*Chrysogonum virginianum*	Trillium	*Trillium grandiflorum*
Hakone grass	*Hakonechloa macra 'Aureola'*	Virginia bluebells	*Mertensia virginica*
Japanese anemone	*Anemone japonica*	Wild blue phlox	*Phlox divaricata*

Perennials for dry shade (*=can become invasive)

Common name	Scientific name	Common name	Scientific name
Bear's foot	*Helleborus foetidus*	Ivy-leaved cyclamen	*Cyclamen hederifolium*
Bishop's cap	*Epimedium x versicolor*	Lamium	*Lamium* spp.
Columbine	*Aquilegia canadensis*	Lily-of-the-valley*	*Convallaria majalis*
Comfrey	*Symphytum grandiflorum*	Lungwort	*Pulmonaria* spp.
Coral bells	*Heuchera americana*	Pussy toes	*Antennaria dioica*
Cranesbill geranium	*Geranium macrorrhizum*	Sedge	*Carex pensylvanica*
Fern, hayscented	*Dennstaedtia punctilobula*	Stonecrop	*Sedum ternatum*
Guinea-hen flower	*Fritillaria meleagris*	Vinca*	*Vinca minor*
Hostas (some varieties)	*Hosta* spp.	Virginia bluebells	*Mertensia virginica*

Note: Many plants recommended for dry shade need moisture to become established before they can tolerate drier conditions. Others can only tolerate temporary or periodic dry conditions. Please research before fully committing to these plants.

Perennials for dry, sandy, coastal soil

Common name	Scientific name	Common name	Scientific name
Bee balm	*Monarda didyma*	Russian sage	*Perovskia atriplicifolia*
Black-eyed Susan	*Rudbeckia hirta*	Salvia	*Salvia officinalis*
Blanket flower	*Gaillardia pulchella*	Sea aster	*Tripolium pannonicum*
Creeping phlox	*Phlox stolonifera*	Sneezewort	*Achillea ptarmica*
Cutleaf coneflower	*Rudbeckia laciniata*	Statice	*Limonium latifolium*
Golden Marguerite	*Anthemis tinctoria*	Steel globe thistle	*Echinops ritro*
Grass pink	*Dianthus plumarius*	Sunflower	*Helianthus* spp.
Iceland poppy	*Papaver nudicaule*	Tickseed	*Coreopsis grandiflora*
Lantana	*Lantana camara*	Yarrow	*Achillea millefolium*
New England aster	*Aster novae-angliae*	Yucca	*Yucca filamentosa*

continued on next page

continued from previous page

Table 15-F. Perennials for specific environments

Perennials for wet soil (*=can become invasive **=can be grown as a water plant)

Common name	Scientific name	Common name	Scientific name
Bee balm	*Monarda didyma*	Joe-Pye weed	*Eupatorium purpureum*
Cardinal flower	*Lobelia cardinalis*	Marsh marigold**	*Caltha palustris*
Eulalia, ornamental grass*	*Miscanthus sinensis*	Pennsylvania or swamp saxifrage	*Saxifraga pensylvanica*
Fern, cinnamon**	*Osmunda cinnamomea*	Swamp rose-mallow**	*Hibiscus moscheutos*
Fern, royal**	*Osmunda regalis*	True forget-me-not	*Myosotis scorpioides*
Fern, sensitive	*Onoclea sensibilis*	Yellowflag	*Iris pseudacorus*

Perennials that require well-drained soil

Common name	Scientific name	Common name	Scientific name
Alpine rockcress	*Arabis alpina*	Maximiliani sunflower	*Helianthus maximiliani*
Beardtongue	*Penstemon laevigatus*	Purple rockcress	*Aubrieta deltoidea*
Foxglove	*Digitalis purpurea*	Sea-holly	*Eryngium maritimum*
German iris	*Iris germanica*	Steel globe thistle	*Echinops ritro*
Globe daisy	*Globularia trichosantha*	Sweet William	*Dianthus barbatus*
Iceland poppy	*Papaver nudicaule*	Tickseed	*Coreopsis grandiflora*

Perennials for poor soil

Common name	Scientific name	Common name	Scientific name
Baby's breath	*Gypsophila paniculata*	Goldentuft	*Aurinia saxatilis*
Cinquefoil	*Potentilla fruiticosa*	Hens and chicks	*Sempervivum*
Creeping speedwell	*Veronica rupestris*	Moss phlox	*Phlox subulata*
Evergreen candytuft	*Iberis sempervirens*	Mullein	*Verbascum thapsus*
Evening primrose	*Oenothera speciosa*	Rock or sun rose	*Helianthemum nummularium*
Geneva bugle	*Ajuga genevensis*	Yarrow	*Achillea millefolium*

Table 15-G. Herbaceous plants for drying

Common name	Scientific name	Common name	Scientific name	Common name	Scientific name
Ageratum	*Ageratum houstonianum*	Coreopsis	*Coreopsis grandiflora*	Marigold	*Tagetes* spp.
Aster	*Aster* spp.	Cosmos	*Cosmos bipinnatus*	Pigweed	*Amaranth* spp.
Bachelor button	*Centaurea cyanus*	Dahlia	*Dahlia* spp.	Salvia	*Salvia* spp.
Baby's breath	*Gypsophila paniculata*	Dianthus	*Dianthus* spp.	Statice	*Limonium sinuatum*
Bells of Ireland	*Molucella laevis*	Globe amaranth	*Gomphrena globosa*	Starflower pincushion	*Scabiosa stellata*
Calendula	*Calendula officinalis*	Globe thistle	*Echinopsis ritro*	Strawflowers	*Helichrysum bracteatum*
Cock's comb	*Celosia cristata*	Gloriosa daisy	*Rudbeckia hirta*	Yarrow	*Achillea* spp.
Corn cockle	*Agrostemma githago*	Love-in-a-mist	*Nigella damascene*	Zinnia	*Zinnia* spp.

Table 15-H. Herbaceous plants with foliage interest

Common name	Scientific name	Common name	Scientific name	Common name	Scientific name
Adam's needle	*Yucca* spp.	Germander	*Teucrium canadensis*	Ornamental onion	*Allium* spp.
Arrow broom	*Genista sagittalis*	Globe thistle	*Echinops retro*	Pachysandra*	*Pachysandra terminalis*
Arum	*Arum italicum*	Goatsbeard	*Aruncus dioicus*	Painter's palette	*Polygonum virginiana*
Avens	*Geum* spp.	Golden lace	*Patrinia scabiosifolia*	Pasque flower	*Pulsatilla vulgaris*
Baneberry	*Actaea rubra, alba*	Hardy century plant	*Agave* spp.	Pearly everlasting	*Anaphalis triplinervis*
Barren strawberry	*Waldsteinia fragarioides*	Hardy ice plant	*Delosperma cooperi*	Plantain lily	*Hosta* spp.
Bear's breeches	*Acanthus* spp.	Iris	*Iris* spp.	Plume poppy	*Macleaya cordata*
Bishop's cap	*Epimedium* spp.	Iron weed	*Vernonia* spp.	Purple heart	*Tradescantia pallida*
Black snakeroot	*Cimicifuga racemosa*	Jack-in-the-pulpit	*Arisaema triphyllum*	Purple shamrock	*Oxalis regnellii* var. *triangularis*
Black-eyed susan	*Rudbeckia* spp.	Jerusalem sage	*Phlomis lanata*	Rodgers flower	*Rodgersia aesculifolia*
Bloodroot	*Sanguinaria canadensis*	Joe-Pye weed	*Eupatorium purpureum*	Russian sage	*Perovskia atriplicifolia*
Blue star	*Amsonia abernaemontana*	Lady's mantle	*Alchemilla mollis*	Saxifrage	*Bergenia cordifolia*
Candytuft	*Iberis sempervirens*	Lamb's-ears	*Stachys byzantina*	Sea holly	*Eryngium planum*
Catchfly	*Lychnis* spp.	Lavender	*Lavandula angustifolia*	Sea kale	*Crambe maritima*
Catmint	*Nepeta* spp.	Lavender cotton	*Santolina chamaecyparissus*	Senecio	*Ligularia* spp.
Cinquefoil	*Potentilla* spp.	Lenten rose, Christmas rose	*Helleborus* spp.	Snow-in-summer	*Cerastium tomentosum*
Comfrey	*Symphytum officinale*	Lily-of-the-valley*	*Convallaria majalis*	Solomon's seal	*Polygonatum odoratum*
Coral bells	*Heuchera* spp.	Lobelia	*Lobelia erinus*	Spurge	*Euphorbia* spp.
Corydalis lutea	*Corydalis*	Lungwort	*Pulmonaria saccharata*	St. John's wort	*Hypericum calycinum*
Cranesbill	*Geranium x cantabrigiense*	Mallow	*Malva alcea*	Stonecrop	*Sedum* spp.
Cyclamen	*Cyclamen* spp.	Mayapple	*Podophyllum peltatum*	Sweet woodruff	*Asperula odorata*
False Solomon's seal	*Smilacina racemosa*	Meadow rue	*Thalictrum aquilegifolium*	Toad-lily	*Tricyrtis hirta*
False spirea	*Astilbe* spp.	Mullein	*Verbascum* spp.	Wild ginger	*Asarum canadensis*
Fern	*Fern* spp.	Ornamental grass	*Carex* spp., etc.	Wormwood	*Artemisia biennis*
Foamflower	*Tiarella cordifolia*	Ornamental rhubarb	*Rheum palmatum*	Yellow wax bells	*Kirengeshoma palmata*
Gay feather	*Liatris spicata*				

*Can become invasive.

AUTHOR

2024 Edition: Esther Mitchell (Prince George's County) and Susan Trice (Frederick County), University of Maryland Extension Home Horticulture Educators and Master Gardener Coordinators

Original author: Steve Allgeier, Carroll County Master Gardener Coordinator, retired.

PUBLICATIONS

Adapted from the *Maryland Master Gardener Handbook, 2016 ed.* and the *Pennsylvania State Master Gardener Manual.*

Armitage, A. 1989. *Herbaceous Perennial Plants.* Varsity Press, Inc., Athens, GA.

Armitage, A. 2006. *Armitage's Garden Annuals - A Color Encyclopedia.* Timber Press, Portland, OR.

Armitage, A. 2001. *Armitage's Manual of Annuals, Biennials, and Half-Hardy Perennials.* Timber Press, Portland, OR. ISBN: 0881926175.

Bloom, A. 1981. *Perennials for Your Garden.* Floraprint USA, Chicago, IL. ISBN: 0903001020.

Brown, M., R. Brown, G. Russell. 1984. *Herbaceous Plants of Maryland.* Port City Press, Baltimore, MD.

Capon, B. 1992. *Botany for Gardeners.* Timber Press, Portland, OR. ISBN: 0881926558.

Clausen, R. and N. Ekstrom. 1989. *Perennials for American Gardens.* Random House, New York, NY. ISBN: 0394557409.

Greenlee, J. 1992. *The Encyclopedia of Ornamental Grasses.* Friedman Publishing Group, Inc. New York, NY. ISBN: 0875634338.

Phillips, E. and C. Burrell. 1993. *Rodale's Illustrated Encyclopedia of Perennials.* Rodale Press, Emmaus, PA. ISBN: 1405077476.

Reich, Lee. 2000. *Weedless Gardening.* Workman Publishing, New York, New York. ISBN: 9780761116967.

Still, S. 1982. *Herbaceous Ornamental Plants.* Stipes Publishing Company, Champaign, IL. ISBN: 0875634338.

U.S. Fish and Wildlife Service. 2001. *Native Plants for Wildlife Habitat and Conservation Landscaping: Mountain, Piedmont, Coastal Regions* (3 volumes). U.S. Fish and Wildlife Service. Annapolis, MD.

WEBSITES

United States Botanic Garden (plant families information). usbg.gov

University of Maryland Extension. *Attracting Wildlife to Your Garden.* extension.umd.edu/resource/attracting-wildlife-your-garden

PHOTOS

Main chapter photo: Stephanie Pully, University of Maryland Extension.

Plant family photos: Wikipedia. Orchidaeceae: Miri Talabac. Bulb photos: Pixabay.

Figures 15-A **Jennifer C** and **graibeard** via Flickr. Figure 15-E: **RichardBH** via Flickr and Miri Talabac.

Figure 15-F: Public domain.

ILLUSTRATIONS

Figures 15-B, 15-C, 15-D by LeAnn Zotta.

16: WOODY PLANTS

Scott Aker

16 WOODY PLANTS

CONTENTS

16.1 Planning and Site Selection 457

16.2 Plant Selection 458

16.3 Purchasing Woody Plants 459

16.4 Planting Woody Ornamentals 461

16.5 Post-Planting Care 464

16.6 Woody Plant Maintenance 465

16.7 Transplanting Woody Ornamentals 468

16.8 Abiotic Problems of Woody Plants 469

16.9 Problematic Trees & Shrubs 473

16.10 Recommended Woody Plants 475

16.11 Ornamental Vines 482

16.12 Groundcovers 483

LEARNING OBJECTIVES

- Criteria for selection of ornamental woody plants
- Forms in which trees and shrubs are sold
- Principles of good planting techniques
- Proper maintenance and cultural practices for woody ornamentals
- Common abiotic problems of trees and shrubs

INTRODUCTION

Woody ornamental plants are key components in a well-designed landscape. This large group of plants consists of trees, shrubs, vines, and woody groundcovers. The following chapter describes how to select, plant, and care for woody ornamentals as well as how to manage common problems.

16.1 Planning and Site Selection

The first consideration when choosing a woody plant is, "Why is that plant going into that location?" In an attractive and functional landscape each plant has a purpose. The document that guides this process is your landscape plan.

You can use plants in a practical way, such as screening off an unsightly view or directing movement through the landscape. A single plant might have multiple functions; placing a flowering tree or shrub for its visual appeal from the kitchen window may also serve to shade a deck or block the view of a neighbor's shed.

In smart landscaping, the function and purpose of a plant comes before selecting the actual plant. For more information, see **Chapter 26, Landscape Design.**

Site evaluation

Prior to planting woody ornamentals, carefully evaluate the intended planting site. Failure of woody plants is most often due to a poor match of plant and site or a failure to correct site problems before planting. Consider the following site evaluation criteria when formulating your landscape plan.

Exposure

Determine whether the site receives full sun, partial sun, or is in full shade. On a clear day during the growing season note how many hours the site is in the sun. If the site receives full sun for six hours or more, it's a sunny location. If it's in the sun for two hours or less, it's a shady location. If it's in between, it's a part-sun location. Also note the prevalence of wind. Some plants, such as broadleaf evergreens, do poorly in windy conditions.

Soil conditions

Soil conditions are determined by soil chemistry and soil structure. Check the soil chemistry by collecting a soil sample and submitting it to a soil-testing laboratory. Use the results to identify pH and nutrient deficiencies. Most woody plants grow satisfactorily with a soil pH between 5.5 and 7.0. Plants such as andromeda, azalea, blueberry, holly, mountain laurel, and rhododendron are exceptions. These plants grow best when the pH is 4.5 to 5.5 (acidic soil). Correct nutrient deficiencies by following the fertilizer and lime recommendations that accompany the soil test results.

Soil texture is determined by the size distribution of the soil particles. Sandy soils have a preponderance of large particles while clay soils have lots of small, plate-like particles. Silt particles are smaller than sand grains but bigger than clay particles. Loamy soils have a balance between sand, silt, and clay that gives them the loose texture of sandy soil along with the nutrient-holding characteristics of silt and clay. Generally, loam and sandy loam provide the best soil structure for plant growth. Soil structure also determines how much lime is needed to raise pH, so an analysis of soil texture is necessary if you want to change your soil's pH.

Another very important characteristic of soil structure is drainage. You can determine the drainage of your soil with a percolation (perc) test. Dig a hole approximately 12 to 15 inches deep and wide. Fill the hole with water and allow all the water to drain. Fill the hole with water a second time and note the amount of time it takes for all of the water to drain. A rate of one-half inch to one inch per hour indicates adequate drainage. A rate of less than one-half inch per hour indicates a potential drainage problem. Correct any drainage issues prior to planting or select a species that thrives in poorly-drained soils.

Potential utility issues

Digging planting holes around your house can be hazardous if you hit a buried utility line. Maryland residents should call "Miss Utility" at 1-800-257-7777 or visit **missutility.net** before digging. Don't forget to check overhead utility lines near your property and avoid planting trees that will interfere with them in the future.

16.2 Plant Selection

Have you ever purchased a new woody plant and then wandered around the yard looking for a place to plant it? Many homeowners plant their landscapes this way but it seldom results in a well-designed or functional landscape. An attractive, functional, and problem-free yard begins with a plan and is developed with a series of plant-selection steps. Always consider the following *before* you plant:

Adaptability to site conditions

In terms of exposure, soil, and wind, is the plant capable of growing satisfactorily?

Hardiness

The **USDA Hardiness Zone Map** identifies growing zones based on average low temperature. You may have a sheltered, slightly warmer location that may allow you to grow some plants aren't reliably hardy in your zone. You may also have exposed, windy areas that require plants that are reliably hardy in the next coldest zone. In Maryland there is a wide range of potential low winter temperatures, ranging from the coldest (in the western part of the state) to the mildest (on the lower eastern shore). If you are considering a plant for which the winter hardiness is either in question or unknown, check with **University of Maryland Extension Gardening** or your local County Extension office for guidance.

Size

What will be the size of the plant in 10 years, 20 years, or at maturity? Do not select a plant that will eventually outgrow its site. If you don't want to wait for trees and shrubs to grow into their designated spaces, you can plant extra, but have a plan to remove them before they crowd the trees and shrubs that will remain.

Maintenance requirements

Does the plant have any special maintenance requirements? These include watering, pruning, fertilization, deadheading, and other maintenance chores. Be sure to match the plants with the care that's necessary (and practical for you) to keep them healthy and looking their best.

Susceptibility to pests and diseases

Does the plant have any specific problems with insects or diseases? Be prepared to address these issues if they arise. Can pest problems be managed without pesticides? Is the plant resistant to any pest or disease problems? These are all important considerations.

Aesthetic qualities

Does the plant provide interesting flowers, fruit, foliage, bark, or other aesthetic quality? When considering one plant versus another, aesthetic qualities can help you make an obvious choice. Use a calendar to chart the period of aesthetic interest and make your plant selections to stagger bloom time and other ornamental characteristics. This will ensure that your landscape is visually pleasing over the course of the entire year.

16.3 Purchasing Woody Plants

Before making any purchase, read and understand the guarantee or return policy should something go wrong. Having a policy in writing eliminates disagreements later. Generally, reputable nurseries and garden centers guarantee a tree or shrub through the first growing season but note that sales promotions and special offers may affect the normal policy.

Trees and shrubs are grown for nursery sales in three different production systems (see Figure 16-A.) There are advantages and disadvantages of each. A few species are best planted as seeds (e.g., hickories and black walnut) because they initially form a deep tap root and cannot be easily grown in nursery production.

Bare-root

Bare-root plants are grown in nursery beds and have had the soil washed or shaken from their roots after digging them up. They are most often sold by mail-order nurseries. Bare-root plants tend to cost less than those produced by other means and are a good option when you want to plant a lot of trees or shrubs in a large landscape. Bare-root plants

Figure 16-A. Types of woody planting stock

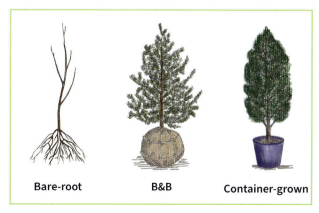

Bare-root   B&B   Container-grown

are one to three years old and are harvested and shipped while dormant.

Bare-root plants tend to establish faster than balled-and-burlapped or container-grown trees and will never have girdled roots.

Never allow the roots to dry out prior to planting. It's a good idea to soak bare-root plants in a bucket of water for 12 to 24 hours just before you plant.

Balled and burlapped (B&B)

B&B plants are grown in a field, in rows. The plants are dug and the root ball is wrapped and secured with burlap, a wire cage, or ropes. B&B plants are available in a wide range of sizes, including large trees with a trunk diameter of up to six inches.

B&B plants can be planted almost any time the ground can be worked. The larger the tree is at planting, the longer the establishment period. Many gardeners choose B&B stock when they want a large tree in a short time. However, a bare-root tree with a one-inch diameter usually exceeds the size of a six-inch caliper B&B after 10 years of growth because B&B trees have lost so much of their root system and may take several years to recover.

When selecting a B&B plant, make sure the root ball is sound and hasn't been broken. Avoid plants that have a loose soil ball or have abrasions or wounds on the trunk or stems. If you're unable to plant right away, be sure to keep the soil ball moist (not wet).

Container-grown

A wide variety of shrubs and small trees are grown in containers. Before buying, ask nursery personnel to remove the container so you can inspect the roots. Roots should be firm, healthy, and visible around the complete circumference of the root ball. Container-grown plants sometimes become root-bound, with their roots circling around the outside of the soil near the wall of the container. These plants need special treatment to loosen the roots when planted.

TIPS FOR PERFECT PLANT SELECTION

Always be on the lookout for:

- A good overall plant appearance, color, leaf size, and vigor. Smaller plants are more likely to survive transplanting.
- Species or varieties that are well adapted to the soil, water, light, heat, wind, and other prevailing conditions present at the intended planting site.
- Plants that, at maturity, will fit into the space allotted for roots and branches.
- Pest-resistant species or varieties.
- A tree trunk that has not been "headed back" or "topped," and is well-shaped.
- Roots, bark, and crown areas that are free of rot, galls, wounds, and insects.
- Roots that are not kinked or encircling the trunk.
- Roots that aren't a solid mass or are disproportionately small compared to its above-ground plant parts.

Source: University of California Division of Agriculture and Natural Resources.

Container plants can be planted any time the ground can be worked, but are often grown in bark rather than soil and may have a difficult time adjusting to your soil conditions.

16.4 Planting Woody Ornamentals

Getting the plant home

Protect your plants as they move from nursery to landscape by keeping the roots moist and covering the tops with tarps or plastic to prevent drying. Avoid damaging the trunks of trees as they are loaded and unloaded.

Plant woody ornamentals as soon as possible after they arrive at the site. If planting is delayed, store plants away from excessive exposure to hot sun and wind. Cover B&B or bare-root plant roots with moist organic mulch, sand, or loose soil. To avoid breaking fine roots, always lift plants by their container or root ball, not by their stems or trunk. Root balls of B&B plants are often very heavy, so take this into consideration when deciding how you will handle B&B plants during the planting process.

Soil preparation

Ideally, the soil should be in good condition over as much of the future root zone of the plant as possible. Mature trees and shrubs develop root systems that may extend three or four times the width of their canopy (see Figure 16-B). For example, a tree with a branch spread of 30 feet may have roots the spread 100 feet from the trunk. Amending only the planting hole in an area of compacted soil will encourage the root growth to stay within the planting hole rather than spreading outward. Plants often "drown" in these holes because organic matter holds water like a sponge and the surrounding heavy soil is slow to drain.

Most woody ornamentals have most of their roots in the top six to 12 inches of soil. If you choose a species that is well-adapted to your existing soil conditions, there is no need to amend the soil. Note that construction activity may bring subsoil to the surface or result in soil compaction. If the soil has been compromised, it is best to amend the entire area of affected soil. Amending only the planting hole will not help the far-reaching roots of trees and shrubs.

Figure 16-B. Typical tree root system (in good soil)

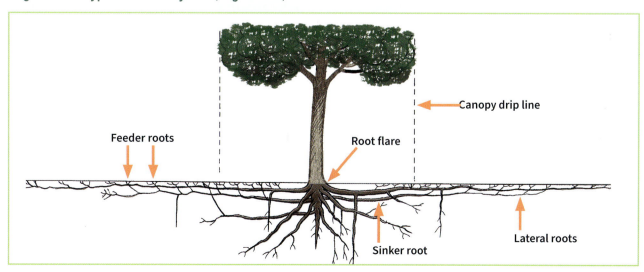

Figure 16-C. Island bed

Where soil conditions are extremely compacted or poorly drained, consider planting in "islands," in which multiple plants share a common area (see Figure 16-C). Island beds create a natural setting that is attractive and easy to maintain. Trees and shrubs grown in "island" plantings tend to be healthier than those planted singly where they have to compete with turfgrass surrounding them.

Soil chemistry

Make sure your soil has the proper pH and no serious nutrient deficiencies. You can find information about soil pH and nutrient levels in your soil test results.

Soil structure

Make sure your soil is not compacted and permits satisfactory aeration and water drainage. Soils are often drastically altered during construction; topsoil is often removed or may be buried under subsoil. If the site evaluation process indicates soil structure problems, correct them prior to planting.

Modifying poorly-structured soils involves:

1. Physically loosening the soil
2. Adding organic matter to maintain and improve structure over time
3. Maintaining an organic mulch layer that improves the soil as it decomposes

When to plant

Late March through April and October through early November are the best times to plant woody ornamentals in Maryland. This time frame corresponds to periods in which root growth is active and the rest of the plant is dormant.

Some plants are best situated in spring because they either don't grow new roots in autumn or they are only marginally hardy in Maryland and need to become established before winter.

Those recommended for spring planting include: birch, camellia, clematis, crape myrtle, cryptomeria, magnolia, oak, and tulip tree. Orchard fruit trees are best planted in early spring as well.

Postpone planting in early fall if the weather conditions are unusually hot, especially if plants are late in losing their foliage. Postpone planting in late winter or early spring if the weather conditions are unusually cold and the ground remains frozen.

The planting process

Bare-root plants

Soak roots in water prior to planting. Inspect roots and remove any dead, diseased, broken, or twisted roots. Dig the planting hole large enough to easily accommodate all of the healthy roots. The hole should be deep enough to allow three or four inches of mounded soil to be placed under the roots. Spread the roots out in the planting hole so they are arranged like the spokes of a wheel. Take care to and place the plant so the point at which the roots flare out from the trunk is at or slightly above the surrounding grade. Fill in soil around the roots and firm the soil to eliminate air pockets. Water thoroughly. (See Figure 16-D.)

Balled and burlapped (B&B)

Field cultivation often results in soil piled up around the trunks of B&B trees and shrubs. Scrape this soil away from the top of the root ball until you can see where the main roots flare out away from the trunk. It is not uncommon for the root flare to be buried under four to six inches of soil.

Dig the planting hole almost as deep as the height of the resulting root ball and twice as wide as the root ball. (See Figure 16-E.) Do not disturb the soil at the bottom of the hole, or the weight of the tree or shrub may cause it to sink into the hole.

Position the plant next to the hole and remove any wire or cords around the burlap. Wire caging left in place won't damage the tree roots, but will present a hazard much later if an arborist is trying to grind the stump after the tree has died or been cut down.

Place the root ball in the hole and rotate the whole tree to lie on its side. Remove all the burlap from the exposed half of the root ball. Rotate the tree to an upright position and remove the rest of the burlap.

Do not be overly concerned about loss of soil or cracking around the root ball. This is a sign that the tree was not properly root-pruned while it was still in the field. Root-pruning causes many fine roots to form near the trunk of the tree that help to hold the root ball together. Chunks of soil that fall away don't contain roots so there is no injury.

Container-grown plants

Remove the plant by sliding it out or cutting the container down the sides to free the

Figure 16-D. Planting bare-root stock (rose)

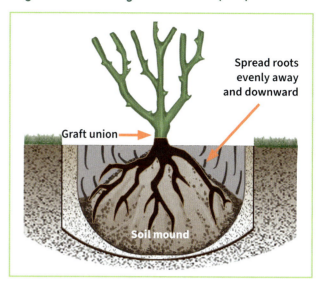

root system. Firm, healthy roots should be visible around the outside of the root ball. The tendency of the roots to grow around the inside of the container may cause girdling to the trunk later if they are not disrupted. Use a sharp knife or blade to cut four or five one-inch-deep cuts the length of the root ball. (See Figure 16-F.) New roots will rapidly grow from the cut areas.

Many conifers grown in containers are planted with multiple seedlings to give the plant a fuller appearance. If you do not remove all but one, your tree will grow with multiple trunks, each with most of its foliage on one side. All will be prone to damage in winter storms.

Figure 16-E. Balled and burlapped (B&B)

Figure 16-F. Container-grown plant preparation

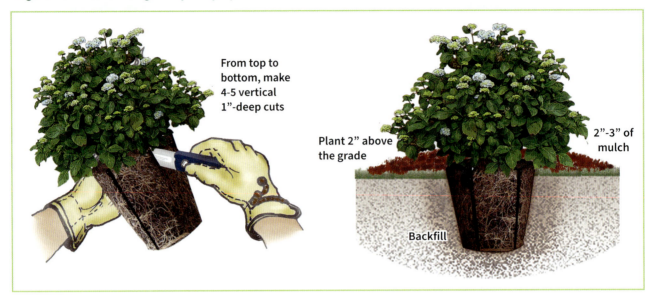

Soil is often added to container grown stock during production. Expose the root flare by removing soil from the top of the root ball until you can clearly see the point at which the roots flare away from the trunk. Dig the planting hole deep enough to accommodate the resulting root ball. If your soil is heavy, it is best to dig a hole that is two to three inches shallower than the height of the root ball. After positioning the tree, fill in soil around the root ball and firm the soil to eliminate air pockets. If the edge of the root ball is higher than the surrounding grade, add soil and rake it to create a gradual slope away from the root ball.

After planting, shape the soil to create a shallow depression one third larger than the diameter of the root ball with a slightly raised berm around the periphery. (See Figure 16-F.) Fill the depression with water. This permits water to go straight to the root zone rather than run off the surface. Thorough soaking after planting eliminates air pockets around roots. Do not place soil on top of the root ball.

16.5 Post-Planting Care

Staking and guying trees

Research has shown that the natural movement of the trunk by the wind stimulates root growth and increases trunk caliper when trees are not staked, so it is not mandatory to stake a new tree. If the tree is unusually large or planted in a windy area, staking or guying may be needed for the first year (see Figure 16-G.)

Staking involves two wooden stakes, driven into undisturbed soil near the base of the tree (but not into the root ball) and secured to the stakes with wires. Cover the wires with short lengths of garden hose where they come in contact with the tree trunk.

Guying uses three equally-spaced wires, anchored with stakes. Loosely loop the wires around the trunk at the lowest branches. Cover the wire with short lengths of garden hose where they contact the trunk. Allow enough slack in the guy wire for some trunk movement. All supports should be removed after one year.

Tree wrap

Tree wrap is used for the first season after planting to reduce sunscald on the bark. Certain trees, such as red maple, littleleaf linden, willow oak, and fruit trees, are prone to sunscald.

Sunscald is physical damage (splitting and cracking) to the bark caused by exposure to the sun and can be life-threatening to the tree. The damage occurs when the side of the trunk that had been oriented to the north or northwest in the nursery is planted toward the south or southwest in the landscape. Tree wraps can also prevent vole feeding and deer injury.

Watering

Check soil moisture around newly-planted trees and shrubs at least once a week. Soil that is moist to the touch is fine. If the soil begins to dry out, water the plant thoroughly. Do not overwater; you can easily drown newly planted trees and shrubs, particularly if your soil has poor drainage. Water only when the root ball has begun to dry out.

Mulch

Maximize the growth of new trees and shrubs by maintaining a mulched area instead of grass under the plants. This reduces competition for nutrients and moisture. Apply mulch as far out as the spread of the branches but no more than three inches deep. Keep mulch four to six inches away from the trunk of the tree.

16.6 Woody Plant Maintenance

Watering

When. Water trees and shrubs according to their needs. Watering depends upon the type of plant, soil texture, and the degree to which the root system is established. Wind, sun, and low humidity may quickly deplete soil moisture. Sandy soils dry out faster than heavy soils or those well-supplied with organic matter.

Some plants tolerate dry conditions better than others, so check all plants regularly because they will dry out at different rates. Extended periods of drought negatively affect all plants. Water trees first, then shrubs, then herbaceous plants.

Watering is not just a summer chore. Trees and shrubs, especially evergreens, can suffer from winter drought damage. Keep an eye on weather conditions in the fall and early winter and if the soil becomes dry, water your landscape evergreens. This is not an uncommon situation from September through November. Water when the ground is not frozen and temperatures are above 40°F.

Where. Water only the landscape. Apply water over as much of the root area of your plants as

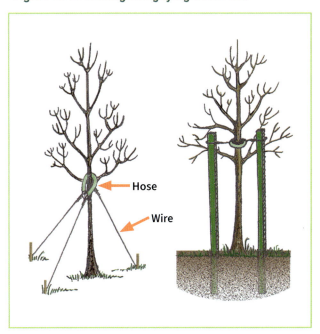

Figure 16-G. Staking and guying a new tree

possible. Watering a small area near the tree trunk does little good because the root system of a large tree extends outward well beyond the drip line.

How. For gardens and low-growing plants, apply water directly to the soil with soaker hoses or drip irrigation. These systems apply water slowly at ground level and only where it's needed. They can supply water beneath plant foliage, which reduces evaporation, an advantage that also keeps leaves dry, reducing the incidence of foliar plant diseases.

If you don't want to invest in soaker hoses, allow a garden hose to run at a trickle. After the ground is saturated to a depth of six inches, move the end of the hose to another dry area.

Water trees and shrubs infrequently but thoroughly. Sprinklers are an acceptable means of watering trees and shrubs during a long dry spell, especially trees. A sprinkler will not wet the foliage, risking fungal disease. Adjust the pressure so the droplet size is large; a fine mist of water will largely evaporate before it can wet the soil. Closely monitor the sprinkler's watering patterns and make sure all parts of the landscape receive adequate water, otherwise much of the root system is still going to experience drought stress.

Use a long screwdriver, shovel, or trowel to see how far water has percolated into the soil. Aim to saturate the top six inches. If your soil is heavy, you may have to water an area until runoff is apparent and water the area again. Avoid watering during midday when the evaporation rate is highest. For established plants, thorough watering does not need to be repeated for several weeks, even with no rain. Avoid frequent watering as it encourages the development of a shallow root system.

Mulch

Mulches can be organic, such as pine bark, or inorganic, such as plastic or stone. Mulch around woody ornamentals to:

- Conserve soil moisture
- Suppress weeds
- Reduce soil compaction
- Prevent soil erosion
- Protect plants from equipment injury
- Create a nice aesthetic

If the purpose of mulching is to improve the growth of your plant's root system, apply mulch over a substantial percentage of the root zone. If you want to protect the plant from equipment damage, apply mulch over as large an area as necessary to create a safety zone around the plant. If aesthetics is your goal, choose mulch to get the look you want. Organic mulches also provide a substrate for beneficial soil microorganisms and gradually release nutrients into the soil as they decay.

Always keep mulch shallow (one to three inches). Deep mulch "volcanoes" not only look bad but can damage your trees and shrubs because they:

- Reduce the amount of water and oxygen available to roots
- Cause roots to grow into the mulch instead of the soil
- May cause decay of the bark around the base of the trunk, leading to death
- Provide a good habitat for voles (rodents that girdle trunks and lower stems)
- Encourage insect and plant problems on the lower trunk and crown

Organic mulches

Bark. Softwood (pine bark) mulches are readily available, slow to decompose and have a pleasant appearance. They are usually more expensive and may be washed away more easily than shredded hardwood. Shredded hardwood mulches are readily available and less expensive. Hardwood bark mulch may contain high levels of manganese, which can be toxic to plants in soils with a pH below 5.0. Apply bark mulches two to three inches deep.

Wood chips. These are often available free or at low cost from local tree removal and trimming companies. Contrary to conventional wisdom, recent research has proven that they may be used immediately without composting or aging. They won't deplete nutrients from soil if the chips average more than a half inch in size and the mulch is no deeper than three inches.

Pine needles. Also called pine straw. Pine needles are slow to decay, attractive, and add fragrance to the landscape. Apply pine needles in a two- to three-inch layer.

Grass clippings. Although it is generally recommended to leave grass clippings on the lawn, there are those who prefer to remove them for aesthetic reasons. Rather than treat removed clippings as trash, compost them or use them as mulch. They decompose quickly and need to be reapplied regularly. Apply in a one- to two-inch layer. Avoid clippings that contain weed seeds and do not use clippings treated with an herbicide or fertilizer-herbicide combination containing dicamba.

Leaves. Leaves make excellent mulch, especially when shredded. They decompose quickly and improve soil structure and fertility. Apply shredded leaves in a two- to three-inch layer.

Compost. Homemade compost makes excellent mulch. It continually decomposes and therefore needs to be replaced annually. Regular additions of compost will significantly improve soil structure. Apply compost in a one- to two-inch layer.

There are many other kinds of organic materials that can serve as mulch, such as corncobs, cocoa shells, or rice hulls. Availability, appearance, and cost are all parameters to consider.

Inorganic mulches

Gravel, stone, and lava rock. These provide long-lasting mulch and are especially useful in special plantings such as rock and alpine gardens. Lava rock is usually red in color and weighs much less than gravel and stone. These materials are often used over plastic or fabric so they don't mix into the soil. Avoid using stone mulches that contain limestone, which can alter soil pH. Apply gravel, stone, or lava rock in a one-inch layer.

Black plastic. While it can provide excellent weed control, plastic may impede movement of rainfall into the soil. Drip irrigation lines are often placed under the plastic to compensate. Black plastic increases soil temperature by about 8°F in the spring, helping plant roots grow earlier but it may cause soil temperatures to rise excessively in mid-summer, damaging roots near the surface. Many gardeners consider black plastic aesthetically unappealing when used alone, and it cannot be recycled. It is often covered with organic mulch. Plastic is broken down by sunlight and should be replaced every two to three years.

Landscape fabrics. These are synthetic, cloth-like materials that are most often used under stone or bark mulch. They come in two forms: woven and spun-bonded. Some woven types look like burlap and others have the texture of fine window screen. Spun-bonded types have a fibrous texture and are more effective on slopes. Unfortunately, soil and debris collect on top of fabric mulches where weed seeds germinate easily. Weeds quickly penetrate the fabric and are very difficult to remove. These fabrics are more permeable than black plastic, but they also inhibit water movement into the soil.

Fertilizing

Woody ornamental plants seldom need fertilization because fungi called mycorrhizae form associations with their roots. The mycorrhizae greatly increase the surface area in the soil for uptake of water and nutrients. In return, carbohydrates are supplied to the fungus by the plant roots. The best fertilizer for woody plants is an organic mulch. This most closely mimics the gradual recycling of nutrients in the ecosystem where woody plants grow.

Fertilizers are only needed if topsoil has been removed from the planting site. Even then, you will only need to apply fertilizer when you prepare the soil. Test your soil so you know how much fertilizer you need to add. Then amend the subsoil with organic matter, fertilizer, and perhaps lime (check the soil test results) before plants will grow well in it. Opt for a granular fertilizer recommended by the soil test and add organic matter at the same time to absorb and hold the nutrients you apply, particularly if the soil is very sandy. If your soil pH is too low for the plants you are growing, add lime at the same time you add fertilizer and organic matter.

Sucking insects such as adelgids, aphids, and scale insects are encouraged by nitrogen fertilization of trees and shrubs. More nitrogen in the plant makes amino acids more abundant in the sap flow and leads to a larger population of pests, so take care not to overuse nitrogen-heavy fertilizers.

Weed management

Weeds compete with plants for both moisture and nutrients and can mar the beauty of your landscape. Don't wait until you have a major weed problem. If a certain type of weed is persistent, properly identify it to determine the most efficient and effect means of eradicating it. Methods to control weeds include:

- Mechanical/hand-removal
- Mulch covers
- Chemical herbicides

See **Chapter 13, Weeds**, for more detailed information. Routinely inspect the landscape and remove weeds as they appear. Do not cultivate deeply because the feeder roots of trees and shrubs are near the surface and deep cultivation can cause irrevocable damage to the plant.

16.7 Transplanting Woody Ornamentals

There may come a time when you decide that a plant must be moved. It is possible to transplant small trees or shrubs from one location to another, but moving large trees with a trunk diameter of two inches or more is difficult and may require a professional.

When to transplant

Transplant trees and shrubs when they are dormant. In Maryland there are two transplanting seasons: mid- to late fall, and late winter to early spring. Always consider weather and soil conditions before you transplant, and postpone it if the weather is hot and dry in the fall. Dormant stock can be planted in late winter or early spring if the soil is not frozen.

Root pruning

At least a year before transplanting a tree or shrub, start pruning roots in early fall. Use a straight-bladed spade to cut the roots at intervals around the circumference of the tree, about four inches inside the edge of the root ball you intend to dig when you move the tree. Cut straight down into the soil and space your cuts six inches apart (see Figure 16-H). Cut the roots to a depth of six to eight inches below the soil surface. The width of the root ball need only be limited by the weight you can manage to move. A shallow, broad root ball will have more intact roots than a round root ball.

Moving and replanting

When you are ready to move your root-pruned plant, dig a trench in a circle starting four inches further out than the root pruning circle. Because most of the roots will be in the top six to 12 inches of soil, opt for a wide, shallow root ball rather than a narrow, deep one. Dig the trench to a depth of eight to 12 inches. When the trench is complete, cut under the plant to sever the roots under the tree. It may be helpful to lift the portion of the root ball you have undercut and position a board under it so you can reach the areas under the center of the root ball with your shovel. When you are sure you have severed all the roots connecting the plant to the underlying soil, slide a tarp under the root ball. Grasp all four corners of the tarp and slide the tree or shrub out of the

Figure 16-H. Root pruning

hole. If you are moving the plant to a site some distance away, wrap the tarp tightly around the soil ball and secure with rope.

Once dug, relocate the plant to its new site as soon as possible. The longer the plant is out of the ground, the greater the chance of failure. Prepare the soil at the new location before you start to dig out the tree or shrub you're moving. Follow the same planting and post-planting procedures used for new woody ornamentals.

16.8 Abiotic Problems of Woody Plants

Issues with woody plants can be biotic—caused by living things such as insects or diseases—or they can be abiotic, i.e., caused by environmental or cultural conditions, poor planting and maintenance practices, or physical or mechanical injury.

Environmental conditions

Drought. Woody ornamentals frequently are damaged by drought. Woody plants don't always wilt in the way annuals and perennials do and the damage caused by drought may not become evident for a year or more after the injury. Symptoms include smaller than normal leaves, branch dieback at the top of the plant, and scorching of leaves. Pay attention to local weather conditions and water plants when rain is deficient.

Lack of oxygen. Insufficient oxygen may cause death of roots and decline or death of the entire plant. Symptoms include reduced growth; wilting during hot weather, even when the soil is moist; smaller than normal leaf size, yellowing of leaves; top dieback; and, when severe, death of the plant.

Compaction is the most common cause of injury to tree and shrub roots. When soil becomes compacted, the pore space available for air and water becomes severely limited. If you find that you have difficulty digging two or three inches into your soil when it is wet, it is likely compacted and requires remediation. The lack of oxygen may also cause the soil to turn grey in color and the anaerobic decay of organic matter in the soil may give it a foul odor. There may be a noticeable absence of plant roots, and if present, they may be rotted.

Improve the soil structure by physically loosening the soil and incorporating organic matter to promote aeration and drainage. The addition of calcium helps chemically bind clay particles into larger aggregates that behave more like sand particles. This can greatly improve the structure of soils that contain large amounts of clay. Use lime to supply the calcium if your soil is acidic and you are growing plants that need a pH between 5.5 and 7.0. Use gypsum as the calcium source if you are growing acid-loving plants. Beneficial fungi and bacteria also produce compounds that chemically bind clay particles together to improve soil structure.

Nutrient deficiency. Plants require certain essential nutrients for growth and development. If one or more essential nutrients is deficient, plants will experience problems. (See **Chapter 6, Plant Nutrition**, for more information on essential nutrients.)

The symptoms of nutrient deficiency vary depending upon which nutrient is lacking and the extent of the deficiency. A common symptom is leaf discoloration. Some nutrients affect young leaves while others affect older, mature leaves. Some nutrient deficiencies significantly reduce growth and cause dieback.

Essential nutrients may be deficient due to:

- Lack of nutrients in the soil
- Improper soil pH that limits nutrient availability
- Drought conditions that limit the uptake of nutrients by roots
- Root injury or death that limits nutrient absorption
- Damage to a plant's vascular system that limits nutrient translocation

Fortunately, most essential nutrients are rarely deficient. Decaying organic matter slowly releases nutrients into the soil that are adequate for the needs of most woody ornamentals.

Salt damage. High salt levels in the soil can damage roots. This can occur due to overfertilization or application of salt for ice and snow removal. Foliage can be directly damaged when high concentrations of fertilizer are applied to plant foliage or road salt is splashed onto foliage by vehicles. Plant roots are more drastically affected by salt than the foliage. Salt damage symptoms are similar to some nutrient deficiencies, herbicide damage, and air pollution injury and often include stunted growth and yellowing foliage. Afflicted conifers' needles turn yellow and progress to brown from the tip downward. In severe cases, plants may die. A soil test for soluble salts can help diagnose salt damage.

Avoid salt damage by fertilizing properly. While a small amount of fertilizer may be beneficial, too much can be damaging. If salt for ice removal accidentally moves into the soil, you can minimize the effect by irrigating with water to leach the salt from the soil. If the soil is frozen, wait until it thaws to irrigate. To minimize foliar salt damage, plant evergreens as far back from roadways as possible. If salt spray is blown onto evergreens, hose them off as soon as possible.

Physical and mechanical injury

Low temperatures. Woody ornamentals are occasionally damaged by freezing temperatures in spring. If a frost occurs after new growth has started, the new growth will be damaged. Broadleaf evergreens are the most sensitive to persistent low winter temperatures, particularly if the ground is frozen and the weather is windy and dry.

New leaves exposed to low temperatures appear water-soaked at first and later turn black. The cold injury sometimes occurs when the leaf is still in bud, prior to opening. Damaged leaves often remain on the plant for an extended period before falling off.

Plants usually recover from late frost damage, although some remedial pruning to remove dead branches may be needed when the extent of damage is apparent. Wait to do any pruning until growth appears to be sure you only remove dead portions of the plant.

Equipment injury. Woody ornamentals are frequently damaged by lawn mowers and string trimmers. Damage can range from minor wounds to death of the plant. Direct impact of equipment injures the bark and underlying vascular system of the lower trunk and stems. Even when there is no visible wound to the bark, the vascular tissue might be damaged.

In most cases, injuries can be seen easily on the lower parts of plants. Symptoms of injured trees and shrubs include foliage yellowing and wilting (especially during hot weather), top dieback, and overall poor growth. You can prevent this type of injury by establishing a wide mulch zone around the plant and keeping the area next to the trunk free of vegetation.

Storm damage. Snow and ice can bend and break branches. Evergreens tend to hold more snow and ice and are more frequently and severely damaged. You can tie shrubs up in late autumn to protect them from damage. Tie a rope or piece of twine onto a branch at the base of the shrub and wrap it in a spiral upward to the top of the foliage. Pull it so there is some tension in it and tie it around the top of the branches. Remember to remove the tie before growth begins in spring. If branches become bent over by heavy snow or ice, don't attempt to knock the snow or ice off the branches. This usually results in breakage and does more harm than good.

Strong winds can break branches and push over trees, especially if the ground is saturated. Straighten/stake the tree as soon as possible. Check the soil to see if there are any obstacles to root growth and correct them so anchoring roots can grow into undisturbed soil. Remove damaged roots or branches.

If a tree has suffered breakage of major branches, you must decide whether the tree should be saved. Consider the following:

- How important is the tree to the landscape?
- Does the tree have sentimental or historical value?
- If all damaged branches are removed, will what remains be a landscape asset or a detriment?
- Will removal of large injured branches cause large wounds on the trunk?

Sometimes the best course of action is to have the damaged tree removed. If you decide to remove only damaged large limbs, call for professional help. If smaller branch damage can be easily reached, remove the branches with straight, clean pruning cuts. (See **Chapter 17, Pruning**, for instructions and techniques.)

Lightning injury. Lightning strikes may kill trees or severely damage branches or portions of the trunk. In some cases, a continuous strip of bark is blown off the trunk resulting in a long vertical wound.

Sometimes there's no visible damage to the trunk. Within a few weeks foliage may wilt, turn yellow, and then turn brown and dry on a section of the top or throughout the entire top. Tall trees and those standing alone in an open area are most susceptible to lightning.

If you are unsure about whether the tree can recover, consult a certified arborist who can install a lightning protection system in any trees that are of special importance.

Root problems

Surface roots. Tree roots may become visible above the soil surface as they grow in diameter or when soil is lost to erosion. This is a natural condition, particularly in heavy, poorly-drained soils. Do not remove the roots or cover them with soil; instead, apply up to three inches of mulch or plant a groundcover that conceals them. See Table 16-A for a list of trees that commonly display surface roots.

As tree roots increase in diameter they can crack or lift sidewalks, driveways, and patios. Removing these roots may result in decline and death of the tree, particularly if the pavement is close to the trunk. The best solution is to select trees that are less likely to develop surface roots or to plant trees further away from paved surfaces. (See Table 16-B for a list of trees you may want to avoid.)

Root barriers can be installed in the soil next to sidewalks, driveways, and patios to block root growth. Place barriers 18 to 24 inches deep along the area to be protected.

Table 16-A. Trees that develop surface roots

Acer platanoides* (Norway maple)	*Metasequoia glyptostroboides* (Dawn redwood)
Acer rubrum (Red maple)	*Platanus occidentalis* (Sycamore)
Acer saccharinum (Silver maple)	*Quercus palustris* (Pin oak)
Betula nigra (River birch)	*Robinia pseudoacacia* (Black locust)
Fagus grandifolia (American beech)	*Taxodium distichum* (Bald cypress)
Liquidambar styraciflua (Sweetgum)	*Tilia cordata* (Littleleaf linden)
*Non-native invasive	

Underground pipes. Roots always grow in the path of least resistance. If they encounter a solid object such as an underground pipe or sewer line, they will change direction. Tree roots cannot invade underground pipes unless cracks or holes are present. Once in the pipe, roots can enlarge and may eventually block the pipe. Blockages must usually be mechanically cleared by a licensed plumber.

Ironically, removing the offending tree usually doesn't stop the problem. It can be difficult to determine which tree is causing the problem, and as long as the damaged pipe remains, roots from other trees will find their way into holes and gaps. The only permanent solution is to replace the pipe itself.

Building foundations. While roots do not grow through solid objects, they can grow into existing foundation cracks. As the roots enlarge, they enlarge the cracks. Avoid planting trees close to walls and foundations.

Septic fields. Leach field pipes are perforated to allow water from the septic tank to escape into the surrounding soil. Tree roots may plug these pipes and cause septic system failure, so avoid planting trees and shrubs nearby.

Girdling roots. Girdling roots encircle and constrict the trunk or other major roots of a tree, limiting growth and damaging the vascular system. The condition originates from root growth in the nursery container. If you don't see a good root flare on your tree or shrub when you dig away the top portion of the container soil, excavate further to determine if there are circling roots in the root ball. Don't be concerned about disrupting the root system. If you don't remove circling roots at planting time, they will ultimately injure the bark at the base of the trunk. If you have chosen a pot-bound plant, slice the root ball up from the bottom about halfway. Splay the two portions of the root ball outward in the planting hole. Trees with girdling roots can sometimes be rescued by cutting a one-inch section out of the girdling root as close as you can to its point of origin.

Construction damage

Trees can be severely damaged or killed by construction activity. Damage can include:

- Removal or addition of soil over tree roots (change in grade)
- Soil compaction caused by heavy equipment
- Severed roots from digging or trenching
- Injured tree trunks and branches from equipment abrasion
- Changes in exposure to sun and wind due to nearby tree removal

It is difficult, if not impossible, to repair tree damage caused by construction. Prevention is always better. Consult a landscape professional to review your plans and assess your property before construction begins. Make use of existing trees and avoid excessive re-grading. Protect desirable trees during construction by fencing off a root-protection zone at least as wide as the canopy of trees.

16.9 Problematic Trees & Shrubs

The trees in Table 16-B have specific problems that should be noted before planting in your landscape.

Table 16-B. Problematic trees and shrubs

Scientific Name	Common Name	Typical Issue(s)
Acer negundo	Boxelder	Attracts boxelder bugs.
Albizia julibrissin	Mimosa	Non-native invasive. Messy (falling twigs/seed pods). Weak growth and branch breakage. Susceptible to fusarium wilt.
Acer platanoides	Norway maple	Non-native that displaces native maples. Difficult to grow grass or other plants inside the drip line.
Acer saccharinum	Silver maple	A large tree with weak wood. Messy (falling branches) and prone to breakage in storms. Surface roots.
Ailanthus altissima	Tree-of-heaven	Non-native invasive. Leaves and stems have a disagreeable odor. Weak wood and frequent branch breakage. Key host for spotted lanternflies.
Betula papyrifera	White birch	Intolerant of hot summers. Prone to bronze birch bark borer.
Elaeagnus angustifolia	Russian olive	Non-native invasive.
Elaeagnus umbellata	Autumn olive	Non-native invasive.
Fraxinus spp.	Ash	Host for emerald ash borer, lilac-ash borer.
Ginkgo biloba	Ginkgo	Female trees produce fruit with an offensive odor.
Juglans nigra	Black walnut	Tree roots produce a toxin that is harmful to other plants. Fallen fruits are messy.
Morus alba	White mulberry	Non-native invasive. Messy fruit.
Paulownia tomentosa	Royal empress tree	Non-native can become invasive.
Populus spp.	Poplars	Weak wood with frequent branch breakage. Short-lived due to canker disease.
Pyrus calleryana	'Bradford' pear	Formerly popular landscape plant that is now a non-native invasive. Self-sterile, but is pollinated by other cultivars.
Quercus acutissima	Sawtooth oak	Non-native that displaces native woodland trees.
Robinia pseudoacacia	Black locust	Messy (falling twigs and small branches). Produces numerous suckers throughout the root zone.
Salix spp.	Willows	Messy (falling twigs and small branches). Susceptible to canker diseases.
Ulmus pumila	Siberian elm	Invasive. Weak wood and frequent branch breakage. Messy (falling twigs and small branches). Susceptible to elm leaf beetle.

16.10 Recommended Woody Plants

The following tables contain non-exhaustive lists of recommended woody ornamentals. Other plants are certainly acceptable provided that they are adaptable to your environment.

Recommended shade trees

The amount of shade produced by a tree can vary from dense to light, depending upon the species. Other characteristics to consider are mature size, growth rate, overall form, leaf shape and size, and autumn color.

Many of the small flowering trees in Table 16-E and 16-F could be used as small shade trees, with flowers as a bonus. Always choose disease-resistant cultivars of crabapple.

Table 16-C. Medium-to-large shade trees (>30′)   ▲=Evergreen   ✪=Maryland native

Symbol	Scientific Name	Common Name	Symbol	Scientific Name	Common Name
✪	*Acer rubrum*	Red maple	▲ ✪	*Pinus strobus*	White pine
✪	*Acer saccharum*	Sugar maple	x	*Platanus ×acerifolia*	London planetree
✪	*Betula nigra*	River birch	▲	*Picea abies*	Norway spruce
✪	*Carya* spp.	Hickory	✪	*Quercus alba*	White oak
▲	*Cedrus atlantica* 'Glauca'	Blue Atlas cedar	✪	*Quercus coccinea*	Scarlet oak
x	*Cercidiphyllum japonicum*	Katsura tree	✪	*Quercus falcata*	Southern red oak
✪	*Fagus grandifolia*	American beech	✪	*Quercus phellos*	Willow oak
x	*Gleditsia triacanthos* var. *inermis*	Thornless honeylocust	✪	*Quercus rubra*	Northern red oak
▲ ✪	*Ilex opaca*	American holly	x	*Tilia cordata*	Littleleaf linden
▲ ✪	*Magnolia grandiflora*	Southern magnolia	x	*Ulmus parvifolia*	Chinese elm
✪	*Nyssa sylvatica*	Black gum	x	*Zelkova serrata*	Japanese zelkova

Table 16-D. Small shade trees (<30′)   ▲=Evergreen   ✪=Maryland native

Symbol	Scientific Name	Common Name	Symbol	Scientific Name	Common Name
x	*Acer buergerianum*	Trident maple	✪	*Hamamelis virginiana*	Common witch hazel
x	*Acer palmatum*	Japanese maple	▲	*Ilex* 'Nellie Stevens'	Nellie Stevens holly
✪	*Carpinus caroliniana*	Ironwood	▲	*Malus* spp.	Crabapple
✪	*Cornus florida*	American dogwood	x	*Sorbus alnifolia*	Korean mountain ash
x	*Cornus kousa*	Kousa dogwood	x	*Syringa reticulata*	Japanese lilac
x	*Cornus mas*	Cornelian cherry			

Recommended flowering trees

Consider differences in flower color, bloom time and succession of blooms.

Table 16-E. Medium-to-large flowering trees (>30′)   ▲=Evergreen   ✪=Maryland native

Symbol	Scientific Name	Common Name	Symbol	Scientific Name	Common Name
✪	*Cladrastis kentukea*	American yellowwood	▲✪	*Magnolia virginiana*	Sweetbay magnolia
✪	*Halesia tetraptera*	Carolina silverbell	x	*Prunus subhirtella* 'Autumnalis'	Higan cherry (fall bloom)
✪	*Magnolia grandiflora*	Southern magnolia	x	*Prunus subhirtella* 'Pendula'	Weeping Higan cherry
x	*Magnolia × soulangiana*	Saucer magnolia	x	*Prunus x yedoensis*	Yoshino cherry

Table 16-F. Small flowering trees (<30′)   ▲=Evergreen   ✪=Maryland native

Symbol	Scientific Name	Common Name	Symbol	Scientific Name	Common Name
✪	*Amelanchier* spp.	Serviceberry	x	*Malus* 'Donald Wyman'	Donald Wyman crabapple
✪	*Aronia arbutifolia*	Red chokeberry	x	*Malus* 'Prairiefire'	Prairiefire crabapple
✪	*Cercis canadensis*	Redbud	x	*Malus sargentii*	Sargent crabapple
✪	*Chionanthus virginicus*	Fringetree	✪	*Oxydendrum arboreum*	Sourwood
✪	*Cornus florida*	American dogwood	x	*Prunus serrulata*	Kwanzan cherry
x	*Cornus kousa*	Kousa dogwood	x	*Prunus ×incam* 'Okame'	Okame cherry
x	*Lagerstroemia* cultivars	Crape myrtle	x	*Styrax japonicus*	Japanese snowbell
x	*Magnolia stellata*	Star magnolia	x	*Syringa reticulata*	Japanese tree lilac
x	*Malus* 'Adirondack'	Adirondack crabapple			

Recommended flowering shrubs

There are thousands of flowering shrubs from which to choose, all easily researched online. The selection listed below features flowering shrubs generally underused in the home landscape.

Table 16-G. Flowering shrubs   ▲=Evergreen   ✪=Maryland native

Symbol	Scientific Name	Common Name	Symbol	Scientific Name	Common Name
x	*Abelia ×grandiflora*	Glossy abelia	x	*Kerria japonica*	Japanese kerria
✪	*Aesculus parvifolia*	Bottlebrush buckeye	▲	*Leucothoe fontanesiana*	Drooping leucothoe
✪	*Clethra alnifolia*	Summersweet	▲	*Pieris japonica*	Japanese pieris
x	*Cotinus coggygria*	Smokebush	x	*Rosa* spp.	Rose
▲	*Daphne odora*	Winter daphne	x	*Spiraea japonica*	Japanese spirea
✪	*Fothergilla gardenii*	Dwarf fothergilla	x	*Spiraea thunbergii*	Golden Thunberg's spirea
x	*Heptacodium miconioides*	Seven sons flower	▲	*Rhododendron* spp.	Rhododendron/azalea
x	*Hibiscus syriacus*	Rose of Sharon	x	*Viburnum ×burkwoodii*	Burkwood viburnum
✪	*Hydrangea quercifolia*	Oakleaf hydrangea	x	*Vitex agnus-castus*	Chaste tree
▲	*Ilex ×meserveae*	Meserve hybrid holly	x	*Weigela florida*	Weigela

Trees with attractive bark

Bark is often an overlooked feature in the landscape. Choosing a variety of contrasting barks can add great interest to a planting area.

Table 16-H. Trees with attractive bark ▲=Evergreen ✪=Maryland native

Symbol	Scientific Name	Common Name	Symbol	Scientific Name	Common Name
x	*Acer capillipes*	Striped maple	x	*Parrotia persica*	Persian parrotia
x	*Acer griseum*	Paperbark maple	▲	*Pinus bungeana*	Lacebark pine
x	*Betula albo-sinensis*	Chinese paper birch	x	*Prunus serrula*	Paperbark cherry
✪	*Betula nigra* 'Heritage'	Heritage river birch	x	*Pseudocydonia sinensis*	Chinese quince
x	*Cornus kousa*	Kousa dogwood	x	*Stewartia monadelpha*	Tall stewartia
x	*Lagerstroemia* spp.	Crape myrtle	x	*Stewartia pseufocamellia*	Japanese stewartia

Plants with attractive fall color

Note that there is always potential for genetic differences from plant to plant, particularly if they were grown from seed. Select plants in autumn when the color can be observed.

Table 16-I. Trees and shrubs with attractive fall color ▲=Evergreen ✪=Maryland native

Symbol	Scientific Name	Common Name	Symbol	Scientific Name	Common Name
TREES			**TREES**		
✪	*Acer rubrum*	Red or swamp maple	x	*Ginkgo biloba*	Ginkgo
✪	*Acer saccharum*	Sugar maple	✪	*Liquidambar styraciflua*	Sweetgum
x	*Acer tataricum*	Tatarian maple	✪	*Nyssa sylvatica*	Black gum
✪	*Chionanthus virginicus*	Fringetree	✪	*Oxydendrum arboreum*	Sourwood
✪	*Cornus florida*	American dogwood	x	*Parrotia persica*	Persian parrotia
✪	*Cornus mas*	Cornelian cherry	✪	*Quercus coccinea*	Scarlet oak
x	*Cornus kousa*	Kousa dogwood	✪	*Quercus rubra*	Red oak
✪	*Crataegus phaenopyrum*	Washington hawthorn	x	*Sorbus alnifolia*	Korean mountainash
✪	*Franklinia alatamaha*	Franklinia	x	*Stewartia* spp.	Stewartia
SHRUBS			**SHRUBS**		
x	*Cornus alba*	Siberian dogwood	✪	*Rhus typhina*	Staghorn sumac
✪	*Fothergilla gardenii*	Dwarf fothergilla	x	*Rosa rugosa*	Rugosa or wild rose
✪	*Hydrangea quercifolia*	Oakleaf hydrangea	x	*Spiraea thunbergii* 'Ogon'	Golden Thunberg's spirea
✪	*Itea virginica*	Virginia sweetspire	✪	*Vaccinium* spp.	Blueberries
✪	*Rhus aromatica*	Fragrant sumac	✪	*Viburnum dentatum*	Arrowwood viburnum
✪	*Rhus copallina*	Shining sumac	✪	*Virburnum lentago*	Nannyberry viburnum
✪	*Rhus glabra*	Smooth sumac	✪	*Viburnum prunifolium*	Blackhaw viburnum

Plants with attractive fruits

Woody ornamentals produce abundant fruit if adequate soil moisture is available through the growing season and the plant remains healthy (i.e., does not suffer serious pest or disease damage). Successful pollination is also necessary. Some plants, like American holly, are dioecious—they bear male and female flowers on separate plants. To produce fruit, there must be a female plant along with a nearby male plant.

A note about the bittersweet vine: Do not mistakenly purchase Oriental bittersweet, which is very invasive.

Table 16-J. Plants with attractive fruits   ▲=Evergreen   ✪ =Maryland native

Symbol	Scientific Name	Common Name	Symbol	Scientific Name	Common Name
TREES			**TREES**		
✪	Cornus florida	American dogwood	▲ ✪	Juniperus virginiana	Eastern redcedar
x	Cornus kousa	Kousa dogwood	x	Malus spp. and cultivars	Crabapple
x	Cornus mas	Cornelian cherry	✪	Oxydendrum arboreum	Sourwood
x	Crataegus spp. and cultivars	Hawthorn (some native)	x	Photinia villosa	Oriental photinia
▲ ✪	Ilex opaca	American holly	x	Sorbus spp.	Mountainash
SHRUBS			**SHRUBS**		
✪	Aronia arbutifolia	Red chokeberry	▲	Nandina domestica	Heavenly bamboo
x	Callicarpa japon...	(Beautyberry)			Pyracantha or firethorn
x	Cotoneaster spp.	Cotoneaster	✪	Rhus glabra	Smooth sumac
x	Elaeagnus multiflora	Cherry elaeagnus	✪	Rhus typhina	Staghorn sumac
▲	Ilex cornuta	Chinese holly	x	Rosa spp.	Rose
✪	Ilex verticillata	Winterberry	x	Symphoricarpos albus	Snowberry
▲ ✪	Myrica pensylvanica	Bayberry	x	Viburnum dilatatum	Linden viburnum
VINES					
✪	Celastrus scandens	American bittersweet			

Figure 14-O. Lawn alternative planting guide

Barrier plants

Note: Some barrier plants have prickly leaves that should be planted away from paths and walkways.

Table 16-K. Barrier plants   ▲=Evergreen   ✪ =Maryland native

Symbol	Scientific Name	Common Name	Symbol	Scientific Name	Common Name
x	Chaenomeles spp.	Flowering quince	▲	Osmanthus heterophyllus	Holly osmanthus
x	Crataegus spp. and cultivars	Hawthorn (some native)	x	Poncirus trifoliata	Trifoliate orange
▲	Ilex spp. and cultivars	Hollies (Am., Ch., Eng.)	▲	Pyracantha spp. and cultivars	Pyracantha or firethorn
▲ ✪	Juniperus virginiana	Eastern redcedar	x	Rosa spp.	Roses

Woody plants that tolerate poor, dry soil

Note that it may be necessary to irrigate these plants during their establishment period.

Table 16-L. Plants that tolerate poor, dry soil ▲=Evergreen ✪=Maryland native

Symbol	Scientific Name	Common Name	Symbol	Scientific Name	Common Name
TREES			**TREES**		
✪	*Betula populifolia*	Gray birch	✪	*Maclura pomifera*	Osage-orange
✪	*Celtis occidentalis*	Hackberry	✪	*Quercus palustris*	Pin oak
▲	*Juniperus* spp.	Junipers	✪	*Robinia pseudoacacia*	Black locust
x	*Maackia amurensis*	Amur maackia	✪	*Sassafras albidum*	Sassafras
SHRUBS			**SHRUBS**		
x	*Chaenomeles* spp.	Flowering quince	x	*Hypericum* spp.	St. John's wort
x	*Cotinus coggygria*	Smoketree	✪	*Itea virginica*	Virginia sweetspire
✪	*Hamamelis virginiana*	Common witch hazel	✪	*Physocarpus opulifolius*	Ninebark
x	*Hydrangea paniculata* cultivars	Panicle hydrangeas	✪	*Rhus* spp.	Sumac
GROUNDCOVERS			**GROUNDCOVERS**		
x	*Hypericum* spp.	St. John's wort	x	*Potentilla* spp.	Cinquefoil
x	*Juniperus conferta* cultivars	Shore juniper	x	*Santolina chamaecyparissus*	Lavender cotton

Woody plants that tolerate shade

Plants which flower will not perform as well in full shade; they prefer some sun.

Table 16-M. Plants that tolerate shade ▲=Evergreen ✪=Maryland native

Symbol	Scientific Name	Common Name	Symbol	Scientific Name	Common Name
TREES			**TREES**		
✪	*Amelanchier* spp.	Serviceberry	▲	*Ilex* spp.	Hollies
✪	*Asimina triloba*	Pawpaw	▲	*Thuja occidentalis*	Arborvitae
✪	*Cornus florida*	American dogwood	▲ ✪	*Tsuga canadensis*	Hemlock
SHRUBS			**SHRUBS**		
x	*Abelia* spp.	Abelia	▲	*Leucothoe fontanesiana*	Drooping leucothoe
✪	*Aronia* spp.	Chokeberry	▲	*Pieris* spp.	Pieris
▲	*Aucuba japonica*	Aucuba	▲	*Rhododendron* spp.	Rhododendron/azalea
x	*Cephalotaxus harringtonia*	Japanese plum yew	▲	*Taxus* spp.	Yew
x	*Chamaecyparis obtusa*	Hinoki false cypress	▲	*Thujopsis dolobrata*	Hiba false arborvitae
▲ ✪	*Kalmia latifolia*	Mountain laurel	x	*Viburnum* spp.	Viburnum
GROUNDCOVERS			**GROUNDCOVERS**		
▲	*Microbiota decussata*	Siberian cypress	✪	*Vaccinium angustifolium*	Lowbush blueberry
▲	*Sarcococca hookeria* var. *humilis*	Sweetbox	✪	*Xanthorhiza simplicissima*	Yellowroot

Plants that tolerate salt air

Most plants will fail in an environment where there is salt air/spray. These woody plants are well-adapted to coastal gardens.

Table 16-N. Plants that tolerate salt air   ▲=Evergreen   ✪=Maryland native

Symbol	Scientific Name	Common Name	Symbol	Scientific Name	Common Name
DECIDUOUS TREES			**DECIDUOUS TREES**		
✪	*Aesculus pavia*	Red buckeye	✪	*Quercus palustris*	Pin oak
✪	*Diospyros virginiana*	Common persimmon	✪	*Quercus rubra*	Red oak
x	*Gleditsia triacanthus* var. *inermis*	Thornless honeylocust	✪	*Robinia pseudoacacia*	Black locust
✪	*Juglans nigra*	Black walnut	x	*Syringa reticulata*	Japanese tree lilac
✪	*Quercus alba*	Eastern white oak	x	*Vitex agnus-castus*	Chaste tree
✪	*Quercus macrocarpa*	Bur oak			
EVERGREEN TREES			**EVERGREEN TREES**		
▲✪	*Juniperus virginiana*	Eastern redcedar	▲	*Pinus thunbergiana*	Japanese black pine
▲✪	*Magnolia grandiflora*	Southern magnolia	▲✪	*Pinus taeda*	Loblolly pine
▲✪	*Magnolia virginiana*	Sweetbay magnolia			
DECIDUOUS SHRUBS			**DECIDUOUS SHRUBS**		
✪	*Aronia arbutifolia*	Red chokeberry	✪	*Rhus* spp.	Sumac
✪	*Baccharis halimifolia*	Groundsel bush	x	*Rosa rugosa*	Rugosa or wild rose
✪	*Clethra alnifolia*	Summersweet	✪	*Rosa virginiana*	Virginia rose
✪	*Cornus sericea*	Redosier dogwood	x	*Spiraea* spp.	Spirea
x	*Cotoneaster* spp.	Cotoneaster	x	*Syringa vulgaris*	Common lilac
x	*Hydrangea macrophylla*	Bigleaf hydrangea	✪	*Vaccinium corymbosum*	Highbush blueberry
✪	*Prunus maritima*	Beach plum	✪	*Viburnum dentatum*	Arrowwood viburnum
EVERGREEN SHRUBS			**EVERGREEN SHRUBS**		
▲✪	*Ilex glabra*	Inkberry	▲	*Prunus laurocerasus*	Cherry laurel
▲✪	*Myrica pensylvanica*	Bayberry	▲	*Taxus* spp.	Yew
▲	*Pinus mugo*	Mugo pine			
EVERGREEN GROUNDCOVERS			**EVERGREEN GROUNDCOVERS**		
▲	*Hypericum calycinum*	St. John's wort	▲	*Juniperus horizontalis*	Creeping juniper
▲	*Juniperus conferta*	Shore juniper			
DECIDUOUS VINES			**DECIDUOUS VINES**		
x	*Hydrangea anomala* subsp. *petiolaris*	Climbing hydrangea	✪	*Parthenocissus quinquefolia*	Virginia creeper

Woody plants that serve as windbreaks

Table 16-O. Plants that serve as windbreaks   ▲=Evergreen   ✪=Maryland native

Symbol	Scientific Name	Common Name
EVERGREEN TREES		
▲	Abies nordmanniana	Nordmann fir
▲	Calocedrus decurrens	Incense cedar
▲	Chamaecyparis pisifera	Sawara false cypress
▲	Cupressus glabra	Smooth Arizona cypress
▲✪	Ilex opaca	American holly
▲✪	Juniperus virginiana	Eastern redcedar
▲✪	Magnolia grandiflora	Southern magnolia
DECIDUOUS TREES		
✪	Carpinus caroliniana	American hornbeam
x	Malus floribunda	Japanese crabapple
x	Metasequoia glyptostroboides	Dawn redwood
SHRUBS		
x	Cephalotaxus harringtonia	Japanese plum yew
x	Ilex cornuta	Chinese holly
x	Ilex crenata	Japanese holly
x	Juniperus chinensis	Chinese juniper
▲✪	Myrica pensylvanica	Bayberry
▲	Rhus aromatica	Fragrant sumac

Symbol	Scientific Name	Common Name
EVERGREEN TREES		
▲	Picea abies	Norway spruce
▲	Picea orientalis	Oriental spruce
▲	Picea omorika	Serbian spruce
▲✪	Pinus strobus	Eastern white pine
▲	Pinus thunbergiana	Japanese black pine
▲	Pseudotsuga menziesii var. glauca	Douglas fir
DECIDUOUS TREES		
✪	Quercus palustris	Pin oak
x	Tilia cordata	Littleleaf linden
SHRUBS		
▲	Taxus spp.	Yew
▲✪	Thuja occidentalis	American arborvitae
✪	Viburnum dentatum	Arrowwood viburnum
x	Viburnum prunifolium	Black-haw viburnum
x	Viburnum tomentosum	Doublefile viburnum
✪	Weigela florida	Weigela

Trees for urban conditions

Table 16-P. Trees for urban conditions   ▲=Evergreen   ✪=Maryland native

Symbol	Scientific Name	Common Name
SMALL TREES (<30')		
x	Acer buergerianum	Trident maple
✪	Celtis occidentalis	Hackberry
x	Cornus mas	Cornelian cherry
x	Crataegus ×lavallei	Lavalle hawthorn
✪	Crataegus phaenopyrum	Washington hawthorn
UPRIGHT (FASTIGATE) TREES		
✪	Acer rubrum	Red maple
x	Carpinus betulus	European hornbeam
x	Ginkgo biloba	Ginkgo
MEDIUM-TO-LARGE TREES (>30')		
✪	Acer rubrum	Red maple
x	Ginkgo biloba	Ginkgo
x	Gleditsia triacanthos var. inermis	Thornless honeylocust
✪	Gymnocladus dioicus	Kentucky coffeetree
x	Parrotia persica	Persian parrotia
✪	Quercus bicolor	Swamp white oak
✪	Quercus coccinea	Scarlet oak

Symbol	Scientific Name	Common Name
SMALL TREES (<30')		
x	Eucommia ulmoides	Hardy rubber tree
x	Lagerstroemia cultivars	Crape myrtle
x	Maackia amurensis	Amur maackia
x	Ostrya virginiana	Hophornbeam
x	Prunus ×incam	Okame flowering cherry
UPRIGHT (FASTIGATE) TREES		
x	Metasequoia glyptostroboides	Dawn redwood
✪	Taxodium distichum	Baldcypress
MEDIUM-TO-LARGE TREES (>30')		
✪	Quercus macrocarpa	Bur oak
✪	Quercus rubra	Red oak
✪	Quercus phellos	Willow oak
x	Sophora japonica	Japanese pagoda tree
x	Syringa reticulata	Japanese tree lilac
x	Tilia cordata	Littleleaf linden
x	Zelkova serrata	Japanese zelkova

16.11 Ornamental Vines

Woody ornamental vines are both functional and decorative. They offer attractive flowers, interesting foliage, ornamental fruits, and outstanding fall color. They can soften harsh architectural features, screen unsightly objects, shade porches and patios, enliven fences and walls, and add form and color to a pergola or trellis. Vines can be particularly useful in forming a cascade of bloom on rough, steep banks while holding the soil in place.

Vine types

Vines can be divided into four groups based on their method of climbing:

Clingers. These vines attach themselves directly to any surface. Examples are Boston ivy, Virginia creeper, and climbing hydrangea. They climb by clinging with small root-like holdfasts to the wall as a means of support. Sometimes these are modified tendrils with small circular discs at the tips. Others, like trumpet creeper, have small rootlets along the stem that firmly attach to a surface. Use brick or masonry walls, not wooden structures, to support clingers, or allow them to grow on a tree.

Grabbers. Grabbers literally grab their supports. They climb by attaching and winding tendrils or leaf-like appendages around the object on which they are growing. Examples of grabbers are grapes and clematis. Use wire or stout twine as supports.

Twiners. These vines climb by twining their stems around their supports. They include honeysuckle, hardy kiwi vine, and wisteria. Each species twines in one direction only, so it is important to start the winding of young vines around their support in the correct direction. Observe how each vine climbs, and then provide the proper means of support (e.g., wires, trellises, and arbors) for the vines you have selected.

Sprawlers. Sprawlers lie on their supports. Examples include Chinese trumpet creeper, jasmine, and roses. To remain tidy, sprawlers need to be tied to their supports.

Vine selection

When choosing a vine, consider the following:

- Does it prefer sun or shade?
- Is it being planted primarily for blooms or foliage?
- Will it be a permanent planting? (If so, select perennial vines hardy for your area)
- Will the vine drop undesirable fruit or other plant material on or near the site?
- Will stinging or other nuisance insects be attracted to the vine?
- Does it exhibit rampant growth that will require frequent pruning to control?

Planting vines

Follow the same set of steps as discussed for trees and shrubs. Prior to planting, evaluate the planting site in terms of light exposure and soil conditions. If necessary, modify the soil chemistry and structure based on your evaluation and soil test results.

Vines are different from other woody ornamentals in that many vines require some kind of support. Exactly what is needed is determined by the type of vine you select. It's important to begin training vines when they are young.

Vine maintenance

As with other woody ornamentals, maintenance includes watering, fertilization, mulching, pruning, and attention to pests and diseases. Unlike other woody ornamentals, vines generally need regular pruning to keep their attractive appearance.

Watering depends upon the vine type, soil conditions, and weather. Check soil moisture periodically and water thoroughly when dry, soaking the soil six to 10 inches deep.

Many vines don't require fertilizer. Excess fertilizer may result in rampant growth at the expense of flowers. Most vines will get the nutrients they need as the mulch around them decays. The exception may be clematis, which does best with a high (alkaline) soil pH. Supply frequent applications of lime.

The benefits of mulch that apply to trees and shrubs also apply to vines. Mulch materials should cover a relatively large portion of the root zone area and should be no more than three inches deep.

Pruning depends upon the type of vine and specific use of the vine. See **Chapter 17, Pruning,** for more information about pruning woody plants.

For pest and disease problems of woody vines, see **Chapter 12, Plant Diagnostics.**

Table 16-Q below provides a partial list of recommended vines for Maryland; there are many others.

16.12 Groundcovers

Groundcovers are relatively low-growing and have a spreading habit so they cover the ground. They are provide color and texture to the landscape. Although lawn grasses are the most commonly used, the term "groundcover" usually refers to plants other than lawn grasses. Most groundcovers are not intended to be walked on and may be damaged by frequent pedestrian traffic.

Table 16-Q. Recommended vines for Maryland   ▲ =Evergreen   ✪ =Maryland native

Scientific Name	Common Name	Climbing Type	Foliage	Hardiness Zone
Actinidia spp.	Hardy kiwi	Twining	Deciduous, but perennial	3 - 7
✪ *Campsis radicans*	Trumpet creeper	Clinging	Deciduous, but perennial	4 - 7
Campsis grandiflora	Chinese trumpet creeper	Sprawling	Deciduous, but perennial	6 - 9
Clematis spp	Clematis	Leaf stalks	Deciduous, but perennial	4 - 7
Gelsemium sempervirens	Carolina jessamine	Twining	Evergreen, perennial	6 - 10
Hydrangea anomala subsp. *petiolaris*	Climbing hydrangea	Clinging	Deciduous, but perennial	4 - 8
Jasminum nudiflorum	Winter jasmine	Sprawling	Deciduous, but perennial	6 - 10
✪ *Lonicera sempervirens*	Trumpet honeysuckle	Twining	Deciduous, but perennial	4 - 9
Wisteria frutescens	American wisteria	Twining	Deciduous, but perennial	4 - 6

In addition to their aesthetic value, groundcovers serve a variety of functions:

- Can be a lawn substitute in areas too shady for lawn grasses or areas where mowing is difficult
- Reduce overall landscape maintenance
- Control erosion, especially on slopes where turf is difficult to maintain
- Provide attractive accents for areas too small to accommodate shrubs
- Obstruct traffic without impeding the view
- Provide vegetative cover for very wet or very dry locations

When skillfully interplanted with trees and shrubs, groundcovers impart a natural-looking textural balance to the area. Groundcovers also give unity to the landscape by tying together multiple elements.

The groundcovers most frequently used are vigorous growers, hardy, and easily propagated. Any slope greater than 12 percent is best planted with a groundcover. Around buildings, groundcovers are superior to paving because they reduce heat, glare, noise, and dust.

Planting groundcovers

Before you plant, consider color, texture, height, required maintenance, and potential pests and diseases (see Table 16-R for a selected list of recommended groundcovers for Maryland).

Because groundcovers usually cover relatively large areas of the landscape, it's important to pay special attention to existing weeds, especially perennials that may be difficult to eliminate. Eradicate them before you plant.

Have the soil tested and correct any pH, nutrient, drainage, and compaction issues. Work the soil eight to 10 inches deep and incorporate any lime, fertilizer, or organic matter required. If the soil is clay, incorporate a three- to four-inch layer of organic matter to improve aeration and drainage.

Plant groundcovers in early spring or early fall when the weather is cool and soil moisture is most reliable. Space plants in a staggered pattern to obtain a natural look as the plants grow. Spacing depends upon plant growth rate, how long you want to wait for the cover to become solid, and your budget. Most groundcovers are spaced between six inches to two feet apart. When planting on slopes, mulch or netting may be required to control erosion until your plants are established.

After planting, check soil moisture weekly and water plants whenever the soil begins to dry out. Apply enough water to thoroughly wet the soil down to the base of the root systems. Keep the areas between groundcover plants weed-free and apply a weed-suppressing mulch between plants.

Groundcover maintenance

Groundcover plants vary in their need for supplemental moisture, but during periods of drought all groundcovers benefit from added water. Apply enough to wet the soil to the depth of the root system.

Fertilize groundcovers only when new growth has begun and apply no more than one pound of nitrogen per 1,000 square feet. When the groundcover has filled in, fertilizer is needed only if nutrient deficiency symptoms appear. Apply fertilizers when the foliage is dry and blow or sweep residual granules off the plants.

Groundcovers planted in the vicinity of trees and shrubs become the depository for fallen leaves and small branches. Accumulations of leaves and twigs may be left on the ground to decay and provide nutrients to the soil as long as they allow sunlight, water, and air to reach the groundcover. Remove excess leaves and debris if needed with a blower or leaf rake. ❄

Table 16-R. Recommended groundcovers for Maryland   ▲ =Evergreen   ✪ =Maryland native

Symbol	Scientific Name	Common Name	Sun/Shade	Height
▲✪	*Arctostaphylos uva-ursi*	Bearberry	Shade	6 - 12 inches
▲	*Cotoneaster dammeri*	Bearberry cotoneaster	Sun	6 - 12 inches
▲	*Juniperus conferta*	Shore juniper	Sun	12 - 18 inches
▲	*Juniperus horizontalis*	Creeping juniper	Sun	4 - 8 inches
▲✪	*Mitchella repens*	Partridgeberry	Sun or shade	1 - 2 inches
▲	*Pachysandra* spp.	Pachysandra	Shade	6 - 12 inches
▲✪	*Sibbaldiopsis tridentata*	Shrubby fivefingers	Sun	2 - 12 inches

AUTHOR

Edited by Scott Aker, Supervisory Research Horticulturist, Gardens Unit, USDA.

Original author: Bob Stewart, Horticulture Educator, University of Maryland Extension, retired.

PUBLICATIONS

Costello, L. R. et al. 2003. *Abiotic Disorders of Landscape Plants: A Diagnostic Guide.* University of California Agriculture and Natural Resources. Publication 3420. Berkeley, CA.

Dirr, M.A. 1998. *Manual of Woody Landscape Plants: Their Identification, Ornamental Characteristics, Culture, Propagation and Uses*. 5th ed. Stipes Publishing Company, Inc. New York, NY. ISBN: 08875638007.

Grimm, W. C. (revised by John Kartesz.) 2002. *The Illustrated Book of Trees*. Stackpole Books. Mechanicsburg, PA.

Harris, R. W. 1992. *Arboriculture: Integrated Management of Landscape Trees, Shrubs, and Vines.* 2nd ed. Regents/Prentice Hall, Englewood Cliffs, NJ. ISBN: 0130442801.

Tripp, K. E. and J. C. Raulston. 1995. *The Year in Trees*. Timber Press. Portland, OR.

Tripp, K. E. and J. C. Raulston. 1997. *The Year In Trees: Superb Woody Plants for Four- Season Gardens*. Timber Press. Inc. Portland, OR. ISBN: 0881925217.

Watson, G. W. and E. B. Himelick. 1997. *Principles and Practice of Planting Trees and Shrubs.* International Society of Arboriculture, Savoy, IL. ISBN: 1881956180.

Wyman D. 1977. *Trees for American Gardens.* Macmillan Publishing Company, Inc. New York, NY. ISBN: 0026322005.

Wyman D. 1969. *Shrubs and Vines for American Gardens.* Macmillan Publishing Company, Inc. New York, NY. ISBN: 0026321602.

WEBSITES

The University of Connecticut Plant Database. **plantdatabase.uconn.edu**

The Missouri Botanic Gardens Plant Finder. **mobot.org/gardeninghelp/plantfinder/alpha.asp**

ILLUSTRATOR

LeAnn Zotta, Berkshire Communications.

Main chapter photo: **littlegemtrees** via Flickr.

17: PRUNING

Ginny Rosenkranz

17 PRUNING

CONTENTS

17.1 Physiology of Pruning 489

17.2 Why Prune? 491

17.3 Pruning Tools 493

17.4 Pruning Techniques & Terms 494

17.5 When to Prune 497

17.6 Training Newly-Planted Trees 498

17.7 Pruning Mature Trees 500

17.8 Pruning Shrubs 502

17.9 Pruning Hedges 502

17.10 Pruning Conifers 504

17.11 Pruning Other Plants 504

LEARNING OBJECTIVES

- Major reasons for pruning
- Physiological effects of pruning
- Pruning techniques
- When to prune
- Types of pruning tools
- Principles of pruning trees
- How to prune hedges, perennials, and ornamental grasses

INTRODUCTION

Pruning is the removal of a part or parts of a plant for a specific purpose. All forms of pruning alter the direction and amount of new plant growth. Understanding the basics of plant growth will help you to consciously direct the pruning cuts.

17.1 Physiology of Pruning

The bud

All new growth comes from buds, and pruning manipulates bud growth. Each bud a plant produces grows into a branch, a leaf, or a flower. Most buds can be classified as either dormant, latent, or adventitious.

Dormant buds form during one growing season and remain dormant until the next growing period when, depending on their type, they grow into stems, leaves, or flowers. Terminal buds arise at the branch tip. Lateral buds are located on the sides of branches. Lateral buds at the base of a leaf, called axillary buds, produce either leaves, stems, or flowers.

Latent buds may remain dormant for many seasons as the supporting branch becomes larger and older. These persistent buds are the plant's insurance for the future.

Adventitious buds develop where no buds previously existed, often after a branch is wounded or cut back to mature tissue. These buds differ from dormant or latent buds in that they are not directly connected to the plant's vascular system. Shoots that develop from adventitious buds, such as water sprouts, are not strongly connected to the trunk or main branches and can be easily broken. A number of years must pass before new layers of wood from annual growth rings can support these branches.

Role of the terminal bud

The terminal bud exerts a strong chemical control over the lateral buds (lower on the stem). This phenomenon, called apical dominance, is directed by a hormone called auxin. Auxin is located in the terminal bud, suppresses the growth of other buds, and slows down their growth.

Figure 17-A. Twig pruning

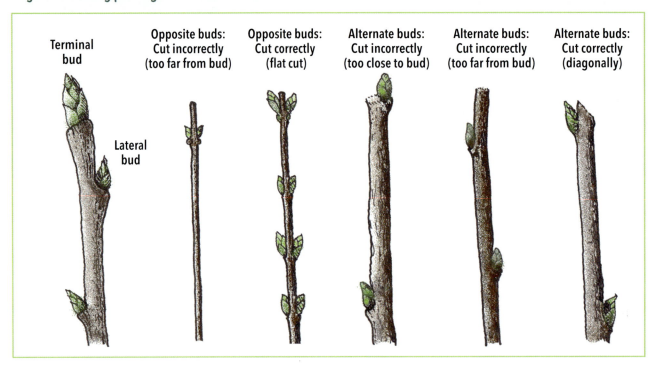

Apical dominance is the reason that few, if any, branches develop from lateral buds close to the tip of the branch. As the branch grows, it sends the terminal bud farther out, away from the center of the plant. When a lateral bud is far enough away from the terminal bud (generally after a seasons of growth), it receives weaker hormone signals until it is released from dormancy and begins to grow. This is why branching on unpruned plants occurs near the base, forming a pyramid shape.

Effective pruning manipulates bud growth to your advantage. (See Figure 17-A.) Removal of terminal buds releases buds from the growth inhibition caused by apical dominance, creating multiple branches. This type of growth response is easily seen on a sheared hedge or a tree cut flat below an electric utility line.

Compartmentalization

Cuts should be well-planned as each has the potential to affect the growth of the plant. A woody plant has to grow over a cut and "compartmentalize" or seal over the wound by forming callus or scar tissue over the cut. Small cuts do less damage than big ones, requiring less repair work for the plant. Avoid unnecessary work by careful pruning and training of young plants or by choosing plants with an ultimate size appropriate to the space and desired end result.

Re-growth response

The nature of re-growth is a function of the amount of material removed. If a small percentage of a young, vigorously growing branch is cut off, there will be re-growth up and down the remaining branch. If a large portion of that same branch is removed, the one or two buds closest to the cut will grow at a very rapid rate. Generally, removing only the growing tips stimulates more branching than the removal of a larger portion of the branch.

17.2 Why Prune?

There are many important reasons to prune!

To establish newly planted trees and shrubs

- Pruning can make young shrubs and trees denser, but do not prune until the year after planting.
- Cutting some shrubs to the ground after the first or second year allows new shoots to develop from the base of the plant.
- Small trees need frequent pruning to establish a strong, stable, and attractive shape after the first year.

Figure 17-B. Reasons to prune

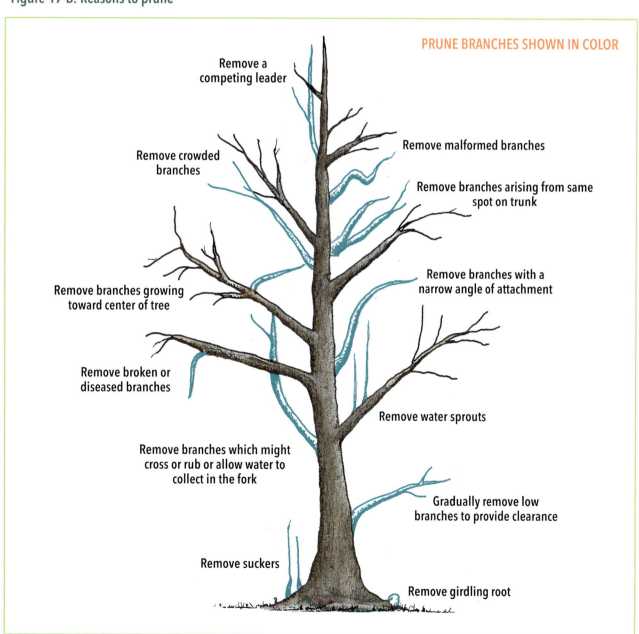

To maintain plant health

- Removing all dead, diseased, damaged, or broken branches helps prevent insects and decay-causing organisms from entering the plant (see Figure 17-B.)
- When removing infected wood, it is important that the cut be made in healthy wood below the point of infection. Always sterilize tools to prevent contamination.
- Badly-crossing branches can damage each other by rubbing and should be removed.
- Pruning can also rejuvenate declining shrubs or perennials. Severe pruning will often produce vigorous new growth in many species that appear to be dying.

To improve the quality of flowers

- Flowers and fruit may become smaller in size as their production increases. Pruning woody parts diverts energy to the production of larger (though fewer) flowers or fruit.
- Removing dead flowers and seedpods may increase blooms for the next year. On rhododendrons, lilacs, and similar plants, seedpods drain energy from the production of new shoots and flower buds and should be clipped off.
- For some perennials, removal of spent blossoms encourages the production of additional blooms. When a perennial has old leggy foliage and lush new growth at the base, the old foliage should be removed to allow newer leaves and stems to develop. If seed heads are removed immediately, biennials or short-lived perennials can sometimes be tricked into another year of flowering.

To promote desired appearance

- Thinning out trees and shrubs lets light into the interior of fruiting plants for better fruiting or to reveal interesting patterns of bark, trunk, or branch structure in specimen trees.
- Pruning or shearing can be used to develop a special form, as in hedges, espalier, or topiary work.
- Green shoots, if they develop, should be removed from a variegated plant to maintain the variegated form.
- Similarly, if a portion of a plant reverts to the wild type, such as strong vertical growth in weeping plants, those portions should be removed.

To restrict growth

- Branches that are hazardous or interfere with power lines should be removed. Homeowners should obtain professional assistance when pruning near power lines.
- Prune overgrown shrubs.
- Thinning can also help reduce storm damage in densely branched shade trees. Multiple shoots growing from a wounded area should be eliminated.
- Remove undesired shoots from the rootstock of grafted plants.
- Water sprouts are soft, rapidly growing vertical shoots that should be removed at the trunk or limb from which they grow.
- Suckers are like water sprouts that grow from the base of the plant or the roots and should be removed if they are not wanted.

17.3 Pruning Tools

- Tools must be sharp to give a good clean cut. Sharp tools leave a smooth surface on the wound with no stubs, split branches, or torn bark to harbor decay-causing organisms.
- Keep cutting edges sharp using a file, diamond sharpener, or whetstone.
- If there is danger of infection, pruning tools should be cleaned with 70 percent alcohol or bleach diluted one part to nine parts water. When bleach is used, tools should be cleaned and rinsed after use, because bleach is corrosive.
- Clean and oil tools regularly by wiping an oily cloth on blades and other surfaces.
- Wooden handles should be painted, varnished, or regularly treated with boiled linseed oil.

Hand pruners

- These cut branches of ¼- to ½-inch in diameter and come in two types: anvil and bypass.
- Anvil pruners have a straight blade that closes against a small anvil or block as the handles are squeezed. Anvil hand pruners should never be used on live plant material because the pressure of the blade against the anvil crushes the plant material.
- Bypass pruners have a curved blade that slides past a broader blade. Bypass pruners are superior to anvil pruners because they reduce tearing or crushing of plant tissues.
- The curved-blade side of the pruner should be toward the plant and should be squeezed up through or across the branch. Moving the blade down through the branch can cause tearing.
- Keep the branch to be cut as deep in the jaws and near the pivot as possible. Cutting branches that are too big for the pruners results in damage to the plant as well as dulling or otherwise damaging the pruners.

Hedge shears should be handled in such a way that they make a straight cut if a formal look is desired. Twisting the handgrips places excessive strain on the joint and creates excessive wear on the shears. Hedge shears should be used to prune hedges and ornamental plants to create a formal look. Regular use of hedge shears creates tight growth with small internodes.

After using hedge shears on hedges and formal plantings, go back with hand pruners to selectively prune out clusters of branches with small internodes so light can penetrate the hedge or formal ornamentals. If a branch is damaged by heavy snow or other injury, the plants can still be salvaged because the sunlight has allowed green foliage growth inside the plant.

Lopping shears with long handles offer better leverage for cutting larger branches and can cut branches up to one and one-half inches in diameter. If a stem is too wide for the blades, the stem cannot be cut cleanly with one cut.

Pruning saws have narrow blades and their teeth are coarser than carpenter saws. The teeth are usually designed to cut on the pull stroke. A small curved pruning saw is useful for working on compact trees or large shrubs and on plants with narrow crotches.

Pole pruners have a hooked blade with a straight blade beneath that is moved by a rope pulled downwards. Fiberglass or plastic poles are lighter than wood and do not conduct electricity, as does aluminum. Pole pruners sometimes have saws. It is important to use great care when using pole pruners to avoid being hit by falling branches. New technology has given us power (gas, battery, and electric) hedge shears and pole saws. Maintenance and disease control for these tools should be the same as for hand tools. Please follow manufacturer's safety instructions when using and cleaning all tools.

17.4 Pruning Techniques & Terms

Deadheading

Deadheading is the removal of spent flowers. Flowers that go to seed consume large amounts of energy that could be used for vegetative growth. Perennials should be deadheaded to a lateral leaf, flower, or bud unless there is a single flower stem nearly bare of leaves, in which case the stem should be cut off close to the base. Rhododendrons, lilacs, dahlias, and peonies are commonly deadheaded.

Disbudding

Disbudding is the removal of small, young, flower buds. Removal of the top (or terminal) bud causes the plant to produce more, but smaller, flowers. Removal of the side or lateral buds will produce a larger flower on a longer stem. Dahlias, carnations, chrysanthemums, and peonies are commonly disbudded.

Espalier

Espalier is a technique that forces a plant to grow in one plane. It is done if space is limited or if a dramatic effect is desired. Special knowledge, artistic skill, and patience are required. Start with young supple plants with a shape that is appropriate for espalier. Plants must be trained gradually by bending branches and tying them to a stiff wire frame, lattice, or hooks in a wall. The branches must be tied loosely and checked regularly to prevent girdling as the branches grow. Branches must be spaced far enough apart to maintain the design. Fruit trees, magnolia, camellia, forsythia, weigela, holly, viburnum, and pyracantha can be espaliered.

Pinching

Pinching is the practice of manually removing the growing tips of plants and the first set of leaves as a way to control plant size and promote bushiness. This technique is most frequently used on annuals and perennials. Chrysanthemums, asters, herbs, and many shrubs, e.g., holly, can be pinched back.

Heading back

Heading back means removing the terminal portion of a branch by cutting back to a bud or another branch. Because new shoots develop from dormant buds, you can control the shape of plants by cutting back branches to a bud or branch that is pointing in the direction of desired growth. Generally, this is an outward-pointing bud. Heading back will stimulate the growth of shoots and increase density.

A good heading cut does not leave a stub and is made about one-fourth inch above an active bud or lateral branch. Prune stems with opposite shoots (stems or buds that are directly across from each other on a stem) just above a strong pair of buds or shoots, making a clean straight cut. Prune stems that have alternate shoots (stems or buds that are not

Figure 17-C. Heading cuts

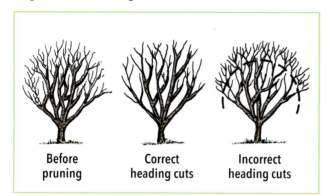

Figure 17-D. Thinning cuts

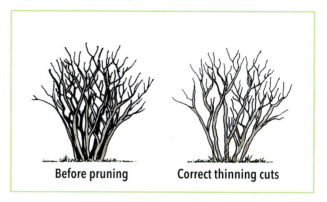

directly across from one another on a stem) by making a clean, angled cut just above the shoot so that the lowest point is opposite the bud base and the top is just above the bud (see Figures 17-A and 17-C.)

Thinning

Thinning is removal of a branch or water sprout to its point of origin, where it joins a main stem, branch, or trunk. This is the least conspicuous method of pruning and results in a more open plant without stimulating excessive growth (see Figure 17-D).

When pruning, cut back to the collar, which is the thickened area at the intersection of branches (see Figures 17-E and 17-F). Do not remove the collar, as it helps the cut heal. If the collar has grown along a dead branch, remove only the dead wood. Cuts should have smooth surfaces, not ragged edges or torn bark.

Renewal pruning

Renewal pruning stimulates the plant to produce new growth and keeps shrubs more compact and vigorous. Remove the weakest and the unhealthiest stems first. Remove the oldest branches of a shrub just above ground level, leaving only the younger, more vigorous branches. Also, remove stems less than a pencil-thickness in diameter. Cut old, poorly developed plants flush to the ground to encourage new branches to develop.

For some overgrown plants it may be advisable to do renewal pruning over several years. Cut out one stem in three each year to the ground to lessen the stress of renewal. Remove other stems to open up the center of the bush or improve its shape. The bush will appear sparse just after pruning, but new growth soon fills in. Bloom may be delayed for a season or more after renewal pruning.

Pruning large branches

Pruning large branches (more than one and one-half inches in diameter) from woody plants requires making three cuts to remove one branch (see Figure 17-F):

- Saw the first cut upward **halfway through the branch,** about a foot from the joint of the branches.

- Saw the second cut downward all the way through the branch somewhat further away from the undercut. This removes the heavy part of the branch,

- Make the final cut perpendicular to the branch next to the collar. If there is no visible collar, make the final cut where the top of the branch makes an

Figure 17-E. Cuts and collars

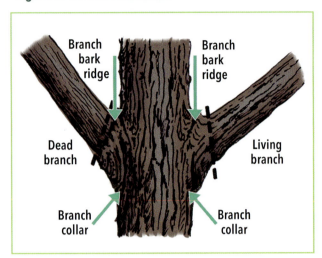

Figure 17-F. Pruning cuts

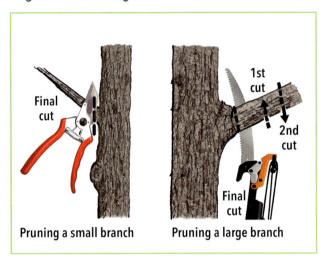

abrupt turn from the trunk so the cut is perpendicular to the top of the branch to be removed.

- Never cut the branch flush with the trunk. The collar is an area of natural chemicals that hinder the spread of diseases, and its presence encourages rapid healing.

- Generally the collar is thicker at the lower portion of the branch intersection. Hence the cut will not be parallel to the trunk, but out from it with the lower edge of the cut farther away from the trunk than the top edge.

- Never use tree-wound dressing, paint, or shellac over the cut surfaces. Contrary to what was once recommended, dressings are no longer used. Dressings may shelter disease organisms and slow the wound-healing process.

Root pruning and transplanting

Root pruning reduces a plant's excessive shoot growth, promotes flowering, and facilitates transplanting. A tree may develop long roots running 15 to 25 feet or more away from the plant, which, along with many-branched side roots, physically support the tree. The area in a three-foot radius of the tree trunk contains very few of the small "feeding roots" essential to gathering nourishment for the tree. These feeding roots are usually located quite some distance from the trunk, branching off the long main roots.

As a consequence, if the tree were to be dug and moved, the necessary feeding roots would be cut off in the balling operation, and the tree might die when transplanted. For this reason nursery operators root prune nursery-grown plants to force them to grow small feeding roots near the base of the plant. These small roots are then moved in the balling operation to ensure growth after transplanting.

To enable safe digging of small trees or shrubs:

- Root-prune plants a year or so before transplanting.

- In the spring, sever half the roots by forcing a sharp spade into the soil around the plant, alternately leaving a shovel width of untouched soil in between cuts.

- The circle of cuts should be slightly smaller than the size of the ball that will eventually be dug.
- In the early fall, sever the other half of the roots, thereby cutting all the roots growing at a depth of a foot or less.
- Move the tree in the following spring.
- Recent research indicates that most new roots grow from the cut end. Therefore, a root ball four to six inches larger in diameter than the root-pruned area must be dug to include the newly developed roots.

Root pruning will also force a vigorously growing fruit tree, wisteria vine, or dogwood into bloom. Using a spade to cut the roots early in spring, as explained above, is all that is sometimes necessary to force a tree, shrub, or vine into bloom the following year. It is important to keep root-pruned plants well watered. Root pruning can also be used to slow the growth of a tree or shrub. It is more commonly used for conifers that do not tolerate pruning of their branches.

Girdling roots

Occasionally roots grow around or across the base of a tree rather than growing away from the tree. As these girdling roots grow, they compete with the growing tree for space and act as a tourniquet, slowly killing the tree. When this happens, it is necessary to remove the root early before it eventually girdles the tree. Pot-bound container-grown plants are prone to root girdling.

Pollarding

Pollarding is a pruning system in which the top of the tree or shrub is headed back severely when young, followed by annual removal of sprouts that arise from the cut area. This maintains a formal appearance and keeps the tree or shrub small. After a number of years pollard heads (also called knuckles or knobs) develop where the sprouts are removed. Care must be taken not to cut into these knobs.

Not all trees or shrubs can withstand pollarding, although it is commonly done on crepe myrtles. Other trees that can be pollarded include: sweet gum, ash, sycamore, beech, catalpa, hawthorn, elm, horse chestnut, oak, maple, pear, and linden. Pollarding was used before smaller cultivars were developed. Now that so many small plants are available, it is better to select a plant that matures at an appropriate size than to undergo the yearly pruning required for pollarding.

17.5 When to Prune

The time to prune is based on a plant's flowering, fruiting, or growth habit:

- When in doubt, prune in early spring. This may mean loss of flowers for one year, but the tree or shrub will not be damaged.
- Do not prune from August to October because the new growth will not have a chance to harden off before winter.
- For plants that flower before the end of June, prune immediately after flowering. Because flower buds develop during the prior growing season, fall, winter, or spring pruning will reduce the spring flowering display.
- For plants that flower in summer or autumn, prune in the winter or early spring before new growth begins; these plants develop flowers on growth produced during spring.

- Delay pruning plants that are grown for their ornamental fruits, such as cotoneasters, pyracanthas, and viburnums, until after the fruit drops.
- If maximum growth is desired, prune in very early spring and avoid pruning during or immediately after the initial spring growth spurt. For minimum re-growth, prune when growth is ending for the season, usually in July.
- Stressed trees should not be pruned because all leaves are important for recovery. Diseased or dead branches should always be removed.
- Prune evergreens, such as pines, in late spring or early summer by selectively pinching off about half of the new growth or candles to promote fullness or reduce growth. (See Figure 17-M.)
- Hollies and some other evergreens can be pruned during the winter if their branches will be used for holiday decorations. Save any severe pruning of evergreens for early spring. New growth at this time will soon overgrow any disfigurement caused by pruning.
- Prune any plants that are damaged by storms as soon as possible, no matter what the season. Minor corrective pruning can also be done at any time.

Sap flow

Some trees, such as birch, maple, dogwood, elm, walnut, and yellowwood exude an excessive amount of sap from pruning wounds made in late winter or early spring. This is not harmful to the tree, but to prevent this, prune these trees in late fall or early winter (November through December) or after new spring growth is finished in May or June.

17.6 Training Newly-Planted Trees

At first, newly planted trees should be pruned only to remove broken or damaged branches. It is a myth that trees should be pruned when planted to compensate for root loss, because leaves and shoot tips provide food and growth substances that stimulate root production (see **Chapter 20, Tree Fruits**, for exceptions).

Roots

- When deciduous trees are planted bare-root, light pruning of the roots may be needed if any are broken, damaged, or dead.
- Shorten longer roots if they will not fit into the hole. Never bend or fold a root into the planting hole.
- Container-grown plants that have become root-bound need to have their roots thinned or cut at planting time. Several vertical cuts, an inch or so deep, down the side of the root ball and across the bottom of the root ball will disrupt the circling root pattern and allow for better root spread in the planting hole.

Temporary branches

- Young trees need their low, temporary branches to provide sustenance for the growing tree. These temporary branches also help protect the trunk and should be kept short enough not to compete with permanent branches.
- As the tree grows taller, the lower branches may be removed gradually over the course of several years (before they become one inch in diameter). As a tree grows taller, branches do not move farther off the ground.

Leader

- Maintain a single dominant leader, which is the tallest, strongest, main trunk of the tree.
- Do not prune back this leader or allow lateral or secondary branches to outgrow the leader.
- If a tree has co-dominant stems or double leaders, remove one, saving the straightest and strongest, to avoid structural weakness.
- Prevent lateral branches from growing larger than half the trunk diameter.

Scaffold branches

- Although some trees, such as conifers and sweet gum, require little or no formative pruning, many young trees need pruning to establish a beneficial branch structure.
- A couple of years after planting, while the tree is still young, establish a strong structure of primary scaffold branches to form the framework of the mature tree.
- Scaffold branches are the primary boughs radiating from the trunk of a tree. Secondary branches stem from the scaffold branches.
- Scaffold branches should not arise from the same point on a trunk.
- Carefully space permanent scaffold branches both vertically and radially.
- The distance between scaffold branches should be three percent of the tree's eventual height. For example, a tree that will be 50 feet tall should have scaffold branches that are no closer than 18 inches apart along the trunk.

Forcing laterals

- If a young tree is failing to produce lateral growth, head back the tip one to two inches during the growing season when the growing point reaches the height that a lateral is desired.
- Select the most vigorous new shoot to become the new leader.
- Choose a new shoot that is growing in the appropriate direction to become the lateral by removing the other shoots that were formed.
- You can pinch back several times per year during the growing season to produce the desired laterals.

One other method that may be used to encourage branching:

- Notch the trunk by removing a slit of bark about a millimeter wide around about fifteen percent of the trunk circumference just above a bud about a month before bud growth.

Crotches

- The angle formed between two branches is called the crotch (see Figure 17-G.)
- Sometimes branches develop with narrow angles of attachment (i.e., with tight crotches). As the tree grows, bark becomes enclosed, which leads to weakness and branch failure or dieback.
- These branches should be removed or forced into a wider angle when the tree is young.
- To achieve branches with sturdy wide crotches, use spacers, sometimes called limb spreaders, or simply bend the branch to a wider angle while it is still supple.

Figure 17-G. Crotches

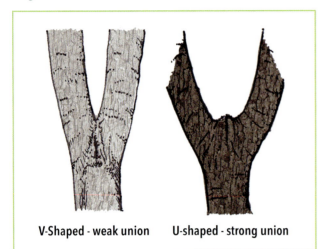

V-Shaped - weak union   U-shaped - strong union

- Spreaders can be made of wire, wood, or plastic and are positioned in a branch intersection to force the angle of intersection to be wider.
- Weights can be tied to young branches to widen the crotch angle. Remove spreaders or weights after one season.
- The spreading and spacing of branches is a long-time practice used on fruit trees that can be applied to any tree.

17.7 Pruning Mature Trees

Crown thinning

Mature trees seldom need pruning, but three techniques can be used when necessary (See Figure 17-H.) Crown thinning is the selective removal of branches to increase light penetration and air movement in the crown of a tree. No more than one-fourth of the living crown should be removed at any one time. Removing a portion of a branch causes the terminal portion of what remains to become dominant. This remaining dominant branch should be strongly attached.

When thinning, it is best to cut to a side branch that is at least one-third the size of the one being cut. Branches smaller than that will not be joined as strongly and are more susceptible to breakage. When cutting back a branch on a mature tree to a lateral branch, remove no more than one fourth of its foliage. Thinning will reduce wind damage by diminishing the degree of wind block.

Crown raising

Crown raising involves removal of the lower branches to allow foot or vehicle traffic under the tree. At least two-thirds of the total height of the tree should have living branches. Street trees should have at least 16 feet of clearance for trucks. Lawn trees should have eight feet of clearance for foot traffic. Trees used for screening or windbreak can have branches near the ground.

Crown reduction

Crown reduction is the removal of upper branches when the tree has become too tall. Branches that are too tall are removed back to the next branch. This procedure should only be used if absolutely necessary. When it is necessary to remove half the foliage from a branch, it is better to remove the whole branch. Never remove more than one-fourth of a tree's canopy. It is better to make several small pruning cuts than one big cut. Avoid cutting large branches if possible.

Topping and tipping

Never "top" a shade tree (see Figure 17-I).

Topping causes the growth of many weak suckers that may break off when they become large branches. Wood rots are more likely to be a problem in topped trees. If a tree must

Figure 17-H. Crown thinning, crown raising, and crown reduction

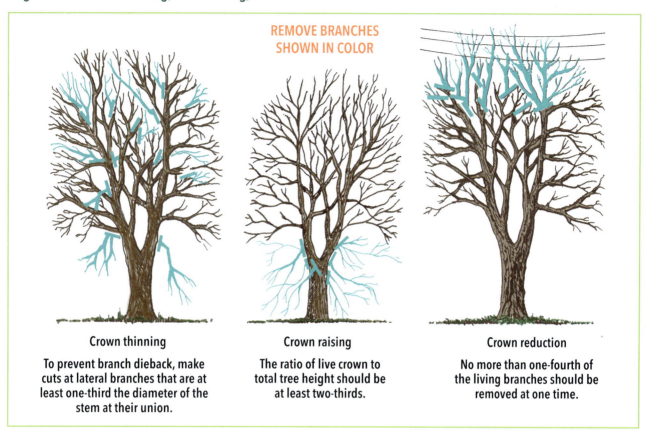

Crown thinning
To prevent branch dieback, make cuts at lateral branches that are at least one-third the diameter of the stem at their union.

Crown raising
The ratio of live crown to total tree height should be at least two-thirds.

Crown reduction
No more than one-fourth of the living branches should be removed at one time.

be reduced in size, thin it by pruning entire branches at their point of origin.

Tipping is the procedure of cutting lateral branches between nodes or buds to reduce crown width instead or cutting back to a node or crotch. Again, thin by pruning entire branches at their point of origin.

Trunk injury

Physical damage to tree trunks requires special attention:

- Trim loose bark from the edges of the wound back to where bark is firmly attached to the sapwood, i.e., the layer of wood under the bark.
- Carefully remove all shredded sapwood and leave a smooth surface to prevent intrusion of insects and disease.

Figure 17-I. Topping and tipping

Do NOT top trees   Do NOT tip branches

- Leave old wounds undisturbed, especially when callus or healing tissue has developed along the outside edge of the wound.
- Trees can protect themselves from invasion by decay-causing organisms through a natural process called compartmentalization. The callus tissue

that forms along the outside edge of an old wound is part of that defense mechanism.

- Replace broken terminal leaders by tying a lateral branch into a vertical position braced with a wooden stick (see Figure 17-J).
- Instead of removing a large limb, it is always better to lighten up the end of the limb and/or cable the limb.
- Pruning very large trees can be dangerous and is best performed by a licensed and certified arborist.

17.8 Pruning Shrubs

The same general principles of pruning trees also apply to pruning shrubs. The bottom of shrubs is usually pruned to be wider than the top so that light can reach the lower branches, except for naturally vase-shaped shrubs.

Figure 17-J. Leader replacement

Small-leaved plants, such as boxwood, can be clipped with shears or a hedge trimmer, but shears can damage large leaves, causing them to turn brown and die. Therefore, on large-leaved plants, such as rhododendron, use pruners, not shears. Maintaining a shrub in a specific shape may require pruning at least once a year. Repeated shearing eventually makes the plant so dense that air circulation is reduced, increasing chances of disease, such as volutella in boxwoods. This can be avoided by use of thinning cuts, or opening small "holes" in the top and sides of the shrub to allow air and light inside.

Hard pruning results in vigorous regrowth. If a shrub is lopsided, hard pruning on the weak side should cause that side to fill in. Sometimes overgrown shrubs can be "elevated" by pruning them up to resemble small specimen trees.

Rejuvenation pruning

To completely rejuvenate neglected or overgrown healthy shrubs in one season, cut all the stems to within one or two inches above the ground before growth begins in the spring. This drastic method can restore an overgrown shrub faster than renewal pruning. Rejuvenation pruning may result in excessive re-growth of stems from the base of the plant or root system. If all the new growth is allowed to remain, plant quality will suffer. Thin new growth and space it to create a plant with proper density. Long stems can be shortened to stimulate branching within the shrub.

17.9 Pruning Hedges

Hedges can be either formal or informal. The formal hedge is pruned with hedge shears to a definite size and shape, one or more times a year. The informal hedge, often a row of shrubs planted close together but allowed to grow normally, is pruned annually to thin out the oldest wood and to maintain a desired height and width, if it is pruned at all (see Figure 17-K.)

The most important step in starting a formal hedge is the first shearing in early spring **the year after planting:**

- Small shrubs one to three years old should be cut back to about three to five inches above the ground. This will force new shoots at the base of the plant to develop into a thick, bushy shrub.
- No additional pruning is needed on newly planted hedges until the next spring.
- When older shrubs are used to start a hedge, about one third can be cut from the top and sides to develop a thick, bushy hedge.

The recommended shape for hedges is a narrow pyramid or inverted "V." For example, a hedge five feet high could be three and a half to four feet wide at the base and about a foot wide at the top. The top of the formal hedge may be slightly rounded or pointed. The rounded top helps the plant to shed snow, which could otherwise break branches.

If the top becomes as wide as or wider than the base, the lower portion will be too shaded and produce sparse, weak growth. (See Figure 17-L.)

Formal and informal deciduous hedges can be kept vigorous for years by annually cutting out one third to one fourth of the oldest branches near or a few inches above the ground before new growth starts. Use hand pruners, loppers, or a curved pruning saw. This method encourages new growth at the base of the plant. Along with regular shearing, formal hedges can also be kept vigorous by thinning out upper branches.

Deciduous hedges that are overgrown, bare-bottomed, or misshapen can be renovated by pruning to one foot below the desired height and trimming frequently for the next few years to the shape and fullness desired.

Narrow-leaf evergreen hedges should not be pruned into bare branches; at least ½ to 1 inch of green foliage must be left. Narrow leaf evergreen plants include junipers, arborvitaes, yews, hemlocks, pine and spruce. Narrow-leaf evergreen plants that grow too large may have to be replaced.

Most broadleaf evergreen hedges should not be pruned into bare wood. There are, however, a number of broadleaf evergreens that can be pruned into bare branches in order to maintain

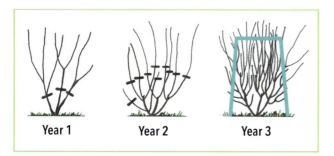

Figure 17-K. Pruning a young hedge

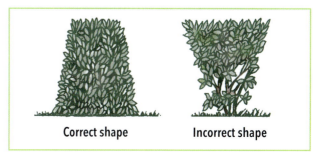

Figure 17-L. Pruning a mature hedge

their shape but reduce their size. These include holly, euonymus, privet, osmanthus and eleagnus. If a holly hedge is too large, it can be pruned down to just a foot off the ground to promote a new hedge if pruned in the very early spring (mid-March). If such pruning is done in the spring the plants will need to be watered as if they were just transplanted for the first full year, at least once a week.

17.10 Pruning Conifers

Plant larger conifers such as fir, spruce, and pine only in areas where heavy pruning will not be necessary, because new shoots will not develop from cuts made in the older wood. Growth can be diminished by root pruning. Conifers do not need pruning for spacing of lateral branches. Whorls of branches emerge close to each other and will not crowd out each other or the leader. Appropriate vertical spacing occurs naturally.

Most conifers used in foundation plantings should be pruned every year. Once they have become overgrown it is usually too late to begin corrective pruning. Yews, junipers, hemlocks, false-cypress, and arborvitae may be headed back in spring or summer. These are the only conifers that will rebound after severe pruning, which should be done in early spring if needed.

Firs and spruces may be lightly pruned in late summer, fall, or winter after growth is completed. Leave the side buds present along the twigs. Never cut the central leader.

Pines may be lightly pruned in early June to increase density by removing the bud plus an inch or so of the young shoots. If large cuts are made, new branches will arise only in the area where needles are present along the stem.

Figure 17-M. Pine candle pinching

To thicken the growth of coniferous trees such as pine, fir, or spruce, pinch out half the candle, which is the new spring growth, when it is about two inches long. (See Figure 17-M.) Use fingers rather than shears.

17.11 Pruning Other Plants

Vines and groundcovers

The general principles of pruning ornamental shrubs also apply to vines:

- Always prune back to a lateral branch, twig, or bud, and do not leave a stub.
- Remove dead and weak wood back to healthy wood.
- Annually thin old and weak stems to encourage new growth.
- Thin any crowded stems by cutting them to the ground.
- Some fast-growing vines can be severely pruned to induce growth close to the ground. If done early in the spring before new growth starts, it causes no harm.

The best time to prune most vines is before new growth begins. Prune early spring-flowering vines soon after they have finished blooming. New growth that develops after pruning will produce buds for the next bloom season.

Some common vines make rapid, vertical growth with few lateral branches except near the top. These vines can be pinched or the leaders pruned back during the growing season to develop more horizontal-growing branches. Then, vertical growth can be allowed to develop where needed. Horizontal branches tend to grow more slowly and produce more leaves, flowers, and fruit than vertical branches.

Perennials

In general, perennials should be deadheaded after blooming unless self-seeding is desired, the seed heads are attractive, or the seeds feed wildlife. Many people allow foxglove, digitalis, columbine, and corydalis to go to seed to generate new plants. Coneflower, Joe-pye weed, sunflower, bee balm, hosta, goldenrod, asters, coreopsis, globe thistle, sedum, native switchgrass and black-eyed Susan seeds are considered attractive in winter and a good food source for birds.

Some perennials are thinned to improve air circulation and reduce the risk of disease, increase flower size, or improve the flowers' appearance. Thinning for perennials means cutting stems at the base of the plant. Phlox, asters, bee balm, and delphinium all benefit from being thinned because they are prone to developing powdery mildew.

Sometimes flowers are removed because they are not considered as attractive as the leaves. Some hostas are an example. In the fall, cutting plants to the ground tidies up the garden and removes debris that might harbor insects or disease.

Pinching

To avoid staking and to produce more compact plants with stronger stems, pinch back perennials (such as chrysanthemums and asters) several times before mid-July. Generally, do the first pinching as soon as there are several sets of leaves on each stem. This pinching delays flowering. Pinching back only some of the stems extends the blooming season, because pinched portions will bloom later. To stagger plant heights or bloom times, perennials such as tall phlox and Autumn Joy sedum can be pruned once or twice until mid-July before the bloom in the fall. Perennials with one leafy stalk, such as a lily, and those with leafless flowering stalks, such as iris, should not be pinched back before bloom.

Ornamental grasses

Grasses that die back in the winter should be cut to the ground in early spring before new growth begins. Dead or diseased foliage on evergreen grasses should be similarly removed. When clumps of grasses become large, cutting them back can be difficult. If two strips of duct tape or string are wrapped around the clump, one at ground level and another a few of inches above it, a chain saw or reciprocating saw can be used to cut the stalks between the strips of tape.

Table 17-A. Pruning guidelines for specific plants

The following table lists common plants and generalized guidelines for their pruning. When in doubt, do not prune; otherwise, use the suggestions below.

Plant name	Botanical name	Symbol	Comments
Abelia	*Abelia grandiflora*	bsg, x, tc	Cut oldest stems to ground each year. Long shoots can be headed back during the growing season.
Andromeda	*Pieris*	af, x	Routine pruning is not required.
Aralia	*Acanthopanax*	bsg	Routine pruning is not required.
Arborvitae	*Thuja*	bsg	Do not cut into old wood that has no leaves or needles.
Ash	Mountain, *Sorbus*	af	For *S. aria* prune previous year's growth by 2/3 in spring. For others routine pruning is not required.,
Aucuba	*Aucuba*	bsg, x	Routine pruning is not required. Prune out black foliage/stems in late spring.
Azaleas and Rhododendrons	Azaleas, Rhododendrons	af, x	Routine pruning is not required. Prune out spent flowers to prevent seed formation. If needed, prune old, non-blooming stems to the ground immediately after blooming.
Barberry	*Berberis thunbergii*	af, bsg, x, tc	Remove old stems to ground each spring. (This plant is listed as a "Plant Invader of Mid-Atlantic Natural Areas" by the US Fish & Wildlife Service.)
Bayberry	*Myrica gale*	bsg, x	When overgrown, cut stems back to the ground.
Beautyberry	*Callicarpa*	bsg, x	Remove 1/3 of oldest stems to the ground each spring.
Beautybush	*Kolkwitzia amabilis*	af, tc	After blooming, cut 1/3 of oldest and weak stems to the ground.
Broom	*Cytisus scoparius*	af	Cut stems to a bud or shoot below spent flowers.
Boxwood	*Buxus*	bsg	Trim boxwood in spring to allow new growth to mature before cold temperatures. Prune out dead branches to the ground any time.
Bush-clover	*Lespedeza*	bsg, x	Cut to ground in spring.
Butterfly Bush	*Buddleia davidii*	bsg, x	Remove crowded stems yearly and cut back remaining stems to 2 or 3 buds above the ground. (Species from Asia and Central America are listed as a "Plant Invader of Mid-Atlantic Natural Areas" by the US Fish & Wildlife Service.)
Camellia	*Camellia japonica*	af	Routine pruning not required. Deadhead after flowering. Renovate by cutting 1/3 of the oldest wood to the ground per year.
Camellia	*Camellia sasanqua*	bsg or af	Fall bloomers; prune in early spring after frost to allow time for next fall's buds to form.
Cherry	*Prunus*	af, hc	Cut overgrown branches back to another branch or the trunk. Prune out water sprouts and suckers.

af=after flowering | **bsg**=before spring growth | **x**=cut to ground when dormant in spring to renew | **hc**=heading cut (Fig. 17-C) | **tc**=thinning cut (Fig. 17-D)

continued on next page

continued from previous page

Table 17-A. Pruning guidelines for specific plants

Plant name	Botanical name	Symbol	Comments
Clematis	*Clematis*		**Group 1:** Non-climbing. Prune hard in winter. **Group 2:** Flowers on year-old wood. Prune immediately after flowering. Cut back previous year's growth (on which flowers just bloomed) to a few centimeters of main framework. **Group 3:** Flowers in summer or fall on current growth. Prune entire previous season's growth to 1 ft. off the ground. **Group 4:** Flowers late spring to early summer on last season's growth. Prune lightly to tidy up plants.
Cotoneaster	*Cotoneaster*	bsg, x	After blooming, prune extension growth to 4-6 buds.
Crabapple	*Malus*	af	Remove suckers.
Crape myrtle	*Lagerstroemia indica*	bsg	Can be trained as a single- or multi-stemmed tree.
Cypress	*Chamaecyparis*	bsg	If pruning is needed, do not cut into old wood with no viable buds.
Deutzia	*Deutzia*	af, tc	Cut 1 stem in 3 of oldest or weakest stems to ground after flowering. Keep center of plant thinned out.
Dogwood	*Cornus*	af	Remove suckers to the ground after flowering. Remove vertical suckers that grow on tops of horizontally-growing branches. Do heavy pruning before spring growth.
Dogwood, Redosier	*Corrnus sericea*	bsg, x, tc	Prune 1/3 of old growth each spring to promote new colorful stems.
Elaeagnus	*Elaeagnus*	bsg	Routine pruning is not required. If rejuvenation is needed cut back whole shrub to 6 inches in late winter..
Euonymous	*Euonymous*	bsg	Routine pruning is not required. Remove solid green stems/leaves from variegated plants.
Fir	*Abies*		Remove only lateral tips. Do not pinch leader or cut into wood without needles.
Forsythia	*Forsythia*	af, x, tc	Cut 1 stem in 3 of oldest/weakest stems to ground after bloom.
Fothergilla	*Fothergilla*	bsg	Routine pruning is not required.
Fringe-tree	*Chionanthus*	af, hc	Prune immediately after flowering to promote next year's flowering.
Goldenrain tree	*Koelreuteria paniculata*	bsg	Prune out old flowering shoots and weak wood right after flowering.
Hawthorn	*Crataegus*	af	Routine pruning is not required.
Hemlock	*Tsuga*	bsg	Can be sheared, but generally requires no pruning.
Hibiscus	*Hibiscus*	bsg	Routine pruning is not required.
Holly	*Ilex*	bsg, x, hc	If plants are bare from the ground, prune to 12 inches in early March. Can be pruned in winter for berries.
Honeysuckle	*Lonicera*	af, x	Prune 1/3 of old branches to the ground immediately after flowering.
Hydrangea, macrophylla	*H. arborescens*	bsg, x	Leave flower heads on during winter and remove in spring. Remove any very thin or very old shoots at ground level in spring if necessary.

af=after flowering | **bsg**=before spring growth | **x**=cut to ground when dormant in spring to renew | **hc**=heading cut (Fig. 17-C) | **tc**=thinning cut (Fig. 17-D)

continued on next page

continued from previous page

Table 17-A. Pruning guidelines for specific plants

Plant name	Botanical name	Symbol	Comments
Panicle Hydrangea	Hydrangea, paniculata	bsg	For larger flowers, cut previous season's growth to 2-4 buds.
Ivy, Boston	Parthenocissus	af, bsg	Prune branches to control spreading
Juniper	Juniperus	bsg, hc	Routine pruning is not required. Avoid pruning to wood without needles. Can be sheared in early spring before new growth.
Kerria	Kerria	af, x, tc	Prune 1 stem in 3 of oldest or weakest stems to the ground after flowering.
Laburnum	Laburnum	af	Prune and shape as a shrub or prune off branches to create a tree in spring.
Lavender	Lavandula	bsg	Cut previous year's growth to within 2-4 inches off the ground.
Leucothoe	Leucothoe	bsg	Cut 1 stem in 3 to the ground if necessary.
Leyland Cypress	x Cupresssocyparis	bsg	Can be sheared. Do not cut into wood with no foliage.
Lilac	Syringa	af, x, tc	In early spring (while still dormant) prune out dead, crossing branches and suckers.
Liriope	Liriope	bsg	Remove old foliage four to six weeks before spring growth.
Magnolia	Magnolia	af	Routine pruning not required.
Mahonia	Mahonia	bsg, tc, hc	Remove 1/3 of leggy growth to the ground. Head back to desired height.
Mock Orange	Philadelphus	af, x, tc	Cut 1 stem in 3 of oldest or weakest stems to ground after flowering. Remove seed pods.
Mountain Laurel	Kalmia latifolia	af, x	Routine pruning is not required.
Nandina	Nandina	bsg, x, tc	If pruning is needed, cut 1 stem in 3 of the oldest to the ground.
Photinia	Photinia	bsg	Routine pruning is not required. Can be sheared mid-season.
Pine	Pinus		See pine pinching diagram (Fig. 17-M). To slow growth remove half to two-thirds of the candle-like terminal growth in spring. Do not cut into wood that has no needles. To reduce size, thin back to laterally growing shoot.
Privet	Ligustrum	af, hc	Can be cut back to two to four inches from ground. (Obtusifolium, L. sinense, and L. japonicum are listed as a "Plant Invader of Mid-Atlantic Natural Areas" by the US Fish & Wildlife Service.)
Pyracantha	Pyracantha	af, hc	Cut longest branches to control size and shape. Old plants can be pruned severely, but berry production will be diminished for a few years.
Quince	Chaenomeles	af, hc	Prune in the spring after flowering. Remove older wood as necessary.
Redbud	Cercis	af	Routine pruning is not required. Major cuts should be made before spring growth.

af=after flowering | **bsg**=before spring growth | **x**=cut to ground when dormant in spring to renew | **hc**=heading cut (Fig. 17-C) | **tc**=thinning cut (Fig. 17-D)

continued on next page

continued from previous page

Table 17-A. Pruning guidelines for specific plants

Plant name	Botanical name	Symbol	Comments
Rhododendron	*Rhododendron*	af, hc	Routine pruning is not required. Do not leave leafless stems inside plant, because they will not develop new growth.
Rose	*Rosa*		Prune tree roses or rose standards as you do hybrid teas, cutting the branches to within 6-10 inches of the base of the crown. This encourages rounded, compact, vigorous growth. Miniature roses do not need special pruning. Just remove dead growth and the rose hips.
			Hybrid tea, grandiflora, floribunda and large-flowered repeat-blooming roses should be pruned before or just after bud break. First, remove branches that are dead, damaged, diseased, weak, and growing inward, and branches that cross other branches. Cut at least 1 inch below damaged areas. If two branches rub, remove 1. On old bushes, cut 1-2 of the oldest canes out each year. Next, cut back the remaining canes at a 45-degree angle, about 1/4-inch above a strong outer bud. Aim the cut upward from the inner side of the bush to push growth outward, promote healthy shoots and quality flowers. Dab the cut ends with a weatherproof glue to prevent rose cane borers. The main guideline for pruning should be to cut down to "good" solid wood. If the cut end shows excessive discoloration or is not firm, cut down further. Cuts all the way to the bud crown are not unusual for Maryland conditions.
			Climbers with blooming habits like hybrid teas are officially classified as large-flowered climbers (LCl) and should be pruned at the same time. Tie the main canes to a horizontal support and cut back to the base when they are diseased, damaged, or unproductive. Do the main pruning on the lateral growth, leaving 4-8 bud eyes. Some LCls are known as "pillar climbers" because they bloom well when the main canes are grown vertically but most do best when horizontally positioned.
			Old-fashioned ramblers and many old garden roses only bloom in the spring. Because all blooms occur on canes at least 1 year old, prune these roses only after the blooming period.
St. Johnswort	*Hypericum*	bsg, tc	Cut 1 stem in 3 of oldest or weakest stems to ground after blooming.
Shadbush	*Amelanchier*	bsg	Only prune in early spring before plants leaf out.
Silk tree	*Albizia julibrissin*	af	Prune to raise canopy in early spring.
Skimmia	*Skimmia*	bsg, x	Cut back to allotted space when necessary.
Smoketree	*Cotinus coggygria*	bsg, x	Prune tree back by half in winter to allow it to flower and "smoke."
Snowball, Japanese	*Styrax japonica*	af	When used as a shrub, remove oldest stems to the ground. When used as a small tree, prune to a single stem and thin crowded branches at the top.
Sourwood	*Oxydendron*	af	No routine pruning. It is difficult to replace lost leader.
Spirea	*Spirea*	bsg	Spring blooming af; summer blooming bsg, tc. Cut oldest stems to the ground.
Spruce	*Picea*		Pruning not generally recommended. If pruning into wood with no needles becomes necessary, remove entire branch. To slow growth, cut new shoots to 1-half when needles are half-expanded in spring.

af=after flowering | **bsg**=before spring growth | **x**=cut to ground when dormant in spring to renew | **hc**=heading cut (Fig. 17-C) | **tc**=thinning cut (Fig. 17-D)

continued on next page

continued from previous page

Table 17-A. Pruning guidelines for specific plants

Plant name	Botanical name	Symbol	Comments
Sumac	*Rhus*	bsg	Cut back oldest and weak stems to the ground to encourage new growth closer to the soil line.
Summersweet	*Clethra alnifolia*	bsg, tc	Oldest and weakest stems can be cut to the ground if necessary.
Sweetshrub	*Calycanthus*	bsg, tc	If needed, cut out oldest stems to the ground or head back longest stems.
Trumpet creeper	*Campsis*	af, bsg	Annually, cut stems back to 3-4 buds to promote new growth. Prune tips during growing season to promote side branching.
Viburnum	*Viburnum*		Spring flowering af; summer flowering bsg, x, hc, tc. Head/thin as needed.
Weigela	*Weigela*	af, x, tc	Prune in late spring. Remove 1/3 of oldest wood at the ground.
Winter jasmine	*Jasminum nudiflorum*	af	Prune in spring after blooming. Prune unbranched stems to a pair of buds to stimulate side branches. Remove weak shoots and crossing growth.
Wisteria	*Wisteria*	af	2 months after flowering, cut back to 5-6 buds from a main branch. In winter cut to 2-3 buds from a main branch. Rejuvenate by removing up to 1/3 of top growth. (Wisterias *sinensis* and *floribunda* are listed as a "Plant Invader of Mid-Atlantic Natural Areas" by the US Fish & Wildlife Service.)
Yew	*Taxus*	bsg	Yews respond best to late-winter pruning (when dormant). Trim back a little on all sides.

af=after flowering | **bsg**=before spring growth | **x**=cut to ground when dormant in spring to renew | **hc**=heading cut (Fig. 17-C) | **tc**=thinning cut (Fig. 17-D)

AUTHOR

Ginny Rosenkranz, Principal Agent Associate, Commercial Horticulture, University of Maryland Extension.

ILLUSTRATOR

Don Wittig, University of Maryland Extension Master Gardener, Montgomery County. Colorization by LeAnn Zotta.

PUBLICATIONS

Brickell, C. 1996. *Pruning and Training.* Dorling Kindersley Limited. London, UK.

Gilman, E. F. and S. Lilly. 2002. *Tree Pruning Best Management Practices.* International Society of Arboriculture. Champaign, IL.

Gouin, F. 1995. *Pruning Ornamental Trees and Shrubs.* Bulletin 150. Updated in 2000 by Bosmans, R. University of Maryland Extension, College Park, MD.

Harris, R. W., J. Clark, and N. Matheny. 2004. *Arboriculture Integrated Management of Landscape Trees, Shrubs, and Vines.* Prentice Hall. Upper Saddle River, NJ.

How to Prune Trees. NA-FR-01-95. USDA, Forest Service. Washington, DC.

Maryland Master Gardener Handbook. 1996. HGIC, University of Maryland Extension. College Park, MD.

Nuss, R. J. 1998. *Pruning Ornamental Plants. Special Circular 235.* Pennsylvania State University. University Park, PA.

Pittenger, D., editor. 2002. *California Master Gardener Handbook.* ANR Publication 3382. University of California Cooperative Extension. Berkeley, CA.

Sweringen, J., K. Reshetiloff, B. Slattery, and S. Zwicker. 2002. *Plant Invaders of Mid-Atlantic Natural Areas.* National Park Service and U.S. Fish & Wildlife Service, Washington, DC.

18: VEGETABLES

Jon Traunfeld

18 VEGETABLES

CONTENTS

18.1 Starting a Vegetable Garden 514
18.2 Garden Types and Techniques 514
18.3 Selecting a Garden Site 516
18.4 Soil Assessment and Testing 521
18.5 Soil Amendments 522
18.6 Cover Crops 523
18.7 Pollination 525
18.8 Vegetable Planting Guide 525
18.9 Planting Seed 534
18.10 Starting Your Own Transplants 536
18.11 Vegetable Garden Maintenance 540
18.12 Harvesting Vegetables 546
18.13 Herbs 548
18.14 Profiles of Selected Vegetable Crops 556

LEARNING OBJECTIVES

- How to start a vegetable garden, including site selection and soil preparation
- Basic techniques for weed management, fertilizing, and watering
- Concepts and practices for intensive vegetable production: raised beds, close planting, succession planting, trellising, interplanting, and season extension
- Characteristics of 31 common garden vegetables

INTRODUCTION

Vegetable gardening is an empowering activity for people of all ages and backgrounds. Growing and sharing fresh produce connects us to the land and each other. Whether you have a few containers, a community garden plot, or a large home garden, you can supply your family and friends with nutritious vegetables for six to nine months of the year. Vegetable gardening is also excellent exercise and can help reduce household food expenses.

This chapter will emphasize organic, sustainable, and intensive gardening practices that improve soil, plant, and human health. The words "organic" and "sustainable" are often used interchangeably to describe a holistic gardening approach that recognizes that soil health, plant health, ecosystem health, and human health are all interconnected. Organic and sustainable approaches are similar and complementary.

The cornerstones of organic gardening are to:

- Improve soil health by feeding the soil food web with organic matter and recycling nutrients
- Grow a large number of different plants and cultivars to expand genetic diversity both above and below ground, attract and conserve beneficial insects, and increase garden resiliency

Farmers must be certified under the National Organic Program of the United States Department of Agriculture (USDA) to sell their products as "organic." The program is administered in our state by the Maryland Department of Agriculture. Unfortunately, there is not a similar program available for organic home gardeners. As a result, "organic" practices vary widely, with the vast majority of home gardeners choosing to avoid synthetic fertilizers and pesticides.

Sustainable gardening means growing vegetables year after year by practicing the 4Rs (reduce, re-use, recycle, re-think), and minimizing any negative impacts to the environment.

Figure 18-A. USDA organic logo

These are best practices for sustainable, organic vegetable gardening:

- Protect and improve the soil
- Recycle plants and nutrients
- Water and fertilize wisely
- Control stormwater
- Increase biodiversity
- Use Integrated Pest Management (IPM)
- Attract and conserve pollinators and natural enemies
- Rely on locally-available materials and resources

18.1 Starting a Vegetable Garden

A wide range of vegetable crops, representing up to 18 plant families, can be grown in all parts of Maryland. Interestingly, none of the most commonly grown vegetables are native to Maryland, although a few, like Jerusalem artichoke, are native to North America.

Most vegetable crops are annuals with a relatively shallow root system that competes poorly against weeds for water and nutrients. Consistent success and high yields are possible when plant needs are understood and satisfied.

Initial planning tips

- Start small and be realistic. Match your garden size with the resources you have for planting, maintaining, and harvesting.
- Test your soil, amend if necessary, and improve it with organic matter.
- Plant vegetables that you and your family like to eat.
- Start off with some of the easier crops to grow like bush bean, cucumber, leafy greens, squash, tomato, and pepper.
- Learn more by using UME resources, visiting area food gardens, and getting tips from experienced gardeners.

Reasonable expectations

- Vegetable crop growth and yields will vary by garden location, growing season, and garden management.
- Even experienced gardeners have crop failures, which serve as valuable learning opportunities. "Doing it right" doesn't always guarantee success. Your crops won't always resemble those pictured in seed catalogs!
- Vegetable gardens require at least a small amount of daily attention. Timely planting, staking, weeding, harvesting, and scouting plants for problems is essential for a productive garden.
- A host of insect, disease, and environmental factors will cause holes in leaves, leaf spots, slow growth, and smaller yields. Learn how to prevent and manage the more serious problems while accepting some level of injury and imperfection.
- All crops have a harvest period; they don't produce food endlessly. For example, bush bean plants produce for about three weeks before declining naturally. Favorable growing conditions and good plant care help extend and increase the harvest.

18.2 Garden Types and Techniques

In-ground traditional rows

In-ground gardens, sometimes called traditional row gardens, have walkways between rows. Soil may be mounded or hilled within rows. Tillers are commonly used in large traditional gardens to prepare the soil and control weeds.

Raised beds

Raised beds are improved areas of soil that are elevated above ground level and often surrounded and contained by wooden boards or other rigid materials. Raised beds create an ideal framework for an intensive garden.

Plant roots grow through the raised bed soil into the native soil below. In this sense, raised beds are in-ground gardens, although they can also be sited on top of hard surfaces. They are usually two to four feet wide, two to 12 inches deep, and as long as desired.

Advantages of a raised bed

- Warms up quickly in spring
- Improves water drainage
- Increases available rooting area
- Reduces compaction and erosion because there is no foot traffic on it
- Provides greater yields per unit area due to high fertility and increased root growth

Disadvantages of a raised bed

- Up-front labor and expense
- Dries out more quickly if weather is hot and dry
- Relatively permanent; garden must be planned around bed dimensions and configuration
- Doesn't work on slopes unless terraced

Raised beds can be built on-site or purchased as a kit. Some of the more common materials include:

- Pressure-treated lumber. Current types contain copper, but not arsenic, and are considered low-risk in food gardens. CCA (chromated copper arsenate) lumber was discontinued in 2004.
- Untreated SPF (spruce, pine, fir) dimensional lumber. SPF is less expensive than pressure-treated and can be painted with exterior latex paint, stain, preservative, or sealer to slow wood decay.
- Cedar or redwood lumber.
- Rough-cut lumber (oak, poplar, locust) from local sawmills.
- Stone, bricks, or concrete blocks.
- Galvanized steel.
- Woven, permeable fabrics supported by a wood, PVC, or aluminum structure.
- Rigid, recycled plastic "boards."

You can forego an enclosure altogether by simply creating a raised bed with sloped or rounded sides.

Soil for raised beds

Raised beds can be filled using the top two to three inches of native soil around the beds. Cover the excavated area with mulch, such as wood chips, to create paths. The soil can then be mixed with an equal volume of compost. Topsoil and topsoil/compost mixtures can be purchased by the cubic yard and used to fill raised beds. Recommended topsoil to compost ratios are 1:1 or 2:1.

Lightweight soilless growing media can also be mixed with compost and/or topsoil. These products are composed of materials such as sphagnum peat moss, perlite, vermiculite, composted bark, and coconut coir. Mixing equal amounts of compost and soilless growing media is recommended for raised beds located on hard surfaces.

Buying topsoil

Topsoil sales are not regulated in Maryland. If you plan to buy topsoil in bulk, go to a reputable nursery or topsoil dealer and ask for soil test results and information about the origin of the soil and on-site mixing and storage. Examine the soil before purchase or delivery. Topsoil should be dark and crumbly with an earthy smell. Do not purchase soil that is very high in sand or clay, foul-smelling, or has grayish mottling or a chalky, sticky, or rough texture. The bags of "organic soil" you may see for sale typically don't contain topsoil (i.e., mineral soil with clay, silt, and sand particles). These products contain various combinations of wood waste, bark fines, compost, peat moss, and other organic materials.

Intensive gardening

The goal of intensive vegetable gardening is to increase the yield per square foot of space. Intensive gardens often have closely-spaced plants which limits the production of individual plants while increasing the total harvest. Reducing wasted space and pathways and using raised beds can also help reduce weed populations.

Intensive techniques described in this chapter include: raised beds, close-space planting, trellising, interplanting, succession planting, and season extension. They work best when based on a thorough knowledge of vegetable plants and a garden plan for continual planting and harvesting throughout the growing season.

Container gardening

Container gardening is an easy and affordable way to get started with vegetable gardening. It's also an excellent option for gardeners who are downsizing, have poor soil, or lack sufficient space or time for a larger garden. These miniature, but productive, gardens can be located on a patio, balcony, driveway, or back step. Edible crops can also be grown in window boxes and hanging baskets.

The amount of sunlight your containers receive determine which crops can be grown. Southern and western exposures are the sunniest and warmest; northern and eastern exposures are shadier and cooler. Portable containers allow you to move them to warmer or cooler spots, depending upon the crop and time of year. Some of the more popular container crops are salad greens, pepper, eggplant, tomato, bean, radish, and cucumber. More challenging container crops include squash, melon, corn, potato, and sweet potato. Look for "bush" or "dwarf" varieties of the crops you want to grow. Refer to **Chapter 26, Container Gardening,** for more information.

18.3 Selecting a Garden Site

Any potential garden site will have benefits and drawbacks. Use the following criteria to select the most suitable location:

- Consider "aspect," the compass direction your garden faces. For example, full-sun gardens have a southern aspect—no trees, hills, or buildings to the immediate south. They warm up earlier in spring, are hotter, and require more watering. The minimum sunlight requirements of garden crops are shown in Figure 18-B.

CLIMATE CHANGE & VEGETABLE GARDENS

The Mid-Atlantic states are experiencing warmer, wetter weather with more extreme temperatures and storms (e.g., two-inch rainfall events). Early spring warm-ups are often followed by late frosts, an intensification of the conditions typical of a Maryland spring.

Climate-change impacts on vegetable gardens include:

- High day and evening temperatures, which contribute to flower and fruit drop (especially on bean, pepper, and tomato), sunscald, and delay or acceleration of plant maturity.
- Elevated CO_2 levels favor weed growth, which requires more attention to weed prevention and management (especially during warm, wet weather).
- Insect pests appear earlier in the season, and have shorter life cycles and more generations per growing season.
- Southern pests are more prevalent due to northward migration and stronger and more frequent storms that carry them to Maryland.
- Disruption of plant-insect and prey-predator relationships, which upsets the natural ecosystem.
- Extreme rainfall can carry pollutants and fecal coliforms into gardens.
- Saltwater intrusion can ruin gardens in coastal areas.
- Dentrification (the loss of soil nitrogen as nitrous oxide) occurs when heavy rains saturate the soil, depriving plant roots of oxygen.

To help mitigate and adapt to the effects of climate change, you can:

- Transition from gas-powered tools to battery-powered tools.
- Reduce or eliminate the use of nitrogen fertilizers produced using natural gas.
- Increase your soil's organic matter to improve carbon storage.
- Reduce the use of plastics to reduce fossil fuel consumption.
- Re-direct stormwater away from your garden.
- Keep garden beds level and covered with plants, mulch, or cover crops to reduce soil erosion and nutrient run-off.
- Select disease-resistant cultivars, and space and prune plants to allow leaves to dry as quickly as possible.
- Switch to drip irrigation to conserve water.
- Increase garden biodiversity; plant locally-adapted cultivars when possible.
- Plant heat-sensitive crops where they receive late-afternoon shade; experiment with shade cloths.
- Experiment with heat- and drought-tolerant crops like sweet potato, okra, southern peas, and amaranth.

Figure 18-B. Light requirements for vegetables

FULL SUN 6-8 hours per day Unfiltered direct sun with little or no shade	
8 hours: Potato, tomato, pepper, eggplant, squash, melon, pumpkin, sweet corn	**6-8 hours:** Cucumber, bean, garlic, onion, broccoli, cabbage, cauliflower

PARTIAL SUN 5-6 hours per day Direct sun with shade or filtered sun for the rest of the day	
6 hours: Carrot, beet, Swiss chard, kale, collards, mustard greens	

PARTIAL SHADE Up to 4 hours per day Indirect or dappled sun with either direct sun or full shade for the rest of the day, or bright shade all day	
4-5 hours: Leafy greens such as spinach, arugula, and lettuce and some root vegetables such as turnips and radishes	

- Find a level, well-drained site. Sloped sites should be terraced first.
- Start small and expand as needed.
- Avoid trees and shrubs. Their root systems may compete for water and nutrients, and their canopy may create too much shade.
- Buildings, sheds, and other structures may also shade sun-loving plants.
- Locate your garden where it is accessible by water hose to an outside spigot.

It's also useful to think about how environmental conditions affect your garden, from regional and national weather to the temperature of just one leaf:

Macro-climate. Thirty-year weather patterns that are independent of soils or topography (e.g., average spring and fall frost dates).

Meso-climate. The effects caused by bodies of water, hard surfaces, and topography (e.g., "heat sinks" in cities, and gardens on dry southern slopes).

Micro-climate. The environmental conditions around a plant, from two feet down in the soil to three to four times the height of the plant (e.g., plants shading one another).

Nano-climate. The leaf or stem surface that extends a few inches out (e.g., morning dew that persists for hours on north-facing leaf surfaces).

Garden layout and preparation

Take the following considerations into account, regardless of the garden design:

- Place tall crops on the north and west sides of your garden so they won't shade short, full-sun plants.
- Group plants by their "days to maturity." For example, plant all lettuces together.
- Place perennial crops on one side of your garden where they will not be disturbed.
- Make a simple garden map. All garden areas should be accessible to make it easy to water, fertilize, weed, and harvest. There are online tools to help you design your garden.
- Incorporate edible plants into ornamental landscapes and beds.

Most vegetable gardens are started on a patch of lawn or weeds. Killing existing vegetation can be accomplished using one of these methods:

- Cover the area with black plastic or black weed barrier fabric (in spring, summer, or fall) for six to eight weeks.
- Lay down untreated cardboard or sections of newspaper and cover with an eight-inch layer of shredded leaves and/or compost. Leave in place for two to three months.
- Cut the turf and weeds with a mower or string trimmer at ground level. Cut and remove the top few inches of turf and soil. Instead of digging downward, slice through the soil horizontally and flip the soil over, turf-side down. Toss the turf pieces in a pile next to the garden. This layer contains valuable topsoil and organic matter so return it to the garden area after the turf dies and decomposes.
- A non-organic method: Apply a non-selective herbicide for vegetable garden use. *Read label directions carefully.* This is the least desirable method because of the potential for crop injury.

Fencing

A variety of wildlife species will feed on unprotected food gardens. These include deer, groundhog, rabbit, squirrel, vole, rat, raccoon, and birds. To a lesser extent, squirrel and opossum will become accustomed to eating garden produce and can be especially difficult to exclude. They are adept at entering gardens via overhanging tree limbs and fencing gaps, or by climbing up fence posts.

Urban and suburban gardeners have as many or more potential wildlife issues as rural gardeners. Even container gardens next to your home are subject to wildlife feeding and often require protection.

ABOUT ANIMAL REPELLENTS

Repellents are generally less reliable than fencing; some work better than others. If you choose to use a repellent, keep these things in mind:

- A rabbit repellent must be used to repel rabbits. A bear repellent will not work. The repellent must match the wildlife species.
- Repellents must be re-applied often.
- Animals eventually adapt to the taste and smell of repellents, so rotate repellents to keep wildlife away.

Don't wait to see which types of wild animals want to share the harvest. If deer are in your area, erect a deer fence before planting the first crops.

Fencing materials and construction

There are many options, ranging from low-cost DIY fences made from scrap and recycled materials to commercial installations. Evaluate the cost, durability, and life span of various materials. For example, steel fence posts will last for decades while untreated wood will only last five to seven years unless protected with paint or a preservative.

Structure. Current types of pressure-treated lumber are safe to use in food gardens. The posts or uprights can be connected at the top using galvanized wire (often 14-gauge or 17-gauge) or other material that can support the weight of the fencing material.

Space fence posts three to ten feet apart and drive them into the ground 12 to 24 inches deep, depending upon the fence's type, height and length, and fencing materials. Steel, wood,

PVC pipe, galvanized conduit, and bamboo are some commonly-used materials for fence posts.

You'll also need a simple garden gate that is wide enough to accommodate your widest garden tool (e.g., cart, wheelbarrow, and lawn mower).

Deer netting. Deer netting is made of black polypropylene. The mesh openings measure one-and-one-half to two inches on each side and the netting is seven to eight feet tall. It is effective, durable, inexpensive, and blends in well with landscapes. It does require monitoring and timely repairs using plastic zip ties or string. Deer netting can be secured to the ground with U-shaped landscape staples.

Fishing line can be strung in a tight vertical pattern as an alternative to deer netting, but requires more repairs and is more easily penetrated by spooked deer. Deer do not willingly jump into confined spaces. They can usually be excluded with a five- to six-feet tall fence if the garden is small or located next to a house or other structure. Deer will, however, push and lean into low fences to reach nearby plants.

Wire fencing. Groundhog, rabbit, rat, and raccoon can chew through deer netting so it is usually necessary to install two- to three-foot tall wire fencing over deer netting. For groundhog, the fencing should be at least three feet tall and hung loosely to discourage climbing. Wire fencing with one-inch or one-by-two-inch mesh is recommended for excluding rabbit. Bury the fencing six to eight inches in the ground to prevent animals from digging under the fence, or secure it to the ground with U-shaped landscape staples.

Welded wire is produced by welding together horizontal and vertical strands of wire. It is galvanized and long-lasting, especially if PVC-coated. Woven wire is also galvanized and is easier to use, but won't last quite as long.

Chicken wire (poultry netting) is another popular woven fencing material. Hardware cloth (one-half inch mesh) is a strong galvanized wire material that can be installed over deer netting and may be required for voles, rats, and young rabbits.

Electric "fencing/netting" (AC, battery, or solar) is actually a strong tape with an embedded electric wire. Three to six strands are typically used to exclude deer and groundhog. It's important to keep vegetation near the fence cut low to prevent the electric wire from shorting out. Keep the fence operating year-'round so that deer don't get accustomed to walking freely in the garden during the off-season.

Bird netting, micro-mesh, and row covers are used to cover individual beds, rows, or plants to exclude birds, squirrels, and other wildlife. Micro-mesh and row covers will also exclude insect pests. Bird netting has the disadvantage of sometimes trapping and injuring birds and snakes, and row covers can cause a heat build-up around plants when used during the summer months. Both require monitoring.

Minimal-till gardening

Most vegetable gardens are started in established turfgrass. Once the grass and weed plants have been smothered and killed, compost can be spread over the area and seeds and transplants can be planted. This can be aptly described as a no-till garden. The University of Maryland has been an international leader in no-till agriculture, which simply means planting crops into the residues of previous crops (including cover crops) without the need for plowing and disking. It minimizes soil disturbance and improves soil health.

Gardeners can adopt a similar no-till approach by not using a roto-tiller or turning soil over by hand, which inverts the soil profile, leaving topsoil below subsoil. No-till garden beds have a year-round soil blanket of cover crops, plant residues, and mulches around and between plants. This method helps build and conserve soil organic matter while keeping weed seeds buried and dormant. No-till gardening is a more complex system to manage, but leads to higher soil quality.

Minimum-till gardeners use a garden fork or broadfork (U-bar) to loosen and fluff soil. These tools are pushed into the top eight to 12 inches of soil and rocked back and forth. This action breaks soil clumps into smaller aggregates. A metal rake can then be used to smooth the surface for planting while removing weeds, rocks, and bits of mulch. This two-step technique can be used any time during the growing season.

The minimal-till technique allows you to:

- Loosen and fluff garden soil, making it easier to plant seeds and transplants.
- Warm up and aerate soil which hastens germination and enhances seedling root growth.
- Uproot and kill weeds without bringing hundreds of weed seeds to the surface.

About machine-tilling

Large (5-8hp) gasoline-powered tillers are designed to till soil six to eight inches deep. Lightweight, narrow tillers cultivate around plants and create seedbeds. In large gardens, strategic and infrequent rototilling can efficiently incorporate compost, manure, and plant residues, and prepare areas for planting. There are, however, significant negative effects of tilling:

- Damages soil structure as the tines pulverize soil crumbs into individual soil particles, reducing pore space and limiting aeration and drainage, which reduces microbial populations.
- Accelerates the decomposition of organic matter (oxidation), releasing CO_2. Tilling causes a large initial increase in oxygen levels that increases microbial activity in the short-run.
- Causes topsoil and subsoil compaction when done repeatedly, especially with heavy machines.
- Brings millions of weed seeds to the surface, where they can germinate.
- Increases erosion risk if an extreme weather event follows.

Whichever soil preparation method you choose, avoid tilling, digging, or fluffing soils when they are wet. This can damage soil structure, which may take years to rebuild.

18.4 Soil Assessment and Testing

Soil test results give you baseline information about soil pH, nutrient levels, and organic-matter content; and recommendations for fertilizing and adjusting the soil pH.

Soil testing helps reduce overfertilizing, which keeps excess nutrients (nitrogen and phosphorus) out of Maryland's groundwater and surface waters. Soil testing labs provide more complete and accurate results than DIY soil test kits. Have your soil tested prior to establishing your garden and then again every three to four years.

- The optimum pH for a vegetable garden is 6.0 to 6.8. If your pH is too high or too low, some nutrients may become unavailable to plants, causing either deficiency or toxicity symptoms.

- Incorporate organic matter and lime (if needed) in the fall to allow time for decomposition and pH adjustment.

- The soil organic matter (OM) level should be higher than 2%, preferably above 5%. (OM is reported on the basis of weight, not volume.)

- All food gardens should be tested for lead. The risk is primarily from inhaling or ingesting contaminated soil dust and particles from tools, hands, clothing, and harvested crops. To minimize soil lead risks:
  - Locate fruit and vegetable gardens away from old painted buildings and heavily traveled roads.
  - Contaminated soil particles can cling to or become embedded in leafy greens and root crops. Lead uptake by fruiting crops like tomato is much less likely. Wash all vegetables and peel all root crops before cooking/eating.
  - Reduce lead availability and plant uptake by maintaining soil pH at 6.5 and incorporating organic matter each year.
  - No food crops should be grown in a soil that is heavily contaminated (over 1,000 ppm). Instead, choose container gardening or raised beds filled with purchased soil.

18.5 Soil Amendments

Soil improvement is essential for developing a productive and resilient vegetable garden. Soil amendments are materials that are applied to or mixed into the topsoil to change the soil's properties and improve plant growth. For example, compost improves soil structure and lime raises soil pH.

Organic matter

Soil high in organic matter is especially important in intensive gardens where plant spacing is closer and water and nutrient requirements are higher. Soils that are rich in organic matter are friable (crumbly), well drained, and biologically active. They contain a large reservoir of slowly released nutrients, have a high water-holding capacity, and increase rooting capacity. Practices that increase organic matter content improve plant vigor, health, and overall garden growth, health, and productivity.

If the topsoil in a new garden area is thin, or the soil is high in clay and/or is compacted, it may need as much as four to six inches of organic matter in the first year or two. After a few years of large additions, you can decrease the amount to one inch of compost per year. To cover an area one inch deep requires three cubic yards of compost per 1,000 square feet, or 8.33 cubic feet of compost per 100 square feet. The goal is to have organic matter comprise ¼ to ⅓ of the top eight inches of soil (by volume).

Homemade or purchased compost can be added to the garden at any time of year. Light incorporation is desirable to prevent it from washing away, but compost can be used as a top-dressing or mulch during the growing season. Plant-based composts have an N-P-K analysis of approximately 1.0-0.5-1.0. Only five to 10 percent of the N (nitrogen) is available to the plant in the year it was applied. Most of the K (potassium) and a small percentage of the P (phosphorus) are available in the first year.

Composted animal manures (sheep, horse, chicken, rabbit, and cow) have a somewhat higher nutrient content than plant-based compost. Manures are fully composted when the pile or windrow reaches at least 131 to 140°F for three consecutive days. This kills most plant and human diseases and weed seeds. Composted manure can be spread and lightly incorporated into the soil at any time.

Aged (uncomposted) animal manures

Fall application and incorporation is recommended for uncomposted manures. Apply no sooner than 90 days prior to harvest if there is no contact between crop and soil, (e.g., staked tomatoes) or 120 days if the crop is in contact with soil (e.g., cabbage). Here are a few tips for working with aged manures:

- Lightly incorporate manure into soil to reduce nutrient losses.
- Horse manure may contain many weed seeds. Be prepared to control weed growth early on.
- Make compost teas from plant-based composts only.
- Never use dog or cat manures in your vegetable garden.
- Wash produce thoroughly after harvest.

Other organic materials, such as plant roots, spent plants, cover crops, tree leaves, food scraps, and organic mulches can also increase the soil's organic matter content. Plant roots are very important for improving soil structure. Cut spent plants off at ground level with pruners or loppers. Compost the tops and leave the root system to decompose in place. Annual weeds can be treated the same way. Food scraps can be buried in trenches in your garden and allowed to decompose, creating a store of nutrients in the root zone.

18.6 Cover Crops

Cover crops, also known as green manures when actively growing plants are incorporated into soil, help prevent erosion in the winter, reduce nutrient losses to leaching, and increase the amount of organic matter. Importantly, cover-crop root systems release sugars and other compounds that feed and increase a soil's microbial populations. Farmers have been growing cover crops for centuries.

Cover crops are mostly small-grain grasses like oats, rye, and wheat; and legumes like clover and vetch (see Table 18-A). These crops are typically planted between late August and late October, depending upon the species and your gardening goals. Research from the University of Maryland and elsewhere strongly supports planting a mixture of two or three different cover crops (usually at least one grass and one legume species) to maximize the benefits.

The soil temperature should be at least 45 to 50°F for germination of cover-crop seed. Winter cover crops should show some growth before the first hard frost. Some species, like oats and forage radish, are killed by cold winter temperatures, but other species go dormant and resume growing in the spring.

Cover crop roots grow deeply into the soil, pulling up nutrients that might otherwise leach out of the soil. The crops are terminated

Table 18-A. Cover crops for vegetable gardens

Type*	Amount (oz.) to sow per 100 sq. ft.	When to sow**	When to terminate	Comments
Alfalfa*	½	Spring or late summer	Fall or spring	Needs warm temperatures for germination. Hardy and drought-tolerant.
Barley	4	Spring or late summer/fall	Spring	Not as hardy as rye; drought-tolerant.
Buckwheat	2½	Spring or summer	Fall	Grows quickly; not cold-hardy. Will reliably re-seed.
Crimson clover*	3	Spring or late summer/fall	Fall or spring	Beautiful spring blooms.
Forage radish†	4	Late summer/fall	Spring	Large white roots break up clay soil. All parts are edible. Monitor for harlequin bugs.
Spring oats†	4	Spring or late summer/fall	Spring or summer	Not cold hardy; tolerates low pH.
Winter rye	4	Late summer/fall	Spring	Very hardy. Produces a massive root system. Can be planted later in fall than other cover crops.
Hairy vetch*	3	Late summer/fall	Spring	Slow to establish. Fairly hardy. Till under at bloom; can become a weed.
Winter wheat	4	Late summer/fall	Spring	Easier to manage/terminate in spring than rye or barley.

* Legumes take nitrogen from air and convert it into a form used by plants. You can help this natural process by using an inoculant (*Rhizobia* spp. *Bacteria*) with your seed. Coat the cover-crop seeds with the inoculant by mixing together in a bag.
** Sow late summer/fall crops from August 15 through October 15, depending upon location, use, and species.
† Will usually winter-kill, leaving a "mat" of dead vegetation that can either be planted over in the spring or turned under.

between mid-April and early May (before going to seed) by cutting them close to the ground with a string trimmer, mower, or sickle. Grasses push out new shoots when mowed, so may require multiple cuttings. Residues and root systems can be incorporated with a tiller or covered with black plastic or weed barrier for two weeks, after which the cover is removed and seeds and transplants are planted through the cover-crop residues.

Buckwheat, Dutch white clover, alfalfa, and sudex (*sudangrass X sorghum*) are some of the cover crops that are sown in the spring or summer to cover and improve bare soil.

Tips for experimenting with cover crops

- Prepare the soil for a cover crop by tilling under or raking off plant wastes and mulch from the summer. The seed must directly contact soil to germinate. Broadcast the seed with a spin seeder, drop seeder, or by hand (preferably before a rain,) and rake seeds evenly into the soil. Combine legumes and non-legumes when possible.

- Sow oats if you want to plant early spring crops. Oats are killed by the first hard freeze, leaving a brown decomposing mat in spring.

- Pull back mulch and sow cover-crop seed between vegetable crops and in the walkways in early September. Your cover crop will get a good start but will not disrupt vegetable plant growth.

- Sow white clover or red clover seed around long-season crops (e.g., squash, pepper, and tomato) after these crops are established. If the soil is fertile, the cover crop creates a living mulch that will not inhibit the growth of the vegetable crops.

18.7 Pollination

Pollination is the movement of pollen from male to female flower parts of sexually-reproducing plants. It is usually accomplished by wind and insects, and results in the development of some type of fruit containing seeds for the species' continuation. Many vegetable crops are grown for their "fruits."

Understanding how flowers are pollinated will help you make gardening decisions and troubleshoot problems. For example, beans are self-fertile and don't require insects for pollination. The plants can be covered to exclude wildlife and insect pests without interfering with pollination and pod set. Summer squash flowers require insect pollination and are only open in the morning, making this species more prone to flower and fruit drop. This is sometimes due to low bee activity during bad weather, insecticide use, and habitat loss. See Table 18-B for information about pollination of common vegetable crops.

Other vegetable crops also produce flowers and fruits containing seeds for future generations. They are not listed because we don't typically consume their fruits. Unless you want to save seeds, don't worry about the pollination requirements of crops like beet, kale, carrot, and onion.

18.8 Vegetable Planting Guide

The growing season (the number of frost-free days) ranges from 150 in far western Maryland to 225 on the lower Eastern shore. Plant growth largely stops when daylight is less than 10 hours per day. For Baltimore's latitude, this occurs between November 15 and January 25. Mild soil temperatures, however, can spur root and top growth into early December and cold soil typically prevents new growth until mid-February. Leafy greens covered by cold frames, greenhouses, and row covers continue to grow slowly in sunny, cold weather.

There is an exciting world of vegetable species and cultivars from which to choose. Some considerations when deciding what to plant:

- Plant vegetables that you and your family like to eat.
- Grow crops that are the most expensive to buy (e.g., garlic, leek, herbs, heirloom tomatoes).
- Start off with easier crops like bush bean, cucumber, leafy greens, squash, tomato, and pepper.
- Plant the crops best adapted to your environmental conditions.
- Select cultivars with disease resistance, especially if specific diseases are a problem in your area.
- "Eat your colors." The nutritional value of your garden increases when the edible plant parts vary in color. The darker the color, the more antioxidants there are in the fruit.
- Some crops have multiple edible plant parts, like beet, sweet potato, garlic, and turnip.

Table 18-B. Vegetable crop pollination (by family)

Cucurbitaceae Family			
Crop	**Flower type**	**Open bloom period**	**Comments***
Summer squash	Imperfect/monoecious	6 hrs. (dawn to noon)	Male flowers open and close 30 min. earlier than female flowers. 8-12 bee visits required.
Pumpkin/ winter squash	Imperfect/monoecious	6 hrs. (dawn to noon)	8-12 bee visits required.
Muskmelon	Perfect, self-sterile, and imperfect male flowers	8 a.m. to dusk	Stigma receptive to pollen grains for only a few hours early in the a.m. 12 bee visits required.
Watermelon	Imperfect/monoecious	8 a.m. to dusk	3 stigmatic lobes. Seedless cultivars require pollination to set fruit, then seeds abort. 8-10 bee visits required.
Cucumber**	Imperfect/monoecious	8 a.m. to dusk	Standard cultivars: staminate flowers appear 10 days before pistillate flowers; stigmas most receptive in a.m. 8-12 bee visits required.
Leguminosae Family			
Lima bean	Perfect/self-fertile	Blooms don't close	Blooms open 7-8 a.m.; fewer flowers set pods than common bean. Bee visits may increase the number and weight of pods.
Common bean	Perfect/self-fertile	Blooms don't close	Blooms open 7-8 a.m.; pollen sheds before flower opens; reliably self-pollinated.
Scarlet runner bean	Perfect/cross-pollinated	Blooms don't close	Attractive blooms for nectar and pollen. Honeybees and bumble bees cross-pollinate the flowers and increase yields.
Pea	Perfect/self-fertile	Blooms don't close	Temperatures >85°F can cause flowers and pods to drop.
Solanaceae Family			
Tomato	Perfect/self-fertile and cross-pollinated	Stigma receptive for up to 8 days	Wind required for pollination. Bumble and other wild bees collect pollen and cross-pollinate a small percentage of flowers.
Pepper	Perfect/self-fertile and cross-pollinated	<1 day	Bees visit for pollen and nectar. 10-30% cross-pollination; varies by species and cultivar.
Eggplant	Perfect/self-fertile and cross-pollinated	2-3 days	Blooms remain open at night. Stigma extends beyond anthers. Cross-pollinating by bumble bees increases yield.

*Seed number and fruit weight increase with more bee visits.
Types of cucumbers: **Standard or monoecious – the first 10-20 flowers are male. For every female flower (which produces the fruit), 10-20 male flowers are produced. **All-female or gynoecious** – have only female flowers; some just have a greater proportion of female to male flowers. Plants tend to bear fruit earlier with a more concentrated set. Standard seeds are added to the seed packet to ensure pollination. **Parthenocarpic** – Very expensive seed; all female and seedless; fruit is produced without pollination. If this type of cucumber is planted near other varieties, pollination will occur and seeds will form.

- Talk to neighbors and friends about which crops and cultivars grow best for them.
- Spend some time with different seed catalogs to evaluate the many options.
- Consult the **Planting Calendar for Vegetable Crops in Maryland** and Plant Profiles beginning on page 556 for specific planting times.

Annual vegetables

Most vegetable crops are annual plants with a life cycle between 25 days (e.g., radish, baby greens) and 110 days (e.g., big pumpkins). Some annuals are actually perennial plants in the regions where they originated (e.g., tomato and pepper). A large number of crops are biennials that are grown as annuals because gardeners are most interested in the edible plant parts rather than the seeds. Carrot, beet, and broccoli are examples of biennial crops that are treated like annuals.

Annual crops can be further divided by the particular part of the growing season in which they are grown and harvested:

Cool-season crops are planted and harvested in spring and early summer, then planted again in summer and early fall for fall harvesting. Planting and harvesting times vary considerably between crops. Cool-season crops include: asparagus, beet, broccoli, Brussels sprout, cabbage, carrot, cauliflower, green pea, leafy greens, leek, lettuce, radish, spinach, and Swiss chard.

Warm-season crops are planted in late spring and summer and grow best in warm weather. Warm-season crops include: amaranth, bean, cucumber, eggplant, okra, pepper, potato, summer squash, Southern pea, sweet corn, sweet potato, Swiss chard, tomato, watermelon, winter squash, and pumpkin.

Garlic and onion foliage grow best during spring and fall. The bulbs enlarge during warmer weather.

Perennial vegetables

Perennial vegetable crops include sorrel, horseradish, asparagus, multiplier onions,

Table 18-C. Vegetable families grown in the mid-Atlantic

Amaranthaceae Family		
Genus	**Species**	**Common name**
Amaranthus	spp.	Leafy amaranth
f	hortensis	Orach
Beta	vulgaris	Garden beet, Swiss chard
Chenopodium	bonus-henricus	Good King Henry
Spinacia	oleracea	Spinach
Amaryllidaceae Family		
Allium	ampeloprasum	Leek, elephant garlic
	cepa	Common onion, shallot, multiplier onion, top-setting onion, potato onion
	fistulosum	Japanese bunching onion
	sativum	Garlic, rocambole
	schoenoprasum	Chive
	tuberosum	Garlic chive, Chinese chive
Apiaceae Family		
Apium	graveolens	Celery, celeriac
Anethum	graveolens	Dill
Anthriscus	cerefolium	Chervil
Coriandrum	sativum	Coriander (cilantro)
Daucus	carota	Carrot
Foeniculum	vulgare	Fennel
Pastinaca	sativa	Parsnip
Petroselinum	crispum	Parsley, parsley root
Asparagaceae Family		
Asparagus	officinalis	Asparagus
Asteraceae Family		
Cichorium	endiva	Endive, escarole
	intybus	Chicory
Cynara	cardunculus	Cardoon, globe artichoke
Helianthus	annus	Sunflower
	tuberosa	Jerusalem artichoke, sunroot
Lactuca	sativa	Lettuce
Scorzonera	hispanica	Black salsify, black scorzonera

continued on next page

continued from previous page

Table 18-C. Vegetable families grown in the mid-Atlantic

Basellaceae Family		
Genus	**Species**	**Common name**
Basella	alba	Malabar spinach
	rubra	Ceylon spinach
Brassicaceae Family		
Armoracia	rusticana	Horseradish
Brassica	juncea	Mustard greens
	napus	Rutabaga (Swede turnip), Siberian kale, rape
	oleracea	Broccoli, Brussels sprouts, cabbage, cauliflower, collards, kale, kohlrabi
	rapa	Turnip, broccoli raab, Chinese cabbage, Chinese mustard
Eruca	sativa	Arugula (rocket)
Lepidium	sativum	Garden cress
Raphanus	sativus	Radish
Rorippa	microphylla	Large-leaf watercress
	nasturtium	Watercress
Convolvulaceae Family		
Ipomea	batatas	Sweet potato
Cucurbitaceae Family		
Citrullus	lanatus	Watermelon
Cucumis	anguria	West Indian gherkin
	melo	Muskmelon, cantaloupe, honeydew, Asian pickling melon, Armenian cucumber
	sativus	Cucumber
Cucurbita	argyrosperma	Squash (green-striped cushaw, white cushaw)
	maxima	Squash (banana, buttercup, Hubbard, turban)
	moschata	Squash (butternut, Tahitian melon)
	pepo	Squash (acorn, crookneck, scallop, small-striped and warted gourds, spaghetti, zucchini), most pumpkins
Lagenaria	siceraria	Hard-shelled gourds
Luffa	acutangula	Angled luffa
	aegyptiaca	Smooth luffa

continued on next page

ABOUT VEGETABLE PLANT HARDINESS

Very hardy perennials can withstand winter extremes in most parts of the mid-Atlantic with minimal protection.

Hardy perennials can withstand winters with protection in colder areas.

Hardy annuals can withstand frosts in spring and fall, but may need protection from heavy frosts or freezing.

Half-hardy annuals can withstand light frosts, but not heavy frosts or freezing.

Tender annuals suffer some tissue damage from a frost.

Very tender annuals are destroyed by frost and require warm weather to grow.

rhubarb, and globe artichoke. They are propagated by seeds and/or root and crown pieces.

See Table 18-C for a chart of common annual and perennial vegetables grown in the mid-Atlantic, grouped by plant family.

Spring and fall frost dates

The last frost in the spring and the first frost in the fall dictate the length of the growing season. Expected last and first frost dates help determine which warm-season vegetable seeds and transplants can be planted in the garden and when to start seeds indoors for transplanting. Frost dates are based on historical temperature data but fluctuate from year to year.

Follow these tips to avoid frost injury:

- Closely monitor extended weather forecasts to make planting decisions, but keep in mind that the likelihood of frost varies between landscapes in the same town or even neighborhood. Factors such as changes in wind, elevation, proximity to buildings and water, and microclimates can all affect the potential for frost.

- Be prepared to protect tender plants if near-freezing temperatures are expected. Blankets and quilts, paper shopping bags, and row covers are all effective.

- Avoid the temptation to plant tender annuals too early. Tomato, basil, pepper, eggplant, and okra are especially cold-sensitive. Wind and rapid temperature swings can injure stems and foliage and the small roots of young plants cannot uptake sufficient nutrients. Large, healthy transplants can better recover from harsh spring weather.

- Plan to gather your final harvest of warm-season crops before the first heavy frost. Pumpkins, winter squash, white potatoes, and sweet potatoes may be injured by a heavy frost. Cold temperatures improve the flavor and texture of kale, collards, cabbage, Brussels sprouts, and turnip greens.

Succession planting is an important tool to maximize food production—simply plant something new in spots vacated by spent plants. For example, sow sweet corn seed after spring peas are finished.

List the crops you plan to grow on paper and draw a map that shows the spacing and location of each crop. Develop spring,

continued from previous page

Table 18-C. Vegetable families grown in the mid-Atlantic

Fabaceae Family		
Genus	**Species**	**Common name**
Arachis	*hypogea*	Peanut
Dolichos	*lablab*	Hyacinth bean
Glycine	*max*	Soybean
Phaseolus	*coccineus*	Runner bean
	lunatus	Lima bean (butter bean)
	vulgaris	Common green or snap bean
Pisum	*sativum*	Garden pea, including edible podded
Psophocarpus	*tetragonolobus*	Winged bean, asparagus pea
Vicia	*faba*	Fava bean (broad bean)
Vigna	*angularis*	Adzuki bean
	unguiculata	Cowpea
Lamiaceae Family		
Ocimum	*basilicum*	Basil
Malvaceae Family		
Abelmoschus	*esculentus*	Okra
Corchorus	*olitorius*	Molokhia, Egyptian spinach
Hibiscus	*sabdariffa*	Roselle
Poaceae Family		
Sorghum	*bicolor*	Sorghum, broom corn
Zea	*mays*	Sweet corn, popcorn, ornamental corn

continued on next page

WHEN IS IT OK TO WORK THE SOIL?

Use this test to determine your soil's suitability to be worked:

Pick up a handful of soil and squeeze it, then bounce it on your upturned palm.

If it easily breaks apart, it's okay to work the soil. If the clump stays together, wait for it to dry out until it crumbles when you perform the "bounce test."

continued from previous page

Table 18-C. Vegetable families grown in the mid-Atlantic

Polygonaceae Family		
Genus	**Species**	**Common name**
Rheum	*rhubarbarum*	Rhubarb
Rumex	spp.	Sorrel

Portulacaceae Family		
Claytonia	*parvifolia*	Miner's lettuce
Portulaca	*oleracea*	Purslane

Solanaceae Family		
Capsicum	*annuum*	Sweet and hot peppers
	baccatum	e.g., Ají
	chinense	e.g., Habanero
	frutescens	e.g., Tabasco
	pubescens	e.g., Rocoto
Physalsis	*peruviana, grisea*	Cape gooseberry, ground cherry
	philadelphica	Tomatillo, husk tomato
Solanum	*lycopersicon*	Tomato
	pimpinellifolium	Currant tomato
	melongena	Eggplant
	tuberosum	Potato

Tetragoniaceae Family		
Tetragonia	*tetragonioides*	New Zealand spinach

Valerianaceae Family		
Valerianella	spp.	Mâche, corn salad

Adapted from: Ashworth, S. 2002. *Seed to Seed: Seed Saving Techniques for the Vegetable Grower* and Buttala, L. and Siegel, S. (editors). 2015. *The Seed Garden: The Art and Practice of Seed Saving.*

summer, and fall maps for each "round" of crops. Cool-season crops (broccoli, lettuce, peas) are followed by warm-season crops (beans, tomatoes, peppers), which then may be followed by more cool-season plants, or a winter cover crop. See Figure 18-C for a sample succession plan.

Tips for successful succession planting:

- Start seeds indoors or in a protected outdoor area. Use transplants, even for crops that are usually direct-seeded. You will gain several weeks of growing time by having transplants ready to go into vacated areas.
- Sow seed outdoors as soon as the soil can be prepared in spring; use transplants of cold-hardy crops if possible.
- Plant warm-season crops as soon as the danger of frost has passed.
- Plant squash, bean, and cucumber following the earlier cool-weather crops.
- Starting in late July, sow seeds of the same crops you direct-seeded in early spring.

Relay planting is the successive planting of one type of crop. For instance, garden beans may be planted at two-week intervals for a continuous harvest. Early crops are likely to get a slower start due to low temperatures, with later crops growing and maturing more quickly. This often results in a glut of produce at the height of the season, so be prepared to process your harvest in advance.

Plan enough time between relay plantings of sweet corn—a crop planted too soon after the previous crop can result in cross-pollination if they bloom at the same time. This can affect kernel color and quality. You can also spread out the harvest time by planting several cultivars with varying maturity dates.

Crop succession is closely related to the concept of crop rotation (moving crop families to different garden locations each season). Vegetable crops have different roots structures and each mines the soil for nutrients at varying depths. They also have different fertilizer needs.

Figure 18-C. Sample succession planting plan

Garden Area 1	Garden Area 2	Garden Area 3	Garden Area 4	Garden Area 5
Nov. 1 - Garlic	Mar. 1 - Peas, favas	Mar. 20 - Lettuce	Mar. 1 - Radish	May 1 - Cucumber
July 1 - Cucumber	June 1 - Squash	May 15 - Green bean	Apr. 15 - Asian greens	July 15 - Green bean
Sept. 20 - Oats, clover	Sept. 1 - Kale	August 1 - Broccoli	June 1 - Eggplant Sept. 15 - Rye	Sept. 20 - Spinach

Companion planting, which includes interplanting, is the intentional planting of two or more plant species close to one another to improve plant growth, increase garden productivity, or repel or suppress pests.

The "Three Sisters" intercropping system, developed by tribes of northeast Native Americans, is a good example. Corn seed was planted in a small circular pattern. Bean seed was planted at the base of the corn, and squash plants sprawled around the corn and beans. The bean plants used the corn for support and improved the soil through nitrogen fixation. The squash plants suppressed weeds and conserved moisture, and their spiny leaves and stems made it harder for animals to feed on the corn and beans.

Consider the following factors when selecting companion plants:

- Length of time to maturity
- Growth pattern above/below ground
- Light, nutrient, and moisture needs
- Planting arrangement:
  - Alternate plants within a row (basil-tomato-basil-tomato)
  - Alternate rows within a bed (a row of peppers next to a row of onions)
  - Plant various species throughout

Maximize yields with companion planting

- Plant low-growing, shade-tolerant salad greens on the north side of corn, tomato, or eggplant.
- Plant peas at the base of tomato cages (north side) in early spring. The pea vines will act as a wind shield.
- Sow long-season (carrot) and short-season (radish) seeds at the same time. Harvest the radishes before they begin to crowd the carrots.
- Plant small plants close to larger plants, like radishes at the base of broccoli.
- Sow cover crop seeds around the base of crops in late summer/early fall. The cover crop will germinate and establish while you continue to harvest crops.

Manage pests with companion planting

Attract beneficial insects by planting mountain mint, anise hyssop, cilantro, basil, dill, buckwheat, and other flowering plants. These plants produce small flowers that are highly attractive to pollinators and natural enemies of garden pests.

- Repel and suppress pests with a border of African marigolds, which will attract beneficial insects and may repel certain pests with chemical compounds found in the foliage and roots.

See **Chapter 10, IPM,** for extensive details.

Crop rotation is the practice of moving crop families to different garden locations each season. Rotating crop location can help even out nutrient removal from the soil, but it is only marginally helpful in lessening insect and disease pressure, especially in a small garden.

Vegetable gardening in the fall

Some gardeners plant a few early spring crops, like lettuce and radish, followed by warm-season crops in May, then spend the rest of the growing season weeding, watering, and harvesting. Other gardeners plant cool-season crops in summer and early fall that will produce food deep into autumn.

Climate change is causing warmer fall weather and later first frosts. This significantly improves and extends the growth of cool-season crops like leafy greens and root vegetables.

The key to fall gardening success is having available gardening space, a planting schedule and map, and the time and commitment to follow through. The idea is to plant fall crops in spaces vacated by spring crops and later warm-season crops like bean, cucumber, and mustard greens that are beginning to decline by late July.

Suggested fall crops

- Hardy (will withstand a hard frost): broccoli, cabbage, lettuce, pea, turnip, kale, spinach, broccoli raab, arugula, endive, escarole, radicchio, Asian greens, spinach, kale, and turnip greens.
- Half-hardy (will tolerate light frosts): beet, carrot, Swiss chard, mustard greens, radish, and cauliflower.
- Alliums: garlic, shallot, and multiplier onion can be planted in October for harvest the following spring/summer.

FALL PLANTING-DATE CALCULATOR

Each vegetable cultivar has a "days to maturity" number, which appears on the seed packet and in catalogs. It refers to the number of days from seeding in the garden to maturity for crops like lettuce, spinach, beet, radish, and leafy greens; and days from transplanting for crops like broccoli, cabbage, cauliflower, and Brussels sprout. This number increases for fall crops due to decreasing light and lower temperatures.

The Short-Day Factor (SDF) helps to compensate for the light and temperature differences, but other environmental factors also affect maturity dates. Use transplants for crops that are normally direct-sown, which will let you plant later into the fall - but don't wait too long.

Fall crops often fail because they are planted too late.* Calculate the proper planting date by including the SDF of two weeks (14 days). Say you want to start harvesting beets on October 1. The seed packet states "55 days to maturity." When should you plant?

October 1 minus 55 days = August 5

August 5 minus SDF (14 days) = July 22

Plant seeds around July 22

*The SDF is especially critical for crops that produce heads or pods; less so for root and leafy crops.

Cool-season crops take advantage of warm late-summer weather to spur strong, early growth. The cooler temperatures that follow benefit these crops as they reach maturity. Frosts improve the flavor and increase the sugars of many cool-season crops. Plants such as looseleaf lettuce, radish, arugula, and

Asian greens grow quickly and can be planted several times from late August through late September for a continuous harvest.

Fall gardening challenges

- Daylength decreases a few minutes each day during the fall gardening season, so it is critical to plant early enough to get plants well-established before temperatures cool down.
- It can be difficult to buy high-quality transplants, so plan to grow your own indoors or outside in a protected, part-shade location.
- Lettuce and spinach seeds are difficult to germinate when soil temperature is above 70°F, so wait until the summer temperatures cool before planting.
- Peas are difficult to grow in the fall because of high soil temperature and insufficient time for plants to produce pods prior to cold weather.
- Seedlings and transplants may need protection from insect pests (use row covers), bright sunlight, and high temperatures (use a shade cloth).
- Heavily-fertilized leafy greens can accumulate excessive nitrate under low-light conditions, posing potential health risks. Use compost and organic fertilizers sparingly on protected leafy greens that will be harvested from December through February.

Fall crop care

- Spread one-half to one inch of compost on beds prior to planting and fertilize as needed once plants are established.
- Keep seedbeds evenly moist.
- Weed regularly and mulch beds to keep new weeds from sprouting.
- Thin plants to the recommended spacing for best results.
- Use cold frames and row covers to foster plant growth and provide some cold protection to extend the harvest period.
- Harvest beet, turnip, and carrot though December by covering the bed with an insulating mulch to prevent freeze damage to the roots.
- Fall crops that overwinter with protection and re-grow in spring include spinach, arugula, kale, mâche (corn salad), parsley, and chicories (radicchio).

Preparing the garden for winter

Garden cleanup and attention to the soil in the fall help ensure a healthy and productive garden the next year:

- Remove stakes, trellises, hoses, temporary fences, plant labels, and other gardening materials.
- Clean up and remove all above-ground plant residues. Instead of pulling plants out of the ground, cut them off at ground level, leaving the root system intact. This reduces soil disturbance while adding organic matter.
- Many diseases can survive over the winter on small pieces of leaves and stems. Some pest insects overwinter under protective layers of dead weeds and crop debris. Either bag up and dispose of these plant wastes or compost them. (All parts of the bin or pile must heat up to >140°F to kill plant pathogens and weed seeds.)

- Don't leave the soil bare. Plant cover crops or cover soil with shredded leaves or some other type of mulch to prevent erosion. The leaves will reduce weed growth and can be retained as mulch next spring.
- Test your soil if has been more than three years since the last test.
- Empty the growing media from containers and store it in a trash can or heavy-duty trash bag. Soilless growing media and compost lose nutrients and break down physically over time, but can be rejuvenated by mixing 50:50 with fresh growing media and/or compost.
- Clean garden tools and sand off any rust. Sharpen the edged tools and rub linseed oil or other vegetable oil on wooden tool handles.

18.9 Planting Seed

Seeds are the amazing living packages that convey genetic information from one season to the next. All of the vegetable crops grown as annuals in Maryland, along with a few perennial crops, are started from seeds. Asparagus, potato, sweet potato, garlic, rhubarb, and horseradish are propagated most often from plant parts other than seeds.

Federal and state laws and regulations ensure that all commercially available farm and garden seeds are properly tested for purity, noxious weed seeds, and germination rate. All seed sold in Maryland or through online seed companies, regardless of price, must meet these standards. Gardeners can also save seeds from open-pollinated cultivars, trade seeds with friends and neighbors, and participate in local seed swaps.

Frequently encountered seed terms

Cultivar: A human-cultivated variety of a specific crop. For example, 'Red Ace' is a beet cultivar. Cultivar is a contraction of "cultivated" and "variety" and is often used synonymously with "variety."

Open-pollinated: An in-bred variety where individual plants in a population cross-pollinate each other and produce nearly identical offspring. When grown using appropriate precautions, these varieties are true-to-type (identical to last year's plants) when seed is saved from year to year.

Hybrid: The controlled cross-breeding of two distinct, inbred, open-pollinated cultivars. The seed of the intentional cross will produce an F_1 (first filial) hybrid. Hybrids tend to be vigorous, uniform, and productive; and many have some disease resistance. Seeds saved from hybrid cultivars are not true to type.

Heirloom: Open-pollinated cultivars that persist because their seed is saved and passed down from one generation to the next. They contain valuable germplasm that would be lost without the efforts of individual gardeners, farmers, small seed companies, seed-saving groups, and the USDA.

Treated seed: Seed that is coated with a chemical fungicide (usually pink or purple) to prevent injury from soil-dwelling diseases after seeds are planted. The most commonly treated crops are corn, pea, and bean. Another treatment is to immerse seeds in hot water to kill pathogens on, and inside of, seeds.

Organic seed: Harvested from crops that are grown and certified according to the USDA National Organic Program (NOP) guidelines. To be certified "organic," seed must be produced and handled by certified organic producers.

Disease-resistant: Has the ability to resist or impede a disease-causing pathogen. The level of resistance may be high or intermediate. This can also apply to insect injury. For example, sweet corn cultivars with long, tight ear leaves resist corn earworm feeding. Cornell University has excellent charts for identifying and selecting disease-resistant cultivars.

Disease-tolerant: The ability of a cultivar to tolerate a disease infection or adverse environmental condition (e.g., drought, cold temperature) without a significant reduction in growth or yield.

Indeterminate/determinate: The shoots of indeterminate tomato cultivars grow and branch throughout the season until frost. The shoots of determinate cultivars reach a certain length and terminate in a flower cluster. Determinate tomato cultivars range in height from less than one foot to five feet and are sometimes referred to as "self-topping."

Days to maturity or days to harvest: The approximate number of days to harvest, either from planting seeds or transplants. For tomato, pepper, eggplant, muskmelon, watermelon, broccoli, cabbage, cauliflower, and Brussels sprouts, the number usually represents days from transplanting. For all other annual crops, the number refers to days from direct seeding.

Parthenocarpic: The flowers are able to set fruit without pollination and fertilization of ovules by sperm cells. These varieties are sometimes referred to as "self-pollinating." Growing a seeded cultivar nearby will lead to seeds forming in the parthenocarpic cultivar.

Gynoecious: The flowers are predominately female, leading to more fruits per plant. Unlike parthenocarpic cultivars, gynecious cultivars require pollination. Some companies include a second cultivar to plant that has both male and female flowers (monecious). Otherwise, you'll need to buy and plant a second variety.

Pelleted: Small seeds (carrot, lettuce, onion) are surrounded by a clay pellet to make handling, spacing, and planting easier.

Primed: Pelleted seeds may also be "primed" to reduce germination time. Seeds receive enough water to almost germinate, and are then dried and stored. These primed seeds break dormancy and germinate quickly when planted. This process, however, shortens the seed's storage life.

Bolting: The plant flowers prematurely and goes to seed, usually due to unsuitable climatic conditions at certain stages of growth. Spinach, lettuce, cilantro, broccoli, and endive are species that are prone to bolting.

Saving seeds

Saving your own vegetable seeds makes your garden more sustainable and self-sufficient, and saves you money. You can also help perpetuate heirloom cultivars that are not available commercially, providing you take precautions to ensure genetic purity.

LOOK FOR DISEASE-RESISTANT SEEDS

Some varieties have resistance to or tolerance of certain diseases and nematodes. You may see one or more of these notations on a tomato seed packet:

V = Verticillium wilt
F = Fusarium wilt
F_1, F_2, F_3 = Races 1, 2, and 3
N = Nematode
T = Tobacco mosaic virus

Heirloom, endangered, and unusual cultivars can be swapped through local, regional, and national seed-saving exchanges.

Keep these considerations in mind when saving seed:

- Second generations of hybrid varieties will not be the same as the parent plant. Use only open-pollinated (or "species") cultivars for home seed-saving. This seed will "come true."
- Save seed from common, self-pollinated annual plants such as lettuce, beans, and peas. Tomatoes and peppers are largely self-fertile, but some crossing may occur if different cultivars are planted in close proximity.
- To save beans and peas, allow seed pods to turn brown on the plant. Harvest the pods, dry them for one to two weeks, shell, and then store.
- To save tomato seeds, pick fruit from desirable plants when ripe. Cut the fruit and squeeze the pulp into a container. Add a little water, and then let seeds ferment for two to four days at room temperature, stirring occasionally. The fungus that grows on the mixture will kill some seed-borne diseases and break down the anti-germination gel coating the seeds. When the seeds settle, pour off the pulp, spread the seeds out, and dry thoroughly.
- Mark your seed storage containers (glass is best) clearly with permanent ink, indicating the cultivar and date.
- Viability increases when seeds are stored in a cool, dry, dark location. The sum of the temperature (°F) and relative humidity (%) should not exceed 100.
- When properly stored, most vegetable seeds will remain viable for at least three to five years. Check references for crop-specific information.
- To test germination, sprout 20 seeds between moist paper towels. If fewer than half of them sprout, either discard the seed or plant enough extra to supply the desired number of plants.

18.10 Starting Your Own Transplants

Seeds can be sown directly into garden soil or started in containers, flats, or pots, indoors or outdoors, and then transplanted into the garden. Cool-season crops benefit from an early spring start indoors so they can mature prior to the summer heat.

Transplants, whether started yourself or purchased, are essential for successful vegetable gardening. They fill a garden space quickly, giving you a head-start on the growing season; and there is no need to thin out extra seedlings. Pest and disease problems are reduced somewhat because the plants are spending part of the growth cycle indoors.

Tomato, pepper, eggplant, cabbage, broccoli, cauliflower, and Brussels sprouts are almost always planted as transplants in Maryland. Many other crops, such as lettuce, melon, squash, onion, kale, collards, and beets, can also be started at home or purchased at garden centers and nurseries. Some gardeners even grow their own bean and corn transplants.

Growing your own transplants gives you unlimited cultivar choices and control of plant production from seed to harvest. Follow these tips for successful transplants:

- Use a lightweight, soilless growing medium that contains ingredients like peat moss, coconut coir, compost, perlite, and/or vermiculite.
- Moisten the growing medium and sow seeds in cells or small pots to the packet's recommended depth.
- Cover the seedling trays with clear plastic to increase heat and humidity for faster germination. Remove the plastic once the seedlings emerge.
- Grow plants under fluorescent or LED lights. Set a light timer so that the lights are on for 14 to 16 hours each day.
- Keep lights no more than one to two inches directly above the plants to prevent legginess. Do not allow leaves to touch the light or they will burn.
- Fertilize with a weak liquid fertilizer only if plants become pale.
- Grow transplants at 70 to 75°F.
- Use a plastic tent to help raise the humidity level and prevent heat loss.
- Bottom watering is recommended. Be careful not to overwater.
- Transplant seedlings to larger containers after "true" leaves appear. Don't crowd plants; use at least a four-inch pot for tomato, pepper, and eggplant.

Hardening-off

"Hardening off" is a term that describes the process of gradually acclimating an indoor plant to the harsh spring conditions in the garden. Hardening-off slows growth and causes soft, succulent tissue to toughen. This can be done over a five to 14-day period, depending upon the crop.

On the first day, place plants outdoors in a shaded, wind-protected area for part or all of the day and bring them back indoors at night. Increase the exposure to sunlight an hour or two each day.

Hardening-off is especially important for cabbage, broccoli, and cauliflower transplants. Stressors, like cold temperature, wind, and cool soil, can greatly reduce the yield of these crops. It is not as important to harden off warm-season transplants (pepper, squash, tomato, eggplant, pepper) if you plant them after any danger of frost, when the soil is sufficiently warm (above 60°F); and give them the water, space, and nutrients they need to grow quickly.

Planting transplants outdoors

Transplants should be stocky, succulent, and insect- and disease-free; and have good green color (see Figure 18-D). When buying transplants, inspect the roots, which should be white and fibrous, but not circling around the container bottom (girdling).

- Be prepared to "hold" plants in a protected location if you need to delay transplanting.
- To prevent transplant shock, transplant late in the day in cloudy, windless conditions. Water your plants several hours before transplanting. Don't let them dry out at any time. Handle plants carefully; avoid disturbing the roots or bruising the stems.
- Turn plants sideways or upside-down to release them from their containers. Plant peat pots directly in the garden, first removing the pot bottom and rim. Do not allow the edge of the pot to stick up out the soil, or it will act as a wick and the transplant will lose moisture.

- Dig a hole large enough to hold the roots of the plant. Tomatoes will develop roots all along the stems. If they are very tall, you can lay the stems horizontally in a trench, leaving only two or three sets of leaves above ground.
- Press soil firmly around the roots of transplants. Water around the base of each plant using a weak liquid fertilizer.
- Protect plants from wind and direct sun for a few days after transplanting by covering with baskets, flower pots, or floating row covers. Water the plants regularly, being careful not to injure stems and roots or dislodge plants. The soil should be uniformly moist, neither dry nor excessively wet.

Planting seeds outdoors

Large seeds, such as pumpkin, squash, bean, and corn, can usually be properly spaced and seeded directly into the soil. It is much more difficult to precisely plant small seeds. Plan to thin out excess seedlings later to achieve the desired spacing. There are several different methods for direct-sowing seed:

Row planting. Drop seeds by hand or from the end of an open seed packet into shallow furrows made by dragging a stick, tool handle, narrow hoe, your hand, or other garden tool through the soil. Cover small seeds just barely with soil or a thin layer of compost; cover larger seeds with one-half inch to one inch of soil or as recommended on the seed packet. Use a hand or garden tool to gently tamp the soil to ensure good contact with the seed and increase the probability of germination.

Broadcast planting. Scatter seeds by throwing them over a designated area. This is also called wide-row planting when the area is rectangular (e.g., eight feet long by two feet wide). Broadcasting is often done with seeds of leafy greens, carrot, beet, radish, and cover crops. This is the least uniform planting method but it can increase food production per square foot by making better use of available sunlight, water, and nutrients. Seed-to-soil contact is critical to germination, so walk on the scattered seeds or gently crisscross the bed with a metal rake.

Hill planting. Pull the soil up into a mound using a spade and metal rake. The mounded soil is somewhat better aerated, which will

Figure 18-D. Transplant tips

Make sure that transplant leaves look healthy and are not so large that the roots inside the container are girdled.

Save and re-use market packs to plant your own seeds for next year's transplants.

hasten seed germination and seedling growth. The hill mimics a raised bed by increasing the available rooting area; and adds some vertical growing space for vining crops like cucumber, squash, melon, and sweet potato. Plant two to four seeds in each hill.

Double-row, block, equidistant, and square-foot planting. These are all interrelated intensive-spacing techniques. Each method can increase food production per square foot by making better use of available sunlight, water, and nutrients. Another benefit is fewer weeds, due to the overlapping canopies of adjacent vegetable plants. The potential drawbacks are crowding, which can stress plants and reduce growth and yields; and reduced air movement around plants, which encourages disease.

For example, bush bean seed can be planted in two five-foot-long rows spaced two feet apart rather than one 10-foot-long row; pepper plants can be planted in two staggered rows with plants spaced two feet apart in all directions. Square-foot gardens are divided into one-foot squares with the crops planted within or between squares based on their eventual size.

A few direct-seeding tips:

- A good rule of thumb is to sow seeds at a depth that is two times their width.
- Use a yardstick or other measuring device to ensure correct spacing.
- Sow seeds deeper in light, sandy soils and shallower in heavier clay soils.
- With cloddy or crusty soils, apply a narrow band of fine compost or vermiculite over the row after seeds are planted. This helps to hold soil moisture and reduce crusting, making it easier for seedlings to push through.

VERTICAL GROWING

Pole beans, some peas, tomatoes, gourds, and most cucumbers can be grown vertically with the necessary support. Eggplant, sweet corn, pepper, and some squash plants can likewise be supported to prevent lodging (falling over) and limit vine sprawl. Some plants entwine themselves onto supports, while others may need to be tied. Plant shade-tolerant crops near vertically-supported crops. Vertically-grown plants are more exposed to the sun and air and dry more quickly.

Stakes, trellises, teepees, cages, and other types of support:

- Increase yields per square foot because plants take up less space
- Decrease fruit problems and make it easier to pick, water, and spray
- Add complex texture to the garden and enhance the ecosystem (e.g., shading, micro-climates)
- Require extra work and expense

- Some gardeners lay boards over newly planted seed during warm weather to keep the bed moist. Check daily for signs of germination.
- Soil temperature has a major effect on the speed of seed germination. In the spring, soil is often cold, and large seeds, such as corn and beans, may rot before they can sprout.

Thinning

Removing excess seedlings is called thinning. It's difficult to plant very small seeds at the desired spacing, so some need to be removed to create space for the plants that remain. Failure to thin seedlings will stunt plant growth and reduce yields. Thinning can be

CLOSE-SPACE GARDENING TIPS

The goal is to space plants at equal distances from each other on all sides, so that leaves will touch at maturity. This saves space, reduces moisture loss from surrounding soil, and reduces weed seed germination.

- Plants should not be crowded so that reduced air circulation leads to disease problems. Also, competition for water and nutrients causes stunting. As you increase the number of plants grown in a given area, you can expect individual plant yields to decline, but the total harvest per area may increase.

- Be observant as you experiment with techniques to maximize garden production. It is tempting to squeeze more seeds or transplants into a small garden. Deep, fertile soil and attention to watering, weeds, and fertilizing may allow you to tighten up plant spacing a bit. But pushing the envelope too far will cause a decline in yield and plant problems. Follow spacing recommendations in the vegetable profiles section guidelines and on seed packets for best results.

done by hand or by dragging a metal rake one inch deep through the planting. This will dislodge excess plants, which you can either remove or leave to decompose. Thinnings of leafy greens can be eaten.

18.11 Vegetable Garden Maintenance

Watering

Vegetable plants and fruits are 75 to 95 percent water. Succulence, eating quality, plant growth, and productivity are all improved when sufficient soil moisture is available.

- The amount of rainfall or supplemental water needed for optimal growth is roughly one inch of water per week (65 gallons per 100 square feet); more is needed for sandy soils, less for clayey soils.

- Keep a rain gauge near the garden and supplement rainfall with irrigation if needed.

- Avoid shallow, frequent watering (except for seed-starting and fast-growing salad greens). This practice encourages shallow rooting which makes plants more susceptible to drought damage.

- When hand-watering, direct water at the base of each plant or along the sides or rows. Water breakers with wands that have cut-off valves are an excellent choice for hand-watering with a hose.

- Overhead watering can foster plant diseases but also helps cool plants and provides moisture for beneficial insects during hot, dry weather. Water early and allow foliage to dry thoroughly.

- Water early in the day. Disease problems are much more likely to get started overnight on cool, wet leaf surfaces.

- Adding organic matter increases a soil's water-holding capacity; mulches will help conserve soil moisture.

- In general, water is most needed during the first few weeks of plant development, immediately after transplanting, and during development of edible plant parts.
- Soaker hoses and drip systems are highly recommended. They minimize water use and deliver water slowly and directly to the root system.

Irrigation techniques

Although climate change is expected to produce more total yearly rainfall in the mid-Atlantic, severe localized droughts will continue to occur during the growing season. Hot, dry conditions in July and August are quite typical and, when persistent, can tax private wells and municipal water systems. Even when rainfall is close to normal during the growing season, your garden will be much more productive if you irrigate regularly.

Sprinklers can irrigate large areas in less time than hand-watering. However, they waste water, make it difficult to work in the garden, and may encourage plant diseases.

Soaker hoses are laid along plant rows or around individual plants and weep water directly to the soil. They are water-efficient, economical, and long-lasting.

Drip irrigation systems are relatively inexpensive, convenient, and easy to assemble and disassemble. Drip irrigation, also known as trickle irrigation, is very efficient compared to overhead watering methods because 90 to 95 percent of the water enters the soil, meaning that less water is required to fully wet the root zone. Walkways remain dry, allowing you to work in your garden without worrying about muddy shoes. Foliage remains dry, preventing disease problems. Drip irrigation

RECORDKEEPING

Take notes based on observations you make through the growing season. How did that new bean cultivar do? Which insect pests and diseases were a problem? What did you learn from planting zucchini in July, or using row covers? How was your garden affected by weather? Did some plants suffer from over- or under-watering?

All of this information can be very useful in preventing problems and improving your future gardening experience. For most of us, it's easy to forget the important details if they are not written down. Develop a system for recording observations that works best for you.

can be easily and inexpensively controlled with mechanical or battery-operated automatic timers.

Affordable kits are available, or you can put together your own customized set-up. Drip irrigation components can be re-used if stored out of the sunlight and away from rodents. The filter, pressure regulator, and connectors should last for many years.

Drip irrigation systems require low water pressure, from 8 to 10 psi (pounds per square inch). A simple filter with a removable strainer is first connected to an outdoor water faucet, followed by a pressure regulator. A backflow check valve is required to prevent contamination of the water source. Typically, a length of flexible three-quarter-inch diameter plastic pipe (header) is laid along the top of each row or bed. Individual runs of drip tubing or drip tape are connected to the header and deliver water from special pressure-compensating emitters inside the quarter-inch tubing or drip tape.

Drip systems deliver about one-half gallon of water per minute per 100 feet of tape or tubing. It can take as little as two to three hours and as long as 24 hours to thoroughly wet the root zone, depending on soil type, temperature, crop, and drip tape or tubing specifications. A single drip line will irrigate a row of plants. For wide beds, drip lines are usually spaced 18 to 24 inches apart, and nine to 14 inches apart on coarse, sandy soils which are more difficult to wet thoroughly. The tubing or tape can be covered with mulch.

Fertilizing vegetables

All vegetable plants grow best with a continuous supply of plant-available nutrients. The nutrient needs of vegetable plants in your garden will vary by:

Species. Cabbage and sweet corn, for example, need more nutrients than beet and pepper.

Point of growth in the crop's life cycle. Plants have critical nutrient needs when getting established and during flowering and fruiting.

Growing conditions. Soil type, plant spacing, rainfall, and weed competition all affect nutrient needs and availability.

"Feed the soil first" is a basic organic gardening principle. Adding organic matter "feeds" soil microorganisms and invertebrates, resulting in the slow and steady release of plant-available nutrients. Fertile garden soil that receives yearly additions of organic matter may have enough nutrients to grow most crops without needing supplements.

It is likely, however, that for certain crops at certain times, sufficient nutrients (especially

---

How to convert synthetic fertilizer recommendations to organic

Synthetic fertilizer recommendation:
Apply 20 lbs. of 10-10-10 per 1,000 sq. ft.
(to supply 2 lbs. of nitrogen)

• • • • •

Organic fertilizer recommendation:
N-P-K of cottonseed meal is 6-2-1
10%/6% X 20 lbs. = 33.3 lbs.

---

nitrogen) will be unavailable. There are four basic reasons:

- Naturally low soil fertility or incorrect soil pH.
- Loss of nutrients from erosion, leaching, and removal by previous crops.
- Release of nitrate in the spring is low because cool soil temperatures limit biological activity. The release rate peaks in late July when soil and air temperatures are high (assuming there is enough moisture and air in the soil).
- In spring, plants growing slowly in cold soil have small root systems that can't adequately mine the soil for available nutrients.

In these situations, plant growth and yields will suffer unless fertilizers are applied.

Fertilizers should be applied based on soil test results and plant needs. Fertilizing lightly in spring with a water-soluble fertilizer will get young plants off to a quick, strong start. If you expect to double- or triple-crop an area, apply compost or fertilizer before each planting. Fertilize eggplant, tomato, and pepper after first fruits form if plant growth is lagging.

Organic and synthetic fertilizers

Synthetic fertilizers are typically referred to as "inorganic" or "chemical" fertilizers. Synthetic fertilizers usually contain relatively high concentrations of nutrients in a readily available (soluble) form for plant uptake, although some, like sulfur-coated urea, are designed to slowly release nutrients. Relatively small quantities are needed and the exact amount of nutrients applied is known and adjustable.

For example:

Muriate of potash:	0-0-60
Potassium nitrate:	13-0-44
Triple superphosphate:	0-45-0
Urea:	46-0-0

Organic fertilizers are typically lower in nutrients than synthetic fertilizers and generally release their nutrients more slowly, although this varies by specific fertilizer. Soil amendments like compost and aged manure that are applied to improve soil and plant health have low nutrient release rates but usually contain a wider range of micronutrients than commercial organic fertilizers.

For example:

Alfalfa meal:	5-1-1
Blood meal:	15-1-0
Cottonseed meal:	6-2-1
Dried poultry litter:	4-3-3
Fish emulsion:	5-1-1

Fertilizing tips

- Always follow label directions. Too much synthetic or organic fertilizer can burn plants or stimulate leaf growth at the expense of fruit.
- One cup (eight ounces) of a synthetic granular fertilizer like 10-10-10 weighs approximately one-half pound).
- One cup (8 ounces) of a dry organic fertilizer like cottonseed meal weighs approximately one-third of a pound (five ounces).
- Apply half of the recommended fertilizer amount at planting time and the remainder later in the growing season. For example, apply the second half when fruits first form on squash, tomato, and pepper.
- Fertilize spring seedlings and transplants with a water-soluble fertilizer.
- Mix dry fertilizers into the top two to four inches of soil. Water in fertilizers if rainfall is not expected.
- Fertilize right before or after a new crop is planted or apply a thin (one-half inch) layer of compost.
- Side-dress plants when needed. Pull mulch away before fertilizing and replace it afterwards.
- Fertilize the actual planting area where roots will be growing, not walkways.
- Use nitrogen-only fertilizers rather than complete fertilizers (which contain N, P, and K) if a soil test report indicates high levels of P (phosphorus) and K (potassium).
- Boron is an important micronutrient that is sometimes deficient in sandy soils. Lack of boron can cause disorders in some vegetable crops. If soil is deficient, incorporate six to seven tablespoons of borax per 1,000 square feet of garden area.

- Slow growth, stunting, pale leaves, and low yields may indicate a need to fertilize. These symptoms can also be caused by other factors, such as crowding, low sunlight, compacted soil, and root-knot nematodes.

Nitrogen (N) fertilizing tips

- Nitrogen is needed by plants in large quantities. The general nitrogen (N) recommendation for vegetable crops is two pounds per 1,000 square feet or 3.2 ounces per 100 square feet.
- Heavy feeders like tomato, broccoli, and beet should receive three pounds of N per 1,000 square feet or 4.8 ounces per 100 square feet.
- High-nitrogen organic fertilizers include cottonseed meal (6-2-1), nitrate of soda (15-0-0), calcium nitrate (16-0-0), blood meal (12-0-0), and fish meal (8-10 percent N) and fish emulsion (5 percent N).

Example of a nitrogen (N) fertilizer calculation:

To apply 3.2 ounces of N per 100 square feet using nitrate of soda (15-0-0), calculate:

3.2 ounces of N ÷ 0.15 (the percentage of N in nitrate of soda) = 21.33 ounces (one-and-one-third pounds) of nitrate of soda.

Applying fertilizer

- Broadcasting: Spreading fertilizer (usually sprinkling by hand) over a large area where plant roots will be growing, either before or after planting.
- Banding: Applying fertilizer in a narrow band next to a line or furrow where seeds or seedlings will be planted.
- Side-dressing: Applying fertilizer around individual plants or along the sides of plants in a row, after plants have become established. Be careful not to pile fertilizer next to the stems.
- Liquid: Applying a mixture of soluble fertilizer and water around plants and/or spraying it on the foliage.

Weed management

Weeds are plants that grow well in disturbed environments and compete with garden plants for water and nutrients. They may also serve as alternate hosts for insect pests and diseases. Have a plan for managing weeds before spring planting. Weed growth can quickly become overwhelming during warm, wet weather, especially if the garden size is more than one can easily manage. Learn about the characteristics and biology of the most persistent and prevalent weed species in your garden. Are they annuals, biennials, or perennials? Do they propagate only by seed or do they spread by rhizomes and stolons? What is the best management approach? Special attention should be paid to difficult perennial weeds such as mugwort, Canada thistle, bermudagrass, yellow nutsedge, and quackgrass. See **Chapter 13, Weeds,** for detailed information.

Beneficial weeds

Weedy plants do have benefits. They can provide shelter, pollen, and nectar for beneficial insects like bees and parasitic wasps. They are a good source of nitrogen for the compost pile if removed before flowering. Many have long roots that bring subsoil elements into their above-ground parts, so when you incorporate the composted weeds into your garden, those elements become available to growing plants. Many weeds are edible and nutritious, such as dandelion, purslane, chickweed, violets, and lamb's quarters.

Cultivation

All types of cultivation, whether with small tools, tillers, or hands, can effectively control weeds under the right conditions—but they all disturb the soil, allowing even more weed seeds to germinate and flourish. The following techniques help minimize soil disturbance:

- Hand-pull weeds when they are young; this is easier following a rainfall. Mature weeds extract large quantities of moisture and nutrients from the soil.
- Slice weeds off at ground level using a hoe or other tool with a sharp edge (see Figure 18-E).
- Use a tool like a stirrup hoe to dig deeply enough in the soil to cut and remove some perennial weeds and deep-rooted annual weeds.
- Use a flat file to keep tool edges sharp.
- Mow and weed-eat around your garden to prevent the spread of weeds.

Mulching

Organic mulches prevent weed growth, moderate soil temperature, conserve soil moisture, and add organic matter to the soil when they rot. After your soil has warmed to 60°F, lay down two to six inches of grass clippings, shredded tree leaves, or newspaper covered with straw or shredded leaves to

Using herbicides in a food garden

Herbicides are generally not recommended in or near the vegetable garden; very few are labeled for this use.

Only use these products exactly according to label instructions and only for crops listed on the label. Organic herbicides like soap and pelargonic acid (fatty acid) and vinegar (4-7 percent acetic acid) can desiccate weed leaves, but they are only minimally effective. Concentrated (20 percent) acetic acid products are highly caustic and potentially harmful. It's best to pull or cut weeds by hand— and better still to prevent them from germinating at all.

Even herbicides formulated to kill lawn weeds can drift and cause damage to vegetable plants. Do not use them around your garden.

Figure 18-E. Proper cultivation depth

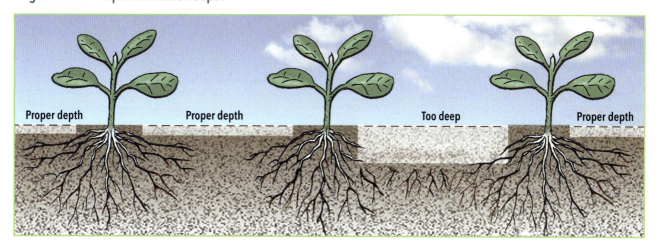

smother weeds. Grass clippings should be allowed to dry before you pile them around plants. Do not use any grass clippings that have been treated with an herbicide. As much as possible, use organic matter generated from your yard and household. Hand-pull any weeds emerging through the mulch.

Organic matter from outside sources carries potential risks. Manure, straw, and hay may be contaminated with long-residual phenoxy herbicides or troublesome weed species. Organic mulches can provide habitat for beneficial animals like spiders and ground beetles, but can also harbor pests like slugs and stink bugs.

Synthetic mulches like black plastic warm the soil for earlier, higher yields of warm-season crops. Research has shown that red plastic mulch may produce higher yields of tomatoes than black plastic. These cannot be re-used. Landscape fabric (weed barrier) warms soil and allows water and air into soil, and it can be re-used. Cut holes in synthetic mulches with scissors or a razor to plant seed or transplants.

Heavy-duty weed barrier material or black plastic tarps can also be used to smother weeds or cover crops that have first been cut to the ground with a mower or string trimmer. The weeds and cover crops are killed in two to six weeks depending upon the species, time of year, and environmental conditions. Completely cover the target area and pin down the edges of the cover with landscape staples, bricks, or soil. If possible, weed-whack or mow the weeds first. DO NOT cover the fabric with any organic material. Weed seeds will germinate on top and grow roots down through the weed barrier.

18.12 Harvesting Vegetables

Vegetables should be harvested when they fall within the optimal range for eating quality. For vegetable crops like muskmelon, the harvesting range is very narrow; fruits can go from underripe to overripe in just a few days. Eggplant, on the other hand, can be harvested over a longer period of fruit development.

Taste and use preferences also dictate when to harvest. Bell pepper can be picked at the green stage or allowed to fully ripen to red. Swiss chard leaves can be harvested at the "baby" stage or allowed to grow so the thick mid-ribs from large leaves can be fried. Small zucchini is excellent when sautéed, while large fruits are perfect for shredding.

Not all vegetables ripen the same way. Fruits that continue to ripen after harvest are called climacteric and include muskmelon, tomato, and potato. Some vegetables stop ripening the instant you pick them, and are called non-climacteric. These include watermelon, summer and winter squash, cucumber, eggplant, pepper, leafy greens, and root crops.

Harvesting tips

- Pick as soon as fruiting vegetables appear to stimulate continuing production. Overgrown fruits can cause plants to senesce early if seed has been allowed to mature inside the fruits.
- If possible, harvest in the early morning before field heat accumulates.
- Use a sharp knife or pruners for harvesting eggplant, pepper, winter squash, and pumpkin.
- Don't leave produce laying on the ground. Freshly harvested vegetables will quickly wilt and get sunscalded.

- Use clean paper bags, plastic buckets, and bushel baskets for harvesting.
- Always wash all produce prior to eating fresh or preparing/cooking. For more harvesting and storage guidelines, consult the individual vegetable profiles at the end of this chapter.

Season extenders

Many vegetable gardeners "put their garden in" after the last spring frost and abandon their garden when those plants stop producing due to natural senescence, weeds, disease, and insect problems.

You can easily extend the growing season in spring and fall by planting and protecting hardy and semi-hardy crops, especially leafy greens. Floating row covers (FRCs) are excellent tools for helping you produce earlier crops in spring, later crops in fall, and even to overwinter some hardy crops. You can also make a "hoop frame" or "low tunnel" from plastic pipe that straddles a garden bed and is covered with clear plastic sheeting or floating row cover material. High tunnels are unheated greenhouses constructed from wood or pipe (plastic or metal) and covered with clear plastic sheeting to extend the growing season. See Figure 18-F for examples.

Cold frames

Cold frames are bottomless boxes with a clear lid that allows sunlight to enter. They can be purchased or constructed at home using readily available materials, such as framing lumber, plywood, bricks, blocks, and plastic sheeting. Resourceful gardeners often build their own using scrap lumber and old storm windows. The back of the frame is higher than the front to increase light interception and shed rainfall and snow. Place your cold frame on level ground facing south for maximum light. Temperature management is critical because heat can build up quickly on a sunny, mild day. The lid should be hinged or removable and easy to open and adjust. You can also cover the lid with a shade cloth to reduce light intensity and heat build-up during the warmer months. This versatile garden tool lets you start seedlings throughout the growing season, hold transplants for planting, and extend the harvest of salad greens.

Cloches and row covers

Cloches are coverings that protect individual plants or a short row of plants from cold temperatures and wind. They may be plastic, wax paper, or glass. Some have vents or openings to exhaust warm, humid air.

Figure 18-F. Common season extenders

Cold frame | Cloche | Row cover

ABOUT ROW COVERS

Lightweight FRCs are often marketed as "insect barriers." They have 85-95% light transmittance and can be left on some crops, like beets, snap beans, and salad greens, from seeding to harvest.

Heavyweight FRCs are usually used to extend the growing season in early spring and late fall and may only have 50% light transmittance.

Advantages:
- Improved plant growth from increased temperature (2-6°F) and humidity
- Frost protection in spring and fall
- Exclusion of insects, birds, deer, groundhogs, and other animals
- Can be reused for two to three years
- Relatively inexpensive

Disadvantages:
- Difficult to manage on windy sites; can tear easily and cause heat stress during hot weather
- Pest insects can become trapped under the cover
- Must be removed or pulled back from blooming crops in the squash family to allow for pollination
- May occasionally abrade or injure tender new growth
- Difficult to use on tall crops

Floating row covers (FRCs) are white, gauzy, lightweight fabrics made from spun-bonded polyester or polypropylene. The covers are draped over plants—individual, rows, or groups—and secured to the ground with landscape pins, boards, bricks, rocks, sandbags, or soil. The cover "floats" directly on top of the crop. With adequate slack, plants push the cover up as they grow. FRCs allow light, air, and water to penetrate while excluding insects and wildlife. They are available in many sizes through mail-order seed and garden supply companies, and at some local garden centers.

Greenhouses

A free-standing or attached greenhouse can dramatically expand gardening interests and activities. A small greenhouse can be used to start seeds, extend the growing season, overwinter tender plants, and dry or cure certain crops.

Shading

Shade cloth is a woven polyester material used to protect plants from excessive sunlight and reduce the ambient temperature around plants. Researchers are exploring systems for using shade cloth to reduce the climate change heat stress of warm-season crops, such as flower and fruit drop. It can also be used to lengthen the harvest period for cool-season crops in late spring, and protect the seedlings of cool-season crops planted in July and August for fall harvest. The most commonly used types exclude either 30 or 50 percent of sunlight.

18.13 Herbs

Herbs bring to mind taste and fragrance; we think of them as the plants that flavor our foods and perfume our homes. Interestingly, more than 25 percent of our modern drugs contain plant extracts as active ingredients. Research continues to isolate valuable medicines from plants used in traditional folk medicine.

Home gardeners' interest in herbs has been increasing for nutrition and health reasons, along with a desire for natural flavors and fragrances. Many herbs also attract beneficial insects. As a group, herbs are relatively easy to grow and don't have as many insect and disease problems as most garden plants.

Start by growing herbs you enjoy using. Choose basil, oregano, and marjoram for Italian-style cooking. Lavender, rosemary, and lemon verbena are great for potpourris; chamomile, peppermint, holy basil, and catnip make wonderful fresh teas. Most herbs have more than one use.

Site and soil

Many of the most familiar herbs—lavender, rosemary, thyme, bay laurel, marjoram, dill, and oregano—are native to the Mediterranean region. These grow best in soils with excellent drainage, bright sun, and moderate temperatures. When growing any herbs, consider the following:

- Improve the drainage of clay soil with organic matter. If you are unable to improve the soil, make raised beds or grow herbs in containers.
- Be sure the site receives at least six hours of direct sun each day.
- Avoid sloped ground where erosion could be a problem.
- Adjust the pH to a range of 6.5 to 7.0.
- Apply balanced fertilizers sparingly. Those high in nitrogen may lessen the concentration of essential oils.

Starting and planting herbs

Herbs are classified as either annual, biennial, or perennial. Be familiar with the growth habits of the plants before you purchase and plant them. In planning your garden, place perennials together to avoid disturbing them when planting annual herbs.

If you want to start seeds indoors, sow them six to eight weeks before setting them out (see **Chapter 24, Plant Propagation**). Perennial herbs are more difficult to begin from seed. Some need chilling treatment or stratification; others may need up to four weeks for germination. Certain herbs—borage, anise, caraway, chervil, coriander, cumin, dill, fennel, and parsley— should be sown directly in the soil as they do not transplant well.

Prepare a hole at least three times the width of the roots, and amend the soil with organic matter. Place the plant into the hole, refill with amended soil, and water frequently until the plant is established and new growth is visible.

Maintenance

Mulch after planting to conserve moisture and prevent mud from splashing onto plants. Use one to two inches of organic material.

Watering tips for herbs

- Watering needs vary, but a rule of thumb is to irrigate once a week to the equivalent of one inch of rain per week (65 gallons per 100 square feet).
- Established perennial herbs are quite drought-tolerant and require less water.
- Annual herbs welcome extra water.
- Herbs should be watered when the surface of the soil feels dry but before the plants look wilted. Do not overwater.

Vegetative propagation

Propagate herbs asexually through layering, dividing, cuttings, or collecting seeds and planting them in the spring. See **Chapter 24, Plant Propagation,** for extensive information about these techniques.

Pest and disease control

When spaced and grown properly, herbs rarely suffer severe disease or insect damage.

- Natural predators and parasites usually keep mite and aphid populations below damaging levels.
- Larger pests, such as beetles and caterpillars, can be hand-picked off of plants.
- Plants that succumb to soil-borne diseases like southern blight should be removed.
- Insecticidal soap can be useful against severe outbreaks of aphids, mites, and whiteflies. Always read and follow pesticide labels.

Harvesting

Herbs grow healthier and fuller if they are harvested frequently. Your method of harvesting depends on which herb you are harvesting and what you plan to do with it.

Guidelines for harvesting herbs:

- Begin harvesting when the plant has enough foliage to maintain growth. Harvest up to three-quarters of the current season's growth each time.
- Harvest in the morning, after the dew dries but before the sun becomes hot.
- Harvest herbs before they flower; otherwise, leaf production will decline.
- For the most intense oil concentration and flavor, harvest leaves after flower buds appear but before they open.
- Pinch out stems at a leaf node to encourage lateral branching, instead of picking off a leaf here and there.
- Harvest herb flowers to dry for craft purposes just before the blossoms open fully.
- Harvest perennials from late spring until about one month before the frost date. Later pruning could encourage tender growth that cannot harden off before winter sets in.
- Harvest often; perennials that are allowed to overgrow and become woody tend to winterkill more easily.
- Harvest tarragon or lavender flowers in early summer, and then shear the plants to half their height to encourage a second flowering period in the fall.

Preservation and storage

Herbs acquire their fragrance and flavor from oils that evaporate into the air when the leaves are crushed. Do not cut or crush the herbs until you are ready to use them. Always use very sharp scissors or a sharp knife to chop herbs for maximum flavor. Herbs can either be used fresh or preserved.

Rinsing herbs for drying and freezing

Remove any foreign matter; insects; and any unwanted bruised, soiled, imperfect leaves and stems. Rinse the herbs under running water without using any soap, bleach, vinegar, or other cleaning agent. Gently shake to remove excess moisture and lay flat on a paper towel to dry thoroughly.

Freezing herbs

The freezer temperature should be 0°F or below (test with an appliance thermometer). Some frozen herbs may develop off-flavors, bitterness, and texture loss; they are suitable only for cooking with heat. The best herbs for freezing are:

To freeze herbs:

- Wrap washed and dried herbs in freezer wrap or place in a plastic zipper bag.

Basil	Lemongrass	Savory
Borage	Mint	Sorrel
Chives	Oregano	Tarragon
Dill	Sage	Thyme

    Chop the herbs first, if you prefer. Label, date, and seal the bag.
- An alternative method: is to lay whole washed and dried sprigs, leaves, or chopped herbs in a single layer on a sheet pan and freeze. Place frozen herbs in a zip-lock bag. Label, date, and seal.

Herbs can be kept in the freezer for one year.

Drying herbs

The best methods to dry herbs are a dehydrator, air, the oven, or microwave. Sun-drying is not recommended because herbs can lose flavor and color, and high summer humidity levels may reduce quality. See Figure 18-G for information about which plant parts to dry.

Air-drying (2-4 days)

- Drying both tender herbs (e.g. basil, oregano) and less tender herbs (e.g. rosemary, sage, thyme) indoors in a clean paper bag will allow any leaves

Figure 18-G. Drying herbs

and seeds that fall to be caught in the bottom of the bag. Drying herbs in a paper bag will also help reduce the potential of dust and pests from landing on drying herbs in your home.

- Punch holes in a clean paper bag to increase air ventilation to dry the herb.
- Tie a small bunch of herbs together by the cut stem end. A large bunch of herbs is more likely to mold.

- Put the bundle in the paper bag and use string to tie the bag closed. Hang it from a structure in your home.
- Dry in a warm, well-ventilated indoor room for the best result.

Dehydrator (1-4 hours)

- Read the dehydrator's instruction manual. Most dehydrators will need to be preheated to 95 to 115°F. In humid locations, preheating to 125°F may be needed.
- After rinsing the herbs, pick each leaf off the stem and lay leaves in a single layer without overlapping on the dehydrator tray(s).
- Check periodically so that the herbs do not over-dry.

Oven-drying (overnight)

- Best for high humidity environments, and for mint, sage, and bay leaves.
- After rinsing herbs, pick each leaf off the stem and lay leaves in a single layer without overlapping on a clean paper towel. Stack another clean paper towel and layer of herbs on top, and repeat for a total of five layers.
- Dry in a very cool oven, either with the oven light of an electric range or pilot light of a gas range, to dry overnight. Leaves will dry flat and hold their color.

Microwave (2-3 minutes)

- Read the microwave's manual for specific herb-drying recommendations. A wattage of 1,000 or higher may be too high to dry herbs.
- Dry small amounts (about a cup) of herbs at a time.
- After rinsing and drying, pick each leaf off the stem and lay leaves in a single layer on microwave-safe paper towels. Timing depends upon the herb type and microwave power level.
- Microwave on high for one minute, mixing after 30 seconds. Continue to microwave, checking at 30-second intervals until sufficiently dry. A total of about two to three minutes is needed per cup of herbs.

Dryness and storage

- Leaves should be crispy-dry and easily crumble between your fingers. Stems should break when bent.
- Store dried herbs whole, crumbled, or ground in a labeled airtight container with a tight-fitting lid.
- Store in a cool, dry, dark location, away from sunlight, heat, moisture, and air.

See the following tables for detailed information about common herbs:

Table 18-D - Common herbs for teas, crafts, medicinal, and other uses

Table 18-E - Common culinary herbs

Table 18-F - Poisonous herbs ❊

Table 18-D. Common herbs for teas, crafts, medicinal, and other uses

Image	Name	Harvest	Uses	Culture	Image	Name	Harvest	Uses	Culture
	Agrimony *Agrimonia eupatoria*	Leaves	Tea, attracts butterflies	Full sun to part shade; moist soil		Elecampane *Inula helenium*	Roots or leaves	Culinary or medicinal	Full sun to light shade; moist soil
	Aloe vera* *Aloe barbadensis* (tender perennial)	Leaves	Balm for burns	Full sun; dry soil		Feverfew *Chrysanthemum parthenium*	Leaves	Potpourri, insect repellent	Full sun; moist soil
	Angelica *Angelica archangelica*	Leaves	Tea, attracts butterflies	Full sun to part shade; moist soil		Geranium, scented* (annual) *Pelargonium graveolen*	Leaves or flowers	Potpourri, insect repellent	Allow to dry out between waterings
	Bergamot *Monarda didyma*	Leaves or flowers	Tea, cut or dried bouquets	Full sun; moist soil		Lavender *Lavandula angustifolia*	Flowers, oil	Sachet, soap, potpourri	Full sun to light shade; moist soil
	Catnip *Nepeta cataria*	Leaves	Tea, cat elixir, attracts butterflies	Full sun; moist soil		Lemon balm *Melissa officinalis*	Leaves	Tea or lemonade, salad, insect repellent	Full sun to part shade; moist soil
	Chamomile (annual/perennial) *Matricaria recutita, Chamaemelum nobile*	Flowers	Tea, skin-cleansing, attracts butterflies	Full sun to part shade; dry soil		Marsh mallow *Althaea officinalis*	Leaves or roots	Poultice, attracts butterflies	Full sun
	Comfrey *Symphytum officinale*	Leaves or roots	Poultice, attracts butterflies	Full sun to light shade; moist soil		Soapwort *Saponaria officinalis*	Leaves or roots	Soap, shampoo	Full sun to light shade; moist soil
	Echinacea *Echinacea* spp.	Roots	Occasional medicinal use	Full sun; moist soil		Sweet cicely *Myrrhis odorata*	Leaves or roots	Salad, cut flower	Full sun to light shade; moist soil

* Tender perennial which may be overwintered indoors in a pot.

Table 18-E. Common culinary herbs

Image	Name	Harvest	Uses	Culture	Image	Name	Harvest	Uses	Culture
	Basil (annual) *Ocimum basilicum*	Leaves	Italian sauces, salads, pizza	Full sun; moist soil		Ginger* (tender perennial) *Zingiber officinale*	Roots	Spice used in teas and Asian dishes	Indirect sun; moist soil
	Bay laurel* (tender perennial) *Laurus nobilis*	Leaves	Stews, soups, *bouquet garni*	Full sun; dry out between waterings		Horseradish (perennial) *Armoracia rusticana*	Roots	Preserved or used in beef dishes	Full sun; moist soil
	Caraway (annual/biennial) *Carum carvi*	Seeds	Sausages, sauerkraut, breads, pickles	Full sun		Lemongrass* (tender perennial) *Cymbopogon citratus*	Leaves or roots	Sautés and stir-fries	Full sun; moist soil
	Chives (perennial) *Allium schoenoprasum*	Leaves or flowers	Leaves for a mild onion flavor; flowers in vinegar for dressings	Full sun; moist soil		Lemon thyme (perennial) *Thymus vulgaris citriodorus*	Leaves	Teas, stews, jellies, soups, and seafood dishes	Full sun to light shade; dry soil
	Cilantro/coriander (annual) *Coriandrum sativum*	Leaves or seeds	Leaves in Asian and Mexican food; seeds for pickling or as a breath freshener	Full sun		Lemon verbena* (tender perennial) *Aloysia triphylla*	Leaves	Teas, salads, cakes	Indirect sun; dry out between waterings
	Dill (annual) *Anethum graveolens*	Leaves or seeds	Leaves for fish, salads, and rice; seeds for pickling	Full sun; well-drained soil		Marjoram (perennial) *Origanum marjorana*	Leaves	Italian and French dishes, soups, and stews	Full sun
	Fennel (perennial) *Foeniculum vulgare*	Leaves or seeds	In cookies, cakes, salads, Mexican, French, and Italian dishes	Full sun; well-drained soil		Nasturtium (annual) *Tropaeolum majus*	Leaves or flowers	Vinegars, salads	Full sun
	Garlic (perennial) *Allium sativum*	Roots	Any savory dish	Full sun; moist soil		Greek oregano (perennial) *Origanum vulgare*, subsp. *hirtum*	Leaves	Mediterranean food; anything with tomatoes	Full sun

* Tender perennial which may be overwintered indoors in a pot.

continued on next page

continued from previous page

Table 18-E. Common culinary herbs

Image	Name	Harvest	Uses	Culture	Image	Name	Harvest	Uses	Culture
	Parsley (biennial) *Petroselinum crispum*	Leaves	As a garnish, in soups and stews; source of vitamin C	Full sun to part shade		Spearmint (perennial) *Mentha spicata*	Leaves	Jellies, teas, as a garnish	Full sun to part shade
	Peppermint (perennial) *Mentha piperaita*	Leaves	Strongest mint flavor; used in jellies and teas	Full sun to part shade		Summer savory (annual) *Satureja hortensis*	Leaves	Vegetables, soups, and stews	Full sun; well-drained soil
	Rosemary (tender perennial) *Rosmarinus officinalis*	Seeds	Adds flavor to roasted meats and vegetables	Full sun; dry out between waterings		Tarragon, French* (tender perennial) *Artemisia dracunculus*	Leaves	In vinegars, sauces, and soups; with fish, poultry	Full sun to part shade, or in pots
	Saffron (perennial) *Crocus sativus*	Stamens	Adds a bright flavor and brilliant yellow color to soups, stews, and rice	Full sun to part shade		Thyme (perennial) *Thymus vulgaris*	Leaves	Seafood, stews, soups, and egg dishes	Full sun to part shade; well-drained soil
	Sage (perennial) *Salvia officinalis*	Leaves or seeds	Adds a strong, earthy flavor to stuffing, roasted meats, and fish	Full sun to part shade; well-drained soil		Winter savory* (tender perennial) *Satureja montana*	Leaves	Vegetables, soups, and stews	Full sun to part shade

* Tender perennial which may be overwintered indoors in a pot.

Table 18-F. Poisonous herbs

Image	Name	Culture	Toxic part	Reaction
	Goldenseal (perennial) *Hydrastis Canadensis*	Prefers shade	All	Respiratory failure
	Lily-of-the-valley (perennial) *Convallaria majalis*	Prefers moist shade	All	Convulsions
	Hyssop (perennial) *Hyssopus officinalis*	Full sun	Leaves, essential oils	High doses are poisonous
	Pennyroyal (half-hardy perennial) *Mentha pulegium*	Full sun to part shade; moist soil	Leaves, essential oils	High doses are poisonous
	Sweet woodruff (perennial) *Galium odoratum*	Part shade	Leaves	High doses cause headache, coma
	Tansy (perennial) *Tanacetum vulgare*	Full sun	Leaves, flowers	High doses cause convulsions

What to do if you eat a poisonous plant

Act fast. While most incidents only cause digestive upset, don't take chances. A quick response could save a life.

Call 911 immediately if you suspect poisoning. Provide the name or a description of the plant, the part that was eaten, and the symptoms. Also provide the weight and age of the patient.

If medical care is not nearby, drink at least 8 ounces of water and induce vomiting. Repeat until stomach contents are clear. Try to get to medical care as soon as possible.

18.14 Profiles of Selected Vegetable Crops

Light

All vegetables profiled on the following page require full sun (direct sunlight for at least six hours per day, preferably eight to ten hours per day). Exceptions are Beet, Swiss chard, lettuce, green onion, radish, spinach, and other tender salad greens, which tolerate partial shade.

Fertility and soil pH

The crops listed here prefer fertile, well-drained soil that is high in organic matter, with a pH of 6.0 to 6.8.

Moisture

Vegetable plants require roughly one inch of water per week. More may be needed for sandy soils; less for clay soils. Okra, Southern peas, watermelon, and sweet potato are the most drought-tolerant crops.

Planting

Denotes whether to plant seed, transplants, or either; and when to start seeds or plant outdoors. Planting dates are for Central MD. Adjust dates as needed for warmer and cooler regions using local weather forecasts and soil temperatures.

Spacing

Two numbers are provided for each vegetable: the first is the spacing between seeds/transplants; the second is the spacing between rows. 12-18" x 24-36" means to space plants 12 to 18" apart in rows that are 24 to 36" apart.

Days to maturity

Indicates the average number of days until the crop can be harvested. Some crops can be harvested early in the "baby" stage (e.g., artichoke, bok choy, greens, squash, carrots, green beans, eggplant, potatoes). Some varieties are specially bred to remain small, even at maturity.

Hardiness terminology

- Very hardy perennial — can withstand winter extremes in most parts of the mid-Atlantic with only slight protection
- Hardy perennial — can withstand winters with protection in colder areas
- Hardy annual — can withstand frosts in spring and fall; may need protection from heavy frosts or freezing
- Half-hardy annual — can withstand light frosts, but not heavy frosts or freezing
- Tender annual — frost will damage plant tissue
- Very tender annual — frost will destroy tissue; needs warm weather to grow

ASPARAGUS

Hardiness	Temperature range	Planting time	Days to maturity	Plant spacing	Approx. yield	Storage
Hardy perennial. Mulch in the fall.	Cool (60°F-65°F)	Plant 1-year-old crowns in early spring. Can also be started from seed.	Begin harvesting lightly in years 2 and 3.	15"-18" x 4' to 5' or wide beds of 3 rows with plants 18" apart in all directions.	(per 10' row) 3-4 lbs.	Process or refrigerate immediately in a plastic bag. Store for 5-7 days.

Planting: Select newer all-male hybrid varieties, which are more productive and disease-resistant. Check crowns for signs of viable buds as well as insects or disease.

- Start asparagus from seed or from 1- to 2-year-old crowns. Crowns are usually set out in March or April.
- Starting plants from seed requires an extra year before harvest. Seeds are slow to germinate and should be transplanted in June. Purchased roots and crowns should be full, slightly moist, and not shriveled. Roots that are dry/brown or soggy/black indicate poor storage.
- Once you have the plants, keep the roots moist (not wet) by misting occasionally. Do not allow them to freeze or dry out. If planting must be delayed for more than a few days, store crowns in a cool place or heel them in a trench of moist soil in a shaded location.
- Traditionally, asparagus crowns are set in a trench 12 in. deep and 12 to 18 in. wide, with 4 to 5 ft. between trenches. A 6-in.-deep trench may be sufficient in high organic matter soils. Space crowns 15 to 18 in. apart. Spread the roots out over a 2-in. soil mound on the trench bottom.
- In high-wind areas, plant rows parallel to the winds so that plants support each other.
- To blanch (whiten) the spears, mound soil around them or otherwise exclude light so they do not form chlorophyll in the stalks.

Fertilizer needs: Medium-heavy feeder. Apply nitrogen annually in early spring. Side-dress after harvest. Asparagus benefits from a yearly top-dressing of compost.

Growing notes: Asparagus is a perennial that lives 12 to 15 years or more and is one of the most valuable early crops.

Choose a site with good drainage and full sun. The tall ferns of asparagus may shade other plants, so plan accordingly. Prepare the bed as early as possible and enrich it with manure, compost, leaf mold, or a combination.

Keep the bed well watered. Weed the bed each spring before the first shoots come up and hand-pull weeds during the season to avoid spear damage.

Harvest: Do not harvest asparagus shoots or spears the first season after crowns are set. Harvest lightly for 3 to 4 weeks the second year. The fleshy root system needs to develop and store food for subsequent seasons. Plants harvested too heavily too soon often become weak and spindly.

If started from seed, do not harvest at all the first 2 seasons, and harvest lightly the third. In the fourth season, harvest daily for 8 to 10 weeks per year. The 6 to 8-in. spears should be snapped off just below the soil surface. If allowed to get much taller, the base of the spear will be tough and require cutting. Do not snap off the spears too deeply; this can injure the crown buds, which produce the next spears.

Allow spears to continue growing once the harvest is over (after 8 to 10 weeks). To extend the harvest period:

- Plant crowns at different depths (4, 6, 8, and 10 in.). The shallower plantings will come up first and can be harvested while spears from deeper crowns are just forming. This method produces a slightly longer harvest, but the plants may be less vigorous.
- Remove mulch from half of the bed. The exposed soil will heat up faster and crowns will sprout sooner. Remove mulch from the other half when spears appear.
- Plant double the amount of asparagus needed for your household. Harvest half the crop in spring/early summer, and let the ferns grow in the other half. In late July, cut the ferns. The crowns will send up new spears, which can be harvested until late in the season. Keep plants well-watered and lightly mulched. Harvest the spring bed only in spring and the fall bed only in fall; otherwise, you risk weakening the crowns.

Winter care: Cut the foliage down to 2-in. stubs after frost and before the red berries fall off (all-male hybrids don't produce berries). Lay down 4 to 6 in. of mulch to prevent weeds.

BEAN

Hardiness	Temperature range	Planting time	Days to maturity	Plant spacing	Approx. yield	Storage
Tender annual, except fava beans (semi-hardy annual)	Warm (65°F-80°F) (except fava beans, which prefer 60°F-70°F)	In spring, after last frost and when soil temperature is above 60°F.	(Direct sow) Snap beans: 50-60 Pole beans: 60-110 Bush limas: 65-75 Pole limas: 85-110	Bush snap: 2" x 24"- 30" Bush limas: 4" x 18"- 30" Pole beans: 4"-8" x 24"-36"	(per 10' row) Snap beans: 3-5 lbs. Lima beans: 4-6 lbs.	Process or refrigerate for up to 1 week in a perforated plastic bag.

Planting: Direct-seed after danger of frost is past. Pre-germinating seed before planting in cool spring soil may help prevent soil rot and seed-maggot problems. (See **Chapter 23, Plant Propagation,** for more details.) Inoculating seeds with nitrogen-fixing bacteria can increase yields on land planted with beans for the first time.

Succession planting: For a continuous harvest, plant snap beans every 2 to 3 weeks from the frost-free date through mid- to late July. Pick regularly to keep plants producing heavily. Cover seed with 1/4 to 1/2 inch of soil or compost. Keep soil moist, but not soaking wet, until the seedlings emerge.

Fertilizer needs: Medium feeder. Beans are legumes and will fix nitrogen once a good root system is established; inoculation will speed the process. Excess nitrogen delays flowering.

Descriptions and growing notes:

Bush beans or snap beans are popular because they mature early and have a compact growth habit. Varieties include standard green, yellow wax, and purple-pod types. Many gardeners prefer flat-pod (Romano) snap beans because of their distinct flavor and texture.

Half-runner beans are a heavy-yielding snap bean with a growth habit between bush and pole beans. Though they have runners about 3 ft. long, half-runners are generally grown like bush beans. Trellising, however, may increase production.

Pole beans produce higher yields over a longer period in less space than bush types. Pole beans are natural climbers but will not weave themselves through horizontal wires. Many types of homemade trellises, including tripods, work well. Trellises should be 6 to 8 ft. tall and sturdy enough to withstand strong winds and rain.

Scarlet runner beans are a fast-growing pole bean that produces delicious beans and beautiful red flowers that attract hummingbirds. Yields increase when more than one cultivar is planted. Harvest as snap beans when young and as green shell beans later. Beans are ready to pick in 75-85 days. The lush 6- to 15-ft. vines can be used to cover arbors, trellises, or fences. Prolonged high temperatures will reduce yield and pod quality.

Lima beans are available in both bush or pole types. Bush limas mature about 10 to 15 days earlier than pole limas, but are less productive. Because the large seeds store considerable amounts of carbohydrates, limas are quite susceptible to soil fungi and bacteria. Cold, wet spells and excessively hot, dry periods can cause lima flowers to drop, reducing crop yields. Baby limas or butter beans are less susceptible to blossom-drop.

Southern peas (black-eyed pea, cream pea, and crowder pea) are neither beans nor peas, but in a separate genus. They are used in the same ways. All are available in pole and bush forms. Southern peas may be harvested in the green shell or dried-pea stage.

Asparagus beans or "yard-long" beans are related to black-eyed peas and have similar flavor, but the pod is 1½ to 2 ft. long. Asparagus beans need a long season to grow well.

Fava beans or broad beans are quite hardy. In cool climates they are often substituted for limas. Sow favas in early spring. Some gardeners have success planting favas in the fall for a spring harvest.

Harvest: Snap beans: Pick before seeds cause pods to bulge. Pods should be tender and break/snap easily when ready. **Lima and green shelling beans:** Seeds should be full-size and pods bright green. The end of the pod will be spongy. For dry beans (of all types), pods should remain on the bush until dry and brown. Keep maturing beans picked to prolong the life of the vines.

BEET

Hardiness	Temperature range	Planting time	Days to maturity	Plant spacing	Approx. yield	Storage
Hardy biennial. Treat as an annual.	Cool (60°F-65°F) Prolonged (30+ days) temperatures below 50°F will cause bolting.	Sow in early spring and successively through late summer.	(Direct sow) 50-60	Plant 2" apart in wide rows or beds. Thin seedlings to a final 3"-4" apart.	(per 10' row) Beets: 2-5 lbs. Yield depends upon the root size.	Very cold (32°F) and moist (95% RH). Store in the refrigerator in a vented plastic bag for 1 week.

Planting: Direct sow beets 2-3 weeks before the last spring frost, throughout the summer, and up until 6 weeks before the first killing frost in the fall.

Seeds germinate at between 45 and 85°F. Cover with ½ in. of soil. Final spacing should be 3 in. all around.

Soaking seed in warm water for 24 hours before planting will aid germination which may help prevent soil rot and seed maggot problems. Fluff soil with a garden fork and smooth with a metal rake before sowing. Grows well with just 4-6 hours of direct light per day.

Fertilizer needs: Heavy feeder. Apply fertilizer before seeding. Boron, a micronutrient, may be deficient in sandy soils and cause development of black spots on the roots. If soil is deficient, apply 6-7 T. of borax/1,000 sq. ft. of garden area.

Growing notes: Beets come in a variety of shapes and colors, including red, golden, white, and striped. Smaller beets are usually preferred for canning and pickling.

Beet seed is actually a fruit or seed ball with several embryos. Unless you buy seed designated as monogerm–one embryo per fruit–you will need to thin the planting when plants are 2 in. tall. The final thinning can be delayed until small beets are large enough for table use.

Water deeply and regularly during dry period, and keep bed free of weeds with shallow cultivation.

Harvest: Harvest beets when roots are 1 to 3 in. across. Thinnings can be used in salads.

BROCCOLI

Hardiness	Temperature range	Planting time	Days to maturity	Plant spacing	Approx. yield	Storage
Hardy biennial. Treat as an annual.	Cool (60°F-65°F)	Start seeds indoors or direct-sow outdoors. Start seed in beds or flats for fall transplants.	(From transplanting) 55-65 (longer for a fall crop)	16"-24" x 24"-30"	(per 10' row) 4-6 lbs.	Very cold (32°F) and moist (95% RH). Store for 10-14 days.

Planting: Start seeds indoors for early spring transplants. Plant seed in beds or flats for fall transplants or direct-sow. Sprouting and raab broccoli are sown directly in spring.

For spring transplants: A month before the last frost, set out 5- to 7-week old transplants. Note that temperatures below 45°F may inhibit heading or encourage seed-stalk formation (bolting).

For a fall crop: Direct-sow seed in mid-July or set out 4- to 6-week-old transplants by the first week in August. Fall-planted broccoli often produces higher yields in the Atlantic region.

Fertilizer needs: Heavy feeder. Use starter fertilizer when transplanting. Fertilize 3 weeks later and after cutting the central head. This encourages side shoots to produce additional small heads.

Growing notes: There are 4 broccoli types: heading, Romanesco, sprouting, and raab. The heading type forms a large central head. Sprouting or Italian broccoli forms many florets, but not a solid head. The spiraling heads of Romanesco are quite dramatic. Broccoli raab is not a true broccoli but a type of turnip cultivated for its flower head. Broccoli has a shallow, fibrous rooting system, so cultivate carefully or use thick mulch.

Harvest: Mature heads measure 3 to 8 in. across. Cut 1 main head before flowers open, then cut small lateral heads (bud clusters) as they develop. Harvest with 6 to 8 in. of stalk.

BRUSSELS SPROUTS

Hardiness	Temperature range	Planting time	Days to maturity	Plant spacing	Approx. yield	Storage
Hardy biennial. Treat as an annual.	Cool (60°F-65°F)	Sow seeds in late June or set out transplants in mid-July.	(From transplanting) 80-100	12"-18" x 24"-30"	(per 10' row) 4-6 lbs.	Very cold (32°F) and moist (95% RH). Store for 3-5 weeks.

Planting: Sow seeds from early to midsummer.

Fertilizer needs: Heavy feeder. Fertilize 2 to 4 weeks after planting or when plants are 12 in. high.

Growing notes: Brussels sprouts are grown for harvest in the fall because cool weather during maturity is essential for good flavor and quality. Plants are tall (sometimes 2 to 3 ft.) and erect. Staking may be necessary if the stalks become heavy.

The sprouts develop in the leaf axils and mature along the stalk. The lowest leaves can be removed to hasten sprout development.

Harvest: Harvest after a frost for the best flavor. Twist or snap off of the stalk when the sprouts are hard, compact, deep green, and about 1 to 1½ in. in diameter. The lowest sprouts mature first. Trim the root end, peel off the top leaf layer and wash well before cooking.

CABBAGE

Hardiness	Temperature range	Planting time	Days to maturity	Plant spacing	Approx. yield	Storage
Hardy biennial. Treat as an annual.	Cool (60°F-65°F)	Start seed indoors for early spring transplants. Sow seed in beds or flats for fall.	(From transplanting) 60-90	Plants: 12"-18" Rows: 24"-30"	(per 10' row) 10-18 lbs.	Very cold (32°F) and moist (95% RH). Store for 4-5 months.

Planting: Start seeds indoors 6 to 8 weeks before the last frost date or sow a few seeds in your cold frame or garden every month to have cabbage until the end of the season.

Plant only the earliest varieties after July 1. It is best not to plant cabbage family crops in the same spot year after year, because diseases and insect pests will accumulate.

Fertilizer needs: Medium feeder. Use starter fertilizer when transplanting, side-dress three weeks later if needed.

Growing notes: Cabbage can be grown in the garden from March to December. It will withstand temperatures as low as 15 to 20°F. Plant spacing affects head size. Close spacing (12 in. apart in the row) produces small heads. Large-headed varieties are spaced wider. Small-headed varieties are fast-maturing and can be succession planted throughout the season. Mature heads can be left on the plant in the garden for about 2 weeks in the summer, 3 to 4 weeks in the fall.

Harvest: When heads become firm; size varies with variety, fertility, and spacing. If unable to harvest at maturity, bend the plant over to break part of the roots, which reduces the incidence of head-splitting.

CABBAGE VARIETIES

Try growing different types of cabbage. Varieties such as bok choy, Napa, savoy, and tatsoi are excellent in salads and stir-fries. Red cabbage adds color and additional antioxidants to your diet.

TIP: Use row covers over seedlings and transplants to exclude flea beetles, caterpillars, and harlequin bugs.

CARROT

Hardiness	Temperature range	Planting time	Days to maturity	Plant spacing	Approx. yield	Storage
Hardy biennial. Treat as an annual.	Best shape/quality when grown between 55°F-75°F.	Direct-sow when the soil temperature has reached at least 45°F.	(Direct sow) 65-75	Thin to 1"-2" apart	2-6 lbs., depending upon row width	Very cold (32°F) and moist (95% RH). Store for 4-5 months.

Planting: Direct seed into loose, friable soil that is free from rocks, clods, or debris. Carrots take several days to germinate, so mark the rows by sprinkling a few radish seeds in with them. Cover seed with ¼ to ½ in. of soil and keep moist. Carrots are best planted in the spring and fall. Temperatures over 70°F reduce root length.

Fertilizer needs: Light to medium-heavy feeder. Incorporate a balanced fertilizer prior to planting.

Growing notes: Use row covers to speed early crops and exclude insects. Hill soil over the tops of the roots to prevent green shoulders. Uniform soil moisture is critical to producing sweet, crisp carrots. There are 5 main types:

Chantenay: Medium to light orange with a red core. Grows to 2 to 2½ in. at the shoulder and 5 to 6 in. long. Medium to large neck. Better for shallow, heavy soils than the long, skinny Imperator types.

Imperator: Deep orange with a lighter orange core. Grows 7 to 8 in. long with a shoulder diameter of 1½ in. Roots become woody when fully mature, but are excellent when harvested at their prime. The main, commercial, fresh-market type.

Danvers: Deep orange with a light center. Conical with a top diameter of 2 to 2-½ in. and length of up to 7 in. Quality is excellent in young roots; becomes fibrous with age.

Nantes: Bright orange with a small core. Cylindrical with a blunt tip, 6 to 7 in. long and 1½ in. in diameter. Tops are often small and require careful digging at harvest.

Miniature and Oxhearts: Consistent medium-orange throughout. Baby carrots are sometimes termed Amsterdam types. Tops are 2 in. and roots are 2 to 3 in. long. Stump-rooted or round carrots are good for heavy soil or containers.

Harvest: Pull or dig when roots reach the appropriate size for the cultivar. Pull the largest roots when they are big enough to eat, leaving the smaller roots to grow. Immediately cut off and compost the tops–this will decrease moisture loss from the roots and help them stay crisp.

For winter harvest, mulch with at least 1 ft. of straw before the ground freezes. Cover the straw with a tarp or sheet of plastic to insulate carrots, and dig them all winter.

CAULIFLOWER

Hardiness	Temperature range	Planting time	Days to maturity	Plant spacing	Approx. yield	Storage
Half-hardy biennial. Treat as an annual.	Cool (60°F-65°F)	Set out transplants 3-4 weeks before the frost-free date.	(From transplanting) 50-80	18"-24" x 2'-3'	(per 10' row) 8-12 lbs.	Very cold (32°F) and moist (95% RH). Store for 2-4 weeks.

Planting: Set out 5- to 7-week-old transplants 3 to 4 weeks before the last frost. Seed in beds or flats for fall transplants or direct-sow.

Do not plant overly mature transplants, which will produce "button heads."

Fertilizer needs: Heavy feeder. Use starter fertilizer when transplanting, and side-dress 3 weeks later if needed.

Growing notes: Blanch cauliflower when the head is 2 to 3 in. across. Pull 3 to 4 large outer leaves up over the head and fasten with a rubber band, or break leaves over the top of the cauliflower and tuck in on the other side. Blanching time is normally 4 to 8 days but may take longer in the fall. If weather is warm during blanching, tie leaves loosely to allow air circulation. Self-blanching cultivars have leaves that grow up over the head to eliminate the need for this practice.

Harvest: Cut before the flower sections begin to separate. The curd should be compact, firm, white, and fairly smooth. Leave a ruff of leaves surrounding the head when harvested to prolong keeping quality. Cauliflower heads become grainy in texture when overly mature.

CUCUMBER

Hardiness	Temperature range	Planting time	Days to maturity	Plant spacing	Approx. yield	Storage
Very tender annual	Warm (65°F-80°F)	Direct-sow after last frost or start indoors.	(Direct sow) 50-65	12"-48" x 6' in rows, or plant in hills (2-3 plants per hill)	(per 10' row) 8-10 lbs.	Medium-cool (45°F-50°F) and moist (95% RH). Store for 1 week.

Planting: Direct-sow or start in containers indoors 3 to 4 weeks before transplanting. Plant a second crop around July 1. Handle transplants gently and disturb the root system as little as possible. Thin seedlings by cutting with scissors rather than pulling them out.

Fertilizer needs: Moderate feeder. Side-dress 1 week after blossoming begins and again 3 weeks later if needed.

Growing notes: Cultivars include the slicer (fresh salad type) and the pickle type (which can also be used fresh), dwarf-vined or bush types, Armenian, and Asian types. Burpless cucumbers are long and slender with a tender skin. Through plant breeding, the bitterness associated with the burp has been removed. There has also been a significant increase in disease resistance in cucumber cultivars in recent years. Try to select resistant varieties when possible.

Members of the Cucurbitaceae family have separate male and female flowers on each plant. For the flower to develop into a fruit, pollen must be carried by bees from male flowers, on the same plant or on different plants, to the female flower (the one with the tiny cucumber fruit attached). Poor cucumber set is common during rainy weather when bees are inactive. Avoid using pesticides during the bloom period. See Table 18-B for more information on pollination requirements.

Trellising: Cucumber vines spread rapidly. Training on a trellis or fence along the edge of the garden will prevent this and also lift the fruit off the soil. Plant 4 to 5 seeds per ft., thinning to 9 to 12 in. apart when plants are 4 to 5 in. high. Benefits of trellising include:

- Increased total yields and yield per square foot
- Longer, straighter fruit (easier for bees to access flowers)
- No soil-borne fruit rot because vines dry faster
- Fruits don't contact the soil so there is less fruit rot
- Easier to pick and a longer harvesting period

Harvest: Pickling cucumbers should be 2 to 3 in. long. Slicing cucumbers should be 5 to 8 in. long, depending upon the variety. Pick by turning cucumber parallel to the vine and giving it a quick snap. Note that working in the vines when leaves are wet may spread disease, so wait until after morning dew or rain evaporates before maintenance or harvest.

EGGPLANT

Hardiness	Temperature range	Planting time	Days to maturity	Plant spacing	Approx. yield	Storage
Very tender annual	Hot (70°F-85°F)	Set out transplants after the last frost.	(From transplanting) 55-80	18"-24" x 30"-36"	(per 10' row) 20 lbs.	Very cold (32°F) and moist (95% RH). Store for 1 week.

Planting: Transplant after all danger of frost, when soil is thoroughly warm. Use 8- to 10-week-old transplants.

Fertilizer needs: Heavy feeder. Apply a balanced transplant fertilizer. Side-dress, if needed, after first fruits form.

Growing notes: There are many eggplant types and cultivars. For example, Japanese eggplant is slender and has thin skin and delicate flavor while standard Italian types are tear-shaped. Warm-to-hot weather and well-drained soil are necessary for good production of all types. Cool temperatures stop plant growth and encourage flea beetles. Nurturing early, rapid root and top growth is critical for high yields. Floating row covers can help promote growth during variable spring weather and protect plants from flea beetles. Reusable black landscape fabric with a soaker hose underneath can increase yield and hasten maturity. When plants are 1 ft. tall, nip back the growing tip to encourage branching. Support plants with cages or a trellis to prevent lodging (plants falling over).

Harvest: Cut fruit stems with a sharp knife or pruners when fruit is not yet fully mature, about 2/3 of maximum size. Skin should be very glossy. Fruit is ripe when pressing lightly with thumbnail leaves an indentation. Discard overripe fruit of dull color with brown seeds. Mature fruit should not be left on the plant as this will reduce overall productivity.

GARLIC

Hardiness	Temperature range	Planting time	Days to maturity	Plant spacing	Approx. yield	Storage
Hardy perennial	Cool (60°F-65°F)	Early to mid-October	250-270	4"-6" apart in double- or triple-wide rows	(per 10' row) 5-9 lbs.	Cool (32°F-38°F) and dry (65%-70% RH). Store for 6-9 months.

Planting: Plant individual cloves in fall, 1 to 2 in. deep, in soil amended with organic matter. Spring plantings produce smaller bulbs because fewer leaves develop prior to bulbing.

Fertilizer needs: Heavy feeder. Apply 4 to 5 lbs. of 10-10-10 per 100 sq. ft. before planting. Use a starter solution for transplants. Side-dress 1 to 2 weeks after bulb enlargement begins (¼ lb. of 10-10-10 or equivalent per 10 ft. of row).

Growing notes: There are 2 main garlic types: softneck and hardneck. Softneck is typically found in grocery stores. Softneck has small cloves but a long storage life. Hardneck cultivars produce an attractive scape that is pinched out to increase bulb size. The scapes are used as scallions. Elephant "garlic" is actually a form of leek that forms large cloves resembling garlic.

Purchase certified, disease-free garlic bulbs for planting from reputable seed sources. Never plant garlic from a grocery store as it may be a symptomless disease carrier. Cultivate very carefully so the shallow root system is not disturbed.

Harvest: Tops begin to die back in late June to early July. Gently lift the plants with a garden fork when the leaves collapse. Do not knock the tops over prematurely. Allow to dry in a well-ventilated location out of direct sun. Cut off the tops after a few days of drying and then lay the bulbs on a window screen in a ventilated area to finish drying. Home-grown garlic will usually last through December if stored in a kitchen pantry.

GARLIC VARIETIES

Reliable hardneck varieties: German White, Music, Siberian, Carpathian, Spanish Roja, Georgian Crystal, and Chesnock Red.

Reliable softneck varieties: Red Inchelium, Nootka Rose, California White, Lorz Italian, Silver Rose, and Silver White.

HORSERADISH

Hardiness	Temperature range	Planting time	Days to maturity	Plant spacing	Approx. yield	Storage
Hardy perennial	Cool to moderate	Plant crowns or root cuttings in spring.	210	24" x 30" in all directions	2-3 lbs. per plant	Dark, cool (35°F-40°F) and moist (90° RH). Store for 6 months.

Planting: Plant root crowns and/or root cuttings (sets) 3 to 5 in. deep in average soil.

Fertilizer needs: Light feeder. Apply manure in the fall. For large roots, loosen the soil to a depth of at least 10 in.

Growing notes: In the home garden, roots can be dug and harvested in the fall and replanted immediately. When making the root cuttings, cut the top straight across and the bottom at a slant so you will know which way is up. Roots may be placed vertically or slanted downward, but the top and bottom should not be reversed. Horseradish can become aggressive if not contained by a large pot or barrier. New plants will emerge from broken roots.

Harvest: Horseradish makes its greatest growth during late summer and early fall, and is typically harvested in October or early November. If you have a large quantity to harvest, cut off the tops 3 or 4 days prior to digging. This will make it easier to find the roots. Small, slender roots are as pungent and flavorful as large roots and less woody.

Processing: Process horseradish outdoors. Peel and grate or blend directly into white wine or white distilled (not cider) vinegar. Do not process with a water bath. Keep refrigerated.

KALE, COLLARD, MUSTARD, AND TURNIP GREENS

Hardiness	Temperature range	Planting time	Days to maturity	Plant spacing	Approx. yield	Storage
Hardy biennial. Treat as annual.	Cool (60°F-70°F)	Direct-sow or start seed indoors for spring or fall planting.	(From seed) 40-80	Kale, collard, mustard: 12"-24" x 30"-36" Turnip: 4" apart	(per 10' row) 5-10 lbs.	Very cold (32°F) and moist (95% RH). Stores 10-14 days.

Planting: Sow directly or start seed indoors for early-spring transplants. Sow seed in beds or flats for fall transplants.

Fertilizer needs: Medium feeder. Use starter fertilizer when transplanting. Side-dress 3 weeks later, if needed.

Growing notes: Closer spacing (2 to 4 in. apart) produces a higher population of small plants that can be harvested repeatedly.

Plant seeds of all 4 types of greens as soon as possible in the spring. You can also germinate seeds indoors and plant 3- to 4-week-old transplants into garden soil. You can either try to keep plants growing through the entire summer or plant twice, in early spring and late summer. Kale and turnip greens are more cold-tolerant than collards, and mustard greens are the least heat- or cold-tolerant. Collards are more heat-tolerant than kale or turnip greens. The latter two don't tolerate temperatures below 15-20°F. All greens can be grown well into the fall in the mid-Atlantic region with a protected garden spot, floating row cover, cold frame, or other protective device.

Frost on the plants will increase the sugar content and flavor of fall greens. Some cultivars of turnip only produce top growth. Most others will also produce turnips that can be harvested throughout the fall.

Greens are relatively high in antioxidants, vitamins, and minerals, making them an important part of home and community gardens. Cultivars with red and purple coloration tend to be higher in antioxidants (e.g., Asian purple mustard).

Harvest: Pick outer leaves, young leaves, or entire plants. For continuous harvests of quick and easy salad greens, sow a raised bed thickly with a mixture of your favorite greens. Shear the plants down to the crown with sharp scissors when they are 6 to 10 in. tall. They will quickly re-grow if watered and fertilized and be ready to cut a second time 2 to 3 weeks later. Remove plants or turn them under when they become overly mature and bitter. Sow a second bed.

LEEKS

Hardiness	Temperature range	Planting time	Days to maturity	Plant spacing	Approx. yield	Storage
Hardy biennial	Cool (60°F-70°F)	Direct-sow or start seed indoors for spring or fall planting.	70-120	5" apart in double- or triple-wide rows	(per 10' row) 5 lbs.	Store for 1 month in the refrigerator, longer in the ground if mulched.

Planting: Start seeds indoors for early spring transplants or later in the summer for a fall crop. Transplant deeply and/or hill up soil around plants to force long, thick, blanched stems with a milder flavor. You can blanch the shanks at the base by transplanting the leeks into a bed of loose soil. Use a dowel with a 1- to 1¼-in. diameter to make holes in the soil about 5 in. deep. Drop a transplant into each hole. Do not fill in with soil, but water gently and the soil will wash in.

Fertilizer needs: Medium to light feeder. Side-dress in June with a balanced fertilizer.

Growing notes: Leeks are related to onions but form a thick stem instead of a bulb. Leeks are a long-season crop, so mulching is essential to keep weeds out and moisture in. In fall, protect the plants with a heavy blanket of straw or leaves so they can be harvested throughout the winter. Leeks left to grow in the spring will go to seed and evolve into a self-perpetuating leek bed. Leeks left to flower may also produce bulblets at the base of the plants. These can be separated and propagated.

Harvest: Dig or pull. Leeks have large root systems, so digging is sometimes easier. They can be harvested any time, from green-onion size to full size, before a killing frost. If covered with mulch, they can be dug throughout the winter.

LETTUCE

Hardiness	Temperature range	Planting time	Days to maturity	Plant spacing	Approx. yield	Storage
Biennial. Treat as an annual.	Cool (60°F-70°F)	Direct-sow leaf and butterhead as soon as soil can be worked. Transplant crisphead and cos in early spring and fall.	(Direct sow) 40-80	Leaf, cos, butterhead: 4"-10" x 12"-24" Crisphead: 12"-15" x 20"-30"	(per 10' row) 2-10 lbs. depending upon type	Very cool (32°F) and moist (95% RH). Store for 2-3 weeks.

Planting: Sow in succession or plant varieties that mature at different times. Install row covers for rapid growth and insect pest protection, and as a sun shield for summer-grown lettuces. Some cultivars (Black Seeded Simpson, Waldmann's Dark Green, Salad Bowl, Winter Density, Brune D'Hiver, Winter Marvel, and Arctic King) can overwinter if healthy 3-week-old transplants are set out around Oct. 15 and protected with a row cover or cold frame.

Fertilizer needs: Medium-heavy feeder. Work in plenty of organic matter prior to planting. Use starter fertilizer on transplants and side-dress as needed.

Descriptions and growing notes:

Lettuce is a cool-season crop that can withstand light frost. Increasing day-length and high summer temperatures usually cause seedstalk formation (bolting) and bitter flavor. Slow-bolting or heat-resistant varieties (e.g., oak-leaf types) extend the lettuce-growing season. Batavia lettuces (a cross between crisphead and butterhead) are the most heat-tolerant.

Plant long-season lettuces so that crops such as sweet corn, staked tomatoes, pole beans, or deciduous trees will shade the lettuce during the hottest part of the day. Some lettuces are even attractive in flower borders. Batavia lettuces (cross between crisphead and butterhead) are the most heat tolerant.

Cultivate carefully, as lettuce is shallow-rooted. Use frequent, light watering to encourage rapid growth, but do not over-water, as this may contribute to diseases. Mulches help to maintain soil moisture and prevent soil-borne diseases.

Crisphead is also known as iceberg. It has a tightly compacted head with crisp, light-green leaves. Crispheads require a long, cool season and "run to seed" as soon as temperatures rise. Select a slow-bolting variety and start seed indoors in late winter or late summer for best results. Transplant in early spring or fall and mulch well to keep soil temperatures from fluctuating and hold moisture in.

Butterheads, such as Bibb and Boston, are loose-headed types with dark-green leaves that are somewhat thicker than iceberg lettuce. Butterheads develop a light-yellow buttery appearance. Small-headed varieties are good for succession plantings. May be started indoors for an even longer season.

Romaine or cos is less commonly grown by gardeners, but is a very nutritious lettuce that deserves attention. It forms upright heads with wavy, attractive leaves.

Leaf lettuces (both red and green) are the most commonly planted. Fast-growing and long-lasting, this type requires little care and grows from March to December. Sow 10 to 20 seeds per ft. in rows 8 to 12 in. apart. Thin plants to 4 to 8 in. apart, depending upon the variety. Leaf lettuce also grows very successfully in a wide-bed arrangement when seedlings are thinned to 4 to 8 in. on all sides.

Escarole, endive, and chicory are grown much the same as lettuce. Follow the seed packet instructions.

Harvest:

- Crisphead is ready when leaves overlap to form a head like those at the supermarket. Heads are compact and firm.
- Bibb lettuce is mature when the leaves begin to cup inward to form a loose head.
- Romaine (cos) is ready when the leaves have elongated and overlapped to form a fairly tight head about 4 in. wide at the base and 6 to 8 in. tall.
- Leaf lettuce can be picked when plants are 5 to 6 in. tall. Use the outer leaves first. You may wish to harvest every other one of the largest plants to thin them.

For continuous harvests of salad greens, sow a raised bed thickly with a mixture of your favorites that have similar maturity dates. Shear plants at the soil level with sharp scissors when they are 6 to 10 in. tall. They will quickly re-grow if watered and fertilized, and be ready to cut a second time 2-3 weeks later. Remove plants or turn them under when they become overly mature and bitter, then sow a second bed.

Storage note: Harvest heads when dry; remove outer leaves, then place in a plastic bag and store in the crisper drawer. Do not wash until ready to use.

MUSKMELON, CANTALOUPE, AND WATERMELON

Hardiness	Temperature range	Planting time	Days to maturity	Plant spacing	Approx. yield	Storage
Very tender annual	Hot (70°F-85°F)	Direct-sow when soil is warm or start seed indoors for spring transplants.	(From transplanting) 80-100	Muskmelon: 18"-24" x 60"-72" Watermelon hills: 6'-8' apart	2-5 fruits per plant, depending upon type	Medium-cool (40°F-50°F) and moist (80%-85% RH). Stores uncut for 7 days.

Planting: Direct-sow outdoors when soil is warm to the touch. For transplants, sow seeds in 3-in. pots 3 weeks before planting. Melons grown from transplants can be harvested up to 4 weeks earlier than if direct-sown.

Fertilizer needs: Medium feeder. Use a starter fertilizer for transplants. Side-dressing with high-nitrogen fertilizer may lower yield and quality, so use a balanced fertilizer. Late-maturing varieties may need additional fertilizer at fruit-set.

Growing notes: Melons are warm-season crops that require a long growing season and considerable space. Muskmelons and watermelons grown on reusable black landscape fabric will produce larger and earlier harvests. If possible, run a soaker hose or drip-irrigation line under the plastic. "Seedless" watermelon varieties have lower germination rates and seedling vigor, and require more careful management.

Arrange vines so they grow in one or two directions. This saves space and keeps your garden orderly. Place cardboard or straw under developing fruits to prevent rot and control weeds.

For the flower to develop into a fruit, pollen must be carried by bees from a male flower, on the same plant or on different plants, to the female flower (the one with the tiny swollen melon). So-called "seedless" watermelons are genetic triploids (3 sets of chromosomes) and require a second diploid (typically 2 sets of chromosomes) variety to set fruit. Poor melon set is common during rainy weather when bees are inactive. Avoid using pesticides during the bloom period.

Although growing plants on a trellis allows closer spacing, each trellised melon (small-fruit cultivars only) must be supported by a sling made of a fast-drying material such as nylon stockings, cheesecloth, or other net-like materials.

Harvest: Muskmelons are harvested at "full slip" (i.e., when the stem separates easily at the point of attachment). Other types of melons, like honeydew and Crenshaw, are cut off the vine after they turn completely yellow. Watermelons should be yellowish on the side that touches the ground and a have a dead tendril near the point where the fruit is attached to the vine. You may also thump the fruit and listen for the dull sound of ripe fruit, rather than a more metallic sound.

OKRA

Hardiness	Temperature range	Planting time	Days to maturity	Plant spacing	Approx. yield	Storage
Very tender annual	Hot (70°F to 95°F)	Direct-sow when soil has warmed to 70°F.	(Direct sow) 50-60	12"-18" x 36"-48"	(per 10' row) 10-15 lbs.	Use ASAP; okra becomes pitted in the refrigerator.

Planting: Soften the hard seed-coat by soaking in buttermilk or a weak vinegar solution for 24 hrs., or scratch the seed-coat with a file. Seeds can also be pre-sprouted.

For an earlier harvest, sow indoors and transplant outdoors after all frost danger has passed.

Fertilizer needs: Heavy feeder. Needs a continuous supply of nitrogen for prolonged pod set. Side-dress at least 1 time after pods begin to form.

Growing notes: Plants can grow to 6 to 10 ft. tall in full, hot sun. Only one flower opens on a single stem in a single day. The fruit can be green, creamy-white, or burgundy-colored.

Okra is only slightly drought-tolerant. Water daily, and try not to get water on the leaves. Mulch will help keep the soil evenly moist while preventing weeds.

Harvest: Most plants are spiny, so wear gloves and use clippers or a knife to cut pods from the plants. Harvest 3-in. to 4-in. pods approximately 1 to 3 days after the flowers open, and before pods get woody. For a continuous harvest, remove any overly-mature pods so plants will continue to bloom.

ONION

Hardiness	Temperature range	Planting time	Days to maturity	Plant spacing	Approx. yield	Storage
Hardy biennial or perennial	Cool during leaf development; medium-hot during bulbing	Early onions: Plant sets in early spring. For perennial or multiplier onions, plant sets in the fall.	85-120	1"-8" x 12"-24" 2" for green onions 4" for med. onions 8" for large onions	(per 10' row) 20-25 lbs.	Very cool (32°F) and dry (65%-70% RH). Store for 6-7 months.

Planting: Use sets, seeds, or transplants in spring for early green onions and bulbs later on. Start seed 8 weeks before setting out. Avoid planting in cold soil, which promotes seed stalk development. Also, do not hill up soil on onions as this encourages stem rot.

Fertilizer needs: Heavy feeder. Use a starter solution for transplants and side-dress 1 to 2 weeks after bulbs start to enlarge.

Growing notes: Hardy biennials include bulb, green, or bunching types. Hardy perennials include Egyptian, tree, walking, or multiplier types. Onions are often grouped according to taste (mild and strong flavored), color (white, yellow, and red), and use (storage or fresh-eating). Globe varieties tend to keep longer in storage.

Onion cultivars also have different sunlight requirements (day-length). If a variety is identified as "long day," it sets bulbs with 15 to 16 hours of daylight and is adapted to Northern summers. Short-day varieties set bulbs with about 12 hours of daylight and are grown in the deep South for winter production. There are also "intermediate" cultivars. Mid-Atlantic gardeners have the best luck with long day and intermediate types. Ensure ample moisture, especially after bulbs begin enlarging. Keep weeds to a minimum with shallow cultivation.

Harvest: Harvest green onions when tops are 6 in. tall and bulb onions when about 2/3 of the dried tops have fallen over. Avoid bruising to help prevent storage rot. Onions may be pulled and left in the garden to dry for several days, then cured in a well-ventilated attic or shaded porch for 1 to 2 weeks. Tops may be left on or cut off; if cut, leave at least 1 in. of the top when storing. Thorough curing will increase storage life.

PEA

Hardiness	Temperature range	Planting time	Days to maturity	Plant spacing	Approx. yield	Storage
Hardy annual	Cool (65°F to 70°F)	Direct-sow when soil temperature has reached 40°F.	(Direct sow) 50-70	1"-3" x 18" or space double rows 8"-10" apart in 18"-24" rows	(per 10' row) 3-5 lbs.	Cool to 32°F right after harvest, then store in refrigerator in vented plastic bag for up to 1 week.

Planting: Growth is inhibited by soils with a pH of 6.0 and lower, so test before planting. Pre-germinate seed for earlier harvests (see **Chapter 23, Plant Propagation**). Plant unbranched types closer together and branching types farther apart.

Seed germination is slowed by soil temperatures below 40°F. Fall-planted peas often do poorly in Maryland because the first killing frost usually arrives before pods can mature.

Fertilizer needs: Heavy user of nitrogen (peas fix little nitrogen). Incorporate a balanced fertilizer before seeding.

Growing notes: Three main types of peas are most often grown in the home garden: English or garden peas, snap peas (edible pods), and snow peas (flat edible pods). Determinate cultivars are bushy and less than 3 ft. tall; indeterminate cultivars will grow to more than 5 ft. Starchy peas have a smooth, round seed. Sugary peas have wrinkled seeds.

Growing plants in double rows on a fence or short trellis will keep the plants erect and productive. Adequate soil moisture is critical for all varieties while pods are filling out.

Harvest: Garden peas: Harvest and shell when pods are plump and full, but before seed becomes starchy. **Snow peas:** Pick when pods are large and flat but before seed begins to enlarge. **Snap peas:** Harvest when pods are succulent and seeds are small. Remove "strings" from along the suture of the pod before cooking or eating.

PEPPER

Hardiness	Temperature range	Planting time	Days to maturity	Plant spacing	Approx. yield	Storage
Very tender annual	Warm (70°F to 80°F)	Start seed indoors 8-10 weeks before last frost. Transplant into warm soil.	65-120 depending upon type	12"-18" x 30"-36" or double staggered rows 2' apart	(per 10' row) 2-8 lbs.	Medium-cool (45°F-50°F) and moist (95% RH). Store for 2-3 weeks.

Planting: Start seeds indoors. Plant transplants when soil has thoroughly warmed. Planting sweet types next to hot types will not make sweet peppers hot.

Fertilizer needs: Light-medium feeder. Use starter fertilizer for transplants. If needed, side-dress after first fruits set.

Growing notes: Pepper types that can all be grown successfully in the mid-Atlantic region include:

- Sweet varieties, such as bell, banana, sweet cherry, Italian frying, and pimiento
- Hot varieties, such as serrano, jalapeño, cayenne, habanero, piquin, and tabasco
- Southwestern/Mexican varieties, such as numex, poblano, pasilla, and mulatto

Peppers generally have a long growing season and suffer slow growth during cool periods. Planting through reusable black landscape fabric helps produce strong, productive plants that will fruit earlier than plants grown in bare soil.

Very warm temperatures, especially at night, will slow or stop pod production. Plant peppers where they will receive some late afternoon shade, and cool down your plants with a water spray during hot, dry weather.

Pinch out early flower buds and small fruits to produce more prolific plants. Plant stems can become brittle and should be supported with cages or short trellises.

Harvest: Harvest sweet peppers when they reach full size. Peppers can either be picked green or allowed to ripen and change color on the plant. When allowed to mature on the plant, most varieties turn red, yellow, purple, orange, or brown; are sweeter; and increase in vitamin A and C content. Cut pods, rather than pulling, to avoid breaking branches. Entire plants may be pulled just before a killing frost and hung upside down in a warmer area, such as a garage, to ripen.

POTATO

Hardiness	Temperature range	Planting time	Days to maturity	Plant spacing	Approx. yield	Storage
Half-hardy annual	Cool (55°F to 70°F)	Plant certified seed pieces from Mar. 15-May 1	90-120	8"-12" x 24"-36"	(per 10' row) 6-15 lbs.	Medium cool (40°F-50°F) and moist (90% RH). Store for 6-8 months.

Planting: Plant 1½ to 2 oz. seed pieces with at least 1 good eye in early spring. Seed pieces will survive a light frost.

Fertilizer needs: Heavy feeder. Apply a balanced fertilizer before planting. If needed, side-dress about 6 weeks later when tubers begin to form. Uniform moisture is required, especially during tuber growth.

Growing notes: Grow an early crop (early-maturity variety) for new potatoes and a late crop (medium-- to late-maturing variety) for storage. Plant potatoes from March 15 to May 1, depending upon your location. Plants grow rapidly with mild spring temperatures and ample soil moisture.

Purchase certified seed stock–never plant potatoes from a grocery store. They could carry symptomless disease. Seed potatoes should be firm and unsprouted. Cut a 6-oz. potato into 4 seed pieces, each with at least 1 good eye. Plant pieces in furrows, cut side down, 3 to 5 in. deep. Plant later crops 5 to 6 in. deep. Pull a ridge of soil over each row.

Keep beds weed-free with shallow cultivation to prevent plant damage. When the tops are fully grown, hill up soil again over potatoes to shield them from sunscald and greening. (Always cut off bitter green areas, which are associated with solanine, a poisonous glycoalkaloid.)

Harvest: Carefully dig early potatoes when tubers are eating size. Harvest potatoes for storage 2 weeks after the vines die or just after the first frost nips the vines. Leave tubers on the ground for a few hours before bringing them in. Do not wash before storing. Avoid long exposure to light.

PUMPKIN

Hardiness	Temperature range	Planting time	Days to maturity	Plant spacing	Approx. yield	Storage
Very tender annual	Warm (70°F to 80°F)	Start seed indoors in 3-in. pots 3 weeks before planting. Set out transplants after last frost.	100+	2-3 seeds every 3'-4'	(per 10' row) 10-20 lbs.	Medium (50°F-55°F) and dry (60% RH). See Harvest section note.

Planting: Mix compost into the soil before planting. Seed or transplants can be planted through reusable black landscape fabric to hasten maturity. Mound up soil in the middle of the planting area and plant 3-5 pumpkin seeds about ½ in. deep. When the plants have their second set of leaves, keep the strongest plant and cut the others at ground level rather than pulling them out to prevent injury to the roots of the remaining plant.

Handle transplants gently and do not disturb the roots. A second crop can be planted between June 15 and July 1 to harvest around the time of the first frost.

Fertilizer needs: Heavy feeder. Fertilize prior to planting; side-dress when fruits first develop.

Growing notes: Pumpkin is a member of the genus Cucurbita and the family Cucurbitaceae. Like other winter squash, pumpkins can be stored intact for carving and eating later in the season. Some varieties are preferable for carving, some for making pies.

Fruits grow on long vines and come in many varieties and colors, but are mostly orange when ripe. Pumpkins produce male flowers for 1-2 weeks before female flowers appear. This is a normal growth habit and varies with cultivars. For a flower to develop into a fruit, pollen must be carried by bees from male flowers, on the same plant or on different plants, to the female flower (the one with the tiny fruit below the flower). Poor fruit-set is common during rainy weather when bees are inactive. Avoid using pesticides during the bloom period to prevent poisoning local pollinators.

Harvest: Pick pumpkins in late September or October before heavy frost. Light frost will not damage the pumpkin skin or flesh, but will kill the vines. Temperatures below 28°F could injure the fruit.

The rinds need to be very firm for pumpkins to store well. Use a sharp knife or pruning shears to cut the fruit from the vine, leaving 3 to 4 in. of stem attached.

Pumpkin seeds can also be cleaned, dried, optionally roasted, and salted for eating.

Note: If pumpkins ripen before Halloween, wash with a weak bleach solution (1 T. of bleach in 2 c. water). Rinse, wipe dry and store in a cool, dry place on a pallet or platform that allows 360° of air circulation.

GROWING GIANT PUMPKINS

Check seed catalogs and garden centers for cultivars such as 'Atlantic Giant,' 'Big Max,' or 'Big Moon'. It will take 4 months to get these pumpkin varieties to produce pumpkins in the 100+-lb. range.

Plant as recommended above. Monitor the growth of the baby fruits, and when they are 6 to 8 in. across, keep the largest and fastest-growing fruit and remove the others. Remove all new blossoms that appear. Place a piece of cardboard under your giant pumpkin to prevent soil rot. You may want to try rolling the pumpkin very gently into a new position each week to keep it from becoming lopsided.

After selecting your single fruit, pinch back the end of the vine to direct the plant's energy into the fruit. Trim main vines and lateral vines as needed again later in the season.

Giant pumpkins need extra nutrients. Apply a water-soluble fertilizer around the base of the plant every week, according to label directions. The fertilizer should contain nitrogen, phosphorous, and potassium. Alternatively, you can sprinkle a dry fertilizer around the base of your plant every 2 weeks. Do not over-fertilize, which can cause excessive vine growth and split the pumpkins.

Water deeply and regularly at the base of each plant, especially during hot, dry weather and once fruits start to form.

Remove all young weed seedlings by hand or with a hoe, and use a mulch around plants to keep weed seeds from germinating.

RADISH

Hardiness	Temperature range	Planting time	Days to maturity	Plant spacing	Approx. yield	Storage
Hardy annual	Cool (55°F to 70°F)	Direct-sow as soon as the soil can be worked.	25-35	1"-2" x 6"-8" or in wide rows	(per 10' row) 3 lbs.	Cool (32°-40°F) and moist (95% RH). Wash, dry, and place in plastic bags. Store for 1-2 weeks.

Planting: Sow seed as soon as the soil can be worked in the spring. Storage roots become spicy-hot and woody with rising temperatures. Can also be planted in the fall.

Fertilizer needs: Light feeder. Avoid excess nitrogen to prevent all growth from going to the tops.

Growing notes: There are several types of radishes: small spring, Asian daikon, and winter storage. Because cool-season radishes grow quickly, plant a small number of seeds every five days for several plantings. Then you'll have a steady supply of radishes, rather than one large harvest.

Because radishes germinate and grow very quickly, they are handy for marking the rows of slower germinating crops, such as carrots, beets, lettuce, and kohlrabi. Simply sprinkle a pinch of radish seed in the row with these other crops as you plant. The radishes will spring up in a few days, defining each row. If you use this method, you will have more than enough radishes without planting an additional row.

Harvest: Radishes will push out of the ground as they grow and mature. Harvest spring radishes when they are about 1 in. across (depending upon the cultivar) and before they crack or become pithy or too spicy. Cut the tap root and stem from the radish before eating.

SOUTHERN PEA

Hardiness	Temperature range	Planting time	Days to maturity	Plant spacing	Approx. yield	Storage
Tender annual	Warm-Hot (65°F to 90°F)	Direct-sow when soil has warmed.	(Direct sow) 50-90, depending upon type	2"-3" x 3'-4'	(per 10' row) 5-10 lbs.	Store unshelled pods in the refrigerator for 1 week. Store dried peas in a cool, dry place.

Planting: Southern peas like warm-to-hot growing conditions. Plant as directed above and cover with 1/2 to 1 in. of soil. For fresh peas all summer, plant every 3 weeks.

Fertilizer needs: Light feeder. Southern peas are legumes and will fix nitrogen once a good root system is established; inoculation will speed the process. Excess nitrogen will delay flowering and encourage top growth at the expense of the pods. Side-dressing is usually not necessary.

Growing notes: The Southern pea (*Vigna unguiculata*) is also known as "blackeye," "cowpea," "crowder," and "field pea."

Control weeds early. Apply an organic mulch to maintain soil moisture and prevent weed-seed germination. Plants are vigorous, and once established, can shade out weeds.

Southern peas are quite drought-tolerant. Irrigate at the base of the plants if they are flowering and podding during very hot, dry weather.

Harvest: For fresh peas, pick the pod when the pea has reached full size and shell it. Each pod may contain 20 or more peas. Fresh peas can be shelled, blanched, cooled in ice water, and frozen. For dried peas, leave pods on the plant until it has died back but before the pods split open. Dried peas can be kept in a cool dry, place for many months.

ABOUT INOCULANTS

The bacterium in legume inoculants is *Rhizobium leguminosarum*, a nitrogen-fixer. These bacteria "infect" peas and beans as they grow, creating nodules where nitrogen in the air is transformed into ammonia and used for plant growth.

When plants die and decompose, the nitrogen produced through nitrogen fixation becomes available and usable by microbes and plant roots.

SPINACH

Hardiness	Temperature range	Planting time	Days to maturity	Plant spacing	Approx. yield	Storage
Hardy annual	Cool (55°F to 70°F)	Direct-sow in early spring when soil temp. reaches 45°F	(Direct sow) 28-55	3"-12" x 18" or 3" apart in wide rows or beds	(per 10' row) 2 lbs.	Very cool (32°F) and moist (95% RH). Store for 2-3 weeks.

Planting: Direct-sow, as spinach does not transplant well. Plants will grow with just 5 hours of sun per day. Make several small plantings in wide rows, several days apart.

Fertilizer needs: Heavy feeder. Incorporate compost prior to planting.

Growing notes: There are 2 types of regular spinach: smooth leaf and savoy leaf. Savoy types have a more crinkly texture allowing soil and sand to catch in the crevices of the leaves and require multiple washings.

Regular spinach bolts as the days lengthen and temperatures rise. Remove spent plants and replant with a new crop. Because spinach tolerates frost, it is a good crop for the fall garden; with protection, it can be harvested into December. In mild areas, spinach sown in late fall will overwinter and make new growth in the spring.

Other types of spinach include perpetual spinach (actually a type of chard), New Zealand spinach, and Malabar spinach. New Zealand spinach prefers hot weather and should be planted after all danger of frost. It will seed itself and come back year after year. Malabar spinach, a vine with glossy green leaves and purple stems and fruit, can be harvested throughout the summer, especially if grown in some shade.

Use floating row covers to exclude spinach leaf miners and to speed the early growth of the plants.

Harvest: Use thinnings when plants are small; cut full-size leaves and new leaves will grow from the crown. Make a final harvest when the plants send up their flower stalk. New Zealand and Malabar spinach can be harvested continuously throughout the summer.

SUMMER SQUASH

Hardiness	Temperature range	Planting time	Days to maturity	Plant spacing	Approx. yield	Storage
Very tender annual	Warm (65°F to 75°F)	Direct-sow when soil has warmed or start indoors 3 weeks prior to setting out.	(From transplant) 50-65	Hills (2-3 plants per hill): 3'- 4' x 4'- 6' Single plants: 2'-3' x 3'-5'	(per 10' row) 20-40 lbs.	Cool (32°-50°F), and moist (90% RH). Store for 5-14 days.

Planting: Start seed indoors in 3-in. pots 3 weeks before the last frost. Plant a second crop July 1-15. Handle transplants gently and do not disturb the roots.

Fertilizer needs: Medium feeder. If needed, side-dress when the first fruits form.

Growing notes: Summer squash grows on non-vining bushes. There are 3 main types: yellow straight-neck or crookneck; white, saucer-shaped, scalloped, or patty pan; and oblong, green, gray, or gold zucchini. Soil containing plenty of compost or well-rotted manure is ideal, although good crops may be grown in average soils with adequate fertilizer. Squashes do not grow well until soil and air temperatures exceed 60°F. Sow seed or set transplants through reusable black landscape fabric to hasten maturity.

Pollination: Many squashes will produce male flowers for 1-2 weeks before the first female flower appears. For a squash flower to develop into a fruit, pollen must be carried by bees from male flowers, on the same plant or on different plants, to the female flower (the one with the tiny squash). Poor fruit-set is common during rainy weather when bees are inactive. Avoid using pesticides during the bloom period.

Harvest: Harvest when immature, about 6 to 8 in. long and 1½ to 2 in. across for elongated types; 3 to 4 in. across for patty-pans; and 4 to 7 in. long for yellow crookneck. Remove hard, overripe fruit to allow new fruits to develop. Check plants daily once they begin to bear. The flowers are also edible.

SWEET CORN

Hardiness	Temperature range	Planting time	Days to maturity	Plant spacing	Approx. yield	Storage
Very tender annual	Warm-Hot (65°F to 95°F)	Direct-sow after last frost. Plant super-sweet types when soil temp. reaches 65°F.	(Direct sow) 63-100	9"-12" x 24"-36"	(per 10' row) 5-10 lbs.	Very cool (32°F) and moist (95% RH). Store for 2-3 weeks.

Planting: Pre-germinate seed before planting in spring to help prevent soil rot, Southern corn rootworm, and seed-corn maggots. Plant a minimum of 3-4 rows side by side to ensure good pollination. Plant early-, mid-, and late-season varieties for a continuous harvest. Successive plantings of the same variety can be made every 2 weeks or when the previous planting has 3-4 leaves.

Plant early types in rows 30 in. apart with plants 8 to 9 in. apart. For medium to large plant varieties, use a 36-in. row with plants spaced 12 in. apart.

Fertilizer needs: Heavy feeder. Incorporate compost prior to planting. Side-dress twice, when plants are 12 to 18 in. tall and again when tassels appear.

Growing notes: Sweet corn is a variety of maize with a high sugar content. Sweet corn varieties differ significantly in days to maturity, kernel color, and sugar content. Pick when immature (milk stage) and eat as a vegetable rather than a grain. Because the process of maturation involves converting sugar into starch, sweet corn stores poorly and must either be eaten fresh or processed before the kernels become tough and starchy.

There are 3 main types of hybrid sweet corn. Many varieties are a combination of more than one type:

- Sugary (su) includes popular cultivars like 'Silver Queen' that have the "good corn flavor" some gardeners believe was lost with the two newer types below. The sugar in the kernels is quickly converted to starch after harvest.
- Super-sweet (sh2) has twice the sugar content of sugary cultivars and converts sugar into starch more slowly, so it stays sweeter longer. Super-sweet varieties may germinate erratically and seedling vigor is low. Plants must be well-watered at all times (especially after seeding), and often benefit from staking/support. When dried, the kernels have a shrunken appearance.
- Sugary enhanced (se) has a sugar content somewhere between the two types above. It is easier to grow and has tender kernels.

Early-maturing cultivars tend to produce relatively small plants. Baby corn is simply immature corn produced from cultivars with a dwarf habit. Harvest when the silks develop but ears are not yet fertilized.

Corn sown in early spring will take longer because of cool soil and air temperatures. Use only the quickest maturing cultivars for July plantings.

It is not necessary to remove suckers or side shoots on sweet corn. With adequate fertility, these suckers may increase yield, but removing them has been shown in some cases to actually decrease yield. Support the growing stalks with one or two strands of heavy string around the perimeter of the planting to prevent lodging (plants falling over) during thunderstorms.

Keep plants uniformly supplied with moisture, especially during establishment, flowering, and ear development. Water deeply and regularly during dry periods.

Hand-pull weeds when soil is moist or slice weeds at the soil line. An organic mulch will help conserve soil moisture.

Several caterpillar pests may be present in great numbers by late summer. Always select cultivars with leaves that form a tight cover at the tip of the ear which will help prevent pests like corn earworms from feeding on it. Cover immature ears with paper bags to prevent insect or bird damage.

Pollination: Corn is wind-pollinated, which is why it should be planted in sections of 3-4 short rows vs. 1-2 long rows. Most corn varieties cross-pollinate readily. To maintain desirable characteristics, extra-sweet and standard sweet corn should be planted at least 400 yds. apart or allow 2 weeks between plantings. Sweet corn must also be isolated from field corn. White and yellow types will cross-pollinate, changing the kernel color.

Harvest: Corn matures 17-24 days after first silk strands appear (more quickly in hot weather). Pick when husks are still green, the silks are brown and dry, and kernels are full-size and either yellow or white at the tip of the ear. Do a "milky-stage" test: Use your thumbnail to puncture a kernel. If the liquid is clear, the corn is immature. If it is milky, it is ready. If there is no liquid at all, it is past its prime and probably inedible.

Keep corn fresh by removing field heat. Plunge just-picked ears into an ice-cold 1-gallon water bath to which 2 t. of lemon juice has been added. Drop just-picked, unshucked ears into the bath for 15 minutes. Drain and store the ears in large plastic or mesh bags until ready to use. Newer hybrids will remain sweet and fresh for 2-3 weeks.

SWEET POTATO

Hardiness	Temperature range	Planting time	Days to maturity	Plant spacing	Approx. yield	Storage
Very tender annual	Warm (65°F to 75°F)	Plant the slips after the soil has warmed to 65°F.	(From transplant) 85-120	12" x 40"	(per 10' row) 15-30 lbs.	Cure (see Harvest section), then keep cool (55°F- 60°F) and moist (85%-90% RH). Store for 6-8 weeks.

Planting: Plant slips in ridges, which improve drainage and give the roots room to expand. Sweet potatoes grow best in light, sandy soils but will also grow well in clayey soils amended with compost.

Fertilizer needs: Medium feeder. Incorporate compost prior to planting. In light, sandy soils, side-dress with a nitrogen source once or twice during the growing season.

Growing notes: The sweet potato (tuberous root) belongs to the family Convolvulaceae; the white potato (tuber) belongs to Solanaceae. They are not related. Sweet potato cultivars with moist flesh ('Georgia Jet,' 'Centennial,' and 'Vardaman') predominate in the U.S. Japanese and Korean types are drier and store better, and are becoming more popular in Maryland.

Sweet potato is sensitive to drought for the first 50-60 days, so water deeply and regularly during dry spells. Overwatering can cause root rots and root splitting. Hand-pull or cut weeds when plants are young and mulch where weed pressure is high.

To grow your own slips: Wash and scrub the roots; cut them in half lengthwise. Lay them cut-side down on top of a few inches of potting soil in a shallow container; cover with more potting soil. Keep the roots moist and warm and grow directly under fluorescent or LED light for 14-16 hours per day. Pull slips from bedded roots and plant; they are rootless so keep them well-watered. You can also take slip cuttings and pot them. 6 weeks from bedding to planting.

Harvest: Young leaves and shoots can be eaten as greens. Check the root size after 80 to 85 days as roots can split if overgrown. Harvest as soon as roots reach eating size and before a frost. Use a garden fork or spade to loosen the soil and gently lift the sweet potatoes. Remove any attached soil clumps but do not scrub or wash roots prior to storing. If there is a frost, dig the roots immediately; if that is not possible, cut away the vines and throw loose soil over the rows to protect the roots. Temperatures below 55°F can cause injury.

Sweet potatoes benefit from optional curing before storing. Curing causes the conversion of starch to sugar and helps heal cuts that could lead to rot. Leave roots on a porch or other covered location (or in a garage), spread out in a single layer on a pallet or screen, for 1 week. Try to harvest in September when temperature and humidity are still relatively high.

SWISS CHARD

Hardiness	Temperature range	Planting time	Days to maturity	Plant spacing	Approx. yield	Storage
Hardy biennial. Treat as annual.	Cool (60°F-70°F)	Start indoors or direct-sow in early spring/late summer	(From seed) 50-70	8"-12" apart	(per 10' row) 8-12 lbs.	Very cold (32°F) and moist (95% RH). Store for 2-3 days.

Planting: Direct-sow or start indoors 5-6 weeks before transplanting. Thin plants to 4 in. apart when 2 in. tall, or 8 to 12 in. for larger plants. Swiss chard will tolerate part-shade and grow vigorously until frost.

Fertilizer needs: Heavy feeder. Incorporate compost or fertilizer before planting. Side-dress as needed.

Growing notes: Swiss chard is also known as silverbeet, perpetual spinach, and spinach beet. It is in the same species as the garden beet, but lacks the edible root. Cultivars can be green ('Lucullus' and 'Fordhook Giant'), red-ribbed ('Ruby Chard'), and multi-colored ('Rainbow Chard'). Keep plants consistently moist. Hand-pull young weeds and mulch along each side of the row.

Harvest: Young leaves can be used raw; mature leaves are typically sautéed and have a more delicate flavor than spinach. The "ribs" can be used like celery. All parts of the chard plant contain oxalic acid.

Regularly snip leaves 2 in. above crowns to rejuvenate plants. New, succulent leaves will quickly be ready to harvest. Swiss chard is extremely perishable and will only keep a few days in the refrigerator. Store in a plastic or mesh bag.

TOMATO

Hardiness	Temperature range	Planting time	Days to maturity	Plant spacing	Approx. yield	Storage
Very tender annual	Warm-Hot (65°F to 85°F)	Start seed indoors 5-6 weeks before last frost or set out transplants.	(From transplant) 65-90	18"-36" x 4'-5'	(per 10' row) 15-45 lbs.	Do not refrigerate tomatoes. Store for 7-14 days (see Harvest section).

Planting: Plant deeply so that only 2-3 sets of leaf branches are above ground. Very tall, leggy plants should be planted horizontally (laid on their side) in a trench and covered with soil, with the top of the stem bent upward and above ground. Roots will form along the buried portion. Mix 2 T. gypsum (calcium sulfate) into each planting hole to help prevent blossom-end rot.

Fertilizer needs: Heavy feeder. Use starter fertilizer for transplants. Additional fertilizer may be needed after first fruits appear, depending upon plant growth, fruit load, and soil fertility. Do not add epsom salts to the soil unless testing shows a magnesium deficiency.

Growing notes: Many tomatoes types are available:

Patio (dwarf) varieties have very compact vines and are best grown in a container. Tomatoes often are cherry-type (1-in. diameter or less); some produce slightly larger fruit.

Cherry tomatoes have small, cherry-sized (or a little larger) fruits often used in salads. Plants of cherry tomatoes range from dwarf ('Tiny Tim') to 7 footers ('Sweet 100'). One standard cherry tomato plant is usually sufficient for a family.

Grape tomato fruits are shaped like grapes and are usually smaller than cherry tomatoes, with thicker skin.

Determinate types are compact varieties that stop growing at a determined height. Many early-ripening varieties are determinate, but will produce tomatoes through the summer.

Indeterminate types have vines that grow until frost or disease kills them. These include many of the long-season tomatoes that are popular with home gardeners.

Beefsteak tomatoes produce a slice that easily covers a sandwich. Individual fruits often weigh more than 1 lb. Fruits are prone to splitting and usually late to ripen.

Paste tomatoes are pear-shaped or oval fruits with meaty interiors and few seeds. They are less juicy than standard tomatoes and are preferred for drying, canning, and sauces.

Colorful cultivars with brown, striped, and multi-colored fruit are available at garden centers and in seed catalogs.

Heirloom tomatoes are older, open-pollinated cultivars grown for exceptional flavor, color, shape, and/or genetic preservation.

Water all varieties deeply during dry periods, at least once a week and more often when blossoms begin to develop. Cultivate carefully to avoid root damage and use a thick mulch.

Pruning: Suckers are shoots that arise from axils (the angle where a plant stem and leaf branch meet). Suckers will eventually produce flowers and fruit, but if you pinch them out, you will get larger tomatoes that ripen faster. Prune staked tomatoes to 1-3 main stems Remove all other suckers weekly.

Support: Staking or caging is strongly recommended to avoid pest and disease issues, and to save space. 1) Install wooden or steel stakes 6 to 8 ft. long and 1½ to 2 in. wide. Drive them 1 ft. into the soil about 4 in. from the planting hole. As it grows, pull the vine toward the stake and tie loosely with stretchy ties or twine. You can also connect fence posts with 4 or 5 horizontal wires spaced 12-18 in. apart, and tie stems to the wires as they grow upward. 2) Wire cages can be purchased or made with 5-ft. wide x 6-in. mesh. Secure cages to the ground at 4-ft. intervals with stakes.

Harvest: Tomatoes can be picked as soon as they begin to color. Doing so can prevent problems like cracking, splitting, insect feeding, and diseases. They will ripen off the vine at room temperature with no quality loss. For longer storage, pick green tomatoes before the first killing frost and store in a medium-cool (50-70°F) and moist (90% RH) place for 1-3 weeks. As you need them, ripen them at 70°F.

GET THE EARLIEST TOMATOES!

Select early season cultivars that ripen in 55-65 days.

Warm the air and soil by laying down reusable black landscape fabric 2-3 weeks before planting.

Surround the transplants with a plastic enclosure that is open at the top. A wire cage surrounded by clear plastic sheeting works well. Another method is to fill water bottles and stand them inside the cage, close to the plants. The water will heat up during the day and release the heat at night. Wall-O-Water is a commercially available plant protector that has produced good results.

Be prepared to cover plants with a blanket, quilt, or other insulating material if temperatures below 35°F are expected.

WINTER SQUASH

Hardiness	Temperature range	Planting time	Days to maturity	Plant spacing	Approx. yield	Storage
Very tender annual	Warm (65°F to 75°F)	Direct-sow or start indoors 3 weeks before planting. Plant a second crop between June 15 and July 1.	(Direct sow) 60-100	3'-4' x 6'-8'	(per 10' row) 10-20 lbs.	Store in 1 layer in a cool (50°F- 55°F), dry place for 5 weeks to 6 months, depending upon type

Planting: Plant groups of 2-3 seeds in warm soil at a depth of 4 times the thickness of the seed, or start transplants in 3-in. pots indoors. Seed or transplants can be planted through reusable black landscape fabric to hasten maturity. After seedlings emerge, remove all but the strongest one by pinching out or cutting excess plants rather than by pulling. Do not disturb the roots. Plant a second crop between June 15 and July 1.

Fertilizer needs: Medium-heavy feeder. Incorporate compost prior to planting and side-dress if needed when fruits begin to form.

Growing notes: Unlike summer squash, harvest and eat winter squash in the mature fruit stage, when the internal seeds have matured fully and the skin has hardened into a tough rind. At this stage, most varieties of this fruit can be stored for use during the winter.

Winter squash grows on long vines and comes in many varieties and colors. Pumpkin, acorn squash, butternut squash, and buttercup squash are among the better-known types.

If you have space limitations, you can select more compact "bush" varieties or grow small-fruited winter squash on a trellis, but be prepared to support the relatively heavy fruit as it grows.

Water deeply and regularly at the base of each plant, especially during hot, dry weather and when the first fruits start to form. Hand-pull or gently hoe weeds, and mulch around plants to keep weed seeds from germinating.

Harvest: Winter squash is typically harvested in September or October before heavy frosts arrive. Use a sharp knife or pruning shears to cut squash from the vine, leaving about 2 in. of stem attached. The rind should be hard and firm for the squash to store well. Unlike summer squash, which yields over a period of time, all of the fruits of winter squash plants are ripe at about the same time.

AUTHOR

Jon Traunfeld, Center Director, Extension Specialist and Center Director, Home & Garden Information Center, University of Maryland Extension.

HERBS SECTION CONTRIBUTORS

UME Family & Consumer Sciences Agents: Beverly Jackey, MS, RDN; Cheryl Bush, MS, RDN; and Shauna C. Henley, Ph.D.

PUBLICATIONS

Adapted in part from the *University of Maryland Handbook (2016 ed.)* and *The Pennsylvania State Master Gardener Manual*.

PHOTOS AND ILLUSTRATIONS

Main chapter photo: University of Maryland Extension.

Figure 18-A: USDA logo. CC License 2.0. usda.org. Figure 18-B: Colorized by Adapted by LeAnn Zotta from Flint, M.L. 1990. *Pests of the Garden and Small Farm.* Publication 3332. University of California, Division of Agriculture and Natural Resources.

Figures 18-C, 18-D, 18-E, 18-F, 18-G: LeAnn Zotta.

Table 18-D: Agrimony: Flickr-**naturemotions**. Aloe vera, Angelica, Bergamot, Chamomile, Comfrey, Echinacea, Elecampane, Lemon balm, Marsh mallow: pixabay.com. Catnip: Public domain. Sweet cicely, Feverfew: pxhere.com. Lavender: pexels.com. Soapwort - wikimedia.org

Table 18-E: Basil, Bay laurel, Chives, Fennel, Ginger, Horseradish, Lemongrass, Marjoram, Nasturtium, Rosemary, Sage, Spearmint, Summer Savory, Tarragon: pixabay.com. Caraway, Cilantro, Greek oregano, Saffron: pexels.com. Dill, Lemon verbena: Miri Talabac. Parsley: Ellen Nibali. Peppermint: kriangphot31 via Adobe Stock. Garlic: Jon Traunfeld. Lemon thyme: Giftmischer87 via Public Domain, Thyme: freefoodphotos.com. Winter savory: **Tangopaso** via Public domain.

Table 18-F: Goldenseal, Lily-of-the-valley, Hyssop: Pixabay. Pennyroyal: **Javier martin** via public domain. Sweet woodruff: pxhere.com. Tansy: pexels.com

Vegetable Profiles: Asparagus, pexels.com. Bean, Sweet Corn: pxhere.com. Beet: **The Farsmstrs** via Wikimedia Commons. Broccoli, Lettuce, Onions: Jon Traunfeld. Brussels Sprouts: **Public domain**. Cabbage, Cabbage varieties, Eggplant, Melon, Tomato: Stephanie Pully. Carrot: Robert Cook. Cauliflower: **Mike Mozart** via Flickr. Cucumber: **Kat Kellner** via Flickr. Garlic: **Forest and Kim Starr** via Flickr. Garlic varieties, Okra, Peppers, Potatoes, Radish, Winter Squash: Pixabay. Kale, Pumpkins, Swiss Chard: Miri Talabac. Southern Peas: Ria Malloy. Spinach, Sweet Potatoes: University of Maryland Extension.

19: SMALL FRUITS

Macarena Farcuh, Ph.D.

19 SMALL FRUITS

CONTENTS

19.1 Cultivar Selection	579
19.2 Site Selection and Preparation	580
19.3 Planting Small Fruits	582
19.4 Small Fruits Maintenance	582
19.5 Blueberries	583
19.6 Brambles	585
19.7 Currants and Gooseberries	588
19.8 Elderberries	591
19.9 Grapes	591
19.10 Hardy Kiwis	593
19.11 Strawberries	595

LEARNING OBJECTIVES

- Factors to consider before planting small fruits
- Basic growth pattern and life cycle of small fruit plants
- Methods of proper soil preparation and planting
- Methods of fertilizing, weed management, and irrigation
- Methods of training and pruning small fruit plants
- Harvesting small fruits

INTRODUCTION

Surprisingly, few Maryland gardeners grow small fruits, although they are well-suited to our growing conditions and can be grown in a relatively small garden plot. Small fruits are excellent choices for many types of landscapes and are good crops for learning about fruit-growing before tackling the more-demanding tree fruits.

Advantages of growing small fruits include:

- Easy and inexpensive to establish and maintain
- Relatively cold-hardy and long-lived
- Quicker than tree fruits to produce a first crop, a special consideration for people who move often
- Fewer insect and disease problems than tree fruits
- Plants produce high yields per square foot
- Integrate nicely into urban and suburban landscapes
- Important source of vitamins, antioxidants, and fiber
- Versatile in cooking, baking, preserving, and wine-making

19.1 Cultivar Selection

Give special attention to cultivar selection. Plants must be adapted to your soil and climate. When possible, select cultivars with the fewest insect and disease problems. See Table 19-D at the end of this chapter for a list of recommended cultivars for Maryland.

Buy only from reputable nurseries that guarantee their plants to be of high quality, true to name, and packed and shipped correctly. Beware of bargains; high prices do not necessarily mean high quality, but well-grown plants are not cheap. Place your order early, specifying cultivar, size, and preferred time of shipment. Purchased plants may be plugs, bare-root, or container-grown. It is best for plants to arrive when you are ready to set them out.

Small fruits are easy to propagate from cuttings and root suckers of established plants. (Always check for plant copyrights before propagating.) Don't propagate wild brambles because they may carry viruses.

19.2 Site Selection and Preparation

Elements to consider before planting include:

Light. Locate your small-fruit patch in full sun. Blueberries, currants, and gooseberries tolerate partial shade. In warmer regions of the state, blueberries and raspberries may benefit from light shade in hot afternoon sun.

Convenience. Locate the patch as close to your home as possible. Space in or near the vegetable garden is usually preferred.

Grade and exposure. Select a site that is free from frost pockets (places where cold air collects), low wet spots, and exposure to strong, prevailing winds. Sites with early morning sun will allow the foliage to dry more quickly, reducing disease problems.

Spacing. Good air circulation helps prevent disease problems. Overcrowding frequently results in poor air circulation, weak plants, and low yields. For best results, small fruit plants should be transplanted no closer than the minimums indicated in Table 19-A.

Soil. Small fruits thrive in deep, well-drained soil high in organic matter, but will yield well on average garden soil with adequate fertilization and care. They tend to have shallow, fibrous root systems and do not tolerate "wet feet" (roots growing in poorly-drained soil). Adding lots of organic matter will improve soil structure and drainage. Six months prior to planting, incorporate compost

Table 19-A. Characteristics of small-fruit plants

Species	Min. distance between rows (ft.)	Min. distance between plants (ft.)	Annual yield per plant (lbs.)*	Years from planting to first crop	Average life span (years)
Blackberry (Thornless)	8	3 - 4	3 - 10	2 - 3	5 - 12
Blueberry**	6	4 - 5	6 - 8	3 - 4	20 - 30
Currant**	8	4	4 - 6	2 - 4	10 - 20
Elderberry**	10 - 12	3 - 5	6 - 10	2 - 3	20 - 30
Gooseberry**	8	4	4 - 6	2 - 4	10 - 20
Grape (American)	8	8	25	3	20 - 30
Grape (French-American)	8	6 - 8	25	3	20 - 30
Raspberry (Black)	8	2.5	1.5	2	5 - 10
Raspberry (Purple)	8	3	1.5	2	5 - 12
Raspberry (Red)	8	2	1.5	2	5 - 12
Strawberry (Day-neutral)	1	1	0.5	1	2
Strawberry (June-bearing)	3	2	1 - 2***	2	4

* Mature plants.   ** Plant more than one variety for best yield. Most small fruits are self-fertile.   *** Per parent plant grown in the matted row system.

Table 19-B. Fertilizer guidelines for small fruits*

Crop	Soil pH	1st Year	2nd Year	3rd Year
BLUEBERRIES				
All varieties	4.3 - 5.3	Do not fertilize the 1st year.	2 oz. of 21-0-0 (ammonium sulfate) per plant during bloom, and 2 oz. 3 weeks later. Scatter in a ring 15 to 18 in. from the plant.	Increase by 1 oz. per year until the 6th year; then use 8 oz. per plant each succeeding year. Avoid fertilizers containing nitrates or chlorides.
BRAMBLES (RASPBERRIES AND BLACKBERRIES)				
All varieties	6.0 - 6.5	½ lb. of 10-10-10 per 10 ft. of row at beginning of bloom.	Same as 1st year.	1 lb. of 10-10-10 per 10 ft. of row in spring and each year thereafter.
CURRANTS AND GOOSEBERRIES				
All varieties	6.0 - 6.5	¼-½ lb. of 10-10-10 per plant in early spring.	Same as 1st year.	Same as the 2nd year and each year thereafter.
ELDERBERRIES				
All varieties	5.5 - 6.5	3-4 T. of high-nitrogen fertilizer per plant in early spring.	1 cup of high-nitrogen fertilizer per plant in early spring.	1½ cups of 10-10-10 per plant in early spring. 4th year: 2 cups of 10-10-10 and each year thereafter.
GRAPES				
All varieties	5.8 - 6.5	3 oz. of 10-10-10 per plant in early spring.	3 oz. of 10-10-10 per plant at flowering.	4 oz. per plant. 4th year: 8 oz. per plant. 5th year: 16 oz. per plant and each year thereafter.
HARDY KIWIS				
All varieties	5.8 - 6.5	Do not fertilize the 1st year.	2 oz. of 10-10-10 per plant in early spring.	4 oz. per plant. 4th year: 6 oz. per plant. 5th year: 8 oz. per plant and each year thereafter.
STRAWBERRIES				
June-bearing	6.0	3 oz. of 10-10-10 per 10 ft. of row, six weeks after planting; repeat in August.	3 oz. of 10-10-10 per 10 ft. of row in August, before new buds form.	Same as the 2nd year and each year thereafter.
Day-neutral	6.0	6 oz. of 15-0-0 (nitrate of soda) per 10 ft. of row once a month from June to Sept.	4 oz. of 15-0-0 (nitrate of soda) per 10 ft. of row once a month from May to Sept.	Same as the 2nd year and each year thereafter.

*Other complete, synthetic, or organic fertilizers can be substituted for 10-10-10 fertilizer.
Note: One-half cup of 10-10-10 fertilizer weighs about 6 oz. Reduce nitrogen rates if plants produce small crops.

or rotted manure. Alternatively, you can grow and turn under a green manure crop like oats, hairy vetch, winter wheat, or winter rye. A raised bed may be well worth the investment if the drainage of your soil is marginal.

Fertilizer and pH. It is much easier to correct nutrient deficiencies before planting than to continually amend the site. Perform a soil test at least six months prior to planting and adjust pH and fertility levels according to test recommendations. A pH of 6.0 to 6.5 is desirable, with the exception of blueberries (see 19.5, Blueberries).

Small fruits are not heavy nutrient users, but timely applications of fertilizer are essential (see Table 19-B). Be careful not to burn foliage with liquid or granular fertilizers. Keep fertilizers eight to 12 inches away from crowns. Organic gardeners can substitute organic fertilizers and soil amendments like alfalfa meal, dried poultry litter, compost, and rotted manure. Working these materials into the soil insures more uniform fertility.

Weeds. Another consideration of pre-plant planning and long-term maintenance is weed control. Don't plant small fruit plants on a site with difficult perennial weeds like thistle, nutsedge, and bindweed until you've controlled them (see Chapter 11, Weeds).

19.3 Planting Small Fruits

When your order arrives, unpack the bare-root bundles and inspect the plants. Roots should be moist and have a bright, fresh appearance. Shriveled roots indicate that the plants have been allowed to freeze or dry out while in storage or transit. Such plants seldom survive. Plant roots must be kept moist and protected from freezing temperatures at all times.

Temporary storage. If the plants cannot be set out immediately, wrap them loosely in a ventilated plastic garbage bag or other material that will prevent their drying out, and store them in a shed or garage at a temperature above freezing. Strawberry and other fruit plants in small quantities may be held in a refrigerator for a few days. You can also remove the plants from the bundle and carefully heel them in a trench of moist soil in a shaded location. Pack the soil firmly around the roots to eliminate all air pockets and prevent the roots from drying out.

Transplanting. Generally, one- or two-year-old plants are set out either one month before the first fall frost or late March-April. Tissue-culture plants are more cold-sensitive and are transplanted after the last spring frost.

The planting hole should be large enough to accommodate the roots when spread out. Large quantities of organic matter should not be added to the planting hole; instead, incorporate modest amounts of well-rotted manure or compost throughout the eventual root zone. Keep young plants well watered. Blueberries, in particular, will not tolerate water stress.

19.4 Small Fruits Maintenance

This section offers general guidelines for maintaining small-fruit patches. Additional details can be found in the subsequent sections for each crop.

Mulch and water

Organic mulches are always beneficial to small fruits. They help to:

- Suppress weeds
- Maintain even soil temperatures

- Hold moisture in the soil
- Add organic matter
- Protect overwintering plant crowns
- Keep fruits clean
- Prevent root damage from shallow cultivation

Straw, shredded leaves, rotted sawdust, untreated grass clippings, newspaper, and compost can all be used for mulch. Wood chips, pine bark mulch, pine needles, and rotted sawdust are good materials to use around blueberries. A winter mulch can be spread around plants to help prevent the freeze-thaw cycle, which can heave and damage plants. Be careful to keep mulch from touching plant crowns to prevent vole feeding.

The rule of thumb for watering is one inch of water (65 gallons per 100 square feet) per week during the growing season. This need increases during flowering and fruiting. Supplement rainfall when necessary. To discourage disease problems, water in the morning and avoid wetting the foliage. Soaker hoses or drip irrigation lines work well in a small-fruit patch.

Pruning and training

Like so many aspects of gardening, pruning and training small fruits is part art, part science. Here are a few general guidelines:

- Prune in late winter or early spring before growth begins.
- Use sharp pruning shears or clippers.
- Always remove twisted, diseased, and broken canes.
- Bury or "hot"-compost trimmings or remove them from the vicinity of the planting area.
- Don't be afraid to prune. Small fruits can produce excessive growth, especially if over-fertilized or neglected.

The following sections detail specific care for each small-fruit crop.

19.5 Blueberries

The blueberry plant is a multi-stemmed shrub, consisting of a shallow root system and woody stems, or canes, that originate from the crown of the plant. The root system is very fibrous but devoid of root hairs. (Root hairs function in most plants by increasing the surface area of the root for water and nutrient uptake.) This characteristic makes the blueberry plant very sensitive to changing soil/water conditions.

A mature, cultivated blueberry usually has 12 to 18 canes. Growth habits vary among cultivars, with some bushes growing very upright and others having a more spreading growth habit. Fruit is borne on buds formed the previous growing season. Some blueberry varieties are self-fertile but all varieties produce more and larger berries when two or more cultivars are planted.

Several native blueberry species grow wild in Maryland. Northern and Southern highbush blueberry cultivars (*Vaccinium corymbosum*) grow well in most regions of the state. Northern highbush should be grown exclusively in far Western MD. Rabbiteye blueberry (*V. ashei*) is a Southern species that also grows well in Southern MD and on the Eastern Shore.

You can select a combination of cultivars to provide a continuous harvest from July through mid-September. Be sure the bloom times overlap and purchase two- to three-year-old plants for best results. See Table 19-D for recommended varieties for Maryland.

Site selection

Blueberries generally prefer full sun, but can tolerate some shade. With Maryland's climate becoming warmer, some light afternoon shade may prove beneficial.

Blueberries need well-drained soil. Soils with poor drainage or which have high clay content can be prepared as a raised bed. Doing so adds gravitational drainage and prevents plant roots from exposure to standing water.

Try to avoid windy, dry sites. Healthy, mature blueberry plants will generally tolerate very cold temperatures, although there is some cultivar variation. Winter injury is more likely when a period of mild winter weather is followed by severe cold.

Most Northern Highbush varieties require 750 hours of chilling between 32 and 45°F. In Maryland, this requirement is usually met no later than early February. After the chilling requirement is met, the plant loses its dormancy and cold-hardiness, making it increasingly susceptible to injury.

Soil preparation

Blueberries are in the heath family and thrive in acidic soils (pH of 4.3 to 5.3) that are high in organic matter. The year before planting, you should increase soil organic matter by incorporating manure or cover crops, then test and amend your soil pH according to the soil lab's recommendations.

The effects of sulfur (to lower the soil pH) and phosphorus (if needed) require time, so these materials should be added the fall before planting. Do not plant blueberries in high pH soils without amending them first. Sulfur does not move through the soil readily, so surface sulfur applications after the plants are in place are not very effective. Excess sulfur can actually cause stress and plant damage.

Soil pH above 6.0 can be lowered ½ unit by incorporating iron sulfate into the soil at the rate of 1.5 pounds/100 square feet. For example, reducing a soil pH from 6.8 to 5.3 would require 4.5 pounds/100 square feet. Sulfur powder or iron sulfate can be used in later years, if necessary.

A soil pH that is too low can result in manganese or aluminum toxicity. Never attempt to lower pH with aluminum sulfate. As the pH decreases, aluminum becomes more available and may be taken up by plant roots at toxic levels. High pH results in the unavailability of certain nutrients like iron, which results in chlorosis of the leaves.

At planting time, amend the entire planting site, not the individual planting holes, with compost, peat moss, or shredded leaves, to improve water-holding capacity. The final growing medium should be above four percent of organic matter (by volume) at planting time.

Mulch and water

Mulch and irrigation are essential for fast establishment, steady growth, and consistently high yields. Blueberry plants require at least one inch of water per week (65 gallons per 100 square feet). Supplement rainfall when necessary.

Trickle or drip irrigation is preferred because it conserves moisture and does not wet the foliage. The trickle line can be placed directly under the mulch. Overhead irrigation has the one advantage of cooling the plants and the berries during extremely high temperatures.

Wood chips, pine bark, and compost are good mulches. Apply mulch two to three inches deep and replenish as necessary. Avoid mulch with a high pH, such as mushroom compost.

Pruning

Immediately after planting: Prune back 50 to 60 percent of the wood. Remove all flowers from two-year-old plants to encourage root growth and good establishment. Do not fertilize at this time. Pruning invigorates the plant, forcing essential new growth from its base. The guiding principle behind blueberry pruning is to constantly renew the older, decreasingly productive canes by cutting them out to force new canes. This is known as renewal pruning and is also done with grapes, peaches, and currants. Pruning will also increase fruit size and improve quality.

Growing seasons two through five: Plants may need light pruning in February or March. Remove a few of the small branches in the center of the bush. Fruit is produced on wood grown the previous year, and the largest berries are on moderately vigorous wood (branches 12 to 18 inches long). Remove all weak growth (see Figure 19-A).

At maturity (six years and older): A healthy plant should be five to seven feet tall and produce three to five new canes each year. In the spring, keep the best two or three new canes and remove some of the oldest canes. (Canes larger than one inch in diameter do not produce the best fruit.) Failure to remove older branches means new canes are likely to be willowy and produce only a few berries. Pruning will ideally result in a plant with 12 to 18 canes of varying ages.

Remove the lowest branches and thin out center branches. The lowest branches often

Figure 19-A. Pruning a four-year-old blueberry bush

A) Before pruning; (B) after pruning. Pruning reduced the fruit buds by about 75%. In very fertile soils, a larger number of fruit buds can be left for a heavier crop.

lay on the ground and are difficult to pick; the center branches produce small, poorly colored and late-ripening fruit. Overly-long canes with many flower buds may be headed back, but do not try to top canes to stimulate growth.

Harvest

A mature blueberry plant will produce six to eight pounds (seven to nine pints) of fruit per year. Harvest begins in June and may continue through mid-September with late varieties. Berries turn blue three to four days before they attain maximum sweetness and flavor. They should be picked every seven to 10 days. Do not pick berries with a reddish tinge; they are underripe and will not ripen after picking.

Blueberries should be picked in the morning. If picked in the afternoon, the berries will contain field heat, which reduces storage life.

19.6 Brambles

Brambles are defined as any species belonging to the *Rubus* genus, which covers a large number of plants found growing wild in the woods and fields in Maryland. Brambles of interest to the home gardener, however, are domestic raspberries (red, black, yellow, and purple types) and blackberries (thornless and thorny types). Wineberry (*Rubus phoenicolasius*) should not be grown in the home garden. It is an invasive non-native plant that is harmful to the natural environment.

Bramble types

Bramble species vary by fruit color, growth habit, pest susceptibility, and other characteristics. Bramble crowns and roots are perennial; canes are biennial. The canes' typical biennial life-cycle is as follows:

- Each spring, canes known as primocanes emerge, grow tall, put out lateral branches, and overwinter.
- In the second growing year, these canes, now called floricanes, produce flowers and fruit.
- Floricanes die after fruiting and must be eventually removed, usually in late winter before new canes come up.

Red raspberries produce new canes as suckers from the root system, so they are usually grown in a hedgerow. They are the most winter-hardy type of raspberry and may be either of two types:

- **Summer-bearing** types have the typical biennial life cycle of a bramble. They fruit from late June through July of their second growing season.
- **Primocane-bearing** types, also known as everbearing, are an exception to the bramble life cycle. Primocane-bearing types have the ability to fruit in the summer and early fall of their first year on their primocanes. They then fruit a second time, in June, on buds below those which fruited the previous year. The first-year crop, however, is more abundant. Gardeners generally treat the canes as annuals, rather than biennials, by mowing the canes to the ground in winter after the fall harvest. This keeps the plants more manageable.

Red raspberries may struggle in our warmer regions; blackberries may be a better choice for these locales.

Black raspberries initiate new canes from the crown of the plant rather than from root suckers. They are grown one plant per hill, with pruning and other maintenance done on a per-plant basis rather than a per-row basis. (Contrary to the definition for "hill" as it relates to potatoes and cucurbits, here "hill" means to space plants rather than allow them to form a hedge. It does not imply that the soil should be mounded up around the plants.)

Unlike with red raspberries, summer tipping is necessary because individual canes grow to unmanageable lengths. Black raspberries bloom from April to May, bear fruit before summer-bearing red raspberries, and are the least cold-hardy of the raspberries.

Purple raspberries initiate new canes predominantly from the crown, but may sucker between plants as well. Bloom time is June, ripening from mid-July to mid-August in Central Maryland. They are essentially grown like black raspberries and are intermediate in cold-hardiness.

Yellow raspberries are also available, although not widely grown. They grow from crowns and are typically primocane-bearers. Cut canes down to the ground each winter like the red primocane bearers.

Eastern blackberries can be of four types:

- **Thorny-erect.** Excellent fruit quality and sweeter than thornless cultivars, but the thorns are brutal. Suckers require containment. Thorny blackberries will tolerate winter temperatures as low as about -5°F.

- **Thornless-erect.** Relatively new cultivars. Despite their name, they require some support.

- **Thornless-trailing.** Much more cold sensitive (to 0°F) and grow best in the southern or warmer areas of Maryland. Because of their trailing growth habit, they require trellising.

- **Primocane-bearing.** New type that has not been tested in Maryland.

Cultivar selection is very important. Purchase virus-indexed, tissue-cultured raspberry plants. If available, use tissue-cultured blackberries as well. Consult Table 19-A for appropriate cultivars.

Planting

Here are the basics for growing brambles:

- Full sun is best; six hours minimum.
- Plant brambles in early spring.
- Black raspberry plants are susceptible to mosaic virus and should not be planted close to red raspberries.
- Avoid poorly drained soils and sites.
- Wild brambles are a principal source of disease, so plant far from wild brambles and remove any within 50 yards.
- Prune bare-root plants after transplanting (see Table 19-D). Healthy potted plants do not require any initial pruning.
- After planting, cut off any old, dead canes attached to the crown as they may harbor disease.
- Remove flower blossoms during the first year to encourage plant establishment.

Training

March is a good time to prune fruit plants in Maryland because you can fully assess any winter damage. Raspberries, however, can be pruned any time canes are fully dormant.

There are several ways to train and manage brambles, depending on their growth habit: erect vs. trailing blackberries, and suckering vs. clump growers (see Figures 19-B and 19-C). Fruiting canes of all brambles (except primocane-bearing types) die soon after fruiting is completed. Remove these dead canes when they are dormant or in late winter.

All bramble plants require heading-back cuts, as well as removal of weak, damaged, and diseased canes. Figures 19-D and 19-E, and Table 19-C summarize the best training and pruning systems for brambles. Refer to the earlier section, Bramble types, for pruning of red and yellow primocane-bearing types.

Harvest

Like all small fruit crops, brambles should be harvested in the morning after dew has dried. This practice allows a minimum of field heat in the fruit and results in longer shelf life.

Ripe berries will detach easily. They should be rolled off the plant, rather than squeezed or pulled, and put in shallow containers. Deep containers tend to crush berries in the lower layers. Blackberries are best picked when the fruit changes from shiny black to a dull black or when the calyx begins to brown. Do not

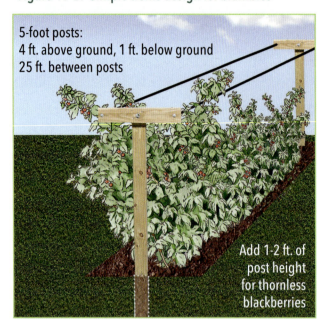

Figure 19-B. Simple trellis design for brambles

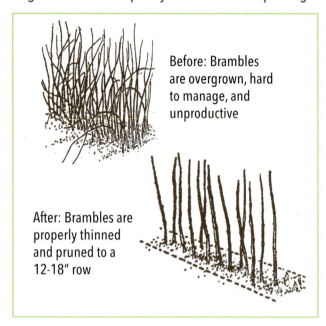

Figure 19-D. Red raspberry: dormant-season pruning

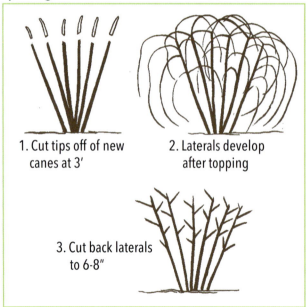

Figure 19-C. Purple/black raspberries: summer pruning

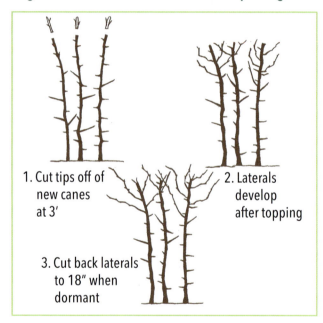

Figure 19-E. Erect blackberries: summer pruning

allow overripe berries to remain on the canes and foster pest problems.

Refrigerate berries immediately, but do not wash them until you are ready to use them. Raspberries can be kept for up to a week, and blackberries will keep several days longer. Bramble fruits will further ripen after harvest, but will not get any sweeter.

19.7 Currants and Gooseberries

Gooseberries and currants (*Ribes* spp.) enjoyed great popularity in the past, particularly in Europe. In the 1800s, enthusiasts could choose from 700 cultivars of gooseberry and would join "gooseberry clubs." Most of the European cultivars were large-fruited and sweet as a result of centuries of selection and

Table 19-C. Pruning guide for established brambles

Species	Cultural systems (hedge or hill*)	At planting	Primocanes: Summer pruning	Dormant pruning: Winter to early spring
Red raspberry Summer-bearing (Figure 19-D)	Hedge; plants tied to a trellis	Head back to ground-level	Narrow the hedge to 18-in. width if necessary.	Select canes of no less than a pencil thickness. Cut back to ¾ of their length. Remove weak canes and dead (fruited) canes. Space canes about 4 in. apart and keep the width of the hedge to 12-18 in.
Red raspberry Primocane-bearing (fall-fruiting)	Hedge	Head back to ground level	Narrow the hedge to 18 in. if necessary; harvest fruit in August and September.	Cut all canes off near ground level in late February or early March.
Black raspberry (Figure 19-C)	Hill	Head back to 2-3 in. above the soil line	Top canes at 36-40 in. to force lateral branches. Remove at least 4 in. of growth.	Head back laterals to 12 in. or no less than a pencil's thickness. Remove weak canes, leaving about 5 per hill. Remove dead (fruited) canes, if this was not done since the previous summer.
Purple raspberry (Figure 19-C)	Hedge/hill	Head back to 2-3 in. above the soil line	Top canes at 40 in. to force lateral branches. Remove at least 4 in. of growth.	Head back laterals to 18 in. or no less than a pencil's thickness. Remove weak canes, leaving about 5 per hill. Remove dead (fruited) canes, if this was not done since the previous summer.
Thorny blackberry (Figure 19-E)	Hill; plants must be tied to a trellis	None (remove dead wood, if any)	Top primocanes to about 42-60 in. to force lateral branches. Remove at least 4 in. of growth.	Remove weak canes. Space canes at about 6 in. within the hedge. Narrow the hedge to 18 in. Head back laterals to 18 in. Remove dead (fruited) canes, if this was not done since the previous summer.
Thornless blackberry	Hill; plants must be tied to a trellis	Head back to 2-3 in. above the soil line	Head back at the top wire of the trellis.	Remove weak canes. Space canes at about 6 in. within the hedge. Narrow the hedge to 18 in. Head back laterals to 18 in. Remove dead (fruited) canes, if this was not done since the previous summer.

* "Hill system" in the context of berries means to space plants and not allow them to form a hedge. It does not imply that the soil should be mounded up around the plants as you might for cucurbits or potatoes.

breeding, whereas American types had less desirable flavor but more disease resistance. Several European cultivars are still available from specialty nurseries. Gooseberries grown today are primarily hybrids of these two types, offering good flavor as well as disease (mildew) resistance.

Gooseberries and currants are woody perennial shrubs that reach a height of three to six feet when mature. Jostaberry is a black currant-gooseberry cross. Plants are vigorous and thornless and grow to five feet tall. Hardy and disease-resistant, the large fruit has a mild black-currant flavor.

Legal restrictions

There is often confusion amongst gardeners about the legality of growing gooseberries and currants. Until 1966, a federal ban prohibited the growing of *Ribes*. The ban was enacted because gooseberries and currants can serve as alternate hosts to white pine blister rust (*Cronartium ribicola*), a destructive disease that kills white pines and their ecosystems. The ban was rescinded in 1966 after it was discovered that other plants could also act as host. In 1933, Maryland passed a law limiting gooseberry and currant cultivation, but the law was not enforced because white pine blister rust is not a significant problem in Maryland.

If you have white pine nearby, you may want to consider growing less susceptible types. Black currant (*Ribes nigrum*) is the more susceptible species, and some areas outside of Maryland still prohibit its cultivation. There are, however, resistant cultivars of black currant. Red and white currants are less susceptible; gooseberries are least susceptible.

Planting

Red currants and gooseberries are self-fertile, but will produce more and larger fruit where more than one cultivar provides cross-pollination. Some black currants are self-sterile and require another cultivar for fruit production. Check before planting.

Unlike most fruiting plants, gooseberry, currant, and jostaberry tolerate partial shade. These plants can all be effectively mixed into a home landscape. You need to know the specific growth characteristics of individual cultivars to make appropriate selection and placement.

Select a cool, moist, partially-shaded site. In fall or early spring, plant well-rooted one- or two-year-old dormant plants. Set plants two inches deeper than they were grown in the nursery. Cut back the top portions of the plant to six to 10 inches. Remove flower blossoms from plants in the first year to encourage plant establishment and growth for future years. Beware of over-watering, which will increase the chances of root-rot diseases. Well-established plants can fruit for 10 to 15 years or more.

Pruning

Prune plants when they are dormant in early spring just before growth resumes. Red currants and gooseberries produce fruit at the base of one-year-old wood, but the greatest production is on spurs of two- and three-year-old wood. Therefore, regularly remove four-year-old wood and choose the best one-year-old wood as replacement canes. Black currants produce best on one-year-old wood. Strong one-year-old shoots combined with two- and three-year-old wood will provide the heaviest yields.

19.8 Elderberries

Because of their unusual taste, elderberries (*Sambucus canadensis*) are popular in wines, jam, jellies, and pies. Most people consider elderberries too tart for eating fresh. This native plant is extremely hardy, seldom frost-damaged, and easy to grow. Landscapers recommend it as an ornamental for its showy white flower clusters and black fruit. Elderberries are also on most wildlife plant lists as an attractant and food source.

Site selection and planting

Elderberries tolerate a wide range of soil conditions, including poorly-drained soils, but they grow best in well-drained silt loam with a pH of 6.5. Elderberries like full sun, but will tolerate some shade. Plant in early spring as dormant plants. Place rows 10 feet apart, and plant six feet apart in the row. Alternate varieties or rows of different varieties to ensure successful cross-pollination and larger yields. Fertilizer application is not recommended in the first year. Because elderberries have shallow, fibrous roots, they are susceptible to drought, especially in the first year. Be sure to provide sufficient water.

Pruning

Elderberries require a yearly dormant season pruning for consistent season-to-season yields. Elderberries fruit most heavily on second-year canes. Seek a balance of second- and third-year canes. Remove third-year canes during the following dormant pruning to stimulate a new generation of first-year canes when growth resumes in spring. Also, regular removal of diseased or insect-infested canes helps eliminate most pest damage and ensures a long-lived, productive plant.

Harvest

Elderberries are best cut from the stem as a cluster and hand-stripped. Harvest is usually between mid-August and mid-September, depending on the cultivar and location. Plants mature between the second and fourth seasons and can yield six to eight pounds per mature plant. Birds are a serious pest in elderberry plantings, so make plans to cover the plants with bird netting when fruits form.

19.9 Grapes

Grapevines adapt relatively well to a wide range of soils and can be grown and manipulated rather easily. Some specialized knowledge of pruning is needed, but the plants will respond well.

Planting and first pruning

During the first year:

- Plant in early spring, three to four weeks before the last frost.
- The planting hole should be wide enough to accommodate the roots once they are spread out.
- After setting plants, remove all but one cane with up to six buds.
- After shoot growth begins from the buds and danger of spring frost is past, remove all but the two strongest shoots.
- Remove all flower clusters.
- Keep a weed-free area 18 to 24 inches wide around the plants.
- Remove all suckers and maintain only the two shoots.
- Keep vines off the ground and tied to either stakes or a trellis.

Subsequent pruning and training

Second year

In early spring, select the best of the two original shoots to become the permanent trunk. Remove the other one. Tie the young vine to a stake. As the vine grows, tie it to the wire. Cut it back right above where you tie it. This promotes straight trunk growth in the vine (see Figure 19-F). Leave four to six buds near the top of the vine and remove the remainder. Remove any flower clusters from the developing lateral shoots.

You can train your grapes to grow on arbors, fences, and trellises. On ornamental structures, prune for a longer trunk and leave more fruiting canes each year.

For best fruit production, the "two-arm system" is the simplest to implement. Heavy (#9) wire stretched between posts, 60 inches above the ground, supports the vine. Use seven-foot posts (three to four inches in diameter) set two feet into the ground, 20 feet apart. Nail or staple the wire to the top of the posts.

Third year

In early spring, select the two strongest lateral shoots from each side of the trunk. Cut them back to five to seven buds and tie them to the wire, extending in opposite directions. Select two other canes, one on either side of the trunk and cut back to two buds. These are called the renewal spurs.

Mature vines

Grapes produce fruit clusters on canes that are two years old. They are non-productive after they fruit and should be pruned out. Prune the four shoots that grow from the two renewal spurs on either side of the trunk. Prune the strongest lateral cane on either side to 20-30 buds each. You can determine the number of buds for fruiting by assessing the vigor of the vine. When the vine is weak, leave no more than 40 buds. Retain 60 or more if the vine is vigorous. Prune the other two shoots to two to three buds; they become the renewal spurs. Each year, remove the fruiting wood from the previous year and select new shoots (renewal spurs) to become next year's fruiting wood.

Prune in March so you can determine the amount of winter damage. Leave more buds after particularly harsh winters. Typically, remove 90 percent of the previous year's growth during dormancy. Ignore the heavy sap flow from fresh pruning cuts made in late spring. This will not weaken or damage your canes. The sap may cause contact dermatitis in some individuals; wear gloves when pruning.

Harvesting

For best quality, bunch grapes should be fully ripe when harvested. Grapes will not improve

> **GRAPE TERMINOLOGY**
> - **Cane:** a mature woody shoot
> - **Cordon:** a horizontal extension off the trunk, trained along a trellis wire
> - **Lateral:** a side branch, either a shoot or a cane
> - **Shoot:** current season's growth spur, a cane pruned to one to three buds
> - **Trunk:** vertical structure of the vine from root system to fruit-bearing wood

Figure 19-F. Training grapes on a two-arm support system

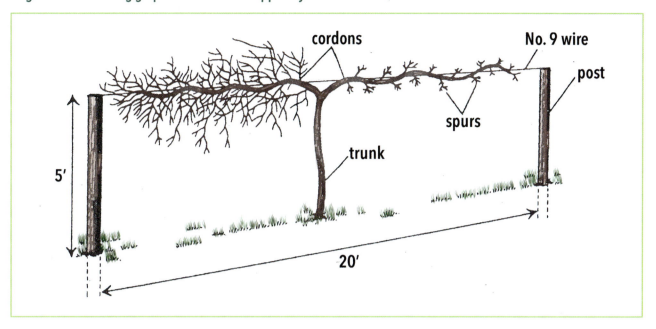

A FEW NOTES ABOUT WINE GRAPES

- Visit wineries and learn before you plant. Wine grapes require special knowledge of site requirements, pruning, cluster exposure to sunlight, and pest management.

- Wine grapes are less cold-hardy and more susceptible to black rot, so research cultivars that are resistant and suitable for your hardiness zone.

- To make wine, grapes must be far more ripe than the table grapes you eat. Follow harvesting recommendations.

- The best home-grown wine grapes are:
  - Chardonnay (only good sites)
  - Vidal Blanc
  - Seyval Blanc
  - Cabernet Franc (only good sites)
  - Chambourcin
  - Foch

in sugar content or flavor after picking. As harvest nears, protect fruit from birds to allow it time to sweeten. Put plastic netting over the vines or small paper bags over individual bunches to exclude birds from the fruit. Cut the bunches off with a knife or shears to avoid bruising the fruit and damaging the vine. Most cultivars should be used immediately, as they do not keep well after harvesting.

19.10 Hardy Kiwis

Hardy kiwifruits (*Actinidia aruguta*) are different from the kiwifruits you find at the grocery store (*Actinidia chinensis*), although they have a similar flavor. Hardy kiwifruit is originally from northeastern Asia, while commercially available kiwis are native to southern China.

In Maryland, the commercial kiwifruit can only be grown in protected spots, while hardy kiwis are more tolerant of our conditions. Hardy kiwifruits, although susceptible to spring frosts, can tolerate up to -25°F. The fruits are

Figure 19-G. Hardy kiwi vs. grocery-store kiwi

not covered with fuzz, and are smaller than the fuzzy types (approximately the size of a large grape). The fruits have small seeds, and can be eaten without peeling. They are sometimes referred to as kiwiberries. From a nutritional standpoint, they have higher levels of vitamin C than most citrus fruits, although some people have reported laxative effects. They have an excellent flavor and can be dried or made into wine.

Cultivar selection

A hardy kiwifruit plant is a vigorous perennial vine that can grow to 40 feet unless pruned. It has small leaves and its stems are bright red. Most hardy kiwi plants are dioecious, meaning they will only bear male or female flowers, but not both, so intersperse female and male plants. Pollen from one male vine will pollinate up to eight surrounding female vines. Male plants flower profusely, but do not produce fruit.

The vines bloom in early summer, bearing small white flowers with chocolate-covered centers on the spur growth of the previous season. Flowers are pollinated by wind or insects, with European honey bees being the preferred pollinator. During the summer, greenish-yellow fruits start to develop and continue into the fall, ripening very late in the season. Generally, hardy kiwi plants will not start to bear fruit until their fourth year. They will bear a full crop by the eighth year. See Table 19-D for cultivar selections.

Site selection and soil preparation

Hardy kiwi cultivars require about a 150-day frost-free season. Plant hardy kiwis on sun-exposed, north-facing slopes. Although they perform best in full sun, they could be prone to break dormancy too early in the spring and suffer damage from late frosts. Avoid planting in frost pockets (places where cold air collects), as early fall frosts can also damage the plants. Hardy kiwi plants are also susceptible to wind damage and hot, dry conditions; and they do not perform well in places with sudden temperature changes. Establish them in protected moderate microclimates.

Hardy kiwis do best on well-drained, loamy soil with a pH between 5.5 and 7. The crop benefits from organic matter incorporation before planting.

Planting and training

Hardy kiwifruits should be planted mid-May onwards, or after the danger of frost has passed. Space plants 10 feet apart, and water frequently until established. Plant one male plant for every eight female plants.

Consider building a trellis system for the vines before purchasing the plants, and set the trellis poles 10 feet apart. Kiwifruit trellises usually are in the form of a T and are called a T-bar trellis. The cross-arm is about seven feet off the ground, with about seven wires across the five-foot-long cross-arm. Trellis wire should have 300 pounds of tension.

After planting, allow the main cane to grow straight up the pole to the height of the cross-arm. It is important to select one or two new canes and train them to grow vertically, not allowing them to twist around the wires; then, train the arms along the center wire. Laterals will grow from these arms, and can be tied to the outside wires. Fruit will develop on shoots from these canes and hang down below the wires, where they are easy to harvest.

Pruning

Kiwi vines need pruning during the dormant and the growing season to maximize production and fruit quality. Two or three times during the growing season, cut non-flowering laterals back to the outside wire on the trellis. Trim flowering shoots back to four to six leaves beyond the last flower. During the dormant season, remove canes that bore fruiting shoots during the previous season, together with any dead, diseased, or tangled canes. Leave the strongest one-year-old lateral canes that have not fruited, spaced about a foot apart along the arms, then trim them back to about eight buds.

Harvest

Only in their fifth year will kiwifruit plants reach maturity and flower. Fruit will generally mature around October, when there is a high probability of frost exposure, so it is difficult to harvest vine-ripened fruit. As soon as the seeds are black, harvest the fruit. Hardy kiwis have a short storage life, so plan to eat or process them within a few days.

19.11 Strawberries

Strawberries are the ideal fruit crop for growers with limited space. The plants are low-growing perennials that succeed in rows, beds, or even pots; and make an attractive groundcover when not fruiting.

A strawberry plant has leaves, a crown (compressed, modified stem), and a root system. In heavy clay, 90% of the roots may be located in the top six inches of soil. This shallow root system is largely responsible for the plant's sensitivity to water deficit or excess.

Runners (or stolons) are the strawberry plant's device for asexual propagation. They arise from buds at the base of leaves in the crown. As the runners grow away from the original "mother" plant, their nodes root and, where they touch soil, produce "daughter" plants.

Cultivar and site selection

Two types of strawberries are grown in Maryland: June-bearing and day-neutral. The June-bearing strawberry is the type most commonly grown in Maryland. Day-neutral strawberry cultivars have two peaks of production: June and late August through frost. Summer production is usually very low due to high temperatures.

A heavy straw mulch helps lower soil temperatures but, even with this precaution, day-neutral cultivars may not perform well during hot weather. For either type of strawberry, always buy registered, disease-free or tissue-cultured plants.

Characteristics of a good strawberry site include:

- Sunny location
- Organic matter enrichment
- Well-drained soil (strawberries will not tolerate "wet feet")
- A raised bed if soil drains poorly

Planting and training

Daughter plants or "runners" can become rampant, so you may want to consider growing strawberries in borders, containers, or restricted beds. Set out field-grown plants in March or early April when the soil begins to warm.

Tissue-cultured plants are grown in a greenhouse and are more cold-sensitive, so plant them only after the last frost date. If they arrive early, store them in the refrigerator until planting time.

Trim roots to within four to six inches of the crown and set plants with half the crown below the soil level, with roots fanned out (see Figure 19-H). Keep new plants well-watered. Broadcast fertilize when foliage is dry, and brush the residual off of leaves. Once plants are in the ground, do not disturb shallow roots by working fertilizer into the soil.

June-bearing varieties typically are trained using either of two systems:

- Hill system: Space plants one foot apart in all directions and remove all runners to encourage more flower stalks.
- Matted row system: Space "mother" plants 18 to 24 inches apart in rows at least 36 inches apart. Allow runners to root freely in all directions and fill in with "daughter" plants. Keep the beds narrow (12 inches) if possible, to maximize sunlight penetration. Plantings will be most productive on the edges. At renovation time, thin the daughter plants to six inches between plants so that they cover the ground but are not crowded (see Figure 19-I).

For June-bearers, remove the flowers for the entire first season. This sacrifices early fruit production to encourage strong growth, runner production, and winter survival.

Day-neutral strawberries do not profusely send out runners, so plant these more closely—about five to nine inches apart. Remove the flower buds and runners through early July of the first year and then allow plants to fruit. They can be treated as annuals, or mulched and overwintered to produce a second year before replacement.

Renovation of June bearers

June-bearing strawberry beds continue to produce for three to five years. Production life can be maximized through renovation. This technique is used in the matted-row system to thin the beds and invigorate the planting.

In the second year, immediately after the end of harvest:

- Mow plants to a height of two to three inches, or just above the crowns.
- Top-dress with one pound of 10-10-10 (or equivalent) fertilizer per 25 plants.
- Thin daughter plants to six inches apart.
- Rototill or spade under runners that strayed beyond the 12- to 18-inch growing bed, leaving a combination of mingled mother and daughter plants.

Repeat the third year: mow, fertilize, and thin daughter plants to six inches apart.

In the fourth year, alter this process. Turn under the mother plants and allow only the strongest daughter plants to form the 12- to 18-inch beds. (Tip: Drive a short stake in the ground at the head of each row during the initial planting so you can identify the mother plants later.)

Figure 19-H. Strawberry planting depth

Figure 19-I. Matted row system

After a period of years, berry yields usually drop due to diseases and environmental stress. You can then start a new berry patch in a new location with fresh plants. Don't move runners from an old patch into a new bed because you may be also relocate insect and disease problems.

Harvest and storage

Strawberries should be left on the plant one to two days after fully red. Berries picked too soon will redden eventually, but not sweeten. Pick early in the day when berries are cool by twisting the stem and fruit from the vine. Do not wash fruit until you are ready to eat it. Process as soon as possible to preserve nutrients and flavor, or refrigerate for three to five days.

Overwintering

Shallow roots make plants prone to winter heaving. To prevent crown heaving and to protect overwintering flower buds, cover the plants and aisles with four inches of straw or other organic mulch. Do this after the soil freezes, when the plants are dormant.

In early spring, pull mulch off of the plants and into the aisles to allow for soil warming and more rapid fruit maturation. When fruits begin to develop, re-apply a thick mulch under the foliage and around the plants to minimize disease, keep weeds down, and maintain even soil moisture.

Floating row covers are useful in preventing winter strawberry damage, promoting early bloom, protecting blossoms from spring frosts, and excluding flying insect pests. Blossoms are pollinated by wind and insects, so be sure to remove the row cover just before flowering begins. ❋

Table 19-D. Recommended small-fruit cultivars for Maryland

BLACKBERRIES

Image	Cultivar	Comments	Image	Cultivar	Comments
	Eclipse *Thornless, semi-erect, floricane-bearing*	Medium-large, dark, firm fruit that ripens early. Sweet flavor.		**Prime-Ark® Traveler** *Thornless, erect, primocane-bearing*	Two crops each season. Medium-large, firm fruits with low acidity.
	Galaxy *Thornless, semi-erect, floricane-bearing*	Larger, sweeter fruit than Eclipse. Ripens a few days earlier.		**Sweet-Ark® Caddo** *Thornless, erect, floricane-bearing*	Large, flavorful fruit. Reliable bearer. Low chill-hours (300 hours).
	Natchez *Thornless, semi-erect, floricane-bearing*	Firm, glossy, oblong berries are very large. Ripens in early summer.		**Sweet-Ark® Ponca** *Thornless, erect, floricane-bearing*	Super-sweet, sub-acid berries from a very prolific plant. Stores well.
	Ouachita *Thornless, semi-erect, floricane-bearing*	Conical fruit with a high-gloss. Ripens mid-season. Stores well.		**Sweetie Pie** *Thornless, trailing, floricane-bearing*	Large, very sweet berries. Heat-tolerant and disease-resistant.
	Prime-Ark® Freedom *Thornless, erect, primocane-bearing*	Two crops each season. Large fruits with good flavor.		**Twilight** *Thornless, semi-erect, floricane-bearing*	Firm, dark fruit that ripens just after Eclipse. Outstanding flavor; a little tart.

BLUEBERRIES

Image	Cultivar	Comments	Image	Cultivar	Comments
	Blue Ribbon *Northern highbush*	Ripens early to mid-season. High-yielding with long storage life.		**Brightwell** *Rabbiteye*	Big yields of deep-blue fruit. Heat- and drought-tolerant.
	Bluecrop *Northern highbush*	A standard for Maryland. Firm, crack-resistant fruit.		**Duke** *Northern highbush*	Early ripening, light-blue berries. Attractive foliage and flowers.
	Blueray *Northern highbush*	A standard for Maryland. Large fruit; heat-tolerant plant.		**Legacy** *Northern highbush*	Evergreen foliage during mild winters. Ripens late mid-season.

continued on next page

continued from previous page

Table 19-D. Recommended small-fruit cultivars for Maryland

BLUEBERRIES (continued)

Image	Cultivar	Comments	Image	Cultivar	Comments
	Lenoir *Northern highbush*	Firm and flavorful. Ripens mid- to late-season.		**Premier** *Rabbiteye*	Compact but prolific plant. High yields of dark berries.
	O'Neal *Southern highbush*	Mid- to late-season. Good pollenizer for other blueberries.		**Reka** *Northern highbush*	Developed in New Zealand. Drought-tolerant.
	Ozarkblue *Southern highbush*	Large, light-blue fruit with very good flavor. Heat-tolerant.		**Top Shelf** *Northern highbush*	Very large and very flavorful fruit. Stores well.

CURRANTS

Image	Cultivar	Comments	Image	Cultivar	Comments
	Baldwin *Black*	Late ripening. Fruit is medium-large, firm to very firm. Very productive. Self-fertile.		**Crusader** *Black*	Resistant to white pine blister rust. Very vigorous, high-yielder.
	Cherry *Red*	Large, vigorous, mildew-resistant. Good for eating fresh and processing.		**Red Lake** *Red*	Vigorous, cold-hardy, and productive. Fruits are large, dark red, and high-quality.
	Consort *Black*	Resistant to white pine blister rust; prone to mildew. Late-ripening fruit has strong, musky flavor.		**White Grape** *White*	Similar to White Imperial with light amber, large, mild-flavored fruit.
	Crandall *Black*	Clove currant (Ribes odoratum); flowers are clove-scented. Large shrub.		**White Imperial** *White*	Fruit is translucent white with a pink blush. Rich, sweet flavor. Cold-hardy.

continued on next page

continued from previous page

Table 19-D. Recommended small-fruit cultivars for Maryland

ELDERBERRIES

Image	Cultivar	Comments	Image	Cultivar	Comments
	Adams	The original cultivar. Strong, productive plants bear large fruit clusters and berries.		Scotia	Medium-sized bushes yield well. Fruit has good flavor with a high sugar content.
	Johns	Very productive. Canes can grow to 10'. Attractive glossy foliage.		York	High yields and the largest berries. Tolerant of both dry and moist soils.

GOOSEBERRIES

Image	Cultivar	Comments	Image	Cultivar	Comments
	Captivator *American/European hybrid*	Thornless, vigorous, with some mildew resistance. Red, sweet fruit is easy to harvest.		**Pixwell** *American*	Nearly thornless; productive. Fair-quality fruit is easy to pick. Good fall color.
	Hinnomaki *European type*	Large, red, and sweet enough to eat raw. Disease- and mildew-resistant.		**Poorman** *American*	Best American cultivar. Vigorous plant grows large, red, delicious fruit.

TABLE GRAPES

Image	Cultivar	Comments	Image	Cultivar	Comments
	Canadice *Seedless*	Early, small-medium red grape with superb flavor. Keeps on the vine. Reliable and productive.		**Neptune** *Seedless*	Very large, yellow-green fruit; some disease resistance.
	Himrod *Seedless*	Golden yellow fruit with fine flavor that keeps well. Very cold-hardy; moderate disease resistance.		**Reliance** *Seedless*	Dependable variety. Very hardy vines. Large, high-quality, red fruit will store 3 months.
	Jupiter *Seedless*	Large, crisp blue fruit. Non-slipskin. Excellent flavor.		**Steuben** *Seeded*	Very large, blue, spicy fruit. Hardy, with some disease resistance.
	Mars *Seedless*	Very hardy, productive, and dependable. Large blue fruit.		**Vanessa** *Seedless*	Brick-red, medium-sized grapes. Firm texture and fruity flavor.

continued on next page

continued from previous page

Table 19-D. Recommended small-fruit cultivars for Maryland

HARDY KIWIS

Image	Cultivar	Comments	Image	Cultivar	Comments
	74 Series (Male and female options)	Large, sweet, oblong fruit on productive vines. Tender, edible skin.		**Issai** (Male)	Compact, with luscious fruit. Harvest in late summer. Excellent pollinator.
	Ananasnaya (Anna) (Female)	Very popular for its extra-sweet 1/2-oz. fruits. Easy to grow.		**Meader** (Male)	Reddish-green fruits have a sweet-tart flavor. An excellent pollinator for female varieties.
	Geneva (Female)	Medium-sized, smooth-skinned fruit with pretty red tinge. Best grown on a south-facing site.		**MSU** (Female)	Lime-green fruits can weigh up to 1 oz. A new and very vigorous variety. Hardy to -25°F.

RASPBERRIES

Image	Cultivar	Comments	Image	Cultivar	Comments
	Anne *Yellow primocane-bearing*	UMD release. Large, pretty fruit with good flavor.		**Encore** *Red June-bearing*	Spineless. Ripens mid-summer between most floricane- and primocane-bearers.
	Bristol *Black*	Large fruit of excellent quality. Erect, vigorous, productive plants.		**Himbo-Top®** *Red primocane-bearing*	Large fruit is firm and bright red. Easy to pick.
	Caroline *Red primocane-bearing*	UMD release; excellent intense raspberry flavor.		**Jaclyn** *Red primocane-bearing*	UMD release; the earliest primocane. Good flavor, heat tolerance.
	Crimson Night *Red primocane-bearing*	Dark purple veins, dark red fruit. Decorative canes are also red.		**Jewel** *Black*	Productive variety. Large fruit with fine flavor; disease-resistant.
	Double Gold *Yellow primocane-bearing*	Attractive, champagne-colored fruit with a deep blush.		**Joan-J** *Red primocane-bearing*	Upright and thornless. Big yields. Mow spring canes to boost fall harvest.

continued on next page

continued from previous page

Table 19-D. Recommended small-fruit cultivars for Maryland

RASPBERRIES (continued)

Cultivar	Comments	Cultivar	Comments
Josephine — Red primocane-bearing	UMD release. Vigorous, with good pest resistance. Stores well.	**Prelude** — Red primocane-bearing	One of the earliest-ripening primocane-bearing varieties.
Latham — Red June-bearing	Cold-hardy, virus-resistant. Flavorful, firm fruit. Mid-season.	**Royalty** — Purple	Large fruit becomes sweeter as it colors. Very vigorous and productive canes.

STRAWBERRIES

Cultivar	Comments	Cultivar	Comments
Annapolis — June-bearing	Medium to large, firm, glossy, light-red fruit. Good flavor.	**Jewel** — June-bearing	Large, bright-red, firm berries. Prone to verticillium wilt and red steele.
Allstar — June-bearing	Very large, elongated, light-colored, flavorful. Productive mid- to late-season berry.	**Seascape** — Day-neutral	Plants produce large, good quality fruits throughout the season.
Cavendish — June-bearing	Very large, firm fruit with good flavor. Mid-season harvest.	**Tribute** — Day-neutral	Vigorous, disease-resistant plants. Medium, slightly acidic berries.
Earliglow — June-bearing	The standard for early varieties and flavor. Small to medium-sized deep red fruit.	**Tristar** — Day-neutral	A UMD release, the day-neutral standard. Sweet, disease-resistant.

AUTHORS

Macarena Farcuh, Assistant Professor and Extension Specialist, Horticulture, Department of Plant Science and Landscape Architecture, University of Maryland, College Park.

PUBLICATIONS

Adapted from *The Maryland Master Gardener Handbook.* 2008.

Bowling, B. and M. Pritts. 2000. *The Berry Growers Companion.* Timber Press. Portland, OR. ISBN 0-88192-489-X.

Eames-Sheavly, M., Pritts, C., Cramer, L., Bushway, L., Merwin, I., Reisinger, R., McKay, S. 2003. *Cornell Guide to Growing Fruit at Home.* Cornell Cooperative Extension. Ithaca, NY 14853. Available online: **ecommons.cornell.edu/handle/1813/67**

Brun, C., DeVetter, L., and Benedict, C. 2016. *Growing Small Fruits in the Home Garden.* Washington State University Extension. Washington, EM103E. Available online: **pubs.extension.wsu.edu/growing-small-fruits-in-the-home-garden-home-garden-series**

Fruit Production for the Home Gardener: A Comprehensive Guide. Publications Distribution Center, The Pennsylvania State University. University Park, PA . Available at: **agsci.psu.edu/fphg**

Reich, L. 2004. *Uncommon Fruits for Every Garden.* Timber Press. Portland, OR. ISBN 0-88192-623-X.

PHOTOS

Main chapter photo: pixabay.com.

Table 19-D cultivar photos courtesy of LeAnn Zotta.

ILLUSTRATIONS

Figures 19-A, 19-C, 19-D, and 19-E by Don Wittig, University of Maryland Master Gardener, Montgomery County, retired. Colorization by LeAnn Zotta.

Figures 19-B, 19-G, and 19-H by LeAnn Zotta.

Figure 19-F: LeAnn Zotta.

20: TREE FRUITS

Macarena Farcuh, Ph.D.

20 TREE FRUITS

CONTENTS

20.1	Tree-Fruit Basics	607
20.2	Planting a Fruit Tree	611
20.3	Mulching and Weeding	612
20.4	Pest and Disease Control	613
20.5	General Pruning Guidelines	615
20.6	Pome Fruits: Apple and Pear	616
20.7	Stone Fruits: Peach, Cherry, Plum, Apricot, Nectarine	623
20.8	Fig Trees	627

LEARNING OBJECTIVES

- Factors to consider before planting fruit trees
- Principles and methods of proper soil preparation and planting
- Principles and methods of fertilizing, weed management, and irrigation
- Principles and methods of training and pruning fruit trees
- Pest and disease control for fruit trees
- Principles and methods of harvesting tree fruits

INTRODUCTION

Home fruit production is time-consuming and demands a year-round commitment by the gardener. It all starts with good planning and site preparation, including identifying the appropriate cultivar(s) that fit your needs. Insects, disease, and weather will test even the most experienced gardener; but picking a juicy ripe peach or a sweet, crisp apple right from your tree and sharing it with loved ones is one of the most satisfying rewards life has to offer.

Most tree fruits suited for the mid-Atlantic region are botanically grouped into two categories: pome fruits and stone fruits. The pome fruits comprise apples and pears, which share many cultural similarities and pest problems. Likewise, the stone fruits—peaches, plums, apricots, nectarines, and cherries—also share cultural similarities and pests. Figs are another option to consider growing in this region.

A number of tree fruits thrive in Maryland home orchards when given proper care. Backyard fruit production allows you to:

- Grow cultivars not readily available in grocery stores
- Control the level of pesticide use
- Enjoy flavorful, nutritious fruits you can harvest at exactly the right time
- Gain a greater understanding of nature's processes while producing wonderful fruits

20.1 Tree-Fruit Basics

Site selection

Choosing the right site is critical to the success of an orchard, and is a task that is generally overlooked. If your site is less than ideal and needs amending, it is significantly easier to amend a site before the trees are planted than trying to do this once the trees are already in the ground.

An ideal location features:

- Good elevation or a slope, to avoid frost pockets (where cold air collects)
- Adequate slope exposure, which influences temperature and wind conditions

- Deep and well-drained soil, but not droughty
- Full sun

Uphill or rolling land is preferred, ideally with a four- to eight-percent slope. A hillside that is too steep to be tilled for gardening usually works well. Cold air will drain down the hill, helping to limit frost damage in the spring.

A gentle, north-facing slope is particularly desirable because it delays early flowering, reducing the risk of tender bud damage from a late spring frost. It also lessens winter injury because the sun will not heat the trunks. Heating causes sap to move up during the day and then freeze at night, splitting the trunk as the sap expands. Plant the trees from the top of the slope to three-quarters of the way down the hill.

Frost problems are common on stone fruits. For this reason, apricots and sweet cherries are not recommended for the colder areas of Maryland. Due to late spring frosts, early-blooming apricots produce a crop only once or twice every five years in most locations.

Sunlight factors

Sunlight is a key consideration because of its effect on fruit trees as they come out of dormancy and begin to bloom. Foliage and fruit dry faster in full sun, reducing disease infection. If temperatures are adequate, fruit will also color better and ripen more evenly in full sun.

Direct southern exposure, however, should be avoided whenever possible. The warmer temperatures on a southern slope force many stone fruits to break dormancy and go into early bloom, increasing the probability of exposure to frost events.

Northern exposures, characterized by slower warming in spring, are usually the right choice, except if the location is additionally shaded by buildings or a taller tree canopy. Light levels will be too low for adequate fruit development on such a site.

In the Mid-Atlantic, west-facing slopes tend to be windier, which can affect pesticide applications during the growing season.

Soil preferences

Deep, well-drained soils are necessary for most fruits. Adequate soil depth allows roots to seek out nutrients and water, and provide anchorage. Ideally, the best soil is a well-drained loam which is a minimum of three to four feet deep. Good drainage should take preference over depth.

Stone fruits, particularly peaches, do not tolerate "wet feet" (roots growing in poorly drained clayey soil). Apples are moderately tolerant, and pears can survive in the more poorly-drained soils. Very sandy soils may drain too quickly, leading to drought stress and nutrient deficiencies.

Although pH and soil fertility are also very important factors to consider when establishing an orchard, soil drainage is most important. The pH of the soil is not usually a limiting factor unless a site is highly acidic. Such soils can be corrected by using a lime application. A soil pH of 6.0 to 6.5 will allow trees to grow well.

Soil fertility can also be corrected by the application of fertilizer or organic matter (which consists of dead and decomposing plant and animal parts). In general, soil fertility should be medium to low as high fertility can lead to overly vigorous tree growth at the expense of fruit production. It is easier to add fertilizer to increase soil fertility than to try to reduce tree vigor.

General water requirements

Pome fruits. For the first five years, regular deep watering may be required to supplement rainfall. Do not let the roots dry out during these establishment years. Create a small ridge of soil around each tree to prevent runoff.

Stone fruits. Stone fruit trees are more shallow-rooted than pome fruits and are less drought-tolerant. Peaches are most sensitive to drought, when the fruit is rapidly increasing in size. Water the tree deeply at this time.

Pollination

Fruit trees are pollinated by insects (mainly bees) that transfer pollen from the flowers of one cultivar to those of another. Cross pollination—the movement of pollen between two different cultivars—is necessary to produce good crops of apple and pear, and most plum, sweet cherry, and apricot cultivars. Peaches, figs, nectarines, some European plums, and sour cherries are generally self-fruitful (see Table 20-A).

Generally, it is recommended to plant two to three different cultivars of apple or pear trees and at least two cultivars of plum, sweet cherry, or apricot. Make sure that the cultivars you select are pollen-compatible and share a similar bloom time. Such trees are referred to as pollenizers, which produce pollen for cross-pollination. A pollinator (often incorrectly used interchangeably with "pollenizer") is an insect or other animal that moves pollen from flower to flower.

Without bees there would be no fruit, so protect your bees and other pollinators. Never spray insecticides on blooming fruit trees,

WHEN IT RAINS TOO MUCH

Excessive rainfall (above average rainfall that stays around for a long period of time) can negatively impact fruit trees.

Roots need water, but they also need oxygen to thrive. There are tiny spaces in the soil that help ensure oxygen flows to the roots. Long periods of rain can fill these pores, blocking oxygen and damaging the root system.

Too much rain and humidity can also increase the susceptibility of fruit trees to disease. Excessive rainfall near harvest time, followed by high temperatures, is often associated with split-pit development in stone fruits (characterized by a hollow center in or around the seed) as well as cracking in stone and pome fruits. Cracked fruit increases the probability of rots and insect pests.

Finally, excessive rainfall can also lessen pollinator activity, which has a critical impact on pollination and fruit set.

and limit pesticide use whenever possible. Fungicides do not interfere with pollination.

Chill hours

Fruit trees must undergo a specific chilling period to break winter dormancy and resume growth. Chill-hour requirements are listed in fruit-tree catalogs for each cultivar. It is expressed as the number of hours of exposure to temperatures between 32 and 45°F. Beware of "low-chill" cultivars which require less chilling. They may begin growing during warm days in February or March and then be damaged by late-spring freezes.

Table 20-A. Fruit tree bearing age, height, and pollination requirements

Species	Bearing age (yrs.)	Tree height (ft.)	Pollination requirement*	Comments
Apple	2 – 10 (See Table 20-B)	6–25 (See Table 20-B)	Mostly self-sterile; requires a pollenizer.	Golden Delicious is self-fertile. Mutsu, Jonagold, Winesap, and Arkansas Black produce sterile pollen and must be grown with 2 additional cultivars.
Apricot	3 – 4	20	Self-fruitful.	Tree blooms early and blossoms are often damaged by late spring frosts.
Fig	2 – 3	5 – 10	Seedless and parthenocarpic.	No pollenizer required. Fruit develops without fertilization or seed.
Peach	3 – 4	20	Mostly self-fruitful.	J.H. Hale is self-sterile and requires a pollenizer.
Pear	4 – 5	15 – 18	Mostly self-sterile; requires a pollenizer.	Asian and domestic cultivars are compatible. Seckel and Bartlett are incompatible. Magness produces sterile pollen and must be grown with 2 additional cultivars.
Plum (Japanese cultivars may not be hardy in western MD)	3 – 5	10 – 20	Mostly self-sterile.	Stanley, Damson, Italian, Lombard, and Reine Claude are self-fertile, European-type cultivars. Most Japanese cultivars listed as self-fertile will produce larger crops when planted with a pollenizer. Plant 2 or more European cultivars or 2 or more Japanese cultivars, but not 1 of each type. Apricot-plum crosses (pluots, apriums, and plumcots) can be pollenized with suitable Japanese plum cultivars.
Nectarine	3 – 4	20	Mostly self-fruitful.	Requires more nitrogen than other stone fruits. Monitor for deficiencies.
Sour Cherry	3 – 5	15	Self-fruitful.	No pollenizer required.
Sweet Cherry	4 – 7	25	Mostly self-sterile; requires a pollenizer.	Stella, Lapins, and Starkrimson® are self-fertile.

*To ensure cross-pollination, make sure the selected cultivars are pollen-compatible and share a similar bloom time. Crabapple trees, callery pear trees (Bradford), and ornamental plum and cherry trees will cross-pollenize their respective fruiting "cousins" if the bloom time is similar. Do not plant callery (Bradford) pear; it is highly invasive.

Frosts and freezes

Whenever temperatures dip below 32°F during spring, the potential arises for frost or freeze damage to fruit tree blossoms. The extent of the damage depends on factors such as the species of the tree, the stage of blossom development, and the degree of cold weather.

In general, frost damage to stone fruits is often more severe than it is to pome fruits. Peaches tend to flower earlier than pome fruits, making them more likely to be impacted by cold nights in early spring. In addition, the anatomy of stone-fruit flowers makes them more susceptible to cold temperatures than the abundant flower clusters of pome fruits.

The later the frost occurs and the more developed the blossoms, the greater the damage potential. Newly-developed peach buds can tolerate temperatures down to 20°F, while open blossoms are injured at around 26°F; flowers that already have dropped their petals and have started to develop fruit are killed at about 28°F.

One way to protect your fruit trees is to cover them with a blanket or sheet (not plastic) during the day so heat can build up before a nighttime freeze. Water the trees before you cover them; as the water evaporates, it will warm the air around the trees and form a protective shield.

20.2 Planting a Fruit Tree

Fruit trees are vegetatively propagated by grafting scion wood (wood of the desired cultivar) onto a clonal rootstock chosen for a specific characteristic, such as hardiness or disease resistance (see Figure 20-A). This is done because seed-grown trees do not have the same characteristics as their parents, lack

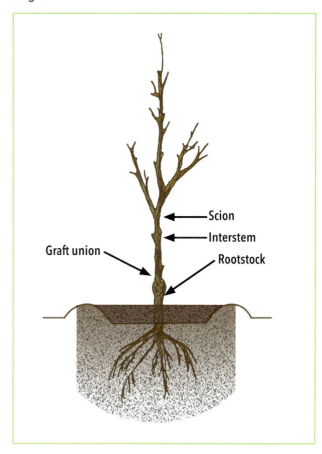

Figure 20-A. Parts of a fruit tree

uniformity, and, in general, are inferior to a grafted tree.

Digging a good hole

Planting is best accomplished in early spring when the soil can be worked. Purchase healthy one- to two-year-old bare-root plants from a reputable nursery.

- Bare-root trees must be planted as soon as they arrive, preferably the same day. Do not attempt this if the ground is frozen.
- If trees cannot be planted immediately, you can keep the trees for a few days outside in a protected location like an unheated garage or shed. Do not uncover the roots, and make sure the tree is not exposed to any frost.

- If the tree needs to be stored for a longer period of time before planting, you can use a method called heeling-in. Dig a shallow hole, remove the covering from the roots, and situate the tree so that the root system is in the hole. Cover the roots with soil and press firmly.
- Hydrate your trees 12 hours prior to planting by placing each one in a large container filled with cold water for four to six hours.
- Do not dig the hole too far in advance of planting so it doesn't have the chance to fill with rainwater. Always avoid planting a fruit tree in standing water.
- The diameter of the hole is much more important than the depth of the hole. The hole should be big enough to lay the roots out without crossing over or bending them, with some extra width and depth for growth.
- Before planting, use sharp pruners to remove any roots that are broken or damaged.
- Generally, set the tree one inch deeper than it was planted in the nursery.
- Plant the tree so that the graft union (the bulge where rootstock meets the scion wood) is two to four inches above the ground after the ground settles.
- Backfill the hole, firmly packing the soil around the roots, and water in well.
- Add a liquid starter fertilizer to the water, but do not add granular fertilizer to the planting hole. This will encourage the roots to grow outward.
- Build a low ridge of soil around tree base to prevent water runoff.
- Water deeply throughout the first season to supplement rainfall.

20.3 Mulching and Weeding

Mulching

Mulch has several benefits for tree fruits, which include:

- Moisture retention and water conservation
- Weed suppression
- Less soil compaction
- Soil structure improvement
- Soil temperature reduction
- Additional organic matter
- Cleaner fruit

The best mulch materials are aged wood chips, bark nuggets, composted leaves, or pine needles. Some gardeners like to use straw, hay, ground bark, sawdust, or untreated grass clippings.

Around May, fruit trees should be mulched to the drip line with a four- to five-inch layer of mulch. Avoid placing mulch against the trunks; it will retain too much moisture, causing it to soften and potentially resulting in disease problems. Mulching is not recommended in soils that tend to remain too wet, as it will aggravate the waterlogged soil by preventing evaporation of excess water.

Apply more mulch periodically through the season, and pull it away from trees in September/October. This allows the trees to harden off and reduces rodent activity around the tree.

Weed management

Weed management starts with site preparation. Treat or remove any persistent perennial weeds. Ideally, cover-crop the site for two years prior to planting. The cover crop crowds out weeds and returns nutrients to the soil while improving soil structure and preventing erosion.

For new orchards, it is critical to manage weeds in the first two to three months. The trees will grow better and produce an earlier and heavier crop. In the case of older, bearing trees, the critical period extends from pre-bloom until four to six weeks after bloom. Weed competition later in the season will mainly affect the water status of the tree, but not the yield.

The primary methods for weed management include:

Mulching. See the previous section.

Cover crops. Plant a cover crop on bare soil to compete with weeds and improve the soil. Covers crops also prevent erosion, particularly important if your fruit trees are planted on a slope.

Physical removal. Hand-pull weeds or use a sharp hoe to cut weeds off at ground level.

Flaming. A portable propane-fueled weed torch fries weeds in a single pass. This is more useful on small weeds or broad-leaf weeds that have growing points at the top of the plant), and less effective on grasses (that have growing points below the surface, protected from heat). Large weeds require more fuel to be killed and have a higher chance of recovering, so always try to address any weed issues while they are young and small.

Herbicides. Herbicides are most effective when applied to emerging weeds that are smaller than two to five inches. Do not allow sprays to land on the tender bark of young fruit trees, which can cause injury to the trees

PREVENT VOLE DAMAGE

Mulch is beneficial in multiple ways for plants, but it also provides ideal habitat for meadow and pine voles. These destructive rodents feed on tree trunks and plant roots. In September and October, pull mulch away from trees. Voles frequently move to other areas where they can be better protected.

and may even kill them. Additionally, consider that young trees have a shallow root system; most of their roots are under the herbicide-treated area.

Always follow the label instructions for application rates, disposal, and safety.

For more information about weed biology and sustainable management, see Chapter 13, Weeds.

20.4 Pest and Disease Control

Domesticated fruit trees are prone to many diseases and pests that can infect tree leaves and fruits. Due to the environmental conditions in Maryland, we have more than our fair share of insect pest and disease issues, especially on apple and peach trees. It is difficult to grow high-quality fruit without some use of pesticides. To minimize problems, consider purchasing disease-resistant cultivars. Pesticides may still be required (particularly in wet seasons), but far fewer applications will be required.

Under normal conditions, you may need six to ten pesticide applications to produce fruit of reasonable quality. A disease-resistant cultivar may only require one to three applications to control pests and still produce high-quality fruit.

Early spray applications are timed to control serious diseases and insect pests, and coincide with stages of fruit bud development (see Figure 20-B). Important stages include:

- Dormant: just before budswell in spring.
- Budswell:
  - Green tip: buds are open at tips, exposing green tissue.
  - Half-inch green: one-half inch of green tissue is projected from bud.
  - Tight cluster: blossom buds are exposed but tightly pressed; stems are short.
  - Pink: blossom buds are pink or white with fully extended stems.
- Blossom: from bloom opening through petal-fall. Do not use any insecticides during the bloom period.
- Petal-fall: petals have fallen.
- Fruit formation: fruit has visibly formed.

Controls include cultural methods, such as removing diseased fruit, as well as organic and non-organic sprays.

Organic pest controls

Careful cultivar selection. Choosing cultivars with high disease susceptibility will doom the success of an organic orchard in this region. Organic growers should select cultivars with disease-resistance (e.g., apple cultivars that are resistant to apple scab, or peach cultivars that are resistant to bacterial spot).

- **Tree size and training system.** Choose smaller trees with an open-vase training system to favor sunlight and air circulation in the canopy. These two factors are crucial for organic disease control.
- Sanitation. A key organic practice in disease control is to remove infected leaves, branches, and fruit. Removal decreases and/or prevents spread.
- Spraying organic disease management materials: these materials will be useful but have limited effectiveness on their own in this area to stop a disease outbreak.

Additional resources:

Chapter 8: Insect Basics

Chapter 9: Plant Disease Basics

Chapter 10: IPM (Integrated Pest Management)

Figure 20-B. Fruit and nut tree bud development

20.5 General Pruning Guidelines

Prune your trees at planting time and yearly thereafter. If you train your fruit trees properly, they will need only moderate pruning in later years to manage growth and correct minor structural weaknesses. A properly trained tree should not require large pruning cuts, which provide an entrance for disease organisms. See Figure 20-C for common terminology that pertains to fruit-tree pruning.

Why prune a fruit tree?

Fruit trees should be pruned for multiple reasons:

- To develop a desired tree shape
- To maintain a desired tree size
- To allow sunlight and spray materials to enter the center of the tree
- To improve tree strength and encourage new shoots
- To improve air circulation within the tree and reduce disease potential
- To remove dead or broken branches

Fruit thinning

The practice of fruit thinning contributes to your orchard's success. It is recommended for apples, pears, nectarines, plums, and peaches. Failure to thin can lead to biennial bearing problems (i.e., over-production one year followed by a year of extremely low yields).

Reasons for thinning are slightly different than those for pruning:

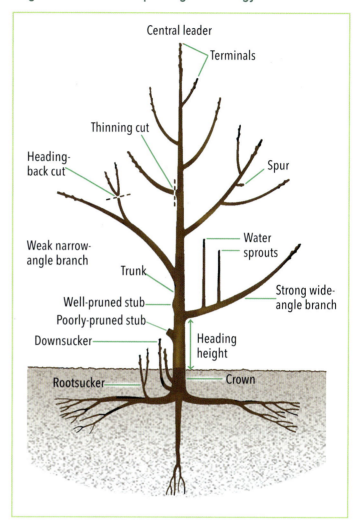

Figure 20-C. Fruit-tree pruning terminology

- A portion of the fruit is removed so that the remainder develops to an adequate size.
- Thinning increases the plant's ability to form flower buds for next year, provided the thinning is done early enough
- Thinning reduces the weight load on the branches, reducing breakage.
- Insects and diseases are easier to access and control.

See specific pruning instructions for pome or stone fruit in the corresponding sections ahead.

20.6 Pome Fruits: Apple and Pear

Apples and pears are excellent candidates for your home garden, as long as you are committed to the attention to detail and pest management that these crops require. To choose a good tree at the nursery:

- Look for a healthy one-year-old whip (an unbranched sapling), approximately four to six feet tall, with a one-half-inch caliper and a good root system.
- Purchase a smaller tree with a good root system rather than a large tree with a poor root system. Avoid trees that have encircling or J-shaped roots that could eventually strangle the trunk.
- Check the label to make sure you are getting the cultivar and rootstock that you want.

Cultivars that do well in Maryland

Deciding which cultivar to plant can be one of the most exciting parts of growing fruit trees, but it can also be frustrating because there are so many cultivars from which to choose. Some of the best pome fruit cultivars for Maryland are described in Table 20-C.

The following tips can help you narrow your choice:

- Look for cultivars with outstanding cold tolerance, disease resistance, and fruit quality. A lower-yielding yet higher-quality cultivar may be the best choice.
- When growing pome fruits, you will need to plant at least two different cultivars to get good pollination and fruit set (see 20.1 Tree-Fruit Basics).

Important terminology you need to know before selecting your cultivar is as follows:

Strains

Some apple cultivars are available in various strains. A strain is a mutation of a certain cultivar that has been selected and propagated for an improved characteristic. A strain may differ in fruit characteristics, growth characteristics, or both.

Spurs

The most common strain difference is between spur strains and non-spur strains. Spurs are short, stubby, slow-growing, modified stems that support multiple fruit blossoms and may remain fruitful for seven to 10 years or more. They are common on apple, pear, and cherry trees.

Spur-strain trees, because of their compact form of growth, are ideally suited for home gardeners with limited space. As a general rule of thumb, spur strains of a cultivar will result in trees only about 60% to 70% as large as the non-spur types of the same cultivar, but they are more productive. Fruit spurs and leaf buds are spaced closer on spur trees, resulting in higher yields per tree.

Rootstock

The two principal plant influences on tree size are the rootstock and the type of strain used (spur or non-spur). Other factors that influence mature tree size include general care, cultivar, soil type, earliness of fruiting, and the time and severity of pruning.

Rootstocks influence not only the size and vigor of the tree, but also the bearing age, winter hardiness, susceptibility to some diseases, and fruit final quality. Apples are the only fruit trees for which a wide range of rootstocks exist (see Table 20-B). A cultivar is grafted onto this special rootstock, so you essentially purchase two plants: the rootstock that anchors the tree and the cultivar that produces the fruit.

Trees on very dwarf, dwarf, and semi-dwarf rootstocks are ideally suited for home growers. Although more expensive, the smaller trees are easier to prune, spray, and harvest; and they begin bearing at an earlier age.

The interstem tree is another category of rootstock that may be available. It has a small stem section of M 9 grafted between an understock, such as MM 111 or MM 106, and the cultivar. (M refers to Malling and MM refers to Malling-Merton rootstock groups.) These trees are slightly larger than dwarf trees but smaller than semi-dwarfs. Because of the extra

Table 20-B. Apple and pear tree rootstocks

Tree size	Approx. mature height (ft.)	Bearing age (yrs.)	Approximate lifespan (yrs.)	Spacing in row (ft.)	Between rows (ft.)	Average yield for trees >10 yrs. old (bushels)
APPLE						
Very Dwarf						
Malling 27[a]*	6 – 8	2	10 - 15	5	13	1 – 1.5
Dwarf						
Malling 9[a]*	8 – 10	2 - 3	15	6	14	1 – 2
Malling 26[a]*	11 – 14	2 - 3	15	8	16	3 – 4
Semi-Dwarf						
Malling 7 or 7A	15 – 18	3 - 4	20	12	20	10 – 12
Semi-Standard						
Malling-Merton 106[b]	18 – 20	3 - 4	20	12	20	20 – 25
Malling-Merton 111[b]	19 – 24	3 - 4	20	12	20	20 – 25
Standard						
Seedling	20 – 25	6 - 10	40	18	26	25 or more
Interstem tree[b,c]	8 – 10	4 - 5	15 – 20	20	28	10 – 12
PEAR						
Seedling			35 – 45	20	28	15 or more
Interstem tree			15 – 20	10	18	5 – 10

* Requires support.
[a] Susceptible to fire blight.
[b] Requires extremely well-drained soils. Do not plant where drainage is slow or the soil is heavy clay.
[c] Apple interstem trees are composed of either Seedling M106 or MM111 roots, a 6- to 8-in. stempiece of M9 or M27, and the scion cultivar on top. Pear interstem trees are composed of Quince root, a 6- to 8-in. piece of Old Home trunk, and the desired scion.

THE BENEFITS OF DWARFING ROOTSTOCKS

- Earlier-bearing
- Can be harvested without a ladder
- Less pesticide is required and there is better coverage
- Improved cold-hardiness and pest-resistance
- Pruning is easier and less is required
- Improved air circulation
- Less space required; can be grown in small yards
- Tolerate clay soils
- Can be spaced closer together than standard trees

propagation needed, interstem trees are the most expensive. Current recommendations suggest planting these trees so that a portion of the M 9 piece is below the soil line.

Two recently developed rootstocks from the Cornell Geneva series that are highly resistant to fire blight are:

- CG-16, which produces dwarf trees similar in size to Malling 9.
- CG-30, which produces semi-dwarf trees similar in size to Malling 7 or 7A.

Fertilizer and pH

Fruit trees have different fertilization requirements than most other plants. Here are some guidelines for fertilizing fruit trees:

- Do not put any fertilizer in the planting hole.
- One month after planting: Evenly broadcast eight ounces of 10-10-10 fertilizer over a two-foot circle around the tree. Keep the fertilizer six inches away from the trunk.
- In June, after planting: Broadcast another eight ounces of 10-10-10 around the tree.
- In subsequent years: Increase the amount of 10-10-10 by 0.25 pound per year up to a maximum of:
  - Two and one-half pounds for a dwarf tree
  - Five pounds for a semi-dwarf tree

Reduce these rates if trees become overly vegetative (producing more than 12 to 14 inches of new shoot growth per year). Maintain the soil pH at 6.0 to 6.5.

Pruning pome fruit trees

The purpose of pruning a tree in the first three to four years after planting is to control its shape and contain excessive vigor. The goal is to develop a strong, well-balanced framework consisting of a central leader with scaffold branches. Apple trees should have a vaguely Christmas-tree shape with the lowest scaffold branches having the widest spread (Figure 20-E). Most apple trees will not grow into this shape without help. Unwanted branches should be removed when small to avoid the necessity of large pruning cuts in later years. During the declining years of the tree, the focus shifts to promote vigor and allow maximum sunlight to penetrate the tree canopy for bigger yields.

At planting time

A one-year-old bare-root whip is ideal to plant. Cut it back to around 30 inches to help reestablish the plant's previous shoot-to-root ratio (see Figure 20-D).

For a branched tree:

- Leave branches that are wide-angled and arranged spirally about six to nine inches apart up the leader (trunk).
- Remove poorly spaced and narrow-angled branches.
- Reduce branches left on the tree by up to one-half their length.
- Cut the leader to about 12 to 15 inches above the top limb.

Second and third years

The most vigorous upright shoot will become your central leader. Create scaffold branches by selecting four to five branches evenly spaced and staggered around the tree (see Figure 20-E). None should be directly above the other. Space them vertically up and down the trunk. This is your first tier of permanent scaffold branches. Head back the central leader so that it is six to 10 inches above the first tier.

Occasionally, a tree does not grow as well as it should during the first year. If this happens, prune the tree back to a whip and start over. You will delay fruiting by a year, but you will have a more manageable tree.

In the third year, branches sprout just below the leader's heading cut that was made the previous year. From these branches, select a second group of scaffold branches. They will be about two to three feet above the first tier; this is the tree's second tier.

Figure 20-E (left) shows a sketch of how the tree in Figure 20-D may look after the second year. Remove branches with broken lines, and tip the central leader if it grew more than two feet.

PRUNING PRINCIPLES FOR POME FRUITS

- Do your pruning in late winter (February or March).
- Prune young trees (up to 10 years old) lightly.
- Older trees (25 years+) produce higher-quality fruit following a vigorous pruning (see Figure 20-F). One or more large limbs may be removed from excessively tall trees. Make large cuts close to the remaining limb. Do not coat the wound.
- Remove branches on the central axis between one-half and two-thirds the diameter of the central axis, especially during the formative years.
- Avoid excessive pruning, which encourages excessive shoot growth/water sprouts, delays fruiting, and reduces quality of fruit on young trees.
- Tip, or pinch off, the terminal one-half inch of new shoot growth in mid-June to encourage lateral branching. Trees from one to four years old are best suited to this practice.
- Make your thinning cuts back to the branch collar—do not leave stubs.
- Make thinning-out cuts (entire limb or shoot removal) to encourage increased flower bud production on apples.
- Make heading-back cuts (shortening the ends of branches) to encourage shoot growth.
- Remove and dispose of prunings away from the orchard area. Dead wood harbors disease organisms that can spread back into the tree.

Figure 20-D. Pruning a one-year-old apple tree

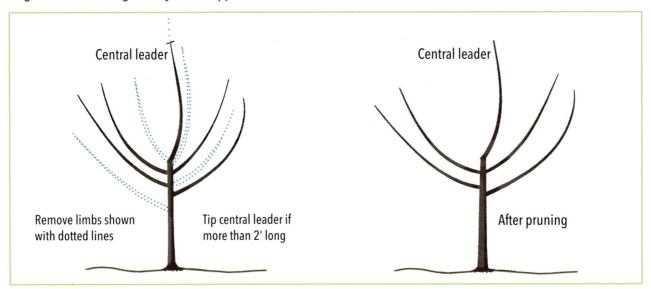

The right side of Figure 20-E illustrates the same tree after proper pruning and spreading of the branches. All limbs in the first tier of branches (A, B, C, and D) have been spread with wooden spreaders, each with a sharp-pointed nail in each end, to illustrate the beginning of the Christmas-tree shape. Limbs E, F, G, and H, in the second tier of branches, have been spread with covered wire.

Pruning in succeeding years

The tree's entire fruit production comes from the permanent scaffold branches you have selected. Because heavy pruning delays bearing, make only necessary pruning cuts during the next few years.

- Continue to head back all new terminal growth by one-fourth each year.

Figure 20-E. Pruning a two-year-old apple tree

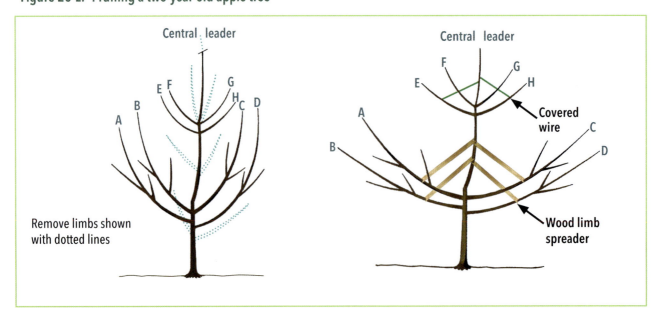

- Remove any upright limbs (suckers at base or water sprouts on branches).
- Remove any broken or diseased limbs.
- Always maintain the central leader as the highest point on the tree. Keep the ends of the primary and secondary scaffolds below the top of the tree.
- Do not allow any major limb off a scaffold branch to be closer than 12 inches to the trunk.
- When two branches grow nearly parallel to each other in a very narrow "V" formation, remove one.
- A scaffold developing a wide "V" is also undesirable; if both limbs are of similar size, the point of attachment is usually weak. Remove one limb.
- If two branches are growing closely parallel one above the other, w one.
- Fruit weight may bend limbs downward. If a limb bends past horizontal, it weakens and grows poorly. On young bearing trees, leave fruits closer to the trunk, but not heavily at the end of the limb to prevent a permanent bend in the branch.
- Stagger severe renovation over a two- to three-year period.

Pruning pear trees

In general, the same pruning and training principles used for apple trees should apply to pears, except that there will not be as much work to do. Wide crotch angles are not essential because pear trees have tougher wood that is less apt to split. Nevertheless, using limb spreaders will encourage flowering and fruiting in young trees.

Figure 20-F. Pruning an old, neglected apple tree

Pruning for fire-blight control

Most apple and pear cultivars are subject to fire blight, a bacterial disease that can kill limbs and even entire trees. Fire-blight infections are more likely to be severe following heavy pruning.

Prune out blighted shoots as soon as possible. New cankers can form around pruning cuts, so sometimes removing an infected branch to the next healthy limb junction can cause the pathogen to move into large, healthy limbs or the main trunk. The "ugly stub" pruning method is a two-step process that prevents the bacterium from moving into healthy wood during the growing season. Prune infected limbs well below the visible blight symptoms, leaving at least a four- to five-inch naked stub below the pruning cut. Fire-blight bacteria will then colonize and form small cankers around the cut. Locate the "ugly stubs" during the dormant season (when temperatures are below 40°F and the bacteria cannot multiply) and cut them back to the branch collar.

Thinning pome fruits

Fruit thinning is necessary for several reasons:

- Improves the fruit size and quality. When a tree sets a heavy crop, fruits will often be small and of poor quality.
- Allows sunlight and air to penetrate the limbs for more even ripening and better airflow.
- Diminishes risk of limbs breaking.
- Prevents biennial bearing (a cycle in which the tree bears excessively in one year and little the next year).
- Reduces the demand on the tree's resources so it can develop viable fruit buds for the next production season.
- Decreases the setback of young trees (which happens in young trees that are cropping too heavily).
- Decreases the spread of pests and diseases.

In pome fruits, all apples, Asian pears, and most European pears require thinning (Bartlett pears often thin themselves). Begin hand-thinning when the fruits are about ½-inch in diameter. Start at one end of a branch and systematically remove fruit, leaving one every six to eight inches. Retain the largest fruits whenever possible, and the ones that have the best exposure to sunlight and air.

Be careful as you thin to avoid damaging spurs (compressed buds that if thinned this year will likely bear a pome fruit next year). Keep in mind that only five to ten percent of the tree's flowers are needed to set a full crop of fruit.

Harvesting pome fruits

Apples. As apples ripen, a series of physiochemical changes take place in the fruit:

- Chlorophyll levels decrease
- Red skin coloration increases
- Seeds turn a darker color
- The flesh begins to soften
- Starch in the flesh converts to sugars
- Acidity levels decrease

Make sure to pick apple fruits intended for fresh-eating when:

- Background color changes from green to yellow

ABOUT LIMB SPREADERS

It is very important to force scaffold branches to grow at a 60° to 90° angle from the trunk. To achieve this, use limb spreaders.

Limb spreaders are devices that can aid in earlier fruit production, improved tree shape, stronger crotch angles, and better fruit color. Spreaders can be either short pieces of wood with sharpened nails driven into each end, wooden spring-type clothespins, or sharpened metal rods. The spreaders will need to remain in place for one to two years until the branch "stiffens up."

Plastic   Wood

- Fruits have reached full size
- A high percentage of red skin coloration occurs

An unripe apple is starchy and leaves a sticky film on your teeth. The easiest way to determine ripeness is to taste the fruit. You might need to harvest from the same tree several times over one or two weeks in order to get all the fruit at the right maturity stage. Be careful not to leave apples hanging too long on the tree as they will overripen, drop, be eaten by birds, crack, and/or rot.

When they are ready to harvest, apples twist off easily from the tree. Gently take the fruit in the palm of your hand, then lift and twist in a single motion. Be careful to not pull off the spur (compressed bud), taking with it next year's flower buds. Apples will shrivel and soften after harvest if left at room temperature, especially when they are tree-ripened. Keep apples in cold storage (33-38°F) in perforated plastic bags or loosely-covered containers to increase their shelf life.

European pears. Do not allow European pears to ripen on the tree. The flesh will become gritty and soft. Pick pears when they still are hard and full-sized, with a slight change in background color. They also twist off the tree quite easily. Store pears in a refrigerator or other very cool location if you don't want to consume them immediately. Pears will soften and dehydrate at room temperature.

Asian pears. These can be allowed to tree-ripen. Again, look for the color change.

20.7 Stone Fruits: Peach, Cherry, Plum, Apricot, Nectarine

Cultivar selections for Maryland

Peaches, nectarines, plums, apricots, and cherries are all closely related members of the Prunus genus. They are commonly referred to as stone fruits because their seeds are very large and hard.

Most stone fruits are native to warmer climates of the world, making them very susceptible to injury from low winter temperatures. They also bloom earlier than pome fruits, and the flowers frequently suffer damage from spring frost. Because of this, the backyard culture of stone fruits has unique challenges:

- Stone-fruit trees require the best sites, with excellent air and water drainage and protection from high winds.
- Peaches, nectarines, and apricots are less hardy than cherries and plums.
- Stone fruits are susceptible to a wide range of insect and disease pests.
- All stone fruits are susceptible to brown rot disease. Apricot, sweet cherry, and peach are very susceptible; tart cherry and plum are less susceptible.
- As harvest approaches, sweet cherries tend to crack if there is excessive rainfall.

Look for cultivars with outstanding hardiness, disease resistance, and fruit quality. A list of some recommended stone-fruit cultivars for Maryland can be found in Table 20-C.

Fertilizer and pH

Key instructions for fertilizing stone-fruit trees are as follows:

- Evenly incorporate eight ounces of 10-10-10 fertilizer into the soil around each tree prior to planting, but do not put fertilizer directly into the hole.
- In subsequent years, broadcast 0.5 lb. of 10-10-10 around each tree in early spring, increasing the amount by 0.5 lb. per year up to a maximum of 5.0 lbs. per tree, regardless of age.
- Never fertilize after July 15. Late fertilization encourages soft growth which may be winter-killed, and interferes with the tree's ability to harden-off for the dormant period.
- Maintain the soil pH at 6.0 to 6.5.

Pruning stone-fruit trees

Like all fruit trees, prune stone-fruit trees to develop a strong, well-balanced framework of scaffold branches.

Remove or cut back unwanted branches early in the tree's life to avoid the necessity of large cuts in later years. The pruning system best suited to stone-fruit trees is called "open center." Pruning and training the trees to this system produces a vase-shaped tree.

Open-center trees allow optimum air circulation and light penetration into the tree's center, both important factors in reducing the development of brown rot on fruit. Because stone-fruits bear on second-year wood, the open-center pruning system also keeps the fruit-bearing surface close to the ground and more accessible for pruning and harvest.

The exception is sweet cherry, which is usually pruned to a central leader system. (See **Pome Fruits: Pruning.**) Apricot and plum can be grown with either a central leader or open center. Spurs (compressed twigs) on plum, sweet cherry, and apricot can bear fruit for more than one year.

At planting time

Cut back a whip or tree with no branches 20 to 30 inches above the soil line to 26 to 30 inches tall after planting. Otherwise, your tree will grow major branches too high above the ground.

For trees with healthy branches 18 inches above the soil line:

- Select three or four scaffold branches, beginning at 18 inches, one at each compass point.
- Choose branches that are growing at a 60° to 90° angle from the trunk.
- Cut these scaffold branches back by one-half to a healthy outside-facing bud.
- Remove all branches that are lower than 18 inches above the soil line.
- Cut the tree off just above the topmost selected branch.
- During the summer, pinch off any shoots that begin to grow toward the center of the tree.

The spring after planting

Stone-fruit trees are very susceptible to a disease called Cytospora canker. If pruned in late winter, trees cannot protect pruning wounds from this disease. Prune your trees from budswell through petal fall in the spring. Your goal is to develop a vase-shaped tree with no branches in the center (see Figure 20-G).

Remove any broken or diseased branches and cut out any vigorous upright shoots that may have developed on the inside of the main scaffolds.

Figure 20-G. Pruning a one-year-old peach tree

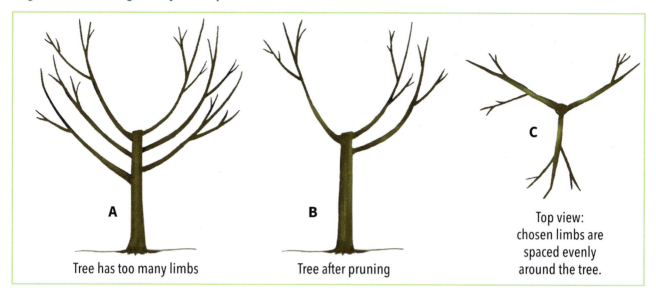

A — Tree has too many limbs
B — Tree after pruning
C — Top view: chosen limbs are spaced evenly around the tree.

Second spring after planting

The second spring after planting, you can begin to develop secondary or sub-scaffold branches on the primary scaffolds.

- From each scaffold branch, select two to three limbs that developed during the previous summer. They should be spaced six to eight inches apart along the branch and 18 to 24 inches from the main trunk.
- Remove all other side limbs.
- Head the chosen side limbs, or sub-scaffold branches, back by one-half.
- Head back the primary scaffolds by one-half.
- Completely remove any large vertical limbs growing on the primary scaffolds, leaving only the moderately vigorous wood for fruiting.

Figure 20-H shows a diagram of a peach tree with corrective pruning cuts, which are needed beginning after the second growing season and continuing through the fourth year. Limbs drooping near the ground or growing toward the center of the tree are removed, as at "B". Also, to keep the tree growing outward rather than up, the highest limbs are headed back to an outward-growing lateral, at "A." (For clear illustration, only two such limbs are shown.)

Figure 20-H. Pruning a two-year-old peach tree

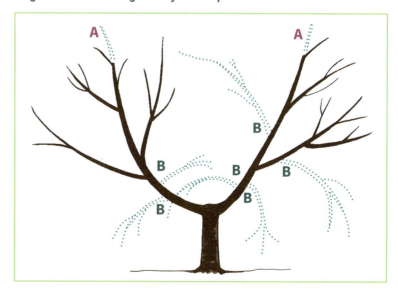

Third and subsequent years

After careful pruning and training the first two years, heavy pruning should not be necessary thereafter. Light, corrective pruning should be enough to maintain the open center.

- Thin out and shorten inside limbs to prevent shading of the center.
- Prune every year to keep the tree within its allotted space and to prevent limb breakage.
- Remove overly vigorous upright branches and leave moderately vigorous ones.
- Remove short, thin shoots and very long shoots which are not as productive.
- Head back limbs to encourage the development of new fruiting wood.

Pruning mature stone-fruit trees

As your peach trees begin to bear heavily, you must prune severely in order to stimulate new growth. Peaches are produced on the previous year's growth, and the best fruiting wood is 12 to 18 inches long.

Limit the height and spread of older mature trees by removing large branches from the upper side of scaffolds, leaving only small fruit-producing shoots. Head back the primary scaffold branches to an outside-growing side branch. Remove or cut back damaged portions of larger branches. Maintain the open center to prevent shading of the interior portion of the tree.

Thinning stone fruits

All stone fruits require thinning. Hand-thinning is the easiest and safest method for removing excess fruit. Begin hand-thinning when the fruits are about ¾-inch in diameter. Thinning too early can result in split pits in stone fruits, especially in peaches; thinning too late reduces the chances for increasing fruit size.

The specific amount of thinning required will depend on the species and the overall fruit load on the tree. In general:

- Thin peaches and nectarines to about three to five inches apart on the branch.
- Thin apricots and plums to about two to four inches apart. If that spring's environmental conditions are ideal, more thinning may be required, as more fruit might set.

Retain the largest fruit whenever possible, and the ones that have the best exposure to sunlight and air. Remove double fruits (two fruits fused together) and small, misshapen, or damaged fruit. If a long branch produces fruit on its entire length, thin more heavily, particularly towards the terminal end.

Harvesting stone fruits

As stone fruits ripen, a series of physicochemical changes take place in the fruit. Some of these changes include flesh softening and changes in skin color from green (high chlorophyll) to purple, red, orange, or a combination of these colors.

Test for ripeness by giving the fruit a gentle squeeze; the fruit should yield to gentle thumb pressure. The easiest way to determine the ripeness is to taste the fruit. The sugar content will not increase after harvest.

Take care not to harm the fruit buds for the next year's crop. The best way to harvest is to simultaneously, and gently, twist and pull. Ripe fruit will easily detach from the stem.

Handle fruit gently, place in the shade, and avoid piling fruit together to avoid bruising and damage that can lead to rotting. Stone fruits will shrivel and soften after harvest if left at room temperature, so refrigerate them at about 32°F in perforated plastic bags or loosely-covered containers to prolong their shelf life.

20.8 Fig Trees

Fig trees (*Ficus carica*) make nice additions to Maryland landscapes. They can be pruned to a shrub or tree form and can be grown in containers or in-ground; they are also virtually pest-free. Choosing the right cultivar (see Table 20-C) and maintaining it correctly can produce quite abundant crops. All figs are seedless, producing their fruits parthenocarpically.

Depending upon your location, fig trees may overwinter or die back to sprout up again in the spring. Gardeners in warmer areas (Eastern Shore, Southern Maryland, and Baltimore City) tend to have the least difficulty overwintering plants and harvesting figs before the first frost.

Purchase plants from a reputable nursery or propagate from spring divisions or summer cuttings from mature plants. Root suckers from established trees can also be pulled and planted in the spring. Pliable branches can be pegged to the ground and tip-rooted or layered. See **Chapter 24, Plant Propagation,** for detailed information.

Site selection and planting

Select a sunny, protected location for planting in the ground; next to a south-facing wall is ideal. Plant fig trees in early spring after danger of frost, or in early fall. Space trees six to eight feet apart. Cut back the top of the plant to force lateral growth.

PHYTODERMATITIS AND FIG TREES

Always wear gloves when handling and pruning your fig trees; they exude a milky latex sap that can get on your skin. Sunlight exposure to skin that has been in contact with fig-tree sap can cause phytodermatitis, a very painful, itchy, blistering skin condition that can last for weeks. These are burns and should be treated as such with cold compresses and NSAID pain relievers. Consult a healthcare provider if the condition is severe.

Figs do very well in a wide range of soils, but will thrive if compost or well-rotted manure is incorporated into the soil prior to planting. Keep the soil pH in the 6.0 to 6.5 range.

Do not cultivate the soil under your plant; figs have shallow roots that can easily be damaged with garden tools.

Fruits form in the leaf axils of the current year's wood. The fruits form from the shoot base towards the tip. Fig trees usually begin to bear in the second or third year after planting.

Harvesting figs

Figs are adored by many animals, not just people. Without netting to throw over your bush, you may find that squirrels and birds dine first on your crop. Figs ripen from mid-September through frost. Figs do not ripen off the tree, so do not harvest them until they are fully-colored and have a slightly soft texture.

Overwintering in-ground fig trees

Unprotected fig plants are often winter-killed back to the crown in Maryland. Sustained temperatures below 10° to 15°F kill above-ground wood. New shoots will spring readily from the roots. In some cases, a plant killed back in the winter will still produce a modest crop the following summer. In most cases, however, the plant will require two to three good growing seasons to return to normal production. The following are suggestions to keep your trees producing an annual crop:

- Grow figs in a bush or shrub habit to make them easier to protect than those in tree form.
- Pin pliable branches to the ground and cover them with burlap, old blankets, or tarps.
- Encircle the tree with chicken wire and fill in with insulating leaves or straw. The top of the plant can be covered with a plastic tarp to shed rain, sleet, and snow.
- In the spring, remove the winter protection after all danger of frost.
- Each spring, prune out ground suckers and remove all dead or weak wood.

Growing fig trees in containers

If you are short on garden space or do not want the trouble of protecting the tree from frost, try planting a fig tree in a large pot, half-barrel, or other 30-gallon container. Placing the container on casters will make it easy to move the tree to a protected area, like a garage or shed, for the winter.

The root restriction created by the confinement of the container may actually improve yields and reduce the number of days to harvest. Most cultivars will perform well in containers.

To pot a fig tree in a container:

- Ensure the growing mix is loamy and well-drained, and contains lots of compost or well-rotted manure. A good growing mix is 50% compost and 50% lightweight soilless potting media.
- Keep fig containers in full sun and water regularly.
- If containers sit on top of soil, fig roots will grow through the drainage holes into the soil making it difficult to move containers.
- When fruits begin to form, apply two to three gallons of water each day.
- After fig leaves drop in the fall, shape the plant by removing suckers and heading back long branches.
- Move it to a protected area, such as a garage or shed. ❋

On the following pages, Table 20-C lists cultivars of a number of pome fruits, stone fruits, and figs that do well in Maryland. Many other cultivars are available that may also be suitable.

Table 20-C. Recommended tree-fruit cultivars for Maryland

APPLE

Image	Cultivar	Comments	Image	Cultivar	Comments
	Antietam Blush	Bred by UMD for hot, wet mid-Atlantic summers. Red with a green-yellow background. Crisp, sweet-tart.		Enterprise	Medium-to-large, red, crisp fruit. Late blooming, moderately vigorous tree; keeps well.
	Bonita	Fruit has pink to bright red color over a yellow green background. Slightly acidic, juicy and crunchy bite. Resistant to apple scab.		Florina	Dark red, large, sweet-tart fruit. Ripens in Oct. Resistant to fireblight, powdery mildew, and scab; but less to cedar-apple rust.
	Cordera	Crimson-rose color. Crisp, sweet, and flavorful. Resistant to apple scab. Honeycrisp parentage.		Galarina	Medium-sized, with orange-red skin on a yellow background. Crisp flesh tastes like Gala. High tolerance to apple scab/powdery mildew.
	Crimson Crisp	Medium-sized, deep-red fruit with crisp, coarse-grained texture. Spreading habit. Resistant to apple scab.		Goldrush	Deep yellow, crisp, firm fruit; upright, semi-spur tree. Keeps well.
	Crimson Topaz	Medium to large fruit with thin, red-and-yellow stripes. Crisp, sweet-tart. Resistant to apple scab/powdery mildew.		MacFree	Large fruit with 90% red blush over tough, green skin. Flavor similar to McIntosh.
	Empire	McIntosh x Red Delicious; dark red fruit, excellent quality. Good keeper; very vigorous, early-bearing.		Redfree	Earliest scab and rust-resistant apple; some fire-blight resistance. Red with creamy flesh. Excellent flavor; ripens mid-late Aug.

* Cultivar names in purple have some resistance to fire blight, apple scab, cedar-apple rust, and/or powdery mildew.

APRICOT

Image	Cultivar	Comments	Image	Cultivar	Comments
	Blenheim	An old favorite. Juicy fruit is especially aromatic. Freestone. Good canning apricot.		Harlayne	Medium-sized fruit with orange, freestone flesh. Productive and cold-hardy.
	Harcot	Early-ripening, productive tree. Adaptable to many different soil types. Ripens in June-July.		Veecot	Medium-to-large fruit with orange freestone flesh.

continued on next page

continued from previous page

Table 20-C. Recommended tree-fruit cultivars for Maryland

CHERRY - SWEET

Image	Cultivar	Comments	Image	Cultivar	Comments
	Hedelfingen	Very productive trees that begin bearing quickly. Good quality black fruit with some crack resistance.		Starkrimson®	Self-fertile tree that only reaches 12-14 ft. Large, red fruit ripens in early June.
	Lapins	Self-fertile, heavy producer. Fruit has good crack-resistance. Ripens mid-July.		Stella	Self-fertile, vigorous large trees (25-30 ft.). Large, dark-red fruit.
	Royal Ann	Very old yellow cherry with a pink blush. Large, productive trees.		Ulster	Medium-sized fruit with dark skin and flesh.
	Sam	Early ripening, large, black cherry. Large, vigorous, upright trees. Blooms later than most other cultivars.		Van	Fruit similar to Bing, but firmer. Vigorous, productive tree can tolerate harsh weather.

CHERRY - SOUR

Image	Cultivar	Comments	Image	Cultivar	Comments
	Danube	Can be eaten fresh; is not as tart as other sour cherries. Ripens a few days before Montmorency.		Montmorency	Very old cultivar. Red fruit with yellow flesh. Tree reaches 15 ft. with a spreading habit. Ripens in mid- to late-June.
	Meteor	Genetic dwarf, reaches 8 to 12 ft. at maturity. Fruit is similar to Montmorency.		North Star	Genetic dwarf, reaches 6-12 ft. Heavy producer bears in 2nd year. Crack-resistant. Hangs for up to 2 weeks.

FIG

Image	Cultivar	Comments	Image	Cultivar	Comments
	Brown Turkey	Medium-sized sweet fruit that ripens to a reddish-purple color. Popular late cultivar.		Chicago Hardy	Drought- and heat-tolerant. Excellent fruit resembles strawberry jam. Sweet and rich.
	Brunswick	Does well in pots/containers. Ripens in July-Aug. Good for preserving.		Marseilles	White fig. Thomas Jefferson's favorite. Fast-growing and cold-hardy.
	Celeste	Closed-eye, pest- and disease-resistant. Heat-tolerant and cold-hardy. Well-flavored early cultivar.		Osborne Prolific	Heavy yields. White to amber flesh, very sweet and fresh-tasting.

continued on next page

continued from previous page

Table 20-C. Recommended tree-fruit cultivars for Maryland

NECTARINE

Image	Cultivar	Comments	Image	Cultivar	Comments
	Arctic Star	Deep red skin with white flesh. Very sweet, low-acid, non-melting. Semi-freestone. Ripens in early June.		Double Delight	The richest flavor among nectarines. Dark red skin, yellow flesh. Freestone. Mid-summer harvest.
	Armking	Large fruit with a red blush. Yellow flesh. Semi-freestone. Ripens in mid-June.		Fantasia	Large, yellow freestone that is firm, but very juicy. Sweet, tangy flavor. Ripens in late August.

PEACH

Image	Cultivar	Comments	Image	Cultivar	Comments
	Bellaire	Large fruit with excellent color and firmness. Trees are vigorous and spreading. Resistant to bacterial leaf spot.		Newhaven	Similar to Redhaven. Very reliable with good disease resistance.
	Candor	Early, medium-sized fruit. Semi-freestone, resistant to bacterial spot but susceptible to pit-splitting.		Raritan Rose	Large, red fruit with white flesh; excellent quality. Vigorous and productive trees.
	Desiree™	Early ripening, medium-size, highly colored fruit. Few split pits. Resistant to bacterial leaf spot.		Red Rose	Medium-sized, red fruit with white flesh. Vigorous, hardy trees.
	Garnet Beauty	A sport of Redhaven. Medium-to-large, fuzz-less, red fruit. Firm, yellow, semi-freestone flesh. Vigorous and productive.		Redhaven	Most popular peach in the Mid-Atlantic region. Semi-freestone, non-browning. Requires thorough thinning.
	Glohaven	Large, firm, uniform fruit. Mostly red with deep yellow ground color. Vigorous grower, bud-hardy. Resistant to bacterial leaf spot.		Redskin	Large fruit, very high quality. Blooms over a long period. Vigorous tree developed at UMD in 1931.
	Loring	Medium-to-large red fruit over a yellow background. Can produce heavy crops but blooms early.		Reliance	Buds are cold-hardy. Good for gardeners in Northern and Western Maryland.

continued on next page

continued from previous page

Table 20-C. Recommended tree-fruit cultivars for Maryland

PEACH (continued)

	Cultivar	Description		Cultivar	Description
	Rich May	Early ripening, medium-size, highly colored, clingstone fruit. Resistant to bacterial leaf spot.		Sunhigh	Large, oblong fruit. Red-over-orange background. Important commercial cultivar.
	Summerglo	Large, yellow fruit. Vigorous and productive trees with above-average cold-hardiness.		White Hale	Similar to J.H. Hale but with white flesh. Large, high-quality fruit; productive trees.

PEAR - ASIAN

	Cultivar	Description		Cultivar	Description
	Hosui	Vigorous, spreading tree with very sweet, russeted fruit.		Shinseiki	Large, vigorous tree; fruit is medium-to-large with little russeting.
	Olympic	Large, upright tree with very large, russeted fruit that stores well.		20th Century (Nijisekki)	Medium-sized tree with drooping habit. Yellow, high-quality fruit. Fruit must be thinned.

PEAR - EUROPEAN

	Cultivar	Description		Cultivar	Description
	Bell	Large yellow fruit with a splash of red. Excellent flavor and fire blight resistance.		Harrow Delight	Juicy, medium-sized fruits. Smooth flesh, no grit cells. Productive trees.
	Blake's Pride	Medium-sized fruit; yellow skin with tan russeting; excellent flavor. Resistant to fire blight and pear scab.		Harvest Queen	Hardier and earlier, but very similar to Bartlett.
	Cold Snap	Large, roundish, fine textured fruit with excellent flavor and fire blight resistance.		Honeysweet	Firm fruit with cream-colored flesh; very similar to Seckel.
	Harrow Crisp	Medium-sized yellow fruit with a splash of red. Excellent flavor. Resistant to fire blight.		Magness	Medium-sized, excellent quality. 2 other cultivars needed. Keep cold for 1 month before eating.

continued from previous page

continued on next page

continued from previous page

Table 20-C. Recommended tree-fruit cultivars for Maryland

PEAR - EUROPEAN* (continued)

Moonglow	Medium-to-large, dull green fruits with pink blush. Smooth, fine flesh; excellent quality.		Seckel	Can be nearly tree-ripened. Very sweet, small fruits. Referred to as the "sugar pear."
Potomac	Medium-sized, fine-grained, aromatic fruit. Trees are moderately vigorous and precocious. Resistant to fire blight.		Shenandoah	Large-sized, late-season fruit. Stores well. Resistant to fire blight.

All cultivars in this section are fire-blight resistant. Bartlett, Bosc, Comice, Anjou, and Clapp's Favorite are fire-blight susceptible.

PLUM - EUROPEAN

Bluefre	Later and larger than Stanley. Yellow, freestone flesh.		Italian Prune	Medium-to-large, purple-black fruit. Excellent quality, freestone flesh. Productive trees.
Damson	Consistent, heavy crops. Fruit is tangy and preserves well. Ripens in August.		Stanley Prune	Medium-sized, dark-blue freestone. Greenish-yellow flesh. Good for fresh eating, drying, and canning. Ripens mid-Aug.

PLUM - JAPANESE

Methley	Round, purple fruit with red blush. Ripens early to mid-July. Vigorous tree.		Santa Rosa	Very large, round, red-purplish fruit. Very high-quality, clingstone flesh.
Ozark Premier	Large, red fruit with yellow clingstone flesh. Harvest early to mid-August.		Shiro	Round, yellow fruit sometimes with pink blush. Very juicy clingstone that ripens late July.

AUTHOR

Macarena Farcuh, Assistant Professor and Extension Specialist Horticulture, Department of Plant Science and Landscape Architecture, University of Maryland, College Park.

PUBLICATIONS

Adapted in part from *The Maryland Master Gardener Handbook*. 1996.

Eames-Sheavly, M., Pritts, C., Cramer, L., Bushway, L., Merwin, I., Reisinger, R., McKay, S. 2003. *Cornell Guide to Growing Fruit at Home.* Cornell Cooperative Extension. Ithaca, NY 14853. **ecommons.cornell.edu/handle/1813/67**

Fruit Production for the Home Gardener: A Comprehensive Guide. Publications Distribution Center, The Pennsylvania State University. University Park, PA. **agsci.psu.edu/fphg**

Otto, S. 1993. *The Backyard Orchardist.* Otto Graphics. Maple City, MI.

Traunfeld, J. 2005. *Home Fruit Production Guide.* Bulletin 125. University of Maryland Extension. College Park, MD.

Whealy, K., ed. 2001. *Fruit, Berry and Nut Inventory, Third Edition.* The Seed Savers Exchange, Inc. Decorah, IA.

Farcuh, M. 2020. *Split Pits in Peaches and Nectarines.* University of Maryland Extension Vegetable and Fruit News #5. August, 2020: 3-4.

Farcuh, M. 2020. *Determining Apple Fruit Maturity and Optimal Harvest Date.* University of Maryland Extension Vegetable and Fruit News #5. August, 2020: 5-8.

Ingels, C., Geisel, P., Unruh, C., and Lawson, P. 2001. *Fruit Trees: Thinning Young Fruit.* University of California, Publication 8047. **growables.org/information/documents/FruitTreeThinningUC.pdf**

Hoover, E., Tepe, E., and Foulk, D. 2018. *Growing stone fruits in the home garden.* University of Minnesota Extension. **extension.umn.edu/fruit/growing-stone-fruits-home-garden**

Hoover, E., Tepe, E., Klood, A., and Foulk, D. 2020. *Growing apples in the home garden.* University of Minnesota Extension. **extension.umn.edu/fruit/growing-apples**

WEBSITES

Backyard Fruit Growers (Southern PA) **byfg.org/**

North American Fruit Explorers Inc. **nafex.org**

Stone Fruit- Frost Protection, University of Florida: **hos.ifas.ufl.edu/stonefruit/production/frost-protection/**

PHOTOS

Main chapter photo: Wikipedia free license. All Table 20-C cultivar photos courtesy of LeAnn Zotta.

ILLUSTRATIONS

All figures courtesy of LeAnn Zotta, Berkshire Communications.

21: NATIVE PLANTS

Mikaela Boley
Sabine Harvey

21 NATIVE PLANTS

CONTENTS

21.1 Why Choose Native Plants? 637

21.2 How to Choose Native Plants 640

21.3 Maximizing Native Plant Performance 640

21.4 Recommended Native Plants for Maryland 641

LEARNING OBJECTIVES

- The definition of "native plant"
- The three physiographic regions of Maryland and how they influence native plant composition
- The importance of native plants for wildlife, pollinators, and biodiversity
- How to properly select native plants for your site
- Maximizing the performance of native plants
- Recommended native plants for Maryland

INTRODUCTION

Let's start with a science-based definition of native plant species and their ecological roles:

Native plants occur naturally in their ecoregion and habitat, where they have adapted to physical conditions and co-evolved with the other species in the same ecosystem.

All plants are native to *somewhere*, but this chapter is primarily concerned with the natural range that includes the Maryland region.

Keep in mind that "native" is something of a relative term. For example, red maple (*Acer rubra*) has a natural ("native") range from Florida north into Canada—but because tree specimens co-evolve with other species in their immediate region, red maples in Florida would likely not survive in Canada because of the dramatic difference in growing conditions.

Even within states or regions, native plants are genetically adapted to local growing conditions. This adaptation is referred to as "local provenance" or "ecotype" subspecies. Ecotype adaptations can be visible variations, such as size, shape, or color. Some ecotype adaptations are undetectable, like drought or moisture tolerance, or even temperature hardiness. Regardless, choosing the correct ecotype is important for any planting site. For more information about habitat fragmentation, see **Chapter 3, Ecology.**

By incorporating locally grown native plants into your landscape, you are essentially preserving and promoting local ecotypes. This is not always an option when purchasing native plants, but it should not discourage you from purchasing them in general.

21.1 Why Choose Native Plants?

Native plants have gained popularity for their low-maintenance nature and simple beauty. They also serve both functional and aesthetic purposes in a landscape. Planting a native garden will:

- Have a better chance of succeeding and flourishing
- Provide habitat for wildlife
- Have a natural and appealing appearance

Conversely, choosing non-native plants can have unintended consequences:

- Most garden-center ornamentals have developed in an alien ecology, and will often fail because they can't adapt to a totally different local ecology.
- For the same reason, "alien" plants don't attract as much wildlife.
- Many landscapes will look and feel artificial because they are influenced by design or maintenance requirements rather than appropriate plant selection for the location and growing conditions.

If you decide to use native plants but don't know where to start, visit a nearby native garden or arboretum to get design ideas and see the plants for yourself.

To conserve biodiversity

Even small backyard gardens impact the natural world and the areas near our home. Plants are primary producers; only they can convert sunlight into usable energy. Therefore, the number of plants and the species of plants will largely determine what other forms of life a particular region can support. Yards that have both a large number of native plants as well as a wide variety of native plants will be able to support more beneficial insects and other forms of wildlife than yards that are planted with just a few species of plants that came from other parts of the world. In addition, planting native species will ensure that their genetic material will be preserved. If a particular plant were to become extinct, so would all the other forms of life that depend on that particular plant. If more gardeners planted native species, together all those gardens would create a large area that could support many different forms of life (Tallamy and Darke, 2009; Tallamy, 2019).

Figure 21-A. Physiographic map of Maryland's three main ecoregions

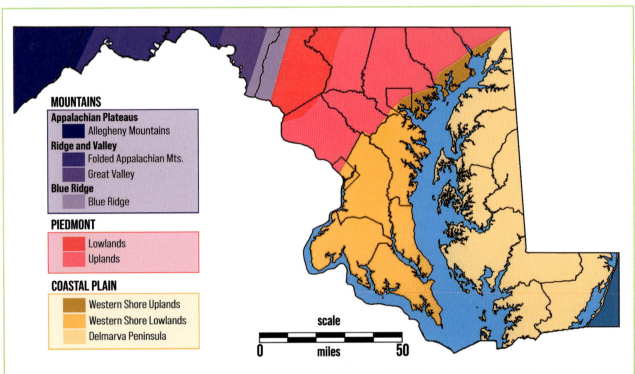

To preserve wildlife habitats

Research has shown that the use of native plants provides the best opportunity for creating habitats for pollinators, songbirds, and other wildlife.

Over millennia, native insects and plants have evolved along with one another, reaching an ecological balance. While there are generalist feeders, many insects are dependent upon one or more plants with which they co-evolved. A good example is the monarch caterpillar, which is entirely dependent on populations of milkweed as a food source.

With an abundance of seeds, berries, and habitats, native plants also support our local bird species as a source of food and shelter. Our native plants also promote a robust population of insects, which indirectly provide the food source that many bird species require.

WHICH IS BETTER FOR WILDLIFE: AN OAK TREE OR A CRAPE MYRTLE?

Oak trees alone provide 534 species of lepidopterans (butterflies, moths, caterpillars) with a food source.

In comparison, crape myrtles, a popular ornamental landscape tree, offer resources to only three species (Tallamy, 2009).

The goal is to choose species that have multiple features or functions that will provide the greatest benefits to our wildlife.

TOP 5 TREES FOR CATERPILLARS

1. Oaks (*Quercus* spp.)
2. Cherry (*Prunus* spp.)
3. Willows (*Salix* spp.)
4. Birch (*Betula* spp.)
5. Poplar (*Populus* spp.)

TOP 5 SHRUBS & VINES FOR BIRDS

1. Gray dogwood (*Cornus racemosa*)
2. Red osier dogwood (*Cornus sericea*)
3. Silky dogwood (*Cornus amomum*)
4. Southern arrowwood (*Viburnum dentatum*)
5. Virginia creeper (*Parthenocissus quinquefolia*)

To create low-maintenance, efficient landscapes

Conventional landscapes are often dependent on maintenance, fertilizers, pesticides, supplementary water, and the use of tools that require high levels of fossil fuels to operate. By choosing plants that are adapted for local conditions, less is required for them to establish and thrive. Native plantings, meadows, trees, and shrubs create self-sufficient landscapes when chosen and planted appropriately, saving water, ecosystems, energy and money.

For example, take a landscape with a wet spot, or an area that gathers water without draining quickly. This would be a challenging location in which to grow traditional turfgrass, so homeowners end up fighting the variety of weeds that thrive in these moist-to-wet soils. Instead of trying to change the topography or drainage slope, consider native plants that thrive in wet soils.

Another alternative could be a rain garden, which also employs native species that are adapted to moister sites.

21.2 How to Choose Native Plants

When you purchase native plants, the primary questions to ask should be:

- Is the site within the natural geographic range of the plant species you chose?
- Where within that range should I get these plants?

The U.S. Forest Service recommends that native plants be sourced within the same **U.S. EPA Level III Ecoregion** for best results.

Growing conditions and characteristics

Because native plants are adapted in specific regions, soils, and cultural conditions, it is important (as with any plant) to consider the following conditions for your natives:

- Light (full sun, partial shade, shade)
- Moisture
- Soil pH
- Soil type
- Salt tolerance
- Flood levels, if applicable
- Elevation, if applicable

Also consider these secondary characteristics, which include aesthetic and wildlife benefits:

- Size: height and spread
- Flowering: color and length
- Fruit: fruiting period, color, and type
- Fall color

21.3 Maximizing Native Plant Performance

The main consideration is to situate native plants in growing conditions similar to those found in the habitats in which they originally evolved. *Remember: Right plant, right place!*

- Select species that are in the mid- to northern portions of their range. Avoid those which have Maryland as the southern end of their natural range, as they will not be able to tolerate the climatic changes. Find the natural ranges of native plants by using the **Biota of North America Program**.
- Purchase herbaceous native plants sourced from local plant populations, if possible. Locally-native plants that are thriving nearby have adapted well to recent climate changes. Find native plant nurseries and sources through the **Maryland Native Plant Society**.
- For help with tree selection, consult the **USFS Climate Change Tree Atlas**.
- If local commercial sources are unavailable, purchase plants sourced from populations in similar ecoregions of the Mid-Atlantic. Avoid plants sourced further north or south of their current natural range, as there can be adverse consequences for both the species itself and local ecosystems.

Find more recommendations on the UMD website's **recommended native plants** or the **Chesapeake Bay Native Plant Center**. ✼

> **INTERESTED IN PROPAGATING NATIVE PLANTS FROM SEED?**
>
> See **Chapter 24, Plant Propagation.**

21.4 Recommended Native Plants for Maryland

Table 21-A. Recommended Native Plants for Maryland

Light: Full sun = ☼   Part-sun = ◐   Shade = ●   Ecoregion: M=Mountain   P=Piedmont   C=Coastal Plain

GROUNDCOVERS & FERNS

Foamflower
Tiarella cordifolia
Soil type: Humus-rich
Soil moisture: Moist, well-drained
Light: ●
Ecoregion: M P

Golden groundsel
Packera aurea
Soil type: Humus-rich
Soil moisture: Moist to wet
Light: ◐ ●
Ecoregion: M P C

Wild ginger
Asarum canadense
Soil type: Slightly acid
Soil moisture: Moist, well-drained
Light: ●
Ecoregion: M P

Christmas fern
Polystichum acrostichoides
Soil type: Adaptable; prefers slightly acidic to neutral
Soil moisture: Dry to moist
Light: ●
Ecoregion: M P C

Lady fern
Athyrium filix-femina
Soil type: Humus-rich
Soil moisture: Moist
Light: ◐ ●
Ecoregion: M P C

GRASSES & SEDGES

Blue sedge
Carex glaucodea
Soil type: Adaptable
Soil moisture: Moist to wet
Light: ☼ ◐ ●
Ecoregion: M P C

Wool rush/Wool grass
Scirpus cyperinus
Soil type: Flood plain
Soil moisture: Moist to wet, acidic to neutral
Light: ☼ ◐
Ecoregion: M P C

Little bluestem
Schizachyrium scoparium
Soil type: Poor
Soil moisture: Dry
Light: ☼
Ecoregion: M P C

Yellow indiangrass
Sorghastrum nutans
Soil type: All, even saline
Soil moisture: Dry to moist
Light: ☼
Ecoregion: M P C

Broomsedge
Andropogon virginicus
Soil type: Adaptable
Soil moisture: Dry to moist
Light: ☼ ◐
Ecoregion: M P C

continued on next page

continued from previous page

Table 21-A. Recommended Native Plants for Maryland

Light: Full sun = ☼   Part-sun = ◐   Shade = ●   Ecoregion: M=Mountain P=Piedmont C=Coastal Plain

FLOWERING HERBACEOUS PLANTS (Forbs)

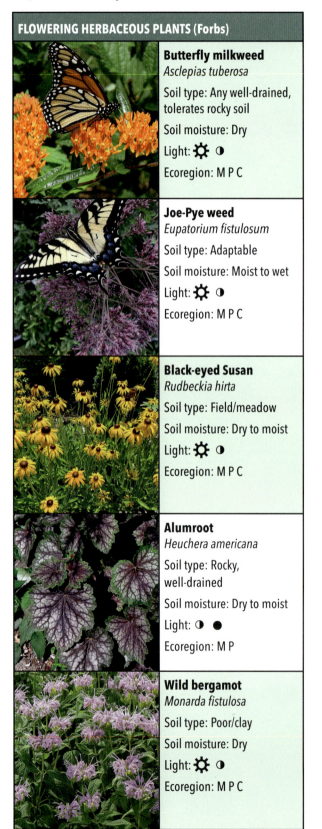

Butterfly milkweed
Asclepias tuberosa
Soil type: Any well-drained, tolerates rocky soil
Soil moisture: Dry
Light: ☼ ◐
Ecoregion: M P C

Joe-Pye weed
Eupatorium fistulosum
Soil type: Adaptable
Soil moisture: Moist to wet
Light: ☼ ◐
Ecoregion: M P C

Black-eyed Susan
Rudbeckia hirta
Soil type: Field/meadow
Soil moisture: Dry to moist
Light: ☼ ◐
Ecoregion: M P C

Alumroot
Heuchera americana
Soil type: Rocky, well-drained
Soil moisture: Dry to moist
Light: ◐ ●
Ecoregion: M P

Wild bergamot
Monarda fistulosa
Soil type: Poor/clay
Soil moisture: Dry
Light: ☼ ◐
Ecoregion: M P C

FLOWERING HERBACEOUS PLANTS (Forbs)

Eastern columbine
Aquilegia canadensis
Soil type: Adaptable, pH >6.0
Soil moisture: Well-drained
Light: ◐
Ecoregion: M P

Foxglove beardtongue
Penstemon digitalis
Soil type: Tolerates poor soil
Soil moisture: Dry to moist
Light: ☼ ◐
Ecoregion: M P C

Great blue lobelia
Lobelia siphilitica
Soil type: Adaptable
Soil moisture: Moist to wet
Light: ☼ ◐
Ecoregion: M P C

New York ironweed
Vernonia noveboracensis
Soil type: Adaptable
Soil moisture: Average
Light: ☼ ◐
Ecoregion: M P C

Rose mallow
Hibiscus moscheutos
Soil type: Loamy, humus-rich
Soil moisture: Moist to wet
Light: ☼ ◐
Ecoregion: C

continued on next page

continued from previous page

Table 21-A. Recommended Native Plants for Maryland

Light: Full sun = ☼   Part-sun = ◐   Shade = ●   Ecoregion: M=Mountain   P=Piedmont   C=Coastal Plain

SHRUBS

Inkberry holly
Ilex glabra
Soil type: Adaptable, pH 4.5-6
Soil moisture: Dry to periodically wet
Light: ☼ ◐ ●
Ecoregion: C

Virginia sweetspire
Itea virginica
Soil type: Humus-rich, pH 5.1-7.5
Soil moisture: Moist to wet
Light: ☼ ◐ ●
Ecoregion: C

Winterberry holly
Ilex verticillata
Soil type: Humus-rich, pH 4.5-6.5
Soil moisture: Moist
Light: ☼ ◐ ●
Ecoregion: M P C

Northern bayberry
Morella pensylvanica
Soil type: Adaptable, pH 5.1-6.5, tolerates salt spray
Soil moisture: Dry to wet
Light: ☼ ◐
Ecoregion: C

Red chokeberry
Aronia arbutifolia
Soil type: Adaptable, pH <6.8
Soil moisture: Dry to wet
Light: ☼ ◐
Ecoregion: M P C

TREES

Blackgum
Nyssa sylvatica
Soil type: Sandy or loamy, pH <6.5
Soil moisture: Average to wet
Light: ☼ ◐ ●
Ecoregion: M P

Eastern redbud
Cercis canadensis
Soil type: Adaptable, humus-rich, pH 4.5-7.5
Soil moisture:
Light: ☼ ◐
Ecoregion: M P C

White oak
Quercus alba
Soil type: Adaptable, pH <6.5
Soil moisture: Dry to average
Light: ☼ ◐ ●
Ecoregion: M P

Tulip poplar
Liriodendron tulipifera
Soil type: Flood plains
Soil moisture: Moist
Light: ☼ ◐
Ecoregion: M P C

Loblolly pine
Pinus taeda
Soil type: Tolerates poor soil
Soil moisture: Dry to wet
Light: ☼
Ecoregion: C

AUTHORS

Mikaela Boley, Senior Agent for Home Horticulture, University of Maryland Extension.

Sabine Harvey, Former Horticulture Program Assistant, University of Maryland Extension.

PUBLICATIONS

Adapted in part from the *University of Maryland Handbook (2016 edition)*.

Runkle, J., K. Kunkel, D. Easterling, B. Stewart, S. Champion, R. Frankson, and W. Sweet, 2017. *Maryland State Climate Summary.* NOAA Technical Report NESDIS 149-MD, 4 pp. statesummaries.ncics.org/chapter/md/

Smith, S. B. and S. R. McWilliams. 2015. *Recommended plantings for migratory songbird habitat management.* Rochester, NY: Rochester Institute of Technology and University of Rhode Island. 2 p.

Tallamy, D. W. and K. J. Shropshire. 2009. *Ranking Lepidopteran Use of Native Versus Introduced Plants.* Conservation Biology. 23 (4): 941-947.

Tallamy, Douglas W. 2019. *Nature's Best Hope: A New Approach to Conservation that Starts in Your Yard*. Portland, OR: Timber Press.

Talllamy, Douglas W. and R. Darke. 2009. *Bringing Nature Home: How You Can Sustain Wildlife with Native Plants, Updated and Expanded.* Portland, OR: Timber Press.

PHOTOS

Main photo, joe pye weed, and black-eyed susan: Stephanie Pully.

Figure 21-A. *Physiographic map of Maryland's three main ecoregions.* Public domain, modified by LeAnn Zotta.

Table 21-A:

Christmas fern: James H. Miller, USDA Forest Service, Bugwood.org.

Golden groundsel: Ria Malloy, University of Maryland Extension.

Wool grass: Mikaela Boley, University of Maryland Extension.

Blue sedge, little bluestem, great blue lobelia: University of Maryland Extension.

Yellow indiangrass: Ajay via Adobe Stock.

Broomsedge: Forest and Kim Starr, Starr Environmental, Bugwood.org.

Wild ginger, foamflower, butterflyweed, alumroot, inkberry holly, winterberry holly, northern bayberry, red chokeberry, eastern redbud: Miri Talabac, University of Maryland Extension.

Lady fern: Courtesy of Andy and Sally Wasowski, Lady Bird Johnson Wildflower Center; used with permission.

Virginia sweetspire: Charles T. Bryson, USDA Agricultural Research Service, bugwood.org

Blackgum: Leonora (Ellie) Enking via Flickr https://www.flickr.com/photos/33037982@N04/

White oak: Joseph O'Brien, USDA Forest Service, Bugwood.org

Wild bergamot: Barbara via Adobe Stock.

Eastern columbine: Rob Routledge, Sault College, Bugwood.org.

New York ironweed: John D. Burd, Mississippi State University, Bugwood.org

Foxglove beardtongue: C. Carignan, University of Maryland Extension.

Rosemallow: Andrew Cannizzaro via Flickr.

Tulip poplar: Pixabay.   Loblolly pines: Pixnio.

22: INVASIVE PLANTS

Ellen Cook Nibali

22 INVASIVE PLANTS

CONTENTS

22.1 About Invasive Species 647

22.2 Invasive Species: Non-Plant 649

22.3 Invasive Species: Plants 652

22.4 Invasive Control Methods 654

22.5 Common Invasive Plants of Maryland 655

LEARNING OBJECTIVES

- The terminology of invasive species, including alien, exotic, native, non-native, and naturalized species
- The damaging impacts of invasive species
- Common characteristics of invasive species
- How to identify and combat invasive species
- Where to report and stay updated on new invasive species

INTRODUCTION

Invasive species are defined as "alien species whose introduction does or is likely to cause economic or environmental harm or harm to human health" (Presidential Executive Order 13112).

These foreign species, also known as exotic or non-native invasive species, can be animal, plant, or other life forms such as viruses. Well-known examples range from snakehead fish, Asian tiger mosquito, and kudzu to diseases such as Dutch elm and West Nile virus. They were brought either accidentally or intentionally from other countries or other regions of the United States into Maryland (or any ecosystem in which they did not evolve).

22.1 About Invasive Species

Most species introduced into a new ecosystem do not become invasive. Even when a few escape into the wild and survive, they do not pose a problem. Invasive species, however, become extremely successful spreaders once they are introduced.

This is possible because they left behind in their land of origin all their natural curbs, such as predators and diseases, which evolved with them and kept their numbers in balance. They capitalize on this advantage, known as enemy release. After gaining a foothold, their populations explode unchecked.

Humans inadvertently contribute to the problem when we alter the natural environment. Some examples:

- Deer populations soar because their natural predators were eliminated by humans and suburban development provides an ideal feeding habitat for them. Because deer evolved eating native plants, they can't digest most non-native invasive plants or don't find them palatable. As deer eat native plants faster than the plants can regenerate, more opportunities open for invasive plants to move in.
- Land-clearing for development alters habitat quality and degrades soil health, allowing invasive species tolerant

UME © 2025. All rights reserved.

22: Invasive Plants   647

of challenging conditions to gain a foothold. Surviving native plants can be stressed by changes and be more vulnerable to attack from non-native pests or diseases.

- Increasing levels of CO_2 spike the growth of many invasive plants at a rate faster than native plants.
- Sometimes, non-native species do not exhibit invasive tendencies or are not seen as invasive until they spread beyond the point of removal.

Why invasive species are important

Since 2010, ash trees (genus *Fraxinus*) in much of the U.S. have been decimated by the invasive Emerald Ash Borer beetle. Ash could become locally extinct if beetle populations don't subside or if trees don't develop resistance. Spotted lanternfly is another example of a high-profile recent invader that is spreading rapidly in the Eastern U.S. This insect can use a wide host plant range.

Invasive species destroy or diminish natural and human environments. Tiger mosquitoes bite aggressively all day, not only in the evening like most native mosquitoes. Invasive plants overrun millions of acres a year, ruining rangelands, clogging waterways, choking agricultural lands, and replacing native plants in parks and natural areas. They alter the ecosystems wildlife depend on, especially threatening many species that depend on a single plant or plant family for survival. Their impact grows until they are stopped.

Why Is this issue emerging now?

Most non-native species that migrated to the U.S. never became a problem —azaleas don't take over neighborhoods, and sheep hordes don't threaten our homes—but invasive species can wreak havoc. Historically, invasive problems were tackled by disparate segments of our society. Farmers attacked weeds, towns replanted street trees killed by Dutch elm disease, park foresters fought woolly adelgid insects killing hemlocks, and doctors developed immunizations. Not until recently did all these impacts get recognized as one problem: invasive species. With Executive Order 13112, a more coordinated approach began.

Why can't nature just handle this?

A few new species have always arrived on our shores naturally (e.g., a storm blew in a bird carrying a seed). A tiny minority of those species was invasive, and eventually brought into balance—maybe a fungus evolved to infect an invasive plant, or a predator evolved new stomach enzymes to digest an invasive insect—but this process can take 100 years or longer. Thousands of species are introduced into the U.S. each year; about 15 percent will become invasive. Their impact is too massive for nature to counter before irreparable damage is done.

What is a Quarantine Protocol?

To restrict the spread of invasive pests and diseases within a state and/or between states, plants or animals may be put under quarantine by state departments of agriculture or the federal Animal and Plant Health Inspection Service (APHIS). Protocols set rules and handling procedures for each quarantined species, such as transport of plants, firewood, etc. A plant infected with sudden oak death or boxwood blight, for example, should NOT be taken to a landfill or moved in an open truck bed, which will spread the disease. Visit the MDA website for information about Maryland quarantines.

22.2 Invasive Species: Non-Plant

The following table is a partial list of non-plant invasive species of concern. See **Chapter 10, IPM** for more invasive pests and diseases.

Table 22-A. Invasive Species: Non-Plant

Invasive Insect Pests of Humans

Image	Insect name	Description
	22A.1 Red fire ant *Solenopsis invicta*	Not currently established in Maryland.
	22A.2 Asian tiger mosquito *Aedes albopictus*	Arrived in Maryland in 1987. Lives in urban and suburban areas. An aggressive daytime biter, it bites quickly and repeatedly. Likes shade and matures in tiny amounts of water in as few as five days. A vector of West Nile virus as well as other diseases. Usually stays within a few hundred yards of the breeding site so eliminating standing water is imperative.

Invasive Insect Pests of Plants

Image	Insect name	Description
Adult / Egg mass	**22A.3 Spotted lanternfly** *Lycoma delicatuma*	First seen in PA in 2014. The large treehopper rapidly spread to several states and is now in many Maryland counties. Lays grayish putty-like egg masses on any surface from trucks to tree trunks, guaranteeing dispersal. Nymphs are spotted black and white, then red, black, and white, maturing into gray-winged adults displaying black, white, and red in flight. Suck juice/sap from a long list of hosts from fruits to native trees. Favors, but is not dependent upon, tree of heaven. Its copious sweet honeydew is repugnant to homeowners and leads to the black sooty mold fungus, which covers leaves and blocks photosynthesis. See HGIC's **Spotted Lanternfly Management for Residents** page for detailed management information.
	22A.4 Asian long-horned beetle *Anoplophora glabripennis*	Kills hardwood trees, including maple, birch, poplar, willow, ash, elm, and black locust. Larval feeding tunnels disrupt phloem and xylem. Look for: 1) perfectly round pencil-sized emergence holes made by adults and 2) unseasonable yellowing or drooping leaves when weather is not especially dry. Not currently established in Maryland.

continued on next page

continued from previous page

Table 22-A. Invasive Species: Non-Plant

Invasive Insect Pests of Plants (continued)

Image	Insect name	Description
	22A.5 Viburnum leaf beetle *Pyrrhalta viburni*	Since 1978, this beetle has killed many native and non-native viburnums. Total defoliation from adults and larvae kills in 1-2 years. Found in Western Maryland in 2020. Prune off twigs with egg masses and destroy them. Eggs are laid in late summer and fall, and may be easiest to find after leaves drop.

Other Invasive Insects	Non-Insect Invertebrates	Vertebrates
Brown marmorated stink bug Hemlock woolly adelgid Spongy moth Oriental beetle Black vine weevil Japanese beetle Pine-shoot beetle (MD quarantine) Spotted wing drosophila	Chinese mitten crab Japanese short crab Green crab Zebra mussel Brown garden snail Asian clam Soybean/corn cyst/root-knot nematodes Virile and rusty crayfish	Canada goose (non-migratory) Northern snakehead fish Grass carp Mute swan Eastern mosquitofish (non-tidal) Nutria

Table 22-A. Invasive Species: Non-Plant

Invasive Diseases of Plants

Image	Disease name	Description
	22A.6 Boxwood blight *Cylindrocladium boxicola*	Fungal disease arrived via Europe in 2011. Fungal leaf spots and narrow black stem cankers lead to rapid defoliation from the bottom up. Fallen leaves remain infectious for years. Sweetbox and pachysandra are also susceptible. Strict sanitation, disease-resistant cultivars, and keeping new boxwood out of established plantings are some management strategies. See the HGIC website for more.
Walnut twig beetles	**22A.7 Thousand-cankers disease** *Geosmithia morbida*	Recently found in East-coast black walnut trees. Fungal disease spread by the walnut twig beetle. The flea-sized reddish-brown beetles make pinhole entries in bark and carry spores into branches and trunks. The fungus makes many small cankers, cumulatively girdling the tree. Scout for crown dieback, bark cracks, branches with yellow or wilting leaves, and tiny exit holes. No cure; Eastern black walnut is highly susceptible and dies quickly once symptoms appear.
	22A.8 Beech leaf disease Caused by the nematode *Litylenchus crenatae*	Only recently discovered to be caused by nematodes. Kills American and other beech in 3 years. First seen in Ohio in 2012 and has already spread to the East coast. Leaves feature banding of dark green between veins. Foliage thins and trees progressively weaken.

continued on next page

continued from previous page

Table 22-A. Invasive Species: Non-Plant

Invasive Diseases of Plants

Image	Disease name	Description
	22A.9 **Sudden oak death** *Phytophthora ramorum*	As of 2020, SOD has been confined largely to the West coast where it was first reported in 1995. It has killed tens of thousands of oaks, but its name is a misnomer. To date, it is known to infect and kill or be host-carried by scores of plants including rhododendron, blueberry, lilac, and viburnum. Stem cankers cause foliage to pale, yellow, brown, and die. On oaks, tip dieback is followed by re-sprouting, dieback, trunk re-sprouting, and death. Leaf spots may have a fuzzier margin than other phytophthora leaf spots. Black or red ooze may bleed from oak bark, staining bark and killing bark moss. Necrotic bark has a black "zone line" under infected bark. Symptoms require confirmation by laboratory tests because other phytophthora diseases exhibit identical symptoms.
	22A.10 **Chestnut blight** *Cryphonectria parasitica*	Early last century this blight wiped out virtually all American chestnuts, once a primary hardwood. The demise began in the early 1800s with ink disease, which killed chestnuts in the south. Chestnut blight appeared in the early 1900s and swept Eastern forests. The American Chestnut Foundation, however, is close to being able to make a blight-resistant American chestnut cultivar available.
	22A.11 **Plum pox virus** *Potyvirus PPV*	Also known as Sharka, this European disease is the most damaging virus of stone fruit in the world. U.S. outbreaks have been contained so far. It is spread by aphids and infected plants, which may show no symptoms. Look for: 1) color-breaking on blossoms, 2) leaves with ring-shaped blotching, chlorosis, or distortion, or 3) ring-shaped blotches on fruit. This disease is not currently established in Maryland.
	22A.12 **Dogwood powdery mildew** *Golovinomyces cichoracearum* & others **Discula anthracnose** *Discula destructive*	An imported version of dogwood powdery mildew is much more infectious and harmful. Resistant varieties have been developed but together these two invasive diseases have tremendously reduced native dogwoods in the U.S., enough to alter ecosystems. Buy resistant cultivars and properly prune them to improve air circulation around branches. Note: Discula is not to be confused with spot anthracnose, which is largely cosmetic.

Other Invasive Plant Diseases

Daylily rust • Southern bacterial wilt • Dutch elm disease

22.3 Invasive Species: Plants

From national and local parks to our own backyards, native plants are being slowly replaced by weeds. Some parks are now 90 percent non-native invasive plants. Master Gardeners can have a profound impact by combating invasive plants on their own properties, whether landscaped or natural, on public lands, and by adding natives. In a backyard, an invasive may seem just a nuisance but in a natural ecosystem, they are devastating.

Damaging impact of invasive plants

Invasive plants out-compete and displace native plants, which are critical links in our ecosystem. All native species, from bacteria to mammals, ultimately need native plants because their food web evolved dependent upon them. Birds, for instance, at some point in their life cycle, feed on insects and insects can eat only those plants that their stomach enzymes evolved to digest. If those plants are not present, the insects die and the birds go hungry. They cannot suddenly "evolve" enzymes to eat non-native plants any more than starving humans can suddenly switch to a diet of plastic. A large percentage of species are dependent on a single plant or plant family. Some invasive plants confuse insects, seeming to be a familiar food source, then poison or starve them.

Invasive species interfere with natural succession, potentially halting the progression of meadows to shrublands and eventually to forests. Human intervention, in the form of controlled burns, selective herbicide use, or other measures to remove invasive species, tend to be needed to reset natural habitat progression.

In addition, native plants are a treasure trove of chemicals with potential uses for humankind. The active ingredient in aspirin, for example, was discovered in willows. Our native plant species have not all been identified yet (much less researched) for possible benefits to humanity.

Characteristics that aid aggressiveness

Besides leaving behind diseases and predators that once curbed their spread, invasive plants share other characteristics which give them an advantage:

- **Fast growth rate.** We don't call it "Mile-a-minute" vine for nothing. Kudzu is the ultimate example.

- **Super-tolerant.** They flourish in a wide range of conditions, especially difficult ones. They thrive in disturbed soils, a by-product of development and human activities.

- **Long growth period.** Many are the first to green up in the spring, last to go dormant in fall, or only go semi-dormant in the winter and continue to photosynthesize.

- **Monopolize water and nutrients.** Their dense root systems out-compete others. Little can grow under a Norway maple, except Norway maple seedlings.

- **Block out the sun.** Their dense foliage shades out plants on the ground. Invasive vines climb over foliage and shade it to death.

- **Strangle/topple other plants.** Invasive vines can girdle trees, and their weight can pull them down.

- **Have multiple means of reproduction.** They sometimes employ several at a time, e.g., multiflora rose multiplies via rose hip seeds, layering, and re-sprouting from roots. Garlic mustard can set seed at the same time it is flowering.

- **Prolific seed production and/or birds spread the seeds.** One purple loosestrife plant can set over a million seeds.
- **High germination rate.** Rates can reach almost 100 percent.
- **Long seed viability.** Mimosa seeds stay viable for 50 years.
- **Hard to eliminate.** This includes mammoth root systems that store huge quantities of energy for regrowth (such as kudzu) or an ability to re-sprout when cut down or from a small piece of root.
- **Monoculture.** Invasives can exclude all native plants. Some monocultures are made up of one invasive plant, such as millions of acres infested with phragmites grass.

Ecological change caused by invasives

Fire regimens. For example, some non-native prairie grasses burn more easily than native ones, causing wildfires to occur more frequently than native plants have evolved to withstand. Other invasive grasses burn more slowly than natives, exposing native plants to fire for longer periods than they can endure. Invasive vines that burn easily can carry fire to tree tops where fire resistance has not developed, killing the tree canopy.

Geomorphologic processes (erosion/sedimentation). Invasives with poor root systems allow soil to be eroded. Conversely, grass that does not decompose like native grass (such as phragmites) can fill in wetlands and create dry land.

Hydrology regimens. Invasive plants with water-greedy roots deny water to native species.

Reproductive ecology. Pollen of invasive plants can be sticky. When spread by pollinators, it can clog native flower reproductive parts. Invasive flowers draw pollinators away from natives. Pollinators may be drawn to foreign pollen and neglect native pollination. Likewise, birds can be attracted more to "junk food" seed/berries of invasives than native plants, slowing the spread of native seeds.

Nutrition. Native wildlife can be drawn to eat "tastier" invasive plant parts that do not provide their necessary nutrition, such as when birds need fat for migration but eat sweet berries instead. Also, invasives out-compete and eliminate wildlife's normal food sources.

Soil ecology. Invasive plants can change the microbes and enzymes in the soil in as little as three months. Their soil changes make the soil more beneficial to the invasive and less beneficial to natives adapted to the original soil. Some examples:

- **Change leaf litter depth.** Invasives may decompose quickly so there is not enough duff to protect tender plant roots, or they may decompose too slowly, smothering small plants and preventing native seeds from germinating.
- **Change pH.** For example, barberry can raise soil pH from 4.5 to 7.6.
- **Change availability of nitrogen in soil.** An invasive plant may decompose faster

or slower, changing normal soil fertility levels as a result.

Ways for Master Gardeners to help

Don't introduce invasive plants

- Don't plant invasive species and don't share their seeds, cuttings, or divisions with others.
- Avoid nursery plants with weeds that might be invasive. Unidentified causes of pest damage or disease symptoms should also be avoided in case those organisms are not already locally established.
- Don't accidentally transport them. Remove seeds on muddy shoes and burrs stuck on clothes.
- Avoid disturbing soils unnecessarily; invasives are quick to colonize. Quickly replant bare soil with desirable plants.

Detect and remove invasive plants

- Learn which plants in your home landscape may be invasive and replace them.
- Watch out for new and emerging invasive species. Save samples and report them to your Extension office.
- Report fast-spreading or unusual plant species, pests, or diseases that raise a red flag.
- Report sightings of invasive plants in parks to the managing agency.
- Support community efforts to clear invasive plants and restore native plants. The effects of a one-time removal can last for decades.

Encourage native plants

- Increase the use of natives in landscapes, which also increases native seed and gene pools. A landscape of at least 50 percent natives makes a huge difference in bird survival.
- Set aside untouched natural areas to preserve native genotypes.
- Support deer control where over-population is decimating native plants.
- Replace invasive plants with natives or, at least, non-invasive plants.

Educate yourself and others

- Encourage local nurseries to stock native plants, particularly local genotypes.
- Learn to identify local invasive plants and how to distinguish them from similar-looking native species.
- Bring nurseries' attention to invasive stock and invasive weeds in pots.
- Keep up with emerging invasives like the bee-bee tree. Check the HGIC and MD Invasive Species Council websites and share news with others.

The Maryland Noxious Weeds program includes some invasive plants. These are agricultural problems, and landowners are legally required to manage them for "effective control." Designated weeds are: Johnsongrass, shattercane, Canada thistle, musk thistle, plumeless thistle, and bull thistle.

22.4 Invasive Control Methods

For complete details and control information, go to invasives.org or the HGIC website.

Mechanical methods

Burn (B). Use controlled fires to destroy above-ground growth. (First contact your local fire department.)

Cut and grind (C&G). Cut down the tree/plant, then grind the stump.

Cut/Mow/re-Cut (C/M/reC). Cut to the ground and re-cut at the first appearance of new growth. This starves the root system. It may require persistence.

Flower/Seed removal (F/S). Do not allow seed development. Cut off flowers before seed forms. Some plants flower and produce seed at the same time. Bag and dispose of seeds in landfills. DO NOT compost.

Girdle (G). Remove the bark and cambium layer around the trunk. Remove (or spray) re-sprouting from roots or below the girdled trunk.

Pull/Dig (P/D). This is especially effective with seedlings or annuals. Mile-a-minute vine, for instance, has almost no root system. For plants that can re-sprout from a tiny root piece, such as Canada thistle, removal of entire root is critical so this method is recommended for only small seedlings. Moist soil helps.

Smother (SM). Cover plants with cardboard, many layers of newspapers, or plastic, then mulch. (Plastic must be removed eventually and, if mulch decomposes on it, this can be an arduous process.)

Weed Wrench™ (WW). This tool can uproot large shrubs and small trees.

Chemical options

Cut & Paint or Spray (C&P/S). Cut down trunk and paint or spray the stump within five minutes with herbicide.

Hack & Squirt (H&S). Slash bark using a saw or hatchet, and squirt liquid herbicide into the wounds.

Post-emergent herbicide (PostE). Spray foliage of perennial/woody plants. Spot-treat in lawns.

Pre-emergent herbicide (PreE). Applied as a granular or liquid herbicide prior to weed seed germination.

Biological controls

Biological controls are organisms from the plant's natural range that feed on it, infect it, or otherwise keep its population in check. The organism undergoes extensive testing before being released here to ensure that it will target only the invasive plant and no other. For example, an insect was located and raised in mass quantities, then released to eat mile-a-minute vine. ❋

22.5 Common Invasive Plants of Maryland

The tables on the following pages contain photos and descriptions of common invasive trees, shrubs, groundcovers/vines, and grasses in Maryland. For a comprehensive list, see the **HGIC** or **Maryland Invasive Species Council** website.

Table 22-B. Common Invasive Trees

Tier 1: Cannot be sold. **Tier II:** Plant requires signage near retail displays. **X** = No restrictions yet. Abbreviations for control methods are fully explained in **22.4, Invasive Control Methods.**

Image	Plant name	Controls	Tier	Description
	22B.1 Bradford, callery, or ornamental pear *Pyrus calleryana*	P/D WW G C&P/S C&G	II	Developed as a sterile cultivar, the Bradford's collapsing branch structure led to the introduction of more cultivars. Cross-pollination resulted in fertile offspring with berry-sized fertile fruit. It spreads rapidly to disturbed and natural areas, displacing natives and disrupting natural succession. Seedlings may grow long thorns.
	22B.2 Empress or princess tree *Paulownia tomentosa*	P/D F/S G H&S P/S C&G PostE	X	Highly valued in Asia, but here its fast growth rate makes wood worthless for export. It invades via seeds (up to 20 million per tree) and persistent suckering from the stump or roots. Astonishing seedling growth rate. Requires some sun, otherwise highly competitive.
	22B.3 Mimosa *Albizia julibrissin*	P/D G H&S C&P/S	X	Native from Iran to Japan, the "silk tree" was introduced for its ferny foliage, pink summer flowers, and fast maturity. Pods produce high seed volume, viable for up to 50 yrs. Nitrogen-fixing pea-family member. Flourishes in poor soils but needs some sun. Primarily a threat to meadows and along water and roadways. Will re-sprout.
	22B.4 Norway maple *Acer platanoides*	P/D C&P/S H&S G	X	Eurasian tree with extremely dense shade and root competition which suppress most growth underneath, except its own seedlings. Milky sap unlike sugar maples, which it out-competes. Its typical paired seeds grow straight out, facing each other. Leaves turn late in fall. Its shade-tolerant seedlings out-compete natives and create monocultures.
	22B.5 Sawtooth oak *Quercus acutissima*	P/D PostE G C&G C&P/S H&S	X	This Asian oak produces acorns at a much earlier age than native oaks. Planted for wild game, it out-competes native oaks. Leaves are entire, not lobed, with spine-tipped serrations. The acorn cap is shaggy. Treat re-growth and replace with native oaks.

continued on next page

continued from previous page

Table 22-B. Common Invasive Trees

Tier 1: Cannot be sold. **Tier II:** Plant requires signage near retail displays. **X** = No restrictions yet. Abbreviations for control methods are fully explained in **22.4, Invasive Control Methods.**

Image	Plant name	Controls	Tier	Description
	22B.6 Siberian elm *Ulmus pumila*	P/D C/M&reC C&G C&P/S G H&S WW	X	This Asian elm was meant to replace American elms killed by Dutch elm disease. (Disease-resistant American elms are now available.) Features rapid growth and copious seeds, taking tough conditions and disturbed soils. It can displace American elms. Inhibits growth under its canopy. Key identifiers are small leaves (1-21/2 in.), even leaf base, and single serrations, unlike the double serrations of native American elm and slippery elm.
	22B.7 Tree of heaven *Ailanthus altissima*	P/D C&P/S H&S PostE See description for details	X	Fast-growing native of China survives the worst conditions. Crushed leaves and all other parts have a rank odor described as "rotten peanut butter." Often confused with native trees. Long, compound leaves resemble walnut, but TOH bark is smooth and gray like sumac. Prominent leaf scars. Yellow-green flowers on female trees produce clumps of papery samara seeds from late summer to early fall. Seed clusters turn brown and hang through winter. Root toxins kill competing plants. Suckers create monoculture colonies. Cutting only stimulates new sprouts. P/D only the youngest trees and get all fragments; C&P/S with maximum-strength triclopyr or glyphosate; H&S (max. 1-in. gap between cuts); PostE (spray re-growth). Also, in Feb./Mar. apply triclopyr or Garlon® to lower trunk bark.
	22B.8 White mulberry *Morus alba*	P/D C/MreC G C&P/S C&G	X	Introduced from Asia during the colonial period as food for silkworms (a failed industry). White mulberry hybridized with native red mulberry (which had far better fruit) and transmitted a fatal root rot. It has both lobed and unlobed leaves. Invades natural areas.

Table 22-C. Common Invasive Shrubs

Tier 1: Cannot be sold. **Tier II:** Plant requires signage near retail displays. **X** = No restrictions yet. Abbreviations for control methods are fully explained in **22.4, Invasive Control Methods.**

Image	Plant name	Controls	Tier	Description
	22C.1 Autumn olive *Elaeagnus umbellata*	P/D (include all roots) C&P/S PostE	X	Large shrub/small tree first planted extensively for wildlife habitat, windbreak, and land reclamation. Flourishes in very poor/disturbed soils. It has invaded fields and open woodlands, out-competing native plants, creating dense shade, disrupting plant succession and nutrient-cycling. Birds feed on the berries; insects and other animals are not known to feed on it.
	22C.2 Japanese barberry *Berberis thunbergii*	P/D F/S WW C/MreC PostE C&P/S	II	Promoted when European barberry was found to host black stem rust on wheat. Its popularity soared with purple and yellow cultivars. Tolerant of shade or sun and produces berries with a germination rate of near 90%. It has spread to most habitats. Sprouts from root pieces or tip roots and alters ecosystems by raising soil pH, changing nitrogen levels and bio activity, and reducing litter depth. Deer avoid it in favor of native shrubs, so it is becoming the main understory plant in parks/natural areas. Barberry host more deer ticks and higher rates of Lyme disease-infected ticks.
	22C.3 Winged euonymus/ burning bush *Euonymus alatus*	P/D F/S C/MreC C&P/S	II	Berries of this Asian ornamental invade sunny or shady habitats where it can form monocultures. Virtually nothing grows underneath except its own seedlings. Do not confuse with native euonymus (strawberry bush or hearts-a-burstin') which does not have corky ridges or "wings" on the stems.
	22C.4 Honeysuckle (Amur, Bell's dwarf, fragrant, Morrow's, Standish's, Tartarian) *Lonicera* species	P/D C/M/reC C&P/S PostE B	I (Amur)	Non-native, hollow-stemmed Eurasian shrubs once planted for flowers, fruit, and erosion control. They displace natives and form monocultures. Birds love the carb-rich berries but they lack the fat needed for long migrations. Flowers compete with natives for pollinators, reducing native seed set. Root toxins may inhibit other plants. Like barberry, infestations promote more deer ticks and Lyme disease-infected ticks.

continued on next page

continued from previous page

Table 22-C. Common Invasive Shrubs

Tier 1: Cannot be sold. **Tier II:** Plant requires signage near retail displays. **X** = No restrictions yet. Abbreviations for control methods are fully explained in **22.4, Invasive Control Methods.**

Image	Plant name	Controls	Tier	Description
	22C.5 **Multiflora rose** *Rosa multiflora*	P/D C/M/reC PostE (with spreader sticker) C&P/S	X	Asian rose that chokes out natives. Flowers are white (native roses are usually pink). It grows impenetrable stands in sun or shade and can climb trees. Disturbed or neglected areas are quickly colonized. Birds spread the seeds. Branches root if they contact soil.
	22C.6 **Privet** All *Ligustrum* species	P/D PostE C&P/S	II (Border)	Grown primarily for hedges, privet has escaped to many habitats. Needs sun to produce berries and multiply from seed. Its dense thickets out-compete native plants.
	22C.7 **Wineberry** *Rubus phoenicolasius*	P/D C/M/reC C&P/S	X	Raspberry-like fruits. Still used as breeding stock. In the wild, it grows fast and forms thickets, crowding out natives over broad areas. Distinguished from other bramble canes by red hairs among small spines, which make the cane appear red and almost furry. Prefers moist soils and sun but is adaptable. Spreads by berry seed and tip-rooting.

Table 22-D. Common Invasive Vines and Groundcovers

Tier 1: Cannot be sold. **Tier II:** Plant requires signage near retail displays. **X** = No restrictions yet. Abbreviations for control methods are fully explained in **22.4, Invasive Control Methods.**

Image	Plant name	Controls	Tier	Description
	22D.1 **English ivy** *Hedera helix*	P/D F/S SM C/M/reC PostE C&P/S	X	Of Eurasian origin, not English. Evergreen vine shades out seedlings and herbs, forming acres of monoculture that attracts rodents. Engulfs tree branches, slowly killing them. Its weight topples trees in storms. Harbors bacterial leaf scorch, a serious disease of maples, oaks, and elms. Mature vines flower and bear toxic berries which birds excrete. Rooted pieces can re-sprout. Waxy leaves repel herbicides so apply in high concentrations with a spreader-sticker.

continued on next page

continued from previous page

Table 22-D. Common Invasive Vines and Groundcovers

Tier 1: Cannot be sold. **Tier II:** Plant requires signage near retail displays. X = No restrictions yet. Abbreviations for control methods are fully explained in **22.4, Invasive Control Methods**.

Image	Plant name	Controls	Tier	Description
	22D.2 Mile-a-minute vine, devil's tear-thumb *Polygonum perfoliatum*	P/D F/S PostE	X	Barbed annual Asian vine can grow in sun/shade to 25 ft. Bright blue berries are spread widely by birds. Quickly shades and smothers plants. Has almost no root system, so pulling it is easy. Releasing insects which feed only on Mile-a-minute slows, but does not stop it.
	22D.3 Kudzu *Pueraria montana var. lobata*	C/M/reC C&P/S	X	"The vine that ate the South" was promoted as livestock forage, an ornamental, and erosion control until the 1950s. Incredible growth rate of 1 ft./day and 60 ft./season. Roots weigh up to 400 lbs. Pods produce some viable seed, but reproduction is primarily vegetative. Up to 30 shoots grow from 1 crown and root where nodes touch soil. Cutting and mowing must continue for two seasons or more. Penned goats can exhaust the root system by grazing. Herbicides are most effective in early fall.
	22D.4 Oriental bittersweet *Celastrus orbiculatus*	P/D F/S C/M/reC C&P/S	X	Asian vine has nearly replaced native species by out-competing and hybridizing with it. Woody vines can smother trees and even topple them. Orange berries are spread by birds and humans who find them decorative. Leaves are both round or with points. Orange-red roots provide fast identification when pulling its myriad seedlings. Can sucker and root where suckers touch soil.
	22D.5 Porcelainberry *Ampelopsis brevipedunculata*	P/D C&P/S	X	Introduced for colorful berries. Woody Asian vine climbs over shrubs and trees, shading and killing them. Leaves resemble grape leaves, but bark does not peel like grape-vine bark. Invades full-sun or semi-shade areas with moist (not wet) soils.
	22D.6 Wintercreeper, creeping euonymus *Euonymus fortunei*	P/D F/S C/M/reC C&P/S	I	Evergreen vine forms dense ground mats, excluding low native plants. Also climbs trees. Tolerant of good or poor soils and both sun and dense shade. Spreads vegetatively and by berries.

continued on next page

continued from previous page

Table 22-D. Common Invasive Vines and Groundcovers

Tier 1: Cannot be sold. **Tier II:** Plant requires signage near retail displays. **X** = No restrictions yet. Abbreviations for control methods are fully explained in **22.4, Invasive Control Methods.**

Image	Plant name	Controls	Tier	Description
	22D.7 **Vinca, periwinkle** *Vinca major*	P/D C/M/reC C&P/S	X	Provides evergreen foliage, quick growth, and lilac-to-white flowers in spring. Crowds out wildflowers and herbaceous natives if it escapes. Spreads by rooting nodes/tips and root pieces. Hard to eliminate.
	22D.8 **Wavyleaf basketgrass** *Oplismenus hirtellus* ssp. *undulatifolius*	P/D PostE	X	Eurasian bright-green shade perennial. Engulfs forest floors in a solid mat. Wide-bladed leaves alternate along low-lying stems. Unusual leaves have ripples like a flag in the wind. Stems and roots where nodes touch soil are visibly hairy (unlike native basketgrass). In fall, seeds with sticky tips attach to animals, humans, even rubber boots.
	22D.9 **Japanese wisteria** *Wisteria floribunda* **Chinese wisteria** *Wisteria sinensis* **Hybrid wisteria** *Wisteria x formosa* *(floribunda x sinensis)*	P/D (when young) F/S C/M/reC PostE C&P/S WW	II	Differences: The Japanese variety flowers in May-June with panicles up to 18 in. long. The flowers can be white, pink, and even pale blue, and appear when the leaves begin developing. The Chinese variety flowers primarily in May with clusters up to 12 in. long. They are usually either lilac-colored or white. The flowers open before leaves appear. The hybrid is usually white or pale pink and feature the longer panicles of the Japanese variety. Leaves/flowers appear together. Because of its spectacular flowers, this ornamental has been widely planted. It has escaped to natural areas and its woody vines strangle and shade out foliage, killing trees. Reproduces from seeds in fuzzy pods, from stems touching the ground, and from any bit of root left in the ground. Cut vines must be bagged and disposed of without touching soil. After cutting down to ground level, vines must be unwrapped from tree trunks or they will still girdle trees. Replace with native wisteria.

Table 22-E. Common Invasive Herbaceous Plants

Tier 1: Cannot be sold. **Tier II:** Plant requires signage near retail displays. **X** = No restrictions yet. Abbreviations for control methods are fully explained in **22.4, Invasive Control Methods.**

Image	Plant name	Controls	Tier	Description
	22E.1 **Canada thistle** *Cirsium arvense* **Bull thistle** *Cirsium vulgare*	P/D (youngest seedling) F/S C/M/reC PostE	X	European thistles, perennial and biennial respectively. Noxious weeds in Maryland. Prefer full sun and quickly form dense patches, possibly aided by root toxins. A threat to agriculture as well as natural ecosystems. Overtake any non-forested area, from dry to wet. Perennial root system holds huge energy reserves. Tap roots send out side roots up to 3 ft. and can regenerate from a 1-in. piece. Hand-pulling only possible with youngest seedlings in moist pliable soil. Pink to purple flowers produce fluffy wind-borne seeds that stay viable for up to 20 yrs.
	Ground ivy, creeping charlie *Glechoma hederacea*	–	X	Lawn weed. See photo **13C.6** in the Weeds chapter and refer to the **Weed Management section** for controls.
	Red (purple) deadnettle *Lamium purpureum*	–	X	Lawn weed. See photo **13C.47** in the Weeds chapter and refer to the **Weed Management section** for controls.
	22E.2 **Garlic mustard** *Alliaria petiolata* *Alliaria officinalis*	P/D F/S (before seed ripens) C/M/reC PostE	II	Biennial Eurasian herb brought by settlers for food/medicine. The first year, it is a low rosette. Second-year stems reach 3-4 ft. White flowers produce skinny seed capsules which propel seeds that are viable for up to 5 yrs. It can also re-sprout from root fragments. Invades woods, stream banks, and roadsides in sun or shade. Crowds out native plants. Especially damaging to spring wildflowers and wildlife dependent on them as sources of nectar, pollen, and foliage. Ignored by deer. Threatens extinction of the rare W. Virginia white butterfly, which feeds on mustard-family wildflowers/foliage. Garlic mustard replaces these native wildflowers and, when the butterfly lays its eggs on garlic mustard foliage, a leaf toxin prevents egg hatch.
	Henbit *Lamium amplexicaule*	–	X	Lawn weed. See photo **13C.46** in the Weeds chapter and refer to the **Weed Management section** for controls.

continued on next page

continued from previous page

Table 22-E. Common Invasive Herbaceous Plants

Tier 1: Cannot be sold. **Tier II:** Plant requires signage near retail displays. **X** = No restrictions yet. Abbreviations for control methods are fully explained in **22.4, Invasive Control Methods.**

Image	Plant name	Controls	Tier	Description
	Indian mock strawberry *Duchesnea indica*	–	X	Lawn weed. See photo **13C.10** in the Weeds chapter and refer to the **Weed Management section** for controls.
	22E.3 Japanese knotweed, Mexican bamboo *Reynoutria japonica*	P/D (young) F/S SM (black plastic) PostE C&P/S	X	Hollow shoots have bamboo-like joints and stems. Aggressive roots penetrate 2-3 ft. and form thickets 6-8 ft. tall. Grows in sun/shade and dry, wet, even salty, soils. Threatens riparian areas where it withstands severe floods. Root fragments spread via fill dirt. Seed travels in shoe treads.
	22E.4 Lesser celandine, celandine buttercup *Ficaria verna*	P/D PostE (must be in leaf)	I	European perennial with 8-petal yellow flowers. Blooms in early spring. Rapidly creates a dense mat that blocks emerging wildflowers. Small bulblets are easily dislodged and carried, with tuberous roots, downstream by high waters. Favors wet areas. Remove entire plant. Caution: Distinguish from native marsh marigold. Similar leaves, yellow 5-9 petaled flower atop 8-in. stem. Same mat-forming habit. No bulblets or tubers.
	22E.5 Mints (herb) *Mentha spp.*	P/D F/S PostE	X	Herb mints (some lawn weeds are also mints) grow rampantly in natural areas, crowding out natives. Spread by seed, roots, and runners, and will sprout from root pieces. Grow herbal mints in containers.
	22E.6 Purple loosestrife *Lythrum salicaria*	P/D F/S PostE	X	"Purple Plague" can grow to 10 ft. Mature plants sprout 30-50 stems that flower June-Sept. and can produce 2-3 million seeds/yr. Invades ANY wetland, forcing out native plants critical to wildlife and habitat, threatening some plants with extinction. Plants sold as sterile are not. Beneficial insects showing some results in the Midwest.
	22E.7 Spotted knapweed *Centaurea stoebe* ssp. *micranthos* **Yellow star thistle** *Centaurea solstitialis*	P/D PostE C/M/reC (below leaf area)	X	Asters of Eurasian and African origin. Strong tap roots and abundant seed. Invades sunny fields and wood edges and out-competes natives. Yellow star thistle not extensive in MD yet. Can cause horse death if ingested. Use certified weed-free hay. Clean seed from clothes, shoes, and tires prior to leaving area.

Table 22-F. Common Invasive Grasses

Tier 1: Cannot be sold. **Tier II:** Plant requires signage near retail displays. **X** = No restrictions yet. Abbreviations for control methods are fully explained in **22.4, Invasive Control Methods.**

Image	Plant name	Controls	Tier	Description
	22F.1 Bamboo *Phyllostachys* and *Pseudosasa* spp.	C&P/S (timing is crucial)	II	Running species (leptomorphs) spread extensively and rapidly with far-reaching rhizomes; clumping types (pachymorphs) remain self-contained. Rhizome barriers can corral running specimens but will not prevent seeding (although rare) and must be carefully monitored for breaches. Do not confuse running bamboo with giant cane (*Arundinaria gigantean*), the native bamboo of Southern Maryland.
	22F.2 Giant reed *Arundo donax*	C/M/reC PostE (after flowering)		Native Indian perennial grass towers up to 20 ft. or more. Once an ornamental and used for erosion control, it tolerates saltwater. Displaces native wetland plants and obstructs waterways. Spread by rhizome and stem pieces transported by water. Digging contributes to spread.
	22F.3 Miscanthus, Japanese/Chinese silvergrass *Miscanthus sinensis*	P/D (young) PostE (fall or late spring)		New cultivars' seed matures earlier, creating more wind-spread. Clumps widen by rhizome and re-sprout from roots. Thickets arise in disturbed soils, neglected fields, roadsides, and other sunny habitats. Flammable/fire hazard.
	22F.4 Phragmites, common reed *Phragmites australis* ssp. *australis*	B PostE (after flowering) C&P/S (after flowering)	X	Non-native reeds have spread along the East Coast for centuries, displacing millions of wetland plants, including native reeds. Natives grow in sparse clumps and easily decompose; European reeds form impenetrable monocultures 15 ft. tall, with old and new canes. Infested wetlands become dry fire hazards and wildlife habitat is destroyed. Roots extend 10 ft./season. Wind/water carry seed and root fragments everywhere. Burning of biomass after cutting benefits reestablishment of natives. Chemical control is currently the only way but biological controls are being explored.
	Japanese stiltgrass *Microstegium vimineum*	–	X	Lawn weed. See **photo** in the Weeds chapter and refer to the **Weed Management section** for controls.

Other Tier I and Tier II plants considered invasive in Maryland

TIER I: Plant cannot be sold
Fig buttercup (*Ficaria verna*)
Shining cranesbill (*Geranium lucidum*)
Yellow flag iris (*Iris pseudacorus*)
Incised fumewort (*Corydalis incisa*)

TIER II: Plant requires signage near retail displays
Scotch broom (*Cytisus scopoarius*)
Bee-bee tree (*Tetradium daniellii*)
Japanese angelica tree (*Aralia elata*)

ADDITIONAL RESOURCES

Mid-Atlantic Invaders Tool: invasive.org/midatlantic/

Maryland Invasive Plants Prevention and Control (Maryland Department of Agriculture): mda.maryland.gov/plants-pests/Pages/maryland_invasive_plants_prevention_and_control.aspx

Common Invasive Plants Easy ID Cards (Maryland DNR): dnr.maryland.gov/wildlife/Documents/Invasive_plants_cards.pdf

Mistaken Identity? Invasive Plants and Their Native Look-Alikes: nybg.org/files/scientists/rnaczi/Mistaken_Identity_Final.pdf

Invasive Species Terminology (Journal of Extension): archives.joe.org/joe/2020june/a3.php

AUTHOR

Ellen Cook Nibali, CPH, Horticulture Consultant, University of Maryland Extension, retired.

PUBLICATIONS

Nibali, Ellen and E. Marlatt. 2003. *Invasive Plant Control in Maryland.* HG #88. University of Maryland Extension.

Swearingen, Jill, K. Reshetiloff, B. Slattery, and S.M. Zwicker. 2002. *Plant Invaders of Mid-Atlantic Natural Areas.* National Park Service and U.S. Fish and Wildlife Service. bugwoodcloud.org/imageSites/pdf/midatlantic-web.pdf

Thompson, Louisa. 1999. *Control of Invasive Non-Native Plants: A Guide for Gardeners and Homeowners in the Mid-Atlantic Region.* Maryland Native Plant Society. mdflora.org/Resources/Publications/control_of_invasive_plants

WEBSITES

Maryland Invasive Species Council (includes "Invasive Species of Concern in Maryland" brochure) mdinvasivesp.org

PHOTOS (+ = BUGWOOD.ORG)

Main chapter photo: + James H. Miller & Ted Bodner, Southern Weed Science Society.

22A.1. Judy Gallagher via Flickr https://www.flickr.com/photos/52450054@N04/

22A.2. Susan Ellis, University of Maryland Extension.

22A.3. + Lawrence Barringer, Pennsylvania Department of Agriculture.

22A.4. + Dennis Haugen, USDA Forest Service.

22A.5. Svetliy via Adobe Stock.

22A.6. David A. Clement, University of Maryland Extension.

22A.7. + Ned Tisserat/Whitney Cranshaw, Colorado State University.

22A.8. Finger Lakes Invasives. Used with permission.

22A.9. + Joseph O'Brien, USDA Forest Service.

22A.10. Pixabay.

22A.11. Jiri Sochor, Petr Babula, Vojtech Adam, Boris Krska, and Rene Kizek via Wikimedia Creative Commons https://commons.wikimedia.org/wiki/File:Viruses-04-02853-g001.png.

22A.12. + Dogwood powedery mildew- John Hartman, University of Kentucky. Discula anthracnose- Terry S. Price, Georgia Forestry Commission

22B.1, 22B.5, 22 B.7 (foliage). + Chuck Bargeron, U. of Georgia.

22B.2, 22C.1, 22C.5, 22C.6, 22D.5, 22D.6. + James H. Miller, USDA Forest Service.

22B.3. + John D. Byrd, Mississippi State University.

22B.4. + Bill Cook, Michigan State University.

22B.6. + Steve Dewey, Utah State University.

22B.7 (Tree of Heaven bark). + Paul Wray, Iowa State University. (Walnut bark) Nahhan via Adobe Stock.

22B.8. Kaitlyn Baligush.

22C.2, 22C.3, 22D.1. + Leslie J. Mehrhoff, University of Connecticut.

22C.4. + Warner Park Nature Center Archive.

22C.7. + Jill Swearingen, USDA National Park Service.

22D.2, 22D.5. + USDA APHIS PPQ Archive.

22D.3. + David J. Moorhead, U. of Georgia.

22D.4. Betty Marose, University of Maryland Extension.

22D.7. + Forest and Kim Starr, Starr Environmental.

22D.8. Miri Talabac.

22D.9. (Chinese wistera) + Whitney Cranshaw, Colorado State University, (Japnese wisteria) Cliff via Wikimedia Commons https://commons.wikimedia.org/wiki/File:Japanese_Wisteria_(Wisteria_floribunda)_%22Nuda%22_(3501616733).jpg#file (Hybrid wisteria) František Pleva, public domain.

23: INDOOR PLANTS

Stephanie Pully
Jean Burchfield

23 INDOOR PLANTS

CONTENTS

23.1 Selecting Indoor Plants 669

23.2 Requirements for Healthy Indoor Plants 669

23.3 Maintenance Tips 674

23.4 Repotting Indoor Plants 675

23.5 Moving Indoor Plants Outdoors 677

23.6 Bringing Plants Back Indoors 678

23.7 Indoor Plant Pest and Disease Diagnostics 678

23.8 Toxic Indoor Plants... 679

LEARNING OBJECTIVES

- How to choose the correct indoor plants for your growing environment
- Optimal growing conditions for various indoor plants
- Proper care and acclimating procedures for indoor plants
- Common issues when caring for indoor plants

INTRODUCTION

Indoor plants are an excellent way for those who lack outdoor space to still experience all the joy and benefits of gardening. There are multiple plant options for all types of indoor growing conditions. Some hearty indoor plants that are good for beginners are cacti, succulents, begonias (*Begonia* spp.), ZZ plants (*Zamioculcas zamiifolia*), snake plants (*Sansevieria*), pothos, philodendron, and pilea.

23.1 Selecting Indoor Plants

When you shop for new indoor plants, remember that your first task is to select plants that can best withstand the particular conditions inside your home. You'll have better success if your plants require the environmental conditions your residence has to offer, rather than to try to alter the environment to suit the plants. Any plant that merely tolerates your environment may do reasonably well, but will likely never thrive.

There are a number of important factors to consider when selecting an indoor plant. Pay particular attention to each plant's light requirements. Make sure that plants are healthy by checking the undersides of the foliage and the axils of leaves for signs of insects or disease.

Select plants which:

- Appear to be free of insects and diseases
- Have new flowers and leaf buds along with young growth
- Show healthy foliage

Avoid plants which have:

- Yellow or chlorotic leaves
- Brown leaf margins
- Wilted foliage
- Spots or blotches
- Spindly growth

While plants with the most open blooms look the most attractive, instead consider selecting plants with buds that are just ready to open. That way you can enjoy the blooms longer before they start to fade.

23.2 Requirements for Healthy Indoor Plants

Light, water, temperature, humidity, ventilation, fertilization, and potting medium are the chief factors affecting a plant's growth, whether it's indoors or outdoors. Excesses of or deficiencies in any one of these factors can prevent a plant from growing properly indoors. See **Table 23-A** for a list of common houseplants and their main cultural requirements.

Light

Light is probably the most essential factor for indoor plant growth. The energy derived from photosynthesis, along with the plant's growth and health, all depend on the amount of intercepted light.

Indoor plants can be classified according to their light requirements: bright, average (sometimes called "medium"), or low. The three important aspects of indoor light are intensity, duration, and quality. Each has a different impact on the plant.

Intensity

- Dependent upon the distance of the light source from the plant.
- Decreases rapidly with increasing distance.

> **About light deficiency**
>
> A geranium will appear spindly or "leggy," with light green leaves and diminished flowering when grown in low light. The same plant grown in bright light will be more compact, better branched, and have larger, dark-green leaves.
>
> Many indoor plants fail after a healthy start because of inadequate light but others are tolerant of a wide range of light intensity. Choose plants according to the light conditions in your home.

Figure 23-A. Indoor Plant Light Guide

Indoor plants require different light intensities and hours of exposure, depending upon where they are placed.

- Influences the manufacture of plant food, stem length, leaf color, and flowering.
- Affected by the direction your windows face. "Low light" is from north-facing windows or artificially-lit rooms; "average light" is from east- or west-facing windows; and "bright light" is through a south-facing window that receives at least six hours of light.
- Influenced by other factors like the presence of curtains, weather, seasons of the year, shade from trees and other buildings, and the cleanliness and type of window.
- Increased by reflective, light-colored surfaces inside the room.

Duration

- The length of time the plant receives light.

670 Maryland Master Gardener Handbook UME © 2025. All rights reserved.

- Important for indoor plants that are photoperiod sensitive. Poinsettia, kalanchoe, and Christmas cactus will bud and flower only when day-length is short (11 hours of daylight or less).
- Plants receiving low-light intensity respond to increased duration of light, as long as the plant is not sensitive to day-length for flowering.
- Most plants require a period of darkness to develop properly, so if you use artificial light, illuminate them for no more than 16 hours each day.

Quality

- Improved by adding an artificial light source.
- Red, far-red, and blue wavelengths are most important for plant development. For healthy plants, supply all three.
- Standard white fluorescent tubes produce mostly blue light.
- Incandescent bulbs produce predominantly red or far-red light.
- Blooming plants require extra far-red light.
- Full-spectrum "grow lights" mimic natural sunlight, and can be fluorescent or LED.
- Remember that excessive light is just as harmful as too little. When a plant gets too much direct light, the leaves become pale, turn brown, and die. Protect indoor plants from excessive direct sunlight during the summer months.

Water

A common question home gardeners ask is, "How often should I water my plants?". The plant itself will tell you. When it's too dry, a plant wilts and turns a dull color; when too wet, a plant may also wilt, or leaves turn yellow and fall off. Avoid both extremes. Plants should not be watered on a schedule, but when they need it. A large percentage of plants are lost due to overwatering or underwatering.

Factors that influence whether or not to water include differences in potting medium, humidity, and temperature. To see if a plant needs water, feel the potting mix at the root zone. Because a plant's roots are usually in the bottom two-thirds of the pot, it doesn't need water until the bottom two-thirds slightly dries out.

Another quick test is to lift the plant, pot and all, to check its weight change. A plant with dry potting medium will weigh much less than a plant which is still retaining ample water. You can purchase an electronic soil moisture reader if desired.

While you're checking watering needs, also check the medium. If your finger can't penetrate two inches, you may need a more porous mix or the plant may be root-bound.

Tips for watering indoor plants:

- Use room temperature water. Water that is too cold may shock or injure the plant.
- When possible, especially for sensitive species like carnivorous plants, use filtered or distilled water to avoid mineral/salt buildup in the soil. Do not use softened water.
- Water thoroughly, until water drains through the holes in the bottom of the pot. Allow all excess water to drain away so salts don't accumulate.
- Water plants that are difficult to access from the top (if they have a lot of foliage or are fragile) by placing them in a

shallow tray or saucer filled with water until you can feel that the top of the soil has become damp (see Figure 23-B).

Figure 23-B. Water plants from the bottom up

Try watering plants using a shallow tray or container to fully water the plant while avoiding damage to foliage.

Soluble salts buildup

Soluble salts:

- Are mineral deposits left from tap or bottled water, or fertilizer residue.
- Stay behind and become concentrated when water evaporates from the growing mix.
- Can inhibit the plant's uptake of water.

A problem of great importance to indoor plants is the buildup of soluble salts in the potting medium, which can be easily avoided with proper watering techniques. Symptoms of this buildup include reduced growth, brown leaf tips, lower-leaf drop, dead root tips, and wilting. A ring of salt deposits may also crust around the pot at the soil line, around the drainage hole, or on the exterior of a clay pot.

If salts build up to an extremely high level in the soil, water is drawn out from the root tips, directly damaging the roots. A weakened plant is more susceptible to attack from insects and diseases.

To prevent the buildup of soluble salts:

- All water contains dissolved minerals, but softened water contains more than others. Avoid using softened water on indoor plants.
- Choose mineral-free water. The next time rain is expected, set some buckets outside and let them fill with rainwater and use it for watering. If you use a dehumidifier, use the distilled water in the drain pan to water your plants.
- Otherwise, draw water for your plants the day before you plan to water them. A day's evaporation should clear the water of chlorine.
- Periodically leach your plants with clear water; how often depends on plant type and other factors. First, remove any salt crust on top of the potting medium. Pour a lot of water—at least twice the volume of the pot—on the potting soil and let it drain completely.
- Leach before you fertilize so that you don't wash away all the fertilizer you just added.
- Repot the plant if the soluble salts level seems high or the pot has poor drainage. Remove as much old potting mix as possible to replace it with fresh mix that is low in salts. Note whether the potting mix contains time-release fertilizer so you don't over-fertilize.

The level of salts that will injure a plant varies with the type of plant and how it's grown. It's a good practice to leach a newly-purchased plant the first time you water it.

Table 23-A. Cultural guidelines for indoor plants (* plant will not do well under this condition)

Scientific name	Common name	Direct/Bright Light	Average/Low Light	Moist or Dry
Saintpaulia ionantha	African violet	B	A	M
Aloe barbadensis	Aloe vera	B	A	D
Pilea cadieri	Aluminum plant	B	A L	M
A. densiflorus "Sprengeri"	Asparagus fern	B	*	D
Nephrolepis exaltata	Boston fern	B	A	M
Sedum morganianum	Burro's tail	D B	*	D
Aspidistra elatior	Cast iron plant	B	A	D
Aglaonema commutatum	Chinese evergreen	B	A L	D
Solenostemon spp.	Coleus	D B	*	M
Schlumergera bridgesii	Christmas cactus	B	A	M
Dracaena spp.	Corn plant	B	A	M
Codiaeum variegatum	Croton	B	A	D
Epipremnum aureum	Devil's ivy, Pothos	B	A	D
Dieffenbachia amoena	Dumb cane	D B	A	D
Dizygotheca elegantissima	False aralia	B	A	M
Ficus lyrata	Fiddle leaf fig	B	A	D
Crassula ovata	Jade plant	D B	*	D
Fatsia japonica	Japanese aralia	B	A	M
Aeschynanthus spp.	Lipstick plant	B	*	D
Adiantum capillus-veneris	Maidenhair fern	*	A L	M
Fittonia spp.	Mosaic plant	*	A	M
Araucaria heterophylla	Norfolk Island pine	B	*	M
Peperomia caperata	Peperomia	B	A	D
Tolmiea menziesii	Piggyback plant	B	A	M
Maranta leuconeura	Prayer plant	*	A	M
Gynura aurantiaca	Purple velvet plant	*	A	M
Ficus elastica	Rubber plant	D B	*	M
Schefflera spp.	Schefflera	D B	A	D
Sansevieria trifasciata	Snake plant	D B	A L	D
Cholorophytum comosum	Spiderwort	B	A	M
Plectranthus verticillatus	Swedish ivy	D B	A	D
Tradescantia fluminensis	Small-leaf spiderplant	D B	A	D
Ficus benjamina	Weeping fig	B	*	D

Temperature

Excessively low or high temperatures may result in spindly or halted growth, dropped leaves, damaged foliage, or plant death.

- In general, foliage indoor plants grow best between 70°F and 80°F during the day and from 60°F to 68°F at night.
- Most flowering indoor plants prefer the same daytime range but grow best at nighttime temperatures of 55°F to 60°F.
- A good rule of thumb is to keep the night temperature 10° to 15°F lower than the day temperature to allow for physiological recovery from moisture loss, intensify flower color, and prolong flower life.
- Indoor plants, especially flowering varieties, are sensitive to door drafts and heat from registers. Protect them from sudden, brief changes in temperature. Do not locate your indoor plants near heat or air-conditioning sources.

Humidity

Most indoor environments lack sufficient humidity for healthy indoor plants, particularly in the winter. With the exception of cacti and succulents, all indoor plants benefit from higher humidity in their vicinity.

Misting foliage does not appreciably raise humidity and may increase the vulnerability of foliage to infection. Wetting leaves can also cause spotting on sensitive species like African violets. Placing pots on a humidity tray doesn't substantially raise humidity, and the tray may develop algae and mold if not regularly cleaned. A room humidifier is the most practical and effective way of boosting humidity and maintaining more consistent levels for the health of both people and plants during seasons with dry indoor air. Grouping plants together can help maintain a pocket of more humid air around their foliage.

Nutrients

The fertilizing goal for growing indoor plants is to supply just enough nutrients so that new growth compensates for leaf loss. The goal should not be the quick growth of a large plant. Large amounts of fertilizer are therefore unnecessary for most indoor plants.

- Fertilizing with a commercial fertilizer containing micronutrients or adding a small amount of well-composted, screened leaf mold or other compost will fill any need for replenishment.
- Plants are not capable of absorbing much through foliage (with the exception of bromeliads/air plants), so refrain from spraying foliage, which would just result in salt deposits on the leaves, which is undesirable.
- Indoor plants don't need fertilizer during the winter months because reduced light and temperature result in less growth. Fertilizing during this time could actually harm some plants by contributing to salt buildup in the potting mix.
- Monthly applications of a diluted liquid fertilizer in the summer months will keep most indoor plants healthy. Worm castings are one organic option.

23.3 Maintenance Tips

Well-groomed plants look their best and will be easier to monitor for signs or symptoms of problems.

- For plants that branch readily, periodically pinch the stem just above the node on new growth to promote denser growth and a fuller plant.

- Thinning overly dense growth improves airflow, which discourages disease and lets inner leaves get sufficient light. Trim irregular growth back to improve symmetry or train the plant into a new shape, such as with bonsai.

- Disbudding means removing selected flower buds to get larger blooms from a few choice buds. It also eliminates flowering in a young plant or recently rooted cutting that should not bear the physical strain of flowering early.

- Removing dead leaves reduces the number of places insect pests and diseases spores can hide. Also remove all spent flowers and dead branches.

- Rinse dust off of leaves in a sink or shower. Avoid flooding the pot (unless the plant needs watering). Do not clean foliage with soap because doing so may remove the protective wax layer and cause damage.

23.4 Repotting Indoor Plants

Although plants can grow in a surprisingly small soil volume if they receive adequate nutrients and water, healthy indoor plants will grow better and benefit from being occasionally repotted. It's time to repot if you see the roots of a foliage plant growing out of the drain hole or if salt buildup is causing plant stress or visible residue.

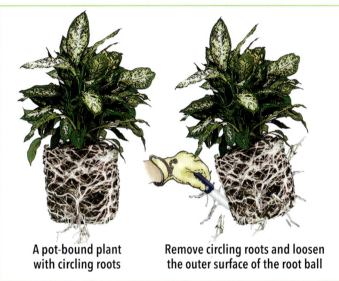

Figure 23-C. Repotting a plant with encircling roots

A pot-bound plant with circling roots

Remove circling roots and loosen the outer surface of the root ball

Prepare your supplies before repotting. Choose a new pot that has drainage holes in the bottom. The diameter of the new pot should be no more than two inches larger than the current pot. Moving a plant to a larger pot with an excessively large volume of soil can lead to waterlogged roots because the plant can't use the available water.

If you're recycling a used pot, scrub soluble salts off with water and a stiff brush. Then wash disease-causing organisms from the pot in a solution of one part liquid bleach to nine parts water. Allow the pot to dry thoroughly before repotting. Purchase a soilless potting medium and moisten the necessary amount ahead of time. The day before you plan to repot a plant, be sure to water it well to reduce possible shock to the root system.

How to repot a plant

- Do not block the drain holes with stones, pottery pieces, or other materials. Once potted, very little soil will fall out of the hole, and as roots grow into the bottom of the pot, they prevent soil loss.

- Place enough new potting mix in the bottom of the pot to support the root ball to an inch or two below the new pot's rim, allowing enough head room for watering.
- Remove the plant from its old pot by knocking the container against a hard surface (or carefully squeezing the sides of a plastic pot) to loosen the root ball. Tilt the pot upside down and gently pull the plant from the pot with your hand covering the soil.
- Using clean, sharp scissors, cut vertically down the root ball about a half-inch into the healthy roots at two- to three-inch intervals. Remove any dead, brown roots or circling roots. (See Figure 23-C.) Alternatively, loosen the roots on the perimeter with your fingers, tweezers, or a hand cultivator. Loosening circling roots is preferable to completely removing them, where possible.
- Place the plant into the new pot and fill in soil around the root ball, gently tamping it in with your fingers to eliminate air pockets.
- Water thoroughly, but avoid further watering until the top inch (or more) of the soil dries out.

Potting media

The potting medium should be porous enough for root aeration and drainage but still able to retain water and nutrients. Some key points:

- Sand is a common additive to improve drainage. Compared to perlite, it will not break down into finer particles over time, nor gradually rise to the surface of the potting mix. Pumice might be used instead of sand by some manufacturers. Keep in mind that using either in a potting mix may substantially increase the container's weight.
- True mineral-based soil (clay, silt, etc.) is relatively dense and water-retentive, so is not used in containers indoors. Instead, potting mix is technically soilless, containing only organic components like peat moss or coco coir and inorganic components like perlite and vermiculite. Although sometimes referred to as 'potting soil,' media for indoor plants should not contain any actual soil.
- Some mixes contain slow-release fertilizers which will meet a plant's nutritional requirements for several months.

The potting medium you buy should have the most efficient combination of elements for the plant you want to grow. Houseplant potting media can be divided into four groups, each of which has slightly different characteristics.

For most indoor plants:

- The mix should be moderately rich, have a loamy base, and adequately hold moisture and nutrients.
- Potting media for flowering indoor plants is often labeled and sold as "African violet potting mix" although it can also be used for other plant groups (e.g., gloxinias, begonias, calla lilies, and other indoor tropicals).
- Should contain about 50 percent humus-rich materials, but not so that it is soggy after watering.

For cacti and succulents:

- Do not need much humus material.
- A high proportion of sand should be present in any purchased mix.

Table 23-B. Indoor plant container comparison

Type of Pot	Advantages	Disadvantages
Terracotta Clay	• Easily absorb and lose moisture • Provide excellent aeration for plant roots • Roots grow near the pot's walls because moisture and nutrients accumulate in the clay pores	• Dry out rapidly • Are easily broken • Are not flexible; it can be difficult to dislodge a plant • Can accumulate surface salt deposits
Ceramic / Stoneware	• Usually glazed to retain moisture longer • Tend to be available in the largest range of colors or patterns • Can be used with a clay or plastic pot inside to allow for drainage	• Frequently lack drainage holes, which encourages moisture to remain in the soil, contributing to the possibility of root rot • Chip/crack/break easily
Plastic / Fiberglass / Resin	• Lightweight and easy to handle • Relatively inexpensive • Easy to clean and sterilize for re-use • Plants require less frequent watering and accumulate fewer soluble salts	• Occasionally lack drainage holes • Can fade in bright sunlight • Can become brittle if left out in cold weather or too much summer (UV light degrades plastic over time)

For orchids:

- Epiphytes, or air plants (e.g., orchids, bromeliads, and some aroids) have roots that attach to tree branches. If grown in regular potting mix, their roots may rot for lack of air. Use a mix of very porous, chunky material that does not retain water very long.

- A typical mix is fir bark or coconut husk chips with charcoal and perlite, sometimes including long-fiber sphagnum for more moisture retention.

Containers

Containers can improve the appearance of plants, especially large floor plants. There are many pots available; each type has advantages and disadvantages (see Table 23-B).

23.5 Moving Indoor Plants Outdoors

Grown under the marginal conditions of most homes, indoor plants can become tired-looking. You can renew your plants by moving them outdoors during the summer months.

Light conditions in the shadiest outdoor spot are usually more intense than the sunniest spot inside. Most indoor plants thrive outdoors in the high humidity of Maryland's summers.

- Put plants out only after night temperatures stay consistently above 60°F. In most of Maryland, this is not until early June.

- Initially place plants in a shady spot and gradually give them more sun (see "Acclimating plants" on p. 678).

- Fertilize and water indoor plants moved outdoors more often to support more vigorous growth.

Acclimating plants

Plants are sensitive to sudden changes in light, temperature, humidity, and other environmental conditions. Take care to slowly acclimate them to outdoor conditions so the plants are not severely shocked.

- Avoid sudden changes in light intensity. When placed in bright sunlight after a winter in a dimly-lit window, your plant will become bleached by photo-degradation of chlorophyll, permanently marring existing leaves. This sunscald can occasionally do so much damage that it kills the plant.
- Gradually increase exposure to sunlight and reverse the process when plants are brought indoors in fall.
- Place a newly-purchased greenhouse plant in a bright-light area of your home; later, move it to a spot that meets its light requirements. Any plants from a garden center will need to be acclimated as well.

Tips for transporting indoor plants from the garden center:

- Take plants directly home; avoid leaving them in a hot or cold car. Even in mild sunny weather, car temperatures can be drastically different than what the plant was accustomed to, causing wilt, leaf damage, bloom drop, water stress, or other problems.
- Shade plants from direct sun while in the car, as foliage can be damaged by the sun shining through the window.
- During winter months, wrap plants thoroughly with newspapers or paper bags before the short run to the car.

23.6 Bringing Plants Back Indoors

Things to remember when bringing plants back inside:

- Check plants thoroughly for insects and treat infestations as necessary. Quarantine them for a few weeks to be sure that overlooked insect infestations don't spread to other indoor plants.
- Gradually move the plants from a sunnier indoor spot to their winter positions, especially if those areas receive low light.
- Cut back fertilization and watering because growth slows.

23.7 Indoor Plant Pest and Disease Diagnostics

As with other plants, diagnosing issues with indoor plants can be challenging. Plants can have issues resulting from environmental conditions, plant pests, or a variety of diseases. It is important to consider all possibilities when diagnosing your indoor plants so you can accurately treat the right issue.

Please refer to **Key 12-Y: Pests and Diseases of Indoor Plants** in Chapter 12 to diagnose a problem with a houseplant.

Remember that when working with indoor plants, it is even more important to avoid using pesticides whenever possible because of the close proximity to people and pets. Additionally, relatively few pesticide formulations are labeled for use indoor. Instead, hand-pick or use a spray of plain water from a sink or shower head to remove pests like mealybugs, scale, aphids, and mites.

23.8 Toxic Indoor Plants

Some houseplants are toxic or poisonous because they contain substances that cause an adverse reaction when touched or ingested. Symptoms and reactions range from eye or skin irritation to death if ingested. Curious pets and children are prone to touch or chew on plant leaves and flowers, so if you have any of the plants in Table 23-C below, take extra care to keep them well out of reach or replace them with non-toxic varieties. ✼

Table 23-C. Toxic indoor plants

Those which are toxic cause injury only if ingested in large quantities. Those which are poisonous can cause extreme injury and sometimes death, even in small quantities. Poisonous indoor plants are marked with an asterisk.*

Scientific name	Common name	Scientific name	Common name
Hippeastrum spp.	*Amaryllis	*Ficus* spp.	Fig (weeping, fiddle-leaf)
Caladium bicolor	Angels' wings, Caladium	*Caryota* spp.	Fishtail palm
Anthurium spp.	Anthurium	*Anthurium andraeanum*	Flamingo lily
Aralia sieboldii, Fatsia japonica	Aralia	*Crassula ovata*	Jade plant
Begonia spp.	Begonia	*Clivia miniata*	Olivia
Aglaonema spp.	Chinese evergreen	*Bougainvillea glabra*	Paper flower
Euphorbia lacteal	*Candelabra cactus	*Philodendron* spp.	Philodendron
Acalypha spp.	Chenille plant	*Euphorbia pulcherrima*	Poinsettia
Nerium oleander	*Common oleander	*Euphorbia* spp.	Various succulents
Aechmea fulgens	*Coralberry	*Ceropegia woodii*	Rosary vine
Codiaeum variegatum	*Croton	*Ficus* spp.	Rubber tree
Euphorbia milii	Crown of thorns	*Cycas revoluta*	Sago palm
Epipremnum aureum	Devil's ivy, Pothos	*Schefflera actinophylla*	Schefflera
Dieffenbachia spp.	Dumbcane	*Sansevieria* spp.	Snake plant
Hedera helix	English ivy	*Monstera deliciosa*	Swiss cheese plant, split-leaf philodendron

AUTHORS

2024 Edition:

Stephanie Pully, Maryland State Coordinator for the UME Master Gardener Program.

Jean Burchfield, Master Gardener Program Management Specialist, University of Maryland Extension.

Original author: Jeanine Smetana, University of Maryland Extension Master Gardener, Harford County.

PUBLICATIONS

Portions adapted from: *The Maryland Master Gardener Handbook*, *The Virginia Master Gardener Handbook*, and *The Pennsylvania Master Gardener Manual*.

Belsinger, S. 1991. *Flowers in the Kitchen.* Interweave Press. Loveland, CO. ISBN-10: 0934026647.

Langer, R.W. 1995. *Grow It Indoors: How to Make Houseplants Thrive.* Stackpole Books. Mechanicsburg, PA. ISBN-10: 0811724808.

Phillips, R. and N. Foy, 1990. *The Random House Book of Herbs.* Random House. New York, NY. ISBN-10: 0679732136.

Simon & Schuster's Guide to Plants and Flowers. 1976. Simon & Schuster. New York, NY. ISBN: 0671222473.

Success with House Plants. 1979. The Reader's Digest Association, Inc. Pleasantville, NY. ISBN-10: 0895770520.

Wyman, D. 1987. *Taylor's Guide to Houseplants.* Houghton Mifflin Company. Boston, MA. ISBN-10: 0395430917.

WEBSITES

Mid City Nursery, Inc. (inventory of house plants, herbs, fruits, berries, herbs and more). midcitynursery.com

University of Maryland Extension. *Growing and Caring for Indoor Plants.* extension.umd.edu/resource/growing-and-caring-indoor-plants

Penn State Extension. *Caring For Houseplants.* extension.psu.edu/caring-for-houseplants

PHOTOS AND ILLUSTRATIONS

Main chapter photo: Pexels.com.

Figure 23-A. Illustration by Jean Burchfield.

Figure 23-B. Photo by Debra Ricigliano.

Figure 23-C. Illustration by LeAnn Zotta.

Table 23-B: terracotta pot- PngXpress via Adobe Stock. Ceramic pot- Marina Lohrbach via Adobe Stock. Plastic pot- Vividz Foto via Adobe Stock.

24: PLANT PROPAGATION

Susan Trice
Courtney Coddington

24 PLANT PROPAGATION

CONTENTS

24.1 Sexual Propagation 684
    24.1a About Seeds 684
    24.1b Preparing Seeds for Germination 687
    24.1c Starting Seeds Indoors 691
    24.1d Starting Seeds Outdoors 696

24.2 Growing Transplants 697

24.3 Asexual Propagation 699
    24.3a Cuttings 699
    24.3b Layering 701
    24.3c Division and Separation 703
    24.3d Grafting and Budding 704

LEARNING OBJECTIVES

- Basic principles of sexual and asexual plant propagation
- Techniques for planting and germinating seeds
- Best practices for growing transplants
- Propagating a plant from a stem, leaf, or root cutting
- Propagation via grafting, budding, layering, division, separation, and tissue culture

INTRODUCTION

Propagation is the controlled process by which plants can be multiplied. Some techniques follow a plant's natural reproductive strategies and some involve a greater understanding of plant physiology. The level of experience required for such techniques ranges from novice to advanced, and the success of each attempt is often dictated by the level of finesse and patience possessed by the propagator.

When preparing to propagate plants it is important to note that each plant has its own specific propagation requirements. Not every method will be successful nor appropriate for every plant. There are two categories of plant propagation:

- **Sexual,** which uses the reproductive morphology of the plant for the development of seeds, which are formed in the flowers of angiosperms, or spores from fungi, from which new plants grow.
- **Asexual** (or vegetative), which occurs by taking a vegetative part of a parent plant (stem, root, or leaf) and causing it to regenerate itself into a new plant or to alter the parent plant. Genetically, the new plant is identical to the parent. Methods include cuttings, layering, division, separation, grafting, budding, and tissue culture.

The advantages of sexual propagation:

- Often requires the least amount of overhead cost
- It may be the only way to obtain new varieties and hybrid vigor
- Transporting genetics in seed form is less expensive and easier than transporting live plants
- In certain species it is the only viable method of propagation
- It may help avoid disease transmission

The advantages of asexual propagation:

- It can be easier and faster for some species than growing from seed
- It may be the only way to perpetuate some cultivars and species if they cannot support sexual reproduction
- It may be easier than certain pollination requirements
- It bypasses the juvenile characteristics of certain species

24.1 Sexual Propagation

Sexual propagation is the union of sex cells in pollen from the anther (male organ) with the egg of the female to produce a seed. Pollen is carried by insects or wind from one flower to another. This process is called pollination. When the pollen lands in a new flower, it travels to the ovary where it fertilizes the ovules (egg cells) to create seeds. This is the fertilization process.

The seed is made up of three parts: the outer seed coat, which protects the seed; the endosperm, a food reserve; and the embryo, the young plant itself. When a viable seed is mature and put into a favorable environment, it will germinate and begin to grow.

The seeds are then dispersed by nature via animals or wind, rain, etc., or intentionally planted by humans.

24.1a About Seeds

To obtain high-quality plants, start with seed of known quality from a reliable source. When selecting your seed source, consider:

- How reputable is the seed source?
- Do you know which type of seed you need to get the result you want?
- Are the seeds compatible with your planting zone and ecosystem? Can you determine their origin?
- What is the viability of the seeds?

Selecting a reputable seed source

Sources may include well-known companies, agencies or private plant breeders/seed-savers. Sources should provide information about how they obtain or breed their varieties. Breeding for purity may also require the isolation or specific spacing between varieties to avoid unwanted cross-pollination, so it is important to note whether the source has a system for assuring varietal identity/quality.

Look on the label for the term "Certified Seed," which means the seed conforms with state, federal, and international seed laws. This certification provides producers and seed buyers with assurance that the seeds have met purity standards though a system of laboratory tests and unbiased field inspections.

Seed types

When selecting your seeds, consider:

- Is it legal to propagate this plant?
- Are you going to save seeds or buy them each year?
- Will future plants be organically certified if you propagate them from saved certified-organic seed?
- If you're propagating plants for a special trait, will this seed produce that result?

Even though the seeds may be available for purchase, they may not meet local and state regulations for species restrictions or bans. In some cases, certain plants may be regulated due to their invasive tendencies, chemical properties, patented genetic information, endangered status, or ability to host potential risks to surrounding agricultural crops.

Start by determining whether the variety of plant in which you are interested may be legally propagated. Certain varieties may be registered under the **Plant Variety Protection Act** or have a patent associated with their genetic information. This not only includes plants produced by genetic modification, but can also refer to certain hybrids or even some specialty heirlooms.

If you intend to save seeds from your propagated plants, and it is legal to do so, you will need to know if your sourced seeds will produce plants that will breed true-to-type and produce seeds that pass on the selected traits of that variety.

Seed sources will describe seeds with terminology such as "open pollinated," "heirloom," "cultivar," "variety," or "hybrid." Some seeds may also be further labeled as "Certified Organic" or "Genetically Modified Organism (GMO)." Knowing the difference between these terms will help you make informed decisions about which seeds to buy, and what outcomes to expect.

Open-pollinated: Plants are pollinated naturally, through wind or pollinators.

Heirloom: An open-pollinated plant line that has been preserved for many years due to its significance in family histories, despite potentially inferior genetics. In some cases "heirlooms" may be considered all named plant varieties developed before hybrids became popular in 1951. Others designate heirlooms as plant varieties maintained by humans and passed down through generations for more than 50 years. Heirloom seeds breed true-to-type and most varieties have been selected for taste and productivity.

Cultivar: A variety of plant selected and cultivated by humans to maintain specific characteristics. The cultivar is identified after the scientific name, capitalized and in single quotations (e.g., *Hydrangea macrophylla* 'Endless Summer®'). Resulting seeds may not stay true to parental traits, therefore vegetative propagation is commonly used.

Variety: A version of a plant with specific characteristics that can occur naturally.

ABOUT PLANTING SEEDS FROM SUPERMARKET PRODUCE

Most grocery-store fruits and vegetables are hybrids, engineered for shipping and long shelf life. Planting seeds from a hybrid will not result in a "true-to-parent" plant, meaning you will not get the same produce from which you saved the seed. Only heirloom (or "open pollinated") seed will grow the same produce as the parent.

Seeds may remain true-to-type. The variety is identified after the scientific name, lower case and in italics. It is common to see varieties associated with specific geographic regions as the plants have adapted to those particular environments.

Hybrid: The cross-pollination of two varieties of plants which produce offspring with desirable traits. Cross-pollination can occur naturally and results in a "variety." Commercially, this process is often initiated by humans, where intentional hybridizing results in a "cultivar," or cultivated variety. Seeds from the propagated cultivar may not produce plants true-to-type, therefore vegetative propagation is commonly used.

Certified Organic: Agricultural products including seeds that are sold, labeled or represented as "organic" must meet the federal requirements and standards enforced by the USDA National Organic Program. Organic seeds are produced by certified operations that do not use genetically modified planting stocks and do not treat their seeds with program-prohibited treatments like fungicides. This term defines the application of practices by which the seed was produced, not necessarily the varietal traits of the plant. Both hybrids and heirlooms can be produced and certified as organic.

Figure 24-A. Typical seed-packet information

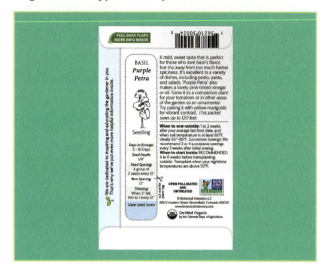

GMO / Genetically Modified Organism / Genetically Engineered / Bioengineered: An organism that has been created through the technological manipulation of genes by adding, removing, or rearranging genes with techniques such as recombinant DNA. Organisms will have heritable traits that create improvements for commercial production, and are not available to the general public. Currently, there are fewer than a dozen types of crops with available GMO varieties.

Seed compatibility

Always choose varieties adapted to your area so they will reach maturity before the earliest anticipated frost. For annuals, this may require selecting fewer "days to harvest" or "days to bloom." For perennials, not only will you want to select for harvest or bloom before the first frost but you will need to determine whether the variety will withstand the winter conditions of your growing zone.

Other factors such as light, nutrient, and moisture requirements are important to identify when matching a variety to your particular conditions. Most of this information can be ascertained by reading the seed packet (see Figure 24-A). The following seed packet information will help you better determine whether or not that seed is right for you.

- **Annual, biennial, or perennial:** The life expectancy of the resulting plant.
- **Planting zone:** Indicates winter and summer hardiness, which is important for perennials. Plants that are suitable for warmer zones may be chosen if planted in containers that can be brought inside for the winter. See the USDA Hardiness Zone Map.
- **Seed count:** The quantity of seeds, either by number or weight. Useful when determining how much to buy, and assessing the value of each seed.
- **Height, variety description, and growing habit:** A description of the mature plant. Especially useful for gauging variety selection for prepared beds or containers as well as identifying aesthetic traits.
- **Days to bloom/harvest:** The number of days to maturity from seeding. This will help determine whether or not there is enough time in your location's growing season for the plant to reach maturity before the first frost. This date will determine whether seeds should be started indoors as transplants or if they can be directly seeded. The description may also provide the method of propagation (transplants or direct sow) which best suits that variety.

- **Packaged date:** The year the seeds were packaged. Keep in mind that seeds will have lower germination rates as they age. This may affect the number of seeds you start in order to obtain a desired quantity of plants.
- **Origin** (not always included): May be listed as the code for the country in which the seed was grown (e.g., DEU=Germany), which may differ from where it was packaged. Origin is especially important when sourcing native varieties, varieties for wildlife, or varieties intended for very specific environments or purposes. The packaged variety may be a species known to exist naturally in your area but many varieties are grown internationally and the resulting "ecotype" of this variety may be better adapted to the country of origin. It may be beneficial to source seeds from local origins in order to best match the plant to your growing environment. See **Chapter 21, Native Plants**, for more information about ecosystems and Table 24-B for native plant propagation techniques.
- **Inert material** (not always included): Inert material is usually debris that cannot be removed from seed processing or that which is added to make spreading easier for very tiny or lightweight seeds. Inert material is often found in seed mixes intended for large-scale broadcast seeding.
- **Weed seeds** (not always included): This is the percentage of weed seeds in the mix. Some weeds seeds may be difficult or impossible to separate out from the targeted seed during processing. The species of weed may or may not be known. The percentage of noxious weed seeds may be listed separately. It is important to consider and anticipate the potential impacts that weed seeds could have for your propagation project.

Seed viability

Although some seeds will keep for several years if stored properly, it is advisable to purchase only enough seed for the current year as the quality and germination rate will diminish over time.

If seeds are obtained well in advance of the sowing date or are stored from a previous year, keep them in a cool, dry place. Paper packets are best kept in tightly-closed containers and maintained at around 40°F with a low humidity. (See **Chapter 18, Vegetables,** for more information about seed-saving and storing techniques.)

24.1b Preparing Seeds for Germination

Viable seeds that are not actively germinating are considered to be in "dormancy." Dormancy prevents a seed from germinating when the surrounding environment is unfavorable. Dormancy prevents a seed from germinating when the environment is unfavorable. The physiological and environmental factors that trigger the seed to begin germination are:

- The removal or breakdown of physical or chemical barriers within the structure of the seed.
- The presence of appropriate environmental conditions such as moisture, temperature, and light. If the requirements cannot be met naturally, it becomes the responsibility of the propagator to simulate conditions to meet those needs.

Table 24-A. Germination table for selected seeds

Plant name	Weeks before last frost date to start	Days required to germinate	Temperature (F)	Light/dark requirement
Ageratum	8	5 to 10	70	Light
Alyssum	8	5 to 10	70	Either
Aster	6	5 to 10	70	Either
Balsam	6	5 to 10	70	Either
Begonia	12 or more	10 to 15	70	Light
Broccoli	8	5 to 10	70	Either
Browallia	12 or more	15 to 20	70	Light
Cabbage	8	5 to 10	70	Either
Cauliflower	8	5 to 10	70	Either
Celosia	8	5 to 10	70	Either
Centurea	6	5 to 10	65	Dark
Coleus	8	5 to 10	65	Light
Cosmos	4 or less	5 to 10	70	Either
Cucumber	4 or less	5 to 10	85	Either
Dahlia	8	5 to 10	70	Either
Dianthus	10	5 to 10	70	Either
Eggplant	8	5 to 10	70	Either
Geranium	12 or more	10 to 20	70	Light
Impatiens	10	15 to 20	70	Light
Larkspur	12 or more	5 to 10	55	Dark
Lettuce	8	5 to 10	70	Light
Marigold	6	5 to 10	70	Either
Muskmelon	4 or less	5 to 10	85	Either
Nicotiana	8	10 to 15	70	Light
Pansy (Viola)	12 or more	5 to 10	65	Dark
Pepper	8	5 to 10	80	Either
Petunia	10	5 to 10	70	Light
Phlox	8	5 to 10	65	Dark
Portulaca	10	5 to 10	70	Dark
Snapdragon	10	5 to 10	65	Light
Squash	4 or less	5 to 10	85	Either
Stock	10	10 to 15	70	Either
Tomato	6	5 to 10	80	Either
Verbena	10	15 to 20	65	Dark
Watermelon	4 or less	5 to 10	85	Either
Zinnia	6	5 to 10	70	Either

Table 24-B. Native plant propagation techniques

Germination technique	Perennials	Trees & shrubs
Seeds can be sown outdoors in the fall or early spring; seeds will germinate after 4 weeks if sown at 70°F.	Asters (*Symphyotrichum* spp.) Wild columbine (*Aquilegia canadensis*) Milkweed (*Asclepias* spp.) Coneflower (*Echinacea purpurea*) Lobelias (*Lobelia* spp.) Black-eyed Susans (*Rudbeckia* spp.)	Sweet pepperbush (*Clethra alnifolia*) Buttonbush (*Cephalanthus occidentalis*) Azaleas (*Rhododendron* spp.) Maple (*Acer* spp.)
Seeds require a cold period (stratification) to germinate; sow outdoors in fall or winter. Or, sow in the spring after artificial cold stratification at 40°F.	Iris (*Iris* spp.) Blue-eyed grass (*Sisyrinchium*) Boneset & Joe-Pye Weed (*Eupatorium* spp.) Beardtongue (*Penstemon digitalis*) Blazing star (*Liatris spicata*) Bee balms (*Monarda* spp.) Goldenrod (*Solidago* spp.)	Chokeberry (*Aronia* spp.) Spicebush (*Lindera benzoin*) Bayberry (*Myrica* spp.) Rose (*Rosa* spp.) Wild plum (*Prunus* spp.) Shrub dogwoods (*Cornus* spp.) Serviceberry (*Amelanchier* spp.) Elderberry (*Sambucus* spp.) Sweetshrub (*Calycanthus florida*)
Seeds need light to germinate; sow on soil surface and leave uncovered.	Lobelias (*Lobelia* spp.) Goat's beard (*Aruncuss* spp.) Monkey-flower (*Mimulus* spp.) Beardtongue (*Penstemon* spp.) Blue vervain (*Verbena* spp.)	Birch (*Betula* spp.) Buttonbush (*Cephalanthus occidentalis*) Laurel (*Kalmia* spp.)
Seeds need an alternating cycle of warm-to-cold-to-warm for germination. Either sown outdoors in spring or summer and will germinating the following year, or sown in a flat in a warm place for three months to a refrigerator for two months, then moved outside in early summer warmth.	Turk's cap lily (*Lilium superbum*) Black cohosh (*Cimicifuga racemosa*)	Viburnums (*Viburnum* spp.) Trumpet honeysuckle (*Lonicera sempervirens*) Ash (*Fraxinus* spp.)
Seeds are hydrophilic (cannot allow to dry out) (sow immediately.	Bloodroot (*Sanguinaria canadensis*) Marsh marigold (*Caltha palustris*) Trilliums (*Trillium* spp.) Wild ginger (*Asarum canadense*) Bellwort (*Uvularia* spp.)	Oaks (*Quercus* spp.) Hickory (*Carya* spp.) Hazelnut (*Corylus americana*) Walnuts (*Juglans* spp.) Spicebush (*Lindera benzoin*) Sassafras (*Sassafras albidum*)
Seeds take two years to germinate. Sow outside in fall or winter and look for germination in the second spring.	Trilliums (*Trillium* spp.) Solomon's seal (*Polygonatum* spp.) False Solomon's seal (*Smilacina* spp.)	Viburnums (*Viburnum* spp.) Witch hazel (*Hamamelis virginiana*) Basswood (*Tilia americana*)
Large seeds (more than 1/4" in diameter) that should be soaked overnight in water or undergo scarification because of an impermeable seed coat.	Iris (*Iris* spp.) Prickly pear (*Opuntia humifusa*) Wild senna (*Senna* spp.) Rose mallow (*Hibiscus moscheutos*)	Witch hazel (*Hamamelis virginiana*) Oak (*Quercus* spp.) Cherry (*Prunus* spp.) Hickory (*Carya* spp.) Rose (*Rosa* spp.) Bayberry (*Myrica* spp.)
Seeds that require cleaning of fleshy exterior or may not germinate in the presence of chemical inhibitors. These species may additionally require one of the techniques above to break dormancy.	Most fleshy fruits Jack-in-the-pulpit (*Arisaema* spp.) Prickly pear (*Opuntia humifusa*) Mayapple (*Podophyllum peltatum*) Trilliums (*Trillium* spp.)	Most fleshy fruits American beautyberry (*Callicarpa americana*) Serviceberry (*Amelanchier* spp.) Chokeberry (*Aronia* spp.) Pawpaw (*Asimina triloba*) Dogwood (*Cornus* spp.) Spicebush (*Lindera benzoin*) Sassafras (*Sassafras albidum*) Rose (*Rosa* spp.)

Occasionally, seeds have additional requirements to break dormancy, such as exposure to cold temperatures or abrasion of the seed coat. Some seeds may also benefit from soaking in water for a period of time to increase germination speed.

See Table 24-A for a list of germination requirements for commonly-planted seeds.

Stratification

Seeds of some perennials and most temperate-climate woody plants require a period of moist, cool conditions before they can germinate. The required period of exposure to these conditions varies by species.

Stratification is used to replicate these naturally-occurring conditions in artificial settings. Seeds can be placed between layers of a moist medium and kept in a cool place, such as a refrigerator or cool shed, for a set period of time. If the temperature outdoors drops low enough and stays low enough for the desired period of time, these seeds can be sown in containers and placed so that stratification can occur with the natural temperature changes outdoors.

To stratify seeds:

Choose and prepare the container. Examples of appropriate containers include clean cottage-cheese cartons, coffee cans, or plastic jars. Plastic storage bags can also be used, preferably with the fold-over tops (rather than zip-lock closures) to encourage air circulation.

Choose and prepare the media. A mixture of peat moss, sand, and/or vermiculite can be used or use several layers of paper towels. Add water to the media mixture or paper towels until they are moist but no additional water can be squeezed out.

Fill the bottom of the container with moistened media. If using paper towels, lay several layers in the container bottom. Place the seeds on top of the media.

Cover seeds. Use a ½-inch of additional media or layers of paper towels to cover seeds.

Seal, cool and wait. Close the container or plastic bag and place in a cool location such as a refrigerator or cool shed. The location should stay between 30°-50°F for the length of time needed for the particular species.

Check moisture. Periodically check to see if the media is still moist. If dry, add moisture using a spray bottle.

Bring to room temperature and plant. After the necessary time has passed, move the container to a room-temperature area (about 70°F) and remove the lid. The seed can remain in the current container to germinate or moved to a different container such as a seed-starting tray. If the seeds begin germinating in the stratification container, wait to move them until they are sturdy enough to be gently handled during transplanting.

Scarification

Some seeds have coats that are tougher than others, which enables seeds in nature to travel away from parent plants to reduce competition for resources. The seed coat wears away the farther the seed travels. In nature, this occurs as seed coats are damaged by contact with soil and mineral particles, interactions with animals, and other physical abrasions incurred during travel.

In a controlled setting, seed coats may need to be mechanically damaged, or scarred, to mimic natural wear before the seed will germinate. Scarification is an artificial process of breaking, scratching, or softening a hard seed coat to allow water to penetrate the seed and initiate germination.

To scarify seeds:

- Use a file or sandpaper to rub the seed coat.
- Place the seed in a bag or container with sand or other coarse, gritty material and shake the bag to mix. Use this method for larger seeds that can be sifted from the abrading material. If the seeds are smaller, it can be difficult to separate the seed from the sand or grit when finished. If using a material that is gravel-sized or larger, this method can be used for smaller seeds and the seeds can then be sifted from the material by falling through a sieve.
- Soak the seed in an acidic solution to dissolve the seed coat.

24.1c Starting Seeds Indoors

When starting seeds indoors, there are many components needed to create a suitable growing environment. These include the selection of containers, growing media, water, temperature control, and a light source. Once you have these components in place, you can begin sowing your seeds.

Containers

Container selection will depend on your own personal propagation process and timeline leading up to when the developed plant will be finally transplanted.

If you intend to "pot-up" seedlings (transplant seedlings into successively larger containers as they grow), you can select almost any clean container, provided it allows for good drainage and is at least two inches deep.

SCARIFICATION BY SOAKING

Before a seed can germinate, it must absorb water from the media in which it is placed. It can take several days for the seed to absorb enough moisture from the soil or other planting media to complete this stage of the germination process, especially if the media dries out.

To speed up the absorption, or imbibition, process, soak the seeds in water for several hours or overnight. Most perennials and woody-plant seeds benefit from soaking. It is unnecessary to soak vegetable seeds but is not harmful to do so. Spinach and cilantro, among others, derive a marked germination benefit from soaking.

Do not leave any seed submerged in water for more than eight hours.

It is common to use greenhouse-style propagation trays or plug flats that are designed for growing one plant per cell. These trays can range in cell size from ½- to one-inch microcells to large two-inch cells with deep-root wells. Using one seed per cell is especially useful when propagating valuable seeds, older seeds, or seeds that grow quickly and require more space immediately. Some seeds can be planted in multiples per cell and then easily thinned to one plant per cell by trimming the seedling at the stem.

By germinating seedlings in separate root wells (vs. an undivided tray), the seedlings will not tangle and there is less risk of root damage during transplant.

If you intend to grow seedlings in containers that will not get potted up or maybe only once, you will need to anticipate the expected size of the plant and its root mass to ensure that it does not get root-bound. Examples of containers that work well for this process include nursery containers, plastic pots, decorative flower pots, or other clean, recycled containers with adequate drainage. Recycled containers are a creative way to reuse clean items such as cottage-cheese cartons, yogurt cups, milk jugs, pie pans, and egg cartons.

Alternative containers

Many planting containers are made of materials intended to biodegrade, allow more air flow, reduce product weight, or alleviate plastic waste. Biodegradable products like compressed peat, coir (coconut husk fiber) or compressed cow manure are available as alternatives to traditional clay or plastic containers. Other alternatives include compressed paper or fibers as well as containers made of sewn fabric.

These alternatives were created to address problems like plastic waste, constricted root growth or root rot, and handling issues due to the weight of the container. Ultimately, your container choice will vary depending on your growing methods and the resources at your disposal.

Media

The material in which the seed is germinated and then grown in is referred to as the medium. Growing media may be different than the initial material used to germinate the seed as well as different from what transplants may be planted in for grow-out. This media is often completely soilless, which is why it is often labeled as "seed-starting mix" or "potting mix."

Good soilless mixes are readily available in garden centers. They are easy to handle, lightweight, and produce uniform plant growth. They usually contain some proportion of sphagnum peat moss, perlite, and vermiculite, which are generally free of diseases, weed seeds, and insects. These mixes are desirable because the peat moss holds water very well, yet the large pore spaces allow excess water to drain easily. Its high porosity also promotes quick and extensive root growth.

Some soilless mixes are produced specifically for seed germination but unless you are starting very fine seeds, a general-purpose soilless mix will be sufficient for most seed-starting projects.

It is a good idea to purchase a commercially-packaged media that has already been sterilized and is free of contaminants. The "home" sterilization process requires the use of an oven, microwave, or industrial steamer. This process is inefficient, arduous and can produce very unpleasant odors and is not a recommended method for the general public.

Even if the media has been initially sterilized, best-handling practices are still advised when using and storing media to avoid contamination. The "damping-off" fungi, *Pythium* and *Rhizoctonia*, can quickly infect media and kill a stand of seedlings if the conditions allow for it. Contamination may occur when the growing medium is too wet.

Always store media in a dry, sealed container and prepare it for planting by wetting and amending it in a separate container. If an infection occurs, discard the affected media, wash containers and implements to remove any debris, and dip them for one to two minutes in a solution of one part chlorine bleach to 10 parts water. Then rinse with clean water.

Make note of the media requirements of specialized plants like cactus, orchid, and bog plants. For these seeds, growers should use media mixes specific to environmental needs of the plant, including drainage, mineral and nutrient content, moisture retention, and airflow. Most specialized media is available for purchase in garden centers and online.

Water

Seed germination begins with the absorption of water. The amount of water available in the germination medium affects the ability of the seed to complete this process. An adequate and continuous supply is essential. Once the process has begun, a dry period will cause the death of the embryo.

Always mix warm water into your growing medium to moisten it prior to seeding. The medium should be uniformly moist to the point of being able to make a ball in your hand, but not so wet as to be able to squeeze water from it. Ideally, seed flats should remain sufficiently moist during the germination period so that watering is not necessary. Lack of uniformity, over-watering, and drying out are problems associated with hand-watering the medium after planting. Additionally, small seeds planted along the very surface of the container may be disturbed with hand-watering.

To assure adequate moisture for germination:

- Cover the container with plastic wrap, purchase matching humidity domes for greenhouse flats, or place the container completely inside a clear plastic bag after an initial watering with a fine-mist spray.
- The plastic should not rest directly on the growing medium; you may need to use items like silverware, popsicle sticks, plant labels, skewers, etc. to prop the plastic up like a tent over the medium.
- Keep the container out of direct sunlight to prevent heat buildup.
- Be sure to remove the covering as soon as the first seedlings appear.
- Water to keep the medium moist, but not wet. It's fine if the surface of the growing medium dries a bit at this stage. You can either mist water onto the media surface or allow your growing medium to wick up water by setting your containers on a shallow pan and adding small amounts of water to the pan.

Temperature

Favorable temperatures are required for germination and optimal growth. Temperature affects not only the number of seeds that will germinate but also the rate of germination. Many seeds have minimum, maximum, and optimum temperatures for germination. Some seeds will germinate over a wide range of temperatures, whereas others fall into a narrow range. For example, tomato seed has a minimum germination temperature of 50°F and a maximum of 95°F, but an optimum germination temperature of about 80°F. Where germination temperatures are listed, they are usually the optimum temperatures.

In some cases, optimum temperature can be reached by placing the germination flat near a sunny window, using the heat produced from an incandescent or fluorescent light bulb, or placing the flat on a warm surface like the top of a refrigerator. These methods are, however, prone to temperature fluctuations and drying

> **ALWAYS LABEL YOUR SEEDLINGS**
>
> You may think you can remember what you planted where, but when seedlings are young, they tend to look very much alike. Label your seedling containers with the variety name and date you planted the seed so that you can check to see if the seeds are germinating as they should.

out. The most reliable way to maintain appropriate temperature during germination is to use a heat mat designed for propagation. These mats are waterproof and designed to maintain growing media at a temperature that is approximately 10°-20°F above the ambient room temperature (about 70°-80°F). Heating mats with adjustable thermostats are also available for seeds that require very narrow temperature ranges.

After germination, seedlings can be given somewhat cooler conditions, with a 55°-60°F night temperature and a 65°-70°F day reading. Note: This temperature refers to the temperature of the growing media, not the air.

Light

The presence of light can either stimulate or inhibit the process of germination, so it is important to know the light requirements for the seeds you intend to germinate. This is often expressed as the planting depth for the seeds. Some seeds will germinate best in darkness, which often requires planting seeds under a thin layer of medium. Calendula, centaurea, annual phlox, verbena, and vinca are examples of plants whose seed germinates best in the dark.

Other seeds, usually the very tiny ones, need light to germinate and should be sown on top of the medium. Examples: ageratum, begonia, browallia, impatiens, lettuce, and petunia.

When sowing light-requiring seed, simulate natural seed dispersal by scattering seeds on the surface of the growing medium and leave them exposed. You may use a fine layer of peat moss or fine vermiculite to hold the seeds in place if that is a concern. These two materials will permit some light to reach the seed and will not inhibit germination.

After germination, seedlings require strong light. The natural light from a window is seldom bright enough for strong seedling growth. Instead, place them one to two inches beneath a fluorescent or LED fixture for 14 to 16 hours a day. An example of an appropriate light setup would be to use two 40-watt, cool-white fluorescent tubes suspended on an adjustable hanger so that they may be gradually raised as the seedlings grow.

Selecting an appropriate light source for indoor germination

- **T- fluorescent bulbs.** Labeled "T" for "tube." The number that follows the T refers to the diameter of the tube (e.g., T-5). They require a ballast fixture like a shop light. These fluorescent bulbs are effective and usually the most economical option for small-scale propagation. They can be placed very close to plants with little damage. Some bulbs produce a light that appears more blue and others may appear as a warmer light, which correlates with the Kelvin rating. A lower Kelvin rating (~5,600 Kelvin) produces a bluer light that encourages stockier growth in seedlings. A Kelvin rating on the higher end (~6,400 Kelvin) produces a warmer light that is suitable for any kind of vegetation.

- **High-output T-bulbs (T5/ HOT5).** These fluorescent tube bulbs are adjusted to produce a brighter light. A full spectrum, high-output light provides a better light source for seedlings through the transplant stage. Note that the narrow bulb requires a special fixture that may not be readily available.

- **Light-emitting diode (LED).** LEDs can emit more than twice the amount of light produced by regular fluorescent bulbs, and with a lower energy-use requirement. They are available in a wide range of prices and come in many shapes and sizes, some of which are designed to maximize growth during different stages of development. LEDs can deliver red and blue spectrums exclusively (which are the main wavelengths required for plant growth) or provide a balanced spectrum in more neutral white-light wavelengths. Either will work for at-home seed-starting.

Pre-germination

Another method of starting seeds is pre-germination, i.e., sprouting the seeds before they are planted in pots or in the garden.

This technique is especially useful when trying to propagate seeds of questionable viability, seeds with high value and limited quantity, or seeds that may be more difficult to germinate otherwise. The germinated seeds are then carefully planted in media as described above.

By closely controlling temperature and moisture you can achieve a higher rate of germination more quickly, while efficiently using planting media for only the seeds that germinate.

ABOUT LED LIGHTS

LED lights will produce much less heat than fluorescent bulbs. The difference needs to be accounted for to maintain the growing environment. The most typical difference when switching from T-bulb to LED would less watering as there is less evaporation and drying caused by bulb heat.

Pay careful attention to the distance between LED lights and seedlings. Because LEDs have a much higher photosynthetic efficiency, they do not need to be as close as a T-bulb. Incorrect placement could result in plant bleaching or death. Eye protection is recommended due the light intensity of some LED lights, which may impact your lighting choice.

- Lay seeds between the folds of a moistened paper towel and place inside a clear plastic bag.
- Keep seeds moist and in a warm place.
- When roots begin to show, plant the seeds into two- to three-inch containers or directly into your garden. Be careful not to break off tender roots.
- Keep the transplants from drying out while they become established.
- Plant the seeds to only half the recommended depth and gently press a little moistened media over the sprouted seed.
- Keep the pots in a warm place and follow steps for seedling and transplant care.

24.1d Starting Seeds Outdoors

Many seeds can be successfully sown directly in the garden. Directions for outdoor sowing are usually found on the seed packet and often you will see them represented by a map graphic which shows the appropriate timing to direct sow according to the state or region in which you live. Use this information, along with the spring frost-free data for your area, to determine the best week to sow your seeds without the risk of a late frost.

The temperature of the soil will be a key factor in determining success with direct sowing, as seeds of warm-season plants will either not germinate or rot in soil that is too cool. You can use a soil thermometer to monitor soil temperature or consult a national database to estimate weekly soil temperatures based on your location. Most vegetables germinate and grow best in soil that is 65°-75°F, however other types of seeds may vary. Use the seed packet information and other available references to determine the most appropriate soil temperature for starting your seeds.

- Determine the best week for sowing based on growing zone and spring frost-free dates.
- Monitor the soil temperature (not the air temperature).
- Prepare the seed bed by removing all debris.
- Plant the seeds according to the instructions on the seed packet. This includes planting depth and spacing between plants and rows.
- Label freshly-seeded areas to avoid over-seeding or accidental foot traffic. If the seeds were broadcast, mark the area in which they were spread or string a border around it.
- After seeding—but prior to germination and emergence—keep the bed moist by using a fine mist of water.
- After seedlings emerge, thin them as prescribed by the seed packet or other reliable reference. Thinning is not necessary in every instance, but it is important to ensure the developing seedlings have enough space to grow and support themselves with the surrounding nutrients.

There are many ways which a gardener can direct-sow besides hand-seeding. The following tools make easy work of the task.

Seed tape

Most garden stores and seed catalogs offer indoor and outdoor seed tapes. Seed tape has precisely-spaced seeds enclosed in an organic, water-soluble material. When planted, the tape dissolves and the seeds germinate normally. Seed tapes are especially convenient for tiny, hard-to-handle seeds, like carrots. The main benefit is that they allow uniform emergence of seedlings, nearly eliminate overcrowding and the need for thinning, and permit sowing in perfectly straight rows. The tapes can be cut at any point for multiple row plantings. They are expensive, but a quick online search will teach you how you can make your own seed tapes.

Seed-spacing ruler

A yardstick with precisely-measured holes to press a dibbler into the ground to make evenly-spaced holes for seeding within a straight row.

Dibbler

A dibbler enables gardeners to quickly create neat rows of holes ready for seeding. A single-hole dibbler is a spike shaped tool that is pressed into the ground to create a hole of the desired depth. Often a dibbler will have a depth gauge marked on the side to assure accurate planting. A plate dibbler has the ability to create multiple planting holes simultaneous with a single punch. It is often a large plank with many evenly spaced dowels on one side that can be pressed into loose soil. The rolling-style dibbler can be single or double and set to roll out holes at varying spacing settings.

Precision seeder

A walk-behind device that combines a dibbler and a seed hopper. Although sizes and designs vary, a typical seeder will have a dibbling wheel leading a seed hopper that disperses seeds as the wheels turn. Seed spacing and quantity are regulated as the seeds leave the hopper and pass through seed-plate wheels before falling into the holes created by the dibbler. Seed plates can be made to accommodate varying sizes of seeds and also varied spacing settings. For larger gardens and beds, this is a very efficient tool for seeding quickly while preventing seed waste.

24.2 Growing Transplants

The term "transplant" for home gardeners typically refers to plants grown in individual cells or small containers that will be "potted-up" into larger containers before eventually being moved outside and planted in the garden. (The term also may refer to the selection of month-old plants that can be purchased from a local nursery or garden center for transplanting.)

Potting-up

If plants have been seeded into small individual containers or cells, they must be potted-up (transplanted) to give them proper growing space, both for their roots and developing leaves.

One of the most common mistakes gardeners make is to leave seedlings too long in the seed flat. The ideal time to transplant young seedlings is when they are small and there is little danger of setback. This is usually about the time when the first true leaves appear above or between the cotyledon leaves. The cotyledons, or seed leaves, are the first leaves the seedling produces. (See **Chapter 4, Basic Botany**.) Failing to pot-up seedlings can result in stunted roots or overall growth or leggy plants as they compete for light, nutrients, and/or water.

To pot-up seedlings:

- Carefully remove the small seedlings from the seed flats or small containers by using a knife or other flat implement to separate the container wall from the root ball.

- Gently squeeze the bottom of the container in order to further loosen the root ball and to push it up and out of the container.

- **Handle small seedlings by their leaves, not their delicate stems.**

- Make a hole in the media into which the seedling will be planted. Set the seedlings so that the leaves and growing point are only slightly above the soil line (most of the stem can be buried).

- Firm the media around each plant and water gently.

- The transplants should continue to grow under grow lights until ready to be acclimated to outdoor conditions.

Fertilizing transplants

Where seed-starting mixes usually do not, soilless mixes may contain a small amount of added soluble nutrients. If your transplants are to be grown for more than six weeks you may need to fertilize with a soluble fertilizer. Follow label directions for indoor plants or transplants. Wash off any liquid fertilizer that contacts foliage. Young seedlings are easily damaged by too much fertilizer, especially if they are under any moisture stress. Alternatively, a high-quality screened compost can be mixed 50–50 with a soilless mix to grow transplants. The compost provides additional nutrients.

Hardening off

This process enables young seedlings to acclimate to the outside environment with gradual exposure to outdoor conditions. It encourages a change from soft, succulent growth to a firmer, harder growth that can withstand elements like wind and natural UV light, as well as changes in humidity and temperature.

To harden-off seedlings:

- Begin hardening transplants one to two weeks prior to setting outside. The easiest way to harden transplants is to place them outside in a shaded, protected spot on warm days, bringing them in at night.
- Each day, increase the amount of sunlight the transplants receive, starting with one hour of exposure.

COLD FRAMES

A cold frame provides an excellent environment for hardening off transplants. It is basically a miniature greenhouse without a bottom and an adjustable clear lid that allows you to regulate the inside temperature. A cold frame insulates your tender transplants from frost, warms the soil and gets your plants off to a strong start.

- Nighttime exposure can also gradually increase to allow transplants to stay outside overnight if the temperature will not fall below 50°F.
- Don't put tender seedlings outdoors on windy days, when heavy rain is expected or when temperatures are below 45°F. (Note: Even cold-hardy plants will be injured if exposed to freezing temperatures before they are hardened)
- Reduce the frequency of watering to slow plant growth, but don't allow plants to wilt.
- The hardening-off process should extend over roughly 7-10 days of successful transitioning. This period may be extended to compensate for days missed due to poor conditions.

- It is important to plant your transplants as soon as they are ready in order to avoid stunting and development issues caused by too small of a growing pot.

24.3 Asexual Propagation

Asexual, or vegetative multiplication, uses a vegetative part of one donor parent plant (stem, root, or leaf) to generate a new plant. Genetically, the new plant is identical to its donor parent.

Asexual propagation, in certain situations, may be the best way to maintain and reproduce specific desirable traits found in parent plants. This is particularly true when an individual plant exhibits characteristics that are not genetically stable enough to be passed on through sexual reproduction. There may be situations where the population of a species is so limited or scarce that it could not support sexual reproduction and using asexual propagation can overcome that hurdle.

Asexual propagation techniques produce clones, which are new individuals that are identical to their one donor parent plant. Many named cultivars of plants have been propagated asexually for years to consistently maintain the distinct characteristic of the specific cultivar for consumers (e.g., Red Delicious apples).

24.3a Cuttings

Many types of woody and herbaceous plants can be propagated by cuttings. A cutting is a vegetative plant part that is severed from the parent plant in order to regenerate itself and form a whole new plant. Plants may be propagated from cuttings of their stems, leaves, or roots, depending upon the plant.

The time of year to take cuttings also varies by plant species. Use reliable references to determine the specific recommendations for the plant you want to propagate.

Stem cuttings

- **Tip cuttings.** Detach a two- to six-inch piece of stem, including the terminal bud. Make the cut just below a node (the part of the stem where the bud arises). Remove lower leaves, leaving one to three leaves closest to the plant tip, ensuring that no leaves are touching or are below the soil surface. Insert the cutting deeply enough into the medium to support itself. At least one node must be below the surface. (See Figure 24-B.)
- **Median cuttings.** Make the first cut just above a node and the second cut just below another node, two to six inches further down the stem. Prepare and

Figure 24-B. Stem-cutting propagation

insert the cutting as you would a tip cutting. Be sure to position it right side up. If uncertain which side is up, axial buds are always above leaves. (See Figure 24-B.)

- **Cane cuttings.** Cut cane-like stems into sections containing one or two eyes, or nodes. Allow to dry several hours. Lay horizontally with about half of the cutting below the medium surface, with the eye facing upward. (See Figure 24-B.) Cane cuttings are usually potted when roots and new shoots appear.

Leaf cuttings

Leaf cuttings (Figure 24-C) are used almost exclusively for a few indoor plants. Leaf cuttings of most plants will either produce a few roots but no plant, or just decay.

- **Whole leaf with petiole.** Detach the leaf and ½ to 1½ inches of petiole. Insert the lower end of the petiole into the medium. One or more new plants will form at the base of the petiole. The leaf may be severed from the new plants when they have their own roots, and the petiole can be reused. This method can be used to propagate African violets.

- **Whole leaf without petiole.** This method is used for plants with sessile (no petiole) leaves. Vertically insert the cutting into the medium. A new plant will form from the auxiliary bud. The leaf can be removed when the new plant has its own roots.

- **Split vein.** Detach a leaf from the stock plant. Make perpendicular slits in the veins on the lower leaf surface. Lay the cutting, lower side down, on the medium. New plants will form at each cut. If the leaf curls, hold it in place by covering the margins with the rooting medium or by using straight pins. A rex begonia can be propagated like this.

- **Leaf (or wedge) section.** This method is often used with snake plant and fibrous-rooted begonias. Cut begonia leaves into wedges with at least one vein. Lay leaves flat on the medium. A new plant will sprout at the vein. Cut snake plant leaves into two-inch sections. Consistently make the lower cut slanted and the upper cut straight so you can identify the top. Vertically insert the cutting. Roots form quickly and a new plant will appear at the base of the cutting. Note that succulent cuttings will rot if kept too moist.

Figure 24-C. Leaf-cutting propagation

Figure 24-D. Root-cutting propagation

Root cuttings

Root cuttings (Figure 24-D) are usually taken from two- to three-year-old plants during their dormant season, when they have a large carbohydrate supply. Root cuttings of some species produce new shoots which then form their own root systems, whereas root cuttings of other plants develop root systems before producing new shoots.

- **Plants with small roots.** Take one- to two-inch sections of roots. Insert the cuttings horizontally about ½-inch below the medium surface. This method is usually done indoors or in a hotbed.
- **Plants with large roots.** Make a straight top cut. Make a slanted cut two to six inches below the first cut. Store about three weeks in moist sawdust, peat moss, or sand at 40°F. Remove from storage. Insert the cutting vertically, with its top approximately level with the surface of the rooting medium. This method is often done outdoors.

24.3b Layering

Layering is a process by which roots will form on a branch or stem while still attached to the parent plant. (See Figures 24-E and 24-F.) Many plants (e.g., vines, brambles) do this naturally.

TIPS FOR PROPAGATING WITH CUTTINGS

- Use a sharp, disinfected knife or razor blade to remove cuttings, which reduces injury to the parent plant.
- Between cuts, dip the cutting tool in rubbing alcohol or a mixture of one part bleach to nine parts water to prevent disease transmission.
- Remove flowers and flower buds from the cutting so its energy is used for root and shoot formation rather than fruit and seed production.
- If desired or recommended, use a rooting hormone to hasten rooting, increase the number of roots, or obtain uniform rooting. To prevent contamination, place a portion of the hormone in a separate container to dip cuttings.
- Dip the stem in rooting hormone and gently tap to remove excess. Do not return unused hormone to the original container to avoid contamination.
- Insert cuttings into a moist rooting medium such as coarse sand, vermiculite, soilless mix, water, or a mixture of peat and perlite. The rooting medium should be sterile, low in fertility, and able to retain enough moisture to prevent water stress. Keep the medium evenly moist while cuttings are rooting.
- Place stem and leaf cuttings in bright, but indirect, light. Root cuttings can be kept in the dark until new shoots appear. Covering the potted cutting with plastic will encourage root growth.

Figure 24-E.   Propagation by layering

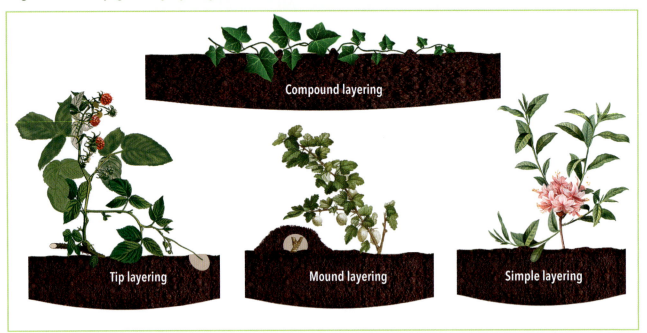

Simple layering

Bend the stem to the ground. Cover part of it with soil, leaving the last six to 12 inches exposed. Bend the tip into a vertical position and stake in place. The sharp bend will often induce rooting, but wounding the lower side of the branch or loosening the bark by twisting the stem can increase rooting success. Examples: rhododendron, azalea.

Tip layering

Dig a hole three to four inches deep. Insert the shoot tip and cover it with soil. The tip grows downward first, then bends sharply and grows upward. Roots form at the bend, and the recurved tip becomes a new plant. Remove the tip layer and plant it in the early spring or late fall. Examples: purple and black raspberries, trailing blackberries.

Compound layering

This method works well for plants with flexible stems. Wound the lower side of the stem sections to be covered. Bend the stem to the rooting medium as for simple layering, but alternately cover and expose stem sections. Examples: heart-leaf philodendron, ivy.

Mound layering

Cut the plant back to one inch above the ground in the dormant season. Mound soil over the cut stems. In the spring, shoots will sprout through the soil mound. Rooting will occur at the shoots' base. The new shoots can be cut and planted in a new location. Examples: gooseberries, apple rootstocks.

Air layering

This process is used most often with tropical houseplants such as dumbcane and rubber plant, especially those that have become too tall or leggy. Cut out a strip of bark just below a node; pack the stripped area with slightly moist sphagnum moss, then wrap securely with clear plastic. When roots form within the moss, the new plant can be severed from the parent and planted. (See Figure 24-F.)

Figure 24-F. Air-layering a houseplant

1. Score a 1-½" strip around the trunk with a clean, sharp knife.
2. Wrap the cut in moist sphagnum moss.
3. Wrap the moss in in plastic and twist-tie the top & bottom.
4. Remove top when roots form and place in a new pot.
5. Repot the original plant and the stump will sprout.

Naturally-occurring forms of layering

Stolons and rhizomes

- A stolon (or "runner") is a slender, above-ground stem that creeps along the surface of the soil, forms a shoot at the end and sends down roots to form a clone of the original plant. Then the process repeats. Examples: strawberry, spider plant.

- Rhizomes grow underground and have less distance between nodes. New shoots and roots can grow anywhere along their length. Plants that produce stolons or rhizomes are propagated by severing the new plants from their parent stems. Plantlets at the tips of runners can be rooted while still attached to the parent, or detached and placed in a rooting medium. Examples: iris, ferns, ginger.

Offsets

Plants with a rosetted stem often reproduce by forming new shoots, or "offsets," at their base or in leaf axils.

New shoots can be severed from the parent plant after they develop their own root system. Unrooted offsets of some species can be removed and placed in a rooting medium. Some must be cut off the parent stem, while others may be simply lifted off. Examples: date palm, haworthia, bromeliads, and many cacti.

24.3c Division and Separation

Division

Division works best with multi-stemmed plants, most notably herbaceous perennials. It involves cutting a plant into segments, each of which must have a bud and some root. Most plants divide best in early spring, before new growth begins or the plant is still very small. Examples: snake plant, iris, prayer plant, and daylily.

Separation

Separation is a form of propagation used with plants that produce bulbs, corms or rhizomes. It involves digging up the parent plant and separating of portions before replanting (see Figure 24-G).

UME © 2025. All rights reserved.

Bulb separation

- New bulbs, called bulblets, form beside the parent plant's bulb.
- Separate these bulb-clumps every three to five years for largest blooms and to increase bulb population.
- Dig up the clump after the leaves have withered. Gently pull the bulbs apart and replant them immediately so their roots can begin to develop.
- Small new bulbs may not flower for two or three years, but large ones should bloom the first year. Examples: tulip, narcissus.

Corm separation

- A large new corm forms on top of the old corm, and tiny cormels (developing corms) form around it.
- After the leaves wither, dig up the corms and allow them to dry in indirect light for two or three weeks.
- Remove the cormels, then gently separate the new corm from the old corm.
- If warranted, dust all new corms with a fungicide (e.g., sulfur) and store in a cool place until planting time. Examples: crocus, gladiolus.

Figure 24-G. Corm separation and rhizome division

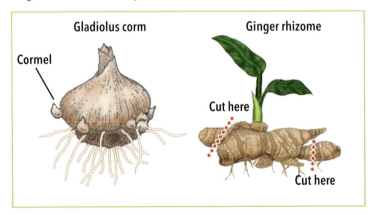

Tubers

- Tubers are fleshy, underground stems with buds that sprout new growth. They can be propagated by planting the whole tuber or cutting it into pieces.
- Each piece must contain an "eye" or bud. Tuberous roots are similarly propagated—make sure each piece has a bud. Example: potatoes.

Rhizomes

- Rhizomes are horizontal stems that grow at or just below the surface.
- Propagate rhizomes by cutting the into sections, each containing an eye or bud, and replant at the same depth. Examples: iris, ginger.

24.3d Grafting and Budding

Grafting and budding are methods that join parts from two different plants so they will grow as one plant. These techniques are used to propagate cultivars that do not root well as cuttings or whose own root systems are inadequate or prone to disease or pests. One or more new cultivars can be added to existing fruit and nut trees by grafting or budding. The portion of the cultivar to be propagated is called the scion. It consists of a piece of shoot with dormant buds that will produce the stem and branches. The rootstock, or stock, provides the new plant's root system and sometimes the lower part of the stem. The cambium is a layer of cells located between the wood and bark of a stem from which new bark and wood cells originate.

Figure 24-H. Cleft grafting

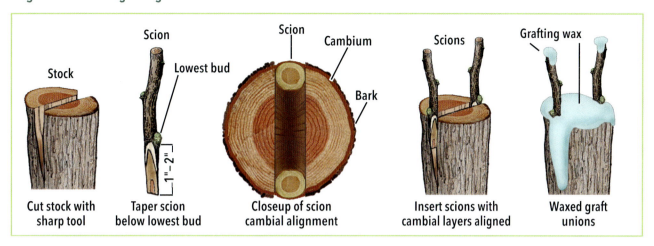

Grafting

Four conditions must be met if grafting is to be successful:

1. The scion and rootstock must be compatible.
2. Each must be at the proper physiological stage.
3. The cambial layers of the scion and stock must meet.
4. The graft union must be kept moist until the wound has healed.

Cleft grafting

Cleft grafting (Figure 24-H) is often used to change the cultivar (top growth) of a shoot or a young tree, usually a seedling. It is especially successful if done in the early spring.

- Collect scion wood that is ⅜-inch to ⅝-inch in diameter.
- Cut the limb or small tree trunk to be reworked perpendicular to its length.
- Make a two-inch vertical cut through the center of the previous cut. Be careful not to tear the bark. Keep this cut wedged apart.
- Cut the lower end of each scion piece into a wedge. Prepare two scion pieces that are three to four inches long.
- Insert the scions at the outer edges of the cut in the stock. Tilt the top of the scion slightly outward and the bottom slightly inward to be sure the cambial layers of the scion and stock touch.
- Remove the wedge, prop the slit open, and cover cut surfaces with grafting wax.

Bark grafting

Unlike most grafting methods, bark grafting can be used on large limbs, although these often become infected before the wound can completely heal.

- Collect scion wood ⅜- to ½-inch in diameter when the plant is dormant, and store the wood wrapped in moist paper in a plastic bag in the refrigerator.
- Saw off the limb or trunk of the rootstock at a right angle to itself.
- In the spring when the bark is easy to separate from the wood, make a ½-inch diagonal cut on one side of the scion, and a ½- to one-inch diagonal cut on the other side. Leave two buds above the longer cut.

- Cut through the bark of the stock a little wider than the scion. Remove the top third of the bark from this cut.
- Insert the scion with the longer cut against the wood. Nail the graft in place with flat-headed wire nails. Cover all wounds with grafting wax.

Whip (splice) grafting

This method is often used for material ¼- to ½-inch in diameter. The scion and rootstock are usually of the same diameter, but the scion may be narrower than the stock. This strong graft heals quickly and provides excellent cambial contact.

- Make a 2½-inch sloping cut at the top of the rootstock and a matching cut on the bottom of the scion.
- On the cut surface, slice downward into the stock and up into the scion so the pieces will interlock. Fit the pieces together, then tie and wax the union.

Caring for the graft

Very little success in grafting will be achieved unless proper care is maintained for the first year or two. If a binding material such as strong cord or nursery tape is used on the graft, it must be cut and removed shortly after growth starts to prevent girdling and eventual death of the graft. Rubber budding strips have some advantages over other materials. They expand with growth and usually do not need to be cut because they deteriorate and break after a short time.

Inspect the grafts after two to three weeks to see if the wax has cracked, and, if necessary, re-wax the exposed areas. Limbs of the old variety that are not selected for grafting should be cut back at the time of grafting. The total leaf surface of the old variety should be gradually reduced as the new one increases. After one or two years the new variety will have taken over. Completely removing all the limbs of the old variety at grafting time causes shock to the tree and excessive suckering. Also, the scions may grow too fast, making them susceptible to wind damage.

Budding

Budding (also known as bud grafting) is the union of one bud and a small piece of bark from the scion with a rootstock. It is especially useful when scion material is limited. It is also faster and forms a stronger union than traditional forms of grafting.

Figure 24-I. Bark grafting

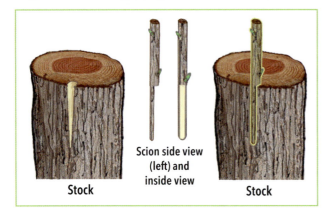

Figure 24-J. Whip grafting

Figure 24-K. Chip budding

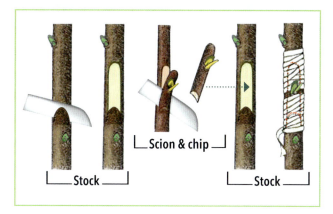

Figure 24-L. T-budding

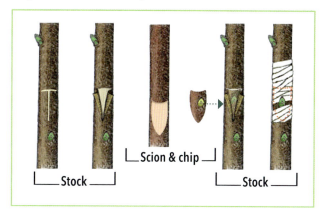

Patch budding

Plants with thick bark should be patch budded. This is done while the plants are actively growing so that their bark slips easily.

- Remove a rectangular piece of bark from the rootstock.
- Cover this wound with a bud and matching piece of bark from the scion.
- If the rootstock's bark is thicker than the scion's, pare it down to meet the thinner bark so that when the union is wrapped the patch will be held firmly in place.

Chip budding

This method can be used when the bark is not slipping (see Figure 24-K).

- Make a ¼-inch cut down into the rootstock stem at an angle of about 45°.
- Start a top cut 1¼-inches above the lower cut and angle it down to join the basal cut; remove the chip.
- Make similar cuts on the scion as on the rootstock, ensuring that the bud is included midway down the chip. Fit the chip to the stock and wrap the union.

T-budding

This is the most commonly-used budding technique (see Figure 24-L).

- When the bark is slipping, make a T-shaped cut through the bark of the rootstock, avoiding any buds.
- Loosen the bark by twisting the knife at the intersection.
- Remove a shield-shaped piece of the scion, including a bud, bark, and a thin section of wood. Push the shield under the loosened stock bark. Wrap the union, leaving the bud exposed.

Caring for buds

Place the bud into the stock in August. Force the bud to develop the next spring by cutting the stock off three to four inches above the bud. The new shoot may be tied to the resulting stub to prevent wind damage. After the shoot has made a strong union with the stock, cut the stub off close to the budded area.

Tissue culture

Tissue culture uses bits of plant material placed in a sterile medium (such as agar) to ultimately grow into new clones of the original. This method allows for the propagation of many hard-to-reproduce plants, making them more widely available. It requires exacting, sterile conditions and is not practical for the general gardening public. ❋

AUTHORS

Susan Trice, Master Gardener Coordinator, University of Maryland Extension.

Courtney Coddington, Home Horticulture Agent Associate, University of Maryland Extension.

Thanks to Mikaela Boley, Senior Agent for Home Horticulture, University of Maryland Extension and Janet Mackey, Talbot County Master Gardener for their contribution of Table 24-B.

PUBLICATIONS

Adapted in part from the *University of Maryland Handbook (2016 edition)*.

Bir, R. E. 1992. *Growing and Propagating Showy Native Woody Plants.* University of North Carolina Press. Chapel Hill, NC. ISBN: 0807843660.

Browning, Sarah. 2011. *What Are Heirlooms?* University of Nebraska Extension in Lancaster County, Lincoln, NE.

Bubel, N. 1988. *The New Seed Starters Handbook*. Rodale Press. Emmaus, PA. ISBN: 0878577521.

Dirr, M., and C. Heuser. 1987. *Reference Manual of Woody Plant Propagation.* Varsity Press. Athens, GA. Hartmann, H.T., D. Kester, F. Davies, and R. Geneve. 2001. *Plant Propagation: Principles and Practices.* 7th Edition. Prentice Hall. Englewood Cliffs, NJ. ISBN: 0136810160.

Hill, L. 1991. *Secrets of Plant Propagation.* Storey Communications. Pownal, VT. ISBN: 0882663704.

U. S. Forest Service. 1974. *Seeds of Woody Plants in the U.S. Agriculture Handbook # 450.* USDA, Washington D.C.

PHOTOS

Main chapter image (cacti): **Pexels,** accessed 3/10/22.

Seed packet: Botanical Interests, Boulder CO. Used with permission.

TABLES AND ILLUSTRATIONS

Table 24-A: Erv Evans and Frank Blazich. *Starting Plants from Seeds.* HIL-8703. North Carolina Cooperative Extension Service. Adapted with permission.

All figures either illustrated or colorized by LeAnn Zotta.

25: CONTAINER GARDENING

Emily Zobel
Ashley Bachtel-Bodkins

25 CONTAINER GARDENING

CONTENTS

25.1 Raised Beds 712

25.2 Choosing Container Plants 713

25.3 Choosing the Right Container 715

25.4 Growing Media for Containers 719

25.5 Potting and Repotting 720

25.6 Caring for Container Plants 720

25.7 Container Plant Pest and Disease Diagnostics 723

25.8 Container Combination Ideas 723

LEARNING OBJECTIVES

- The advantages and disadvantages of container gardening
- The types of plants that can be grown in containers
- The types of containers which can be used to grow different types of plants
- The types of growing media and their uses
- How to maintain a container garden
- Container combination design ideas

INTRODUCTION

Container gardening is the space-saving practice of growing plants in a pot or other vessel instead of in the ground. Containers can be placed on a deck or patio or even in the ground or another pot.

There are many reasons to start a container garden:

- A yard may be unavailable, but there may be balcony, deck, or patio space.
- If there is a yard, the soil may not be suitable for growing due to soil-borne diseases, nematodes, or poor soil conditions.
- Container gardening is a perfect way to teach children about growing plants.
- Container gardens include raised beds, which make gardening easier for those with physical limitations.
- A container can be used to add height or interest to an in-ground garden.
- Containers are a great way to grow aggressively-spreading plants that would otherwise take over your garden.

The advantages of container gardening include:

- It doesn't require any long-term changes to the landscape.
- Container gardens tend to have fewer weeds than in-ground gardens and are easier to maintain.

Figure 25-A. Balcony garden

Container gardening is ideal for people without a yard. "Vertical gardening" using hanging baskets and railing planters is perfect for areas with limited space.

- Containers can be placed almost anywhere—culinary herbs can be located close to the kitchen or plants can be situated on a deck, porch, patio, or balcony.
- Plants are movable to locations with more sun or shade for better growth, or simply to keep things interesting.
- You can take plants with you if you move.

The disadvantages include:

- The extra cost of potting mix and containers versus planting directly in the ground.
- Container gardens require more frequent watering than in-ground plants.
- After the growing season, containers must be stored, which requires space.
- There are some limitations to what you can plant. For example, trees (except dwarf/compact varieties) have a root system that is simply too large for most containers. Even if you find a container large enough, the plant will quickly outgrow it. The container will also be very difficult to move due to its weight.

25.1 Raised Beds

Raised beds are plots of soil that are constructed above ground level. They can be free-standing mounds or supported and enclosed with boards or other rigid materials.

Gardeners like raised beds because they:

- Warm up quickly in spring
- Drain well
- Less like to get compacted because the beds aren't walked upon

Figure 25-B. Raised-bed garden

Permanent paths typically border raised beds so you can stand or kneel in the path instead of compacting the soil in the bed. Use mulch, wood chips, or gravel to prevent weeds and allow rainwater to drain away.

- Don't erode/lose soil because the bed boundaries are contained
- Can produce greater yields due to high fertility, better soil structure, and more room for vigorous root growth

Raised beds do have a few disadvantages:

- There is up-front labor and expense to create the beds
- The beds dry out more quickly
- They are relatively permanent
- You must plan your garden around the bed's dimensions
- Raised beds don't work on slopes unless they are terraced

While most people think of raised beds as rectangles, they do not have to be. Design and build them in whatever shape and size you like—it's up to you. When considering your bed dimensions, make sure you can reach the middle of the bed to weed and care for plants without stepping on the soil.

Because raised beds are more permanent than other forms of container gardens, also consider sunlight patterns and access to water when choosing a location.

There are many suitable enclosure materials for raised beds, including stone, bricks, concrete blocks, wood boards (e.g., oak, locust, poplar, or cedar), recycled plastic "boards," and metal. Using a metal border will cause the soil to heat up faster, which means more frequent watering, but metal will last longer than wood or plastic. Rot-resistant lumber, such as redwood or cedar, is popular for food-growing beds. The option you choose will depend on the bed size, material cost, and what you want the end result to look like.

Unlike individual containers, raised beds are typically filled with a mixture of compost and garden soil (or purchased topsoil) in a 1:2 or 1:1 ratio. If using existing garden soil, have a soil test performed first, and if you plan to grow food, have a lead test done as well.

25.2 Choosing Container Plants

It is possible to grow almost any type of plant in a container, as long as its size is adequate for the plant at maturity. Some exceptions would be plants that have a long tap root, are very large at maturity, or have unique needs that cannot be met in a container environment.

Containers are also a good option for plants you'd like to grow that may not be hardy in your USDA growing zone. When the temperatures start to drop, you can simply move the container to a protected area.

Above-ground containers are more susceptible to weather changes because they're not insulated. They warm up more quickly in the spring but freeze faster in the fall and

About pressure-treated lumber

People are often concerned about growing food in beds bordered with pressure-treated lumber. The worry is that toxic chemicals from the treated lumber will leach into the soil.

Before 2004, pressure-treated wood was made with chromated copper arsenate (CCA), which contained arsenic, copper, and chromium. This wood is no longer available for residential use.

Alkaline copper quaternary (ACQ) is currently the most widely available type of wood preservative for residential use. It does not contain arsenic, but it does contain copper (at levels that are considered low in toxicity). For information on the health risks associated with ACQ-treated wood, see the **National Pesticide Information Center website.**

Treated wood can also be painted with exterior latex paint, or a heavy plastic liner can be installed to minimize soil contact and further reduce any potential risk.

winter. Perennials (plants that come back year after year) may need some additional care to overwinter and protect the root system. Provide a wind break or move them into an unheated building. If feasible, cover the containers or wrap them in insulating material. The goal is to provide protection but not keep the plants growing all year. Perennials need to go dormant for a period of time each year.

Which plants are good for containers?

- Bulbs and tubers, such as begonias and spring-flowering bulbs make interesting container displays. Depending upon the species they may need to be dug up in the fall, stored in an unheated garage or shed and then replanted in the spring.

Figure 25-C. Vining plant in a container

A cucumber plant grown in a terracotta pot, with some help from a trellis.

- Ornamental grasses can be a good fit for containers as well as other aggressively-growing plants that you want to keep from spreading to your landscape.

- Fruit trees and bushes can be grown in containers with the caveat that they will be smaller and not produce as much fruit. Consider fruit plants that are bred for container gardening, such as columnar apple trees, compact varieties, and dwarf citrus varieties that require a heated environment during cold months.

- Vines, both foliage-only and flowering, make great additions to containers. They can cascade over a tall container or climb a trellis to add height to a garden space.

- If growing vegetables, use container-specific varieties. These are sometimes marketed as "bush," "patio," "dwarf," or "compact." Full-sized vining vegetables such as squash, pumpkins, watermelon, or gourds, and tall crops like sweet corn, will not grow well in containers. You can, however, use a trellis for smaller vining crops like peas and cucumbers. Leafy greens do very well in shallow containers.

- Herbs (both perennial and annual) do well in containers and are a great option for restricting the growth of the aggressive mentha (mint) family.

- Annual flowers, the most common container plants, last for one growing season and are a great option for beginning container gardeners. Avoid buying fully-grown annual planters from greenhouses and nurseries. They're very expensive and will be tired-looking at the end of the season. Try your hand at creating your own combination planters using cell-pack transplants—you'll save considerable cost and create a look that's unique to your space. (See Table 25-B for inspiration and ideas.)

You can either plant seeds directly in a container or use transplants. If you choose transplants, it is more cost-efficient to use plants from a cell-pack rather than 4" or quart-sized pots. The cell-pack plants will fill in the container in no time for much less money.

Indoor plants that can be moved outdoors during warm weather can be a stunning addition to your container-garden design. Incorporate different sizes, textures, and heights for visual interest.

See the **Chapter 23, Indoor Plants**, for more information about growing indoor plants in containers and moving them outdoors for the summer.

25.3 Choosing the Right Container

Once you've decided which plants you'd like to grow, you'll need to find suitable containers. There is a wide variety of shapes and sizes available at local garden centers and through mail-order catalogs. There are also many everyday objects that can be recycled or repurposed into suitable containers.

When choosing a container, it is essential to consider the purpose of your garden. Is it to grow vegetables and herbs for cooking? Maybe you want to add a splash of color to your deck or porch. Did you receive a nice pot as a gift that you want to display? Or is there a specific plant that you have always wanted to grow? Identifying your garden's purpose will help you figure out which plants and containers to use.

Consider the following before you buy:

- What is the mature size of the plant(s) intended for the container? Consider both top growth and the root system.
- How long will the plant be in this container? A month? A growing season? A year? Multiple years?
- What are the plant's growing needs?
- Where is this container garden going to be located? Are there any limitations to that location or space?

Containers gain and lose heat faster than the ground. During the summer, the soil could heat up enough to injure tender roots and prevent the full development of a plant's root system. Avoid placing dark-colored containers or those made from materials that absorb heat, such as metal, in full-sun areas. Avoid sitting containers directly on a surface that retains and radiates heat, such as stone, concrete, brick, or asphalt. Instead, use either pot feet or a brick to raise the container, which will allow air movement beneath the pots and prevent direct contact with the hot surface.

Containers made from porous materials (like clay, ceramic, concrete, and wood) will dry out more quickly than containers made from plastic or metal, so they will need to be watered more often.

Container material

The material from which a container is made will affect the microclimate for the plants in the container. Below is some information about common materials used to make commercially-produced containers.

Clay

Terracotta clay pots are a common choice for container gardens. They come in a wide range of sizes and are relatively inexpensive. Clay will chip, crack, or break if dropped and over time can develop unsightly salt or moss stains. Be prepared to water plants in porous clay pots more often because they dry out more quickly.

Ceramic

Glazed ceramic containers are simply clay pots that have been glazed and fired. This process makes them less porous, so while they will still absorb heat, they don't lose as much water as unglazed clay pots. They can be found in a wide array of colors and designs; many are hand-painted. Glazed ceramic pots are usually pricier and heavier than standard clay pots.

Tip: Don't situate a plant in a decorative pot; plant it in a plain plastic pot that is slightly smaller than your decorative container. This practice is called double-potting and it's done because most ceramic containers don't have drainage holes. Double-potting allows the interior pot to drain, likely saving the plant (see Figure 25-D).

Plastic, resin and fiberglass

Plastic pots are inexpensive, easy to find, and come in various sizes, shapes, and colors. They are lightweight and relatively durable but will fade in time if left in direct sunlight. They are non-porous, so they retain soil moisture. Plastic pots can crack if soil freezes in them, so insulate these pots over the winter months.

Resin is low-density polyethylene that is poured into a mold and baked. Resin containers often look like stone but are very lightweight and durable. They will fade over time but are weather-resistant and good insulators.

Fiberglass is made from plastic embedded with glass fibers. This allows it to be molded into different shapes. It will often look like concrete, stone, or glazed ceramic but will be lighter and less expensive than the real thing. Fiberglass tends to be fairly durable but will crack if dropped.

Wood

Wood containers can be purchased, or you can make them. Barrel planters are popular if your goal is a rustic feel. Choose redwood, cedar, or locust for the best result.

Wood containers range in price but are usually more expensive than plastic and terracotta clay. They are relatively weather-tolerant but will need replacing after a few years.

Metal

Metal containers can be made out of copper, galvanized metal, steel, stainless steel, iron, or

Figure 25-D. Double-potting

Use this pot-in-a-pot method to create drainage in a ceramic container without holes in the bottom.

aluminum. They are long-lasting and durable but are susceptible to dents if dropped or hit with garden tools. Metal containers absorb heat better than other materials and can harm plants if temperatures get hot enough. The plant can easily dry out, wilt, develop sun scald, or even die if it's not monitored.

Concrete

Concrete containers are hard to damage and suitable for long-term use. They are weather-resistant and good insulators, but they are quite heavy, so place them on a plant dolly if you plan to move them.

Repurposed items

Using repurposed items can be a fun, cheap, easy way to add some whimsy to a garden space (see Figure 25-E). When using repurposed items make sure they meet the container requirements below; if they don't, consider double-potting.

- Do they hold the correct volume of soil for your plants?
- Are they made out of appropriate material?
- Can extra water easily drain out of them?

Repurposed items are great for flowers but consider double-potting if you are planting food plants, because items that are not food-quality may leach chemicals into the soil. Don't plant anything edible in anything older than the 1980s because it may contain lead-based paint or asbestos.

Weight

Remember that any container you choose will be heavier when filled with damp potting mix. This may make it hard to move or could add extra strain to the container's structure. Putting large, heavy items on a plant stand with wheels or a plant dolly solves this issue.

Drainage

Whichever type of container you choose, it is critical to provide adequate drainage or you risk the loss of your plants. All containers must have a way for excess water to drain out to keep plant roots from rotting or drowning.

Drainage also allows excess fertilizer and salts to be washed out. If a container doesn't have drainage holes, consider double-potting so that the plant can be removed to be watered and then replaced once it has finished draining. After watering, don't forget to empty the saucers or your plant will be standing in water, which can cause a myriad of problems.

Most commercially-sold garden pots will have drainage holes, but not all. Make sure to check before you buy. Depending upon the materials used to make the container, you may be able

Figure 25-E. Repurposed containers

to drill holes in it yourself. Do not attempt this with ceramic pots, as they are likely to crack.

Contrary to popular garden lore, adding rocks, gravel or broken pot shards in the bottom of a container will not improve drainage. It may actually raise the water table, which can contact plant roots and cause rot.

Size

The correct container size depends upon several factors, including the garden's purpose, the plant(s) you choose, the garden's lifespan, and the amount of time you want to spend caring for it.

A basic rule of thumb: Go a little larger than you think you'll need. If roots are restricted by a container that's too small, the plant won't thrive. Smaller containers take up less space, weigh less, and are easier to move compared to larger ones—however, they hold less potting mix, which means they can't hold as much water, so they will need more frequent watering. They will also require less fertilizer but will need it more often. Because there is less space for roots, plants can become stunted and yield less if they outgrow the container.

The opposite is true for larger containers. They take up more space and weigh more but can hold more potting mix, water, and nutrients. Their size, space, and weight might limit how many you have and where they can be placed. Storing them during the winter might also be more challenging.

Always choose a container based on the mature size of the plant (unless you plan to transplant it later in the growing season. Also, match the volume and depth of the container to what you're planting (see Table 25-A).

Table 25-A. Potting guide for container plants

Plant type	Examples	Amount of potting medium	Minimum pot depth
Large vegetables	Tomato, pepper, eggplant, cucumber, winter squash	8-10 gallons	12" - 16"
Medium vegetables or flowering plants	Dwarf/bush varieties of pepper, eggplant, tomato, summer squash, plus cole crops, beans, beets, chard, carrot, cabbage, larger herbs (rosemary, parsley, lavender, fennel), flowering and foliage perennials, and ornamental grass	4-6 gallons	8" - 12"
Small vegetables or flowering plants	Herbs (garlic, basil, cilantro, thyme, mint, marjoram), radish, scallion, spinach, salad greens, Asian greens, mustard greens, pea, bean, and small flowering annuals	1-3 gallons	4" - 6"
Other plants	Potato Strawberry Dwarf fruit tree Shrub	6 gallons 1 gallon 25-30 gallons 25 gallons	6" 8" 20" 18"

25.4 Growing Media for Containers

After choosing the container, the next most important decision is what to use as growing substrate. It is very important to choose good-quality growing media. Do not use soil that you dig directly from the ground or bagged top soil, as your container plants will not thrive in it. Compost and compost-based products are rich and full of nutrients but they can cause stains on decks as water leaches through the planter.

For the best chance of success, purchase potting mix (also known as soilless potting mix) or potting soil. Both are lightweight, easy to handle and drain well. Potting soil contains some soil; potting mix does not.

Potting mixes can be made of many different combinations of ingredients, depending upon the brand. Most mixes have peat moss as the main ingredient. Other components can include coconut fiber (coir), vermiculite, sand, perlite, pine bark, and/or compost.

Soilless growing mixes can get expensive, but they are:

- Sterile (free of pathogens)
- Weed-seed-free
- Optimally blended to provide good tilth and water retention
- Specifically formulated for use in containers

There are also specialized mixtures available, such as for seed-starting (a lighter, finer mix), young trees and shrubs (a higher percentage of sand or pine bark), and succulents and cactus (a sandy or gravelly mix). You can tailor the mix even more by adding a silica gel, which absorbs water and reduces the need for daily watering.

Homemade compost as growing media

Remember that if you choose to use homemade compost as your medium, it may be a source of contaminants (fungus, bacteria, diseases), especially if the temperature in the compost pile did not get hot enough to kill them.

You really cannot go wrong with potting soil or potting mix. If you're sure your compost was "hot" and killed all weed seeds and pathogens, add a little to the potting medium to enhance it.

Figure 25-F. Growing media for container gardening

Various soilless potting mixes   Pine bark   Succulents/cactus mix

Use one of the growing media above for containers rather than ground soil or purchased topsoil.

Lastly, adding a slow-release fertilizer will extend the nutrients that are available at planting time and will help prevent plants from fading in mid-season.

Never use a potting mix if it has a foul smell, is heavy, dense, or clumped together as it may contain mold. Never add lime, wood ashes, or gypsum to any commercial growing media or compost as it may change the pH of the media.

The best practice is to replace potting soil each year to eliminate pests and diseases. If cost is an issue, replace at least half of the growing media each year and replenish it with a slow-release fertilizer. You can also add used potting soil to the compost pile, where it will be rejuvenated and ready for next season.

25.5 Potting and Repotting

Repotting is the term used when a plant is removed from one container and placed into a different, usually larger container.

Plants are usually repotted to expand the space available for root growth so the plant can grow larger. More space also means the container can make more nutrients available.

It's time to repot if ...

- The plant appears stunted or stops producing new shoots.
- The plant looks too big for its pot.
- The plant keeps wilting.
- The roots are growing through the drainage holes of the pot.
- Water just sits on the top of the potting medium and doesn't soak in.
- You haven't repotted the plant in several years.

Figure 25-G. Root-bound plant that needs repotting

Repotting also gives you a chance to loosen encircling roots and get rid of salt and mineral buildup around the bottom of the root ball. Perhaps you just want to put the plant in a more decorative container.

When repotting, don't place the plant deeper than it was in its original container. (The exception is a tomato plant, which will root from the stem if planted under soil.) Identify where the plant's soil line is so that you don't cover it and kill the plant. Cover the entire root system with soil to prevent it from drying out. The space between soil and the top of the container allows for water infiltration, so allow at least two inches of headspace.

25.6 Caring for Container Plants

Providing proper care for your container garden will ultimately determine whether it will either thrive or simply limp along. The biggest issues that arise in container gardens are due to lack of water, too much water, lack of nutrients, and inadequate over-winter care.

Watering

Improper watering (either too much or too little) is the number one reason for a container plant to fail. Plants will need more water as the plants get larger and the temperatures get hotter, but tendency to overwater during periods of heat stress often leads to fungal and bacterial diseases. The key is to know your plants, what they require, and when they've had enough water.

The amount and frequency of watering varies based on the plant type and size of the container. To see if a plant needs water, simply check the soil by pressing your finger into it. If the soil is dry then water it; if not, wait until it feels dry to the touch. Always apply water at the base of the plant—not on the leaves—to help prevent diseases. Avoid quick, shallow watering. Instead, water containers until the water starts to run out of the drainage holes.

If containers go too long without water you might see a gap develop between the soil and the edge of the container. Water flows through the gap, avoiding the soil. Repeated watering will be needed to rehydrate the soil. The container can also be immersed halfway in a bucket or sink filled with water and left until the surface of the soil is moist.

If there is one, empty the saucer under the container after watering or a significant

Check plants under overhangs

Containers that are located up against the wall of a home, a shed, on a porch, or a covered balcony will likely not receive much natural rainfall. Check these containers often to make sure they're getting the right amount of water.

Figure 25-H. Standing water in plant saucers

Remove standing water from plant saucers to avoid root rot and mosquito breeding. A turkey baster works well for plants that are hard to lift.

rainfall. A bulb-type baster works well if the pot is heavy or awkward to move. Use pot feet or bricks to raise containers out of the saucer for better drainage.

Self-watering containers

Self-watering containers are a great way to help conserve water and nutrients and make it possible to leave your containers unattended for a few days. Self-watering pots are designed to provide a consistent level of moisture directly to the plant's roots by connecting the plant to a water-storage system. The bottom section has an overflow hole on the side to prevent overfilling and flooding the growing medium. Instead of watering the plant, just fill the storage tank, which can typically hold a few days to a week's worth of water.

There are several commercial models available, or you can make your own. Simply place a saucer under a pot and fill it with water. The water will wick up into the media or be pulled up by roots that reach the saucer. Be sure not to leave any standing water.

Fertilizing

Watering leaches nutrients from containers, so the nutrients must be replenished. The amount of fertilizer needed will depend on many factors, including plant type, fertilizer type, container size, and watering frequency.

Long-season vegetable crops, such as tomato, cucumber, eggplant, and pepper, may need to be lightly fertilized every two weeks to produce a continuous harvest. If there is fertilizer already mixed with your growing media, then your plants should have enough for few weeks, after which additional fertilizer will be needed. Always read and follow the label on the fertilizer package because using too much can burn the plant and cause excessive salts to build up in the soil.

There are several types of fertilizer available for containers, but the easiest and most effective options are slow-release granular and dry powder that is water-soluble.

Figure 25-1. Add slow-release fertilizer to potting mix

Slow-release fertilizers can be mixed into the growing media (note that some media already contain it). They are made of water-soluble pellets encased in a semi-permeable resin coating. When the pellets come in contact with water, small amounts of nutrients are released to the soil for use by the plant. Each time you water, the plant is "automatically" fertilized.

Dry-soluble fertilizers are normally sold as a powder that can be mixed with water and applied as directed.

Overwintering

After the season is over, discard/compost any undiseased annuals grown in containers. Empty out the containers and store the pots upside-down to prolong their life. If possible, keep them in an unheated garage or shed.

Many perennial and evergreen container plants can survive the winter if proper precautions are taken. Prune back perennials in the fall just like you would if they were growing in the ground. Check the USDA cold hardiness zone for your area and compare it to the plant's cold hardiness. Because above-ground containers cool faster and may end up being the same temperature as the winter air if not insulated, go two hardiness zones colder with container plants. You may need to store containers in an unheated garage, shed, cold frame, or basement if the plants do not meet the hardiness zone requirements.

Dry soil freezes faster than moist soil, so don't let plants dry out, but don't water if freezing temperatures are forecast for the next 24 hours.

Prevent soil and container freezing by insulating outdoor containers with bubble wrap, burlap, straw, or by double-potting. Group containers together. Move them out of windy areas, closer to a building.

Figure 25-J. Protect containers from freezing

Containers that overwinter outdoors needs to be protected from freezing. Wrap in burlap, bubble wrap, straw, or other insulating material.

25.7 Container Plant Pest and Disease Diagnostics

Container gardens are affected by the same kind of insect pests and diseases as in-ground gardens but usually not to the same extent. The most common issues are lack of water, lack of nutrients, overcrowding, and improper overwintering. Plants can also suffer root rot from too much water, especially if the growing mix does not drain well or if drainage holes are clogged. See **Chapter 12, Plant Diagnostics**, for more information about insect and disease management.

25.8 Container Combination Ideas

Reference the plant tag on greenhouse-grown transplants or the seed packet to understand the plant's needs before you plant. Grow plants in containers with other plants that like similar environments. For example, grow sun-loving plants with other full-sun plants and shade plants with other shade plants, or you may risk losing one or the other.

Designing your own containers is a fun project. As you gain experience you will learn what looks good, what grows well together, and what thrives in your own landscape.

Here are some general design tips and tricks to get you started:

- Whether it is the number of plants in a container or the number of containers in a group, odd numbers always look best. Example: Plant one dracaena spike, three geraniums, and five marigolds.

- Specialized container varieties like trailing or spreading plants can create a full, beautiful mini-garden. More upright plants will be required to fill space. Foliage vines and spikes give your planter dimension by changing up the leaf textures, shapes, and colors.

- Tailor the container with a theme, such as pollinator-friendly, salad, salsa, cottage, or culinary herbs.

- Consider grouping three or five containers to create depth. It's especially pleasing if the containers are different sizes. Add height by elevating a container with bricks.

- A classic container design includes a thriller, a filler and a spiller:
    - Thriller: A tall plant that provides height and a focal point. Examples: dracaena, red-hot pokers, fountain grass.
    - Filler: The short plants that fill in around the thriller should be ½ to ¼ the size of the thriller to balance the arrangement. Examples: pansy, marigold, geranium, dwarf bee balm, aster, hosta, zinnia, begonia, cosmos, angelonia, ornamental hot peppers.
    - Spiller: The plant that's placed at the container edge and spills over. Examples: sweet potato vine, fuchsia, gold moneywort, dichondra.
- Make a dramatic statement by using plants with different leaf textures and complementary colors. Create a more soothing mood by using a more monochromatic scheme with only one or two similar colors.
- Warm colors (red, orange, and yellow) can be seen from afar while cool colors (blue, violet, purple, and bright greens) blend with the foliage from a distance but appear more defined and colorful when in close proximity.
- If the container will only be seen from one side, plant the tallest plant(s) in the back. If seen from all sides, the tallest plants should be placed in the center.
- Consider planting vegetables and herbs along with flowers to create an edible garden. Examples: Parsley, basil, and rosemary with kale, hot peppers, and cherry tomatoes.

See Table 25-B below for design ideas. ❋

Table 25-B. Container combination ideas

Full-sun/part-sun combinations

ELEGANT 25K.1
Silver-purple scheme
Full sun
Tolerates hot weather

Components:
Dusty Miller
Petunia
Dichondra

CONTEMPORARY 25K.2
Green-white scheme
Full sun
Survives year-'round in warm climates

Components:
Queen Mum Agapanthus
Weeping White Lantana
Trailing rosemary

Some photos in Table 25-B are used with expressed permission from BalconyGardenWeb.com. See the References section.

continued on next page

continued from previous page

Table 25-B. Container combination ideas

Full-sun/part-sun combinations (continued)

CLASSIC
25K.3
Pink-purple scheme
Full sun
Occasionally pinch back petunias to keep them bushy

Components:
Wave petunia
Purple fountain grass

DRAMATIC
25K.4
Green-orange scheme
Full sun, part-sun

Components:
Gazania
Dichondra
Mexican feather grass

WHIMSICAL
25K.5
Purple-green scheme
Full sun
Keep soil moist

Components:
Tri-color sedum
Joey
Lemon Ball sedum

ENGLISH GARDEN
25K.6
Pink-purple scheme
Full sun, part-sun

Components:
Miniature rose
Dracaena
Campanula
Variegated ivy

BUTTERFLY MAGNET
25K.7
Pink-purple scheme
Full sun
Attracts butterflies
Fertilize regularly

Components:
White calibrachoa
Butterfly bush

PRIMARY COLORS
25K.8
Bright, cheerful mood
Full sun
Keep evenly moist

Components:
Blue petunia
Yellow biden or marigold
Red verbena

continued on next page

continued from previous page

Table 25-B. Container combination ideas

Shade combinations

VICTORIAN COTTAGE 25K.9
Pink-green scheme
Dappled shade
Keep evenly moist

Components:
White Queen caladium
Whopper begonia
Variegated creeping fig

WINDOW BOX 25K.10
Orange-coral-green scheme
For north- or east-facing window boxes (part-shade)
Keep well-fertilized

Components:
Maidenhair fern
Dragon begonia
English ivy
Croton

COOL SHADE 25K.11
Green-purple scheme
Shade
Replace torenia when temps drop in fall

Components:
Variegated spike
Autumn Frost hosta
Blackberry Ice heuchera
Violet torenia

ONE OF EVERYTHING 25K.12
Peach-white scheme
Shade

Components:
Boston fern
Hydrangea
Hyacinth or tulip
Begonia
Variegated ivy
Fittonia
Maidenhair fern

Winter combinations

NO-WATER URN 25K.13
Red-green scheme
Any location

Components:
(Cuttings)
False cypress tree
Arborvitae
Red dogwood
Winterberry holly
Gold winterberry

NO-WATER WINDOW BOX 25K.14
Mostly-green scheme
Any location

Components:
Evergreen cuttings
Holly berries
Red dogwood cuttings
Pinecones

continued on next page

continued from previous page

Table 25-B. Container combination ideas

Edible combinations

ITALIAN
25K.15
Festive mood
Full sun
Keep soil moist

Components:
Cherry tomato
Basil
Bi-color marigold
Variegated thyme

HERBS I
25K.16
Blue-green scheme
Full sun
Do not overwater the rosemary

Components:
Rosemary
Parsley
Pansy
Viola

PEPPERS
25K.17
Bold mood
Full sun
Keep watered and fertilized

Components:
Bell peppers
Angelonia
Celosia
Creeping Jenny

HERBS II
25K.18
Fragrant green scheme
Full sun
Do not overwater

Components:
Dill
Cilantro
Rosemary
Lavendar
Thyme

SALAD TABLE
25K.19
Full sun
Keep watered and fertilized

Components:
Basil
Thai Basil
Use any lettuce, greens, or herbs of your choice

APPLES
25K.20
Full sun
Keep watered and fertilized

Components:
Columnar apple tree
(Do not plant anything else in the container to preserve nutrients and water for the tree.)

UME © 2025. All rights reserved.

25: Container Gardening   727

AUTHORS

Ashley Bachtel-Bodkins, Senior Agent Associate, Garrett County Master Gardener Coordinator.

Emily Zobel, Agent Associate, Dorchester County Master Gardener Coordinator.

WEBSITES

University of Maryland Extension Gardening. *Growing Vegetables in Containers.* extension.umd.edu/resource/growing-vegetables-containers

University of Illinois Extension. *Successful Container Gardens.* extension.illinois.edu/containergardening/

Virginia Cooperative Extension. *Container and Raised-Bed Gardening.* pubs.ext.vt.edu/426/426-020/426-020.html

Colorado State University Extension. *Container Gardens.* extension.colostate.edu/topic-areas/yard-garden/container-gardens-7-238/

PHOTOS AND ILLUSTRATIONS

Main chapter photo: Amanda Slater via Flickr. www.flickr.com/photos/pikerslanefarm/

Figure 25-A-B, 25-K.15. Created by Stephanie Pully using Adobe Firefly.

Figure 25-C. Andres via Adobe Stock.

Figure 25-D by LeAnn Zotta.

Figure 25-E. Assembled from Pixabay photos (wal_172619, pasja1000, James DeMers, Chrstian Neff).

Figure 25-F. From left to right: Christa Carignan, Dave Clement, Stephanie Pully, Madeline Potter, Christa Carignan.

Figure 25-G. Keith Williamson via Flickr. https://www.flickr.com/photos/elwillo

Figure 25-H. Pixabay.

Figure 25-I. Petra Richli via Adobe Stock.

Figure 25-J. Gold Picture via Adobe Stock.

Table 25-B: Figures 25-K.1-25-K.7, 25.9, 25-K.11-25-K.13, 25-K.16-25-K.17: Used with permission from balconygardenweb.com.

Figures 25-K.8. daryl_mitchell via Flickr. https://www.flickr.com/photos/daryl_mitchell/

Figure 25-K.10. dbvirago via Adobe Stock.

Figure 25-K.14. Kristen via Adobe Stock.

Figure 25K18. Stephanie Pully, University of Maryland Extension.

Figure 25K-19. University of Maryland Extension.

25-K.20: hcast via Adobe Stock.

26: LANDSCAPE DESIGN

Maria Malloy
Stephanie Pully

26 LANDSCAPE DESIGN

CONTENTS

26.1 What Is Landscape Design? 732

26.2 Site Analysis and Blob Design 733

26.3 Functional Uses of Space 734

26.4 Elements of Design 736

26.5 Principles of Composition 738

26.6 Plant Selection 739

26.7 Finalizing Your Design 740

26.8 Installation 742

LEARNING OBJECTIVES

- The importance of designing the landscape before you buy the first plant
- How to create a residential landscape plan using basic principles of design and composition
- How to evaluate an existing property and prioritize tasks
- Choosing the right plants for the right place
- Hiring a pro vs. DIY for installation

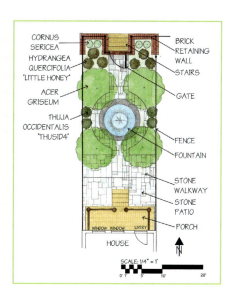

INTRODUCTION

Landscape design is the process of improving your outdoor surroundings by incorporating fine art, applied art, and natural sciences.

Different forms of landscape design have been around for ages, and you can see many of these influences of the past in garden features today. Parchment drawings show landscaping plans and irrigation systems from ancient Egypt. Their walled cities influenced the Persian paradise gardens, which created a shady, lush oasis in the harsh heat of the desert. Their use of water and fountains in the landscape was translated in large scale by the Greek gardens, and the walls were carried into Medieval period gardens where the land supported those who lived and worked on it. The Italian Renaissance brought a whole new dimension to the use of water and water features. Gardens became very symmetrical and geometrically planned. The idea of perspective was introduced into the landscape in alignment with the art of the time. Parterres became common garden features during the Italian Renaissance, but they were made even grander during the French Baroque era. This

Figure 26-A.   The gardens of Versailles

The gardens at Versailles embody the grandeur and detail of the French Baroque style of landscape design. Allees, parterres, fountains, water features, topiaries, and more are arranged expertly, using perspective to emphasize the magnificence of the castle.

period featured landscapes that were incredibly grand and detailed. Common features in Baroque design included allees, bosquets, and topiaries (see Figure 26-A). These gardens were meant to exemplify the power and wealth of those who commissioned them.

While some of the grand ideas of the Italian Renaissance and French Baroque gardens remained, landscapes in 18th and 19th century England were more focused on the existing natural beauty of an area. The idea of the "Picturesque" was introduced, and the landscape was planned to look like a serene painting. These ideas carry more into modern landscape designs. Many of the Mid-Century modern designers kept their focus on a more naturalistic design, but they began to design more with the architecture on site in mind as part of the landscape. Their designs complemented the buildings on the site and incorporated them into the design. It is helpful to look at designs of the past as they may help inform what you might like to see in your own garden!

26.1 What Is Landscape Design?

Landscape design is a subset of landscape architecture. Landscape architecture addresses large-scale projects that can be implemented over time. Landscape architecture is the art, planning, design, management, preservation, and rehabilitation of the land and includes construction of related features.

The scope of the profession includes architectural design, site planning, estate development, environmental restoration, urban planning, parks and recreation planning, regional planning, and historic preservation. Specifically, landscape architecture includes garden design; and landscape management, engineering, detailing, assessment, and all subcategories of landscape planning.

Landscape design deals with the land on a more personal level. The relationship is analogous to designing for the construction of a home versus designing the interior spaces.

You can create an outdoor environment for residential use that is functional and efficient, as well as visually appealing, by using a few basic principles that form the cornerstones of landscape architecture and design.

You can implement your landscape design over a period of time as long as you have an overall game plan. This chapter will help you sort out the components that go into creating a landscape that meets your needs and is aesthetically pleasing and environmentally responsible.

Landscape design objectives

What objective or purpose do you want to accomplish with your design? Give yourself a personal questionnaire and conduct an inventory of your property. "Form follows function" will be your guiding principle. Ask yourself these questions to help determine your needs and wants:

- Do you want to create an outdoor setting that extends your living space?
- Do you need to direct visual, pedestrian, and/or vehicular traffic?
- Do you want to create a variety of areas for activities such as casual entertaining, children's sports, or gardening?
- Are there specific views, plants, or architectural features you want to showcase?
- Do you have site problems that need to be corrected, such as excessive slopes or areas that are too wet or too dry?
- How much property do you want to devote to regular gardening activities?
- How much time do you want to devote to regular gardening activities?
- Do you want a passive garden that you can view with pleasure from various vantage points in your home?

- Do you enjoy looking at beautiful surroundings, but don't have the time or desire to do the work yourself?
- Do you just want to give your landscape a facelift?

26.2 Site Analysis and Blob Design

Here are some tips for performing an analysis of your site before you start digging:

- Take an inventory of the features/areas of your property.
- Make a photocopy of the plat plan for your property. If you don't have a copy, you can get one from your county government offices (see Figure 26-B for a sample plan.)
- Draw in all existing hardscapes or structures such as the home, shed, deck, walkways, pool, fence, or retaining wall. (A hardscape is defined as a feature in your landscape that is not plant material and is not easily relocated.)
- Include the natural compass orientation to establish sun, shade, and wind direction. This will help determine appropriate plant species for each part of your property.
- Locate existing plants and/or planting beds. Also include the soil type, if known, and general slope of property. This will help to determine microclimate situations for future plant selection.
- Identify any drainage issues related to excessive slopes or high water tables. You want to avoid maintenance nightmares by not locating plants with high water requirements on the top of a hot, dry slope that is far away from a water supply.

Figure 26-B. Plat plan

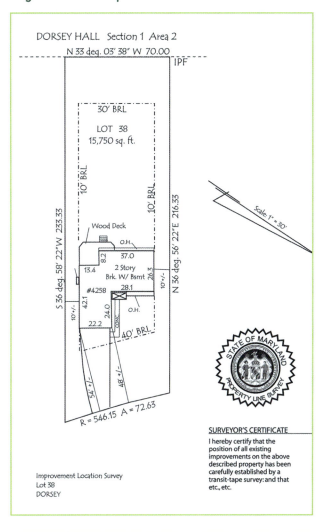

CALL BEFORE YOU DIG

Before you start digging, always contact Miss Utility to mark your utility lines.

Call 811 or 800.257.7777

Monday through Friday

7:00am to 5:00pm

You can also visit their website and submit a "locate request" online:

missutility.net

Please schedule a minimum of 48 hours in advance, excluding weekends and holidays.

- Include the location of utilities and other major features of your property. Call "Miss Utility" to mark utility lines before beginning any major construction project involving digging.

- Place tracing paper on top of a copy of your plat plan. Using a pencil, draw basic shapes or blobs to designate the general use you intend for the areas on the property (e.g., patio or deck, vegetable gardens, turf, perennial/shrub borders, water gardens, and foundation plantings). Using a pencil and tracing paper make changes simple (see Figure 26-C).

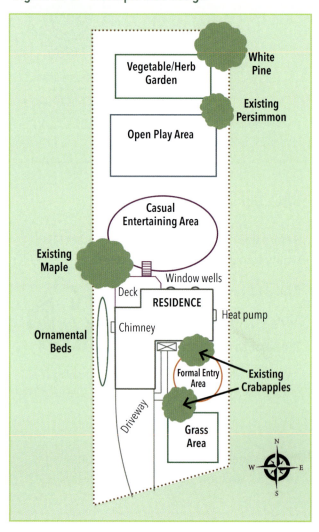

Figure 26-C. A sample blob design

26.3 Functional Uses of Space

Function will determine what you plan for your available spaces (i.e., which functions you will incorporate into your design).

Activities

Who will be using the spaces for which activities, and how much space is needed for each? For example:

- Children—sand box or swing set
- Pets—just enough room to "take care of business," or for exterior living
- Wildlife—which types would you like to attract
- Gardening—ornamental, food production, cut flowers
- Sports—putting green, soccer field, or basketball court
- Water features—a magic drawing card for wildlife, no matter the size

Consider how outdoor activities will impact the environment. If you live near a water source, incorporate buffers into your design to prevent nutrient and pesticide run-off.

Always design with nature in mind. The existing features of a property might naturally suggest an activity. For example, a low area with a high water table might be the perfect location for a water feature with moisture-loving plant species in the existing surrounding soil. Conversely, the natural features of a property might eliminate certain activities due to functional incompatibility. For example, a steep grass slope can be a mowing nightmare. Consider terracing the slope and selecting plants that have stabilizing root systems to avoid soil erosion.

Outdoor entertaining

- At a minimum, each person needs 25 square feet for passive small-group activities. That translates to a minimum of 100 square feet for four people and furniture, plus additional access space. About 140 square feet will accommodate a sitting area for four people and adequate circulation space.

- Slope is defined as the ratio of the change in rise over the change in run. A 30-foot driveway that is three feet higher at the top than the base has a ten percent slope. Most people won't notice a six percent slope. An 11 percent slope should be the limit for a sidewalk or path. A one to six percent slope is best because it will allow for drainage without causing erosion or chemical runoff.

- Do you need visual screening or a sound barrier for privacy? Consider a vertical or overhead enclosure using either a structure or plants. The enclosure can be real or implied. A real enclosure might be a physical structure, such as a fence or a deck, enclosed to create a sunroom or screened porch. An implied enclosure would use plants to emulate walls and ceilings, using evergreens to vertically screen a wall and shade trees for the overhead enclosure of a "ceiling." A large shade tree planted in close proximity to the viewer gives the sense of both overhead and vertical enclosure.

A vertical element that blocks your view creates spatial enclosure. A vertical element that is at least at eye level and twice as far away as the height of the viewer creates implied enclosure (see Figures 26-D and 26-E).

Figure 26-D. Design with no overhead enclosure

Figure 26-E. Design with an implied enclosure

Creating visual interest

- Walk around the exterior of your home clockwise and counterclockwise, close to the structure and farther away from the structure.

- Assess the view of your home from the street and from the driveway.

- From inside the home, view the landscape through all of the windows.

- Consider the view of guests as they approach your front door.

- If you want guests to appreciate a particular specimen plant, you can direct the pedestrian approach and visual attention with the use of walkways and plant material.

- Visually draw the observer through the landscape by designing intrigue. Use curved lines and partially obscured views. People aren't naturally drawn into a large open space; they need a reason to venture into the yard.

- Be thoughtful about large, open spaces; they are equivalent to a visual barrier. They provide no refuge and no sense of security. A forest invokes more of a sense of comfort than an open meadow.

Design for energy conservation

- Plant shade trees on the south or southwestern exposure to shade your house in the heat of summer, but allow light to help heat your house in the winter.

- Plant shade trees to shield your air conditioner in the midday summer heat.

- Plant evergreen trees and shrubs to deflect the prevailing winds in the winter, which are usually from the north.

- Direct wind movement with strategically-placed plantings.

26.4 Elements of Design

Mass

Mass is volume of space, both occupied and empty. It must relate, in size, to its surrounding features. Mass can be a structure, plant material, or an open area.

When selecting plant material, you must consider mature size, the space it will occupy, and how it will relate to the surrounding structures or landscape features. A two-story house on flat, unplanted property will look

Figure 26-F.   The "golden rectangle" concept

out of place if surrounded by a foundation planting composed exclusively of low-growing plants. Conversely, planting a combination of tall, medium, and low-growing plants will help the house transition into the surrounding landscape. The mass of each component will bring it into scale with the others and the surrounding space.

There is a formula for determining the appropriate complementary dimensions for plants adjacent to structures, structures in relation to each other, or plants in relation to each other. The "golden rectangle" concept can be used to determine the ideal rectilinear shape. It can also be applied to adjacent spaces (see Figure 26-F).

The sides of an ideal rectilinear shape should have a ratio of 1:1.618, or roughly 3:5. That gives the most visually pleasing proportion. Picture frames, area rugs, and index cards are all examples of common items with standard sizes that reflect the golden rectangle concept. This is not an absolute necessity but, rather, a guideline.

Form

Form is a three-dimensional shape in the landscape. There are hard geometric forms and soft, flowing, natural shapes.

Forms evoke emotions. Hard geometric forms, such as squares, triangles, and rectangles, connote strength, rigidity, tension, and stability. Soft, flowing shapes, such as circles, ovals, or free-form shapes, connote quiet, imperfect, casual, and unbroken emotions.

Although you may like a certain type of form, too many of any single form is monotonous. Conversely, too many different forms is confusing to the eye. Plants can be put into the following categories of form or shape:

Columnar. Points skyward, attracts attention, leads the eye upward, and provides an uplifting feeling. Use this form to create a dominant focal point and direct the eye.

Pyramidal or conical. Less stiff than columnar, with a wide base that is visually heavy and formal-feeling. Use sparingly, as accents. A row of pyramidal plants is very formal and stiff.

Round. Spherical or rounded on top. The majority of plants are round because they are neutral in the landscape and are good fillers.

Spreading or horizontal. Low spreading or branching structure that guides the eye along and creates the illusion of width without being too dense. A good balance for columnar or pyramidal plants.

Vase-shaped. Graceful and eye-pleasing. A good tree shape because it provides space underneath its canopy for additional plantings. Helps to bring large structures into scale with the surrounding space.

Weeping. Fluid feel, with a graceful silhouette. Pulls the eye downward. Place near low or horizontal plants, but not vase-shaped plants.

Irregular. Informal shape, rugged look/feel. Makes good specimens, especially if backlit.

Lines

Lines are one dimensional—length only. The line is a dynamic design element that makes visual and physical movement through the landscape. You can have formal, straight, and rigid lines; or informal, curved, and relaxed lines (see Figures 26-G and 26-H).

Lines direct the eye and define an edge. They can also define the style that you want to create in your landscape, or even evoke an emotion. A combination of both straight and curved lines is typical and pleasing to the eye.

Figure 26-G. Informal/curved lines

Figure 26-H. Formal/straight lines

Texture

Texture can be fine, coarse, visual, or tangible. All are suitable for incorporating into your landscape design.

Fine texture. Small leaves, compound or deeply-cut leaf margins. Creates an airy quality that appears to recede from view and makes the area appear restful or calm.

Coarse texture. Large, solid leaves that seem heavy. Makes the plant seem to jump forward and grab attention, and is a good focal point. Can make small spaces seem overwhelmed.

Visual texture. How the light plays on plants or structures and the visual impression it makes. Leaf size, the outline of a plant, or growth habit can visually suggest texture.

Tangible texture. The physical sense of touch you feel as you go through the landscape.

A balanced combination of textures might include hardscapes and planting areas. Imagine a curved pebble driveway bordered with low-growing ornamental grasses, leading up to a house framed by oaks with an understory of dogwoods and shade-loving groundcovers. A flagstone path leads from the parking area to the front door, directing the eye through the landscape to specimen planting areas.

Color

Color contributes to the emotional feeling of your design.

- Warm colors, like red, orange, and yellow, will appear closer and larger and will make the planted area appear to advance toward the viewer. Overuse of warm colors will make your yard appear smaller and more enclosed.

- Cool colors, like blue, green, and violet, will appear more distant and will make the planted area recede, giving the appearance of a larger space.

- Complementary colors, like red-green, blue-orange, and yellow-violet, are opposite on the color wheel and create a dramatic, showy effect. You can use them quite effectively on a large scale.

- Analogous color schemes, like red-violet-blue, blue-green-yellow, and yellow-orange-red, make use of neighbors on the color wheel and create the feeling of harmony and restfulness.

- Monochromatic color schemes, including various tints and hues, can make a dramatic statement. However, they are best used on a small scale to avoid being monotonous.

- Polychromatic schemes create a bright, cheery, festive atmosphere, but be aware that they can also make your landscape appear random, scattered, and disorganized.

26.5 Principles of Composition

Scale = relative size. It is more visually pleasing when plantings are in scale with their surroundings (see Figure 26-I).

Figure 26-I. Proper scale of tree to house

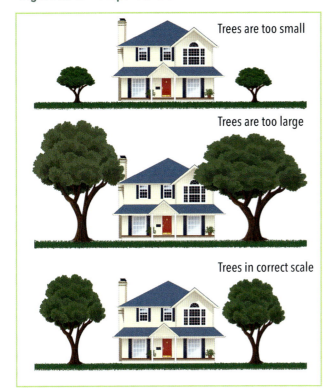

Figure 26-J. Symmetrical balance vs. asymmetrical

Figure 26-K. Draft design layout (refined blob design)

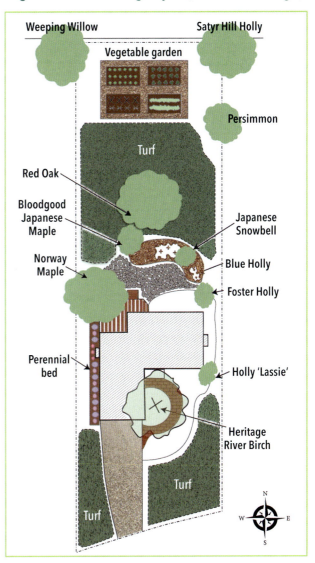

Balance = visual weight. This concept is similar to furniture arrangements inside the home. Balance the sizes, colors, and textures of the evergreen, deciduous, annual, and perennial plants throughout your landscape (see Figure 26-J).

Rhythm = repetition of elements. Although balance and variety are good, too many different elements appear confusing. The best approach is to repeat the same element in your design as a backdrop to create unity.

Emphasis = unique character. Once you have established rhythm, punctuate it with a completely different plant to draw attention to the unique character of that plant. Examples of unique characters are exfoliating bark, a weeping growth habit, a striking floral or fruit display, or multiple trunks.

Simplicity = less is more. Visualize a solitary weeping willow at the edge of a pond. Its gentle flowing branches swaying in the breeze conjure a peaceful image. As in all art forms, it is a matter of personal preference. If your passion is displaying your plant collections, consider a design that has complementary species together for the best transition.

With these concepts in mind, now you can further define your design with more detail (see Figure 26-K). Use a pen and heavier weight paper to draw in features, and use colored markers to help visualize the design.

26.6 Plant Selection

Right plant, right place! Many maintenance issues can be minimized or avoided by choosing plants that are appropriate for the location. Make sure the plants' requirements coincide with the site's characteristics—available sunlight, planting zone, soil conditions, and available space. Select plants that are disease- and pest-resistant.

Whenever possible, select plants that are native to your planting region and avoid planting non-native invasive plant species. See **Chapter 22, Invasive Plants**; **Chapter 15, Herbaceous Plants**; and **Chapter 16, Woody Plants** for more information.

Trees are the backbone of your landscape design. Shrubs are the second most important plant element in your landscape. Whether evergreen or deciduous, these plants set the stage for all of the other plants in your design.

Selections of annuals and perennials for your landscape will change over time as your trees and shrubs grow and provide shade. The main initial focus should be on tree and shrub selection, as they take the longest to mature.

26.7 Finalizing Your Design

Be sure these important elements have been considered in your design:

- Clearly defined specific areas like planting beds, entertainment areas, and activity areas. Determine how they will connect with each other.
- Circulation for everyday and formal entry, utility access, and easy access to trash and recycling bins.
- Sufficient access to the rear of the property for future projects and/or maintenance.

You may also want to make an optional perspective drawing; it can often help visualize the final result (see Figure 26-L).

Figure 26-L.   Perspective drawing

Now it's time to complete your design. At this point, your "blobs" should have morphed into well-defined lines representing structures, planting beds, and open areas (see Figure 26-M).

Figure 26-M. Final landscape design

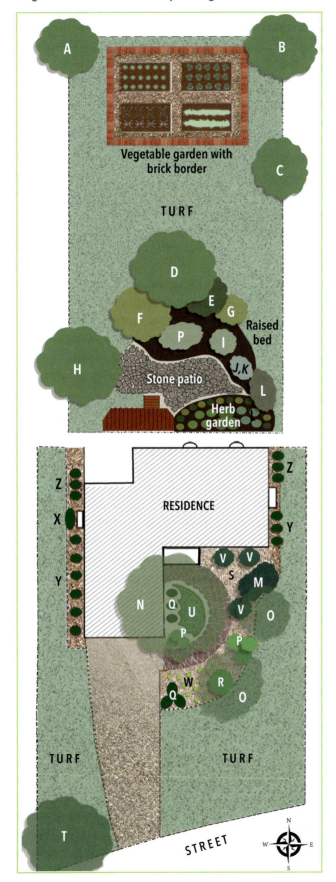

Table 26-A. Plantings key

	# of plants	Common/botanical name
A	1	Weeping willow (*Salix babylonica*)
B	1	Satyr Hill American holly (*Ilex opaca* 'Satyr Hill')
C	1	Common persimmon (*Diospyros virginiana*)
D	1	Red oak (*Quercus rubra*)
E	1	Flowering dogwood (*Cornus florida*)
F	1	Bloodgood Japanese maple (*Acer palmatum* var. *atropurpureum* 'Bloodgood')
G	1	Korean spice viburnum (*Viburnum carlesii*)
H	1	Eastern redbud (*Cercis canadensis*)
I	1	Japanese snowbell (*Styrax japonicus*)
J	2	Blue Princess blue holly (*Ilex x meserveae* 'Blue Princess')
K	1	Blue Prince blue holly (*Ilex x meserveae* 'Blue Prince')
L	1	Foster holly (*Ilex x attenuata* 'Foster #3')
M	1	Lassie Koehne holly (*Ilex x koehneana* 'Lassie')
N	1	Heritage river birch (*Betula nigra* 'Heritage')
O	2	Japanese flowering crabapple (*Malus floribunda*)
P	9	Buttonbush (*Cephalanthus occidentalis*)
Q	6	Doghobble (*Leucothoe axillaris* or *L. fontanesiana*)
R	1	Oak leaf hydrangea (*Hydrangea quercifolia*)
S	6	Wild ginger (*Asarum canadense*)
T	1	Pin oak (*Quercus palustris*)
U	1 flat	Allegheny pachysandra (*Pachysandra procumbens*)
V	3	English yew (*Taxus baccata* 'Repandens')
W	12	Green and Gold (*Chrysogonum virginianum*)
X	1	Climbing hydrangea (*Hydrangea anomala* subsp. *petiolaris*)
Y	9	False Blue Indigo (*Baptisia australis*)
Z	6	Foxglove Beardtongue (*Penstemon digitalis*)

UME © 2025. All rights reserved.

26: Landscape Design

Add your plants, drawn to scale at their mature size. Make a separate plant list and include the quantity of each (see Table 26-A).

As much as you would like to have immediate "curb appeal," beware of installing hardscapes or plants that will be damaged or have to be removed to access the back yard or install a pool. Consider planting slow-growing shade tree species first. Divide your plan into smaller projects that can be completed in a reasonable amount of time for you.

It is reasonable for it to take five to 10 years to complete your entire plan, but the rewards are many. A well-designed and properly installed landscape design will not only add value to your property, but taking an active role in the design and installation will give you great personal satisfaction.

26.8 Installation

Timing

Whether or not you intend to hire a landscape company to install your design, plan for the process to take place slowly over time. Start with a small portion of your design that you know is manageable to maintain. Once that section has been established, you can then move on and install another section.

Fall, early winter, and early spring are the best times to plant trees and shrubs. The soil should not be frozen. Summer planting, when plants are in full leaf, can be stressful and should be avoided if possible.

Some trees have fleshy roots and should be planted or transplanted in the spring: dogwoods, magnolias, willow oaks, tulip poplar, and yellowwood.

While broadleaf evergreens are best planted in the spring, some like mountain laurel, boxwood, and hollies can be transplanted in the early fall if they are watered deeply and regularly, and mulched.

Most balled-and-burlapped (B&B) and container-grown trees can be planted any time the soil isn't frozen.

About hiring professionals vs. DIY

The size and scope of the project may determine whether this will be a DIY project or if you will need to hire a professional.

Landscape designs with grade changes, construction of hardscapes, or electrical work will require specific expertise and permits to ensure that local codes are followed. Contractors must be insured and licensed by the state.

You might save money by designing and doing the work yourself. However, if you are planning a large-scale design or renovation, consider hiring a professional to develop a plan that can be implemented over time. You can do some of the work yourself but hire contractors for tasks that require special equipment and permits.

If you plan to hire professionals, here are a few points to keep in mind:

- Are they licensed by the state for the services you want them to provide?
- Ask which professional associations they belong to and whether employees receive ongoing training to maintain professional certifications.
- Are they local? Have they done other projects in the area?
- Do they have examples of previous projects they can show you? Ask for

references and call them with your questions.

- Do they use environmentally-friendly and sustainable practices?
- Ask them to select locally-sourced native plants when possible.
- Will they provide you with a maintenance guide so you can take care of your own landscape?
- Do they offer a guarantee on their installation?

Maintenance

It is important to pay close attention to newly-planted plants. They may need more water in the beginning than they will when they become established, so make sure to check every day and water them regularly.

It is possible that buried seeds of various weeds were unearthed and caused to germinate during the planting process, so be sure to check for and remove any weeds that come up around your new plants so they don't have to compete for water or nutrients.

There may also be new pests or diseases that appear on your new plants, especially if you have not had them before. Be sure to monitor your new plants for problems so you can treat them as early as possible.

AUTHORS

Maria Malloy, Certified Professional Horticulturist, University of Maryland Extension, retired.

Stephanie Pully, Master Gardener Program, University of Maryland Extension.

PUBLICATIONS

Portions adapted from Master Gardener Handbooks of Texas, Virginia, Illinois, and Arizona.

Armitage, A. A. 2000. *Armitage's Garden Perennials: A Color Encyclopedia.* Timber Press. Portland, OR. ISBN-10: 0881924350.

Armitage, A. A. 2006. *Armitage's Native Plants for North American Gardens.* Timber Press. Portland, OR. ISBN-10: 0881924350.

Dirr, M. A. 1990. *Manual of Woody Landscape Plants: Their Identification, Ornamental Characteristics, Culture, Propagation and Uses.* Stipes Publishing Company. Champaign, IL. ISBN-10: 0875637957.

Holmes, R. and R. Buchanan. 1998. *Home Landscaping Mid-Atlantic Region.* Creative Homeowner. Upper Saddle River, NJ. ISBN-10: 1580110029.

Ricigliano, D., E. Nibali, S. Hill, and R. Malloy. *Maryland Master Gardener Advanced Training Landscape Design Module.* Unpublished. 2005.

Simonds, John Ormsbee. 1961. *Landscape Architecture: The Shaping of Man's Natural Environment.* McGraw-Hill. New York, NY. ASIN: B0006AWTIA.

Wirth, T., and J. Howland. 1984. *The Victory Garden Landscape Guide.* Little, Brown and Co. Boston, MA. ISBN-10: 0316948462.

PHOTOS

Main chapter photo: Flickr free license.

Fig. 26-A: pxhere.com.

ILLUSTRATIONS

Fig. 26-B: Maria Malloy, Certified Professional Horticulturist, University of Maryland Extensions, retired.

Fig. 26-C, 26-I: LeAnn Zotta.

Figs. 26-D, 26-E, 26-F, 26-G, 26-H, 26-J: Don Wittig, University of Maryland Extension Master Gardener, Montgomery County, retired. Colorized by LeAnn Zotta.

Fig. 26-L: Stephanie Pully, University of Maryland Extension.

Figs. 26-K, 26-M, 26-N: Maria Malloy, Certified Professional Horticulturist, University of Maryland Extension, retired. Modified by LeAnn Zotta.

27: WILDLIFE AND WOODLANDS

Annette Cormany

Jonathan Kays

Mikeala Boley

27 WILDLIFE AND WOODLANDS

CONTENTS

27.1 Woodlands 748

27.2 Principles of Forestry 751

27.3 Property Inventory 752

27.4 Land Care Practices 755

27.5 Managing a Wildlife Habitat 765

27.6 Attracting Beneficial Insects 771

27.7 Attracting and Feeding Birds 772

27.8 Managing Wildlife Damage 776

27.9 Nuisance Animals 777

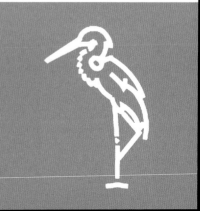

LEARNING OBJECTIVES

- The benefits and disadvantages of wildlife
- How to inventory your woodland property and develop a Land Care Plan
- How to create and manage a wildlife habitat
- Learn which plants are most wildlife-friendly
- How to attract birds/hummingbirds, pollinators, and other beneficial insects
- How to manage wildlife damage and nuisance animals

INTRODUCTION

Birds, bees, butterflies, and other wildlife are welcome creatures in our landscapes and enhance our quality of life. We appreciate their beauty, companionship, pollination services, and role in a healthy ecosystem. Wildlife is part of the larger web of life that connects us and every other living thing.

Wildlife have many benefits, both essential and aesthetic. One in three bites of food we eat depends upon pollinators—from bees and wasps to moths and bats—so protecting pollinators protects our food. Birds, toads, beneficial insects, and other wildlife help control damaging insects.

But with wildlife's benefits come challenges. While we enjoy desirable wildlife, sometimes we may find other wildlife such as deer and groundhogs to be destructive. Raccoons and squirrels raid our bird feeders, deer-related car accidents have increased, and hungry wildlife damage our gardens.

Humans' coexistence with wildlife has become increasingly less peaceful. As human populations grow, so has encroachment

Figure 27-A. Pollinators sharing milkweed nectar

into undeveloped areas that wildlife need to survive and thrive. Loss of habitat is the single biggest threat to wildlife. According to the National Wildlife Federation, one-quarter to one-half of all vertebrates and more than 9,000 native species are at risk for extinction.

Maryland is home to more than 90 mammals, 93 reptiles and amphibians, more than 400 species of birds, and untold numbers of insects and other invertebrates. Of these thousands of species, more than 300 are rare and more than 100 are threatened or endangered.

So how do we balance our desire to create a wildlife-friendly landscape with the need

> **"THE WOODS IN YOUR BACKYARD" ONLINE COURSE**
>
> This 10-week non-credit course is built upon a cloud-based system and is compatible with Windows, Mac, and Linux systems. For more information, visit **the UME website.**
>
>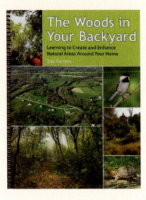
>
> The course is approved by the Maryland State Master Gardener and Master Naturalist offices to meet their respective continuing education requirements.

to protect our gardens and ourselves from damage? The answer lies in learning how to manage our landscapes such that they welcome the wildlife we want and limit less desirable wildlife.

27.1 Woodlands

A woodland is a natural area large enough to serve as both a habitat and an ecological system. It has enough plant and animal diversity to contribute natural system functions to the environment. While planting two or three trees on your property has definite environmental benefits, those plantings do not create an ecological system.

Most residential and commercial properties have natural areas associated with them, such as abandoned old fields and pastures, young and old woodlands, wetlands, and the associated wildlife. Most people feel a sense of responsibility to care for the natural areas on their property but are unsure how. *The Woods In Your Backyard* (WIYB) guide was designed to help those interested in the stewardship of their woods. (See the Publications section at the end of this chapter.)

In Maryland, private landowners with 10 or more acres of woodland (or land they want to convert to woodland) can use the Maryland Department of Natural Resources (DNR) Forest Service to prepare a written forest stewardship plan. This plan identifies landowner objectives for the property. It provides a map of the property that identifies similar woodland areas or "stands;" an inventory of the composition, soils, and other land features; and recommendations on woodland management practices for each stand. It ends with a timeline for activities to be implemented over the next 10 years.

In Maryland, 85% of the woodland parcels are from one to nine acres and make up 22 percent of the woodland acreage. This means small acreage landowners have limited access to assistance from professional foresters.

"The Woods In Your Backyard"

The *Woods In Your Backyard* partnership was developed in 2006 by extension organizations in Maryland, Pennsylvania, and Virginia. The aim is to provide self-help to landowners with smaller parcels to be more proactive in managing existing natural areas or converting existing lawn into natural areas. The WIYB guide will help you develop a plan for your land. It also provides a series of lessons and activities that are conducted on your own property. An online course is available (see the inset box to the upper left).

Dividing property according to use

While most gardeners focus on intensive-use areas, the WIYB guide focuses on existing natural areas and converting intermediate areas to natural areas. When assessing a property for ways to expand or create natural areas, divide the land into three categories:

- Intensive-use areas include buildings, decks, patios, paved areas, driveways, roads, and gardens.
- Intermediate-use areas include lawns, orchards, Christmas tree plantations, pastures, and other semi-natural areas (see Figure 27-B).
- Natural areas include wooded/shrubby areas, waterside areas, and other areas that are not regularly managed or maintained.

Creating and enhancing natural areas

Many of the land care practices and activities discussed in WIYB address converting intermediate-use (mostly lawn areas) into natural areas. Most people like having a lawn, but in some cases it is too much to care for and so many benefits accrue from less lawn-mowing. These include:

- Improved wildlife habitat through increased plant diversity
- Decreased reliance on fertilizers and herbicides
- Reduced oil and gas consumption
- Reduced air and noise pollution
- Saved money and time
- Enhanced sense of land stewardship

If you stop mowing grass, nature will slowly create a woodland over several years, or you can jumpstart the process by planting

Figure 27-B. Three land parcels with different uses

These three-acre lots were developed at the same time. The property at the right has intermediate use areas that could be converted to natural areas.

trees. Regardless, invasive species need to be controlled.

Mapping your property

You can gain new insights about your property by putting its features on a map. You can hand-sketch your property or use online digital resources. Google Maps makes it easy to zoom in on your property, but almost all of its photography is taken during the growing season, making it hard to distinguish landscape attributes such as pine and hardwood trees, size, streams, and ponds.

A better choice is MDMerlin.net, an online resource that allows you to map your property and apply many different layers (e.g., wetlands, parcel boundaries) using high-resolution images taken during the dormant season. The landscape view is open, without tree cover (see Figure 27-C). Another option is ForestsForTheBay.org, a site that allows you to put a boundary around your property. The mapping tool then provides information on soils and other features, as well as available landowner assistance programs.

Aerial maps are available using Web Soil Survey, an online resource provided by the National Resources Conservation Service. Some forestry and soil information is available.

The concept of habitat units

Most people can draw a general sketch of their property that identifies such main features as the house, sheds, trees, and vegetation. A closer look will likely show you that the property is not uniform and you will find a variety of trees, shrubs, terrain, and other features. For management purposes, we call sub-areas with similar vegetation "habitat units," because wildlife is attracted to them. Habitat units could include:

- Lawn or other intermediate areas you want to stop mowing and convert into natural area.
- Shrubby areas.
- Stands of hardwood trees.
- Stands of pine trees.
- Mixed areas of pine and hardwood.
- Specific groups of specimen trees.
- Old fields or pasture land.
- Streams, rivers, ponds, or other riparian areas.
- Wetlands.

Figure 27-D shows five habitat units for a sample property.

Figure 27-C. Growing season vs. dormant season

Compare views of the same property on Google maps (left) with MDMerlin.net (right). The dormant-season high-resolution photography, along with GIS layers for wetlands and parcel boundaries makes it easier to distinguish landscape features and habitat areas.

Figure 27-D. Sample habitat-unit property map

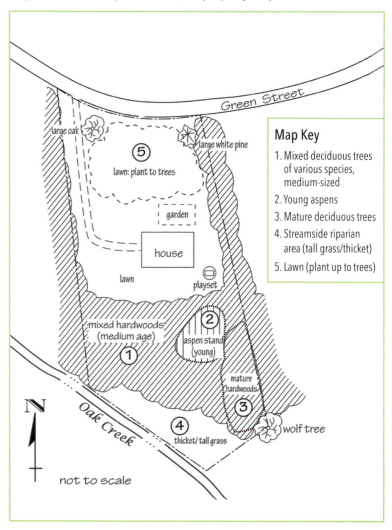

750   Maryland Master Gardener Handbook

Create a stewardship journal

A stewardship journal will help focus your thoughts about your land and will become a record of your progress and observations. A stewardship journal can be done in any way you choose, using paper and pen, a computer, or video. Consider the following items:

- Basic facts about your property, such as when you acquired the land and the story behind it
- Motivations for the purchase

SAMPLE STEWARDSHIP JOURNAL ENTRY

Stewardship Journal – October 3

Last weekend, we finished figuring out our habitat units on the property and updating our map. The hardest part was distinguishing the areas of different tree species in the woods. When we started, I could probably identify four or five different trees by their leaves, but that's about it. I joke that Tim can identify two trees—one is an oak and the other isn't—but now I think both of us agree on what trees we do have, even if we don't know all the names. There were more aspens than we thought at first, so we gave them their own unit number. And we had to be careful about judging the age of a tree by only its height when figuring out the border between the mature hardwoods and the medium-aged ones.

We almost had a problem when we were going between units 3 and 4 where we found some poison ivy. We caught Annie before she started to pick it because she found the leaves "pretty." — EK

- What you enjoy most about the land and what you enjoy least
- What you want from the natural areas you enhance or create
- Which projects you have already undertaken

A journal entry might look something like the inset box to the lower left.

27.2 Principles of Forestry

Distinct principles govern the growth, health, and maturation of trees. The following describes seven basic principles of forestry and silviculture (the development and care of forests):

1. Tree size is not directly related to age. A tree's final size depends on its genes, the site quality, and the quantity and quality of light. You may have heard that if you remove all the big trees from a site, the little ones will grow up to replace them. That is not always true. After years of being suppressed in the understory, a tree often loses its ability to grow large.

2. Different tree species require different conditions to thrive. Some factors in a site's suitability for a tree species include soil depth and composition, precipitation, wind, slope direction and position, and species range. All these site characteristics define site quality and what will grow there.

3. Different species grow at different rates, depending on site quality and competition. On a given site, the mix of tree species reflects site quality as well as individual tree and species competition for light, nutrients, and water. Some trees will benefit, while others will have slow growth rates and lose vigor. Thinning (cutting down select trees) reduces the competition, reallocates resources, and produces more vigorous trees.

4. Healthy forests are three-dimensional. Openings in the forest canopy develop naturally as trees die from crowding, attacks by insects and disease, or weather events. Gaps in the canopy change the light conditions on the forest floor and stimulate new growth. The result is the development of plants of different heights, known as vertical stratification.

5. Trees reproduce from seeds or stumps. While pine trees grow only from seeds, deciduous trees can regrow from stumps or root sprouts, depending on the size, age, and species. Deciduous species are more difficult to establish by planting seedlings than conifers because deciduous trees are more susceptible to weed competition and wildlife damage.

6. Snags are valuable for wildlife and soil. It is always good to leave some deadwood standing for wildlife. Decomposing dead trees also feed the soil and related soil food web.

7. It is important to control invasive species (see Figure 27-E and **Chapter 22, Invasive Plants,** for more information).

Figure 27-E.   Ivy overtaking a tree

Native wildlife species complement native plants. The result is well-developed relationships between plants (especially native plants), insects, and animals that are healthy, vibrant, and mutually beneficial.

27.3 Property Inventory

Your place in the landscape

As you look around your property, your neighbors', and beyond to the larger landscape, evaluate how much habitat diversity is around you. Is the landscape dotted by isolated stands of trees? Are almost all the trees around you large? Are there any open fields or brushy areas? In suburban and even some rural environments, a single property usually cannot meet all the habitat needs of many wildlife species. You might attract the most wildlife by providing specific habitat that is absent from your landscape.

Many landowners have natural areas, but these areas are so overgrown that their owners can never enjoy them. Building a trail to access your natural areas is critical. Be sure it is wide enough to minimize ticks and proximity to things like poison ivy. You may want to create a natural haven in the woods, providing a place to hunt, or just creating a visual screen. Try to minimize narrow hard-edge areas (those less than 50 feet deep) and maximize interior space away from the edge of a habitat type (see Figure 27-F).

Wildlife managers refer to an area that contains a single kind of habitat, like an old field, as a "patch." You may have everything some species need on your property for at least part of their life cycle, but often you cannot meet all needs all the time. The basic premise of managing patches is to make them as large and as close together as possible, or to physically link them. For example, if you have an existing natural area on your property, adding to that "patch" will likely provide the most value for wildlife (see Figure 27-G).

Because animals do not observe property boundaries, your neighbors' land provides an extension of the habitat on your land. If a neighbor's property includes a water source, you will see a greater wildlife variety.

Figure 27-F.   Soft-edge vs. hard-edge patches

Use aerial imagery available on MDMerlin.net and other sites to identify your habitat patches and see which elements are missing.

Create a firewise landscape

The vegetation that enhances wildlife habitat may also become fuel for wildfire that could damage your home or property. In many regions or communities, wildfire is a real concern from spring through fall.

Create a firebreak by removing fuel from areas within 30 feet of your home. This should increase to 75 feet near pine forests. Firebreaks consist of mowed lawn or widely-spaced trees and shrubs that could not carry a fire from vegetation to buildings (see Figure 27-H).

"Firewise" is a national program designed to help individuals and communities learn how to landscape in ways that reduce wildfire risk. For more information pertaining specifically to Maryland residents, visit the MDNR website.

Figure 27-G.   Habitat-patch positioning

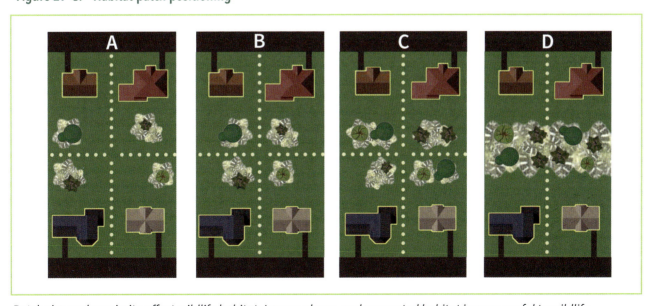

Patch size and proximity affect wildlife habitat. Larger, closer, and connected habitat is more useful to wildlife. Arrangement (B) is better than (A) because the habitats are closer. (C) is better than (B) because the habitats are larger. (D) is better than (C) because the habitats are connected.

UME © 2025. All rights reserved.   27: Wildlife and Woodlands   753

Figure 27-H. Make your landscape "firewise"

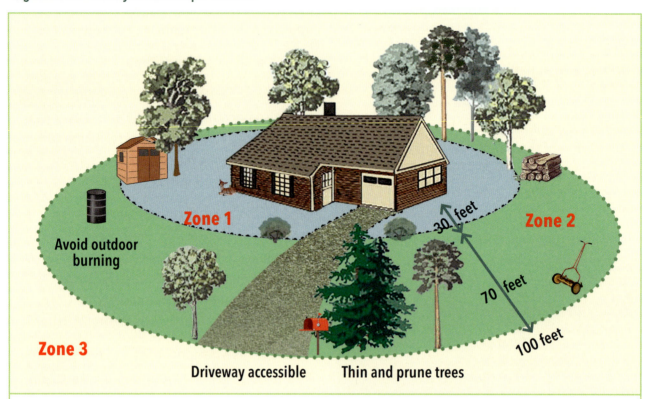

Zone 1

- Carefully space low-growing plants that are free of resins, oils, and waxes that burn easily.
- Mow the lawn regularly. Prune trees up six to ten feet from the ground.
- Space conifer trees 30 feet between crowns. Trim back trees overhanging the house.
- Create a "fire-free" area within five feet of the home, using non-flammable landscaping materials and/or high-moisture-content annuals and perennials.
- Remove dead vegetation and leaves from under decks and within 10 feet of the house.
- Consider fire-resistant material for patio furniture, swing sets, etc.
- Remove firewood stacks and propane tanks from this zone.
- Water plants and trees regularly.
- Consider xeriscaping in climates with water-use restrictions.
- Leave 30 feet between clusters of two to three trees, or 20 feet between individual trees.

Zone 2

- Maintain a mix of deciduous and evergreen trees.
- Create "fuel breaks," like driveways, gravel walkways, and lawns.
- Prune trees up six to ten feet from the ground.
- Remove smaller conifers growing between taller trees. Remove heavy accumulation of woody debris.

Zone 3

- Reduce tall tree density so canopies are not touching.

Constraints to land management

As you formulate goals for your natural area, it is important to be realistic. Economic, physical, biological, and ecological factors may constrain your options. It is also important to identify social and legal constraints.

Economic and physical constraints. If you and/or your family and friends plan to do most of the work, you will still need some basic equipment, skills, and strength. Consider hiring people to help you implement your land management plan.

Ecological constraints. These are the most difficult to overcome. The quality of your land depends upon these factors:

- Does the land slope or is it flat?
- Does the land flood or does it have drought conditions?
- What is the site's past land use?
- What is the land use around your property?
- What are the latitude, altitude, and aspect (the compass direction a slope faces)?
- What is the soil type?

Social constraints. These are not officially codified into law, but they can still cause tension with neighbors. Changing neighborhood aesthetics by cutting trees, allowing grass to grow, creating excessive noise with chain saws, and other issues are best handled by explaining to your neighbors what you are planning—and why—before you begin.

Legal constraints. Laws and regulations may affect how you manage your natural land. Before you begin work, check your property deed to see if an easement, right-of-way, or homeowner association covenants might affect your plans.

Identifying trees and shrubs

Managing natural areas on your property is very difficult without identifying the existing trees and shrubs. A few simple tree characteristics are used in most tree and shrub identification keys. If you learn these, you will be able to better identify all trees.

- Is the plant deciduous or evergreen?
- Are the branches opposite, alternate, or whorled? (Alternate is most common.)

IDENTIFYING HARDWOOD TREES

Only a few hardwood species have opposite branching and can be remembered by the phrase "Mad Cap Horse." They are:

- **M**aple
- **A**sh
- **D**ogwood
- **Cap**rifoliaceae (a family of large shrubs or small trees that includes honeysuckles, coralberry, nannyberry, and elderberry)
- **Horse** chestnut

- Are the leaves simple or compound?
- What do the leaf shape and margin look like?

Examples of each characteristic can be found in the Leaf Identification section of Chapter 4, Botany.

Other good tree and shrub resources with keys to help even novices identify species include:

- Common Native Shrubs And Woody
- Vines Of Virginia and Tree Identification
- Virginia Tech Tree ID Dendrology

Once you have identified a specimen tree, flag it so you can go back and compare it with other trees you want to identify.

27.4 Land Care Practices

Any time someone plants a garden or prunes a tree, he or she is taking an active part in managing the landscape. *The Woods in Your Backyard* guide uses the term "land care practices" to describe a number of techniques that you or a service provider can perform to

Figure 27-I. Plastic trunk guards vs. mesh

make changes to natural areas. Some land care practices, such as planting trees, will take time; others, such as choosing to stop mowing an area of lawn, will have more immediate effects on your goal achievement.

We group these practices into four types:

1. Converting lawn to natural areas
2. Modifying or improving existing wildlife habitat
3. Improving privacy and aesthetics, or farming your woodlands
4. Controlling invasive plants and insect pests

Converting lawn to natural areas

This endeavor involves planting tree seedlings of three or four difference species, 10 to 12 feet apart. Protect hardwood seedlings with plastic tree guards (do not use these on pine seedlings; instead, use mesh guards) (see Figure 27-I). This planting technique is cost-effective and the seedlings will adapt to the site conditions if competing vegetation is controlled.

Convert lawn to woodland over time using **natural succession.** Desirable tree seedlings can be identified and protected with tree guards and released from unwanted competing vegetation as the site develops.

Establish and manage warm-season grasses and wildflower areas to create a unique habitat for a variety of wildlife species. Be aware that complete removal of the existing ground cover, a two- to three-year establishment period, and annual maintenance can be challenging for many landowners.

Mow occasionally. If you are unsure about committing to reforesting an area, consider the following:

- Do not mow tall grass from mid-April to late July, when birds and small mammals use the habitat for nesting and rearing their young.
- Mow smaller blocks annually to develop diverse vegetation. Divide the mowed area into thirds and mow only one-third once each year. This frequency maintains lush grassland habitat, but discourages trees and shrubs. Control of invasive species will need to be addressed annually.

Figure 27-J. Riparian buffer

Modifying or improving existing wildlife habitat

Establish a riparian buffer around a stream, lake, or pond using either tree planting or natural succession. A riparian buffer (also called a riparian forested buffer or riparian zone) is a woodland area that is adjacent to a water body, such as a stream, river, or pond (see Figure 27-J). Riparian areas protect water quality by filtering out sediments, and support greater plant and animal diversity.

Many properties have streams with eroded banks or lawn mowed right to the edge of the waterway. These areas would benefit from establishing a streamside woodland. Vegetation, such as trees, shrubs, grasses, and forbs, in riparian zones helps improve waterways by buffering impacts from upland areas. The general concept for all buffers remains the same: use the natural functions of a plant community to trap and slowly release runoff water before it reaches the stream.

There are a number of considerations when establishing or improving a riparian buffer:

Buffer width. A width of 50 to 100 feet on each side of the water is ideal, but the landowner's goals and available land will determine the width. Ten feet is better than nothing.

Limit vehicle, equipment, and foot traffic beyond established trails. These practices can preserve the soil porosity and maintain the buffer's effectiveness. Cover trails with wood chips or gravel, and locate trails along the contour of the land to avoid erosion.

Stabilize the stream bank. Stabilization may stop or reduce erosion. Stop mowing and plant trees and shrubs, if possible. If the stream has already eroded and shows undercutting, seek advice from your local soil and water conservation district.

Chosen-tree management

This practice is used to enhance the growth of individual trees, usually hardwoods. It increases growing space around selected trees by removing adjacent trees competing for resources, mainly sunlight (see Figure 27-K).

The increased growing space allows the chosen tree to occupy a "dominant" position in the canopy. Favoring chosen trees improves mast production (fruits or nuts for wildlife), produces larger diameter trees in a shorter period of time, increases diversity, and provides more light for trees in the understory.

Figure 27-K Chosen-tree management

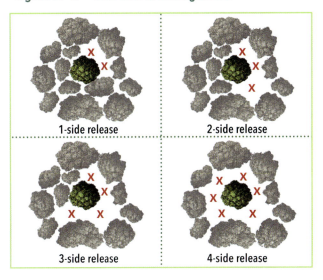

UME © 2025. All rights reserved.

27: Wildlife and Woodlands   757

Chosen-tree management differs from traditional forest thinning. Thinning is done uniformly across larger acreages and is designed to increase the growth of all remaining trees. In chosen-tree management, only trees with canopies that touch the canopy of the chosen tree are removed.

Typically, up to 25 chosen trees per acre is sufficient. Three to four sides of the canopy are opened by either felling or killing the competing trees. Chosen trees can be selected based on the species, crown class, form, and/or overall tree health and vigor. The chosen trees may grow significantly in the first growing season after the crown release; maximum growth usually occurs several years later following crown expansion.

Create and manage den trees

Den trees have a natural hollow, or cavity, in the trunk or limbs. A snag is a standing dead tree. Both are essential habitat for many kinds of woodland wildlife throughout the year for nesting, feeding, perching, cover, and protection from weather. Many opinions exist about how many snag trees are desirable per acre for wildlife. We suggest leaving or creating five to seven snags or living den trees per acre if improved wildlife habitat is an objective. Snags should be at least six inches in diameter.

If snags are absent from the property, they can be created by mechanical girdling or applying herbicide to undesirable trees, such as invasives, those with a broken canopy or poor form, or those unlikely to flourish.

Create wildlife openings

To create a wildlife opening, cut all but a few large, well-formed trees. The size of the area can vary from one-quarter acre to more than two acres, depending on the size of the property. Retain some mast-producing tree species to improve wildlife habitat.

Plant food plots

Some people like to plant food plots for wildlife in woodland openings. These may be unharvested grain fields or perennial herbaceous crop fields (e.g., alfalfa, clover) left unharvested or semi-harvested to attract deer, turkey, ducks, geese, rabbits, and songbirds. Wildlife biologists favor managing native vegetation for wildlife habitat when possible. If food plots are desired, locate them between two different habitat types and near cover.

Make brush piles

Creating brush piles is an easy way to improve wildlife habitat using readily available materials: the trees or limbs you cut in releasing chosen trees, pruning, or clearing storm damage; and discarded Christmas trees. Brush piles provide cover for amphibians, reptiles, birds, and small mammals. Providing winter cover will improve the likelihood that wildlife will stay on the property year-'round. Use large-diameter materials as the base of the pile and cover them with finer material. The larger the pile, the better.

Hinge-cut selected trees

Hinge-cutting provides cover and browsing opportunities for wildlife while removing undesirable/competing trees. Use a handsaw or chain saw on small trees to cut through halfway, and then push them over so that they stay alive but their top touches the ground. The tree or shrub will produce vertical shoots that provide cover close to the ground.

Improving privacy and aesthetics, or farming your woodland

The orientation of small-acreage properties in open subdivisions can result in residences being close to each other even though the combined acreage is substantial. The addition of security lights, sheds, access roads, and other structures create noise and annoyance. Natural vegetative barriers can immensely improve the enjoyment of a property. Options for creating barriers include:

- A privacy line of trees or shrubs along the property line. Plant at least two rows of trees set back 10 to 15 feet from the property line (see Figure 27-L).

- Create fenceline vegetation. Install a piece of fence wire for birds to perch on about 10 to 15 feet back from your property line. Birds will deposit seeds, and trees and shrubs will grow along the fence line. Remove undesirable species.

You may to want to create a peaceful place to rest and relax in a private part of the property. Campfire away from the house in keeping with the fire prevention guidelines previously covered in this chapter.

A road or trail system makes it easier to monitor the health of the natural area and identify management concerns (see Figure 27-M). Lack of good access in a woodland or old field is a common problem for landowners. Best management practices for woodland trail and road construction and maintenance offer widely accepted methods to reduce soil erosion and prevent or control water runoff.

A trail is more appealing if it meanders, especially through a small property. It should follow natural contours and cause minimal site disturbance. Keep the trails below a 10 percent grade whenever possible to prevent erosion.

Consider growing food in your woodland such as native mushrooms (e.g., morels, chicken of the woods, and oyster mushrooms), mushrooms grown on oak logs (shiitake), paw paws (a fruit tree native to much of the eastern U.S.), ginseng, black walnuts, blackberries, mulberries, or maple-syrup trees. If this type of "forest farming" is of interest, contact your local extension agent or other groups that specialize in woodland farming.

Figure 27-L. Create a privacy screen with conifers

Figure 27-M. Trails make it easy to monitor property

Controlling invasive plants and insect pests

Most woodland owners recognize the presence of at least a few plant species that are either competing or invasive. In many cases, these plants become overly abundant to the point that they must be controlled. We recommend an approach called integrated vegetation management (IVM) (see Figure 27-N). IVM uses cost-effective control techniques with the lowest environmental impact.

Cultural control

Cultural control practices enhance the growth of desirable plants and make the environment less suitable for competing and invasive plants. A few practices include:

- Preventing over-browsing by deer by opening the property to hunting.
- Removing soil and vegetative material from equipment and footwear before entering sites.
- Monitoring and destroying small infestations before they become major problems.

Figure 27-N. Integrated Vegetation Management (IVM)

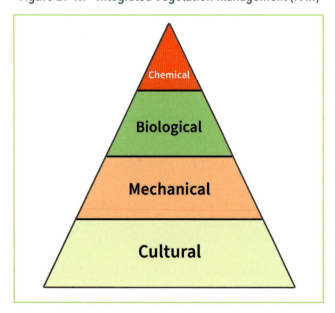

Mechanical control

Mechanical control involves hand, animal, or machine removal of competing and invasive plants. This method is usually neither practical nor effective, and personal injury is always a concern. A few control options include:

- Hand-pulling, cutting, or digging individual plants for small infestations.
- Mowing or disking fields on a three-year cycle.
- Hiring a forestry mulcher and attaching it to a skidsteer machine to remove dense understory.

Biological control

Biological control involves one type of organism preying on another. The most common approach is to release insects or diseases to target the pest. Biological control measures reduce undesirable plant populations to manageable levels, rather than eradicating them. The options include:

- Prescribed grazing by goats.
- Browsing by deer. This is a form of biological control, but not a positive one. Deer will typically browse the native plants, shifting species composition toward less desirable invasive exotic plants.

Chemical control

Herbicides are a type of pesticide designed to control plants. Today's forestry-labeled herbicides are an effective method of controlling vegetation. They are used in woodland management to:

- Control undesirable vegetation, including trees, shrubs, vines, forbs, and grasses.

- Increase woodland productivity.
- Prepare sites for natural tree regeneration and planting.
- Boost tree seedling survival and growth.
- Remove competing trees.
- Free naturally established and planted trees from weed competition.

No single herbicide, application rate, or method works for all vegetation management needs. Plant species, distribution, time of year, density, and size all affect herbicide recommendations.

Selective herbicide application methods target individual plants, with little or no impact upon desirable vegetation. Selective application methods include:

- Directed foliar spray
- Basal bark
- Hack-and-squirt
- Cut-stump

When treating large areas, broadcast treatments using tractor-mounted equipment may be necessary. These treatments are generally nonselective applications in which all vegetation is destroyed.

Choosing an herbicide

Herbicides can provide a valuable method for enhancing woodland health. Always carefully read and follow the product label directions, precautions, and restrictions before applying any pesticide.

The U.S. Environmental Protection Agency (EPA) approves pesticide use and establishes restrictions. Only certified applicators can apply "restricted use" pesticides which have a prominently displayed statement on the product label. If a pesticide is not labeled "restricted use," it is for "general use" and does not require certification for use on private property. Virtually all vegetation control in woodlands can be accomplished with general-use herbicides.

For more information on using pesticides and herbicides, with safety information, please see **Chapter 11, Pesticide Use and Safety.**

Common woodland herbicides

Herbicides commonly used in woodlands are available under a variety of trade names (see Table 27-A, which lists the most commonly used woodland herbicides). Check with your state regarding specific regulations on herbicide use.

Woodland herbicide application methods

Before applying any herbicide, it is important to properly calibrate the equipment. A calibration check involves making a trial run over a known area and measuring the amount of material applied to see if the correct amount and proportions are being distributed.

Directed foliar spray method. Used to control small woody plants, herbaceous weeds, grasses, and vines from mid-summer through December. Using aerial or ground spray application equipment such as a tractor, ATV, backpack sprayer (see Figure 27-O), or spray bottle, evenly mist herbicide mixture onto the foliage. Do not spray to the point of runoff.

Basal bark method. Generally used to control thin-barked trees, woody trees, and shrubs less than six inches in basal diameter. Using a low-pressure backpack sprayer, thoroughly wet the lower 12 to 15 inches of the stem completely around the tree, including the root collar area. Do not spray to the point of runoff. This method can be done any time of year.

Table 27-A. Common herbicides for woodlands use

Active ingredient (common name)	Trade name (partial list)	Manufacturer	Application equipment options	Application method
Glyphosate	Accord XRT II	Corteva Agriscience	Backpack sprayer Hatchet and spray bottle Vehicle-mounted Mist blower	Foliar Hack-and-squirt Cut stump
	Roundup Pro Concentrate	Bayer		
	Rodeo	Corteva Agriscience		
	Generic	Various		
	Escort XP	Bayer		
Imazapyr	Arsenal AC	BASF	Backpack sprayer Hatchet and spray bottle Vehicle-mounted	Foliar Hack-and-squirt Cut stump
	Polaris AC	Nufarm		
Caution: Imazapyr (e.g., Arsenal and Polaris) has considerable soil activity and can injure nearby trees through root absorption. Follow label directions.				
Metsulfuron-methyl	Generic	Various	Backpack sprayer Vehicle-mounted	Foliar
	Oust XP	Bayer		
Sulfometuron-methyl	Generic	Various	Backpack sprayer Vehicle-mounted Mist blower	Foliar Pre-emergent soil
	Oust Extra	Bayer		
Sulfometuron-methyl and metsulfuron-methyl	Garlon 3A	Corteva Agriscience	Backpack sprayer Vehicle-mounted	Foliar
Triclopyr	Vastlan	Corteva Agriscience	Backpack sprayer Hatchet and spray bottle Vehicle-mounted	Foliar Hack-and-squirt Cut stump
	Garlon 4 Ultra	Corteva Agriscience	Backpack sprayer Hatchet and spray bottle Vehicle-mounted	Foliar Cut stump
	Pathfinder II (Ready-to-use)	Corteva Agriscience	Backpack sprayer	Basal bark Hack-and-squirt Cut stump
	Generic	Various		

* Some herbicides can be purchased in a generic form at lower cost.

Cut-stump method. Used from mid-summer through December to control resprouting of cut hardwood stumps. For water-soluble herbicide mixtures, spray or paint the living tissue or sapwood (the outer area of lighter-colored wood) of stumps immediately after cutting. If using an oil-soluble mixture, apply up to one month after cutting. If spraying is delayed, spray the sides of the stump to the root collar and the sapwood around the entire circumference of the cut surface until thoroughly wet.

Hack-and-squirt method. Generally used from mid-summer through December to control individual trees one inch in diameter and larger (see Figure 27-P). Use a hatchet, machete, or similar sharp device to make cuts at a downward angle at proper spacing, following label recommendations. Cuts should

Figure 27-O. Backpack sprayer

Figure 27-P. Hack-and-squirt method

penetrate the bark into the living tissue or sapwood (the outer area of lighter-colored wood) and produce a cupping effect to hold herbicide. Spray a measured quantity into cuts with a squirt bottle. Do not allow the solution to run out of the cuts. This method is not recommended for use during heavy sap flow in spring. Safety is critical with hack and squirt, so have a file with you in the field to make sure your instrument stays sharp. Sharp tools are safer tools because dull blades will bounce off trees and increase the risk of injury.

Vine management

Vines can be classified as woody or herbaceous, hanging or climbing, or native or nonnative. Hanging vines include grapevines, greenbrier, and Japanese honeysuckle. They tend to hang from trees and grow into the crown either by growing over from adjacent trees and shrubs or growing up with the tree as it matures. Climbing vines, such as Oriental bittersweet and English ivy, attach themselves to the trunk of the main stem and grow up into the crown. They spread to adjacent trees by growing along the ground as well as from tree to tree in the crown.

Grapevine is a widespread native vine and grows aggressively in many woodlands. Grapevines and Oriental bittersweet damage trees by growing into crowns; breaking tops and limbs, especially as snow and ice accumulate; and blocking sunlight to leaves. Other vines cause similar damage.

Vines should be removed from the crown. Fortunately, vines can be treated by simply cutting them at the base. They will die, dry out, and fall out of the crown over time. Herbicide can be applied to the cut stump to prevent resprouting. Basal bark or hack-and-squirt herbicide applications are effective for larger hanging and climbing vines.

Common invasive insect pests

Invasive plants are not the only invaders affecting Mid-Atlantic woodlands. We also have a host of invasive insects. Some are so lethal that all trees of a certain species in a woodland can be affected. Controlling invasive pests is not really possible in extensive woodlands or natural areas, but methods like injecting insecticide into tree trunks, soil drenching, foliar spray, and bark sprays have been tried. Common invasive insects affecting woodlands in Maryland:

- Hemlock Woolly Adelgid
- Emerald Ash Borer
- Spotted Lanternfly
- Spongy Moth
- Southern Pine Beetle

Detailed information about these insects pests is available in **Chapter 8, Insect Basics.**

Putting your knowledge to work

Choosing and implementing projects

The Woodlands in Your Backyard (WIYB) guide will help you identify objectives for natural area improvement, forest products, wildlife habitat elements, water resources, recreation, and aesthetics. Case studies provide project schedules and timetables to serve as examples. Always record your project(s) with photos taken each year from set points on the property to document landscape changes.

Creating a Land Care Plan (LCP)

An LCP includes the following components (see Table 27-B):

Table 27-B. Land care plan

Habitat goal	Project description	Start/finish	Cost estimate
Lawn (Convert to trees)	Kill turf and weeds in the fall before spring planting with a non-selective herbicide like glyphosate. Alternatively, smother the vegetation in areas to be planted using heavy-duty black weed barrier. Use trees and shrubs that flower/have great fall color/produce wildlife food to reforest lawn in front of the garden. Seedlings will include yellow poplar, black walnut, red oak, black cherry, and white pine. Order bare root seedlings from state nurseries in late fall. Plant on a 10' x 10' spacing in this 3/4-acre area (~225 trees). Install a tree shelter and a wooden stake around each seedling to protect it from deer browsing. Re-spray the grass between the rows with herbicide in the summer after planting, if needed. Mow between the rows until forest canopy closes because of homeowner association rules.	Start in the fall and end in the spring, 3 years later. Split plot into thirds so the cost and time required per year are less. Start closest to the road.	$300 for plants at $1.35 per plant $100 for Round-up or other herbicide and backpack sprayer $900 for shelters $4-$5 each for stakes
Entire property (Create a trail)	Design and clear a trail that rings the property and touches each of the habitat units. Highlights will include Oak Creek (although most of the trail will be back from the water) and the wolf tree in the back corner that will provide a natural haven for solitude. Talk more with neighbors about the trail idea.	Start fall and finish by spring	Have chain saw; ~$15 for fuel, $40 for herbicide
Riparian area (Plant a buffer)	Plant trees and shrubs (~440) recommended for riparian buffers throughout area currently in tall grass and thorny shrubs (1 acre). Plants will include river birch, green ash, sycamore, red maple, dogwood, and buttonbush. Use tree shelters. Mow grass before planting and frequently thereafter until trees establish. Use herbicide label for use near the stream.	Next fall and end of following spring	$600 for plants; $2,200 for tree shelters and stakes

- The landowner's goals, such as improving woodland health, enhancing wildlife habitat, improving growth of trees, less mowing, creating new natural areas, and/or improving access.
- A property summary and map, including acreage, how much land is lawn and natural area, and features of this and surrounding properties.
- A summary and identification of areas of highest concern
- Recommendations outlining projects for each habitat unit.

Additional resources

Additional wildlife and woodlands resources can be found **here.**

Up-to-date soil maps and photographs are available **here.**

DNR foresters are located in each county and can provide information on forest stewardship. Find a consulting forester here:

Maryland Department of Natural Resources Forest Service

27.5 Managing a Wildlife Habitat

A habitat is what wildlife need to survive: food, water, cover, and a place to raise young. To attract a specific type of wildlife to your landscape, you must know which type of habitat it needs and then provide it.

A habitat can be large or small and should vary with the life stage of the animal(s). A monarch butterfly caterpillar needs only a patch of milkweed; a chipmunk a half-acre of habitat; and a squirrel up to 10 acres. Building many different habitats in your landscape will attract the widest variety of wildlife.

Food

When we think of feeding wildlife, we most often think of bird feeders, but planting trees, shrubs, grasses, and perennials provides birds and a broad range of wildlife with seeds, berries, nuts, pollen, and nectar. It also provides cover and nesting sites while beautifying a landscape.

Wildlife-friendly plants include:

- Nut-producing plants, such as oak or hazelnut
- Berry-producing plants, such as winterberry or dogwood
- Seed-producing plants, such as pine trees and coneflowers
- Nectar-producing plants, such as salvia and coral honeysuckle

Native plants are an excellent choice for attracting wildlife. Well-adapted native plants require less care and have co-evolved with native wildlife. They also provide the most nutritious food. For example, a native oak feeds the caterpillars of more than 500 butterflies and moths, which in turn feed the rest of the food chain. Look for native plants at local nurseries or find them at online sources and native plant sales. Avoid invasive plants which threaten habitats. Tables 27-C and 27-D list some of Maryland's native plants and the wildlife they benefit.

Wildlife need food year-'round, so plan a landscape where varied food is always available. Include plants that provide pollen and nectar from spring to frost, berries in summer, and nuts and seeds in fall and winter.

Butterflies often only lay eggs on one type of plant that feeds their caterpillars. Providing that particular plant—called a host plant —

Table 27-C. Native plants for wildlife   FS = Full sun • PS = Part-shade • S = Shade

Name	Mature height (ft.)	Value to wildlife	Light	Soil	Fruiting period
SHRUBS					
American cranberry (*Viburnum trilobum*)	17	The beautiful red berries are often left uneaten by birds until winter, when the fruit quickly disappears.	FS-PS	Moist, well-drained	Fall to spring
Coralberry (*Symphoricarpos orbiculatus*)	6	The purple fruit is eaten by numerous songbirds, ruffed grouse, and wild turkey. Useful for cover and nesting.	FS-S	Moist, well-drained	Fall to winter
Serviceberry (shrub form) (*Amelanchier* spp.)	6-10	One of the first native shrubs to flower in the early-summer woods. Excellent for shady yards. Provides fruit for many woodland birds, squirrel, chipmunk, raccoon, and red fox. Eastern cottontail and whitetail deer browse the twigs.	FS-S	Moist	Early summer
Highbush blueberry (*Vaccinium corymbosum*)	12	Native shrub with fruits taken by many songbirds. Its dense form provides cover and nest sites.	FS	Acidic, moist	Mid to late summer
Common elderberry (*Sambucus canadensis*)	13	Provides food, cover, and nesting sites.	FS-S	Moist	Late summer
Common spicebush (*Lindera benzoin*)	12	Red aromatic berries are eaten by many birds and mammals. Whitetail deer and eastern cottontail browse twigs. Host plant for Spicebush swallowtail.	FS-S	Moist	Late summer to fall
Brambles (raspberry and blackberry) (*Rubus* spp.)	6	Provide cover and nest sites, and produce berries that are eaten by nearly all birds and mammals.	FS	Moist	Early to late summer
Winterberry (*Ilex verticillata*)	10-15	A deciduous holly with red berries, providing both winter interest and food for more than 48 species of birds and small mammals. Requires male and female plants for fruit.	FS-S	Adaptable, prefers moist	Fall to winter
American hazelnut (*Corylus americana*)	9-12	Produces nuts eaten by songbirds and upland gamebirds, such as grouse and wild turkey. Also valuable to mammals. Its dense foliage creates shelter/habitat.	FS-S	Moist, well-drained	Late summer to fall
American euonymus (*Euonymus americanus*)	4-5	Foliage and twigs are a favorite for white-tailed deer. Strawberry-red seeds are eaten by songbirds. Native alternative to the invasive burning bush (*Euonymus alatus*).	PS-S	Rich woodland soil	Late summer to fall
Blackhaw viburnum (*Viburnum prunifolium*)	12-20	Host plant for azure butterflies. Fruits are eaten by songbirds and small mammals. Provides shelter.	FS-S	Moist, some dry	Late summer to winter
Arrowwood viburnum (*Viburnum dentatum*)	10-15	Fruits are eaten by songbirds, grouse, turkey, and small mammals.	FS-S	Moist	Late summer to fall
Black chokeberry (*Aronia melanocarpa*)	3-6	Fruits are edible for wildlife and humans. Attracts birds, butterflies, and pollinators. Suckering habit.	FS-PS	Moist	Late summer to fall

continued on next page

continued from previous page

Table 27-C. Native plants for wildlife FS = Full sun • PS = Part-shade • S = Shade

Name	Mature height (ft.)	Value to wildlife	Light	Soil	Fruiting period
SHRUBS (continued)					
Silky dogwood (*Cornus amomum*)	10-12	Blooms provide nectar for butterflies. Fruits are eaten by songbirds and mammals. Supports specialized native breeds.	FS-S	Moist	Summer to fall
Bayberry (*Morella cerifera*)	15-20	Winter cover. Host for red-banded hairstreak butterfly, as well as a nectar source for pollinators. Fruits are eaten by birds in fall and winter. Salt-tolerant.	FS-PS	Adaptable	Late summer to winter
SMALL TREES					
Choke cherry (*Prunus virginiana*)	30	The purple fruit is favored by songbirds, gamebirds, and many mammals.	FS-S	Moist to dry	Late summer
Red mulberry (*Morus rubra*)	40	Long fruiting season. Berries provide food for birds and mammals.	FS-PS	Moist to dry	Early summer
Serviceberry (tree form) (*Amelanchier* spp.)	15-30	One of the earliest shrubs to flower in the early-summer woods. An excellent choice for shady yards. Provides fruit for many woodland birds, squirrel, chipmunk, raccoon, and red fox. Eastern cottontail and whitetail deer browse the twigs.	FS-S	Moist	Early summer
American crabapple (*Malus coronaria*)	30	Both native and cultivated varieties exist. Select trees with small fruits that are available into winter.	S	Moist to dry	Fall and winter
Eastern red cedar (*Juniperus virginiana*)	40	This hardy native provides food, cover, and nest sites. The small blue fruits are eaten by at least 54 species.	FS	Dry	Fall to spring
Flowering dogwood (*Cornus florida*)	40	As ornamental as it is valuable to wildlife. Unfortunately, it is currently being attacked by dogwood anthracnose so it is not now recommended. Consider planting Tartarian dogwood (*Cornus alba*), red osier dogwood (*C. sericea*), or Cornelian cherry (*C. mas*).	FS-PS	Dry	Fall
American holly (*Ilex opaca*)	30	The evergreen foliage provides winter cover for birds. The red fruit is available throughout winter.	FS-PS	Acidic, moist	Late summer to spring
American mountain ash (*Sorbus americana*)	40	Orange fruit of this native ornamental is often available through winter.	FS	Dry	Late summer
Persimmon (*Diospyros virginiana*)	50	The orange fruit is eaten by nearly all birds and mammals.	FS-PS	Dry	Late summer to fall
Smooth sumac (*Rhus glabra*)	9-15	Host for red-banded hairstreak caterpillars and luna moths. Provides nectar for butterflies. Fruits eaten by songbirds and mammals, as well as upland birds.	FS-PS	Well-drained, moist	Late summer to fall

continued on next page

continued from previous page

Table 27-C. Native plants for wildlife

FS = Full sun • PS = Part-shade • S = Shade

Name	Mature height (ft.)	Value to wildlife	Light	Soil	Fruiting period
SMALL TREES (continued)					
Staghorn sumac (*Rhus typhina*)	35-50	Winter food and nectar source for native bees. A larval host plant for luna moths.	FS	Dry to moist	Late summer to fall
Black willow (*Salix nigra*)	35-50	Stabilizes stream banks; preferred food of ruffed grouse and pine grosbeak. Has some salt tolerance.	FS-PS	Moist to wet	Fall
TALL TREES					
American elm (*Ulmus americana*)	100	Buds, blossoms, and winged seeds invite birds during spring when little else is available. Susceptible to Dutch elm disease.	FS-PS	Moist, well-drained	Spring
Black cherry (*Prunus serotina*)	60	Superb choice for attracting birds. At least 47 species eat the fruit of this native tree.	FS-S	Dry	Summer to fall
Eastern white pine (*Pinus strobus*)	100	The large cones provide highly nutritious seed that is eaten by 38+ bird species. The evergreen foliage provides cover throughout the year and nest sites in summer.	FS-PS	Moist	Fall
Sour gum (black gum) (*Nyssa sylvatica*)	100	Blueberry-like fruit is preferred by more than 30 species of birds.	FS-S	Moist	Late summer to fall
Eastern hemlock (*Tsuga canadensis*)	70	Provides food, cover, and nest sites. Twigs browsed by whitetail deer and eastern cottontail. Susceptible to woolly adelgid.	FS-S	Moist	Fall
Oak (*Quercus* spp.)	60-100	Provides nest sites and food for a variety of mammals, birds, and caterpillars.	FS-S	Moist to dry	Late summer to fall
Bitternut hickory (*Carya cordiformis*)	60-100	Nuts are consumed by squirrels, birds, and other small mammals. A wide variety of moths and butterflies use the tree as host.	FS	Moist, rich soil	Late summer to fall
Hackberry (*Celtis occidentalis*)	40-100	Larval host for butterflies and moths. Small fruits are consumed by many birds and mammals. Cover and nesting for songbirds, gamebirds, and rabbit (young trees).	FS-S	Dry	Summer to fall
Virginia pine (*Pinus virginiana*)	50-80	Many birds feed on the seed. Evergreen branches provide good winter cover.	FS	Dry to moist	Fall
VINES					
Virginia creeper (*Parthenocissus quinquefolia*)	N/A	The blue berries are favored by 35 bird species.	S	Moist	Late summer to spring
Wild grape (*Vitus* spp.)	N/A	At least 52 species of birds and mammals eat the fruit. Grape tangles are also nest sites.	FS-PS	Moist	Late summer to fall
Trumpet honeysuckle (*Lonicera sempervirens*)	N/A	Long bloom period, providing nectar and food source for butterflies, hummingbirds, songbirds, pollinators, and small mammals. Larval host for some butterflies and moths.	FS-PS	Moist	Late summer to spring

continued on next page

continued from previous page

Table 27-C. Native plants for wildlife

HERBACEOUS PLANTS				
There are dozens of species of the following plants that benefit wildlife; this is a general list.			
Common name	Scientific name	Common name	Scientific name
Goldenrods Purple coneflower Coneflowers Milkweeds	*Solidago* spp. *Echinacea purpurea* *Rudbeckia* spp. *Asclepias* spp.	Little Bluestem Big Bluestem Switchgrass Indiangrass Broomsedge	*Schizachyrium scoparium* *Andropogon gerardi* *Panicum virgatum* *Sorghastrum nutans* *Andropogon virginicus*

helps attract those species. For example, plant milkweed for monarch butterflies and parsley or dill for swallowtail butterflies.

Birds, toads, and other wildlife eat insects, providing natural pest control. Create an insect-friendly landscape with a wide variety of plants for pollen and nectar, and avoid using insecticides and herbicides that can harm not only insects but the wildlife that eat them.

Water

As with all living things, wildlife need water. Supplement natural sources from streams to ponds with birdbaths and water features, which also boost your landscape's appeal.

Wildlife feed and drink at different heights. Pedestal and ground birdbaths attract different birds and other wildlife, from squirrels to toads. Add a rock to allow beneficials such as wasps to get water safely.

Moving water is irresistible to wildlife. A fountain, birdbath dripper, mister, or pond waterfall entice abundant wildlife. Make your own dripper with a bucket with a nail hole hung above a birdbath or clay pot saucer.

Cover

Wildlife need cover for protection from the elements and predators; and for nesting sites, travel routes, and camouflage for hunting prey.

Trees and shrubs provide good cover. A combination of evergreens and deciduous trees and a variety of native shrubs have wide appeal. Perennials, grasses, and meadows also provide cover. Hedges and thickets (a tangle of fast-growing thorny plants, such as wild roses and raspberries) attract myriad wildlife. Consult the **Audubon Society website** to find natives in your zip code.

"Messy is beautiful" to wildlife. A brush pile of tree and shrub trimmings provides cover for rabbits, chipmunks, turtles, foxes, birds, and other wildlife. A dead standing tree (also known as a "snag") can be home to squirrels, a nest site for owls and bats, and a food source for woodpeckers. Groundcovers, leaf litter, and fallen logs also provide good habitat for hunting and cover. One in four local birds need snags, den trees, and felled logs. Letting a corner of your property go a bit wild greatly benefits wildlife.

Wildlife travel along natural corridors. Hedgerows, fence rows, streams, woods, and soft edges between lawns and woods are used as wildlife expressways. Create corridors by linking natural areas on your own property or joining neighborhood plantings and pathways.

Lawns have limited appeal for wildlife. Shrinking turf areas in favor of groundcovers or meadows, trees, shrubs, and perennials is much more appealing to wildlife.

A place to raise young

Wildlife need safe places to lay eggs, raise young, and gather materials to build nests. Monarch butterflies lay eggs only on milkweed and birds most often nest in trees. Mud dauber wasps need mud to make nests and bats need caves, barns, or bat houses.

Some wildlife nest and raise young in meadows, brush piles, conifers, thickets and hedges, den trees, and ponds. Again, the secret is to find out exactly which wildlife you want to attract and provide what they need.

Wildlife landscape design

The next time you walk through the woods, notice the layers of trees, shrubs, perennials, wildflowers, leaves, and moss. Natural habitats have layers, and wildlife feed and live at different heights within those layers. Adding layers to your own landscape will attract more wildlife naturally. Tuck shrubs under trees. Incorporate everything from low groundcovers to tall trees. Large, freeform plantings that mimic nature also boost appeal to wildlife.

Survey your landscape for wildlife habitat, making an inventory of available resources and noting opportunities to build habitat:

Figure 27-Q. Landscape succession: wildlife

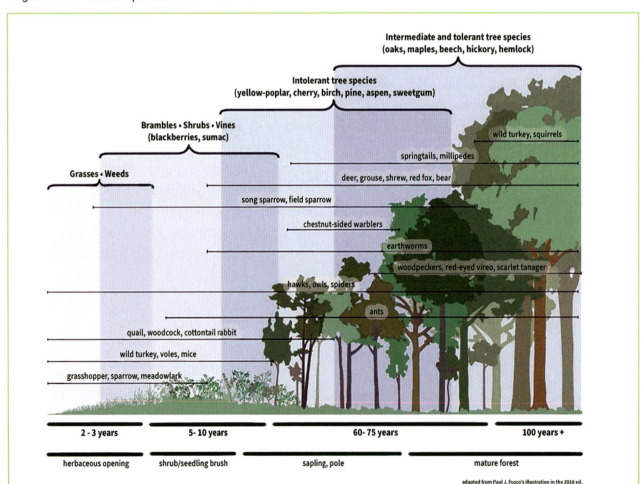

- Do you have trees and shrubs, tall grasses and perennials?
- Have you included plants that bloom from early spring to frost, including native plants?
- Are there "messy" areas, such as brush piles and leaf litter?
- Are there water and food from feeders and natural sources?
- Is your landscape richly layered to feed and shelter a wide variety of wildlife?

Understanding succession is important to managing your landscape for wildlife. Succession is the natural replacement of one plant community for another. Unmown grasses become meadows which develop shrubs and small trees, then evolve into forest. At each of these steps, different wildlife thrive as habitat changes (see Figure 27-Q).

Accelerating the succession process by planting trees and shrubs or holding it back by repeatedly mowing a meadow helps to control habitat.

Remember to design enjoyment into your landscape. Much of the pleasure in creating a wildlife garden lies in being able to see and enjoy wildlife more closely. Build pathways and trails. Create comfortable seating areas to observe wildlife. Invest in field guides, binoculars, a camera, and a hand lens. You'll see, learn, and appreciate wildlife even more.

27.6 Attracting Beneficial Insects

Nine out of 10 insects are beneficial and help to control destructive insects. Attracting these allies provides natural, chemical-free control of harmful insect pests.

Beneficial insects are either predators or parasites. Predators eat damaging insects, while parasites use pests as food for their young. Lacewings, ladybugs, praying mantids, predatory mites, and ground beetles are just a few of many predators. Wasps, aphids, and beneficial nematodes are types of parasites. Together they number in the thousands, ranging from specialists that control one type of insect to generalists that control many different insects.

Several strategies work to attract beneficial insects to your landscape. Provide a constant source of pollen and nectar for them with plants that bloom from spring to fall. Be sure to include native plants, which offer superior nutrition.

Certain types of flowers have greater appeal to beneficial insects. Coneflowers and other daisy-shaped composite flowers are attractive, as well as umbrella-shaped flowers such as yarrow or dill. Herbs and other plants with small flowers lure small beneficial insects.

Beneficial insects need water, cover, and nesting sites, just like other wildlife. Provide water in shallow containers or add rocks to bird feeders and fountains for safe sipping. Some beneficials have specific nesting and cover needs. Orchard mason bees (among others) nest in tubes or holes drilled in wood. Such bee houses are available at garden centers and online. Many insects overwinter in hollow or soft stems, so cut down perennials to a foot in the fall to provide habitat.

Other insects nest or pupate in leaf litter, so allow some fallen leaves to lie undisturbed and avoid cleaning up garden debris until spring.

Protect beneficials by avoiding chemical products. Broad-spectrum and systemic insecticides can't tell the difference between harmful and beneficial insects. If needed, use organic and cultural controls instead.

27.7 Attracting and Feeding Birds

Birds are welcome in our gardens for their beauty, songs, entertainment value, and impressive insect control. Just one pair of black-capped chickadee feeds 6,000 to 9,000 caterpillars to one nest of young.

While birds may uproot the occasional seedlings or feast on your blueberries, the damage is usually minimal and temporary. Many birds come seasonally or migrate through the area.

To increase the number of birds in your yard, improve the habitat with access to more food, water, cover, and places to raise young.

Food for birds

Bird feeders are the most common way to feed birds. Find out which type of food your favorite birds eat and provide it in the right feeder. A sunflower seed feeder and winter suet feeder attract a wide variety of birds, but many have preferences (see Table 27-E).

Place feeders where you can see the visiting birds. Situate them within 20 feet of trees and shrubs for shelter, then install them at a height of five to six feet, at least 10 feet away from jumping-off points to deter squirrels. Add squirrel baffles for extra protection. Clean bird feeders regularly with soap and water.

Bird feeders are most helpful in winter, but can be used all year. Supplement feeders with natural food sources by planting a variety of native plants to produce seeds, berries, and nuts. Birds feed on seeds from ornamental grasses, perennials, and deciduous and evergreen trees. Instead of cutting back perennials or grasses in the fall, leave them standing so the seedheads can feed the birds in winter.

Water for birds

Birds need water for drinking and bathing. Adding a birdbath to your landscape will draw many more birds. They are particularly crucial in times of extreme heat and drought when natural water sources such as ponds, streams, and puddles dry up.

Pedestal birdbaths help to thwart predators while ground birdbaths appeal to certain birds and small mammals, such as chipmunks and rabbits. Avoid ground birdbaths if predators are active in your area.

Birdbaths can be store-bought or handmade. A clay pot saucer makes a simple, affordable ground birdbath. Purchased birdbaths are available in every material and price point.

The best birdbaths have sloping sides and are no more than three inches deep. The surface should be rough, such as stone or concrete, for good traction and have an edge for perching. Place your birdbath near a tree so birds have a place to sit and preen after bathing, but away from dense shrubs where predators may lurk.

Moving water is irresistible to birds. They love drippers and fountains. Add a birdbath heater in winter so birds have fresh water all year.

Replace the water in your birdbath every few days to keep it fresh and thwart mosquitoes. Clean it regularly with soap and water. Never use harsh chemicals.

Some birds such as doves dust-bathe rather than bathe in water. Create a dust-bathing area by leaving a small area of soil bare.

Table 27-D. Seeds and feeders for attracting birds

Species	Food preference	Feeder preference**
Mourning dove	Cracked corn, millet	Ground, low tray*
Red-bellied woodpecker	Suet, orange/apple halves, peanuts	Almost all feeders
Yellow-bellied sapsucker	Suet	Suet feeder
Downy and hairy woodpeckers	Suet, sunflower seeds, peanuts	Suet feeder, hanging feeder
Northern flicker	Suet, orange/apple halves, peanuts	Suet feeder
Blue jay	Corn, sunflower seeds, suet, peanuts	Platform feeder*
Black-capped chickadee	Sunflower seeds, suet, peanuts	Almost all feeders
Tufted titmouse	Sunflower seeds, suet	Small hanging feeder
White-breasted nuthatch	Sunflower seeds, suet	Almost all feeders
Red-breasted nuthatch	Sunflower seeds, suet	Suet feeder, hanging feeder
Brown creeper	Suet	Suet feeder
American robin	Apple halves, raisins	Ground, low tray*
Eastern bluebird	Peanuts, suet, raisins, apple halves	Suet feeder, tray*
Northern cardinal	Sunflower seeds, cracked corn, millet, raisins, peanuts	Ground, tube feeder with tray, low tray*
Song sparrow	Sunflower seeds, millet, peanut hearts	Ground, low tray*
White-throated and white-crowned sparrow	Millet, cracked corn, hulled sunflower seeds, peanuts	Ground, low tray*
Dark-eyed junco	Millet, cracked corn, hulled sunflower seeds, peanuts	Ground, low tray*
Purple finch	Sunflower, niger, peanuts, suet, millet	Hanging tube, niger feeder
House finch	Sunflower, niger, millet, fruit, suet	Tube, niger feeder, ground
Pine siskin	Niger, hulled sunflower seeds, millet	Tube, niger feeder
American goldfinch	Niger, sunflower seeds, nutmeats	Niger feeder, hanging tube, ground
Ruby-throated hummingbird	Sugar water	Hummingbird feeder
Northern oriole	Sugar water, orange halves, millet, grape jelly	Oriole feeder

*Food in platform feeders or open trays can become spoiled from bird droppings and moisture. Put out only enough food for one day and regularly clean the feeders. Drill weep holes in the bottom to help drain rain and melting snow.
** Information about feeder placement: **allaboutbirds.org/news/where-to-put-your-bird-feeder/**

Cover and nesting sites for birds

Birds are attracted to woodland and meadow habitats and to a mix of evergreen and deciduous tree and shrub plantings. They use these for food and shelter, protection from the elements, travel, and nesting.

Particularly attractive are dense shrubs like viburnum and evergreens that provide safe shelter from predators. Locating trees and shrubs near birdbaths and feeders also boosts their appeal. Brush piles, den trees, and dead standing trees (snags) are also attractive to birds as food sources, nesting sites, and safe cover.

Birdhouses shelter adult birds and young. Some birds have distinct housing preferences. Bluebirds like tall, narrow boxes with one and three-eighth inch entry holes; purple martins like high-rise communal apartments. A Carolina wren will nest in anything from a boot to a fishing creel. Consider installing roosting boxes, which birds use for shelter, warmth, and protection from the elements.

Landscaping for hummingbirds and butterflies

Hummingbirds

These tiny birds add grace and beauty to the landscape. While there are over a dozen hummingbird species in America, only one lives in the eastern half of the U.S.: the ruby-throated hummingbird. It annually migrates to the U.S. from Mexico and Central America. It arrives in our area in mid-April and departs for warmer climes in mid-October.

Weighing about the same as a dime, the ruby-throated hummingbird is a miniature powerhouse. It can fly up, down, forward, backward, sideways, and hover, all while beating its wings 50 times per second. Its vigorous metabolism makes it especially vulnerable to chemicals. Avoid pesticides whenever possible.

To fuel their active lifestyle, hummingbirds need the nectar of more than 1,000 blooms a day. The liquid diet is supplemented with insects and sap. Plant a layered floral landscape that blooms from spring to fall to provide a constant food source. Hummingbirds have long skinny beaks and tongues, ideal for sipping nectar from tubular flowers. Plant red and orange tubular blooms and other flowers that are rich in nectar (see Table 27-F.)

Help hummingbirds find your garden with a specialized feeder. Fill it with a solution of one part sugar to four parts boiled water. No red dye is needed, and is actually discouraged. Clean and refill the feeders weekly.

Hummingbirds prefer showers to baths. Birdbath drippers and fountains are appealing, as are hummingbird misters.

Butterflies

Aside from their aesthetic qualities, butterflies are essential pollinators and an important food source for birds, reptiles, frogs, and bats. Bringing butterflies to your landscape is as easy as providing nectar for adult butterflies and plants for their larvae (see Table 27-G).

Plant nectar-rich annuals and perennials in large groups according to color to make it easier for butterflies to spot them. A succession of blooms provides an ongoing food source. Choose plants of varying heights to add interest to your butterfly garden, and locate them in full sun for the most/best blooms.

Table 27-E. Flowers that attract birds

Status: N = Native • E = Escaped cultivation • C = Cultivated
Light: FS = Full sun • PS = Part-shade • S = Shade

Common name/ scientific name	Description	Height (ft.)	Status	Light	Soil	Summer flowering
Cardinal flower (*Lobelia cardinalis*)	Woodland perennial with red tubular flowers	2 - 5	N	FS - S	Moist or wet	Late
Bee balm (*Monarda didyma*)	Perennial with clusters of bright red tubular flowers	1 - 5	N	FS - PS	Moist or wet	Mid
Columbine (*Aquilegia canadensis*)	Woodland perennial with drooping bell-like flowers	1 - 3	N	FS - PS	Rocky, well-drained	Early to mid
Bleeding heart (*Dicentra eximia*)	Perennial with drooping heart-shaped flowers	1 - 2	N	S	Moist	Early
Black-eyed Susan (*Rudbeckia hirta*)	Tender perennial with bright yellow flowers and dark center	1-3	N	FS-PS	Moist to dry	Mid to late
Turkscap lily (*Lilium superbum*)	Perennial with a tall, flowering stem and drooping orange flowers	3 - 8	N	FS - PS	Wet	Mid to late
Hollyhock (*Althaea rosea*)	A perennial plant with bell-shaped flowers borne on tall stalks	4 - 6	C	FS	Moist to dry	Mid
Buttonbush (*Cephalanthus occidentalis*)	Shrub with round white flowers	6-12	N	FS-S	Moist to wet	Mid to late
Coralberry (*Symphoricarpos orbiculatus*)	Shrub with bell-shaped purple flowers	to 3	N	FS - PS	Moist	Mid
Weigela (*Weigela florida*)	Shrub with white, pink, or red tubular flowers	to 10	C	FS - PS	Well-drained	Early to mid
Trumpet honeysuckle (*Lonicera sempervirens*)	Vine with yellow to red tubular flowers	10 - 20	C	FS - PS	Well-drained	Early to mid
Trumpet creeper (*Campis radicans*)	Vine with orange trumpet-shaped flowers	30 - 40	E	FS	Widely adapted	Mid to late
Tulip poplar (*Liriodendron tulipifera*)	Native tree with large tulip-shaped flowers	to 100	N	FS - PS	Well-drained to moist	Early

Table 27-F. Flowers that attract butterflies

Status: N = Native • E = Escaped cultivation • C = Cultivated
Light: FS = Full sun • PS = Part-shade • S = Shade

Common name/ scientific name	Description	Height (ft.)	Status	Light	Soil	Summer flowering
Cosmos (*Cosmos* spp.)	Annual garden flower	to 6	C	FS - PS	Moist to dry	Mid to late
Heliotrope (*Heliotropium arborescens*)	Clusters of small, fragrant blooms; select those with purple flowers	2	C	FS - PS	Moist	Mid
Marigold (*Calendula officinalis*)	Annual plant provides food for caterpillars and nectar for butterflies	2	C	FS - PS	Moist to dry	Mid to late
Zinnia (*Zinnia elegans*)	Annual garden flower	1 - 2	C	FS - PS	Well-drained	Mid to late
Dogbane (*Apocynum* spp.)	Field wildflower with milky juice, long tubular flowers	1 - 4	N	FS	Dry	Mid

Most larvae do not feed on the same plants as adults, so provide plants that are attractive to females for laying their eggs. Favorites of larvae include dill, fennel, cabbage, and tomato. Plant a few extra of these for the caterpillars.

Some weeds, such as clover, serve as both a nectar source and food for larvae. If a perfectly weed-free lawn is not a priority, leave the clover to grow and attract a myriad of butterfly species to your yard.

Butterflies, just like birds, need shelter. You can create natural windbreaks with ornamental shrubs, evergreens, and tall grasses as well as hardscape items like low stone walls and trellises. Use the latter to grow flowering vines, which provide cover and food. Locate windbreaks on the north and west sides of your garden area and allow some fallen leaves to remain over the winter for protection against the cold.

In addition to flowers, create an area of wet sand or mud in the ground or in a shallow container to attract butterflies. They love to sip water in a behavior called puddling.

Butterflies and other beneficial insects are extremely susceptible to broad-spectrum insecticides. Employ integrated pest management (IPM) strategies to lessen the need for insecticides to manage insect pests See **Chapter 10, IPM,** for more information.

27.8 Managing Wildlife Damage

Traditional wildlife management has focused on improving wildlife habitat for certain species or groups of species, but as wildlife becomes more abundant and human populations continue to expand into natural areas, human-wildlife conflicts have increased.

Some wildlife species cause damage to landscapes, buildings, and other property; whereas other conflicts can raise safety concerns.

Some wildlife damage can be costly and discouraging, and no single, quick, guaranteed solution exists. The following principles will help improve your success:

- Identify the species responsible for the damage.
- Determine the monetary cost of the damage and the level of damage you are willing to accept.
- Educate yourself regarding the control options and their cost and practicality.
- Select and implement the options and monitor the results, adjusting your options as needed.

There are basically five solutions to most animal problems:

- Change the habitat to make it less attractive, or improve access to predators.
- Trap and relocate or kill the problem animal.
- Construct a barrier to prevent animal access.
- Use repellents to discourage animal activity (see Table 27-G).
- Learn to live with the situation.

Many people think that relocating animal pests such as squirrels, rabbits, or groundhogs is a humane way to deal with the problem. In fact, relocating most animals requires a permit from the state wildlife agency. More importantly, research shows that relocated animals tend to die more quickly because the relocation process causes damaging physiological stress; they are unfamiliar with the area, less prepared to deal with predators, and must compete with other wildlife in an area where habitat is already limited. It is usually more humane to euthanize an animal, if that is allowed by law. Effective control depends upon the following factors:

Timing. Install barriers around gardens before an animal problem occurs. If left unattended, some animals will destroy a garden in a very short time. It is important to act at the very first indication of their presence.

Persistence. Many animals can foil your various attempts to discourage them. A single attempt at constructing a barrier or using a repellent may not work. Keep trying until you find an effective control or a combination of control strategies.

Integration. A single approach to control may not work, and no single control method continues to be effective just because it worked before. Animals differ in their habits and can use their ingenuity to get into a garden. Typically, you will need to integrate a variety of strategies and devices for effective control.

27.9 Nuisance Animals

Even though we want to build our gardens and landscapes to sustain wildlife, we may often encounter problems with some of the wildlife. Following are some strategies to handle these problems.

Crows

Crows can cause considerable damage to fruit and vegetable gardens by eating seeds, fruit, and young transplants. They also eat the eggs and young of songbirds. They thrive in areas with large trees that adjoin open fields where they can search for food. Because crows are omnivorous, they will eat almost anything and can readily adapt to seasonal food supplies.

Controls

- Drape nylon netting over plants and small fruit trees.

Table 27-G. Nuisance-animal repellents

Mode of action	Active ingredient	Longevity	Name brands
Odor/taste	Putrescent egg-based	7 weeks or more, less with cold temperatures and persistent snow cover	Deer-Away, Liquid Fence, Deer Guard
Odor/taste	Edible animal protein, fish oil	Same as above	Repellex, Bobbex, Plantskydd
Taste	Benzyldiethyl ammonium benzoate (Bitrex®)	Same as above	TreeGuard, Ropel, Repel
Odor/taste	Combination preparation: egg-based, garlic, mint oil, pepper, Bitrex®, etc.	Same as above	Deer Stopper, Deerbuster, Deer 1
Taste	Fungicide (Thiram-based): not recommended due to fungicide impacts	Same as above	Shot-Gun Deer Repellent, Chew-Not

Figure 27-R. Crow

- Place paper sacks over individual ears of corn until the silk turns brown.
- Install various "scare" techniques such as loud noises, lights, and bright reflective objects. Crows can become accustomed to loud noises over time and learn to ignore them.

What not to do

- Ultrasonic sounds are not effective because birds cannot hear them.
- Toxic baits and shooting are less safe (and may be illegal) for homeowners and desirable wildlife.

Pigeons

The common pigeon found in Maryland and Delaware is a descendant of the European rock dove, originally introduced into America as a domesticated bird. The pigeon is now probably the most important bird pest in human habitations in cities and around farms.

Pigeons feed on grain, garbage, and other food associated with humans. The average life span for a typical city pigeon is only about three or four years, but in captivity they may live longer than 15 years. They produce several broods each year and both the male and female care for the young. The female feeds the young a special liquid called pigeon milk.

Pigeons are attractive birds and feeding them entertains many people. The problem arises when there are large numbers of them and their droppings deface and damage buildings and statues. They may also carry diseases to humans through their droppings (e.g., encephalitis, Newcastle disease, toxoplasmosis, and salmonella food poisoning.) In addition, their many parasites, such as mites, ticks, and lice, also bite people.

Control

Because pigeons are so accustomed to living around people, "frightening tactics" often do not work. Block pigeon access to roosts and nesting sites. Use heavy hardware cloth or stainless steel porcupine wire, which fastens to ledges and window sills. The sharp wires inflict temporary discomfort and cause pigeons to avoid landing on these surfaces. Naphthalene moth flakes are registered as a pigeon repellent and work well when spread on an attic or shed floor.

Figure 27-S. Pigeon

What not to do

Toxic baits will cause distress in the bird without killing it. The ailing bird sends out distress calls that frighten other members of the flock away. These products can only be bought and applied by licensed, certified pest control operators.

Woodpeckers

Woodpeckers belong to a group of birds that also includes flickers and sapsuckers. There are 22 species of woodpeckers in the U.S. Among the species in Maryland are the downy woodpecker, red-headed woodpecker, flicker, and yellow-bellied sapsucker.

Because woodpeckers depend on trees for shelter and food, they are found on the edge of wooded areas. Many woodpeckers utilize man-made structures for nesting and have extended their habitat to include wooden fence posts, utility poles, and buildings.

One commonly-held misconception is that they only peck holes in search of insects. Many species drill holes in sound wood where no insects exist. Sapsuckers will drill many quarter-inch holes in healthy trees to feed on sap.

Occasionally, woodpeckers will try to nest in a person's home. Wooden buildings in the suburbs or rural wooded settings are most apt to suffer pecking and hole damage because woodpeckers favor this habitat. Generally speaking, damage to a house is caused by one or two birds. Houses with expensive cedar and redwood siding are singled out for woodpecker damage. Some birds even peck on aluminum siding!

Control

One of the most effective methods to prevent woodpecker damage to siding beneath the eaves is to cover the area with lightweight netting. Apply metal barriers over the pecked areas as soon as it begins. Toy whirligigs and plastic reflective strips have been successful. Loud noises such as hand-clapping or banging on metal trash can lids have also been useful. Many bird watchers place beef suet near buildings and trees that are attacked by woodpeckers, providing an attractive alternative to pecking.

Figure 27-T. Yellow-bellied sapsucker

What not to do

- Model owls and snakes are ineffective.
- Don't offer suet in warmer seasons because it may become rancid and harm woodpeckers.

Bats

Bats are the only mammals that can truly fly. Contrary to folklore, they are not related to mice; the latter belong to the order Rodentia, whereas bats belong to the order Chiroptera.

Figure 27-U. Bat

According to the Maryland Department of Natural Resources, 10 bat species live in Maryland. Probably the two most common species in Maryland are the big brown bat (*Eptesicus fuscus*) and the little brown bat (*Myotis lucifugus*).

Both species live in colonies in buildings, hollow trees, and caves. Day roosts are dark and secluded. They are insect feeders, foraging around water, forests, fields, ravines, and buildings. They consume up to half their weight in insects each night. In cold weather, bats migrate or hibernate in caves, mines, and sometimes in houses. Many gardeners have built roosting boxes to help encourage their presence in the garden.

Bats, however, may become a nuisance to people when they roost in houses, revealing their presence with fecal droppings and stains near eaves, beneath entrance holes, and below roosts. In old, loosely constructed buildings with an attic roost or a space between a wall and a chimney, bat guano may seep through cracks and stain ceilings and walls.

Bats commonly enter houses under the overhang of the roof or eaves. They are often found in attics, ceiling or roof spaces, and cornices; and behind shutters, fascias, or small openings.

Rabies is the most important public health hazard associated with bats, but its impact has been greatly exaggerated. Rabies in bats is quite similar to rabies in other carnivores but is less dangerous because bats fly and are rarely aggressive. Misleading information often brings on intense public reactions and demands for complete bat destruction.

Control

The best control for bats that have entered attics or wall voids is exclusion. They must be evicted before bat-proofing so they won't be sealed inside. The best time to start is in the fall after young bats have learned to fly and before the onset of cold weather. Block holes after dark, or in the early evening, after the bats have gone to feed. The following evening, remove plugs to allow any remaining bats to leave before the last exit is sealed. This routine must be repeated if any bats are left inside.

REPORT A WILDLIFE PROBLEM

The Maryland Department of Natural Resources Wildlife and Heritage Division and the U.S. Department of Agriculture (USDA) have teamed up to provide a toll-free number to report nuisance, injured, or sick wildlife. They can provide advice and some resources to help you with wildlife damage problems, but they do not handle problems with deer, bear, and other larger species.

Operators are available from 8:00am to 4:30pm, Monday through Friday, except state holidays.

1-877-463-6497

Exclusion entails caulking, and application of weather stripping, flashing, and screening of any openings. Bats can squeeze through openings with diameters as small as half an inch. Bright lights in the attic may be helpful to chase them out. Drafts from a fan will also chase bats from their roost. For severe infestations, contact an exterminator or a member of a conservancy group in your area.

Cats and dogs

Although most cats and dogs bring joy to their owners, these same animals can be a nuisance for neighbors. Dogs can sometimes become a safety concern when they roam in packs, which can kill small livestock. Cats and dogs can become a nuisance when they tear open trash bags, dig holes in gardens, destroy plants, kill native wildlife, and defecate and urinate on other people's property. Large dogs are particularly destructive if they "mark their territory" on shrubs.

State and local regulations help to protect people and property. County and municipal laws vary so always consult with local authorities to help solve a recurring problem.

Control

The control of nuisance cats and dogs can be a very uncomfortable problem because the aggrieved party has to inform the owner of the pet. If there is a recurring problem, approaching the pet's owner with tact is the best solution. Many times, the pet's owner may not even be aware that their animal is causing a problem. Responsible pet ownership is the only real solution.

What not to do

Various brands of commercially-available cat and dog repellents can be bought at pet shops

Figure 27-V. Cat and dog

and garden centers, but they are not always reliable. When they do work, it is in a very localized or confined area. Large-scale use is expensive, impractical, and not very effective. Additionally, most commercial repellents cannot be used in vegetable gardens.

Deer

Deer are the most widely distributed and best-recognized large mammals in North America. The deer in our area are white-tailed deer. They are creatures of the forest edge rather than the dense, old-growth forest. They thrive in agricultural areas interspersed with woodlots. Deer browse on leaves, stems, and buds of woody and herbaceous plants, and fruits and nuts in season; and are most active in the early morning and evening. In the fall, male deer (bucks)rub their antlers on sapling-sized trees and shrubs to remove the velvet, destroying the bark in the process. One or two deer can destroy an entire garden in one visit.

Figure 27-W. Deer

Deer populations are overabundant throughout much of Maryland, especially in urban and suburban environments. Deer have adapted quite well to people, with many losing their fear of humans. This has raised serious safety concerns because overabundant deer populations are associated with increases in deer-vehicle collisions and Lyme disease.

Overabundant deer also cause serious ecological damage to forests by browsing many of the tree, shrub, and herbaceous species we value. Over time, deer browsing removes most vegetation up to about five or six feet high. This creates a conspicuous "browse line" and eliminates wildlife habitat.

Control

There are four main options for homeowners:

1. Fencing. The only sure way to eliminate deer damage in rural or suburban areas is to install an eight-foot tall fence. The cost of expensive deer fences limits construction to areas of intensive agriculture, such as orchards and private gardens. You can install a wire-mesh fence (sturdy and long-lasting, but expensive) or plastic mesh (light, inexpensive, easy to handle).

Many homeowners have had excellent success using an electric fence charger connected to two strands of polywire or polytape on posts with a maximum height of about three feet. Polywire is a plastic filament interwoven with strands of metal wire to carry an electric charge. The fence is baited every 20 to 30 feet with aluminum foil or metal flashing strips with peanut butter halfway between.

Curious deer touch the fence, get shocked, and learn to stay away. It is not very effective in the winter when snow insulates the deer from getting a shock and the lack of other food sources causes deer to compromise the fence. The polywire fence is low-cost, easy to install, and very effective for small acreages.

Bird netting can be placed over shrubs to stop winter browsing but must be removed before new growth begins in the spring. New netting must be installed each year.

2. Scare tactics/repellents. Scare tactics and repellents are most effective if they are used at the first sign of a problem. It is difficult to break deer behavior patterns or movements once they are established.

In the home landscape, repellents are best suited for use in orchards and gardens or on ornamental plants (see Table 27-G).

Some of the basic facts of repellents:

- They have a limited time before they fail. Winter longevity is usually from seven to 13 weeks in Maryland.
- New growth requires frequent application.

- They work by odor, taste, or a combination.
- Deer tend to change their feeding patterns in the fall and spring. For winter damage, apply repellent in October before deer start establishing their winter feeding pattern.
- Repellent that works in one area may not work in another.
- Change repellents annually because deer get used to the same smells.
- Repellents must be kept fresh for maximum effectiveness.
- During the winter when other foods may be scarce, repellents may not be as effective. Repellents tend to fail more quickly in areas with cold temperatures and persistent snow cover.
- The long-term costs of repellents are high; seriously consider fencing.

3. Disruption of deer's feeding habits. Deer are selective feeders. By interfering with their preferences, they may leave the area in search of better food.

- Plant less-preferred species or establish susceptible plants only in protected areas. No plant is "deer-proof." Most damage occurs when winter snow or extreme cold has reduced food supplies. Rather than starve, deer will eat most anything.
- Deer are creatures of habit, and prior movement patterns or foraging experience can foretell where damage will occur. Plan accordingly.
- New plantings in an area already severely damaged by deer will likely suffer from browsing. Use extra protection on new plants.

Figure 27-X. Wildlife Damage Management (WDM)

The principles of WDM are the same as IPM (Integrated Pest Management), but apply to vertebrates: Identify the problem; consider a variety of solutions; implement the least harmful, most cost-effective strategies; monitor the problem to ensure that it has been solved; and evaluate the effectiveness of the solution you used.

4. Population management. Deer population quickly gets out of balance with habitat and humans. Traditional hunting is the most cost-effective method to reduce high deer numbers, but this is usually not possible in urban and suburban environments. As deer populations have increased in urban and suburban areas, new strategies have been developed to address the need for population management (see Figure 27-X).

In many communities, citizen task forces have been organized by local agencies or organizations. The charge of these task forces is to bring in experts to learn about the effectiveness of the options available to manage deer, complete a survey of citizens to determine the magnitude and scope of the problem, share what they learn with their stakeholders, and provide a report with recommendations on options. Local governments can then work with the educated stakeholders to implement population management strategies using managed hunts and sharpshooters, along with an educational program on non-lethal options.

House mice

Mice can cause considerable damage outdoors to bulbs and young tree bark during winter. During fall, many common house mice move into homes in search of warmth and food.

These small, slender rodents are generally grayish-brown with a gray belly. Similar mice include white-footed mice and harvest mice. House mice will eat any kind of food, but prefer seeds and grain. They may nibble on other foods high in fat, protein, or sugar, even when grain and seed are available. Because they nibble on many foods and discard partially eaten items, mice ruin considerably more food than they actually eat. Mice are also known to damage house insulation and may gnaw on electrical wiring.

Control

Mouse control involves a multi-faceted approach that includes sanitation, habitat modification, traps, and selective bait placement:

Sanitation. Remove all sources of food, including food crumbs behind and underneath kitchen appliances. Don't leave pet food out overnight and store it in closed containers.

Habitat modification. Seal all openings around the house, such as spaces near vents, basement doors, and under the bottom edge of siding.

Traps. Ordinary snap traps are economical and work quite well. Set them along walls, in cabinets, and in suspended ceilings, perpendicular to the wall with the trigger next

Figure 27-Y.   House mouse

to the wall. One house usually has several mice, so place several traps out in one evening. Good baits include peanut butter, cheese, and bacon. Get mice used to feeding from the traps by baiting the traps for two or three nights without setting them.

Baits. Larger infestations may require bait containing an anticoagulant. A high enough dose will kill after one feeding. The anticoagulant, warfarin, is very effective against both rats and mice. To prevent non-target animals from getting into the bait, place the bait inside a bait station along a wall.

A newer type of bait delivers a lethal dose of vitamin D, which causes a calcium imbalance in the blood. Mice die in a few days after ingesting it. This bait is toxic only to rodents.

Consult with a professional pest control service if the infestation is severe.

Rats

The rat species most commonly found in city and country settings is the Norway rat. It is sometimes called the wharf rat, sewer rat, or brown rat.

Rats are accustomed to living near people although they are usually only active at night. Rats burrow under buildings, sidewalks, and other structures, where they rear their young. Rats stay within a 150-foot diameter area of their nest. In that space, they memorize every object, passage, and location of food and water. Rats will eat nearly any type of food but prefer cereal grain, meat, fish, nuts, and some fruits. Unlike mice, rats need to drink water if they are feeding on dry materials. Food items found in household garbage will offer a fairly balanced diet that can also satisfy their moisture needs.

If a rat eats a sub-lethal dose of toxic bait and becomes ill, it will stay away from that bait for weeks, or even months. Pre-baiting an area with a non-toxic bait can fool the rats into eating the bait prior to placement of a toxic bait.

Control

- Physical barriers that are "gnaw-proof" can prevent both rats and mice from entering a building. Holes of one-half inch or larger are big enough for rats to squeeze through.
- Improving sanitation and eliminating hiding places in urban areas is key. Good sanitation will not always eliminate rat populations in rural areas, but it will prevent them from flourishing.
- Unusually loud and novel sounds, including ultrasonic sounds, will frighten them and disrupt their behavior, but this approach lasts only a few weeks or months.
- Baiting, in conjunction with sanitation and habitat modification, is the recommended control technique. When used according to directions, anti-coagulant baits are an effective part of a rodent control program. The baits are also relatively safe to use around livestock, pets, and humans.

Figure 27-Z.   Rat

Moles and voles

Moles and voles can be troublesome for homeowners. Their peak activity is in June and again in the fall. Although these animals are often mistaken for one another, they pose two different problems in the lawn and garden and require different mitigation remedies.

Moles

Moles live underground and feed on earthworms, beetles, and grubs. Moles eat 70 to 100 percent of their body weight each day. Moles do not eat bulbs, plants, or roots, but damage lawns and gardens as they tunnel through plant roots in search of food.

Moles differ in appearance from voles:

- They have naked, pointed snouts and small, almost hidden eyes.
- They lack external ears.
- Their powerful forefeet are very large and broad, designed for digging.
- Their feet, noses, and tails are light pink and their fur is velvety.

Figure 27-AA. Mole

Seldom seen above ground, moles prefer to live in underground burrows. Moles must cover a wide area to satisfy their food requirements. A mole's runway system is a network of shallow burrows dug just beneath the surface of the ground. Some slightly deeper burrows are highways leading from the mole's home to its feeding grounds. The shallow burrows may or may not be used again. Old tunnels are eventually abandoned when they become blocked with soil, especially after heavy rains.

Voles also use these tunnels to feed on seeds, roots, and tubers exposed by the mole.

Control

Beetle grubs are their preferred food, but moles subsist on a wide range of soil invertebrates. Products containing castor oil or other repellents may prove effective in some instances. Always follow label directions and be persistent.

What not to do

- Applying grub-control insecticides to the lawn in hopes of eliminating the mole's food source doesn't work because moles eat many other invertebrates, not just grubs.
- Poison bait pellets do not work because moles rarely eat grain or seeds.
- Don't use a lethal mole trap unless you are committed to it. They are hit-or-miss unless you tamp down all the tunnels, then place the traps in the new tunnels that reappear (those are now the active tunnels). Traps take precise placement and daily attention, and aren't to everyone's liking.

Voles

Voles, also called meadow or field mice, are also members of the rodent family. The two species of vole are the meadow vole and the pine vole. The meadow vole is a small, compact rodent approximately four-and-a-half to seven inches long, with small round ears and a tail about twice the length of the hind foot. Meadow voles live in grassy habitats where they construct a complex network of surface runways. To identify active runways, look for clipped grass and small droppings that resemble green or tan grains of rice.

The pine vole, also called the pine mouse, lives in burrows one inch to two feet below ground. The adult pine vole is smaller than

Figure 27-BB. Vole

the meadow vole, approximately four to five inches long, with a shorter tail, smaller eyes, and a more blunt nose. All voles are brown or gray, though many color variations exist.

Voles are becoming increasingly common in the home landscape. They eat mostly succulent green tissue during the growing season; but in the late summer and fall, they may store seeds, tubers, bulbs, and rhizomes for the winter. During the fall and winter, they eat woody tissue and can girdle the stems and devour the roots of ornamental plants and young trees, as well as eat bulbs. Homeowners usually notice vole feeding damage in the spring when trees, shrubs, and bulbs fail to sprout. Voles are active day and night and throughout the year, as they do not hibernate.

Control

Limit mulch depth to two to four inches. Pull mulch away from tree trunks and ornamentals to prevent voles from chewing bark.

Voles will avoid digging in pea gravel. Lay it at the base of fruit trees before winter.

Use snap mouse traps or sticky traps on a grid pattern in the landscape. Place the trap perpendicular to the runways with the trigger end in the runway. A peanut butter-oatmeal mixture or apple slices make good baits. Cover with a shingle or scrap wood.

Rabbits

The most common rabbit in Maryland is the Eastern cottontail. They are very abundant and quite adaptable, making them equally at home in rural areas, suburbs, or cities. Rabbits do not distribute themselves across the landscape but prefer to live in bushy fence rows or at the edge of fields.

Figure 27-CC. Rabbit

In the garden, rabbits love to eat peas, beans, lettuce, beets, and a variety of flowers. They don't bother corn, squash, cucumbers, tomatoes, peppers, or potatoes. Much more serious is the damage that rabbits do to trees and shrubs when they gnaw bark during the winter. Rabbit feeding leaves clean, diagonal cuts vs. the ragged, stringy cuts left by deer feeding.

Control

Enclose the area by constructing a two-foot high fence of chicken wire with the bottom tight to the ground or buried a few inches. Cylinders of quarter-inch hardware cloth, plastic tree guards, or tree wrap will protect young tree trunks. The cylinders should be two to three feet taller than the expected snow depth.

Effective rabbit repellents act upon their senses of taste and smell. Dried blood can be used as a scent repellent. Repellents are available in hardware stores as formulated products. Sprinkling these mixtures around plants helps keep rabbits away until rain dilutes their effect.

Some gardeners have reported effective results with sprinkling vinegar, hot pepper flakes, and liquid chile-pepper sprays on and around plants. Try soaking corn cobs in vinegar for five minutes and scatter them throughout the garden. After two weeks, re-soak the cobs with the vinegar.

Another technique is to sprinkle soiled cat litter around the edge of the flower garden, shrub beds, or trees. The smell of a natural predator can be quite effective. Do not apply cat litter to any edible gardens.

Some gardeners plant a border of marigolds around their vegetable gardens. Rabbits hate the smell of them.

Raccoons

Raccoons are familiar to homeowners throughout rural, suburban, and urban areas. These very adaptable animals can grow up to three feet long and weigh between 10 and 30 pounds. In nature, raccoons live in hollow trees, under large logs, and in underground burrows. In urban neighborhoods, they readily make their homes in storm drains, under porches and sheds, and even in chimneys.

Wild raccoons should always be treated with caution as they will fight fiercely when cornered or trapped. Raccoons are nocturnal, and if a raccoon is seen wandering during the day, it might have been flushed from its den, injured, or possibly sick with rabies.

Their typical diet includes fruit, vegetables, and carrion; dog and cat food; and small animals, including crayfish, snails, insects, turtles, snakes, mice, and rabbits. Their favorite foods include fish, poultry, and eggs. Sweet corn grown in home vegetable gardens is frequently damaged by raccoons,

Figure 27-DD. Raccoon

as evidenced by torn-open ears revealing partially eaten corn. The stalks may also be broken from the weight of the raccoon climbing on them.

Control

Repellents and scare-devices are ineffective once raccoons become accustomed to them. The best way to keep a raccoon out of a garden, attic, shed, or garbage cans is exclusion with proper screening or fencing.

A two-strand electric fence, positioned six inches above the ground, helps keep them out of vegetable gardens and fish ponds.

Stop garbage-can raids by using metal cans or tough plastic containers with tight-fitting lids.

To keep raccoons out of a chimney, install a tight-fitting screen cap. A cap will also keep rain and birds out. If you remove a raccoon from an attic or chimney in the spring or summer, be sure no babies are left trapped inside. Do not attempt exclusion practices until you know that all the raccoons are out of the structure.

When all deterrents fail, the only solution is to trap and remove the troublesome animal from the property. Raccoons are usually easy to trap with a large cage trap. It must be large enough to comfortably hold the raccoon, about 10 x 12 x 32-inches. Use raw fish, chicken, sardines, or canned cat food as a bait. Trapped raccoons should not be released but turned over to local animal-control authorities.

Skunks

Skunks, large members of the weasel family, can grow to be about 30 inches long (tail included), and weigh about eight pounds. Their natural habitat is around clearings and pastures, and along the edges of forests where they live under hollow stumps or logs. In suburban areas, they often live under low porches and decks, or behind stone walls.

Skunks are primarily carnivorous and will eat plant or animal matter and pet foods, but their favorite foods are insects and their larvae. To find insects, skunks dig small cone-shaped holes in lawns and gardens, usually smaller than three inches across and deep.

Skunks become a concern to homeowners when they damage lawns in search of grubs or when they release their scent near the house. Rabies is occasionally carried by skunks; abnormal behavior towards people or activity during the day should be viewed cautiously.

Control

Skunks can usually be controlled without harming them. Prevent them from making a den under structures by sealing off all foundation openings with heavy hardware cloth. Because skunks are poor climbers, fencing will prevent them from entering areas you want to protect. Stop skunks from invading trash cans by putting garbage bags into containers with a tight-fitting lid. Repellents are a temporary help.

Figure 27-EE. Skunk

Skunks may also be successfully caught in live traps that are set close to their den. Use fish-flavored cat food or bread with peanut butter as a bait. Cover the trap with a heavy cloth to make the trap appear more secure to the skunk and to reduce the chances of it discharging its scent. Turn the caged skunk over to local animal control authorities. Many people are not aware that, in keeping with state law, most trapped mammals like skunks are not released but destroyed to prevent the spread of rabies. The exceptions are squirrels, opossums, moles, voles, and non-mammals such as snakes.

Squirrels

The common species of squirrel found throughout Maryland and Delaware is the Eastern gray squirrel. They eat tree fruits, seeds, nuts, buds, shoots, insects, and fungi. In their search for food, they often destroy the growing tips of young trees and shrubs, strip bark from trees, and dig up flowers and bulbs. Squirrels are most active in the early morning and late afternoon.

Homeowners have problems with squirrels chewing through siding and tearing open attic vents to gain access into the house. Once inside the attic, they can ruin insulation by

Figure 27-FF. Gray squirrel

digging through it. Squirrels also chew on wiring and damage stored items. Garden-related problems include damage to bulbs, fruits, tomatoes, and flower buds of rhododendrons.

Control

Securely cover attic vents with half-inch hardware cloth. Leave a light on in the attic or in other hiding places to discourage nesting.

A live box or cage trap is useful for catching nuisance squirrels. Bait the trap with apples, seeds, or peanut butter. Put the baited trap out but do not set it for a few days so that the squirrels will become accustomed to feeding from it. After a few days, set the baited trap for capture. Turn captured squirrels over to animal control or release them at least five miles from your home, or they will come back. Wear gloves and do not touch the squirrel.

In the garden, squirrels will dig up newly planted bulbs. To prevent this, soak bulbs in a repellent, such as Ropel, before planting. It smells and tastes very bad to them. Construct metal barriers or apply Tanglefoot on trunks to prevent squirrels from climbing trees. This only works if they can't jump from tree to tree.

Chipmunks

Chipmunks are small ground-dwelling rodents with distinctive stripes on their rusty-red to chestnut-brown fur. Five dark-brown stripes line the back with a creamy-buff stripe separating them. Mature chipmunks are nine to 10 inches long and weigh about three ounces.

Chipmunks are omnivorous, eating both plants and animals. Acorns, hickory nuts, beechnuts, cherry seeds, Juneberries, raspberries, dogwood seeds, corn, and plant bulbs are favorites. The main animal foods are birds' eggs, insects, snails, and occasionally mice and young birds. Chipmunks gather food in the fall. Hard foods are stuffed into their cheek pouches and stored in food caches.

Figure 27-GG. Chipmunk

When chipmunks move into an urban setting, they dig seeds from the garden, feed on flower bulbs, and burrow into lawns, especially near rock walls. In lawns, the two- to three-inch burrows descend almost vertically. Burrow openings cut neatly through the turf and lack excavated soil at the entrance.

Control

Homes with wooded lots, thickets of ornamental shrubbery, and dry rock walls are very attractive to chipmunks, but most people value their trees and shrubs too highly to drastically modify the landscape. Chipmunks can seldom be eliminated from an area unless their living conditions are radically changed, so people opt to tolerate the chipmunks.

Chipmunks are not protected by law and may be trapped in any season. Live trapping with small commercial or homemade box traps can reduce their numbers. Once trapped, release them at least a mile from the capture area.

Snap traps are only effective because they kill the animal. Should you choose this route, bait the trap with peanut butter, nut meats, sunflower seeds, or rolled oats. Place the trap in areas where chipmunks travel or feed.

Chipmunks occasionally enter homes where they are generally more bothersome than destructive. Prevent entry by closing holes in foundation walls and screening windows, vents, and other ground-level openings.

Groundhogs (Woodchucks)

Groundhogs are common in rural areas but are also at home in the suburbs near open land. Also called woodchucks, furry brown groundhogs are very large members of the squirrel family, growing to a length of almost two feet and weighing five to 10 pounds. Their powerful claws are well-adapted for digging burrows as deep as five feet. Entrance holes, about a foot wide with a mound of soil around them, are usually well hidden. The network of tunnels can cover an underground area as large as 59 square feet.

Groundhogs become a problem when they feed on trees, shrubs, flowers, and vegetables. The mounds of soil and large holes present a hazard to people; and groundhog tunneling can undermine porches, decks, and sheds.

Figure 27-HH. Groundhog

Control

In rural areas, homeowners shoot groundhogs when they become numerous and destructive. This is neither a safe nor legal method of control for suburban homeowners. A strong, three- to four-foot high wire fence buried 10 to 12 inches in the ground will help keep them out of a garden. Groundhogs are good climbers, but if the top of the fence is loose, they will fall backwards. An electric wire placed four to five inches off the ground and the same distance outside the fence will prevent climbing and burrowing.

Live-trap groundhogs using apples, carrots, or lettuce. Locate the trap at the main entrance of a burrow. Contact local animal control for proper removal.

Groundhogs will often burrow under garden sheds or other outdoor structures. Strong repellents can discourage them. Fencing around the base of the shed is also useful.

Snakes

Snakes are considered the most highly-evolved reptiles. All snakes are predators and can swallow food larger than their head. The larger species of snakes in our area, such

Figure 27-II. Poisonous Maryland snakes

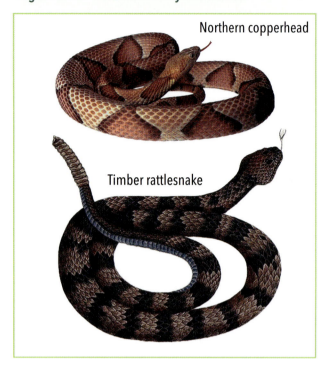

The Northern copperhead is a pit viper, found in rural areas. Its venom is less toxic than other rattlesnakes and fatalities are rare. Nevertheless, a bite is serious. It causes severe pain and needs immediate medical attention.

The timber rattlesnake, also a pit viper, is relatively rare because of human intrusion on its habitat. Its bite can be fatal.

Because both poisonous snakes in Maryland are pit vipers, they can be identified easily. Pit vipers have eyes with vertical pupils, and have a "pit," a heat-sensing hole, on each side of their head. Pit viper heads are large and triangular in shape. Copperhead juveniles have a sulfur-yellow tail.

Certain other native snakes, such as hog-nosed snakes, water snakes, and corn snakes, also partially fit this description, and people will misidentify them. Most snakes will broaden their jaws when alarmed, making their head an almost perfect triangle. The hog-nosed snake can put on a tremendously convincing show, flaring its neck and hissing loudly, mimicking a cobra. The best advice for the general public is to leave all snakes alone. All snakes are protected by law in Maryland.

as rat snakes and king snakes, eat rodents. Other smaller species, such as garter snakes and ring-necked snakes, feed on a range of earthworms, insects, and amphibians.

Areas that are attractive to snakes include firewood stacks, old lumber piles, heavily-mulched planting beds, cluttered basements, barns, outbuildings, unmowed lawns, and attics where there is a rodent population.

There are only two species of dangerous snakes in our state: the Northern copperhead and the timber rattlesnake. Water moccasins and other rattlesnakes are not found here.

AUTHORS

Annette Cormany, Horticulture Educator, University of Maryland Extension (Washington County).

Jonathan Kays, Forestry Extension Specialist, University of Maryland Extension.

Mikaela Boley, Senior Agent for Home Horticulture, University of Maryland Extension.

Andrew A. Kling, Faculty Extension Assistant, Western Maryland Research and Education Center.

PUBLICATIONS

Adapted from the *Maryland Master Gardener Handbooks*. 2012 and 2016 eds. University of Maryland Extension. College Park, Maryland.

Bourne, R., Ed. 1974. *Gardening with Wildlife*. National Wildlife Federation. Washington, DC. ASIN: B000KUI9U8.

Dennis, J. V. 1985. *The Wildlife Gardener*. Alfred A. Knopf, Inc. New York, NY. ISBN-10: 0345348605.

Henderson, C. L. 1987. *Landscaping for Wildlife.* Minnesota Department of Natural Resources. St. Paul, MN. ISBN-10: 788123181.

Jackson, D. and J. Finley. *Herbicides and Forest Vegetation Management: Controlling Unwanted Trees, Brush, and Other Competing Forest Vegetation.* Penn State Extension, State College, PA.

Kays, J., J. Drohan, A. Downing, and J. Finley. 2006. T*he Woods in Your Backyard: Learning to Enhance and Create Natural Areas Around Your Home.* Natural Resource Agricultural Engineering Service (NRAES). Ithaca, NY.

Kays, J. S., A.,Downing, J. Finley, A. Kling, C. Highfield, N. Dawson, and J. Drohan. 2016. *The Woods in Your Backyard: Learning to Enhance and Create Natural Areas Around Your Home.* 2nd ed. Plant and Life Sciences Publishing. Ithaca, NY.

Kays, J. S., A. Kling, D. Jackson, A. Downing, A. Kedmenecz, C. Highfield, J. Schieffer, J. Lehnen, S. Gill, and J. Drohan. 2020. *Woodland Health Practices Handbook: A Practitioner's Guide for Creating, Enhancing, and Maintaining Natural Areas.* Virginia Tech Publishing, Blacksburg, VA.

Kays, J. S., A. Kling, D. Jackson, A. Downing, A. Kedmenecz, C. Highfield, J. Schieffer, J. Lehnen, S. Gill, & J. Drohan. 2020. W*oodland Health Practices Handbook: Woodland Health Assessment Checklist & Management Actions.* Virginia Tech Publishing, Blacksburg, VA.

Kress, S. W. 1985. T*he Audubon Society Guide to Attracting Birds.* Charles Scribner's Sons. New York, NY. ISBN-10: 0684183625.

Newcomb, L. 1977. *Newcomb's Wildflower Guide.* Little Brown. Boston, MA. ISBN-10: 0316604429.

Petrides, G. A. 1986. *A Field Guide to Trees and Shrubs.* Houghton-Mifflin. Boston, MA. ISBN-10: 039535370X.

Picone, P. M. 1995. *Enhancing Your Backyard Habitat for Wildlife.* Connecticut Department of Environmental Protection, Bureau of Natural Resources Wildlife Division. Hartford, CT.

Slattery, Britt E., Kathryn Reshetiloff, and Susan Zwicker. 2003, 2005, 2009, 2012. *Native Plants for Wildlife Habitat and Conservation Landscaping: Chesapeake Bay Watershed.* U.S. Fish & Wildlife Service, Chesapeake Bay Field Office, Annapolis, MD.

Mizejewski, David. 2004, 2019. *Attracting Birds, Butterflies and Other Backyard Wildlife.* Fox Chapel Publishing Company, Inc., Mount Joy, PA.

Tallamy, Douglas W. 2007. *Bringing Nature Home: How You Can Sustain Wildlife with Native Plants.* Timber Press, Inc. Portland, OR. ISBN-13: 978-0-88192-992-8.

Tallamy, Douglas W. 2019. *Nature's Best Hope: A New Approach to Conservation that Starts in Your Yard.* Timber Press, Inc., Portland, OR. ISBN 978-2-60469-900-5.

Petrides, G.A. *A Field Guide to Eastern Trees: Eastern US and Canada.* Houghton-Mifflin. Boston, MA. ISBN-10: 0395904552

Virginia Department of Forestry. 2009. *Common Native Trees of Virginia: Tree Identification Guide.* Virginia Department of Forestry, Charlottesville, VA. Available online.

Virginia Department of Forestry. 2009. *Tree and Forest Health Guide.* Virginia Department of Forestry, Charlottesville, VA. Available at: Available online.

Additional reading:

Kays, J., M. V. Bartlett, and L. Curtis. 2003. *Resistance of Ornamentals to Deer Damage.* Fact Sheet 655. University of Maryland Extension. College Park, MD.

Kays, J. 2003. *Managing Deer Damage in Maryland.* Extension Bulletin 354. University of Maryland Extension. College Park, MD.

Kays, J., and E. M. Dutky. 2004. *Reducing Vole Damage in Nurseries, Orchards, and Landscapes.* Fact Sheet 654. University of Maryland Extension. College Park, MD.

Tregoning, D. and J. Kays. 2003. *Using Commercial Deer Repellents to Manage Deer Browse in the Landscape.* Fact Sheet 810A. University of Maryland Extension. College Park, MD.

WEBSITES

Cornell Lab of Ornithology: birds.cornell.edu/home/

Maryland Department of Natural Resources: dnr.maryland.gov/Wildlife/Pages/plants_wildlife/home.aspx

Maryland Native Plant Society: mdflora.org/

Michigan State University: canr.msu.edu/resources/building_and_managing_bee_hotels_for_wild_bees_e3337

National Wildlife Federation: nwf.org/garden-for-wildlife/create

Pollinator Project: pollinator.org/

University of Maryland Home & Garden Information Center: extension.umd.edu/resource/pollinator-gardens

Xerces Society for Invertebrate Conservation: xerces.org/

Internet Center for Wildlife Damage Management: ic.org

Maryland Dept. of Natural Resources - Maryland Bat Identification Dichotomous Key: dnr.maryland.gov/wildlife/Pages/plants_wildlife/bats/bat_key.aspx

University of Maryland Natural Resources Program: agnr.umd.edu

University of Maryland Woodland Stewardship Education Program: extension.umd.edu/woodland

PHOTOS

Main chapter photo: USFWS Miwest Region via Flickr https://www.flickr.com/photos/usfwsmidwest/.

Fig. 27-A: Public domain. Figs. 27-B, 27-C, 27-E, 27-F, 27-I, 27-J, 27-L, 27-M, 27-O, and 27-P are courtesy of Jonathan Kays.

ILLUSTRATIONS

Fig. 27-Q: LeAnn Zotta, Berkshire Communications. Adapted from Recovering Northern Bobwhite Quail: A Guide to Habitat Management by UME, PSUE, & VA Cooperative Extension.

Figs. 27-D, 27-R, 27-V, 27-AA, 27-CC, and 27-GG, by Ray Bosmans. Colorized by LeAnn Zotta except 27-D.

Figs. 27-G, 27-H, 27-K, 27-N, 27-S, 27-T, 27-U, 27-W through 27-Z, 27-BB, 27-DD, 27-EE, 27-FF, 27-HH, and 27-II by LeAnn Zotta.

28: CONSERVATION LANDSCAPING

Wanda MacLachlan
Andrew Lazur, Ph.D.

28 CONSERVATION LANDSCAPING

CONTENTS

28.1 The Bay-Wise Philosophy 798

28.2 The Hydrologic Cycle 801

28.3 Groundwater 803

28.4 Water Pollution 805

28.5 Water Conservation 806

28.6 Stormwater Management 809

LEARNING OBJECTIVES

- Grasp the principles of conservation landscaping and the Bay-Wise philosophy
- Understand the hydrologic cycle
- Learn how ground and surface waters can become contaminated, and how to protect them
- Encourage on-site rain infiltration with a rain garden
- Learn how to conserve water in the landscape

INTRODUCTION

Over the years, land development has transformed our ecosystem into unconnected fragments. Removal of forests to build communities has benefitted humans, but it has been at the expense of the plants and animals that lived there before us. We now realize the detrimental effects of development on the ecosystem and are finding ways to successfully coexist with flora and fauna. One way is to create a little piece of native habitat on our home landscape, which can help restore local natural environments for our native wildlife.

Landscaping can increase property values, and, if done intentionally, can improve water quality and conserve nature—all while using only minimum resources. Terms like BayScapes, Bay-Wise, sustainable, low-impact, and conservation landscaping have been used to describe these intentions.

- **BayScapes** promotes a holistic approach that benefits people, wildlife, and the Chesapeake Bay, while promoting the use of native plants (see Figure 28-A).

Figure 28-A. "BayScaping" instead of expansive turf

- The **Bay-Wise landscape management** program's long-term goal is to improve water quality in the Chesapeake Bay, which in turn enhances local environments.
- **Sustainable landscaping** highlights the practice of working with nature to maximize the environment's value. Its principles consider local climate and environmental factors; preserve local wildlife habitat; reduce waste; and prevent water, air, and soil pollution. Best practices in plant selection and maintenance methods are key.

- **Low-impact development** is defined by the EPA as "systems and practices that use or mimic natural processes that result in the infiltration, evapotranspiration, or use of stormwater in order to protect water quality and associated aquatic habitat."
- **Conservation landscaping** focuses on reducing turfgrass areas, strives to improve water quality, promotes and preserves wildlife species, and protects native wildlife habitat. It is based on eight essential elements.

A conservation landscape:

1. Is designed to benefit the environment and function efficiently and aesthetically for human use and well-being.
2. Uses local native plants that are appropriate for site conditions.
3. Institutes a management plan for the removal of existing invasive plants and the prevention of future non-native plant invasions.
4. Provides habitat for wildlife.
5. Promotes healthy air quality and minimizes air pollution.
6. Conserves and cleans water.
7. Promotes healthy soils.
8. Is managed to conserve energy, reduce waste, and eliminate or minimize the use of pesticides and fertilizers.

28.1 The Bay-Wise Philosophy

The misdirection of stormwater runoff, misuse of pesticides and fertilizers, lack of soil management, and poor plant selection can all contribute to the degradation of Maryland's streams, rivers, and the Chesapeake Bay. The

Figure 28-B. Bay-Wise program sign

Bay-Wise landscape management program aims to overcome these damaging practices with a holistic approach.

The Bay-Wise philosophy was first introduced to Maryland Master Gardeners in 1996. Its main tenets recommend that gardeners:

- Manage yard pests with integrated pest management (IPM)
- Plant wisely
- Water efficiently
- Mow properly
- Control stormwater runoff
- Mulch appropriately
- Recycle yard waste
- Fertilize wisely
- Encourage wildlife
- Protect the waterfront

The Bay-Wise program has synthesized all of these principles into one program that teaches Maryland residents how to maintain their landscape while protecting the Chesapeake Bay, local streams and rivers, and, ultimately, the environment.

Manage yard pests with IPM

It's unrealistic to strive for an insect- and disease-free landscape. Pesticides can provide effective treatment for serious problems, but they should not be used routinely or indiscriminately. Improper use of pesticides can result in pest resistance and can harm humans, pets, beneficial organisms, and the environment (see Chapter 11, Pesticide Use and Safety).

IPM is a comprehensive, environmentally-conscious way to manage pests. It involves an understanding of the life cycle of the pest, other organisms (e.g., beneficial organisms, pets, and humans), and the effects of a given pesticide on these untargeted organisms. When confronted with a pest, consider all possible alternatives, and use a pesticide only as a last resort. Always read the label before using any pesticide. See Chapter 10, IPM, for more information on pest management. Other chapters/chapter sections that might be of interest include:

Chapter 8: Insect Basics
Indoor Pest Identification
Lawn Insect Identification

Plant wisely

Select the right plant for the right place. Plants suited to your site, especially native plants, will require minimal amounts of water, fertilizer, and pesticides; and may provide significant benefits. Plant deciduous shade trees on the southern and western sides of your house to cool it during summer and warm it during winter. Reduce the lawn area and replace with low-maintenance ornamentals. Plant a variety of flora (trees, shrubs, perennials, grasses, and groundcovers) and group them according to their water and maintenance needs. When the opportunity arises, replace problem-prone plants with natives. Consider soil type and light conditions when selecting replacements.

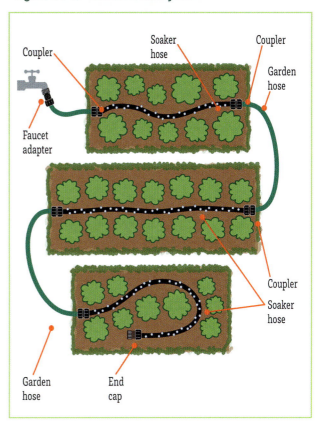

Figure 28-C. Soaker hose layout

Water efficiently

Limit watering to reduce runoff and maintain healthy waterways. Drought-tolerant plants, once established, require less water. Use rain barrels, soaker hoses, and drip irrigation to water landscape plants (see Figure 28-C). Cool-season grasses (e.g., fescues, bluegrasses, and ryegrasses) naturally go into a semi-dormant state during summer's heat and drought. Tall fescue lawns are more drought-tolerant than Kentucky bluegrass. Conserve water and mimic seasonal patterns by not watering during summer. If you must keep your lawn growing during this time, water only when your lawn and landscape really need it.

Figure 28-D. Correct mowing height (right)

Figure 28-E. Correct mulch placement (right)

Mow properly

Taller grass shades out weeds, cools the soil, and encourages a deeper, more drought- and pest-tolerant root system. Maintain the lawn at a height of three to four inches (see Figure 28-D). Use a reel (push) mower when possible or opt for an electric rather than a gas-powered mower to reduce air pollution. Sharpen the mower blades to maintain a healthy lawn.

Control stormwater runoff

Any rain and irrigation water that runs off your yard carries soil, debris, fertilizer, and pesticides into neighborhood storm drains. These drains lead to local streams, rivers, drinking water reservoirs, and the Bay. Runoff elements can harm living organisms, habitats, and water quality, so reduce runoff at every opportunity. Ways to reduce stormwater runoff include:

- Directing downspouts to the lawn or garden
- Using porous surfaces or stepping stones for paths rather than impervious walkways
- Using rain barrels to temporarily store water for use in the landscape after a rain event
- Installing a rain garden
- Improving soil health to increase permeability

Mulch appropriately

Mulching retains soil moisture, moderates soil temperature, and helps prevent erosion and weeds. Around trees it helps prevent mechanical injuries from mowers or weed whackers. Spread mulch two to three inches deep and never allow it to touch the bark of woody plants (see Figure 28-E). Never use freshly-chipped organic material, like brush or hardwood bark, as mulch because it robs nitrogen from the soil and can cause plant yellowing. Allow these materials to age for at least six months before using.

Recycle yard waste

If municipal ordinances allow it, grass clippings, leaves, yard trimmings, and organic kitchen scraps (e.g., vegetable and fruit peels, egg shells, and tea and coffee grounds) should be composted rather than sent to the landfill or down the kitchen disposer. Many communities collect yard waste if composting isn't possible.

Fertilize wisely

Healthy lawns can protect soil and water quality by holding soil in place with their roots, which can be strengthened with fertilizers; however, synthetic fertilizers can be harmful to the environment if used improperly. When applied at the wrong time or over-applied, fertilizers can create salt problems in the soil, affect winter hardiness, exaggerate pest problems, and make plants grow excessively fast (which can mean more mowing!) Fertilize only as needed to maintain the health of the lawn. The University recommends using no more than 0.9 pound of total nitrogen (which can include 0.7 pound of soluble nitrogen) per 1,000 square feet of lawn per application, and no more than two to three applications per year (see **Chapter 14, Lawns,** for more information). Excess nitrogen and phosphorus (two primary components of fertilizer) can leach out of the soil, pollute groundwater, or run off landscapes. If heavy rain is forecast, avoid using fertilizer to prevent runoff. Do not apply lawn fertilizer between November 15 and March 1 (that is Maryland law).

Encourage wildlife

Maryland has a great diversity of wildlife—some desirable (e.g., birds and pollinators) and some not so desirable. (See **Chapter 27, Wildlife and Woodlands,** for information about nuisance animals.) Provide adequate food, water, and shelter to increase the number and variety of wanted species that visit your yard.

Local wildlife relies on native plants for food and shelter. Leave some "mess" in garden beds (spent flowers, branches, some fallen leaves) over the winter to provide shelter for overwintering native bees, butterflies, and other insects. Local and migrating birds will appreciate the extra food the following spring.

Protect the waterfront

Waterfront property owners realize the special contribution our waterways and the Bay make to our quality of life. It is important they understand how fragile these natural treasures can be. Waterfront property includes those properties that border even the smallest streams. Permits may be required to modify properties within Maryland's critical area. Urban areas may also be considered waterfront because the street gutters empty directly into the nearest stream. Keep nutrients (grass clippings, yard waste, and animal waste) away from waterway portals.

28.2 The Hydrologic Cycle

To understand how your gardening practices can affect water quality, you must first understand how and where surface water and groundwater moves. This movement is part of the hydrologic cycle. Water travels through the atmosphere into or onto the ground and back into the atmosphere, moving through solid, liquid, and gaseous states, in a never-ending cycle called the hydrologic (or water) cycle (see **Chapter 3, Ecology,** for a visual diagram).

When water falls to earth as rain, sleet, or snow, it eventually does one of three things: it infiltrates the ground, runs across the surface, or evaporates back into the atmosphere. Water that infiltrates the ground evaporates from the soil, be used by plant roots; or percolates further underground until it reaches a zone of saturated water called groundwater or aquifer. Groundwater makes up 1.7 percent of the total amount of water on earth and 30 percent of our fresh water. Ground and surface water is connected with about 54 percent of Maryland streamflow coming from groundwater.

Maryland receives an average of more than 40 inches of precipitation per year. The problem is that we don't always get rain when and where we want it. Precipitation can vary by 50 percent from month to month and year to year and still be considered "normal."

Figure 28-F. Infiltration and runoff

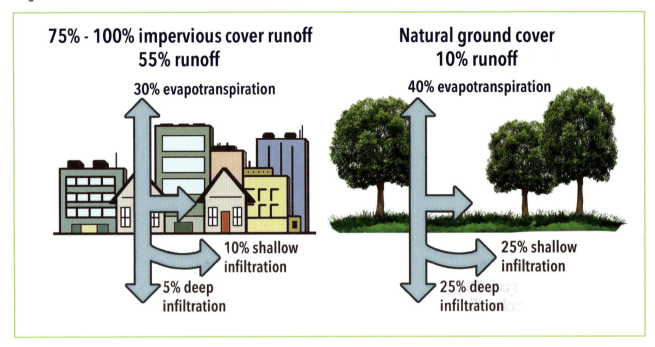

Infiltration

Infiltration is water that flows through the soil. It may or may not pass all the way through the root zone to the groundwater table (percolation). Infiltrating water that doesn't move to the water table is taken up by roots, stored for later use, or moves rapidly and shallowly to a nearby stream. This is called interflow or lateral flow.

Water infiltrates into the soil through the path of least resistance. That may be where pores between grains of soil are largest or through larger pores (macropores) made by:

- Cracks from the shrinking and swelling of the soil due to drying and wetting cycles
- Roots dying and rotting away
- Insects burrowing into the soil
- Worms, small rodents, and other living creatures that move through the soil

When you disturb the soil (e.g., compaction), these surface-connected pores are destroyed. Water moves more slowly into the soil and more rainfall becomes surface runoff rather than infiltration. This is how urban and suburban development results in more surface runoff (see Figure 28-F).

Runoff

Rainfall can lead to runoff under certain conditions:

- Interception by dense covers of forest or shrubs commonly amounts to 25 percent of the annual precipitation. Trees such as willows may intercept nearly a half-inch from a long, gentle storm.
- Runoff will occur only when the rate of precipitation exceeds the soil infiltration rate. Water then fills depressions on the soil surface. As the depressions are filled, overland flow begins. The water eventually infiltrates or evaporates.

- Water that runs across the earth's surface will travel to the lowest point, normally into a stream, river, pond, lake, ocean, or reservoir. As this water moves across the surface, it can pick up nutrients in the form of nitrogen and phosphorus; sediment in the form of soil eroded from bare ground; and toxins in the form of motor oil and antifreeze (from roads), pesticides, and heavy metals. These pollutants harm organisms living in the surface bodies of water. If they occur in the watershed east of the Eastern Continental Divide, they eventually end up in the Chesapeake Bay.

Evapotranspiration

Evaporation is water that escapes as vapor from soil, water, and leaf surfaces. Water moving up through plants and out through their stomata into the atmosphere is called transpiration. About 90 percent of the water taken up by plant roots is lost through transpiration. The combined water loss from plants through evaporation and transpiration is collectively called evapotranspiration (ET).

When water evapotranspires from the earth's surfaces, the moisture collects in the atmosphere in a gaseous state as clouds. When enough accumulates in the clouds, it turns to a liquid (condensation) or solid in the form of rain, ice, or snow; and falls back to the earth's surface as precipitation. This completes the hydrologic cycle.

28.3 Groundwater

Groundwater (aquifer) accounts for 13 percent of total water usage in Maryland. Whereas the Eastern Shore depends almost entirely on groundwater, greater Baltimore relies more heavily on surface water.

Cities and towns that obtain drinking water from surface water often have to deal with the problem of groundwater pollution. If your house is not connected to a public water system, you probably use groundwater from a well. Private wells are not regulated like public water supplies, so it is the homeowners' responsibility to test the water for safety and quality.

Because so many Marylanders rely on groundwater, it is crucial that we protect and replenish it by directing stormwater to drain into the ground rather than directing it off the property. Proper storage and recycling chemicals (not flushing them down the toilet or putting them in the trash), practicing home water conservation (e.g., fixing leaks, using water-saving appliances), and pumping a septic tank every three to five years are also important homeowner stewardship practices.

Water table

When water infiltrates and moves through the root zone, it percolates to a place where water fills all of the pore spaces. This condition is called "saturated." The upper point of the saturated zone of groundwater is called the water table. This "first" section of saturated soil and geologic material is called the water table aquifer. Once the porous media is saturated, the water then moves from higher water pressure to lower pressure. Near the surface, particularly in the water table aquifer, this may be lateral movement to a stream or river. As it travels through the soil, water can take on the characteristics of that soil. Water from soil full of iron ore tastes like metal. Water from soil full of sulfur smells like rotten eggs.

Figure 28-G. Confined and unconfined aquifers

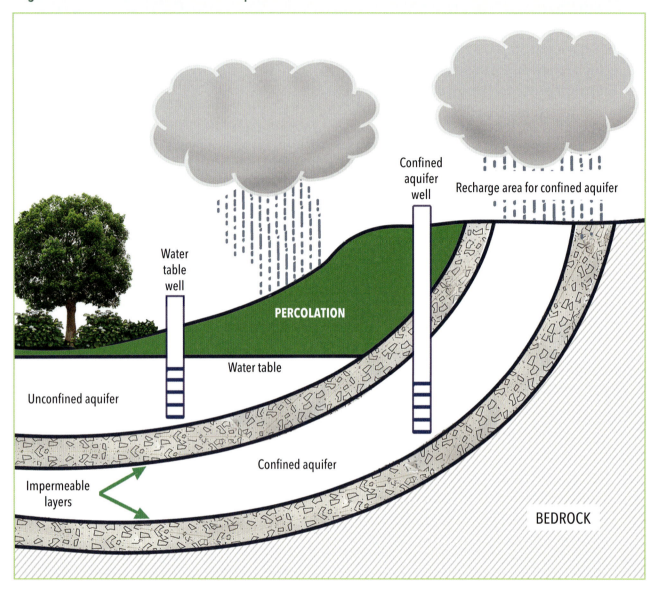

Water from limestone soils is "hard water," high in pH, calcium, and magnesium.

Aquifers

An underground area of soil or rock that can yield a significant quantity of groundwater to wells is called an aquifer. Aquifers can vary in length and width from a small area to more than several thousand square miles. They can be a few feet to several thousand feet deep. Water flows at different rates in different aquifers—faster in sand and slower in clay. All movement is relatively slow. Unconfined aquifers are usually found close to the land's surface and are at higher risk of being contaminated because of our activities on the soil's surface.

Aquifers may be separated by layers that do not transmit much water. These layers are called confining or impermeable layers. If a confining layer exists above an aquifer that is fully saturated, the aquifer is called a confined or artesian aquifer (see Figure 28-G).

28.4 Water Pollution

In 1607, when Captain John Smith began exploring the Chesapeake Bay, he could look into the water and see fish swimming around. The fish were so plentiful that he and his crew tried to scoop them up with frying pans. Today, our water is far from the clear, pristine water Captain Smith wrote about in his journal. We have polluted our water through our everyday actions.

Contaminants can enter groundwater through several different routes:

- Rain carries contaminants on the soil surface into the soil as it seeps into the ground.
- Liquid contaminants released on the soil flow down into the groundwater.
- Hazardous substances leak from buried storage tanks without anyone ever seeing it.

Sometimes, beneficial soil microorganisms can break contaminants down into harmless components. In many instances, contaminants enter the groundwater and remain for long periods and not much can be done other than abandoning that aquifer or implementing a treatment system to remove the contaminants. Remediation of contaminated groundwater is nearly impossible, so the best practice is to reduce or eliminate contamination in the first place.

The three main forms of water pollution are excess nutrients, sediments, and toxics.

Excess nutrients

In a balanced ecosystem, nutrients are consumed by algae. Many organisms, like small fish and shellfish, feed on the algae.

Figure 28-H. Algal bloom from fertilizer runoff

Larger fish consume the smaller ones, and animals, such as bears and humans, consume the larger fish. This is the natural food chain.

In highly populated areas, fertilizer from farms, lawns, and gardens; and nutrients from wastewater treatment plants, private septic systems, and other organic materials overload the water with far too many nutrients. This overabundance creates an overpopulation of algae, called an algal bloom (see Figure 28-H). Large amounts of oxygen are consumed when the excess algae die and decay. Aquatic life dies off when dissolved oxygen levels decline.

When excess nutrients encounter the soil and microorganisms and plant roots are unable to use them before they infiltrate the soil, they eventually reach the groundwater. In some cases, nitrogen from fertilizers and manures can increase groundwater nitrate levels, posing human health risks.

Sediments

Sediment is soil that washes off the land into the water. It comes from bare farm fields, especially during the winter months; from land that is being developed, and from bare soil in our landscapes.

When soil erodes into our local streams and rivers and settles on the bottom, it raises the water level and can lead to flooding. Before it reaches the bottom, sediment suspended in water can block light from getting to the bottom of the stream or river, thus preventing underwater plants from photosynthesizing. The suspended sediment can also clog the gills of fish.

Sediment is responsible for carrying phosphorous into the water because phosphorous is tightly bound to soil particles. Like nitrogen, excess phosphorous can promote algal blooms.

Toxics

Toxic substances, such as heavy metals from industry and atmospheric deposition, and pesticides used by gardeners and farmers, can poison aquatic life and humans when runoff washes into our surface water supply. Referred to here as toxics, this term should not be confused with the term "toxin," which is a poison or venom produced by living organisms. The Maryland Department of the Environment periodically issues advisories about eating fish caught in Maryland waters because of toxics such as methylmercury and polychlorinated biphenyls (PCBs).

Toxics can also percolate down into the soil where microbes break many of them down into harmless substances. Other synthetic toxics are too complex for soil microbes to decompose; these toxics infiltrate through the soil and into our groundwater.

The amount of toxic substance that reaches groundwater depends on its persistence and solubility, as well as the geology between the surface and the groundwater supply. Persistence is defined as the length of time a substance remains active before breaking down; it is measured by its half-life. A half-life is defined as the time it takes for the original amount of substance to be degraded to half its original amount. Substances with a long half-life remain active for a longer time and are more likely to contaminate groundwater. Solubility is defined as how readily the solute (the toxic) dissolves in a solvent (soil water). The more soluble a substance is, the greater its ability to move into the groundwater.

Many other groundwater contaminants, like gasoline, oil, road salts, and chemicals, can get into the groundwater and make it unsafe and unfit for use. Many types of soil bacteria help remove contaminants from the water as it infiltrates to the groundwater, but some bacteria, like fecal coliform, are harmful to humans and can contaminate groundwater.

28.5 Water Conservation

Summer months in Maryland are often hot and dry, causing significant plant stress. Hotter temperatures evaporate more water from leaves, causing drier soils. Global warming is predicted to increase the length and severity of summer drought. With greater numbers of people living in the Chesapeake Bay watershed, fresh water is becoming more in demand than ever before. Water conservation principles and techniques are vitally important to ensure sufficient water for plants, animals, and people.

Plant selection

By carefully selecting the plants you choose for your landscape, you can decrease the amount of water needed to maintain it.

- Plants vary widely in their drought tolerance. Native plants often tolerate drought better than many popular non-native ornamental plants, so always choose native plants when you can.

- Strive to design and maintain a landscape that, once established, will survive on natural rainfall.
- Leaves have many adaptations that reduce transpiration:
  - Small, fine, needle-shaped leaves have less surface area, which minimizes transpiration.
  - Hairy leaves reduce wind flow and silver leaves reflect sunlight which lower heat, both reducing transpiration.
  - Succulent leaves contain unique water storage features. Leaves are covered with a layer of wax called a cuticle. Thicker cuticles lower the transpiration rate.
- Plants with deep, spreading roots increase the chance of the plant finding water in dry soils.
- Roots that develop a symbiotic relationship with soil-dwelling fungi called mycorrhiza are able to pick up more nutrients and minerals. Mycorrhiza presence can be enhanced by adding a live inoculant to the soil.

Rain barrels

Rain barrels, which collect water from downspouts, have multiple benefits (see Figure 28-I). They:

- Reduce stormwater runoff
- Reduce your water bill
- Provide a free source of natural water that is better for your plants (tap water contains chlorine and fluoride)

Rain barrels of all kinds can be purchased online or you can make one yourself. All you need is a food-grade container (the larger

Figure 28-I.   Rain barrel with downspout diverter

the better), an overflow hose (at least one to two inches in diameter), mesh screen for any opening (to prevent mosquitoes), and a downspout diverter. A rain barrel with brass fixtures will last longer than plastic ones.

Precautions should be taken when using harvested rain water for edible plants. Certain roofing materials, like asphalt and cedar shingles, can release asbestos and fungi (mold), respectively. Limit rain barrel water to use on ornamental landscape plants.

Gray water

Gray water is wastewater generated by washing dishes, doing laundry, and bathing. It makes up 50 to 80 percent of residential wastewater. Other water classifications include:

- Black water: Wastewater contaminated with feces or toxic chemicals.
- Dark-gray water: Wastewater that contains significant food residues or high concentrations of toxic chemicals from household cleaners.
- White water: Potable fresh water.

Gray water is fine for watering outdoor plants such as trees, shrubs, ornamentals, and even non-root crop vegetables. Be careful to apply water to soil only; avoid splashing the water on the leaves. Use gray water only on well-established plants, not seedlings or young plants.

Water wisely

- During the hottest part of the day in low humidity, 50 percent of sprinkler water can evaporate and be wasted. Water in the morning whenever possible. Morning watering also reduces potential disease problems because water on leaf surfaces will dry before nightfall. Water that stays on leaf surfaces overnight encourages plant diseases.
- Avoid watering turf if at all possible. One inch of irrigation water over 10,000 square feet of grass uses 6,234 gallons of water. That is 20 days of water for a family of four. Turf-type tall fescue will go dormant when the weather becomes too hot and dry. It will be brown but not dead. When rain returns in the late summer and fall, the turf will green up again and thrive
- Water infrequently, slowly, and deeply. Deep and infrequent watering encourages a deep root system and makes plants more tolerant of future droughts. Frequent light watering encourages weak, shallow root growth.
- Avoid overhead watering. Drip irrigation and soaker hoses deliver water slowly and directly to the root system (see Figure 28-J). A soaker hose is made from recycled rubber and weeps water slowly from tiny pores along the length of the hose. Lay the soaker hose in place just after planting flowers and vegetables to prevent damage to plants. Covering the soaker hose with soil or mulch will further conserve water. Drip irrigation systems can be inexpensively automated with a timer.
- There is one exception to the "avoid overhead watering" rule: when the weather is very hot and dry, an occasional overhead watering can actually help cool plants and provide moisture for beneficial insects and spiders.

(See **Chapter 17, Vegetables,** for more information about irrigation systems.)

Additional information about water use and conservation can be found in **28.1 The Bay-Wise Philosophy.**

Figure 28-J.   Avoid overhead watering

28.6 Stormwater Management

Development, whether new or old, greatly affects the natural hydrologic cycle. In a naturally forested area, rainwater is intercepted by trees, shrubs, and herbaceous plants before reaching the ground. This plant cover prevents runoff and erosion by absorbing energy from falling raindrops, slowing runoff, and keeping the soil surface porous. The greater the plant cover, the lower the amount of runoff.

This principle also holds true in your own landscape. An impervious surface like asphalt has 100 percent runoff. Bare soil has slightly less runoff, but a great amount of erosion. Healthy lawns absorb or infiltrate water better than weak or stressed lawns. Land covered by layers of vegetation yields the lowest amount of runoff.

Rainwater picks up and carries many types of pollutants as it runs across lawns, driveways, sidewalks, and roads. Nutrients from fertilizer, pet waste, and organic yard waste; toxic components from pesticides, oil, antifreeze, and heavy metals; and sediment from exposed soil as well as trash are all carried to the nearest ditch or storm drain. The ditches or storm drains in the Chesapeake Bay watershed lead to local streams, rivers, drinking water reservoirs, lakes, and the Bay.

Climate change is predicted to increase the severity of major storms, and, in turn, tidal and inland flooding in Maryland. Sea level rise is the main cause of tidal flooding while impermeable surfaces that reduce stormwater infiltration cause inland flooding. Managing stormwater on developed land can help moderate climate change's resulting effects.

Slow down the water flow

Your goal should be to slow the flow of water from your landscape. In many older suburban developments, stormwater is directed off the landscape into the nearest street gutter, and then down a storm drain that empties into a nearby stream. During light rains, this design works fine because not much runoff occurs; but, during heavy rainfalls, the runoff can overflow banks and wash out creeks and streams. The fast-moving water carries loose soil, leaves, twigs, trash, and other debris it picks up along the way.

The rapid expansion of impervious surfaces (e.g., rooftops, driveways, walkways, parking lots, and roads) limits groundwater recharge because less water is able to percolate through soil. It also deprives tree roots of aeration, reduces ecological productivity, and interrupts atmospheric carbon cycling. Pervious surfaces allow water to naturally penetrate the soil for plant use or groundwater recharge. Community planners now use swales and stormwater retention ponds to minimize water runoff and recharge groundwater.

Tips for managing residential stormwater

- Guide stormwater from downspouts into pervious surfaces such as garden beds or lawns instead of impervious areas like sidewalks and driveways; or direct downspouts into rain barrels. Protect the soil at the base of the downspout by using a splash block.

- Create level terraces and build retaining walls to slow run-off and increase water infiltration and percolation. For paths and walkways, install pervious surfaces where possible such as gravel, pavers, bricks, or mulch.

Figure 28-K. A barrier garden to prevent runoff

- Swales (natural or man-made depressions) catch stormwater so that it has time to infiltrate instead of running off. You can take advantage of a swale by either leaving it alone or locating a rain garden at its lowest point.
- If your property slopes down from your house to the street, establish a mulched bed of plants between your property and the road to create a buffer (see Figure 28-K). The planting bed will intercept runoff before it goes off-site.

Rain gardens

Rain gardens are becoming more prominent as we look for ways to replenish groundwater and reestablish habitat for displaced wildlife (see Figure 28-L). A rain garden is simply an infiltration technique—a way to capture water in a slightly sunken area that features native plants, where the water can slowly filter into the ground rather than run off.

Rain gardens can range in size and scope from a small planting in a residential landscape to a highly engineered project on a large site. For a residential site, locate the rain garden at least 15 feet away from your house, sizing the rain garden to the amount of expected runoff, selecting proper native plants, and making sure the garden is sunk deep enough (usually 6 to 8 inches). Direct the downspout so stormwater flows onto the grass before entering the garden. This prevents the runoff from washing away the mulch.

The key to a successfully functioning rain garden is good drainage. If your soil is heavy clay, use compost as the backfill after excavating to the proper depth. You can mix some of the clay soil with the compost, but too much clay as backfill will slow infiltration.

Erosion

During the natural process of erosion, wind, water, and ice work to displace soil, mud, and rock. Natural erosion is normal; the problem arises when the local ecosystem is overwhelmed with excess sediment.

Erosion is happening in your landscape if:

- Soil is splashing onto walls or windows
- Gullies are beginning to show (see Figure 28-M)

Figure 28-L. A rain garden to catch runoff

Photo courtesy of gardenarchitecturellc.com

- Muddy water is running down your driveway
- Bare spots are appearing in the lawn
- Small stones are rising to the surface

Streams that become wider and deeper and fallen trees from stream banks are also signs of erosion. If the streambed is actually rising, erosion deposition is occurring. It is only a matter of time before that stream overflows, creating a flood plain.

These simple actions can minimize or prevent soil washing off your property:

- Construct paths along the contour of a slope instead of straight up and down.
- Encourage a healthy, thick lawn to provide erosion control, especially on steep, sunny slopes and ditches.
- Plant groundcovers or spread mulch in areas where grass won't grow.

Figure 28-M. Soil erosion in neighborhood

- If planting woody or herbaceous plants on a slope, use straw mulch or erosion-control matting until vegetation is established.
- Plant gardens on level areas. If you must plant on a slope, plant along the contours and then enclose the bed with a terrace, where possible. ✻

Additional resources

Sustainable/conservation landscaping:

Tips for sustainable landscaping
Creating a sustainable landscape
Stormwater practices
8 essential elements of conservation landscaping

BayScapes:

Riversmart Homes: Landscaping
Chesapeake Bay Watershed geography and facts

Rain barrels and rain gardens:

Rainscaping.org
Backyard makeover
Montgomery County Dept. of Environ. Protection
Rain gardens

AUTHORS

Wanda MacLachlan, Senior Agent/Bay-Wise Program Coordinator/Master Naturalist Program Coordinator, University of Maryland Extension, retired.

Andrew Lazur, Ph.D., State Extension Specialist - Water Quality, University of Maryland Extension.

PUBLICATIONS/WEBSITES

Duttle, M. 1994. Safe Use of Household Grey Water. College of Agriculture and Home Economics, New Mexico State University. Las Cruces, NM. cahe.nmsu.edu/pubs/_m/m- 106.html

EPA. Urban Runoff: Low-impact development. epa.gov/nps/urban-runoff-low-impact-development

Frazer, L. 2005. Paving Paradise: The Peril of Impervious Surfaces. Environmental Health Perspectives, Vol. 113, No. 7. ehponline.org/docs/2005/113-7/focus-abs.html

The Groundwater Foundation. Information on groundwater and citizen actions. groundwater.org/

McClure, S. 2000. Water: A Practical Guide to Using and Conserving Water in the Garden. Workman Publishing. New York, NY.

Ross, B. and T. Dillaha. 1996. Rainfall Simulation/Water Quality Monitoring for Residential Landscape Alternatives in Lynchburg, Virginia. Virginia Polytechnic Institute and State University. Lynchburg, VA.

PHOTOS

Main chapter photo: Julie Weisenhorn, UMN Extension. https://extension.umn.edu/water-wisely-start-your-own-backyard/rain-barrels

Figures:

28-A: pxhere.com.

28-B, 28-D (right), 28-E (Correct Technique): University of Maryland Extension.

28-C: Image courtesy of Gardener's Supply Company/gardeners.com.

28-D (left): **rocklights** via Adobe Stock.

28-I: **Milos** via Adobe Stock

28-E (Incorrect Technique Photo): Mary Ann Hansen, Virginia Polytechnic Institute and State University, Bugwood.org.

28-H: Paul Terrio, USGS, Public domain.

28-J: pexels.com compilation.

28-K: Center for Neighborhood Technology, Flickr. https://www.flickr.com/photos/centerforneighborhoodtechnology/

28-L: Garden Architecture, LLC; used with permission.

28-M: Jon Traunfeld, University of Maryland Extension.

ILLUSTRATIONS

Figure 28-F: Ria Malloy, University of Maryland Extension, retired. Modified and colorized by LeAnn Zotta.

Figure 28-G: LeAnn Zotta.

29: GARDEN TOOLS AND EQUIPMENT

Doris Behnke

29 GARDEN TOOLS AND EQUIPMENT

CONTENTS

- 29.1 Choosing the Right Tools 815
- 29.2 Hand Tools 817
  - 29.2a Cutting Tools 818
  - 29.2b Digging Tools 821
  - 29.2c Raking Tools 823
  - 29.2d Maintenance of Hand Tools 824
- 29.3 Power Tools 825
  - 29.3a Mowers 826
  - 29.3b Tillers/Cultivators 827
  - 29.3c String Trimmers 829
  - 29.3d Leaf Blowers 830
  - 29.3e Lawn Edgers 831
  - 29.3f Chipper-Shredders 831
  - 29.3g Maintenance of Power Tools 833
- 29.4 Garden Accessories 833
  - 29.4a Wheelbarrows and Carts 833
  - 29.4b Trellises, Cages, and Stakes 834
  - 29.4c Watering Equipment 837
  - 29.4d Sprayers 841
  - 29.4e Maintenance of Watering Equipment and Sprayers 842
- 29.5 Other Tools and Accessories 842
  - 29.5a Composting Tools 842
  - 29.5b Other Accessories 845
  - 29.5c Maintenance of Other Tools and Accessories 847

LEARNING OBJECTIVES

- Become familiar with the variety of hand and power garden tools and how to choose the right tool for the job
- Understand the pros and cons of gas-powered tools versus electric and cordless
- Know what to look for when buying garden tools
- Learn how to use hand and power garden tools
- Know how to maintain and store your garden tools

INTRODUCTION

A successful garden requires a sunny location, fertile soil, a water supply—and a properly appointed tool shed. Have your tools seen better days, or are they not as functional? Take an occasional inventory to see what may be missing or what needs replacing. Your shopping trip may even reveal a previously undiscovered tool that could make your gardening life simpler and easier.

You may need a power tool or two to get a new garden installed, but beyond that, most home gardeners do very well with a set of good hand tools. A larger property generally requires a few basic power tools to keep things manageable. Gas and electric options are available for most power tools these days, even tillers and chipper-shredders.

Literally hundreds of gardening tools are available for purchase, ranging in length, weight, head size, and handle material. Some are for everyday use; some are for more infrequent, specialized tasks; some are simply gimmicky gadgets. The key is to determine what will work for your garden.

Figure 29-A. Invest in high-quality tools

29.1 Choosing the Right Tools

It's easy to go overboard at the garden center when you see all those shiny new tools. To keep your wallet and storage shed from becoming unmanageable, stay focused on the basics. The number one rule for tools of any kind is to buy the best-quality tools your budget will allow, and maintain them in good condition. A tool that is made well and properly cared for will last many years.

Find out the material(s) the tool is made from, how it is constructed, how it works, and its "heft" factor. The way a tool fits your hand is important, so shop in person.

How to identify high-quality tools

Manufacturing materials

Many garden tools are now made from plastic or composite materials. They are much lighter than wood or steel, but tend to be more brittle and can crack from high-impact activities. Traditional wood handles absorb the shock of impact better than steel, but wood is not as strong as steel (or even heavy-duty fiberglass), and wood can splinter as it ages. That said, a high-quality wood handle that is kept oiled and protected from the elements can last for decades.

Tools with metal parts, like shovels and spades, should be manufactured from either stainless steel or high-carbon steel. Stainless has the benefit of being rust-resistant and lower-maintenance, but is also more expensive.

The grip should be made from a material that will still look good—albeit pleasantly weathered—as it ages. Soft-molded, ribbed plastic may not be entirely UV-resistant, but it is better than hard plastic, which can fade, warp, and split. Soft-molded grips also feel secure, even when your hands get wet from sweat or water.

Construction method

The connection between the handle and the head of the tool is more important than the shaft material because it is at this junction where most tools break. Good tools have a socket fitting so that the shaft slides into the socket and is fixed in place with rivets or bolts.

Always look for forged tools, which are stronger and longer-lasting because they are heat-tempered. Tools that are stamped from

THE IDEAL GARDEN TOOL LIST

Power tools:
- Mower
- Tiller or cultivator
- String trimmer
- Leaf blower

Hand tools:
- Bypass pruners
- Snips or scissors
- Hand cultivator or hand fork
- Hand trowel
- Loppers
- Telescoping pruner
- Pruning saw
- Hedge shears or trimmer
- Round-point shovel
- Spade
- Hoe
- Garden rake
- Leaf rake
- Garden fork
- Wheelbarrow or garden cart
- Garden hose
- Soaker hose
- Watering can

Composting tools:
- Compost fork or pitchfork
- Thermometer
- Aerator
- Sifter

Nice to have:
- Lawn edger
- Chipper-shredder
- Hori Hori knife or soil knife
- Compost tumbler

Figure 29-B. Ergonomic cultivator (left) vs. standard

Figure 29-C. T (pistol)-grip (left) and D-grip snap-ons

metal sheets can break under pressure and have a shorter lifespan.

Design

Tools that are ergonomically designed (i.e., made to work smoothly and comfortably in conjunction with the human body) are a must in the garden. If you have ever worked for any length of time with a non-ergonomic tool, you know well the discomfort it can cause.

A tool should never feel awkward in your hand. The handle shouldn't be too short; it should always cross the full length of your palm. The handle should be comfortable, which is usually the result of a handle/shaft with a wider diameter, even for small hands (see Figure 29-B).

Look for tools and equipment that are designed to allow your back, elbows, and knees to remain in a stable, untwisted position. For example, push-pull tools like cultivators and garden rakes put the least stress on the body when the shaft is long enough for you to stand up straight while working. Tools with a pistol grip, also known as "P" or "T" grips, keep your wrist straight and unpressured.

Look for oversized, adjustable D-grips that let you dig with both hands, minimize bending, and give you a lot of extra leverage. If your budget is tight, you can buy ergonomic T- and D-grip attachments for your existing tools (see Figure 29-C). These snap-on grips are far less expensive than buying a entirely new shovel or rake, and you can use them interchangeably on a variety of tools.

Some of the better-quality brands have replaceable parts, which will greatly extend the life of your tools. They cost a bit more up front, but have greater longevity and pay for themselves over time.

29.2 Hand Tools

Hand tools are usually manually operated, although some grass clippers, mini-saws, pruners, and other garden tools are battery-powered.

The following are some general guidelines and buying tips to help you purchase the right hand tool. Buying tips are also included for Power Tools (29.3)

Which shaft length is best? Short-handled tools include trowels and pruners; long-

Figure 29-D. Left-handed pruners

Which type of grip is best? For heavier digging work, a "D" shaped handle is easier to grip than a straight shaft. You can also attach ergonomic grips to your existing tools, as mentioned in the previous section.

Make sure you choose the right tool for the job, one that fits you well and is not too heavy. A left-handed tool (see Figure 29-D), a shovel with a shorter handle, or a tool with an ergonomic design might suit you better. Tools are now available for small, large, and even arthritic hands.

handled tools include shovels and rakes. Short-handled long tools such as shovels and rakes with shorter handles are designed to encourage a better body stance for moving heavy material. Most gardeners use standard long-handled tools, which require less bending but can be problematic if you need to lift heavy loads. Putting weight out in front of you and then twisting sideways to move the load can cause severe muscle pulls or back injury.

Shafts also come in different diameters. Smaller-diameter shafts are easier to use for smaller hands; conversely, larger-diameter shafts are more ergonomic.

29.2a Cutting Tools

Pruners

Once the planting phase of the season is complete, pruners will become your most indispensable garden helpers. All summer, you'll need them to prune, deadhead, and snip to keep your plants growing and thriving. Pruners are primarily built to cleanly cut tender and woody stems, but can also be used for cutting out deadwood and harvesting crops.

Hand pruners come in four styles: bypass, anvil, ratchet, and straight-blade snips (short and long), each designed for particular uses (see Figure 29-E).

Figure 29-E. Pruner types

Bypass   Anvil   Ratchet   Snips (short)   Snips (long)

Bypass. Bypass pruners have a curved top blade that actually "passes by" to the lower curved blade in a scissors-type motion. These will be go-to pruners, so keep them sharp for consistently clean cuts.

Uses: Pruning live plants and green/young wood less than one-quarter-inch in diameter.

Anvil. Most gardeners consider anvil pruners to be clumsier to use and not as effective as bypass pruners because the two blades meet at their respective edges, leaving ragged cuts.

Uses: Anvil pruners are best for dead wood. Do not use on live stems or branches as they can be easily crushed.

Ratchet. Ratcheting pruners use torque to create power, which can be helpful for anyone with a weak grip or arthritic condition. By repetitively squeezing the handles together, the blade slowly (but surely) makes its way through the branch. Some gardeners say the work of repeatedly squeezing the handle hurts more than their arthritis, but some people find them very useful.

Uses: Pruning out deadwood and woody plants between one-half inch to one-and-a-half-inches in diameter.

Buying tips: Consider buying a few high-quality pruners for woody plants and several inexpensive ones for everyday tasks. With pruners, you really do get what you pay for.

- Choose those that open and close smoothly and have thick padded or rounded handles for comfort. Good pruners should have a blade lock that flips shut for safe storage.
- Pruners should feel comfortable and cross the full length of your palm. Get the handle length and blade size that work for your hands.

Straight-blade (snips). Snips are essentially small bypass pruners with straight blades, designed for detailed maintenance. Use them to get into hard-to-reach spaces and to clip small-diameter stems (e.g., roses, perennials, and herbs). Cutting larger branches will quickly dull the blades. Some snips come with a blade cover, which lets you safely tote them in a pocket.

Uses: Cutting flowers to bring indoors, fine pruning, nipping buds, and deadheading spent flowers.

Loppers/telescoping pruners

Loppers are essentially super-sized bypass pruners (see Figure 29-F). Their extra-long handles let you get to places that are out of your normal reach, and their blade mechanisms are designed to cut through thicker branches with one swift movement. Some loppers have extendable/telescoping handles that provide a little bit of extra reach without having to get up on a ladder. A bypass

Figure 29-F. Lopper types

Hand loppers   Telescoping - closed (left) and open

Figure 29-G. Pruning saw types

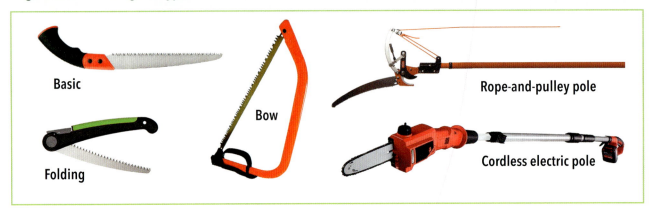

lopper is preferred by most gardeners, but anvil versions might be preferable if the majority of your pruning chores are cutting out deadwood.

Uses: Choose loppers over pruners for larger woody branches and hard-to-reach spots.

Buying tips: Because loppers require more arm strength than pruners, choose a ratchet type. Look for tempered carbon steel blades and ergonomic grips, and be sure the loppers are not too heavy for you to lift in the air.

Pruning saw

When hand pruners are too small to handle the job, use a pruning saw. Pruning saw blades are shaped like a large knife rather than a wood saw, but have teeth like a wood saw. Some models conveniently fold in half (see Figure 29-G).

Some newer pruning saws are motorized, including those mounted on a long pole for cutting very high branches. These "chain saws on a stick" require some skill and dexterity to use, and are not for beginners.

Uses: Hand saws are generally designed for use on branches measuring no more than one-and-one-half inches thick. Pole pruners with a rope-pulley system and "chain saws-on-a-stick" can cut branches up to eight inches thick.

Buying tips: Have a few different sizes of pruning saws on hand to tackle shrubs and trees in various stages of maturity.

Hedge shears/trimmer

Hedge shears are giant scissors that require two hands to operate (see Figure 29-H). A good pair of hedge shears is sufficient if you just have a few shrubs that need cutting back once or twice a year. Corded and cordless electric hedge trimmers can shear a large number of shrubs in a short amount of time. Pole trimmers have a telescoping shaft so you can safely reach tall shrubs and hedges.

Figure 29-H. Hedge shears/trimmer

820   Maryland Master Gardener Handbook

Avoid standing on a ladder when using an electric trimmer. Reaching forward to trim an outlying spot a could result in a fall or serious injury from the trimmer itself.

Uses: Shearing back small-branched shrubs and hedges, large perennials, ground covers, and overgrown grass and weeds. Do not use when material you want to cut is wet as it will significantly dull the blade, which is tedious and time-consuming to sharpen.

Buying tips:

- Assess your yard and make a list of the plantings that require trimming, how often they need it, and the obstacles you encounter. The proper tool will make any trimming task easier.
- If you have fewer than 10 shrubs that need regular trimming and none of them is taller than about five feet, you can use manual shears.
- If you have 10 or more shrubs under five feet tall, electric trimmers are a good investment. (Gas-powered hedge trimmers are usually only used by professionals.)
- For taller shrubs, choose a telescoping pole trimmer.

29.2b Digging Tools

Round-point shovel

A shovel is a little more versatile than a spade. Shovels have a rounded edge that comes to a point; instead of a flat blade, they have a funneling function to help place soil, mulch, or amendments in the right place. All shovels should have a ledge along the top of the blade so you can push down on it with your foot.

Uses: Digging shallow holes and moving soil, mulch, and other loose material.

Buying tips: For a shovel that will last for years, buy one made of forged steel. Forged blades are thicker at critical stress points and gradually thin toward the edge, which improves the cutting performance. Fiberglass and steel handles will last the longest, but wood will age well with proper oiling.

Spade

A spade looks like a shovel, but has a square edge for straight cutting and digging plant holes. It disturbs less soil and is more maneuverable than a round-point shovel, making a spade the digging tool of choice in an established garden. Narrow-blade spades are specifically made for digging in tight places.

Figure 29-1.   Shovel, spade, and fork types

Figure 29-J. Hoe/cultivator types

Paddle   Stirrup or shuffle   Dutch or Warren   Onion   Rolling cultivator   Hand cultivator

Uses: If a perennial needs transplanting, use a spade to dig a destination hole, then precisely "cut out" the plant and transport it to its new home. A spade also works well for removing deep-rooted weeds that are too hard to pull by hand; and does a good job of transporting small loads of mulch, soil, or amendments.

Garden fork

Garden forks (sometimes called pitchforks) come in several lengths and types of tines. If you need to turn soil with less disruption to the ecosystem, a garden fork is more efficient than a spade or shovel. Garden forks are also better at digging into clay or rocky soil. Hand-sized forks work well for smaller tasks.

Uses: Gently turning the soil; moving piles of mulch, compost, and leaves; and turning compost piles. A garden fork can also serve as a turf aerator for small areas.

Buying tips:

- A good garden fork has a D-grip hardwood handle and four square tines with diamond-shaped points.

- Buy according to your height and the amount of bending that feels comfortable to you. A short-handled long tool may be more comfortable than a full-length shaft.

- Choose fork tines with a slight curve if mulching and composting are frequent chores. Straight-tine forks are better for digging.

Hoe

A garden hoe consists of either a paddle, stirrup, or blade attached at an angle to a long handle (see Figure 29-J).

- A paddle hoe is the most familiar type, and has been around for centuries. The rectangular flat blade is attached to the handle at a 90° angle, making it easy to chop, mound, and level the soil. A hoe with a similar structure but with a triangular blade is called a Dutch or Warren hoe.

- A stirrup hoe (also called a shuffle hoe) looks like just the stirrup on a horse saddle. It slices through rather than chops down on weeds and is most effective when used in a back-and-forth motion.

- An onion hoe has a long, thin blade that is meant for narrow spaces and detailed cultivating. The hand-sized version gets into even tighter spots.

Uses: Shallow cultivating, weed-chopping, breaking up soil, and leveling; mounding up planting hills for potatoes, onions, and cucurbits.

Buying tips: Choose a hoe with a shaft of either steel or fiberglass, and one that feels comfortable as you push-pull it. A tempered steel blade will make it last and a cushioned grip will take the stress off your hands.

Trowel

A trowel is a hand-sized shovel. The handle should be easy to grip and the trowel blade and extension should be one piece versus two. Trowels with a narrow blade are easier to use than those with a wide blade, but the job at hand may require a wider blade.

Uses: Chopping through roots, adding soil around the base of a plant, digging transplant holes, weeding, and working in rocky soil.

Buying tips:

- Invest in thick-gauge stainless steel digging tools that will not bend or rust.
- Look for a padded grip and an ergonomic handle to take pressure off the wrist.
- Choose one-piece construction instead of two for strength and durability.

Hand cultivator

Think of a cultivator as a small-scale garden rake (see Figure 29-J). Cultivators come with long and short handles, and each type rakes through/breaks up soil with three curved tines that are narrower than those of a garden rake.

One type of cultivator has a long handle and a rolling spike-studded drum (a mini-tiller) that chops up small weeds and breaks up the soil using a push-pull motion. Powered cultivators are larger still and serve as mini-tillers (see the section on Tillers, 29.3b).

Uses: Disturb/chop small weeds, gently break up the top layer of soil, smooth and level soil, create furrows for seed-planting.

Buying tips: Same as for trowels.

29.2c Raking Tools

Garden rake. These are usually made of iron and have a long wooden handle and one row of straight, short tines with a parallel bar

Figure 29-K. Rake head types

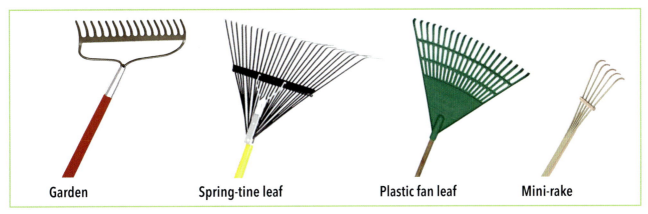

Garden — Spring-tine leaf — Plastic fan leaf — Mini-rake

above the tines; when you turn the rake over and drag it across the soil, it has a leveling effect.

Uses: Loosening and leveling soil; raking up gravel, stones, and debris on top of bare soil.

Buying tip: Garden rakes are usually well-made and similarly designed, so choosing one is a matter of preference and feel.

Leaf rake. Leaf rakes can be made of flexible aluminum (spring-tine) or rigid plastic, and are not as durable as garden rakes.

Uses: Raking leaves, grass clippings, and garden debris; and fine-tuning mulch applications. Mini-rakes, often made of bamboo, are perfect for getting leaves out of and underneath shrubs and other hard-to-reach spots.

Buying tip: Many leaf rakes are cheaply made and will only last a couple of seasons. Look for a sturdy wide-fan plastic rake or a well-made spring-tine rake if you have an uneven lawn.

29.2d Maintenance of Hand Tools

Properly maintained quality garden tools are easier to use and can last for generations. Regular cleaning, sharpening, and oiling will keep your hand tools in great condition.

End-of-season maintenance

At the end of each growing season, take some time to clean and preserve your tools so they will be ready to use the following spring. For annual maintenance, you will need the following:

- Cleaning supplies: detergent, garden hose, sponge, and old rags or towels.
- Cleaning tools: steel wool, scrub brush, wire brush, and a rotary wire brush attachment for your drill.
- Sandpaper: 80 and 120 grit, made to work on both wood and metal.
- Sharpening tools: a fine metal file and a sharpening stone.
- Lubricating oil: boiled linseed oil, tung oil, motor oil, lamp oil, or cooking oil are all suitable.
- Safety equipment: gloves, eye protection, and a dust mask.

Step 1: Cleaning

Scrub off any mud or grit from the blades and handles and wash with soapy water. Dry with an old towel and leave tools to dry overnight. This is an important step because oiling tools that have not thoroughly dried can trap moisture and damage the tools.

Step 2: Rust removal

With some steel wool or a wire brush, gently whisk off all rust from metal blades and tool parts. Do not use a bench grinder for this task or you will risk weakening the metal.

Step 3: Sanding

Use some medium-grit sandpaper to smooth any splinters or superficial stains on wooden handles. Sandpaper also removes rust in crevices and will give metal a nice polish. Wipe off any sanding dust with an old towel.

Step 4: Sharpening

Use a metal file or sharpening stone to even out nicks and burrs, and sharpen blade edges. You will need to disassemble your pruners to properly do this. Pruners should be sharpened several times a season as well as in the fall.

Step 5: Oiling

Using a clean rag, apply lubricating oil to both the wooden handle and the metal blade. Rub the oil into the surface, then wipe off any excess. The oil conditions the wood and will prevent it from cracking, and will also help keep the blade from rusting. After the wooden handle has dried, apply a second coat if the first coast was absorbed. Tools with fiberglass or composite handles only need a good cleaning.

Daily maintenance

At the end of every gardening day, spend a few minutes to:

- Rinse off mud or soil with a garden hose and leave tools to dry in the sun.
- Scrub away stubborn mud with a scrub brush.
- Use paint thinner to remove sap and tar.
- Hang tools off the ground rather than stand them on their edge.

29.3 Power Tools

Many gardening purists choose to use only manual tools, whether for the sake of tradition, simplicity, or just energy savings. Technically, any gardening chore can be done with a manual tool. Pioneers used a horse and plow instead of a rototiller; their sod cutter was a sharp garden spade.

Most gardeners find a happy medium, using power tools when manual tools are beyond their physical capabilities or just take too much time to use. For example, if you're converting turf to garden space, a gas-powered sod cutter would make relatively quick, easy work of removing the grass.

THE ADVANTAGES OF GAS-POWERED TOOLS vs. ELECTRIC CORDED/CORDLESS

GAS:

More powerful

No waiting for a battery to charge

Large coverage area

Less expensive up front

Sturdier manufacturing

Lower emissions on newer models

ELECTRIC:

Quiet

Clean (no gas or oil)

Lightweight/portable

Environmentally-friendly

Low maintenance

Less expensive to operate

About gas-powered tools

Gas-powered lawn equipment like mowers, string trimmers, and leaf blowers has always been the standard for professional landscapers, though some cities are adopting air-quality and noise ordinances that ban gas-powered lawn equipment. As a result, many are having to turn to electric and cordless options. For tough jobs like cutting brush, dense weeds, or large expanses of lawn, the engine power and durability of a gas-fueled garden tool is still unmatched. Thankfully, innovations in battery technology, product design, and construction materials have made the switch very easy for the typical homeowner—eventually the technology will catch up on the commercial side.

Figure 29-L.   Mower types

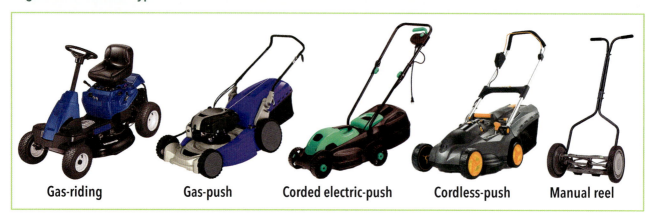

Gas-riding   Gas-push   Corded electric-push   Cordless-push   Manual reel

About electric/cordless tools

Cordless garden tools are designed to let you roam freely around the yard and garden without being tethered to a power source. Lithium-ion batteries have become popular because they deliver a consistent level of power throughout their runtime, but there is a concern about discarded batteries and lithium mining.

If your property measures less than half an acre, electric tools can likely save you some money. Cordless electric equipment can be used on larger yards, but the tool is likely to run out of power after 30 to 60 minutes of use. Keeping a second battery charged up will double your mowing time.

Electric versions of most gas-powered tools are now available, including tillers. The following sections provide details about specific tools, including buying tips and a comparison of gas and electric versions.

29.3a Mowers

An old-fashioned manual reel mower is the ultimate in "green" gardening, as it has no carbon footprint. An electric mower, even including the factory emissions generated by its manufacturing, reduces carbon dioxide by 38 percent over a gas mower, according to the National Gardening Association. Gas mowers (riding and push-style) emit the most hydrocarbons. The size of your yard, the amount of power you need to do the job, and your level of environmental concern should dictate your mower purchase.

Gas mowers can often be less expensive to buy, but over time the ongoing maintenance expense will add up. Buying and storing gasoline, two- or four-cycle oil, air filters, and spark plugs is necessary for gas equipment. You must check the oil each time you mow. See Figure 29-L for different mower types.

Buying tips

- Choose a gas mower for large lawns, and a cordless model for lawns of 12,000 square feet or less.
- If you have physical limitations, consider a lightweight cordless mower. They are easy to push (some are self-propelled) and cover uneven ground smoothly.
- Corded electric mowers may be less expensive, but they can be difficult to manage because they limit your range. There is also a risk of cutting through the cord while mowing.

Figure 29-M. Choose the right tiller

29.3b Tillers/Cultivators

If you are gardening directly in the ground, you may need a sod cutter and/or a rototiller to clear and prepare the area. It isn't cost beneficial to own either piece of equipment, so most people just rent them. As an alternative, you can install a raised-bed garden, which will eliminate the need for a rototiller; or use cardboard and newspaper to "solarize" and kill the turf and weeds, eliminating the need for a sod remover.

Tillers quickly and efficiently turn the soil, simultaneously mixing in organic matter, fertilizer, and soil amendments. Doing these chores by hand could take days if your garden is at all sizable. For any area too large to turn with a garden fork (100 square feet or more, depending on your level of fitness), a tiller is a good solution. The key is to not over-till, as you will disrupt the crucial ecosystem that plants thrive in (see the section on **minimal-till gardening** in the Vegetables chapter).

Heavy-duty tillers often come with attachments such as wood chippers or wagons. They're ideal for the person who has a large yard and many projects. Medium-size tillers work well for breaking up loam or sandy soils and for yearly garden maintenance. Small tillers make easy work of preparing established beds. Many small tillers also have attachments, such as a lawn edger.

There are four main types of tillers (see Figure 29-N):

Cultivator. These mini-tillers are narrow enough to get between rows and dig out weeds without disturbing plant roots. In addition to removing weeds, cultivators are good for breaking up the soil surface and mixing in compost or other amendments prior to planting. They are not the right tool, however, for breaking up hard soil that has never been tilled.

Front-tine. These light-duty tillers are larger and have more power than a cultivator. Their soil-churning tines are located at the front, and help propel the machine forward; but require considerable upper body strength to keep moving in a straight line. For difficult soil or large areas, a front-tine tiller will likely give you more of a physical workout than you want. Despite its detractions, a front-tine tiller is a good all-purpose, affordable option for a medium-sized garden plot.

Rear-tine. For heavy-duty jobs, a rear-tine tiller is needed. The wheels (which are powered by the engine) are in front, while the tines are in the back. This design makes the machine much easier to operate for long stretches. Because a rear-tine model is more powerful, it is necessarily larger and heavier, so it still requires some strength to maneuver. Use a rear-tine tiller when you need to break heavy soil for the first time, or turn soil that is full of roots/rocks. A well-made rear-tine tiller is pricier than a front-tine model, but it is still less expensive than a tractor. These tillers are popular with truck farmers and other small-scale commercial gardeners who can't justify the tractor investment. Gardeners with small plots often rent a rear-tine tiller to do the initial hard work, and then buy a cheaper front- or mid-tine model to keep the soil workable with an annual tilling.

Mid-tine. The tines are directly under the engine, which helps push the tines into the soil. The wheels are very widely spaced compared to the other tiller types, and provide good stability. Mid-tine tillers are used for the same tasks as front-tine models, but require significantly less strength to operate.

TYPES OF TILLER TINES

Most tillers are designed with interchangeable tines to tackle different soil conditions. If the soil is especially hard or clayey, it may be necessary to take a pass with each type, in succession. The three main tine types are:

Bolo: Curved or L-shaped blades are standard on most models. They work best when deep tilling is needed and where rocks, vegetation, and roots are minimal.

Slasher: The best choice for cutting through roots and heavy vegetation, slasher tines are designed to prevent debris from wrapping around the tines and jamming the machine, a common complaint with bolo tines.

Pick-and-chisel: These heavy-duty tines are made to break up hard, rocky ground.

Buying tips

- The type of tiller you buy depends mostly on the size of the garden and its intended use. When choosing a tiller, opt for a well-known brand backed by at least a one-year warranty.

Figure 29-N. Tiller types

Cultivator   Rear-tine   Front-tine   Mid-tine

Figure 29-O. String trimmer types

Gas-straight   Corded-curved   Cordless-straight

- Consider the weight of the tiller and how manageable it is for you. A petite woman will have difficulty using a cumbersome 200-pound machine. The alternatives are to either buy a lighter machine or hire someone to use the bigger machine if you need it to dig through hard soil. See Figure 29-M to determine which size tiller you need.

29.3c String Trimmers

A string trimmer is needed when you can't get to a patch of grass with your mower. String trimmers have either a curved or a straight shaft. Curved shafts are usually shorter and more maneuverable; straight shafts have a longer reach. Professional landscapers like the straight-shaft type because they can do more trimming in a shorter time.

There are three types of string trimmers: gas, electric (corded), and battery-powered (see Figure 29-O):

Gas-powered string trimmers will do a good job on any property size. Traditionally the best string trimmer for large properties, a gas-powered model goes anywhere and can run indefinitely, as long as there's fuel in the tank. They're not as popular as battery-powered string trimmers anymore, but there still are plenty of options. Look for models with an adjustable handle and a translucent gas tank so that you can see when fuel is low.

Gas-powered string trimmers with a four-cycle engine run cleaner and use regular gas, but cost more. Models with a two-cycle engine cost less, but you'll need to add oil to your gasoline. All the gas-powered string trimmers in our tests are loud enough to require hearing protection (earplugs or earmuff-style headsets) for users.

A corded string trimmer is perfect for budget-conscious homeowners with a small yard (up to one-quarter acre). While a corded trimmer limits your work area, you can always purchase extension cord(s) to extend your reach. In addition to up-front savings, you won't require gasoline, oil, or a charged battery.

Cordless battery-powered string trimmers have improved in design, and many of them cut as well or better than gas trimmers. They also have the benefit of no carbon emissions, quiet operation, easy startup, and very little maintenance. The battery is also likely to be interchangeable with batteries of other cordless tools of the same brand. Cordless trimmers will run for about half an hour on a single charge and are ideal for a property of up to one-half acre. They can cover much more area if you have spare charged batteries ready to go.

All string trimmers can cause serious injury. Always put on protective eyewear, gloves,

Figure 29-P. Leaf-blower types

Hand-held   Walk-behind   Backpack vac/mulcher

29.3d Leaf Blowers

If your yard has many trees, cleaning up leaves in the fall can take days. Choosing the right kind of blower can save you a significant amount of time and energy (see Figure 29-P).

Gasoline-powered leaf blowers deliver maximum mobility and runtime. These models are suited for properties of a quarter-acre or more. Hand-held leaf blowers are the most common kind for typical

heavy shoes or boots, and long pants before you start using your trimmer.

Uses: Trim grass/weeds in difficult-to-reach places, along borders, buildings, around tree trunks (carefully), and hardscape structures. Also serves as a short-term grass edger.

Buying tips:

- Look at the spot where the cutting head meets the shaft. If there is a big gap, tall grass can get wrapped around the trimmer. A small gap will prevent entanglements, as will a trimmer head that easily detaches for cleaning.

- Some manufacturers offer a standalone "base." It is essentially an engine that can power different attachments, such as a pole saw, lawn edger, hedge trimmer, or cultivator. A base tool is a good choice if you don't want to buy all of those tools separately.

- Choose trimmers with a warranty of three to five years that covers the battery.

SAFETY FIRST!

- Wear safety goggles, work shoes or boots, and long pants to prevent injury when using power tools and equipment.

- Protect your hearing when using machinery. If you have to raise your voice to talk to someone who is an arm's length away, the noise can be potentially harmful to your hearing.

- Wear gloves to protect your hands.

- Follow the operating instructions and warning labels on lawn and garden equipment.

- Regularly check your equipment for loose parts/connections to avoid injury.

- Don't operate machinery or climb ladders if you take medications that might make you drowsy or impair your judgment or reaction time.

- Do not pour oil or gasoline into storm sewers or on turf areas.

830   Maryland Master Gardener Handbook   UME © 2025. All rights reserved.

yards. Walk-behind blowers with wheels and backpack blowers are gasoline-powered, and provide more power and comfort for prolonged use in large areas.

Some blowers can convert to a vacuum so you can collect leaves and small twigs without bending over, and dump the contents on your compost pile. Deluxe models will even mulch the debris as it goes into the attached bag.

Electric leaf blowers are low-maintenance machines. They're lighter and quieter than gasoline-powered blowers and easier to start. Use a smaller model to blow debris off of a walkway, driveway, patio, or deck; and choose a high-powered electric blower for fast fall leaf clean-up of areas up to a quarter-acre. Additional extension cords may be required to reach the areas that need attention.

Cordless blowers have always been easier to use than corded versions, but until recently the short battery life made them less desirable. Now, high-voltage lithium-ion batteries provide longer runtimes and better mobility in the yard. Batteries need regular recharging, so depending on the size of your landscape, you may want to keep a spare battery (or two) charged.

29.3e Lawn Edgers

Lawn edgers are different from string trimmers in that edgers use a fixed metal blade to create clean, sharp edges by slicing through grass roots. String trimmers only neaten up the grass blades, and the "crisp" edge disappears within a week or two. For perfect-looking edges all season, you will probably need to use a slicing edger two to four times per season.

Figure 29-Q. Edger types

Manual   Cordless   Corded walk-behind

Lawn edgers can be gas-powered, corded, or cordless; there is also a manual version (see Figure 29-Q). All will give your landscape a crisp, manicured look. Most gardeners prefer either the cordless or hand-tool version, as gas-powered edgers are noisy and inconvenient to maintain, and corded edgers are awkward to use.

Uses: To create a crisp line through turf along walkways, driveways, curbs, and garden beds. Some models will also dig up to a four-inch deep trench for outdoor lighting or fencing.

Buying tips: Most corded edgers are for light-duty. If you need to cut through clay to edge a lawn or planting bed, move up to a heavier-duty gas machine. Also, if you choose a corded model, look for one with a cord-retention mechanism to keep you from tripping over the cord or cutting through it.

29.3f Chipper-Shredders

A property with even a few large trees will create a constant shower of twigs, broken branches, and fallen leaves that demand year-'round pick-up. Instead of spending money

Figure 29-R. Chipper-shredder

Shredder only   1.5" capacity   3" capacity

on boxes of plastic lawn-and-leaf bags (that some local landfills may not accept anyway), consider buying a chipper-shredder. Not only will you be able to quickly get through yard chores, but by reducing piles of yard waste to mulch, you will be creating excellent free fodder for your compost pile and garden beds.

The size of your property and the type of debris your yard generates will determine which machine to buy. You may find that you only need a shredder for leaves, grass, and small twigs. Larger machines are usually overkill for the typical property of one acre or less unless it is heavily treed.

A motor that is somewhere between 15-amp and 7-hp will address what the average homeowner needs.

Gas-powered chipper-shredders offer more power to handle larger-diameter yard waste. Some models can chip branches up to four inches in diameter. These machines aren't limited by cord length, so they're practical for use around large landscapes.

Corded chipper-shredders are the most common type. If the debris from your medium-sized yard (less than an acre) consists primarily of leaves, small twigs, and small branches (up to two inches), this type of machine will handle it.

Cordless chipper-shredders are new to the market. They are less powerful than corded models, but fine for small jobs like shredding leaves, yard debris, twigs, and branches up to about one-and-one-half inches in diameter.

A chipper-shredder is very easy to operate: simply feed the material into the chute/hopper and let the rotating blades shred it up. The processed material is automatically discharged onto the ground, into your wheelbarrow, or into a bag. Always wear protective gear (gloves and safety glasses) when using a chipper-shredder.

CHIPPER-SHREDDER TERMINOLOGY

- **HP:** The horsepower number indicates the rate at which energy is expended (power). If you need to chip-shred branches larger than two inches in diameter, you will need a machine with a higher horsepower number.

- **Chipper capacity:** Indicates the branch-diameter limit for that machine.

- **Reduction ratio:** The level of efficiency at which the machine reduces the content being fed into the hopper. A 5:1 ratio means the machine reduces five bags of yard waste to one bag of shredded material.

Uses: Chopping/shredding dry fallen leaves, yard debris, twigs, and branches up to two inches thick. Note: Do not use fresh wood chips as plant mulch as they will burn plants.

Buying tips:

- For extra safety, look for a model that is equipped with a paddle to assist the feeding process, keeping your hands away from the machine.
- Look for a wheeled model that can be easily moved around your yard.
- Some models have a hopper that tilts downward, allowing you to rake material directly into the shredding mechanism.
- Sharpening shredder blades is difficult, time-consuming, and potentially dangerous. Look for a model with self-sharpening blades.

29.3g Maintenance of Power Tools

Contractors always say, "take care of your tools and they'll take care of you." That is no less true for garden tools.

During the season:

- Sharpen mower blades after every 20 hours of use.
- Keep the mower deck, undercarriage, and blade free of debris by cutting only dry grass. (This practice also helps keep the blades sharper.)
- Store your mower in a sheltered garage or shed between mowings.
- Hose off the mower's undercarriage only when the engine has cooled. No water should touch the engine compartment. The same goes for string trimmers.
- For gas mowers, check the oil level before each mowing, and check/clean the air filter every four mowings.

At the end of the season:

When your grass has been cut for the last time that season, always winterize lawn movers, trimmers, and blowers to extend their life.

- Drain gasoline from gas-powered tools or add a fuel stabilizer to the tank. Do not pour gasoline on grass, in drains, in toilets, or in the street. The best way to dispose of old gas is to pour it into a full tank of fresh gas in a car or truck. Otherwise, take it to a recycling station that handles hazardous materials. If using fuel stabilizer, follow the instructions on the container.
- Change the engine oil, change or clean the air filter, and replace the spark plug. Sharpen the blades once more and your mower will be ready for the following spring.
- Check the fuel filter, fuel line, cables, and connections.
- Clean the outside of the carburetor and fan blades.
- For electric mowers, disconnect the battery to prevent corrosion and clean the terminals. Wipe down the mower with a damp cloth and store in a sheltered garage or shed for the winter.

29.4 Garden Accessories

29.4a Wheelbarrows and Carts

A wheelbarrow or garden cart is indispensable for hauling bags of soil, compost, leaves, mulch, gravel, and other landscaping materials; as well as tools and plants.

THE IDEAL GARDEN ACCESSORIES LIST

- Wheelbarrow or garden cart
- Trellises for flowers and vegetables
- Bamboo/wooden stakes, or metal/plastic cages for tomatoes and peppers
- Twist-tape, zip-ties, or twine
- Bulb planter or auger
- Weed pail
- Garden hoses/nozzles
- Sprinkler for large areas
- Watering can
- Dedicated hand sprayers
- Garden gloves
- Kneeling pad or padded kneelers
- One-foot ruler and a yardstick or tape measure
- Measuring spoons/cups
- Moisture/pH meter
- Row covers/netting

Wheelbarrows have metal or wood handles, and there are plastic versions. Utility carts, made more deep than wide, are compact and easy to maneuver. Rolling, ground-flush canvas totes let you rake right into the bag.

Garden carts are far less like to tip over, but tend to make hauling heavy loads more difficult because of the way the weight is distributed. Conversely, traditional two-handled, single-wheel wheelbarrows tend to tip/flip over and require more arm and back strength to move, but carry heavy loads better than a garden cart. One person of average strength can tote 200 pounds in a wheelbarrow. Try out several models to see what you can handle comfortably.

Buying tips

- Stick with steel parts for durability. Exposure to the elements can make plastic crack and degrade wood frames and handles.
- Large tires roll more easily on uneven ground and distribute load weight better. Models with airless tires eliminate periodic refills.

29.4b Trellises, Cages, and Stakes

Trellises

Trellises are used to support climbing or vining plants. Situate your trellis first, then place the plant so that it will immediately start growing vertically. Check periodically to keep the plant trained on the trellis, attaching vines with stretchy ties to keep them off the ground.

Figure 29-S. Wheelbarrow and cart types

Garden wheelbarrow   Contractor's wheelbarrow   Garden cart   Utility cart

Figure 29-T. Trellis types

Teepee A-frame Arbor Obelisk Wire mesh Post-and-twine

Use a trellis to:

Save space. Growing vertically takes up less square footage, allowing you to grow more.

Enjoy a bigger harvest. Growing fruit or vegetables on a trellis will give you a bigger crop because more of the plant is exposed to sunlight.

Reduce disease and insect damage. Trellising improves the air flow around your plants and keeps fruit off of the ground, away from soil-borne diseases. Trellising also keeps vining fruits and vegetables much cleaner.

Harvest easily. Your harvest is easier to see and reach, and spares you having to bend down to pick.

Trellis types

You can buy trellises at a garden center or online, or you can easily make your own with stakes, garden netting, or wire or twine (see Figure 29-T). If you have a chain-link fence, you have a built-in trellis! The following are descriptions of common trellis types.

Bamboo teepee

A bamboo teepee is a classic, easy-to-build trellis that is ideal for pole beans, peas, cucumbers, and vining flowers. Use five eight-foot bamboo posts, evenly spaced around a four-foot diameter section. Push the posts ten to 12 inches into the ground at an angle so the posts all meet in the middle. Bind the tops of the posts together with heavy-duty twine and cover with netting, if desired.

A-frame

A-frame trellises can be bought or built. Set two rectangular trellis panels at a 45° angle so they form an "A." A-frame trellises are typically very sturdy and can be used for beans, peas, gourds, and cucumbers as well as heavier fruits like melons and squash.

Arbor or arch

To have vining plants grow over the shape of a rounded entrance arbor is very pleasing to the eye—and can also support edible plants. The Internet has plenty of plans for arbors; if you are the least bit handy, this is a fun project and considerably less expensive than buying one or having one built for you. Look into building an arch out of birch, willow, or hazel branches for a charming rustic look.

Obelisks, towers, and pyramids

Obelisks, bean towers, and pyramids are ornamental trellises often made from wrought iron, which can add some personal style to your garden. The height of the structure adds dimension and interest to your landscape and also creates more horizontal space for you to grown another crop.

THE BEST VEGETABLES FOR TRELLISING

Pole bean
Scarlet runner bean
Pea
Cucumber
Summer squash (non-bush types)
Indeterminate tomato
Hops*
Pumpkin*

THE BEST FRUITS FOR TRELLISING

Trailing brambles
Grape
Hardy kiwi
Melons*

THE BEST FLOWERS FOR TRELLISING

Climbing rose
Sweet pea
Climbing nasturtium
Morning glory
Clematis
Wisteria
Carolina jessamine
Chocolate vine
Climbing hydrangea
Honeysuckle
Trumpet vine
Virginia creeper

*Require very strong support. Heavy individual fruits require a sling. These can be made from old pantyhose or cheesecloth.

Wire mesh

Framed wire mesh panels can support any number of fruits, vegetables, or flowers. Most any homeowner can make one simply by making a "picture frame" of wood; overlaying it with one-inch hardware cloth, mesh, or fencing; and sandwiching the mesh between another frame. In the off-season, the frame can be used as a compost sifter.

Posts and netting or twine

The easiest type of trellis to build yourself is one made of posts and twine or wire. Pound in posts or stakes at intervals of at least four feet to enclose the growing space, then secure netting or twine between the supports. These work well for peas and pole beans.

Cages

Like stakes and trellises, cages serve the purpose of keeping foliage and fruit off the ground and less prone to soil-borne diseases (see Figure 29-U).

Cages come in many shapes and sizes, but the small ones are really only useful for pepper plants that might need a little extra support. Tomatoes, even determinate varieties, need something more substantial.

Square tomato cages are structurally stronger and usually made of a heavier-gauge metal than the ubiquitous round types. To save space, they fold flat at the end of the season. Place the cages immediately before planting so as not to damage roots.

Stakes

Use multiple stakes to make a teepee for vining crops like peas and cucumbers, or a single stake to help hold tomatoes and

Figure 29-U. Cage types

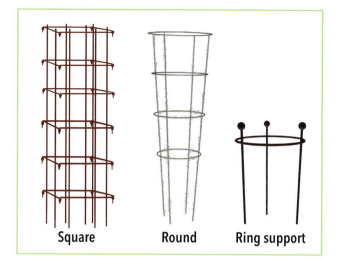

Square Round Ring support

Figure 29-V. Stake types

Wood Bamboo Fiberglass Spiral

peppers off the ground (see Figure 29-V). Alternatively, space stakes two to three feet apart in a straight line, and affix netting or chicken wire to make a "wall" up which fruits and vegetables can grow.

29.4c Watering Equipment

One of the biggest mistakes novice gardeners make is to install a new garden where a water supply is not readily available. This necessitates hauling hoses and watering cans to keep plants alive and thriving. Plan for your water supply and watering equipment before you dig, and learn about the watering tools you will need to keep soil moisture levels where they ought to be.

Hoses and accessories

The hose and sprayer type you choose—and the way you use them—can actually have an effect on the production of your garden.

A garden hose is what most people use to get water to their garden, but not all garden hoses are created equal. Here are some of the more common types:

Vinyl. Easy on the budget, but not long-lasting, a vinyl hose is usually reinforced with nylon mesh to make it more durable; however, the fittings need regular replacement and they tend to kink. Use a vinyl hose in a place where it can be left, like a distant planting bed.

Rubber. Durability is the main feature of a good rubber hose. The walls are thicker, more flexible, and less likely to kink than vinyl hoses. Rubber is also less susceptible to UV damage over time.

Polyurethane. If you have to regularly travel around the yard with your hose, this is a good choice because it is lighter than vinyl or rubber. Polyurethane can be hard to coil, so look for a pre-coiled version you can hang up.

Expandable. These polymer hoses are advertised on TV as a lightweight, flexible alternative to "heavy, bulky" garden hoses. A coiled expandable hose can be held in your palm, yet expands to 25 feet (or more) when filled with water. When the water is shut off, the hose returns to its original size. Consumer complaints about the cheap fittings and tendency for the hose to snag on brick and concrete forced a redesign, and now these

Figure 29-W. Hose types

Vinyl   Rubber   Polyurethane   Expandable   Soaker

hoses are of much better quality. Look for the brands with a good warranty.

Soaker. Saving water and getting moisture to plant roots at ground-level are the two main reasons to use flat soaker hoses in your beds. It will take some experimentation to learn how long to leave the water running in order to water deeply enough. Pre-drilled hoses are available at garden centers and online, but you can make your own with a drill or an ice pick, an old garden hose, and a set of connectors.

Buying tips: Always look for:

- A good manufacturer's warranty.
- High-quality brass fittings.
- A kink-proof feature.
- An octagonal connector that can be connected/disconnected with pliers, if necessary.
- A burst-pressure rating of more than 350 PSI. The higher the PSI, the less chance there is of the hose leaking when stepped on or driven over.

Nozzles and connectors

Nozzles are available for every kind of watering requirement, from a light shower to a pavement-cleaning power jet. Be mindful that different plants need different watering methods. For example, always water tomato plants as low as you can to prevent fungus and disease, and spray on the mist setting if you're watering delicate flowers.

Pistol-grip. As the name indicates, this is an easy-grip model shaped like a pistol. Just aim and squeeze. Most models have an adjusting screw or knob to let you control the strength of the water flow, from a broad mist to a sharp jet stream. This type of nozzle has limited spray patterns, but can be had for just a couple of dollars. Higher-end pistol models are also available.

Multi-pattern revolver. Similar to a pistol nozzle, but with a more ergonomic grip and up to nine spray patterns (e.g., jet, center, shower, mist, flat). It is lockable so you don't have to hold the trigger down to keep the water flowing.

Fan or flat. When a gentle, fine spray is needed over a broad area, choose a fan nozzle. These are useful for small gardens, container groups, and other more delicate watering tasks.

Twist. This type is probably the most familiar kind of nozzle from childhood. The barrel is straight, with a narrower spray end. To control the amount of water, twist the nozzle to the right or left. The resulting spray patterns

Figure 29-X.   Nozzle types

Pistol   Revolver   Fan   Twist   Wand

are very similar to the pistol-grip nozzle—anything from a fine mist to a narrow, hard stream. Some models are designed such that the stream can be considered "power-wash" strength, although it cannot be equally compared to an actual power washer.

Wand. Wands allow you to extend your reach to maximize water distance and flow. Place water exactly where needed for hanging baskets, deep garden beds, shrubs, and flowers. A telescoping shower head delivers a gentle spray, sometimes adjustable, that won't harm tender plants or wash away soil.

Quick-connect couplings

Two-piece quick-connectors are quite ingenious. Instead of threading hose ends onto a faucet, simply connect the female piece to the faucet and the male piece to the hose end, sprinkler, or power washer; then snap the two together/apart. Excellent for arthritic hands, they are made by multiple manufacturers.

Buying tips: Plastic and aluminum are cheaper but brass is best. Look for models that are crack-resistant in cold weather.

Sprinkler

Lawn sprinklers deliver an overhead shower to lawns, gardens, and flower beds. Stationary sprinkler heads are fixed in the landscape to direct water onto a specific area. Rotating lawn sprinkler heads whirl, oscillate, or turn to provide a wider area of coverage (see Figure 29-Y).

If possible, try to limit overhead watering, especially late in the day. Prolonged moisture on foliage can lead to fungal and bacterial diseases. Always try to water at ground level, if possible. When you must use a sprinkler, there are a number of different types:

Stationary. This doughnut-shaped device sprays like an upside-down shower head, covering up to a 360° radius. Just move it to cover another area, which eliminates overwatering areas that don't need it. Stationary sprinklers can be set at varying radii. Best for small applications.

Impact. The tchik-tchik-tchik is a familiar sound during the summer, made by an impact sprinkler. It is mounted on a spike, which can easily be moved from place to place. It is well-suited for large areas but not delicate flower gardens. The radius is adjustable.

Oscillating. An oscillating, or overhead, sprinkler is simply a stable rectangular base with an overarching perforated metal tube that moves back and forth as it dispenses water. The rectangular spray pattern can be adjusted to be shorter or longer.

Figure 29-Y. Sprinkler types

Stationary   Impact   Oscillating   Rotary   Irrigation head

Rotary. Water pressure turns the three-pronged device like a whirligig, covering a full circle with three streams of water. Use a rotary for slow-draining soils because it delivers less water than an overhead sprinkler.

Irrigation system. An irrigation system is a set of underground PVC pipes and pop-up sprinkler heads intended to cover the entirety of the watering area. The system is wired to a control box that allows you to program the time of day and length of time the system runs, or you can program selected sprinklers to run. It is possible to DIY this, but a project this complex is almost always better left to a professional.

An irrigation system uses an incredible amount of water and people have a habit of setting it to water shallowly every couple of days, which opens the door for poorly-rooted grass and fungal diseases. To save water and money, opt for planting drought-resistant turf cultivars—or better yet, native groundcovers—that do not require an irrigation system.

Buying tips:

- Know the size of the area you need to cover and the kind of spray pattern needed to cover it. Some sprinklers are designed to water smaller spaces, like gardens and flower beds, while others can cover most or all of your lawn.
- Make sure the sprinkler has a "gentle" setting to water delicate flowers, new grass seed, and other areas where a heavier shower might be disruptive.

Watering can

Size is the most important consideration when considering a new watering can. A small-spout sprinkler can is best for seed-sprouting and tiny plants; a two-gallon can is adequate for spot-watering and hitting those places beyond your hose's reach (see Figure 29-Z).

The best way to choose a watering can is to hold a full one in your hand so you can feel how the water weight is distributed. Some cans are "top-heavy" and pull you forward when full, spilling water before you're ready to pour.

Watering cans are usually made of either plastic or metal. Plastic is less expensive and reasonably durable, but UV rays will eventually fade, crack, and deteriorate plastic.

Metal cans are more durable provided they are galvanized to resist rust. A good one may be a bit heavier to haul around but it can last for many years.

Figure 29-Z. Watering can types

Seedling   Plastic short-neck   Plastic long-neck   Galvanized

Buying tip: Look for a removable spout-end (also called a rosette) so it can be cleaned.

29.4d Sprayers

If you have plants that are suffering from a fungal disease, insect pest invasion, or nutritional deficiency, a garden sprayer is the right tool to apply a liquid treatment (see Figure 29-AA). Choose the sprayer you need based on the problem you have and the size of the area you need to cover.

Hose-end

A hose-end sprayer is an inexpensive option for applying treatments to your lawn and garden. The two hose-end sprayer types are:

Fixed-rate. Set the sprayer control to the product package's recommended amount of dilution and open the valve to spray. The rate of siphoning is usually described in ounces of product per gallon of water. The product is mixed with water at the nozzle.

An option for a water-only setting lets you switch between solution and plain water, and an anti-siphon device prevents chemicals from being pulled back into your water supply.

Adjustable rate. Some sprayers have a dial on the nozzle that allows you to siphon at an adjustable rate. Be sure the follow the instructions on the product container.

Adjustable-rate sprayers also have a "water only" setting that allows you to stop spraying solution. This is especially convenient when the product must be "watered in" after application.

Use hose-end sprayers to apply herbicides, fertilizers, fungicides, or pesticides to your lawn.

All-in-one

All-in-one sprayers are lightweight, usually holding one gallon or less of solution. To use them, add the correct amount of product and water, then hand-pump the sprayer to pressurize it. To distribute the spray, just press

Figure 29-AA. Sprayer types

Hose-end   All-in-one   Tank   Backpack

the release tab (or squeeze the pistol-grip handle). To adjust the spray type, twist the nozzle right or left to go from a fine mist to a jet stream. *Uses:* A good all-around sprayer for small applications of fertilizer, fungicide, insecticide, or herbicide.

Tank

Tank sprayers have a hose wand that siphons solution from a one- or two-gallon (or larger) tank. The vacuum-pressure function is just like the all-in-one sprayer; pump the handle until the tank is pressurized and use the hose wand to aim the spray where you want it.

Backpack

Backpack sprayers keep your hands free for reaching areas that require a ladder to access, such as a roof or eaves. They also place the weight distribution across your shoulders rather than you arms, which lessens fatigue if you have a large ground area to cover. The two types of backpack sprayers are:

Piston pump. Choose this type for handling liquid disinfectants, herbicides, and pesticides.

Diaphragm pump. Choose this type when using wettable powders or bleach.

29.4e Maintenance of Watering Equipment and Sprayers

At the end of the season:

- Disconnect, drain, and store your garden hoses in a dry, protected place.
- Disconnect plastic nozzles from hoses and store them with your hoses. Leaving them outdoors over the winter will likely result in cracked nozzles the following spring.
- Drain your irrigation system to prevent the lines from freezing/bursting.
- While you should not store mixed solution in the sprayer, it's easy to forget to spray out all solution after each use. If you have any leftovers, spray an area the product was originally intended for. Do not empty sprayers into storm drains, onto driveways, or down household drains.
- Store all watering cans and sprayers in a sheltered location for the winter to prevent damage from the elements.

29.5 Other Tools and Accessories

29.5a Composting Tools

For complete information about starting and maintaining a compost pile, please see **Chapter 7, Composting.** For images of common composting tools, see Figure 29-BB.

Compost thermometer

A large, well-constructed compost heap creates its own heat. The mesophilic microorganisms that fuel the composting process thrive in temperatures between 68 and 113°F. Thermophilic microorganisms like the pile even hotter, but not higher than 150° or the heat will begin killing the microorganisms. To keep a compost pile "cooking," it's important to monitor its temperature, moisture level, and carbon-to-nitrogen ratio (see inset on the following page). Too much (or too little) of any of these elements will throw off the balance that makes the process work.

A compost thermometer looks very much like a candy thermometer (but has a 12- to 14-inch probe that can reach deeper into the pile) and a stainless steel and glass read-out dial.

Figure 29-BB. Composting tools

Thermometer   Plunger aerator   Crank aerator   Compost fork   Rotary sifter   Pan sifter   Frame sifter

Compost aerator

A compost pile, especially if it has not been turned for a while, can compact and become surprisingly heavy. It may be difficult for some people to use a compost fork or pitchfork, but a compost aerator can easily introduce oxygen into the pile. Plunger-types have two tines that open when you start to pull it out of the pile. Crank-types work like a corkscrew to "drill" through the pile and create air pockets.

Compost fork

You can turn compost with any garden fork or pitchfork, but a compost fork will make the job easier. The larger (but lighter) head provides additional leverage for turning; and the long, thin tines penetrate the compost materials rather than cutting into them. Compost forks come with long or short shafts. Choose the length that fits your height, stance, and working style.

Compost sifter/screener

Once your compost is finished, it can usually be used straight from the pile. If, however, you have been composting twigs, branches, or other wood, you may find many chunks remaining. A little bit of solid wood in compost is good and will help to harbor beneficial fungi, but if there is too much, it will rob the soil of nitrogen. You may need to do a little sifting.

The three types of sifters are: a hand-crank rotary model that works like a food mill to

IS "COMPOST STARTER" NECESSARY?

A compost starter is an additive you can buy that supposedly "kickstarts" your compost pile and makes it process faster. A starter is not necessary if you have the right carbon-to-nitrogen ratio of "green" to "brown" (1 part green, 2 parts brown).

If the ratio of your pile isn't ideal, you can make your own starter:

Mix the following in a bucket and let stand for two to three hours.

- One gallon of water
- One-half cup of liquid ammonia
- One bottle or can of non-diet cola
- One bottle or can of cheap beer

Dribble the liquid over the pile and add three shovelfuls of soil. Toss the pile to distribute the starter.

Figure 29-CC. Composting tumbler types

Single-chamber　　Dual-chamber　　Galvanized　　Plastic/sifter　　DIY

push through finer particles, trapping the larger ones; a pan (like gold prospectors use, only with a much bigger mesh); and a framed-screen type. For large amounts of compost, you can buy or make a lean-to screen and shovel the compost right onto the screen.

Compost tumblers

A compost tumbler is typically a drum, barrel, or similar container with a crank-type handle. It is affixed to a stand that allows the container to be rotated on an axle. It is essentially a compost-turning device that retains heat and aerates the compost, allowing microorganisms to thrive. The types and designs of compost tumblers are as follows (see Figure 29-CC):

Single-chamber. One compartment holds all of the materials.

Dual-chamber. Includes two compartments, one for "maturing" compost and one for new additions. Most gardeners prefer this model.

Metal construction. Unless it is galvanized, it will rust. Metal tumblers also require additional insulation to keep heat in during cold months.

Plastic construction. Unless UV-ray-protected, plastic will degrade from the sun and heat of the contents, but hold in heat far better than metal during colder months. Plastic tumblers are lighter, much less expensive, and preferred by most composters.

DIY. You can make one from a 55-gallon drum and some PVC pipe. Dozens of building plans are available on the Internet, if you are so inclined.

Compost tumblers are something of a luxury item—they can get expensive ($70 to $400 and up), but they dramatically speed up the composting process and are neat, compact, and efficient. Wildlife will also be deterred from snacking on your composting scraps if you have a tumbler.

Buying tips

- The most frequent complaint of tumbler owners is that they have far more composting material than tumbler space and can't make compost fast enough. If you're planning to buy, get the largest drum size you can afford.

- For some yards, a mobile tumbler can be a great time and energy saver. Just wheel the tumbler to wherever you need to pick up raw materials or deliver finished compost.

- Look for a tumbler with a built-in sifter, which will give you a fine enough texture for seed-sowing.

Figure 29-DD. Garden glove types

Nitrile | Canvas | Leather | 3/4 Length | PVC nibs | Claw | Waterproof

29.5b Other Accessories

Gloves

Gardening gloves are essential to protect your hands from scratches, scrapes, splinters, and even soil-borne bacteria. Canvas, deerskin, and leather used to be about the only material choices, but now there are garden gloves with water-resistant nitrile palms, claw fingers, super-gripping capability, and multiple lengths. Materials range from ABS plastic to polyurethane to nylon (see Figure 29-DD). There are even gloves for arthritic hands.

Buying tips:

- Rose gardeners need longer, elbow-length gloves to protect arms from thorn scratches.
- Check the fabric content—many people are allergic to latex and some gloves are either lined or coated with it.
- If you are continually hanging up your fabric gloves to dry at the end of your gardening day, consider a pair of waterproof gloves for "wet chores."

Kneelers and knee pads

Gardening frequently requires bending, which can get more difficult with age. Kneeling helpers are an inexpensive and useful solution. They protect knees against scrapes, rocks, and dirt; and can give you more hours of gardening time without knee or back pain.

Three types of kneeling accessories are as follows (see Figure 29-EE):

- Kneeler-seat: a folding kneeling pad with side supports that flips upside-down and converts to a seat.
- Flat high-density foam kneeling pad (some models are waterproof).
- Foam or gel knee pads with Velcro® straps

Buying tips: Kneeling pad/knee pad density can vary widely among models. Some have too much "give" and end up not being comfortable. Try before you buy.

Figure 29-EE. Kneelers and knee-pad types

Kneeler seat | Foam kneepads | Kneeling pad

Figure 29-FF. Bulb-planter types

Bulb planter/auger

Bulb-planting can always be done by digging out the entire area where you want to plant, but it is often easier and more precise to plant bulbs individually.

Three tools to plant bulbs and plugs are as follows (see Figure 29-FF):

- A short plunge-and-twist model with a wood handle
- A step-on model with a long shaft
- An auger attachment for your power drill

For a few dozen bulbs, the short model will do a nice job. The long-shaft model gives you much more leverage and is easier on the hands, wrist, and back. If you are planting many bulbs, the auger attachment will "dig" your holes very quickly.

Buying tips

- Stainless is always the best choice because it won't rust. Avoid plastic models as they do a poor job of cutting through tough soil and crack/break easily.
- Choose a model with serrated "teeth" around the bottom circumference to make cutting through soil easier.
- Look for models that are marked with measuring depths on the plunger.

Weed pail

Most gardeners take yard waste and pulled weeds to the compost pile. As a rule, that is fine as long as your compost pile is hot enough to kill any weed seeds or diseases that might be clinging to spent leaves, plants, or prunings.

If you are not a regular pile monitor, it's best to sort your yard waste into "dispose of in trash" and "dispose of in compost pile." Using two weed pails (five-gallon buckets work well), sort what you pick up as you go and dump it accordingly, and your compost pile will remain free of issues.

A wheeled pail is helpful for those who have trouble carrying or lifting weight.

Measuring tools

If you have any gas-powered tools, you probably have a measuring cup and spoons to mix gas and oil for your two-cycle machines. In addition, it is helpful to have the following handy to measure spacing between plants, borders around beds, or the square footage of a particular area:

- A one-foot ruler
- A yardstick or tape measure
- A laser-measuring app on your phone

Moisture/pH meter

A meter is no substitute for a lab soil test, but it is good enough to help you diagnose immediate plant issues and make amendments as needed. Moisture-pH meters have a readout dial at the end of a probe which indicates the soil pH and moisture level. Most of these meters require no battery. Newer models also include a light sensor to detect light intensity. The moisture meter will help prevent you from over- or underwatering plants, especially those in containers.

Row covers/netting

Row covers are lengths of very light, opaque fabric that protect against frost, insect pests, and, to some degree, small rodents. They "float" over your garden rows and are secured to the ground with landscape pins. Material grades differ in their level of protection against frosts and freezes; some row covers claim to protect against a killing frost. Be sure to remove row covers during pollination periods or your crop will yield less.

Standard UV-resistant polyethylene netting with a two-inch mesh will keep birds out of your fruit bushes and trees. Drape the netting over plants before the fruit begins to ripen. To keep out larger insects like grasshoppers, cicadas, fruit wasps, and other nuisance insects, choose a three-quarter-inch mesh.

Frames/hoops for structuring row covers are available in varying shapes and heights, as are clips for holding netting pieces together.

Gardening journal

Keeping a garden journal is an excellent way to track plants you have purchased, where you got them, what thrived (and what didn't), formulas for your sprayers, frost dates, what the weather was like and how your plants responded, and whatever else you want to document or remember.

29.5c Maintenance of Other Tools and Accessories

Composting tools

- Clean off compost aerators, compost forks, and sifters with a hose and let them air-dry prior to storing them in a shed or garage for the winter.

- Clean off compost thermometers with a moist rag and store them in a sheltered location for the winter. The same goes for pH/moisture meters. Do not allow them to freeze.

- Compost tumblers don't require regular maintenance but it is a good idea to periodically clean out the drum and inspect for insect pests or rodents that may have found their way in.

- Cotton and canvas garden gloves can be machine-washed and dried. Vinyl will be damaged by laundry detergents, so rinse gloves with vinyl components in a solution of water and plain dish soap, rinse, dry, and store in a shed or garage.

- Hose off kneeling pads and knee pads, and air-dry before storing for the winter.

- Remove all cages, stakes, and trellises (unless permanently installed) and brush them off prior to storage. Do not use a wire brush on enameled cages or you will damage the paint.

- Hose off your bulb planter/auger attachment after each use and oil the handle and metal to extend the life of the tool. ❋

AUTHORS

Doris Behnke, Principal Agent Associate, Cecil County, University of Maryland Extension.

PUBLICATIONS

Cromell, Cathy, and National Gardening Association. 2010. *Composting for Dummies.* For Dummies, a Wiley Brand. New York, New York.

Laws, B. 2014. *A History of the Garden in Fifty Tools.* University of Chicago Press. Chicago, Ill.

WEBSITES

"25 Garden Tools and Essentials for Year-Round Care." HGTV. **hgtv.com/outdoors/gardens/best-garden-tools-and-essentials**

"Garden Tools - Gardening Tools." Gardeners Supply. **gardeners.com/buy/gardening/garden-tools/**

"Garden Tools – the Home Depot." The Home Depot. **homedepot.com/b/Outdoors-Garden-Center-Garden-Tools/N-5yc1vZbx6x**

"Gardening Health and Safety Tips." Centers for Disease Control. cdc.gov (article no longer available online)

"Lawn & Garden - Harbor Freight Tools." Harbor Freight Tools. **harborfreight.com/lawn-garden.html**

"Lawn & Garden Hand Tools " Lowes. **lowes.com/c/Lawn-garden-hand-tools-Outdoor-tools-equipment-Outdoors**

"The Best Gardening Tools of 2022." Bob Vila. **bobvila.com/articles/best-gardening-tools/**

PHOTOS

Main chapter photo: Flickr free license.

ILLUSTRATIONS AND PHOTO ILLUSTRATIONS

Figures 29-A through 29-FF, except 29-D (Envato Elements license), 29-T and 29-V (illustrations by LeAnn Zotta): Photo illustrations by LeAnn Zotta.

30: RESOURCE APPENDIX

30 RESOURCE APPENDIX

CONTENTS

Glossary of Terms 851

Table 30-A. Measurement Conversions 885

Freeze Dates and Hardiness Zones 886

Glossary of Terms

A

Abdomen The posterior section of the three main body divisions of an arthropod.

Abiotic Non-living (or non-biological) components of the habitat, such as climate, water, and light.

Abscise To separate, as a leaf from the stem.

Abscisic acid (ABA) A complex natural growth inhibitor, involved in the dormant (resting) stage of buds, and leaf and fruit abscission.

Abscission zone One or more layers of cells where transverse divisions and weakening of middle lamellae cause separation of an organ from the plant (abscission).

Absorption The process by which a substance is taken into and included within another substance. Example: intake of gases, water, nutrients, or other substances by plants.

Acclimate To adapt to new environmental conditions.

Acervulus (pl. acervuli) Saucer-shaped or cushion-like fungal fruiting body bearing conidiophores, conidia, and sometimes setae.

Achene A simple, one-seeded fruit in which the seed is attached to the ovary wall at only one point, such as the "seed" on the surface of a strawberry.

Acid-forming A term applied to any substance that tends to make the soil more acidic.

Acid soil A soil with a pH value below 7.0; a soil that has a preponderance of hydrogen over hydroxyl ions in the soil solution.

Adaptation An inherited characteristic that improves an organism's ability to survive and reproduce in its habitat.

Adsorption The increased concentration of molecules or ions on a surface, including exchangeable cations and anions on soil particles.

Adventitious Produced in an unusual position or at an unusual time; can refer to any plant organ (bud, root, or shoot).

Aeration The process of incorporating air (oxygen) into water, soil, or decaying green waste.

Aerial root A root produced above ground, often for climbing.

Aerobic In the presence of oxygen.

Aesthetic threshold A level of injury to an ornamental plant considered unacceptable to the grower, which triggers a control action.

Aggregate, soil A group of small soil particles such as clay particles that are chemically bonded together such that the resulting larger particle has physical characteristics of a silt or sand particle.

Aggregate fruit Fruit made up of two or more carpels from a single flower, plus the stem axis. Example: blackberry.

Air drainage The flow of cold air down a hill.

Air layering A propagation method whereas cut is made three-quarters of the way through the stem to promote new roots. The cut surface is encased in a material such as coir or peat that is kept moist to encourage the root growth from the callus that grows from the wound on the stem.

Algae An aquatic plant that lacks a vascular system. Some are microscopic; others are large. Examples: pond scum, kelp, red tides.

Alkaline soil A soil with a pH reading above 7.0.

Allelopathy The ability of a plant species to produce substances that are toxic to certain other plants.

Alternate branching A branching pattern where side branches, leaves, and leaf scars do not grow directly across from each other.

Alternate host A secondary host that becomes infected and is necessary for the life cycle completion of a disease-causing organism.

Alternate leaf arrangement Leaves are arranged at one leaf per node on different sides along the stem.

Amendment Any material, such as lime, gypsum, or compost, that is worked into the soil to improve plant growth or soil health.

Anaerobic Able to live and grow where there is no air or free oxygen.

Anamorph The asexual form in the life cycle of a fungus, in which asexual spores (e.g., conidia) or no spores are produced.

Angiosperm A flowering plant whose seed is enclosed in an ovary.

Anion A negatively charged ion, such as sulfate (SO -) or phosphate (PO).

Annual A plant that germinates, grows, flowers, produces seed, and dies in one growing season.

Antagonist An organism that releases toxins or otherwise changes conditions so that activity or growth of other organisms (especially plant pathogens and pests) is reduced.

Antenna (pl. antennae) A pair of segmented appendages located on the head above the mouthparts and usually sensory in function.

Anther Upper part of the stamen where the pollen is produced.

Anthesis The expanded or full-bloom stage of flowers, marked by shedding of pollen or receptiveness of the stigma.

Anthocyanin Any of a class of water-soluble pigments, including most of those imparting red, purple, or blue color to fruits or flowers.

Anthracnose A type of leaf- or fruit-spot disease caused by acervuli forming fungi and characterized by sunken lesions and necrosis.

Antibody A protein formed in the blood of warm-blooded animals in response to the injection of an antigen.

Antigen Any foreign substance (normally a protein) that induces antibody formation in animals.

Anvil pruner Pruner with a straight blade that closes against a small anvil or block as the handles are squeezed.

Apex The tip or distal end of a leaf.

Apical bud A bud at the apex or terminal position on a plant or branch.

Apical dominance The tendency of an apical (terminal) bud to produce hormones that suppress growth of the buds below it on the stem.

Apothecium (pl. apothecia) Open, cup-shaped, spore-bearing structure produced by certain types of fungi such as *Sclerotinia*.

Appressed Fitting closely against.

Appressorium (pl. appressoria) Swollen, flattened portion of a fungal filament that adheres to the surface of a host plant, thus providing anchorage for invasion by the fungus.

Arthropod An invertebrate animal (insect, arachnid, or crustacean) that has a jointed body and limbs and usually a hard shell or exoskeleton that is molted periodically.

Artificial selection The selection and reproduction of individual plants to favor desirable traits.

Ascocarp Sexual fruiting body (ascus-bearing organ) of an ascomycete.

Ascomycete Member of a class of fungi that produce sexual spores (ascospores) within an ascus.

Ascospore A spore produced within the sac-like cell (ascus, pl. asci) of the sexual state of a fungus.

Asexual Vegetative; without sex organs, sex cells, or sexual spores (e.g., the anamorph of a fungus).

Asexual propagation The duplication of a plant from a cell, tissue, or organ of the parent plant.

Asymmetrical leaf base The base is not formed the same on either side of the petiole; it is uneven.

Auricle A small ear-like projection from the base of a leaf or petal.

Auxin A plant hormone that stimulates plant cell growth and suppresses the growth of axillary buds.

Available nutrient The quantity of a nutrient element or compound in the soil that can be readily absorbed and assimilated by growing plants.

Available water The amount of water held in the soil that can be extracted by plants.

Awn A slender bristle at the end or on the back or edge of an organ.

Axil The angle formed by a leaf or branch with the stem.

Axillary bud A bud formed in an axil, situated along the sides of a branch, and not at the tip.

B

***Bacillus thuringiensis* (Bt)** A bacterium that produces a protein crystal that damages the gut of insects (mostly caterpillars), formulations of which are used as insecticides.

Bacterium (pl. bacteria) A single-celled, microscopic, plant-like organism that lacks a nucleus. Most bacteria obtain their nitrogen and energy from organic matter; some bacteria cause plant or animal diseases.

Balled and burlapped (B&B) A tree or shrub, grown in a field, dug with an intact ball of soil around the roots and wrapped in burlap and cordage for shipment, holding, and transplanting.

Band application An application in which a material such as fertilizer is applied in a narrow line along a row of plants or in a circle around individual plants.

Bare root (BR) A small, dormant tree sold with soil removed from the roots for shipping and transplanting.

Basal Arising from the base of a stem; relating to or being essential for maintaining the fundamental vital activities of an organism.

Basidiomycete Member of a class of fungi that form sexual spores (basidospores) on a basidium.

Beak The protruding mouthpart structures of a sucking insect; proboscis.

Beneficial (noun) Organism that provides a benefit to plants; applied especially to natural enemies of pests and to pollinators such as bees.

Bentgrass A high-maintenance grass used on putting greens that requires frequent cutting with a reel mower, and frequent fertilization and watering; highly susceptible to several diseases.

Berry A simple fruit derived from one flower, in which the parts remain succulent; it may be derived from an ovary (e.g., grape) or from an ovary plus receptacle tissue (e.g., blueberry).

Biennial Plant that completes its life cycle in two years or growing seasons, with a dormant period in between. It produces leaves the first year and flowers and seeds the second.

Bilateral symmetry Symmetry in which there is only one axis dividing the object into two equal, mirror-image parts.

Binomial nomenclature The two-part scientific Latin name of a plant or animal, consisting of the genus and the specific epithet (i.e., species).

Biodegradation The breakdown of a human-made chemical by organisms in the environment.

Biological control The action of parasites, predators, or pathogens in maintaining another organism's population density at a lower average level than would occur in their absence. Biological control may occur naturally or from manipulation or introduction of biological control agents by people.

Biological diversity Presence of many different types of living organisms.

Biotic The living (plant and animal) components of the habitat.

Biotic disease Disease caused by a pathogen, such as a bacterium, fungus, mycoplasma, or virus.

Biotype A strain of a species that has certain biological characteristics separating it from other individuals of that species.

Bipinnate (twice pinnate) A tree with two orders of leaflets, each pinnately compound. Example: honey locust.

Blade The flattened, green portion of the leaf.

Blanch Protecting plant stems (leeks), bulbs (fennel), or heads (cauliflower) from sunlight and the elements. This enhances succulence and prevents discoloration.

Blasting A process in which buds and flowers may fail to develop or blacken because of disease or extreme environmental conditions.

Blight A disease characterized by sudden, severe, and extensive spotting, discoloration, wilting, or destruction of leaves, flowers, stems, or entire plants. Usually attacks young, growing tissues. "Blight" is often coupled with the name of the affected host part (e.g., leaf blight, blossom blight).

Bolting (running to seed) Flowering prematurely, usually due to unsuitable climatic conditions at certain stages of growth. Spinach, lettuce, broccoli, and cilantro are species particularly prone to bolting.

Bone meal Cooked bones, ground to a meal without any of the gelatin or glue removed. Steamed bone meal is steamed under pressure to dissolve part of the gelatin. A slow-release organic fertilizer that is about 15% P (phosphate).

Bonsai A potted plant dwarfed by frequent and extensive pruning of both root and shoot growth.

Bordeaux mixture A fungicide made of a mixture of hydrated lime and copper sulfate.

Botanical Derived from plants or plant parts.

Botany The scientific study of plants.

Botrytis blight A gray, felt-type mold that covers parts of a plant and causes stunting, dieback, and distorted growth.

Bract A leaf-like structure associated with flowers and fruits.

Bramble Any shrub with thorns in the rose family; usually refers to blackberries and raspberries.

Branch collar The raised area surrounding the base of a branch where it attaches to the trunk or main stem.

Bristle-tipped leaf A leaf tip that is sharply pointed with an extended hair or bristle.

Broadcast application The application of a fertilizer or herbicide to the entire surface of a bed, lawn, or field; or the sowing of seed by scattering it uniformly or randomly over the soil or container surface, rather than sowing in rows.

Broad-leafed Shrubs and non-coniferous trees with flat leaves. Conifers have needles or scales. Broad-leafed trees are also called deciduous trees or hardwoods.

Broad-spectrum pesticide A pesticide that kills a large number of unrelated species.

Brood All the individuals of a generation that hatch at about the same time.

Bud An undeveloped stem, consisting of a tiny bundle of cells, from which leaves, lateral buds, flower parts, or all three, arise. On trees and shrubs, leaves form from either terminal buds at the ends of twigs or lateral buds along the sides of twigs. Most buds have protective scales that enclose the leaf tissue. Buds without scales are called naked buds.

Budding A type of grafting in which a bud is placed into a stem on the rootstock plant.

Bud scale A small, modified leaf or stipule (there may be one, a few, or many) that covers the terminal bud and embryonic leaves of a plant during winter.

Bud-scale scar A mark on the stem where a bud scale was attached. Growth rings are formed when the terminal bud sprouts and its scales fall off. The portion of a stem between two sets of growth rings indicates one season's growth.

Bud union The location of a graft that was performed by budding.

Buffer capacity of soils The ability of the soil to resist a change in its pH (hydrogen ion concentration) when acid-forming or base-forming materials are added to the soil.

Bulb An underground storage organ made up of enlarged and fleshy leaf bases enclosing a bud.

Bulbil A small bulb that forms along the stems of certain plants. Examples: tiger lily, bladder fern.

Bulblet A small bulb that develops around a parent bulb that can be removed to propagate additional plants.

Bulk density The ratio of the mass (weight) of water-free soil to its bulk volume, expressed in pounds per Cu. foot or grams per Cu. centimeter.

Bundle trace Dot-like scars within a leaf scar, representing the broken ends of vascular bundles that once led to the leaf stalk.

Button The small heads of broccoli or cabbage that form as a result of seedlings being exposed to cold spring temperatures.

Bypass pruner Pruner with a curved blade that slides past a broader blade.

C

Calcareous soil Soil containing high levels of calcium carbonate.

Calibrate To standardize/correct the measuring function of instruments, as on fertilizer spreaders.

Callus tissue A thin layer of meristematic cells formed in response to wounding that gives rise to new phloem and xylem cells or new roots.

Calyx The united green sepals of a flower that lie just below a flower or flower bud and enclose its base.

Cambium Thin layer of undifferentiated, actively growing tissue between phloem and xylem; the tissue in a plant that produces growth that increases the girth of branches and trunks of trees.

Candle The new shoot growth on pines and some other conifers before the needles expand.

Cane The flexible stem of a plant such as raspberry, blackberry, or grape.

Canker A localized dead, discolored, often sunken area (lesion) on a root, trunk, stem, or branch that is caused by a pathogen, usually a fungus.

Cannibalistic Feeding on other individuals of the same species.

Canopy The top layer of a tree including branches and foliage.

Capillary action A force that causes liquids to rise or fall when inside very small spaces due to surface tension of water. Occurs when adhesive forces between a liquid and a substance are greater than the cohesive forces between liquid molecules.

Capsule A dry, dehiscent fruit that splits open into two or more parts at maturity. Example: sourwood.

Carbon dioxide (CO_2) A colorless, odorless gas found in the air that is absorbed by plants and exhaled by animals.

Carbon:nitrogen ratio (C:N) The ratio of the weight of organic carbon to the weight of total nitrogen (mineral plus organic forms) in soil or organic matter.

Carotenoid Any of a number of orange-red or yellow pigments similar to carotene found in leaves, fruits, and flowers.

Carpel The female part of a flower consisting of the stigma, style, and ovary.

Carrying capacity The number of individuals a habitat can support at any given time.

Caterpillar The larva of a butterfly, moth, sawfly, or scorpionfly.

Catfacing Disfigurement or malformation of fruit, caused by low temperature at or before flowering, insects, and other factors.

Cation An ion carrying a positive charge of electricity. Soil cations include calcium Ca++ and sodium Na+.

Cation exchange capacity (CEC) The capacity of a soil to exchange cations with the soil solution, determined by surface area on soil particles and organic matter; a measure of potential soil fertility.

Catkin A cluster of unisexual flowers that forms a long, skinny, caterpillar-like shape. Catkins are typical of aspen, willow, oak, birch, walnut, and chestnut.

Causal agent Organism or agent that causes a given disease or plant problem. Examples: fungi, stinkbugs, drought, air pollution.

Cell The unit of plants that makes up tissues. Cells have a cell wall that encloses the protoplasm.

Cellulose A highly insoluble compound; the primary material giving plants their physical structure.

Cell wall The protective covering that surrounds a plant cell and is composed primarily of cellulose.

Cephalothorax A body region consisting of head and thoracic segments of arthropods.

Certified seed or planting stock Seeds, tubers, or young plants certified by a recognized authority to be free of or to contain less than a minimum number of specified pests or pathogens.

Chambered pith Pith formed by a series of tiny chambers that can be seen if the twig is sliced open. Example: walnut.

Chilling injury Damage to certain horticultural crops, such as banana, papaya, cucumber, and sweet potato, resulting from exposure to temperatures that are cold but above freezing.

Chilling requirement A cold period required by certain plants and plant parts to break physiological dormancy or rest, expressed in terms of the required number of hours at 45°F or less.

Chlamydospore Thick-walled or double-walled asexual resting spore formed by modification of a hyphal segment.

Chlorophyll The green pigment of plants that captures the energy from sunlight necessary for photosynthesis.

Chloroplast The organelle in which photosynthesis takes place.

Chlorosis Yellowing or bleaching of normally green plant tissue usually caused by the loss of chlorophyll.

Chlorotic Lacking chlorophyll, with a yellow color often most pronounced in areas between leaf veins.

Chrysalis The pupa of a butterfly.

Circadian rhythm A biological cycle that is approximately 24 hours in length.

Clay A minute mineral soil particle less than 0.002 millimeter in diameter and generally plate-like in shape.

Cleistothecium (pl. cleistothecia) Closed ascus-containing structure, usually spherical, with distinctive appendages, of powdery mildew fungi.

Cloche A portable glass or plastic cover for a plant or row of plants to protect them from cold.

Clone A group of plants originating from one individual, as from buds, cuttings, or division; they are genetically identical because the reproduction occurred without flowers and seeds.

Clubbed With the distal part (or segments) enlarged. Example: clubbed insect antennae.

Clustered Multiple leaves, flowers, or fruits seemingly arising from a common juncture; because they are crowded, it is difficult to determine if they are alternate or opposite.

Cocoon A sheath, usually of silk, formed by an insect larva as a chamber for pupation.

Cold frame A low structure with a translucent top, used for protecting plants from the weather and for hardening-off young seedlings.

Cole crops Members of the species *Brassica oleracea*, including cabbage, broccoli, cauliflower, and Brussels sprouts.

Collar 1) A band of material used as a mechanical barrier to protect a plant from damage by insects. 2) The swelling where a branch joins the trunk of a tree or another branch.

Collar region 1) In grasses, the region where the leaf blade and sheath meet; it is used in identifying species. 2) In trees, the area where the roots and the trunk are joined.

Colloid Very small organic and inorganic soil particles that carry a negative electric charge and are the primary reactive sites for cation exchange.

Compaction A state where soil particles are forced closely together, reducing pore space.

Companion planting The practice of interplanting different plant species to reduce pest problems or improve plant growth.

Compartmentalization The process by which plants wall off woody tissue against insect or decay-organism invasion by depositing tannins and phenolic compounds in injured wood.

Complete fertilizer A fertilizer that contains nitrogen, phosphorus, and potassium.

Complete flower Flower composed of a short axis or receptacle from which arise four sets of floral parts (i.e., sepals, petals, stamens, and pistils); a flower that contains both male and female parts.

Complete metamorphosis Changes in body form of insects that include egg, larva, pupa, and adult.

Compost The stable, earthy smelling end-product of aerobic animal and plant decomposition.

Compost tea A low-nutrient liquid fertilizer that results from placing a mesh bag of compost in water for 1 to 2 days.

Compound eye An eye composed of many individual elements, each of which is represented externally by a facet.

Compound leaf A single leaf with numerous leaflets. Ash, boxelder, and walnut display this characteristic. Double compound is when each leaflet is also made up of secondary leaflets.

Compound umbel A type of flower structure in which a series of simple umbels (a flower cluster with pedicels that are about equal in length; see Umbel) arise from the same point on the main axis.

Compressed Flattened from side to side.

Cone A reproductive structure of a conifer that has scales arranged spirally around an axis.

Conidiophore Specialized fungal hyphae on which conidia are produced.

Conidium (pl. conidia) A type of asexual fungal spore.

Conifer A cone-bearing tree.

Contact insecticide A poison that must contact the body of the insect to be effective.

Continuous pith The pith or inner spongy portion of twigs that contains no lines or division and appears solid.

Cool-season crop A crop that grows best during the cool temperatures of spring and fall.

Cool-season grasses Turfgrasses that thrive in northern areas, including Canada, and that grow actively during the cooler spring and fall weather. These include Kentucky bluegrass, the fescues, ryegrasses, and bentgrass.

Cordate leaf Heart-shaped leaf with a basal sinus. Example: catalpa.

Cordon Horizontal branches of a fruit plant trained along a trellis; also called arms.

Core aeration Increasing air penetration of the soil by removing plugs of soil, usually with a special, heavy machine.

Corm A short, fleshy, underground, upright stem in which food is stored. Gladiolus and crocus are cormous plants.

Cormel A small corm that forms around the parent corm; it can be removed and planted to propagate a new plant.

Cornicle Two tubular structures located on the posterior of an aphid's abdomen.

Corolla The petals of a flower, collectively.

Cortex Tissue between the phloem and the epidermis in roots and stems.

Corymb Type of raceme flower cluster in which the pedicels of the lower flowers are longer than the pedicels of the upper flowers, resulting in a flat-topped flower cluster.

Cotyledon The leaf or leaves of the embryo, also called seed leaf or first leaf. The "true leaves" are the larger leaves that emerge next.

Cover crop A crop that covers and improves the soil in which it is grown; usually grasses and legumes sown in late summer or fall.

Crawler The active first instar of a scale insect.

Crenate leaf margin A leaf margin with scalloped, rounded teeth. Example: cottonwood.

Crochets Tiny hooks on the prolegs of caterpillars.

Crop rotation Growing crops of a specific family in different areas of the garden each year to avoid diseases and nutrient depletion.

Cross-pollination The movement of pollen from one flower to another, either on the same plant, between different plants of the same cultivar, between plants of different cultivars, and sometimes between plants of different species.

Crotch angle The angle measured from the trunk of a tree to the upper surface of a branch.

Crown The part of a plant where the roots and stem meet, usually at soil level. Also used to refer to the shortened stem of a strawberry plant, from which roots, leaves, and fruit arise. On a tree, all the branches that hold the leaves are collectively called a crown.

Crown raising Removal of lower tree branches.

Crown reduction The removal of upper branches when the tree has become too tall.

Crown thinning The selective removal of branches to increase light penetration and air movement in the crown of a tree.

Culm The jointed stem of grasses.

Cultivar Cultivated variety; a selection from a wildtype of a species or from another cultivar; a result of human selection.

Cultivation Preparation of the soil for growing plants; tilling or hoeing soil to eliminate weeds.

Cultural control The use of gardening techniques to manage diseases and pests.

Curing Holding potato tubers or sweet potato roots under warm, humid conditions that favor wound healing.

Cuticle 1) Continuous layer of a structureless, waxy substance on leaves/fruit that protects the tissue against excess moisture loss. 2) The non-cellular outer layer of the body wall of an arthropod.

Cutin The waxy or varnish-like material that makes up the cuticle.

Cutting Detached vegetative plant part which, when placed under conditions favorable for regeneration, will develop into a complete plant with characteristics identical to the parent plant.

Cyme A broad, more-or-less flat-topped determinate (i.e., having a fixed number) flower structure in which the central flowers bloom first.

Cytokinins A class of plant hormones that stimulates cell divisions and delays senescence (e.g., benzyl adenine, zeatin, kinetin).

D

Damping-off A complex of water molds that attacks seedlings, causing them to wilt and die. These fungus-like pathogens—Phytophthora, Pythium, and Rhizoctonia—thrive in wet, humid conditions and are the causal agents.

Day-neutral plant A plant that will flower under any day length.

Days to maturity The number of days between planting and first harvest.

Deadhead To remove spent blossoms of herbaceous plants.

Deciduous Trees or shrubs that drop their leaves at the end of each growing season.

Decomposer (detritovore) An organism that breaks down (feeds on) organic matter.

Decurrent habit A plant form typical of angiosperm trees and shrubs, which are more round-headed and spreading, lacking a main leader to the top of the plant.

Decussate A situation where opposite leaves at any two consecutive nodes on a stem are oriented at 90-degree angles to one another.

Degree-day A unit combining temperature and time used in monitoring growth and development of organisms.

Dehiscent Possessing carpels (a simple pistil) that split along seams at maturity to release mature seed.

Dehydration An abnormal loss of fluids.

Delayed dormant In fruit tree crops, the period when buds begin to swell until the beginning of green tip development.

Deltoid leaf Triangle-shaped leaf. Example: cottonwood.

Dendrology The science of dating trees and assessing past climate conditions by studying growth rings of trees.

Denitrification Process by which nitrates or nitrites in the soil or organic deposits are reduced to lower oxides of nitrogen by bacterial action. The process results in the escape of nitrogen into the air.

Dentate Leaves having marginal, sharp teeth that are roughly perpendicular to the margin (leaf edge).

Desiccation Drying.

Determinate Growth that is limited; "self-topping" type of tomato plant having a terminal point that stops growing and sets fruit.

Detritus Dead plant and animal material.

Diameter at breast height (dbh) the diameter of a tree trunk at a height of 4.5 feet above the ground.

Diapause A period of physiologically controlled dormancy in insects.

Diaphragmed pith When the pith or inner spongy area of the twig contains visual lines (stripes) or divisions and the pith is continuous.

Dichotomous key An aid to plant identification in which each question has two possible answers. Each answer then leads to another question with the process continuing until the species is identified.

Dichotomous veined leaf A leaf with forking veins. Example: ginkilogramo.

Dicot (also dicotyledon) Flowering plants with embryos that have two cotyledons or seed leaves.

Dieback Progressive dying from the extremity of the plant or plant part.

Dioecious The condition of male and female flowers on separate plants. Example: holly.

Direct sow ("in situ") Sowing seed in the ground where the plant will grow to maturity.

Disbudding The removal of small, young, vegetative or flower buds.

Disease Any disturbance of a plant that interferes with its normal structure, function, or economic value.

Disease resistance The tendency not to be infected by a particular pathogen.

Disease tolerance The ability of a plant to continue growing without severe symptoms despite being infected by a pathogen.

Distal Near or toward the free end of an appendage; that part of a segment or appendage farthest from the body.

Diurnal Active during the daytime.

Dolomite A natural material used for liming soils in areas where both magnesium and calcium are needed. Made by grinding dolomitic limestone, which contains magnesium carbonate (MgCO) and calcium carbonate (CaCO).

Dominant gene A parental character that has the ability to express itself in the resulting hybrid offspring.

Dominant leader The tallest main trunk of the tree that is generally widest in diameter and from which other branches grow.

Dormancy A state of quiescence or inactivity.

Dormant Alive but in a state of suspended animation until all conditions are right for growth.

Dorsum The back or top (dorsal) side.

Double-dig Method of soil preparation used by bio-intensive gardeners. Requires removing the soil to the depth of one spade blade and then digging down an equal distance, and breaking up and mixing organic matter into the subsoil.

Doubly serrate leaf margin A leaf margin having teeth that are divided into smaller teeth.

Drainage The movement of water through the soil.

Drift The aerial dispersal of a substance, such as a pesticide, beyond the intended application area.

Drill A shallow furrow in which seeds are sown.

Drip irrigation A water-conserving irrigation system of plastic tubing with small holes that allows water to drip out, filter through the soil, and reach the root zone of plants.

Drip line A line encircling a tree corresponding to the furthest extent of its branches.

Drought A prolonged period of dryness that can cause damage to plants.

Drupe A one-seeded, fleshy fruit with the seed enclosed in a stony pit. Examples: cherry, plum.

Drupelet A small drupe, the unit making up the fruit. Examples: raspberry, blackberry.

Duff Partly decayed organic matter on the forest floor.

Dwarfing A stunting of normal growth characterized in plants by smaller than normal leaves and stems.

E

Economic threshold A level of pest population or damage at which the value of the crop damage exceeds the cost of the control action, such as a pesticide application.

Ecosystem The biological communities occupying a given habitat where energy is used, stored, and transferred. Examples: your garden, a woodlot.

Ectoparasite A parasite that lives on the exterior of its host.

Elbowed antenna An antenna having the first segment elongated and the remaining segments coming off the first segment at an angle.

Elliptical leaf Football-shaped leaf, usually more than twice as long as it is wide. Example: American beech.

Elytron (pl. elytra) A thickened, leathery or horny front wing present in beetles, earwigs, and some bugs.

Embryo A stem and root axis within a seed that may develop into a plant upon maturation and germination.

Endocarp The stony part of the pit containing the seed(s) of stone fruits.

Endoparasite A parasite that lives inside its host.

Endophyte 1) A plant living within another plant. 2) In turfgrasses, a fungus living within the grass plant secreting substances that repel insect pests.

Endoskeleton A skeleton or supporting structure on the inside of the body.

Endosperm Seed tissue surrounding the embryo. It contains stored food used by the embryo in the process of germination as an energy and protein source.

Entire leaf margin A smooth leaf margin without teeth; may or may not be lobed. Example: magnolia.

Entomophagous Feeding on insects.

Environment The complete surroundings of an organism.

Enzyme A protein substance produced by living cells that can change the rate of chemical reactions.

Epicormic branches Branches that develop from one of two types of buds after the stem is injured or energy reserves are reduced: 1) from dormant buds that develop when the twig is still small and move outward with the cambium as the diameter of the branch enlarges; or 2) from new buds that develop within the cambial zone as needed.

Epicotyl The part of an embryo or seedling above the attachment point of the cotyledon(s).

Epidermis The outermost layer of living cells on the surface of a plant or animal.

Epigynous Having floral parts that arise conjointly from above the ovary. Examples: apple and pear flowers.

Epiphyte A plant that usually grows on another plant and gets its nutrients from the air and water.

Erosion The gravitational loss of soil by the action of wind, water, and ice.

Espalier A plant trained to grow flat against a wall or trellis.

Ethylene A gas produced by plants that acts like a hormone (e.g., speeds aging).

Eutrophication Oxygen depletion of a water body as a result of excess nutrients feeding large algal blooms. Large amounts of oxygen are required by bacteria to decompose the algae when it dies.

Evapotranspiration The combined evaporation of water from soil, water, and plant surfaces; and the transpiration of water through the plant and out through leaf stomata.

Everbearing An imprecise term applied to some strawberry and bramble cultivars that implies the ability to flower and fruit for an extended period.

Evergreen plant Tree or shrub having needles or leaves that remain alive and on the tree through the winter and into the next growing season.

Exchangeable ion An ion held on the soil complex that may be replaced by other ions of like charge; called non-exchangeable if held so tightly that it cannot be exchanged.

Excurrent habit The cone-shaped form typical of many conifers and a few angiosperms having a clearly identified central leader and growing point at the top of the plant.

Exfoliating bark Bark that peels or is shed in plates or sheets from a branch or trunk.

Exocarp The outer layer of fruits derived from an ovary. Example: skin of a peach.

Exoskeleton A skeleton or supporting structure on the outside of the body.

Exposure The intensity, duration, and variation in sun, wind, and temperature that characterize any particular planting site.

Eye A collection of several buds on the surface of a potato tuber, one of which will sprout and form a new stem when conditions are favorable.

F

Fallow To allow cultivated land to lie idle to accumulate moisture and restore nutrients.

Family A taxonomic division of an order. Usually a family comprises two or more genera, but one genus possessing sufficiently distinctive characters may form a family.

Fanned compound See "palmately compound."

Fascicled Leaves grouped in small, tight bundles, as in the needle leaves of pines.

Feces Excrement, the waste material passed from the alimentary tract through the anus of an animal.

Feeder roots The youngest roots with root hairs, important in absorption of water and minerals.

Femur The third segment of a leg.

Fertilization 1) The union of the male cell with the egg. 2) The application of nutrients to the soil.

Fertilizer Any natural or manufactured material added to the soil in order to supply one or more plant nutrients.

Fertilizer burn The browning or wilting, and in extreme cases, killing of plants from exposure to excessive fertilizer salts on the leaves, stems, or roots.

Fertilizer grade An expression that indicates the weight percentage of plant nutrients in a fertilizer. A 10-20-10 grade contains 10 percent nitrogen (N), 20 percent phosphate (P_2O_5) and 10 percent potash (K_2O).

Fibrous root A root system with finely divided, thin, thread-like roots, often without a primary root.

Field capacity The moisture level in soil after saturation, gravitational drainage, and runoff.

Filament The part of the stamen that holds the anther in position for pollen dispersal.

Filiform Hair-like or thread-like, as in filiform antennae.

Fine fescues Fine-leaved turfgrasses that grow well in shade, low soil moisture, low-fertility and low-pH soil; includes red, hard, and chewing fescues.

Fissured A bark characteristic describing grooves and ridges. They may be fairly deep and sometimes look like cracks or splits.

Floating row cover Lightweight, gauzy, non-woven polyester fabric laid directly over a crop to accelerate growth and exclude pests.

Floret A small flower, usually one of a dense cluster.

Floricane Two-year-old cane on raspberries and blackberries that flowers and fruits, and then dies.

Flower A shoot of determinate growth with modified leaves that is supported by a short stem; the structure involved in the reproductive processes of plants that bear enclosed seeds in their fruits.

Flower bud A bud in which flower parts are contained.

Foliage Leaves in general, such as on a branch.

Foliar Applied to or affecting the foliage (i.e., foliar fertilizers, foliar nematodes).

Food chain A sequence of organisms in a community in which each chain member feeds on the member below it (e.g., fox, rabbit, and grass).

Force To manipulate environmental factors to make a plant blossom out of season or earlier than usual.

Frass Plant tissue mixed with excrement produced by boring insect larvae. It often resembles wet sawdust.

Frond The leaf of a fern or a palm.

Frost pocket A depression in the terrain into which cold air drains but cannot escape, thereby subjecting plants to freeze injury more frequently than surrounding areas.

Fruit An expanded and ripened ovary with attached and subtending reproductive structures.

Fruiting body In fungi, reproductive structures containing spores (pycnidium, acervulus, apothecium, cleistothecium).

Fruiting wood On fruit plants, the canes, shoots, and spurs that will produce the current year's fruit.

Full sun A site that receives at least six to eight hours of direct sun each day during the growing season.

Fungicide Chemical or physical agent that kills or inhibits the growth of fungi.

Fungus (pl. fungi) Saprophytic and parasitic organisms that lack chlorophyll and include rusts, mildews, smuts, mushrooms, and yeast.

Furrow A shallow trench made in garden soil for planting seeds or transplants.

G

Gall Localized swelling or outgrowth of plant tissue, often formed in response to the action of a pathogen or other pest.

Gaster The rounded part of the abdomen posterior to the node-like segment or segments in ants.

Gene The portion of the chromosome that transmits a characteristic from parents to progeny.

Genus (pl. genera) 1) Groups of closely related species clearly distinguished from other plants. 2) The first name of an organism in the binomial system of classification.

Germination The initiation of active growth by the embryo, resulting in the rupture of seed coverings and the emergence of a new seedling plant capable of independent existence.

Gibberellin A plant hormone involved in seed germination and cell elongation.

Girdle To damage or remove vascular tissue as in a canker that encircles a plant stem.

Girdling root A root that grows around the base of a tree rather than growing out and away from the tree.

Glabrous Having a smooth surface without hairs or projections.

Glaucous Covered with a whitish, waxy bloom. Examples: plum, blueberry.

Glume One of the pair of bracts at the base of a spikelet.

Glycoalkaloid A bitter-tasting compound present in potato foliage and in the epidermis of potato tubers.

GMO A genetically-modified organism.

Grade The degree and direction of slope on an area of ground.

Grafting The joining of two separate structures, such as a root and a stem or two stems, so that by tissue regeneration they form a union and grow as one plant.

Graft union Place where the rootstock joins the scion or top part of a grafted tree or vine.

Grasscycling The process of recycling grass clippings by leaving them on the lawn to decompose instead of collecting them.

Green manure A cover crop that is turned into the soil before it flowers to decay and enrich the soil.

Greensand A natural source of potassium containing about 7% potash plus trace elements.

Ground cover A plant, such as Allegheny spurge, used to cover the soil and form a continuous low mass of foliage. Often used as a substitute for turf grass, especially in shade, on embankments, or on other areas where turf grasses perform poorly or are difficult to maintain.

Growing point The tip of the plant's stem. It can be nipped to encourage the development of side shoots.

Growing season The period from the last spring freeze until the first freeze in the fall.

Growth regulator Any of several classes of natural or synthetic chemicals that regulate plant growth.

Grub Short, fat, worm-like larva, especially of beetles.

Guano The decomposed, dried excrement of birds and bats, used as a fertilizer.

Guard cell A specialized, crescent-shaped cell that controls the opening and closing of a stoma.

Gummosis A general disorder (nonspecific), particularly of stone fruits, in which exudation and deposit of gum occurs.

Gymnosperm A non-flowering plant that produces seeds that are not enclosed.

Gynoecious Species or cultivars that produce mostly female flowers.

Gypsum ($CaSO_4 \cdot 2H_2O$) The common name for calcium sulfate, a mineral used by gardeners and farmers as a source of calcium and sulfur.

H

Hardening The result of many changes that occur in a plant as it develops resistance to adverse conditions, especially cold.

Hardening off The process of gradually acclimatizing a plant that has been raised indoors to lower temperatures or more severe conditions, so that it is not severely checked when planted outside.

Hardiness The ability to withstand harsh environmental conditions.

Hardpan A hard, compacted layer of soil that cannot be penetrated and that restricts root penetration as well as movement of air and water.

Hardwood A tree or shrub with broad leaves (not needles or scales) that drop in the fall. Hardwood trees can also be called "broad-leafed" trees or "deciduous" trees.

Hardwood cutting A mature, woody piece of a woody plant that is removed to asexually propagate a new individual plant.

Hardy Term used in the Temperate Zone for plants that survive outside every year without protection.

Haustorium (pl. haustoria) A specialized outgrowth of stem, root, or hyphae of certain parasitic plants that serves to draw food from the host plant.

Head 1) An inflorescence in which small flowers all arise from a common receptacle, as in a sunflower. 2) The inflorescence of many grass plants, including small grains.

Heading back Also called stubbing, dehorning, or lopping. Main branches are cut back to stubs with little regard for their location. Re-growth from below the cuts is dense, vigorous, and upright.

Heartwood The older rings of xylem at the center of a tree that no longer function in transporting water, and are often dark in color due to the deposition of tannins and other compounds that prevent decay.

Heat unit Synonym for degree-day.

Heave To lift out of the soil, as a plant or stone, caused by alternating cycles of freezing and thawing, which can make the soil expand and contract.

Heavy metals The heavy metals of concern to gardeners are lead, zinc, chromium, arsenic, copper, and cadmium. These metals can be toxic to plants (and a potential risk to humans) when they accumulate to high levels in the soil.

Heeling in Covering the roots of a dormant plant with soil or mulch for short periods while awaiting planting in its permanent location.

Heirloom plants Cultivars of flowers, fruits, and vegetables that are open-pollinated, in use prior to 1945, and preserved by farmers and gardeners.

Hemelytron (pl. hemelytra) The front wing of true bugs (Hemiptera).

Herbaceous A non-woody plant.

Herbaceous perennial A plant with soft, succulent stems whose top is killed back by frost in many temperate and colder climates, but whose roots and crown remain alive and send out top growth when favorable growing conditions return.

Herbarium A collection of plant specimens that have been taxonomically classified, pressed, dried, and mounted for reference.

Herbicide An agent that stops plant growth or kills a plant.

Herbivore An organism that feeds on plants.

Hibernation Dormancy during the winter.

Hilling-up The process of pulling soil up and around stems to encourage rooting and protect plant parts from the sun. Examples: potato, leek.

Hilum Scar on the surface of a seed, marking the point of its attachment to the seed stalk.

Honeydew Sugary plant sap that is excreted by aphids and other juice-sucking, plant-feeding insects. It makes leaves shiny and sticky, and leads to the growth of sooty mold.

Hormone Organic compound directing growth and development in plants and animals.

Horny Thickened or hardened.

Horticultural oils Highly refined petroleum-based or seed-derived oils that are manufactured specifically to control pests on plants.

Host A plant that is invaded by a parasite and from which the parasite obtains its nutrition.

Hotbed A cold frame with soil heated by electric cables or decomposing animal manure. Used for growing seedlings and forcing vegetables early in the year.

Humus Long thought to be the end-state of organic matter decomposition in the soil. Current research suggests otherwise. Recalcitrant organic matter is protected from decomposition by soil aggregates.

Hybrid Plant or animal derived from a cross between genetically different parents. F_1 (first filial) hybrids are seeds harvested from the crossing of two pure inbred lines to produce plants with desirable traits, such as increased vigor, uniformity, and disease resistance.

Hyperparasite A parasite whose host is another parasite.

Hypha (pl. hyphae) Tubular filament or threads making up the mycelium of a fungus.

Hypocotyl The portion of an embryo or seedling between the cotyledons and the developing root tip.

Hypogynous Having stamens, petals, and sepals attached at the base of the ovary.

I

Immune Exempt from infection by a given pathogen.

Included bark Occurs at branch attachments when bark becomes embedded between the branch and stem. Included bark creates a weak branch attachment that is susceptible to breakage.

Incompatibility A state in which sex cells or graft components are not compatible.

Incomplete flower Flower lacking one or more of the four sets of floral parts.

Incomplete metamorphosis Gradual growth of an arthropod that involves change in size, but not form.

Incubation period The time between infection by a pathogen and the appearance of symptoms.

Indehiscent Type of dry fruit in which the fruit wall does not split at any certain point or seam at maturity.

Indeterminate Often used to describe a type of tomato plant with a vegetative, terminal growing-point that does not set fruit and continues to grow through the season.

Indexing Testing a plant for a virus infection, usually by grafting tissue from it onto an indicator plant.

Infection The stage when a pathogen is growing in a host and causing symptoms.

Inferior ovary Flower parts are attached at a site above the ovary.

Infestation The presence of a large number of pest organisms in an area or soil, on the surface of a host, or on anything that might contact a host.

Inflorescence The arrangement of the flowers on the floral axis; a flower cluster.

Inner bark In woody plants, the living part of the bark, the phloem.

Inoculant A microorganism that is introduced into the soil or applied to seeds to improve growth of legume crops.

Inoculation 1) The introduction of a pathogen to a host. 2) The process of coating legume seeds with a special bacteria enabling these plants to "fix" atmospheric nitrogen.

Inoculum Pathogen or pathogen part (e.g., spores, mycelium) that infects plants.

Inorganic Being or composed of matter other than plant and animal (carbon-based); often of mineral origin.

Instar The stage in the life of an arthropod between molts. These are usually numbered, such as "2nd instar."

Integrated pest management (IPM) A pest management strategy that focuses on long-term prevention or suppression of pest problems through a combination of techniques such as cultural, physical, biological, and chemical control practices; it involves monitoring pest populations and environmental conditions to develop an effective and integrated approach for preventing economic or aesthetic damage to crops.

Internode The area on a stem between nodes.

Interplant To grow two different intermixed crops to maximize space usage or manage pests.

Interstem (interstock) An intermediate stem piece that is grafted between the scion and the rootstock.

Invasive A species of plant, animal, or insect that is 1) alien to an ecosystem, and 2) whose introduction causes or is likely to cause economic or environmental harm or harm to human health.

Invertebrate An animal with no internal skeleton.

Ion An electrically charged particle. In soils, an ion refers to an electrically charged element or combination of elements.

J

Joint An articulation of two successive segments or parts.

Juglone A toxic, natural, chemical defense mechanism of certain trees (e.g., walnut, butternut) to reduce competition for resources.

June drop The final post-bloom shedding of fruits, especially peaches, often occurring in late May or June.

Juvenile The stage of a seedling plant in which floral initiation is not possible, often accompanied by leaf or stem morphology distinct from that of the adult or reproductive form of the plant.

K

Kelp Any of several species of seaweed harvested for use as a fertilizer or plant-growth activator.

Key An outline or shortcut for identifying a specimen by the process of elimination.

L

Lanceolate leaf Lance-shaped, tapering from a broad base to an apex, much longer than it is wide. Example: black willow.

Landscape This is "the lay of the land," which includes plants and other physical features such as lawn or meadow areas, waterways, pavement, utilities, and structures. Mistakenly used in many instances to refer only to plantings.

Landscape fabric A loosely intertwined fabric that is placed over the soil as a mulch to inhibit weed growth.

Larva (pl. larvae) The immature form of insects that develops through the process of complete metamorphosis, including egg, several larval stages, pupa, and adult. In mites, the first-stage immature is also called a larva.

Latent Producing no visible symptoms (often refers to an infection or a pathogen). Latent buds on plants are dormant and invisible.

Latent period 1) The time between when a vector acquires a pathogen and when the vector becomes able to transmit the pathogen to a new host. 2) The time between infection of a host plant and production of inoculum the infection.

Lateral A side shoot or branch coming off a main shoot or twig.

Lateral bud Buds found along the length of the twig, not at the tip. See "axillary bud."

Lateral meristem A tissue of meristematic cells responsible for secondary growth in woody plants.

Layering A method of propagation in which adventitious roots form before the new plant is severed from the parent plant.

Leaching The movement of salts, nutrients, and other materials in water through the soil profile or other growing medium. Leaching accounts for nutrient losses but can also be beneficial in ridding a soil or growing medium of excess salts.

Leaf The primary organ of photosynthesis in plants.

Leaf base The bottom of the leaf at the stem. The angle at which the leaf base joins the stem is helpful in tree identification.

Leaf-bud cutting A cutting consisting of a leaf blade, leaf stalk, and a short piece of the stem.

Leaf cutting: Entire leaf with or without the leaf stalks.

Leaflets Individual parts of a compound leaf which look like individual leaves but are not. The leaf starts where the woody twig tissue ends. Examples: ash, boxelder.

Leaf margin The outer edge of the leaf; leaf margins may be a variety of shapes, such as smooth, lobed, or indented.

Leaf miner An insect that lives in and feeds upon the leaf cells between the upper and lower surfaces of a leaf.

Leaf scar The mark left on a twig after the leaf drops in the fall. Each leaf scar has a particular pattern of "bundle scars," which is where the leaf vessels were connected to the twig.

Legume A dry fruit with two seams in the outer wall. Example: black locust. Also used to refer to plants in the family Fabaceae (Leguminosae).

Lenticels Small, corky spots on the surface of stems and roots made of loosely packed cells, providing gaseous exchange between the inner tissues and the atmosphere. Also, small bumps or spots on twigs that serve as "breathing" holes for the twigs.

Lepidopterous Of or pertaining to the Order *Lepidoptera*, the moths and butterflies.

Lesion Localized area of diseased or discolored tissue.

Ligule In many grasses, a short membranous projection on the inner side of the leaf blade at the junction where the leaf blade and leaf sheath meet.

Lime A white or grayish mineral compound (limestone) used to reduce soil acidity and to supply calcium for plant growth. Ground limestone (calcium carbonate), hydrated lime (calcium hydroxide), and burned lime (calcium oxide) are types of lime.

Linear leaf Long, narrow leaf with nearly parallel sides. Example: willow oak.

Loam The textural class name for soil having a moderate amount of sand, silt, and clay. Loam soils contain 7 to 27 percent clay, 28 to 50 percent silt, and less than 52 percent sand.

Lobed leaf margin A segmented leaf having pointed or rounded extensions separated by sinuses that do not extend more than halfway to the midrib. Example: oak.

Lobes Lobes are "fingers" or "peninsulas" that make an irregular leaf shape. Maples and oaks are best known for their lobed characteristic. The indentations between lobes are called "sinuses." Margins can be smooth or toothed.

Locule One of the seed chambers in the ovary.

Lodging When high winds push over tall, top heavy plants like corn or hollyhock.

Long-day plant A plant that requires a night shorter than its critical dark period (usually 12 hours or less) to flower.

Looper A caterpillar that moves by looping its body, that is, by placing the posterior part of the abdomen next to the thorax and then extending the anterior part of the body forward.

M

Macroclimate 30-year weather patterns that are independent of soils or topography (state and regional level). Example: Average spring and fall frost-dates.

Macronutrient A nutrient needed in large amounts by plants: oxygen, hydrogen, nitrogen, phosphorous, potassium, magnesium, calcium, and sulfur.

Maggot A legless larva without a well-developed head capsule. Example: true flies, Diptera.

Mandible Jaw; the forward-most pair of mouthparts of an insect.

Mature (plant) Able to produce flowers (reproduce); contrast with juvenile, which is unable to reproduce.

Maxilla One of the paired mouthpart structures immediately posterior to the mandibles.

Maxillary palp A small, feeler-like structure arising from the maxilla.

Membranous Like a membrane; thin and more-or-less transparent (wings); thin and pliable (cuticle).

Meristem A region of cell and tissue initiation (cambium or the tip of a growing shoot or root); cells that do not mature but remain capable of further growth and division.

Mesocarp The middle of three layers of the fruit wall.

Mesoclimate Climate at an intermediate geographical scale, such as that found near bodies of water, impervious surfaces, and topography (neighborhood and town/city level). Examples: heat islands in cities; dry, southern slopes.

Mesothorax The middle or second segment of the thorax.

Metamorphosis The changes of form insects go through in their life cycle, from egg to immature stages to adult.

Metatarsus The basal segment of the tarsus.

Metathorax The third or posterior segment of the thorax.

Microbe Microorganism; an organism of microscopic size.

Microbial pesticide Pesticide that consists of bacteria, fungi, viruses, or other microorganisms and is used for control of weeds, invertebrates, or plant pathogens. Example: *Bacillus thuringiensis* (Bt)

Microclimate Environmental conditions around a plant from two feet down in the soil to three to four times the height of the plant. Example: plants shading one another.

Micronutrient A nutrient needed in small amounts by plants; also called a trace or minor element.

Microorganism An organism of microscopic size, such as a bacterium, virus, fungus, viroid, or mycoplasma.

Micropropagation Generation of new, disease-free plants from tiny pieces of meristem tissue.

Midrib The central or main vein of a leaf.

Miticide A pesticide that kills mites.

Mollusk Invertebrate animal with a soft, unsegmented body, usually enclosed in a calcium carbonate shell. Examples: clams, snails.

Molting The process of shedding the exoskeleton.

Moniliform Antennae which are bead-like with rounded segments.

Monocot or monocotyledon Flowering plant that has an embryo with only one cotyledon.

Monoecious A plant that has separate male and female flowers on the same plant. Examples: pumpkin, walnut.

Morphology The study of structures in living things.

Mosaic Disease symptom characterized by foliage discoloration, with a more or less distinct intermingling of normal and light green or yellowish patches, usually caused by a virus.

Moss Small plant that does not produce flowers or seeds. It grows in moist, shaded areas where fertility is low.

Mottled Spots or blotches of different colors or shades of color interspersed with the dominant color.

Mulch A material applied to the surface of a soil to conserve moisture, stabilize soil temperature, suppress weed growth, protect plant roots from heat or cold, or keep fruit clean.

Multiple fruit Fruit formed by fusion of carpels from many flowers, plus stem axis and accessory tissues. Examples: mulberry, fig.

Mummy 1) Unharvested shriveled fruit (often resulting from disease). 2) The dried skin of an aphid whose inside has been consumed by the larvae of wasp parasitoids.

Mutation The abrupt appearance of a new, heritable characteristic as the result of a change in the genetic material of one individual cell.

Mycelial mat A macroscopic surface layer formed by fungi that produce hyphae, often used to identify the plant disease organism. In nature, it may form between the bark and wood of trees or over the surface of the plant tissue.

Mycelium (pl. mycelia) Mass of interwoven filaments or hyphae that make up the vegetative body of a fungus.

Mycoplasma Unlike viruses, mycoplasmas can reproduce in the absence of a host and are the smallest free-living organisms.

Mycorrhizae Beneficial associations between plant roots and soil fungi.

N

Naiad An aquatic, gill-breathing nymph.

Native A plant or animal that occurs naturally in a particular region and was not introduced from some other area.

Natural enemies Predators, parasites, or pathogens that are considered beneficial because they kill organisms normally considered to be pests.

Naturalized Species that is not native to an area, but has been introduced by humans and now widely reproduces. Example: Queen Anne's lace.

Natural selection The natural process in which individuals best suited to the environment are more likely to survive and reproduce.

Necrosis Death of tissue accompanied by dark brown discoloration, usually in a well-defined part of a plant (e.g., the portion of a leaf between leaf veins or the xylem or phloem in a stem or tuber).

Nectar guides A pattern in flower petals that points the way to the nectar, often seen only by insects sensitive to ultraviolet light.

Nectary A gland that secretes nectar.

Needle The narrow leaf of a conifer, adapted for cold and dry conditions.

Nematodes Microscopic, unsegmented, parasitic roundworms that live in water, soil, and plants; usually not visible to the naked eye.

Niche The functional role of a population in a community.

Nitrification The formation of nitrates and nitrites from ammonia (or ammonium compounds), as in soils by microorganisms.

Nitrogen fixation In soils, the conversion of free nitrogen from the air by soil microorganisms to nitrogen compounds that eventually become available to plants.

Node The point on a stem where a leaf or bud is attached.

Nodules Swellings on the roots of legumes where nitrogen-fixing bacteria live.

Nut A hard-shelled, dry fruit, sometimes with an outer covering or husk. Example: hickory.

Nutlet A small nut. Example: beech.

Nutrient Substance needed by an organism for growth and reproduction.

Nutrient cycle Path of a macronutrient such as nitrogen through the environment.

Nymph A stage or series of size changes between egg and adult in the life cycle of insects that go through incomplete or simple metamorphosis (e.g., aphids, grasshoppers).

O

Oblique leaf base A leaf base that is asymmetrical and unequally sided. Example: elm.

Oblong leaf The prefix (ob) means reverse or opposite. Long and wide leaf with nearly parallel sides. Example: persimmon.

Obovate leaf Upside down, egg shaped with the broadest part of the leaf near the tip. Example: black gum.

Ocellus (pl. ocelli) A simple eye of an insect or other arthropod.

Ocrea A papery sheath that encloses the stem at nodes.

Offset Plant produced at the base of the parent plant and easily detached from it.

Offshoots Short, horizontal stems that occur in whorls or near whorls at the crown of stems.

Open-pollinated Arising from natural pollination. Open-pollinated cultivars come true to type when seed is saved and replanted.

Opposite branching A branching pattern where side branches, leaves, and leaf scars grow from the stem directly across from each other. Examples: dogwood, viburnum.

Order A subdivision of class or subclass containing a group of related superfamilies or families.

Organ A group of tissues working together to perform a function.

Organic Of plant or animal origin; containing carbon compounds.

Organic matter Plant and animal residues, such as leaves, yard trimmings, and manure, in various stages of decomposition.

Organic soil A general term applied to a soil or to a soil horizon that consists primarily of organic matter, such as peat soils, muck soils, and peaty soil layers.

Outer bark In older trees, the dead part of the bark that protects living tissues such as the cambium.

Oval leaf Widest part of the leaf is in the center. Example: dogwood.

Ovary Swollen bottom part of the pistil that contains the ovules or immature seeds.

Ovate leaf Egg shaped with the broadest part of the leaf near the base. Example: Osage orange.

Overseeding Sowing seed over established turf.

Oviposit To lay or deposit eggs.

Ovipositor The egg-laying apparatus; the external genitalia of the female.

Ovule The portion of the ovary that contains the embryo sac and the egg cell, and which, after fertilization, develops into a seed.

Oxygen (O_2) A colorless, tasteless, odorless gas that is 1/5 of the volume of the atmosphere and shields the earth from UV radiation.

P

Palmate compound leaf A compound leaf with all the leaflets arising from one point at the end of the leaf stalk, named after the shape of a hand with the fingers spread wide. Example: buckeye.

Palmately veined leaf A leaf with veins radiating from a center point. Example: maple.

Panicle Type of flower cluster with a cluster with either racemes or corymbs (see definitions); distinctly branched.

Parallel venation Leaves with large veins that are essentially parallel to one another and are not connected by lateral veins.

Parasite, parasitoid An organism that lives on or in another living organism (called a host) and obtains its food supply from the host.

Parent material The unconsolidated mass of rock material (or peat) from which the soil profile develops.

Parthenocarpic Species or cultivar that produces fruits without pollination/fertilization.

Parthenogenesis Development of the egg without fertilization.

Pathogen A disease-causing organism.

Pedicel The stalk that directly supports a flower or fruit.

Pedipalps The second pair of appendages of an arachnid.

Peduncle The short, main supportive stem of the flower or fruit cluster.

Pelletized Covered in a substance that weathers away, as for very small seed, lime, or fertilizer, for ease and safety of distribution.

Pellicle The covering (skin) that encloses the kernel; it is white during development but becomes brown at maturity.

Pendulous Hanging or drooping. It can refer to plant form or parts, like branchlets or inflorescences.

Perennial A plant that does not die after flowering, but lives from year to year.

Perfect flower A flower that has both a pistil (or pistils) and stamens.

Perfoliate With the petiole appearing to run through the center of the leaf.

Perianth Structure consisting of sepals and petals.

Pericarp The fruit wall, consisting of three distinct layers: the exocarp, the mesocarp, and the endocarp.

Periderm A secondary protective tissue replacing the epidermis of woody plants; made up of cork, cork cambium, and phelloderm.

Perithecium (pl. perithecia) A flask-shaped or subglobose, thin-walled ascocarp (fungal fruiting body), containing asci and ascospores and having an ostiole (spore) at the apex, through which spores are expelled or otherwise released.

Pesticide Any substance or mixture intended for preventing, repelling, or killing insects, rodents, weeds, nematodes, fungi, or other pests.

Pesticide resistance The genetically-acquired ability of an organism to survive a pesticide application at doses that once killed most individuals of the same species.

Petals Structures collectively making the corolla, which protect the inner reproductive structures and often attract insects either by their color or their nectar, thereby facilitating pollination.

Petiole 1) The leafstalk that connects the blade(s) to the twig. 2) The narrow stalk or stem by which the abdomen is attached to the thorax (Hymenoptera, wasps). 3) In ants, the node-like first segment of the abdomen.

Petiolule In compound leaves, the attachment structure between a leaflet and the stem-like structure of the compound leaf (rachis).

pH A measure of acidity or alkalinity of a medium. A pH value of 7.0 indicates neutral; lower values indicate acid; and higher values indicate alkaline.

Phenotype A type or strain of organisms distinguishable from others by some characteristic, due to heredity or environment.

Phenoxy herbicides A group of herbicides derived from phenoxy-acetic acid; includes 2,4-D; dicamba, and MCPA.

Pheromone A substance secreted by an organism to affect the behavior or development of other members of the same species; sex pheromones that attract the opposite sex for mating are used in monitoring certain insects.

Phloem The vascular tissue responsible for the movement of starches and sugars from their site of manufacture (photosynthetic tissue) to the entire plant.

Photoperiodism Response of plants to the relative length of light and dark cycles.

Photosynthate The products of photosynthesis, used to support growth, respiration, and fruit production.

Photosynthesis The chemical process that green plants use to produce sugars (and oxygen) from carbon dioxide and water, thereby capturing solar energy for use in other chemical processes and tissue-building activities of the plant. Formula: $6\ CO_2 + 6\ H_2O \rightarrow$ Sugar $(C_6H_{12}O_6) + 6\ O_2$

Phototropism The bending of a plant toward the direction of more intense light.

Phylum (pl. phyla) One of the major divisions of the biological kingdoms.

Physiological disorder A disorder caused by factors other than a pathogen; an abiotic disorder.

Physiology The study of functions and processes in living things.

Phytochemical A chemical found in plants that provides human health benefits, including disease prevention.

Phytophagus Feeding on plants.

Phytoplasma Round-to-elongate organism similar to bacteria, but lacking cell walls; it invades the phloem and causes disease symptoms.

Phytotoxicity The ability of a material such as a pesticide, air pollutant, or fertilizer to cause injury to plants.

Pinching Manual removal of the growing tips of plants and the first set of leaves as a way to control plant size, to promote bushiness, and increase density.

Pinnately compound The arrangement of leaflets attached laterally along the rachis of a compound leaf. A leaf is "even" pinnately compound if the leaflets are in pairs with none left over (e.g., honeylocust), and "odd" pinnately compound if the leaflets are in pairs except one is left over (e.g., black walnut).

Pinnately veined leaf A leaf with veins similar in appearance to a feather. Example: beech.

Pioneer species A plant species that colonizes a disturbed habitat.

Pistil One carpel or a group of fused carpels.

Pith The center or inside of a twig, branch, or stem. The kind of wood in the pith often differs from the kind of wood around the outside. See also "chambered pith" and "continuous pith."

Plugs Young perennials or grasses used to cover large areas of beds or lawns; so-called because they are "plugged" into small holes drilled or dug into the soil.

Plumose Feather-like (e.g., plumose antennae).

Pollarding A pruning system in which the top of the tree or shrub is headed back severely when young, followed by annual removal of sprouts that arise from the cut area.

Pollen Dust-like male bodies capable of fertilization of ovules. Each pollen grain contains two cells: the vegetative cell from which the pollen tube develops, and the generative cell which produces sperm.

Pollenizer The producer of pollen or the cultivar used as a source of pollen for cross-pollination.

Pollination The transfer of pollen from the anther to the stigma.

Pollinator An insect or other source by which pollen is carried from one flower to another.

Polygamous Bearing both unisexual and perfect flowers on the same plant or different plants of the same species. Example: pawpaw.

Polymorphic Being able to assume different forms.

Polytunnel A structure covered with plastic films used for plant protection. Walk-in polytunnels (high tunnels) are approximately six to eight feet tall at the ridge; low polytunnels are rarely more than two feet high.

Pome fruit A simple fleshy fruit, the outer portion of which is formed by he floral parts that surround the ovary. Example: apple.

Post-emergent herbicide A pesticide that kills plants after they have grown to seedling stage or beyond.

Pot-bound Having a restricted and circular pattern of root growth, caused by a too-small container.

Potting medium (pl. media) Material used for growing plants in containers. It may include vermiculite, perlite, coir, sand, peat, compost, bark, or soil.

Predator Any animal (including insects and mites) that kills and feeds on other animals (prey).

Preemergent herbicide A pesticide that kills plants as they germinate.

Prepupa A quiescent stage between the larval period and the pupal period.

Pre-sprout To germinate seeds indoors, sometimes between moist paper towels, rolled up and placed inside a perforated plastic bag. The sprouts are planted in the garden after radicles develop.

Pricking out To transfer thickly-sown seedlings from the pot, pan, or seed tray in which they were sown into larger containers, giving them more space to develop.

Prill A coated form of water-soluble fertilizer, such as urea, that allows nutrients to be released slowly as the coating degrades. The timing of the breakdown is determined by coating type, thickness, and soil conditions.

Primary infection The first infection of a plant, usually in the spring, by a pathogen that has overwintered.

Primary inoculum The initial source of a pathogen that starts disease development in a given location.

Primocane New, first-year cane on raspberries and blackberries.

Proboscis The extended beak-like mouthparts of some insects.

Procumbent Having stems that trail along the surface.

Prognathous Having the head horizontal and the mouthparts projecting forward.

Proleg A fleshy, unsegmented leg of caterpillars.

Propagules Any part of a plant from which a new plant can grow, including seeds, bulbs, and rootstocks.

Protandry A state in which pollen is shed before the stigmas are receptive.

Protectant Agent, usually a chemical, applied to a plant surface in advance of a pathogen to prevent infection.

Prothorax The anterior of the three thoracic segments of an insect.

Protogyny A state in which stigmas are receptive before pollen is shed.

Protozoan Organism made up of a single cell or a group of basically identical cells.

Pubescent Covered with fine, soft, short hairs.

Pupa (pl. pupae) The non-feeding, inactive stage between larva and adult in insects with complete metamorphosis.

Puparium (pl. puparia) A case formed by the hardening of the next to last larval skin, in which the pupa is formed (true flies, Diptera).

Pupate To molt from the larval stage to the pupa.

Pustule Small, blister-like elevation of epidermis from which fungal spores emerge.

Pycnidium (pl. pycnidia) Small, spherical or flask-shaped structure formed by certain types of fungi, inside which spores are produced.

R

Raceme Type of flower cluster in which stalked flowers are on pedicels approximately equal in length on a single floral axis. Example: snapdragon.

Rachis The midrib of a compound leaf.

Radicle The part of a plant embryo that develops into the root system.

Raised bed A technique where the soil in the planting bed is elevated above ground level; it is often used where drainage is poor.

Rasping Mouthparts that are rough and used to scrape a surface on which to feed. Example: thrips.

Raster pattern Distinct pattern of hairs, spines, and bare spaces located on the underside of the abdomen of white grubs and used in the identification of the species.

Receptacle The apex of the flower stem that bears the organs of the flower.

Recurved Curved upward or backward.

Renewal pruning A technique for reviving old, overgrown shrubs by cutting them down to the ground in early spring. Peach, blueberry, grape, and currant, require renewal pruning to stimulate new fruiting canes/wood.

Renewal spur On grapevines, the cane pruned to one or two nodes on the cordon; it becomes the fruiting cane the following year.

Renovation Removing an old planting and putting in a new one or removing and replacing only part of a planting.

Reservoir The site where a pest population or quantity of inoculum can survive in the absence of a host crop, and from which a new crop may be invaded.

Residual activity The persistence of a pesticide and its ability to control pests or weeds for several weeks or months after application.

Resin Clear to translucent yellow or brown, solid or semi-solid, viscous substances of plant origin; used to defend plants from attack. Example: rosin.

Resistance The genetic ability to prevent or impede disease development.

Respiration The process where food is oxidized (burned) to release energy for cellular activity.

Rest A state of suspended growth or outwardly visible activity due to internal physiological factors; also referred to as physiological dormancy.

Resting spore Temporarily dormant spore, usually thick-walled, capable of surviving adverse environments.

Reticulate Net-like appearance; for example, referring to a leaf having veins that branch many times in a dense pattern.

Rhizome Horizontal underground stems that serve as storage organs and a means of vegetative reproduction. An underground stem, unlike a root, may have nodes, buds, and primitive leaves; and may give rise to new plantlets.

Rhizosphere Area of soil immediately surrounding roots.

Ring spot Disease symptom characterized by yellowish or necrotic rings enclosing green tissue, as with some plant diseases caused by viruses.

Root Vegetative plant part that anchors the plant, absorbs water and minerals in solution, and often stores food. It is distinguished from a rhizome by not having nodes.

Root flare In trees or shrubs, the point at which the roots meet the trunk; generally marked by a gradual curve of woody tissue that flares out from the base of the trunk into the major roots.

Root hairs Tubular outgrowths of surface cells of the root.

Rooting hormone A chemical that stimulates the growth of roots from the base of the cuttings it is applied to.

Root prune To cut back the roots of a plant to encourage them to develop more fibrous roots, reduce the root mass, limit growth, or stimulate flowering and fruiting.

Rootstock The plant onto which a scion or bud is grafted or budded.

Rosette A cluster of leaves arranged in a compact circular pattern, often at a shoot tip or on a shortened stem at the surface of the soil.

Rostrum Beak or snout.

Rot Softening, discoloration, and often disintegration of succulent plant tissue as a result of fungal or bacterial infection.

Rotation The practice of purposefully alternating crop species grown on the same plot of land.

Row-cover fabric A spun-bonded polyester fabric used to protect plants from pest damage or harsh climate, or to speed plant growth.

Rugose A rough appearance of leaves in which veins are sunken and interveinal tissue is raised. Could be a natural characteristic or caused by pests or pathogens.

Runner 1) A slender stolon with elongated internodes that grows vigorously across the ground. These root at the nodes that touch the ground (e.g., strawberries). 2) Stems (vine) of certain types of vegetable plants that grow vigorously across the ground (e.g., runner beans).

Russeting Thickening of the periderm on tubers of russet potato cultivars that occurs after vine senescence. Also seen on apple and pear fruits.

Rust A type of fungal disease that often gives a rusty appearance to the plant. Many rusts require two hosts to complete their life cycle. Example: Cedar-apple rust alternates between Eastern red cedar and apple.

S

Salts The soluble salts in soils are mostly combinations of the cations (positively charged ions) (e.g., sodium, calcium, magnesium, and potassium) and the anions (negatively charged ions) (e.g., bicarbonate, chloride, and sulfate). When dissolved in water, these compounds separate into their respective cations and anions. For example, calcium sulfate (gypsum) will separate into calcium cations and sulfate anions.

Samara An indehiscent dry fruit with either one or two seeds, in which the pericarp bears a flattened wing-like outgrowth. The "helicopters" of the maple trees are double-samaras. Ashes and elms also have samaras.

Sand Individual rock or mineral fragments in soils having diameters ranging from 0.05 millimeter to 2.0 millimeters. Usually, sand grains consist chiefly of quartz, but they may be of any mineral composition.

Sanitation Any activity that reduces the spread of pathogen inoculum, such as removal and destruction of infected plant parts or cleaning of tools and propagation supplies.

Saprophyte An organism that obtains nutrition from dead organic matter such as carrion, dung, or dead logs.

Sapwood Active xylem of a woody plant, often light in color.

Scab The generic name for several diseases that cause similar scab-like leaf symptoms.

Scaffold branches The primary boughs radiating from the trunk of a tree or the structural branches of vines that bear the fruiting branches.

Scales Modified leaves that protect structures.

Scaling A type of propagation that separates bulb scales from the mother bulb to induce the formation of bulblets.

Scalping Removing an excessive quantity of functioning, green leaves of turfgrasses at any one mowing; exposes crowns, stolons, dead leaves, and even bare soil, resulting in a shabby appearance.

Scarification The chemical (soaking in buttermilk) or physical treatment (rasping with file or sandpaper) given to some seeds to break or weaken the seed coat sufficiently for germination to occur.

Scavenger An animal that feeds on dead plants or animals, decaying materials, or animal wastes.

Scientific name An internationally recognized Latinized name of a species or subspecies. The scientific name of a species consists of the generic and specific names and the name of the describer of the species.

Scion The upper part of the union of a graft; the shoot portion of a rootstock-scion graft.

Sclerotium (pl. sclerotia) A compact mass of hardened mycelium that serves as a dormant stage in some fungi.

Scorch Leaf injury (leaf-tip and margin browning) due to insufficient water, excessive transpiration, contact with fertilizers or pesticides, or injury to the water-conducting system of the plant.

Secondary infection Infection by microorganisms that enter the host through an injury caused by previously by another pathogen, insect, or physical injury.

Secondary inoculum Inoculum produced after primary infection by a pathogen.

Secondary metabolites Chemical compounds that are not necessary for the growth and reproduction of a plant, but may protect against insect feeding or infections. The four major groups of secondary metabolites are the alkaloids, phenylpropanoids, flavonoids, and terpenoids.

Secondary outbreak The increase of a non-target pest to harmful levels following a pesticide application, caused by poisoning of natural enemies that normally control the non-target pest.

Secondary roots The network of fine roots that develops from the primary roots of a plant and that picks up water and nutrients from the soil.

Sedges A group of grass-like, herbaceous plants that differ from grasses by having unjointed, usually solid stems that are often triangular in cross section.

Seed Plant embryo with associated stored food encased in a protective seed coat.

Seed leaf The leaf formed in a seed and present on a seedling at germination; cotyledon.

Seed piece Portion of a potato tuber containing at least one eye that is planted to produce a new potato plant.

Segment A subdivision of the body or of an appendage, between joints or articulations.

Selective herbicide A pesticide that kills only one type of plant. Example: Broadleaf herbicides only kill broadleaf weeds, not turfgrasses.

Self-fertile (self-fruitful) Plants that set seed without cross-pollination.

Self-pollination The process by which pollen is transferred from the pollen-producing part of the plant to the pollen-receiving part of the same flower.

Self-sterile Unable to produce seed when self-pollinated.

Semi-aquatic Living in wet places or partially in water.

Semi-evergreen Having some deciduous leaves and some leaves that persist throughout the winter, with the degree of persistence determined by the harshness of the winter season.

Semi-hardwood cuttings Cuttings of new tip growth with partially matured wood, usually taken in early summer to propagate woody plants.

Senescence Natural process of decline and death of an entire plant or plant part.

Sepals Structures that usually form the outermost whorl of the flower; collectively, the calyx.

Septum (pl. septa) Cross-wall present in fungal mycelia.

Serrated (toothed) leaf margin A leaf margin that has pointed teeth that are directed upwards. Example: American basswood.

Sessile Without an obvious attachment structure, such as a leaf attached to a stem without an obvious petiole.

Seta (pl. setae) A bristle.

Sexual reproduction Production of new generations involving the exchange of chromosomes from both a male and female parent.

Sharp sand A coarse sand used in building.

Sheath The part of a grass leaf that encloses the stem below the collar region.

Shoot A stem that is one-year-old or less and possesses leaves.

Short-day plant A plant that requires a night longer than its critical dark period, usually 12 hours or more, to develop flowers.

Shrub A woody perennial plant. Different from a perennial herb or a tree in its size and general absence of a well-defined stem. Some species, however, can grow as trees or shrubs, depending on climate and site conditions.

Side-dress To apply fertilizer to the soil on the side(s) of growing plants to promote fruiting or more vigorous plant growth.

Sigmoid Shaped like an S.

Signs The visible parts or products of a pathogen, insect, or other pest, seen on the host that can be used to identify the pathogen or pest.

Silt (1) Individual mineral particles of soil that range in diameter between the upper size of clay, 0.002 mm, and the lower size of very fine sand, 0.05 mm. (2) Soil of the textural class silt containing 80 percent or more silt and less than 12 percent clay. (3) Sediments deposited from water in which the individual grains are approximately the size of silt, although the term is sometimes applied loosely to sediments containing considerable sand and clay.

Simple Unmodified, not complicated; not forked, toothed, branched, or divided.

Simple bud Bud containing either leaves or flowers, but not both.

Simple fruit Fruit developing from one carpel. Examples: acorn, bean.

Simple layering A method similar to tip layering, except that the stem behind the end of the branch is covered with soil and the tip remains above ground.

Sinus Leaf sinuses are the areas between lobes. Maples and oaks are typical examples of trees with "lobes" and "sinuses."

Skeletonize To remove leaf tissue between the veins, leaving the network of veins intact.

Slice seed A technique used to fill a thinning lawn by using a machine to sow seed; it slices grooves into the lawn or soil and drops seeds directly into the grooves.

Slow-release fertilizer A fertilizer that is made by coating the particles with a wax, clay, or other material to provide a predictable, slow release of the encapsulated nutrients.

Softwood cuttings Cuttings taken from soft, succulent, new spring growth of deciduous or evergreen species of woody plants to asexually propagate a new individual plant.

Soil The outer, weathered layer of the earth's crust that supports all life on the planet.

Soil block A cube of compressed soil (or growing medium) made with a blocking tool. A single seed or sometimes a group of seeds is sown in the block.

Soil buffer compounds The clay, organic matter, and compounds such as carbonates and phosphates that enable the soil to resist appreciable change in pH.

Soil conditioner Any material added to soil to improve its structure, tilth, or drainage.

Soilless mix Potting medium that contains a mixture of peat, vermiculite, perlite, coconut coir, compost, or other materials, but no mineral soil.

Soil permeability The quality of a soil that enables water or air to move through it.

Soil profile A vertical section of the soil extending through all its horizons.

Soil structure The arrangement of individual soil particles.

Soil texture The relative proportions of sand, silt, and clay of a mass of soil.

Solarization The practice of heating soil to levels lethal to pests and pathogens by tarping the soil surface with clear plastic for four to six weeks during sunny, warm weather.

Soluble salts Salts from fertilizers, manure, compost, and tap water that are dissolved in water.

Solvent A liquid that can dissolve a substance.

sp. (pl. spp.) Species (spp. used after a genus name refers to several species without naming them individually).

Species A group of individuals that look the same and can breed with each other but not usually with individuals of another species.

Specific epithet The descriptive second name of the binomial given to a species. Example: "rubrum" is the specific epithet of *Acer rubrum*.

Spike An inflorescence in which flowers are sessile and arranged on an unbranched axis. Example: liatris.

Spikelet Diminutive type of spike inflorescence found in grasses.

Spine 1) A sharp-pointed woody structure, usually a modified leaf or leaf part. 2) A thorn-like outgrowth of the insect's cuticle.

Spinneret A structure on an insect by which silk is spun, usually finger-like in shape.

Spiracle An external opening of the system of ducts, or tracheae, that serves as a respiratory system in insects.

Sporangium (pl. sporangia) A fungal structure in which asexual spores are produced.

Spore 1) The microscopic reproductive unit in fungi, ferns, and other lower plants; it is analogous to the seed of green plants. 2) A bacterial cell modified to survive an adverse environment.

Sport A variety or strain arising from bud mutation.

Spreader-sticker Substance added to pesticides to make them spread over and stick to a surface more readily.

Sprout (tree) Some trees reproduce by sprouting from dormant buds located around the root collar, near the ground. Sprouts that grow from dormant buds on the root system are called suckers.

Spur Compressed woody stem that is the primary fruiting structure for some fruit trees. Examples: apple, sweet cherry.

Stamen The male, pollen-bearing part of the flower consisting of the anther and the slender filament that holds it in position.

Staminate flower Flower in which only the stamens (male reproductive parts) are present.

Stele The central cylinder inside the cortex of the roots and stems of vascular plants which contains the vascular or conducting tissue.

Stem The main trunk of a plant that develops buds and shoots.

Sterigma A woody peg that holds evergreen needles.

Stigma The pollen-receiving site of the pistil.

Stipules Bumps or growths at the bottom of a leaf stalk, sometimes leafy-looking, common in members of the rose family.

Stolon An aboveground stem that reclines or becomes prostrate and may form roots where nodes contact with the ground. Called a "runner."

Stoma (pl. stomata) A pore in the epidermis of a leaf that is regulated by two guard cells and exchanges water vapor, CO_2, and O_2.

Storage root A root modified to store large amounts of water, carbohydrates, or starch. Example: carrot.

Strain A subgroup of a species; the descendants of a common ancestor.

Stratification Storing seeds at low temperatures under moist conditions in order to break dormancy.

Style 1) The slender part of a pistil between the stigma and the ovary. 2) A bristle-like projection at the apex of an antenna; a short, slender, finger-like projection.

Stylet A needle-like structure; one of the piercing structures in sucking mouthparts.

Subclass A major subdivision of a class, containing a group of related orders.

Suberin A waxy substance, resistant to microbial attack, formed in the corky cells of periderm layers.

Subfamily A major subdivision of a family, containing a group of related tribes or genera. Subfamily names end in -inae.

Subgenus (pl. subgenera) A major subdivision of a genus, containing a group of related species. Subgeneric names are capitalized, italicized, and placed in parentheses following the genus name.

Suborder A major subdivision of an order, containing a group of related superfamilies or families.

Subphylum (pl. subphyla) A major subdivision of a phylum, containing a group of related classes.

Subsoil Soil layers of varying consistencies found beneath the topsoil.

Subspecies A grouping within a species used to describe varieties isolated geographically.

Succulent 1) Having tender, new growth. 2) Composed primarily of thick, fleshy tissues that store water, such as cactus.

Sucker A shoot arising from the root or lower part of the plant stem. If suckers grow from stumps or around the bottom of the trunk, they are called stump sprouts. Common with species such as oak, elm, and birch.

Superfamily A group of closely related families. Superfamily names end in -oidea.

Superior ovary Flower parts are attached to the receptacle beneath the ovary. Example: squash.

Susceptible host An organism that can be infected by a pathogen.

Symbiont An organism living in symbiosis with another organism.

Symbiotic A relationship in which two or more dissimilar organisms live together in close association with a resulting mutual benefit.

Symptom Evidence of disease or damage. An unnatural change in plant growth or appearance.

Systemic Capable of moving throughout a plant or other organism, usually in the vascular system.

Systemic insecticide or fungicide Absorbed into the tissues of plants, thereby poisoning the organisms that feed on the plant.

T

Tall fescue A coarse, clump-forming turfgrass that tolerates low fertility, heavy wear, heat, and drought; and has good insect- and disease-tolerance.

Tannin A brown-colored defensive chemical found in plants; used to soften animal hides for use as leather.

Taproot A stout, tapering primary root that has limited side branching or fine roots.

Target pest The pest species at which a control action is directed.

Tarsus (pl. tarsi) The leg segment immediately beyond the tibia, consisting of one or more "segments" or subdivisions.

Taxonomy The science of naming and classifying species of plants and animals.

Teliospore Thick-walled, dark spore of rust and smut fungi that is able to survive adverse conditions.

Temperate fruit A fruit plant that requires a cool period (chilling hours) and is deciduous. Examples: apple, pear, peach.

Tender Plants that can be injured by cold or frost.

Tendril A slender, coiling, modified leaf or leaf part that helps plants climb.

Tensiometer A device for measuring soil moisture, consisting of a buried tube of water that develops a partial vacuum as surrounding soil dries out.

Terminal The growing tip of a stem, especially the main stem. Terminal buds are large, vigorous buds at the tips of stems.

Terrace A flat platform of soil on a slope.

Thatch An intertwined layer of dead and living roots, stems, and blades of grass plants that holds water, pesticides, and fertilizer like a sponge, preventing them from reaching the roots.

Thinning 1) Pulling or clipping the weak seedlings in a pot or row in order to leave the others room enough to develop. 2) Removing a branch or water sprout at the point where it joins a main stem, branch, or trunk.

Thorax The middle of the three major divisions of the arthropod body. The body region behind the head, which bears the legs and wings.

Thorn A short, sharp-pointed woody stem.

Tiller Aboveground sideshoot arising from the crown of some types of grass plants.

Tilth The physical condition of a soil (e.g., aggregation, porosity) and its ability to support seed germination and plant growth.

Tip layering Layering in which rooting takes place near the tip of the current season's shoot when it contacts soil naturally.

Tipping Cutting main stems or laterals between nodes to reduce plant size or induce branching.

Tissue A group of cells performing the same function.

Tissue culture The growing of masses of unorganized cells on agar or in liquid suspension; useful for the rapid asexual multiplication of plants.

Tolerance Capacity of a plant or crop to sustain disease or endure adverse environment without serious injury or loss of yield.

Toothed margin Leaf margin with variously sized and shaped "teeth" that help identify the species. "Single-toothed" means all teeth are about the same size and shape. "Double-toothed" means a fewer number of larger teeth with many smaller teeth that sometimes are in between the larger teeth. "Serrated" refers to a pattern resembling that of a hand saw.

Top dressing A fertilizer or soil amendment applied to the soil or surface; usually incorporated by raking or irrigating.

Topiary Training, cutting, and trimming of plants into ornamental shapes.

Topping The procedure of cutting off the top of a tree by cutting mature branches back severely. Usually not recommended.

Topsoil Uppermost layer of soil, usually darker and higher in nutrients than the subsoil.

Toxin A poisonous substance produced by a living organism.

Trachea A tube of the respiratory system, ending externally at the spiracle.

Translocation The movement of food or other materials from one part of a plant to another.

Translucent Allowing light to pass through, but not necessarily transparent.

Transpiration The process in which water vapor is lost through the leaves, pulling water up from the roots.

Trap crop A crop or portion of a crop intended to attract pests so they can be controlled by treating a relatively small area or by destroying the trap crop and the pests together.

Triploid An individual with three sets of chromosomes.

Trochanter The second segment of the leg in an insect, between the coxa and the femur.

True leaves The first leaves to emerge after the cotyledon(s) or "seed leaves."

Truncate leaf base or tip A leaf base or tip that is squared or abruptly cut off.

Trunk The main stem of a tree, shrub, or vine.

Tuber A short, thick, usually (but not always) subterranean stem or branch bearing buds or "eyes" and serving as a food-storage organ.

Tubercle A small knob-like or rounded protuberance.

Turgid The condition of a cell, tissue, or plant when it is filled with water so that it is swollen to firmness; not wilted.

Turgor The normal distention or rigidity of plant cells resulting from the pressure exerted from within against the cell walls by the cell contents.

Twig Small, thin terminal branch or stem.

Tympanum A vibrating membrane; an auditory membrane or eardrum.

Types Forms designated, when a species or group is described, to be the most representative or typical, to serve as the reference if there is any question about what that species or group includes. The type of a species or subspecies is a specimen; the type of a genus or subgenus is a species; and the type of a tribe, subfamily, family, or superfamily is a genus.

U

Umbel Type of flower cluster in which the pedicels arise from a common point and are about equal in length. Example: dill.

Understock The part of a plant to which a scion or bud is attached.

Understory Forest vegetation is arranged in layers from the ground to the top of the forest canopy. Sapling trees and shrubs constitute the understory portion of the forest.

Undulate leaf margin A leaf margin that is wavy. Example: witch hazel.

V

Variegated Plant parts having different pigments, resulting in foliage of more than one distinct color or shade.

Variety An identifiable strain within a species. Usually refers to a strain that arises in nature as opposed to a cultivar, which is specifically bred or selected for particular properties. Sometimes erroneously used in the place of "cultivar."

Vascular bundle A strand of the conducting system of a plant tissue containing xylem and phloem. See bundle trace.

Vascular system The system of plant tissues that conducts water, mineral nutrients, and products of photosynthesis through the plant, consisting of the xylem and phloem.

Vector An organism that transports and transmits a disease-causing pathogen.

Vegetable The edible portion of an herbaceous garden plant.

Vegetative Plant parts and processes concerning growth and nutrition but not reproduction.

Venation The pattern of veins.

Ventral Lower or underneath, pertaining to the underside of the body.

Véraison Beginning of fruit ripening, recognized by berry-softening and beginning of pigmentation in colored varieties.

Viability The ability of a seed to germinate, which diminishes with age.

Virulence The relative infectiousness of a bacteria or virus, or its ability to overcome the resistance of the host metabolism.

Virulent Pathogenic, capable of causing disease.

Virus A very small organism that can multiply only within living cells of other organisms and is capable of producing disease symptoms in some plants and animals.

Volatilization The evaporation or changing of a substance from liquid to vapor.

Volunteer crop The emergence of a stand of a self-seeded, previously-planted crop in a garden or field.

W

Warm-season crops Crops that are harmed by frost and do not grow well until average daily temperatures are in the 70s.

Warm-season grasses Grasses that grow best in southern regions, thriving in the heat of summer. Examples: Bermuda, zoysia.

Water sprout A vigorous, vertical shoot arising from the trunk or main branch of a tree.

Water table The upper surface of groundwater.

Weed 1) A plant growing where it is not wanted. 2) A plant that grows in a disturbed site.

Wet feet A condition where plants are exposed to excess soil moisture caused by flooding, a high water table, or compacted soil.

Whip A very young tree with a flexible trunk.

Whorl Leaves arranged three or more per node. Example: catalpa.

Wilt Loss of rigidity and drooping of plant parts caused by dry soil conditions or interference with water conduction inside the stems (e.g., boring insects, pathogens).

Wilting point The amount of water in a soil when a plant cannot obtain enough water to remain turgid.

Windowpane A symptom of insect feeding marked by the removal of all but the epidermal layer of leaf tissue, leaving small transparent areas.

Winter annual A plant that germinates at the end of the summer and overwinters as a small, dormant, but green plant. It usually completes its life cycle by late spring of the following year. Examples: henbit, hairy bittercress.

Witches' broom A dense, bushy growth of branches and foliage caused by a parasitic fungus, virus, mites, or poor pruning techniques.

Woody plant A plant having secondary (woody) growth due to a lateral meristem; trees and shrubs.

X

Xylem The principal strengthening and water and nutrient conducting tissue of branches, stems, and roots. The wood of woody plants.

Y

Yellows A type of disease, common among some flowers, that is caused by a virus or phytoplasma-like organism. This disease causes stunting and a yellowish appearance.

Z

Zonate Marked with zones or bands; belted or striped.

Zone of cell division The area of the root that contains meristematic tissue and is responsible for cell division.

Zone of elongation The area of the root where cells increase in size and length.

Zone of maturation The area of the root where cells differentiate into cell types and root hairs form from the epidermal cells.

Zoophagus Feeding on animals.

Zoospore Fungal spore with flagella, capable of locomotion in water.

Table 30-A. Measurement Conversions

Cu.=Cubic   cm=centimeters   Tbsp.=Tablespoons

Multiply:	x:	To convert to:	Multiply:	x:	To convert to:	Multiply:	x:	To convert to:
Bushels	8	Gallons	Cu. meters	1000	Liters	Liters	0.2642	Gallons
Bushels	1.24	Cu. feet	Cu. meters	2113	Pints (liquid)	Liters	2.113	Pints (liquid)
Bushels	4	Pecks	Cu. meters	1057	Quarts (liquid)	Liters	1.057	Quarts (liquid)
Bushels	0.04545	Cu. yards	Cu. yards	22	Bushels	Meters	100	Cm
Cm	0.3937	Inches	Cu. yards	27	Cu. feet	Meters	3.281	Feet
Cm	0.01	Meters	Cu. yards	46.656	Cu. inches	Meters	39.37	Inches
Cm	10	Millimeters	Cu. yards	0.7646	Cu. meters	Meters	0.001	Kilometer
Cu. cm	0.00003531	Cu. feet	Cu. yards	202.0	Gallons	Meters	1.094	Yards
Cu. cm	0.06102	Cu. inches	Cu. yards	764.6	Liters	Miles	5280	Feet
Cu. cm	0.00001	Cu. meters	Cu. yards	1616	Pints (liquid)	Miles	1.609	Km
Cu. cm	0.000001308	Cu. yards	Cu. yards	807.9	Quarts (liquid)	Miles	1760	Yards
Cu. cm	0.0002642	Gallons	Feet	30.48	Cm	Ounces	0.0625	Pounds
Cu. cm	0.001	Liters	Feet	12	Inches	Ounces	2	Tbsp. (liquid)
Cu. cm	0.002113	Pints (liquid)	Feet	0.3048	Meters	Ounces	6	Teaspoon (liquid)
Cu. cm	0.001057	Quarts (liquid)	Feet	1/3	Yards	Ounces	3	Tbsp. (dry)
Cu. feet	0.0002832	Cu. cm	Gallons	3785	Cu. cm	Ounces	9	Teaspoon (dry)
Cu. feet	1728	Cu. inches	Gallons	0.1337	Cu. feet	Ounces	28.349527	Gram
Cu. feet	0.02832	Cu. meters	Gallons	231	Cu. inches	Ounces (fluid)	1.805	Cu. inches
Cu. feet	0.03704	Cu. yards	Gallons	0.003785	Cu. meters	Ounces (fluid)	0.02957	Liters
Cu. feet	7.48052	Gallons (liquid)	Gallons	0.004951	Cu. yards	Pecks	0.25	Bushels
Cu. feet	28.32	Liters	Gallons	3.785	Liters	Pecks	2	Gal.
Cu. feet	59.84	Pints (liquid)	Gallons	8	Pints (liquid)	Pounds	16	Ounces
Cu. feet	29.92	Quarts (liquid)	Gallons	4	Quarts (liquid)	Pounds	453.5924	Grams
Cu. feet	0.8	Bushels	Gallons (water)	8.3453	Pounds (water)	Pounds (water)	0.01602	Cu. feet
Cu. inches	16.39	Cu. cm	Grams	0.01	Kilograms	Pounds (water)	27.68	Cu. inches
Cu. inches	0.0005787	Cu. feet	Grams	1000	Milligrams	Pounds (water)	0.1198	Gal.
Cu. inches	0.00001639	Cu. meters	Grams	0.03527	Ounces	Quarts (dry)	67.20	Cu. inches
Cu. inches	0.00002143	Cu. yards	Grams	0.002205	Pounds	Quarts (liquid)	47.75	Cu. inches
Cu. inches	0.004329	Gallons	Inches	2.540	Centimeters	Tbsp. (liquid)	0.5	Ounces
Cu. inches	0.01639	Liters	Kilograms	2.205	Pounds	Tbsp. (dry)	0.3333	Ounces
Cu. inches	0.03463	Pints (liquid)	Kilograms	1000	Grams	Tbsp.	3	Teaspoon
Cu. inches	0.01732	Quarts (liquid)	Kilometer	0.6214	Miles	Teaspoon (liquid)	0.1666	Ounces
Cu. meters	10000	Cu. cm	Liters	1000	Cu. cm	Teaspoon (dry)	0.1111	Ounces
Cu. meters	35.31	Cu. feet	Liters	0.03531	Cu. feet	Teaspoon	0.3333	Tablespoons
Cu. meters	61.023	Cu. inches	Liters	61.02	Cu. inches	Tons (metric)	1000	Kilograms
Cu. meters	1.308	Cu. yards	Liters	0.01	Cu. meters	Tons (metric)	2205	Pounds
Cu. meters	264.2	Gallons	Liters	0.001308	Cu. yards	Tons (short)	2000	Pounds

Freeze Dates and Hardiness Zones

Spring frost and freeze dates by zip code:

https://go.umd.edu/mdfreezedates

The likelihood of frost will vary between landscapes in the same town or even neighborhood, due to many factors such as changes in wind, elevation, proximity to buildings, and water.

Avoid the temptation to put tender annual plants in the ground too early. You might be eager to plant warm-season tomatoes, basil, peppers, and annual flowers that are set out early at the garden centers, but you take a gamble if you put them in the ground when it is too cold. Tender plant roots may not be able to absorb nutrients from cold wet soils, which will lead to poor growth later on. In most areas of Maryland, it is generally safe to plant tender annuals by the second week of May.

Interactive/predictive map of plant hardiness zones:

https://go.umd.edu/futurezones

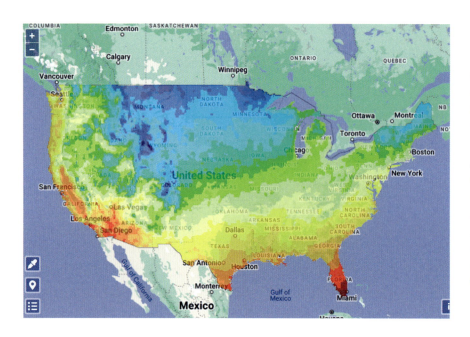

The data used to generate these maps are sourced from this publication of the U.S. Forest Service: Mathews, S.N., L.R. Iverson, M.P. Peters, and A.M. Prasad. 2018. Assessing potential climate change pressures across the conterminous United States: mapping plant hardiness zones, heat zones, growing degree days, and cumulative drought severity throughout this century.

LIST OF FIGURES

LIST OF FIGURES

3: ECOLOGY

Fig. 3-A.	The physiographic regions of Maryland	37
Fig. 3-B.	Elevation change: Friendsville-Ocean City	38
Fig. 3-C.	Average yearly air temp. across Maryland	38
Fig. 3-D.	Average yearly rainfall across Maryland	38
Fig. 3-E.	Stormwater infiltration and runoff	41
Fig. 3-F.	Forest fragmentation	42
Fig. 3-G.	Water gain/loss in plants and animals	44
Fig. 3-H.	The food web	53
Fig. 3-I.	The hydrologic cycle	54
Fig. 3-J.	The nitrogen cycle	55
Fig. 3-K.	Trapped debris	58
Fig. 3-L.	Standing water	58
Fig. 3-M.	Immature bald cypress	59
Fig. 3-N.	Fallen tree, diminished roots	59
Fig. 3-O.	Skunk cabbage	59
Fig. 3-P.	Beaver damage on tree	61

4: BASIC BOTANY

Fig. 4-A.	Monocot and dicot stems	68
Fig. 4-B.	Arrangement of leaves on stem	71
Fig. 4-C.	Leaf shapes	72
Fig. 4-D.	Leaf margins	72
Fig. 4-E.	Leaf bases (top) and tips	73
Fig. 4-F.	Simple and compound leaves	73
Fig. 4-G.	Root and shoot terminology	74
Fig. 4-H.	Meristems	74
Fig. 4-I.	Tap root (left) and fibrous root	75
Fig. 4-J.	Root anatomy	75
Fig. 4-K.	Modified stems	76
Fig. 4-L.	Tuber (left) and corm	77
Fig. 4-M.	Cross-section: woody dicot stem	77
Fig. 4-N.	Vein patterns in leaves	78
Fig. 4-O.	Attachment of leaves to stem	78
Fig. 4-P.	Stoma	79
Fig. 4-Q.	Cross-section of a bud	79
Fig. 4-R.	Flower anatomy	80
Fig. 4-S.	Flower symmetry	81
Fig. 4-T.	Position of the ovary	81
Fig. 4-U.	Inflorescences	82
Fig. 4-V.	Pollination and fertilization	82
Fig. 4-W.	Monocot vs. dicot seed cross-section	82
Fig. 4-X.	Pericarp of the peach	83
Fig. 4-Y.	Photosynthesis reaction	88

5: SOILS AND FERTILIZERS

Fig. 5-A.	Composition of topsoil when drained	96
Fig. 5-B.	The 12 soil textural classes	96
Fig. 5-C.	Continuum of organic matter in soil	97
Fig. 5-D.	The soil food web	98
Fig. 5-E.	Protected organic matter (PrOM) formation	99
Fig. 5-F.	The five soil-forming factors	102
Fig. 5-G.	Soil-forming processes	103
Fig. 5-H.	Example of a soil profile	104
Fig. 5-I.	Soil mosaic east/west of the Fall Line	105
Fig. 5-J.	The hydrologic cycle (soil perspective)	106
Fig. 5-K.	A simplified version of the N cycle	109
Fig. 5-L.	A simplified version of the P cycle	111
Fig. 5-M.	Positive effects of liming on the soil	113
Fig. 5-N.	Extractability of soil nutrients	114
Fig. 5-O.	Sample soil analysis report	115
Fig. 5-P.	Nutrient guarantee of a fertilizer	116
Fig. 5-Q.	The soil health paradigm	120
Fig. 5-R.	Cover crops mulching vegetable beds	121

6: PLANT NUTRITION

Fig. 6-A.	Liebig's Law of the Minimum	128

7: COMPOSTING

Fig. 7-A.	Simplified composting equation	142
Fig. 7-B.	The compost-pile food web	144
Fig. 7-C.	A three-bin compost setup	146
Fig. 7-D.	Typical compost tumbler	147
Fig. 7-E.	Trench composting	148
Fig. 7-F.	Vermicomposter	148
Fig. 7-G.	Pitchfork	150
Fig. 7-H.	Compost sifter	150
Fig. 7-I.	Figuring the application rate	154

8: INSECT BASICS

Fig. 8-A.	Dung beetle	158
Fig. 8-B.	Insect exoskeleton layers	159
Fig. 8-C.	Grasshopper structure: Head, thorax and abdomen	159
Fig. 8-D.	Insect head with chewing mouthparts	160
Fig. 8-E.	Mandible types	160
Fig. 8-F.	Modifications of insect mouthparts	161
Fig. 8-G.	Insect antennae types	162
Fig. 8-H.	Leg adaptations of selected insects	162
Fig. 8-I.	Insect wing types	163
Fig. 8-J.	Gradual vs. complete metamorphosis	164
Fig. 8-K.	Dragonfly and damselfly	164
Fig. 8-L.	Earwig	164
Fig. 8-M.	Grasshopper, katydid and cricket	165
Fig. 8-N.	Cockroach and termite	165
Fig. 8-O.	Praying mantis	166

Fig. 8-P.	Brown marmorated stink bug	166
Fig. 8-Q.	Cicada and leafhopper	167
Fig. 8-R.	Aphid	167
Fig. 8-S.	Thrip	167
Fig. 8-T.	Adult lacewing	168
Fig. 8-U.	Vine weevil and carrion beetle	168
Fig. 8-V.	Pipevine swallowtail butterfly	168
Fig. 8-W.	Promethea silkmoth	168
Fig. 8-X.	Black onion fly	169
Fig. 8-Y.	Insects from the order *Hymenoptera*	170
Fig. 8-Z.	Common landscape pests	170
Fig. 8-AA.	Pest caterpillars (maximum length)	171
Fig. 8-BB.	Common borers	172
Fig. 8-CC.	Stinging caterpillars	172
Fig. 8-DD.	Butterfly vs. sawfly larva	172
Fig. 8-EE.	Scarab beetles and larvae (grubs)	173
Fig. 8-FF.	Asian longhorned beetle/damage	173
Fig. 8-GG.	Metallic wood borer and damage	174
Fig. 8-HH.	Leaf beetles	174
Fig. 8-II.	Boxelder bug	175
Fig. 8-JJ.	Firebrat	175
Fig. 8-KK.	Flying ant vs. termite swarmer	175
Fig. 8-LL.	Flea	176
Fig. 8-MM.	Bedbug	176
Fig. 8-NN.	Carpenter bee	176
Fig. 8-OO.	Hornworm covered with wasp pupa	177
Fig. 8-PP.	Adult ladybird beetle and larva	178
Fig. 8-QQ.	Two-spotted stink bug	178
Fig. 8-RR.	Lacewing larva	178
Fig. 8-SS.	Flower fly	179
Fig. 8-TT.	Spider mite webbing	179
Fig. 8-UU.	Deer tick	180
Fig. 8-VV.	Garden spider	180
Fig. 8-WW.	Centipede (top) and millipede	180

9: PLANT DISEASE BASICS

Fig. 9-A.	Close-up of chestnut blight	188
Fig. 9-B.	Examples of disease symptoms	189
Fig. 9-C.	Examples of disease signs	189
Fig. 9-D.	Examples of plant disease causes	190
Fig. 9-E.	Plant disease triangle	191
Fig. 9-F.	Mushroom mycelium	191
Fig. 9-G.	Asexual / sexual fungi reproduction	192
Fig. 9-H.	Boxwood blight	194
Fig. 9-I.	Southern blight on delphinium	195
Fig. 9-J.	Volutella blight on pachysandra	195
Fig. 9-K.	Cedar apple rust on juniper and apple	196
Fig. 9-L.	Botryosphaeria canker on rhododendron	197
Fig. 9-M.	Ganoderma fungi	197
Fig. 9-N.	Powdery mildew on a squash plant	198

Fig. 9-O.	Powdery mildew on lilac	199
Fig. 9-P.	Bird's nest fungi on mulch	200
Fig. 9-Q.	Bacterial leaf scorch on maple and elm	201
Fig. 9-R.	Fire blight on apple tree	201
Fig. 9-S.	Aster yellows	202
Fig. 9-T.	Root knot nematode on a tomato plant	203
Fig. 9-U.	Common viral plant diseases	205
Fig. 9-V.	Dodder (cuscuta) on ground cover	207
Fig. 9-W.	Common diseases/disorders caused by environmental factors	208

10: INTEGRATED PEST MANAGEMENT (IPM)

Fig. 10-A.	Ladybird beetle (ladybug, lady beetle)	217
Fig. 10-B.	Lacewing life cycle	218
Fig. 10-C.	Syrphid (hover fly, flower fly)	218
Fig. 10-D.	Praying mantid	218
Fig. 10-E.	Ground beetle	218
Fig. 10-F.	Predatory mite	219
Fig. 10-G.	Other natural predators	219
Fig. 10-H.	Parasitic wasp and aphid host	219
Fig. 10-I.	Life cycle of a parasitic wasp	220
Fig. 10-J.	Parasitic nematode - borer host	220

11: PESTICIDE USE AND SAFETY

Fig. 11-A.	Sample pesticide label	231
Fig. 11-B.	Pesticide caution label	236
Fig. 11-C.	Phytotoxicity on cucumber leaf	239

12: PLANT DIAGNOSTICS

Fig. 12-A.	Normal vs. abnormal needle drop	245
Fig. 12-B.	Canopy loss and branch death	246
Fig. 12-C.	Leaf damage pattern - chemical injury	246
Fig. 12-D.	Shoot dieback	246
Fig. 12-E.	Heat damage (l) and frost damage (r)	248
Fig. 12-F.	Plants affected by chemical factors	249
Fig. 12-G	Fungal disease	251
Fig. 12-H.	Bacterial disease	251
Fig. 12-I.	Viral disease	251
Fig. 12-J.	Chewing damage (sawfly)	252
Fig. 12-K.	Sucking insect damage (mealybug)	252

13: WEEDS

Fig. 13-A.	Plant succession (section elevation)	348
Fig. 13-B.	Life cycle of annual weeds	349
Fig. 13-C.	Life cycle of perennial and biennial weeds	350
Fig. 13-D.	Adaptations that aid weed seed dispersal	351
Fig. 13-E.	Shallow cultivation	368
Fig. 13-F.	Systemic herbicide translocation	372
Fig. 13-G.	Residual barrier	373

14: LAWNS

- Fig. 14-A. Parts of a grass plant ... 381
- Fig. 14-B. Leaf blade shapes and textures ... 382
- Fig. 14-C. Leaf sheath types ... 382
- Fig. 14-D. Vernation types ... 382
- Fig. 14-E. Collar types ... 382
- Fig. 14-F. Ligule types ... 382
- Fig. 14-G. Auricle types ... 383
- Fig. 14-H. Grass growth habit ... 383
- Fig. 14-I. Tall fescue ... 384
- Fig. 14-J. Fine fescue ... 384
- Fig. 14-K. Kentucky bluegrass ... 385
- Fig. 14-L. Perennial ryegrass ... 386
- Fig. 14-M. Bermudagrass ... 386
- Fig. 14-N. Zoysiagrass ... 387
- Fig. 14 O. Lawn alternative planting guide ... 414

15: HERBACEOUS PLANTS

- Fig. 15-A. Leggy vs. stocky annual ... 428
- Fig. 15-B. Types of underground stems ... 432
- Fig. 15-C. Corm with cormlets ... 436
- Fig. 15-D. Perennials that may bloom again after deadheading ... 441
- Fig. 15-E. Properly-spaced iris vs. overgrown clump ... 444
- Fig. 15-F. Dahlia garden completely from cuttings ... 444

16: WOODY PLANTS

- Fig. 16-A. Types of woody planting stock ... 459
- Fig. 16-B. Typical tree root system (in good soil) ... 461
- Fig. 16-C. Island bed ... 462
- Fig. 16-D. Planting bare-root stock (rose) ... 463
- Fig. 16-E. Balled and burlapped (B&B) ... 463
- Fig. 16-F. Container-grown plant preparation ... 464
- Fig. 16-G. Staking and guying a new tree ... 465
- Fig. 16-H. Root pruning ... 469

17: PRUNING

- Fig. 17-A. Twig pruning ... 490
- Fig. 17-B. Reasons to prune ... 491
- Fig. 17-C. Heading cuts ... 495
- Fig. 17-D. Thinning cuts ... 495
- Fig. 17-E. Cuts and collars ... 496
- Fig. 17-F. Pruning cuts ... 496
- Fig. 17-G. Crotches ... 500
- Fig. 17-H. Crown thinning, crown raising, and crown reduction ... 501
- Fig. 17-I. Topping and tipping ... 501
- Fig. 17-J. Leader replacement ... 502
- Fig. 17-K. Pruning a young hedge ... 503
- Fig. 17-L. Pruning a mature hedge ... 503
- Fig. 17-M. Pine candle pinching ... 504

18: VEGETABLES

- Fig. 18-A. USDA organic logo ... 513
- Fig. 18-B. Light requirements for vegetables ... 518
- Fig. 18-C. Sample succession planting plan ... 531
- Fig. 18-D. Transplant tips ... 538
- Fig. 18-E. Proper cultivation depth ... 545
- Fig. 18-F. Common season extenders ... 547
- Fig. 18-G. Drying herbs ... 551

19: SMALL FRUITS

- Fig. 19-A. Pruning a four-year-old blueberry bush ... 585
- Fig. 19-B. Simple trellis design for brambles ... 588
- Fig. 19-C. Purple/black raspberries: summer pruning ... 588
- Fig. 19-D. Red raspberry: dormant-season pruning ... 588
- Fig. 19-E. Erect blackberries: summer pruning ... 588
- Fig. 19-F. Training grapes on a two-arm support system ... 593
- Fig. 19-G. Hardy kiwi vs. grocery-store kiwi ... 594
- Fig. 19-H. Strawberry planting depth ... 597
- Fig. 19-I. Matted row system ... 597

20: TREE FRUITS

- Fig. 20-A. Parts of a fruit tree ... 611
- Fig. 20-B. Fruit and nut tree bud development ... 614
- Fig. 20-C. Fruit-tree pruning terminology ... 615
- Fig. 20-D. Pruning a one-year-old apple tree ... 620
- Fig. 20-E. Pruning a two-year-old apple tree ... 620
- Fig. 20-F. Pruning an old, neglected apple tree ... 621
- Fig. 20-G. Pruning a one-year-old peach tree ... 625
- Fig. 20-H. Pruning a two-year-old peach tree ... 625

21: NATIVE PLANTS

- Fig. 21-A. Physiographic map of Maryland's three main ecoregions ... 638

23: INDOOR PLANTS

- Fig. 23-A. Indoor Plant Light Guide ... 670
- Fig. 23-B. Water plants from the bottom up ... 672
- Fig. 23-C. Repotting a plant with encircling roots ... 675

24: PLANT PROPAGATION

- Fig. 24-A. Typical seed-packet information ... 686
- Fig. 24-B. Stem-cutting propagation ... 699
- Fig. 24-C. Leaf-cutting propagation ... 700
- Fig. 24-D. Root-cutting propagation ... 701
- Fig. 24-E. Propagation by layering ... 702
- Fig. 24-F. Air-layering a houseplant ... 703
- Fig. 24-G. Corm separation and rhizome division ... 704
- Fig. 24-H. Cleft grafting ... 705
- Fig. 24-I. Bark grafting ... 706
- Fig. 24-J. Whip grafting ... 706

Fig. 24-K. Chip budding 707
Fig. 24-L. T-budding 707

25: CONTAINER GARDENING

Fig. 25-A. Balcony garden 711
Fig. 25-B. Raised-bed garden 712
Fig. 25-C. Vining plant in a container 714
Fig. 25-D. Double-potting 716
Fig. 25-E. Repurposed containers 717
Fig. 25-F. Growing media for container gardening 719
Fig. 25-G. Root-bound plant that needs repotting 720
Fig. 25-H. Standing water in plant saucers 721
Fig. 25-I. Add slow-release fertilizer to potting mix 722
Fig. 25-J. Protect containers from freezing 723

26: LANDSCAPE DESIGN

Fig. 26-A. The gardens of Versailles 731
Fig. 26-B. Plat plan 733
Fig. 26-C. A sample blob design 734
Fig. 26-D. Design with no overhead enclosure 735
Fig. 26-E. Design with an implied enclosure 735
Fig. 26-F. The "golden rectangle" concept 736
Fig. 26-G. Informal/curved lines 737
Fig. 26-H. Formal/straight lines 737
Fig. 26-I. Proper scale of tree to house 739
Fig. 26-J. Symmetrical balance vs. asymmetrical 739
Fig. 26-K. Draft design layout (refined blob design) 739
Fig. 26-L. Perspective drawing 740
Fig. 26-M. Final landscape design 741

27: WILDLIFE AND WOODLANDS

Fig. 27-A. Pollinators sharing milkweed nectar 747
Fig. 27-B. Three land parcels with different uses 749
Fig. 27-C. Growing season vs. dormant season 750
Fig. 27-D. Sample habitat-unit property map 750
Fig. 27-E. Ivy overtaking a tree 752
Fig. 27-F. Soft-edge vs. hard-edge patches 753
Fig. 27-G. Habitat-patch positioning 753
Fig. 27-H. Make your landscape "firewise" 754
Fig. 27-I. Plastic trunk guards vs. mesh 756
Fig. 27-J. Riparian buffer 757
Fig. 27-K Chosen-tree management 757
Fig. 27-L. Create a privacy screen with conifers 759
Fig. 27-M. Trails make it easy to monitor property 759
Fig. 27-N. Integrated Vegetation Management (IVM) . . . 760
Fig. 27-O. Backpack sprayer 763
Fig. 27-P. Hack-and-squirt method 763
Fig. 27-Q. Landscape succession: wildlife 770
Fig. 27-R. Crow 778
Fig. 27-S. Pigeon 778

Fig. 27-T. Yellow-bellied sapsucker 779
Fig. 27-U. Bat 780
Fig. 27-V. Cat and dog 781
Fig. 27-W. Deer 782
Fig. 27-X. Wildlife Damage Management (WDM) 783
Fig. 27-Y. House mouse 784
Fig. 27-Z. Rat 785
Fig. 27-AA. Mole 786
Fig. 27-BB. Vole 786
Fig. 27-CC. Rabbit 787
Fig. 27-DD. Raccoon 788
Fig. 27-EE. Skunk 789
Fig. 27-FF. Gray squirrel 790
Fig. 27-GG. Chipmunk 790
Fig. 27-HH. Groundhog 791
Fig. 27-II. Poisonous Maryland snakes 792

28: CONSERVATION LANDSCAPING

Fig. 28-A. "BayScaping" instead of expansive turf 797
Fig. 28-B. Bay-Wise program sign 798
Fig. 28-C. Soaker hose layout 799
Fig. 28-D. Correct mowing height (right) 800
Fig. 28-E. Correct mulch placement (right) 800
Fig. 28-F. Infiltration and runoff 802
Fig. 28-G. Confined and unconfined aquifers 804
Fig. 28-H. Algal bloom from fertilizer runoff 805
Fig. 28-I. Rain barrel with downspout diverter 807
Fig. 28-J. Avoid overhead watering 808
Fig. 28-K. A barrier garden to prevent runoff 810
Fig. 28-L. A rain garden to catch runoff 810
Fig. 28-M. Soil erosion in neighborhood 811

29: GARDEN TOOLS AND EQUIPMENT

Fig. 29-A. Invest in high-quality tools 815
Fig. 29-B. Ergonomic cultivator (left) vs. standard 817
Fig. 29-C. T (pistol)-grip (left) and D-grip snap-ons 817
Fig. 29-D. Left-handed pruners 818
Fig. 29-E. Pruner types 818
Fig. 29-F. Lopper types 819
Fig. 29-G. Pruning saw types 820
Fig. 29-H. Hedge shears/trimmer 820
Fig. 29-I. Shovel, spade, and fork types 821
Fig. 29-J. Hoe/cultivator types 822
Fig. 29-K. Rake head types 823
Fig. 29-L. Mower types 826
Fig. 29-M. Choose the right tiller 827
Fig. 29-N. Tiller types 828
Fig. 29-O. String trimmer types 829
Fig. 29-P. Leaf-blower types 830
Fig. 29-Q. Edger types 831

Fig. 29-R.   Chipper-shredder 832
Fig. 29-S.   Wheelbarrow and cart types 834
Fig. 29-T.   Trellis types 835
Fig. 29-U.   Cage types 837
Fig. 29-V.   Stake types 837
Fig. 29-W. Hose types 838
Fig. 29-X.   Nozzle types 839
Fig. 29-Y.   Sprinkler types 840
Fig. 29-Z.   Watering can types 841
Fig. 29-AA. Sprayer types 841
Fig. 29-BB. Composting tools 843
Fig. 29-CC. Composting tumbler types 844
Fig. 29-DD. Garden glove types 845
Fig. 29-EE. Kneelers and knee-pad types 845
Fig. 29-FF. Bulb-planter types 846

LIST OF TABLES

LIST OF TABLES

3: ECOLOGY
Tab. 3-A. Food/shelter requirements for common native pollinators 46
Tab. 3-B. Typical early and late successional species in Maryland 47

4: BASIC BOTANY
Tab. 4-A. Differences between monocots and dicots ... 68
Tab. 4-B. Same plants—different common names 69
Tab. 4-C. Different plants—same common name 69
Tab. 4-D. Classification of tomato/purple coneflower .. 70
Tab. 4-E. Plants categorized by lifespan 88
Tab. 4-F. Wild cabbage/mustard by selection 89
Tab. 4-G. Major categories of transgenic plants 90
Tab. 4-H. Issues relating to transgenic plants 90

5: SOILS AND FERTILIZERS
Tab. 5-A. Major mineral classes in a soil 96
Tab. 5-B. Effect of soil texture on soil properties 97
Tab. 5-C. Adverse conditions due to soil acidity 101
Tab. 5-D. Atmospheric and soil-air gases after rain.... 101
Tab. 5-E. The four soil-forming processes 104
Tab. 5-F. Important hydrologic cycle processes 107
Tab. 5-G. Textural class, clay content, and CEC 108
Tab. 5-H. Processes in the nitrogen cycle............. 110
Tab. 5-I. Processes in the phosphorus cycle 112
Tab. 5-J. Common liming materials 113
Tab. 5-K. Likelihood of improved plant growth 114
Tab. 5-L. Nutrient guarantee of synthetic fertilizers .. 117
Tab. 5-M. Nutrient guarantee of organic fertilizers 118
Tab. 5-N. Pros and cons of nutrient sources 119
Tab. 5-O. Features of cool-season cover crops 120

6: PLANT NUTRITION
Tab. 6-A. Terms to remember 129
Tab. 6-B. Macronutrients and micronutrients 137

7: COMPOSTING
Tab. 7-A. Compost measurement conversions 145
Tab. 7-B. Composting system comparison 149
Tab. 7-C. C:N ratios of common ingredients 150
Tab. 7-D. What (and what not) to compost 151
Tab. 7-E. Troubleshooting compost issues 153

8: INSECT BASICS
Tab. 8-A. Examples of arthropod classes 157
Tab. 8-B. Examples of insect-flower pollination 177
Tab. 8-C. Insect characteristics by order 182

10: INTEGRATED PEST MANAGEMENT (IPM)
Tab. 10-A. Plants with flowers that attract/feed beneficial insects 221

11: PESTICIDE USE AND SAFETY
Tab. 11-A. Common pesticide formulations 229
Tab. 11-B. "Signal words" on a pesticide label 230
Tab. 11-C. Terminology: pesticide application 235

13: WEEDS
Tab. 13-A. Production of weed seeds per plant 350
Tab. 13-B. Longevity of buried weed seeds 350
Tab. 13-C. Common lawn and garden weeds 352
Tab. 13-D. Vegetative identification of weedy grasses .. 364

14: LAWNS
Tab. 14-A. Characteristics of turfgrass species 387
Tab. 14-B. Seed rate for new and established lawns ... 389
Tab. 14-C. Sod vs. seed comparison 391
Tab. 14-D. Starter vs. slow-release fertilizer content ... 395
Tab. 14-E. Low-input turf fertilizer recommendation... 397
Tab. 14-F. Optional turf fertilizer application 397
Tab. 14-G. Mowing-height guide...................... 398
Tab. 14-H. Common lawn weeds 404
Tab. 14-I. Moss causes and controls.................. 405
Tab. 14-J. Lawn insect identification and control...... 406
Tab. 14-K. Insect-caused turf problems (by symptom) 408
Tab. 14-L. Common turf diseases..................... 409
Tab. 14-M. Disease-caused turf problems (by symptom) 409
Tab. 14-N. Abiotic turf problems (by symptom) 412

15: HERBACEOUS PLANTS
Tab. 15-A. Planting guide for flowering bulbs 433
Tab. 15-B. Traits of flowering-plant pollinators 438
Tab. 15-C. Perennial bloom times (by season) 445
Tab. 15-D. Perennial planning and planting guide 446
Tab. 15-E. Annuals for specific environments 450
Tab. 15-F. Perennials for specific environments 451
Tab. 15-G. Herbaceous plants for drying 452
Tab. 15-H. Herbaceous plants with foliage interest..... 453

16: WOODY PLANTS
Tab. 16-A. Trees that develop surface roots 472
Tab. 16-B. Problematic trees and shrubs 474
Tab. 16-C. Medium-to-large shade trees (>30')........ 475
Tab. 16-D. Small shade trees (<30') 475

Tab. 16-E.	Medium-to-large flowering trees (>30')	476
Tab. 16-F.	Small flowering trees (<30')	476
Tab. 16-G.	Flowering shrubs	476
Tab. 16-H.	Trees with attractive bark	477
Tab. 16-I.	Trees and shrubs with attractive fall color	477
Tab. 16-J.	Plants with attractive fruits	478
Tab. 16-K.	Barrier plants	478
Tab. 16-L.	Plants that tolerate poor, dry soil	479
Tab. 16-M.	Plants that tolerate shade	479
Tab. 16-N.	Plants that tolerate salt air	480
Tab. 16-O.	Plants that serve as windbreaks	481
Tab. 16-P.	Trees for urban conditions	481
Tab. 16-Q.	Recommended vines for Maryland	483
Tab. 16-R.	Recommended groundcovers for Maryland	485

17: PRUNING

Tab. 17-A.	Pruning guidelines for specific plants	506

18: VEGETABLES

Tab. 18-A.	Cover crops for vegetable gardens	524
Tab. 18-B.	Vegetable crop pollination (by family)	526
Tab. 18-C.	Vegetable families grown in the mid-Atlantic	527
Tab. 18-D.	Common herbs for teas, crafts, medicinal, and other uses	553
Tab. 18-E.	Common culinary herbs	554
Tab. 18-F.	Poisonous herbs	555

19: SMALL FRUITS

Tab. 19-A.	Characteristics of small-fruit plants	580
Tab. 19-B.	Fertilizer guidelines for small fruits	581
Tab. 19-C.	Pruning guide for established brambles	589
Tab. 19-D.	Recommended small-fruit cultivars for Maryland	598

20: TREE FRUITS

Tab. 20-A.	Fruit tree bearing age, height, and pollination requirements	610
Tab. 20-B.	Apple and pear tree rootstocks	617
Tab. 20-C.	Recommended tree-fruit cultivars for MD	629

21: NATIVE PLANTS

Tab. 21-A.	Recommended Native Plants for MD	641

22: INVASIVE PLANTS

Tab. 22-A.	Invasive Species: Non-Plant	649
Tab. 22-B.	Common Invasive Trees	656
Tab. 22-C.	Common Invasive Shrubs	658
Tab. 22-D.	Common Invasive Vines and Groundcovers	659
Tab. 22-E.	Common Invasive Herbaceous Plants	662
Tab. 22-F.	Common Invasive Grasses	664

23: INDOOR PLANTS

Tab. 23-A.	Cultural guidelines for indoor plants	673
Tab. 23-B.	Indoor plant container comparison	677
Tab. 23-C.	Toxic indoor plants	679

24: PLANT PROPAGATION

Tab. 24-A.	Germination Table for selected seeds	688
Tab. 24-B.	Native plant propagation techniques	689

25: CONTAINER GARDENING

Tab. 25-A.	Potting guide for container plants	718
Tab. 25-B.	Container combination ideas	724

26: LANDSCAPE DESIGN

Tab. 26-A.	Plantings key	741

27: WILDLIFE AND WOODLANDS

Tab. 27-A.	Common herbicides for woodlands use	762
Tab. 27-B.	Land care plan	764
Tab. 27-C.	Native plants for wildlife	766
Tab. 27-D.	Seeds and feeders for attracting birds	773
Tab. 27-E.	Flowers that attract birds	775
Tab. 27-F.	Flowers that attract butterflies	775
Tab. 27-G.	Nuisance-animal repellents	777

30: RESOURCE APPENDIX

Tab. 30-A.	Measurement Conversions	885

INDEX OF DIAGNOSTIC KEYS

INDEX OF DIAGNOSTIC KEYS

Key 12-A. Abiotic Problems of Herbaceous Ornamentals and Vegetables 255
Key 12-B. Abiotic Problems of Woody Ornamentals, Small Fruit Plants, and Fruit Trees 262
Key 12-C. Seedling and Transplant Problems 272
Key 12-D. Pests and Diseases of Shade Trees 275
Key 12-E. Pests and Diseases of Evergreen Trees 282
Key 12-F. Pests and Diseases of Evergreen Shrubs 285
Key 12-G. Pests and Diseases of Deciduous Shrubs 292
Key 12-H. Pests and Diseases of Annuals and Perennials 297
Key 12-I. Pests and Diseases of Solanaceous Crops (Tomato, Eggplant, Pepper, Potato) 300
Key 12-J. Pests and Diseases of Cucurbits (Cucumber, Squash, Melon) 302
Key 12-K. Pests and Diseases of Brassicas (Broccoli, Cabbage, Collard) 305
Key 12-L. Pests and Diseases of Legumes (Bean, Pea) 307
Key 12-M. Pests and Diseases of Sweet Corn 309
Key 12-N. Pests and Diseases of Sweet Potato 311
Key 12-O. Pests and Diseases of Alliums 311
Key 12-P. Pests and Diseases of Asparagus 313
Key 12-Q. Pests and Diseases of Other Vegetable Crops 314
Key 12-R. Pests and Diseases of Pome Fruits (Apple, Pear) 315
Key 12-S. Pests and Diseases of Stone Fruits (Peach, Cherry, Plum, Apricot) 319
Key 12-T. Pests and Diseases of Small Fruits 323
Key 12-U. Pests and Diseases of Nut Trees 328
Key 12-V. Pests and Diseases of Turfgrass 330
Key 12-W. Pests and Diseases of Indoor Plants 334
Key 12-X. Identification of Indoor Pests 336
Key 12-Y. Identification of Wood-Destroying Pests 339
Key 12-Z. Identification of Bees and Wasps 340

INDEX

INDEX

Bold caps denotes a chapter title

A

Abiotic factors 247, 248
About this handbook 3
Air layering 703
Annuals 88, 221, 349, 403, 419, 421, 422, 427, 428, 429, 430, 431, 438, 439, 440, 442, 450, 470, 527, 528, 529, 534, 586, 596, 686, 774. *See also* HERBACEOUS PLANTS
   Annuals for specific environments 450
Anthracnose. *See* Plant diseases, common fungal
Ants. *See* Insect pests, common household
Aphids. *See* Insects, common landscape
Apple. *See* TREE FRUITS
Apricot. *See* TREE FRUITS
Arachnids
   Predatory mites 218
   Spider mites 50, 178, 179, 215, 218, 276, 278, 282, 285, 297
   Spiders 45, 52, 177, 217, 219, 220, 337, 546, 808
   Ticks 179, 180, 351
Arthropods, common non-insect 179–183
   Centipedes 180
   Millipedes 180
   Mites 179
   Spiders 180
   Ticks 179

B

Bacillus thuringiensis (Bt) 238, 275, 853, 869
Bacterial diseases 251, 301. *See also* Plant diseases, common bacterial
Balcony gardens. *See* CONTAINER GARDENING
Bay-Wise landscape management 797, 798
Bees. *See* Insects, beneficial; *See also* Diagnostic Keys
Beetles 168, 177, 182, 184, 406, 438. *See also* Insects, common landscape
Biennial bearing, def. 269, 329
Biennials 349, 350, 431, 454
Biotic factors 246, 247
Birds, seeds and feeders for 773
Blueberries. *See* SMALL FRUITS
Bolting 258
Borers. *See* Insects, common landscape
Boron 133, 134, 137, 250, 260, 329, 543, 559
BOTANY 65–92
   Classification of Plants 69–73
      Horticultural designations 70
      Latin binomials 69
      Leaf identification 71
      The classification system 70
   Groupings of Plants 67–69
      Plant growth patterns 68
   Plant Growth & Development 86–87
      Environmental growth regulators 86–87
      Growth factors 86
   Plant Selection & Modification 89–91
      Artificial selection 89
      Current GMO information 91
      Genetic modification 89
      Genetic modification issues 91
      Natural selection 89
   Pollination 83–84
      Attracting pollinators 84
      Pollination strategies 84
      Self-pollination 84
      Special pollinators 85
   Regulation of Plant Growth 87–89
      Life cycles 88
      Metabolic processes 87
   Reproductive Structures 80–83
      Anatomy of a flower 80
      Angiosperms and gymnosperms 80
      Cones 81
      Flowers 80–81
      Fruit 83
      Seeds 82–83
   The Structure of Plants 73–80
      Buds 80
      Cells, tissues, and organs 73
      Grasses 74
      Leaves 78–79
      Meristems 74
      Roots 75
      Stems 76–78
Botrysphaeria fungi 284
Brambles. *See* SMALL FRUITS
Bt (Bacillus thuringiensis) 90, 209, 217, 232, 238, 275, 283, 291, 296, 298, 305, 306, 308, 309, 310, 315, 331, 853, 869
Budding, chip 707
Budding, patch 707
Budding, T- 707
Bulbs. *See* HERBACEOUS PLANTS • Underground Stems
Butterflies. *See* Insects, beneficial

C

Calcium 108, 111, 112, 113, 115, 129, 130, 131, 208, 250, 256, 259, 270, 329, 470, 574, 804, 855, 856, 860, 864, 868, 869, 876
Carbon 127, 128, 142, 143
Cation exchange 107, 108, 111
Cherry. *See* TREE FRUITS
Chesapeake Bay 35, 39, 40, 57, 59, 60, 61, 62, 63, 132, 239, 377, 381, 398, 400, 640, 793, 797, 798, 803, 805, 806, 809, 811
Chlorine 134, 137, 256, 332, 412
Climate change 36, 50, 106, 517, 541, 548, 809
CLORPT (soil formation) 103
Cold frames 547, 698

COMPOSTING 139–154
  6 Factors of Effective
        Composting 142
  Basic Composting Steps 151–153
      Finished compost 152
  Compost Ingredients 143–146
      Composting system
          comparison 149
  Composting tools 149–150.
          See also Garden Tools and
          Equipment
  Compost measurement
          conversions 145
  Five ways to handle leaves 152
  How Is Compost Made? 142–143
      The composting process 142
  Making "fast compost" 152
  Starting a Compost Pile 146–150
      Composting methods 146
      Locating your pile 146
      Trenching and incorporation 148
      Vermicomposting 148
  The compost-pile food web 144
  Tips for Using Compost 153–154
      As a mulch 153
      For potting 154
      Soil application 153
  Troubleshooting Compost 153
  What Can Be Composted? 150–151
  Why Make Compost? 141–142
  Composting Tools. *See
          also* COMPOSTING
**CONSERVATION
        LANDSCAPING 795–812**
  Groundwater 803–804
      Aquifers 804
      Excess nutrients 805
      Sediments 805–806
      Toxics 806
      Water table 803
  Stormwater Management 809–811
  The Bay-Wise Philosophy 798–801
      Control stormwater runoff 800
      Encourage wildlife 801
      Fertilize wisely 800–801
      Manage yard pests with IPM 799
      Mow properly 800
      Mulch appropriately 800
      Plant wisely 799
      Protect the waterfront 801
      Recycle yard waste 800
      Water efficiently 799

  The Hydrologic Cycle 801–803
      Evapotranspiration 803
      Infiltration 802
      Runoff 802–803
  Water Conservation 806–808
      Gray water 807–808
      Plant selection 806–807
      Rain barrels 807
      Water wisely 808
  Water Pollution 805–806
CONTAINER GARDENING 709–728
  Caring for Container
          Plants 720–723
      Fertilizing 722
      Overwintering 722
      Watering 721–722
  Choosing Container
          Plants 713–714
  Choosing the Right
          Container 715–718
  Combination Ideas 723–727
      Edible combinations 727
      Full-sun/part-sun
          combinations 724–725
      Shade combinations 726
      Winter combinations 726
  Container Plant Pest and Disease
          Diagnostics 723
  Growing Media for
          Containers 719–720
  Potting and Repotting 720
  Potting guide for container
          plants 718
  Raised Beds 710, 712–713. *See
          also* VEGETABLES • Raised
          beds
Copper 134, 137, 138, 147, 202,
          266
Currants. *See* SMALL FRUITS
Cuttings, leaf 700–701
Cuttings, root 701
Cuttings, stem 699–700

D

Damping off 274
Day length 87, 420
Deer 46, 48, 50, 51, 61, 221,
          273, 281, 284, 288, 294,
          310, 324, 351, 414, 415,
          465, 519, 520, 548, 647,
          654, 658, 662, 747, 758,
          760, 764, 766, 767, 768,
          780, 781, 782, 783, 787
Deer feeding 281, 288, 294, 324
Diagnosing Plant Problems.
          See Diagnostic Keys
  Common signs and symptoms 189
**DIAGNOSING PLANT
        PROBLEMS 243–245**
  Biotic vs. Abiotic Causes of Plant
          Problems 247–251
      Distinguish among abiotic
          factors 248–251
      Distinguish among biotic
          factors 247–248
      What causes plant
          problems? 247
  Common signs and symptoms
      Bark stripped 284, 288, 294
      Blossom drop 257, 269
      Blossom-end rot 259, 440
      Branch death 246
      Branch dieback 267
      Catfacing 259, 270, 856
      Cauliflower "buttoning" 257
      Chlorosis 130, 131, 134, 135,
          136, 137, 247, 249, 250,
          331, 420, 584, 651
      Corn silk chewed 310
      Cracked or split fruit 270
      Damaged buds/blooms 268, 319
      Damaged fruit (external) 271
      Deformed fruit 270, 318, 322
      Deformed spears (asparagus) 313
      Drooping spears (asparagus) 313
      Failure of graft union 266
      Failure to bear nuts 329
      Failure to establish 262
      Failure to flower 257, 268
      Failure to fruit 258, 269
      Failure to ripen 261
      Frothy mass 291, 296
      Fruit discoloration 259, 260,
          261
      Fruit drop 258
      Fruit oozing sap 270
      Fuzzy mold on fruit 324
      Girdling roots 267, 473, 497
      Grass blade tips, ragged 333
      Hairy carrot roots 260
      Holes in Brassica heads or
          florets 306

Holes in fruit 304
Holes in leaves 253, 273, 306, 308, 514
Holes or tunnels in Brassica roots 306
Kernel damage 310
Leaf cupping 290, 302
Leaf curl 290, 302
Leaf damage 290, 302
Leaf discoloration 290, 302
Leaf distortion 290, 302
Leaf drop 290, 302
Leaf margin browning 266
Leaf mottling 287, 293, 297, 334
Leaf scorch 256
Leaf stippling 297, 307
Leaf-tip burn 256
Leaf yellowing 255, 278, 292
Leaves chewed 273
Leaves eaten 273
Leaves/needles turn brown 287
Leaves/stems chewed 273
Leaves turn black 293
Needle browning 264
Needle drop 283
Needle yellowing 263, 282, 285, 286
Orange pustules on leaf 325
Pale green leaves 273
Pesticide burn 256, 264, 266, 271
Plant canopy damage 245
Poor germination 272
Poor nut quality 329
Premature fall color 265
Purple leaves 273
Root tunneling 315
Serpentine trails 279, 282, 287, 293
Shoot dieback 340
Split stems 257
Stunted growth 137, 260, 274
Sudden death of plant 263
Thousand cankers 291, 292, 294
Tops yellow (asparagus) 313
Tree bark problems 267
Tree oozes sap 267
Trunk problems 267, 320, 321
Undersized fruit 270

Vascular browning 278, 292, 297
Water-soaked spots 312
Webbed or tented foliage 291, 296
White coating on leaves 287, 293, 307
Wilting 247, 265, 284, 290, 295, 299, 306, 307, 311, 335, 883
Winter burn 257, 264
Yellow leaf tips (alliums) 311
Define the problem 243
Determine the causes of the problem 244–245
Finalizing the diagnosis 244
How plants show symptoms 245–247
  Needle damage 245
  Normal vs. abnormal needle or leaf drop 245
  Plant canopy damage 245
  Shoot dieback 246
Look for patterns 244
Normal vs. abnormal needle or leaf drop 245
Symptoms and Signs of Insect Pests 253–255. *See also* Common signs and symptoms (above)
  Chewing damage 253
  Other insect damage 254
  Sucking or rasping damage 253
Symptoms and Signs of Plant Diseases 251–253. *See also* Common signs and symptoms (above)
  Bacterial diseases 251–252. *See also* Plant diseases, common bacterial
  Fungal diseases 251. *See also* Plant diseases, common fungal
  Nematode diseases 252. *See also* Plant diseases, common nematode
  Phytoplasma diseases 252–253. *See also* Plant diseases, common phytoplasma
  Viral diseases 252. *See also* Plant diseases, common virus

Diagnostic Keys 254–340
Abiotic Problems of Herbaceous Ornamentals and Vegetables 255–261
Abiotic Problems of Woody Ornamentals, Small Fruit Plants, and Fruit Trees 262–271
Diagnostic Keys, index of 898
Identification of Bees and Wasps 340
Identification of Indoor Pests 336–338
Identification of Wood-Destroying Pests 339
Pests and Diseases of Alliums 311–312
Pests and Diseases of Annuals and Perennials 297–299
Pests and Diseases of Asparagus 313
Pests and Diseases of Brassicas (Broccoli, Cabbage, Collard) 305–306
Pests and Diseases of Cucurbits (Cucumber, Squash, Melon) 302–304
Pests and Diseases of Deciduous Shrubs 292–296
Pests and Diseases of Evergreen Shrubs 285–291
Pests and Diseases of Evergreen Trees 282–285
Pests and Diseases of Indoor Plants 334–335
Pests and Diseases of Legumes (Bean, Pea) 307–309
Pests and Diseases of Nut Trees 328–329
Pests and Diseases of Other Vegetable Crops 314–315
Pests and Diseases of Pome Fruits (Apple, Pear) 315–318
Pests and Diseases of Shade Trees 275–281
Pests and Diseases of Small Fruits 323–328
Pests and Diseases of Solanaceous Crops (Tomato, Eggplant, Pepper, Potato) 300–301
Pests and Diseases of Stone

Fruits (Peach, Cherry, Plum, Apricot) 319–322
Pests and Diseases of Sweet Corn 309–310
Pests and Diseases of Sweet Potato 311
Pests and Diseases of Turfgrass 330–333
Seedling and Transplant Problems 272–274
Dichotomous keys 71
Dicot 68, 77, 82, 364
Dogwood anthracnose 188
Dollar spot 330, 409
Downy mildew 193, 303, 305, 307, 312, 327
Dutch elm disease 188, 648, 651, 657, 768

E

ECOLOGY 33–64
Ecosystems 52–56
  Biodiversity in the landscape 56
  Disrupting food webs 52
  Nitrogen cycle 55
  Recycling in the garden 56
  Water cycle 54
  What are food webs? 52
How to Preserve Wetlands 61
  Community involvement 62
  Reducing human Impact 61
Maryland's Ecology
  Appalachian Plateau 37, 38
  Biomes 36
  Blue Ridge 37
  Coastal Plain 38, 39, 134, 641, 642, 643
  Piedmont Plateau 39
  Ridge and Valley 37
  The biosphere 36
  The region 37
Maryland's Landscape 39–42
  Forest fragmentation 42
  From forests to farms 40
  Urbanization 41
  Watersheds 39–40
Plant and Wildlife Communities 42–45
  Energy and nutrients 44
  Microclimates 43
  Physiology 45
  Water gain/loss 44
  What organisms need to survive 42–43
Species and Populations 48–52
  Evolution and adaptation 48–49
  Human influences on evolution 49–50
  Plant breeding 51–52
  Population dynamics 50
  Population genetics 51
  Rare plants in Maryland 52
  What are species? 48
Species Interactions 45–48
  Changing interactions 46
  Functional groups 45
  Native pollinators 45–46
  Natural disturbances 48
  Succession 47
Wetland Regulations 60–61
  Chesapeake Bay Critical Area Act 61
  Federal Clean Water Act 60
  MD Nontidal Wetlands Act 61
  Maryland Tidal Wetlands Act 61
What Is a Wetland? 56–59
  How to recognize a non-tidal wetland 57
  Wetland plant categories 58
  Wetland types 57
Why Are Wetlands Important? 59–60
  Benefits of wetlands 60
  Chesapeake Bay Critical Area Act 61
  MD Nontidal Wetlands Act 61
Elderberries. *See* SMALL FRUITS
Espalier 494, 861

F

Federal Clean Water Act 60
Fire blight 201, 279, 281, 289, 316, 318, 319
Flies 45, 169, 177, 182, 199, 438
Floricanes 326, 586
Flowers, commonly grown
  Begonia 433, 441, 450, 669, 679, 688, 726
  Caladium 432, 433, 679
  Calla 433, 445
  Canna 432
  Crocus 357, 431, 432, 434, 437, 704, 858
  Cyclamen 335, 433, 445, 451, 453
  Daffodil 432, 433, 437, 445
  Dahlia 432, 433, 444, 445, 452, 688
  Foxtail lily 433
  Freesia 433, 445
  Fritillaria 433, 451
  Gladiolus 432, 433, 437, 445, 704, 858
  Glory-of-the-snow 433
  Half-hardy annuals 427, 528
  Hardy annuals 427, 528
  Hyacinths 433, 445, 529, 726
  Impatiens 427, 428, 429, 694, 726
  Iris 58, 77, 81, 255, 415, 425, 431, 432, 433, 437, 444, 445, 447, 452, 453, 505, 665, 689, 703, 704
  Lilies 432, 433
  Narcissus 433, 445
  Ranunculus 354
  Roses 18, 206, 293, 482, 509, 659, 769, 819
  Scilla 433
  Snapdragons 85, 427
  Spanish bluebell 433
  Tender annuals 428, 450, 528
  Toad lily 433, 445, 448
  Tulip 59, 69, 177, 279, 433, 445, 643, 644, 775
  Windflower, Grecian 433
Food web 158, 368, 513, 752
Frass 281, 288, 295, 863
Freeze damage 255, 259, 533, 611
Freeze Dates 886
Fruiting bodies 189, 194, 245, 246, 248, 251, 278, 406, 408
Fruit tree problems. *See* Diagnostic Keys
Fruitworms 318
Fungal diseases 251, 272, 309, 650. *See also* Plant diseases, common fungal
Fungi 35, 44, 45, 87, 132, 143, 144, 174, 180, 187, 191,

192, 193, 194, 196, 197, 198, 199, 200, 203, 204, 217, 227, 236, 238, 245, 246, 247, 251, 277, 278, 280, 281, 284, 288, 295, 297, 298, 334, 387, 407, 411, 422, 468, 470, 558, 692, 789, 807, 843
Fungicides 199, 202, 209, 234, 238, 266, 279, 322, 326, 371, 411, 685, 841
Fusarium wilt 300, 307, 313, 535

G

Galls 171, 179, 196, 247, 254, 281, 290, 291, 292, 294, 297, 310, 316, 321, 324, 327, 328, 460
   Cane galls 324
   Crown gall 210, 251
   Eyespot gall 279
   Flower gall 290
   Grape tumid galls 327
   Stem galls 291, 292, 294
   Tulip tree spot gall 279
Garden pests. *See* Insects, common landscape
GARDEN TOOLS AND EQUIPMENT 813–848
   Choosing the Right Tools 815–817
      How to identify high-quality tools 816–817
   Garden Accessories 833–842
      Sprayers 841–842
      Trellises, Cages, and Stakes 834–836
      Watering Equipment 837–841
      Wheelbarrows and Carts 833–834
   Hand Tools 817–825
      Cutting/Pruning Tools 818–821
      Digging Tools 821–823
      Maintenance of Hand Tools 824
      Raking Tools 823–824
   Other Tools and Accessories 842–847
      Composting Tools 842–844
      Maintenance of Other Tools and Accessories 847
      Other Accessories 845

Power Tools 825–833
   About electric/cordless tools 826
   About gas-powered tools 825
   Chipper-Shredders 831–833
   Lawn Edgers 831
   Leaf Blowers 830–831
   Maintenance of Power Tools 833
   Mowers 826
   String Trimmers 829–830
   Tillers/Cultivators 827–829
   The ideal garden accessories list 834
   The ideal garden tool list 816
Germination, seed 82, 392, 403, 687, 688, 689
Glossary of Terms 851
Glysophate injury 290
GMOs. *See* Botany • Plant Selection & Modification
Gooseberries. *See* SMALL FRUITS
Grafting, bark 705–706
Grafting, cleft 705
Grafting, whip (splice) 706
Graft union 266, 267, 612, 705
Grapes. *See* SMALL FRUITS
Green shoulder 260
Groundcovers. *See* WOODY PLANTS
Grow lights (for seed-starting) 694–695
Gummosis 267, 321

H

Habitat 41, 42, 46, 60, 63, 164, 165, 166, 167, 168, 169, 183, 454, 750, 753, 764, 765, 784, 793
Hardiness zones 68
   Freeze Dates and Hardiness Zones 886
Hardy Kiwis. *See* SMALL FRUITS
HERBACEOUS PLANTS 417–454.
   See also NATIVE PLANTS; INVASIVE PLANTS; LAWNS
   About Herbaceous Gardens 420
   Annuals 427
      Annuals for specific environments 450–452
      Guidelines for purchasing annuals 428
      Life cycle of annuals 427

      Planting annuals 428–429
      Types of annuals 427–428
   Asexual Propagation of Herbaceous Plants 443
      Cuttings 444
      Division 443
   Biennials 431
   Herbaceous Garden Maintenance 439–441
      Mulching 439
      Preventing weeds 439
      Pruning, deadheading, and pinching back 440
      Watering 439–440
   Herbaceous Plant Families 421–427
      Asteraceae 421
      Cacti 425–426
      Euphorbiaceae 423–424
      Lamiaceae 424
      Liliaceae 424–425
      Malvaceae 426
      Orchidaceae 422
      Poaceae 422–423
      Solanaceae 426–427
   Herbaceous plants for drying 452
   Herbaceous plants with foliage interest 453
   Landscape Design with Herbaceous Plants 436–439
      Assess and amend the planting site 437
      Selecting plants 437
      Tips for arranging plants 438
   Perennials 429
      Life cycle of perennials 429
      Perennial bloom times 445
      Perennial planning and planting guide 446–449
      Planting new perennials 430–431
      Transplanting established perennials 431
      Types of perennials 429
   Sexual Propagation of Herbaceous Plants
      Starting seeds indoors 442
      Thinning 443
      When to plant seeds 442
   Traits of flowering-plant pollinators 438
   Underground Stems 431–436

Bulb maintenance 435–436
Planting bulbs 434
Planting guide for flowering bulbs 433
Spring-flowering bulbs 432
Storing bulbs 436
Summer-flowering bulbs 434
The life cycle of underground stems 431
Types of underground stems 431
Herbicide damage 255, 264
Herbs 548–552
Common culinary herbs 554
Common herbs for teas, crafts, medicinal, and other uses 553
Harvesting herbs 550
Pest and disease control 550
Poisonous herbs 555
Preservation and storage 550–552
Drying herbs 551–552
Freezing herbs 551
Site and soil 549
Starting and planting herbs 549
Hornets 170, 288, 294, 318, 322
Horticultural oil 217, 222, 271, 276, 277, 282, 283, 285, 286, 287, 288, 289, 290, 292, 293, 294, 296, 298, 307, 315, 319, 321, 323
Hummingbirds 45, 253, 273, 306, 308, 514, 773, 774
Hybrids 51, 534
Hydrogen 127, 128, 131, 420

I

INDEX OF DIAGNOSTIC KEYS 897–898
Indoor pests. *See* Insect pests, common household
Indoor plant problems. *See* Diagnostic Keys
INDOOR PLANTS 667–680
Bringing Plants Back Indoors 678
Cultural requirements for indoor plants 673
Indoor Plant Pest and Disease Diagnostics 678–679
Maintenance Tips 674–675
Moving Indoor Plants
Outdoors 677–678
Acclimating plants 678
Repotting Indoor Plants 675–677
How to repot a plant 675–676
Potting media 676–677
Requirements for Healthy Indoor Plants 669–674
Humidity 674
Light 670–671
Temperature 674
Water 671–674
Selecting Indoor Plants 669
Toxic Indoor Plants 679
Inoculants 570
INSECT BASICS 155–184
Beneficial Insects 176–179. *See also* Insects, beneficial
Common Household Pests 175. *See also* Insects, common household
Common Landscape Pests 170–174. *See also* Insects, common landscape
Common Non-insect Arthropods 179–181
Examples of insect-flower pollination 177
Insect characteristics by order 182
Insect Classification 164–170
Insects with complete metamorphosis 168–170
Insects with gradual metamorphosis 164–167
Insects as Part of a Natural System 158
Insect Structure 158–163
Abdomen 163
Exoskeleton 158–160
Head 160–162
Legs 162
Mouthpart structure 160–161
Thorax 162–163
Wings 162
Insecticidal soap 217, 222
Insect pests, common household 175
Ants 84, 164, 169, 176, 182, 216, 338, 339, 344, 863, 872
Bedbugs 176
Box elder bugs 175
Brown marmorated stink bugs 175
Cockroach 165, 338
Crickets 165, 175, 182, 335, 336
Fleas 175–176
Ladybird beetles 175
Mealybugs 171, 334, 335
Silverfish and firebrats 175
Termites 165, 175, 183, 339
Whiteflies 170, 273, 286, 292, 334, 335
Insects, beneficial 47, 176–179, 771
Assassin bugs 219
Bees
Bumblebees 45, 161, 170, 177
Ground bees 333
Honeybees 45, 526
Mason bees 177
Solitary bees 46
Braconid wasps 178
Butterflies 35, 42, 45, 46, 84, 164, 168, 169, 176, 177, 182, 232, 553, 639, 725, 747, 765, 766, 767, 768, 769, 770, 774, 775, 776, 801, 868
Damselflies 219
Dragonflies 164, 182
Garden spider 180
Green lacewings 178
Ground beetles 407, 546, 771
Lacewings 217, 218, 771
Ladybird beetles (ladybugs) 45, 175, 217, 338
Paper wasps 176
Parasitic wasps 219
Praying mantids 166, 182, 218
Predatory stink bugs 178
Spined soldier bug 178
Syrphids (flower flies) 179, 218
Tachinid flies 178
Insects, common landscape 170–175
Adelgids 167, 468
Alderflies 168
Allium leafminer 312
Antlions 168, 182
Aphids 43, 170, 215, 253, 276, 277, 283, 299, 301, 302,

305, 308, 314, 315, 323, 334, 335
Apple aphids 43, 170, 215, 253, 276, 277, 283, 299, 301, 302, 305, 308, 314, 315, 323, 334, 335
Apple maggots 317
Bagworms 275, 283, 291, 296
Beetles 85, 168, 177, 182, 406, 438
   Bark beetles 284
   Bean leaf beetle 308
   Cucumber beetles 43, 45, 302, 304
   Elm-leaf beetles 275
   Flea beetles 273, 314, 327
   Japanese beetle 173, 252, 254, 275, 310, 319, 406, 650
   Leaf beetles 174
   Longhorn beetles 173–174
   Metallic wood-boring beetles 174
   Mexican bean beetles 43
   Sap beetles 310, 328
   Scarab beetles 173
   Squash beetle 303
Borers 169, 172, 174, 220, 246, 254, 278, 280, 284, 286, 288, 289, 292, 294, 295, 297, 299, 304, 310, 317, 320, 326, 440, 509
   Cane borers 326
   Clearwing borer larva 288
   Clearwing borers 295
   Corn borers 310
   Emerald ash borer 46, 174
   European corn borer 309
   Peach tree borer 278, 320
   Peach tree borers 320
   Shothole borer 321
   Squash vine borers 4, 5, 168, 177, 304, 315, 766, 769
Brown marmorated stink bugs 175
Butterflies 35, 42, 45, 46, 84, 164, 168, 169, 176, 177, 182, 232, 553, 639, 725, 747, 765, 766, 767, 768, 769, 770, 774, 775, 776, 801, 868
Caterpillars 171–172, 184, 214, 275, 314
Chafers 275, 406

Chinch bugs 332, 407
Cicadas 167, 280, 289, 294
Corn ear worms 310
Cutworms 273, 274, 328
Dobsonflies 168
Earwigs 164, 182
Fall webworm 275
Fishflies 168, 182
Four-lined plant bugs 297
Grape cane girdlers 327
Grape phylloxera 327
Grasshoppers 159, 162, 163, 165, 298, 308
Green peach aphid 320
Ground bees 333
Grubs 168, 173, 220, 274, 279, 309, 313, 315, 333, 340, 385, 394, 406, 408, 785, 786, 789, 875
Harlequin bugs 297
Hemlock woolly adelgid 283, 650
Holly berry midge 290
Juniper tip midge 289
Juniper webworm 291
Katydids 165, 182
Lacebugs 276
Leafhoppers 171, 276, 297, 299, 300, 308, 314, 315, 323
Leaf miners 254, 314
Leafrollers 253, 275
Lecanium scales 317
Mealybugs 171, 334, 335
Mimosa webworm 275
Moths 46, 84, 85, 160, 170, 172, 176, 232, 253, 254, 275, 285, 327, 331, 407, 408, 426, 639, 747, 765, 767, 768, 868
   Codling moth 317, 318
   Grape berry moths 327
   Oriental fruit moth 321, 322
   Pine tube moth 283
   Spongy moths 253, 275
Oakworm 275
Owlflies 168
Pear leaf blister mite 316
Pine tortoise scale 283
Pine webworm 283
Plant bugs 276, 314
Plum curculio 318
Potato leafhopper 300, 308
Potato tuberworm 301

Psyllids 167, 171
San Jose scale 171, 316, 317, 318
Sawflies 169, 170, 182, 275, 283
Sawfly 169, 170, 182, 275, 283
Sawfly larvae 172
Scales, armored (hard) 171, 278, 280, 285, 289, 292, 294
Scales, soft 171, 277, 278, 285, 292
Slugs 273, 274, 298, 313, 328
Snakeflies 168
Spittlebugs 277, 291, 296
Spotted lanternflies 253, 474
Spotted-wing drosophila 325
Squash bugs 302
Swallowtail caterpillar 4, 5, 168, 177, 315, 766, 769
Tarnished plant bug 314, 328
Thrips 167, 182, 296, 312
Ugly nest caterpillar 291
Walnut caterpillars 328
Walnut curculios 329
Walnut husk fly 329, 344
weevils 168, 253, 254, 291, 298, 315, 327, 329, 335, 407
Whiteflies 170, 273, 286, 292, 334, 335
White pine weevil 285
Wireworm 311
Woolly aphids 295
INTEGRATED PEST MANAGEMENT (IPM) 211–224. *See also* **INSECT BASICS**
Healthy Plants = Fewer Problems 215–216
IPM Steps 214–215
Plants that attract/feed beneficial insects 221
Taking Action 216–222
   Beneficial organisms 220
   Biological control 217
   Chemical strategies 222
   Common insect parasites 219–220
   Common insect predators 217–219
   Cultural strategies 221–222
   Physical strategies 221
   When to act 222
What is IPM? 213–214
INVASIVE PLANTS 645–666

About Invasive Species 647
   What is a Quarantine Protocol? 648
   Why invasive species are important 648
   Common Invasive Plants of Maryland 655–664
   Common Invasive Grasses 664
   Common Invasive Herbaceous Plants 662–663
   Common Invasive Shrubs 658–659
   Common Invasive Trees 656–657
   Common Invasive Vines and Groundcovers 659–661
   Other Tier I and Tier II plants 665
Invasive Control Methods 654–655
   Biological controls 655
   Chemical options 655
   Mechanical methods 654
Invasive Species: Non-Plant 649–651
   Invasive Diseases of Plants 650–651
   Invasive Insect Pests of Humans 649
   Invasive Insect Pests of Plants 649–650
   Other Invasive Insects 650
Invasive Species: Plants 652–654
   Characteristics that aid aggressiveness 652–653
   Damaging impact of invasive plants 652
   Ecological change caused by invasives 653
   Ways for Master Gardeners to help 654
IPM. See INTEGRATED PEST MANAGEMENT (IPM)
Iron 134, 137, 250, 263, 273, 331, 374, 386, 412, 413, 420, 453

L

LANDSCAPE DESIGN 729–744
Elements of Design 736–738
   Color 738
   Form 737
   Lines 737
   Mass 736
   Texture 738
Finalizing Your Design 740
Functional Uses of Space 734–736
   Activities 734
   Creating visual interest 735–736
   Design for conservation 736
   Outdoor entertaining 735
Installation 742
   About hiring professionals vs. DIY 742
   Maintenance 742
   Timing 740–742
Principles of Composition 739–740
   Draft design layout 739
   Final landscape design 740–741
Site Analysis and Blob Design 733–734
   A sample blob design 734
What Is Landscape Design? 732–733
with Herbaceous Plants 436–439
Lawn and garden weeds, common 352–363
LAWNS 379–416
Cultural Practices for Turf 393–400
   Aeration 401–402
   Grasscyling tips 399
   How much fertilizer will you need? 396
   Liming 402
   Mowing 398–400
   Nitrogen sources 394–395
   Thatch management 400
   Turf fertilizers 393–394
   Watering 400
Lawn Alternatives 413–415
   Groundcovers recommended for Maryland 415
   Lower-maintenance options 414
   No-mow/natural areas 414
   Ornamental grasses 414
Lawn Establishment 389–393
   Renovation and overseeding 393
   Seeding 390–391
   Site preparation 389
   Sod 392–393
   Soil testing 389–390
   Lawn insect identification and control 406
   Organic Lawn Care Tips 413
   Sod vs. seed comparison 391
Turfgrass Identification 381–383
   Auricle 383
   Collar 382
   Leaf blade 382
   Leaf sheath 382
   Ligule 382
   Turfgrass terminology 381
   Vernation 382
Turfgrass Problems 402–412
   Abiotic disorders of lawns 411–412
   Common lawn weeds 404
   Common turf diseases 409–410
   Diseases 408–412
   Insects 406–408
   Lawn insect identification and control 406
   Moss 405–406
   Mushrooms 406
   Types of herbicides 403–404
   Weeds 402–403
Turfgrass Species 383–389
   Bermudagrass 386–387
   Fine fescues 384–385
   Kentucky bluegrass 385–386
   Perennial ryegrass 386
   Tall fescue 383–384
   Turfgrass cultivars recommended for Maryland 388–389
   Zoysiagrass 387
Liebig's Law of the Minimum 127
Limb spreaders 622
LIST OF FIGURES 887–892
LIST OF TABLES 893–896

M

Magnesium 101, 104, 108, 111, 113, 115, 117, 129, 130, 131, 250, 255, 263, 271, 329, 344, 402, 574, 804, 860, 868, 876
Manganese 135, 137, 250
Measurement Conversions 885, 895
Media, for seed-starting 692–693

Micronutrient deficiency 329
Micronutrients. *See* PLANT NUTRITION
Molybdenum 135, 137
Monocot 92
Moss 333, 405, 412, 452, 869
Moths. *See* Insects, common landscape
Mulches, inorganic 467
Mulches, organic 467
Mushrooms 191, 194, 199, 248, 278, 281, 288, 295, 333, 344, 376, 406, 408, 410, 759, 863
Mycorrhizae. *See* PLANT NUTRITION

N

NATIVE PLANTS 635–644
  How to Choose Native Plants 640
  Maximizing Native Plant Performance 640
  Recommended Native Plants for Maryland 641–643
    FLOWERING HERBACEOUS PLANTS (Forbs) 642
    GRASSES & SEDGES 641
    GROUNDCOVERS & FERNS 641
    SHRUBS 643
    TREES 643
  Top 5 native trees for caterpillars 639
  Top 5 shrubs and vines for birds 639
  Why Choose Native Plants? 637–640
  To conserve biodiversity 638
  To create low-maintenance, efficient landscapes 639–640
  To preserve wildlife habitats 639
Native plants, propagating 689
Nectarine. *See* TREE FRUITS
Nematodes 187, 190, 203, 204, 206, 217, 220, 227, 247, 250, 252, 284, 292, 295, 297, 302, 323, 335, 349, 406, 535, 544, 650, 711, 771, 863, 872. *See also* Plant diseases, common nematode
  Pine wilt nematodes 284
  Root knot nematodes 203, 252

Nickel 135, 137
Nitrogen. *See* PLANT NUTRITION
Nitrogen deficiency 131, 263, 273, 320, 331
Nuisance animals. *See* WILDLIFE AND WOODLANDS

O

Open-pollinated 51, 442, 534, 536, 574, 685
Oxygen 128, 136, 142, 144, 146, 207, 249, 256, 381, 400, 411, 466, 470, 517, 521, 609, 805, 843

P

Peach. *See* TREE FRUITS
Pear. *See* TREE FRUITS
Pecan scab 328
Perennial grasses 47, 76, 348
Perennials 203, 205, 257, 299, 349, 350, 419, 421, 429, 430, 431, 438, 439, 443, 492, 505, 528, 549, 550, 567, 686, 691, 703, 722, 754. *See also* HERBACEOUS PLANTS
Perennial bloom times (by season) 445
Perennial planning and planting guide 446
PESTICIDE USE AND SAFETY 225–240
  Managing Pesticide Risk 233–234
  Organic Pesticides 236–238
    Biopesticides 236
    Minimum-Risk Pesticides 236
  Pesticide application terminology 235
  Pesticide Basics 227–228
  Pesticide Formulations 228
  Pesticides and groundwater 240
  Pesticides in the Environment 238–240
    Pesticides and groundwater 240
    Pesticides and surface water 239
    Spills and misapplication 239
  Proper Application 234–236
    After you apply 235
    Before you apply 234
    During application 235
    Storage and disposal 236
  The Pesticide Label 228–233
pH 101, 110, 112, 113, 115, 129, 130, 131, 132, 133, 135, 136, 215, 250, 256, 259, 260, 262, 263, 367, 384, 389, 390, 395, 400, 401, 402, 413, 420, 421, 428, 437, 457, 458, 462, 467, 468, 470, 483, 484, 521, 522, 524, 542, 549, 556, 567, 581, 582, 584, 585, 591, 594, 608, 618, 623, 624, 627, 640, 642, 643, 653, 658, 720, 804, 834, 846, 847
Phloem 68, 250, 872
Phomopsis 284, 289
Phosphate 111, 112, 115, 116, 118, 132, 135, 206, 390, 394, 395
Phosphorus 108, 109, 110, 112, 113, 115, 116, 117, 129, 130, 131, 132, 136, 250, 389, 390, 394, 521, 523, 543, 584, 801, 803
Photosynthesis 44, 53, 67, 76, 78, 79, 128, 134, 135, 198, 252, 277, 399, 435, 649, 670. *See also* Metabolic processes
Phytodermatitis 627
Phytoplasma diseases 252. *See also* Plant diseases, common phytoplasma
Piedmont Plateau 39, 105
PLANT DIAGNOSTICS.
  See DIAGNOSING PLANT PROBLEMS
PLANT DISEASE BASICS 185–210
  Basic Plant Disease Concepts 189–191
    Host-pathogen interactions 191
    Inoculum and pathogen spread 190
    Pathogen survival 190
    Plant disease causes 189
    Signs 189
    Symptoms 189

Biological and Integrated Pest Management Controls 210
Classification of Plant Pathogenic Fungi 192–199
  Ascomycete: the Sac Fungi 193
  Basidiomycetes 194
  Common fungal diseases 194–200
  Fungi-like organisms 192
  Zygomycetes: the Bread Molds 193
Common fungal diseases. *See also* Plant diseases, common fungal
Environmental Diseases 207–208. *See also* Diagnosing Plant Problems • Common signs and symptoms
  Air pollution 208
  Moisture effects 207
  Nutritional effects 208
  Temperature effects 207
Fungi and Plant Diseases 191–192
  Fungi 191
  Fungi reproduction 192
Impact of Plant Disease 187
Parasitic Plants 206–207
  Broomrape 206
  Dodder 45, 202, 205, 206, 207, 364
  Mistletoe 206
  Witchweed 206
Plant Diseases Caused by Bacteria 200–202. *See also* Plant diseases, common bacterial
Plant Diseases Caused by Nematodes 203–205. *See also* Plant diseases, common nematode
  Beech leaf disease 188, 650
  Ectoparasites 203
  Endoparasites 203
Plant Diseases Caused by Phytoplasmas 202–204. *See also* Plant diseases, common phytoplasma
Plant Diseases Caused by Viruses 204–206. *See also* Plant diseases, common virus
Principles of Plant Disease Control 208–210. *See also* INTEGRATED PEST MANAGEMENT (IPM)
  Chemical controls 209
  Exclusion 209
  Inoculum reduction 209
  Resistant plants 209
Plant diseases, common bacterial
  Bacterial leaf blight 289, 293
  Bacterial leaf scorch 200, 201, 279
  Bacterial spot 300, 320
  Bacterial wilt 252, 310, 651
  Blackleg (potato) 301, 306
  Fire blight 201
  Plum leaf spot 320
  Shepherd's crook 317
Plant diseases, common fungal
  Anthracnose 188, 209, 216, 245, 246, 279, 325, 411, 651, 767
  Bitter rot 318
  Black knot 321
  Black rot 305, 316, 326
  Black spot 293
  Botrytis (gray mold) 251, 296, 312, 324, 325, 326, 854
  Boxwood blight 188, 194, 286, 650
  Brown rot 251, 322, 343, 623, 624
  Brown spots 135, 137, 195, 304, 311, 318
  Cankers 189, 196, 266, 278, 280, 284, 320
  Cedar apple rust 196, 284, 316
  Cenangium twig blight 285
  Cercospora 293, 314
  Cherry leaf spot 320
  Chestnut blight 46, 188, 651
  Choanephora rot 304
  Gray mold (botrytis) 251, 324
  Gummy stem blight 303
  Late blight 301
  Leaf spot 190, 251, 287, 300, 303, 314, 316, 320, 323, 344, 386, 409, 410, 631, 632
  Lima seed rot 309
  Mummy berry 325
  Needle cast 282
  Ovulinia petal blight 290
  Phytophthora 272, 278, 280, 320, 651
  Plum pockets 322
  Powdery mildew 188, 189, 198, 199, 238, 277, 287, 298, 307, 315, 319, 323, 411, 505, 629, 651, 856
  Procera root rot 284
  Red thread 330, 410
  Rhizopus soft rot 322
  Root rot 251, 263, 292, 323, 335
  Rose rosette (RRD) 206
  Rust 179, 187, 188, 193, 194, 196, 238, 251, 282, 284, 307, 309, 313, 315, 316, 325, 331, 344, 366, 410, 534, 590, 599, 629, 651, 658, 816, 823, 824, 840, 844, 846, 876, 881
  Scab, apple 316
  Scab, peach 322
  Scab, pear 316, 632
  Septoria leaf spot 190, 300, 314
  Smut (corn) 310
  Southern blight 195, 297, 299, 301
  Southern blight on groundcovers 195
  Sphaeropsis tip blight 284, 285
  Spur blight 326
  Verticillium wilt 278, 289, 292, 294, 297, 299, 320, 325, 344, 535
  Volutella blight on pachysandra 195
  Wood-decaying fungi 197
Plant diseases, common nematode
  Foliar nematodes 204
  Root knot nematodes 203
Plant diseases, common phytoplasma
  Aster yellows 202, 314
Plant diseases, common turf
  Brown patch 330, 409
Plant diseases, common virus
  Cucumber mosaic 205, 302
  Impatiens necrotic spot 205
  Ringspot 302
  Rose rosette 206
  Tobacco mosaic 205, 535
  Tobacco ringspot 206
  Tomato ringspot 205, 206

Tomato spotted wilt 205
PLANT NUTRITION 125–138
  Beneficial Non-Essential
      Nutrients 136–137
    Cobalt (Co) 136
    Silicon (Si) 136
    Vanadium (V) 136
  Macronutrients 129–133
    Calcium (Ca) 129
    Magnesium (Mg) 130
    Mycorrhizae 132
    Nitrogen (N) 130
    Phosphorus (P) 131
    Potassium (K) 132
    Sulfur (S) 133
  Micronutrients 133–136
    Boron (B) 133
    Chlorine (Cl) 134
    Copper (Cu) 134
    Iron (Fe) 134
    Manganese (Mn) 135
    Molybdenum (Mo) 135
    Nickel (Ni) 135
    Zinc (Zn) 136
  Nutrient Availability 129
  Nutrient Types 128–129
    Mineral nutrients 128
    Non-mineral nutrients 128
  Nutrition Essentiality 127–128
    Liebig's Law of the Minimum 127
  Plant problems. *See* DIAGNOSING PLANT PROBLEMS
PLANT PROPAGATION 681–708
  Asexual Propagation 699–708
    Cuttings 699–702
    Division and Separation 703–704
    Grafting and Budding 704–707
    Layering 702–703
    Tissue culture 708
  Germination table for selected seeds 688
  Growing Transplants 697–699
    Fertilizing transplants 698
    Hardening off 698–699
    Potting-up 697–698
  Native plant propagation techniques 689
  Sexual Propagation 684–687
    About Seeds 684–687. *See also* BOTANY; VEGETABLES
    Preparing Seeds for Germination 687–691

Starting Seeds Indoors 691–696
Starting Seeds Outdoors 696–697
Plum. *See* TREE FRUITS
Pollination. *See* BOTANY
Pollinators 35, 42, 43, 45, 46, 52, 79, 84, 85, 121, 169, 170, 176, 202, 221, 232, 258, 259, 269, 333, 340, 407, 414, 436, 438, 514, 531, 569, 609, 637, 639, 653, 658, 685, 747, 766, 767, 768, 774, 801
  Traits of flowering-plant pollinators 438
Pome fruits. *See* TREE FRUITS
Potash 115, 116, 117, 390, 395, 543
Potassium 108, 115, 116, 117, 129, 130, 131, 132, 133, 137, 250, 260, 331, 389, 394, 523, 543, 569
Pressure-treated lumber, about 713
Primocanes 326, 589. *See also* SMALL FRUITS
PRUNING 488–510
  Physiology of Pruning 489–491
    Compartmentalization 490
    Role of the terminal bud 489–490
    The bud 489
  Pruning Conifers 504
  Pruning guidelines for specific plants 506–510
  Pruning Hedges 502–503
  Pruning Mature Trees 500–502
    Crown raising 500
    Crown reduction 500
    Crown thinning 500
    Topping and tipping 500
    Trunk injury 501–502
  Pruning Other Plants 504–505
    Ornamental grasses 505
    Perennials 505
    Vines and groundcovers 504–505
  Pruning Shrubs 502
    Rejuvenation pruning 502
  Pruning Techniques & Terms 494–497
    Deadheading 494
    Disbudding 494
    Espalier 494
    Girdling roots 497

    Heading back 494–495
    Pinching 494
    Pollarding 497
    Pruning large branches 495–496
    Renewal pruning 495
    Root pruning and transplanting 496–497
    Thinning 495
  Pruning Tools 493–494
  See also GARDEN TOOLS AND EQUIPMENT
  Topping (shade trees) 500
  Training Newly-Planted Trees 498–500
    Crotches 499–500
    Forcing laterals 499
    Leader 499
    Roots 498
    Scaffold branches 499
    Temporary branches 498
  When to Prune 497–498
  Why Prune? 491–492

R

Rabbits 273, 274, 314, 787, 788
RESOURCE APPENDIX 849–886
Root pruning 469, 496, 497
Row covers, about 548

S

Scarification (seeds) 690–691
Seed bank 50, 351, 375
Seedling and transplant problems. *See* Diagnostic Keys
Seed-starting 691–696
Seed tape 696
Seed types 684–686
Senescence 255, 262, 547, 859, 876
Shallow cultivation 368
Shoot dieback 898
Slime mold 330
SMALL FRUITS 577–603
  Blueberries 583–585
  Brambles 585–588
    Pruning guide for established brambles 589
  Characteristics of small-fruit plants 580

Cultivar Selection 579
Currants and Gooseberries 588–590
Elderberries 591
Fertilizer guidelines for small fruits 581
Grapes 591–593
   About wine grapes 593
   Grape Terminology 592
   Harvesting 592–593
   Planting and first pruning 591–592
   Subsequent pruning and training 592
   Training grapes on a two-arm support system 593
Hardy Kiwis 593–595
Planting Small Fruits 582
Recommended small-fruit cultivars for Maryland 598–602
Site Selection and Preparation 580–582
Small Fruits Maintenance 582–583
   Mulch and water 582–583
   Pruning and training 583
Strawberries 595–597
Soil compaction 121, 405, 473

SOILS AND FERTILIZERS 93–124
Important hydrologic cycle processes 107
Soil as Entities of Nature 102–104
   Soil horizons 104
   Soils across the landscape 104–105
   The five soil-forming factors 102–103
   The four soil-forming processes 103
Soil Health 119–122
   Characteristics of healthy soils 119
   Practices that develop and maintain a healthy soil 120–121
   Soil productivity beyond nutrients 121–122
Soil Pores 100–102
   Aerobic and anaerobic conditions 101
   Soil air 101
   Soil pH 101

Soil solution 100
Soils as Biochemical and Chemical Reactors 107–112
   Adsorption 108
   Cation exchange 108
   Nutrient cycling 109–110
   Soils as filters 110
Soils as Hydrologic Buffers 106–107
Soils as Media for Plant Growth 112–114
   Liming material 113
   Optimizing soil pH for plant nutrition 112
Soils as Natural Capital and Ecosystem Services 105–107
Soil Solids 96–100
   Biomass 97–98
   Mineral solids 96
   Organic solids 97
   Protected Organic Matter (PrOM) 99
   Texture and structure 96
   The role of humus 100
Soil Testing 114–119
   Choosing a nutrient source 119
   Commercial, synthetic, and organic fertilizers 117
   Nutrients for plant growth 116
   Sample soil analysis report 115
   Understanding a soil test report 114–116
   The 12 soil textural classes 96
   The soil food web 98
   What is a Soil? 95–96
Spiders. *See* Arachnids
Squirrels 280, 789, 790
Stone fruits. *See* TREE FRUITS
Stratification (seeds) 690
Strawberries. *See* SMALL FRUITS
Succession 40, 47, 48, 348, 396, 414, 437, 476, 513, 516, 530, 531, 560, 565, 656, 658, 756, 757, 770, 771, 774, 828
Sulfur 133, 137, 237, 249, 268, 395, 397, 420, 584

T

TEACHING AND COMMUNICATION 7–32
Age-Appropriate Teaching 11–12
Communication Methods 13–20
   Casual conversation 18
   Email 14
   Formal speech 18
   Graphics and visual aids 17
   Multimedia 15
   Phone 18–19
   Printed materials 16
   Published articles 17
   Social media 15
   Writing 13
Communications Overview 12–13
Giving a Great Presentation 20–24
   After your presentation 16
   Assessing the room 22
   Before your presentation 15
   During your presentation 16
   Organizing your presentation 20–21
   Practicing your presentation 23
   Presenting your material 23
   Visual aids 22
Licensing and fair use 12
Online content reliability 12
Teaching Online 27–29
   Best practices for online instruction 29
   Method of delivery 28
   Planning an online program 28–29
Teaching Overview 9–11
Using Mass Media 24–27
   Advertising 25–27
   Appearing on-air or live recording 27
   Building your local audience 27
   Producing your content 26–27
   Publicity 24–25
Using technology to communicate 12
Terminal bud 250, 489, 699, 854, 855
"The Woods in Your Backyard" online course 748
Ticks. *See* Arachnids
Tip layering 702
Toxicity 129, 130, 131, 132, 133,

134, 135, 136, 230, 231, 233, 234, 236, 237, 238, 250, 256, 266, 290, 298, 373, 374, 522, 584, 713
Tree and shrub problems.
　See Diagnostic Keys
TREE FRUITS 605–634
　Fig Trees 627–628
　　Growing fig trees in containers 628
　　Harvesting figs 627
　　Overwintering in-ground fig trees 627–628
　　Phytodermatitis and fig trees 627
　　Site selection and planting 627
　General Pruning Guidelines 615
　　Fruit thinning 615
　　Why prune a fruit tree? 615
　Harvesting pome fruits 622
　Harvesting stone fruits 626–627
　Mulching and Weeding 612–613
　Pest and Disease Control 613–615.
　　See also INSECT BASICS
　　See also INTEGRATED PEST MANAGEMENT (IPM)
　　See also PLANT DISEASE BASICS
　Planting a Fruit Tree 611–612
　Pome Fruits: Apple and Pear 616–623
　　About limb spreaders 622
　　Apple and pear tree rootstocks 617
　　Benefits of dwarfing rootstocks 618
　　Cultivars that do well in Maryland 616
　　Fertilizer and pH 618
　　Harvesting pome fruits 622–623
　　Pruning pome fruit trees 618–623
　　Pruning principles for pome fruits 619
　　Rootstock 616–618
　　Spurs 616
　　Strains 616
　　Thinning pome fruits 622
　Pruning, pome fruit trees 618–622
　Pruning, stone-fruit trees 624–626
　Recommended tree-fruit cultivars for Maryland 629–634
　　APPLE 629

　　APRICOT 629
　　CHERRY - SOUR 630
　　CHERRY - SWEET 630
　　FIG 630
　　NECTARINE 631
　　PEACH 631–632
　　PEAR - ASIAN 632
　　PEAR - EUROPEAN 632–633
　　PLUM - EUROPEAN 633
　　PLUM - JAPANESE 633
　Rootstock, about 616
　Stone Fruits: Peach, Cherry, Plum, Apricot, Nectarine 623–627
　　Cultivar selections for Maryland 623
　　Fertilizer and pH 623
　　Harvesting stone fruits 626–627
　　Pruning stone-fruit trees 624–626
　　Thinning stone fruits 626
　Thinning pome fruit 622
　Thinning stone fruits 626
　Tree-Fruit Basics 607–611
　　Chill hours 609–610
　　Frosts and freezes 611
　　Fruit tree bearing age, height, and pollination requirements 610
　　General water requirements 609
　　Pollination 609
　　Site selection 607–608
　　Soil preferences 608–609
　　Sunlight factors 608
True bugs 166
Turf and lawn problems.
　See Diagnostic Keys

U

"Ugly-stub" pruning method 319
Underground Stems 431–436
　Bulb maintenance 435
　Bulbs 431–432
　Corms 432
　Planting bulbs 434
　Planting guide for flowering bulbs 433
　Rhizomes 432
　Spring-flowering bulbs 432–433
　Storing bulbs 436
　Summer-flowering bulbs 434

　Transplanting bulbs 435
　Tubers 432
　Types of underground stems 431–432
University of Maryland Extension Master Gardener Program 4–5
　About your volunteer responsibilities 30

V

Vegetable crop problems.
　See Diagnostic Keys
VEGETABLES 511–576
　Climate change & vegetable gardens 517
　Cover Crops 523–525
　　Cover crops for vegetable gardens 524
　Garden Types and Techniques 514–516
　　Container gardening. See also CONTAINER GARDENING
　　Container gardening (vegetables) 516
　　In-ground traditional rows 514–515
　　Intensive gardening 516
　　Raised beds 515–516
　Harvesting Vegetables 546–548
　　About row covers 548
　　Season extenders 547–548
　Mulching a vegetable garden 545–546
　Planting Seed 534–536
　　Disease-resistant seeds, about 535
　　Saving seeds 535–536
　　Seed terminology 534–535
　Pollination 525. See also BOTANY • Pollination
　Recordkeeping 541
　Row covers, about 548
　Selecting a Garden Site 516–520
　　Fencing 519–521
　　Garden layout and preparation 518–519
　Soil Amendments 522–523
　Soil Assessment and Testing 521–522

912　Maryland Master Gardener Handbook　　　　　　　　　　　　　　UME © 2025. All rights reserved.

Starting a Vegetable Garden 514
Starting Your Own
    Transplants 536–540
    Hardening-off 537
    Planting seeds outdoors 538–539
    Planting transplants
        outdoors 537–538
    Thinning 539
Using herbicides in a food
    garden 545
Vegetable families grown in the
    mid-Atlantic 527
Vegetable Garden
    Maintenance 540–546
    Cultivation 545–546
    Fertilizing vegetables 542
    How to convert synthetic
        fertilizer recommendations to
        organic 542
    Minimal-till technique 521
    Mulching 545
    Watering 540–542
    Weed management 544
Vegetable Planting Guide 525–534
    Annual vegetables 527–528
    Fall planting-date calculator 532
    Perennial vegetables 527–528
    Preparing the garden for
        winter 533–534
    Spring and fall frost
        dates 528–529
    Vegetable gardening in the
        fall 532–533
    Vertical growing 539
    Watering a vegetable
        garden 540–541
**VEGETABLES (profiled by
    name) 556–575**
    ASPARAGUS 557
    BEAN 558
    BEET 559
    BROCCOLI 559
    BRUSSELS SPROUTS 560
    CABBAGE 560
    CARROT 561
    CAULIFLOWER 561
    CUCUMBER 562
    EGGPLANT 562
    GARLIC 563
    HORSERADISH 563
    KALE, COLLARD, MUSTARD, AND
        TURNIP GREENS 564

LEEKS 564
LETTUCE 565
MUSKMELON, CANTALOUPE, AND
    WATERMELON 566
OKRA 566
ONION 567
PEA 567
PEPPER 568
POTATO 568
PUMPKIN 569
RADISH 570
SOUTHERN PEA 570
SPINACH 571
SUMMER SQUASH 571
SWEET CORN 572
SWEET POTATO 573
SWISS CHARD 573
TOMATO 574
WINTER SQUASH 575
Vines. *See* WOODY PLANTS
Viral diseases 252, 308. *See
    also* Plant diseases, common
    virus
Voles 288, 317, 321, 324, 613,
    786, 787

W

Walnut wilt 265
Wasps 45, 164, 169, 172, 176,
    177, 178, 182, 219, 220,
    254, 277, 281, 299, 324,
    544, 747, 769, 770, 847.
    See also Diagnostic Keys
    Gall wasps 277, 281
Water sprouts 267, 883
WEEDS 345–378
    Sustainable Weed Maintenance
        Plan 374–375
        Implementation 374
        Lawn weeds 375
        Prioritization 374
        Site analysis 374
    Vegetative identification of weedy
        grasses 364–365
    Weed Biology 349–352
        Life cycles 349
        Means of reproduction 350
        Seed dispersal mechanisms 351
        Seed longevity (dormancy) 350
    Weed Identification 352–364

Weed Management 366–374
    Biological management 366
    Chemical management 370
    Cultural and mechanical
        management 366
    Herbicide types 371
    Why Are Weeds a
        Problem? 348–349
    Weeds, common lawn and
        garden 352
Weevils. *See* Insects, common
    landscape
Wetland plants. *See* ECOLOGY
White pine blister rust 188
White pine decline 262, 284
**WILDLIFE AND
    WOODLANDS 745–794**
    Attracting and Feeding
        Birds 772–776
        Flowers that attract birds 775
        Landscaping for hummingbirds
            and butterflies 774
        Seeds and feeders for attracting
            birds 773
    Attracting Beneficial
        Insects 771–772
        Flowers that attract
            butterflies 775
    Attracting wildlife with native
        plants 766–770
    Land Care Practices 755–765
        Controlling invasive plants and
            insect pests 760–764
        Converting lawn to natural
            areas 756
        Improving privacy and
            aesthetics, or farming your
            woodland 759
        Land care plan 764
        Modifying or improving existing
            wildlife habitat 757–758
    Managing a Wildlife
        Habitat 765–771
        A place to raise young 770
        Cover 769
        Food 765
        Water 769
        Wildlife landscape
            design 770–771
    Managing Wildlife
        Damage 776–792
    Nuisance Animals 777–792

Bats 779
Cats and dogs 781
Chipmunks 790
Crows 777
Deer 781
Groundhogs (Woodchucks) 791
House mice 784
Moles 785
Nuisance-animal repellents 777
Pigeons 778
Rabbits 787
Raccoons 788
Rats 784
Report a wildlife problem 780
Skunks 789
Snakes 791
Squirrels 789
Voles 786
Woodpeckers 779
Principles of Forestry 751–752
Create a firewise landscape 753–754
Your place in the landscape 752–753
Property Inventory 752–755
Constraints to land management 754–755
Identifying trees and shrubs 755
Woodlands 748–749
Creating natural areas 749
Dividing property by use 749
Mapping your property 749–750
The concept of habitat units 750
"The Woods In Your Backyard" 748
Witches' broom 179, 281, 295
Wood-destroying pest problems. *See* Diagnostic Keys
WOODY PLANTS 455–486
Abiotic Problems of Woody Plants 469–472
Construction damage 473
Environmental conditions 470–471
Physical and mechanical injury 471–472
Root problems 472–473
Groundcovers 483
Maintenance 484–485
Planting groundcovers 484
Planning and Site Selection 457–458
Planting Woody Ornamentals 461–463
Getting the plant home 461
Soil preparation 461–462
The planting process 462
When to plant 462
Plant Selection 458–459
Post-Planting Care 464–465
Staking and guying trees 464
Problematic trees and shrubs 474
Purchasing Woody Plants 459–462
Balled and burlapped (B&B) 460
Bare-root 459–460
Container-grown 460–461
Recommended flowering shrubs for Maryland 476
Recommended flowering tree s for Maryland 476
Recommended groundcovers for Maryland 485
Recommended shade trees for Maryland 475
Recommended vines for Maryland 483
Transplanting Woody Ornamentals 468–469
Moving and replanting 469
Root pruning 469
When to transplant 468–469
Trees for urban conditions 481
Trees with attractive bark 477
Vines 482–483
Planting vines 482–483
Vine maintenance 483
Vine selection 482
Vine types 482
Woody Plant Maintenance 465–468
Fertilizing 468
Mulch 466
Watering 465–466
Weed management 468
Woody plants that serve as barriers 478
Woody plants that serve as windbreaks 481
Woody plants that tolerate poor, dry soil 479
Woody plants that tolerate salt air 480
Woody plants that tolerate shade 479
Woody plants with attractive fall color 477
Woody plants with attractive fruits 478
Worms (pests). *See* Insects, common landscape

X

Xylem 76, 77, 130, 133, 134, 135, 136, 167, 171, 250, 254, 649, 855, 865, 870, 876, 882

Z

Zinc 136, 137